The
TRANSCENDENTALISTS
and
THEIR WORLD

The
TRANSCENDENTALISTS

Monument at Concord

and
THEIR WORLD

ROBERT A. GROSS

FARRAR, STRAUS AND GIROUX

NEW YORK

Farrar, Straus and Giroux
120 Broadway, New York 10271

Art on title page and part openers courtesy of the Concord Free
Public Library.
Art on chapter openers from Vector Hut / creativemarket.com.

Library of Congress Cataloging-in-Publication Data
Names: Gross, Robert A., 1945– author.
Title: The Transcendentalists and Their World / Robert A. Gross.
Description: First edition. | New York : Farrar, Straus and Giroux,
    2021. |Includes index. | Summary: "The eminent and award-
    winning historian Robert A. Gross presents his long-awaited,
    immersive journey through Concord in the age of Emerson and
    Thoreau" —Provided by publisher.
Identifiers: LCCN 2021025273 | ISBN 9780374279325 (hardcover)
Subjects: LCSH: Transcendentalism (New England) |
    Transcendentalists (New England)
Classification: LCC B905 .G76 2021 | DDC 141/.3—dc23
LC record available at https://lccn.loc.gov/2021025273

Designed by Janet Evans-Scanlon

For Ann

Who shared and sustained this journey

Of books and life

CONTENTS

———•———

Maps ix
Preface xiii

Part I: *A Community in Change*

Prologue: A New Beginning 3

1. A Day of Good Feelings 15
2. Community and Conscience 43
3. The White Village 83
4. The Curse of Trade 113
5. Husbandmen and Manufacturers 147
6. Knowledge Is Power 185
7. Internal Improvements 219
8. Privilege and Conspiracy 259

Part II: *Transcendentalists and Their World*

9. Freedom of Mind 305
10. A Little Democracy 345
11. The Philosopher of Modern History 379
12. Young Men and Women of Fairest Promise 405
13. *The* Man of Concord 449
14. Famine in the Churches 483
15. The Spirit of Reform 509
16. The Iron Horse 541
17. Walden and Beyond 569

Notes 609
Acknowledgments 789
Index 805

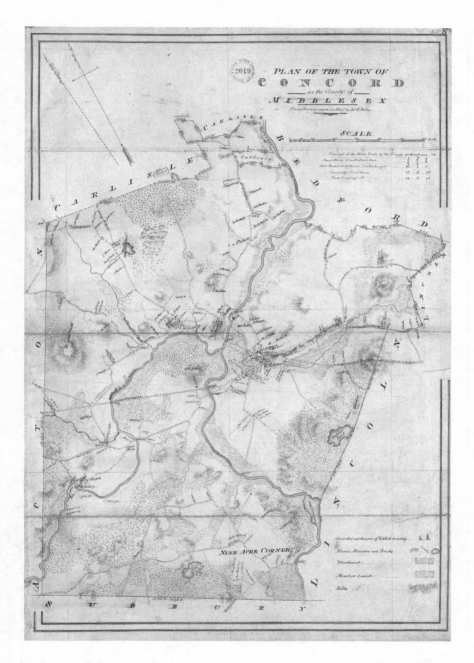

JOHN G. HALES, "Plan of the town of Concord, Mass. in the county of Middlesex" (1830). This map of Concord in 1830 highlights the thickening of settlement in the central village, the extension of highways east into Cambridge and Boston and west and north into the countryside, and the growth of water-powered manufacturing along the Assabet River in the southwest. Note the prominence of Walden Pond in the southeast. (Courtesy Massachusetts Archives)

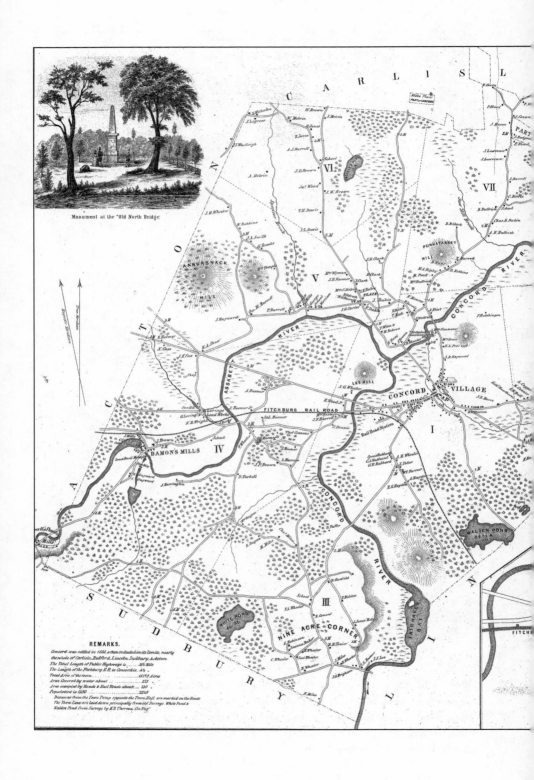

Ṃᴀᴘ

OF THE TOWN OF

CONCORD

MIDDLESEX COUNTY MASS.

Surveyed by Authority of the Town.

H.F. WALLING CIVIL ENG.ʳ

Nᵒ.81 Washington Street Boston

1852.

SCALE OF RODS.

CONCORD
VILLAGE

RIVER

Map of the Town of Concord, Middlesex County, Mass. (1852), surveyed by H. F. Walling, a civil engineer. The coming of the railroad is evident on this map of Concord, showing the route of the Fitchburg line as it enters the town at the edge of Walden Pond, heads north into the central village, and then turns west to pass the Damon textile mill before crossing into neighboring Acton. The map indicates each of the school districts, and the inset image highlights the association of Concord with the monument at the Old North Bridge.
(Courtesy Concord Free Public Library)

Preface

There can be no true history written until a just estimate of human nature is holden by the historian.

—Ralph Waldo Emerson,
"Philosophy of Modern History," December 8, 1836

Wherever men have lived there is a story to be told, and it depends chiefly on the story-teller or historian whether that is interesting or not.

—Henry David Thoreau,
March 18, 1861

American individualism found its strongest voices in the nineteenth century among the New England Transcendentalists, and none more so than Ralph Waldo Emerson and Henry David Thoreau. From his ancestral home of Concord, Massachusetts, Emerson summoned his countrymen to free themselves from bondage to the past and refuse unthinking conformity to contemporaries. "Trust thyself," he urged; seek inspiration in nature; realize your infinite potential. Through such spiritual journeys, people of all sorts—women as well as men, Blacks as well as whites, poor as well as rich—could tap their inner genius and build together an original American culture, independent of the errors and injustices of the Old World and true to the ideals of liberty and equality at the heart of the democracy that the break with Britain had left unfulfilled.[1]

Starting in the mid-1830s, Emerson preached this stirring message in Boston and vicinity and at home in Concord, and over the ensuing decade he extended his reach on the lecture circuit to audiences across New England, in the leading port cities of the Northeast, and as far south as Baltimore. He was not alone nor initially in the forefront of the Transcendentalist movement; well into the 1840s, even as his literary reputation was growing in England, he remained a provincial figure in his native land.[2]

No one attended to his words or felt his influence more fully than his younger townsman Thoreau, the only native son among the Concord writers, who, after graduating from Harvard in 1837, became his disciple and protégé. Coming of age a generation after Emerson, Thoreau heeded the master's call for self-reliance, cultivated his own voice and vision by the shores of Walden Pond, and fashioned a classic account of how to live simply and sincerely, in harmony with nature. *Walden* continues to inspire today as a model of Transcendentalist individualism and a foundation text of the environmental movement. Although he "lived alone, in the woods, a mile from any neighbor," Thoreau never lost sight of his townspeople, and through his strenuous critique of their way of life, he put his birthplace on the literary map. He tightened the link between Transcendentalism and town that his mentor had initiated. As Emerson gathered thinkers and reformers in his orbit, as Margaret Fuller arrived for extended stays, and as Nathaniel Hawthorne and the Alcotts took up residence, Concord gained notice as a literary center, and it soon came to symbolize the social ferment and the intellectual iconoclasm of the age. The town has been celebrated as the seat of the American Renaissance in literature and art during the decades before the Civil War. The writer Henry Adams dubbed Transcendentalism "the Concord Church." It sheltered a faith he could not adopt but whose appeal he could not deny. So it was for many New Englanders then and now, within and beyond the town, and for readers all over the United States and the world.[3]

Why Concord? Was it simply the accidents of birth and geography— Emerson's familial antecedents, Thoreau's native origin, plus proximity to Boston—that made the town a literary center? Or was the community fertile ground for novel ideas? One popular account has it that Concord was the home of two revolutions—the first on April 19, 1775, when Minutemen clashed with Redcoats at the North Bridge and fired what Emerson called "the shot heard round the world"; the second in the intellectual awakening the Transcendentalists sparked with their rejection of European hierarchy and inequality and their vision of free individuals realizing the promise of democracy in everyday life. In this telling, the "embattled farmers" waged a successful war for political independence and self-government; their heirs in the 1830s and 1840s built on that achievement with an intellectual campaign to liberate American minds. The Transcendentalists thus extended what the Minutemen began, and their idealistic legacy has posed a vital challenge to our culture ever since.[4]

That story misses a profound transition in American life. The Revolutionary generation fought for collective ends. It defended the right of towns and provinces to tax and govern themselves, and it founded a republic on the duty of citizens to serve the public good. In New England the ideology of civic republicanism merged with Puritan traditions to emphasize the interdependence of individuals and families within a common way of life. This worldview was compatible with a host of inequities—slavery, white racism, class privilege, patriarchy and the subordination of women—and it was never without challenge, especially by libertarian arguments in favor of free markets and the right of individuals to pursue their own interests, whether in business or in religion. Nonetheless, a half-century after independence, the social web was still binding—as an idea, if not always in practice. In principle, everyone belonged to the community; none lived alone, independent of established institutions and without obligations to the neighbors.

The Transcendentalists rejected this intellectual heritage. Combining Romantic notions from Europe with the Protestant stress on personal salvation, and infusing these influences with a democratic faith in liberty and equality, Emerson put the individual first and foremost. As he saw it, every person comes into this world with a divine soul, infinite in possibility. It is the highest calling in life to dive into this "inner ocean" and give it expression. No other duty takes precedence, not the demands of elders, not the claims of church or state, not the obligation to be useful to society. An institution is merely "the lengthened shadow of one man." Emerson's purpose was to break the hold of ancient traditions and involuntary associations, so that every person could take the journey of self-discovery and be an inspiration to others along the way. "Former generations acted under the belief that a shining social prosperity was the aim of men: and sacrificed uniformly individuals to the nation," he declared. "The modern mind teaches that the nation exists for the Individual;—for the guardianship and education of every man." Thoreau, characteristically, carried these convictions to excess. "I am not responsible for the successful working of the machinery of society," he exclaimed. "I am not the son of the engineer." "I love mankind," he added during his sojourn in the woods. "I hate the institutions of their forefathers."[5]

How do we explain this revolution in social thought and practice? Why did individualism come to the fore as a cultural ideal, and why in this time and place, Concord and the Boston area during the second quarter of the nineteenth century? In this book, I address these questions through a community study of Concord, with the aim of tracing the connections between Transcendentalism and the society from which it emerged and to which it spoke. This inquiry places the Concord writers in the context of the town in which they lived and wrote; it explores how the unfolding life of the community formed their understanding of the broader society and culture; it sets forth the responses of the townspeople—some favorable, others dubious, many uncomprehending—to the radical ideas of their intellectual neighbors. *The Transcendentalists and Their World* is at once a social history of a storied New England community and a cultural history of major American writers and the ideas they professed; it highlights the interplay between the two, the links between literature and life.

A common myth about Concord in the era of Emerson and Thoreau portrays the community as a simple country town, shaped by the seasonal routines of farmers tilling the land and supporting their families. Though the town lay along two rivers, it lacked sufficient waterpower to drive large-scale manufacturing, and so the industrial revolution passed it by. Supposedly remote from the progress of the age, Concord retained an agrarian landscape, formed by generations of mixed husbandry since the beginnings of English settlement back in 1635: an attractive blend of gardens and cornfields, meadows and pastures, woodlands and orchards. The slow-moving rivers made for pleasant boating; the pristine ponds, nestled in the forests, offered recreation and solitude in nature. In this picturesque view, Concord enjoyed a reputation as a quiet, pastoral place, fit for poets and philosophers. Safe from the conflicts and stresses of the wider world, the town nourished Emerson's muse and energized Thoreau's quest for a simpler mode of life.

This vision of the ideal small town, combining nature and culture in harmony, is a fiction. It was created in part by the Transcendentalists themselves, who liked to contrast the simpler ways of the town with those of the mass society taking shape in the nation's cities. For Emerson, individuals could still thrive in the small community, could know and engage their neighbors, and could make their voices heard in public affairs. The pastoral image of Concord was popularized in the Civil War era and for long afterward to attract tourists and armchair travelers in search of an imaginative escape from the pressures of urban-industrial existence.[6] But in the heyday of the Transcendentalists, Concord offered no haven from the times, as Emerson and Thoreau well knew and told us in their most searching works. Although its population numbered little more than two thousand souls, the town was as profoundly affected by the upheavals of the age as any booming metropolis. It was a community in ferment, whose small, ordered society, founded by Puritans and defended by Minute-men, was dramatically unsettled by the expansive forces of capitalism and de-mocracy. During the several decades around Thoreau's childhood, youth, and coming into maturity (1815–1847), his hometown was economically dynamic, religiously diverse, racially heterogeneous, politically divided, and receptive to social and political reforms. It stood in the mainstream of Jacksonian America with an excellent vantage on a society undergoing rapid change.[7]

If Concord was in many respects a representative town, it also had claims to uniqueness, including its origin as the first inland settlement of the Mas-sachusetts Bay Colony, its preeminence at the start of the Revolutionary War, its significance as a commercial and political center in the early republic, its close connections with Cambridge and Boston, and its longevity as a religious body under the watch of one dominating figure in the pulpit for more than six decades. From 1778 to 1841, Rev. Ezra Ripley embodied the old order of eighteenth-century Massachusetts for his parishioners, preaching a social ethic designed to hold the community together, even as it was increasingly un-dercut by change. When Emerson rejected this philosophy, he was repudiating the legacy of his own step-grandfather. Transcendentalism was a personal as well as a public fight for individual freedom.

In the Concord version, this intellectual movement differed from its Bos-ton counterpart. There such radical thinkers as Orestes Brownson and George Ripley linked self-culture to social reform. In their perspective, a new age was possible only when free men and women cooperated to remove the barriers of inequality and oppression to individual fulfillment. Their colleagues in Con-cord disagreed. They stood apart from the moral crusades of the day. Emerson long resisted a public stand on behalf of abolitionism. Thoreau preferred to go his own way. For them, the route to reform ran through individual conscious-ness, one soul at a time. Individualism was the banner of Concord Transcen-dentalism, and it is to this theme that this book attends. Formulating their ideas in a community where older customs were waning, social ties fraying, and people asserting greater freedom to make their own choices and direct their own affairs, Concord writers spoke to contemporary experiences and offered fresh ways to make sense of change. In so doing, they wrestled with the same issues as their neighbors, while bringing cosmopolitan knowledge to bear on local life. The America of their lectures and writings had its origins in Concord.

Emerson, a native of Boston, opted to make Concord his home in 1835, as he sought to carve out a new path after resigning from the ministry. As he was settling in, Thoreau was in Cambridge for his sophomore year at Harvard. It would be two years before they met. By then, the ongoing transformation of Concord was provoking a profound crisis in the social and political order. In this milieu, the newcomer Emerson would compose and deliver his most influential statements of Transcendentalist individualism—*Nature*, "American Scholar," the Divinity School address, and the various lecture series at Boston's Masonic Temple. Thoreau, growing up amid the changes, would absorb the new ideas about individual possibility into his worldview and exhort his neighbors to resist the constraints of capitalism and conformity by living deliberately and making their every act a conscious choice.

The social transformation of Concord and New England had its roots in the Puritan foundations of the community and in the heritage of the Revolution, and the legacy of that past was epitomized by the long-serving Parson Ripley. The stirring of change was felt at the dawn of the American republic, but it was in the 1820s to the 1840s that a new order, built on greater individual freedom, voluntary association, economic innovation, social mobility, and integration into the wider world, challenged inherited ways and created new tensions and contradictions for the town and its people. These were the years when Emerson forged his role on the public platform and set forth his best-known ideas and when Thoreau laid the basis for his most influential work, *Walden*. This book thus concentrates on the quarter century from 1825 to 1850 to tell their stories.

It has taken many years of research to construct this picture of the town and its writers. *The Transcendentalists and Their World* is the sequel to my earlier account of Concord in the era of the American Revolution. *The Minutemen and Their World* appeared in 1976, just in time for the Bicentennial, with an approach that was then still young. It was a work of the "new social history," which widened our view of the past beyond the elite white men who had typically dominated the stage and took in groups long ignored. This would be a novel history "from the bottom up," recovering the thoughts and actions of common folk. Inspired by that agenda, *Minutemen* encompassed all levels of society and every walk of life. It placed people who were usually on the margins—notably, women and people of color, enslaved or free—in the narrative as actors in their own right. The aim was to capture the ongoing life of the town, with its issues and conflicts, as the inhabitants encountered the tumultuous forces of a revolutionary world.

The new social history, once an insurgency, has long since been tamed and absorbed into the scholar's toolkit. It has been challenged, in turn, by other initiatives, especially, by a "new cultural history" attentive to the ways social roles are informed by cultural ideas (such as race and gender) and by a transnational perspective linking the local and the global. Academic readers will discern the impact of these innovations in the work that follows.

Yet this book is true to its scholarly origins. It builds on the database assembled for *Minutemen* to identify significant patterns in collective life. But where the documentary record for the colonial town was manageable by a single scholar, with the aid of a few research assistants, the nineteenth century burgeoned with manuscript and printed sources in tandem with an explosion of activity in economy, politics, and society. Concord abounds in materials documenting the vigorous growth and movement of the population, the expansion of economic production and exchange, the splintering of churches and the rise of new sects, the proliferation of voluntary associations, the mobilization of the grassroots in political parties and moral crusades, the increased enrollment and impact of colleges and schools, and the publication of books, newspapers, and magazines in vast profusion. Emerson professed disdain for "the cheap sublime of magnitude and number," but he recognized the uses (and abuses) of statistics to illustrate his portrait of the contemporary world. So too has this historian been enticed by the opportunities such sources offer for systematic, quantitative analysis—a labor spread over several decades and made possible by a dozen or more undergraduate and graduate data gatherers and computer consultants.

The counterpoint to these records of an emerging mass society are the many personal documents left behind by individuals with heightened awareness of their public and private selves. The autobiographies, diaries, memoirs, and letters used in this study provide ample testimony to the new consciousness of self and society Emerson considered the hallmark of the age. As Concord became more deeply integrated into the wider world, its sons and daughters were constantly on the move in search of employment in the countinghouses of Boston, the mills of Waltham and Lowell, and farmlands and rising towns on the expanding Western frontier. Newcomers, in turn, flowed in and out of town, reducing the native-born to a minority. The Yankee migration deposited the personal papers of onetime Concordians across the continent, from Maine to Massachusetts and Connecticut, south to North Carolina, west to Texas, and across the Rockies to the West Coast. Chasing all these people down is a job never done, as online genealogical databases are continually updated with new details. But I have followed their trails far and wide to make unexpected discoveries about life in the wide-ranging world of Emerson and Thoreau.

Like its predecessor, this book is addressed both to students of American history and literature and to the general public. The narrative aims to present the story of Concord and its writers fluently and accessibly; the endnotes take up details of evidence and debates among scholars. The study began as an investigation into how the close world of the Minutemen, with its communal ethic and its inclusive institutions, gave way to the fragmented and individualistic society of the Transcendentalists. Over the last few years, as I wrote the bulk of these pages, Concord and Massachusetts in the mid-nineteenth century have seemed uncannily close to the United States in our own times.

Theirs was an era of globalization, as exhilarating and unsettling as our own. Political democracy was then new; so, in the Bay State, was religious choice. The issues with which we struggle today—fake news, electoral fraud, sloganeering, personal attacks, and conspiracy theories—drove the partisans and sectarians of small-town Concord into mutually suspicious enclaves. Yet confidence in progress remained high, far more so than it does today. Moral reformers campaigned to rid the earth of sin; school reformers strove to bring education up to date. And though the flood of information from mass media could seem overwhelming, libraries and lyceums offered guides to understanding. As a public intellectual, Emerson took up the charge of canvassing the ever-increasing world of learning and digesting it for others.

Most important, through their efforts to make sense of a rapidly changing society, the Transcendentalists and their neighbors struggled for ways to reconcile the new freedom of individuals with the older claims of interdependence for the common good. Their legacy resides not in their answers but in their attempts.

Part I

A COMMUNITY
IN CHANGE

A New Beginning

Early in August 1822, a Boston schoolmaster and his wife gathered up their four young children for a trip to the country. Their destination was Concord, sixteen miles west of the city and a four-hour journey by stage. The weather was perfect for the expedition, "so fine, clear and cool," one newspaper noted, that the usual toll of deaths in the hot season was surprisingly light and the crops in the fields and orchards promised an abundant harvest. The children, ranging in age from nine to three, were undoubtedly excited by the open, rural landscape, so unlike their neighborhood atop Beacon Hill, with its continuous rows of houses and brick-lined streets. The highlight of this outing was not the farms under cultivation but rather a pond in the woods a mile from Concord center—a scene seemingly so solitary and untouched by man that it caught the imagination of the five-year-old boy in the little entourage and aroused a lifelong love of the wild. Nearly a quarter-century later he would remember that day as a turning point in his life. "That woodland vision for a long time made the drapery of my dreams," Henry David Thoreau recalled not long after taking up residence by the shores of Walden Pond in the summer of 1845. "Some how or other it at once gave the preference to this recess among the pines where almost sunshine & shadow were the only inhabitants that varied the scene, over that tumultuous and varied city—as if it had found its proper nursery." The encounter would prove fateful not just for the aspiring writer but for the place where he dwelled. It was a signal moment in the making of Concord, Massachusetts, into a literary landmark and of Thoreau, its native son, into an enduring force in American culture.[1]

In the summer of 1822, that visit to Walden was little more than an excuse for John Thoreau, age thirty-four, to get out of the city and escape his troubles.

The father of four was at a low ebb in his fortunes. A native of Boston, he was the son of a self-made merchant of French Protestant origins from the Isle of Jersey, who had arrived in the colonial capital in 1773 and prospered in the Revolution. The sire's story was the stuff of American myth. A mariner on a vessel that shipwrecked off the Massachusetts coast, Jean Thoreau showed up in Boston with little but his skills as a seaman, yet somehow, through wartime service on a privateer under the command of Paul Revere, he obtained the capital to enter trade in the new nation. His import house on Long Wharf in Boston harbor thrived in the 1790s; his home in the North End teemed with eight children. This upward course was upset by the death of his wife, and after remarrying a woman with ties to Concord, he relocated his family in 1800 to a house on the town common, only to die within a year. The orphans were left to the care of a new stepmother and the guidance of the court-appointed administrator of the paternal estate.[2]

John Thoreau, the eldest son and fourth child, spent his teenage years training to follow in his father's footsteps and enter a countinghouse. His first store in Concord was ill-starred; launched in 1809, when he was just twenty-one, it soon fell victim to the pressures on American commerce in an Atlantic world at war. A second try, in the town of Chelmsford ten years later, succumbed to the Panic of 1819 and the ensuing depression. Amid these setbacks, in 1812 the unlucky merchant wed another newcomer to Concord, Cynthia Dunbar, and struggled to support their growing brood. For more than a decade he was in and out of the town, doing whatever was available to make ends meet. He peddled goods to Indians in Maine, clerked in others' stores when he was not failing in his own, and farmed on his mother-in-law's land. Nothing took. At thirty-five, he was reduced to instructing boys and girls in a Boston school not far from the former site of his father's once-booming business. The summer outing to Walden in 1822 was surely a welcome distraction. In the splendor of the woods and pond, he could forget for a few hours his meager prospects in the city.[3]

His wife Cynthia's family had also known better days. Mary Jones, her maternal grandmother, was born into the colonial elite of Weston, fifteen miles south of Concord. Her father, one of the largest landholders in Massachusetts Bay and among the most politically influential, resisted popular pressure and fought for king and country, as did six of his eleven adult sons. That action resulted in the loss of the family's vast holdings and permanent exile for five sons in Canada. Grandmother Mary, who stayed behind, expressed her political sentiments by marrying men with misgivings about the Patriot cause. Her first husband, Harvard graduate Asa Dunbar, gave up a pulpit in Salem for a law office in Keene, New Hampshire, where he proved his loyalty sufficiently to be chosen selectman and town clerk. At his death in 1787, he left behind five minor children, including his one-month-old daughter Cynthia. Mary struggled to support her growing brood, keeping a tavern in Keene and then a boardinghouse in Boston, before marrying Capt. Jonas Minot, a substantial Concord farmer and once lukewarm Patriot, in June 1798 and settling into his homestead on the Virginia Road in the eastern quarter of the town. The union supported a genteel style of life for the Dunbars, but stepfather Minot was spending as much as he took in, and when he died in 1813, his estate afforded little ready money for the widow. Mary's daughters had to rely on their manners and minds to make their way. Louisa Dunbar briefly won the affections of future senator Daniel Webster in a short-lived courtship; younger sister Cynthia found her life's partner in the struggling John Thoreau.[4]

Ironically, Cynthia's ne'er-do-well older brother gave her family a route back to Concord and the middle class. Charles J. Dunbar was legendary for barroom tricks and wrestling feats; he could toss his hat high in the air and catch it on his head without fail over and over again. But he possessed little knack for earning a living. It was to everyone's surprise, then, that in October 1822 he finally did something useful. On a tour of the New Hampshire countryside, he stumbled upon gold—"black gold"—on a farm in the Lakes Region not far from the White Mountains. His find was a lode of "plumbago," better known today as graphite, well suited to use in lead pencils. Dunbar readily grasped its commercial potential and with good reason. Though often on the road, he considered Concord home, and he was well aware that the town was the birthplace of American pencil making. Local cabinetmaker William Munroe had pioneered the infant industry, and after 1819 he steadily improved the technology, reduced its costs, and built the market. About the same time Dunbar was acquiring rights to the graphite in the Granite State, Munroe was advertising his ability to furnish all the pencils his countrymen could want and at a lower price than those long imported from Britain.[5]

That was no deterrent to Dunbar. Rather than supply the raw material to Munroe, he went into the business himself, with two Concord investors as partners. Within a few months the company was floundering for lack of a steady hand at the helm. The call went out to Dunbar's brother-in-law to step in. In March 1823 John Thoreau returned with his family to Concord, rescued the enterprise, and made it his own. Munroe notwithstanding, there was room for more than one firm in the growing industry. Pencil making enabled Thoreau to obtain a fresh start in the town he had departed five years before and to stay there for good. Instead of importing and selling foreign commodities, he pursued a new strategy for economic success: producing high-quality items from domestic sources for the citizens of an extensive republic. What the father did with pencils, his literary son would do with books.[6]

John Thoreau returned to a community facing its own economic challenges. The small town of nearly eighteen hundred inhabitants in the early 1820s had been as buffeted by the ups and downs of the wider economy as had the aspiring merchant-turned-pencil-maker. In the first decades of the republic, America quickened with new motion, its trade expanding across an Atlantic world disrupted by revolution and war, its population spreading onto once-Indian lands across the Appalachians. Concord shared in the boom. From its farms flowed wagonloads of barreled beef and pork destined for West Indian plantations and oxcarts heaped with rye, hay, and wood to sustain the bustling seaports on the Massachusetts coast. The central village filled up with stores and taverns catering to rural customers with money to spend on the latest textiles and tableware, spices and lemons, rum and wine from abroad. Craft shops multiplied, and the area in the center known as the milldam, where waterpower was channeled to grind corn and rye into flour and to saw lumber into boards, took shape as a manufacturing district. It supported a little clock industry, which assembled timepieces in mahogany cases and equipped them with brass movements from the foundry across the road. The makers advertised their goods for shipment anywhere in the country.

The financial bubble burst abruptly at the close of 1807, as the Jefferson administration imposed an embargo on trade with the outside world. In the contracting economy, John Thoreau's "yellow store" at the head of the common was doomed. An exodus of workingmen began; so many poured out that Concord registered a small loss of population in the census of 1810. The unsettlement continued into the War of 1812, though the suspension of commerce with Britain did give a boost to American manufacturers. Free from competition from cheap imports, local entrepreneurs devised substitutes. This was the moment when Munroe shifted from making clock cases to pencils; blacksmith Joshua Jones produced nails and wire. One of the earliest cotton mills in New

England began operating along the Assabet River, in the western part of town. Protected by war and profiting from scarcity, these industrial start-ups faded with peace. The clockmakers departed; the cotton factory survived only by suspending production for a year and a half. Munroe looked yet again for new products to sell. In the uncertain times, people did the bookkeeping of their losses with imported pencils. By the early 1820s, the milldam was adrift and run-down. In a young nation that was doubling its population every twenty-five years, the ancient town of Concord, founded in 1635, was barely holding its own. Between 1790 and 1820 it grew by just 12 percent, well below the statewide increase of 38 percent. Concord was in need of a new direction to stave off further decline.[7]

Changes were stirring. The revival of pencil making in Concord was one sign of the economic expansion gathering force in the Bay State. In his address to the legislature at the start of 1823, Gov. John Brooks took pride in the advance of manufacturing; of the 149 companies chartered by the Commonwealth in recent years, with a capital exceeding $16 million, "nearly all" were in "successful operation." The modern textile factories started at Waltham in 1814 and Lowell in 1823 put Middlesex County at the forefront of the industrial revolution. Located at the geographical center of the county, Concord felt the stimulus to enterprise and innovation. The modest mill on the Assabet became as capable of converting cotton into cloth as the more famous complex on the Merrimack. Half a mile downstream another establishment, begun in 1819, produced lead pipes for aqueducts. The town center hummed with the activity of William Whiting's carriage works, Alvan Pratt's gun shop, and James Adams's "furniture warehouse."[8]

Concord was well connected to wider markets. Long a hub of communications, the town was linked by highways east to Boston, west into the interior, and south to Hartford and New Haven. The most popular route to the coast, however, ran through Lexington and Medford to Charlestown, then across a toll bridge into the capital. It was far preferable to the Cambridge and Concord Turnpike, constructed with great hopes in 1803. The private toll road cut a straight path to the city, climbing up and down hills and passing through marshes. But its steep grades proved tough going for ox-teams pulling great loads of farm produce. In Concord the turnpike got off to an embarrassing start. One section of the road, crossing the wetlands along the mill brook, was built up, layer by layer, from planks of wood topped by piles of gravel. After a few days' use, it sank out of sight, beneath seventeen feet of water. By the early 1820s the turnpike was so neglected, according to one wag, that it housed a "nest of young birds among the long grass in one of the ruts."[9]

Townspeople could also take a water route to the coast via the Middlesex Canal, which joined the Concord to the Merrimack and Medford rivers in the late 1790s. It was suitable for freight such as wood, bricks, and iron ore, too heavy for overland carriage. Around 1812 Col. Amos Wood, whose farm lay along the Sudbury River, tried the experiment of floating "long flat boats of small draft," laden with lumber, down the waters. The venture lasted only two or three years. An occasional canal boat could still be glimpsed a decade later, trailing an aura of romance in its wake. To young Henry Thoreau, the sight of a vessel "stealing mysteriously through the meadows and past the village" stirred a sense of wonder:

> It came and departed as silently as a cloud, without noise or dust, and was witnessed by few. One summer day this huge traveller might be seen moored at some meadow's wharf, and another summer day it was not there. Where precisely it came from, or who these men were who knew the rocks and soundings better than we who bathed there, we could never tell . . . They were a sort of fabulous rivermen to us.[10]

Enthusiasm for technological change spread to local farms. Starting in October 1820, the town played host to the annual fair of the Society of Middlesex Husbandmen and Manufacturers, founded to "promote improvements in agricultural knowledge" and to advance "the interests of manufacturers and mechanics." Forget the antiquated customs of the past, its speakers urged; follow the lessons of science and the best practices of the day, as demonstrated by the winners of the yearly competitions. Local farmers vied for the cash prizes that went to the biggest crops, the largest livestock, and the best-kept fields, while manufacturers displayed the results of their mechanical ingenuity. Pencil maker Munroe led the way; he was the first person in Concord to join the new group. John Thoreau put his products to the test in the fall of 1823, just seven months after returning to town—and, remarkably, received a two-dollar premium "for a specimen of excellent Lead Pencils, manufactured from American Plumbago." He became a member the next year.[11]

The agricultural society soon had allies in the cause of improvement.

Knowledge was progressing in many fields, not just in husbandry, and to keep up with the advances, townsmen got together in 1821 and formed a social library, whose collections would provide access to "the useful and popular works of the day." A private academy opened the next year with the purpose of offering a richer curriculum and better instruction than was available at the town's grammar school. For those whose schooldays were over, a Debating Club began meeting to examine the pros and cons of various issues and initiatives. "Would the establishment of a Bank in this town be beneficial to the community?" The members considered this question at their first recorded session in November 1822, as a newly chartered Middlesex Bank was trying to raise enough capital to launch. These voluntary associations strove to foster a modern intellectual outlook: curious about the world, eager for the latest knowledge, critical of tradition, and hopeful of progress. Arguably, these were the mental habits essential to republican government and economic growth.

Not everyone agreed. A "Middlesex Rustic" objected to the arrogance of learned gentlemen presuming to lecture "worthy yeomen" on how to farm. Such "pompous agricultural declamations" constituted "a palpable indignity," as "destitute . . . of the principles of farming as a Hottentot of civilization." Others saw no reason for the households of farmers, mechanics, and laborers to alter their way of life. Why chase after the fashionable goods in growing profusion at local stores? On the Sabbath the meetinghouse was already filled with too many women bedecked in the popular taste, making "an ocean of ribbons and plumes." Obliged to pay the bill for such unnecessary expenses, the mechanic should remember that his was "a life of care," requiring unceasing "prudence and economy . . . If a mechanic would thrive, he must rise with the lark, go to bed with the whip-poor-will and eat the bread of carefulness." Consumerism was a threat to his well-being. In competing agendas for the economy lay fundamental disagreements about how to live.[12]

IN THE EARLY 1820S CONCORDIANS WERE LIVING IN THE TWILIGHT OF THE Revolution. Most of the local heroes who had turned out on April 19, 1775, to confront the king's troops at the North Bridge had gone to their rest in the town's burial grounds or departed in quest of land and opportunity on New England's frontiers and in the expanding West. But veterans of the War of Independence still guided the republic. James Monroe, the last of the Revolutionary fathers, sat in the White House; Continental Army officer John Brooks, a veteran of Lexington and Concord, Bunker Hill, and Saratoga, was in his eighth and final term as governor of Massachusetts in 1823. The eighteenth century was well represented in Concord's seats of power. Reverend Doctor Ezra Ripley was celebrating his forty-fifth anniversary in the pulpit of the established Congregationalist church, his salary funded by the taxpayers. His secular counterpart, the physician Abiel Heywood, had served as selectman and town clerk since 1796. The two clerks, graduates of Harvard College, ministered to the townspeople in a distinctive style. Both continued to wear the knee breeches and high stockings of the colonial era well after every other man in town had discarded them for pantaloons. Then in 1822, when he was sixty-two, Squire Heywood astonished his neighbors by abruptly changing his life and his dress. In one burst of enthusiasm, he got married and put on pants. His new appearance was saved for the wedding day. In preparation, he nervously consulted a neighbor. How do you put these newfangled trousers on? The quick-witted advisor drolly replied that "he believed that people generally drew them on over their heads." The elderly groom presumably learned by trial and error.[13]

The townspeople professed inordinate pride in their Revolutionary heritage and never lost an opportunity to assert Concord's priority in the War of Independence. How could they forget? In their midst were thirty "surviving patriots" from the town's famous day, rehearsing their "stories and traditions" in the taverns and stores to admiring audiences of young boys. So familiar was the presence of this aging band that the town did little to commemorate their glorious moment in the nation's history. The Nineteenth of April came and went year after year without ceremony. Independence Day was the focus of patriotic celebration, and even that anniversary was observed intermittently. An 1822 effort to mark the "national Jubilee" never materialized, prompting Asa Biglow, editor of the *Middlesex Observer*, to rebuke his readers. "Shall we suffer it to pass unaccompanied by demonstrations of . . . joy?" Dare we "expose ourselves to the reproach of undervaluing this precious legacy of our forefathers?" The chastened townspeople got the message and honored July 4, 1823, with appropriate exercises, including a public dinner "under an awning near the field, rendered memorable by the events of the 19th of April, 1775." But no monument stood on the sacred ground to distinguish the "scenes of British aggression and American resistance." The North Bridge itself was gone. It had been pulled down in 1793, its planks recycled for a new crossing a few hundred yards downriver.[14]

While Concord took the past for granted, the town could not shed its hold. Even in 1823, local politicians were still carrying on the fights that had gripped the republic ever since Thomas Jefferson ousted John Adams from the presidency. Over the two decades of competition between Federalists and Democratic-Republicans, the voters of Concord usually sided with the latter, though by narrow margins. By the early 1820s, most of the country had grown weary of the conflict, but not Massachusetts. In 1823 Federalists reignited partisan passions by nominating the aristocratic Harrison Gray Otis to succeed the retiring Brooks as governor. Despite the ongoing movement to set aside old divisions, no one in the opposite camp was willing to forgive Otis's hardline support for the Hartford Convention of 1815, which had sought to mobilize New England against the War of 1812. Republicans challenged him with another Continental Army veteran, William Eustis. The contest was conducted under a new constitutional provision extending suffrage in all Massachusetts elections to male taxpayers without regard to race. Any man, age twenty-one and older, qualified if he had resided in the state for at least a year and the town where he wished to vote for at least six months. So polarized were the voters that the editor of the local paper feared to take a stand. "Think you that we are so reckless of consequences as to lift our feeble voice in support of any man or measure when it cannot be done without peril to our list" of subscribers? Turnout in Concord soared by nearly half over the year before, from 170 to 250; roughly 70 percent of eligible voters cast ballots, as high as at the peak of the partisan struggle over "Mr. Madison's War." (John Thoreau arrived too late to qualify.) When the votes were counted, the Republican won handily, with Concord in the victor's column by a margin of 60 to 40 percent.[15]

The eligible voters were not the only residents to be excited by the contest. Every spring the boys of Concord waited impatiently for the first Monday of April, when Election Day brought a school holiday. While the adult males were exercising the democratic right of suffrage, the youth organized a masculine competition of their own. Taking up their shotguns, they declared open season on birds. Anything with wings was a fair target, even if it hadn't hatched from its shell. Points were assigned to every sort, with the fine discrimination of *Peterson's Guide*: "The crow was considered the highest, afterward the hawk and down to the smallest; the eggs were counted lowest." Dividing into two teams, the boys raced into the woods on their mission of avian doom. At an appointed time, they reassembled, displaying their "ill-gotten trophies" in numerous bloody heaps. The victors proved their prowess as future hunters and farmers. Crows damaged crops; ducks and pheasants supplied food. In pursuit of such fowl, the hunt was practical preparation for life on the farm and in the woods. But killing hawks or destroying eggs exceeded any useful purpose, except to express an adolescent urge to absolute power. On Election Day, winning candidates eliminated rivals and captured office, relying upon ballots, rather than bullets, to accomplish their will. In emulation of the adult world they would someday join, the schoolboys employed the only weapons at hand—deadly shotguns—and enacted their own exercises of power. Combining camaraderie, competition, and cruelty, the day's events were a dress rehearsal for adulthood in the male republic of violence.[16]

The murderous ritual no longer went unquestioned. Following the vote for governor, a little debate erupted in the *Middlesex Observer* about the practice. A writer styling himself "Humanitas" condemned the wanton killing of "innocent and harmless birds." What kind of person could look on such conduct with indifference? One reader was not ashamed to admit the pleasure he enjoyed in "taking a partridge on the wing." The sport of hunting, he insisted, encouraged "cheerfulness, health and soundness of nerve," in sharp contrast to the "sickly sensibility" that "Humanitas" had evidently absorbed from "some boarding school Miss." In this war of words, the newspaper's editor, Asa Biglow, urged an end to the annual bird hunt on both practical and moral grounds. The reckless destruction of avian life, he argued, was no good for farming. It eliminated the natural predators of the insects and vermin that damaged crops. It led to disastrous accidents, as children raced through the woods with firearms and "in very many instances filled the hearts of parents with the deepest anguish." Worst of all, the competition blunted the "finer feelings of our nature." If a child could exult over his bloody pile, heedless of the "last agonies" of his victims, would he not grow up "indifferent" to the needs of others and learn to set aside those "sympathies and affections" that are the "cement of society"?[17]

A new cultural outlook was on the rise. It took aim at a wide variety of targets, rooted in customs inherited from previous generations. Its enemies were inefficiency, ignorance, and inhumanity. Its immediate campaigns would push for better schools, broader diffusion of knowledge, more productive farms, and kinder treatment of the dependent and the poor. It would eventually inspire a crusade against slavery. But the prospects of such progress depended on who led not only the government but also society at large.

In the wake of the election of 1823, the *Middlesex Observer* discerned no "era of good feelings" in the Bay State. "There now exist two parties in Massachusetts without the prospect of an amalgamation of feelings or union in sentiments." Yet just a month later, the people of Concord celebrated the Fourth of July "by a union of all parties." The event promised to unite the inhabitants in common citizenship and patriotism and thereby "draw more closely those cords of love and brotherly affection which bind together the whole human family." At the public dinner near the battlefield, that hope was affirmed in two of the toasts. One expressed civic pride: "The plains of Lexington and Concord: Here commenced that drama, which in its bloody course, brought forth the purest and most exalted characters." The second marked the progress of the times: "America in 1776, and America in 1823: No imagination of the heart could then have conceived her present glory and prosperity."[18]

Nor could anyone have foreseen the age of improvement that was about to unfold. But the choices to be made by such men as John Thoreau and his wife Cynthia Dunbar would give rise to a new social order and cultural climate in the years to come. In that formative milieu, their literary son would grow up, and the radical outlook of Transcendentalism, voiced by Boston transplant Ralph Waldo Emerson, would find a home.

A Day of Good Feelings

John Thoreau brought his family back to Concord at a propitious time. The fiftieth anniversary of the American Revolution was approaching, and from their new home in the center of town, the pencil maker's family was well situated to join in the festivities. The planning began early in 1824, when President Monroe invited the aging Marquis de Lafayette, the comrade-in-arms and "adopted son" of George Washington, to return to the United States as "the nation's guest" and receive the thanks of a grateful people. The next year, as the French aristocrat made a triumphal progress throughout the republic, John Quincy Adams, Monroe's successor in the White House, ushered in the celebrations. "The year of jubilee since the first formation of our Union [the First Continental Congress] has just elapsed," Adams announced at his inauguration; "that of the declaration of our independence is at hand."

Concord was quick to partake in the commemorative fervor. On the Nineteenth of April 1824, for the first time since 1776, the townspeople observed the "illustrious" day with a military parade and drill, a public dinner, and a visit to the battlefield; the following September they held an elaborate reception in honor of the visiting Lafayette. The climax of these ceremonies was the jubilee of the Concord Fight. "We cherish with gratitude the recollection of those patriotic actions by which our independence was declared and achieved," the townspeople resolved, "and deem it our duty specially to commemorate by a public celebration . . . the fiftieth anniversary of Concord Battle, in which the enemies of freedom were first met and forcibly repulsed by brave Americans." Held on a "warm and pleasant" day, attended by hundreds from Middlesex County and Boston, the commemoration was a gala of national patriotism and local pride.[1]

Civic rituals can serve more than one purpose, and so it was with the affair in Concord. Designed to pay homage to the selfless souls who had answered the call of duty a half-century before, the remembrances were also exercises in self-promotion, asserting the town's precedence in the annals of the American republic and showcasing the local elite. Here brave Patriots first fired upon the king's troops; here the American Revolution had its start. The claims proved controversial, particularly in nearby Lexington, where the first American blood was shed on that fateful morning in April 1775. But the townspeople were unwilling to share credit. On the long-held conviction that Concord was the birthplace of the Revolution, they constructed a civic identity, through which the citizens could overcome differences of age, politics, religion, and class and cherish a common bond. Or so they hoped. At age seven, Henry Thoreau witnessed both Lafayette's reception and the fiftieth-anniversary celebration. A dozen years later, on the eve of his graduation from Harvard College, he boasted of his local origin in an autobiographical essay for the yearbook. "To whatever quarter of the world I may wander, I shall deem it my good fortune that I hail from Concord North Bridge."[2]

IT WAS NO EASY FEAT TO ASSEMBLE CONCORD'S CITIZENS UNDER ONE PATRI-otic roof. For a quarter-century, the townsmen had been divided politically be-tween rival parties. As elsewhere in the early American republic, they took sides as Federalists or Republicans in an ongoing contest for power. The dispute originated early in the administration of George Washington, as leaders of the new nation clashed over the economic program of Treasury secretary Alexan-der Hamilton, which resembled the policies of the mother country from which the United States had only recently broken free. In the late 1790s, the divisions intensified and spread to the people at large, as a result of the French Revolu-tion and the worldwide upheaval it unleashed. Split over sympathies with the warring powers, Britain and France, Americans debated foreign policy with an ideological fervor that led neighbors with opposing opinions to see one an-other as enemies in unholy alliance with foreign despots. The conflict peaked in intensity during the years of embargo and war (1807–15)—the tumultuous era that doomed John Thoreau's initial entry into trade—with Republicans and Federalists trading charges of betraying liberty and jeopardizing national independence. No wonder, then, that the competing parties in Concord and beyond could seldom sit down together and celebrate the Fourth of July. Partisans opted for separate commemorations when they marked the day at all.[3]

The fierce rivalry between the parties brought Concord's voters to the polls in unprecedented numbers. Although voting was restricted to property holders, most adult males qualified (except for laborers and paupers), and—spurred by county conventions, local rallies and speeches, and appeals in the press—they exercised the right of suffrage with growing enthusiasm. At the height of the partisan conflict, 72 percent of eligible men turned out, more than in the state as a whole.[4] Such commitment turned virtually every election for federal, state, and county office from 1800 to 1816 into a close contest. Republicans won more often than not, typically by narrow margins, but in the wake of Jefferson's embargo and Mr. Madison's war, which generated Federalist tides in the Bay State, Concord floated between the parties. In 1802 the poll for governor was a dead tie until the Federalists dragged a man from his sickbed and captured the election. A dozen years later the town abandoned the effort to elect a representative to the state legislature, after no candidate, on two successive ballots, could command an absolute majority. This narrow division over two decades was unusual in Massachusetts, where most towns went reliably for one side or the other, and it set Concord apart from its neighbors in Middlesex County, a Republican bastion. In the intensity of its party division, Concord was as conflicted a community as could be found anywhere in the Bay State.[5]

But the partisanship was ambivalent. Even as the townsmen mobilized for victory at the polls, they had reservations about their conduct. To the men who won independence and created the republic, political parties were unwelcome. Ideally, government should be conducted under the helm of enlightened gentlemen cooperating for the common good. That was impossible whenever "factions" entered the scene to pursue their own selfish interests. Nobody envisioned such associations as useful means of informing and motivating voters, conducting elections, and carrying out the popular will. Both Federalists and Republicans yearned for harmony and consensus, and they blamed opponents for stirring up discontent and disorder for personal gain. Time and again they reminded the citizens of the biblical injunction: a "house divided against itself shall not stand" (Matthew 12:25). Were everyone to heed that counsel and disavow "party spirit," Massachusetts would enjoy liberty and prosperity under what Concord's minister, Ezra Ripley, upheld as a "free, elective government; a government of laws, and not of men; a government guided by definite constitutions, deliberately formed, and watched by ten thousand penetrating eyes."[6]

Parson Ripley longed to speak for such a unified community. But in an age of bitter political conflict, he often fell short. Born in 1751, the descendant of English Puritans who had crossed the Atlantic in the Great Migration of the 1630s, Ripley grew up on hardscrabble farms in northeastern Connecticut and on the central Massachusetts frontier, one of nineteen children in a household noted more for faith than for wealth. (An astonishing seventeen survived to adulthood.) With a precocious piety and "a strong desire for learning," the youth escaped the farm for Harvard College and the "gospel ministry," thanks to a charity scholarship. His senior year was spent in Concord, where the college had found a haven in 1775–1776 while American troops used the Cambridge campus as a base for military operations against the British in Boston. Two years later, after Concord's fiery patriot minister William Emerson died in service as an army chaplain, Ripley returned to the town and assumed his predecessor's pulpit, married his widow, and moved into his manse overlooking the North Bridge. (He would thereby become Ralph Waldo Emerson's step-grandfather.) There he stayed put for the next sixty-three years, preaching a clerical version of republicanism meant to unify the community and inspire Christian faith.[7]

That mission worked for Ripley's first two decades as head of the religious establishment. The Revolution, as he saw it, was no radical break with the past. The United States had simply taken over from New England as God's chosen people, in sacred covenant to accept "the divine word and ordinances" and "profess godliness" before the world. Freed from the British yoke, Concordians would continue their ancestors' ways. This complacent scenario was shattered by the reverberations of the Old World uprisings in the New. Ripley feared the spread of French radicalism into his parish. "The great object of the enemy," he told the congregation, "is to destroy religion and morals among the people. This done, they have confidence, and with reason, that civil government must fall." With reverence for Providence gone, what would bind the community together and enforce order? "Disrespect to the authorities over us and disunion among ourselves," he warned, "are at the bottom of our political troubles and danger."[8]

In the late 1790s, as the United States engaged in a naval "quasi-war" with France, and then again in 1813, with the onset of hostilities with Great Britain, the Concord minister took to the ramparts in defense of the New England way.

Suspending his "regular preaching" of Christ, he laid out his entire social philosophy in twenty-one sermons on "the social virtues and moral duties." His central theme, indeed his only theme, was duty in every sphere of life. There were the duties that made for community: candor, charity, friendship, peaceableness, "civility and condescension," public spirit. And there were the duties that ensured order: reverence for authority, obedience to law, subordination to superiors. Some duties, like charity, cut across the social ranks; others varied with one's station. Ripley invoked "the duty of parents to children" in one sermon, "the duty of children to parents" in the next. He moved from "the duty of parents to restrain their children from vice" to "the duty of children to honor their parents." "The duty of servants" was matched by "the duty of masters," that of "subjects" by that of "magistrates and rulers." Always there was "the duty of gratitude to God." Through the several pairs of sermons, all integrated to advance a single, unified theme, Ripley gave rhetorical expression to his worldview. Like the linked units in his series, society constituted a great chain of interdependent parts, organized by mutual duties and privileges and sustained by common interests and affections.[9]

The "ambassador for Christ" did not shy away from outright political engagement. His antipartisanship was unmistakably partisan. He preached the Federalist message of "liberty with order," and he readily associated himself with that party, even as his congregation was split down the middle. In the summer of 1812, several months after Congress declared war against Great Britain for violating American rights on the high seas, the Concord minister welcomed to his meetinghouse a Middlesex County convention of "the Friends of Independence, Peace, and Union" and petitioned "the Throne of Grace" to bless the antiwar gathering, which urged the defeat of the Republican administration in the upcoming November election. Ripley was on the winning side in Concord, but his partisan stance would long be remembered and held against him.[10]

Two years later, as the war dragged on, with British forces occupying eastern Maine (then a part of the Bay State) and threatening the Massachusetts coast, the parson turned his annual Thanksgiving sermon into a political screed. Taking in his words were his Emerson grandsons, including eleven-year-old Ralph, who spent the fall and winter of 1814–1815 at the manse, safe from the threat of enemy warships to Boston. It was customary on this occasion for the pastor to assay the condition of his flock and thank the Lord for their good fortune. But so distracted and disordered were the American people in 1814, so faithless to divine commandments, that Ripley was at a loss for blessings to count. Taking his text from the Book of Ezra, he likened Americans to the Israelites of the Old Testament, who had strayed from their covenant with God, engaged in "abominations" with strangers, and been punished less than they deserved. Had not the citizens of the United States done the same? Had they not "indulged partialities for other nations of a political and moral nature, which are both sinful and injurious"? Such biases had wreaked havoc on national life. Their "tendency" was "to darken counsel, alienate the affection of fellow citizens, excite a party spirit, promote factions, weaken authority, convulse the states and endanger the freedom of government and the just liberties of the people."[11]

Ostensibly evenhanded, the parson's strictures were actually directed at the followers of Jefferson and Madison. Why was xenophilia distorting U.S. foreign policy? Ripley pinned the blame on immigrants from Europe and Great Britain, especially from Ireland. The newcomers, streaming into the new republic in search of economic opportunity and political liberty, were critical to Republican victories at the polls. Many of these "foreigners" were radicals in exile for revolutionary activities abroad, and they were now propagating their dangerous ideas in the American press. As political writers and newspaper editors, these "fomenters of sedition [and] leaders of insurrections" exercised an undue influence over public opinion. Owing to them—and to the many American merchants who had been tainted by stays overseas—"our politics have been confused, our morals corrupted, our national faith ruined, and our religious principles weakened." Ripley took pains to disavow hostility to immigration altogether; it was "the glory" of America to be "an asylum for the oppressed of all nations." But "for want of judgment or principle," he complained, the country was admitting the wrong sort of people—"rogues, renegadoes . . . and those who have merited the halter or the dungeon." By failing to distinguish between "the precious and the vile," America was being taken over by godless men aiming "only to enrich and aggrandize themselves." Under this onslaught, "the free, religious, young and inexperienced" republic was at risk of losing its identity as a special people singled out by God for a unique mission.

Ripley was not simply a nativist, though his fear of foreigners would resound across the centuries. His early version of American exceptionalism was meant to preserve Concord and New England from alien influences. Excessive importation of foreign goods, ideas, and people threatened a way of life reaching back to the Puritans. "The piety, morality, and simple manners of our fathers have been contaminated, if not lost. We are become like the nations about us, to whom we were unlike, and which likeness from such affinity is our sin, and is now a heavy curse upon us." Let the people repent, change their ways, and come together in unison to obey God's laws. Only then would Concord be back on track. The ideal town was homogeneous, its members true to the past, bound together in mutual dependence, and of one mind.[12]

The Federalist parson spoke for roughly half the town, including nearly all of the local elite, but his desire for consensus cut across party lines. Republicans too worried about unpatriotic factions that were at odds with the common good. When war was declared, they rallied in support, raising volunteers for the army and awarding enlistment bonuses from the town treasury.[13] To their mind, the opposition in Massachusetts was doing everything possible to obstruct the military effort. The suspicions were not without merit. For even as Ripley preached against "partialities" to foreign powers, a convention of New England states was set to meet in Hartford, Connecticut, with the aims of opposing the Madison administration's conduct of the war and demanding redress of the region's grievances. Secession loomed as a threat to the American union. In late October 1814, Middlesex County Republicans assembled in Concord to denounce Massachusetts's participation in the upcoming convention. Watch out for "the insidious intrigues and conspiracies of domestic traitors, who boldly triumph in the prospect of their country's ruin," they warned. The schemers were bent on replacing the federal compact, "the great pillar of our Independence," with a government "more congenial to the views and feelings of a powerful and restless aristocracy." As it turned out, the Hartford Convention eschewed extreme measures. But the conclave did share Ezra Ripley's distrust of immigrants and advocate the exclusion of naturalized citizens from public office. To Republicans, the proponents of such measures were "a relentless and powerful faction" ambitious to rule unchecked over a virtuous people. The cause of republicanism—America's mission to the world—required their defeat.[14]

The party divisions continued well after the shooting had stopped. On April 13, 1815, both sides in Concord gathered in the meetinghouse to join in the "national thanksgiving" proclaimed by President Madison to mark the end of hostilities. Amid the general relief, Parson Ripley could not refrain from disparaging the late conflict as "a distressing, corrupting, and unprofitable war." The next Fourth of July, only 150 "ladies and gentlemen" turned out to celebrate American independence at the Concord battle site; though not "a word of party politics" was permitted, the event, featuring yet another speech by Ripley, evidently had little appeal for those still upset by Federalist reluctance to defend American independence.[15]

Old enmities died hard. The Federalists waned as a national political force after James Monroe won overwhelming election to the presidency in 1816, but in the Bay State the parties continued to vie for power. In the summer of 1817 the new president visited Boston—but not Concord—during a goodwill tour of the nation, and he was so warmly greeted by "eminent men of all political parties" that a Federalist editor dubbed the reception "an era of good feelings." Even so, in state and national elections the rivalry went on, though with diminishing intensity. In Concord, turnout for congressional elections plummeted. Where 218 voters cast ballots in 1814, only 116 did so in 1818, and four years later a mere 50 citizens bothered to come out and endorse Republican Timothy Fuller for a fourth term over token opposition. The annual elections for statewide offices (governor, lieutenant governor, and state senate) remained far more competitive and engaging. Concord went for the Federalists in close contests between 1817 and 1820 and then turned into a Republican stronghold. When Federalists nominated Harrison Gray Otis, the spearhead of the Hartford Convention, for governor in 1823, the deep-seated passions revived and enjoyed a last hurrah. By the mid-1820s the party faithful were waging battles over symbolic issues with little relevance to the present.[16]

When state and national issues were not involved, Concord's leaders found it easy to cooperate, doing everything possible to insulate local government from the party wars. The principal officials of the town—a board of three selectmen, one of whom doubled as town clerk—were elected year after year without opposition. The typical selectman in the 1820s served five or six terms, usually consecutively, before stepping down; the town clerk, Dr. Abiel Heywood, was a fixture in office from 1796 on and, having caught up with the times by switching from small clothes to trousers, had no plans to retire. The same families that had governed the colonial community still ruled, with greater dominance than ever; over 90 percent of selectmen descended from Puritan founders of the town: Barretts, Heywoods, Hubbards, and Woods, names identified with the local landscape. Every year the town met on the same schedule, doing its business chiefly in spring (March to May) and late fall (November) in four or five sessions; in between, the selectmen gathered once a week in local taverns to monitor affairs over dinner and drinks. The basic obligations of town government—seeing to roads and bridges, supporting schools and the poor, paying the minister's salary, collecting taxes—were handled without partisan rancor. For thirty years, from 1796 to 1825, town meeting voted by acclamation, rarely tallying the results. In a wider world of political conflict, the town meeting was a haven of consensus.[17]

When Concordians were offered the chance to change, they largely stuck with familiar ways. In mid-November 1820, Massachusetts convened a constitutional convention in Boston to reconsider the frame of government devised for the Commonwealth in 1780 by John Adams together with his cousin Samuel Adams and James Bowdoin. The first state in the new nation to choose a representative body to draft a constitution and submit it for popular ratification, Massachusetts was also the first to convene a convention to revise its plan of government. The Constitution of 1780 rested on the will of the people (actually, only the adult males), but it curtailed democracy by setting property qualifications for voting and officeholding, and it restricted freedom of worship by requiring the inhabitants of each town to support an official church and minister with local taxes, an arrangement known as the Congregationalist Standing Order. The citizenry was also enjoined to attend public worship on the Sabbath. These provisions, set forth in article three of the constitution, were designed to harness the religious legacy of the Puritan past to the needs of the new republic. What better way to instill a respect for law and love of morality than through religious establishments?

Many people resented the demand to fund churches whose doctrines or mode of worship went against their beliefs. In principle, dissenters, such as Baptists and Quakers, could apply their tax money to whatever religious institutions they preferred, but local authorities often denied that option. Nonbelievers had no choice but to pay for preaching they disdained or ignored. These requirements gave rise to mounting dissatisfactions, which conservatives succeeded in blocking until the separation of Maine from the Bay State made it necessary to adjust the fundamental law of the state. Here lay an opportunity to enhance liberty and equality and extend popular power.[18]

Concord sent two delegates to play important parts in the conclave. The lawyers Samuel Hoar and John Keyes, one Federalist, the other Republican, belonged to a new generation of leaders assuming power in the postwar political climate. In 1820 they were still early in an ascent that would carry them to prominence well beyond the town; the rivalry between them would charge local affairs for the next two decades. Neither was native to Concord. The older of the two, Hoar, born in 1778, came from Lincoln, the adjacent town to the southeast, which had broken off from Concord in 1754. Keyes, born in 1787, had his origins in nearby Westford, seven miles northwest. Both grew up in farming families of old Puritan stock that had taken seriously the biblical injunction to be fruitful and multiply. Hoar, the eldest son and namesake of his father, had nine siblings; Keyes had eight, of whom he was the firstborn in his father's second marriage. Both were sons of the Revolution whose fathers had turned out for the skirmish at the North Bridge and gone on to serve in several campaigns of the war.

The similarities of background ended there. Whereas Hoar built on a notable heritage of education and leadership, Keyes enjoyed few inherited advantages and was obliged to sacrifice for his schooling. Harvard College had a long association with the Hoar family, one of whom had served as its president in the 1670s. Hoar's father, Samuel, "a farmer of great respectability" and political eminence, intended his firstborn son for higher learning; while working on the family farm, the youth prepared for college with unusual thoroughness, then entered Harvard (Class of 1802) at the relatively late age of twenty. So greatly did he excel at his studies that four years after graduating, Hoar was offered the professorship of mathematics at his alma mater, an opportunity he declined in favor of a career in law.

The bookish Keyes, by contrast, escaped a life of farming only because of "a severe accident incurred by upsetting a cart in his fifteenth year"—a convenient mishap that rendered him unsuitable for manual labor. Though the father was "hardly able to afford it," Keyes attended the local academy, a daily three-mile walk each way. At seventeen, he rode on horseback through the woods to Dartmouth College in Hanover, New Hampshire, selling his mount on arrival to help pay expenses. By dint of severe economy and schoolteaching during winter vacations, Keyes got by, and whatever the hardships, they did not deter him from graduating as salutatorian in the Class of 1809 and going on to forge a career in law. Rising in the world with few advantages, he knew firsthand the value of self-discipline and hard work.[19]

College education in the eighteenth century was designed to produce gentlemen as well as scholars. Hoar and Keyes absorbed those lessons in distinctive Yankee style. Tall and slender at six feet three inches, austere and formal in appearance, Hoar (nicknamed "Cato" by his classmates for his Roman severity) had the dignified way of a minister, marked by "great courtesy" and grace, especially to women and children. Keyes, somewhat above average height, was "rather spare and erect," dressing neatly but "without display" and carrying himself in a "courteous and gentlemanly" manner. Having polished their social skills—Hoar through two years as a tutor in the sophisticated household of the prominent Virginia planter John Tayloe—the two moved easily in polite circles and made advantageous marriages. Hoar waited till age thirty-four to wed Sarah Sherman, the twenty-nine-year-old daughter of Connecticut's most distinguished Revolutionary leader, Roger Sherman, a signer of the Declaration of Independence, the Articles of Confederation, and the Constitution. Keyes at twenty-nine found a wife in Ann Stow Shepard, stepdaughter of the late sheriff of Middlesex County; descended from a royal official in Boston who decamped with British troops for Halifax, Nova Scotia, in 1776, she was nonetheless the child of a Patriot home, which had grown rich from wartime privateering. Through marriage, Keyes secured advantages that Hoar had possessed from birth.[20]

The two attorneys practiced their profession in contrasting ways. Hoar arrived in Concord first, around 1807, renting a room for his law office in the yellow store, where John Thoreau was just setting up his short-lived business. Hoar's trenchant mind and winning way with juries soon attracted a growing clientele. In the courtroom he would start with a simple principle and proceed earnestly and systematically to expound its logic "with almost mathematical precision" to a conclusion he would cap with a rural saying or lively story. His impact became legendary; one admirer swore that "if he should kill a man, he would have no fear of being hung, if he could get *Esq. Hoar* to plead his case." In one criminal trial where he presented the defense, the story goes, the jury reached a deadlock.

> *The presiding judge asked whether their difficulty was with the law or the evidence. The foreman replied that it was not in either, but in the plea; that the law and the evidence seemed to show that the man was guilty, but that Squire Hoar had said in his plea that he believed his client was innocent, and as Squire Hoar always told the truth, most of the jury did not see how they were to get over it.*

Through such triumphs, Hoar soon dominated the county bar. During the 1820s, by one count, he served as counsel in a third of the Middlesex cases before the state supreme court. He was sometime associate and occasional opponent of the legal giants of Massachusetts, Daniel Webster and Rufus Choate. And like them, he became the advocate of vested interests and great corporations, particularly the powerful cotton manufacturers, whose cause he advanced by developing into "the highest authority in Massachusetts upon the law pertaining to mills and water power."[21]

Focused on his legal practice, Hoar bided his time before seeking public office. Though his father was an ardent Republican who had represented Middlesex County in the state senate during the War of 1812, he opted for the Federalist politics of his in-laws. His wife's uncle, Roger Minot Sherman, was a leading figure in the Hartford Convention, for which Hoar was said to be an apologist—a charge that haunted his political career. Within Concord, the erudite lawyer commanded respect for his fairness, and he was regularly chosen to moderate town meetings. By the mid-1820s he monopolized the post as thoroughly as he dominated the courts. Occasionally someone else presided, perhaps because Hoar was unavailable. The alternative was often John Keyes.[22]

Few attorneys could rival Hoar's record; Keyes never tried. The Westford native could not afford to devote years to legal study. Obliged to pay his own way, he financed his professional training by teaching school. That brought him to Concord around 1812 and to the notice of the town's leading lawyer, John L. Tuttle. Under his wing, the young man not only qualified for the bar but also learned how to use the law for political advancement. Tuttle, a Harvard graduate (Class of 1796), took up the cause of "the people" against the aristocracy and rose to leadership of the local Republicans; he captured the post of county treasurer, added a seat in the state senate, and secured the patronage plum of U.S. postmaster in Concord. Upon his mentor's death in 1813 while in military service, Keyes followed a similar course. He became a Republican activist, took over the treasurer's job, and acquired the post office. His legal practice grew in turn. Although he earned "a good rank" in the profession, he was respected mainly for "his zeal and faithfulness to clients," rather than for expert knowledge. Through diligence at the treasurer's office in the courthouse, he seized on the numerous business opportunities that came his way and built a "lucrative and respectable practice." In the mid-1820s, he held some $7,000 in personal and real property. Ranking twelfth on the list of polls and estates, he was not yet in Hoar's bracket. The older, more accomplished attorney was the town's third-richest man, with an assessment of $11,637—eight times the average taxpayer's worth. The well-educated Federalist and Republican representatives were securely in the economic as well as political elite.[23]

The two delegates thus went down to the constitutional convention in Boston with divergent outlooks and experiences. Though newcomers to such assemblies, each made an impact on the proceedings. Hoar took the more active part. In his view, the 1780 constitution was "a nearly perfect system of government," and he allied himself with Daniel Webster, Josiah Quincy, and other pillars of the Boston Federalist elite to uphold the "old Fabrick." Preserving the Standing Order of Congregationalist churches was his top priority. The faithful Federalist was a longtime member of Ripley's church, and as he carried on the campaign to retain the church establishment, Hoar invoked the same moral vision of social life preached in Concord every Sabbath. Speaking "only as a citizen and not as a divine," he insisted on the indispensability of religion to law and order. Individuals were not free agents, apart from society. Just the opposite: people derived their social and moral being through public institutions. "Much has been said about inalienable rights," but Hoar demanded to know "if this meant that society could not do what was most for its good? If a man could not give up any rights for his greatest benefit?" The corporate community took priority over the autonomous individual. "If we could trust to anything in history, it was to this, that our prosperity, and what distinguishes Massachusetts, is owing to our provision for the support of religion and morality." Without article three, how would social order be maintained? The only alternative he saw was "to support it by religion and morality, or by a standing army."[24]

The other delegate from Concord had nothing on the record to say about this subject. At thirty-three one of the youngest members of the convention, Keyes "sat and listened and learned rather than acted." But one issue engaged his attention. The Republican lawyer was determined to expand the right to vote. In 1811, under his party's control, the Massachusetts legislature had enacted a version of taxpayer suffrage for local elections. Keyes now proposed to go further. A month into the proceedings, he introduced a resolution "to amend the constitution, [so] as to provide that no pecuniary qualification shall be required for electors of any officers under this government." With this revision, voting for the state senate would no longer be restricted to men possessing estates worth $200—a longtime Republican goal. Such a change, Keyes explained, would be purifying. The current system was "pregnant with much evil," because by inducing citizens to lie about their property holdings and selectmen to manipulate voter lists for partisan advantage, it "had often been the cause of moral perjury."

Two days later, while Keyes was out of the hall, the delegates took up and endorsed the measure, by a vote of 185 to 157, without any debate. No sooner had the convention voted than the members had second thoughts. Could paupers qualify under the amendment? Yes indeed, explained one opponent of the change; Keyes's resolution "introduced a new principle into the constitution. It was universal suffrage." The floodgates of criticism now opened in a move for reconsideration. One of the leading voices in that effort was that of Samuel Hoar.

Undeterred by loyalty to his fellow Concordian, Hoar assailed the plan to end all property qualifications for voting. In his characteristic mode, the Federalist lawyer announced the fundamental principle at stake: universal suffrage would "sap the foundations of society." Then he set forth his reasoning. Voting constituted not an individual right but a social privilege, awarded under designated conditions for particular ends. For Hoar, the test of any law was its "moral tendency," that is, its effect on the character of the citizens. Voting requirements should be set high enough to encourage "industry and economy." Consider the lessons of experience. Young men were frequently motivated to work hard and acquire property, in order to obtain the franchise; hence the qualification must be sufficient for the purpose. Even a taxpayer suffrage was too liberal. Then Hoar added a second ground of opposition: universal suffrage was an "anti-republican principle." The citizen must possess the means of moral and social independence. If the propertyless could vote, they would be tempted to sell their support to the highest bidder. Were not the poor "destitute of character"?

Hoar carried his defense of classical republicanism too far. The convention was not a jury but a gathering of politicians, sensitive to public opinion. Having returned to the hall and heard the debate, Keyes read the delegates' shifting mood and added new language to his amendment: "paupers and persons under guardianship" would be denied the vote. With that exception, the proposal effectively incorporated the 1811 suffrage law into the constitution, expanding the electorate for offices at every level of government, from town and county to state and nation, and putting Massachusetts in tune with the democratic trend of the times. Taxpayer suffrage for white men was already the norm in neighboring Connecticut and New Hampshire, as well as in the Middle Atlantic states, parts of the South, and on the Western frontier. Why not the Bay State? The con-vention eventually endorsed Keyes's revised proposal, without racial restrictions, and submitted it for ratification by the current voters.[25]

Even on seemingly minor items, Hoar was attached to tradition. He op-posed a plan to open the Massachusetts "political year" with a January session of the General Court, instead of the customary one in May. The change was advocated for the sake of economy, but that was not reason enough. "A session in May, was an institution of an antiquity of nearly two centuries," Boston's Josiah Quincy instructed the delegates; it should not be discarded lightly. Hoar agreed and voted with the conservative minority against the move. Such change did not trouble Keyes. But on the major social issue before the convention—whether to retain the taxpayer-supported religious establishment—the Repub-lican joined with his Federalist colleague and opposed any change in article three. Apart from extending the franchise, Keyes was no force for expanding democracy or toleration. "He had great reverence for law, both human and divine," his son later recalled, "and but little patience with those who attacked or ridiculed institutions founded in either."[26]

Delegates Hoar and Keyes read public opinion in Concord accurately—or at least the minority of men who cared enough to vote on the constitutional changes submitted by the convention to the citizenry. Back in 1780, when con-stitution making was new, close to half of Concord's adult males (47 percent) showed up at town meeting and voted overwhelmingly to ratify the new frame of government. Four decades later the exercise aroused little excitement. Only 128 men—a mere 29 percent of eligible males—cast ballots in the April 1821 referen-dum on the proposed amendments. They displayed a limited desire for change. The town welcomed the extension of voting privileges to all male taxpayers (pau-pers and wards excepted) and grudgingly approved the right of militia members, even those under twenty-one, to vote for company officers. Popular participation in elections claimed broad support, perhaps because it had long been the norm. Holding on to tradition, the townsmen refused to countenance any liberalization of the Standing Order; 63 percent turned down a catchall amendment that ended compulsory attendance at public worship and allowed greater choice in the use of taxes for supporting ministers. They also rejected measures to adapt government to the needs of an expanding state. The convention proposed to reduce the size of an unwieldy House of Representatives. Concord, fearful of losing representation, said no. Another amendment addressed the dilemma of communities whose populations grew too large for efficient town meetings. Was city government the solution? Not in Concord's opinion. Nor was the alteration of the political year, endorsed by the vast majority of convention delegates, acceptable. On these and other issues, the fluctuating majority in town meeting, ranging from sixty-five to eighty men, proved more conservative than voters statewide. The inhabitants—or rather, the small cohort active in politics—were reluctant to leave behind the corporate ideal of the unified, homogeneous town.[27]

The constitutional convention was a turning point in Keyes's political career. Having expressed his townsmen's will on every issue, he won their gratitude. In May 1821 he was elected representative to the legislature, a post he held for two years before moving up to the senate—promoted by an electorate he had helped to expand. Hoar fared less well at the polls. In 1822 and 1823 he was a losing Federalist candidate for the senate; even in his hometown, he came in next to last. The Republican politician was, in the mid-1820s, Concord's representative man and—as postmaster, county treasurer, state senator, moderator of town meetings, justice of the peace, and judge advocate in the county militia—its most ubiquitous official.[28]

A NEW ERA OF POLITICAL UNITY OPENED IN CONCORD JUST IN TIME FOR THE national jubilee. Following their defeat in the spring elections of 1824, Federalists gave up and "amalgamated" with the Republicans. This fresh spirit of harmony animated that April's inaugural ceremony marking the anniversary of the Concord Fight. Assembling where "once the embattled farmers stood," the townspeople listened to an "instructive address" by Doctor Ripley rehearsing "with great minuteness the scene and circumstances" of the glorious day. A "high tone of national feeling . . . pervaded" the gathering. On this patriotic day in 1824, there were neither Federalists nor Republicans but only Americans.[29]

Four months later Concord welcomed a famous visitor, the Marquis de Lafayette. In late August 1824 the "nation's guest" kicked off his American tour in the Boston area, where he attended the annual commencement of Harvard College, from which he had received an honorary degree back in 1784.[30]

Following that event, the Frenchman received visitors in Boston, and a delegation from Concord came calling. It included an heir of Maj. John Buttrick, bearing the musket that supposedly killed the first British regular at the North

Bridge. The group achieved its purpose; six days later the General traveled out to Lexington and Concord.

It was an honor for Concord to host the hero of the Revolution, but the last-minute scramble to put together a proper reception had unforeseen consequences. With no time for a formal town meeting to plan the event, the local notables took it upon themselves to organize a welcome "calculated to make a fine impression on the mind" of the valiant soldier. Every aspect of the day was orchestrated, though surprisingly, the Frenchman never was taken to view the celebrated battlefield. When Lafayette's party neared the town line, it was greeted by a cavalcade of forty gentlemen, headed by John Keyes—"the first and only time" his son ever saw the dignified lawyer on horseback. The procession set out for the village with an escort of five military companies on parade, drums beating and fifes playing, and their arrival was heralded by a crescendo of sounds: the blast of cannons, a twenty-four-gun salute, the ringing of the village bell, the cheers of the waiting crowd.[31] In front of the meetinghouse stood an open tent, decorated with flowers and evergreens, inside which the ladies of the town had set an elaborate table with refreshments for the distinguished guest— the first time, the local newspaper boasted, that women "have come forward to share the honor of preparing a welcome for the companion of Washington."

Standing before the bower, the selectmen offered greetings before turning the ceremony over to Samuel Hoar, who was given the closing speech to match Keyes's performance at the day's start. "You, Sir, now behold *the spot on which the first forcible resistance* was made to a system of measures calculated to deprive the whole people of these States of the privileges of freemen." This was the conventional wisdom in Concord, which Lafayette graciously received. Then the guests, the officials, the ladies, and the committee retired into the bower for the repast. Afterward a select group of Revolutionary veterans was invited to meet the Frenchman and shake his hand. Everybody else had to glimpse the festivities from behind the ropes that cordoned off the tent and were patrolled by soldiers in arms.

A chorus of discontent rose from the dense crowd. In their eagerness to see Lafayette, many inhabitants pressed against the barriers, the guards pushed back, and tempers flared. Some people complained aloud at the favoritism: "although they were not as well dressed nor as educated in society . . . as those within . . . their fathers had served the country, some had fought with Lafayette in the battles of the Revolution, and they were as grateful for his services." Luckily, the town escaped a riot, and Lafayette's party did not notice the disturbance.

An angry backlash soon swirled through town. The Lafayette affair exposed the personal jealousies and social resentments that periodically erupted against would-be "aristocrats," Federalist or Republican. "Well do I remember the insulting treatment I received," one inhabitant recalled ten years later, "when, among others, I attempted to look at Lafayette; we had to stand back then at the point of the bayonet, whilst the great folks sat and drank at our expense." The outrage boiled over after the organizers of the reception, oblivious to their neighbors' hurt feelings, asked the town meeting to cover their costs, which amounted to eighty dollars for the ample refreshments of wine, coffee and tea, and fancy cakes. A broadside addressed "To the Inhabitants of Concord" and emblazoned with an emblem of "EQUALITY" derided the self-serving conduct of the arrangements committee. "The persons who were for excluding their neighbors from . . . the ceremonies, were now not so very anxious to exclude the same neighbors from paying the bill." The statement clearly expressed the common feeling. The town meeting "dismissed" the request for reimbursement. The privileged could party at their own expense.[32]

The Lafayette reception also soured relations between Concord and its neighbor Lexington. When Samuel Hoar proclaimed Concord "the first site of *forcible resistance*," he was saying nothing new. But Lexingtonians deemed the remark an insult to their forefathers' courage and their town's honor. How dare Concord claim credit for "having raised the first standard of an armed opposition to the unjust and tyrannical measures of the mother country!" That glory belonged rightly to Lexington, whose militiamen had not tamely suffered the unprovoked assault of the king's troops but returned fire in self-defense. On their village green, *not* at the North Bridge, "the revolutionary war commenced." The competing claims were fought out in the press. Concord mocked little Lexington's bid to convert a "massacre" into a "battle." Lexington answered with jibes at Concord's "caprice," which reflected the vanity of the larger, richer town.[33]

As these controversies were stirring, commemorative events began unexpectedly to affect political fortunes. In the summer of 1824, the incumbent Republican congressman from Middlesex, Timothy Fuller, announced he was stepping down after four terms. The Honorable Senator Keyes seized the chance to continue his political ascent. County Republicans gathered in convention and unanimously endorsed his choice. With no Federalist opposition in sight, Keyes had every reason to anticipate victory in November. As it happened, this scenario was just beginning to unfold when the "nation's guest" paid his visit to Concord. Keyes undoubtedly counted on using his prominent part on that occasion to advance his candidacy. Unhappily, the reception was a political fiasco. With angry inhabitants attacking "aristocrats" who liked to "*display their own personal consequence to advantage*," no smart politician would brag of his role in the debacle. To make matters worse, a young lawyer who had recently settled in Concord devoted himself to Keyes's defeat. Refusing to "submit to the domination of the old Concord clique," Elisha Fuller, a twenty-seven-year-old Harvard graduate, had limited influence. But as the youngest brother of outgoing congressman Timothy Fuller, he could employ the family name and connections to considerable effect.[34]

Keyes's enemies had a candidate of their own: Edward Everett, the Harvard professor of Greek literature whose eloquent speech welcoming Lafayette at the 1824 commencement propelled him to admiring public notice. With Daniel Webster working behind the scenes on his behalf, a convention of citizens claiming no partisan affiliations nominated the distinguished scholar for Congress. In this competition, Keyes's conventional assets—efficiency, experience, familiarity with the district—suffered by comparison with Everett's stature as "an elevated American statesman" and an eminent "literary character."

Within eastern Massachusetts, Everett was building his reputation as secretary of the Bunker Hill Monument Association (BHMA), founded in 1823 by leading figures in the Boston elite. Just as the race for Congress was heating up, the association went public with its campaign for a colossal monument on the famous hill in Charlestown, where on June 17, 1775, two months after the Concord Fight, Yankee soldiers stood up to the king's troops and once again rebuffed British military power in Massachusetts. Through his activities as the group's secretary, Everett's name was identified with its patriotic enterprise. There was no way Keyes could match these advantages. Everett, a scion of Boston Federalism who charted a nonpartisan course, triumphed easily, with 58 percent of the vote; even in Concord the result was a dead tie (90–90). After a decade of uninterrupted political advancement, Keyes had hit a bump in the road.[35]

Plans for the Charlestown monument intersected with Concord's preparations for the jubilee. In mid-October 1824, as part of its fundraising campaign, the BHMA made an unexpected proposal. To win support from Concord, which had tried and failed twice before to secure state aid for its own monument, the group pledged to contribute to a memorial in the town where "the first conflict was had." The offer was pending as Concord set about organizing its own half-century celebration.[36]

Could the town hold an impressive commemoration without triggering another outburst of social tensions? Mindful of the botched Lafayette affair, local leaders began preparations early in 1825 with a determination to be inclusive and transparent. The event was authorized by a unanimous town meeting, in response to a petition of ten citizens, including John Thoreau. "We cherish with gratitude the recollection of those patriotic actions by which our independance [sic] was declared and achieved," the town voted, "and deem it our special duty" to hold a "public celebration" of the fiftieth anniversary of "Concord Battle, in which the enemies of freedom were first met and forcibly repulsed by brave Americans."[37]

This would be a community celebration and not a top-down affair. Two committees were named by the town: one to organize the commemoration, the other to select the monument site. The committee of arrangements consisted of fifteen members, who were born in the 1780s and 1790s; these were the sons of the Revolution, charged with organizing a display of gratitude to the fathers. To this end, they honored the aged survivors of the Concord Fight, sixty altogether, with "badges of distinction" and included them, at town expense, in the public dinner following the ceremonies. The committee acknowledged the military services of Concord's neighbors, too, and appointed representatives of those towns—even Lexington—as honorary "vice presidents" of the day. Finally, the committee sought out the new congressman, the eloquent Edward Everett, to deliver the official address—a decision that won almost universal approval, except for one "Old Farmer" from Keyes's native town of Westford, who grumbled that "he must be a great man to command the suffrages, as a free offering of voters, with whom he could boast of but little or no personal acquaintance."[38]

The monument committee, by contrast, was a thirty-man council of elders. Made up of magistrates and veterans of the Revolution, the body included the leading men of both political parties who had guided the town over the last half-century and who still controlled much of its wealth. The typical committeeman was sixty-eight years old; born in 1757, he had been a youth of eighteen on April 19, 1775, and had fought for independence. Who could have been more appropriate to decide on a monument than the actual participants in the Concord Fight and their compatriots in the ensuing war? So large a committee was potentially unwieldy. To ensure that it operated efficiently, the town turned to the thirty-eight-year-old John Keyes, who was still respected despite his loss to Everett, to guide the deliberations.

The project was controversial from the start. For one thing, it was tied to the grand plan of the BMHA, whose organizers were not simply disinterested Patriots. Men of considerable wealth and influence in Boston, they had an ideological agenda, born of Federalist politics. Through public commemoration of such landmark events as Forefathers' Day, when the Pilgrims supposedly stepped onto Plymouth Rock, and of Lexington, Concord, and Bunker Hill, they hoped to gather a deferential populace behind a conservative elite in shared "patriotic feelings" on "sacred ground." That would hardly have pleased the antiaristocratic Republicans on the Concord committee. To some critics, the huge sums the association planned to raise for "a useless pile of stones" would be far better spent on "hospitals and charitable institutions" and on the poor "suffering for want of assistance." Worse, the association's promise of $500 to aid the Concord monument came with two strings attached: first, the structure had to be a smaller-scale version of the obelisk planned to ornament Bunker Hill—a provincial chip off the metropolitan block; second, it had to be located in the village center. The style requirement raised no objection, but the site was a very different matter. It provoked "much conversation" at town meeting, resulting in the unusual thirty-man committee to resolve the dispute.[39]

In principle, there was a good case for the village site. On April 19, 1775, the British had occupied the center all morning, ransacked the area in search of military supplies, seized and destroyed armaments and provisions, and made a bonfire of the liberty pole, sparks from which spread to the courthouse and stirred alarm that the British were burning the town down, thus prompting the Minutemen on the high ground above the river to launch their fateful march toward town "to defend their homes, or die in the attempt." The resulting skirmish at the North Bridge took but two to three minutes, and in its wake, the Minutemen spent far more time and blood harassing the enemy's flight. Measured by casualties, prisoners of war, and property losses, the village could rightly claim recognition for its sacrifices. With a monument at the center, it would surely gain compensation from the many visitors to its stores, shops, taverns, and hotel—not to mention the aid from the Bunker Hill Monument Association.

The alternative site, the battlefield, had a fatal flaw: the Great North Bridge no longer "arched the flood," having been taken down some thirty years earlier. Built back in 1660, it had been the victim of a nasty political struggle that set one section of town against another. At the center of that conflict was Parson Ripley, whose manse looked out over the battleground. The minister took a proprietary pride in the scene. It was said that whenever an out-of-town dignitary came calling, he would summon the hired boy. "Jeremiah or Nicodemus, the cow-boy, would deferentially approach and inquire, 'Into what pasture shall I turn the cow to-night, Sir?' And the old gentleman would audibly reply: 'Into the battle-field, Nicodemus, into the battle-field!'" As Ripley saw it, the Revolution had begun in his own backyard.

Actually, the property on the opposite side of the river belonged to the Brown and Buttrick families, who were none too pleased by the scheme to remove the ancient bridge and reroute the road. The minister strongly advocated the change; in his view, it would provide direct passage into town for residents of the distant northeast, enabling them to get to Sunday meeting more easily.

The proposal caused "much altercation" over a year and a half, from 1791 to 1793, followed by appeals to the county court. In the end, Ripley and his supporters got their way. More than that, the minister engaged in a private land-taking of his own. He quietly appropriated what remained of the old road to the North Bridge and incorporated it into his back pasture. That unauthorized act of private enclosure eliminated public access to the site where the British soldiers fell. Some aggrieved residents never forgot nor forgave what one called "the Second Great North Bridge Battle." Owing to Ripley's act of "vandalism," no convenient route led to the battle site in 1825. This was no place to put a monument.[40]

Reaching a decision was a protracted and painful process. On March 2, 1825, Edward Everett came out to Concord for an informal conversation about the jubilee. It was five days before town meeting was to vote on whether to commemorate the anniversary. Would he give the official address? Without him, the noted orator was told, "there would be no celebration." To Everett's distress, nothing was said about a monument. "I found more difficulty at Concord than I expected; nor is the thing yet settled." The situation was not much clearer when the monument committee was appointed on April 4. The thirty

members huddled together for several days, then reported their recommendation. On April 8, the town opted for a monument in the village, located "at or
near the Guide post and town pumps," where the liberty pole had been moved.
The vote was a decisive one, but for the first time since 1796, a division was
recorded in the town book: 65 in favor, 25 against. Three days later the opposition obtained one concession: the cost of laying the cornerstone would be paid
by private subscription, not by taxes.[41]

On April 19, 1825, the townspeople put all these differences behind them.
The village awakened to the sounds of a thirteen-gun salute and the ringing
of the meetinghouse bell. It went to bed to the music of fiddles playing at the
"splendid ball" in the Middlesex Hotel. The centerpieces of the festival were
the laying of the monument cornerstone in the town square and the public
address by Everett in the meetinghouse.

The first event was conducted in a ceremony that had become a familiar sight
in the new nation. With the creation of a republic based upon popular consent
came the need for appropriate buildings in which to carry on the essential work
of self-government. From the 1780s on, state capitals and county seats all over
the nation experienced a construction boom, as a host of civic structures rose
on the landscape, such as Concord's new courthouse on the common, erected
in 1794. Such buildings were meant to be temples of the republic, sustaining
liberty and law, and for this purpose they required an impressive dedication. The
Freemasons, the fraternity of gentlemen, merchants, and artisans, answered the
need. Claiming to possess the secrets of architecture dating back millennia to
King Solomon's Temple, one of the wonders of the ancient world, Masons os-
tentatiously devoted their knowledge to the service of virtue and enlightenment.
Laying cornerstones—"christening" a structure at its birth—was their specialty,
performed with a ritual combining the pleasures of pageantry with the rules of
reason. But the Masonic method was not the only way to dedicate a building, so
Concord's town meeting told the committee of arrangements to decide whether
to go with "Masonic or civil order" in the ceremony. With Keyes serving in yet
another leading role as junior warden—the third-ranking official—of the Massachusetts Grand Lodge of Freemasons, and with Ripley and other magistrates
longtime members of the local Corinthian Lodge, the decision was an easy call.

Lined up on the common, dressed in fraternal garb of lambskin aprons and
white gloves, and bearing the lodge's jewels and swords, the Masons made a
stately procession to the site, where the foundation was hurriedly made ready to

support the projected monument. For centuries, Catholic bishops had conse-crated churches by placing the sacred relics of saints within altar stones. In the new civil religion of America, a variety of secular objects was more appropriate for deposit: Continental currency and U.S. coins; the federal and Massachusetts constitutions; a list of town officers; newspapers of the day; and the "Order of Proceedings" printed up for the event (and the source for this account)—a "time capsule" of items attesting both to the rational origins of the republic and to the aspiration of participants to transmit evidence of their experiment in self-government to the future. With these lay an inscribed silver plate:

> *Here on the 19th of April, 1775 began the war of that*
> *Revolution which gave Independence to America.*
> *Our fathers will it, and their will be done;*
> *The world now admires what their valor won.*

Sealing the stone, the Masonic officers took out the tools of their craft—square, level, and plumb—and gauged the foundation before declaring it sound. The fledgling structure was then anointed in corn, wine, and oil, traditional symbols of "plenty, joy, and peace." Tapping the stone with a mallet three times, the grand master of the lodge signaled the ceremony's end. Together the breth-ren clapped their hands, lifted their arms to the sky, and raised their voices in song and prayer. Perhaps for a moment, the troubled beginnings of the Con-cord monument were forgotten in the solemnity of the occasion.[42]

From the middle of the town square, the official parade assembled at noon for the march to the meetinghouse, five minutes away. In a tangible display of the hierarchy that gave legitimate order to the republic, participants took their places according to assigned rank: the various officers of the day (from the mar-shal and orator to the committee of arrangements) and "invited strangers," suc-ceeded by high public officials (judges, senators, and councilors); clergy right in the middle, the symbolic center of this republic in epitome; then rows of public men, in civil and military roles—Masonic brethren, sixty veterans of the Concord Fight and other Revolutionary soldiers, representatives and justices of the peace, military officers—and finally the "citizens at large," in whose name the others ruled. Led by a military escort and twelve-piece band, the parade set off with the "citizens at large" ahead of the rows of magistrates extending back to the officers of the day, and made its way past the millpond and along the

Lexington road. At the meetinghouse, painted a fashionable yellow, with clock, bell tower, and ninety-foot spire, the assemblage turned and reversed order, entering with the magistrates at the head and the common citizens bringing up the rear, a proper emblem of social order. The ladies of the town, having arrived early, looked down on the scene from reserved seats in the gallery above. Here was the Federalist ideal on view: liberty and order proceeding in harmony to the meetinghouse. In the spirit of the day, perhaps it pleased Republicans as well.[43]

It was time for music and prayer. The exercises at the meetinghouse opened with an anthem in praise of "laws, religion, and *LIBERTY*," then a "fervent prayer" offered up by Parson Ripley from his accustomed pulpit eight feet above the meetinghouse floor, followed by an original hymn for the occasion, sung by the parish choir to the tune of "Old Hundred," sacred in New England since the Puritans. Together, words, music, and setting conveyed the point: a covenanted people was gathered to remember with gratitude the blessings they had received.[44]

At exactly 1:40 p.m., as Edward Everett rose to speak, expectations ran high. "The popularity and eloquence of the orator cannot fail to give the house a crowded audience," the *Concord Gazette and Middlesex Yeoman* had predicted. The congressman, known for his elegant manner and musical voice, did not disappoint, holding forth for two hours to a rapt audience without ever glancing at his text. He opened with a sweeping survey of the American nation, whose growth and grandeur "almost exceed the grasp of the human mind." Only seventy years ago, he recalled, the Connecticut River Valley of Massachusetts was the scene of vicious war, with "the savages of the wilderness" ravaging homes and shattering families; now it supports "a numerous, increasing, refined, enterprising population." Having survived and overcome the Native threats, America, as seen from Massachusetts, has become a strong and prosperous state. What accounted for the "unexampled rapidity of our national growth"? Everett sought the answer in the "agency of individual events and men" that had won for America "a new and original political life, a fresh and hopeful national existence."[45]

The American Revolution—"that great, that astonishing incident in human affairs"—had taken place on a universal stage. It had a long preparation, starting with colonization, that formed "the political national education of America." Even so, everything depended on the actions of a single day. Had "our forefathers" submitted to British force, "then the Revolution had been at an end, or rather never had been begun." Everett then turned to the immediate circumstances behind the

Nineteenth of April. One imperial act of tyranny followed another in rapid succession down to 1775. The British forces of General Gage planned their attack, under the watchful eyes of the "vigilant sons of liberty." By the time the regulars set out for the countryside, the provincial express-riders Paul Revere and William Dawes were spreading the alarm. Now "the momentous hour arrives, as big with consequences to man, as any that ever struck in history."

That moment posed something of a problem for the speaker. How to handle the competing claims of Lexington and Concord? Everett devised an ingenious solution. His narrative took its time at the Lexington green, devoting fifteen minutes to the "furious" British assault and the brave stand of the "self-devoted heroes" who, in Everett's telling, did not disperse until they had returned the enemy's fire. Only after this tribute did the advance to Concord resume. Everett was now on page thirty-one, more than an hour into the discourse; so he refrained from rehearsing the incidents in Concord so familiar to his audience. Pleading "the reasonable limits of a public discourse," he dispatched this part of the story, including the clash at the North Bridge, in four pages.

Actually, it was not the constraints of time but the expansive theme that dictated the orator's choice. Everett wanted to move on to the longest section of his speech, which recounted the rallying of "the indignant yeomanry" in response to the Concord alarm: "unprepared husbandmen, without concert, discipline, or leaders," drove the "picked men" of the British Army back to Boston in defeat. In this view, the glory of the day belonged not to Lexington or Concord alone or in twain, but to the citizen-soldiers who poured forth from every Middlesex village and farm. When visitors ask where "the first battle of that great and glorious contest was fought," Everett benignly suggested, we can "with honest complacency" direct them "to the plains of Lexington and Concord." With even deeper truth, we can point to the character of the people, "as citizens and as freemen, starting from their beds at night, from their firesides and from their fields, to take their own cause into their own hands . . . It was one of those great days, one of those elemental occasions in the world's affairs, when the people rise, and act for themselves."

Everett's address sounded a surprisingly democratic chord to balance the elitist notes of the day. In contrast to the tiered ranks of magistrates and citizens in procession to the meetinghouse, the scene on the Nineteenth of April '75, as the speaker painted it, offered a "spectacle" of "the people struggling for their rights, moving . . . in spontaneous action, man for man, and heart for heart." These were freemen, sprung from the soil of Middlesex County, inspired by liberty, capable of thinking and acting for themselves. With that soaring tribute to the yeomanry of Middlesex County—the very constituency that had recently elected him to Congress—Everett employed a new Romantic rhetoric to make the Revolution live again in the hearts and minds of the people.[46]

Then it was off to the public dinner, where five hundred men gathered to feast and celebrate the day. On such festive occasions, the high point was the toasts, through which Americans often made political statements, intended not just for the immediate audience but also for distant readers of the public prints. In keeping with this custom, Concord's committee of arrangements composed thirteen toasts, to be delivered by invited dignitaries and supplemented by volunteers. Once more, as in the parade, officialdom was at the helm, followed by ordinary citizens. The prepared toasts gave convivial voice to the themes of the day. They saluted the great event—"the first scene in the progress of universal emancipation"—and its principal actors. Lexington got its due, as did the Concord Fight and Bunker Hill, "co-heirs of the early glories of the revolution; the patrimony is equal to all claims."

Local notables claimed their due as toastmasters. Overshadowed by Everett on this occasion that might have been his, Keyes was reduced to a platitude: "While the page of history and the marble records and the Orator paints in glowing colours the noble deeds of our fathers, the hearts of their children should, nay, will feel the debt of gratitude they owe them." Ripley, the once-strident Federalist always calling for unity, hoped "the monument this day founded" would serve as "a powerful check to the spirit of faction and tyranny." That desire was repeated in a toast to "Party Spirit—Dying of old age—may it have an easy death and rest from its labors." And New England's covenant with the Lord was reaffirmed in a toast from a young divinity student who was just beginning to compose sermons. Twenty-two-year-old Ralph Waldo Emerson, recently enrolled in Harvard Divinity School, was back in Concord, staying with Grandfather Ripley, for the gala. He rose with a reverent offering: "The little bush that marks the spot where Capt. Davis fell—'Tis the burning bush where God spake for his people."[47]

On April 19, 1825, Concord replaced partisanship with patriotism and fully entered into the spirit of "good feelings." Just a month before, John Quincy Adams had assumed the presidency, hopeful that the "baneful weed of party strife" had been uprooted for good. Early the following month Levi Lincoln, a onetime

Republican, was elected governor of Massachusetts on a nonpartisan basis and without opposition, while Middlesex County voters sent both Keyes and Hoar to the state senate on a "Union" ticket. The trend culminated in May, when Concord chose Nathan Brooks for a third term as representative in a "unanimous" vote.

The Concord jubilee at once symbolized and advanced the new era. At long last the townsmen could set aside old conflicts, balance authority with democracy, and rally behind a virtuous, nonpartisan elite. If only for a day, the unity that had eluded the Revolutionary fathers was achieved by the sons.[48]

ONE MORNING IN THE WINTER OF 1825–1826, THE VILLAGERS AWAKENED TO discover an unusual sight. Atop the cornerstone of the monument, still unbuilt, was a fantastic formation: a heap of tar barrels and boards, twenty feet high, raised in mockery of the site. "This monument is erected here," explained an accompanying inscription, "to commemorate the battle which took place at the North Bridge." Evidently the minority had not reconciled to its defeat. The satirical display did not last long. The following night "some of the rowdy element," aggressively defending village honor, set the sham monument on fire. It was a "great illumination," one witness recalled years later. Unluckily for the assailants, their action proved self-defeating. The cornerstone was ruined. No shaft ever rose above the base.[49]

And in succeeding years the crack in the foundation of community widened.

Community and Conscience

John Thoreau came back to Concord to make pencils. Cynthia Thoreau was returning to her spiritual home. A dozen years earlier, age twenty-four and single in the summer of 1811, she had joined Ezra Ripley's church. A resident of Concord since 1798, the young woman was on the verge of matrimony and motherhood. Perhaps for that reason, she decided it was time to declare her faith and enter the Christian communion. She was at once taking responsibility for her spiritual well-being and looking out for the family she was soon to form.[1]

In a society whose custom and law dictated that women be subordinate to men, where a woman's social standing derived from her father or husband and where wives had no independent relation to the state, this was one decision Cynthia Dunbar could make for herself. As an inhabitant of Concord, she belonged to its single parish and attended Sabbath services, in conformity with the law and community expectations. Joining the church entailed a deeper commitment. In the Puritan tradition, it represented a voluntary choice to unite with fellow believers and uphold the cause of Christ.[2] And so, in accord with the rules of the First Church, she sought out Parson Ripley for a private interview, displayed sincerity in her religious beliefs and in her dedication to a moral life, and won approval. The church members readily went along and welcomed her into the fold. The community she entered was largely female, with women comprising close to three-quarters of the body, among them her sisters-in-law-to-be, the "Misses Thoreau," Elizabeth, Jane, Maria, and Mary. All of these members, men and women alike, covenanted with one another to uphold the faith, carry on its rituals, and support one another in their daily walk.[3]

That support must have been sorely lacking in the years following her marriage to John Thoreau and their displacement from Concord. After struggling for a living in Boston and Chelmsford while raising four young children, Cynthia was undoubtedly relieved to be back in the place where she could count on obtaining moral and religious support. Her hopes would soon be shattered. By the mid-1820s, the First Parish provided no sanctuary from worldly turmoil. The congregation was rocked by dissent, and Ripley struggled to hold it together. As it turned out, among his most forceful opponents were the Thoreau women and even, for a time, Cynthia Dunbar Thoreau herself. Theirs was a bid for a truer faith and a richer spiritual experience. Little did they anticipate that the conflict thus set in motion would prove to be a crucible for Transcendentalism.

EZRA RIPLEY WAS INTENT ON CREATING AN INCLUSIVE CHURCH, POTENTIALLY embracing every soul in town. On assuming the pulpit in 1778, he took over a congregation that had been fractured for a generation and had only recently been reconciled. The conflict had its origins in the Great Awakening of the 1740s, when religious revivals had shattered the peace of communities throughout the colonies and undercut clerical authority and social order. Concord's minister, Daniel Bliss, had been an enthusiast of this movement, and he alienated many with his emotional sermons and disregard for established forms. Opponents withdrew from communion to worship on their own, and not all came back after Bliss's death in 1764. Under his successor, William Emerson, the division was revived in a prolonged fight over a controversial applicant for church membership. The squabbling ended only with the Revolutionary crisis. By the time Ripley came up for consideration as the next pastor, the church had renewed its covenant, and harmony prevailed. A lone skeptic objected to the appointment, on the ground that the short and slender candidate looked so "feeble" that he would not last for long. A half-century later the aged minister enjoyed telling this tale.[4]

The new parson was well suited to his task. Early on he showed a disposition for the pulpit. At five, he liked to imitate ministers and preach to his playmates. On one occasion little Ezra was discovered "in a flood of tears, and inconsolable," because his brother had told an untruth. Recalling biblical warnings against the sin of lying, the boy was in agony over the "divine displeasure" sure to await his sibling. At sixteen, he felt called to the cloth after lightning struck, quite literally, "in a terrible storm" and, as he put it, "licked up the spirit" of a man standing nearby. That traumatic moment was, for the country youth, a sign from Providence, singling him out for God's cause. He was soon on the road leading to Harvard and the "gospel ministry." His college years coincided with the outbreak of the Revolution. In the "unsettled state of the times," politics occupied students; academic discipline relaxed; and the fast crowd indulged in irreverent ideas and fashionable wit. But not "holy Ripley," as he was known to the Class of 1776. A mature student who had made enormous sacrifices for an education, he never skipped a class or missed daily prayers, and though he could tell a good story and enjoy a sociable evening, he shunned every "appearance of vulgarity or impurity."[5]

The minister's personal life signified the new harmony of the town. In November 1780, two years into his tenure, he married Phebe, daughter of one Concord minister, Daniel Bliss, and widow of another, William Emerson. At twenty-nine, Ripley was arriving late to the altar—the typical groom in that era was twenty-five—and the bride was ten years older, a struggling single mother with five growing children. The unconventional union astounded at least one member of the congregation. Not long before the wedding, a distraught mother called on Ripley for advice about her son, who planned to marry a woman two years his elder. This was, she lamented, "a highly improper act . . . as the man should always be older than the wife." She pressed the minister to approach the youth and show him the error of his ways. After hearing her out, Ripley inquired, with a sly wit, what she would think of a man's marrying a woman nearly eleven years older than himself. She "could not think it possible."

"It is not only possible," Ripley said, "but certain to happen within a short time."

"Who is it?"

"It is your minister."

The mother's response went unrecorded. Whatever the shock to her sensibilities, the marriage brought real advantages to the campaign to reintegrate the town. It linked Ripley to his immediate predecessors in an act of continuity that registered his deep reverence for the past. Genealogically as well as institutionally, he could legitimately claim the mantle of the church.[6]

Ripley presided over the community with boundless energy and a relentless will. "In this town," he once declared, "I am placed a watchman and a monitor." True to that trust, he plunged into the life of the parish with zeal, as if the character and conduct of every individual were his personal responsibility. For all his humility before God, Ripley was "an active, urgent, imperative man," as one admirer recalled, "always doing, as I supposed, just right; but doing just as he pleased." When duty called, there was no stopping the parson, who proved to be as headstrong as his horse Caesar, a beast "so willful and vicious that none but Dr. Ripley could control him. The violent creature trembled at the voice of his master." Few inhabitants escaped his scrutiny. "My people," he called them with proprietary pride. The minister participated in the vital events of their lives: he married the couples, baptized their babies, prayed at the funerals of young and old. He composed epitaphs for the gravestones and obituaries for the press. Year after year, he assiduously recorded the deaths of parishioners in a private register, gauging the causes in the medical and moral categories of the day—apoplexy, consumption, dysentery, fever, mortification, old age and "natural decay," suicide, intemperance, and excess of all sorts—and reporting the toll every November in his Thanksgiving sermon. He was sure to pay an annual call on every household, and he catechized the children twice a year at the district schoolhouses. "It was a great moment, when we stood up, for the first time [before the minister], at the call of our name," recalled one survivor of the inquisition. "Those who did not know their catechism, were made to feel that they must know it before the next parochial round." As they grew up, he counseled the young on the choice of a calling and penned countless letters of recommendation on their behalf. Like a modern college professor, he was forever endorsing applications to schools, for jobs, even for pardons from jail.[7]

In the course of his pastoral rounds, parishioners of every age and rank suffered Ripley's blunt honesty and constant determination to do good. One little boy miscalculated when he accompanied his mother on a visit to the parsonage. As the woman chatted with Madam Ripley, "the young rogue took advantage of [her] desire to have peace, in the minister's house at least, and played off his naughtiness." Not for long. The parson took matters into his own hands. He seized "the culprit, carried him away, and whipped him; causing much grief and indignation to the poor mother, and not a little fear . . . to the young rebel." ("The back of the body," he once said, "was made to whip.") So long as a person required it, Ripley volunteered his advice, however unasked for. At the funeral of one farmer, Ripley offered condolences to each of the mourners, until he approached the eldest son, a man notorious for "intemperance," who was about to inherit the estate:

Sir, I knew your great-grandfather. When I came to this town, your great-grandfather was a substantial farmer in this very place, a member of the church, and an excellent citizen. Your grandfather followed him, and was a virtuous man. Now your father is to be carried to his grave, full of labors and virtues. There is none of that large family left but you, and it rests with you to bear up the good name and usefulness of your ancestors. If you fail, Ichabod, the glory is departed. Let us pray.[8]

Ripley's interventions in his parishioners' lives, his charities and severities, were not just the product of a vital but meddlesome personality. They enacted an ideal of community that was tied to the distinctive role of the minister in the legal system of Massachusetts and the religious principles by which Ripley steered his course. Under the state constitution of 1780, the minister held office as a "public protestant teacher of piety, religion, and morality." In that position, he was charged with preaching the virtues necessary to orderly civic life; he was, in effect, a higher schoolmaster, supported by the taxpayers to provide instruction in God's commandments to men. (In 1816 the Concord minister became "Doctor Ripley" after the new theological seminary at Harvard awarded him an honorary degree in divinity.) At the same time, within the congregational system of church government, the minister carried out sacred duties as an "ambassador for Christ." Ordained over a particular gathered church, he exercised his powers within a strictly voluntary association, whose members looked to him for spiritual guidance, the administration of the sacraments, and the impartial conduct of internal business. As town minister, then, Ripley served two masters, the parish that paid his salary and the church that sustained his holy mission, though he clearly thought himself accountable only to the Lord.[9]

Ripley spent much of his time writing sermons in the manse. Christianity, as he interpreted it, constituted "a system of doctrines and morals, of articles of faith and practical duties." Twice every Sabbath—once in the morning, again in the afternoon—he ascended the high pulpit in the meetinghouse and expounded the scriptures, rehearsed the life, teachings, and sacrifice of Christ, and enjoined obedience to divine law. By the mid-1820s, he had composed and delivered some 2,500 sermons, written in little hand-sewn notebooks and numbered and dated carefully until in June 1812 he reached 1,500 and stopped counting. Following a model set by the Puritan clergy, he keyed each text to a passage from the Old or New Testament, explicated its meaning, and prescribed its lessons. On the annual thanksgiving day, he reviewed the blessings of the Lord; on the annual fast day, he indicted the sins of the people. The topics ranged from "the importance of religion in early life" to "aged people exhorted to practical goodness" and from "the covenant of grace explained" to "the faults of christians exposed and guarded against," to name but a few. Whatever the subject, one theme always came through: the moral duties of men. For Ripley, the mission of the minister was fundamentally ethical. To teach Christianity, as he did it, was to convey "all things requisite . . . to incline [people] to virtue, and qualify them for usefulness, to render them good members of society, and sincere worshipers of the true God."[10]

In the gospel according to Ripley, the fundamental value was community. "Who could live alone and independent?" he asked the congregation. "Who but some disgusted hermit or half crazy enthusiast will say to society, I have no need of thee; I am under no obligation to my fellow-men?" The good life consisted of living thickly among family and neighbors, subject to the support and supervision of common institutions. It could not be taken for granted. In Ripley's scheme, society did not arise out of spontaneous cooperation; nor did it follow natural laws of its own—a view to which his grandson Waldo would eventually take sharp exception. Maintaining community required active, continuous effort. The parson employed the language of politics to portray the task: "order and regularity" were essential to the "government" of every institution, especially the family. "We must regulate, govern, and command our children and household." Otherwise anarchy could result. "A community of people grown up without government, without the habits of subordination, could not subsist with any order, virtue, or happiness."[11]

The church that put Ripley at its head was Calvinist in belief and congregational in governance. It still held with its founding Puritan fathers that humanity was irredeemably corrupted by original sin, the consequence of Adam's fall, and hence alienated from God and doomed to "miseries in this life" and "the pains of hell forever." Yet through the sacrifice and intercession of Jesus Christ, the "eternal son of God," the Lord had chosen to spare some souls from his wrath and admit them into a "covenant of grace." No one deserved such selection; no one could do anything to bring it about. The only way to enter the company of saints was to experience the unmerited gift of saving grace, which could come at any moment and lay utterly beyond human control. Born again in "God's Spirit," the fortunate few repented their sins, received divine pardon, and inspired by love of Christ and "the Moral Law," set about "sanctifying" their lives in the pursuit of "righteousness." Who better, then, to compose the churches of New England? In Concord, as elsewhere, the Church of Christ was founded on the elect. It was an independent congregation, subject to no higher authority and ruled by those admitted into the fold. They formed the membership, chose the leaders, set the policies, admitted newcomers, and enjoyed the privileges of attending communion and baptizing their children. Everyone else in the parish stood on the outside looking in, paying taxes for the meetinghouse and minister and attending public worship, if not faithfully every Sabbath, then as it suited their convenience.[12]

Ripley was no fan of the Calvinist scheme of salvation. Though he had been raised on "the principles of Calvin," he claimed to have shed them as soon as "I became of age to think and act for myself." It was an easy decision: in his experience, Calvin's system of predestination and original sin was no more than a formal dogma, recited by rote but never explained nor urged. At his ordination, nobody even asked him about this creed, and he wisely kept his doubts to himself. He inclined to an alternative version of theology, known as Arminianism (for its resemblances to the thinking of a sixteenth-century Dutch cleric), which was staked out by such prominent critics of the mid-eighteenth century Awakening as Boston ministers Charles Chauncy and Jonathan Mayhew.

The Arminians recoiled from the anticlericalism and emotional "enthusiasm" of revivalists like Daniel Bliss, and over the second half of the eighteenth century, they coalesced into a network of like-minded ministers in Boston and environs, who eschewed sermons about original sin, predestination, and the urgent need to be born again through a soul-ravishing influx of divine grace. Instead, these liberal clergymen took a generous view of human nature. In their optimistic assessment, human beings had the capacity to do good as well as evil, and with God's help, faithful Christians could lead moral lives and gradually perfect their characters. Should holiness result in worldly success, that was no cause for concern. Far from rejecting the corruptions of this world—a familiar refrain of the Calvinist "New Lights"—the Arminians took satisfaction in the "riches, honours, and pleasures" of society. That message went over well with their comfortable congregations of merchants and ship captains, magistrates and professionals, and landed gentry. Ezra Ripley was drawn into their orbit, and so was his stepson, Rev. William Emerson, the father of the Transcendentalist.[13]

As Ripley interpreted the gospel, Jesus Christ was the "promised Messiah" for *all* humanity and not just for a righteous remnant. Thanks to His sacrifice on the cross, the way to salvation was open to every individual who sincerely repented of sin, experienced "a moral change of heart and life" through "faith in Christ," and displayed "charity and holiness" in daily life. As "the minister of reconciliation [of man] to God," Christ could no more forget a soul than Ezra Ripley could overlook a parishioner.[14]

Rather than rehearse objections to Calvinist dogma, Ripley preferred to ignore theology and concentrate on "practical preaching" of "the leading and essential doctrines of the Gospel." This was a short list of the requirements for salvation: belief in God, Christ, and revelation; adherence to the Ten Commandments and the Bible; and commitment to a "heavenly minded and holy" life. Why bother with anything else? Nobody expected him to address such matters, certainly not his ministerial colleagues, who in the late eighteenth century generously extended the hand of fellowship to their peers without ever inquiring into their doctrinal correctness. "Orthodoxy, at that time," he later remembered, "was so undefined, that it was not easy to say, whether the real creed of one agreed with that of another." Calvinists read and recommended their critics, and vice versa. A diversity of opinions coexisted among the Congregationalist clergy. Perhaps the greatest reason for Ripley to downplay controversial issues was the state of harmony in the Concord church. Why risk a unity that was so hard-won and so recently achieved?[15]

Despite this policy of studied silence, Ripley's opinions evolved over the years, and attentive listeners could not miss his drift away from Calvinism. Initially, he appeared sympathetic to the spiritual fervor that had flared in Concord under Daniel Bliss. Too young to have witnessed the Great Awakening, he was prepared in 1792 to accept the testimony of aged members of the congregation that the revivals had been true seasons of grace, "days of God's power upon men's hearts," when "many were made willing to receive and obey the Lord Jesus Christ for ever." Still, he worried that "the charges of enthusiasm and disorder alleged by some . . . were [not] wholly groundless." A decade later he expressed skepticism about instant conversions. Don't look for "any miraculous influence" nor "any irresistible compulsion on the mind or heart," he counseled. God employs "the rational use of suitable means"—Bible study, guides to piety, sermons, prayers, and rigorous self-scrutiny—and saves those who have labored long and hard to ready their hearts for the divine spirit to come in.[16]

This broad-minded outlook, dubbed "liberal" for its tolerance of diverse views and its openness to new ideas, as opposed to Calvinist insistence on strict orthodoxy, inspired fundamental changes in church governance. In the Puritan dispensation, local churches were assemblies of the elect, whose piety and holiness were evident to all. Admission to their company was no simple matter. Aspirants had to prove their spiritual and moral fitness. Had they truly felt saving grace? All applicants were required to give testimony of God's working in their souls. These "spiritual relations" put the candidates' private experiences on public view, to be judged for their authenticity; in principle, no aspect of an individual's life, outer or inner, was exempt from the prying eyes of neighbors. The demands did not stop there. Each would-be member had to assent to an official creed, set forth in a catechism drawn up in 1647 by a religious council in England (the Westminster Assembly of Divines) and endorsed by the Puritan fathers. A code of conduct was also imposed. Subscribers to the church covenant pledged to live together by God's law, in peace, equity, and Christian love, and to shun a host of sins, including ostentation in dress, false dealings in business, and disturbance of the peace through "slandering, back[bit]ing, and reproaching our Neighbor." To ensure such good behavior, the church extracted one final commitment: submission to its moral oversight and "discipline." Let a brother or sister stray from the path of virtue, and their fellow members would be ready to step in and right the course. No one in the covenant ever acted alone.[17]

With his zeal to bring every inhabitant within the church, Ezra Ripley eventually turned against these restrictive policies. A decade and a half into his ministry, he carried through a wholesale revision of the rules for baptizing children and admitting new members. "I am far from saying or thinking, 'the former times were better than these,'" he once opined. In this progressive spirit, he effected an end to a long-standing practice known as "owning the covenant." In the Puritan regime under founding minister Peter Bulkeley, the rite of baptism had been available only to the children of church members, who had subscribed to the covenant. This arrangement was acceptable so long as most people experienced conversion and joined the fellowship. But what to do when the rising generations failed to enter the fold? Rather than let the majority of children go unbaptized, the Concord church, like many others, had come up with a halfway measure. If parents were willing to come forward and "own the covenant"—that is, accept the creed, agree to church discipline, and promise to "train up" the young in Christian faith—their infants could be brought to the baptismal font. This policy had satisfied the townspeople for more than a century when Ripley intervened. "All children born in a christian land," he told the church, "ought to be baptized." This "privilege" was "their birthright," and it "ought not to depend on the good or bad conduct of their parents."

The push to open up baptism, the ritual introduction of children into the Christian community, became the entering wedge in Ripley's bid to alter the bases of church membership. In 1795, under the minister's deft leadership, the church undertook a comprehensive reform of the procedures it had inherited from the forefathers. These policies, it concluded, were neither warranted by the Bible nor beneficial to the community. Rather than draw a sharp line between saints and society, the church should invite all sincere believers to participate in its collective life. Every child now became eligible for baptism. No longer required to own the covenant, its parents needed only affirm faith in Christianity and promise a religious education for the offspring. That declaration carried a reward for the adults as well: invitation to the communion table. That ceremony, restricted by Puritans to the elect, carried a sacred aura, and many conscientious Christians, in Ripley's observation, felt "apprehensions of unpreparedness for that ordinance." To calm their worries, the church invited reluctant souls to be present at the sacrament but refrain from the commemorative feast. Gradually, it was hoped, the hesitant would shed their doubts and take their place.[18]

Access to church membership became easier as well. Where once the church had subjected candidates to a thorough review of their moral and spiritual fitness, it now refrained from such intrusive inspection. No longer were applicants required to give "spiritual relations" of their conversion experience. The church abandoned its claim to be a body of "visible saints." Demands for intellectual and moral conformity were relaxed as well. The Westminster catechism was deleted from the covenant; thereafter members were asked only to give broad assent to the Trinity and the gospel. Applicants were also freed from the long-standing requirement of making "public confession" of their sins, and although they were still subject to discipline for moral lapses, the church voted to replace the "fearful engagements" of the 1776 covenant with a general pledge to do right. From a lengthy contract, full of details, the covenant was transformed into a limited membership pledge.[19]

These root-and-branch changes in church policies derived from a universalist principle. If Christ had atoned for all humanity, then surely the Concord Church of Christ should draw every inhabitant within its embrace. To attain this goal, the minister redrew the boundaries between the individual and the group. Baptism became the right of every child, independent of the parents' status in the church. The creed sidestepped controversial issues and deferred to individual judgment. Each person's "spiritual relation" with God was sacred— and nobody else's concern. A new premium on privacy distinguished Ripley's church.[20]

For all the rhetoric of community, these reforms came at the cost of collective life. Throughout the colonial era, the full members of the church, all visible saints, had played a vital role in its corporate affairs, running admissions, enforcing discipline, mediating disputes, and at times fighting with the minister and among themselves. Under the new rules, they had little to do. Applicants for admission, like Cynthia Thoreau, were now interviewed in private by Ripley, and if he approved, they would be "propounded" for a vote. Church members were limited to tacit consent. The power of disciplining wayward members slipped away, too. Not a single infraction came before the church until 1816, and then it was handled by the minister and deacons behind closed doors. Enforcing morality became a confidential act. With little business to transact, the church met infrequently. A few times a year the brothers and sisters would convene after public worship and handle such chores as electing deacons, appointing delegates to councils and ordinations in other towns, and contributing money to the parson's favorite causes. The minister called the members together, and he kept the records of their occasional actions. Intentionally or not, by relaxing the rules to attract members, he enhanced his own power. With good reason, the Church of Christ in Concord came to be known as "Doctor Ripley's church."[21]

NO FAMILY WAS MORE ENGAGED THAN THE THOREAUS IN THE CHURCH. As soon as they settled into their new home at the west end of the common, newcomers Jean and Rebecca Thoreau were introduced into Ripley's village circle. The family attended public worship, hosted the parson for tea, and enlisted in his Federalist crusade against radicalism and "infidelity." The connection formed easily; Rebecca's sister and next-door neighbor Esther was married to Deacon John White. Following Jean Thoreau's death in March 1801, Ripley hastened to comfort the thirty-eight-year-old widow, left in charge of eight minor stepchildren (the oldest nineteen, the youngest four). "The care of heaven for widows and fatherless children is matter of great consolation and encouragement to them," he preached on the Sabbath immediately after Thoreau's passing. In the ensuing years, four of the Thoreau daughters entered the church under the liberalized rules. (Two others joined churches elsewhere.) They belonged to a large cohort of young, single women professing faith and sealing religious identities during the passage to adulthood. Submission to Christ must have been a source of strength, as they courted and prepared for lifelong subordination to husbands, or perhaps it furnished consolation, a sense of purpose, and an alternative community for those who never wed. Church membership also deepened family ties. When Cynthia Dunbar joined in 1811 on the verge of marriage, she became a "sister in Christ" with three of her soon-to-be sisters-in-law. Piety bonded the Thoreau women together.[22]

The widow Thoreau was particularly close to the pastor. Daughter of a deacon of the Congregationalist church in Charlestown, she displayed a precocious piety in childhood, preferring "sobriety to mirth" and "things virtuous to vanity and needless play." By her teenage years, she was absorbed in "religious conversation and reading" but hesitated to profess her faith for want of "clear evidence of regeneration." Hers was an agonizing uncertainty that plagued a good many conscientious souls; it was partly to eliminate such uncalled-for suffering that Ripley's church stopped asking would-be members for "spiritual relations." "Whether [believers] can tell you when or how they were converted," the parson explained, "is not material, so long as they now feel and manifest their concession to God." Rebecca was a case in point, imbued with the divine spirit before she even knew it, and so virtuous that she had no "wicked dispositions to overcome, no vicious practices to renounce." Eventually, at eighteen she gained the confidence to unite with the Charlestown church. Two decades later she arrived in Concord as the wife and then widow of Jean Thoreau, and she bore up under her trials with such "meekness, charity, and patient submission to the will of God" that Ripley was prompted to pen a tribute to her character after her death in 1814. She was "the best of mothers," raising the orphans as if they were her own. She enjoyed "easy circumstances," thanks to the substantial Thoreau estate, and was unstinting in charities. Hers was a model Christian home, with daily prayers and Bible-reading. Amid these responsibilities, she retained the spiritual aspirations of her youth. "She sought heavenly-mindedness and to be more and more holy in heart and life. Her walk with God was close, constant, humble, and cheerful."[23]

Rebecca Thoreau never transferred her church membership from Charlestown to Concord, perhaps because she craved a deeper spiritual experience than was on offer from Ripley's pulpit. Shortly after the New Year in 1810, Concord felt the stirring of a minirevival, as members of the congregation, anxious about their salvation, gathered in one another's homes for "religious conferences." The first session took place at the manse, where, under the minister's guidance, some fifty people discussed the topic "Wisdom is the principal thing" (Proverbs 4:7). It went so well that participants were eager for more. The meetings convened in private homes every two weeks. With her relish for religious inquiries the incipient awakening held immense appeal for the middle-aged widow. She hosted a conference where "as many attended as the house could well accommodate." Usually, Ripley took charge, leading prayers and hymns, preaching short sermons, reading from the Bible and from contemporary divines. But he could not always be present, and twice the participants went ahead without him, perhaps glad of a rare opportunity to exercise initiative.

In other communities, such lay assemblies spread like wildfire, gathering emotional force and, with their minister's encouragement, bursting into full-fledged revivals. Not in Concord. As the meetings progressed, Ripley grew alarmed at their potential for producing "disputations and irregularities." It was the biggest test of his three decades in the ministry, a time of "singular trouble and divine merciful interposition." Ultimately, following a seventh session he was unable to attend, the parson called a halt. No more gatherings of laypeople would occur on his watch and outside his control. "If the people are disposed to hear private lectures at convenient times and places," he declared, "the pastor is ready to hold them, and to regulate them in such manner as shall seem to him best calculated to promote the great interests of religion."[24]

Under close pastoral scrutiny, the Concord church experienced a rational, orderly awakening. From 1810 to 1818, admissions surged to new highs of fifteen, sixteen, eighteen a year; there were more young, single members than ever, men as well as women. Whereas the events of 1810 struck Ripley as "more a work of man than of God—more the effect of human passions and policy than of divine influence," the conversions of succeeding years appeared authentic signs of the Holy Spirit.[25]

Cynthia Dunbar entered the communion early in July 1811, as this movement was gathering force. Her decision for Christ was prompted as much by her impending union with John Thoreau as by an experience of saving grace. In ten months the twenty-four-year-old woman would give up her legal independence and subsume her identity within the Thoreau family. At a time of religious fervor in the community, why not seize the moment, align herself with her future kin, and declare her intention to establish a Christian household? Perhaps she was anticipating not just motherhood but also the perils of pregnancy. "Prepare for Heaven": that was the traditional Puritan counsel. Confronting mortality, many mothers-to-be felt new urgency about the state of their souls. Would they die in the faith, assured of Christ's blessings for themselves and the little ones they left behind? As it turned out, six months after joining the church, the fiancée of John Thoreau became pregnant; the wedding took place five months later; and Helen Louisa Thoreau arrived in October 1812. Premarital pregnancies, once common in pre-Revolutionary Concord, were still frequent enough to cause no stir; under Ripley's new regime, they escaped church discipline. Nobody questioned Cynthia Thoreau's status among the elect.[26]

In a church dominated by female members, Ripley attended to the sisterhood. As he saw it, New England's women, like "the famed daughters of Israel," were naturally pious. Their minds were "peculiarly formed for the exercise of friendship and generosity, and sweetly vibrating to the impressions of religion." This testimonial stressed mild emotions and social service, at the expense of spiritual intensity and intellectual speculation.[27] It suited the parson's temperament and seemed satisfactory to his listeners. Even teenagers absorbed the message.

Consider the case of Mary Merrick, who would become a close ally of Cynthia and Helen Thoreau in the ranks of reform. In 1820 the nineteen-year-old was considered "the fairest of the fair" among the village belles and was eagerly pursued by young men. Her social credentials added to the personal charm. Her father Tilly graced the local elite. A Harvard College graduate (Class of 1773), he had seen the wider world as a diplomat in Amsterdam during the Revolutionary War and then as a merchant and planter in Charleston, South Carolina, before failing in trade and retreating to his native town. There he tended a small country store with "ill grace and modest" profit and dabbled in Federalist politics. At forty-two, he formed a family with a cousin fifteen years his junior and persevered until her death in 1816, after which his business steadily decayed. Daughter Mary, the eldest of three children, benefited from his connections. She was an intimate of Sarah Ripley, the minister's daughter, went to parties at Squire Hoar's, and delighted in visits to "the good old parson's house."

The social calls and compliments were balanced by domestic duties. Following the loss of her mother, Mary assumed the burden of running the household for her father and two brothers. Amid the endless chores, she found time to read the latest books, including the novels of Walter Scott, participate in the singing school, go stargazing to learn astronomy, savor moonlight walks on summer evenings ("I can hardly suppose a person has a soul who does not love it . . . Nature . . . is my favorite theme"), and maintain a daily journal of her thoughts and feelings, which she sent in letters to a cousin. Like many teenagers then and now, Mary had her emotional ups and downs, one moment laughing at awkward suitors, the next dolefully predicting she would never leave her father for a husband. She was easily wounded and prone to feel sorry for herself, "confined" as she was to the home "as much as any old tame housewife of sixty." Fortunately, she had a ready source of consolation: "the moment any thing troubles me, that moment I begin to think of eternity."[28]

The young woman had learned well her lessons from the Concord pulpit. Under the weight of her mother's early death and her father's sad decline, she saw life as a trial and steeled herself against adversity. "The dearest friends," she knew, "may in an instant be snatched from us by death and we left to mourn the loss which can never be repaired." Why, then, chase after passing pleasures in a world of "sorrow and suffering, and sin"? "If I seek happiness here, I shall be most egregiously mistaken." The wisest course was to practice "self-denial," improve "fleeting time," and pursue "piety to God and usefulness to man." Such "moralizing," the stuff of sermons heard week after week, runs through the correspondence of this lively teenager, along with her witticisms and talk about books. She had made the parson's discourse her own. "Who that studies their own heart attentively will deny the depravity of human nature?" Not Merrick, who struggled with "vanity" and "egotism" and was startled by how easily "evil passion should find its way into my heart."

Despite her aspiration to "prepare for Heaven" and her recognition of the "comparative nothingness of all terrestrial objects," she was as earthbound as anyone else. "I sometimes despair and think it impossible."[29]

Three and a half years later, in June 1824, Mary Merrick "made peace with God." Feeling "dependence on that Being on whom [rests] our life, and our breath, and all our comforts," she entered the fellowship of the Concord church. If the struggle to find grace was personal, the timing followed a similar schedule to Cynthia Dunbar's. Eleven months earlier, at twenty-two, Mary had found a way out of Tilly Merrick's house by marrying a widower of her own, the lawyer Nathan Brooks. (Just a month before the wedding, the Republican Brooks had defeated Federalist Merrick for Concord's representative to the state legislature; presumably the father-in-law held no grudges.) Now, as she subscribed to the covenant, she was an expectant mother, with an infant due in a couple months. Her practice of religion, like Cynthia Thoreau's, conformed to a familiar social script.[30]

A few church members burned with a fierce, unconventional piety. The parson's own stepdaughter, Mary Moody Emerson, chafed at his constant counsel of duty to society and submission to the "Government of God," with good reason. She was a toddler in 1776 when her father died in service as an army chaplain, and to ease the burden on her grieving mother, she was shipped off to the care of relatives in Malden, some fifteen miles away. Even after Phebe Bliss Emerson remarried in 1780 and became Madam Ripley, the girl did not return to the manse. She endured childhood as a domestic drudge in the bleak home of an economically hard-pressed aunt. When she finally got the call back to Concord as a teenager, it was to assist in the chores at the parsonage. Even so, she welcomed the reunion and in 1794, at twenty, joined the church in company with her younger sister.

But the long separation had left its mark. As a lonely girl suffering a miserable "orphanship," Mary Moody Emerson had cultivated a solitary relation with God, whose "electing love for me" she "presumed" as given from birth, and the move to Concord, though it immersed her in family and friendships, did not alter that interior life. "Alive with God is enough—'tis rapture," she declared in her spiritual diary. No human relationship could take its place. Having been shut out of "the pales of the initiated by birth wealth talents & patronage," she spurned marriage and social convention for the pursuit of holy passion. This religious calling, pursued through wide reading and contemplation of sublime nature, propelled her out of Concord and into a peripatetic existence among kinfolk from the Boston area to the backwoods of Maine. Her "spiritual Journey" demanded an unfettered soul. She "danced to the music of my own imajanation" at "the throne of my Master." Not surprisingly, Stepfather Ripley, with his communal ideology and devotion to institutions, could not comprehend that wayward choice. Give up this roving life, he urged, and come back "nearer the place of your nativity and the land of your ancestors," where "all the grand and pleasing varieties of nature" could be found, along with "books and solitude, or society, at your option."

Why then fly into the wilderness, or bury yourself in the desert? Surely, it cannot add to your happiness or improvement to hear the screaming of loons, the hooting of owls, and the howling of wolves. The wildness and simplicity of nature you may see and enjoy without being surrounded by that in her which is savage, terrible, and unsocial.

Mary Moody Emerson resisted such counsel. She could not bear to be around Ripley for long. During one visit to the manse in 1821, she despaired over the uninspiring sermons of "Dr. Reason." "Why, o why . . . am I never to reach the goal of perfection here? Never to pick a bone of metaphysics,—sweeter than the marrow of social life." "I could not stand it," she added, "nor pray." She was soon confiding these complaints to nephew Waldo, on the cusp of his training for the ministry, and influencing him to seek a more ambitious role in the pulpit, where he could change hearts and minds through the eloquence of his words.[31]

As Ripley entered the fifth decade of his ministry, for all his efforts at inclusion, the Concord church had fewer members in full communion than it had had at the start. The upsurge of admissions during the wartime crisis (1810–1815) was followed by a slow decline (1816–1825). The church was particularly wanting in appeal to men; by the mid-1820s, it took in just one out of every ten male taxpayers. Altogether, six out of ten households contained no member of the church for which all were obligated to pay. The aging Ripley was well aware of the problem: the church was losing the young. The new members admitted from 1816 to 1825 constituted the oldest cohort in its history; the average woman was forty-three, her male counterpart forty-nine. Even then, the parson estimated unhappily in 1816 that "there are . . . more than 200 persons in this town, above 40 years old, who are not open communicants"—individuals for whom he held out little hope, since "at their time of life, it is less likely than in years past, they will ever become really better." One consolation remained for the pastor, afflicted with gout but soldiering on in his seventies. "My people are in peace and harmony," he exulted in 1823 on his forty-sixth anniversary in the pulpit. "They appear to be respectful, affectionate, and kind towards me."[32]

IN THE FALL OF 1825 THE "MISSES THOREAU"—ELIZABETH, JANE, AND Maria—helped set in motion a series of events that would create a permanent rift in the community. Driven by the desire "for a more active spiritual life" than was available in the Concord church, they joined with a handful of like-minded souls to revive the "religious conferences" that had briefly stirred the parish and enlisted their stepmother back in 1810. But this time the partici-pants were determined to act on their own "in a very quiet way," without Ezra Ripley's approval. Word of their meetings got around, and one evening, when these seekers came together to pray under the guidance of a visiting deacon from Boston, they were startled by an unexpected visitor. At the appointed hour, Doctor Ripley entered the room and took charge.

> *After adjusting his glasses to the right focus [one witness recalled decades later,] [he] read a hymn, which was sung by the audience, then led in prayer, then read a chapter in the Bible, then read another hymn, which was sung; then selected a passage of scripture upon which he commented for about thirty minutes; then read another hymn, which was sung, followed by a prayer, and the benediction. After which the glasses were returned to their steel case, and to the pocket. After adjusting the broad brim hat upon the head, with cane in hand, bowing his re-spects to the audience he walked out.*

Everyone suffered the intervention in silence; the venerable minister could still exact respect. But as soon as Ripley departed, the worshipers returned to their original purpose. By March 1826, the "little band" of dissenters was taking steps to organize a church and build a meetinghouse. Within a month fourteen townspeople pledged to support "a Calvinistic teacher of piety, religion, and morals" according to "the means with which God has blessed us." The final step was to withdraw formally from Ripley's congregation and constitute a new body of Christ. The Thoreau sisters led the way, petitioning with five others—

three women and two men—for a formal "dismission" from the liberal communion. They were following their own consciences, and owing to their initiative, the era of one town, one church—which had endured in Concord for nearly two centuries, apart from the disruption of the Great Awakening—came to an end.[33]

Why did discontent produce a formal division in 1826 but not in 1810? Rebecca Thoreau and her fellow seekers had gone along with Ripley and given up private meetings at his behest, but her stepdaughters would not. Rather than set aside their religious convictions for the sake of community, they acted on conscience and decamped. The dissent was of long standing, but the context had changed. A battle was now raging for control of Congregationalist churches throughout the Bay State. On one side were champions of Calvinist orthodoxy, intent on upholding "the faith once delivered to the saints"; on the other were the liberal clergy, who dominated the pulpits of Boston and vicinity and the faculty of Harvard College, ancient nursery of the New England ministry. Both parties claimed to be true heirs of the Puritan fathers, though in fact they were remaking the legacy of the past. At the center of debate were the reforms of church admissions and the downplaying of Calvinist "doctrines of grace" by such entrenched ministers as Ripley, whose alliance with the liberals was signified by his honorary doctorate of divinity from Harvard. For years the Concord minister had deftly avoided conflict over these issues, but by 1825 his luck had run out.

The opposition to his regime was no longer merely local. Moved by a desire for strict Calvinist preaching and a more intense mode of worship, the Thoreau sisters and their associates acted quietly on their own in withdrawing from the established church. But their separation reverberated beyond the town. It was seized upon by outside forces to advance the cause of the orthodox party in the struggle for power within Massachusetts Congregationalism. As a result, what began as a small, parochial dispute became part of the Second Great Awakening, a revival of religion that swept across the republic in the 1820s and 1830s with new doctrines and methods to convert people to Christ. Like its precursor in the previous century, this movement unsettled existing churches, introduced competition for believers, sharpened distinctions between rival faiths, and spawned the rise of new sects. The proliferation of choices enhanced the power of individuals to determine their religious fates—a development ratified in theology as well. The Massachusetts Standing Order could not survive the upheaval. Even Unitarians felt the urge for a deeper spiritual experience, and out of their discontent with liberal Protestantism would emerge the Transcendentalists, who took it upon themselves, as did Henry Thoreau, to preach the "prospect of awakening or coming to life" through the experience of the divine in nature.[34]

The ringleader of this fight was Rev. Jedidiah Morse of Charlestown, in whose church Rebecca Thoreau had worshiped before coming to Concord. The Yale-trained minister was determined to expose apostates from Calvinism, counteract their influence, and drive them from the pulpit. He was the leading force behind the establishment of Andover Divinity School as a counterweight to Harvard and the inauguration of *The Panoplist* as the periodical voice of orthodoxy. Morse tolerated no cooperation with liberal clergy, and he was prepared to jettison tradition to get his way.

It was customary for Congregationalist ministers to visit in one another's pulpits. By this means, they gained relief from the burden of composing and delivering fresh sermons every Sunday, and at the same time their congregations got to hear different voices and views. Ezra Ripley delighted in such exchanges. Over the four decades of his ministry, he was frequently out of town on the Sabbath, holding forth in churches throughout Middlesex County and occasionally beyond. At seventy, he vowed to cut back and concentrate on "my own people" in "the gospel ministry." Despite that pledge and his gout, he harnessed up Caesar to the chaise and took to the road at least twenty-six times in 1823. He delivered his sermon "Conscience, Its Design, Use, and Obligations" in sixteen places, including the adjacent town of Bedford, where the severe Calvinist Samuel Stearns presided. In turn, Ripley welcomed orthodox preachers, even graduates of the Andover seminary, to Concord. Those who truly loved God, he observed, did not "exclude from communion christians who differ in opinion on some private points," nor bar "the gate of heaven against all but [their] own sect." Such catholicism was anathema to Morse and his allies, who insisted on an exclusionary rule. By the mid-1820s, the Calvinist party got its way: orthodox pulpits admitted only the like-minded. Ripley would thenceforth journey to Bedford, once part of Concord, in vain; in 1824 Stearns closed his pulpit to liberals, abruptly ending nearly three decades of friendly exchanges with his next-door neighbor.[35]

The breaking of clerical ties often led to the breakup of churches. Over the 1820s close to one hundred new Congregationalist churches were founded in the Bay State, nearly two-thirds resulting from Trinitarian secessions from established congregations. (A minority were started by liberals departing orthodox churches or parishes.) Six separations took place in 1823, nine in 1824, then ten in 1825 and ten again in 1826. The acrimony split Concord's neighbors Bedford and Lincoln. Secessions were thus unmistakably on the upswing when the little orthodox band in Ripley's parish quietly decided to boycott the meetinghouse on the Sabbath and worship on their own.[36]

No sudden innovation in church policy nor any struggle over admissions drove the Thoreau sisters and associates from the pews. The immediate aim was to restore "sound doctrine" and recover "vital godliness" in the practice of faith "according to the dictates of their own consciences." Starting a new church was not on the agenda.[37] But the separation played out on a larger stage. The orthodox party had made steady gains in the Boston area since Jedidiah Morse launched his crusade. It planted its standard in the heart of the capital at Park Street Church, within the shadow of the Massachusetts State House, and from this citadel it conducted the campaign against liberalism in the weekly *Boston Recorder*.

The Calvinist cause had also acquired a powerful spokesman in Rev. Lyman Beecher, who took charge of the Hanover Street Church in Boston's North End the year of the Concord church split. The Yale-trained newcomer from Connecticut set out to expel the "enemy out of the temple they have usurped and polluted." His was a more dynamic approach to promoting faith than ever contemplated by Morse, a traditionalist fighting a rearguard action to uphold the Puritan system as he had inherited it. Beecher took the Calvinist creed and applied it dynamically to win souls for Christ. In the evangelical spirit of the Great Awakening, he labored tirelessly to stir mass conversions in large-scale religious revivals. He also allowed for greater human agency in the work of salvation—in effect, employing Arminian means to achieve Calvinist ends. Don't sit around and wait for the holy spirit, he told listeners; strive actively to be born again. His preaching was designed to speed the process. He "pricked" hearts with dire warnings of the terrible fate in store for the unregenerate, then urged on "the sudden anxieties, and deep convictions of sin," essential to achieving grace and experiencing "sudden joy in believing." Redemption culminated in "reformation and a holy life." In this view, church membership was reserved for the elect, and just to be sure that only the saints came marching in,

Beecher demanded a return to the strict admission requirements abandoned by the liberals, notably, testimony of saving grace. His outlook was in keeping with that of the defectors from Ripley's church.[38]

The prayer meetings in Concord had barely gotten started before word of the dissent reached orthodox leaders in Andover and Boston. Immediately an emissary was dispatched from "Brimstone Corner"—aka Park Street Church—to assess the situation and dispense encouragement and advice. The "little band" in the village could not believe their good fortune. They were few in number, counting the Misses Thoreau and a dozen others, and, with only a couple exceptions, "poor in this world's goods." The aid of outsiders would surely be a boon to their cause. But the help came at a high price. The "Higher Powers" in Boston moved to take control of the separatist effort and steer it in a direction useful to the larger sectarian cause. Concord, in their estimation, would be a prize catch, and its accession into the orthodox ranks had to be done carefully. The fledgling congregation required "men of wealth and influence" in its leadership. To attract such figures, it was necessary to appeal to secular as well as religious motivations. Tell them, advised the Bostonians, that an orthodox "establishment would add greatly to the growth and popularity of the town,—gentlemen of the city, would be induced to come and take up residence here." Hire a "popular preacher" capable of drawing inhabitants away from the "old and uninteresting" incumbent. And build a house of worship to promote the true faith and publicize the town. The Bostonians would gladly lend the money to make all this happen. The one condition was that the men and women in the nascent church set aside their own plans and accept the outsiders' guidance.[39]

This intrusion into the parochial affairs of Concord outraged one member of the "little band," a twenty-six-year-old tradesman named Joseph C. Green, who published an anonymous exposé of the behind-the-scenes maneuvering that gave rise to the Trinitarian church. The Bostonians' plan of action, according to his account, was "directly contrary to the clear convictions of the greater part" of the emerging congregation. The Misses Thoreau could not have been pleased. The orthodox power brokers swept into Concord under cover of night, excluded women from their closed-door meetings, and swore all the participants to secrecy. Objections to their suggestions were brushed aside, on the ground that the locals were "ignorant and inexperienced, not correctly indoctrinated in divine truth and christian expediency." Concord ought to be grateful to the outsiders for doing so much for the cause. These arguments silenced his female colleagues, but not Green. He could not care less about the material benefits a new church would bring to the town: "A fine house, a good orator, or a very learned minister was [not] necessary to the conversion of souls or the revival of pure and undefiled religion among them." The only reason to start a new church was to "worship God in a free country, according to the dictates of their own consciences."[40]

The "Higher Powers" in Boston were not the only group holding back Green and the hesitant women. Ripley's church had to approve the dissenters' withdrawal from communion, and it was in no hurry to grant this "dismission." In May 1826 the impetuous Green, one of the few men of his generation to enter the First Parish Church in his teens, forced the issue. He joined with nine other dissidents to ask for leave to depart. The petitioners comprised seven women, including the Thoreau sisters, and three men. If not poor, most were in modest circumstances, except for the wealthy leather dealer John Vose and his wife. Veterans of the religious establishment, totaling 164 years in the communion among them, they wished to separate on good terms. But their former brothers and sisters reacted coolly to the request. It was "sudden and unexpected," Ripley recorded in the minutes. The church "thought best not to reply without further consideration."[41]

A decision could not be put off for long. Two weeks later the members convened after public worship and heard a report from a committee chaired by Samuel Hoar, a communicant since 1806. He had been grappling with the orthodox-liberal split within his own family since his brother-in-law, Jeremiah Evarts, signed onto Jedidiah Morse's Calvinist crusade as editor of *The Panoplist*. At the 1820 state constitutional convention, the squire had fought mightily to preserve the Standing Order, with its compulsory religious taxes, and to limit the freedom of individuals to pick and choose where their money would go.

> *What would be the situation of our towns? [he asked.] A minister becomes unpopular; some of his society leave him. The burden thereby becomes heavier on the others, and this induces some of them to leave; so that half a dozen only, or still fewer remain. The law compels the town to support public worship; is this small remainder then to be punished because public worship is not maintained in that town?*

In one of those droll stories for which he was famous, the squire invoked the case of a man who had deserted a Congregationalist parish for a Baptist society; after undergoing immersion, the convert was asked if he had "washed away his sins." "He had washed away his taxes," the man replied, and that "was his principal concern."[42]

Now Hoar was faced with a similar challenge within his own town, and he was forced to concede the right of dissent. "Our brethren & sisters . . . [have] the same right of private judgment which we claim for ourselves," Hoar began, and in their spiritual quest, "they may have been more successful or highly favored than we have been in acquiring the knowledge of religious truth." Nonetheless, "we are not aware of any such difference of opinion as ought to induce them to separate themselves from us . . . We do not believe that there exists sufficient reason for a division of the church." The dissidents bore the blame for the schism. By attending preaching "separate from the established place of worship of this church," they have acted "erroneously and inconsistently with their engagements to attend religious worship & ordinances with us." But though they were misguided, the petitioners were well intended, and the church could not stand in their way. Accordingly, Hoar bade them farewell with "deep regret" and "sincere" wishes for success. Ripley agreed. Brother Hoar's speech, the parson added to the minutes, was "very pertinent, judicious, and interesting."[43]

The grant of dismission could not have come too soon. The next day Concord witnessed another cornerstone-laying ceremony. Even before formally organizing a church, the Trinitarians began construction of a Federal-style meetinghouse modeled on Lyman Beecher's Hanover Street Church. It stood just across the millpond from the official house of worship. The project, contrary to the wishes of Joseph Green, attested to the orthodox party's influence over the separation; the cost was well beyond the means of the new congregation's founding members.

The speaker at the dedication ceremony, Rev. Asa Rand, a rising figure in orthodox circles, extended an olive branch to the Concord neighbors. "It is not in our hearts to set up 'altar against altar,' from any spirit of contention or animosity. Though we separate from our brethren, we rejoice that the separation is accomplished in a regular and peaceable manner." To this end, the new church disclaimed any desire to challenge its liberal rival. Our goal is simply "to procure the ministration of the gospel, and the ordinances of [God's] covenant, for ourselves and our children, according to our views of duty; and to open a house, where the same gospel will be preached to all, who may voluntarily choose to come in." Sounding "the gospel trumpet," they aspired to "rouse slumbering souls around us, to attend to the things of their everlasting peace."

The First Parish reciprocated this display of "charity" by allowing use of its meetinghouse for the formal organization of the Trinitarian church. Just two weeks after the cornerstone laying, a remarkable assemblage of orthodox ministers gathered there to confer official blessings on the new congregation. The group included Bedford's Samuel Stearns, Waltham's Sewall Harding, and neighboring Carlisle's Paul Litchfield, all of whom had only recently declined to exchange with Doctor Ripley. Occupying the pulpit was the preacher for the day, Lyman Beecher, already taking Boston by storm. The prominence of the delegation suggests the importance attached to this addition to the orthodox ranks. But nobody was disposed to gloat. In its account of the ceremony, Concord's *Yeoman's Gazette*, whose editors John C. Allen and Herman Atwill would join the Trinitarians, said nothing about orthodoxy, Calvinism, or sectarian sentiment. Concord was simply acquiring "a new church."[44]

The goodwill did not last long. Under the headline "Encouraging Prospects," the *Boston Recorder*, of which Rand would shortly become coeditor, trumpeted the organization of a "little band" in Concord "professing the primitive faith of the New England pilgrims." The report noted briefly the main facts—the number of members, the participants in the ceremony, the construction of a meetinghouse—before adding a concluding remark: "The necessity of this measure will be readily apparent, when it is understood, that more than half the people of that populous town are not in the habit of attending the preaching of the word."

That jibe stirred a quick and surprising response. While their meetinghouse was being built, the Trinitarians were without a place of their own for public worship. Late in April, they had asked Squire Heywood, the town clerk, for permission to use the courthouse. "By no means," he had replied. "You shall not have the house for that purpose." Eventually the town relented and granted use of the brick schoolhouse on the common. On Sunday, June 11, two days after the appearance of "Encouraging Prospects," the Trinitarians proceeded to that meeting place, only to find that someone had gotten there first and nailed the doors tightly shut.

Who would carry out so unneighborly an act? No one ever came forward to receive credit or blame. Many years later a member of the Trinitarian congregation discovered the perpetrator's name, which he inscribed on a clipping of the *Recorder* story buried in the church archives. The vandal was none other than the Hon. John Keyes, apparently retaliating for the newspaper's insult to the reputation of his town.[45]

Charge and countercharge soon followed in the Boston and Concord press. One defender of Concord's establishment denounced the *Recorder* report as a "gross slander" and "willful and malicious misrepresentation." In a communication to the local *Yeoman's Gazette*, "No Friend to Hypocrisy" disputed the claim that over half the townspeople were seldom seen in the meetinghouse on the Sabbath. To the contrary, absentees were rare exceptions; there are "few towns in the Commonwealth where the people are more united, more regular and constant in their attendance" at public worship than the inhabitants of Concord. That assertion was challenged, in turn, by a penetrating "Observer" in the orthodox paper. In an informed critique he surveyed the seating capacity of the pews and galleries in the meetinghouse and concluded that only one out of three inhabitants—and no more than a quarter of all households—could be accommodated for public worship. The problem involved more than numbers. Even those who were "strict and punctual" in observing the Sabbath practiced a superficial faith, devoid of true piety; "it is feared that this is all they do to make their 'calling and election sure.'" For some, religion was merely a social convention, performed on rare occasions. "It is true that there are few, if any, that never went to meeting in their life, but there are some that go only when they have a note to put up for the death of friend, or on some other special occasion." In the eyes of the orthodox, Concord's Standing Order lacked spiritual vitality, and that was the chief cause and justification of the split.[46]

"No Friend to Hypocrisy," the self-appointed champion of the establishment, ignored the substance of Trinitarian criticisms and concentrated on their betrayal of community. He had gotten wind of the external influences operating behind the scenes to bring the new church into existence, and he used this information to challenge the legitimacy of the enterprise. Where had the "little band" of dissenters obtained the funds for a meetinghouse? And why were Andover divinity students and Boston ministers so active in Concord's affairs? The division, he insinuated, had been cooked up by outside agitators for sectarian ends. Not so, answered the "Observer"; the Trinitarians had organized on their own initiative and recruited preachers from Boston "not so much to gather, as to feed them." If anybody deserved condemnation, it was surely those who turned to "hammers and nails" to stop their neighbors from meeting.

"No Friend to Hypocrisy" became even shriller in response. "The tongue of a slanderer is an abomination," he thundered in biblical language. "Attack not the people who live in Concord, when they give no reason for offence." Invoking the prophecy of the "last days" in the second book of Timothy (3:5–7), he likened the disturbers of Concord's peace to the false pretenders to godliness "who are seen creeping into houses leading captive silly women" into their unholy camps. With that statement "No Friend to Hypocrisy" revealed his identity—at least to a later historian. He was none other than John Keyes, who made a habit of deriding opponents for taking advantage of "captive silly women." Patriarchy was the traditionalist's last line of defense. The "Misses Thoreau" and their sisters had not acted on their authentic desires; according to Keyes, they had been seduced by religious rakes. In the face of competition, liberalism contracted into parochialism. In a theme familiar in Concord history, supporters of the historic church were defending a local establishment against external attack. Appropriately, they took to the hometown *Yeoman's Gazette* to press their case; the orthodox aired their defense in the *Boston Recorder*.[47]

RIPLEY TOOK THE SECESSION BADLY. HE HAD TRIED SO HARD TO AVOID CONtroversy and maintain good relations with orthodox colleagues. He had served on the executive board of the Middlesex Bible Society from its founding in 1814, collaborating with Jedidiah Morse at the start and with Samuel Stearns and other Trinitarians down to 1826. And he kept his distance from Unitarianism, a word that does not appear in his sermons through 1825. When he heard a rumor that Unitarians in neighboring Acton were actively recruiting their own minister, he advised one potential candidate to steer clear of the town. Its settled minister, though orthodox, was "a man of piety and good sense" who got along well with liberals and deserved support. "We condemn the orthodox for stirring up divisions and organizing churches of a few disaffected and ignorant persons," Ripley told Rev. James Walker, a future president of Harvard College. "Let us do nothing which we condemn in others."[48]

Once the critics of his pastorate withdrew from communion, Ripley geared up for battle. At his study in the manse, "its walls . . . blackened with the smoke of unnumbered years," and surrounded by "grim" visages of George Whitefield and other famous divines, he furiously composed several dozen new sermons restating the "things essential to christianity and salvation." On the Sabbath he lashed out at opponents. "I was in hopes of living & dying in peace & harmony with my people," he said sadly. "But those have risen up who are dissatisfied, & are endeavouring to propagate sentiments & opinions injurious to my reputation & usefulness as a teacher of religion, & tending to alienate christian brethren & divide our religious society." Not that he took personal offense at the attacks. But Ripley could not be true to his "conscience" if he did not correct the errors in circulation.

He thus undertook "a strain of preaching to which I am not much used": a series of doctrinal sermons on "disputed subjects," delivered over the winter of 1826. The opening salvo assailed the "hyper-Calvinist" position known as "Hopkinsianism" for its readiness to condemn the mass of men to eternal punishment for sins they were incapable, by divine plan, of avoiding. Another appraised the doctrines of Calvin and Arminius, as laid out in Hannah Adams's *View of Religions*, a work with a liberal bias by an author famously at odds with Jedidiah Morse. Arminianism won. "The present is an age of inquiry and improvement," as well as "an age of contention and controversy about religion," Ripley told the congregation. Every individual had the duty to examine the competing positions and exercise rational judgment. Under the guidance of the parson, the right choices would be made.[49]

The orthodox defection came at a particularly difficult time for the old man, increasingly isolated and gout-ridden in the manse. The septuagenarian was still grieving over the recent deaths of wife Phebe, a sickly woman long confined to her bedchamber, and of their forty-year-old son Daniel in distant Alabama Territory, where he had moved to rebuild his reputation and legal career after fighting a duel in New England. In the winter of 1826, as the division of his church was accelerating, Ripley was alone in the parsonage with his daughter, Sarah. She had become her father's right arm but was now ailing herself and could provide little comfort in his distress over the separation. Then in November 1826 she died suddenly at forty-five. Only one child, the Waltham minister Samuel, remained to come to his father's aid. The personal losses compounded those from the church. "My dear and only daughter died—," he noted in his journal, "and at this time a sectarian spirit is dividing my beloved church and people."[50]

There was nothing Ripley could do to stop the schism. As the new church organized, hired a minister, and erected a meetinghouse, he was reduced to laments about the loss of unity. "Well, it is all an unhappy and wicked business," he exploded to the orthodox minister Rand, "and has been brought about by this exclusive spirit that has crept into the churches. We are breaking to pieces, and going to ruin, all for the want of a little liberality of feeling."[51]

As it turned out, desertions from the First Parish were fewer than the beleaguered parson feared. The original ten dismissions were followed by another two in 1826 and eight in 1827, including the parson's "good friend and neighbor," Deacon John White, and the wealthy merchant Josiah Davis. Thereafter, only a handful trickled away. Altogether, the First Parish limited its losses to twenty-two communicants through 1833, amounting to one out of seven church members. But it recouped them with a sudden accession of sixty new brothers and sisters, who were perhaps moved to declare themselves by the Trinitarian secession. The vast majority of townspeople—some 85 percent of all polls—remained within the First Parish, seemingly content to pay for a liberal mode of religion.

Crucially, the political and social elite, almost to a man, rallied behind Ripley's leadership, as did its daughters and wives. Liberalism defined their sensibilities. Mary Merrick Brooks stuck with him; so did Cynthia Thoreau, after briefly vacillating. Even the fervent Mary Moody Emerson, who burned with a spiritual passion her stepfather would never fathom, sent a message of consolation. "To be rid of fanatical narrow minded christians is a blessing," she wrote from faraway Maine. ". . . The sole clue to their feelings and understanding is—'the church I belong to is the only true one' . . . Oh I am sick to the very heart when I see long faces and high orthodoxy, where it is united with exclusive salvation and canting declamation."[52]

With the departure of the orthodox faction, the First Parish was free to press forward with a liberal agenda and affiliate with the new Unitarian denomination, formed in 1825. A new hymnal was introduced to replace Watts's old standby, no longer acceptable for its Calvinist sentiments. A clear-cut statement of belief in the Trinity silently disappeared from the church covenant. A fresh style of preaching was heard when Waldo Emerson, now a minister himself, began appearing in the pulpit. From 1827 to 1830, Ripley's grandson traveled out from Boston to deliver at least sixteen sermons to the congregation. One contemporary deemed them "some of the purest & best I have ever heard in Concord," though he allowed that they were "sometimes too refined & intellectual" for the locals. Another new voice was that of Hersey B. Goodwin, hired in 1829 as the aging parson's assistant and anointed successor; he won unanimous admiration for his liberal sentiments, sweet temper, and earnest manner. As for Ripley himself, he was soon publishing sermons in the new denominational periodical *The Liberal Preacher* and his reminiscences in the *Unitarian Advocate*. Within a few years, Ripley and thirty-four parishioners organized a local chapter of the American Unitarian Association.[53]

Harmony had returned to the First Parish Church, and in testament to the new liberal consensus, the members completed the reforms that Ripley had initiated back in the mid-1790s. On the last day of August 1832, they adopted and signed a covenant designed to "return [the church] as far & as fast as is practicable . . . to the simple methods of the primitive Christians." Dropping formal tests for membership, the new agreement invited affiliation. Aspirants need only declare a broad belief in "One God, the Father of all, and in Jesus Christ his Son, our Saviour, the One Mediator between God & man" and in the Bible as divine revelation. (Evidently this was flexible enough to appease orthodox believers while allowing for reservations about the Trinity.) The church did not question their knowledge or probe their conduct. It accepted at face value the intention to live in accord with the scriptural "rule of faith and practice." The compact between individual and church was mutual and voluntary, similar in spirit to other associations.

These changes won acceptance from all but one member. Altogether, 125 people—eighty-seven women, thirty-eight men—endorsed the new covenant, twenty-nine fewer than in 1815. They included Squire and Madam Hoar; Mary Merrick Brooks; Mary Moody Emerson, back in Concord for a while; Ripley's step-grandson Edward Bliss Emerson, younger brother of Waldo; and Cynthia Dunbar Thoreau. This simple fellowship, on the model of the "primitive Christians," confirmed the parson's confidence in free inquiry. Concord was enjoying the "forward march of intellect" and the "higher cultivation of moral powers" Ripley had always anticipated from the progress of liberal principles. In 1832 he envisioned "the eventual triumph of the Unitarian and Liberal cause." Little did he anticipate that Unitarianism would soon suffer still more conflict with the rise of Transcendentalist dissent from within.[54]

THE TRINITARIAN CHURCH GOT OFF TO A QUICK START. THE MEETINGHOUSE, built at a cost of $5,000 to $6,000, was ready for use in December 1826, some six months after the cornerstone was laid. Andover graduate Daniel South-mayd assumed the pulpit in April 1827 in a ceremony that brought Lyman Beecher back to Concord along with other orthodox luminaries. The biblical text for the ordination sermon, "But we preach Christ crucified" (1 Corinthians 1:22–24), was a declaration of evangelical zeal. Ironically, the same passage had inspired Ezra Ripley's discourse at his ascension to the pulpit back in 1778. Building on its core of defectors from Ripley's congregation, the roll of saints expanded quickly. Starting from its original base of sixteen founders, the church added twenty-two souls in its first year and thirty-one by its second anniversary. Most of those recruits were already professors of religion, whose spiritual qualifications were attested by the letters of dismission they carried. Women dominated the ranks; eleven of the charter members were female, about the same proportion (70 percent) as in the liberal rival. The break with the First Parish Church was not as stark as first appeared.[55]

In the core of the new church were a few pillars of the establishment. The most prominent were the numerous and contentious Davis clan, village merchants all. Fifty-three-year-old Josiah, the second-richest taxpayer in 1826, was exactly the sort of man the "Higher Powers" in Boston urged the Trinitarians to recruit: a figure "of wealth and influence" in the town. Joseph C. Green, a jack of various trades, paled in comparison, with but a half share of a house and garden to his name. The circumstances of the Thoreau sisters were similarly straitened. They made ends meet from their share of the family inheritance—rents from the real estate in Boston and interest on the money bequeathed to them—and by taking in boarders at the house they occupied on the common. One by one other members of the extended Thoreau clan joined them in communion. In the summer of 1826, thirty-six-year-old sister Sarah moved to Concord from Boston, where she had been converted to Christ under the guiding hand of Lyman Beecher. In ensuing years, other kin of Henry Thoreau became loyal Trinitarians, including his maiden aunt, Louisa Dunbar, who had also belonged to Beecher's church in Boston, and his ne'er-do-well bachelor uncle Charles.[56]

Cynthia Dunbar Thoreau was conflicted in her religious loyalties. Her husband, John, was content to worship in the family pew at the established church, but she felt a pull to the dissenting congregation. In late April 1827, the forty-year-old mother of four obtained a letter of dismission from the First Parish

Church so that she could join her relatives in the new body. Her plan was buttressed by a growing friendship with the new Trinitarian minister Southmayd and his wife Joanna. Arriving that spring, the couple was steered to the boardinghouse Cynthia kept in the village center. In her parlor and around her dining table, talk about religion and the state of the churches must have been intense. "We are boarding in a very gentile [genteel] pleasant family," Joanne Kent Southmayd wrote her mother in September 1827. "The worst I fear is that this society is so enjoyable that it will beguile us of too much of our time."

Undoubtedly the minister's wife was glad to see her landlady at Sabbath worship. But to her consternation, Cynthia hesitated to unite with the Calvinist church. She was simply not in complete accord with Trinitarian beliefs and could not keep her doubts to herself. "There are few subjects," Southmayd noted, "upon which we can converse together without some little collision of feeling." At issue was the nature of Christ: was he God "manifest in the flesh," as the Trinitarians contended, or a creature of God's will, whether his son or some other sacred being, as the Unitarians claimed?

> *I had a very serious conversation with Mrs. T., in which I told her my views and feeling respecting the Saviour. She said her views were the same, yet acknowledged that she could not see how he was Divine. She could not receive Him as such. I told her I saw a vast difference between her views and mine. It would make a vast change in my mind to believe that I must reserve a higher homage for another being than Jesus Christ. I warned her with as much tenderness and faithfulness as I could, of that pride of reasoning which she exhibited much of . . . I am afraid she is blind to the truth—yet she takes up sermons, which hold forth the character of Christ & professes to agree with them . . . She says she prays to Christ without any feeling that he is inferior.*

Joanna Southmayd was skeptical of such assurances, and she was right. Despite all the arguments and pleadings from her tenants and her relatives, Cynthia Thoreau could not swallow her reservations or go against her conscience. (Her ten-year-old son David Henry must have taken notice.) By February 1828, the Southmayds were keeping house on their own, aided "by presents and sewing" from the Misses Thoreau, and six months later Ezra Ripley was pleased to note in the church record book that the stray sheep had "changed her mind" and returned to the flock. The only trace of her presence among the Trinitarians was a folio edition of Brown's *Self-Interpreting Bible*, which rested on a reading stand long after its donor had taken herself and her doubts back to Doctor Ripley's meetinghouse.[57]

The new church filled up with a great many newcomers, who acquired an anchor in Trinitarianism as they drifted in and out of town. On the model of the Standing Order, the orthodox religious body comprised two groups: the "visible church," mostly female, embracing all those admitted into the covenant, and the largely male "society," consisting of all who joined in Sunday worship and paid for its support. The society counted ninety-one members through 1829, most of whom were just passing through. Only one out of four was born in Concord; the great majority (over 60 percent) came from places unknown and after a few years picked up for destinations equally unknown.[58]

These birds of passage were typically young men—the very constituency Ripley could not reach—such as the hatter's apprentice Marcus M. Cushman, who "labored under instruction" in a shop opposite the law office of Squire Hoar. "I saw him often," recalled Cushman five decades later, and knew he disapproved of the new church. But the "wandering boy" had no taste for Doctor Ripley's preaching; "to me his sermons were dry." Notwithstanding the frowns of his elders, Cushman had no intention of going without spiritual refreshment; he attended Trinitarian services for the seven months he resided in Concord before moving on to Boston, completing his training, and eventually becoming, at twenty-three, a "country preacher." Likewise, the journeyman cordwainer Nathan Robbins was quick to enlist in the orthodox flock. In the judgment of Doctor Ripley, as Robbins felt it, "we, who were young, had no right to pretend to know more about the Bible than he did, and leave his preaching, and go away to hear others, without his permission." Out of a "feeling of individual responsibility," the youth screwed up his courage and disregarded such pronouncements. He found ready reinforcement among his peers. "We seldom met anywhere," another participant in the early Trinitarian prayer meetings related, "when religion was not the principal theme of conversation."

The reward of nonconformity was admission to an intense community of faith. For these "young Christians and anxious inquirers," the doctrines that liberals dismissed as inessential opened the way to a personal relation with God. The terrors of hell and damnation, set against the promise of eternal life, drove fearful souls to seek salvation and to win welcome among the elect. For entry into that communion, the Trinitarian church required aspirants to surrender the privacy that Ripley was so determined to protect. All those Puritan practices the First Parish Church had abandoned—spiritual relations, creeds, confessions, moral discipline, and "public propounding" of candidates for membership— were reinstalled by these claimants to Peter Bulkeley's mantle, implementing an agenda strongly advocated by Lyman Beecher. These policies emphasized the equality of the saints, all bound together in common obedience to divine law. In this spirit, the Trinitarians abandoned Saint Paul's command that "women keep silence in the churches" (1 Corinthians 14) and, in a striking reversal of Puritan precedent, granted female communicants the vote. A fierce communalism and egalitarianism set the orthodox apart from the liberal church.[59]

Surprisingly, the rapid expansion troubled Joseph Green and other founding members. In their view, the church was relaxing its admission standards for the sake of growth. Already put off by the interference of outsiders in local affairs, the prickly mechanic resented the flow of unqualified strangers into communion. It was bad enough that the little band had been pressured into starting a church prematurely, building an expensive meetinghouse it could not afford, and setting aside reservations about the hiring of Southmayd as minister. Now the very purity of the faith was being compromised to increase membership. The "Higher Powers" from Andover and Boston seemed "more anxious to get people into the *church* than to *save* souls." Worse, the new pastor appeared to be a man of dubious orthodoxy, who failed to "preach the truth" as Green knew it. Pouncing on the minister's every word, Green detected too much allowance for human will in the holy work of conversion. He was right: Southmayd inclined to the energetic brand of New Divinity identified with Beecher, as his supporters conceded. Deacon Moses Davis, a village merchant, admitted that the preacher's outlook was "not the *old* fashion sort of Calvinism—it was a new kind, that was pretty generally adopted throughout the New-England states, and was considered to be better than the old Calvinism." Just as Green suspected! "I fully believe that Mr. [Southmayd's] intention has ever been, (since he has been among us,) to destroy the existence of Calvinistic sentiments in this church, and establish those of a more liberal character." It was the same fight all over again.[60]

The outrage had an edge of class resentment. Green saw outsiders of wealth and influence bringing in their own favorites and stealing the church from its pious founders. The mechanic had his own flaws. He was said to abuse his wife, neglect family prayers, and cheat on his debts—charges he countered by accusing his critic of being "a liar, or a hypocrite." Whatever his misconduct, he was not alone in distress over the course of the church. By September 1827, twenty-six individuals were apparently ready to demand a "reformation," and a petition was being circulated to this end. The core of the opposition consisted of the original members; as Nathan Robbins remembered fifty years later, Green claimed to have the sympathy of the female founders, who "perhaps did not enter into their duties with that cordiality, which their deep piety would have rendered most influential." (If the Misses Thoreau were in that number, as seems likely, their alienation must have contributed to sister-in-law Cynthia's decision not to join.) To many others, the issues at stake were unfathomable. "To unlearned hearers, it was hard to see the difference which some thought they detected in the Doctrine, as presented by different preachers . . . [But] Christians of that day were very jealous of compromising the Truth."[61]

Word of the developing conflict quickly got around town. One day in February 1828, Ripley paid a call on the wife of his Trinitarian colleague and offered condolences on her move to Concord. "He said to me, rather feelingly, 'you have come to a stormy part of the world,'" Joanna Southmayd, herself a minister's daughter, wrote her sister in Vermont. Although Southmayd tried to minimize the difficulty, the fight had burst into open warfare, particularly after Green began exposing Concord's troubles in the Boston press. That act was denounced as a betrayal of community, and it was compounded when Green began disparaging the intelligence and faith of his female allies with a contempt similar to John Keyes's. Soon he stood nearly alone before a committee admonishing his unchristian conduct. Rather than accept church discipline, Green counterattacked, and for his defiance, he was put on trial for disturbing the church's peace and excommunicated. A month later he paid a further price for dissent; at the insistence of Deacon Davis, he was briefly incarcerated in the local jail for failing to pay an overdue debt. Upon his release, Green recruited a preacher and hosted rival worship services in a shop near the new meetinghouse. By 1831 he was spending the Sabbath at a Baptist church in nearby Sudbury. His wife, Lucy Prescott Green, had her own quarrel with the orthodox congregation. She was expelled two years after her husband in a case that she publicized in the Universalist *Trumpet*.[62]

The conflict exposed the dynamic logic of dissent that Ripley had tried so hard to contain. As in the First Great Awakening, so in its sequel: one person's orthodoxy was another's heresy. In the insistence on purity of faith, some believers felt compelled to separate from others time and again, and they could end up, like Joseph and Lucy Green, "holier than thou," isolated in self-righteous sects appealing to nobody but themselves. This was a dilemma of the Trinitarians' own making. They had obeyed Christ's command to "come out" of the world and pursue truth when they established their church. Why should not others do the same? As followers of Christ, they claimed to be bound by a higher law, and as much as they disliked division, they were obligated to act on "the great and sacred principle of conscience . . . There is a point where compromise with error, whatever be the inducement, is treason against heaven." That was the message from the pulpit when the Trinitarian meetinghouse was dedicated early in December 1826. Heeding those words, Joseph and Lucy Green seceded from one institution after another and took sanctuary in conscience. Their example would be followed by other, better-known Concordians in the years to come.[63]

Relieved to be rid of the Greens, the Trinitarian church still labored under difficulties. The new body staggered under the burden of debt incurred in the ambitious bid to compete with Ripley's church. It was denied the fruits of the established church's endowed funds for the support of public worship. It enjoyed no town money for the upkeep of its meetinghouse. Barred from the brick schoolhouse and other municipal buildings, it spent another $500 on a chapel for its meetings. "We do not complain," Southmayd protested unconvincingly. "*Power, we know, is law.*" The orthodox also had to endure gratuitous insults. In 1827 both the First Parish church and the Trinitarian church inaugurated "Sabbath schools" for the children in their flocks; and the teachers of the orthodox school had the friendly idea of inviting their colleagues across the pond to bring their pupils over for a common class. The Unitarians were having none of it. It would be "improper to take our children there," the Sabbath school committee decided, "to join in any sectarian measures, or listen to discourse calculated to alienate the children's affection from their present mode of worship and instruction." A wall of hostility separated the churches, though they were only one hundred yards apart.[64]

At least the orthodox could take pride in their 1,172-pound bell. With a strong, pleasant sound, it was as superior to its cracked counterpart atop the First Parish meetinghouse as its purchasers deemed their heartfelt worship to the dull services of the liberals. Concord's official bell-ringers thought so; they jumped at the opportunity to toll the hours properly, only to return to their

duty as soon as the town bought an equivalent instrument. On Sabbath mornings, each church competed to outlast its rival in a ringing affirmation of faith;
at the height of enthusiasm, both bells would peal for a full hour. The sound
of the dissenters' bell so offended one follower of Ripley, the septuagenarian
farmer Ben Hosmer, that once, after mistaking its peal for the nightly nine
o'clock tolling from the official meetinghouse and going to bed, he dragged
himself out from under the covers and got dressed all over again. "Do you suppose," he grumbled, "I'm going to bed by that condemned old bell?"[65]

Southmayd answered the call to duty with diminishing enthusiasm. His
ministerial salary was a frugal $600, less than Hersey Goodwin earned as Rip-
ley's assistant. The Trinitarian society fell behind in its payment, despite his
faithful delivery of three sermons every Sabbath. After two years of overwork,
he cut back on pastoral visits to members' homes in order to devote his spare
hours to "meet the pressing demands of his creditors." The retrenchment made
matters worse. "Many became dissatisfied with my want of devotion to the work
of a gospel minister," Southmayd realized, "supposing the fault to be in my
disposition rather than in my inability." The cash-strapped clergyman was in an
impossible bind. He had borrowed from the church's trustees to buy his home
in the town center, but the very parishioners who had encouraged him to settle
in Concord were rendering him incapable of keeping up payments on the loan.
Eventually he and Joanna abandoned the struggle, forfeited the house, and departed in 1832 for the thriving mill city of Lowell, from which he wrote plaintively to his lawyer, Nathan Brooks, that "I have not two dollars in the world"
and no means of ending "my embarrassments." His successor, Rev. John Wilder,
hired after two others turned down the job, endured similar trials, as did many
of their Calvinist colleagues.[66]

Overshadowed by the establishment, hobbled by debts, and enmeshed in
internal quarrels, the Trinitarians soldiered on as martyrs for their faith. Occasional bequests from faithful members offered a measure of relief. Sarah
Thoreau followed her stepmother Rebecca's example and at her death in
1829 endowed the church's first trust fund with fifty dollars; Deacon White
left a generous $700 to support the ministry—too late to rescue Southmayd.
None of this saved the hard-pressed congregation from the necessity of seeking financial aid from the Massachusetts Home Missionary Association. But
worldly troubles could be a spur to spiritual renewal. In the late summer and
fall of 1831, Concord joined in the great revival of religion sweeping across

the Northeast. For three straight days in the Trinitarian meetinghouse, anxious souls were battered with warnings from Southmayd and others about the punishments awaiting the unredeemed in the afterlife. "Sinners were . . . threatened, much more than they were invited and won, by the presentation of a Redeemer's Love," Robbins recalled. The harvest of converts that season numbered fifteen, returning the church to the fervor of its founders.[67]

Under Southmayd's preaching the orthodox acquired a fighting faith. The immediate targets of attack were the apostates of liberalism close by. "The whole system of Unitarianism is one which . . . would be acceptable to any unregenerate heart . . . Who ever heard of a Unitarian bowed down beneath the overpowering sorrows of a heart broken for sin?" Certainly not in Concord, where the establishment employed its power to cut down the orthodox. "Many have been our trials," which the preacher saw no need to rehearse. Whatever the difficulties, the faithful could take heart from the correctness of their doctrine and the purity of their church. No matter their small size nor their fragile finances, the Trinitarians shored up their identity by contrast to the so-called First Parish Church. *They* were the true heirs of the Puritans, *not* the false pretender across the way. Within their house of worship could be found the "city set on a hill" of ancient Puritan longing.[68]

IN AN UNWONTED WORLD OF RELIGIOUS DIVERSITY, THE TWO CHURCHES coexisted uneasily and competed unequally. Having lost almost two dozen members to the orthodox, Ezra Ripley clung to his remaining followers with tenacity. When one of his parishioners, a man suffering from consumption, experienced a sudden sickbed conversion, Ripley suspected Trinitarian meddling. The parson was frequently looking over his shoulder. In May 1830 the female "apothecary" Betty Nutting, who was something of a town institution, died at fifty-eight, just as Ripley was planning to set out for a wedding in Plymouth. Who would conduct the funeral? Unfortunately, Hersey Goodwin was bound for the same affair as his "venerable father." The old warhorse found himself in a quandary. "If I do not stay," he wrote Ruth Emerson, "Mr. Southmayd stands ready; and . . . some will raise a cry to my disadvantage. 'Two ministers in one parish, and yet by both a wedding is preferred to a funeral!'" The dilemma made plain the everyday challenges for all Congregationalist clergymen, young and old, of living in the new age.[69]

At the peak of conflict from 1815 to 1830, the orthodox and liberal parties in Massachusetts, heirs to a common Puritan tradition, took their differences over theology and constructed irreconcilable identities. Crucial issues were certainly at stake regarding the nature of spiritual experience and the character of the Christian community. Paradoxically, the champions of the Standing Order, rooted in particular towns, cultivated a broad-minded, cosmopolitan style, while the rank and file of orthodoxy consisted of mobile men and women in quest of temporary communion. Such contrasts in orientation and ideology fueled the sectarian wars. In retrospect, the contending parties resembled one another as feuding branches of the same family tree, like the brothers-in-law and lawyers Jeremiah Evarts and Samuel Hoar. Both factions in Concord claimed the Puritan mantle of Peter Bulkeley; both stood forth in defense of "the faith once delivered to the saints." The contending parties claimed to be faithful to scripture and true to principle. No more than the Misses Thoreau or their sister-in-law Cynthia would Ezra Ripley or Daniel Southmayd submit to demands for intellectual conformity or violate conscience to satisfy others. The discussions at the Thoreau dinner table had long-term reverberations.

When they stopped talking about ideals, these ecclesiastical politicians could put their secular counterparts to shame. They made and kept crucial decisions in secret. They employed flattery, pressure, and money to get their way. They called for deference and appealed to community, while engaging in whispering campaigns and ad hominem attacks. They were quick to blame the troubles of Congregationalism not on honest differences among sincere believers but on dark conspiracies of evil men. And although they demanded intellectual freedom for themselves, they could be dismissive of dissent. Perhaps the greatest challenge facing the participants in this dispute over theology was ethical: reconciling not with God but with the neighbors. The principle of compromise had failed.

In the wake of the sectarian struggle, the Massachusetts religious establishment, approaching its bicentenary, was barely standing. The contest had undermined popular respect for the ministry and the authority of its word. In 1833 the state legislature finally decided to put the Standing Order, the last in the nation, out of its misery. Orthodox Congregationalists, shut out of the meetinghouses, trust funds, and historic title that had come with official status, joined Baptists, Methodists, and other dissenters who had long been clamoring for disestablishment. In November a proposed amendment to the state constitution, guaranteeing equal status to all religious groups "demeaning themselves peaceably and as good citizens of the Commonwealth," was submitted to the voters. It won easy ratification, with nine out of ten in favor. Even Concord went along, albeit grudgingly, with a substantial minority of the 132 men who turned up at town meeting (43 percent) supporting the establishment to the last.[70]

The conflict within Congregationalism shattered the traditional role of the churches as integrating institutions. In the New England ideal, religion bound inhabitants together in common duty and faith. On the Sabbath, neighbors were expected, indeed mandated by law, albeit one laxly enforced, to gather in the meetinghouse; though separated by worldly distinctions—age and gender, status and wealth, education, occupation, residence, and race—and divided by interests and politics, they subsumed their differences in the public worship of God. That was the vision Ezra Ripley had enjoined on his people year after year, despite its utter impracticability, given the price of pews and the shortage of free seats. "No man lives to himself or dies to himself," the parson was still affirming as he entered his eighth decade. "He is necessarily connected with others, with society, and is obligated to contribute of his powers and worldly good for the benefit of his fellow creatures." But contention among Christians endangered community. When neighbors became "cold and alienated," they stayed away from the meetinghouse and ignored their minister.

The controversy took a heavy toll. The bitter dispute had tarnished the moral claims of liberals and orthodox alike. At the very moment when local leaders were celebrating the end to the generation-long conflict between Federalists and Republicans, ministers and churches were drawing new lines of division and contending for advantage with the relentless partisanship of seasoned politicians. Such conduct bred skepticism about organized religion. No wonder that half the townspeople were seldom seen at Sunday meeting. Some of them were looking beyond the church for spiritual refreshment. In the summer of 1831, Doctor Ripley was dismayed to learn that "there are men and boys among us, who on the sabbath wander about and play in the fields and woods. This is a shameful abuse of liberty." Their ranks would only grow larger in years ahead.[71]

The White Village

In 1823 the Thoreau family moved into a neighborhood in transition. The brick house it rented at the corner of Main Street and the road to Watertown (now Walden Street) stood at the heart of a central village with uncertain prospects. The dwelling had once belonged to the blacksmith Joshua Jones, whose death three years earlier, along with those of several other businessmen, put the immediate future of the local economy in jeopardy. Jones had owned not only the wherewithal of his trade—a "large Smith's Shop," with four furnaces, trip-hammer, and grindstone—but also an adjacent gristmill, which had been grinding corn, rye, and wheat into grain since Puritan settlement. The water to power that mill was channeled from a modest brook flowing into town from a source some three miles to the east and draining into the Concord River nearby. The backwash of its operation generated a considerable pond running past the meetinghouse and a quarter-mile beyond. The gristmill provided a crucial nexus between village and farm and an emblem of the rural economy that had sustained Concord for nearly two centuries.

The pond gave a distinctive character to the center. It was a watering hole for livestock in fall and spring, a skating rink for youths in winter, and a fishing hole in summer; in the dog days of July and August, when the water ran low, the grass along the banks was cut for hay. Starting only a few yards from the Jones house, it engaged the interest of the new family in residence. From ages five to eight, David Henry Thoreau grew up by the shores of a pond made not by nature but by man. He would soon witness its disappearance from the landscape. Rather than let the milldam decay, local entrepreneurs stepped in and took steps to invigorate this business district and give the center a new look.

The remaking of the environment to suit the needs of commerce was a dominant force in the Concord of Thoreau's boyhood.[1]

Not many towns in Massachusetts looked like Concord. Most rural communities sprawled across the land, scattering farms in clusters of settlement populated by neighbors and kin. By contrast, from its start in 1635 Concord was organized around a compact village. In the colonial period, public life centered on the common. It was where the militia trained, town meetings assembled, and courts convened. It was the locus of the grammar school, the meetinghouse, and the burial ground. The principal routes into town from all directions converged there. Stores, shops, and taverns lined the king's highway from the east (known as "the Bay Road" or the "Lexington road"). The mill and the millpond lent a rustic appeal to this scene; in 1775 the Redcoats encountered a village that blended into the surrounding countryside.[2]

The center gained even greater importance in the opening decades of the republic. A new civic landscape advertised the town's stature as an urbane county seat, with an elegant courthouse on the common (1794), its octagonal tower rising sixty feet into the air; a stone jail (1789) just off the common on the opposite side, a formidable fortress, three stories high, guarded by a twelve-foot stockade; and an enlarged meetinghouse (1792), painted bright yellow, enhanced with a clock and bell tower, and capped by a ninety-foot spire pointing all eyes to heaven. Concord strengthened its long-standing position as a hub of communications. Highways ran east to Boston, west to the interior, and south to Hartford and New Haven; new turnpikes put the village on a continuous route from the hill towns of the Connecticut River Valley all the way to Boston. Seven bridges, built at local expense, spanned the two rivers—the Assabet and the Sudbury—that merged into the Concord River at the ancient Indian campsite of Egg Rock above the center. Stage lines began running from Concord to the capital several days a week; a post office, authorized by the federal government in 1795, opened in William Parkman's "little one-story box" of a store familiar to passersby for the salt cod, so withered that no one could tell "whether it be animal, vegetable, or mineral," that the merchant hung at its entrance "as the insignia of his calling." These initiatives spurred the local economy and advanced integration into metropolitan markets. Even as Ezra Ripley preached the virtues of stability and order, his parishioners sought their livelihoods in movement and change. The pathway lay through the central village, geared to the flow of people, goods, and news through the town.

The hive of the expanding village was the milldam. Over the years the passage across the dam had been widened into a highway, and along its borders a variety of enterprises had sprouted. No longer was the section merely an adjunct to agriculture. It filled in with mechanics' shops and became an industrial park. It was also a place for trade. A little grocery store, popular for sales of rum by the glass, lay across a narrow alley; to its east, heading toward the common, was Stephen Wood's tannery (he owned the store as well), an extensive operation for turning hides into leather, with a long yard containing vats of lye, lime, urine, and dung, hidden behind a five-foot fence, and also with a two-story mill, where a workhorse, plodding in circles hour after hour, turned a stone wheel that crushed oak bark into tannin. Then came a foundry, which made bells for horse-drawn sleighs and cast brass parts for the clockmakers on the other side of the street. There, propped up on pilings and resting on the dam walls, an assortment of shops—cabinetmakers, clockmakers, hatters, printers—employed state-of-the-art technology to produce fashionable goods.[3]

At its peak as an industrial district, clockmakers dominated the milldam. Trained in the innovative shop of the entrepreneurial Simon Willard in the town of Roxbury, just outside Boston, Daniel and Nathaniel Munroe produced eight-day clocks with the aid of seven or eight journeymen and apprentices; their cabinetmaker brother William furnished the polished mahogany cases. Theirs was no traditional enterprise fabricating goods to order one by one. The Munroes were *manufacturers*, who gathered standardized parts from several sources—dials and glass covers made in Boston, brass movements from the nearby foundry, wooden cases by brother William and other cabinetmakers—and assembled them into finished goods for sale at wholesale or retail. The firm offered clocks "by the Dozen, at a reduced price," to customers in any part of the United States; the biggest sales, as it turned out, were to wealthy planters in the South. Thanks to the Munroes and their successors, Concord emerged between 1812 and 1822 as the "largest timepiece manufacturing center" outside the Willard base in Boston and Roxbury.

The Munroes were not unique. Ingenuity flourished on the milldam, especially in the blacksmith shop, where Joshua Jones applied water-powered machines of his own invention to turn out nails and wire, and in the cabinet-making shop of William Munroe, who put his talent for clock cases and side-boards to an unexpected purpose—producing common pencils—and thereby launched a new American industry. On its slender stretch of land above the brook, at once an industrial center and a conduit between the common and the main street, the milldam constituted a small-scale version of the manufacturing village in Roxbury perched at the gateway to the capital over the narrow Boston neck.[4]

The shops along the milldam were a constant source of fascination to the boys in the village. Henry Thoreau never recorded his reactions, but it is likely that he felt the same curiosity and wonder that Edward Jarvis recalled when he looked back at his childhood and remembered watching the mechanics at their work a few minutes away from his father's house on the common. Born in 1803, Jarvis grew up during the heyday of the milldam, and in old age he lovingly recollected the street shop by shop, occupant by occupant, over the decade from 1810 to 1820, during which he had gone from a seven-year-old schoolboy with a mechanical turn of mind to an aspiring college student. His greatest interest lay in the novel machines introduced to improve efficiency and expand production. After observing the process of casting at Munroe's foundry, the boy hurried home to try it himself; from molds of flour, he cast lead hatchets and plummets for ruling lines in blank books. He could not get over Jones's massive trip-hammer: "We could not imagine that one could wield a hammer that was bigger than a man's head and weighed more than a hundred pounds."

Sometimes the mechanics themselves provided the spectacle. The only residence on the dam was a small house occupied by an Englishman named Samuel Platt, a "good and industrious" journeyman clockmaker for the Munroes, who dissipated his daytime labors in the shop with heavy drinking and domestic strife at night. Platt's marriage was a stormy one, with husband and wife frequently embroiled in loud, drunken fights that sounded through the village. Local boys, Jarvis included, peered into the windows of Platt's house to watch the couple at war. They looked "like fiends, sitting on opposite sides of the fireplace, holding each a shovel or tongs or broom, threatening and yelling." There was not much privacy on the milldam—or anywhere else in the village.[5]

If the milldam put nature to work for manufacturing, it also afforded splendid recreation, especially in winter. Skating on the frozen pond was a favorite pastime in the village; it was likely on that surface that Henry Thoreau took the first steps toward the "dithyrambic dances and Bacchic leaps on the ice" that later impressed Sophia Hawthorne. Gliding was made all the more challenging by the daily operations of the mill. As water flowed through the milldam, the ice rose and fell, and inevitably, in response to changing temperatures, it became dangerously thin in places. The boldest youths tempted fate by creating a game out of the hazard and competing to be the last to make it safely across. As the pond broke up in March, another feat was to leap onto a huge cake of ice and float about, as on a raft, with a long pole to steer by. These escapades were "dangerous play," Jarvis observed, and he cautiously avoided them.[6]

For all its attractions, the milldam fell into difficulties by the early 1820s. Born in a boom, the manufacturing district then benefited from the cutoff of imports during the era of embargo and war, only to suffer with the return of peace, when British goods flooded back into the country and swamped infant industries. Still, the clockmakers met the challenge and even expanded, their ranks reshuffled with the departure of Daniel and Nathaniel Munroe and the arrival of such fine craftsmen as Lemuel Curtis, designer of the luxurious girandole clock, made for display in the parlor. Four years later the survivors of the postwar crisis were jolted by yet another economic upheaval, the Panic of 1819, the nation's first collective encounter with the boom-and-bust cycle of modern capitalism, which brought slumping markets and falling prices in its wake. By 1822, the lively corps of clockmakers, roughly a dozen workers at its peak, had shrunk to the small crew of Samuel Whiting, who soldiered on with a couple of apprentices to turn out timepieces for John Thoreau and a good many others. Joshua Jones was gone, as was the tanner Stephen Wood, the two dying insolvent within six weeks of each other early in 1820. The gristmill and blacksmith shop were auctioned off to pay Jones's debts; the property went to three wealthy farmers from leading families with deep roots in Concord's agricultural way of life. The new owners rented out the premises, "one of the best places for mechanics that can be found in this county," to a succession of tenants. In April 1825, weary of the business, the partners were ready to sell. Before they could do so, disaster struck. One proprietor died in August, another a month later. The future of the mill and blacksmith shop remained as uncertain as the Wood tannery, which languished on the dam.[7]

This patchy, vernacular landscape of one- and two-story shops, shacks, and store yards all crowded together on a narrow dam was ripe for renewal. With the stench of hides and offal from the tanyard, the creak of the mill wheel, the pounding of the trip-hammer, and the curses of the Platts, the area had never been genteel. At one point the pond teemed with so many bullfrogs that Joshua Jones could not get a good night's sleep. Tired of the endless trumping, he sent out his apprentices in a rowboat to eliminate the noise. Knocking the frogs on the head, the assiduous laborers filled a "good-sized tub" with them almost to the brim. But insects were not so easily driven away. The scene was most noisome in the summer. In the eighteenth century the gristmill suspended work every May to September, and the brook was allowed to run free. As the pond dried up, farmers dug into its bottom and carted off the muck to fertilize their fields; the surrounding meadows, drained of water, sprang back to life, imparting the sweet smell of grass to the air. But early in the nineteenth century that practice ceased. When the road across the dam was extended, the sluiceway meant to keep the water flowing below clogged up, and the consequence was unavoidable: a large, fetid "quagmire" thick with weeds and festering with mosquitoes stretched through the heart of town every summer. It was, recalled one townsman three decades later, a "great nuisance."[8]

But it was commercial stagnation, rather than still waters, that spurred Concord's entrepreneurs into action. The county road across the dam had long been a bottleneck to the efficient movement of goods and people in and out of the village. If nothing were done soon about the "narrow and inconvenient" route, local firms would suffer, and the milldam would deteriorate still more. It was imperative to widen the highway, and to this end, at the start of 1826, forty-five villagers submitted a petition to the county court. The project won support from every economic interest in the center: merchants and craftsmen, hotel and tavern keepers, stage drivers and hostlers, doctors and lawyers, and inevitably, real estate speculators. Concord had plenty of the last group: would-be developers with extensive experience in buying and selling land. Full of ambitions for the town, they possessed the capital to finance their schemes and the power to realize them. Theirs was a vision not just for the milldam but for the center as a whole. The first step was to upgrade the highway, which the county court readily approved; the second was to take down the idle mill at the heart of the village and transform the area extending from the town common all the way to the brick house occupied by the Thoreau family into a modern, attractive place to do business.[9]

The principal figures in this effort came from the economic and political elite. One was the merchant Daniel Shattuck, whose store at the northwest corner of the common facing the central square had on offer the largest assortment of English, American, and West Indian goods in town; another was his rival Samuel Burr, running a close second in the "green store" (so called for its painted color) at the crossroads of town right next to the old burial ground on the Bay Road. The physician Isaac Hurd, a Harvard classmate of Ezra Ripley, had come to Concord in 1789 and during the next quarter-century built a port-folio of real estate as impressive as his roster of patients; his valuable holdings included two stores (one rented to Burr), two taverns, and a considerable stretch of the main street beyond the mill brook. No one had a better opportunity to gauge potential investments than deputy sheriff and jail keeper Abel Moore, whose official duties entailed seizing property for unpaid taxes or debts and auctioning it off to the highest bidder. Cultivating a reputation as a "sharp and hard" bargainer, Moore thrived as a land speculator. And wherever a good deal was in view, the ubiquitous lawyer Keyes could be found. These men, along with the carriage maker William Whiting and the soap and candle manufac-turers Cyrus and Nathan Stow, came together in the early months of 1826 to address the decline of the milldam. Although they had grown up on farms, they were successful men of the village, their personal prospects bound up with its growth—a common bond transcending partisan and sectarian differences. They were linked generationally as well; with the exception of the aged Hurd, they had been born after the Revolution, came of age during the first decades of the new nation, and were now, in their midthirties to early forties, in the prime of life. Seizing the initiative as a self-appointed chamber of commerce, they were ready to create a new blueprint for Concord's future.[10]

The project was not designed to set the mill wheel turning. In March 1826 the investors bought the gristmill and blacksmith shop, with the associated water rights, from the various heirs for just over $1,200. Five months later they transferred "the right to flow" the stream through town to a public-spirited band for the token sum of one dollar. The thirteen grantees—mechanics on the dam, meadow owners along the brook—pledged to abandon the prac-tice of "raising a head of water to drive a mill." The arrangement reflected a broad agreement among Concord's residents: it was finally time to clean up the central village. In a gesture combining civic-mindedness with economic self-interest, the milldam partners took the lead, advanced the funds, and carried out the legal measures to make this possible, all in concert with their neighbors. Once the water right was given up, the flumes were removed from the dam and the brook set free. No longer would bream, hornpouts, shiners, and perch swim in the town center; no more would bullfrogs disturb sleep on summer nights. Waterpower—the engine of the industrial revolution—was banished from the village to outlying parts of the town.[11]

A new business district gradually took shape under the guiding hand of the milldam proprietors. The ramshackle collection of shops and shacks was pulled down; the noxious tanyard was no more. In their place rose several buildings in the Federal style, behind whose symmetrical facades were conducted various craft and retail activities, including the "hat factory" of the poetic mechanic Comfort Foster, who advertised hats "strong and warranted to last / Till the present fashion's past," and the barber shop of Emerson Melvin, combining "hair dressing" with razor sharpening and cures for baldness. With its array of craftsmen, the renovated street fulfilled the developers' intention to "promote the mechanic interest of the village in which . . . our prosperity mainly depends." The ten enterprises active in 1830—one store and nine shops—catered largely to local consumers rather than producing for distant markets, as had the clockmakers. Some traditional crafts were altogether unwelcome. When the milldam proprietors sold lots to potential builders, they took pains to forbid the establishment of "any blacksmith shop nor any shop or building in which any filthy or offensive business shall be carried on." By 1844 carpenters, cabinetmakers, and wheelwrights were added along with stables to the list of banned businesses. A distinct aesthetic was emerging for the town center: the making and selling of goods were to be conducted in a clean, well-ordered, and attractive environment.[12]

No building was better suited to the remodeled district than the Greek Revival temple housing the offices of the Middlesex Mutual Fire Insurance Company and the Concord Bank. Erected in 1832 at the west end of the milldam, the "beautiful" two-story brick edifice, with its imposing portico, boldly asserted Concord's bid to become a center of finance in Middlesex County. Standing on the site of the old blacksmith shop and next door to the former gristmill, the building signaled the ascendancy of money and credit—and of the men who controlled them—in the advancing capitalist economy. Banks furnished an essential medium of exchange for the conduct of commerce beyond the local community, and together with insurance companies, they were rapidly developing into a key source of capital for enterprising individuals ambitious to turn an innovative idea, an ingenious invention, or a valuable resource into a business capable of supplying a wide market and generating substantial profits—just the sort of "industrious mechanics" the milldam associates hoped to encourage. In fact, the principal figures behind the Concord Bank and the insurance company were the same individuals redeveloping the milldam: Burr, Keyes, Moore, and Shattuck, along with the lawyer Nathan Brooks and the town factotum Abiel Heywood. These were Concord's leading venture capitalists, an interlocking directorate at the helm of the new corporations accelerating the growth of the local economy.[13] It was thus fitting that the milldam project, launched at the same time as the insurance firm and chartered as a company in 1829, literally paved the way for the headquarters of its sister institutions. All grew out of a shared aspiration to provide "a public benefit," to promote Concord's interests as a town, and to make "a profitable investment of capital" in the process. In the 1820s and early 1830s this outlook was widely held in the central village.[14]

The remaking of the milldam was but the first step in a broader campaign to beautify the town. The common, a plain, unbroken expanse of grass extending from the First Parish meetinghouse to Shattuck's store and largely unshaded by trees, had long served utilitarian needs. It was a convenient pasture for cattle and sheep and an open training ground for militia. Its only ornament was the liberty pole that had once boldly asserted colonial rights atop a gravel hill. Rescued from that crumbling mound, it was relocated next to the town pump on the square, where it proudly displayed the symbol of the new nation, the American flag. Livestock were barred from grazing the ground in the 1790s, but it took three decades more before residents began to display concern over the uninviting aspect of the public space.[15]

In the spring of 1829 the *Yeoman's Gazette* called attention to "improvements" in the town, singling out the "goodly number of spacious and elegant houses" built by such notables as Samuel Hoar and the many shade trees recently planted, which did more than anything else to "ornament . . . and give a rural appearance, which country villages ought to possess." Four years later these various efforts took on a more systematic character, when John Thoreau joined with forty-seven other villagers to form the Concord Ornamental Tree Society. "Knowing that a variety and abundance of well arranged and thrifty trees" not only add to "the pleasantries, health and comfort of a country village but enhance the value of property in their vicinity and indicate good taste and refinement among the people," the founders set about planting elms, sycamores, maples, and ashes along the main streets, around the central square, and in front of the meetinghouses. First among the members was Daniel Shattuck, joined by the other directors of the Mill Dam Company. The society enlisted every merchant in the village, the three innkeepers, the ministers of the two churches, lawyers Hoar and Keyes, the physician Edward Jarvis (the chronicler of the milldam), and a number of mechanics. Meanwhile a town committee was taking note of the disgraceful condition of the village burial grounds, where cattle grazed freely and trampled over graves and "heedless" boys made tree houses out of memorial locusts. "Let us . . . remove the impression that has gone abroad that the bones of our dead are strewed upon the highway and bleaching in the sun," advised the committee, on which Shattuck sat alongside the newspaper editor Herman Atwill. Let us "beautify the graves of our friends with appropriate shrubbery." An obliging town meeting set aside one hundred dollars for the purpose.[16]

Through such initiatives Concord gained favorable notice as a trendsetter, its ornamental tree society reputedly the first in the region. Such distinctions mattered, for by the 1820s Concord no longer stood out as the rare town with a vigorous center. Commercial villages now dotted the map of Massachusetts, organizing production and exchange and giving focus to social and political life. Linked together through an expanding network of transportation routes leading to Boston, Worcester, Providence, Hartford, and New York, these town centers were attuned to the fashions and standards of the metropolis. Self-consciously cosmopolitan, they were in but not of the countryside. In this spirit they distanced themselves from the rural surround and took on the picturesque look that has come to be seen as the classic New England town: an appealing cluster of stores, shops, and homes, all centered around a neat village green and an elegantly simple meetinghouse. These "white villages"—so called for the hue of their Federal and Greek Revival buildings—combined a neoclassical aesthetic with the traditional virtue of community. Through the austere geometry of columns and pediments, through balanced forms and rational designs, town improvers projected republican values of simplicity, moderation, and order. No place incarnated the white village ideal more fully than Concord, exactly as Shattuck, Keyes, and their associates hoped. By raising a canopy of trees "stretching out their arms . . . to protect the citizen and the traveler from the summer's heat," these boosters aimed to "render Concord one of the pleasantest villages in New England."[17]

One unfortunate blemish on the village remained: the forlorn cornerstone with the embarrassing crack in its foundation. Instead of supporting a noble monument, the granite block on the square supplied a handy mount for getting on horseback. It also served as a humble goalpost in schoolboy games. Yet no one appeared in a hurry to make repairs and get on with the work of raising a memorial to the Concord Fight.

One inhabitant was so upset by the inaction that he took up his pen and submitted a series of columns to the *Yeoman's Gazette* in March and April 1826 urging relocation of the projected monument from the village to the vicinity of the battlefield. Public opinion had changed on this subject, the writer insisted. It was now clear that the decision to place the monument in the center was intended to serve the economic interests of businessmen and homeowners near the common: "If the monument were of consequence, as was expected and intended, would it not affect real estate, public houses, mercantile business, mechanic shops, &c?" The site also appealed to many farmers on the outskirts, their days a constant round of chores. For them, a trip to town, whether to trade at the store or to go to Sunday meeting, would be enlivened by the chance "to see & gaze at a fine monument . . . With a certain class of people . . . curiosity goes a long way."[18]

Worse still, argued "Middlesex," the village was unworthy of a monument. On April 19, 1775, many of its inhabitants had fled the Redcoats, while those trapped in the center surrendered to superior power. Not a shot was fired against the invaders. "What claim then has the centre of town to the monument?"

In short, the central village was no place to put a shrine. To command notice in a busy village, a monument would have to tower over its surround; unless it was "very costly & magnificent," it would appear "contemptible." The setting too defeated the purpose. It lacked the solitude and calm essential to a lofty scene. With the noise and the smells, the hubbub of commerce, the "teams [and] the dust," the area would be "very unpleasant" to tourists. Strangers in town would attract attention from busybodies, suffer unsolicited "confusion, stares, & remarks," and be interrupted in their patriotic mission. Under these circumstances, the monument would be off-limits to women; no "lady" would expose herself to such insults. Instead of a sacred space, the village was profane ground.[19]

In effect, everything remarkable about the town center—its bustling trade, its busy streets, its dense population—was an argument against its suitability. Far better to place the memorial on historic ground, if not on the exact spot where American forces had first clashed with British regulars, inaccessible since

1792 owing to the removal of the North Bridge, then on the high ground north-west, where the Minutemen had held their "Council of War" before undertak-ing the fateful march to the North Bridge. That site had practical advantages as well: a granite column atop that hill would be "conspicuous" throughout town and accessible from the road. Guarded by a "handsome" fence, planted with "ornamental and shady trees," providing seats on which visitors could rest, "the spot [would be] easily made one of the most inviting, delightful, & venerable." Its charms would draw genteel "persons of sentiment" and polite "parties of amusement," whose leisure would be purified by their presence on "almost holy ground." A pilgrimage to the monument would be at once a touristic and a transcendent experience.[20]

This sustained case against the village halted progress on the monument. "Middlesex" evidently spoke for a good many inhabitants, and as it happened, his dissent came from the heart of the establishment. The writer was none other than the proud proprietor of the manse overlooking the battleground and the self-appointed custodian of the town's heritage. The newspaper series bore the stamp of the cleric's characteristic style, with its careful consideration of principles and applications. More than that, the originals of the columns, preserved in the archives, are in Ezra Ripley's own handwriting, and his very words were reproduced the next year in a pamphlet titled *History of the Fight at Concord* attributed to the parson.[21]

With Ripley pushing one way and the proponents of the village—Burr, Moore, Shattuck, and Keyes doubtless among them—pulling in the opposite direction, the monument project fell into limbo, its huge granite block an un-avoidable eyesore and a distressing witness to local divisions. "How long will it be," the *Yeoman's Gazette* asked plaintively in May 1831, "before we shall en-joy the proud pleasure of announcing the completion of the Monument, in commemoration of Concord Fight and Bunker Hill Battle?" The query went unanswered. In the politics of development, village interests could not always impose their will.[22]

WITH ITS COMPACT SETTLEMENT, COMMERCIAL DEVELOPMENT, AND STRATE-gic location at the crossroads of major highways, the village was the most visi-ble section of Concord. But the town had been diversifying since the beginning of the nineteenth century. By 1820 one man was engaged in manufacturing for every two in agriculture. Distinct neighborhoods were taking shape around specific economic activities. Banished from the center, industrial production migrated to outlying areas where waterpower was available to turn mill wheels and run machines. Along the Assabet River, in the western part of town, a cotton factory had been producing yarn and cloth since 1808, and it was joined by lead pipe manufacturing in the 1820s. Some three miles from the center and near the border with the town of Acton, the district was emerging as a factory village with interests of its own and a distinct way of life. Elsewhere manufacturing blended into the countryside, as in the Barrett's mill area, where William Munroe relocated his pencil-making operation in the early 1820s. These enterprises, along with Elijah Wood's production of cheap shoes, destined for Southern slaves and Western pioneers, on his family farm, and William Whiting's carriage-making works in the village, prompted one observer in 1835 to boast that "the manufacturing and mechanical business of the town is increasing, and promises to be a great source of wealth."[23]

The textile mill on the Assabet put Concord in the forefront of the industrial revolution. One of the earliest cotton factories in the country, it was launched in 1808 by a local family long established in the clothier's trade. Jefferson's embargo was the spur to the enterprise, opening up a market for domestic cloth to replace imports from abroad. The Concord firm seized the moment in pursuit of patriotism and profit. "It behooves us, as a commercial people," the partners Ephraim Hartwell and John Brown, Jr., proclaimed, to turn the native "growth of our own country"—the cotton crop produced by the labor of slaves—into an item Americans could buy at home rather than purchase from overseas. For a decade and a half, the manufacturers set to the task in good times and bad. The business prospered during the War of 1812, when foreign competition was nonexistent, faltered with the rest of the infant industry upon the return of peace, hung on through the lean years following the Panic of 1819, and then embarked on a new, more vigorous career. In its formative period, the mill was restricted to the machine production of cotton yarn. In the mid-1820s it expanded into a state-of-the-art facility for converting raw cotton into woven cloth through the efficient operation of the latest technology and the disciplined labor of young women from the surrounding countryside. On the banks of the slow-moving Assabet, Concord raised a small-scale counterpart to Lowell, then springing into existence as an industrial behemoth along the powerful Merrimack.[24]

The mill operated on a scale unmatched by any other enterprise in town.

Set over a raceway, the factory occupied a long wooden building (100 by 28 feet) with three stories, capped by a tower and facing the road. It took in bales of cotton on the ground floor, where they were broken up, loosened, picked by hand, and then released to the upper levels for carding and spinning into yarn. The resulting spools went on to a dye house for coloring before returning to be woven into cloth on power looms. The complex included a separate woolen mill with its own water-powered equipment, and a blacksmith's shop, where machine parts could be made and repaired. Some thirty-five acres of land supported the operation with food for the workers and wood for fuel and construction. The manufacturing establishment represented an immense investment of capital, amounting to $25,000 in 1820, and that was several years before the power looms were installed. No other business in Concord came close.[25]

The labor force at the mills was as unprecedented as the physical setting. The pioneering textile mill in the new nation, inaugurated in 1790 by Samuel Slater in Pawtucket, Rhode Island, relied upon entire family units—men, women, and children—to perform the variety of tasks, most of them calling for limited skills, necessary for producing yarn from machines. That was the practice Slater had learned back in England, and it became the model for the early mills he founded and inspired all over the Blackstone River Valley during the first decade and a half of the nineteenth century.

In Concord, Hartwell and Brown gathered up two dozen children, teenagers, and twentysomethings and settled them in a large boardinghouse a few minutes away from the factory. This unconventional household stretched the definition of family to its limits. The assistant marshal who took the federal census of Concord in 1810 struggled to fit the inmates into the categories he was assigned to record. At the head of this household was neither a single patriarch presiding over an intimate set of dependents—wife, children, apprentices, and servants—nor a widow taking charge of a family bereft of a male provider. Instead, a business, Hartwell & Brown, held sway over what was simply a dwelling with twenty-six persons, most of whom were on their own, apart from parents or other adult kin. Five were children under age ten—one boy, four girls—tasked with cleaning cotton, piecing threads, and running errands. Another five— three boys and two girls approaching or just entering adolescence (ages ten to fifteen)—fed carding machines and tended the jennies and frames, as did the ten workers, three males and seven females, between the ages of sixteen and twenty-five. Their ranks were supplemented by another dozen children and teenagers—seven of them female—living next door. Ten years later the vast majority of the twenty-six employees were teenagers and young women between ten and twenty-five. Well before the Lowell mill girls gained national fame, Concord was relying on a largely female workforce on its factory floors. But these laborers remained obscure: anonymous on the census returns; unnoticed in the press; and confined to a noisy, dusty factory six days a week, ten hours a day, without a break, their lives governed by the clock, with slender ties to the central village three miles away. Appropriately, their little district, with some fifty or sixty inhabitants, carried a separate designation: "Factory Village." It was a place where few lingered for long.[26]

Textile manufacturing demanded resources beyond the means of the original partners. In 1813 they recruited a twenty-one-year-old kinsman from New Hampshire, Ephraim H. Bellows, to join in the management, and within four years the company was operating under his name. But if the venture were to survive, it required more capital, and so like other small mills, it turned for financing to the dry goods dealers who supplied its cotton and distributed its yarn and cloth. Soon the Boston textile merchants Thomas Lord and Elisha Parks were in control, though Bellows remained the public face of the firm. With this infusion of funds, the mill expanded its productive capacity by adding more spindles and installing twenty power looms. Even then the business struggled to stay afloat. The available waterpower constrained the operation, and the partnership was unsettled time and again by the sudden deaths of principals and by family feuds. At one point Bellows left Concord for a new job as superintendent of a much larger manufactory in the western part of the state, only to return six months later, when he inherited a new share of the firm. The only long-term solution for the shortage of capital was to become a joint-stock corporation. In 1832 the Concord Manufacturing Company secured a charter from the Massachusetts legislature "for the purpose of manufacturing cotton and woollen goods and machinery." Authorized to hold up to $100,000 in real and personal property, the business at long last appeared to have achieved a solid foundation.[27]

Amid these vicissitudes the factory gradually increased production and employment. In the early 1830s it relied on thirty female hands, mostly teenagers and women in their twenties, to tend its 1,100 spindles—up from 660 ten years before—and twenty looms. A few boys and girls worked alongside them, and another nine men—carpenters, blacksmiths, wheelwrights, machinists—kept the works in order. The disparities in pay were striking: the female workers, whatever their age, earned only thirty-eight cents a day, compared to ninety cents for the men. No sign of discontent appears in the records; the women went from boardinghouse to mill without leaving any hint of protest.

The industrious community of factory village kept busy from dawn to dark, transforming 52,000 pounds of cotton, obtained from the slave plantations of Georgia and Alabama, into 188,000 yards of cloth over the course of the year. Plain, coarse shirting and stripes were the principal product of those twenty power looms, along with handmade calicos, checks, and ginghams. With revenues of $18,000, this enterprise was tiny, compared to the giants of Lowell and Waltham with their production of cloth by the millions of yards. Yet it tied Concord's fortunes to the southwestern march of the Cotton Kingdom. In the 1820s and early 1830s this entanglement with the slave system provoked no comment; nor was it addressed in later years when the abolitionist movement got going. Nor did Emerson or Thoreau ever visit the mill and remark on the condition of the operatives. The factory remained apart from the mainstream of local life. Nonetheless, it helped to make Concord a more mobile, changeable, and impersonal place, with a floating population of laborers coming and going in a distant corner of the town and living and working on an industrial scale unprecedented in a society of small shops, stores, and farms.[28]

BEYOND THE TOWN CENTER AND THE MILL VILLAGE, FARMS EXTENDED AS far as the eye could see: roughly two hundred homesteads, sixty acres on average, about the same number as fifty years earlier. Devoted largely to growing fodder for livestock and cereals for people, the fields were a sea of yellow and green in an open landscape fringed with apple orchards and steadily dwindling woodlots. But substantial swaths of territory remained largely untouched by the plow or the hoe. To the north of the town square, the "great wild tract" that Thoreau would later dub "Estabrook Country" encompassed five to ten square miles of forest, rocky pastures, a lime kiln, brooks, and swamps, through which the Old Road to Carlisle ran to accommodate the few farms scattered deep in the woods. To the south, roughly two miles from the center, lay the Walden woods, a pine-oak forest comprising some 2,680 acres (four square miles) in Concord and its daughter town Lincoln, with the gem of Walden Pond at its heart. The route through these woods had once been a busy thoroughfare, when the best way to Boston ran across the narrow Roxbury neck, but after a bridge opened in 1785 connecting Charlestown to the capital, farmers deserted the Great County Road, as it was known, and carried their crops to market along the Bay Road east through Lexington to the coast. Like the Estabrook country, it was bypassed by travelers and valued chiefly by locals owning woodlots therein. Here, in the years after the Revolution, gathered a little settlement of ex-slaves on infertile land nobody was in a hurry to improve.[29]

With its sandy acidic soils, steep, rocky ledges, and inaccessible wetlands, the area surrounding the kettle pond made famous by Thoreau was best suited to hunting, fishing, and appreciating scenic views. It was a tough place to get a living from the land. For this very reason it had been passed over by the Puritans and their descendants in the agricultural development of the town and hence was available to men and women of color seeking new lives in freedom at the dawn of the republic.[30]

Colonial Concord had never been a nursery of slavery; its modest farms could not repay the investment. But enough members of the local elite found the ownership of human "property" to be useful or prestigious that the town was home to some two dozen "servants for life" before the war. Professional men—lawyers, doctors, ministers—were especially partial to slaveholding. Rev. Daniel Bliss, the evangelist of the Great Awakening, had no objections to human bondage, and his more liberal successor, William Emerson, not only took in stride the inheritance of two enslaved women from his clerical father-in-law's estate but added a third manservant on his own. Ezra Ripley, in turn, assumed control over these dependents with his succession to the manse.[31] But just as the new parson was doing so, slavery was collapsing in the Bay State, in large measure through the initiative of people of African descent seizing upon the rhetoric of the Revolution to demand liberty and equality for themselves. As Loyalist masters fled the fury of Patriot neighbors, as Black men won manumission through military service, as still other people of color walked away from bondage and emancipated themselves, the system dissolved. When Massachusetts Supreme Court justice William Cushing in 1783 declared slavery to be a violation of the state constitution's founding principle, that "all men are born free and equal" and hence entitled to liberty, he was ratifying a development well under way but still incomplete. The settlement in the Walden woods was testimony to that change.[32]

It was one thing for Massachusetts to disown slavery, quite another for it to embrace free people of color, even Black veterans of the Continental Army, as equal citizens. In March 1788 the General Court prohibited inhabitants from engaging in the "unrighteous commerce" of the African slave trade; it then passed a companion measure barring residence to any "African or Negro" from out of state who lacked proof of citizenship. The two laws were clearly meant to build a Commonwealth as white as the columns of the Bulfinch-designed statehouse and the private mansions on Beacon Hill. Just to be sure, the legislature banned matrimony between whites and "Negroes, Indians, or Mulattoes." Ignoring the sacrifices made by Patriots of color on the battlefield, the lawmakers excluded the same racial minorities from militia duty, a fundamental obligation of citizenship. No one could mistake the state's repudiation of slavery and the slave trade for inclusive and tolerant humanitarianism.[33]

Marginal in the law, free people of color existed on sufferance at the edges of town. In the generation following the Revolution, no one went to the woods in order to live deliberately. Walden attracted squatters who had no place else to go. As many as fifteen people of color made homes there down to the 1820s. The earliest pioneers were refugees from the Lincoln estate of a wealthy Loyalist who fled the fury of Revolution for a plantation in the Caribbean, leaving his servants to fend for themselves. At war's end they were joined along the Great County Road by several Black veterans. In colonial Massachusetts, slaves could legally contract marriages, but after the vows were exchanged, bride and groom remained as subject to the rule of white patriarchs as before. Now such former soldiers as Brister Freeman, once held in bondage by Col. John Cuming, the leading figure in the local elite, returned home from Continental service intent on enjoying the independence for which they had fought. That meant marrying, raising children, and living apart from the supervision of whites. In principle, Freeman possessed the resources to do so. In 1785 he joined with a fellow veteran to purchase an "old field" in the Walden woods, on which they built a house to share. Several years later Freeman received a substantial bequest of £35 sterling from his late master Cuming's estate. The land and the legacy seemingly put Freeman in a privileged position, but there was a catch. The money did not go to him directly. Under the terms of Cuming's will, its management was entrusted to Concord's selectmen. Freeman enjoyed little benefit. After he failed to pay his taxes for several years, the authorities refrained from the usual practice of seizing and selling the delinquent's land. Instead, they dipped into the trust fund to purchase enough of his paltry real estate to cover the exact amount of the debt. Freeman was left with a half-acre of infertile land, plus whatever the trustees of his money were inclined to dispense, on which to support his wife Fenda and three children.[34]

Despite the obstacles, Brister Freeman was not alone in his bid for autonomy. As early as 1790, two out of every three people of color in Concord resided in a household with a Black person as the head. Three decades later that figure was approaching three out of four, and in these homes most of the town's young people of color (67 percent) were being raised. But the Walden woods were uncongenial to self-sustaining families. Brister and Fenda Freeman were lucky; two of their three children reached adulthood and wed. Other denizens of the area succumbed to poverty and disease, some falling victim to ailments associated with malnutrition. Instead of developing into a neighborhood of families, the struggling settlement remained a forlorn place of isolates and outcasts, with a few white ne'er-do-wells among them. One of the best-known residents was an aged Black woman named Zilpah White, who occupied a small house by the corner of what would become Thoreau's bean field, where "she spun linen for the townsfolk" and startled passersby with her "shrill singing" and loud cackling. "Ye are all bones, bones!" she was heard to mutter like a witch "over her gurgling pot." So fearsome became the reputation of the area that anxious travelers raced through it as fast as they could. Yet it was surely a haven from a hostile world.

In the village a Black man was always vulnerable to the whims of malicious whites. On one occasion around 1812, Brister Freeman was asked to go into Peter Wheeler's slaughterhouse and fetch an ax. Little did he know that only minutes before, a ferocious bull had been driven inside. The old soldier opened the door and faced another fight for his life, to the great amusement of Wheeler and his men watching the action through knotholes. It was later said that when the Black man emerged victorious, his face was "literally white with terror." In the face of such casual cruelty, he understandably gained a reputation as "a very passionate man [who] often got into quarrels with the boys who loved to insult and plague him."[35]

By the early 1820s the little Black community at Walden was dying out. The "hermitess" Zilpah died in 1820 at seventy-two, "nearly blind" but independent to the end. Then in January 1822 Freeman and his fellow Continental veteran Case Feene passed within a week of each other, the last people of color to inhabit the woods. Few traces of their presence remained on the landscape, except for the cellar holes Thoreau investigated with so much curiosity during his sojourn at Walden. Why had "this small village, germ of something more," failed, "while Concord keeps its ground?" he mused. "Were there no natural advantages,—no water privileges, forsooth?" Actually, the demise of that village was just one of the transitions Concord was undergoing at the time. The future of the milldam hung in the balance; the cotton factory had to expand or expire. The local world of African Americans was even less secure than that of whites.[36]

Amid the pressures of racism and poverty, Black Concordians persevered. They not only maintained their presence but deepened their participation in local life. Their numbers were small but stable. Every decade from 1790 to 1830 saw anywhere between two and three dozen individuals of color in residence, about as many as before the Revolution. In 1820 they made up just under 2 percent of Concord's 1,788 people—a larger share than was the case for the state as a whole.[37] Elsewhere in Massachusetts, African Americans were picking up stakes and heading for Boston, the hub of the state's free Black population, and New Bedford, seat of the whaling industry. As a result of that exodus, the countryside whitened: the number of towns claiming not a single Black resident rose fourfold, from twenty-one in 1790 to eighty-one in 1830.[38]

Concord resisted the trend. While the Walden woods were emptying out, other areas beckoned. In the central village, Blacks boarded in white households. Artisans in various crafts—blacksmiths, clockmakers, and cordwainers—took African American apprentices and journeymen into their homes and shops; innkeepers furnished lodging for the Blacks they hired to wait on tables and clean stables. In the out-districts, too, some farmers provided room and board to laborers of color just as they did for whites.[39]

For the most part, these Black Yankees were native to Massachusetts or New England, with deep roots in the colonial slave regime. Only a couple arrived in Concord from points south. Thomas Dugan, a man in his forties, appeared in the late 1780s from somewhere in Virginia, his days under slavery behind him, and made a new life as a farmer. He eventually acquired a seven-acre homestead and a reputation as a skilled agriculturalist, who introduced the first rye cradle into the Bay State and won admiration for his talent at grafting apple trees. In 1817 the aging yeoman was anxious to secure the future of his younger sons, and so integrated was he into his rural neighborhood along the Old Marlborough Road that he turned confidently to white neighbors for a solution. "Two boys of colour wish for places in good families, one eighteen years old, the other eleven," he advertised in the *Middlesex Gazette*; "said boys are used to farming." The 1820 census shows two youths of the Dugan boys' ages in nearby homes.[40]

The other newcomer was Jack Garrison from New Jersey, whose hope of freedom had been blasted after that state passed a gradual emancipation law in 1804, from whose benefits he was excluded. Six years later, at forty-one, he showed up in Concord and found a place on a farm along Virginia Road in the eastern part of town. The property belonged to Capt. Jonas Minot, stepfather of Cynthia Dunbar. Garrison dwelled in close quarters with the family, which took his place among them for granted. Nearly fifty years later, in a reminiscence of the "Cold Friday" of January 19, 1810, when the temperature suddenly plunged to thirty-three degrees below zero, Cynthia Dunbar Thoreau recalled the little group huddling for warmth in the kitchen, among whom was the fugitive from New Jersey. He would soon marry and be off on his own, but the experience arguably laid the foundation for the young woman's later antislavery activism. Neither Dugan nor Garrison was deterred from settling in Concord by state or federal laws meant to keep slaves in place and out of Massachusetts. They lived and mixed freely in the small town, apparently without concern that an unfriendly neighbor would take steps to send them back into bondage. Concord was the last stop on their journey to freedom.[41]

In November 1812 Garrison wed a widow of African descent, Susan Robbins Middleton, and left the Minot farm for her father's place a couple of miles west. There at the far edge of a sandy plain, once an Indian cornfield and then enclosed as a common planting ground, known to the English settlers as the Great Field, Caesar Robbins had lived since the 1780s. Born into bondage around 1742 in the nearby town of Chelmsford, he had come to Concord as a free man after brief service in the Revolutionary War and settled on two acres that had likely been made available by his former master. It was a lonely spot, two miles north of the high ridge bordering the Bay Road and overlooking the Great Meadow along the Concord River. But it enabled Caesar and his wife, Catherine Boaz (who may have been enslaved in the Bliss and Emerson households), to eke out a living and raise four children to adulthood. The aspiring yeoman was obliged to supplement the produce from his land with day labor for whites, handouts from the female charitable society, and favors from a wealthy farmer named Humphrey Barrett, who made his woodlot freely available for Robbins's needs.

One year the benefactor unexpectedly sent loggers to a section of woods that Caesar had come to regard as his own. The Black veteran raced to inform his patron of the incursion. "Master Barrett," he supposedly said, "I have come to let you know that a parcel of men and teams have broke into *our* wood-lot, and are making terrible destruction of the very best trees, and unless we do something immediately, I will be ruined." Moved by the appeal, Barrett recalled his men without ever divulging the truth. Like his Yankee neighbors, Caesar Robbins sustained independence with a good deal of help.[42]

The little hamlet by the Great Field succeeded the Walden area as the center of Black life. In May 1822 the paterfamilias of the budding settlement died at seventy-six, two days after his wife. Caesar Robbins was Concord's last living link to slavery in colonial Massachusetts, but later generations would remember him neither for his odyssey from bondage to freedom nor for his contribution to the Revolution but for his place on the physical landscape. In little more than a decade, "Caesar's woods" was a familiar spot for a winter's walk, the land at long last in his name. Caesar's thirty-year-old son Peter took up the challenge of building on the father's legacy. In April 1823 he turned to the family benefactor, Humphrey Barrett, and arranged to purchase two pieces of real estate for $260. One parcel consisted of "a dwelling house and barn" plus five acres near the Great Meadow; the other encompassed eight acres of pasture and woodland. This was an unusual purchase. It is doubtful that Robbins had the cash in hand; the cost of the property was equivalent to a year's steady wages for a laborer. Yet the buyer did not follow the common practice of financing the acquisition with a loan from the seller. Nor did Barrett transfer title as a gift in token of his regard for the recipient, as he did in other cases. Even so, he set a restriction on the sale indicative of a charitable intent. The deed reserved to Peter's sister Susan "the right to occupy by herself & family the easterly half of the house and the easterly half of the cellar during her natural life." Evidently Barrett meant to secure the future of the Garrisons and their five young children in the place where they had lived for a decade. A year and a half later, in December 1824, Peter Robbins married Fatima Oliver, a woman of mixed racial origins, from neighboring Acton. Thanks to Barrett's generosity, the two families of color came to share a dwelling in a pattern of co-residence seen in many Concord households. And they could look forward to establishing their own neighborhood of kin, a "Robbinsville" similar to "Hubbardsville" in the south of town, Meriam's corner in the east, and the Barrett's mill district in the west.[43]

The one-and-a-half-story house (about 544 square feet) into which the Robbins and Garrison families moved was a new building constructed for their use: a typical yeoman's dwelling of the sort that had dotted the landscape throughout the eighteenth century, with two rooms on the main floor, plus attic lofts for sleeping and cellar for storage. Its clapboards were unpainted and left to weather with the seasons. A central chimney was designed for heating and cooking in both rooms. It was plain, neat, and respectable, with a bed, tables and chairs, a looking glass, and a teakettle in case guests came calling. Used for cooking, dining, working, and sleeping, each room was a crowded hive of activity, especially for the Garrisons with their growing children. A barn stood nearby to house the farming tools and the two oxen Peter owned by 1826.[44]

The expanding farm at the edge of the Great Field was the base from which these Black families ventured into the mainstream of local life. Each Garrison child walked the proverbial mile to the brick schoolhouse on the common, following "Peter's path" for a half-mile to its terminus at the river road to Carlisle, catty-corner from Ripley's manse, then heading south into the village. Jack Garrison was a familiar figure along the same route, "with his saw-horse over his shoulder and his saw on his arm," off to do a job for Nathan Brooks or Waldo Emerson. He was widely esteemed for his industry and for his skill at cutting, sawing, and splitting wood.[45]

Susan Garrison created her own social network. Not only did she make contact with village families, who hired her to do laundry; she also took sides in the church split. Early in the nineteenth century, she had lived in Boston, as did her siblings Obed and Catherine, and she helped to establish the African Baptist Church on Beacon Hill. After returning to Concord, she apparently maintained that connection. Then in the fall of 1828, as the liberal and orthodox churches competed for members, the pious woman opted for the Trinitarian congregation. Her profession of faith, backed by a letter of recommendation from Rev. Thomas Paul, pastor of the African meetinghouse, won her quick admission into the fold. It also brought her still closer to the Thoreau family and, in particular, to her sisters in communion, the Misses Thoreau. So respectable was the Garrison family that some whites did not hesitate to walk out to the Great Field and pay a social call. One April afternoon in 1836, the Garrisons welcomed a neighbor from just down the river road, eighteen-year-old Martha Prescott, daughter of an up-and-coming politician. Jack Garrison and his son William periodically did chores on the Prescott farm, but that did not keep Martha from visiting a laborer's cottage. The young woman was impressed by the family, especially the mistress of the household. "Mrs. G. is really quite agreeable, her colour is all that draws the line between her & many of our aristocratic dames, for in sound sense she far surpasses many of them." On such positive encounters, Concord's antislavery movement would be built.[46]

For all these gains, severe obstacles stood in the way of economic opportunity and social equality. Racism was pervasive in the press, and white benevolence too often slid into condescending paternalism. One stark reminder of persisting hostility to Black aspirations lay in the hill burying ground. Back in December 1772 a memorial was erected at the grave of John Jack, an African native who had succeeded, by dint of assiduous labors as a shoemaker, in purchasing his freedom. It was inscribed with an eloquent epitaph indicting the injustice of slavery. Composed by the Loyalist lawyer Daniel Bliss, who was executor of the Black man's estate, the lines captured notice on both sides of the Atlantic after a British officer climbed up into the graveyard on the morning of April 19, 1775, to survey the town and happened to notice the stirring words. "God wills us free; man wills us slaves," the eulogy began. "I will as God wills; God's will be done." Then the poetic tribute turned into an elegant assault on the hypocrisy of Patriots who demanded liberty for themselves while holding fellow human beings as slaves. Bliss observed of the Africa-born Jack that

> *Tho' born in a land of slavery,*
> *He was born free,*
> *Tho' he lived in a land of liberty,*
> *He lived a slave.*
> *Till by his honest, tho' stolen labors,*
> *He acquired the source of slavery,*
> *Which gave him his freedom;*
> *Tho' not long before*
> *Death, the grand tyrant*
> *Gave him his final emancipation,*
> *And set him on a footing with kings.*

Touched by the accomplished form and the pertinent sentiments, the Redcoat copied the verse into a letter back home, and Bliss's lines soon appeared in the British press. American newspapers did not reprint them until safely after the war had been won. The "ingenious epitaph" periodically surfaced in Northern publications during the first decades of independence, usually at the instance of a reader who had been in Concord and visited John Jack's grave.

Then in June 1819 the *Middlesex Gazette* reported the distressing news that two years earlier "some person . . . from evil disposition, no doubt" had "entirely demolished" the tombstone, and it lay on the ground in ruins. In an earnest desire to preserve the poetic protest against slaveholding, the newspaper put the verse back into circulation. (No copy of that issue survives; the story is known only from a reprint elsewhere.) For the next decade or so, the rubble went unattended in the burial ground, a forlorn symbol of indifference to slavery and contempt for Blacks. Like the neglected cornerstone of the monument to the Concord Fight, it was a memorial to small minds and mean spirits.

At least a few townspeople were appalled. Around 1830 another lawyer, Rufus Hosmer, whose father Joseph had debated fiercely against Daniel Bliss in the run-up to Revolution, gathered up contributions from townspeople and paid for the erection of a facsimile memorial by Jack's deserted grave, set amid "a cluster of beautiful young locust trees." The last remains of Concord's involvement in slavery would not be expunged. And perhaps a better future for Revolutionary ideals lay in store.[47]

FROM THE MID-1820S TO THE LATE 1830S, CONCORD FLOURISHED IN THE regional economy, as the United States recovered from the downturn precipitated by the Panic of 1819 and then surged on a long wave of growth. No longer did foreign trade set the nation's direction; the premium was now on internal development. Settlers poured onto the Western frontiers; the Cotton Kingdom marched forward on the backs of slaves; New England led the way to industrial revolution. The Erie Canal, completed in 1825, opened the rich agricultural lands of the interior to northeastern markets; the factories of Lowell started up in 1823 and quickly raised mass production of cotton and woolen goods to new heights. The quickening trade spurred demand for the products of Concord's farms and shops, even as it heightened competition for sales at local stores and in expanding urban markets. The town grew over the 1820s to more than two thousand inhabitants—the fastest pace in any decade between Jefferson's election and Lincoln's.[48]

The village garnered the biggest share of that growth. Within a mile of the center lived a thousand people, approximately half of the town, and in their ranks were Concord's wealthiest men, including, as the *Yeoman's Gazette* reported in 1826, sixteen of the seventeen largest taxpayers. Altogether, residents of the center paid two-thirds of the annual tax bill. The future of the renovated village appeared buoyant, prompting one optimistic citizen to draw up a commercial directory for the town, in anticipation of an urban future. It listed some nine stores, forty shops, four hotels and taverns, four doctors and lawyers each, and a variety of county associations, nearly all in the center. John Thoreau's pencil-making shop, in its seventh year, claimed notice along with that of his rival William Munroe. Unfortunately, the guide went unpublished. Even so, for a brief moment, many in Concord could look around the village and imagine themselves at the leading edge of change.[49]

In this age of villages, Concord center dominated the town so thoroughly that it is now hard to see local life beyond its limits. The archives are rich in diaries, letters, autobiographies, and memoirs covering the decades from the dawn of the republic down through the Civil War—nearly all of them written by onetime residents of the village. Likewise for the voluminous account books of stores and shops, the files of old newspapers, and the records of numerous voluntary associations. The center was the base and vantage point of the writers most closely associated with the town. When Emerson made Concord his home in 1835, he settled down in "Coolidge castle" at the terminus of the Cambridge Turnpike with the Bay Road from Lexington, ten minutes from the schoolhouse and meetinghouses that hosted so many of his lectures. In the spring of 1826, the peripatetic Thoreau family left the brick house at the head of the milldam, perhaps to escape the noise and dust of construction, but it stayed put in the center for two decades before taking up residence in 1844 behind the railroad tracks in the first home of their own. Six years later they would be back on Main Street. "He [father] belonged in a peculiar sense to the village street," Henry reflected, "loved to sit in the shops or at the post-office and read the papers." The son was equally a habitué of the village. Apart from a brief stay in Manhattan and his sojourn at Walden, the writer was seldom far from the milldam. To tell the story of Concord in the era of Emerson and Thoreau is to write a history of the central village, and that is the narrative of a changing way of life.[50]

Concord village was an outpost of urban civilization in the countryside. With all the tasteful improvements of the landscape, it projected an appearance of calm, order, and stability. But everyday life was in constant ferment, exposing the townspeople to the same experiences of novelty and change, mobility and uncertainty, diversity and disorder that were the norm in Boston and its sister cities. A constant stream of strangers passed through the town. Some came to clerk in the stores, practice crafts in the shops, or perform domestic service in private homes. Few stayed for long; seven out of ten laborers were gone within five years. There was little to hold them; between 1801 and 1826, the ranks of landless laborers swelled from 156 to 255, an increase of 63 percent, and rose again by a fifth to more than 300 in 1835. Where once the majority of taxpayers possessed the stake in society—the ownership of land—that their Revolutionary fathers deemed essential to republican citizenship, now more than half (56 percent) held none, and with no expectation of ever acquiring title to any land, they quickly moved on. The jubilee of the Concord Fight was celebrated by more newcomers than natives; a decade later, when the town commemorated its bicentennial, those born in Concord made up little more than a third (35 percent) of all adult males.[51]

To this floating population of laboring men were added scores of strangers coming and going daily for the purpose of conducting business, attending a meeting, performing a concert, or perhaps even intruding into local disputes. Starting in 1825, three stage lines ran regular routes through Concord, carrying as many as 150 passengers in a day and 350 a week. On Mondays, Wednesdays, and Saturdays, an early riser could depart Concord around five a.m., arrive at Hanover Street in Boston's North End (not far from the Paul Revere house) at nine a.m., get in a good day's work, take the return stage at four p.m., and be home for supper by eight. The fare from the capital cost one dollar, more than a day's wages for a laborer. One line stopped at the Middlesex Hotel, another at William Shepherd's inn. The Concord Accommodation Stage, co-owned by Shepherd, was true to its name, picking up passengers anywhere in the village and taking them wherever they wished along a route through Lexington, West Cambridge, and Charlestown into Boston, with side trips to Cambridge as needed. The ride required patience, owing not only to the various out-of-the-way stops but also to the famously deliberate pace of the driver; Shepherd's partner Leonard Brown was dubbed "the Deacon" for his "slow, sober" conduct at the reins. The stage line ensured a steady supply of guests at Shepherd's establishment, which won a reputation for its carriage trade. The Middlesex Hotel also thrived on the traffic, as did Hartwell Bigelow's tavern on the main street, a favorite of teamsters and working people. When the census was taken on June 1, 1830, all the inns were full, with twenty persons lodging at Bigelow's, nineteen at Shepherd's, and seventeen at the Middlesex Hotel. No one counted all the horses put up for the night in their stables.[52]

There were good reasons to visit Concord. It was the regular meeting place for political conventions in the county and a frequent venue for annual gatherings of groups from the Middlesex Bible Society to the Middlesex Medical Association. It drew all sorts of traveling attractions and "dealers in wisdom": ventriloquists, elocutionists, and exhibitors of lions, monkeys, elephants, and camels. The town was plugged into the latest fads; in 1833, not long after blackface minstrelsy burst onto the stage in the major Eastern cities, a printer's apprentice reported that "Jim Crow" was being performed in Concord "pretty slick"—a sign of the vibrant white workingmen's culture sustained by the local mechanics. In the area known as "Sleepy Hollow" northwest of the town center, the Society of Middlesex Husbandmen and Manufacturers held its annual cattle show every October from 1820 on, attended by hundreds of people eager to view the exhibits of fat cattle and swine, merino sheep, homemade tablecloths and factory-made broadcloth, and the ever-popular displays of strength and command at the plowing matches.

Four times a year the courthouse on the common was packed with litigants, lawyers, judges, jurors, witnesses, and spectators, all assembled for the sessions of the Middlesex County Court of Common Pleas in March, June, and September and of the supreme judicial court riding circuit in April. Court week in September was an annual holiday on the village calendar, "the Mecca," as one inhabitant recalled, "to which the people of the county repaired for their law business and pleasure." While the leading lawyers and judges of the state were trying cases, "the stores and taverns did a rushing business," and country folk gambled, wrestled, raced horses, ate and drank at booths set up on the common, and caught glimpses of such occasional distinguished visitors as John Quincy Adams and Daniel Webster (with whom Samuel Hoar was at times associated as co-counsel). Each term left a good many people behind in its wake, including at least a few arrested in drunken brawls while court was in session. In the mid-1820s the massive stone jail, kept by Deputy Sheriff Moore, held 160 inmates over the course of a year, with debtors outnumbering criminals two to one; by 1833 that number had jumped to 187. Containing eighteen whitewashed "apartments," the jail had the capacity to hold as many as thirty-six prisoners at a time; in June 1830 the census found eighteen in residence. But a fair number of miscreants got away. Counterfeiters often passed through town with fake banknotes and IOUs. Burglaries were common enough to prompt formation of a society for "detecting rogues and thieves" in 1830.[53]

Concord could not take its status as shire town for granted. In 1812 it tried and failed to become the sole county seat in Middlesex.[54] Sixteen years later its official status was in jeopardy. Early in 1828 a coalition of citizens to the west petitioned the state legislature to break up Middlesex and Worcester counties and carve out a new jurisdiction with courts and offices closer to the residents. The authorities responded by calling for a vote on the plan in all the affected communities. As with previous such proposals, Concord's inhabitants readily set aside differences and united to defend the local economic interest. Were the scheme for a new county to go through, the town would surely see fewer litigants and lawyers in its courts and fewer customers in its taverns and stores. Hardly anyone welcomed that prospect; by a vote of 144 to 1, the town meeting rejected the change. So did most voters in Middlesex and Worcester, even in towns that would presumably benefit most.

Within two years another and more serious threat loomed to the northeast. Lowell was rising fast as a manufacturing center; by 1830, its population was 6,200 and expected to double again in a few years. Those growing numbers put a heavy burden on the courts. Lowell and its neighbors, it was estimated, accounted for a quarter of all cases on the Middlesex dockets. No wonder, then, that the editor of the *Lowell Journal* was already floating ideas for a new county with the city of looms and spindles as its hub. Concord's leaders were quick to disparage any notion of "amputating" Middlesex County. Lowell's claims were exaggerated, the *Yeoman's Gazette* insisted, its demands for recognition premature. While "the great manufacturing city" was entitled to "every advantage, which of right appertains to it," it was not yet "the *true center of the universe*" around which "all other created things" must revolve. Let its citizens wait patiently until that time came and do more to stay out of court. Meanwhile the Middlesex justices concentrated on refurbishing the courthouse on Concord common. So comfortable and "elegant" was the new courtroom, the Concord paper boasted in 1834, that the judges and lawyers would likely be tempted to linger longer in the center than ever.[55]

For two decades the white village enjoyed unprecedented wealth and comfort and fostered widening horizons and cosmopolitan views. The stage lines, like the post office whose mail they delivered and the newspapers they carried, were advance agents of a changing way of life, extending the reach and accelerating the speed of communications and commerce and integrating the country towns of Massachusetts more tightly than ever into regional, national, and international markets. But the expanding economy also subjected the inhabitants of Concord to forces beyond their control: the ups and downs of the business cycle, the whims of supply and demand, competition from rivals in the same trade, fluctuations of currency, changes of public policies, the shifting movements of people, the arrival of unwelcome ideas.

Life in Concord was at once more open and less certain, more promising and less stable. No one could count on staying in the same place. By the time the Mill Dam Company was incorporated in 1829, Dr. Isaac Hurd, once the richest man in town, had fallen from grace, forced by his son's crushing debts and his own overspeculation to sell off his real estate holdings to his erstwhile partners and retreat into an embittered old age. A victim of changes he had helped set in motion, Hurd could take little satisfaction from the progress on the milldam. And if the septuagenarian struggled to comprehend the unsettled times, he was not alone. As Concord grew more diversified and differentiated, as inhabitants came and went with little attachment to its institutions, as new interests competed with older commitments, the bonds of community frayed still more, and the inherited ideology of interdependence underwent further strain.[56]

The Curse of Trade

David Henry Thoreau grew up in the heart of a business community whose devotion to buying and selling, getting and spending, he came to loathe. "Trade curses every thing it handles," he would write in *Walden*, "and though you trade in messages from heaven, the whole curse of trade attaches to the business." Yet he was a child of commerce himself, grandson of a self-made merchant who had built up a fortune in trade, and son of a storekeeper who had lost his share of that wealth. John Thoreau's early years in business were an unhappy story of repeated failures, brought on by bad timing and risky choices that burdened his household for decades; only after giving up the countinghouse for the manufactory and concentrating on making pencils did he gradually climb his way back to prosperity. Even then he could not just produce a useful writing implement and count on customers at his door. He had to employ the arts of marketing and salesmanship and compete successfully against rivals. That was a challenge the pencil maker accepted with little relish and that his proud son deplored.

The merchants and manufacturers who rose to prominence in Concord readily tackled the demands of a changing marketplace. Achieving success in business required paying close attention to shifting needs and tastes, and it rewarded efficiency and innovation in meeting them. It also called for less worthy talents. It could demand the pursuit of self-interest at the expense of others. It could mean breaking one's word in an economy built on trust and cheating partners to get out of a deal. It could devalue labor and skill in favor of price and profit. In these ways and more, it tested the norms of neighborliness and the injunction to interdependence. With good reason Emerson would complain that "we eat and drink and wear perjury and fraud in a hundred com-modities." The Transcendentalists were not alone in making such criticisms. Many of their contemporaries worried about the ways money was being made in a society where all values, moral as well as economic, appeared to be in flux. The business history of Concord in the early republic helps to explain why.[1]

IN THE FALL OF 1808, JOHN THOREAU WAS A YOUNG MAN IN A HURRY. THAT October he marked his twenty-first birthday and legally came of age. Ever since his father's death seven years before, his inheritance had been in the hands of a legal guardian, who doled out money for his upkeep and oversaw his training for a mercantile calling. The youth had spent his teenage years clerking in John White's store next door to his home on the common and then in a dry goods house in Salem, perhaps to learn the China trade. With his days of dependency at an end, he was determined to go into business on his own. No matter that American commerce was disrupted by federal embargoes on trade, with the prices of imports shooting up and earnings from exports dwindling. Nor that Concord's population was declining, along with that of many of its neighbors.[2] Thoreau was undeterred, too, by the prospect of competing with a half-dozen other village retailers, the latest of which had started up a year earlier in the well-known green store on the square. That establishment was operated by twenty-five-year-old Isaac Hurd, Jr., the wealthy doctor's son, just back from four years as a supercargo on trading voyages to Canton, and its shelves were stocked with chests of Souchong tea and bales of Nankeen cloth. It stood just forty or fifty feet away from the yellow store where the ambitious Thoreau now proposed to do business. His landlord was Dr. Hurd.[3]

Despite all these reasons for caution, the aspiring merchant plunged ahead. Two days after his birthday, he turned to his widowed stepmother and bor-rowed $1,500, pledging as security part of his inheritance, a one-eighth share in Boston real estate that his father had owned and that now generated a regu-lar rental income for the heirs. He took that loan, added another $600 that he could immediately claim from the paternal estate, and invested in goods for the store. He had no partner with whom to share the risk—a normal arrangement of the time. He never advertised his business in the Boston press. He lacked the capital to sustain himself if it took a while to build a clientele. And he strug-gled to collect from customers who did not pay their bills on time. Hardly had he opened for business than he was in court suing for nonpayment of debts.[4]

Among the delinquents was Isaac Hurd, Jr., himself, who had failed to redeem a promise to pay $130 on demand in exchange for "value received." Just as John Thoreau was impatient to enter trade, so he could not postpone his need for cash. The crisis came quickly. The yellow store closed in under two years. By the spring of 1811 John Thoreau was in Bangor, Maine (then part of the Commonwealth of Massachusetts), peddling goods to the Penobscot Indians.[5]

He had not given up on a life in trade. In and out of Concord, he clerked at Josiah Davis's store on Main Street and had a brief stab at being a Boston merchant. By 1817, the year of David Henry's birth, his prospects looked dim. Following his stepmother's death, he was called upon to settle his accumulated debt to her estate, and when he proved unable to do so, his mortgaged share in the Boston house was sold at auction. Even then an outstanding balance of $290 had to be written off "on account of [his] poverty." A year later, after the assets in his late father's estate were finally disbursed to the heirs and he had received just under $900 as his due, he was ready to test fate with another venture, this time in the town of Chelmsford. Once again his timing was unlucky. The Panic of 1819 set off a prolonged depression, claiming among its victims the fledgling store. The business lasted two and a half years, six months longer than the yellow store. His career as a merchant at an end, the thirty-four-year-old father of four had to start over yet again.[6]

John Thoreau had many counterparts. In the eighteenth century, Concord imported merchants from the coast or raised its own, shipping sons to work in countinghouses in Boston or Salem or to sail the seas on trading voyages across the globe. Thoreau and Hurd followed those routes. In the early republic, the town itself became a commercial destination. From the hill country along the central Massachusetts–New Hampshire border, a steady stream of ambitious young men flowed into the place from which their forebears had emigrated a generation or two before in search of land. With the thin, rocky soil of the upcountry wearing out, they were now looking for alternatives to the family farm. So were a handful of newcomers from nearby Acton and Lincoln as well as natives born and bred in Concord. From wherever they hailed, nearly all were destined for disappointment. Years later Henry Thoreau would estimate that "a very large majority, even ninety-seven in a hundred," were "sure to fail." Well aware of his father's ill fortunes in trade, he was not wide of the mark.[7]

Numerous hopefuls passed through the six or seven stores in Concord village. Of some thirty-four men in business between 1808 and 1835, only a dozen lasted more than five years.[8] The personnel behind the counters turned over faster than the goods on the shelves. Lysander L. Bascom came from Ashby to clerk in the green store, and in November 1826, when his service was over, he set out on his own at twenty-one, launching a new dry goods outlet with one Aaron Thompson on the milldam. But an "unforeseen" fire in the shop—a suspected arson—obliged the partners to sell off what they could and close within a year. Undaunted, Bascom started over in February 1828 with a fresh associate, William Cole from Lincoln, in the same place—an arrangement lasting a mere six weeks, owing to his partner's sudden death. With one Cole gone, Bascom recruited another, and Bascom & Cole was revived. Eleven months later the sheriff seized the store's goods for nonpayment of debts, including some fifteen hundred books put up for public auction. By the summer of 1829, Bascom was back in Ashby, once more a dependent in his uncle's household, hiding from creditors and desperate for funds. "My situation at present is very unpleasant," he advised his lawyer, Nathan Brooks.

Bascom's failure was due only in part to the accidents of fire and death. It owed much to the inexperience or imprudence of youth. Bascom entered trade shortly after reaching maturity, with partners no older than he. His situation was typical of the transients coming and going as proprietors, few of whom could call on the ample resources of a wealthy father like Hurd. Rather than bide their time clerking for a merchant and slowly amassing start-up capital, the country youths who flocked into Concord center were eager for independence and impatient to make their mark. Seldom did they possess the means to persevere when business proved slow and debts piled up. Better to make way for another overoptimist and try again in a different town.[9]

Samuel Burr and Daniel Shattuck beat the odds and prospered in trade. In the mid-1820s their rival stores were fixtures on the common, offering the largest and most varied stocks of European, West Indian, and American goods in town. Yet when they started out a decade and a half earlier, there had been little to distinguish them from the other hopefuls who made brief stops before moving on. Both merchants, some two years apart in age, grew up on modest farms in the Massachusetts–New Hampshire borderland, and for the most part, they had to make their own way in the world. Shattuck arrived in 1806 as a teenager to clerk in the Davis brothers' store; Burr showed up five years later after completing his training in Boston. Each launched into business in his early to midtwenties, Burr in combination with Moses Prichard, a clerk for Hurd at the green store, and Shattuck in partnership with Bela Hemenway, a native of Groton twenty miles to the northwest. Going into business signaled their coming of age.

How did these young men acquire the means to open their own stores? Their partners undoubtedly helped; it was doubtless in recognition of the family money they supplied that the firms were originally known as Moses Prichard & Company and Hemenway & Shattuck. But the key to the new businesses was a fortunate combination of patronage and timing. At the very moment Shattuck and Hemenway were hoping to get into trade, the veteran merchant John White, at sixty-three, was looking to retire from the store he had run at the northwest corner of the common for nearly forty years. The older man achieved his goal by making the younger ones an offer they could hardly refuse. His entire stock of goods, consisting of British textiles, crockery, hardware, glassware, hollow ware (pots, kettles, Dutch ovens), paints, books, and West Indian rum and sugar, many "of the latest importations," was theirs for the sum of $5,000—a figure White estimated, to Shattuck's astonishment, without even taking an inventory. The two-story building in which all these items were sold was available for an annual rent of $100. In exchange, the novice partners would assume White's debts to his Boston suppliers and provide IOUs for the rest of the assets. White required only $1,000 as a down payment. Hemenway and Shattuck could pay the bulk of their obligation in notes due on a staggered schedule eighteen months or more in the future. Not a penny in interest was charged.

In effect, White was turning over a business ready to go, with a well-established clientele and a central location, and thanks to his generous credit terms, he was financing his successors' entrance into trade. But the bargain nonetheless involved considerable risk. In November 1812, when the new partners signed the agreement, the United States was at war with Britain, and prices for imported goods had soared. If peace had come quickly, bursting the bubble, Hemenway & Shattuck would have been ruined. Luckily for them, the war was prolonged. Aggressively advertising "as great a variety of Goods as is to be found in any store in the country" and promising "the lowest Boston prices" for cash sales, the new firm reaped wartime profits on White's old stock. When the conflict ended, British exporters dumped a huge backlog of goods on the American market, and following Hemenway's death early in 1816, Shattuck faced hard times. Once again he turned to White, who reentered business in partnership with the younger man and furnished the resources to ride out the postwar slump. Shattuck continued his ascent to the top of the economic order. By the mid-1820s, his estate was assessed at some $13,000—the biggest in town.[10]

Burr & Prichard harvested a similar bounty, having acquired Hurd's inventory at peacetime rates, doubtless on credit. They quickly secured a further advantage. In 1811 the green store became the headquarters of the post office under the auspices of Republican politician John L. Tuttle and his successor Keyes. It was common practice to locate post offices in village stores, and smart politics as well. Attentive to the many newspapers and magazines passing through their hands, Burr and Prichard were among the first to learn the latest news and to pass it along to their patrons. As they listened to conversations among townspeople picking up mail, the merchants regularly took the political pulse of the village. Running a post office was a job that never let up; seven days a week Burr, Prichard, or their clerks rose early to meet the mail stage, then kept the store open late to accommodate people who were expecting letters or anxious for the news. But the rewards were considerable, far exceeding the modest annual rent the postmaster paid for the use of the premises. Situated at the heart of the village and performing a vital public service, the green store developed into the town's communications hub. Within two years of operation, Burr & Prichard had some two hundred customers on the books. No wonder the firm seldom bothered to advertise its wares in the press. Why waste the money when virtually everyone in town had occasion to visit the store?[11]

The country store was an emporium of goods from around the world. It brought tea from China, coffee from Java, spices from the Indies, lemons from Spain, sherry from Portugal, chocolate from Caracas and Chiapas, rum and sugar from Jamaica, and cigars from the Caribbean and carried them deep into the American hinterland, to be enjoyed on tableware from the factories of Josiah Wedgwood and other English exporters. It outfitted Yankee men and women in clothes made from fabrics spun and woven by machine in the burgeoning factories of Britain and by hand in sweatshops from Italy to India and China. By the second decade of the nineteenth century, textiles from New England mills, including the manufactory in western Concord, were also on offer.

Whatever their origins, these amenities were regularly available throughout the year; confident of steady supplies, townspeople bought such goods in modest quantities—two or three pounds of coffee, a gallon of wine, a few yards of cloth at a time—and returned often to replenish their cupboards.

Also available was the produce of local farms—eggs and butter, veal and pork—and the output of nearby shops, ranging from almanacs and primers to boots and shoes. From beyond New England came the bounty of the fertile lands in the West. In a sign of changes impending in the local way of life, "Genesee white wheat flour" from western New York, shipped down the Erie Canal, went on sale in local stores at the very moment the old gristmill on the dam was on its way to extinction.[12]

The country store taught lessons in consumerism to rural folk who liked to boast of their self-sufficiency when they were not out shopping. Textiles of every variety and source—used for clothing, curtains, tablecloths, and bed hangings—dominated the curriculum. They constituted a merchant's largest investment, roughly a third to a half of his outlay on inventory.[13] It was their imposing presence on the shelves, in neatly folded piles behind the counter, that identified a commercial establishment as a *dry goods* store. At home, in fields, or in shops, Concordians were content to wear "linsey-woolsey," made of flax and wool from their farms. But when company came calling in the parlor, when families assembled for Sunday meeting, or when couples danced in the ballroom of the Middlesex Hotel, fashionable people put on their best clothes, cut from silks, cottons, and woolens bought at the store and tailored according to the styles popular in London and Paris. Merchants were keenly aware of those preferences, filling the press with advertisements in large, bold type to catch the eye.

A preference for imported fabrics prevailed through the 1820s, long after the spindles and looms of New England's mills began producing a profusion of cheap textiles. Even the "rogue" who broke into Burr & Prichard's store in August 1827 was discriminating. "From its well filled shelves," reported the *Yeoman's Gazette*, he "purloined a fine piece of black broadcloth, containing ten or twelve yards, worth sixty or seventy dollars." The thief was surely a local resident. For how else could he have selected his cloth "with so much judgment"? It was "one of the finest pieces in the store."[14]

The advance of consumerism met occasional resistance in the press. Self-styled bachelors and workingmen prepared the way for Henry Thoreau with acerbic commentaries on the follies of fashion and the wastefulness of luxuries. Usually women got the blame for this misbegotten economy. Why had he rejected the "noblest inheritance this world affords, that of a beloved rib," and opted for a life of "single blessedness"? Not for lack of interest, claimed one penny-pinching bachelor. Rather, "to marry and maintain a wife agree-ably to their notions of gentility" requires "the wealth of a Nabob." Back in his grandmothers' time, nearly all men found mates who were committed to "prudence and domestic economy." Sadly, now young ladies were so "indulged in idleness, fine dress and all the vanities" that if a man declined to "provide her with silks, Laces, Leghorns and a thousand other expensive knicknacks," he was rejected as an "unfeeling stingy brute."[15]

Not all anticonsumerism was fueled by misogyny. Some observers discerned in the new plethora of goods a threat to hierarchies of all sorts, class as well as gender. Status-seeking workingmen were as tempted as women by the allure of fancy clothes and furnishings. Forgetting that "the life of a mechanic is a life of care," requiring "prudence and economy," they sought a quick path to upward mobility in fashionable manners and dress. No one was fooled by such store-bought pretensions. "To endeavor to compete with the rich in the display of . . . dress, furniture and other extravagances," observed "A Mechanic," was a guaranteed "road to ruin." Whatever he wore, a laboring man intruding into cultivated circles was out of place and sure to suffer the fate of the frog in Aesop's Fables, "who endeavored to swell to the size of an ox" and ultimately burst to death, in a "foolish example of ignorant pride." The lesson was simple: do not "attempt an impossible thing." Clothes do not make the man.[16]

The warnings against conspicuous consumption dissipated when custom-ers stepped inside the stores, surveyed the goods on display, and encountered the blandishments of merchants. Shattuck was a keen observer of salesman-ship, and in the memoirs he wrote late in life, he took the measure of the store-keepers he had known in youth. His patron and sometime partner, Deacon John White, was "not a well-educated merchant"; nor was he stirred by compe-tition. His fortunes were made during the boom years of the 1790s and early 1800s, when it took no great skill to buy goods "with ordinary care" and sell them at the "desired profits." White counted on his prime location on the common and his reputation for "integrity and fair dealing" to keep the cus-tomers coming. Skeptics did suggest that White sold liquor "so weak that it would not run down hill" and gunpowder with so little spirit that after a cask caught fire, "more than half of it was burned" before the flames were put out. But who could doubt the sincerity of the retailer, who welcomed the boys and girls of the village into his store every New Year's Day and, after receiving their polite greetings, presented them with "little books"? If some parents abused the kindness and dispatched Johnny or Sally to the store with a shameless message—"Deacon, I wish you a happy New Year, and mother says I may take a primer, and the rest in sugar"—the merchant paid no mind. His acts of neighborliness and charity tempered suspicions of self-interestedness.[17]

In his own practice as a merchant, Shattuck cultivated a friendly acquaintance with one and all. Though trade was his second choice—he had been preparing for college when his father's health broke and money fell short—the New Hampshire farm boy was "eminently fitted" for the countinghouse. In the view of one contemporary, "he had a gift for trade." With an ingratiating manner, he made his store a welcoming place for leisurely shopping and conversation. He could talk easily and wittily on any subject, and "no man was more polite" to the ladies. He also was a packrat, who collected "all manner of 'odds and ends'" in his store and barn for sale or loan. His public spirit was undeniable. No one served on more town committees or supported civic improvements more earnestly. But he never lost sight of business. He remained "cool" and "sharp" in the hardest bargaining. The patina of neighborliness did not win everyone over. "There might perhaps have been some question of the frankness and sincerity of his cordial smile and greeting." But who could complain when the genial storekeeper concluded every large sale with a friendly alcoholic "treat"?[18]

In contrast to Shattuck, anecdotes about Burr are wanting. He and Prichard embodied the genteel style that the goods in their store were meant to furnish. The former was remembered as an "active, courteous, pleasant, gentlemanly, well-dressed, but reserved, dignified, and sensible man," while the latter left behind a reputation as "a thorough gentleman of the old school, with those good manners, kind and deferential, which are fast taking their place among the lost arts." When the success of a store was built on personal relationships, sociability and politeness mattered. The storekeepers were walking advertisements for the consumer revolution.[19]

For all the shows of neighborliness, Shattuck and Burr kept an eye on the bottom line. Their store accounts recorded every customer's purchases and payments. On the first of April, the start of a new business year, Shattuck consulted the books and drew up a statement of his financial condition. By that date, customers were expected to pay their bills, either in cash or in commodities. Just about anything from farm and shop was acceptable, with values set by prevailing prices in Boston. Most mingled such "country pay" with banknotes and coins.[20]

At some stores charges could remain on the books for years without incurring interest. But Shattuck obliged delinquents to sign formal notes promising to pay outstanding sums on demand at 6 percent interest, the limit set by law. He regularly classified these IOUs into three categories: "good," "doubtful," and "bad," and when necessary, he dunned the debtors and took them to court.[21]

Building up capital, the traders branched out as creditors, lending money to local businesses and providing mortgages on farms. Foreclosure was one way to amass real estate; speculation in distressed property was another. Shattuck emerged as a leading landlord, from whom the Thoreau family rented a house on Main Street from 1827 to 1835. (He would later sell John Thoreau the "yellow house" farther down that street, taking a thousand-dollar mortgage in July 1850 to secure payment.) The storekeepers were familiar figures at public auctions, bidding on dwellings and farms seized for back taxes or debts. Steadily, more and more property gravitated into their control. In the 1820s close to half of Concord's 354 adult male taxpayers (47 percent) depended on others for housing, whether in parents' or employers' homes, in boarding-houses kept by such women as Cynthia Thoreau, or in rentals supplied by such village grandees as Hurd, Shattuck, and Josiah Davis.[22]

Shattuck's influence extended to all corners of town, including the little hamlet overlooking the Great Meadow where the Robbins and Garrison families dwelled. In 1823 Peter Robbins acquired his house and thirteen-plus acres free from debt, but the returns from the farm, supplemented by earnings from day labor, proved insufficient to keep up with expenses. In March 1827 he lacked the money for a butcher's bill for $18.83, so he signed a note pledging to pay the amount "on demand with interest." Three years passed, and his financial needs grew more urgent. Like so many other townspeople, the Black yeoman turned to Shattuck for aid. The merchant was forthcoming with a mortgage loan of $200, less than the property had originally cost. Not long afterward he paid the outstanding note to the butchers, in exchange for the right to cut "what wood he thinks proper" from Robbins's lot. All the while the charges to the farmer's account at the creditor's store accumulated. Shattuck did not wait long for payment. In April 1832 he foreclosed on the house and land and months later won a court judgment of $68.50 for the unpaid grocery bills. The title to all Robbins's real estate, except for his wife's dower right, was transferred to Shattuck. The potential independence of an African American family faded, as the richest man in town added to his holdings. The

Robbins and Garrison families now became, like the Thoreau household, tenants of the sharp-eyed investor.[23]

Diversification was the way to wealth. Gathering up surplus crops from the countryside for sale to the growing population of the village or for shipment to the rising industrial center of Lowell and the busy port of Boston, Concord's merchants operated as independent agents in the organization of economic life. But the earnings from country stores were limited and uncertain.[24] Financial investments and ancillary enterprises promised to cushion merchants against the vicissitudes of trade. Shattuck bought stock in banks from Boston to Lowell, and in 1822 he joined with Burr and other local business and political leaders to push for the incorporation of a Middlesex Bank in Concord, with an authorized capital of $100,000. (The enterprise was stillborn; apparently the promoters were unable to raise the necessary funds.) By the early 1830s, Shattuck was as active in banking as in storekeeping, serving as director of banks and insurance companies in Boston, Lowell, and Concord and as president of the Concord Bank at its organization in 1832. Meanwhile Burr & Prichard were running "a sort of savings bank" out of their store, taking deposits from a good many townspeople and paying interest without fail on even "the smallest amount."[25]

The merchants undertook entrepreneurial ventures of their own. Burr shipped 1,060 "bunches" of onions to Haiti in 1823 and twenty-five barrels of cranberries to New Orleans a few years later (the latter at a loss of $150). Shattuck put his energies into cottage industry. In January 1831 he advertised for workers to braid "1,000 Palm Leaf hats." In an elaborate network of production, he and other storekeepers, including Josiah Davis, acquired palm leaf from Cuba and the Virgin Islands from import merchants in Boston and put the raw materials out to rural households for women and children to braid into hats. The headwear was destined for slaves on Southern plantations and farm laborers in the West. Shattuck profited from the venture in two ways at once: first, from the sale of the hats, and second, from increased demand at his store, since the workers were paid in credits for goods. Burr & Prichard took a direct role in Concord's own industrial revolution; they invested in David Loring's lead pipe manufactory along the Assabet River and were among the four incorporators of the company in 1828. No sector of the advancing economy of New England went unnoticed by Concord's wide-awake merchants. Agriculture, commerce, manufacturing, finance: Burr and Shattuck had their hands in them all.[26]

The quickening of economic life to which Burr and Shattuck contributed made business more competitive and the position of established merchants less secure. Until the War of 1812 cut off transatlantic commerce, these country retailers ordered their goods from leading countinghouses in Boston, which dealt, in turn, with well-established exporters in Britain. The system rested on long-term credit and trust. But in 1815, with the resumption of trade, these arrangements were undercut, after London merchants, needing to unload the immense inventories that had piled up in their warehouses during the conflict, bypassed long-standing partners to sell their commodities to one and all at public auction. This cash business, conducted by American firms specializing in the marketing of dry goods, led to reduced prices throughout the supply chain. No longer dealing in credit, auction houses passed on savings to small-town traders, who, in turn, offered unprecedented bargains to customers with ready money.

The innovation took hold alongside the older way of doing business. It reflected the ethos of the auction: fast-paced, impersonal, and a little shady, with buyers well advised to beware. And it challenged the loyalty of patrons at Concord's stores. Concord got its first "Cheap Store" in the spring of 1822, when a new firm advertised "a complete assortment of ENGLISH, INDIA, FRENCH, AMERICAN & WEST INDIAN GOODS" for sale "LOW for CASH." "As they will receive their goods direct from the importers," Adams & Potter explained, "they can afford and will sell as cheap as can be obtained at retail in Boston." That store turned out to be a fly-by-night operation, but the strategy of low prices for cash quickly spread, and Shattuck could ill afford to ignore the competition. In December 1823 he too placed a notice of "Cheap Goods" in the press, under which he listed "an extensive variety of STAPLE and FANCY" articles always on hand—unlike other stores, he insinuated, which attracted shoppers with false promises. Shattuck & Company continued to sell goods on the traditional basis "for Cash or credit," but the firm also promoted its "large assortment of SPRING & SUMMER GOODS."[27]

The premium on cash payment was made possible by the astonishing growth of American banking. Nearly two hundred banks were in operation in 1815, some 321 by 1830. The Concord Bank joined the ranks two years later. These financial institutions, chartered by state governments, took deposits, granted loans, and issued notes that gave the new nation's expanding economy an indispensable medium of exchange. Banknotes were, in principle, equivalent to hard money in the vault. Simply present a ten-dollar note to the cashier and receive the same in gold and silver coins. That was the promise carried by the tens of thousands of notes circulating across the countryside in the 1820s and 1830s and facilitating trade at Concord's stores. Capitalism—the buying and selling of goods and labor on free markets—was already, by 1800, the norm for most production and exchange in the Boston region. Banks fueled its further advance with liberal supplies of money.

The promises printed on banknotes could prove illusory. The bills were institutional IOUs, no different in principle from personal notes signed by individuals pledging payment in cash. Their value rested, at bottom, on trust. Did a bank actually possess the specie reserves to redeem its notes? And were those notes actually authorized by that bank? Wherever banknotes circulated, counterfeits were quick to follow. As early as 1818, *Niles' Weekly Register*, the *Wall Street Journal* of its day, worried that the United States was in danger of becoming "a nation of counterfeiters."[28]

The periodical could have taken Concord as a case in point. In December 1818 the townspeople were shocked by the news that Daniel Smith, who had succeeded John Thoreau in the yellow store on the common, was accused of counterfeiting. The charge was instigated by Burr, who had seen Smith passing ten-dollar notes on the Bank of Auburn in New York State and suspected they were phony. A search of Smith's premises found further evidence of monetary fraud, including "a great number" of counterfeit notes, ninety-one in all, purporting to be from the Phoenix Bank of Connecticut, and equipment to mint five-, ten-, and twenty-cent silver coins. If that was not bad enough, Smith also had to answer complaints that he had rigged the scales in his store to produce short weights.

Daniel Smith was yet another country boy come down from the New Hampshire hills to try his luck in Concord. Trained as a tanner, he had labored as a journeyman for Stephen Wood before venturing into selling patent medicines and groceries. With a winning way and free glasses of rum at the store, Smith got himself elected a captain in the militia and rose to master of the local Masonic lodge. Soon he was calling himself "gentleman." But his character was as trustworthy as his freshly minted coins. Found guilty by the state supreme court on three counts of counterfeiting, the forty-five-year-old felon was sentenced to five years' hard labor in the state prison at Charlestown.[29]

As it turned out, confidence in Smith's accuser, Samuel Burr, was also misplaced, with far more damaging consequences. In the mid-1820s the merchant was seemingly thriving in trade. The green store was the crossroads of the community, with some five hundred customers of every rank and order on the books, a good many of whom had entrusted their savings to the firm. Burr was also a rising figure in politics. A major in the county militia, he was elected in 1827 to the first of three terms as Concord's representative to the legislature. His personal affairs were looking up, too. In November 1828 the most eligible bachelor in Concord, at forty-one, finally wed a "very pretty, agreeable, and lively" schoolmistress a dozen years his junior, and he set about building "an elegant Cottage" for his new bride befitting their high standing in the local elite.[30]

Appearances were deceiving. The Burr & Prichard partnership scrambled to stay afloat, as it coped with the new developments that were simultaneously increasing sales and undermining rural retailers. Where once the Concord store ordered its inventory from Boston suppliers and paid with goods and cash from the local clientele, it was now pinched for funds to pay buyers and sellers alike. The cheap stores siphoned off some business. Worse was the defection of farmers, who drove cattle to Brighton and teamed commodities to Boston in order to bargain with merchants there for higher prices and larger profits. Not that the wholesalers on whom the green store depended—the urban distilleries of rum, refineries of sugar, suppliers of crockery, hardware, and textiles—had any interest in the foodstuffs from Concord's farms. These firms demanded cash and soon, within sixty or ninety days.[31]

As the pressures mounted, the green store continued to take payment in local butter and eggs, beef and pork, and barrels of cider, most of it destined for consumers in the village. It was also a regular outlet for the fine red pencils John Thoreau produced at his shop. The merchants took as many as one hundred gross at a time, plus the quires and reams of paper the manufacturer obtained in the course of trade. But Thoreau was an exception; after 1819 William Munroe sold his pencils in the city.[32]

Ultimately, Burr & Prichard required capital, for which they turned to banks in Boston and Cambridge, borrowing substantial sums from $150 to $1,000 on short-term loans at 6 percent interest. The proceeds went to repay their suppliers. Juggling the bills was a constant balancing act. No sooner was one debt paid off than another was contracted. Getting customers to settle their accounts was a top priority, though Burr was surely inclined to go easy on patrons whose votes he needed for reelection.

Amid these pressures, Burr's personal circumstances worsened. In mid-

March 1829 a sudden fire reduced the new house he was building to ashes; it was uninsured. Eleven months later a thief broke into the green store on "a bright moonlit night" and, "in full view of nearly a dozen dwelling houses," got away with fifty dollars in silver coins and a counterfeit bill on a Boston bank. Burr was distracted by family matters, too. His forty-six-year-old brother, who suffered from mental illness, escaped notice, got drunk, and ended up in the county jail. Not even the birth of a son dispelled the gloom. The merchant's health failed, and on doctor's orders, he made plans to depart Concord during the winter of 1830–31 and seek relief in the warm air and mineral waters of St. Marys, Georgia.

In preparation for the trip and under financial distress, Burr and Prichard dissolved their business and turned over the store to a newcomer, who paid with an IOU. The ailing Burr sold or mortgaged nearly all his real estate and Mill Dam holdings to the same gentlemen—Shattuck, Brooks, Hoar, and Prichard—with whom he had collaborated over the years. Perhaps he hoped to start over once his health revived. Upon arriving with his wife at the Georgia spa, Burr was initially upbeat. St. Marys "is the land to heal all diseases—you would be astonished to see the variety of invalids here," he reported. But he could not deny the evidence before his eyes. "They are seeking this place from all parts of the country and droping [sic] along and many that even reach here live but to see their place of exit."[33]

So it was with Burr. News of his death in "a remote region" reached Concord on April 23, 1831, nineteen days after the event. In a short obituary, the Yeoman's Gazette paid tribute to the "enterprising merchant" who was "for many years . . . one of the most valued inhabitants," a man noted for "sterling integrity, sound judgment, liberal sentiments, and untarnished reputation . . . The death of such a man is a loss to the community, a misfortune not readily repaired." That statement proved prescient. Four months later Burr's estate went into probate, and the appraisers discovered that the seemingly prosperous businessman had died deeply in debt. He was hardly poor, with an estate valued at $10,280, but the homestead was mortgaged, as was the furniture. Most of his wealth consisted of IOUs, signed by thirty-one persons; unfortunately, nearly half of it was owed by the purchaser of the green store, who had already gone out of business. The other side of the ledger was a disaster. Burr owed an astounding $18,488 to some forty-eight claimants. The estate was insolvent.

The probate report provided a postmortem on Burr & Prichard. The firm, it turned out, was in as ill health as the senior partner. The biggest debts were owed to the Boston wholesalers, who had supplied hardware, groceries, and rum to the store. The Lowell Bank held an outstanding note; the Middlesex Mutual Fire Insurance Company, of which Burr had been a director, another. Many of the claims, accounting for over half the obligations, came from Burr's neighbors and particularly from prominent figures in the village, including Hoar, Keyes, and Abel Moore. Leading institutions in Concord—the First Parish, the Trustees of the Ministerial Fund—were also entangled in Burr's web of debts. Unlike the Boston merchant houses, most of these local creditors were not seeking payment for goods supplied to the green store. They simply wanted the return of the hard-earned money they had entrusted with the partners in expectation of obtaining a safe harbor for their surplus funds.

No one had an inkling of the gathering storm, perhaps not even Burr. To many townspeople, the informal bank at the green store had been a community service provided by the generous partners. In reality, the biggest beneficiaries had been Burr and Prichard themselves. Their customers' savings had rescued the firm from bankruptcy time and again. Subject to no reserve requirements, the storekeepers welcomed deposits, mingled the money with their own, and paid bills, loans, and interest as they came due. So long as no one lost confidence, there was no cause for concern, and no one in town was the wiser. Behind the scenes, the merchants were constantly robbing Peter to pay Paul, and the day of reckoning came when Burr's time ran out. His pretense of prosperity proved no more reliable than the scales at Daniel Smith's store.[34]

As Burr's fortunes crumbled, Shattuck rose to new heights in the economic and political order. In 1824, after operating on his own for a few years, he recruited his younger brother Lemuel, a sickly schoolmaster in the frontier city of Detroit, back to New England and took him into the business. Daniel Shattuck & Company flourished for the next eight years, meeting the challenge of the cheap stores, keeping up with the latest fashions, advertising regularly for customers throughout Middlesex County, and attracting the trade of backcountry farmers eager for a convenient alternative to Boston as an outlet for their goods. When the new firm started up, its stock in trade was valued at $10,000—double the amount with which Shattuck had begun in 1812—and the senior partner estimated his net worth at $21,635. Eight years later, when the partnership was dissolved, that figure had increased to $32,000.

This fortune rested less on the country store than on shares in bank and insurance companies, mortgage loans, and real estate. By the mid-1830s the Concord Bank and the Mill Dam Company were occupying his attention far more than crockery and yard goods, and Shattuck was glad to hand over the daily conduct of the store to a new partner. He was busy with politics, too. A frequent member of town committees, he joined with Burr and Josiah Davis in managing the town fund for constructing the still-unfinished monument to the Concord Fight. The voters rewarded his service with election to succeed Burr as representative in the statehouse; several years later he was elevated to the senate. His wealth and standing stood out on the landscape. His "Mansion House" on the common, a new two-story hip roof structure, claimed the notice not only of visitors to the village but also of readers of John Warner Barber's 1839 survey of the "history and antiquities of every town in Massachusetts." An engraving of "Colonel Shattuck's residence" prominently illustrated the section on Concord. There he and wife Sarah raised four children and socialized often with the village elite. The suave financier, who grew "stout" and "rather florid" over the years, was well on his way to becoming one of "The Rich Men of Massachusetts"—a status he was granted, in an 1851 book of that title, in recognition of possessing an estate said to be worth $100,000. To judge by his fortune, Shattuck was virtually without peer in the town. His only real rival was Squire Hoar.[35]

In Shattuck's case, appearances matched reality. But in a fluctuating economy and fluid society, where the facade of wealth too often rested on a flimsy foundation, where fashionable dress and polite manners could conceal lowly origins, and where upstart merchants turned out to be counterfeiting gentlemen, who would be the next Daniel Smith or Samuel Burr? As business grew more impersonal and population more transient, that question gained urgency. Even in a small town of two thousand, whom could you trust?

JOHN THOREAU COULD NOT HAVE BECOME A PENCIL MAKER BUT FOR WILliam Munroe, and Munroe never expected to make pencils. The industry did not even exist in America during the 1790s when he was apprenticing to the craft of cabinetmaking in his hometown of Roxbury. Like so many other finished goods, pencils were made abroad and imported into the United States. England had long dominated the trade, thanks to the discovery of graphite in the Cumberland Hills of the Lake District back in the sixteenth century. The crucial ingredient in lead pencils, the mineral made possible the development of a writing implement that over the next two and a half centuries gained widespread use in everyday life. The common pencil was employed by clerks and surveyors, artists and diarists, schoolboys and goodwives for scribbling notes and sketching pictures. But its availability could not be taken for granted. As the republic drifted toward war with Britain in 1812, the supply threatened to dry up.[36]

The nation's need was Munroe's opportunity. In 1800, not long after completing his apprenticeship and coming of age, the journeyman cabinetmaker had settled in Concord, where he fashioned mahogany cases to house the clocks assembled by his brothers on the milldam and made ordinary bureaus, tables, chairs, cradles, and coffins for other customers. He did well enough in the good times before the embargo of 1807 to marry and start a family, but in the ensuing years work for cabinetmakers and "every other business of a common mechanical kind" fell to "its lowest ebb." In 1811, around the same time John Thoreau was shutting his store, Munroe took stock of his situation, and the future looked dim. After a decade of laboring over furniture, the thirty-three-year-old father of three had accumulated only a few hundred dollars' worth of property. "Unless I could start some project where I could earn money faster," he reflected, "I should, in a few years at most, even if I should have my health, be poor."

Munroe cast about for "a useful article" well suited to his expert hand at woodworking and certain to be scarce once commerce with Britain was cut off. The answer lay right at hand. "If I can but make lead pencils," Munroe reasoned, "I shall have less fear of competition, and can accomplish something." Somehow the resourceful mechanic obtained a source of English graphite, and in a little shop on the milldam, he devised a technique for grinding lead and encasing it in cedar. Although the product was of "poor quality," it was bought up right away by Benjamin Andrews, a hardware merchant in Boston intent on encouraging "almost every species of American manufacture" that could be had "at a fair price."[37]

Arriving on the market two weeks after the U.S. declaration of war, Munroe's pencils garnered quick sales, and soon Andrews was taking everything the Concord shop could turn out. But the Boston merchant, who insisted on the exclusive right to vend the product, proved an unreliable partner. Within six months his business failed, leaving Munroe out of pocket for over half of the $1,000 in pencils he had supplied. The determined craftsman quickly enlisted another distributor, and free from competition under the artificial conditions of wartime, he profited handsomely. The pencils commanded an inflated price of $5 per gross, and over a year and a half, some 1,200 gross were sold, with Munroe enjoying a surplus of $4,000 above his costs. Then the market collapsed. With British men-of-war outside Boston harbor, demand became "very dull" and money scarce. Worse still, Munroe's remaining stock of plumbago ran out. So did the funds of the new buyer he had found to replace Andrews. Instead of receiving cash, he was obliged to take possession of a farm in the backcountry, which he rented out for a few years. The income was surely welcome following the return of peace. With the resumption of English imports, Munroe's infant industry was erased from the landscape.[38]

A decade later Munroe was back in pencil making, seemingly stronger than ever. The cabinetmaker had tried other expedients after the war, even toothbrushes and watch brushes, but nothing offered the returns he had once enjoyed from pencils. In late 1819 he made the fateful decision to take the plunge and resume the manufacture. Soon he was selling pencils not only in Concord and Boston but as far away as Louisville, Kentucky. Production at first grew slowly—400 gross in 1819; 800 in 1820 and 1821; 565 in 1822—then jumped dramatically to 4,000 in 1823 after the Boston dry goods merchant Hervey Bates took over the marketing. At $1.50 per gross, the price paid for the pencils had plummeted far below its wartime peak. That was no problem, thanks to the "great improvements" Munroe had introduced "in the facility of manufacturing" pencils and "in the perfection of their goodness." The Concord shop could now turn out as many pencils in four days as had once taken a month to produce. In an advertisement in Boston's *Columbian Centinel*, Munroe boasted that his "black Lead Pencils" were now cheaper than the English alternative and just as good. The argument worked—so successfully that in 1825 an optimistic Bates came up with a new offer that was a manufacturer's dream. The merchant contracted to take 20,000 gross of pencils over the next four years. With an assured revenue and guaranteed sales, Munroe was free to concentrate on manufacturing pencils even more efficiently and to anticipate large profits from the economies of scale. Let Bates worry about the marketing. Munroe had eliminated his risk.[39]

In 1825 the forty-seven-year-old pencil maker was living comfortably with his family—wife Patty and now six children ranging in age from two to fifteen—on an extensive farm two and a half miles northwest of the village along the road to Barrett's mill and the town of Acton beyond. There he had moved his pencil-making operation a few years earlier after two decades of residing and working in the village, and there he would remain for a quarter-century. When he first came to Concord, local officials worried that he would become a public charge and once exempted him from taxes in "a very nice precaution" to keep him from gaining legal residency. Now they enlisted his aid in managing the schools and conducting parish affairs. With a distinguished Revolutionary pedigree—one grandfather had participated in the Boston Tea Party, the other was wounded on Lexington green—he was a natural choice for the committees running the jubilee of the Concord Fight and overseeing the laying of the cornerstone for the projected monument. He now ranked in the top 10 percent of property holders, with eighty-seven acres of land, a shop in the village, and a total estate worth $4,287—a position well below Shattuck and Burr but seemingly as sturdy as his pencils.[40]

The remarkable rise of William Munroe in the local hierarchy owed much to his ascent from mechanic to manufacturer. The cabinetmaker had learned his trade during the 1790s as an apprentice in a traditional craft. When his term was up, he took work as a journeyman and eventually rose to master of his own shop. This was the customary plan, derived from English precedents and bequeathed to the new republic, and it provided the framework for the organization of labor and the transmission of skills in every craft. Carpenters and masons, coopers and shipbuilders, shoemakers, hatters, and weavers: they were mechanics all, earning a living by the sweat of their brows and the dexterity of their hands. Munroe took great pride in the skills he had acquired, and in later years, while regretting the "very limited education" he had obtained from intermittent attendance at school, he still cherished his reputation as "the best workman in the shop," to whom was assigned "all extra work that required nicety, carved work or any new fashion that had not been made in the shop before."[41]

Munroe's pencil-making enterprise had little in common with the shop in which he was trained. There were no teenage apprentices, no troublesome young men requiring paternal supervision and expecting instruction in the "mysteries" of the trade. Instead, Munroe hired one or two workers as needed, initially for five to ten weeks during his first stab at pencil making, later for extended periods to fulfill large-scale orders. Just as he had fabricated clock cases for his brothers, so he put out work to other mechanics, one independent contractor to another. Nor was he obliged to earn a living by making goods to order—a chest here, a coffin there—to satisfy patrons as they came in. His business consisted of manufacturing pencils for general sale. Munroe was happy to do so through a single distributor—one mammoth patron—assuring payment at a fixed price, an arrangement that surely enabled him to raise working capital from wealthy neighbors, including Squire Hoar, who furnished a substantial loan of $600. As for the actual work, Munroe delegated the labor of pencil making to others and concentrated on improving his manufacturing methods. It was his mechanical ingenuity, according to his son, that "enabled him readily to contrive the means of doing whatever was required in any process of his by inexpensive methods that had directness and simplicity."[42]

Munroe was glad to leave the traditional craft shop behind. When he remembered his teenage years as an apprentice, he did not recall fondly a community of workers joined together in useful labors and entertaining frolics. Nor did he tell stories of sharing drinks with his comrades and master in convivial moments of bonding across the social ranks. He dwelled on the miserable food and the humiliating rituals of the meals. One "very hard" master furnished an unending diet of "mush, salt fish & potatoes for dinner and nothing else"; another "kept very meanly as to food." The fare improved somewhat in his final berth but not the conditions under which it was served. It was the custom in the home of Deacon Nehemiah Munroe, the cabinetmaker (and second cousin) under whom William served, to set two tables for dinner in a "long narrow" kitchen, one for the family, the other for the apprentices. The food was ladled out from the master's table. As soon as he finished carving and readying the meal, the deacon summoned the boys: "hand your plates." The oldest apprentice rose first, crossed the ten feet separating the tables, and held out his platter; his fellows followed, one by one in order of age, until the youngest lad completed the procession. At a time when republican ideas of liberty and equality were breeding discontent among the lower orders, the boys simmered with resentment over the daily lessons in hierarchy and subordination.

One day a stonemason's apprentice from the neighborhood was invited to dine at the master's table, obliging young Munroe and his workmates to perform the infuriating parade in front of their peer. Mortified by the experience, the boys conceived "a desperate undertaking": the senior apprentice was delegated to confront the deacon and demand an end to the practice. "What do you mean?" the nonplussed master replied. Eventually, he got the message. If the boys would not defer to his authority at dinner, he would banish them to a separate room. Thereafter the deacon dined with his family in the sitting room; the apprentices remained in the kitchen, where they filled their trenchers with the roasts and stews fetched by the youngest. Even as they challenged the deacon, the boys enforced their own pecking order.[43]

One little rebellion led to another. Morning and evening, day in, day out, breakfast and supper consisted of bread and milk. Sabbaths were the one exception, when chocolate was served. Why not every day? the boys demanded, to no effect. Flush from their first victory, they staged a hunger strike, leaving the monotonous rations untouched: "Some hard words pass'd on the subject, but we formed our resolution and meant to succeed or leave." The master relented, and chocolate became the breakfast beverage. When the situation called for it, William Munroe acted on his own. The ingenious youth was restive under the rigid rules of the shop, which taught the skills of cabinetmaking as they had always been performed. As he gained in ability, he lost patience with the constraints imposed by custom on his developing talents. Seeing a better way to hang a table leaf by its hinges, he quietly introduced it without asking permission. A "tell-tale" detected the change and informed the master, who ordered an immediate stop. Could he just finish what he had started? The youth begged until the deacon gave in, "and the result was such that no other way of hanging a table leaf but his was the rule of the shop from that time." Munroe was set on the independent-minded course that eventually led to inaugurating the pencil industry.[44]

A novel trade in the United States, pencil making was free from traditions, so Munroe could innovate as he wished and with no one to answer to but himself. He also enjoyed a broad latitude in decision-making, thanks to the rapid advance of the cash economy. When he resumed the manufacture in 1819, he had no choice but to accept "barter pay" from the storekeepers and stationers who took his product. In 1821 two-thirds of the earnings were paid in goods. As sales expanded, the situation reversed, and more and more cash flowed in. In 1824, when deliveries to Bates reached a new high of $4,350 worth of pencils, Munroe collected half the bill in cash and half in dry goods, the latter for use at home or readily exchangeable in trade.

Just five years after resuming production, Munroe had good reason for optimism. In the spring of 1825, with ample money in hand, the pencil maker set about expanding his operation in order to fulfill the agreement with the wholesaler Bates to supply 20,000 gross in four years. To carry out this job, he contracted with Ebenezer Wood, a "smart" cabinetmaker previously in his employ, and guaranteed him work through 1829 at a wage of 32½ cents per gross. Assisting Wood was Joseph C. Green, the firebrand of the Trinitarian church. The effort progressed quickly; by the Fourth of July, Munroe had shipped $1,700 in pencils—well over a thousand gross—to Boston. But two weeks later production abruptly stopped when Munroe received unexpected news. Bates's firm had failed, in a reprise of the experience with Benjamin Andrews a dozen years earlier. Once again the manufacturer was the victim of an overconfident merchant whose promises could not be trusted. Munroe found himself "in a very uncomfortable and critical position," at a time when "business of every kind" and particularly the pencil business was "remarkably dull." He faced the prospect of losing his investment and lapsing back to a mere mechanic.[45]

The crisis came at the very moment Munroe was having to adjust to a new reality. He was no longer the only pencil maker in town. His very success in the business attracted rivals, who aspired to follow the trail he had blazed. John Thoreau was the first and most serious challenger.[46] Half a year after starting production in Concord, the newcomer was winning prizes for "a specimen of excellent Lead Pencils, manufactured from American Plumbago," at the county and state agricultural fairs. With that endorsement, the Thoreau pencils won a ready reception at Burr & Prichard's store, which immediately took six gross. Although the early pencils were "greasy, gritty, brittle, [and] inefficient," the firm established a strong reputation; the next year the Massachusetts Agricultural Society deemed them "superior" to any shown in recent years, presumably including Munroe's. The newcomer posed a real threat to the pioneer's monopoly.[47]

How did John Thoreau achieve such quick results? In just six months, the merchant entered an entirely new field, set up operations, and despite his lack of experience, won awards for his product. He must have had help, and he likely found his assistants among the mechanics who had labored for Munroe. (Joseph C. Green, the unreliable ally of the "Misses Thoreau," is the best bet.) The father of the industry evidently thought so. In 1839, as he composed his autobiography, he was still nursing his grievances against those who, "envying my prosperity," copied his methods and went into competition against him. If he had Thoreau in mind, he never said. The rival's name never appears in his manuscript. Nor did Concord's second pencil maker ever recount his early days in the trade. He kept his secrets to himself.[48]

John Thoreau & Company was not Munroe's only problem. Even worse was betrayal by his employees. One workman secretly connived with the miller who ground Munroe's lead to siphon off the dust and use it for "very good" pencils of their own, which they then had the effrontery to exhibit at a state fair in competition with the boss's. (Munroe took the award over his double-dealing rivals.) Joseph C. Green, whose mechanical "genious" the pencil maker admired, was hired to devise a trimming machine. Amid his labors on the project, he went behind Munroe's back and solicited funds from Daniel Shattuck to start a competing business. The merchant evidently agreed to the proposal, to Munroe's lasting resentment. It was an "ungenerous" act, he sniped, entirely "characteristic of the man." The plan soon collapsed, as Green displayed the same erratic character in business as he did in the church dispute. Munroe got his revenge by keeping the trimming machine as compensation for a debt owed by its inventor.[49]

As he coped with all these adversities—unreliable merchants, dishonest employees, rising competition, falling prices, and dwindling sales—Munroe confronted a harsh truth. "The manufacture of lead pencils had nearly run out" by 1826, and unless he came up with a better business plan, he was sure to fail. The solution was to make improved pencils from "lead of the best quality" ground "more finely" than ever and to package them in "a neat fancy box." They could then be sold as "a much superior article." That strategy succeeded by dint of a clever marketing campaign. The new, improved pencils were unveiled to the public for the first time at the Massachusetts Agricultural Society's annual exhibition in Brighton and at the "great fair" sponsored by the New England Society for the Promotion of Manufactures and the Mechanic Arts, both held in October 1826. Munroe won plaudits at the events, including a silver medal at the latter. These endorsements were immediately turned to advantage with an advertisement prominently placed in the Boston *Commercial Gazette* for his "Superior Lead Pencils," available at wholesale or retail from a new distributor, Isaac W. Goodrich of State Street in Boston, and other stationers. This time Munroe did not make the mistake of relying on one exclusive agent.

The next step was to "graduate" the pencils according to the degree of "hardness"—a "difficult" labor of two years. The new line went on the market in late 1828. Munroe's pencils were now available in three varieties: "best quality," "premium," and "common." The "best" commanded $4 to $5 per gross at wholesale, as much as during the wartime boom; the common earned $1.25. Six inches long, a centimeter (0.39 inches) in diameter, "MUNROE'S BEST PREMIUM Lead Pencils, For Drawing or Writing" came in a box with a proud patriotic label depicting an American eagle carrying a banner with the slogan "e pluribus unum." Munroe's pencils would write the future of the American union.[50]

No sooner had Munroe introduced these innovations than the business was again in jeopardy. Back in 1825, he had contracted with Ebenezer Wood for four years' work on the order of 20,000 gross of pencils for Boston merchant Hervey Bates. When the distribution deal collapsed within a few months, the pencil maker renegotiated the arrangement. Enough wood and lead were on hand for 7,000 gross of pencils—close to two years' labor for Wood and an assistant—and he proposed they go ahead on that basis. The mechanic accepted, and in Munroe's mind the original contract was a dead letter. However, in an uncharacteristic "great want of prudence," he had omitted to put that understanding in writing. Four years later, long after Wood had removed to Acton, where he was operating a gristmill, making hundreds of timepiece cases for clockmakers in Boston, grinding graphite for John Thoreau, and neglecting Munroe's pencils for months at a time, the wayward cabinetmaker suddenly resurfaced at the worst possible moment to demand payment of the money due. By the spring of 1829, Munroe had exhausted his raw materials and capital and was $1,400 in debt. Fulfilling the obsolete promise to Wood was not on his agenda. But if the erstwhile contractor filed a lawsuit, as he threatened, the pencil maker expected to lose as much as $1,000 in damages. Not only were the facts against him, but so was Concord's ablest attorney and Munroe's own creditor Samuel Hoar, representing Wood. An onerous judgment, on top of the outstanding debts, could set the pencil maker back severely, if not put him out of business altogether.[51]

"Who . . . would think that Wood would have the ingratitude and inconsistency" to take his unfair and unjustified claim to court? Munroe felt betrayed by the mechanic with whom he had worked amicably, off and on, since 1813. A native of the central Massachusetts town of Lunenberg, Wood had come to Concord at fifteen to train as a cabinetmaker, and even before his apprenticeship was over, he had joined the new venture of pencil making. Over the next dozen years, he labored for Munroe, sometimes on timepiece cases, other times on pencils, and occasionally boarded in his home. In September 1819 Munroe made it possible for Wood and James Adams to launch their own cabinetmaking firm by selling them his shop on the milldam, along with tools and supplies, in exchange for an equivalent "woodwork of lead pencils." That partnership dissolved in the spring of 1823, and Wood was soon back in Munroe's employ. Unfortunately, the talented cabinetmaker spent money as fast as he earned it—"and a little faster." By 1828, his debts were mounting and his creditors importunate. When word got around that Wood had a valid claim on Munroe, they pressured him to sue. The cautious pencil maker was being dunned for his employee's imprudence—and for his own neglect of details.[52]

Anticipating that he would lose in court, Munroe agreed to arbitration. Three referees were chosen: one by Wood, a second by Munroe, and the third by the other two. Munroe was confident that the case would be decided in the spirit of equity and "not on strict principles of law." He laid out the facts plainly to his lawyer Rufus Hosmer, and on them "I depended for my defense." But the attorney proved a great disappointment: he "did not bring [the facts] forward with that force & perspicacity that I anticipated." The result went against Munroe, who was held strictly accountable to his original contract and ordered to pay $465 in damages. The losing party suspected bias. Wood had belonged to Concord's Corinthian Lodge of Masons since 1819 and had served as its master in 1826. For his referee, he had selected the prominent lawyer John Abbot of nearby Westford, one of the highest-ranking Freemasons in the state. Even Munroe's own lawyer Hosmer, who had presented such an ineffective case, was a Mason. In his account of the dispute Munroe refrained from crying conspiracy, but that was no doubt his thought: "Whether this [the fraternal bond] influenced Mr. Abbot in favour of Wood, is more than I can say; but I can safely say that in another & similar case, I should not consent to the principal referee being a free mason."[53]

Despite the loss, Munroe was relieved to be done with the dispute, and having prudently collected a few debts "to provide for the worst," he turned down the generous offer of another loan from Samuel Hoar, who was "far from being my enimy [sic]," and he paid the judgment quickly. The case "had interfered with my business, and taken up considerable time," and when it ended, Munroe predicted that "should Mr. Wood and myself both live four years [longer], neither myself would be one cent the poorer, or he one cent the richer . . . I have not the least doubt that it was strick'dly [strictly] and literally true." In short order, the pencil maker was free and clear of debt, had surplus funds to lend, and took satisfaction that "my business was fair." Wood was no better off than before.

Luckily for Munroe, the case concluded just as his new business plan was taking hold. The three grades of pencils turned around his fortunes and ensured his success. Endorsed by painters, lithographers, and engravers, they found ready markets up and down the east coast and as far away as New Orleans, and he no longer needed an exclusive marketing agent. Wholesale orders now came in from booksellers, stationers, and general merchants across the republic, to whom he shipped on short-term credit for prompt payment in cash. By the early 1830s, "my sales began to be more like a regular business," Munroe reflected, and the "manufacture of lead pencils was pretty fairly established . . . My reputation as a manufacturer stood fair."[54]

Munroe was taking nothing for granted. By the early 1830s, having set aside his resentment of Wood's "ingratitude," he regularly took his plumbago to the former employee's mill in Acton for grinding. So did the Thoreau shop, which had increased its output substantially. The two firms together were manufacturing 3,000 to 6,000 gross of pencils annually. Although the market was expanding, Munroe evidently worried about overproduction and a collapse of prices. To avert another downturn, he took aggressive steps to limit the supply. According to one contemporary, he approached Wood and urged him to refuse Thoreau's business. Once again Munroe overestimated the loyalty of his longtime associate. Instead of complying, Wood turned around and afforded Thoreau exclusive access to the mill. Like it or not, Munroe would have to compete.[55]

By the early 1830s, Concord's manufacturing enterprises opted for the same business model as Munroe's pencil-making enterprise. Theirs were wholesale firms producing goods "principally sold abroad." Whiting's "Coach and Chaise Manufactory" operated on a scale unimaginable when its owner, another country boy from central Massachusetts, came to Concord in 1803 and apprenticed with a harness maker and carriage trimmer. In response to the expanding market for riding vehicles, the manufacturer took on new activities and incorporated all aspects of carriage production into a single coordinated process. Passengers rode in his horse-drawn carriages all over New England and even in distant New Orleans. Priding himself on using only "the very best" materials and hiring only "first rate workmen," as many as a dozen to eighteen at a time, including four to six apprentices (whom he presumably treated well), he earned up to $18,000 a year for his harnesses, chaises, sleighs, wagons, stages, and carioles—four times as much as Munroe realized from his pencils.[56]

By contrast, custom work hung on in those areas of the economy where people still treasured personal service and fine craft. Tailors and dressmakers continued to fashion bespoke items of apparel. In the 1820s the London-trained tailor James Weir competed for men's business with John C. Newell, born and bred in rural Westford, amid a changing cast of mantua makers and milliners serving female customers; all set up shop on the common and milldam close by the leading stores. The widow Elizabeth Willis lasted the longest; in May 1826, seven months after losing her husband, the mother of three rented a room opposite the Middlesex Hotel and advertised her dress-making services—one of many such female-run enterprises starting up all over the New England countryside. Two years later she took up quarters inside the Fiske brothers' store, right at hand to cut and sew the latest woolen, cotton, and silk fabrics into gowns fit for polite society. Down to 1834, in various locations, she and several assistants successfully plied needles and shears; her rivals seldom survived more than one or two seasons.

Willis readily ceded the ordinary jobs of tailoring to the spinster Mary Minott, "a rather stern, business like woman," who seized on new terrain for a "tailoress" and made clothing for men as well as women, often at their homes. The Thoreau men were steady customers for coats, suits, vests, and pantaloons, although Minott's fashionable taste was not to the liking of every member of the family. On one occasion she balked at David Henry's request for a garment in a specific style, perhaps the coat she made for him in October 1838. "They do not make them so now," she informed the demanding customer. Years later Thoreau vented his frustration and outrage in a passage in *Walden*. How dare the tailoress invoke the gods of fashion "as if she quoted an authority as impersonal as the Fates"! Who are "They" to dictate what he should wear? "It is true, they did not make them," insisted the uncompromising writer, "but they do now."[57]

Even traditional crafts were departing from time-honored practices and stirring with the spirit of innovation. James Weir trained as a tailor under his father in London, before enlisting in 1806 at thirteen in the British Navy and sailing on military and mercantile missions during the Napoleonic Wars. The lad participated in victories over the French fleet in the Indian Ocean and the Mediterranean; he witnessed Napoleon's exile to Elba. His adventures over in 1815, he went back to tailoring in London, where he learned state-of-the-art techniques for diagramming a man's body and calculating its proportions. Tape measure in hand, the tailor no longer needed to rely on just eye and experience to size up a client; now he could make an abstract of anyone's body, dividing it up into discrete sections—shoulders, waist, hips—measured exactly in a blueprint for a precise fit. With the new methods, a gentleman's coat or suit could be made to order quickly, efficiently, and at reduced cost. Custom clothes thus became affordable to a much wider market. When Weir, at twenty-five, arrived in Concord in 1817, the fourth tailor to practice in town since 1775, specialists in the clothing trades were only just becoming aware of these advances. He quickly gained renown for introducing into Massachusetts "the square rule of cutting garments by inch measure." The same thing was happening elsewhere, most notably in Lower Manhattan, where a modern garment industry took shape rapidly in the 1820s, pioneering mass production of cheap ready-made and custom clothing for the nation at large.[58]

A calculating mentality, geared to markets and gain and at odds with older practices of trade and community, ran through Concord's shops as well as stores, affecting masters, journeymen, and apprentices alike and driving incompetents out of business. (Weir's rival John C. Newell abandoned the tailor's trade for the Universalist ministry and ended up in an insane asylum.)[59] William Munroe absorbed this outlook over the course of two decades dealing with unreliable merchants, disloyal employees, deceitful competitors, and defaulting debtors. By disposition, he was "cautious, methodical, [and] exact," averse to risk and pinching every penny; three decades after the event, he still smarted over the two days' wages he had lost on leaving Deacon Munroe's furniture shop and coming out to Concord. Still, he had learned to set aside hurt feelings and to separate business from friendship. Despite his anger at Ebenezer Wood's "ingratitude," he continued to hire the cabinetmaker, whom he deemed "a good workman," for pencil jobs, though he was now careful to spell out their agreements in detail and to record them in his memorandum book. "I have never suffered my resentment or my anger," he explained, "to run away with my interest."

Actually, he profited greatly from Wood's labors. According to one contemporary, the improvident mechanic was the secret of Munroe's success. An "inventor of a high order," Wood devised a series of original machines that transformed pencil making from a handicraft into an industry. "His hand and brain largely helped to make Munroe's fortune," claimed the sometime pencil maker Horace Hosmer. But Wood never gained credit for those contributions; no patents were ever attached to his name. No one would ever know that this literary-minded craftsman, who recited poetry by heart while on the job, stood "in the very front rank of American pencil makers." Far from rewarding Wood's mechanical genius, Munroe appropriated its fruits to his own advantage. That ill-starred contract with Bates had fixed the price of pencils at $1.50 per gross; Wood received a mere 32½ cents—a fifth of that amount—for doing much of the work. To be sure, the costs of supplies, credit, and transportation had to be covered as well, but if the arrangement came close to Munroe's first foray into pencil making back in 1812–1813, the profit would be immense, as much as 80 percent. It apparently never occurred to Munroe to give Wood a bonus or to offer a partnership. Why should he? Perpetually in debt, Wood was glad for the work the manufacturer gave him, especially in the wake of their legal dispute, and he was willing to accept a cut in pay, earning less than ever. Munroe exacted his revenge for nearly six years—the contract, he acknowledged, was "much in my favour"—then, after the price of foodstuffs soared, he felt sorry for the hapless employee and restored the original wage. Even then Munroe took pains to add the raise, an extra five cents per gross, to the wholesale price of his pencils.[60]

Munroe took to capitalism well. By the early 1830s, he was no longer plowing all his profits back into pencils but was putting some surplus funds into financial investments. Having experienced the benefits of doing business on a cash basis, he was quick to enlist in the plan to establish the Concord Bank. In 1832, when the state legislature granted a charter for the institution, the manufacturer was among the original six incorporators. No matter that his onetime lawyer, the untrustworthy Rufus Hosmer, was also a founding member of the bank, nor that the unneighborly Daniel Shattuck immediately assumed the presidency. The pursuit of gain trumped hard feelings. Soon Munroe would be serving on the board of directors with Shattuck, where he would make decisions over whether to grant loans to his competitor in pencil making, Thoreau.

In his own affairs Munroe was a prudent investor. He resisted the lure of quick money from land speculation during the boom years of the 1830s and put his funds into banks, insurance companies, steamboats, and railroads, the well-capitalized agents driving economic growth. Those investments, recorded in a separate "book of stocks," would eventually outstrip his commitment to pencil making and make him one of the richest men in town. More than a cabinetmaker, a mechanic, or a pencil maker, Munroe developed into a businessman first and foremost, and he came to see life from that limited perspective. His autobiography was restricted to a narrow account of business trials and successes. It said nothing about religion, though Munroe and his wife Martha had joined the First Parish Church in 1806, three months before the birth of their first child. It omitted any mention of his civic services to town, parish, and schools or of his political involvements. Munroe measured his achievements by the accumulation of property and by his ability to provide for his children.[61]

Money talked in Concord, but it did not monopolize the conversation. Even as business carved out an autonomous realm with its own code of conduct, townspeople upheld ideals of neighborliness in economic affairs and put them into practice. Munroe thrived in the cash economy, and he bought and sold what he required. Yet the prosperous manufacturer was reluctant to cast aside familiar practices binding him to households along the road to Barrett's mill. In the conduct of his farm, Munroe operated as a traditionalist, boarding laborers in his home, furnishing rum and molasses to hay makers in the field, and loaning various items—a team of oxen and cart here, a patent plow there—to neighbors in need and expecting to borrow from them in turn. If he no longer relied on Samuel Burr to distribute his pencils, he nonetheless paid his bills at the store with eggs, chickens, pork, beans, and sausages.

Even in his dealings as a pencil maker, Munroe trusted in his neighbors' goodwill and was outraged when they let him down. One incident never ceased to trouble him. In the fall of 1837 the manufacturer got word that pencils stamped "N. Munroe, Concord, Mass." were being sold in the South. How could that be? A clue soon appeared in the form of an order for pencils from a hardware merchant in Boston, whom Munroe considered not very "honorable and fair." Stopping by the store, he discovered the owner away on a trip to the South and the man's son in charge; on the counter prominently displayed was "a lot of pencils that appeared as my manufacture" but that were no longer in their fancy case—a "singular" circumstance arousing unease. His suspicions grew stronger after he departed for a few minutes and then returned: the pencils were nowhere to be seen. The next day Munroe paid yet another surprise visit; this time he caught a clerk alone packing pencils into a box. Could he inspect them? The innocent young man held out a set of pencils resembling Munroe's, with the "same kind of paper" and the same printed labels, including the "small eagle," but reading "N." rather than "W. Munroe." Unfortunately, the clerk explained, they were not for sale. The boxes were being shipped to the store's owner in the South, and no others were in stock.

On his return to Concord, the distressed manufacturer investigated further, calling on an impoverished (and unrelated) shoemaker named Nathan Munroe in the northern part of town and demanding an explanation. How had his name gotten on those pencils? The poor man reluctantly divulged that at the request of a Concord "friend," acting as agent for a Boston merchant, he had allowed the use of his name on pencils to be sold far away. But he refused to say just who had conducted this "base and mean transaction."[62]

Under the circumstances Munroe moved to stem his losses, placing a running ad in the *Boston Courier* and including notices in his packing cases warning against "DECEPTION—IMPOSITION—FRAUD." The counterfeiting of the pencils took a heavy toll; sales in 1837 fell by more than a fifth—"more than could reasonably have been expected" from "the general prostration of business." Munroe had a good idea who among his townsmen had betrayed him so unscrupulously, and he recorded the name in his autobiography. Shattuck is a likely suspect. But the offending party can no longer be known; in 1903 eighty-four-year-old Mary Munroe read over her father's narrative and removed the page with the accusation from the manuscript, lest the charge someday become public and bring "grief" to innocent descendants.[63]

CAPITALISM AND THE INDUSTRIAL REVOLUTION WERE IN FULL SWING WELL before Emerson and Thoreau appeared on the Concord scene to indict the acquisitive practices of the townspeople and the subordination of their intellectual potential and spiritual growth to the daily demands of making a living. John Thoreau and his generation knew all too well the promises and pitfalls of the expanding economy: the allure of riches, the likelihood of failure; release from custom and constraint, submission to an impersonal market; the excitement of innovation, the necessity of salesmanship; the spur of competition, the temptations to cheat; greater comfort, heightened inequality; widening horizons abroad, narrowing ties at home. These changes were gaining rapidly in Concord by the nineteenth century, and they were in full swing by the time Henry Thoreau was helping out in the pencil shop. Propelled by a cultural drive for wider individual freedom and choice, the transformation of the town formed the mi-lieu in which the future Transcendentalist grew up. As he observed its effects on family and neighbors, he would decry the costs of the new way of life and cast about for alternatives. Perhaps the farms beyond the village offered the simplic-ity and sincerity he craved.[64]

Husbandmen and Manufacturers

Bulkeley, Hunt, Willard, Hosmer, Meriam, Flint,
Possessed the land which rendered to their toil
Hay, corn, roots, hemp, flax, apples, wool, and wood.
Each of these landlords walked amidst his farm,
Saying, "'Tis mine, my children's and my name's."

. . .

Where are these men? Asleep beneath their grounds:
And strangers, fond as they, their furrows plough.

—RALPH WALDO EMERSON,
"Hamatreya" (1846)

Jean Thoreau had made his fortune from the sea, his son John earned his living in the village, and there his famous grandson belonged in turn. The longest David Henry ever spent beyond a town center, before the sojourn at Walden, was his first eight months of existence, when his parents lived on the homestead of the late Capt. Jonas Minot in the eastern section of town. Yet the farms and fields were never far away from Concord center—a five-to-ten-minute walk in every direction from the meetinghouse. For all the dynamism and urbanity of the village, agriculture remained the mainstay of the local economy and way of life. It was thus natural for John Thoreau, following his failure in trade, to move to his widowed mother-in-law's portion of the Minot estate and attempt to support his young family on the land. The collapse of that effort was due less to inexperience than to the crop-killing cold facing everyone in 1816, the legendary "year without a summer."

Tending plants and animals continued long after returning to the center. The Thoreau household raised flowers, fruits, and vegetables in a kitchen garden and periodically kept chickens, cows, and pigs for dairy and meat. Like the other village boys, Henry trudged barefoot through mud and water to drive the family cow to pasture, and he raised his own chickens for sale. On one occasion, after delivering a basket of the birds to the Middlesex Hotel, he was obliged to watch as Tom Wesson, the customer, took hold of the "darlings" and wrung their necks, one by one. The sensitive child "wept inwardly, but did not budge." In Concord, town and country blended into one another, and as the author of *Walden* learned early on, one could experience nature not just by the solitary shores of a pond but also in one's own backyard.[1]

The infant David Henry Thoreau began life on a homestead that had been cultivated by Jonas Minot for over a half-century, from the late 1750s to his death in 1813. At eighty-six acres, it was 40 percent bigger than the average farm in Concord, but its management was much the same, carrying on familiar practices from the mid-eighteenth century. From the tilled fields came a variety of crops: corn and rye for daily bread and potatoes for dinner, plus oats for two horses, cornstalks for cattle, and surplus ears for swine. The land also grew flax for linen fiber, to be mixed with fleece from sheep and made into homespun "linsey-woolsey" garb. The meadows and pasture yielded the grass and hay necessary to sustain the herd of cattle—a yoke of oxen, a couple of steers, and half a dozen cows—that supplied meat and dairy for the table. The hogs added pork.

The value of the livestock went beyond contributions to family meals, though the captain did love his milk, waking up repeatedly each night to guzzle a quart fresh from the cow. Draft animals furnished the motive power to plow arable land and to carry heavy loads back and forth to the fields and woods. Manure from the barn was essential to restore the fertility of the soil, so that the annual cycle of planting, hoeing, and harvesting could begin again. "No grass, no cattle," farmers told one another; "no cattle, no manure; no manure, no crops." Minot thus devoted nearly all his improved land—nine out of every ten acres—to the animals' needs. An orchard on rocky land unsuited to the plow provided cider to drink and apples to roast over the hearth. Fuel for the fire, as well as timber for fencing and building, was cut from Minot's woods and unimproved land. Every acre of the farm had its uses in affording a comfortable subsistence for the household and surpluses of commodities for sale in Boston and beyond. The cash and credits the produce earned paid for imported goods at the stores.[2]

There was little to distinguish Minot's farm from its neighbors, apart from size. In middle age he could call on the labor of four sons in field and forest, and five daughters and his wife in barn, garden, and kitchen; by the time he wed Mary Dunbar in 1798, nearly all those children were far from Concord, and by 1810, the seventy-five-year-old farmer was relying on Jack Garrison and other hired help to support a household of eight, including his wife's unmarried daughters Louisa and Cynthia. Once a man of influence in town—scion of a rich father and a Loyalist-leaning militia captain before the Revolution— Minot ranked just below the top tenth of taxpayers a year or so before his death. But the social distance between him and the middling and lesser folk was easily bridged. In the early nineteenth century, Concord farmers, whatever their wealth and scale of production, were joined together by common pursuits, raising the same crops and livestock—cereals, garden vegetables, grasses, and cattle. Theirs was at once a market-oriented business and a domestic way of life.[3]

The Minot farm was old-fashioned and probably run-down by the time John Thoreau took charge of his mother-in-law's dower—though not as decrepit as the place his literary son would later long to acquire. It represented an age of husbandry that would soon be on the wane. In the countryside change was stirring, in tandem with the currents roiling the village stores and shops, and from the mid-1820s on, it was transforming the conduct of agriculture and altering social life on the farm. As population burgeoned in the mill towns springing up all over New England and in the metropolis of Boston, and as a "transportation revolution" eased the movement of people and goods north and south, onto the Western frontiers, and between the interior and the seaboard, farmers in Concord entered a new world of unprecedented opportunities, uncertainties, pressures, and risks. Old routines faced stiff competition. Why grow "rye and Injun" for brown bread when flavorful Genesee wheat could be had cheaply at Shattuck's store? Why raise flax and wool in the fields and devote endless hours to the spinning wheel and loom when machine-made fabrics and ready-made clothes were available in abundance?

Far better to jettison outdated activities and concentrate on profitable commodities that were in greater demand. Doing so meant abandoning time-honored practices, passed on from father to son for generations, and it impelled a strenuous search for new crops, better tools and techniques, enhanced efficiency, and expanded productivity. Well-off farmers, often with money from trade or professions, prospered by adapting to shifting markets and rationalizing their methods. But not everyone wished or could afford to join in this quest; a good many were stymied by shortages of capital, scarcities of labor, and stresses on the land. In the process, the ties that once bound together the rural community frayed, and new lines of division separated a successful minority of progressive agriculturalists, attuned to the latest science and responsive to markets, from struggling neighbors hanging on by traditional means and from a transient class of landless laborers arriving from elsewhere, spending a few seasons on local farms, and then moving on. In the village and in the hinterlands both, society fractured into competing groups, shaped by different experiences of progress and privation, inequality and insecurity. The harvest of the new agricultural capitalism was decidedly mixed.[4]

HIGH ABOVE TOWN, NEAR THE CREST OF THE "BROAD-TOPPED HILL" THAT the Massachusett Indians had called Punkatasset, about a mile and a half northeast of the village, stood the ancestral farm of the Hunt family. Acquired by the Puritan settler William Hunt in the mid-seventeenth century, it had passed down from father to son for five generations without a hitch. In 1825 the latest heir, Daniel Hunt, twenty-nine and newly married, with an infant on the way, was assuming the mantle from his father, Nehemiah, retiring at sixty-two. The homestead was rich in history and natural beauty. On this site, in the early morning hours of April 19, 1775, as British regulars marched into town, the local Minutemen had repaired for safety before making their fateful march to the North Bridge. Comprising some sixty acres of tillage, meadow, pasture, and woodland and sloping one hundred feet down to the banks of the Concord River, the Hunt farm offered an "always attractive" prospect of the landscape. "The view from the house and fields," Daniel's son recalled, "was fine . . . It made at times a beautiful picture," especially when the river overflowed the meadows to form a broad lake and the forest trees burst forth in autumnal colors. At such moments, the proprietors could pause from their labors and briefly forget that to get a living from this stony soil was a constant struggle "between brain and muscle on one side and rocks on the other." But not for long. This ancient seat of the Hunt family remained a battleground in an "unending" war that had

begun long before the famous Concord Fight and that was still enlisting combatants a half-century after that event.[5]

Daniel Hunt entered the field under considerable disadvantages. His grandfather Nehemiah had been blessed; in the 1740s, while still in his twenties, he
received a portion of the paternal estate "in consideration of [his father's] Love,
good will and affection." Such gifts reflected an era of abundance long gone,
when Concord's patriarchs had possessed sufficient acreage to settle all their
sons and daughters on lands close by. Nor had Daniel inherited the homestead
at an early age. That had been the good fortune of his father Nehemiah, who
had received the property shortly after coming of age in 1785. The eldest son
among ten surviving children, Nehemiah assumed ownership following his father's sudden death. With no last will and testament to direct the division of the
property, the estate went into probate court, where the authorities determined
that the patrimony could not be split up "without spoiling the whole." The
dilemma was widespread; so prolific had been the Puritan families of Massachusetts Bay that on the eve of the Revolution, most farms in long-settled towns
had been repeatedly broken up to provide for the rising generations and had
reached their lower limits. In such cases, the real estate went to a single heir,
on condition that he pay his brothers and sisters their respective shares of its
market value in due course, plus 6 percent annual interest. Nehemiah Hunt fulfilled the obligation, but at a heavy price. He was land rich and cash poor, and
to meet his commitments, he had to sell off bits and pieces of his birthright over
the years. By the mid-1820s, when the homestead passed on to Daniel, it was a
fraction of its former self: an old house, barn, sheds, and sixty acres. The Hunts
were the "lords of Punkatasset" no more.[6]

Ownership did not come easily to the new proprietor. Initially, the property was divided between Daniel and his older brother, yet another Nehemiah,
"the eldest and most favored son." The firstborn male inherited a name but
not much aptitude for agriculture; he soon retreated to a smaller, more manageable plot, where he divided his time between farming and pump making.
The way was clear for Daniel to take charge. In January 1827 he purchased
the ancestral home and land from his parents for $2,000. Although he had
labored for his father for decades, postponing marriage until he was nearly
thirty, the price was not cheap; Daniel paid nearly $500 over the assessed value,
presumably in promissory notes that he would eventually have to redeem. The

transaction was a business arrangement designed to meet family needs. Two of Daniel's brothers remained minors, one training to be a carpenter, the other a mason; and with their apprenticeships about to end, both would soon be expecting their portions. By these arrangements, Concord's large rural families—the elder Hunts had eleven children, ten of whom reached adulthood—sought to ensure financial security for young people coming of age in communities where only one or two sons could succeed to the homestead and the rest of the siblings would have to take up trades or professions, labor for others, marry well, and more often than not, move away. On such terms, Daniel Hunt, having waited patiently for years, came into possession of the land that had been farmed by his forebears for 175 years and took responsibility for keeping it in the family name. His estate came steeped in tradition and encumbered with debt.[7]

Life continued on the Hunt homestead in familiar ways. In mid-December 1825, a few months after taking charge of the farm, Daniel wed Clarissa Flint Cutter, a twenty-eight-year-old widow with a three-year-old daughter. The newlyweds had probably known each other from childhood, since Clarissa had grown up along the river road to Carlisle, less than a mile from the Hunt farm, and their families had kin in common. When Clarissa became pregnant sometime in 1825, she and Daniel quickly tied the knot. The premarital conception stirred no scandal; since the mid-eighteenth century, sex had frequently preceded wedlock among rural youth impatient to assume the prerogatives of adulthood. Should pregnancy occur, a wedding would soon follow, sometimes under the gun of the bride's father. Like the union of John and Cynthia Thoreau a decade before, the marriage of Daniel and Clarissa Hunt followed this script, though by the 1820s the laxity of the past was gradually giving way to a strict standard of propriety among the village middle class. The new family moved into the old Hunt house, where they shared quarters with Daniel's parents and probably his widowed sister and her six-year-old son as well. Immediately adjacent was the fashionable white house with green shutters recently built by Nehemiah Jr. for his young family—a signal of the social ambitions he would never achieve. The three intertwined generations were living thickly according to an extended family pattern deeply rooted in the New England past.[8]

Built before 1700, the Hunt house had originally affirmed the family's elite status, rising two stories high on its hilltop at a time when nearly every other dwelling had only one floor. One hundred twenty-five years later, it had become a vernacular remnant of the colonial past, with its long, unpainted clapboards weathered with age, its low lean-to in back, its unfenced yard, and most of all, its great fireplaces dominating the two rooms that constituted the first floor. The large east chamber served variously as "kitchen, dining room, living room, and parlor," depending on the need. (The west room was the bedroom and living room of the aging Nehemiah and Mary Hunt.) There Daniel, Clarissa, and their growing brood would gather for meals three times a day—breakfast between six and seven, dinner at noon, supper at six—and welcome visitors around the open hearth in a communal setting that would soon become an object of nostalgia throughout the region. Dinners followed a regular round: baked beans one day, boiled dish another, and a roast next, in strict succession. The "plain, simple" diet resembled the fare in the Minot home, and it too was largely supplied by the farm. A few items from Burr & Prichard's store—salt and pepper, sugar and molasses, baking soda, Chinese tea, and New England rum—added variety and taste, but as much as possible in the 1820s and 1830s the family supplied its necessities from "within." Maintaining the old ways, the Hunts ate locally and lived locally in a neighborhood dense with kin.[9]

That stability was hard-won, and it contributed to the image of Concord as an "old" town populated by farmers fixed in the ancestral soil. In fact, Daniel and Nehemiah Hunt belonged to a select minority of descendants from the Puritan fathers. In a premodern world where disease or accident could destroy a family overnight, their forebears had, by the grace of Providence, persisted on the land, at least long enough to propagate potential heirs. But in most families the rising generations had to look elsewhere for land to farm. From the 1720s on, Concord's youth departed in an accelerating exodus that carried Flints and Hunts, Minots and Meriams, onto New England's frontiers to settle central Massachusetts, New Hampshire, Vermont, and Maine. The prospect of freeholds on which to enjoy independence and raise a family drove them on, despite the hardships of pioneering. As the eldest son, Nehemiah Hunt, Daniel's father, was the presumptive heir to the paternal estate, prompting every one of his nine younger siblings, male and female, to make a new start elsewhere. Alternatively, the youngest son in a family might be tapped to stay home, care for aging parents, and take over the estate, as was the case with Abishai Flint, Clarissa's father; all but one of his seven older siblings took off well before that happened, some landing in the same towns with the Hunts. The family relocations, with neighbors and kin often settling together, laid a genealogical trail from Concord across the countryside.[10]

The Hunt family was still holding its own in local life when the next generation succeeded to the Punkatasset estate. With his stylish house on the hill, Nehemiah, the eldest son, claimed a place on the landscape in keeping with his aspirations to office. Captain of the Concord Light Infantry Company in the early 1820s, he gained a place on the jubilee committee in recognition of the Revolutionary service of his grandfather and namesake. The burden of the family farm fell on Daniel. He shunned the civic roles Nehemiah seemed to crave; one term as a highway surveyor was enough. Caring for the land and livestock, supporting his aging parents, and meeting the needs of the ten children whom Clarissa would bear over seventeen years demanded every waking moment. As he entered his thirties, Daniel Hunt was a hardworking husbandman seeking nothing more than to carry on the "old style of farming." But that was becoming ever more difficult. In a time of rapid change, it proved no easy matter to follow in the footsteps of the forefathers.[11]

The problems began with the land. The Hunt farm could just barely feed all its occupants, human and animal alike, on its sixty acres. Nearly all of the homestead was being cultivated with grains, vegetables, fruits, and grasses for the Hunts, their cattle, and their swine. On the typical Concord farm of the day, seven out of ten acres were being "improved" for crops to feed both people and livestock; the Hunts were approaching nine out of ten. A mere eight acres of woodland lay in reserve for future expansion—an undesirable option, since it would deprive the household of needed lumber and fuel. Daniel Hunt had no choice but to press the ancient homestead to the limit.[12]

This was a difficult balancing act. To be sure, thanks to the spread of "cheap stores" with their discount fabrics and to the surging production of the Lowell mills, Hunt no longer raised sheep for wool or planted flax for linen. The spinning wheel ceased its hum, although his mother continued to work her loom and weave cloth and carpets for the neighbors. The shift from homegrown to store-bought textiles was a limited gain. It reduced the burden of domestic labor, especially for women, but it added to the family's expenses while releasing little land on which to grow more food. Caught in a tight bind between the family's needs and the farm's capacity, Hunt "kept things moving," as his son William Henry recalled life on the homestead as late as the 1840s and early 1850s, "and provided liberally for the necessities," but "there was nothing left for luxuries, and not very much for comforts." At times family members must have cut their brown bread thin.[13]

The predicament of the farm ran deeper still. Though "industrious" and "abstemious" (but not always totally abstinent), Daniel Hunt was not a vigorous man. Unfortunately, he had to perform nearly all the hard field labor by himself. A newlywed when he took charge in 1825, he would have to wait a decade before any of his children could lend a serious hand with the most physically demanding chores. As it happened, the delay proved even longer. One infant daughter after another filled up the Hunt house; not until the spring of 1831, five years after the marriage, did the first son arrive. Nor did Daniel's kin furnish an alternative labor pool. His father had retired in his early sixties, earlier than usual, perhaps for health reasons; his three younger brothers were laboring as mechanics in the village. Only Nehemiah, the firstborn son, was close by, and although he must have helped out from time to time, he had his own land to improve, some twenty acres, along with his new business of pump making. He had already proved ineffective at managing the homestead; two enterprises now competed for his attention. Hired men—or at least live-in help—were no option either, undoubtedly for lack of money. When the census taker came by in 1830 and 1840, he found no one but Daniel, Clarissa, and the children in the household.[14]

Occasionally, a neighbor must have joined in the farmwork, especially during the hectic haying season, in the expectation that Daniel would repay the service at a later time. Such exchanges, known as "changing works," were of long standing in rural New England, as the account book kept by another Concordian attests. Widowed at thirty-five with three young children, Eunice P. Wyman managed a farm of twenty-two acres inherited from her wealthy merchant father. Luckily, she could call on two brothers close by for help. Just a few minutes away, in the area known as "the Plains," George and Jonathan Hildreth plowed her garden, mowed the meadow, and carried loads of rye and corn to the mill. Their oxen were at her service. The assistance did not come for free. As much as they cared for Eunice, the brothers expected to be compensated in kind. Their contributions created debts, painstakingly recorded in her account book and conscientiously repaid with diverse goods—butter, milk, and cheese from the dairy, pork and sausages from the pigpen—and with the labor of her teenage sons. Franklin and John were regularly on call from spring plowing to fall harvest; they hoed corn, mowed grass, shoveled gravel, laid stone walls, and carted manure. And not just for their uncles: the boys redeemed their mother's obligations to the several neighbors with whom she "changed works." Only daughter Laura was spared. By the early 1830s, none of the Wyman children were content to remain the family dogsbody. On coming of age, all promptly departed for new lives in the booming city of Lowell. Eunice Wyman carried on by herself for another decade without the benefit or burden of "changing works."[15]

The labor shortage at the Hunt farm set strict terms on the operation. It took more than thirteen weeks to raise the grains and grasses necessary to sustain life on Punkatasset Hill. Daniel was hard-pressed to get everything done in season.[16] In the mid-decades of the nineteenth century, before agriculture entered the machine age, it was a rule of thumb that a farmer in the Northeast could handle twenty acres of tilled crops and mown grass at most. Add pasture and woodlands to the mix, and the maximum rises to sixty acres. With his twenty-three acres of tillage and meadow and sixty-six acres in total, Hunt had all the land and livestock he could manage and little leisure to contemplate the sublime view from the hillside. Until his sons became teenagers, he got hardly any relief from sunup to sundown except on the Sabbath.[17]

"Old-style farming" could not survive without change. For generations Concord's yeomen had enjoyed the natural bounty of the river that was known to the Indians as Musketaquid or "grass-ground." The sluggish waterway abounded in native grasses beneficial to cattle and sheep. Reaping that harvest required intensive labor: ditching and draining wetlands, removing shrubs and brush, sowing with edible plants, and "taking time by the foretop" to race against heat and rain and get in a seasonable crop. It was a collaborative effort among neighbors, who created on the Great Meadow and along the town's many streams a "rich, organic soil" furnishing sufficient fodder to sustain the livestock essential to New England husbandry.

The Hunt farm boasted a number of acres along the river, a dozen in 1801, yielding nine tons of hay to keep the cattle over the winter. Nehemiah Hunt set aside a mere four acres of upland to cultivate with timothy, redtop, and clover. But those English grasses were claiming increasing attention in Concord just as Daniel was taking over from his father. The plants were more nutritious than the coarse fodder from the river meadows, and they produced higher yields per acre. Most important, clover fixed nitrogen in the soil, thereby improving the land as it grew and enabling constant use without the need to fallow. Clover was the miracle crop of the eighteenth century; it helped to drive the English agricultural revolution, and its benefits were touted far and wide to farmers in the new American nation. But English hay had disadvantages. Unlike the meadow crop, which nature provided for free, timothy and clover seeds had to be bought at the village stores. Sowing uplands with English grasses was labor-intensive; the land had to be plowed, manured, and seeded, with the burden falling on individual farmers rather than on neighbors working together in the Great Meadow. River meadows were replenished by seasonal flooding, which returned nutrients to the soil; English mowing, without enough fertilizer or lime, degraded the land over time. And although an acre of upland could produce a ton or more of excellent hay, that crop was vulnerable to the ravages of grasshoppers. English hay was thus not a sure winner for a hard-pressed farmer like Daniel Hunt, strapped as he was for labor and capital.

And yet switch he did. Over the late 1820s and 1830s he converted one acre after another to English meadow, until by 1840 he had reversed his father's pattern. Now fourteen acres were cultivated for English hay; only three remained in river meadows. Hunt was not alone in making the change. During the same period, his neighbors were expanding their acreage of English meadows by more than a third. Even so, the typical farmer in 1840 still depended more heavily on fresh meadow (thirteen acres on average) than on cultivated uplands (nine acres) for his hay. For all his traditional inclinations, Daniel Hunt stood in the forefront of Concord's own agricultural revolution.[18]

Hunt was driven to the change by necessity, not choice. The Hunt farm had long reaped the fruits of its location along the banks of the Concord River. Every spring, as winter snow and ice melted, water flowed onto the surrounding meadows, revitalizing the grasslands with valuable nutrients before receding to allow a new growth of fresh meadow hay. But about a decade before Hunt took over the farm, that seasonal cycle was disrupted. The spring floods no longer retreated as before; year after year the waters remained on the meadows at ever-higher levels, killing off most of the standing grass and making what little survived inaccessible. When a farmer could cut grass from these wetlands, it was of no use as fodder and served merely as bedding in cattle stalls. In 1840 Concord's selectmen pinned the blame for the "flowage" problem, as it came to be known, on the Middlesex Canal Company, whose dam at Billerica downstream obstructed the river's flow and backed up water onto the meadows along the banks. But farmers may well have contributed to the dilemma through their own excesses, clearing too much woodland for cultivation, erod-ing the capacity of the soil to hold water, and thereby adding to the runoff into the river and streams. That does not appear to have been the case on the Hunt farm. It was more victim than agent of the decline. As Daniel Hunt faced the future, the same waters that had long been the lifeblood of Concord agricul-ture now jeopardized its very existence.[19]

Hunt rose to the challenge but not through his efforts alone. Clarissa and the girls were equally indispensable to the economic survival of the enterprise. Every ton of English hay wrested from the waterlogged meadows and every acre of pasture rescued from weeds was channeled into the milk produced by the half-dozen cows regularly kept on the farm and then transformed by the la-bors of the females of the family into the principal cash crop: butter. While the spinning wheel was being relegated to the attic, the wooden churn was gaining heightened importance in the household economy. The Hunt women spent endless hours during the summer months milking, straining, skimming, and churning to produce the butter that the boys regularly delivered to customers in the village.

In the eighteenth and early nineteenth centuries, butter was the chief means by which New Englanders enjoyed the produce of the dairy; they consumed between thirteen and fifteen pounds per capita each year. By the mid-1820s, demand must have been strong in Concord's two villages; nearly 60 percent of taxpayers and probably 30 percent of households lacked a cow. In 1835 eight out of ten taxpayers, including John Thoreau that year, were without their own source of milk and butter. The Hunts helped meet the need by selling 350 pounds of butter annually. "Always a hard worker," Clarissa Hunt "gave herself without reserve to her duties," according to her son, and took great pride in the quality of her butter, sparing "no pain" to maintain a high standard. She may also have acted as the business manager of the farm, since, in the opinion of William Henry, her husband lacked the knack for "making good trades."[20]

The joint efforts of husband and wife and of parents and children in the fields and barn, the kitchen lean-to and dairy, thus yielded a living for the Hunt household, supplemented perhaps by extra income from braiding palm leaf hats for Daniel Shattuck or other "outwork." It was enough to keep the family out of debt and the family farm intact. But success exacted a heavy price. While brother Nehemiah went riding in his horse and chaise, Daniel, Clarissa, and the children stuck close to the land, toiling tirelessly and living frugally. The parents were "law-abiding, church-going members of the community," intent on performing their "full duty to God and man." There was little margin to their lives in the constant struggle to get by. Who could blame them—and especially the children—for feeling dissatisfaction and even envy if they occasionally compared their straitened existence on the homestead to the rising standards of comfort in the village and found it wanting? As a boy, William Henry Hunt noticed the frustration of his sisters with their "cramped" situation. Clarissa Cutter, his half-sister by his mother's first marriage, got away only by entering domestic service in the village home of Ebenezer Rockwood Hoar, the squire's lawyer son, where she remained a spinster and honorary "Aunt" for the rest of her days. The six daughters of Daniel and Clarissa stayed behind, waiting to marry and yearning for larger lives beyond the river's shores.[21]

As Daniel Hunt was succeeding to his ancestral farm, Abel Moore was assembling a very different agricultural enterprise along the Bay Road a half-mile east of the meetinghouse. The deputy sheriff had no long-cultivated land on which to follow in the footsteps of his forefathers. Born in 1777, the fourth of eight children and third son of a farming family in Sudbury, Moore abandoned the land to enter trade as a storekeeper. In 1812 he was doing business in Stow, next door to his hometown, when he caught the notice of the well-connected lawyer Rufus Hosmer. Through the attorney's influence, the retailer gained appointment as a deputy sheriff of Middlesex County. Soon he was recruited to Concord and put in charge of the local jail. His days behind the store counter were over. The middle-aged Moore became a well-known figure in the village, as famous for his affability and neighborliness as for his energy and efficiency in enforcing the law. For more than a quarter-century, from 1815 to 1843, he attended to the work of the courts. He served writs; summonsed witnesses; attached, seized, and sold property; and arrested and incarcerated criminals and debtors alike. He was also frequently called on to auction goods at public sales. A functionary of the legal system, Moore dealt in paper—warrants, bonds, summonses, and executions—rather than dry goods and earned a fine living in the process. But the lure of the land remained strong. As he approached his fiftieth birthday, Moore set about building a modern farm at odds with the tradition Daniel Hunt sought to preserve and on a scale that old-style yeoman could never hope to reach.[22]

The site of Moore's venture was unpromising. Comprising one hundred acres, it extended on both sides of the Bay Road, stretching north above the ridge to the Great Meadow and Great Field and running south to the Cambridge Turnpike. The property had once been the pride of the Prescott family, one of the wealthiest in colonial Concord, whose patriarch had combined the profession of medicine with the practice of farming. But the Prescott clan was cut down in the Revolution, with two sons dying for the cause. The heir to the estate was a physician like his father, but he neglected the farm over the years, and in old age, plagued by debts, he lost the patrimony to his colleague Hurd, who, in turn, sold it to Moore. The deputy sheriff paid just $613 for the property; one year later the assessors valued the Prescott "home farm" at nearly $2,000. It would be worth a lot more once Moore set about improving it.[23]

On paper, the farm included seventy acres of improved land. In reality, it was "completely run down" after many years of disrepair. In its degraded condition the place was an embarrassing eyesore. Travelers into the village saw "an unsightly swamp" overgrown with wild shrubs and coarse grasses, where "the muskrats and bull frogs seemed to hold undisputed possession." Moore, a canny real estate speculator, knew what he was getting. "I had on my hands a large quantity of unproductive land," he reported some years later, "part of which would produce nothing, because it was so wet and marshy, and the rest would produce nothing because it was so dry and sandy." But this "active and successful business man" had an ambitious plan to revive his new holdings, and as he carried it out, he led the way in a far-reaching transformation of the agricultural landscape.[24]

The stream that wound its way through the old Prescott farm was the source of the difficulty. Its waters had been channeled to create the milldam in the center. Unfortunately for the Prescotts and then for Moore, the backwash inundated their meadows in a miniature version of the flowage problem afflicting Daniel Hunt and his neighbors along the banks of the Concord River. But where those victims of rising waters lacked the political clout to remove the supposed cause of their troubles—the dam at Billerica—the deputy sheriff had the connections and the capital to resolve his. It was easy to persuade his fellow entrepreneurs—Burr, Hurd, Keyes, Shattuck, and the Stow brothers—of the urgent need for action. Everyone already agreed that the millpond during the summer months was an offensive breeding ground for weeds and mosquitoes. But no one had the will to effect a remedy.

Enter Abel Moore, who recognized that in helping to eradicate a long-standing town problem, he could alleviate a new one of his own. The Mill Dam Company proved a brilliant answer to both. It harnessed the solution of one man's dilemma—the need to drain his wet meadows—to the larger development of the central village. As the driving force behind the project, Moore served the public and the private interests at once. No wonder that he gained a reputation as an unprincipled businessman, who pressed his own cause "to the very verge of honesty." The deputy sheriff made light of those suspicions. He liked to say that when he first came to Concord, he and several new acquaintances pledged to "get their living honestly, but that after a short trial they found the thing utterly impossible, and were obliged to give it up." The truth lay hidden in plain sight.[25]

Pulling down the milldam was just the first step in Moore's agricultural plan. Next came a herculean campaign to convert the wetlands into productive meadows. Moore began by digging an extensive series of ditches to drain off the accumulated water. Then his men bent their backs to the arduous challenge of cutting the accumulated brush and pulling up weeds and bushes by the roots. Yet the land remained "too miry" for plowing and planting. Ultimately the solution lay in "an interchange of soils" between the sandy uplands and the boggy meadows. Moore's laborers loaded up their oxcarts with peat and mud from the wetlands, dragged them over the ridge, and laid the fertile muck onto fields "hardly considered worth cultivating." On the return trip, the teams carried piles of sand and heaps of manure—four hundred cartloads of the one, twenty of the other per acre—to apply on the lowlands and build up a solid, productive soil. The results proved extraordinary. Sown with herdsgrass and redtop, the reclaimed meadows yielded an abundance of English hay, roughly three tons per acre, with nary a blade of wild grass to be seen. They were the gift that kept on giving, year after year, requiring only occasional manuring to continue bearing fruit.[26]

The reclamation project was costly in capital and labor, well beyond the resources of Daniel Hunt. Moore had ready access to the cash needed to finance his ambitious design. His public office was lucrative: every time he exercised his duties, he earned a fee—twenty cents for issuing a bail bond, thirty cents for serving a warrant, fifty cents for attaching property or seizing a debtor, and seventy-five cents for every twelve hours spent guarding prisoners in criminal cases and attending proceedings in court. As keeper of the Concord jail, he boarded debtors and earned eighteen cents a day for each one. As auctioneer, he received 1 percent of the value of the goods he sold. The misfortunes of his neighbors were Moore's bread and butter.

The sums, though small, steadily mounted. The deputy sheriff was well rewarded by the local lawyers. John Keyes paid $134 for his services between July 1829 and December 1830; Nathan Brooks owed $262 in accumulated charges over a comparable period. From all sources, Moore told the assessors in 1826, his income from public office came to $600 a year. And that didn't count the free lodging his family obtained in the county house, the free meals he enjoyed on the road, and the extra income he took in from various sidelines, including making and repairing boots and shoes, renting out his horse and chaise, and fattening one or two hogs a year for sale as bacon and sausages, pork, and lard. His was a comfortable and secure life in the public service. At fifty in 1827, Moore had no pressing reason to launch his venture on the old Prescott farm, except for a desire to return to the land, contribute to the progress of agriculture, and reap a profit.[27]

Although Moore claimed credit for the improvements, the bulk of the work was done by hired men. The deputy sheriff was too busy with official duties and too often on the road to supervise the project on site; in fact, he continued to live in the county house on the common not only during the early days of the farm but for more than a decade after it was growing crops and raising livestock. He regularly commuted from the village to his fields. Nor did his six children contribute much to the enterprise. When he launched the operation, three of Moore's four sons were young men in their prime, but all were headed for lives off the land: Henry, age twenty, for law; Reuben, eighteen, for trade; and George, fifteen, for Harvard College and the ministry. Only nine-year-old John would find his calling in agriculture. Moore expected everyone in his household to help out in the jail—George kept his father's records, as did daughter Harriet, who also attended to the inmates and read to them on the Sabbath—and all were on call to respond to sudden demands, such as the unexpected arrival of prisoners after dark. "This getting up, I do not like," grumbled George, whose sleep had been interrupted one time too many. "I shall soon wish to have a law to prevent people from coming to gaol in the night." The county house of detention was a greater family effort than the farm. Appropriately, the 1830 census treated the "gaol" as a household with seventeen members, of which Moore was the head.[28]

With his sons unavailable for the job, Moore looked elsewhere for labor.

One supply lay close at hand. The shrewd jailer marched inmates of the county lockup out to his sodden meadows and set them to ditching and draining for what one suspicious observer guessed were "little or no wages." Moore once boasted that the reclamation of his wetlands was accomplished by "my men and teams" during down times, when "foul weather" interfered with other chores, and in the winter, when the waterlogged meadows froze over. That was undoubtedly cold comfort to the exploited prisoners. Other laborers were volunteers enticed by a good deal: whatever peat they dug up, Moore promised, they could take away. What thrifty Yankee could turn down the offer of free fuel?

With such "helps," Moore made his uplands and meadows ready for cultivation in a few short years. By the early 1830s, he was reaping forty to fifty tons of English hay annually on land that had once been capable of supporting only a single cow on its coarse produce. Ten years later the operation was bigger still, consisting of one hundred acres of improved land, including eighteen in tillage and thirty-one in English meadow. It took as many as eight hired hands to manage all the work, at a cost of $550 a year. By then, John B. Moore, the youngest son, was twenty-three years old and eager to join his father in the cause of agricultural improvement.[29]

So successful was Moore's renovation of the run-down Prescott farm that he was eager to promote his methods far and wide and win recognition from his countrymen. Following the fall harvest in 1833, he entered the county agricultural society's contest for best farm in Middlesex, touting his techniques for reclaiming wetlands and showcasing the profitable returns. Seven years before, he noted, the income from his meadows had been not even a penny an acre. Now, after intensive treatment, the same land exceeded $100 to $150 per acre. Moore measured his success by a financial calculus, according to which the "best farm" produced the greatest yield and the largest profit; he never reckoned the environmental costs of eliminating all those wetlands. The same was true for the committee awarding the prize, which gave the Concord farmer second place. As it happened, there were only two entrants in the competition. Moore pocketed his twenty-dollar premium and renewed his bid. The next year he faced five rivals and again fell short, though the judges singled him out for doing "the most of any man in the county" to reclaim wetlands. His "enterprise and perseverance" were "an example for all our farmers."[30]

As he increased production and added improvements, Moore's reputation soared. He built a "commodious and substantial barn" with wide doors for carts and chaises to pass through, with ample storage for the immense crops of English hay, seventy-five to eighty tons a year, he was getting in, with comfortable stalls for the livestock, and with a cellar carefully designed to capture and preserve manure. So much for the skepticism of neighbors who had asked, "What are you going to fill it with?" Seven yoke of oxen, thirteen cows, four young cattle, and four horses usually occupied the stalls; thirty-three head of cattle wintered over. The casual sideline of fattening a couple hogs a year had grown into a major business; in 1840 Moore was breeding a mix of Berkshire and Mackay pigs for sale, some fifty to seventy-five a year, and slaughtering a ton of pork. All of these animals subsisted on the copious supplies of hay, corn, potatoes, turnips, and other root crops raised on the farm. The dairy yielded six hundred pounds of butter a year, more than Daniel Hunt's, along with fresh milk for sale in the village from November to January. Moore also dedicated considerable attention to his orchard, which contained two hundred apple, ten pear, ten peach, eight plum, and six cherry trees destined for consumers in the village and in the Boston area. This was a commercial enterprise, geared to the market, conducted with hired labor, and sustained with large infusions of capital. No "old-style" farm ever operated on such a scale.[31]

Every aspect of Moore's farm, from his up-to-date barn to his specialized breeds to his grafted apple trees, followed the best practices of the day. Moore was no longer just an expert at converting unproductive wetlands into bountiful meadows. He had developed into a master of several branches of husbandry (tillage crops, hayfields, livestock, and orchards) practiced in New England. In 1839 the *New England Farmer* featured the enterprise as one of the top two in the county; the next year the Massachusetts Society for Promoting Agriculture declared it the "best cultivated" farm in the Commonwealth, for which Moore walked away with a $200 prize. When Rev. Henry Colman issued his *Fourth Report on the Agriculture of Massachusetts* in 1841, he praised Moore as an example of "what magic power there is in skillful cultivation." He has "raised [the worn-out land of the Prescotts] from the dead and adorned [it] with life and beauty."

Perhaps the most lavish tribute came from the pen of Moore's neighbor, Ralph Waldo Emerson, who took to his journal to celebrate the progressive farmer as "a musician . . . who knows how to make men dance for him in all weathers, & all sorts of men, paddies, felons, farmers, carpenters, painters, yes, and trees, & grapes, & ice, & stone, hot days, cold days." The philosopher was as attuned to Moore's achievements as the Middlesex Agricultural Society's committee on farms. "His are the woods & the waters, the hills, & meadows. With a stroke of his instrument he danced a thousand tons of gravel from yonder blowing sand-heap on to the bog-meadow beneath us, where now the English grass is waving over countless acres." In his enthusiasm, Emerson spared Moore the fate of the "earth-proud" yeomen in his poem "Hamatreya," "Who steer the plough, but cannot steer their feet / Clear of the grave."[32]

Unlike Emerson, Henry Thoreau said nothing about Moore, but he was clearly taking careful note of the captain's assault on the wetlands. In *Walden* he would single out English hay as the epitome of the cash crop: an artificial product of science, reduced to a commodity, and antithetical to the wild freedom of nature. Who needed these so-called improvements?[33]

IN 1820 CONCORD THREW ITSELF INTO THE DEVELOPING MOVEMENT FOR agricultural reform. In response to a law passed by the state legislature encouraging the formation of county-wide associations for "the encouragement or improvement of agriculture or manufactures," the townspeople took the lead in starting the Society of Middlesex Husbandmen and Manufacturers. The new organization superseded an earlier venture, which had been confined to towns west of Concord, and it differed as well from the Massachusetts Society for Promoting Agriculture (MSPA), launched three decades earlier by leaders of the Boston elite. Once an exclusive conversation among landed gentlemen, the campaign for change was expanding its sights and reaching out to working farmers, "the bone and gristle" of the country.[34]

The chief activity of the county association was the sponsorship of an annual "cattle show," where common people could not only view the expensive agricultural experiments of their well-to-do neighbors but also vie for awards in a wide variety of areas, from plowing contests to fat cattle and swine and from orchards, cider, and butter to domestic manufactures. The prizes were funded by the state, which matched local contributions with anywhere from $200 to $600 annually. With that financial incentive, the exhibitions and competitions popularized the push for improvement. They recruited yeomen to seek out new crops, new breeds, and new techniques of cultivation and, in a "spirit of emulation," to surpass their neighbors in the quality and quantity of their productions. Farmers' wives and daughters were encouraged to do the same with the products of their domestic industry, from carpets and blankets to stockings, straw bonnets, and ribbons.

The new Society of Middlesex Husbandmen and Manufacturers launched its first gathering in October 1820, and it continued without fail thereafter for decades. Drawing large crowds to the displays of well-bred livestock and well-cultivated crops and to the thrilling tests of strength and skill in plowing contests and ox pulls, the fair became a fixture on the annual calendar, a "farmer's holiday" and harvest festival. Hosting the event stimulated civic pride in the ever-ambitious county seat. It was popularly known as the *Concord* cattle show and embraced by the townspeople as a local institution.[35]

The name of the organization was a calculated act of public relations. Husbandry evoked an ancient tradition in English culture, sanctified by religion, honored by the Crown, and perpetuated in folklore. In this outlook, the land longed for the husbandman as did a wife for her spouse. He planted the seed and made her fertile; their union brought forth fruit from the earth. This was an organic, reciprocal relationship, maintained by practices transmitted from father to son across the centuries. But the new Middlesex society meant to overturn that tradition and to substitute science and progress in its stead. It viewed the soil not as a willing partner but as an inert resource to be used, manipulated, and improved for maximum profit in the market. The master of the land was the farmer, equipped with the latest knowledge and the most efficient techniques, though this agenda for change was played down in the title and imagery of the association. The elaborately engraved certificate of membership projected the ideal: a gentleman and a workingman rest contentedly under a fruit tree. They are surrounded by the tools of husbandry (plow and scythe) and the bounty of the harvest (sheaves of wheat, pumpkins, ears of corn). A beehive symbolizes their industry, and in the distance a windmill and factory thrive on the products of the farm. Peace and harmony reign. Industry, commerce, and agriculture prosper together.[36]

Joining the agricultural society was virtually an act of patriotism, both local and national. "In Agriculture," declared the *Middlesex Gazette* in 1819, "America will ere long stand pre-eminent, as she already does in every thing that is great and good." In that optimistic faith, Concord's inhabitants entered their names on the membership rolls in remarkable numbers. Thirty men signed up in the society's first year, 1819–1820, followed by eight more up till the fall of 1824.

Then as that year's cattle show was opening, seventy-nine Concord men joined the ranks on a single day, in a sudden wave of enthusiasm that resembled a religious revival, and another ten in the succeeding weeks. "An impulse favorable to the Society seems to have seized the great body of our citizens," observed the local newspaper, under fresh ownership and emphasizing its identification with agriculture in a new title, *Concord Gazette and Middlesex Yeoman.*

By 1826, one out of every four male taxpayers belonged to the group. The vast majority were men of property from the upper ranks of the town; nearly all owned a farm. Newcomers like Abel Moore signed up along with scions of ancient families; traditionalists like Daniel Hunt stayed away. The typical member was a modest landowner in his late thirties, farming around forty acres, considerably less than Hunt or Moore. Not surprisingly, few laborers were found among them; hired men participated in the agricultural society chiefly by driving their masters' plows and teams in the annual competitions. Even so, this was an organization made up mostly of working farmers rather than village gentlemen and country squires. Fired up with reforming zeal, they shared the conviction that "the cause of agricultural improvement is the common cause of all."[37]

The new society lived up to its name: it was a partnership of *manufacturers* and *husbandmen*. Indeed, it appealed to everyone in town with an entrepreneurial bent. The pencil maker William Munroe was the first in Concord to belong; he was soon joined by his faithless employee Ebenezer Wood and his business rival John Thoreau. Bookbinders, clockmakers, shoemakers, carriage makers, and other craftsmen added to the list. The principal village storekeepers took an interest, as did the doctors and lawyers. So popular was the society during the first half of the 1820s that Concord residents dominated the membership. In October 1824, when enthusiasm was at a fever pitch, the group took in more than one hundred new members throughout Middlesex; eight out of ten lived in Concord.

The leading figures in the shire town quickly filled top offices in the organization. Though "not much of a farmer"—his greatest achievement was a seventy-three-pound squash—Daniel Shattuck served as treasurer for a decade (1821–1830) before rising to trustee, vice-president, and president for two terms (1835–1836). Concord residents invariably filled the positions of secretary and treasurer and served among the trustees. Abel Moore took a place on the board just as he was achieving the distinction of model farmer. The organization was dominated by the men who had formed the Mill Dam Company, built the insurance company, and launched the Concord Bank.[38]

Every October, as the fall foliage was displaying its annual show of colors, the Middlesex fair put on a man-made spectacle of its own. Into the center rumbled the finest specimens of cattle, sheep, and swine on their way to temporary pens on hilly, uncultivated ground in "Sleepy Hollow," several hundred yards northeast of the common. They were followed by crowds of onlookers, as Henry Thoreau once observed, eager "to see the procession of a hundred yoke of oxen, all as august and grave as Osiris, or the droves of neat cattle and milch cows as unspotted as Isis or Io." The day began promptly at nine o'clock with the plowing match, in which contestants vied to turn over the soil of an allotted tract, an eighth of an acre of smooth, light grassland, as quickly and thoroughly as possible—a competition often accompanied by the shouts and oaths of drivers intent on speeding up their plodding teams. The winners invariably finished in under half an hour. By ten the committee of arrangements was herding participants and spectators in a procession across the common, over the milldam, and into the meetinghouse, where Doctor Ripley, as ready as any farmer to seek a premium for the fruits of his orchard, sought divine blessing on the occasion, after which the speaker of the day held forth on the progress of agriculture and the continuing need for improvements. An hour later it was time for "the trial of strength and discipline of Working Oxen." Teams of oxen were put to grueling tasks, such as hauling a load of more than three and a half tons up "a steep ascent, of half a dozen rods in length."

As the animals heaved and strained, the committees appointed to view and judge the numerous items submitted for premiums went about their work at the courthouse, where the growers of fruit, the weavers of carpets and coverlets, the makers of boots and shoes, gloves, and hats displaced plaintiffs and defendants for a day in the contest for advantage. Here was the opportunity for entrepreneurs to showcase their manufactures; both William Munroe and John Thoreau looked to build their businesses with prizewinning displays of pencils. The competitions reached broadly through the community. Waldo Emerson treasured his apples and pears and put them in contention for premiums, though rarely with success. One year a distinguished committee of the Massachusetts Horticultural Society unexpectedly asked to visit his orchard. Of course, he replied, expressing "modest pride" at the honor, only to be quickly disappointed. "Mr. Emerson, the committee have called to see the soil which produces such poor specimens of such fine varieties." Young people too gladly showed off their accomplishments. Helen and Sophia Thoreau won awards for their artwork; Henry took a premium for "a monstrous squash" he had grown, "so coarse that nobody could eat it."[39]

By two p.m. everyone was ready for dinner; as many as two hundred people filled the Middlesex Hotel for the repast, following which the leaders of the society and various "volunteers" stood up and offered toasts in an unofficial competition to present the wittiest puns and the slyest hits on agriculture, politics, and fashion. Nathan Brooks was particularly esteemed for his "keen sense of humor" as toastmaster. In a typical play on words, Brooks raised a glass to the cause of temperance among "the Farmers of Middlesex": "May they have that *spirit* of industry and prudence, which will keep them from being knock'd down by ardent spirit, or hauled up by law or physic." When the feasting and toasting were over, the group reassembled at the courthouse to hear the announcement of the prizes. The winners celebrated; the also-rans returned home and prepared to try again the following year. In a ritual that grew ever more elaborate over the years, the cattle show celebrated the unity and productivity of rural society even as it accelerated the transformation of agriculture under the leadership of a commercially minded elite.[40]

The annual orations at the cattle show laid out the agenda for change. In Middlesex as elsewhere in Massachusetts, the speakers were gentlemen with white shirts and smooth hands; of the eleven men chosen to give the address between 1821 and 1831, seven were lawyers, four ministers. All but two had attended Harvard College. (The exceptions went to Dartmouth.) The men of the cloth sided with Unitarians in the bitter sectarian politics of the day. Working farmers of all persuasions furnished the audience.[41] The talks themselves were full of praise for the farmer as the backbone of the republic: "the yeomanry are the strength and safeguard of almost every nation," Rev. Charles Briggs of Lexington declared in 1825, and their way of life is the envy of all, with "so few evils" and "so many of the substantial comforts and real enjoyments of life."

The optimistic rhetoric was belied by apprehensions about the future of farming in a fast-changing world. "We are rapidly becoming a manufacturing nation," the Framingham lawyer Josiah Adams told the society in 1823, "and need little stimulus to effect that object." Not so for agriculture, which was "strangely neglected" and falling behind the times. Unless it stepped up the pace and took on the enterprising spirit of the age, husbandry would not just stagnate—it would hold back the progress of the entire country. Agriculture and manufactures must "advance hand in hand, or they will both go backward," warned the editor of the *New England Farmer* Thomas G. Fessenden. "Agriculture without manufactures would give us farmers without tools, manufactures without agriculture would produce mechanics without bread."[42]

Agricultural and industrial revolutions thus went together. To advance this partnership, the speakers urged farmers to gear their production to the needs of manufacturing. New England's textile factories demanded raw materials of all sorts and not just cotton from Southern slave plantations. Woolen mills were hungry for fleece to convert into yarn and cloth. If Yankee farms were abandoning homespun "linsey-woolsey" in favor of store-bought fabrics, that was no cause for concern. Let them devote their hilly, rocky pastures to support flocks of Merino and Saxony sheep, imported from Europe, whose long-staple wool was well suited to keeping people warm in New England winters. The "craze" for these animals was bolstered by high tariffs protecting American-raised wool against foreign competition.

Wool growing appealed only to men with money to burn. Back in the colonial period, over half of Concord's farmers had kept sheep, averaging six to nine head, for a total of 713 just before the Revolution. Six decades later that number had increased to over a thousand, valued at $1,500 for the wool. But only three farmers took the risk of this precarious trade. One was Joseph Barrett, the gentleman farmer who served as a trustee of the agricultural society through the 1820s and rose to president in 1830. Hundreds of finely bred Merino and Saxony sheep ranged over his nearly five hundred acres atop Nashawtuc Hill, on the southern outskirts of the village. The "largest wool grower" in Middlesex, Barrett took inordinate pride in his flock, which "repeatedly" won first prize in statewide and county competitions. In a relentless quest for ever-finer fleece, he pressed selective breeding to dangerous extremes. So delicate became the lambs that they fell quick victims to disease and "died by hundreds," to the inexpressible grief of their owner, who had taken personal charge of their care and invested affections as well as dollars in their well-being. "The sheep would come at his call more quickly than at that of any other," recalled his son. Barrett suffered greatly, both emotionally and financially, from their loss. The disaster served as a warning to the neighbors, who saw no future in wool growing. By 1837 roughly one hundred common sheep remained in Concord. Woolen factories would have to look beyond Massachusetts to the rolling hills of Vermont for fleece.[43]

When one form of textiles did not work out, agricultural reformers recommended another. Instead of sickly sheep from Europe, why not try an even more exotic crop: mulberry trees and the silkworms that fattened on the heart-shaped leaves? From the cocoons spun by the small creatures, it was predicted, would arise a new domestic industry. Silk, a luxury good associated with both Europe (France and Italy) and China, could be as American as cotton and wool. The trade dated back to the mid-eighteenth century, when Connecticut lawmakers voted a bounty to encourage the planting of native white mulberry orchards, and thanks to that aid, it took root in the town of Mansfield, where, it was estimated in 1826, three-quarters of households were raising worms and furnishing raw silk to local mills. The Concord *Gazette* took notice and began promoting the enterprise in 1827, confident that "this is well-calculated for a silk growing country."[44]

The campaign escalated in 1830, when a new variety of mulberry from China, *Morus multicaulis*, was introduced with great fanfare. The Chinese import promised easy money for modest effort. The speaker at the 1831 Concord cattle show, banker John M. Cheney, caught the silk "fever" and passed it on. In his enthusiastic endorsement, silk cultivation seemed to solve two pressing problems for the farmer at once: it offered a new source of income at a time when cheap Western grains were pouring into the Northeast via the Erie Canal and driving down prices for local corn and rye, and it furnished "a pleasant and profitable employment" for women and children in homes where "the music of the spindle and the loom has ceased to be heard." Silk could provide an add-on crop readily fitted into rural routines. Mulberry orchards would thrive on "dry, sandy" soils that were ill suited to other purposes, and their leaves could be gathered, chopped, and fed to the voracious caterpillars by "the daughters of Middlesex" in free hours. Caring for the worms would be a "fireside" occupation for girls anxious to avoid "the hard alternative of going into disagreeable and dangerous service abroad, or of remaining in a useless and burdensome idleness."

The toughest labor was performed by *Bombyx mori* itself, spinning its silk cocoon before departing the larval state for new life as a moth. The filaments of the cocoons were drawn out and wound onto reels, twisted into raw silk, and piled into heavy bales weighing up to 150 pounds for sale to manufacturers. Silk cultivation thus had the potential to boost rural incomes, pay for goods at village stores, and guarantee manufacturers a steady supply of raw materials for thread, ribbons, and cloth. Through such collaboration, agriculture and industry, the twin pillars of Middlesex society, would join forces to advance the common wealth. "Know that every improvement you make upon your lands," enjoined Cheney, "adds to the permanent riches of your country." But few working farmers were convinced. The industrial crops of wool and silk proved passing fads.[45]

The future of commercial agriculture lay in more familiar areas: in the drained meadows that Abel Moore was converting to English hay; in the tilled fields yielding substantial harvests of oats for the many horses pulling omnibuses in Boston and Lowell, regular stages between the city and the country, and the chaises carrying a fortunate fifth of Concord's inhabitants around town; in the dairies furnishing butter to customers in the village; in the woodlots that were steadily being stripped of oak, chestnut, and pine to provide pastures for local livestock and to build and fuel the expanding cities; and in the orchards and vines whose economic potential was beginning to be explored in the 1820s, as the agricultural society was launching its annual fair.[46]

In the eighteenth century and after, farmers had typically devoted an acre or two to growing apples for cider, sauce, and pies; fresh apples and other fruit contributed little to the daily diet. Around 1820, soon after coming of age, Nathan Barrett, Jr., a neighbor of Daniel Hunt on Punkatasset Hill, set out "a large quantity of young apple trees of the best varieties" on the family farm, to the consternation of old-timers, who saw only "rashness" in the venture. It was confidently predicted that "he would never find a market for such a quantity of nice apples." There was good reason for skepticism. The young man was known for "an easy, somewhat indolent disposition," and in his early years on the farm, he preferred to supervise operations rather than undertake the hard labor himself. As it happened, he lost big on sheep raising and then on butchering beef. But he was prescient about the market for fruit. Popular tastes were changing in the 1820s and early 1830s, with demand rising for apples, pears, peaches, plums, and watermelon. The agricultural society was quick to award premiums to orchards that grafted saplings in the nursery and pruned the growing trees. "Much of the excellence, as well as the beauty of an orchard," a committee declared in 1826, "depends on this." Members of the Barrett family won the top prizes year after year, and others, such as Daniel Hunt's brother Nehemiah, were tempted to try. He was surely disappointed when the judges recommended "a little more attention to trimming and shaping" his trees. Not so Doctor Ripley, who in his eighties received one dollar for a "sweet pound pear." That success in the orchard inspired Rufus Hosmer to offer a special toast to the parson at the 1833 fair: "He has given additional evidences this day [that] in old age he produces the best fruit."[47]

To agricultural improvers, the fruit of the vine also called out for cultivation. When John Cheney delivered the address to the cattle fair in 1831, he noted that nature had bestowed on Middlesex a "rich and delicious product . . . in almost wasteful profusion." Why should New Englanders be so eager to import "exotics from every climate under heaven" when the native wild grapes of the region could be converted into wine "equal in richness and flavor to the choicest that France, Spain, or Italy can boast"? Such a beverage would advance the cause of temperance, replacing "villainous" ardent spirits with a "pleasant and salubrious" drink. With this endorsement and the encouragement of premiums, the race was on to be the first to develop the sweet of the vine that came to be known as the Concord grape.[48]

The quest for new crops was a response both to the challenges of Western competition and to the opportunities of emerging urban markets. More than that, it aimed to transform not just the output of the farm but more importantly the consciousness of the farmer. "Because an article has been cultivated by our Fathers, and has been profitable to them," the *Gazette* advised readers in March 1827, "is no reason why it should still be cultivated . . . The condition of the world changes, so do its wants, and the farmer must endeavor to supply them in some degree as the merchant supplies the fashions." In speeches to the agricultural society, in the annual *Farmers' Almanac*, in the weekly issues of T. G. Fessenden's *New England Farmer*, and in the "Agricultural Miscellany" of Concord's *Gazette*, reformers pressed home the same theme: every aspect of Yankee husbandry demanded rethinking and remaking for the changing times. For one thing, farms were too big to run in the existing mode of production. The typical yeoman, it was charged, attempted to cultivate far more land than he had the labor or capital to manage with any success. His supply of manure was insufficient to fertilize all his fields; he scattered it "as if it were Calomel," an overused remedy for constipation. With too few hands for the work, he had no choice but to plow shallowly and hoe carelessly before racing to bring in an inadequate crop. Everything was done "by halves"—"half-farming, half-cultivating, and half-manuring"—without any foresight or plan. Farmers labored hard, it was acknowledged, far harder than they ought, but "to no kind of good purpose." "Their work hurried them on," lamented a New Hampshire critic reprinted in the *Middlesex Gazette*, "and they have not time to make the necessary retrenchments and improvements, but continue . . . 'slashing on, heels over head,' without consideration . . . [and] without improvement." Like Daniel Hunt struggling on his sixty acres, they pressed to the limit and beyond and made "perfect slaves of themselves," passing "through the world without enjoying the sweets of living—they follow their fathers' paths and swerve not."[49]

In that blind deference to the past lay the fundamental source of the problem. Reformers called on their countrymen to break "the power of habit and the charm of hereditary custom" and abandon the time-honored ways of their fathers and grandfathers before them. Just because your forebears had sowed crops and slaughtered hogs according to the phases of the moon—an astrological notion of the seventeenth century—did not mean you should, too. The modern farmer consulted the experts, adopted the best practices, and sought to improve upon them with his own experiments. "He who adheres to old customs while everybody about him is adopting newer and better," advised attorney Albert H. Nelson, junior partner of Keyes, "will fall behind the age."[50]

The key to success resided in the rule of reason. The "wise farmer" applied the lessons of science to all his operations: he chose "the best kinds of grains, grasses, and roots," sowed them on soils best adapted to their growth and enhanced by the most effective fertilizers, and cultivated them with "the best modes" and tools available, such as the cast-iron plows sold at Burr & Prichard's store. The modern age of agriculture, driven by science and dependent on chemical fertilizers and advancing technology, was on the rise, and the speakers at the Concord cattle shows were intent on promoting its cause. Even if, as they conceded, "all farmers cannot be Chymists and experimental Philosophers," everyone could organize his affairs rationally and efficiently. The well-run enterprise followed a careful plan. Everything was done in proper order, with fields fenced before they were plowed and manured before they were sown. No one ever heard "the shocking sounds of *hogs in the corn! sheep in the mowing lot! cows in the cabbage yard!*" Performing his chores thoroughly and on schedule, the "good farmer" enjoyed a composure lacking in his harried neighbors, who "spin round and round like a top" in "perpetual motion," constantly in a hurry to "attempt every thing without accomplishing any thing." There was consequently always time to review and record the activities of the farm and to keep its finances in order.

Like every other businessman, the yeoman was well advised to maintain an exact record of his transactions, to note down all his credits and debts, and to pay every obligation as it came due, whether it was demanded or not. At the end of each year, having paid all bills and settled all accounts, he should draw up a statement of his financial condition, just as Shattuck and Munroe invariably did. Let "economy and industry" be the watchwords. Don't "run into debt," the farmer was told, unless you are confident of repaying the loan on time; don't buy goods at auction because they are cheap, unless you actually require what is on offer; and "never hire a man to do a piece of work, which you can do yourself." Self-reliance was the best course.[51]

That caution against depending on others posed a sharp challenge to the social norms and cooperative customs of old-style husbandry. Since the colonial period, the practice of farming had been enmeshed in the conduct of community. When Eunice P. Wyman and Jacob B. Farmer "changed works," they did not merely assist in the completion of necessary farm tasks; they enacted a widely held commitment to "good neighborhood." Agricultural reformers condemned the tradition as a waste of time. How often did farmers come over to their neighbors' fields for the chance to gossip rather than pull weeds! "There are some," complained Thomas's *Farmer's Almanack* in 1821, "who cannot bear to work alone. If they have a yard of cabbages to hoe, they must call in a neighbour to change work. Now this is very pleasant, but it tends to lounging and idleness, and neglect of business, for we cannot always have our neighbours at work with us." Far better to do all essential chores on one's own.

Even worse were the periodic gatherings of rural folk for the ostensible purpose of husking corn, paring apples, and raising barns. In the eyes of critics, they commonly degenerated into drunken frolics, which could cost the poor host as much in rum, biscuits, and "apple platter pies" and in damaged crops as he gained in shucked ears of corn and skinned fruit. By the 1820s, these seasonal events were going out of fashion, and when a contributor to the Concord *Gazette* in 1825 recalled wistfully the "joyous huskings" of the past, he was roundly denounced for peddling immorality in the press. To the champions of the new order of agricultural capitalism, labor and leisure no longer belonged together. In the realm of work, the priorities were productivity and profit. The chain of community was giving way to the claims of cash.[52]

Agricultural reform was Janus-faced. On the one hand, its advocates worked tirelessly to effect far-reaching social and economic changes; on the other hand, they were anxious to preserve the yeomanry as the bedrock of New England. The ideal farm, in their view, was a small-scale enterprise, intensively managed to realize the maximum return for the most intelligent effort. Who needed eighty to one hundred acres? Lexington's Reverend Briggs was confident that with "wise and improved cultivation," yeomen could harvest "more produce and greater profit" on half as much land. But for all the talk about markets and profits, the speakers at the Concord cattle shows had a higher purpose. Yankee farms, they stressed, were as important for cultivating virtue as for making money. "Nations that have been the most agricultural," Briggs preached, "have commonly been the most virtuous." Labor on the land fostered "intelligence, frugality, and temperance." It bred Patriots, who identified their "paternal inheritance" with the well-being of the country and were quick to rally to its defense, as did their fathers and grandfathers on the nineteenth of April in 1775. And it inspired religious reverence for "the great Author of all things." "When we walk among the works of nature," the Unitarian minister opined, "we seem to hear the voice and feel the presence of Divinity."[53]

The trouble was that not many sons and daughters of Yankee farms were heeding that message. From the hills of New Hampshire and Massachusetts, they were streaming into the commercial villages springing up all over the region—as did Shattuck, Burr, and the Davis brothers of Concord—into the textile factories of Waltham, Lowell, and smaller mill towns, and into the urban entrepôts of all this growth. Concord contributed its share to the vast population flow, including a good many migrants drawn to the fertile lands of the West. Why toil so long and hard to wrest a living from the stony soil of New England, when bountiful land was beckoning across the Appalachians to the banks of the Mississippi? Western grains were already winning the day in the Boston market, and the newspapers abounded with accounts of "vegetable wonderments" on the frontier, such as the "prolific" watermelon vines, nearly seventy feet long, grown by Tilly Brown, son of the Concord saddler Reuben Brown, who had settled in southern Indiana along the Ohio River by the early 1820s. Brown anticipated that his extravagant report would be "the very [death] knell of my veracity" among the folks back home, and he was right. The *Middlesex Observer* responded with a satirical tall tale of a Yankee migrant to "the land of milk and honey" in the West, who, lacking the means to build a house for his family, grew their shelter from pumpkin seeds. The biggest gourd was ample enough, after being scooped out, to "form a very commodious house, with numerous apartments"; the smaller ones afforded "convenient stables and out-houses."

Sarcasm alone could not stem the exodus. So the spokesmen for agricultural reform came up with various reasons why the farmers of Massachusetts should stay at home. Yes, the banker Cheney admitted, the Massachusetts climate could be severe, the soil "hard and stubborn," but such challenges built "strong" bodies and "manly" character. To bridle at the imperative of arduous labor was to "murmur at the decrees of Providence." It was true, too, that no one was getting rich from farming in Massachusetts, certainly not as easily as people had done back in the boom years of the 1790s and early 1800s. That "age of dazzling successes" was over. In a new era of free trade and international competition, Yankee farmers would have to lower expectations and settle for modest rewards, many of them immaterial. Surely the benefits of living "thickly" in long-settled communities, close to the meetinghouse and schools, and connected to neighbors and kin, outweighed the hardship and isolation of the frontier, no matter how prodigious the melons and plentiful the harvests. Sustained by a supportive community and his own hard work, the "honest and intelligent" Yankee yeoman could stand proudly "erect and unabashed, amidst the foremost of the land."[54]

For all its advocacy of markets, efficiency, and innovation, agricultural reform was conservative in intent. Under the guidance of progressive merchants, manufacturers, and commercial farmers, the "corn and pumpkin" husbandry of the past would fade. But sober, frugal Yankee men and women would remain on the land, still enmeshed in an interdependent community, and gather together every thanksgiving to appreciate the sacrifices of their ancestors and the blessings of Providence.

GEORGE MINOTT WAS "THE MOST STAY-AT-HOME BODY IN CONCORD."[55] THE old-style farmer never attended the annual orations at the cattle show, nor did he ever compete for a premium. Then again he did not participate in town meeting, never held office, never served on a special committee, and never sought admission into Doctor Ripley's church. His name is absent from the membership rolls of the many voluntary associations that proliferated in Concord during the two decades following the War of 1812. Even the spelling of his surname, with the extra *t*, set him apart from his distant kinsmen. Family obligations were not the excuse for his unsociable life. A lifelong bachelor, he kept house with his spinster sister Mary, the tailoress, and her employees in a small, weathered dwelling on the hill overlooking the main road into the village. Unlike Daniel Hunt, Minott had neither a growing family nor a big farm to sustain. In 1826 he was tending a mere six acres, with only one in tillage and another in English meadow, on the opposite side of the Bay Road. His time was his own to improve in any way he chose, and as it turned out, that did not include the civic duties, the religious squabbles, or the reform campaigns preoccupying so many of his neighbors. Living near the heart of town, Minott quietly withdrew into himself and made no demands on anyone else. His solitary example showed that a man could be a hermit in the village just as easily as in the woods.

Minott boasted as illustrious a lineage as anyone in Concord. Born in 1783, he was a scion of the colonial elite going back to the Puritan settlers. His paternal grandfather rose to eminence as a longtime member of the royal governor's council. On his mother's side, he descended from the Prescott clan, landed magnates and political luminaries themselves. The Prescott domain, comprising 145 acres of improved land in 1771, was the very property that fell into Abel Moore's hands in the mid-1820s.[56]

Ephraim Minott, George's father, inherited the bulk of the estate but did not enjoy it for long. A fervent Patriot, he enlisted in the Continental army for as long as the war lasted, but after being wounded at the Battle of Trenton, he was commissioned lieutenant of a company of invalids. Returning home "lame" with diminished prospects, he struggled on for a decade, hampered not only by his injury but also by excessive drinking; his death in 1794 was blamed on both "intemperance" and "consumption." Three of his five children with Abigail Prescott were still at home, including eleven-year-old George and his sister Mary, twenty-one. The two siblings stuck with their mother in the four-room cottage so neatly situated above the Bay Road that it struck one observer "as if it had grown up there in a night a century ago."[57]

With her widow's third and a handsome legacy from her father, Abigail Prescott lived genteelly with her adult children in a home furnished in the elite style of the eighteenth century, with cherry and mahogany tables, china and pewter plates, tea service, and looking glasses. George cultivated the twenty-five valuable acres in the center that were once part of his grandfather's estate; Mary plied her needle and thread. At twenty-one, George signed on as a laborer at a farm in nearby Lincoln, and after seven years, he was ready to strike out on his own and start an independent life. The widow Minott would not countenance the move. She "required him to stay" at home. George gave in on the condition that he receive $120 a year, plus room and board, for his pains. This was the going rate for a farm laborer, which was credited to George's account year after year with 6 percent interest until it had accumulated into a tidy sum.

On the tax lists, George Minott appeared to be one of the many landless men flowing in and out of town. As he approached middle age, he doubtless expected to inherit most of his mother's land and eventually to obtain his back wages. But when Abigail Prescott died at seventy-seven in February 1825, a widow longer than she had ever been a wife, the son was upset to learn that the estate could not pay its $3,116 in debts. All of the household goods and farming tools went up for auction, along with a good bit of the land, in a legal process overseen by the late widow's own nephew, Samuel P. P. Fay, judge of the Middlesex County Probate Court. The Minott siblings faced a shrunken future as the last representatives in Concord of a family that was downwardly mobile and at the end of the road.[58]

Ironically, the financial plight of the estate was due to two creditors: George and Mary Minott themselves. When the court-appointed officials gathered to appraise the assets and liabilities, they were handed bills from the two siblings: $1,100 claimed by George, the equivalent of nearly nine years' wages, and $1,000 by Mary, together amounting to 60 percent of the total obligations. There was no way the estate could meet such demands. So the executor appointed a committee to appraise these claims. Unfortunately for George, the members were those dedicated agricultural reformers Abel Moore, John Cheney, and Reuben Brown, Jr., who looked skeptically at his bill. Did his labor on so small a farm really deserve the $120 a year promised by the widow Minott? "An able man would do all he did in half the time," opined Brown, who thought Minott "not worth more than $5 a month." Moore agreed; Cheney proved more liberal, allowing $6 a month. The arbitrator went with the more generous estimate, discounting George's bill by a third to $740. Mary got less than half of her claim for domestic labor.

A good part of that money did not stay in the siblings' purses for long. When the property came under the auctioneer's hammer, Mary had to pay $565—more than she was allowed on her bill—for the house in which she lived; George obtained the barn and nine acres south of the Cambridge Turnpike for $490, two-thirds of his payment due. Luckily, not all of the inheritance was sold off. The two siblings were granted nearly eleven acres of woodland in nearby Lincoln. But none of the Concord property came as a bequest, and most of it passed into the hands of such neighbors as Moore, who was then building his model farm on the ruins of the Prescott estate.[59]

If leading figures in the Society of Middlesex Husbandmen and Manufacturers scorned his deliberate approach to farming as a waste of time, Minott was not concerned. He consulted only himself. For just this reason, he won the admiration of Henry Thoreau. The two were almost kin, through their relation to Jonas Minot. As a boy and then as a college student, Thoreau used to walk up the steep path to the Minott house to be measured and fitted for his coats, jackets, and pantaloons by the tailoress Mary. Once out of Harvard and back home, he continued to follow that route to seek out George for conversation, intermittently in the 1840s and then frequently over the next decade.[60] Their talks ranged over the woods and fields of Concord, taking in the habits of foxes, rabbits, and squirrels, of pigeons and bluebirds, the cultivation of corn and potatoes, haying in the Great Meadow, the best way to cut trees in a forest, the signs of the seasons, and blizzards and hurricanes in times past. The youth, thirty-four years junior, seldom tired of the stories, which Minott, sitting in a corner by the stove with a cat in his lap and chewing tobacco, related in a Yankee accent as antique as the two-hundred-year-old clock ticking behind him.

Visits with the old farmer, some eighty altogether, fill the writer's journals; Minott appears in his pages more often than anyone in Concord except the Transcendentalist poet Ellery Channing, who penned his own portrait of the "local, homely, rustic" as one of the last of the Yankee husbandmen from the eighteenth century. For Thoreau, Minott represented more than that: he was at once a trusted guide to the natural history of Concord and a defector from a modern world "turned upside down." His alienation from the times undoubtedly reached a peak in the 1850s, as he entered his seventies and saw the Concord he once knew and loved disappearing before his eyes. But Minott's resistance had deep roots. He was fixed in his ways early on, and by the time he came into his inheritance in 1827, the middle-aged bachelor stood apart from his neighbors, treasured his independence, and refused to budge in the conduct of his farm or of his life, no matter what the annual orators at the cattle show had to say.[61]

Minott's dissent was silent but emphatic. Mary participated actively in church, charity, and reform, but George made a deliberate choice to avoid all these entanglements. Why didn't he go to Sunday meeting as she did? "I don't want to," he declared; "blast em!" Nor did he see any point in voting: "it will not stay," he told Waldo Emerson, "but what you do with the gun will stay." Aloof from both church and state, Minott steered clear of the economic concerns of his neighbors. In an era of restless mobility, he stayed put. He went down to Boston only once in his life; that was during the War of 1812, when his militia company marched to defend the capital against the threat of British warships. Hardly had he arrived than he fell victim to homesickness and "promptly deserted." He never saw the sights of the city again. Why bother? He had nothing to buy or sell in the metropolis; it was his boast that he had never taken goods to market. The small farm along the Bay Road satisfied nearly all his needs, and his sister's tailoring paid for the few items—tea, sugar, salt, flour, and wine—they bought at Burr & Prichard's store. Minott was content with this simple existence. He had not the slightest interest in the so-called improvements pushed by the agricultural society nor in the commercial ventures that drove so many others to incessant labor. To be sure, he had nothing saved up for old age and without Mary's earnings might well end up in the almshouse. That prospect troubled him not at all. "He is not poor," observed Thoreau, "for he does not want riches."[62]

Thoreau idealized Minott as "the most poetical farmer" in Concord, "who most realizes to me the poetry of the farmer's life." His few acres were cultivated skillfully, according to a plan the agricultural society would certainly have approved, had it not been so time-consuming. Minott did not take on more land than he could manage successfully; nor did he hire anyone to assist him. He required no lessons from "book farmers" to recognize the wisdom of careful and thorough husbandry. "He is never in a hurry to get his garden planted," his literary admirer reported, "and yet it is always planted soon enough and none in town is kept as beautifully clean." So it was with his harvest. When Minott gathered in his corn, he took pains to remove the entire plant—ears, husks, and stalks—from the ground, unlike the "speculating, money-making farmers," who left the stubble behind to turn "dry and dingy and black as chips." After drying on the "braces and timbers" of the barn, the stalks furnished nutritious fodder for Minott's cow. This thoughtful regimen was economical, but Minott did not pursue it for the sake of profit. In contrast to Abel Moore or even Daniel Hunt, he treated the land tenderly and received its bounty with reverence: "He handles and amuses himself with every ear of his corn crop as much as a child with its playthings—and so his small crop goes a great way." No wonder the reviewers of his mother's debts were so dubious of his bill. The independent-minded farmer performed his labors for their own sake and *not* for the money his crops and livestock yielded: "He gets out of each manipulation in the farmer's operations a fund of entertainment which the speculating drudge hardly knows." If anyone deserved the title of model farmer, it was Minott and *not* Moore.[63]

The old man would surely have rejected that distinction. In his youth, he had preferred to spend his time in the rivers, swamps, and woods rather than labor on the land. "Should you be fond of the *chase*, or the sport with the *hook*, indulge occasionally," the *New England Farmer* advised, "but never to the injury of more important concerns." Minott paid no heed. From early on, he delighted in hunting the abundant game around Concord, and in later years he took equal pleasure in recounting his exploits to Thoreau half a dozen times and more. Rabbits and squirrels; pigeons, partridges, ducks, and geese: all were easy prey to his keen eye and steady finger on the fowling pieces he treasured as affectionately as his hunting dogs. "Minott has a story for every woodland path . . . Where we walked last, he had once caught a partridge *by the wing*!" He could recall when pickerel and trout ran free in the mill brook and bear, moose, and wildcats roamed the Walden woods. Those days were back in the 1790s and early 1800s, when Minott was growing up, and by the time Thoreau was coming of age, they were long gone.

Minott thus served as a living link to a wilder, rougher, less domesticated world. As he never wearied of repeating, winters had been colder and longer, summers shorter, fish and game more profuse, and crops bigger in the "holy days" of his boyhood. The men were as outsize as the creatures: they flocked to impromptu turkey shoots in the woods, where the rum flowed as freely as the shots; they gambled over dice on Concord common during court week; and they took every opportunity to challenge one another to wrestling matches. Their masculine world was free from the restrictive rules of respectability that constrained the educated, middle-class young men and women of Thoreau's generation.[64]

That was the message Minott conveyed to his Transcendentalist admirers. He came from a time when men lived closer to nature, with a sharper sense of its seasonal rhythms and a greater respect for the teeming life it sustained, and he retained his youthful habits into maturity. But there was little room for such free souls in the Concord of the 1820s and 1830s. As the woods steadily retreated before pastures and meadows and as commerce overtook the countryside, Minott went his own way, content with the "competency" his small farm provided. The careful husband, cultivating his few acres with a devotion approaching piety, found contentment in his native town.

Ironically, Minott fulfilled the ideal of the agricultural reformers, but for a goal they would never approve. His intensive labor enabled him to remain apart from the market. Refusing to enter the world of agricultural capitalism, the bachelor farmer preserved the traditional ways of the household economy without ever forming a family, and he kept his place in a community in which he seldom took part. He spurned both the old and the new, the dense social web inherited from the past and the self-seeking materialism that was tearing it apart. Living independently and simply in harmony with the land, he became an inspiration to Thoreau: "Minott adorns whatever part of nature he touches; whichever way he walks he transfigures the earth for me."[65]

Knowledge Is Power

While John Thoreau threw himself into pencil making and Cynthia set up housekeeping, took in lodgers, and vacillated between churches, their four children went to school. Just a five-minute walk from their home at the corner of Main and Walden streets stood an "old unpainted weather beaten" house by the shore of the millpond, where a maiden lady in her thirties named Phoebe Wheeler ran an "infant school" for little boys and girls. There David Henry[1] and his siblings John and Sophia spent day after day reciting their letters at the knee of the severe Miss Wheeler, to whose dress they were "pinned" by their aprons to keep them close. Noisy children were "shut up" in the dark behind the door to the steep garret stairs, where they cowered in "mortal fear" of disturbing the wasps buzzing around the windowpanes. This early nursery school was an unforgettable experience; one survivor never got over the "continuous drilling" in the ABCs. "The alphabet," he recalled many decades later, "is the hardest lesson a child ever learns." It was also the ticket of admission to the brick schoolhouse on the common. Without reading readiness—the ability to recognize letters and identify syllables—no child could begin formal instruction in the town schools. And so parents provided the lessons themselves or turned to "dames" like Phoebe Wheeler to take on the assignment for a small fee.[2]

Thus began the exposure of Henry Thoreau to the varied arrangements in Concord for the education of the young. From Miss Wheeler's little venture, the boy would go on to the public grammar school on the common and then to the private academy in the village. Singled out early for his bookish disposition and precocious intellect, he was following a conventional course to college and a learned profession, like the sixty-plus lads from Concord who had blazed the trail to Harvard since the seventeenth century.

But his preparation took place in a dawning era of change. A wave of school reform was rising in Concord and the Bay State that would eventually broaden the methods and purposes of education. The movement strove to improve instruction by updating curricula and texts, upgrading teacher training, and softening discipline in the classroom. By these means, it aspired to enhance the abilities of the young to contribute to the wider society. In this progressive blueprint for change, the schools would pull away from the older way of life in which they were enmeshed and enlist in the cause of economic progress and technological innovation. Reform also added to the strains and divides in the community. Townspeople contended for control of education; the young drew apart from the old; and Thoreau's generation splintered along lines of occupation, gender, and class. As greater opportunities for some individuals opened up, the ties of interdependence loosened still more.[3]

The future writer observed the changes swirling around him and pondered his books.

IN THE WANING DAYS OF SUMMER IN 1825, A BAREFOOT EIGHT-YEAR-OLD Henry accompanied his brother John across the milldam and past the Middlesex Hotel to the grammar school on the common—the same school that eleven-year-old Ralph Emerson had attended for "six short months" in 1814–1815.[4] As the bell tolled the start of day, children lined up to enter the schoolroom. One by one, each boy paused at the threshold to bow to the master, each girl to "courtesy" in a gesture of respect; the obeisance was met with "a mark of attention" in return. The daily ritual of deference enacted the mission of the school to inculcate religious faith and moral virtue in the young. Under the tutelage of the instructor, the Thoreau boys and their classmates would be imbued with a "love of social order and obedience to laws," "reverence for the literary, civil, and religious institutions of our country," and "supreme regard to the name and will of God and to virtue." Along the way, they would also come to read and write correctly, cipher numbers, and know a little geography and history. This was the curriculum Concord's "scholars" had been pursuing since the late eighteenth century, and it was taught through texts that had changed little over the years. Who could doubt that the schools were a bastion of tradition, when the very books the pupils studied were often tattered and worn from use by parents and siblings before them?[5]

In principle, the school was a well-regulated realm, where everything was done by rule and enforced by authority. But things did not always work out according to plan. An obstreperous classmate of Henry Thoreau refused to truckle to his superiors. Not even Squire Abiel Heywood could command a gesture of respect. One day when the veteran magistrate and his colleagues visited the schoolhouse, each pupil was called on to offer a polite greeting. The ritual went smoothly; then it was the rebel's turn. The squire waited and waited until, his patience running out, he cleared his throat audibly. "You need not hem, Doctor," declared the brazen boy, "I shan't bow." Henry Thoreau never forgot that lesson in resistance to civil government.[6]

Discipline could never be taken for granted. Built in 1820, the brick grammar school on the common had space for eighty children. Boys sat on one side of the classroom, girls on the other in four opposite rows of ten each. All faced the master's desk, which was elevated on a raised platform to ensure that no one escaped notice. Enrollment exceeded capacity. As many as 125 students were entered on the rolls for a twelve-week term. Luckily, attendance was irregular; on average, some fifty to sixty scholars were in their seats, though not necessarily on time, on any given day. Managing that number proved a formidable test, as children from ages six to seventeen restlessly waited their turn to stand before the teacher and recite their lessons. The space was poorly ventilated; in winter it was heated by a rickety old stove that choked the room with smoke. Those seated close by wilted in the heat; those in the back rows shivered in the cold.[7]

To keep themselves awake and relieve the tedium, mischief makers developed their creativity. A boy might drop his slate and ruler on the floor, "apparently accidently but probably intentionally," setting off an avalanche of falling objects. Another would raise the wooden lid of his desk and carelessly let it drop with a thud; a loud volley would follow, the "rough music" of the schools. As instruments of disorder, the rows of desks, arranged in pairs, had many uses. By abruptly leaning back in his seat, a boy could jostle the desk behind him and shake its occupant, whose pen would inevitably scratch the page and veer from the rules. "He is joggling, sir," the frustrated victim would cry out. Soon everyone was joggling. Or in a familiar ploy, some of the boys in the smoke-filled room could not stop coughing, in what became an unstoppable epidemic; "it seemed as if almost every boy was seized with an irrepressible coughing."[8]

Charged with maintaining discipline was a succession of schoolmasters nearly as transient as the pupils. From 1721 to 1762, the grammar school had been ruled by a single figure, the "celebrated Master" Timothy Minot (Harvard Class of 1712). After independence and the formation of the Commonwealth, that position turned over year after year, but it was nearly always held by a recent graduate of the college in Cambridge. The novice teachers, often just out of their teens, were especially challenged during the winter months, when rough farmhands and mechanics crowded into the schools for a few months' learning and tested the mettle of so-called authorities not much older than themselves. One instructor failed the first day when he was unable to locate an "obscure river" on the map; for that misstep, he was memorialized by one wag in a piece of doggerel posted behind his desk:

> Mr. — is a stupid fool,
> Of neither wit or knowledge,
> He came to keep old Concord's school
> And then went back to College.[9]

Resourceful schoolmasters deployed a vast arsenal of measures to punish troublemakers. The official regulations, approved in 1799, advised instructors to be "mild" to the children, in a spirit of "parental affection," and "as far as it is practicable [to] exclude corporal punishment from the schools." But in the day-to-day struggle for control, high-minded sentiments gave way to the ferule, a wooden stick eighteen to twenty-four inches long, that was inflicted on the palms of rowdy boys and caused "great suffering." It was a little more humane than the alternatives of flogging backs, boxing ears, and shaking collars. One way or another the body of the boy had to be forced into submission. (Girls were exempt from such abuse.)

The very symbols of learning were turned into instruments of torture. A youth could be ordered "to stand on the floor and hold out [one arm] horizontally, at extreme length, with a heavy book in his hand, and if from weariness the arm should fall from its horizontal position, the master with a blow of his ferule would remind him of his delinquency." Or he might be made to subordinate himself to the physical emblem of the master—either by bending from the waist and tucking his head under the desk, or by sitting right under it, in a painful posture that threatened injury to the spine. These were extreme measures; successful teachers earned goodwill for their dignity and learning, and they reciprocated by showing respect for the intelligence of the young. But on occasion the classroom could dissolve into a war zone, where instructor and pupils fought an unequal contest for mastery, sometimes coming to blows. Thoreau's first year at the grammar school was fraught with violence. The master, James Furbish (Harvard Class of 1825), was "very liberal with his ruler," and not surprisingly, he "was not liked very much." The turbulent scenes left a lasting impression; the schools Thoreau taught would sustain a very different ethos.[10]

Despite the deficiencies, Concord was justly proud of its commitment to education. The town schools were tuition free, and they consistently exceeded state requirements. Elementary lessons in reading and religion were available at neighborhood schools in the village, which boasted three, and in six outlying districts. The brick grammar school afforded more advanced instruction in English, mathematics, and history to any child in town, and under its master, teenage boys could acquire sufficient Latin and Greek to pass the entrance examinations into Harvard. In the early 1820s, Concord spent $1,400 annually, about two dollars per child, to keep the grammar school running year-round and the district schools in winter and summer sessions of ten or more weeks each. The winter schools were usually taught by college students on break, the summer schools by local women for a year or two before marriage, at a quarter to a third of the men's pay.[11]

Starting in 1800, an official committee, elected at the annual town meeting, was charged with overseeing the schools, approving instructors, and checking on the performance of students; in 1825 it numbered fifteen members, two from each of the rural areas and three from the center, with representatives assigned responsibility for their respective districts. Parson Ripley joined them in looking out for the young. He wrote the "rules and regulations" for the schools in 1799 and periodically oversaw revisions. He regularly visited the schools for which he prescribed. As "public protestant teacher of piety, religion, and morality," he took care to ensure that instructors had "good moral and religious character" and fulfilled their primary duty to instill "virtue and religion" in the youth.[12]

Not every community supported its schools as generously as Concord. In the colonial era, the General Court had required every town with one hundred

or more families to maintain a grammar school at which young men could prepare for college and the ministry. That mandate was unpopular, and in the first
decades of the republic, it was steadily relaxed and lightly enforced. Workingmen resented paying taxes for schools their sons would never attend. Of what
use was advanced learning for the rising generation of mechanics, fishermen,
and mariners? Destined for lives of hard labor on land and at sea, they needed
little more than the three *R*s. Responding to such sentiments, many towns
refused to fund grammar schools; others kept them open for a few months
and not for the entire year, as state law prescribed. In 1824 the legislature diluted the commitment to public education still more by exempting towns with
fewer than five thousand inhabitants from the burden of sustaining grammar
schools. Only Boston and six other seaports fell under the mandate. The future
of the public grammar school, funded by local taxes, looked as uncertain as the
Standing Order in religion it was meant to support.[13]

Concord—and eastern Massachusetts more broadly—stood out as oases in a
parched educational landscape. Their leaders worried that the 1824 law would
hurt all the state's children and not just college-bound youth. In this conviction, a reform movement gradually took shape with the goal of reviving public
education. Ironically, it was the preceptor of a private institution who touched
off the campaign. James G. Carter (1795–1849) had gone from poor farm boy
to Harvard graduate (Class of 1820) via Groton Academy, and after completing
his collegiate studies, he opened a proprietary school of his own in the town of
Lancaster. Despite this background, he condemned the state's new direction as
a betrayal of equal educational opportunity.

In an open letter to a prominent state legislator, Carter insisted that grammar schools were the linchpin of Massachusetts society. Where else could ambitious young men gain the knowledge to rise in the world? Private academies
could not do the job; with their exorbitant tuition, they were "out of the reach
of precisely that class of people" who needed them most. "Not one in twenty,
if one in fifty" deserving youth would ever pass through their doors. But it
was not only the "mute inglorious Miltons" of New England who would suffer
from the recent law. Children generally would be the victims. Teaching was
already in a low state at the district schools; it would only get worse when "the
mass" of instructors had "no other opportunities for improvement, than are
afforded in the very schools" where they themselves had barely learned to read
and to cipher. Such ill-trained teachers knew little more than their pupils and

were ignorant of the wider world. Their manners were rude, their prejudices narrow. No one was uplifted by their example. By contrast, the masters of grammar schools, with their academy and college training, brought "refined" manners and enlarged views into a community. They elevated the character of the countryside and eased social tensions as well. Instead of "mutually hating and despising each other," the educated few and the unlettered many came to appreciate "their mutual worth and dependence" "as members of the same body politick."[14]

Under Carter's prodding, Massachusetts reversed course and imposed a new framework of public education. In March 1826 the state legislature required every town in the Commonwealth, no matter how small, to establish an official school committee, like the ones in Boston and Concord. Consisting of no fewer than five members elected annually, the new body was tasked with certifying teachers, inspecting schools, and assessing the achievement of students. The duties were familiar, but the pace of oversight was stepped up. Previously, local officials had checked on the "regulation and discipline" of the schools and the "proficiency of the scholars" every six months; now school committeemen carried out these duties and on a more frequent schedule— quarterly at grammar schools, during the first and last two weeks of district schools—and "at least once a month" without advance notice.

The instructors themselves came under closer scrutiny. No one could be employed by a district without an official "certificate of fitness" from the general school committee. Once they were hired, masters and mistresses had to be always on their toes, in case of a sudden spot check. Not even the books used in the classroom were the teachers' choice. In a striking innovation, school committees were authorized to make the selections and obtain the required texts for parents to purchase; for those too poor to pay, books would be supplied at town expense.

Power over local schools was thus shifted upward, away from the districts and into the hands of a potentially strong supervisory body. The towns, in turn, were answerable to the state. The law required local officials to submit annual reports to the secretary of the Commonwealth about key aspects of school management, from the number of schools, public and private, in a town and its annual appropriations (including teachers' wages) to the length of school sessions, the level of enrollment, the extent of nonattendance, and the incidence of illiteracy among young people. What state officials would do with this information went unsaid. But the future could be glimpsed: the start of school reform saw the birth of school bureaucracy, with demands for data to measure effectiveness and ensure accountability that have waxed and waned in public education ever since.[15]

The push for better schools touched a responsive chord in Concord. The local newspaper kept a close eye on the progress of reform legislation on Beacon Hill. "If there is any thing for which New England has just cause to boast," opined the *Gazette* in March 1826, "it is her common schools . . . Established by the wisdom of our ancestors, on a liberal system, they have placed the means of education within the reach of all." But there was no denying that these institutions were falling short of their potential because of "the defect in the systems of instruction—the incompetency of teachers—and the inattention of the people to their schools."[16]

The *Gazette* filled its columns with editorials, local contributions, and reprints from other newspapers indicting a trio of obstacles to better schooling: inept teachers, outdated schoolbooks, and retrograde parents. The three problems were interconnected. "No station in our whole grand republic, from its chief magistrate, to its humblest village official, is more important . . . than that of a teacher of children and youth," posited a correspondent styling himself "Septentrion" (for the northern region of the earth and sky). But did school committees look to hire the best instructors? Not at all. Yankee farmers lived up to their reputation for thrift, asking not "how well qualified" a candidate was but "how cheap." This pinchpenny standard was a recipe for educational failure. First, "a man of liberal education," hired for the going rate of $500 a year, was "shut . . . up for six or eight hours in a day, to teach 60 or 80 half starved, half clothed, half witted urchins." Then if he actually tried to inspire the scholars with a desire to learn, he was told to stick to the beaten path and drill the same "dull lessons" into them "word by word," as had always been done. Should he take a break from the routine and give the children an hour to play, with a view to refreshing their bodies and renewing their spirits, he would be accused of cheating the town of its pay. "He must not vary a minute from his time . . . , must cause his scholars to stand in a straight line—jerk their heads nearly off by a mechanical bow." Discipline—"by the tongue, ferule, whip or by a flagellatory steam-engine"—took priority over actual learning.[17]

The movement for school reform was as impatient with tradition as the campaign for agricultural improvement, and the rustic targets of criticism resented the jibes directed against them. "A Parent" was so angry at "Septen-trion's" animadversions that he composed a sarcastic rebuttal, the only piece critical of school reform published in the *Gazette* during the 1820s. Mocking the notion that instructors needed higher pay to add "a few more shirts or dickies to the small number already sadly worn" and suggesting that a "jerk of the head" in a show of deference could never replace the missing "jerk of the back" in a master's spine, the writer was most upset by the charge that school committees were overly concerned to reduce costs and demand results. He rightly sensed that the barrage of complaints about ill-informed, miserly parents and their tightfisted representatives was meant to discredit the famil-iar arrangements for governing local schools and to shift power upward to the educated elite—far better judges, in their own opinion, than rural folk who rely on "hearsay, and the tales of children." That suspicion was well founded. In 1827 the school committee was reduced to seven members, with Ripley as chair and villagers Brooks, Keyes, and Prichard invariably in the majority.[18]

Young Henry Thoreau directly benefited by the reforms. When the eight-year-old entered the grammar school in 1825, he was too young for some stud-ies. Children were not taught how to make quill pens until they reached age ten. Arithmetic commenced at twelve and composition at fourteen. Was the precocious boy frustrated by the slow pace? If so, he must have been pleased by the school committee's decision in December 1826 to abandon arbitrary age limits and let the scholars take up subjects whenever they were ready. No longer did the future writer and surveyor have to put off inquiries that would be at the heart of his life's work. And there were new incentives to perform well; "industrious and good scholars" were to be rewarded with prizes and praise. Individual initiative and merit thus claimed greater recognition in motivating students. Girls could take heart from the changes, too. Previously excluded from the grammar school from December through March, "misses" over age ten could now join boys during the winter sessions so long as there was room. Age fourteen in 1826, Helen Thoreau, the eldest of the siblings, may well have accompanied her brothers to class—an early pioneer of coeducation.[19]

At the start of September 1826, Henry began his second year at the gram-mar school under an instructor eager to promote educational reform. The new master was, like nearly all his predecessors, a recent Harvard graduate. Edward Jarvis, at twenty-three, was no stranger to the residents. A Concord native, he had grown up in the center of town and at the heart of the establishment. His father, Francis, ran a bake house in the former Wright tavern on the square, a stone's throw from the grammar school Edward had attended and now headed. The elder Jarvis had arrived in Concord in 1778 as an eleven-year-old apprentice from Dorchester with nothing to his name and had risen to become "a man of substance" in trade and a figure of influence in town and parish. For over a quarter-century he was a deacon of the First Parish. The businessman compensated for little schooling with constant reading, devouring books "of a grave cast": history and biography, geography and travels, the Bible daily, and lots of sermons. Devoted to education, he served seven straight terms on the school committee. His children benefited from this commitment; Edward, the third son and fifth child, went to school continuously from ages three to sixteen.[20]

For all these intellectual advantages, the youth's passage from pupil to master was not smooth. For one thing, the deacon declined to encourage Edward's ambitions for "a literary profession." As he saw it, the boy's insatiable curiosity about the shops along the milldam with their ingenious technology showed a strong mechanical aptitude. He was surely well suited to a career in manufacturing. In addition, the baker was already putting one son through Harvard, and he could not afford tuition for two. (He was too proud to seek financial aid.)

Against his inclinations, Edward at sixteen was apprenticed at a textile factory in the nearby town of Stow. The heretofore-dutiful teenager seethed with resentment. He clashed with his employer—"My mistress was a virago. My master a tyrant and conceited squire"—and quarreled with fellow workers. Instead of concentrating on the job, he retreated into books. Eventually the boss accused him of "laziness" and "ingratitude," and the boy angrily rehearsed his own complaints. There was no alternative but to take him home, where, after consulting with Ripley, the deacon reconciled himself to the expense of sending Edward to a private academy in Westford and then to join his brother in Cambridge. The young man had learned a valuable lesson in self-assertion.[21]

As a college student and aspiring professional, Edward Jarvis strained against ancient customs and pressed to be recognized as an individual in his own right. His father was enmeshed in the local community, glad to form reciprocal ties with neighbors and to assist those in need. The businessman invariably had a little surplus cash on hand, which he freely loaned out at no interest. He was equally generous with his books. He amassed an ample supply of tools for virtually every purpose, on which his neighbors made frequent calls. Through such charity, Jarvis built an extensive network of mutual benefits and obligations. Long after he had ceased to deliver bread personally to his customers, he still checked in with them every few months, in the belief that "those who dealt together . . . [should] have a mutual knowledge of each other, and . . . retain a personal as well as business connection." Loaf by loaf, loan by loan, Deacon Jarvis enacted the ideology of interdependence Ripley preached.[22]

Edward Jarvis resisted such bonds and flouted tradition, both before and after he took charge of the grammar school. As a college student, he took advantage of Harvard's long winter break by keeping school to earn money for expenses. His first job was in familiar territory, the town of Acton on Concord's western border. Much to his employers' surprise, the new schoolmaster disdained the usual practice of visiting among the farming families of his rural district. "I was thought proud, aristocratic," he admitted; "indeed I was." He was no more disposed to the company of mariners and fishermen when he taught in the Mackerel Creek district of Beverly on the North Shore; although he enjoyed his status "as a superior sort of being" in this "obscure" district, he confined his calls to the "most genteel" and to the fashionable homes of Harvard classmates in Salem across the bay.[23]

This self-conscious superiority to "lesser" folk stirred resentment, and it might well have fueled opposition to Jarvis's appointment as grammar schoolmaster. During senior year, his older brother and his mother had died within months of each other, and the grief-stricken deacon was anxious to have Edward back home for comfort. Would he keep the school? After initially demurring, the young man applied for the post, only to encounter strong opposition. Many townspeople doubted that a youth, who had only a few years earlier been reciting lessons in the brick schoolhouse, could now take command as master. "The money would be lost," it was said, "the time worse than lost, the school had better be shut up."

Actually, there was ample precedent for hiring locals straight out of college to conduct the school. The stated objection to Jarvis might have masked personal dislike. Whatever the reasons, the choice divided the three-man hiring committee. Although Deacon Jarvis was no longer on that body, he pushed hard for his son's selection and won the influential support of John Keyes. His colleague Nathan Brooks was willing to go along, but Moses Prichard, co-owner of the green store, professed "great doubts and fears" about the candidate. He was overruled. Thanks to the father's lobbying and political connections and *not* to his personal credentials, Edward Jarvis got the nod. In the eyes of some parents, he assumed the position under a cloud.[24]

With his disdain for rural customs, the new master of the grammar school was in step with the calls for educational change. Two months into the job, he penned his "thoughts on Schools" in three anonymous contributions to the *Gazette*. "In our times," he began, "the cry is improvement and reform" in agriculture, manufactures, and other arts. But education lagged far behind. "The same men who would throw aside an old tool the moment they could purchase a better, are content that their children at school should go on in the old beaten path, and with much toil glean a little knowledge from books almost worthless, though better ones might easily be obtained."

In parody of Yankee parsimony, the author presented a conversation between a penny-pinching guardian and an inquisitive youth. The boy pleaded for the purchase of a new geography text "far superior" to the one in common use. Nothing he could say would open his master's purse. Why acquire a new book, demanded the curmudgeon, when "the old one isn't half worn out yet. I used it myself, and your cousin Sam after me; it was good enough for us and it shall be for you." But the latest work had an atlas, the lad pointed out, and that feature would enable him to learn faster and locate places on the map more readily. The guardian was unmoved. He had "larnt geography" from the old title in six weeks, and "I never was called a fool." One book would lead to another; the next thing he knew, his savings would be gone. "Haven't you cost me much, you foolish boy! Why it costs me a dollar a year for books for all of you,—I bought year before last a new testament, last year a new spelling book, this year three slate pencils, and I am obliged to buy twenty sheets of paper or more for your writing and ciphering books every winter. Your aunt complains that . . . the poor old gander's wings are almost stripped for quills."[25]

This satire on stingy, narrow-minded guardians wedded to outdated ideas and incorrect information revealed an irreverent young man with no tolerance for rural prejudices. The grammar schoolmaster ridiculed opponents as country bumpkins, ruled by ignorance and selfishness. His dismissiveness was typical of progressive reformers, and it might well have appealed to the Thoreau boys and their classmates. To judge from Jarvis's diary, the only account of his year in the classroom, everything went swimmingly at the outset. The novice was understandably nervous, considering all the opposition to his appointment. Happily, his first contingent of students was "exceedingly gentlemanly in their deport-ment" and thrived under his tutelage. "They showed me that deference of re-spect, a willingness and alacrity in obedience that they would have shown to one they liked." Confounding the skeptics, the school performed well at the public exhibition: "I had trained them to run at my beck, to go at my nod." Apparently even Henry Thoreau wore the harness without complaint.

This easy success did not survive into the winter term. The next group, packed with "large and less learned" boys, was "harder to govern," and al-though the final examination pleased the school committee, the instructor was losing heart. By the summer term, attendance on some dog days was down to as few as twenty students with barely any "literary spirit"; the boys "prefer going into the fields and even so do I." Though his labors were light, Jarvis found the entire business "exceedingly tedious" and could not wait to be fin-ished. His only satisfaction lay in the "very good discipline" he maintained and the "deference, cheerful obedience, and respect" he received. Even so, well be-fore his year's contract ran out, the twenty-four-year-old had decided to move on and commence the study of medicine. Keeping a school, he concluded, is a "wearisome, perplexing, care-requiring, stupefying, unsatisfactory business." So disgusted was he that at the final exhibition, where the schoolmaster re-ceived "unqualified praise" for his accomplishment, Jarvis once again flouted expectations and declined to give the customary valedictory speech: "I despise speaking merely for effect."[26]

Not once in all these teaching experiences did Jarvis record a moment of intellectual engagement. He merely ran the scholars through their paces and despaired over "the futility of human expectations" when they stumbled. No student was singled out in his diary for special attention or praise, not even the Thoreau boy, though later in life he would praise the author of *Walden* as having been "a good scholar" with a taste for natural history. If only Jarvis had shared with the students his enthusiasm for botany and taken them outdoors to collect specimens as a lesson in science! But the deacon's son stayed in the schoolhouse, where he was nobody's mentor. If girls were in his classroom, as they undoubtedly were, there is no hint in the private records he kept. Winning the respect of scholars and receiving displays of deference were the principal rewards he craved. His greatest accomplishment was to maintain order with minimal resort to the ferule. In his opinion, he applied the rod only for good cause and when not doing so "would do wrong to the boy, to the school and the cause of good order." For all his enthusiasm for reform, he *kept* school rather than *taught* it, and that was all employers everywhere in the mid-1820s required.[27]

Despite his dissatisfactions, Jarvis did not give up on school reform. Six years later, after training as a doctor at Harvard Medical School and practicing briefly in the Connecticut River Valley town of Northfield, he was back in his birthplace. In November 1832 he was chosen to replace Lemuel Shattuck, a departing member of the school committee, and would go on to serve three full terms as a zealous advocate of change. In that role he carried on the agenda of his immediate predecessor—for it was in Shattuck, the younger brother of the leading village merchant, that Concord had found the principal architect of its schemes for educational progress.[28]

LEMUEL SHATTUCK ARRIVED ON NEW YEAR'S DAY 1822, AFTER A DECADE-long effort to build a career as a professional educator. Twenty-eight and single, he had followed a long, circuitous route from his hometown of New Ipswich, New Hampshire, to Concord common. He had spent his youth on the unforgiving farm from which his brother Daniel, three years older, made an early exit to seek his fortune in trade. Teenage "Lem" and two sisters were left behind to manage the homestead and care for their ailing father in an atmosphere made oppressive by a constantly scolding stepmother. The youth was desperate to get away but had no idea how. He found escape neither in trade nor in manufacturing; a trial run at a woolen mill was nearly his financial undoing. Farm labor proved a dead end.

The only thing Lem excelled at was school. Though his opportunities had been spotty, three or four weeks each winter, he had regularly stood at the head of the class. "Don't you think he is a remarkable good reader?" one teacher enthused. Following a couple months at the local academy, Shattuck made a bid for independence. In 1811, shortly before his eighteenth birthday, he left home to keep a winter school in the town next door. Despite his inexperience, he took pride in his performance. For the first time, he held "a highly honorable occupation" and enjoyed deference from others; he had never felt so important before. Education opened a way out of a rural backwater and into the mainstream of American life.[29]

Shattuck was looking for more than a means of making money. For this idealistic youth, deciding on a life's calling was an ethical choice. "To benefit my fellow being as well as myself," he later affirmed, "was then and ever has been considered a part of my duty." To this end, the youth set his sights on higher learning, for which he prepared in further stints at the New Ipswich academy and through a relentless regimen of reading. For twelve to fourteen hours a day, he pored over books "without a stop in an unbounded ambition to absorb and know everything all at once." His health broke under the strain; instead of tempering his pace, Shattuck rashly abandoned all hope of college. He settled for a career as a schoolmaster.[30]

Following his father's death in 1815, there was nothing to keep the twenty-two-year-old on the farm. Hearing that year-round teaching jobs were plentiful in the Hudson River Valley of upstate New York, Shattuck headed for the rising manufacturing city of Troy in Rensselaer County. He was a real-life Ichabod Crane: a provincial Yankee schoolmaster in Dutch New York, with a mere seventeen dollars in his pocket, certificates of his piety, morals, and teaching ability, and trust in a "kind and gracious Providence" to guide a stranger "in an unknown land." His faith was promptly rewarded. A position opened up, combining low pay—just a dollar more a month than in rural New Hampshire—with access to genteel and wealthy circles. It was a life-changing experience. The awkward youth seized every chance to acquire "intellectual and social knowledge . . . I saw more of the world than I had done during my whole previous life."[31]

In Troy, Shattuck was exposed to a new mode of instruction, the monitorial system, then rapidly gaining popularity in leading urban centers. Developed by the English Quaker Joseph Lancaster for teaching children of the poor, the scheme furnished an innovative blueprint for mass education. In conventional schools, the pupils were supposed to sit at their desks silently conning their books. One by one they would come before the master to recite what they had absorbed; seldom were they asked to show they actually understood what they had read. Much time was wasted in this arrangement and even more in enforcing order.

Lancaster reorganized the regimen to keep the students active and engaged through mutual instruction. Under his plan, individuals were assigned to small groups of ten or twelve, ranked by their proficiency in basic subjects. Each "class" was drilled in its daily lessons by a student "monitor" from the one immediately above it. As the pupils progressed, they moved up the educational ladder. Everyone learned at his own pace, and competition drove the process. To motivate the students, prizes were bestowed for achievement and penalties for misconduct. A Lancasterian schoolhouse was a hubbub of activity kept on course by the master, who planned the curriculum, set the lessons, classed the students, chose and supervised the monitors, and orchestrated the entire operation like a factory manager coordinating workers and machines to produce goods as efficiently and cheaply as possible. Shattuck liked what he saw. The monitorial scheme elevated the schoolmaster into an expert, capable of educating at low cost hundreds of pupils according to uniform principles and rules set forth by Lancaster and transmitted by his disciples. It thereby promised to raise his income and enhance his standing as a professional.[32]

Shattuck was soon in Albany, training in the new pedagogy under a former student of Lancaster himself. There he lucked into another opportunity. The "University of Michigania" was looking to hire a teacher versed in the monitorial method for an "English school" it was starting in the frontier outpost of Detroit. Would Shattuck be interested? Barely a year and a half out of New Hampshire, he was receptive to the idea, even though his siblings back in Concord and New Ipswich expressed dismay that he would be going "almost out of the world." When it turned out that his salary would be $800 a year—four times his current earnings—there was no question. At twenty-four, he embraced the chance to go west and grow up with the country.[33]

In the Western settlement, with some 1,100 people in 1818, Shattuck conducted his school with characteristic intensity and perfectionism. The Lancasterian system had originally been designed for large groups of children in the laboring class. He adapted the plan to win over elite parents; soon top figures in the territory, including Gov. Lewis Cass, were enrolling their young. In a remarkable coincidence, one of his students was an eight-year-old boy from Concord whose father, a hatter and fur trader, had recently moved his family close to his source of supplies in the West. To little Ben Williams, the Yankee schoolmaster made a welcome contrast to the "old drunken brute" and to the "small, waspish, violent-tempered man" under whom he had previously suffered. Shattuck managed the school, which at its peak had 150 students, with calm authority and efficiency. Williams appreciated the unusual freedom students enjoyed to progress "according to their industry and application to their studies" without being "held back by duller scholars."[34]

The frontier school proved a great success. Shattuck won praise from the trustees for his "indefatigable assiduity to improve the minds, correct the manners, and inculcate the principles of sound morality among your pupils." But once again he pushed himself to exhaustion. He devoted nearly every waking hour to the school: thirteen to fourteen hours in class and a couple more outside of it. Rather than rest on the Sabbath, he started a Sunday school and invested "considerable time" in it. Always he read voraciously in a tireless program of self-education: "I felt unwilling that any one should know more than I did or any thing that I did not know."[35]

Beneath all this hectic activity were growing misgivings about the move to the West. The schoolmaster's $800 salary was eaten up by the high cost of living on the remote frontier. His employer did not live up to its name or to its word. The University of Michigania was merely a board of trustees authorized by the territorial legislature to receive and disburse public funds for schools. It lacked educational stature and was straitened for cash. Before departing for Detroit, Shattuck had shelled out $100 of his own money to purchase books, slates, and other supplies for his new venture; two years into the job, he was still waiting for reimbursement. His salary was far in arrears. By November 1819, Shattuck was already contemplating a return to the East. But he hung on until the summer of 1821, when he was laid low by the "most terrible fever" he had ever endured and nearly died. He lay in a sickbed for four weeks, and then, on doctor's orders, took a vacation, heading back to New England.

The temporary leave became a permanent move. In Concord, he was urged to put the frontier behind him and start over yet again in the town where his brother had done so well. His health would surely improve, and so would his financial situation. Shattuck was racked with doubts. He had obtained a "station of influence and respectability" in Detroit; his prospects there were "very good." Why not bet on "a new and growing city . . . in a new country just then emerging into existence and importance"? But the mentor of youth was not much of a risk taker. Against his better instincts, he took the safer course and opted for Concord. It was another misstep to be recorded in the volume of regrets he would call his "autobiography." Shattuck consoled himself with the thought that "it is not for a man to direct his steps."[36]

The move to Concord brought Shattuck's teaching career to a disappointing end. Sadly, he put the classroom behind him and turned his mind to trade. After clerking in brother Daniel's store for two years, he became junior partner in Shattuck & Company. But he could not stop thinking about education. To the new man behind the counter, teaching was a higher calling than selling goods and making money. If he had to give it up, he would at least pass on what he had learned, in hope of inspiring others. Little did he anticipate that his ideas would drive the agenda of school reform in his adopted town.

In mid-November 1822, eleven months after settling in Concord, Shattuck composed a detailed statement of his credo as a pedagogue, in which he distilled the lessons of his six years' experience as a "teacher of youth," and dispatched it to the *Boston Recorder*, the periodical voice of orthodox Congregationalism. At the time Boston had no magazine or newspaper devoted to the subject of education, so Shattuck turned to the religious publication. "Education is intimately connected with the great subject of religion," he explained, "and in proportion as the former is understood the latter will be promoted." The article found a ready reception. Signed by "S" of Concord, the "Resolutions of a Teacher of Youth"—thirty in all—appeared in the January 25, 1823, issue, two months after submission.

The contribution was not out of place. It affirmed a statement of faith that was as fervent as the vows Ezra Ripley wrote out on the eve of his ordination to the ministry and renewed on the annual anniversary of that event. "I engage in the profession of a teacher of youth," he began, "because it is one which affords a greater opportunity for contributing to the happiness of my fellow beings, and the prosperity of religion, than I could have, with my present qualifications and acquirements, in any other situation of life." So exalted was the calling, so demanding the duties, that Shattuck pledged "my whole self" to the work and forswore "every personal gratification" that might distract from its pursuit.

The lengthy set of resolutions, drawn from a memo book containing his classroom observations and insights, offered a systematic view of teaching. Every instructor was expected to possess "thorough acquaintance with all the branches of knowledge," plus a grasp of "the most simple and best method" of conveying them. Shattuck presumed such command and put his emphasis on personal qualities. An instructor needed a sound mind in a healthy body; his religious piety would be manifest in holy living. His temperament was equable, his judgment deliberate. Honest and steadfast, he kept his word and fulfilled his promises. He was a perfect gentleman, with "a native ease, sobriety, and dignity of manner." Most important, he embodied self-reliance: "the resources of his own mind [were] sufficient to enable him to act without the advice of others." Unmoved by pressure, he followed his own judgment in "complete self-possession and self-government." Appropriately, he granted every child the same respect and dignity he claimed for himself. And he was answerable to God for his performance.

At the heart of Shattuck's pedagogy was a generous view of how children learned. He treated students not as subjects to be ruled with the rod, nor as vessels to be filled with information for absorption by rote. In his schoolroom, the young were active participants in the educational process. The instructor adapted his lessons to the capacity of each student, taking into consideration the differences among them in "natural genius, age, previous acquirements, and discipline." To this end, he spoke clearly and distinctly in "perfectly simple, but strictly grammatical language." His style was animated, his lessons enlivened with "frequent familiar similes and examples."

Shattuck laid out a long list of dos and don'ts. Don't overawe the pupils with all your knowledge; "give no more instruction at one time than can be well understood and retained, but give it in the most vivid and impressive manner." Don't ask questions a child cannot "reasonably" be expected to answer; don't ridicule "ignorance or weakness"; don't put anyone on the defensive by asking "why don't you do better"; and, on the other hand, don't overpraise. Rather than dictate a course of action, present options and let the individual choose. By that means, you will "cultivate his faculties of taste and reason." Be accessible without being overly familiar; issue few orders, but do so "in candor and solemnity," so as to "win the affections, and control the will." Authority should rest on love and respect.

Most striking was Shattuck's commitment to each and every child. Self-educated himself, from modest origins, he followed a rule of equality. Everyone deserved encouragement and respect, whatever his station in life. "Show the same mildness and attention to the poor as the wealthy," and appreciate "worth" wherever it appears. How else could the teacher "give full scope to the exercise of the genius of the child"? Therein lay the innovative thrust of Shattuck's thought. Schooling, as he saw it, was meant to foster both the development of the individual and the progress of society. Cultivating the one would advance the other.

The object of education and of all the discipline and instruction of the school shall be to bring all the powers and faculties of our natures to the highest perfection of which they are capable; to fit the scholars to perform justly, skillfully, and magnanimously the duties of every station in life, both public and private; to secure to them the greatest possible happiness, taking in the whole life; to elevate their minds from the degradation of sin, to the love, worship, and favor of God; and to qualify them for the eternal enjoyments of heaven.

Here was a pedagogy for a society about to embark on numerous campaigns of self-improvement. Just as agricultural reformers hailed the "immense productive power of a perfectly cultivated acre," so the instructor of youth yearned to develop the moral and mental power of each perfectly cultivated scholar.[37]

This Shattuck would do, after a hiatus of six years, during which he toiled in the store, not altogether successfully. The reluctant merchant resented the claims on his time for "weighing out sugar and tea by the pound, and measuring out bombazine, nankeen, or tape by the yard." So uncongenial was he behind the counter that when children went on errands to the store, they were instructed by parents "not to buy anything of Lemuel if he was in . . . but to return and wait until Daniel arrived." Despite a "very precise and pompous" manner, he was welcomed into elite circles, and until his marriage in 1825 to the daughter of a wealthy Boston merchant, he was considered among the most eligible bachelors in town, even catching the interest of twenty-seven-year-old Maria Thoreau, who deemed him "in every way . . . superior" to his brother.

In April 1829 the storekeeper got another chance to improve education when he was chosen for the school committee. His election was in recognition not only of his experience as a teacher but also of his new status as head of a growing family, with a toddler at home and another child on the way. He served a total of three annual terms, the first two (1829–1831) under the chairmanship of Ezra Ripley, the last (1832–1833) under Ripley's junior minister, Hersey Goodwin. Appointed secretary of the eight-man board, Shattuck promoted his long-standing educational ideals and pedagogical practices. It was as a policy maker, rather than as a teacher, that he would form the minds and morals of Concord's youth.[38]

The first initiative of the committee in 1829–1830 was to revisit the school regulations. Just four years earlier the rules had been liberalized to let the "scholars" advance at their own pace and to reward individual achievement—practices that Shattuck had introduced back in Detroit. Now, under the secretary's influence, the body went beyond piecemeal changes and undertook a systematic revision of all its procedures. The result was a comprehensive document that would be recognizable in any school system today. *Regulations of the School Committee of the Town of Concord* was printed for annual distribution to managers of the district schools and every new teacher at the start of the academic year; it also appeared in the *Gazette* to inform parents. The little volume bore the stamp of authority. The rules were arranged under four main chapters, each in its own appropriate section. Underscoring the new power in school governance, "the Board of the School Committee" came first, with its duties to certify teachers, visit schools, examine students, work with district officials, and hold semiannual meetings all painstakingly spelled out. Rules for instructors and scholars followed, including separate units for the grammar school and for the districts. Even the local schools were renamed. No longer were they identified with specific families and neighborhoods rich in historic associations. Each was assigned a number: one for the "centre," two for the East district, and so on to number seven (the old Buttrick district). Logically organized and conveniently available, the regulations could now be enforced efficiently and impersonally. Bureaucracy ruled.

Information was a key desideratum for improving schools. Under the new provisions, teachers were required to record the attendance and progress of every student; "the names of all obstinate and refractory scholars, who may be guilty of improper conduct in school," were to be taken down as well, along with the disciplinary measures applied. These details were meant to guide the school committee in its assessment of student achievement. Like educational authorities today, the members evaluated the performance of pupils at final examinations, holding teachers to account. This scrutiny applied to the committee in turn. The regulations directed the board to issue an annual account "of the general state of the schools." By this means, the committee aimed both to educate and to engage the townspeople. "Though the people of Concord are not behind most towns in imbibing the 'spirit of the age,'" it explained, "yet a deeper interest is desirable even here on the subject."

The initial report, composed by Shattuck and submitted in March 1830, created a new literary genre. It set forth the "amount spent on public instruction" ($1,450), the number of school districts (7), the cumulative length of time all schools were in session (74 months), the level of enrollment (779), the equivalent data on academies and private schools, and the number of persons between fourteen and twenty-one who were unable to read or write (0)—all particulars that school committees were obligated to transmit each year to the secretary of the Commonwealth. It appraised the "progress of the scholars," the performance of the teachers, and the introduction of new technology (blackboards and slates). Thanks to Shattuck, the committee counted whatever it could in order to determine how the schools were doing and whether the town's money was well spent.

The school report was not merely a numerical survey. It also served as a public relations document. It was designed to show "the amount of good" the town's expenditure on education had achieved and "to excite in the minds of every one a desire to do all in his power to improve the condition, elevate the character, and promote the usefulness of our schools"—in other words, to rally public support for the school committee. In this inaugural report, the first ever to be submitted by a local school committee in Massachusetts, secretary Lemuel Shattuck deftly met the challenge of supplying information and giving it a positive spin. He had the soul of a school superintendent. And with the annual school reports issued by Concord's committee, he set a precedent for the rest of the Commonwealth to follow.[39]

These innovations were in service to an expansive vision of education. If schools were to fulfill their noble purpose and nurture the "genius" of every child, as Shattuck had long held, they required a new philosophy of instruction. The secretary found that approach in the works of Swiss educator Johann Pestalozzi, then gaining currency in the early republic. This pedagogy was child-centered. Building on the Romantic ideas of Jean-Jacques Rousseau, it assumed that children were innocent and curious by nature, and rather than beat lessons into a pupil's head (and body), it adapted itself to the learning style of the young. Boys and girls, according to Pestalozzi, absorbed information through the senses; they learned inductively from encounters with the physical world, gradually advancing, step by step, to form generalizations in words. No one gained by heeding authority and memorizing rules from a book. Real education was grounded in experience.[40]

The new pedagogy rendered the old schoolbooks obsolete. A fresh set of texts incorporating Pestalozzi's approach provided lessons in spelling, reading, composition, elocution, arithmetic, geography, history, and science. Shattuck led his colleagues to adopt them. Taking advantage of its expanded authority under the 1826 state law, the school committee prescribed books on nearly every subject for the district and grammar schools. When some parents objected, the members insisted on the advantages of uniformity. It was more "economical" for an official body to set the titles than to depend on "the caprice of teachers who are constantly changing." But saving money was not the principal motive. Through the books it selected, the committee was endorsing the cutting-edge pedagogy of its day.

Schoolbooks in the new vein started from the standpoint of the young learner and worked upward and outward. Take the study of geography. The Massachusetts legislature had just directed each town and city in the Commonwealth to commission a detailed survey of its natural topography and settlement pattern, and the school committee eagerly awaited the arrival of the map of Concord. Geography "would then begin, as it always ought to, at home." For just this purpose, one Cambridge publisher issued *A Geography of Middlesex County; for Young Children* in 1830. In the same spirit, the study of the past would start with local history and ripple beyond to state and nation; hence the winter schools introduced the "History and Constitution of Massachusetts, and the United States." The list of required and recommended titles scrapped the standbys of the past—Noah Webster's speller and grammar, Jedidiah Morse's geography, Lindley Murray's *English Reader*—and substituted recently published works. Under the new regime, the boys and girls of Concord would be up-to-date with current knowledge, acquired as much as possible from firsthand experience. Learning by seeing and doing, they would thereby develop into adults capable of contributing to agricultural experiments and technological progress—exactly as the Society of Middlesex Husbandmen and Manufacturers hoped.[41]

The school committee proudly affirmed its reforming outlook in the opening lines of the 1830 regulations. The phrase "KNOWLEDGE IS POWER" was emblazoned on the title page.[42] The text itself began with a paragraph declaring in vaulting rhetoric the "great object of all education." It was a lightly edited version of the statement of faith Shattuck had penned seven years before. Infusing the document with idealistic purpose, the preamble charted a new direction. Under the rules drawn up in 1799 and revised twice thereafter, education had served conservative ends. Schoolmasters and -mistresses were charged with inculcating respect for authority, hierarchy, and established institutions, obedience to law, and reverence for God. Shattuck never questioned these priorities; indeed, they were repeated in the new code. But the committee secretary subordinated these familiar goals to a progressive emphasis on the individual. His personal credo as a teacher—"to bring all the powers and faculties of our nature to the highest perfection of which they are capable"—now became the official mission of Concord's schools.

Shattuck did not prize self-development for its own sake. As a youth, he had aspired "to benefit my fellow beings as well as myself." In this spirit, the schools retained their social purpose, as was evident in another addition he made to the rules: education was to "qualify us for *the greatest usefulness in the world*" as well as for "the eternal enjoyments of heaven." By that means, Shattuck expected, individuals would realize "the greatest possible happiness" and rise above "every unholy influence." With its message of interdependence, this language was sure to appeal to chairman Ripley. At the same time, it carried the committee and the town across a crucial cultural divide. The goal of common schools had been to fit individuals into community. Now each student stood front and center with unique talents to be nurtured and personal goals to be honored. A tension between self and society, so evident in the economic and political initiatives of the townspeople, was written into the mission statement of the schools. If Shattuck had not articulated a doctrine of self-reliance, he had nonetheless helped open the way for the self-made man and for the pursuit of self-culture by Emerson and Thoreau.[43]

The earnest educator did not get to witness the full results of his innovations. In June 1832, after spending a decade in town, he ended his partnership with his brother Daniel and entered business as a publisher and bookseller, first in Cambridge, then in Boston. There was no better fit for this devotee of libraries and expert in schoolbooks. His departure opened up a vacancy on the school committee, which the town filled with a like-minded soul. Edward Jarvis was a worthy successor in the crusade for reform.[44]

HENRY THOREAU BARELY SAMPLED THE IMPROVEMENTS IN PUBLIC EDUCATION. In late November 1828 the eleven-year-old was enrolled at Concord Academy, a short walk west from the house his family was renting on Main Street from Daniel Shattuck. Opened six years earlier, the school was one of many such private institutions proliferating in the 1820s to meet a rising demand for knowledge geared to the needs of a fast-changing modern world. This learning came at a steep price: a tuition of five to eight dollars per quarter, as much as thirty-two dollars a year. No wonder the Thoreau family, struggling to build the pencil business, could afford to send only one child at a time. As Henry entered the school, his brother John left it, and as the future writer departed for college, his younger sister Sophia took his place. The academy equipped all three (and perhaps older sister Helen as well) for the family vocation of schoolteaching. But Henry was there for a larger goal. Singled out for a liberal education, the bookish youth spent five long years at the academy parsing Greek and Latin and studying math, among other subjects, in order to obtain admission to Harvard. The preparation was almost for naught; Henry just cleared the bar set by the admissions exams. With good reason, he disparaged that training: "I was fitted, or rather made unfit, for college, at Concord Academy & elsewhere, mainly by myself, with the countenance of Phineas Allen, Preceptor."[45]

Whatever its failings as a prep school, the academy met important needs within and beyond the classroom. The impetus for its founding had come at the beginning of the 1821 school year, when eight-year-old Willy Whiting, son of the carriage manufacturer, started out at the grammar school. Day after day the boy was beaten up in the schoolyard; at the close of the first week, "his body was quite speckled with black and blue spots caused by blows from his schoolmates." Shocked by the abuse, his father sought out the master, a recent Williams College graduate named Abner Forbes, to express concern, only to be stunned by the response. A "fair-talking fellow" with "a smooth tongue," Forbes sympathized with the boy's plight but doubted anything could be done to stop the bullying. Better to withdraw his son from the school than subject him to further rough treatment. "He [Forbes] would as soon put a child of his on board a man of war as send him to that school."[46]

With no alternative close by, William Whiting set out to create one. Determined to afford his three children "as good an education as could be obtained within a reasonable distance, let the expense be what it might," he turned to several prominent neighbors—Nathan Brooks, Josiah Davis, Abiel Heywood, and Samuel Hoar—for support. The five residents of the village, all middle-aged fathers except for the sixty-two-year-old bachelor Heywood (who would shortly don trousers and marry), quickly formed a partnership.

The venture was well suited to their personal circumstances. Each of the parents was in the early stages of child-rearing; none had a son or daughter over eight. The proprietors shared Whiting's reservations about the village school, and they all wanted to educate their children "more thoroughly" than could be done in town. They were ambitious, too, to enhance Concord's standing in Middlesex County. Soon "a neat, commodious building" similar to the brick grammar school was rising in "a pleasant part of town," not far from their

homes on land aquired from Daniel Shattuck. The two-and-a-half-story building was equipped with desks, chairs, and "apparatus" for instruction. A row of
elms lined the passageway to the school. Hiring a preceptor and recruiting students, the proprietors were ready to open in September 1822. Altogether the
educational enterprise cost about $2,400. It was worth the investment. "Their
intention," Lemuel Shattuck noted in 1832, as the academy entered its second
decade, "has always been to make the school equal to any other similar one."[47]

This was not Concord's first effort at academy making. In March 1806 the
state legislature had approved a charter for an all-girls school to be based in
Concord. Proposed by Ezra Ripley and twenty-two of his parishioners, the
Middlesex Female Academy would be devoted "exclusively for the instruction
of females in learning, virtue, and religion." The institution was conceived as a
pioneering "experiment" in female education: the first "public establishment
of the kind in the United States." For this benevolent purpose, the petitioners raised $2,000, obtained donations of land, designed a handsome Federal-
style building with three wings, began assembling a library, and organized a
thirteen-man board of trustees. The Middlesex Female Academy would clearly
put Concord on the map as a magnet for aspiring young women and their ambitious parents. For some reason, it never got off the drawing board. Like the
Middlesex Bank, incorporated by the state in 1822, it existed only on paper, a
testament to the disappointed ambitions of the local elite.[48]

With no academy inside its borders, Concord was obliged to send its sons
and daughters elsewhere for higher education. In the decades before the 1820s,
local parents had a good many options: Middlesex County supported five academies all within a day's journey of Concord. Westford Academy, where John
Keyes and Edward Jarvis prepared for college, was two towns and ten miles
to the north. Groton Academy, started in 1793, the same year as Westford, afforded education to both sexes, albeit in separate classrooms. It proved a major
draw for Concord's young through 1820, enrolling more than thirty individuals in an institution twenty miles northwest of home. Squire Hoar served as
one of the trustees. As the academy building was going up in Concord, a rival
school, the sixth in the county, was winning a state charter in nearby Lexington. William Whiting's plan was thus not an obvious solution for the troubles
at the Concord grammar school. Better and safer facilities for education were
available not far away.[49]

An academy in Concord center was even more desirable. It would enable the proprietors to educate their children, sons as well as daughters, close to home in a setting with considerable advantages over the town school. William Whiting's initial purpose was to shield his son from contact with local toughs. That could be accomplished through a private institution serving a restricted clientele: the supposedly well-behaved children of families with above-average financial means. The propertied could afford the tuition; the laboring class would be kept away. The academy catered to young people who relied on words, not fists, to get their way, and to ensure this result, disturbing elements were removed in advance. Social stratification—the solidarity of youth from similar backgrounds—would preserve peace at the price of diversity. In yet another arena, the townspeople were pulling apart from one another and erecting separate enclaves for their young.[50]

The academy was not just a safe space for the privileged: it carried larger educational ambitions. It would be not merely as good as any in the area but "superior" in its "advantages of instruction," as the sponsors boasted fifteen months after it opened. Like its public counterpart, the academy was in session throughout the year, offering classes in twelve-week quarters, each followed by a one-week break. Girls were welcome in every season, with no restrictions. At the new school the "misses" could take up Latin or Greek and gain entrance into the world of classical learning, from which they were excluded at the all-male colleges of the day. French was available as well—a subject not on offer at the grammar school; likewise the new science of botany. With these curricular innovations, the academy sought to keep step with the progress of knowledge, rather than limit itself to passing along time-worn skills and the wisdom of the ages.[51]

The most important competitive advantage of the private school was its size. The Concord Academy marketed itself as a small, selective institution, where students would get the personal attention essential to lasting educational achievement. Its advertisements stressed that "the number of students is limited" and urged the submission of applications as soon as possible, before all the seats were filled. Enrollment in the fall of 1828, the earliest year it is known, was thirty-two—twenty-one girls, eleven boys—under a single instructor; it slipped to a mere twelve scholars in December 1829, before rebounding four years later to fifty-six, with equal representation of males and females. To handle the expanded numbers, the school hired two assistants to the head teacher. Such small classes must have been the envy of the eighty to one hundred students packed into the village grammar school during the fall and winter sessions. At a time when the Lancasterian method was being touted as an educational panacea and practitioners of the system took pride in overseeing the instruction of as many as 150 or 200 students at a time, the academy charted an opposite course. Class size and class status were inversely related: the lower the one, the higher the other. Setting itself off from the public school, with its large, heterogeneous population, the private institution conferred its benefits on a favored few in an educational strategy that would be familiar in the twenty-first century.[52]

Like most academies, the Concord enterprise was an entirely private affair. Lacking a corporate charter or any other state aid, it made its way in the world on its own. The proprietors financed the schoolhouse and hired the head teacher, who drew the students whose tuition fees covered his salary and other operating costs. Such schools were typically as short-lived as the stores and shops of the parents who paid the bills. Of the thirty-five academies incorporated in the Bay State between 1780 and 1821, only a dozen were still welcoming pupils the year the Concord institution was conceived. In the minds of its sponsors, the new enterprise constituted a civic endeavor, supplementing the tax-supported district and grammar schools with a privately supported form of secondary education—a precursor to the high school. The proprietors were actually strong supporters of public education, with years of service on the school committee.[53] No one accused them of having divided loyalties or feared a loss of commitment to common schools. This moment of easy coexistence was not destined to last.[54]

The academy, like the grammar school, hired its preceptors from the same pool of recent college graduates, nearly all from Harvard. It got off to an auspicious start with George Folsom (Harvard Class of 1822), a future diplomat and historian, under whose tutelage an expanding cadre of students thrived. "Such a variety, extent, and accuracy of knowledge, connected with the politer accomplishments . . . are rarely equaled at seminaries of the kind in this country," the *Gazette* enthused after one public exhibition. So successful was Folsom that after three years on the job, he was stolen away by an academy in Framingham, just at the start of a new school year. The proprietors found a Yale man—the son of trustee Josiah Davis—to replace him, then returned to a Harvard graduate the next year.[55]

The academy regained its footing in the fall of 1827 with the recruitment of Phineas Allen as preceptor. Another Harvard graduate (Class of 1825), the twenty-five-year-old Allen, son of a selectman and deacon in the town of Medfield, was in education for the long haul. He had already spent two years as master of the Latin Grammar School in Brookline, outside of Boston, and won praise for his pedagogical skills. Crucially, he was willing to run the enterprise in Concord at his own risk and expense. Under his leadership, the school gained stability for the first time in its existence. For eight straight years, it provided instruction both in the classics and in the "different branches of [modern] learning" commonly on offer at such institutions. It became the gateway to college for local youth, cutting the brick grammar school out of the field.[56] In September 1830 Allen introduced a third division of studies: training in "the art of School Keeping" with lessons in "the newest and most approved methods of managing schools." Although the academy catered primarily to local residents, it drew a growing contingent from Boston and other Middlesex towns, and one pupil even hailed from distant Claiborne, Alabama. Out-of-town parents could confidently send their children to live in Concord. The preceptor married Clarissa Fiske in 1827, and as the newlyweds set up housekeeping, they took students into their home as boarders, with a promise to monitor closely the "moral" and "intellectual improvement" of their charges. Not incidentally, they added to their income as well.[57]

By these means, along with free publicity in the *Gazette* and a steady drop in tuition to as low as three dollars per term for children under twelve in the English branch of study, the academy developed into an ornament of the village. When the preceptor arrived in Concord, he lodged for a few months in the Thoreau home; after marrying, he and Clarissa resided on "School Street." There they sank roots in the community. Allen lectured to his neighbors about natural philosophy and astronomy; he worshiped with Clarissa at Doctor Ripley's church and helped to choose books for the Sunday school; he became secretary of the Concord Mozart Society, a new group devoted to "improving in the practice of Music." The couple celebrated the birth and grieved the death of their first child in 1830, then, following the arrival of two sons by early 1833, began raising their children in Concord. The family and the academy appeared to be fixtures of the town. In contrast, the grammar school remained a turnstile through which one college graduate after another passed on the way to a better-paying, more engaging vocation.[58]

For all its advantages of small size and select clientele, the academy did not necessarily afford a superior education. Thoreau might have done as well at the grammar school, despite its succession of instructors, and saved the tuition. Both institutions drilled future collegians on the texts used for Harvard's entrance exams. From Greek and Latin to algebra, geography, logic, and natural philosophy, many of the titles were the same. Both the public and private school offered "the common branches of an English education." What distinguished them was the higher-level curriculum. With his lifelong love of language, Thoreau could have gotten an early start on French and Italian with Allen, and he must have been glad for the chance to study botany and chemistry. On the other hand, he could have explored astronomy at the town school and acquired the practical skill of surveying that proved so valuable in his later life. The developing writer enjoyed numerous opportunities to compose essays on such assigned topics as "The Seasons," "Cruelty to Animals," and the motto, "Knowledge Is Power." Had he been at the grammar school, he could have joined the future journalist William S. Robinson in taking on the theme "Learning is better than house and land." Both schools prepared boys to engage in public speaking through declamations and debates—anticipations of their future role as male citizens of the republic. Practicing the arts of eloquence, Thoreau gave voice to political and military heroes, both ancient and modern, at dramatic moments of their careers. Such performances were not to his taste. Affirming that "it require[s] more talents to make a good writer than a good extemporaneous speaker," the twelve-year-old lost his first trial in forensics to Rockwood Hoar, who would later gain fame in the courtroom and on the hustings.[59]

Nor was steadiness at the helm of the academy a decisive advantage over constant change at the grammar school.[60] Phineas Allen devoted his life to teaching, and he was later remembered in his family as "a representative of the old-school pedagogue . . . as regular as the sun, the personification of faithfulness." That was not how Concord youth experienced his tutelage during the years Thoreau attended. John Shepard Keyes, son of the "honorable" statesman, left Phoebe Wheeler's dame school at age six and began seven long years of study under the "nervous, irritable" Allen, whom he deemed "the poorest teacher . . . I ever knew anything about personally." He got nowhere in Latin or Greek and spent his days in the schoolhouse "waiting impatiently" for recess. In the winter of 1834, he played hooky every afternoon without ever receiving a "rebuke" or being reported to his parents. Caroline Brooks, daughter of Nathan and Mary Brooks, was usually quiet and obedient, but Allen failed to earn her respect. It was said that the master once "boxed her ears," perhaps in frustration over her mispronunciation of the Latin word "itàque" (i.e., therefore). Time and again, as the girl was reciting, Allen played the pedant and made her repeat the word over and over until she got it right, ultimately requiring her to stay after school for further practice. When he finally had to let her go, the young girl paused at the door, turned around, and "with a courtesy" offered the salutation "itàque, Sir!" in her original rendition.

No greater regard was forthcoming from Caroline's future husband, Rockwood Hoar, who challenged the preceptor's attempt to correct his spelling. "Where do you find authority for that spelling?" the boy asked. Allen cited his source, only to have young Hoar counter with his own. The master was unbending. "Well, you can spell it as I say on my authority." "The least of all," snapped the future lawyer and judge. The verbal contests occasionally degenerated into physical combat. Refusing to take his punishment, one insubordinate youth grabbed the ferule from the master's hand, broke it over his head, and smashed his spectacles, whereupon "the little discipline there had been in the school [dissolved] with a single blow."[61]

Why, then, did the academy not simply survive but actually flourish under Allen? The answer may lie less in the formal curriculum and mode of instruction than in its social function. The sons and daughters of the leading village families attended the private school together and thereby strengthened the close bonds already existing among their parents through neighborly visits and political and business alliances. Their ranks were supplemented by scions of such Middlesex gentry as the county register of probate Isaac Fiske and Groton's veteran statehouse representative, Luther Lawrence. To be sure, not every student was a child of privilege, certainly not the Thoreau siblings, whose parents had slid down the social scale. Even so, the little knot of bright boys and girls living close by each other was tightened by their years together chafing under Allen. In the younger Keyes's recollection, the Main Street set considered themselves an "uncommon lot," a term that embraced social as well as intellectual distinction. Perpetual tenants on that street, the Thoreau children accrued status by association.[62]

The in-crowd at the academy was visible to less fortunate contemporaries, such as Thoreau's chum Willy Robinson, the son of an impoverished journeyman hatter. Though "the wheel of the family fortune had reached the lowest point in its descent" in his boyhood, the Robinsons were proud and independent.

Willy excelled at the grammar school, where he studied Latin, parsed Alexander Pope's *Essay on Man*, and formed his writing style. His head was always in a book. But he had no chance of attending the "Catermy," as the private institution was known to the village mechanics and laborers. His hard-drinking father had no money for the tuition and no desire to see his son in genteel company. A local physician, impressed by the boy's talents, offered to subsidize his preparation for college; once admitted, Willy could work his way through Harvard by sweeping floors and building fires. The elder Robinson would hear nothing of it. "He shall never take a broom there: if he can't get a living without rubbing against that college, he may beg." Instead, Willy was apprenticed to a printer and set on the course that would employ his Concord-honed literary skills to good advantage in a notable career as a reform-minded, antislavery journalist.[63]

The academy was thus seen by insiders and outsiders alike as an instrument of social distinction, setting apart the sons and daughters of privilege from the rest of the community and forging them into a separate and self-serving upper class. That was exactly what early school reformers feared and what Henry Thoreau disliked. Nearly all his boyhood pals—Ben and Joe Hosmer, Willy Robinson, among them—spent their days at the grammar school, cut off from the college-bound companion with whom they rambled in the woods, fished in the rivers, and skated on the ponds. In later years the Transcendentalist eschewed the self-styled "bon ton" of the town for the company of plainspoken workingmen and ne'er-do-wells. The process of segregation was incipient in Thoreau's youth, and reformers meant to check its advance. The public schools provided a space where boys and girls of all classes mixed and where Ellen Garrison, granddaughter of slaves, could claim a seat alongside her white peers and carry away prizes for "superiority of learning," in contrast to Boston, which assigned students of color to a separate and unequal school. Reformers elevated this inclusiveness into a democratic ideal. "The children of rich and poor, of the prosperous and the unfortunate, all meet together, and drink at the fountain of knowledge," boasted the *Gazette*. "The children of the humblest stand side by side with those of the proudest, and the Master knows no distinction but what consists in aptness to learn;—and this distinction is quite likely to be in favor of the indigent." If the vision of one town, one church was no longer feasible, Concord could still aim to embrace all children in *common* schools.[64]

By the mid-1830s, the campaign for school reform was a work in progress. Enrollment was nearly universal. In a typical year, the names of 750 pupils appeared on the rolls. That figure included just about every child between four and sixteen, plus many two- and three-year-olds whose parents were caught up in a short-lived burst of enthusiasm for "infant education," the early nineteenth-century precursor of pre-K. Concord's record was typical for towns of its size, but it outstripped even the big cities in the length of the school year.[65] The school bell rang an average of 231 days, and though it was heard most often in the village, it increasingly summoned boys and girls from the farms.[66]

Spending began to grow as well, and to ensure equal access to public education, the "school money" was distributed in a new way. No longer did each district receive a sum equal to its proportional share of local taxes; now the town gave the poorer areas "extra" funds with which to extend the school calendar. "Money is raised by the towns and thrown into their treasuries," reasoned a committee headed by Shattuck, "not for the purpose of conferring a greater privilege on one section of the town than another, but to be used as a common fund for the equal and greater good of the whole, without distinction of wealth." The annual budget from 1826 to 1832 stayed constant at $1,400, before reformers mounted a campaign for more generous funding. In 1835 the town raised the amount to $1,800. Jarvis, then in his third term on the school committee, took credit for the close to 30 percent raise. His goal, he recalled decades later, was to "extend these schools so that with merely long vacations in spring and fall, they would be almost continuous." Not everyone was enthusiastic about this agenda. "Some of the economists" rose in town meeting to object; Daniel Shattuck, in particular, characterized by Jarvis as "noted for sharp trading," asked "if the Doctor would not take a little less." But the appropriation carried by "a great majority, and the people seemed to be happy that so much more opportunity of education was offered to their children."[67]

The drive for improved schools strove to revive an inclusive community. But it was geared to transforming the local culture and society. Urging townspeople to break with tradition, scrutinize inherited institutions, and adopt the best practices of the day, as urged by experts and proven by experience, reformers hoped to bring about improvements gradually and without conflict. The trouble was that the world they ushered in looked very different from what had come before. By the early 1830s, Concord's transient schoolmasters seldom lodged in their districts or visited among the scholars' families. They were, for the most part, agents of the expansive villages, tightly linked to Boston and beyond, which were ever more forcefully asserting sway over the countryside, to the growing dismay of farmers and mechanics in the rural out-districts. It was the signal achievement of the school reformers and their compatriots in the cultural field that they reacted against the forces of social distinction and strove for a more inclusive society. Emerson and Thoreau would share these concerns. But to preserve the community they valued (if only in retrospect), the reformers had to break it apart.[68]

Internal Improvements

J ohn and Cynthia Thoreau belonged to the future. They readily set aside outdated practices and customs when new and better ways became available. The pencil maker was quick to join the society of husbandmen and manufacturers and to enter the products of his workshop, pigpen, and garden in the competition for prizes at the annual cattle show. Both parents scrimped to afford culture for their children. For years such luxuries as coffee, tea, and sugar were absent from their table; the money they saved went for a piano for Helen and Sophia and for tuition at the academy and, for Henry, at Harvard. Education was a top priority in their drive for self-improvement.[1]

Beyond the schools, Concord abounded in opportunities for residents to participate in an expanding world of knowledge. It gained a circulating library in 1821, a debating club the next year, and a lyceum in 1829. "Thanks to our local situation almost in the suburbs of the city," the *Gazette* observed in May 1825, "our own town is seldom [for] long . . . without the benefits" of visiting lecturers on the scientific progress of the age. "That we are a great sight wiser, happier, and richer, by reason of these foreign lights, there can be no reasonable doubt." The Thoreau family heartily agreed. Both the older and younger members of the household took advantage of the new organizations; the Concord Lyceum was the one institution Henry unhesitatingly endorsed. Having slipped in social status from their eighteenth-century forebears, the parents undoubtedly hoped to recover standing through culture. But learning had broader uses. Through the ideas and information disseminated in books and periodicals, lectures and debates, the Thoreaus and their neighbors distanced themselves from tradition and obtained the resources to forge a new way of life.[2]

Intellectual innovation and social reform went together. As these pioneers of change added to their stock of knowledge, they set out not only to alter the economy and the society but also to remake themselves. They aspired to live on a higher and purer plane. One youth from an impecunious farm, after boarding for a while in the Thoreau home, was astounded by what he saw. The parents encouraged the curiosity of their children and fostered their aspirations: "Mrs. T loved Nature, and Mr. T Art, and one interpreted for the other." Even the food and drink at their table reflected refined tastes: the "abundance of fruit and vegetables" from their garden, the "delicious brown and white bread and butter," and most notably, the entire absence of liquor, even hard cider, as a beverage. Though John had once sold rum at his stores and Cynthia had served up drinks at her family's New Hampshire tavern, the couple did not imbibe. Quick to embrace the temperance cause, they withdrew from the culture of drinking that had been central to neighborliness and sociability in Concord. This mode of life proved a revelation to the newcomer from the backcountry. The Thoreaus, he later opined, were "20 years ahead of the Concord people in almost everything, intelligence, civilization, religion."[3]

They were also in the mainstream of an emerging middle class. As they shared intellectual interests and pursued self-improvement with like-minded villagers, the Thoreau family was helping to draw new lines of social and cultural difference. Reform separated cosmopolitans from locals, the one attuned to the latest discoveries in the wider world, the other faithful to the lore of previous generations, and each committed to its version of community. Temperance rallied the abstinent to associate in self-conscious sobriety and to exclude even the moderate drinker from their midst. In a community riven by factions and sects, the very advances of the age at once opened new prospects for personal fulfillment and weakened the bonds of interdependence still more. These changes would also prepare the social and cultural ground for the individualism of Emerson and Thoreau.

IN THE WINTER OF 1821, AS JOHN THOREAU WAS CLOSING HIS CHELMSFORD store and moving his family to Boston, the leading men of Concord village were initiating a civic enterprise destined to evoke both pride and disappointment in its Transcendentalist native son. Born of a commitment to the improvement of the town, the Concord Social Library was a hybrid organization. It was not funded by local taxes; nor was it free to residents. Nonetheless it was considered a *public* library. In the Commonwealth of Massachusetts, all sorts of entities—banks, canals, and turnpikes; charities and fraternal societies; academies and libraries—were deemed public if they served a common good. Accordingly, the legislature awarded them the special privilege of operating as legal corporations, with rights of property holding and self-government.

The Concord venture qualified. A joint-stock company, it consisted of fifty shares, available at the substantial price of five dollars each, equal to one term's tuition at the academy soon to come into being. Perhaps for this reason the venture was not a runaway success. It attracted thirty-nine subscribers within ten months but took another seven years to dispose of the remaining shares. In exchange for that sum, investors obtained the right to borrow one book at a time for up to four weeks. (Overdue fines were one or two cents per day.) Initially, that was a limited privilege, for the collection was small. But the proprietors' ambitions were large. They aimed to "diffuse useful information among the young, and afford instruction or rational amusement to all classes."[4]

Concord already had a library. It was started in 1795, with Parson Ripley the driving force. The institution was known as the Charitable Library Society, in testimony to its benevolent intent. The fifteen charter members meant to serve both their neighbors and themselves by assembling a collection freely available to anyone in town. All a would-be reader had to do was apply to the officers for permission to borrow a title and be approved. Some deserving individuals would even receive books as outright gifts.[5]

The choice of titles was limited. The collection reflected the outlook of Ripley and his associates, including Rebecca Thoreau's second husband, Jonas Minot, who served four terms as president. The library was top-heavy in works on religion, most of them authored by English divines from the mid-eighteenth century and by their New England counterparts. Virtually all presented Christianity as Ripley preached it, short on doctrinal debates and focused on matters of faith, ethics, and spiritual experience. Comprising 40 percent of all titles, this miscellany of sermons, prayers, conversion narratives, biblical commentaries, and theological treatises formed a literary tabernacle for the propagation of Christian morals. The library also eschewed the freethinkers of the Enlightenment and counteracted the irreverence of a revolutionary age. Among its acquisitions were the leading English and American rejoinders to *Age of Reason* (1794), Thomas Paine's slashing attack on established churches and revealed religion as bulwarks of tyranny. These broadsides were distributed gratis to the inmates of the Concord jail. Paine's incendiary pamphlet was not.[6]

As in religion, so in politics: the books dispensed lessons in republicanism with a lowercase *r* from a Federalist perspective, which grew increasingly shrill as the struggle against Jefferson and French radicalism reached a fever pitch in the run-up to the presidential election of 1800. But relief from these ideological battles lay at hand in the literature on offer, consisting chiefly of poetry and essays by the leading lights of England's Augustan age: Alexander Pope, James Thomson, Samuel Johnson, Addison and Steele. Like the curriculum in the local schools before the stirring of reform, the charitable library upheld the existing order of government, religion, and morality. "Every member of the community is obliged to seek and promote the public good," the constitution affirmed in language that echoed the parson's own. Ripley's little group aimed to fulfill this duty one book at a time.[7]

By the early 1820s, the charitable library was a graveyard of works buried in the past, with little of interest to the rising generation. Few current publications refreshed the collection. Of the 237 titles, the great majority—seven out of every ten—were the handiwork of authors abroad, more than half from the former mother country, who had first appeared in print when the Province of Massachusetts Bay was proudly celebrating its membership in the British Empire.[8]

As the son of a charitable library member, young Edward Jarvis looked with awe on "the huge [octavo] volumes" bulging in a case at Stephen Wood's store. Here, he was told, were "the best books in the English language—sermons—Divinity—History—Philosophy—with a few travels, and very few tales." Sadly, "almost the whole" of them were "beyond the comprehension of boys." Though Jarvis yearned for tales of adventure and romance, he made the best of the situation. He borrowed a few books of travel and devoured *Robinson Crusoe* several times. But after he took one book out for a fourth time, "my mother told me, I must not do it again, for four times was enough to read any book." Thereafter he was obliged to settle for heavy adult fare, including such unrewarding tomes as James Burgh's *The Dignity of Human Nature* (1754), his father's favorite, which promised "a Brief Account of the Certain and Established Means for Attaining the True End of Our Existence." But what was good for one generation was not good for all.[9]

The charitable library was on its deathbed when the plan for another library was set in motion. Its rationale for existence had disappeared with the ideolog-ical climate that brought it into being. Bowing to the inevitable, the older body joined forces with the challenger, contributing its antiquated collection and throwing in a bookcase as well. The new group matched that donation with a promise to purchase "as many books in value as those now in the library." Each member of the expiring institution got a share in its replacement. Leadership was divided among both factions. Ezra Ripley shepherded the transition, mov-ing from secretary of the charitable society to president of the membership library. The new organization was not bound by a lofty mission statement, and it welcomed into its ranks anyone willing and able to buy a share. A conven-tional subscription library, the Concord Social Library put proprietorship on a democratic basis. Money, rather than status or opinion, opened the door.[10]

Launched on a fresh wave of enthusiasm for social libraries throughout New England, the Concord group cut a broad swath through the village and beyond. It enlisted lawyers and doctors, established storekeepers and their short-lived rivals, husbandmen and manufacturers. The charter members were far wealthier than their neighbors, but a good number of middling men joined their ranks. Interest in books was not confined to a narrow elite.[11]

John Thoreau never bought a share in the social library—he didn't have to. The collection was open to anyone in town willing to pay for the privilege. Un-like its predecessor, the social library was not a charitable venture run by benev-olent gentlemen for the benefit of less-privileged neighbors. This enterprise was meant to be self-sustaining, and to that end it collected annual dues from share-holders and lent books to nonmembers for a modest sum. Charges were set on a sliding scale, with discounts offered for longer-term commitments: $1.25 for twelve months, seventy-five cents for six, fifty cents for three. Over the course of a year, an active reader could gain access to as many as fifty-two volumes for the same cost as the purchase of a single new work. And that was precisely the ap-peal of the venture. Where the charitable library had found intellectual fodder in the past, its successor looked for nourishment in the writings of contempo-raries, in "the useful and popular works of the day."[12]

And what an abundance of reading was now available! In the 1820s the business of publishing was booming, with books, magazines, and newspapers pouring from the press. By 1834 the country supported 125 publishers, con-centrated chiefly in Boston, New York, and Philadelphia, who turned out some fifteen hundred new titles and reprints a year. A day trip to Boston by stage or foot, Concord benefited from its proximity to the literary emporia of Washington, Cornhill, and Court streets, which occasionally advertised their new offerings in the local gazette. The town supported its own bookstore, run by John Stacy first in the old Wright tavern, then in a fashionable building erected by the Mill Dam Company. Surely, the books in the social library should be as up-to-date as their surroundings. "A Citizen" took to the local press on Christmas Day 1824 to urge that priority. New England's libraries, he complained, were weighed down with "volumes venerable for their antiquity, as well as valuable for their solid contents." But these did not contain the sum of human wisdom. "Great advances and discoveries have been made of late years in almost every branch of knowledge, which it would be clever" to make available "through the medium of a public Library."[13]

"A Citizen" knew the prevailing winds. From the start, the social library set about acquiring the latest titles as they came off the press. In its first phase of operation (1822–27), it added an average sixteen titles a year, then raised that annual harvest to twenty (1828–33)—quadruple what the charitable library had been able to acquire. The selection committee credited this growth "in great measure, if not entirely," to the addition of "the popular works of the day." Each annual report beat this refrain. If circulation went up, the officers reaffirmed the purchasing policy, and if it slumped, they apologized for not adding enough new books. "It is evident that without a constant increase of new and popular books," the committee observed in January 1830, "the number of volumes which shall be read will decrease." And that would undermine the business model of the enterprise. For without the fees from nonproprietors, how would the social library pay its bills? Should the collection no longer appeal to townspeople at large, the burden would fall entirely on the stockholders. These investors were already paying fifty cents each in annual assessments, and they were unlikely to welcome an increase. It was thus imperative to keep up the supply of new books.[14]

It was also a cultural choice. The very year the social library was inaugurated, the Concord newspaper described Americans of the time as a "reading generation"; within a few years Supreme Court justice Joseph Story would christen the era "the age of reading," marked by "the general diffusion of knowledge." These pronouncements were testimonies of faith more than descriptions of social fact. They articulated a dynamic ideology of moral reform through reading.

To the promoters of this crusade, reading was a fundamental social good. Protestants, of course, had long insisted that every man and woman be able to read the Scriptures. The founders of the republic were certain that popular self-government required an informed citizenry. The sponsors of social libraries affirmed these two goals but put their emphasis on a third: reading as a means of personal advancement. How else but through the "useful information" contained in books could a common person rise in the world? Agricultural reformers urged farmers to consult the latest experts in print; the same counsel was given in every field of endeavor. Through self-education, an individual could expand his intellectual capital, increase his efficiency at work, and raise his status in the world. For women and men alike, to be ignorant and out of touch was to become a social outcast. Lemuel Shattuck, for one, took this message to heart. "Any person, by having a judicious plan for saving the odd moments of life and appropriating them to reading good books or the acquisition of useful information," he once reflected, "may obtain a large fund of knowledge, which will be a qualification for greater usefulness in any station." As clerk of the social library and member of its selection committee, the merchant put this faith into practice and encouraged the upward striving of his neighbors, exactly as he prescribed for the schools.[15]

The project of reform through reading could not be imposed. Dependent on willing payments by nonproprietors to buy new books, the social library had to consider what townspeople wanted to read rather than what they should read. No longer could the managers fill the shelves with sermons and books of divinity, lest they offend any sect. The social library likewise avoided partisanship with its slim offerings on politics.[16]

It was not always possible to sidestep controversy, even in an effort to avoid giving offense. In 1830 the selection committee ordered the recently published four-volume *Works of Thomas Jefferson*, the first full edition of the late president's papers to be issued after his death. So eager were they to have the writings of "so eminent a patriot and statesman" that the committee bought the set sight unseen. As soon as the publication arrived in Concord, one member, Moses Prichard, took a quick look and was shocked. One of Jefferson's letters "contained sentiments which he was sorry to see." That letter touched on the vital subject of religion, and as the committee explained in its annual report, it "served to ridicule St. Paul and to call into question the truth of that part of the gospel relative to the birth of our Saviour." What should be done?

The committee came up with a seemingly obvious solution. It cut the offensive pages out of the book. That action stirred unease, and the committee was clearly on the defensive for its arbitrary act of bowdlerization. "Whether the act of taking away these leaves is right or wrong," the committee pleaded in self-justification, "the motive which prompted it was good—for it is better that a work should loose [*sic*] two leaves" than that anyone lose his eternal soul by encountering them![17]

With its premium on "useful knowledge," the social library sought out books that were filled with "matters of fact": histories, biographies, travels, practical science, the latest discoveries about the past and about the contemporary world. Surprisingly, few of the titles disseminated practical information about agriculture, astronomy, or other advances in science and technology, though Lemuel Shattuck did donate Rev. Charles Briggs's address at the 1825 Middlesex cattle show. The biographies, histories, and travels ranged far across time and space in an impressive display of cosmopolitanism. A determined reader could canvass the centuries from the ancient Greeks and Jews and the "decline and fall of the Roman empire" through the age of chivalry and the crusades, the Reformation, and the Thirty Years' War down to European expansion into the Americas, the growth of the English colonies, especially Massachusetts and New England, the English, American, and French revolutions, the triumphs of Napoleon and his defeat, and the rise of modern nation-states. Biographies featured famous figures on the throne, in war, in affairs of church and state, on voyages of discovery, and in the republic of letters. But this was not merely a galaxy of "greats," leading lives unimaginable to ordinary folk. The collection also supplied models of self-education and upward mobility in the autobiography of Benjamin Franklin, in the lives of "Eminent Men" in Great Britain who had engaged in the "Pursuit of Knowledge under Difficulties" (1830), in "memoirs of the most eminent American mechanics" (1840), and in a British disquisition *On the Improvement of Society by the Diffusion of Knowledge* (1831). Through the volumes it collected, the social library propagandized for itself.[18]

Far from dictating to readers, the social library accommodated changing tastes. The charitable library had made little room for fiction on its shelves. Its leaders had shared the conviction, widespread in late eighteenth-century New England, that novels disordered the imagination, fostered luxury and corruption, and distracted people from attending to the state of their souls. Such works had to be judiciously chosen and sparingly used. But hostility to fiction was dissipating by the time the social library went into operation. As a member of the charitable society, Squire Hoar had professed a "great dislike to fiction of all sorts," and he banned novels from his home during the first two decades of his marriage. Then, according to his son, on a winter day in 1832, the lawyer was stranded at a country inn by a sudden snowstorm; with nothing to read, "time hung heavy on his hands," until out of sheer boredom he asked the landlord if there were any books. The only thing to be found was the first volume of Sir Walter Scott's *Redgauntlet*, recently issued in a revised edition. "Father read it with infinite delight," related George Frisbie Hoar. "His eyes were opened to the excellence of Scott." And he could hardly wait to finish the plot. As soon as he returned to Concord, he sent to Stacy's bookstore for the second volume. He was "a great lover of Scott ever after." The squire was very late to the party. By the time the lawyer had discovered the Scottish novelist, the social library owned twenty-five of his works.[19]

With Scott opening the dike, a deluge of novels flooded into the social library. As the officers were well aware, they were the key to increasing circulation. Fiction dominated the selections, approaching half of the accessions in the 1820s and 1830s. But this was fiction of a special sort—what the managers deemed respectable, wholesome tales. The preference was for the host of British and American counterparts to Scott, who had eased fears of fiction by yoking the imagination to the hard world of historical fact. Half of the novels ordered by the social library committees in the 1820s were written by their countrymen, including not only Washington Irving and James Fenimore Cooper but also such female chroniclers of New England as Catherine Sedgwick and Lydia Maria Child. They safely instructed in morals while they delighted the imagination. Deriving from families similar to the library proprietors, these novelists conjured up social worlds in the throes of change, along lines that were being charted by Yankee readers themselves. They were the next best thing to historians—romancers of New England's and America's past and projectors of the future.[20]

Edward Jarvis shared these tastes in reading and helped to enforce them as well. During his year as grammar schoolmaster and then as a medical student, the young man was hardly ever without a book in hand during his waking hours. In the spring of 1827, while teaching his classes, he made his way through fifteen volumes of Scott's novels, two or three of David Hume's *History of England* (1754), and most of Daniel Neale's five-volume *History of the Puritans*

(1732). The years that followed were similarly ambitious. He even courted Almira Hunt with books. One "perfect" spring day in Concord, "a day that God had made for man," the couple sat outside and dipped into *Curiosities of Literature* (1791) together. He could not have been happier that his fiancée liked this anthology, assembled by the English writer Isaac Disraeli, as much as he. "She is disposed to cultivation," he observed with pride, "and reads and thinks to that purpose."[21]

In December 1832 Jarvis, having succeeded to his father's share in the library, was elected to the selection committee. He was a good fit for the position. "It was our object to get books of as high character as the people would read," he reflected. "Not so dull & heavy as to fail to attract their attention & secure their taste—nor so light as to be unprofitable. History—Novels—a few novels of the best kind—and works of morality, religion & philosophy—we got." Jarvis gauged his intentions more accurately than the results. When it came to picking items for the collection, he went for novels and travel narratives (the close companion of fiction) with as much gusto as his colleagues. His literary preferences were an epitome of the Concord collection.[22]

By the mid-1830s, a decade and a half after its founding, the social library was stronger than ever. It was adding more than thirty titles a year, nearly fifty in 1835 alone, and lending was at a peak, with well over two thousand volumes in circulation, more than double the rate at the institution's start. A rich store of reading was available for the Thoreaus and their literary-minded neighbors. The standing committee of 1834, on which Jarvis served, was cheered by the "flourishing condition" of the library and the "incalculable benefit" it brought to the town in the form of "solid instruction" and "rational amusement." Indeed, this modest country town, with some two thousand inhabitants, stood out in the Commonwealth for the strength of its collection. The social library possessed one book for every two inhabitants, according to a survey taken in 1837; by contrast, in Middlesex County as a whole, the ratio was one to five, and in largely rural Worcester County, one to ten. The selection committee could rightly boast of Concord's intellectual riches, well before Emerson and Thoreau made the town a literary mecca.[23]

For all its public-spirited intentions, the social library accentuated differences among the townspeople. Like the addresses at the annual cattle fairs, the books in the collection were apostles of progress, summoning readers to break with custom and improve their lives with innovations advocated by experts and tested by experience. Those who heard and heeded this message would be welcome in local parlors; those willfully ignorant would be shut out, as the writer who styled himself "Concord" made plain in his contribution to the local *Gazette*: "Ladies, have you read Hamilton [the author of Cyril Thornton] and [Maria] Edgeworth? No. The history of your own State? No. Of Rome, of Greece, or of England? No, of course." Anyone so benighted should clearly be ashamed. A new norm of respectability, founded on education and culture, was taking hold.[24]

WITHIN A YEAR AND A HALF OF ITS FOUNDING, THE CONCORD SOCIAL LIbrary had a companion in the pursuit of enlightenment. The Concord Debating Club began holding weekly meetings in the brick schoolhouse sometime in the late fall of 1822. Similar groups had recently started up in Boston, New Bedford, and Newburyport. Now Concord was leading the way in the countryside and introducing a new pastime for the winter season. There in the central village, on most Wednesday or Thursday evenings from December through March, a half-dozen or more men engaged in animated discussion of current issues from economics and politics to religion, society, and culture, while fellow club members, female relatives, and neighbors looked on to weigh the pros and cons of the opposing sides and to enjoy the thrust and parry of verbal combat.[25]

What need did the residents of Concord and other towns have for lessons in forensics? For two centuries, Puritans, Minutemen, and their descendants had been holding forth at town and parish meetings with learned rhetoric and vernacular speech. During the Great Awakening and the Revolution, the plain-spoken voices of common people made themselves heard, often in blunt confrontation with authorities. In the party battles of the early republic, political talk could be vehement, even violent, and calculated not to persuade but to polarize for the sake of winning elections. In schools and academies, boys and girls imitated the great orators of the ancient world and of the American Revolution with practice in declamation. Nonetheless, as political passions subsided, a good many people who were never comfortable with factional fighting hoped to impose a new order on public speech. In an "era of good feelings," they maintained, public discourse should center on measures, not men, and it should do so with moderation, impartiality, respect for others, and concern for the common good. Debating societies could be valuable means to that civic end.

Public speaking was also a route to individual advancement. During the

1820s and 1830s opportunities to vote and hold office were expanding in a major step forward for democracy, at least for white men. Massachusetts extended these rights to all male taxpayers, irrespective of race. Under these circumstances, "where every honor is in the gift of the people" and "where the humblest citizen may aspire to the highest honors," how would young men without education and privilege acquire "the power of rapidly, extemporaneously, and . . . *correctly* conveying ideas" to their fellow citizens? Reading by itself was not enough; those with "strong marks of intellect" needed to "exercise their minds" in contact with others. Too often individuals were blinkered by their callings—lawyers "shackled and confined to tedious facts and dry questions of law," merchants indifferent to anything "of more value than silver and gold"—and hence were ill-equipped to cross the gulfs separating the various classes of society. Debating societies could remedy this problem by serving as schools of eloquence, wherein the future Ciceros of the republic would gain experience speaking "promptly and elegantly" on "questions of great public importance."[26]

This agenda naturally appealed to ambitious men, especially the young. The typical member of the Concord Debating Club was in his midthirties, still single or about to wed, and with the free time to devote to improving his oratorical skills. Debating was so popular among bachelors that it became a standing joke; it was said that the club in Fall River fell apart after nearly all its members got married and did their debating "at home." Residents of the village, the participants in the Concord group were tradesmen, teachers, and lawyers, who earned their living with their words. The debating club was small in size—only fourteen were on the rolls in 1829—and membership was apparently by invitation only. Rather than take all comers, the club insisted on vetting applicants and formally electing new members.[27]

The members of this small circle ranged over a vast territory in their debates, from local issues before the town to great philosophical questions about history, nature, and the human condition. The first topic on record addressed an ongoing economic initiative: "Would the establishment of a Bank in this town be beneficial to the community?" The debating club took up the question in November 1822, ten months after the state legislature granted a charter to the Middlesex Bank. The outcome of the discussion is unknown, but as things turned out, the negative side won. The bank never went into operation. Other ventures to come under scrutiny were the annual cattle show ("Do Manufactures and Agriculture derive any advantage" from the effort?) and the plan to raise a monument to the

Concord Fight (should it be placed on the battleground or in the village?). The conflicts roiling the Congregationalist establishment drew repeated attention; no sooner did the "little band" of dissenters from Doctor Ripley's church begin worshiping on their own than the debating club considered whether "an established religion [is] beneficial to a Country." The value of religious pluralism remained an open question. So too did the usefulness of political competition. As Federalists and Republicans gave up the fight and banded together under the label "National Republican Party," the disputants in Concord looked warily at the political scene ("Are two distinct political parties beneficial to a republic?") and were troubled over popular initiatives to control government ("Are Representatives in Congress bound by the instructions of their constituents?"). The policies and practices of democracy in the Commonwealth and the nation were always up for debate.[28]

No shift in society, no development in culture was outside the club's purview. This band of bachelors and married men saw fit to argue the merits of female education and to weigh the relative influence of "ladies" and "gentlemen" in "forming the character of the age," while their sisters and wives looked on in silence, barred by custom from speaking in public. These white men had no hesitation to speculate about the intellectual capacities of the races, though the way they framed the question—are whites "superior"?—made plain an implicit bias for their own kind. Native Americans garnered greater sympathy, with the disputants asking whether "civilized nations [have] a right to take possession of newly discovered countries inhabited by savages?" Turning literary critics, the club members debated the benefits of reading novels, the usefulness of "critical Reviews," and whether "Novels or History" do more to shape morals, all questions of immediate interest to the social library. The members took the measure of recent history—Did Napoleon do more harm than good? Was the French Revolution good or bad for the cause of liberty?—and stepped back for a long view across the centuries. "Are mankind morally better at the present age than at any former period?" The disputes could turn philosophical and inquire into human nature: "Have we good reason to think that mankind possesses an innate moral sense of right and wrong?" Or they could question the point of even raising such issues. "Are Debating Clubs beneficial to the Community?" they asked one evening in November 1827. In this case we can presume the result was positive. The group continued to meet.[29]

In public, the debating club presented a high-minded model of deliberation. Behind the scenes, club meetings could be rancorous. During his stint as master of the village grammar school, Edward Jarvis was elected to membership and shortly after became the recording secretary. The Harvard graduate was quickly displeased with the way the group was run. The president was the lawyer Elisha Fuller, brother of the retired congressman Timothy Fuller and uncle of the future Transcendentalist thinker Margaret Fuller. The censorious Jarvis considered him "somewhat eccentric and variable in his humour, temper, and feelings." That was hardly the temperament needed to guide the club, yet Fuller invariably got his way over protests by Jarvis and his few allies. "This was a cause of a great deal of wrangling and dispute," Jarvis noted. "Almost every meeting we saw something in the ruling party to censure." The recording secretary made no friends with the minutes he took. "They were offended . . . and often charged me with keeping improper though not false records." When he stepped down from the post, the members declined to offer the customary vote of thanks, even though, Jarvis grumbled, "no one had done more for them . . . nor had any one given a more exact account of the proceedings."

Surprisingly, Jarvis was chosen as the debating club president at the next election, enjoyed a successful term, and continued to participate in the group while pursuing medical studies in Boston. But decades later he was full of regrets for the time wasted in forensic competition. "It was simply a trial of skill at mental gladiatorship. Reason and sophistry, truth and error, were alike to be employed if they seemed to favor the part assumed. This was not well for mental discipline, nor did it aid the search for truth, nor was it always productive of good feeling and harmony." That was not his opinion at the time. Despite repeated defeats in the winter of 1828, he took satisfaction in the effort. "I think I have improved much. My thoughts are more ready and connected. I reason more closely though by no means well." Thanks to debate, he could sometimes be as critical of himself as he was of others.[30]

Enthusiasm for debate trickled down to the schools. In 1827 grammar schoolmaster Horatio Wood initiated a young men's debating society, and over the three years of its existence, it engaged as many as forty-eight schoolboys and others wrestling with such questions as "Ought Negroes be allowed to vote." The name of Henry Thoreau is absent from the roster of participants, but after he switched to the academy, the twelve-year-old was drawn into the Concord Academic Debating Society, started by Phineas Allen to keep up with the public institution. The youth was a reluctant participant. Fittingly, his first debating assignment was to take the affirmative position on the question, "Does it require more talents to make a good writer than a good extemporaneous speaker?" Thoreau lost the argument to Rockwood Hoar, though neither debater was "very animated." The next outing was a fiasco. The topic for discussion, "Is a good memory preferable to a good understanding in order to be a distinguished scholar at school?," proved uninspiring. The spokesman for the question forgot to prepare anything; Thoreau, taking the negative, did "not much more." No one else was moved to speak. "Such a debate, if it may be called so . . . I hope never again will be witnessed in this house, or recorded in this book," the club's secretary commented in disgust. "It is not only a waste of time, but of paper to record such proceedings." Based on this experience, Thoreau had good reason in later years to deem authors superior to orators. The orator, he jibed in *Walden*, "yields to the inspiration of a transient occasion, and speaks to the mob before him . . . , but the writer . . . speaks to the intellect and heart of mankind." Here, as in so many other areas, he marched to a different drummer.[31]

Debate, in the end, was not just about proper political discourse. To participate actively in a debating society was to forge a distinct identity as a citizen of the world. Members were not confined to town and parish; nor were they bound by custom. They took notice of events and trends anywhere, in the past or the present, and set out confidently to master them through study and debate. Far from being fearful of change, they expected to impose intellectual control over an expanding nineteenth-century world teeming with fresh discoveries and exciting inventions. One week a young man had no idea whether "the South American republics [were] sufficiently enlightened for a permanent republican form of Government"; the next, after looking into the matter, he was forcefully maintaining yea or nay. Debates were a form of mutual education, by which peers instructed one another through the contest of arguments and ideas—a Lancasterian school for adults. In the process, the participants became cosmopolitans, seeking out knowledge from far-flung places as readily as they pursued markets for their products in Louisville, New Orleans, and Cuba. "Are the habits and manners of the present age more favorable to good morals and long life," they asked in January 1824, "than were the habits and manners of our forefathers?" Debating the question, they detached themselves from tradition, surveyed their world critically, and prepared to be agents of change.[32]

IN LATE OCTOBER 1828, A VISIONARY CONNECTICUT SCHOOLMASTER NAMED Josiah Holbrook was in Concord lecturing on geology to "a large audience" eager to hear about the fashionable new science. But the speaker had larger goals in mind. He was on the road to promote a scheme for the diffusion of useful knowledge in all the sciences and in other fields as well. A forty-year-old Yale graduate, Holbrook had developed a passion for science after attending Benjamin Silliman's lectures on chemistry and geology in New Haven. Intent on putting the lessons into practice, he opened an Agricultural Seminary on his family's farm in nearby Derby, where young men combined manual labor with study of the natural sciences. As that venture was collapsing, Holbrook read an article about the British mechanics' institutes, which aimed to expose workingmen to the branches of science so that they could cooperate more effectively with employers in the pursuit of technological progress and thereby raise their wages and status. He seized on the idea, adapted it to American circumstances, and made it the mission of his life.[33]

The plan called for the establishment of "associations for mutual instruction in the sciences, and in useful knowledge generally." The target audience was young men in need of "an economical and practical education," who would come together for lessons in "Mechanics, Hydrostatics, Pneumatics, Chemistry, Mineralogy, Botany," and "any branch of the Mathematics, History, Political Economy, or any political, intellectual, or moral subject." The benefits of such instruction were not limited to the young; "rational and useful information" would be diffused through the community at large. For one thing, as skilled craftsmen applied scientific knowledge "to the domestic and useful arts, and to all the common purposes of life," new ideas and inventions would multiply to ease the burdens and expand the comforts of everyday existence. For another, the associations would uplift "the moral and intellectual taste" of the community; instead of haunting taverns and risking "dissipation" and "ruin" for lack of anything better to do, young people would gain a wholesome and productive outlet for their leisure time.

To achieve these important aims, Holbrook proposed a variety of activities. Besides offering opportunities for mutual education, the associations would sponsor lectures "in any subject of useful knowledge" and assemble the essential means of scientific instruction: books, laboratory equipment (then called "apparatus for illustrating the sciences"), and collections of minerals. Following the pedagogy of Pestalozzi, the lessons combined theory and practice on the principle that all real learning derives from firsthand experience. At Holbrook's associations, that would be achieved by listening, speaking, and doing.[34]

Holbrook wrote up his scheme, published it in an educational journal, and then took to the road in a campaign to promote his plan. His "associations for mutual instruction" now carried the shorter and snappier title "lyceums" in honor of the Yale building where Benjamin Silliman had conducted his "scientific demonstrations." The name possessed the added advantage of evoking the site in ancient Athens where Aristotle had taught. It quickly caught on to signify the new venture in popular education for aspiring Americans.[35]

The lyceum movement got its start in Worcester County, Massachusetts, a hive of industry with hundreds of skilled craftsmen concentrated in more than a dozen villages, the very people most likely to appreciate Holbrook's plan. In November 1826 the appropriately named town of Millbury, a center of arms manufacturing, was the first to sign on as "Branch No. 1 of the American Lyceum." Within a year Holbrook claimed to have inspired the creation of fifty to sixty more.[36]

Concord marked his first foray into Middlesex County, and the town was well prepared to receive him. In August 1828 the *Gazette* gave favorable notice to the lyceum plan; two months later, when he came to lecture, Holbrook enjoyed a warm welcome. "Would it be expedient to establish a lyceum in this town?" the Concord Debating Club asked in his wake. The affirmative side won. The momentum accelerated when Doctor Ripley endorsed the idea at the close of his Thanksgiving sermon and announced a meeting in the brick schoolhouse to rally public support for the measure. The organization of a lyceum appeared to be a done deal.[37]

Then the initiative faltered. When a "large and respectable" body of citizens came together to implement Holbrook's design, it confronted two stumbling blocks. One major hurdle was the supposition that Concord could never come up with "a sufficient number of lecturers, especially among our own people," to accomplish the worthy goal of disseminating useful knowledge. The second disagreement turned on the question of dues. Under Holbrook's model, the annual membership fee would be two dollars for adults and half as much for men under eighteen. That policy did not go over well with people who lived outside Concord village. Surely, they argued, heavy snows and storms in the winter would prevent some of them from attending all the lectures. It was unfair to impose the same dues on them as on residents of the town center.

The plea went nowhere. Only after the lyceum fell short in its initial bid for subscribers were fees set at half-price for inhabitants in the outer districts. No matter where they lived, each member was entitled to bring "two ladies" to the lectures and, "if married, his children in addition." The rules were soon loosened to allow entire families like the Thoreaus—parents, children, and a female guest—to attend together. Before the lyceum had finished its first year, the cost of membership was reduced still more: one dollar in annual dues for villagers, fifty cents for everyone else. Any resident could obtain a free ticket to a single lecture upon request.[38]

The Concord Lyceum was no mechanics' institute. By the time it got going in January 1829, five months ahead of Boston, the group had fifty-seven charter members, nearly all of whom belonged to the propertied classes. The commercial and professional men of the village comprised half of the initial subscribers. The craftsmen in the ranks were all masters of their own shops; not a single journeyman and just one laborer were among them. Remarkably, fifteen of the founders were farmers, scattered around the town, including the struggling husbandman Daniel Hunt. Nor was this an assemblage of young men just starting out in the world. Their average age was thirty-five, with only one out of three in his teens or twenties. The oldest was a toughened saddler of eighty-one, the youngest the twelve-year-old son of Squire Hoar.

The lyceum developed into a community-wide affair, attracting as many as 111 dues-paying members over the first three seasons. The rapid growth was undoubtedly due to the strong backing of the local political and economic elite. Eschewing sectarianism, the group picked Doctor Ripley, in his late seventies, as president in the early years and elected his clerical colleagues, the Unitarian Goodwin and the Trinitarian Southmayd, as fellow officers. In its constituency and leadership, the new association resembled the agricultural society and the social library. Ultimately, to its advocates, the endeavor amounted to a patriotic project befitting the descendants of Minutemen. "Those whose ancestry were among the foremost and boldest assertors [sic] of civil and political liberty," argued one supporter, "should stand in the first rank of men, whose purpose is to establish moral and mental freedom, to effectuate an emancipation from vice and ignorance."[39]

A mere two weeks into its existence, the group took steps to avoid competition with the debating club. A merger took place in March 1829, following a final weighing of the question, "Will the general establishment of Lyceums in the Commonwealth be productive of good to the community?" Over the next five years the lyceum conducted fifty-seven public debates involving some fifty-one participants. Forensic exercises were secondary to the main business of the lyceum: sponsoring a public lecture every week or two from fall to spring. The Concord Lyceum, like its counterparts elsewhere, was essentially a lecture bureau and a debating club.[40]

For all the support it garnered, the lyceum had no guarantee of success. It had to compete against a steady stream of "lectures, exhibitions, shows, experiments, musical machines," and other displays of "human ingenuity" seeking Concordians' leisure time and dollars. Who would pass up the opportunity to see the exotic animals on display in front of the Middlesex Hotel: elephants, lions and wildcats, monkeys, and camels? In this rivalry the lyceum possessed considerable advantages. Freelance lecturers came and went on their own schedules, as suited their self-interest, and they could be expensive. One teacher of astronomy sold tickets to a course of sixteen lectures for $2.50, more than membership in the lyceum ever cost. The lyceum season was varied, covering a wide range of subjects, and the program was put together by local curators acting not for private profit but for the higher interests of the townspeople. "There are few institutions," the *Yeoman's Gazette* insisted, "where so much amusement and instruction can be procured for so little expense."

Most important, the lyceum was founded on the principle of mutual instruction. In both lectures and debates, members would do their part to advance knowledge for the benefit of both their fellows and themselves. "There is scarcely a man among us of any intelligence, who is not better acquainted with some one or more subjects than his neighbors," the curators reported after the opening season, "and will a majority of such persons be so wanting in benevolence as to confine their knowledge to their own breasts for want of a little confidence?" Self-improvement and the general good went hand in hand.[41]

As it turned out, the members disproved the skeptics and strode up to the platform. Of the 143 lectures given between 1829 and 1834, twenty-eight local residents delivered well over half of them (58 percent). The group took pride in this accomplishment. Year in, year out, with few exceptions, the curators underscored the achievement in their reports. When local contributions slumped, the members exhorted themselves to "use more exertions to prepare themselves to lecture." Some individuals confined themselves to their own area of expertise. The textile manufacturer Ephraim Bellows held forth on protective tariffs—favorably, one assumes. Farmer Anthony Wright optimistically advocated "the culture of silk worms." Schoolmaster Cyrus Hosmer discoursed on education, his clerical brother George on the Protestant Reformation. Dr. Josiah Bartlett, having presumably treated many cases of dyspepsia, offered his thoughts on "indigestion." Lawyer Henry Moore took up "trial by jury." Other members were willing to step outside familiar territory, explore a new area of knowledge, and report back on what they had found. Phineas Allen lectured on astronomy, Reverend Goodwin on "animals and body temperature," Lemuel Shattuck on entomology. In taking up scientific subjects, these and other speakers were being true to the original design of the lyceum. Nearly half of the lectures by Concord residents in these formative years were devoted to science and technology, the single largest category by far.[42]

No one was more enthusiastic about the lyceum than Nehemiah Ball, a tanner who assumed the podium repeatedly from 1829 to 1834. Ball had grown up on an old-style farm, learned the craft of tanning without going through a formal apprenticeship, and entered the leather business with his brother-in-law. Luckily, he married well, and he parlayed that good fortune into lucrative investments. One contemporary recalled him as a pompous, calculating, formal man who was "never known to make a joke," and insofar as he ever appreciated the wit of others, he could summon up little more than "a grim smile" or "a feeble chuckle." The one thing about which Ball felt passionate was education, both for his eight children and for himself. A charter member of the lyceum, he served as a curator for three terms from 1830 to 1833, booking himself often as a speaker on the topic of natural history.

One of his lectures, on the animal kingdom, was illustrated with a magic lantern projecting images of "every known species of ape, monkey, and baboon" onto a white sheet, as Ball set forth "a very precise and accurate statement of their length from the tip of the nose to the insertion of the tale." To one teenager in the audience, the irreverent son of the Hon. John Keyes, the presentation was ludicrous. "This is a ferocious animal," Ball would supposedly say as the image of a lion appeared before everyone's eyes. The speaker punctuated his remarks with a frequent refrain: "I apprehend." That "I apprehend," John Shepard Keyes recalled decades later, "became a byword among the young people of the day, who could hardly keep from laughing in his face at its constant repetition, notwithstanding the eminent gravity with which it prefaced his conclusions." This self-taught citizen might not have diffused as much useful information as Josiah Holbrook had hoped. And why sit through Ball's tedious descriptions of exotic animals when the actual creatures could be seen up close in the traveling menageries so frequently on display in the village?[43]

When lyceum lecturers turned from the laws of nature to those governing man and society, they addressed fundamental questions troubling people, young and old, in a world of increasing competition and mobility. What personal habits and skills were necessary to achieve a productive, useful, and happy life? What methods of education were best designed to cultivate those capacities in youth? What were the defining qualities of a good society? These were issues of central concern to local and outside speakers alike. The lyceum purported to engage these matters free from partisan or sectarian bias.

Even so, Unitarian ministers assumed its platform more often than clergy from other denominations; Doctor Ripley was never reluctant to hold forth.[44] Politically, the list of lecturers was top-heavy with National Republicans and Whigs, who were occasionally tempted into outright partisan advocacy. One newcomer to Concord in December 1833, the widow Prudence Ward, who boarded with the Thoreau aunts, found discourses on such topics as "the Tariff Laws, or the American System," hard to take. The meetings "have not been interesting, nor as useful as they might be," she complained. "The speakers came very near saying hard things on politics & religion. I am quite surprised to find how far you [men] will sometimes stray." If the lyceum were to succeed as family entertainment, it had to appeal to the ladies.[45]

Avoiding controversy was more than wise policy for the novice institution. It enacted a vision of the lyceum as an instrument for building consensus in a diverse community. In the fall of 1832 the *Yeoman's Gazette* reflected that "it is the coming together upon common ground of men of different opinions and occupations, that will wear off some of the rough edges that human nature is so liable to acquire in these times of suspicion and discord . . . The remark is generally true that the more we know of one another—the more room we shall find for mutual forbearance, respect and love."

The rhetoric of community was undercut by the many lectures urging listeners to shed older ways of thinking and acting, such as the various "superstitions" decried by Reverend Bernard Whitman in his inaugural lecture, stretching from the foolish faith in lucky days and credulous fear of ghosts to the ill-considered practice of slaughtering swine and timing other farm chores by the phases of the moon. "The moon has no more to do with hogs," the faithful shepherd opined, "than the Pope of Rome." Forget the traditional lore of your fathers and grandfathers, the speakers urged; attend to experts, cultivate a scientific mentality, and put a premium on individual self-improvement and upward mobility, no matter how much family friction and neighborly conflict such behavior may cause.[46]

Taken together, the miscellany of lecture topics at the lyceum was as eclectic as the mix of genres at the social library (but without the excitement of historical romances). The "character of Indians" was on view one week, the "life of Sir Walter Raleigh" the next; practical accounts of tariffs and manufactures were followed by treatments of "the conditions of [modern] Greece," the history of Poland, and Egyptian hieroglyphics.[47] Equally variegated were the wide-ranging questions the members of the lyceum put up for public discussion during the 1830s after absorbing the debating club. As before, the agenda for discussion combined issues of public policy on local, state, and national levels with long views of history, literature, and philosophy.

More surprising than the topics were the participants. A taste for debate was commonly associated with the young, and accordingly, men in their twenties made up a quarter of the discussants. One recent college graduate found Concord's cultural scene so enticing that he neglected his legal training under Squire Hoar and eventually abandoned the law. "To me," Jonathan T. Davis (Harvard Class of 1829) later recalled with regret, "the book of nature, the Lyceum, and the Debating Club afforded more than Blackstone and Bacon." Concord's elders were also drawn to forensics. A dozen men did most of the talking in the debates held by the lyceum in the 1830s, and they included the notables whom residents were accustomed to hear at town meetings and Sabbath worship. Why did such veteran leaders of the town as Ripley and Keyes enlist so enthusiastically in debate? Surely not for the experience of speaking in public. These eminent men never lacked for opportunities to address the inhabitants from the pulpit, at the courthouse, and on the hustings. But they did possess a strong sense of duty. If the lyceum were to succeed, all members had to make "efforts to improve their own minds and impart knowledge to others," as the curators urged in 1832. Through lectures and debates, Concord's leaders could briefly step out of their superior roles in church and state and collaborate with their fellows in high-minded, impartial disquisitions meant to advance the common good. Debates thus contributed to the development of a more open and inclusive public sphere.[48]

Then again, some participants may simply have enjoyed the sound of their own voices. The merchant Josiah Davis considered himself a man of authority, and he deemed it his responsibility to offer his opinion in every public forum. "Though public speaking was not his forte," recalled Rockwood Hoar, "he did not incline to let his light be hid under a bushel, and at town meetings, church meetings, and the like, could not easily be brought to regard silence as consistent with his duty to his fellow-men." Once in a debate over whether "a fertile soil [is] best calculated to call forth the energy of a people," the native of New Ipswich invoked a litany of "eminent men" from New Hampshire to whom the Bay State was "indebted." At the close of this "enumeration," the self-important merchant could not resist a personal reference. "Why, in this town, Mr. Prichard and Colonel Shattuck, and I, all came from New Hampshire." It was not a winning point.[49]

The lyceum hit its peak of activity and popularity during the first half of the 1830s. The lecture season typically commenced in late October, after the cattle show had come and gone and the trees had largely shed their leaves; it ran through the snow and frost of winter and lasted into apple blossom time. In these years a dedicated member could attend anywhere between twenty and thirty lectures annually and witness twenty debates as well. (The fad for forensics soon waned to a dozen a year around 1835 and about half as many into 1838.) With so many programs on offer, the curators could rightly assert that "there is no way of accomplishing so much good for a trifling expense as by Lyceums." Membership in the society soared. This was the heyday of the lyceum movement in Massachusetts, with Middlesex County rivaling Boston for the lead. In 1832 two-thirds of the county's thirty-five towns supported lyceums. Only Boston and its surrounding communities in Suffolk County outpaced that record.[50]

To Ezra Ripley, the Concord Lyceum carried on the same educational cause as his prior endeavors but in a new, improved form. An inveterate reformer into old age, the Doctor welcomed enterprises that treasured the achievements of past generations and added to them. No sooner had the plan for the lyceum been set in motion than he vowed "not to spare any trouble or labor" to ensure its success. Besides serving as founding president, he joined in fifteen debates and lectured a dozen times, right up to age eighty-seven, on a wide range of topics, from "mental effort," "formation of character," and "government of the temper" (always an issue for the testy parson) to the "means of preserving health," "economy," and caring for an orchard. Barely a year after the launch of the lyceum, he was hailing the enterprise as a key agent in the progress of the age. Here "we may

hear respectable lectures on Geography, Astronomy, Agriculture, and other subjects, by mechanics and farmers." Through this medium, knowledge was advancing, "accompanied by benevolence," and he foresaw a society where "all classes
of citizens" would gain in "information and virtue," in "sincere piety and moral
goodness." For all his insistence on authority and his vision of community as
composed of ranks and orders, the minister had come by the 1820s to embrace a
society open to the ambitions and striving of all.[51]

THE APPEAL OF THE LYCEUM MOVEMENT SPANNED THE GENERATIONS, AND
for Ripley, it was something of a family affair. His Emerson grandsons welcomed
the opportunity to share their knowledge with the citizens of their ancestral
town. At age twenty-three, Edward Bliss Emerson was the first of the brothers
to lecture in Concord; he spoke in the lyceum's inaugural season the week after
his grandsire. The topic was "the geography and history of Asia," an adaptation
of his prizewinning Harvard essay on the Chinese empire. Charles Chauncy Emerson, three years younger, followed with four lectures between 1830 and 1834;
his talks dealt with classical antiquity ("the Life of Socrates"), geography ("the
West Indian Islands"), social customs ("the History of Popular Amusements"),
and philosophy ("the Constitution of Man"). The two speakers prepared the way
for their older brother Waldo, whose Concord debut did not come until May
1834, when the thirty-one-year-old former pastor of Boston's Second Church
traveled out from the city to expound on his recent travels in Italy. His address
presented "an account [of his] tour, and of the cities, the country, the people, and
the works of art" he encountered along the way. Later that year, as he was moving
into Ripley's manse, he offered his reflections on "Society" and then, on New
Year's Day in 1835, a discourse on "the Uses of Natural History." These talks fit
the bill; there was little to distinguish them, at least by titles and topics, from the
expected fare of the lyceum.[52]

Waldo's lecture on natural history was not entirely conventional. The discourse had originally been composed in a hurry, just four weeks after his return from Europe, and had been delivered to the aptly named Boston Society
for Natural History in November 1833. In his repeat performance for the Concord Lyceum, Emerson bore a superficial resemblance to Nehemiah Ball by
presenting an extended survey of the animals he had seen at Paris's Jardin des
Plantes, the vast botanical and zoological garden displaying the "inexhaustible, gigantic riches of nature." First came the "camelopard [i.e., giraffe] nearly

twenty feet high," followed by "lions from Algiers and Asia" and "elephants from Siam," after which appeared "our own countrymen, the buffalo and the bear from New Hampshire and Labrador," and, of course, who could forget "all sizes and all stripes of tygers, hyenas, leopards, and jackals, [and] a herd of monkeys." All Emerson needed was a magic lantern for an audience experience of déjà vu.

The similarity of content disguised a fundamental difference of approach, however. Unlike Ball and his fellows, Emerson did not aim at an objective description of a world beyond himself. His aim was to establish a relation between listeners and subject. He thus began with the proposition that humans were drawn, by the very circumstances of their being, to study the natural world. How else could they get a subsistence? And how could they resist nature's aesthetic appeal? "The beauty of the world is a perpetual invitation to the study of the world": Emerson had experienced that connection, emotionally and aesthetically, during his visit to the French zoo. There he had felt profoundly, at the core of his being, the interconnection among all living things, from "the very worm" and "the crawling scorpion" to himself. A relation to nature was thus not so much utilitarian—the premise of the lyceum movement—as fundamental, built into the very constitution of man.

On this basis, Emerson proceeded to lay out the various "advantages" to be gained from the study of natural history. For one thing, it was good for your health to be outdoors in the "fresh and fragrant fields"; it was equally good for your "mind and character," training the intellect to be "exact, quick to discriminate between the similar and the same, and greedy of truth." The knowledge thereby gained would directly serve "the economical needs" of mankind for "food, clothing, fuel, furniture, and arms." Most lyceum lecturers would have ended there. Not Emerson. For him, the great reward from studying nature was the sheer delight that springs from the discovery of truth: "the knowledge itself, is the highest benefit," for it promised to "explain man to himself." The aims of the lyceum, Emerson implied, were too low. The truths of science mattered for their own sake and not merely for the technological advances and the economic benefits they conferred. The speaker was rehearsing the argument he would make in the Transcendentalist manifesto *Nature*.[53]

THE RISE OF THE LYCEUM COINCIDED WITH THE DEVELOPING CAMPAIGN against another social ill, the scourge of intemperance, and not by accident. From the start, Holbrook had envisioned his "associations for mutual instruction" as a high-minded alternative to the tavern. Young people, in his view, needed "places of resort for social enjoyment," and in the absence of other options, they gravitated to alehouses. Give them the better choice of the lyceum, with its ample resources for studying "the works and laws of [the Creator]," and the "shelves of loaded decanters and sparkling glasses, so richly filled, and so neatly arranged . . . for their enjoyment" in the barroom would lose their appeal. Who would not prefer informative lectures and spirited discussions to "the merry song, the vulgar wit, and the loud laugh" of an inebriated crowd? In that conviction, the carriage manufacturer William Whiting was always glad to raise funds for the Concord Lyceum. As he went about town seeking donations for a new season of lecturers, he took "much satisfaction" in asking "the keepers of the drinking places and other resorts of idle youth in the neighborhood" for money. Although he never got a penny, he was delighted with the reason why. The lyceum, he was told, "interfered with their business." To Whiting, that excuse was "the best testimony" possible "to the wisdom and success of [the] enterprise."[54]

The lyceum featured only an occasional program about the evils of alcohol and the best means of combating them. The burden of this social reform fell on other do-gooders. And what a load they had to bear! Drinking was a social custom as well as an individual choice; it was as embedded in the familiar way of life as changing works on the farm and haggling at the village store. To decline a sociable glass was to break the rules of hospitality; to refuse grog to laborers was to violate the accepted terms of employment; to shun the tavern was to cut oneself off from a vital hub of community and news. The movement for temperance thus introduced yet another solvent of social ties. In the name of purifying morals, it could set neighbor against neighbor in irreconcilable conflict.[55]

There was good reason for alarm over popular drinking. At the jubilee of the American Revolution, the citizens of the young republic enthusiastically toasted the spirit of liberty—again and again and again. Alcohol use was at an all-time high in the nation's history. Annual consumption of distilled liquor reached five gallons per capita—three times greater than today. Concordians imbibed at the same pace as their countrymen. The typical townsman over fifteen drank four to six ounces a day (the Sabbath included), roughly the same amount Continental soldiers had enjoyed as their daily ration. But New Englanders remained a peculiar people in their choice of poison. In the decades after 1790, whiskey, once little known, captured the market as the national drink, thanks to the cheap production of grain on the rich farmlands of the West. But Yankees from New Hampshire to Rhode Island continued to cherish their mugs of rum, as had their fathers and grandfathers before them. Whether imported from the West Indies or distilled in Boston, rum won favor in various forms, including grog (mixed with water), toddy (sweetened and watered), flip (a warm concoction of rum, sugar, and beer), and "new rum" (flavored with caramel and aged in the barrel). For alternatives, gin and brandy were widely available. Where spirits didn't suit, wine from Lisbon and Madeira appealed to gentlemen with money to spend. And then there was cider, as constant a presence on the farm table as bread and milk for breakfast and a pot of beans at noon. Packing a strong punch from long fermentation, the free flow of cider added to the intoxicating mix. From dawn to dark, at home and abroad, strong drink fortified men for labor, stimulated social gatherings, and comforted many a lonely night.[56]

Alcohol was omnipresent in the workplace. Convinced that intense physical effort could not be sustained "without the aid of spirit," farmers supplied rum to their men in the fields; twice daily, at ten in the morning and three in the afternoon, work would stop for grog and toddy, in a rural version of the modern coffee break. Arduous tasks required ardent spirits, especially during haying season, when everyone labored furiously under the hot sun. The physician Josiah Bartlett, who moved to Concord in 1820, could never get over the shock of seeing "almost every substantial farmer . . . drunk, with all his farm hands, in haying-time and on holidays." Masters doled out drinks to mechanics in their shops. Militia companies paused during drills on the common so that pails of toddy could be brought out to the men. Nobody dared defy these customs. Deacon Jarvis seldom touched liquor himself, but it was always available for his hired hands. "My father would not confine their diet," his son Edward recalled.[57]

Drinking forged bonds across social ranks. In shared moments of conviviality, employers cultivated the loyalty of workers and politicians the support of voters. Winning candidates celebrated victory at the taverns, with free toddy and crackers for all. Traders sealed bargains with a glass of rum, while auctioneers stimulated bids with open decanters. The neighborly spirit was enhanced by drink. A man was considered mean if he did not bring out wine, rum, and brandy when visitors came calling. Even funerals required a libation, with special provisions for pallbearers. In December 1815, twelve-year-old George Washington

Hosmer joined several other boys in carrying the coffin of a little schoolmate to the grave. Before the ceremony, the "young bearers" received the customary hospitality. Gathering at the home of the deceased, they waited in a room reserved in their honor, amply supplied with decanters of spirits, sugar, water, and tumblers. According to Hosmer, no one dared taste a drop. Even so, they got the message: adult responsibilities brought adult rewards. No official drinking age separated boys from men.[58]

Ezra Ripley was no teetotaler. He enjoyed wine and spirits in moderation and furnished them generously to guests. His accounts at local stores attest to his purchases over the years; in one ten-month period, from March to November 1812, he bought four and a half gallons of rum, three and a half of brandy and one of cognac, and one and a half of wine. When he made pastoral calls, he felt obligated to share drinks with his hosts. He took advantage, too, of a special privilege accorded the town minister. Whenever the church celebrated communion, a little wine and bread were usually left over; with Yankee frugality the remnants were turned over to the pastor for his use. The trouble was that Ripley disliked the Malaga wine that was always used and that Deacon Jarvis, who was responsible for the service, was unwilling to change. To accommodate everyone, the conscientious deacon devised an ingenious solution. Every Monday morning one of his sons would go to the store, swap the Malaga for Lisbon, the reverend's favorite wine, and deliver two quarts to the manse. All of these liquid benefits the parson accepted as gifts of Providence for "our comfort, health, and happiness." Used properly, he was convinced, alcohol "preserves health, strength, and activity of the body; it promotes calmness and tranquillity of mind, a happy temperature of the passions and affections; all of which is favourable to calm and correct thinking, to dispassionate and impartial judging, and to pious and virtuous dispositions and conduct."[59]

To satisfy the thirst of townspeople and travelers, Concord supported six stores and four taverns in the mid-1820s, nearly all concentrated in the central village. Under Massachusetts law, taverns were authorized to sell spirits for consumption on the premises, while retailers were restricted to take-away service, but in practice the line between them blurred. Merchants relied on liquor to build business. "New rum," the most popular beverage, was priced as low as possible to attract bargain hunters into a store; whatever was lost on that "leading article" would be made up in broadcloths and bombazetts. Once a purchase was complete, the grateful trader would express thanks by offering his customer a glass of grog, ready for mixing from the tumbler of rum, pitcher of water, and bowl of sugar on the counter. Daniel Shattuck was always glad to do so. "Liberal in his habits of life, given to good living, fond of a social glass," he was said to "always be ready to take a little something, and not always quite little enough for his own good." Selling, shopping, and socializing went together. Though dry goods were the key to commercial success, wet ones contributed importantly to the bottom line.[60]

The several village taverns were rightly known as "public houses," for they hosted a variety of civic events and rivaled the meetinghouse and courthouse as venues for local gatherings. Constables posted notices of upcoming town meetings at both churches and taverns, confident that those who failed to visit the former would surely spend time at the latter. The selectmen and town committees regularly convened at the Middlesex Hotel to conduct official business; Squire Abiel Heywood held court there as a justice of the peace. Public service was unpaid, but it carried a valuable perk: drinks and meals at town expense. Members of town committees took full advantage of the privilege. In the spring of 1826, the reform-minded school committee, chaired by Ripley, launched its campaign for improvement over bottles of wine and gin and mugs of beer. Another appointive body downed bottles of brandy as it considered how to cut the costs of poor relief. Altogether, over the ten months from March 1826 through mid-January 1827, the tab for refreshments run up by local authorities came to almost fifty-two dollars—equivalent to the annual poll taxes collected from the same number of inhabitants. Other groups repaired to the inns for convivial moments after finishing their official duties. Federalists and Jeffersonians, National Republicans and Democrats raised glasses to victory at the polls. The Concord Light Infantry Company, the "crack corps" of the town, made its "headquarters" at Shepherd's Hotel; the Concord Artillery opted for the rival Middlesex. The two competed to make as dazzling an appearance each winter in their respective hosts' ballrooms as they did on the muster field.[61]

The taverns were hubs of community, where diverse inhabitants mingled in the barroom and eavesdropped on travelers passing through, glanced at newspapers from the landlord's subscriptions, and joined in the talk of the town. Each drinking place catered to a distinct clientele, easily identified by manners and station. The Middlesex Hotel, at the crossroads of the village, was the local establishment. Every morning at eleven (except for the Sabbath), workingmen flowed into the cheery barroom on the first floor, its "huge stove" in the center casting "a glow of brightness" on the patrons pausing from their labors to en-joy a pick-me-up. The routine was repeated each afternoon at four. On the sec-ond floor, "the more respectable of the citizens and town officials" did business in a quieter, more secluded atmosphere. Shepherd's Hotel, opened on Main Street in the late 1820s, quickly became a resort of the carriage trade. A regular stop for the stage lines in which its owner had invested, the tavern could afford to discourage teamsters and tipplers from lingering at the bar. Made to feel unwelcome, the "low and rowdy element" took its trade to Bigelow's Tavern a few rods up the road, where anyone could enjoy a few tumblers—or more—without interruption. All night the sounds of drinkers—"their jokes, their sto-ries, their mutual banterings and their loud and merry laugh, and sometimes their quarrels, and rarely a fight"—could be heard from the street, onto which they would eventually tumble. Townspeople stepped lightly, lest they trip over a drunk. Happily, most people could avoid the company of the rough-hewn and the besotted. In a community increasingly split into segments by religion, wealth, and interests, the public houses did their part to differentiate among the inhabitants. Men of color labored in the stables; women might serve food and drink. Neither enjoyed the hospitality of the barroom. The public house was a place of prejudice and an instrument of class distinction.[62]

For all its services to officialdom and its accentuation of social divisions, the alehouse furnished an alternative to the piety and moralism of the churches, the dry lectures on improvement at the lyceum, and the relentless work ethic of the town's energetic entrepreneurs. It was a refuge for those looking to idle their time, rather than to improve it, and to escape the burdens of family in a boisterous, all-male space. Fueled by alcohol, men could release their emotions in curses and jests, mock authority, and perhaps indulge in other vices outside the notice of the magistrates.

With good reason, then, public authorities were wary of liquor dealers, lest they lubricate antisocial behavior with rum and gin. Nobody could sell intox-icating drinks without a license from a county court, and that was granted only to individuals endorsed by the selectmen of the town where they did business. When John Thoreau left Concord to start his store in Chelmsford, he carried with him a recommendation from Ezra Ripley. "I have been long ac-quainted with him," the parson affirmed. "He has sustained a good character, and [I] now view him as a man of integrity, accustomed to store-keeping, and of correct morals." The language was as formulaic as the practice was routine.

Over the decades since the Puritans introduced licensing in the 1680s, the supervision of inn-holders and retailers had grown lax. Justice of the peace Abiel Heywood tried 179 cases between 1798 and 1825; just two involved public drunkenness, and both were dismissed. Nor did Concord's selectmen exercise their authority to bar sales of intoxicating beverages to habitual drunks. That responsibility was left to the discretion of barkeeps, few of whom had the social standing or the local knowledge to do the job well. Like storekeepers and schoolmasters, most were new to town and quick to move on.[63]

Not that anyone in the first decades of the republic was clamoring for strict controls over liquor sales. Concord was thriving as a market center and transportation hub, and local officials had no intention of curbing this trade. Far from it. They often imbibed as much as or more than the common folk they were meant to police. During court week in September, when people from all over Middlesex crowded onto the common to gamble and drink, Deputy Sheriff Abel Moore welcomed colleagues in law enforcement to his sitting room with open decanters of brandy, West India rum, and gin; the company, normally about twenty men, would run through more than three bottles a day, a quart's worth in each. At that rate, the average guest imbibed a daily dose approaching a half-pint. A good many officials must have appeared in court inebriated—or with very bad hangovers. Moore did not need a special occasion to indulge. He was famous for his talent at tricking bartenders into providing free drinks. Once the lawman stopped by Stephen Patch's Main Street tavern with a gift for the landlord: a large tub for use in the tavern yard. The grateful barkeep incautiously asked how he could repay the favor. Waving money aside, the deputy proposed to "take a little something" from the bar from time to time "by way of interest." Patch fell for the trap. Moore drew upon his account often, to the amusement of all; it was said that "wine enough had been drawn on account of that old tub to fill it to the brim." But perhaps the bartender had the last laugh. When Moore came for the final payment of interest, he was served his liquor straight or "doctored so that the Captain took more than he could carry." Unable to make it home on his own, the "short, stout" Moore was unceremoniously "tumbled" into a laundry basket full of soiled linen and delivered to his official residence as Middlesex County jailer.[64]

There was a darker side to the tippling, as Ripley was all too aware. Year after year the parson tracked the ravages of liquor in the lives of his people, as he recorded their deaths in a manuscript notebook. Between 1778, when he assumed the pulpit, and 1828, a half-century later, he documented the passing of 1,333 souls. For many of these losses, he assigned a cause, from cancer and consumption to dysentery and fever, measles and whooping cough, accidents and old age. His diagnoses mixed together physical ailments and symptoms with moral failings, among which the abuse of alcohol stands out. Such deaths were not frequent at first: five or six per decade from the 1780s through the 1810s; as tragic as they were for the unhappy individuals and their grieving families, nobody would have taken alarm. In the 1820s, the toll of ardent spirits mounted; not a year went by without a death from "intemperance." The parson listed forty losses from this cause through 1827, and the numbers keep rising thereafter, peaking at five deaths in 1830 alone. In all, fifty individuals came to untimely ends from excessive drinking. Nearly all were men; just two women shared their miserable fate. Some deaths were blamed on intemperance alone; in others, a medical condition, notably consumption, was made worse by drink, as had happened to Lt. Ephraim Minott, father of the solitary farmer George. Sometimes the cause was said to be an unfortunate accident, but Ripley suspected that drunkenness was the real culprit. In 1814 two parishioners died suddenly on the same street within months of each other, one "crushed by the wheel" of his wagon, the other taking a fall and lying "bruised, bleeding, and cold" on a freezing January night. Shocked by their passing, the pastor ascended the pulpit and spoke the blunt truth. Were not ardent spirits at fault? "It pains my heart to bring these things to view," he told the congregation, "but it ought to be more painful to neglect endeavours to reform and save the living."[65]

Ripley had always been a force for moderation, and in 1814 he inspired the formation of a local auxiliary of the Massachusetts Society for the Suppression of Intemperance (MSSI). That effort was born in the frantic political climate during the War of 1812, when anxious Federalists blamed the political plight of the nation on a host of sins, including "the too free use of ardent spirits, and its kindred vices" of gambling, cursing, and Sabbath breaking. Ripley rallied his people to "discountenance and prevent . . . by [their] own example and influence, every kind of vice and immorality." Altogether, 126 men, roughly 40 percent of male property holders, answered the call by pledging to remove alcohol from elections, militia musters, and funerals, but not from the farm or shop. "Great reformations are to be expected only by slow degrees," Ripley counseled. Drinking in private life remained respectable, so long as it was not carried to excess. Every person was free to set his own standard of moderation.[66]

Flexibility compromised the moral crusade. The group could not muster a quorum for its second annual meeting; the final entry in its record book was inscribed in January 1817. Nine years later Ripley was plaintively regretting the absence: "Where is [the MSSI auxiliary] now? It has fallen into neglect."[67]

Despite that torpor, a deep change in drinking practices set in. In 1827 the Fiske brothers, new storekeepers in the village, tried the experiment of eliminating West Indian rum from their stock in trade and concentrating exclusively on the sale of dry goods; little more than a year later they held a going-out-of-business sale. That failure did not dissuade Moses Davis from a similar course; in May 1829 he thanked the public for its patronage, "notwithstanding our discontinuance of the sale of distilled liquors." His brother Charles successfully followed suit. Even retailers still carrying ardent spirits stopped promoting their sale. Advertisements dried up in the press; in September 1832 the *Gazette* reported running just six such notices over the previous five years and a mere three over the last two. The "good sense" of local merchants won the editors' praise. Meanwhile the Middlesex Mutual Fire Insurance Company announced that it would no longer underwrite policies for "any person who is habitually intemperate." So many farmers decided to withhold rum during haying season that the society of husbandmen and manufacturers considered awarding a premium to the man "who shall manage his farm best without the use of ardent spirits." The proposal was discussed at length but rejected, for fear that it would be hard to recruit or retain laborers without the customary rations.[68]

These decisions signaled a wider shift in popular demand. In 1834, as the reaction against rum was gaining momentum, the two reform-minded physicians, Bartlett and Jarvis, set out to gauge the change. At the doctors' request, the proprietors of local stores and taverns looked over their account books for 1828 and 1833 and calculated how much spirits and wine of different kinds they had sold in those two years. The survey was a pioneering work of social statistics. It showed that in 1828 five stores and three public houses sold well over eleven thousand gallons of distilled spirits and took in $6,760; six years later four stores sold hard liquor in competition with the three taverns, but sales slumped to 7,850 gallons and earnings to $4,608. That was a decline of over 30 percent. On a per capita basis, Jarvis calculated, consumption of ardent spirits was 5.4 gallons in 1828; in 1833, it was 3.5. Years later Jarvis looked back over these numbers and reflected on the social revolution they disclosed. It was "a moral and intellectual epidemic—one of those silent, unrecognized changes in public opinion that creep over a community, [when citizens] occasionally find their views of things, and the motives of action which had governed them, giving way and other [views and motives] taking their places."[69]

The turn away from ardent spirits owed nothing to the government nor to any voluntary association. It began while the MSSI was moribund, and it was rapidly growing in the fall of 1829, when an agent of the newly formed American Temperance Society (ATS) arrived with a call for total abstinence from distilled spirits. Though they agreed with the goal, the sober citizens of Concord declined to join the crusade. The problem lay less with the message than with the messenger. The ATS agent was Rev. Justin Edwards, an orthodox Congregationalist who belonged to the inner circle of evangelical conservatives who were at war with the liberal Protestants of the Bay State. These were the very troublemakers who had meddled in local affairs to provoke the Trinitarian split, and they conducted the assault on demon rum in the same uncompromising spirit they had displayed toward the Unitarian enemy. "It is not quite certain," the skeptical *Gazette* opined, "that the preaching of lectures, and spinning long yarns about the odious vice of drunkenness," were the best ways to win people over. Edwards did instigate the formation of a temperance society in the Trinitarian parish, but the group vanished from view the moment it was announced. By 1830 the ATS claimed over two hundred affiliates in the Commonwealth. Concord was not among them.[70]

How, then, did popular opinion about drinking change? The press was the principal agent of reform, supplemented occasionally by the lyceum. Under a succession of printers and titles, the *Gazette* regularly opened its pages to animadversions on ardent spirits. The arguments rehearsed the same themes over and over. Intemperance injured health, shattered families, sapped industry, and burdened communities with poverty and crime. The challenge was to formulate the most persuasive statement of the case. Some contributors entered the debate as self-styled economists, calculating the money wasted on rum and estimating the labor lost to liquor on and off the job. Others calculated the costs of poor relief borne by the taxpayers. These claims were abstract and impersonal, appealing primarily to rational self-interest. They lacked emotional force and did nothing to demonstrate the imperative of total abstinence.[71]

Far more compelling were the fictional sketches and mini-narratives that put human faces on intemperance. Drinkers in every social station were subject to caricature and condemnation: striving farmers flush with prosperity and then with rum; heedless heirs growing up in comfort and without self-discipline, ultimately succumbing to early death, while their youthful companions from laboring families rose to eminence through "industry, frugality, and temperance"; a smug landowner in Maryland shamed into sobriety upon witnessing two boys of color imitate his "staggering reeling, hiccupping, [and] tumbling," to the amusement of the domestic servants; an Irish immigrant mother lying drunk in the street with her beautiful two-year-old son in tow, yet refusing to give the boy up to a generous gentleman's care. "No! by faith and St. Patrick," she exclaimed in a thick brogue, "my fortune is not at so low an ebb as to force me to abandon my child to the hands of a stranger." It was; she died; the orphan ended up in the man's home. The numerous tales of intemperance portrayed a mobile, segmented society much like Concord itself, made still more fluid and insecure by gin and rum. One step off the straight and narrow could plunge an incautious young man or woman on a downward spiral to an ignominious end.[72]

The most ingenious arguments against the use of ardent spirits were made by the very medical authorities who had once freely prescribed brandy as a medicine to aid digestion, quicken blood flow, supply energy, and relieve such ailments as headaches, gout, and bad breath. It was also commonly believed that spirits distilled from grain were nutritious. And so, having spread these misconceptions, it fell to the selfsame experts to dispel them and to make the case for total abstinence. Concord's physicians played a prominent part in this campaign, none more so than Josiah Bartlett. A native of Charlestown and Harvard graduate (Class of 1814), he opened his practice in Concord on New Year's Day 1823, at twenty-three, and he kept at it for some fifty-seven years, almost to the day of his death. A man of firm principles, "absolute honesty," and indomitable energy, the doctor would be treasured in old age as "the true type of the New England country physician." In his prime he braved controversy in the temperance cause.[73]

Working closely with his junior colleague Jarvis and with a new physician catering to Trinitarian patients, Bartlett took to the press in the winter of 1834 with a five-part series setting forth in painstaking detail the immense harm done to body and mind by "the evils of intemperance." Submitted over the pseudonym "X.Y.Z.," the pieces eschewed moral and religious arguments and invoked the authority of science in their stead. Appealing to "reason, and interest, and justice, to the feelings of every man," the author expounded on the physiological and psychological consequences of alcohol use. The case rested on a simple proposition: distilled spirits were a poison—"a vegetable poison"—as deadly as arsenic, as devastating as opium. Potentially therapeutic in very small doses and when diluted with water, hard liquor could not be digested, and so it supplied nothing in the way of nutrition. An unnatural substance, it traveled through the human frame as an alien invader wreaking havoc on whatever it touched. "There is scarcely a disease either of mind or body which is not either produced or aggravated by the habitual use of Ardent Spirit." As for the supposed stimulus—the surge of energy, the lifting of spirits injected by a shot of whiskey or a dram of rum—that was an illusory gain. The tonic inevitably proved toxic, as the craving for alcohol unsettled the mind. With his judgment impaired, the drinker acted erratically, at one moment "hasty and rash," at another "negligent and irresolute." He "lost the government of himself."

The science of "X.Y.Z." purported to derive from observation and experience, but as the author recounted the consequences of intemperance, the lessons began to sound familiar. No one trusted the drunkard in business; his family despaired. Once the "habit of intoxication" was fixed, the passions took over, sacrificing every semblance of humanity—"intellect," "conscience," and "heart"—every consideration of self-interest, every loyalty to kin, every tie to community. Reduced to a brute, the inebriate ended up a social isolate, utterly cut off from his fellow beings. "His heart feels no friendship, no human sympathy, no love to wife or children, to its own self." Ardent spirits not only poisoned the individual who became its slave; they also sapped the life of the community in which he was once enmeshed. The drunkard represented the ultimate outcast. His disorder was characteristic of a society where people withdrew from their neighbors and did more and more things on their own, including drinking themselves to death.[74]

The medical case against ardent spirits joined its supposed empirical knowledge to the inescapable ethic of interdependence. To refrain from rum was to be a good neighbor. In this spirit, townspeople finally overcame sectarian differences and enlisted in a county temperance society, inaugurated in March 1832 with Samuel Hoar at its head. Eighteen months later Doctor Ripley took the helm of the Concord Temperance Society. The group welcomed everyone, liberal and orthodox, men and women alike, who shared its goals; the only requirement for admission was to subscribe to the constitution and thereby "express [oneself] in favour of entire abstinence from ardent spirits as a drink."[75]

That move brought female influence to bear on the cause. For who was injured more by the "curse" of strong drink than the unhappy wives and mothers struggling desperately to feed and clothe innocent babes while husbands ignored farm and shop for the barroom and poured their last few dollars down their throats? Let women join the crusade for total abstinence, and entire families would be redeemed. The inclusion of women as fellow (if not equal) participants in a public movement for social reform was a striking departure from past practice. It affirmed the significance of every individual in the community, whatever her gender, and it asked her to make a public choice on an issue of immense importance to all. From the expansive effort to line up commitments to the temperance cause would come crucial lessons in grassroots mobilizing.

Temperance drew a new line of distinction in the town, gathering the abstainers from ardent spirits and separating them as moral exemplars from everyone else. The new faith in sobriety won adherents from all denominations. The campaign did not merely seek out individuals to endorse the cause; it put considerable pressure on them to conform. Who dared to decline an invitation to subscribe? To refuse was to court a reputation as a potential drunkard. Some men, well known for their sobriety, would not be intimidated. William Munroe drank neither brandy nor rum, shunned the company of those who did, and starting in 1835, would not hire any man expecting toddy at noon. Rather than sign a temperance pledge, he counted on the power of personal example: he would be "a law unto himself." Ripley appreciated his objections. "Men are not willing to be driven like children, and to be accused as intemperate," he conceded in a temperance society report, "because they see no need of signing a pledge that they will never taste a drop of spirit nor keep it in their house." Even so, the campaign moved steadily forward. As the officers of the temperance society carried subscription papers door to door, one after another resident fell in line. Within four months of its founding, the group claimed 389 adherents; after a year in operation, it counted 550, roughly a quarter of all Concordians and one out of every two adults. Six out of ten were women, in a pattern not unlike church membership.[76]

The temperance movement drew on the same progressive spirit that energized the lyceum. Where one expanded the mind by adding to its stock of knowledge, the other penetrated more deeply within the self in a bid to control appetites and passions and purify morals. Temperance was the ultimate *internal* improvement. But its advocates formed an uneasy coalition. Evangelicals kept raising the bar of acceptable conduct and imposing it on others. In December 1833 the Trinitarian Church added another stringent requirement for admission; new communicants had to pledge themselves to lives of total abstinence from ardent spirits. By contrast, the Unitarian congregation merely asked its members to "seriously endeavor . . . by all reasonable measures" to end the use of distilled liquor as "a common drink." Controversy intensified after the most ardent reformers pushed to extend the list of banned beverages: were not wine, beer, and hard cider intoxicating? Ripley's earnest assistant, Hersey B. Goodwin, had to admit the force of this claim: "How can I ask the poor man to give up his cheaper stimulant while I use the more costly and desirable one?" The liberal minister immediately joined Dr. Bartlett in repudiating all intoxicating drinks.[77]

But many in town saw nothing wrong with moderate consumption of any sort, especially wine, and others resisted the demand to commit the temperance society to an all-inclusive ban.[78] The debate roiled the meetings of reformers. One critical observer condemned the movement's own intemperance. It was bad enough that the activists slandered innocent individuals as drunkards for declining to embrace total abstinence or condemned the honest retailer as "a thief and murderer" for continuing to sell liquor at his store. Such violent rhetoric not only turned off potential supporters; it was also destructive of community. The inevitable tendency was "to unsettle society, to break up social and friendly intercourse; make men displeased with each other when they meet." In their demands for conformity and their intolerance of dissent, the reformers were poisoning the town with a spirit far more deadly than brandy or rum. Partisans of all stripes could invoke the ideal of interdependence to support their cause.[79]

No wonder, then, that the growth of the movement stalled. At the end of 1834, the town ranked a little above average in its support for temperance. Twenty-seven percent of its 2,017 inhabitants (as of 1830) belonged to the society—a far cry from such towns as Framingham and East Sudbury (a little over half) but about the same as neighboring Lincoln and Carlisle. The Middlesex County average was just over 25 percent. Dissenters from pledges of total abstinence stood for a large contingent of the county population, perhaps even a silent majority. Meanwhile Concord's stores and taverns continued to sell drinks to locals and strangers alike, though in diminishing quantities of brandy and rum. Voluntary actions and moral suasion remained the norm.[80]

BY THE MIDDLE OF THE 1830S, CONCORDIANS WERE ASSOCIATING WITH ONE another in new ways. Since 1826 they had no longer been going to Sunday meeting all together; with disestablishment, they fanned out to a variety of churches or none at all. Children no longer all suffered indifferent instruction from a peripatetic crew of ill-trained teachers at common schools; private academies beckoned to the sons and daughters of privileged homes. Public houses were losing hold as gathering places for gentlemen and workingmen to mingle in the barroom. In growing numbers, respectable residents shied away from drinking establishments out of principle, for fear of tainting their reputations or to avoid unpleasant company. Social relations grew more fluid and fleeting. On the farm, cooperative activities diminished: fewer neighbors "changed works"; husking bees, notorious for carousing and courting, faded into nostalgic memories; and many employers were loath to share drinks with laborers who would be gone the next season. Customers haggled less frequently with storekeepers, who offered fewer "treats" in gratitude for purchases and preferred to charge fixed cash prices, based on the impersonal mechanisms of supply and demand. As the inhabitants drew apart into separate enclaves of occupation and class, their ties with one another became more contained, more formal, and thinner.

Community was not so much declining as shifting forms. Less bound to inherited institutions and involuntary associations, the townspeople put a fresh premium on free choice and extended their connections beyond the town—and with good reason, since so few would live there all their lives. In the books and newspapers they read, the lectures they heard, the debates they conducted, the school curricula they approved, and the organizational affiliations they formed, the men and women of Concord integrated themselves ever more deeply into the wider world. The temperance movement introduced a dynamic mode of association. Town, county, state, and national units were tightly bound together on the platform of total abstinence from ardent spirits. The Concord Temperance Society was founded on a common conviction and a shared code of conduct, in which it labored to enlist everyone in town. Its statement of purpose was modeled on that of the county association, which conformed, in turn, to the policies of the parent society of the state. If the arena was local, the agenda was not. Armed with publications and petitions produced by a well-organized apparatus, temperance supporters in Concord would soon be coordinating with activists elsewhere to push uniform policies on the Commonwealth. Social reform fostered cosmopolitan outlooks at the same time as it made for more standardized lives.[81]

The terms in which people thought about themselves, their communities, and the republic were changing slowly. Concordians were behaving differently, seeming strangers even in a small town, pulling apart in everyday affairs while expecting adherence to familiar norms. When conflict erupted, as it inevitably would in a world of so much change, neighbors could suddenly turn against one another with a fury abetted by all the internal improvements they had wrought in their lives.

Privilege and Conspiracy

John Thoreau was not much of a joiner, and when he did participate in civic life, he was typically a follower, not a leader. He belonged to the agricultural society, paid dues to the lyceum, and enlisted in the volunteer fire company. But he was content to let others run the show; the only office he ever held was secretary of the Concord Fire Society, keeping a neat record of the group's proceedings for two years. Nor was the pencil maker ever called to public duty. He was never chosen for local office, and not once in his long residence in Concord was he asked to serve on an ad hoc committee of the town. Despite the success of his business, no one welcomed him into the economic or political elite.[1]

That was apparently his preference. Though he regularly went to town meeting and cast his ballot at the polls, Thoreau had no desire for power, and he steered clear of the quarrels that rocked the village in the 1820s and 1830s. Perhaps he was too busy making pencils to get involved, or perhaps he was more inclined to spend his leisure time with his family. Even so, he attended closely to the bustling life in the town center, and by his death in February 1859, according to his writer son, "he remembered more about the worthies (and unworthies) of Concord village" than anyone around. It was one thing to be a sympathetic bystander, quite another to take public stands. John Thoreau was no model of civic leadership for the rising generation at home.[2]

There was not much call for his political involvement during the 1820s. With the end to electoral contests between Federalists and Republicans, Concord entered an era of political consensus. The town gave nearly unanimous support to John Quincy Adams in his two runs for the presidency, and it paid no heed to Andrew Jackson. With equal devotion, the voters backed the Friends of the National Administration—Edward Everett in Congress, Levi Lincoln in the governorship—and like-minded candidates for the General Court. No longer a swing district, Concord became virtually a one-party regime from 1824 to 1832.[3]

During these years of National Republican ascendancy, local leaders closed ranks behind "the American system," a program of public support for private economic development. Under this plan, state and federal governments would charter corporations, protect domestic industry with tariffs, expand credit and regulate currency through a well-organized system of banks, and ease the flow of goods to market through aid for the construction of highways, canals, and railroads. Here was a scheme that Concord's ambitious entrepreneurs—the merchants and craftsmen of the village, the cotton manufacturers along the Assabet, the progressive farmers all over town—could get behind, almost to a man. Pencil maker Thoreau shared in the enthusiasm, and when the National Republicans rebranded themselves Whigs, he cheered for their standard-bearers Henry Clay and Daniel Webster, booed Jackson and Martin Van Buren, and passed these sentiments along to his sons.[4]

Even so, social tensions simmered beneath the facade of unity. The changing economy eroded familiar bonds of interdependence. Farmers turned away from cooperative practices; merchants pressed for cash payment; manufacturers jettisoned older structures of employment. An expanding army of transients passed through town. The premium was now on innovation in the pursuit of self-interest. In the spirit of improvement, neighbors withdrew from inherited institutions and involuntary associations and sought common cause with fellows sharing their ideas or interests. The new organizations made for a more diverse community but also a more segmented one, with townspeople divided into enclaves of family and neighborhood, occupation and class, faction and sect, custom and reform.

This voluntary social order was itself a breeding ground of conflict. For not all groups were alike. Some—the lyceum, the social library, the Society of Middlesex Husbandmen and Manufacturers—were open to all who endorsed their purposes and paid the membership fees. Others were closed companies into whose ranks admission was tightly restricted. And where temperance and other reformers conducted their affairs in public according to well-defined rules, two influential groups operated behind closed doors and revealed little to outsiders. The Social Circle, a self-selecting club of the local elite, and the

Corinthian Lodge of Freemasons, a secretive branch of a fraternal hierarchy run by higher officials, with counterparts in every state and overseas, were particular sources of unease. Did these bodies serve the public good or just the selfish interests of members? Were they consistent with a republic based on equal rights and the rule of law? John Thoreau, a member of neither, could no more avoid these questions than any of his neighbors.

Such issues grew urgent by the late 1820s, and as they burst into the open, they disrupted the political scene. The National Republicans hoped to guide the economy, like the society, on a well-ordered course of gradual progress. But many chafed at the restrictions that program imposed, from close supervision of the money supply by the Second Bank of the United States to protection of corporate privileges by the government of Massachusetts. The rise of Andrew Jackson's Democratic Party was fueled, in part, by resentment of a paternalistic state. It gained little support in Concord. There the National Republican coalition was fractured by a fight over a bridge that rocked state and county politics for years and eventually went all the way to the U.S. Supreme Court in a landmark ruling.

Under these growing strains over economic issues, the National Republican coalition confronted a crisis in the social order: an insurgency from a rising Anti-Masonic movement over the supposed threat to the republic posed by the secretive Masonic fraternity. The ensuing fight was a watershed in civic life. It shattered older habits of deference to established leaders. It inaugurated a new populist style in politics. It established fresh ground rules for a liberal social order. And it proved a crucible of Jacksonian Democracy.

DURING THE NATIONAL REPUBLICAN ERA, CONCORD, A TOWN OF JUST TWO thousand people and 320 families, played an outsize role in Massachusetts politics.[5] That was partly owing to its strategic place in the civic landscape. As a Middlesex County seat, the town was integral to the conduct of government in the Commonwealth. The courthouse on the common hosted regular sessions of the civil and criminal courts; here also county officials convened twice a year to lay out highways and bridges, license taverns and inns, and handle other matters, for which they levied taxes on the forty-plus towns under their jurisdiction.[6] County treasurer Keyes oversaw the finances at his courthouse office, next door to his home. With so many public servants and lawyers congregating in the village, it is not surprising that Concord developed into a political beehive, to which the ambitious gravitated to win notice, obtain patronage, form alliances, and build followings in pursuit of higher office. Fittingly, the town became a hub of communications: it was the invariable venue of political conventions, which were held at the Middlesex Hotel, and the home of the principal county-wide newspaper, issued under various titles as the *Gazette* by a changing cast of printer-editors and with little competition until the mid-1830s. Located at the geographic heart of the county, with a vibrant commercial center, Concord—the eighth most populous town in Middlesex—furnished a strong base for someone to build a political career.[7]

Local politicians put these advantages to good use. A Concord clique rose to power in Middlesex with the Jeffersonian Republicans, and under the leadership of John Keyes, it remained in control after the amalgamation of parties in 1824. From his office as county treasurer—a sinecure to which he was elected year after year, from 1814 to 1837—Keyes laid the foundations for statewide power. He earned two terms as Concord's representative to the legislature, then won a place among the Middlesex members of the state senate, served six successive terms, and became a leading candidate for president of the upper house. Ambitious townsmen aspired to join him on Beacon Hill, and between 1823 and 1835, they almost always succeeded. On several occasions, two townsmen vied for seats in the five-man county delegation, and in 1825 both prevailed. These "honorable" gentlemen were the erstwhile rivals and near neighbors Keyes and Hoar, who represented the two wings of the National Republican coalition in its years of ascendancy, and in their official roles had a significant impact on government in state and nation.[8]

These ambassadors to the wider world ranked among Concord's wealthiest, best-educated, most cosmopolitan men. As lawyers, Hoar and Keyes advised and advocated for the textile manufacturers driving the industrial revolution, and as investors, they were stockholders and directors of the enterprises transforming the village. They also took prominent roles in promoting social and cultural reform. And when neither man was in the legislature, other key figures in these projects—notably, the lawyer Nathan Brooks and the merchants Burr and Shattuck—took their places on Beacon Hill as representatives of the town or spokesmen for the county. All had long experience in the metropolis, trading goods to and from Boston or riding circuit with the courts.[9]

Commitment to improvement inspired affinity with the National Republican agenda. The Federalist Hoar and the Republican Keyes buried their former antagonism in support of economic policies beneficial to their town and state. Neither statesman had any doubts about the constitutionality or the wisdom of protective tariffs to promote manufacturing, and when Southern planters demanded repeal of the so-called Tariff of Abominations, with South Carolina threatening nullification of federal law, Concord's leaders rallied in its defense. Hoar was one of sixty-three Massachusetts delegates to a September 1831 gathering of "the Friends of Domestic Industry" in New York City, and on his return, he helped to instigate grassroots support for protectionism. In June 1832 a convention of "Farmers, Manufacturers, Mechanics, and others, interested in the Protection of American Industry" assembled in Concord to make that case. Its report, drafted by a committee including Keyes, laid out an economic philosophy that won enthusiasm from small-scale businessmen like John Thoreau.

The convention forcefully challenged the notion, put forward by free traders, that the "protective system" constituted a government handout to special interests at the expense of working people and consequently was "oppressive, unequal, and unjust"—nothing less than "a tyranny the most odious." Not so, insisted the delegates at the Middlesex Hotel, who were said to include "many of the [county's] most upright, intelligent, and patriotic citizens." Far from favoring one class over others, tariffs benefited all. Under their aegis, textile mills expanded, the economy diversified, incomes rose, and individuals "of every class" gained from "the increasing confidence and facility in doing business." The good times were evident everywhere: "in the thrift of the farmer, the success of the dry goods dealer, grocer, baker, tailor, shoemaker, hatter, and other tradesmen which have clustered around our manufactories, till their vicinity has slowly risen into villages and great towns." Young men were no longer forced to depart their ancestral homes to seek opportunity "in the unreclaimed forests of the West"; they could now remain to "cultivate our fields or enliven our villages by their activity and enterprise." From Middlesex, "the largest manufacturing county" in the country, the products of all this labor went forth to shower "blessings" on the Commonwealth, on New England, on the entire republic. Who could doubt that this was truly "the American system"?[10]

The vision of an integrated economy, joining all sections and classes together in a scheme of mutual betterment, rested on familiar ideas. It was the outlook of the Society of Middlesex Husbandmen and Manufacturers writ large. Agriculture, commerce, and manufactures, in this view, marched forward together.

Economic growth strengthened the bonds of interdependence. For material gain was not an end in itself. It served higher purposes: the progress of communities and the cultivation of individual character. According to the Concord convention, textile manufacturing aided education by supporting schools; it supplemented lyceums by "diffusing sound knowledge." It inspired "a spirit of industry, frugality, and economy"; it nurtured "a love of order, and self-respect among all classes." Unlike the "dark Satanic mills" of Great Britain, with their degraded workers, the manufactories of Middlesex took a sound society and made it even better. The "American system" was ultimately a plan for internal improvement in all aspects of life.[11]

Beneath the rhetoric of unity lay a fierce resolve. When the state of South Carolina "nullified" the tariff of 1832, the descendants of Minutemen were prompt to react. To their minds, the opponents of protective tariffs were threatening the people of Middlesex with ruin. Trusting in the promises of the federal government, enterprising citizens had built up "the agricultural, commercial and manufacturing interests" not just of the county and the Commonwealth but of "the whole country." To rescind that pledge of support and repeal import duties now was a profound betrayal of "the faith of the People." It portended a "war of extermination" by Southern extremists against their Northern countrymen. To that threat the Concord convention issued a cry of defiance. If South Carolina or any other state was so antagonistic to national policy as to contemplate secession from the Union, then these Massachusetts Yankees were prepared to let them go. Secession was preferable to "the sacrifice of the principle of the protective system." But the delegates hoped the conflict would not come to that unhappy end. Better to defend their interests "by all constitutional means" and "with untiring zeal and unshrinking boldness."[12]

For all the divisions it sowed in the republic at large, the National Republican program elicited broad agreement in Concord. Year after year the party prevailed in elections that were foregone conclusions; as late as November 1832, with Andrew Jackson on the ballot for a second term as president, local Democrats could muster no more than thirty-five votes for the incumbent (18 percent). Then again, with so little competition, many citizens stayed home on Election Day. The era of good feelings was the age of little voting. In 1821 Massachusetts eliminated its long-standing property-holding requirement for suffrage and granted the vote to all adult male taxpayers. The change did not spur a rush to the polls. No more than one out of three voters—125 or so men—regularly cast ballots while Adams was in office, and although turnout occasionally approached 50 percent during Jackson's ascendancy, it could not match the fervor of the Federalist-Republican battles during the War of 1812. From 1825 on, Town Clerk Abiel Heywood did not even record the votes for town representative to the state legislature at the annual May election. Why bother?

So pronounced was the general "apathy" and "indifference" that in the spring of 1826, the *Gazette* abandoned the practice of printing detailed, town-by-town results of the state elections: "We presume they would be uninteresting to our readers." The editors correctly gauged the popular mood. Six months later Edward Everett's bid for reelection to Congress attracted little interest. In many Middlesex towns, turnout fell below 20 percent; in Concord, a mere seventy-one men voted, a level of participation that the *Gazette* deemed a dispiriting display of civic irresponsibility. "It is hoped that the people are not becoming inattentive to the things that make for peace," the paper opined. "The right of suffrage is one that ought not to be neglected, and wherever it is for any length of time, there intrigue and corruption will be seen and felt."[13]

Actually, the *Gazette* deserved a share of the blame for the political torpor. Under the management of printers John C. Allen and Herman Atwill (1826–1828) and then of Atwill on his own, the weekly did little to encourage debate over public policy. It played down dissension within Concord and advocated for the pet projects of the local elite. Its columns were filled with editorials and letters urging economic initiatives and cultural improvements. Seldom did critical voices gain space to defend the rustic customs of the past or challenge the schemes of reformers.[14] The same was true of the political coverage; the *Yeoman's Gazette*, as the paper became known in 1826, was essentially a house organ of the National Republicans. It carried the party's cause in election season, announcing meetings, publicizing candidates, and disseminating addresses to the voters. During the 1832 presidential campaign, the paper repeatedly denounced Jackson's veto of the Second Bank of the United States. Absent from its pages were opposing points of view. As an instrument of electioneering, the *Gazette* did not provide a forum for controversy. It addressed the party faithful and ignored those outside the fold.

It was certainly in the editors' interest to follow the party line. The printers were bound by undisclosed ties to Concord's richest man, biggest merchant, and most active speculator in real estate. In 1826 or before, the senior partner

Allen borrowed $300 from Daniel Shattuck, apparently to finance the purchase of a house in the town center, and over the next two years, the debt rose to $500 and Allen fell into arrears. By April 1828, when the merchant did his annual review of assets and liabilities, the outstanding loan demanded attention. "550 J. C. Allen dun," the astute creditor recorded in his memorandum book. A few months later Allen was gone, having sold his interest in the printing office to Atwill and moved north to Vermont. Atwill's note to Allen for that share likely ended up in Shattuck's hands, payable on demand.[15]

Under these circumstances, the prudent course was to align the newspaper with the views of its principal backer. Shattuck kept a close eye on the operation; indeed, for a time he had his own man on the inside, his brother Lemuel, who served behind the scenes as an anonymous "subeditor," selecting copy and penning comments on public affairs while the printers set the type, pulled the press, and ran the shop. Always on the lookout for opportunities "to benefit my fellow beings as well as myself," the onetime schoolmaster quietly worked out a political alliance with Edward Everett, the former Harvard professor who had defeated Concord's favorite son for a seat in Congress. Upon the representative's reelection in November 1826, Shattuck penned a congratulatory note with an assurance that "it is the determination" of the *Gazette*'s proprietors to conduct the newspaper "decidedly in your interest."[16] Both sides benefited from the arrangement. Everett sent his speeches to the *Gazette* soon after their delivery on the House floor; he showered the printers (and the social library) with loads of congressional documents; he even contributed an unsigned weekly letter on "Affairs at Washington," one of which praised "an able report" he himself had presented. The newspaper reciprocated with extravagant praise for his performances ("as great an effort of the human mind, as we have witnessed on the floor of Congress," enthused one observer the *Gazette* quoted) and defended him against criticism from Keyes, still bitter about his loss and sniping from the sidelines. The attachment to Everett continued even after Shattuck departed the subeditor's post; his successor was the lawyer Elisha Fuller, the nemesis of Keyes and occasional challenger for the office of county treasurer. Through the election of 1832, Atwill was solidly in the congressman's camp.[17]

The National Republican coalition was an uneasy amalgam of discordant elements, and the tensions among them occasionally burst to the surface and threatened to dissolve the alliance. That was the case in the mid-1820s, when a campaign for a toll-free bridge into Boston across the Charles River shook up the political scene in Middlesex and adjoining counties and unleashed populist attacks on chartered monopolies and special privilege. The scheme was devised to circumvent the existing crossing between Charlestown and the capital. Constructed in 1785–1786, the Charles River Bridge was the first route to allow travel over the river by carriage, cart, or foot since the founding of Boston in 1630. It was an immediate success, improving access to the Boston market for communities in the vicinity and tightening links between the country and the city. Indeed, it did too well for its own good. The project was undertaken by a private corporation, which received a charter from the Commonwealth and the exclusive right to charge tolls. Awarded to reimburse the company for its construction costs and to provide a fair return on investment, the privilege was originally limited to forty years but was later extended to seventy. Secure in its monopoly, the Charles River Bridge Corporation enjoyed a virtually guaranteed income. The more trade along the route, the greater income from tolls, which remained unchanged long after the original expenses were recouped. Not until the mid-1850s would the bridge become a free public highway.[18]

Many people, especially businessmen in Charlestown, were unwilling to wait. Not only were the tolls a daily irritant to residents going back and forth into the capital; they were also a bottleneck to continuing growth of the area. With no relief in sight, leading merchants came up with an alternative. They would erect a rival thoroughfare a short distance from the existing crossing. This Warren Bridge, as it became known, would have wider access roads, handle more traffic, and most important, eliminate tolls as soon as the start-up costs were recovered and the investors compensated. It would be "free forever," in contrast to the "burdensome, vexatious, and odious" monopoly. This plan finessed the rights of the existing bridge company. That body would continue to enjoy its toll privilege uninterrupted, but with a nearby competitor offering free passage, the franchise would quickly become worthless.[19]

The controversy thus put two National Republican priorities at odds: on the one hand, respect for established property rights; on the other, public support for internal improvements. Could the state legally vacate the charter privileges of the Charles River Bridge Company by authorizing a rival with a better business plan to enter the fray? If so, was it wise to do so? The issues exposed the strains in the ruling party, as advocates of the Warren Bridge raised the banner of free trade and equal rights, while the other side urged respect for law and precedent. At the center of this debate and the ensuing political maneuvering were Concord's two leading men, Hoar and Keyes, both serving in the state senate during the 1825–1826 session, when the bridge issue came to the fore. Once again foils for one another, they articulated positions that reflected both their ideological predispositions and the mixed sentiments of the townsmen they represented, caught between the drive for economic progress and the lingering attachment to inheritance and custom.

In 1825, when a petition for a "free bridge" was submitted to the lawmakers on Beacon Hill, Hoar, now forty-five, was in his first term in the senate. Twice defeated as a Federalist candidate for the office, he finally prevailed on a "Middlesex Union" slate with nominees from the two former parties. Even then he was not the people's choice. In the April 1825 election, he lagged behind his running mates and fell short of the absolute majority required for election. It was thanks to the members of both houses, acting together to fill vacancies, that he was ultimately chosen for the seat.[20]

The new senator was not hobbled by the lack of an electoral mandate. Noted for his legal learning, Hoar assumed the chair of a joint house-senate committee on bridges and took charge of the hearings on the Warren Bridge petition. After a painstaking review of the cases for and against the memorial, the body issued a lengthy report in February 1826 rejecting every argument for the free bridge. Its practical advantages were negligible. It would not shorten the trip from the Charlestown square to the Boston market; it would not improve "communication between the country and the city." It would actually pose "a greater obstruction to navigation of the river" than currently existed. And it was not needed. The existing bridge was sufficient for the current traffic and could, in fact, handle twice as much.

The objections were not simply practical. The Warren Bridge would not serve "the public good," as Hoar saw it. It was true, he acknowledged, that residents of Charlestown would save money through the elimination of tolls. But their gain was the Charles River Bridge Company's loss. The "whole community" would gain "nothing" at all. The new bridge would also inflict harm on the many people and businesses that had sprung up along the existing route since its debut in 1786. The thoroughfare was more than a physical means of crossing the river from one point to another. It was the focus of an entire social and economic environment. Stores and shops, boardinghouses and inns congregated in its vicinity. People adapted their "arrangements for business and pleasure" to its availability. To draw passengers away from this well-established route and attract them to another with the promise of free passage was to "inflict an evil of considerable magnitude." Public policy had encouraged people to invest and settle in the area. By what right did government now undo those decisions? Although the squire served as legal counsel to the textile manufacturers of Lowell, he was no blind enthusiast for progress. His skepticism about economic development offered a rare dissent from the American political mainstream.[21]

Hoar's report laid out a principled defense of vested interests and established institutions. It honored choices made in the past and upheld their claims on the present. It saw economic enterprises not as collections of individuals pursuing personal gain but as social networks linking people in chains of interdependence. It put a premium on continuity. The senator's outlook was consistent and comprehensive. He defended the Charles River Bridge Company on the same premises he had sustained the Standing Order, with its religious taxes and mandatory Sabbath observance, and had championed the rights of ancient parishes against present-day dissenters. In this Yankee brand of conservatism, Squire Hoar resisted the rising economic individualism of the times and erected tollgates against sudden, disruptive change.[22]

Ultimately, the noted attorney put his trust in the law. The corporate charter awarded in 1785, he maintained, was a contract between the Massachusetts General Court and the Charles River Bridge Company, and the government was bound by its terms. To allow a new bridge so close to the old one and to afford the new one an unfair competitive advantage constituted "a breach of good faith." Neither "public convenience" nor "necessity" could justify such an act. The scheme unjustly abridged the rights of "the more ancient owner" and expropriated property without compensation. It thus violated the contract clause of the U.S. Constitution, as set forth by John Marshall's Supreme Court in *Fletcher v. Peck* (1810). This argument affirmed the position of the beleaguered corporation; in much the same terms, Daniel Webster would take it to Washington and present it to the nation's highest tribunal. It was a losing case. In 1837 the Supreme Court ruled in favor of the upstart bridge company and put its imprimatur on new enterprise over old.[23]

Hoar's conscientious brief for the past over the present would be challenged within a decade by the new school of thought with which Concord would eventually be identified. But in 1825 Transcendentalism was not on the horizon. Squire Hoar put a premium on backward glances, and he spoke for a good many of his countrymen. His report stalled the drive for the Warren Bridge; in the next legislature, with the senator gone from the upper chamber, the plan revived and passed both houses, albeit by a single vote in the senate, only to be rejected by Gov. Levi Lincoln in the first exercise of the veto power by a chief magistrate in the history of the Commonwealth. A strong supporter of state aid to internal improvements, Governor Lincoln nonetheless accepted Hoar's reasoning that the proposed law unfairly deprived the Charles River Bridge Company of its property ("the right to toll") and hence violated the state's obligation to honor the contract it had made. After an override vote failed, champions of the free bridge appealed to the voters and won such strong support, especially in Middlesex County, that Lincoln, reelected for a third term and eager to restore consensus, reversed course and endorsed the plan. The Warren Bridge quickly underwent construction and opened on Christmas Day 1828. Its beleaguered rival, bereft of traffic and tolls, turned to the courts in a protracted quest for compensation and justice that would eventuate in a landmark decision in American constitutional history.[24]

Much of Concord—at least its politically active community—applauded Hoar's position. The town declined to join Charlestown's petition for a free bridge. The *Gazette* praised the senator's report as "long and able" and endorsed the governor's veto. "We are in favor of having the avenues to Boston *free*," the paper commented, "but the statements of the Governor against the erection of a new *free* bridge are conclusive in our minds." In the spring 1827 elections, the townsmen resisted the "excitement" sweeping through Middlesex and gave overwhelming support (88 percent) for Lincoln's reelection. A month later they chose two representatives to the state assembly who held firm against the Warren Bridge to the bitter end.[25] But sentiment for a free bridge was strong in this commercial hub, and such entrepreneurs as John Thoreau were eager for cheap access to the Boston market.[26] The political spokesman for their cause was Keyes, who voted as consistently for a free bridge as his Concord colleagues in the legislature went against it. The former Republican presented a powerful counterweight to his ex-Federalist neighbor in the senate.

Keyes was certainly on the popular side in Middlesex County, if not in his hometown. In the election following the bridge report, Hoar was not on the National Republican ticket for senate, and in the next two years (1827 and 1828) he was a candidate on a breakaway slate opposed to the party's official nominees. The dissidents were soundly defeated, even in Concord, while Keyes went from one success to another in an unbroken political ascent.[27] Leader of the Middlesex delegation in the upper chamber, he embodied a more dynamic side of Concord. Unlike Hoar and Ripley, who always seemed to uphold the established order, he served the ambitions of men on the make, eager to profit from the opportunities of the expanding economy—men, that is, very much like himself.[28]

The fight over the Warren Bridge hastened the breakup of the National Republican Party in the Bay State. In this contest, Keyes had allied himself with the antimonopoly faction led by David Henshaw, a nouveau riche businessman turned politician and owner of the Boston *Statesman*. By early 1828, the publisher had switched his support from Adams to Jackson in the upcoming presidential election and turned his newspaper office into headquarters for a new "Republican Jackson" party. Keyes, it was suspected, sympathized with this move. "A favorite with the old republican party," he was wary of the ex-Federalists in the National Republican coalition. In June 1827 he opposed the choice of Daniel Webster for U.S. senator, preferring a lesser-known politician who defected to Jackson the next year. Keyes also was in no hurry to pass legislation favorable to Adams's cause in the Electoral College. To David L. Child, editor of the pro-Adams *Massachusetts Journal* as well as a fierce opponent of the Warren Bridge, the senator from Concord looked to be a closet Jacksonian, nominally committed to the present administration but working against its interests behind the scenes. "He is always between wind and water," the editor charged. "No one can safely depend upon him. He does you all the mischief he can covertly, though if he is compelled to unmask he shows himself a friend." The Harvard-educated lawyer (and husband of writer Lydia Maria Child) determined to expose the hypocrite and destroy his influence.[29]

On March 29, 1828, nine days before the state elections, in which Keyes looked forward to winning another term, the *Massachusetts Journal* published explosive allegations against the "honorable" gentleman. Since 1825 the Concord politician had headed the committee on accounts, a joint body of the house and senate responsible for awarding contracts for printing the state laws and other government documents. The committee was supposed to oversee a competitive bidding process, issuing a public call for sealed proposals by a set date and then selecting the lowest bidder capable of performing the work. Under Keyes's superintendence, the contract went to the printers of Henshaw's *Daily American Statesman*, despite complaints about the actual cost of their work. That choice raised suspicions of political favoritism, but nothing could be proven. Then at the close of the spring 1827 session of the General Court, the chairman showed his hand. With all the members assembled to review the bids, Keyes suggested continuing the existing agreement with the *Statesman* printers so long as their offer came within $500 of the others. This was "no more nor less" than a gift of $500 from the state treasury to *"that reprobated Jackson press,"* exclaimed Child. Then, after the envelopes were opened, the chairman glanced over the proposals and peremptorily concluded that the *Statesman*'s was the lowest. One member objected to this high-handed procedure, and he painstakingly went over the bids to show that the *Statesman*'s price was the highest by far, $1,100 above any other. At this disclosure, the chairman became visibly distraught. It was obvious that he could no longer favor his political friends, yet "his feelings" would not allow him to decide against them. So rather than make a choice, he abruptly rose from his chair and "fairly bolted" the room with a bustle that belied his usual dignified manner.[30]

Although Child had heard about these questionable proceedings soon after they occurred, he waited nine months to air his charges, until they could inflict the most political damage. Here, at long last, was proof to out Keyes as a Jacksonian! The candidate would be hard-pressed to rebut the allegations before voters went to the polls. The exposé went beyond an electoral tactic. In his exaggerated tone of outrage over the committee chairman's readiness to set aside agreed-upon procedures and give away public money to partisan allies, the editor insinuated something far more damaging: Keyes was not merely inconsistent or insincere; he was corrupt. He was guilty of the very abuses of power he claimed so vociferously to oppose: working secretly to subvert the rules of equal competition and dispense special privileges to his political friends.

In the face of this "unjust attack" on his character, Keyes hurried into Boston and made his way directly to the *Massachusetts Journal* office. There, "a little in a passion," he confronted the editor, denounced the "obnoxious piece" as utterly false, and demanded an immediate retraction. The censure of his political conduct, Keyes emphasized, was not his concern. Nor was he worried about the imminent election. But the accusations of impropriety could not go unchallenged: "My reputation was at stake."[31]

After an angry exchange of words, the meeting ended with an empty promise by Child to look into the matter and correct any errors. He never did, despite his antagonist's parting threat to take legal action should no retraction be forthcoming. "I will make sure you are put on trial before a jury in Middle-sex County, where I am known," the outraged politician warned, "and where I hope to make you better known."[32]

To clear his reputation, Keyes called on committee colleagues and solicited public statements on his behalf. Within Concord, his friends—Shattuck, Prich-ard, and Brooks—got up handbills defending his character. The *Gazette* opened its columns to his cause, though it also gave space to critics. Unfortunately, this public relations campaign provoked Keyes's opponents into broadening their attack and targeting his steady accumulation of offices and fees. One lo-cal critic likened the National Republican magistrate to an Old World tyrant, "clinging to the offices and distinction of ruling the People as [his] undoubted and *perpetual* right." Who would challenge this "caucus-created Despot"? asked "an elector of Middlesex." "What individual is bold enough to do that which all desire—approach the tyrant in his sable and secret hall, and though sur-rounded by his sycophants and dependants [*sic*], boldly push him from this throne"?[33]

Keyes needn't have worried. The regular Republican nominees easily won the county over a ticket of Adams men. The four incumbent senators earned another year in the statehouse. Keyes could take satisfaction in the result. In Concord, his total vote actually increased from 106 the previous year to 131. The senator prevailed with 65 percent of the ballots at home. Within the county as a whole, the last-minute charges in the *Massachusetts Journal* put a dent in his overall popularity, as he fell from first to fourth on the winning list. Keyes thus remained securely on the throne, but he had good reason to keep a watchful eye over town meetings and county conventions for potential claimants to his crown.[34]

The victorious candidate craved more than vindication at the polls. True to his word, on the day after the election, before the results were known, Keyes acted on his threat to Child. With the Massachusetts Supreme Court in Con-cord for its regular April term, he approached the state prosecutor and laid out his complaints against the reckless editor. The case was promptly presented to the grand jury and an indictment just as speedily returned. Child was to be prosecuted for the crime of publishing "a false, scandalous, and malicious libel." He would get his chance to "become acquainted with the good citizens of Middlesex."[35]

This resort to the law to punish an outspoken critic was not unique to

Keyes. Civil suits and criminal prosecutions for libel had not disappeared from American courts following the repeal of the notorious Sedition Act of 1798. In the states, authorities continued to prosecute individuals for publishing offensive statements, and they did so with greater latitude than the lamented federal law had allowed. As political competition quickened in the late 1820s, a new tide of prosecutions was rising in the courts. The editor of the *Massachusetts Journal* was a defendant so often that he acquired the nickname "David *Libel* Child." His prosecutor in the Keyes affair, Massachusetts solicitor general Daniel Davis, deemed legal action imperative to curb rampant abuse of the press. "If I were a candidate for popular election," he declared, "I should expect to have my character ripped and torn all to pieces by lawless writers for the popular press." Determined to protect themselves against journalistic assault, Massachusetts legislators enacted a new libel law in March 1827. It followed the standard of the day: truth was not enough to excuse a libel; the accused had to show he was acting sincerely for the public good. Among those voting for the bill was Middlesex senator Keyes.[36]

The trial of David Child in January 1829 was a gripping political spectacle. Conducted over two days in a Cambridge courthouse "thronged with spectators," it put many of the state's leaders under the intense spotlight of a criminal proceeding. The presiding judge was Massachusetts Supreme Court justice Marcus Morton, a Jacksonian Democrat who had shown the flag for his emerging party as a nominee for governor in the same election roiled by Child's attacks on Keyes. Solicitor General Davis conducted the prosecution, assisted by the complainant Keyes; Child's defense was presented by two members of the Boston bar. A parade of witnesses from the state's governing class took the stand, including five current and two former senators and four representatives, plus Keyes himself. The secretary of the Commonwealth testified, along with clerks for various government offices. The atmosphere was electric with excitement. "During the most important parts of the testimony," the Concord *Gazette* reported, "almost a breathless silence pervaded the house, and everyone present seemed to consider his own political rights and privileges at issue."[37]

The trial itself was straightforward. Child readily admitted to composing and publishing the alleged libel. Under the law, his actions were justifiable if the article in question was true and had been put into circulation out of a sincere concern for the public good. Those were difficult claims to sustain. Child had gotten critical details wrong. Witnesses disagreed, and their testimony was suspect because of personal ties to Child or Keyes.[38] So the jury was instructed to rest its judgment less on the truth of the editor's allegations than on his motives for making them. Did the defendant confine himself to what he was told? Did he give "any authority for the information"? Did he attempt to investigate the truth before going to press? Did his other publications suggest "malicious intent"? The jury had no trouble answering those questions. It soon returned a guilty verdict, and Morton sentenced the unapologetic editor to six months in the state prison at Charlestown. Keyes had secured his vindication.[39]

The case had significance beyond the conduct of Child and reputation of Keyes. The trial exposed the inner workings of the state legislature in unparalleled detail. From the testimony of current and past members of the committee of accounts, it became evident that top officials on Beacon Hill conducted the state's business in a casual manner ripe for abuse. Important decisions were being made outside public view. Keyes ran his committee informally, with private conversations leading to tacit understandings that never came up for critical scrutiny or open debate. Rules and procedures were adapted for the convenience of favorites; when the *Statesman*'s printers missed the deadline for submitting a written bid, they were allowed to enter the committee room and request that their previous year's proposal be considered. No transcript of discussions was kept, so with conflicting memories, it was impossible to determine who had said what and when. No formal votes were taken or recorded. As chairman, Keyes preferred to operate by consensus, and the members usually deferred to his judgment. He thrived in the backrooms, where leaders could negotiate agreements without the glare of public scrutiny. This style of elite management was losing credibility in the rising democratic age. To many citizens, the libel trial exposed an appalling truth: an elite of self-serving officials had rigged the government to benefit themselves. Equal opportunity—the chance to obtain a government contract on the basis of merit—was losing out once again to special privilege.[40]

Despite the verdict, Child prevailed in the court of public opinion. An enterprising court reporter took down the proceedings of the trial and gathered them into a volume whose publishers, ironically, took the state printing contract away from the *Statesman*. The trial record was widely reviewed. Newspapers from Maine to Manhattan hailed Child as "a faithful sentinel upon the walls of the Republic," fearlessly exposing "foul corruptions" and "petty thefts" by dishonest politicians. In publishing what he believed to be the truth,

he "behaved as an Editor should behave." How else could government officials be held accountable to the citizenry? The prosecution and conviction of
the uncompromising journalist crystallized opinion in favor of more liberal
libel laws, so that editors could do their jobs "fearlessly and promptly . . . Who
needs the protection of the law, so much as the *honest* editor? If *he* is afraid,
who will have the courage to speak out?" By contrast, Keyes was regarded with
contempt. As chairman of the committee on accounts, he had shown "gross
negligence" and wasted the taxpayers' money in pursuit of his own ambitions.
But he could no longer conceal this betrayal of the public trust.[41]

Even the hometown weekly turned against Keyes. The *Gazette*, of which
twenty-four-year-old Atwill had become sole proprietor in June 1828, initially
proceeded cautiously and tracked the progress of the libel case without editorial comment. After the guilty verdict and the prison sentence, the editor
made plain his sympathy with the persecuted Child. The newspaper advertised
and recommended the book-length report of the trial, from which it printed
copious extracts, and in the issue of May 16, 1829, it weighed in with a favorable unsigned review, in all likelihood composed by subeditor Fuller, who was
trained in the law. The piece opened on a judicious note, urging everyone to
read the testimony and decide for himself. Then it hastened to prejudge that
inquiry. "There can hardly be a doubt" that Child's accusations were correct.
The contract for the state printing was awarded in violation of the rules, at a
cost to the taxpayers of "some thousands of dollars." The man responsible for
that egregious act was the chairman of the committee on accounts. For telling
the truth, the editor of the *Massachusetts Journal* had paid a severe price: "great
pecuniary losses," much labor, and "large abuse, little present praise and less
thanks," not to mention an involuntary, six-month sojourn in the state facility at Charlestown. But eventually, his sacrifices would be requited. "Let him
persevere:—the public will finally reward him. The people will not—cannot—
must not forget him." As for Keyes, no defense of his conduct ever appeared in
the *Gazette*.[42]

Thanks to the revelations in the *Massachusetts Journal*, there were fresh hopes
for political reform. The reviewer in the *Gazette* credited Child with opening
people's eyes to the abuses that ensued when honest citizens, for the sake of
"tranquillity and ease," eschewed "the strife of Caucuses and the bustle and
dust of Elections." It was time for the people to rise up and take government
away from the politicians. John Keyes had inadvertently catalyzed a populist

awakening. He got the message. After seven years in the state senate, still professing his "consistent" support for Adams and opposition to Jackson and attributing "insinuations" to the contrary to "the worst of passions," he declined in 1829 to be a candidate for reelection.[43]

Keyes was not out of state government for long. At the start of 1832 he returned to the statehouse as one of Concord's two representatives to the assembly and retained the post the next year. With his extensive experience, he was soon managing legislation and was viewed as a potential house speaker. Ironically, as Keyes was taking his seat in the people's chamber, Samuel Hoar was back in the senate, having finally won office as a National Republican candidate by popular acclamation in what the *Gazette* hailed as a victory for "the friends of the American system." Once again the two rivals from Concord were power brokers on Beacon Hill and in party circles. As the uproar over his conduct subsided, Keyes appeared secure in his ample domain as federal postmaster, state representative, county treasurer, town moderator and committeeman, justice of the peace, militia adjutant, and king of the Royal Arch Chapter of Freemasons.[44]

But the suspicion of privilege and the demand for equal rights could not be stifled, and they would soon challenge the foundations of the Concord elite's rule.

THE THOREAU FAMILY MINGLED WITH THE LEADERS OF CONCORD POLITICS and society. In their peripatetic life in the village, they rented homes at various times from Josiah Davis, Daniel Shattuck, and Nathan Brooks and finally settled in the handsome "Yellow House" on Main Street in a purchase financed by Shattuck. The children attended the academy with the sons and daughters of the Hoar, Keyes, Prichard, Shattuck, and Whiting clans; teenage Helen Thoreau enjoyed the privilege of practicing musical pieces on the "very elegant new piano" at Squire Hoar's. The Main Street set welcomed the Thoreaus, young and old, into their parlors and, in turn, snapped up invitations to the annual summer "melon sprees" hosted by John and Cynthia. But for all the mixing, the pencil maker never belonged in the elite. He was neither considered for nor admitted into their social circle.[45]

The phrase "social circle" was more than a metaphor. It designated an organization dating back to the Revolutionary era, when town leaders regularly got together to discuss local affairs, work out disagreements, and forge a united front. So effective was this informal effort at consensus-building that after a few false starts, it was put on a permanent foundation in 1794 with the constitution of the "Social Circle in Concord" with a mission to "strengthen the social affections and diffuse useful communications among the members." The club, limited to twenty-five, gathered every Tuesday evening from the start of October to the end of March. Meeting in one another's homes, the participants enjoyed lively conversation and "moderate" refreshments. Here, in a private setting safe from eavesdroppers, men could speak freely about issues facing the community. Here proposals could be hammered out to bring to town meeting; here projects for civic betterment could be vetted. The Social Circle was, in effect, an unofficial caucus of the local elite, operating behind closed doors to set the agenda for the town, build support for particular measures, and preconcert votes before the ballots were ever taken. By 1828, the group was still going strong and celebrating its own jubilee.[46]

The inauguration of the Social Circle marked a striking departure from the New England way. The colonial community rested on a quartet of institutions—town and church, militia and schools—embracing and serving all. Boston, Salem, and other port cities offered more diversity and choice. Not so Concord, which was as unitary and inclusive on the eve of the Revolution as it had been at its founding. This social landscape formed the framework for the ethic of interdependence preached by the religious establishment, from Peter Bulkeley to Ezra Ripley. In practice, the town was less inclusive than it pretended; all sorts of barriers—based on age, gender, wealth, neighborhood, and race—kept individuals from full participation in local life. Even so, an alternative model of institutional life was slow to develop in the countryside. The Social Circle was a harbinger of change. It tapped a select set of individuals for membership in a restricted association, gathered them together outside public view, and charged them with formulating policies for the general good. Within the comradely circle would develop a self-conscious elite bound together by loyalties forged in the friendly evenings and holding distinctive interests of its own. Set off from the neighbors, this exclusive association posed a potential challenge to the interdependence of the inhabitants and the moral unity of the town.[47]

Nobody protested this break with custom, and for four decades, from the 1790s to the 1830s, the organization went about the business of discreetly managing local affairs. Federalists could vie furiously with Republicans for control of state and national offices; within the circle, the rivals would chat amiably over drinks and agree to insulate town government from partisan divisions. Consensus was easy, since the members overwhelmingly supported the party of John Adams and later that of his National Republican son.[48] With no fear of publicity, the group could exercise a free and hidden hand to govern for the common good—or its version of the same. Hardly a project for civic improvement went forward without its blessing. From the Social Circle came the plan to celebrate the jubilee of the Concord Fight.[49] Its members were prominent in the agricultural society, the lyceum, and the social library. The Concord Bank constituted a pet project. The group furnished the original incorporators, officers, and directors of the enterprise, and twenty members subscribed to the initial stock offering. If the circle endorsed a proposal, the members went into action. Thanks to its efforts, Concord maintained considerable unity in town politics and enlisted in the social and cultural improvements of the age.[50]

Admission to the Social Circle was a badge of distinction, for which would-be aspirants could apply at their own initiative. That was the procedure from 1795 down to 1827, when the rules were changed to allow only current members to nominate candidates. It took just two blackballs to kill a bid; despite this high bar, elections proceeded year after year without rancor. Between 1804 and 1828, thirty-three individuals knocked at the doors, and every single one was let in. Presumably, unwelcome applicants were steered away to avoid the stigma of rejection. The circle cultivated the harmony it aimed to foster in the town.[51]

Whatever the path taken, successful applicants to the Social Circle fit a type: they were family men in their midthirties, on a quick ascent into the top stratum of the town. The circle concentrated the economic elite. With good reason, John Thoreau never sought entrance; he lacked the economic standing. Nor did he possess a record of public service, unlike the prominent members, such as Keyes and Shattuck, who governed the town. Many were newcomers from nearby Middlesex towns and from other parts of the New England countryside. The circle was open to Yankees of talent and civic spirit no matter where they started out. The Tuesday-evening gatherings brought together the leading merchants (Burr and Prichard, the Shattuck brothers, Josiah Davis), successful manufacturers (Munroe and Whiting), substantial farmers (Joseph and Nathan Barrett, Abel Moore), and respected professionals (lawyers Brooks and Keyes, doctors Bartlett and Hurd). Doctor Ripley, an honorary member after 1787, could drop in whenever he pleased.[52]

Acceptance into the Social Circle was highly prized. The typical member stayed for twenty years, and some endured for five decades, such as Moses Prichard, at twenty-three the youngest man ever elected, and Daniel Shattuck, who entered at twenty-five. In some instances, affiliation was a family tradition. In the mid-1820s, two father-son pairs—Dr. Hurd and his China-trading son; the saddler Reuben Brown and his farming namesake—and the brothers Shattuck combined family and the circle. Old money mingled with new; the upwardly mobile sat alongside fortunate sons of privilege. A small minority struggled to get by or left town in search of better prospects.[53]

Yet this self-perpetuating society of the elite was out of step with the times by the 1820s. Its secretive sessions in private homes contrasted sharply with the open meetings of the new voluntary associations for social improvement. Like Keyes's committee on accounts, the Social Circle lacked transparency; meeting behind closed doors, it claimed to foster the common good without any input from or accountability to the public it presumed to serve. It managed to keep a low profile amid a gathering revolt against caucuses and coteries, but the placid surface was misleading. In March 1829 the circle rejected a nominee for membership for the first time in its history. He was the merchant Charles B. Davis, put forward under the new procedures by his wealthy brother Josiah. The candidate had little to his credit except money, but the real objection was to his religion. As a defector from the First Parish to the Trinitarian church, he had exacerbated discord in the town. He was thus deemed unworthy to enter a body committed to consensus. It would be another twenty years before a religious dissenter was allowed in. The Davis case was a sign of the growing unsettlement of Concord life. With partisan competition rising and class differences sharpening, the Social Circle could not escape change. In the years to come it was more likely to reflect the divisions in town than to heal them.[54]

THE SOCIAL CIRCLE HAD AN EARLY COMPANION IN PUBLIC SERVICE. JUST three years after it was organized, the Corinthian Lodge of Ancient, Free and Accepted Masons set up in Concord to promote knowledge and virtue for the general good. Animated by the Enlightenment ideal of an orderly universe designed by a benevolent creator for rational men, the lodge claimed unique access to ancient mysteries and timeless truths essential to the progress of humankind. In Concord, as elsewhere, it targeted fit candidates for this wisdom, inducted them into its arcana and lore, and prepared them to apply the lessons for the benefit of their fellow men. Within the Masonic sanctuary, members learned the arts of self-government and tried on the challenges of leadership. They were instilled with the principles of morality. And they formed loyalties and forged bonds on which they could call in the world at large. So disciplined and trained, the Masonic brethren would constitute an aristocracy of virtue ready to take the helm at every level of the republic—or perhaps qualify for a place in the Social Circle.[55]

Freemasonry was distinct from that select coterie and from all the other voluntary associations active in town. The Social Circle was born and bred in Concord, its horizons confined to that precinct. The lodge was a branch of a fraternal order that was cosmopolitan in outlook and international in reach. Originating in late seventeenth-century Britain and spreading to Europe and across the Atlantic to the North American colonies, the organization took on new life during the Revolution and adapted itself to the political culture of the rising republic. Who could doubt the patriotism of a society to which the illustrious names of Franklin, Washington, and Lafayette were forever attached? The fraternity enjoyed a surge of popularity during the first decades of the new nation. The Corinthian Lodge arrived at the peak of a wave of expansion into the Massachusetts countryside. Based in Concord village, it covered a broad territory in central and northern Middlesex County, drawing close to half of the founding members from a distance of eight miles or more.[56]

Little about the fraternal order was local. The Concord branch owed its very existence to a charter from the Grand Lodge of Massachusetts. Every aspect of its operation—its constitution and bylaws, its hierarchy of officers, its ladder of degrees, its rituals and oaths, its costumes, tools, and jewels—followed rules and models made in Boston and London. To ensure conformity with its directives, the state body dispatched officials to visit each lodge annually and review its conduct, and it supported a "Grand Lecturer" who went from town to town dispensing lessons in Masonic doctrines, rituals, and history. Freemasonry was a top-down institution intent on imposing uniform rules. Wherever a brother went, the order would always be the same.[57]

For all these formative differences, the cosmopolitan fraternity was as conflict-averse as the local notability. Admission to a lodge required a unanimous vote—a stricter standard than was upheld by the Social Circle, where it took two negative votes to reject a candidate. "No question shall be asked," Masonic rules prescribed, "or secret divulged respecting the refusal." Only once in its first three decades did the lodge formally reject an individual, and in that case it did so "by every vote," as the secretary scrupulously recorded in the minutes. Within the group, gentlemen of diverse political and sectarian views came together to eat and drink, engage in polite conversation, and forge new bonds of friendship. Talk of politics and religion was forbidden. The only faith required of a Freemason was "that religion in which all Men agree," a nondogmatic outlook broad enough to encompass Protestants and Catholics, deists and Jews. Only "stupid Atheists" and "irreligious Libertines" needed not apply. The Social Circle never embraced such diversity. Rooted in the First Parish and hostile to Trinitarians, it eschewed latitudinarianism.[58]

Both select societies put a premium on confidentiality. But where the Social Circle counted on gentlemen to keep its affairs to themselves, the fraternal lodge relied on more stringent measures to ensure secrecy. Its mysteries were imparted to novices through solemn and sometimes fearsome rituals conducted in darkened rooms. Members advanced in Masonic knowledge by going through a sequence of initiations into ever-higher degrees of wisdom. These occult proceedings were known only to participants and were never to be revealed to outsiders. To ensure their silence, Masons took sacred oaths of fidelity, which they violated on pain of the most terrifying punishments. Let "my throat [be] cut across, my tongue torn out by the roots, and my body buried in the rough sands of the sea" should I violate my word, the entered apprentice agreed. The higher the level, the more appalling the sanctions. Even ordinary sessions for the sake of electing leaders and reviewing finances were held behind closed doors, safeguarded by the "tyler," the lodge security officer, with drawn sword.[59]

Freemasonry was a maze of contradictions. Its devotion to reason and enlightenment was belied by its mystical rites and opaque proceedings. The order purported to serve the public but confined its benefits to members and answered only to its own hierarchy. It boasted of universality but excluded women from the ranks and rejected men of color (who founded their own brotherhood, African Lodge No. 1, in Boston). Its secretive ceremonies aroused lurid fantasies of "bacchanalian frolics and abusive behavior." It caused parents to fear for the morals of sons and wives to beg "beloved husbands" to steer clear of "the sin of Masonry." But these objections did little to slow the growth of the institution. With some eighty thousand brothers collected in hundreds of lodges from the seaboard to the frontier (roughly 5 percent of the adult white male population), Freemasonry was in the mid-1820s the most popular and influential voluntary association in America.[60]

No set of men assumed a larger role in the public sphere than Freemasons. The fraternity proudly counted on its rolls "men of rank, wealth, office and talent . . . in almost every place where power is of importance." One out of every four governors and U.S. senators between 1797 and 1801 belonged to the order; in the South, more than half. During the War of 1812, James Madison stacked his cabinet with Freemasons; Andrew Jackson, a brother himself, did the same after ousting John Quincy Adams from the presidency in 1829. And what official ceremony would be complete without a featured role for the brethren in full regalia? The temples of the republic—the Massachusetts and Virginia statehouses, the U.S. Capitol in the District of Columbia—were consecrated in Masonic rituals. So too was the cornerstone of the uncompleted monument to the Concord Fight. With compass and level in hand, the masters of the craft symbolically presided over the public square.[61]

Concord readily acknowledged Masonic claims to public notice. The Corinthian Lodge occupied a prime piece of real estate on the town common: the upper floor of the brick schoolhouse, whose construction it helped to finance in 1820 with a contribution of $400. Freemasons' Hall, as it became known, was hailed as the start of "a new era, a new order of things." In this sacred space, the fraternity could conduct its affairs in security, though it could not stop inquisitive boys in the grammar school below from occasionally creeping up the stairs and peering through the keyhole to spy what they imagined were "coffins and scaffolds."[62] Here as many as five hundred brothers from county and state assembled in June 1824 to observe the Masonic festival of St. John's Day and to parade through the town center in celebration of the craft. The *Gazette* filled its columns with reports of such gatherings, as if the fraternity's doings were matters of general interest; it accorded space even to its after-dinner toasts, especially when they praised the "Concord Chapter—Located on the spot where their fathers in the revolutionary struggle first met the enemy and beat them." With good reason, the newspaper offered friendly coverage. In mid-December 1826, editor Atwill accepted lodge master Lemuel Shattuck's invitation to embark on the steps leading to enrollment as a "Master Mason."[63]

Freemasonry boasted of the prominent public officials in its ranks, and in Concord the Corinthian Lodge claimed the affiliation of influential figures in church and state alike. A member since 1798, Doctor Ripley regarded the fraternity as a "handmaid" to Christianity, reinforcing the lessons of the gospel and adding incentives to perform acts of "benevolence and charity to our fellow men." The parson frequently preached this message in sermons to the brethren and in his role as "Grand Chaplain" of the Massachusetts Grand Lodge. John Keyes, for his part, worked the Masonic connection to his political advantage. After serving as master of the local group, he advanced to the third-highest position in the state hierarchy. Through the fraternity, he formed alliances across town borders, particularly with government figures in Middlesex County, where Masons were strongly represented.[64] But few fellows in the Concord elite followed this lead. Only six members of the Social Circle joined the lodge in its first years; a quarter-century later that number had risen by one. The agricultural society, the Mill Dam Company, and the Concord Bank elicited far more enthusiasm. Freemasons were also conspicuous by their absence from local government. After 1800 no lodge member held a top office in town; only two—Keyes and Deacon Jarvis—represented Concord in the state legislature.[65]

The fraternity sought candidates of high character from every rank and order—in particular, individuals "of sober life, of industrious and good moral habits, and of an occupation by which [they] can obtain a decent and honorable living." As it turned out, such worthy souls preponderated in some occupations and classes more than in others. Locating in commercial centers, lodges drew a mix of merchants, artisans, and professionals across the economic ranks; farmers and laborers were few and far between. So it was in Concord. Young men just starting out in life formed a sizable cohort. New recruits were typically in their midtwenties. With apprenticeships, clerkships, or professional training behind them and marriages just made or on the horizon, these novices evidently saw in Freemasonry a portal to prosperous adulthood. They were men on the move, sojourners in Concord en route to other destinations. But they now had engraved certificates of membership and letters of reference to carry with them into new communities. Such introductions were a major benefit of the brotherhood, as Ripley liked to point out. Let a stranger come into a new place and declare "I am a Free and Accepted Mason," and he would secure "friends and needed favours" wherever members of the order were found. The social profile of the Corinthian Lodge was no more unique than its table of organization and its fraternal rituals.[66]

If anyone should have joined the fraternity, it was John Thoreau. Starting out in trade just as he came of age, without a father to guide him, the young merchant could have used the help of the lodge's veteran businessmen. All the more so, as he soon failed and then spent the next decade floating among towns and callings. The struggling husband and father was well aware of the benefits Freemasonry could confer. His wife Cynthia's late father, Rev. Asa Dunbar, had been a devotee of the order; founder and master of a lodge in Keene, New Hampshire, he hailed the institution as an instrument of enlightenment and unity with a fervor similar to Ripley's. At his death just one month after Cynthia's birth, he was buried with full Masonic honors. A quarter-century later the brotherhood proved a godsend to his widow, Mary. Once again bereft of a helpmeet and in financial straits following the death of her second husband, Jonas Minot, in 1813, she appealed to "the benevolence and charity of the Masonic Fraternity." The assistance helped tide her over the crisis.[67]

None of this mattered to son-in-law John Thoreau: he never sought affiliation with the Corinthian Lodge or any other branch. Perhaps, in the struggle to support his young family, he could not spare the funds for membership. It cost a total of fifteen dollars to go through all the ceremonies to qualify as a master mason, plus a one-time tax of four dollars to join and two dollars in annual dues. Or maybe he had no interest in an all-male body, whose demands would take him away from the domestic life he preferred. With its secrecy, its aura of mystery, and its occult symbols, the "surrogate religion" of Freemasonry never stirred the soul of this prosaic supporter of Doctor Ripley's church. The fraternity in the mid-1820s meant various things to its adherents. It was a sacred temple, a pillar of republicanism, a refuge from partisanship, a political network, a bank of friendship, a fund of charity, a school and lecture hall, a masculine retreat. But for John Thoreau and many others in Concord and beyond, it was a waste of time and money and a meaningless spectacle.[68]

In 1826 Freemasonry was at a peak of influence, both nationally and locally. In its new headquarters, the Corinthian Lodge was flourishing with forty-five members, and in August of that year, a Royal Arch Chapter of Freemasons, the next level up in the fraternal hierarchy, was installed to great fanfare. This branch of the fraternity was reserved for a "chosen few" who were willing to suffer a strenuous ordeal and bear considerable expense to gain deeper access to the "ancient mysteries" of the sacred order. In a two-hour ceremony initiates were blindfolded and tied together by a rope, then subjected to a series of tests, including crawling on hands and knees over a large pile of stones and debris and through a gauntlet of officials pummeling them with "knuckles, knees, and feet." Participants endured an intense ride through uncertainty, fear, and pain to an emotional catharsis, as they entered a loving community of cognoscenti. "Exalted" as

"Mark Masons," they were now truly in the Masonic elite, entitled to recognition as "companions" and eligible for such distinguished offices as high priest, king, and master of the veils. Among those who qualified were Keyes and Ripley, who made the unusual decision to sacrifice their dignity to struggle through a corridor of fists and kicks. The state senator was immediately chosen king of the forty-six-man chapter, ruling in partnership with high priest William Whiting. Fittingly, the septuagenarian minister assumed the post of chaplain. He also got off without charge; clergymen were admitted for free.[69]

At just about the same moment the Concord brethren were raising their triumphal arch, forces were gathering hundreds of miles away in western New York to pull it down. In the town of Batavia, fifty miles from Buffalo, a workingman named William Morgan, on the outs with his lodge, was preparing to expose the secrets of the fraternity in the local press. As rumors of the plan circulated, outraged Masons did everything possible to stop it. A club-wielding mob tried unsuccessfully to burn down the printer's office. Morgan himself was briefly jailed for unpaid debts, then released into the hands of unknown agents, who snatched the malcontent from the street, forced him into a waiting carriage amid cries of "Murder! Murder!," and ferried him from one hiding place to another before ending up at Fort Niagara on Lake Ontario, the last place he was seen alive. Eventually his body washed up on its shore; like so many in the order, Morgan died, as he had lived, on the move.

Finding the kidnappers and bringing them to justice proved more elusive. Masonic sheriffs showed little interest in pursuing the matter; neither did their brethren on the bench, nor the grand juries handpicked for loyalty to the order. The evident cover-up aroused popular outrage that soon swirled into a political movement designed to break the supposed Masonic stranglehold on government. Critics suddenly discovered that the fraternity was an antirepublican institution, whose adherents were bound by secret pledges to prefer brothers over others, in flagrant disregard of the public good. And far from being a "handmaid" to Christianity, the barbarous order, with its "bloody initiation oaths," threatened the very existence of true religion. In the name of equal rights, opponents mobilized to expose the Masonic conspiracy, drive it from power, and prevent future incursions by outlawing "extra-judicial oaths" and barring anyone bound by such vows from public office. The firestorm of Anti-Masonry quickly burned over western New York and then scorched the rest of the Northeast and parts of the South and West. Eventually, even Concord, a stronghold of the institution, felt the populist fury.[70]

The *Yeoman's Gazette* ignored the rumblings. Having been told that membership in the lodge would be in "our pecuniary interest," editor Atwill dismissed the reports from western New York and underwent the process to become a master Mason. For years the newspaper carried only good news about the fraternity. After downplaying the rumors of Morgan's murder, it treated the "diabolical" crime as a violation of "the benevolent principles for which the institution is proverbial." Determined to see no evil, Atwill strove to keep the "contemptible Morgan fever" not only out of the *Gazette* but out of New England altogether. Letters to the editor for or against the order were unwelcome. Readers learned little about the progress of Anti-Masonry as a political force. But Atwill could not always keep his promise "never to indite a word" about the "selfish" and "unprincipled" insurgency. In November 1831 Massachusetts held the first election of state officials under its newly revised constitution, with members of the Anti-Masonic Party putting up candidates against the National Republican and Democratic tickets. Warning against the upstart party, the editor insisted that the "friends of good order and correct principles" had no choice but to support the National Republican slate. Anti-Masonry was a distraction from the battle against a corrupt "King Andrew" in the White House. Anyone not repulsed by the "wickedness, corruption, contradictions and absurdities of Gen. Jackson and his Administration," Atwill inveighed, was "fairly entitled to the flattering cognomen of a stupid A.S.S [antisecret society]."[71]

For all the bluster, Concord's Freemasons were reeling from the attacks. Admissions to the lodge slowed to a trickle. An organization that had boasted forty-five members in 1826 was down to thirty-four in 1830 and shrinking fast. Attendance at monthly meetings plummeted. Time and again the officers were reduced to the symbolic act of opening and closing the lodge. It limped along, with token sessions or none at all for months at a time, though occasionally morale was lifted when "Reverend Brother" Ripley made "some useful and interesting remarks." At least the group stayed in existence; all over the country many of its counterparts were closing their doors. So dire was the situation that in the spring of 1831 a committee chaired by Shattuck briefly considered selling the forlorn meeting hall before concluding to rent out the room for "lyceum lectures, public meetings, and concerts." On Sabbath mornings Freemasons' Hall was filled with Methodist or Universalist worshipers, whose payments were sorely needed to fill a depleted treasury.[72]

Massachusetts Freemasons were still in a fighting mood at the end of 1831, when twelve hundred brothers signed a public declaration rejecting the charge that the fraternity was an antirepublican state within a state and insisting that it was a true voluntary association, whose members enjoyed "freedom of thought and speech," followed their conscience in religion and politics, and took no oath that was at odds with "the fundamental principles of morality" and the duties of "a good and faithful citizen." Twenty-four men of Concord subscribed, including Keyes, Moore, Ripley, Lemuel Shattuck, and their companions of the Royal Arch. Joining them on the list was Atwill, who printed the statement on the front page of the *Gazette*.[73]

Eleven months later, following the 1832 presidential election, the editor abruptly changed his tune. Searching for an explanation for Andrew Jackson's victory, Atwill took his cue from Congressman Edward Everett and pinned the blame on the Freemasons, whose refusal to address the reasonable concerns of their fellow citizens split the opposition to the president and awarded him a second term. Reform of the fraternity was thus imperative to "allay public excitement." Let the lodges and chapters open their doors to outsiders; let them give up "their uncouth, barbarous, and unmeaning Oaths and Obligations." These proposals were meant to strengthen the anti-Jackson coalition, but Atwill miscalculated. As he charted a new course, publishing a series of letters by ex-president Adams on Freemasonry and its oaths, he stirred a backlash from lodge brothers. He was "immediately assailed with letters," some anonymous, others signed, demanding that he cancel the series or face "masonic indignation." The editor held firm, and in just three months he shattered the National Republican consensus, ignited a populist uprising against the local elite, and plunged Concord into the new age of Jacksonian democracy.[74]

Once he embarked on the Anti-Masonic course, Atwill never looked back; nor did he provide any explanation for his change of mind, other than that suddenly he had seen the light. Instead, he pummeled his new enemies with the same gusto that he had directed at the old. The *Gazette* could not run enough exposés of "Masonic outrages," calls for lodges to surrender their charters, extracts from the proceedings of Anti-Masonic Party conventions, and denunciations of so-called neutrals who hypocritically claimed that "I am neither a

Mason nor an Antimason." Many of these pieces came straight from the *Boston Daily Advocate*, the official organ of Anti-Masonry in the state, which hailed the Concord editor's courageous decision to end his long embargo on articles friendly to the cause. For a time, Atwill claimed to be open to contributions on both sides of the issue. "Our columns like ourselves are free." But this pretense of neutrality was blasted when the editor betrayed his solemn vow and divulged the "oath, obligation, and penalty" imposed on him and others by the Corinthian Lodge. "I, H—A—, of my own free will and accord, in presence of Almighty God," the pledge began, in language repeated thousands of times a year all over the republic. The renegade editor had become Concord's counterpart to William Morgan.[75]

Atwill was soon fighting for economic survival. Following a playbook used by Masons elsewhere, his adversaries set out to wreck his business and ruin him financially. One angry reader after another canceled his subscription and pulled his ads. The editor cleverly exposed them in print. The boycott backfired, and the newspaper soon added more customers than it had lost.[76] In a more direct assault on his finances, Atwill was suddenly pressed to pay outstanding debts. Daniel Shattuck drew up his bill against the printer and, before there was time to pay, dispatched Deputy Sheriff Prichard with a legal demand, prepared by Keyes, for immediate settlement (plus court costs). Abel Moore followed suit and added insult to injury by spreading word that the *Gazette* proprietor was "in failing circumstances." That rumor provoked a swarm of additional creditors to descend with their claims; in the week before the Middlesex County Court of Common Pleas met in Concord for its March 1833 term, a dozen suits for debt were filed against Atwill. It was, he protested, the first time in his nearly eight years of doing business that he had been taken to court. "The spirit of Shylock seemed to be abroad to exact the pound of flesh," the *Boston Daily Advocate* observed sympathetically.

No one desired vengeance more than King Keyes, who had surely resented the editor's failure to support his return to the state senate in 1828. Worse still, Atwill had endorsed David Child's stand against persecution, and he reaffirmed that praise in December 1832, when the state supreme court overturned the editor's conviction for criminal libel. In the very issue of the *Gazette* in which he broke his silence on Freemasonry, Atwill ran tributes to the exonerated journalist as "an independent and fearless editor"—a role model for himself. Still, there was good reason to placate the powerful politician. The editor's home stood on land under a five-hundred-dollar mortgage held by Keyes, who was prepared to use that leverage to his advantage. When Atwill declined to submit to Masonic pressure, the lawyer sent a curt note simultaneously canceling his subscription and calling in the loan. "I do not feel secure," he explained. Having helped to ignite panic among the printer's creditors, he was now first in line to be paid.[77]

To counter the Anti-Masonic diatribes of the *Gazette*, Keyes and Shattuck recruited an editor to start a competing weekly. Boston native William W. Wheildon was well suited to the task. The young man had trained as a printer in the office of the *Boston Statesman*, where he must have set type for government documents under the contract awarded by Keyes's committee. In 1827, at twenty-one, he launched the *Bunker-Hill Aurora* in Charlestown as an advocate for the Warren Bridge. The next year he campaigned for Keyes's reelection to the state senate while the *Gazette* opted to remain neutral. The *Aurora* had been the politician's editorial organ—and the *Gazette*'s rival—ever since.

In February 1833 Wheildon opened an office in Concord village, ostensibly as a business decision to make the *Aurora* "more of a *County Paper*." Situated at the center of Middlesex, the enterprise aimed to "extend its circulation and usefulness and to afford facilities for advertising legal and other notices." The editorial formula of the challenger resembled the competition. It supported National Republican candidates and policies and promised to serve "the Farming, Mechanic, and Manufacturing Interests" of the county with "the Politics, News, and Literature of the day." Wheildon was as committed as Atwill to "the diffusion of useful knowledge, and correct principles, in politics, morals, and manners." The two weeklies cost the same, two dollars a year, and came out every Saturday, with the *Aurora* waiting to appear until the evening, in order to answer stories in the morning *Gazette*. But in one key respect the newcomer offered a welcome alternative: it would be free of anti-Masonry. Though not a lodge member himself, the Charlestown editor was closely tied to the fraternity by his half-brother, the author of the 1831 declaration in defense of the order. He was thus well positioned to battle Atwill on his home ground; soon, his backers expected, the *Gazette* would fold. To ensure that result, Keyes wielded his influence with county officials to get the advertising of the probate court, presided over by Samuel P. P. Fay, Concord native and onetime grand master of the state lodge, transferred from the *Gazette* to the *Aurora*; likewise for many notices from the county commissioners.[78]

After kowtowing to the Concord elite for so long, Atwill fought to sustain his new independence. The editor portrayed himself as a man of conscience upholding press freedom against "a palpable combination." He would not be silenced for "daring to tell truths which these men were determined should be kept from the view of the community." The motto of the *Gazette* henceforth would be "PRINCIPLES, NOT MEN."

In fact, Atwill was as quick as his opponents to play the politics of personality. His enemies were a "Press Gang," like the British navy before the War of 1812, intent on forcing men into its service; he called them out by name, impugned their honesty, and reviled their records. Wheildon was their "supple tool," seeking to "crush our press" out of a "desire of gain" and petty "personal malice." Keyes was singled out for special abuse. "King John" had enjoyed a "considerable salary" from the taxpayers for too long, but his "Masonic Throne" was "tottering" and would soon come crashing down. In the name of transparency, every private act of aggression against Atwill was brought before the "All-Seeing Eye" of a "jealous public" and condemned.[79]

The exchange of insults went from the printed page to the streets. In April 1833 a new apprentice in the lodge—the first in more than a year—was understandably infuriated when the *Gazette* exposed him as a bankrupt and mocked his "long ears," "vulgar tongue," and "empty head." On running into Atwill in the village, the man exploded in anger. "* * you," he exclaimed, according to an eyewitness. "If you have said anything about me in your paper I'll slap your * chops." Somehow a fight was averted, though the antagonist promised to "thrash" the editor within the week. Atwill let it be known that he regularly carried a pistol. A year and a half later the dispute with Keyes turned physical. One day in December 1834 Atwill stood in the post office at the green store inspecting the list of letters available for pickup, when Keyes arrived to oversee his federal domain. Absorbed in his reading, the editor did not realize that he was blocking the passageway, nor that the impatient postmaster was trying to get by. He was thus thrown off balance when Keyes stormed ahead and shouldered him out of the way. The victim reached out to break his fall, only to put his hand into the scalding water in a basin atop the store's large wooden stove. Whether the injury was intended or not, Keyes showed no concern for Atwill's condition: "His majesty passed on." The Freemasons did succeed in one formal retaliatory measure. On a motion by brother Reverend Ripley, the lodge expelled Atwill from membership for revealing the "secrets of the Craft" and prohibited him from ever visiting again.[80]

In the end, what saved the *Gazette* was not principle but partisanship. Atwill's public defiance of the "Press Gang" won the endorsement of the *Boston Daily Advocate*, which highlighted his "moral courage" in an article, "The Yeoman's Gazette vs. Masonry." That praise amounted to money in the bank. With the backing of the *Advocate*, Atwill put his press in service to the Anti-Masonic Party of Middlesex County. In late February 1833, just two months after breaking its silence about the fraternity, the *Gazette* announced an upcoming Anti-Masonic convention to be held in the Concord courthouse. The notice appeared over the name of Herman Atwill, secretary. The editor took the rostrum at the convention and laid out in detail the misbegotten measures of the Masons to destroy him. The delegates responded not only with anger at this "open and palpable attack on the Liberty of the Press" but also with pledges of financial support. Supposedly, in return for the aid, the *Gazette* became "the property" of the party committee and subject to its dictates—a rumor the *Aurora* was quick to spread and Atwill to deny ("Our press is our own," he repeatedly asserted; he was "alone responsible" for its conduct). Whatever the reality, the newspaper became an integral part of the county organization, its counting room doubling as party headquarters, its editor a valuable functionary in delivering the Anti-Masonic message.[81]

With this turn to politics, the era of one-party government came to an end. As the *Gazette* urged voters to shun every candidate "whose mind, and soul, and body, are under the enslaving and pernicious bondage of Masonic Oaths," Anti-Masons contested elections for every office up and down the ballot, from selectman and town clerk to governor and congressman. Presented with meaningful choices for the first time in a decade, the townsmen exercised the right to vote with an enthusiasm not seen since the Federalist-Republican battles during the years around the War of 1812. Turnout in the November state elections surged from 195 in 1832 to 292 two years later—a 50 percent jump. Urged on by dueling newspapers, virtually every voter—seven out of ten male taxpayers—went for a straight party ticket.[82]

Concord entered the new era of popular politics with gusto. Anti-Masons threw themselves into mass petition drives to influence the state legislature; at home, partisans sought advantage through the manipulation of voter rolls and outright fraud. The populist insurgency put the demand for equal rights and justice at the center of public life. It replaced entrenched "fathers of the town" with upstarts valued chiefly for ideological correctness. By those means, Concord underwent its own democratic revolution.

Petitioning was key to the transformation. The act itself was nothing new. In the early republic, as in the colonial period, individuals and communities commonly sought favors from government, such as charters for banks and bridges or grants of authority to form new parishes or towns. Such requests followed the rules of hierarchy; framed in the deferential language of prayer, they were the supplications of subjects to sovereign. Seldom did they set an agenda for public policy or coordinate with others. But starting in the late 1820s, the tone and purpose of such requests altered dramatically. Instead of offering pleas to magistrates, they pressed demands upon them for passage of specific measures for the general good. Evangelical Protestants led the way in national campaigns to persuade Congress to end the delivery of mail on Sundays and to honor treaties with the Cherokee Indians. Gathering up scores and hundreds of subscribers in communities across the republic, these memorials at once formed and expressed public opinion. Each person's signature appended was an equal individual unit of a larger democratic whole.[83]

Perhaps in reaction against the evangelical sponsorship, Concord's citizens had stayed aloof from these earlier grassroots campaigns. Anti-Masonry ended that detachment and incorporated townsmen of all faiths into a statewide effort with a distinctive political purpose. Each winter from 1833 to 1835, the partisan adversaries of the fraternity drew up "memorials"—*not* petitions—for submission to the state house of representatives. These addresses pressed an escalating set of demands. The first statement called for an official inquiry into the Grand Lodge, the second urged passage of a law to ban all "extra-judicial oaths" in private life, and the final one in 1835 advocated an annual registry of "secret societies" with the names of members and the pledges they had made. Well before the anti-Communist crusades of the twentieth century, anxious activists were on the hunt for disloyal neighbors in their midst.

Nothing about these documents was unique to Concord except for the signers' names. The texts were composed and printed in Boston and distributed all over the Commonwealth through a well-oiled machine. Every county had its committee, and every town a representative on it, in charge of canvassing for signatures. The state party was up front about its leading role; the 1834 memorial stated explicitly that it was "prepared by the direction" of the September

1833 Anti-Masonic State Convention. Anti-Masons boasted of their organizational prowess, extensive reach, and numerous supporters; taking advantage of the ongoing improvements in communication, the friends of "equal rights" and "the supremacy of the laws" worked assiduously to give voice to public opinion. Ironically, Anti-Masonry was as uniform in its message and as standardized in its methods of operation as the cosmopolitan foe it sought to slay. But unlike Freemasonry, its activities were visible for all to see.[84]

Petitioning and electioneering went together. The memorials identified and mobilized the rank and file of the fledgling party. Like public opinion surveys today, they provided a show of grassroots support in advance of elections and made it easy to target voters and get them out to the polls. Toppling Keyes from his throne furnished ample incentive. In 1832, with the scandal of the rigged bidding seemingly behind him, the county treasurer won his twentieth term in office without opposition. The next year Middlesex Anti-Masons put up a candidate against him, and while Keyes's vote barely changed in Concord, sixty-seven townsmen suddenly came out and cast ballots for the challenger. Eight months later, with John Quincy Adams the Anti-Masonic nominee for governor, the insurgency made a clean sweep of the town. "ANTIMASONRY TRIUMPHANT IN OLD CONCORD!" the *Gazette* crowed. Registering a dramatic shift of opinion, the new party came out on top with 148 votes, more than double its earlier total and a decisive majority of 57 percent over National Republican and Democratic nominees. The Anti-Masonic senate slate enjoyed a comparable victory. Once indifferent to Anti-Masonry, Concord now ranked among its banner towns in a state and county that still favored the longtime political establishment.[85]

Nothing pleased local Anti-Masons more than defeating Keyes as town representative. He was removed from office along with the wealthy farmer Joseph Barrett in an election Atwill compared to the famous Nineteenth of April 1775. Under the headline "THE OLD BATTLE GROUND," Atwill reprinted a tribute from the *Boston Advocate*: "Concord has proved itself worthy to have been the first battle ground of the revolution. It put down King *George* then, and it has now put down King *John* . . . The little King David of the Yeoman's Gazette with the *sling of truth*, has struck to the ground the Goliath of Masonry, who threatened to ruin him by foreclosing a mortgage."[86]

The Anti-Masons carried the fight into local elections, heretofore exempt from partisan battles. In March 1834 the insurgents fielded a slate for selectmen, town clerk, treasurer, and overseers of the poor and won every contest. To everyone's astonishment, Concord Academy preceptor Phineas Allen ousted Abiel Heywood from the town clerk's post that he had held since 1796. It took two ballots, the first a tie, to reach a decision; the *Freeman* proudly reported the victory—126 to 119—in a break with precedent. Intent on fostering an image of consensus, the outgoing clerk had never reported an official tally. To take the sting out of the rejection, the town unanimously passed a resolution thanking Heywood for "the skill, diligence & fidelity" with which he had served the town for thirty-eight consecutive years. Even so, the election was a rebuff to the Masonic elite. "High Priest, King, Grand Chaplin [*sic*], and a retinue of *subjects*, were put to rout, and totally defeated by the persevering Antimasons of Concord," Atwill exulted.

Not entirely: in the separate vote for county treasurer, Keyes hung on but by a smaller margin than ever. His base remained static, while the opposition continued to grow. The veteran officeholder actually did worse in his hometown than in the county as a whole. The entire election was carried off with "great harmony and good feeling," according to Atwill; only a single "ill-natured" remark was heard. That was not how Keyes's son remembered it decades later. "It was a revolution, and how the antis hurrahed and the masons groaned and gnashed their teeth . . . How mad I was [too] and how even we boys quarreled like our fathers over the result."[87]

Ezra Ripley was not on the ballot in these elections, but he was as big a loser as Heywood and Keyes. The parson had curtailed his involvement in the fraternity during the 1820s, becoming an honorary member and rarely attending meetings. Then, as "an exterminating warfare" was being waged against the institution, he returned to the fray to "let the world see that he was not ashamed of the profession of Masons." He prayed at important celebrations, including the ceremony held in October 1830 to lay the cornerstone of the new Masonic Temple on Beacon Hill, signed the 1831 declaration, and assumed the office of grand chaplain in the Grand Lodge at the height of the popular excitement. On June 24, 1833, the Corinthian Lodge braved popular disapproval and commemorated St. John's Day with a parade through the streets and speeches at the First Parish meetinghouse. There the defiant minister assumed his accustomed place to offer words of welcome and warning. Anti-Masonry "has become a political and party spirit," Ripley advised, "and if successful may become a radical and revolutionary spirit." The minister went on to charge the leaders of that opposition with spreading lies. "They are a self-constituted, self-created inquisition . . . Their claims are unjust and unreasonable." Anti-Masonry posed a threat everywhere, even in the home. "Our domestic peace has been invaded; discord has been sowed between husband and wife; the parent has been set against his children, and children against their parent." Ultimately, freedom of thought was under siege. No one had the right "to enter into his soul," the eighty-two-year-old minister asserted with uncharacteristic passion, "and dictate what he shall say or believe, or swear"—"provided he do nothing contrary to the laws and religion." The assembled brothers applauded these "appropriate, forcible, and eloquent" remarks; Atwill, who sat with his new comrades in the meetinghouse, heard them "with painful emotions."[88]

The aged minister miscalculated. His public defense of the fraternity alienated many in the congregation, and it brought him notoriety just months before the voters were to decide on whether to amend the Massachusetts Constitution and eliminate the tax-supported religious establishment. Concord was clearly split on the question. In the state legislature, Joseph Barrett opposed the change, Keyes approved, and it is a good bet that Samuel Hoar cast a no vote in the senate, as he had done back in 1820. With the *Gazette* on record as favoring an end to public funding of religion, if only to remove "a perpetual theme of party and sectarian declamation," the November election would determine whether Ripley would remain a public officer of the town. In the state as a whole, the outcome was a foregone conclusion, with 90 percent of voters in favor. Even in Concord, Ripley could not rally his parishioners. The referendum evoked apathy, with just 132 men expressing their opinion, not quite half as many as voted for governor, and when the ballots were counted, the measure prevailed. Just as his Federalist preaching had pushed people into the Republican camp a generation before, so Ripley's strident defense of Freemasonry appears to have generated support for the separation of church and state. Starting on January 1, 1834, the old man would no longer be Concord's "public protestant teacher of piety, religion, and morality." After fifty-five years looking out for the well-being of "my people," he would now minister to a voluntary association and speak for a diminishing part of the town.[89]

The crusade against Freemasonry was somewhat of a religious struggle. Trinitarians could not abide the fraternity's openness to all believers in a Supreme Being, Jews and Muslims included; they distrusted the secrecy and mysticism of the rituals and worried about the immoralities taking place behind closed doors. The new church was also in competition with the lodge for the allegiance of the many rootless young men passing through town. But the worshipers in the new religious society did not throw themselves into the protest movement until Rev. John Wilder assumed the pulpit in the summer of 1833.[90] Under his leadership, nearly two-thirds of the men in the parish embraced the insurgency. Among their number was a recent addition to the rolls, Herman Atwill, who had attended Doctor Ripley's church since settling in town but had abandoned the religious establishment soon after turning on the political one.[91]

The insurgency found proportionately less support in the First Parish. Even so, close to one hundred men of the First Parish took a public stand against the fraternity, outnumbering Trinitarians in the protest by three to one. One such defector from Ripley's camp was Deacon Reuben Brown, Jr., a fifty-year-old bachelor farmer who turned against the fraternal connection that had long joined his aged father and his pastor together. Ripley perhaps had such generational tensions in mind when he deplored Anti-Masonry's assault on "domestic peace."[92]

Still, it was less religion than occupation and neighborhood that impelled men into Anti-Masonry or inured them to its appeal. The conflict did not pit rich against poor, nor old wealth against new. Anti-Masonry was *not* a revolt of the dispossessed. Rather, it mobilized property holders against one another; the more advantaged the group, the more likely it was to oppose the fraternity. The economic elite was the most polarized class of all. And in a community where residents of the center held a lion's share of top offices and committee posts and where villagers led the way in organizing voluntary associations, the protest movement broke the mold. It drew supporters from all over the town, and in some of the farming districts a solid majority joined the political uprising. By contrast, the friends of the fraternity congregated in the center, where Freemasons' Hall stood as the citadel of the beleaguered group, in the factory village, and in the eastern district. In the early 1830s a Freemason was as scarce as sheep and silkworms on Concord's farms.

Anti-Masonry was thus a populist revolt of a sort that would reverberate across the centuries. It brought together farmers of the out-districts with mechanics and men-on-the-make in the center and sealed their alliance in shared grievances against the merchants and professionals in the village. Here was a cause that united the overworked farmer Daniel Hunt and his kin atop Punkatasset Hill with Phineas Allen at the academy and Atwill in his printing office above Charles B. Davis's store. It was a movement of the disenchanted, not the deprived.[93]

A good many townsmen, numbering around 125 voters, were neither Masons nor Anti-Masons. John Thoreau was among them, withholding his signature from the several memorials circulating in Concord during these years. Silence could have indicated a variety of positions, from indifference to indignation over the attack on the fraternity. Ralph Waldo Emerson, still a resident of Boston, preferred to ignore the upheaval entirely. In January 1834 he expressed relief that the demands of lecturing about natural history provided a distraction from the agitated political scene: "What a refreshment from Anti-masonry & Jacksonism & Bankism is in the phenomena of the Polar Regions or in the habits of the Oak or the geographical problem of the Niger."[94]

It is likely that Ripley's grandson and his parishioner John Thoreau shared the view of Samuel Hoar. An admirer of John Quincy Adams, the Concord statesman ran into the ex-president in Boston one day in 1833. The disputatious *Letters on the Entered Apprentice's Oath* had just been published as a pamphlet. Had Hoar read it, the author asked, and if so, what was his opinion? "It seems to me, Mr. Adams," the squire politely replied, "there is but one thing in the world sillier than Masonry. That is Anti-Masonry." Who could believe that such prominent figures as Keyes and Ripley were secret conspirators against the common good? For every Reuben Brown, Jr., repudiating the fraternal affiliation of his father, there was a Daniel Shattuck unwilling to regard his public-spirited brother, or a John Thoreau his late father-in-law, as an enemy of the republic.[95]

Partisanship mattered, too. With Andrew Jackson back in the White House overturning the banking system and unsettling the national economy, it was urgent to put National Republicans, newly rebranded as Whigs, into state and national offices. In November 1834, Squire Hoar was the party's candidate for Congress, whom the *Gazette* assailed for his past opposition to Adams's bid for governor and for his pleas to "the poor, miserable, despised, fanatical Antimasons" to "save the '*Great* National Republican party' from ruin." To Atwill, neutrality was unacceptable; one was either for or against the monstrous "Institution." But John Thoreau and others refused this view, and in November 1834 they not only voted to send Hoar to the U.S. Congress but also returned Keyes and Joseph Barrett to the statehouse as representatives of the town. It took two rounds of voting before Hoar won an absolute majority in the district, and by the time the ballots were counted in December, his support at home had fallen from a strong majority to a thin margin of four votes more than his Anti-Masonic opponent. Concord's favorite son went to the nation's capital without the clear endorsement of his neighbors. At the height of Anti-Masonry, the sentiments of the townspeople remained split. Concord was once again a swing town, its majority up for grabs.[96]

The Social Circle could not smooth over these divides. The Anti-Masonic crusade disrupted the exclusive coterie and hindered its ability to guide the town from behind the scenes. After the circle denied admission to Trinitarian Charles B. Davis in 1829, it had recovered its former amity, with five candidates entering in 1832. Then came the insurgency. The group rejected three nominees in a row, all of them Anti-Masons. In the fevered atmosphere, it was an achievement that the society met at all to cultivate the "social affections."[97]

Ultimately, the battle lines in this Concord fight were most sharply drawn among the sons of the Revolutionary generation, as they contested the character of the social and political order.[98] Did Freemasonry betray the heritage of liberty and equality, or was it a rightful legacy of such Patriots as Joseph Warren and Paul Revere (who had issued the charter of the Corinthian Lodge)? Anti-Masons embraced the ethos of the new voluntary associations for social and cultural improvement. Open to all who shared their purposes and paid their dues, these civic groups held public meetings, often published their proceedings, and freely offered their services to fellow citizens. Freemasonry, by contrast, was opaque, its knowledge secret, its membership exclusive, its initiation rites out of sight. Who needed Masonic learning when lyceums and libraries were so active in disseminating the scientific and technological advances of the day? Of what use was Masonic character building when the fraternity tolerated moderate drinking, unlike the new temperance societies campaigning for total abstinence from ardent spirits? And why rely on Masonic charity in times of need, when mutual insurance policies gave better protection against disaster? The fraternity was obsolete. So argued Edward Everett in calling on the lodges to open their doors, abandon their oaths, and let the people in. In this spirit, Atwill identified the insurgency with the progress of the age. "The life and soul of antimasonry is information. Diffuse information" and "show the people what masonry is, and they will rise up in their strength, and destroy it. Information—information—information. Nothing else is needed."[99]

Anti-Masonic activists were forward-looking in their worldview.[100] In their minds, the Masonic order stood in the way of progress. It jeopardized the heritage of liberty and equal rights that the Puritan and Revolutionary fathers had sacrificed so much to achieve and that had made possible continuing moral and material advancement. Born into an Old World of bishops, nobles, and kings, the fraternity stood out as an anomaly in a new age of expanding participation in politics and society. By what right did it claim a special status in the republic? On what ground did it enjoy pride of place in the public sphere? It was no more entitled to such privilege than were banks and bridges to exclusive charters and churches to official favor. If an organization wished to attract members and influence society, it should come forth openly, conduct its affairs transparently, and compete for its place. Likewise for individuals in a democratic society, who rose and fell according to their merits.[101]

Anti-Masonry was thus a force for equality of opportunity and individual possibility in a community where norms of hierarchy and interdependence still had compelling advocates in church and state. As a political party, it peaked in 1834–1835 and soon vanished from the scene, merging in Concord and the Bay State with the democracy of Jackson and Van Buren. But as a social movement, it had more lasting effects. Rather than brave public disapproval, the Corinthian Lodge went into retreat for a decade, its dwindling membership rarely meeting but still clinging to its charter; the Royal Arch Chapter folded altogether.[102]

With Freemasonry's withdrawal from the public sphere, Ezra Ripley lost an indispensable "handmaid" at the very moment when the religious establishment was being dismantled and one-party rule was coming to an end. A unitary society could no longer be sustained. Competing newspapers and parties, linked to wider political forces, were diversifying and democratizing civic life. Rival churches and sects, tied to larger denominations, introduced a new era of religious pluralism and choice. Various voluntary associations pushed different agendas for improvement and reform. The fraternal order beloved by Ripley was at odds with this modern order. Its organization was top-down, its decisions made by consensus. It treasured ancient wisdom in old books and imparted lessons dictated by authority and tradition. It located in commercial centers and associated with ruling powers. It was a cornerstone of the minister's institution-minded worldview. Now under attack, that outlook suffered fissures as damaging as the cracks in the base of the monument Concord was still struggling to erect in the town center.

At just this moment, a very different way of seeing the world was coming into view. This new philosophy urged Americans to free themselves from the dead hand of the past, put politics and business aside, and seek out spiritual truths through firsthand experience in nature. It elevated individuals over institutions and celebrated self-trust. From this new perspective, an institution was merely "the lengthened shadow of one man." Nothing could be more antithetical to Transcendentalist individualism than Masonic fraternalism—and, thanks to Anti-Masonry, that ideological opponent had lost its punch. The stage was set for a new chapter in Concord's history. In this community in change, Emerson and Thoreau would find their intellectual home.[103]

Part II

TRANSCENDENTALISTS AND THEIR WORLD

Freedom of Mind

Ralph Waldo Emerson was a man at loose ends early in October 1834, when he arrived at his step-grandfather Ripley's home and moved in. At thirty-one, the scion of six generations of New England ministers going back to Peter Bulkeley had not yet become the Sage of Concord or anywhere else; nor was the house the legendary "Old Manse" that would be conjured up by Nathaniel Hawthorne a dozen years later. Emerson came to Concord in large part because he had nowhere else to go.

Among contemporaries constantly on the move, he had led a more peripatetic existence than most. Born in Boston, he spent his early years in the parsonage of the city's "prestigious" First Church, where his father presided as pastor. Then in 1811, Rev. William Emerson suddenly died, leaving behind a widow, five sons, and an infant daughter to make their way in the world. (The girl did not survive beyond age three; one son, Robert Bulkeley, was intellectually disabled and in need of lifelong care.) Never again did the family enjoy a settled place.

Obliged to support her boys by running a boardinghouse, Ruth Emerson shuttled them among rentals in the capital. In October 1817, at fourteen, Ralph entered Harvard as a scholarship student from one address and graduated four years later, now calling himself Waldo, from yet another. By then, he had resided in half a dozen or more dwellings, not counting the college dormitories. The peregrinations continued as he taught school in various towns, journeyed south for his health, and prepared for the ministry back in Cambridge. Even ordination as minister of Boston's Second Church and marriage to eighteen-year-old Ellen Tucker, both in 1829, brought only brief stability. The new bride died of consumption seventeen months after the wedding; a year and a half later Emerson resigned his pulpit and resumed the roving life, traveling to Europe and Britain for ten months before returning to Boston in hopes of charting a new direction. Soon Concord beckoned, if only for the free lodgings he could enjoy while his mother kept house for the ailing Doctor Ripley. After so many moves and so much unsettlement, the town offered a temporary haven from constant change.[1]

Emerson's mind and spirit were restless, too. Though he had fulfilled familial expectations by following his forefathers into the Congregationalist ministry, he recoiled from the pastoral duties: the never-ending visits to parishioners' sickrooms and deathbeds, the formulaic prayers he was expected to offer during Sabbath worship, and the conduct of rituals in which he gradually ceased to believe. For the young minister, the fundamental mission of the clergyman was to preach the truths of religion as he knew them personally, not from the Bible, not from authority or tradition, but from the sanctuary of his soul and the experience of everyday life. The longer he served, the less authentic conventional Christianity felt. The administration of communion proved the breaking point. Both orthodox and liberal Congregationalists deemed the ceremony indispensable; in Concord, Ezra Ripley had opened up access to the Lord's Supper and invited all believers to the table. Emerson, by contrast, rejected the practice as a dead form with no hold on his religious sentiments. Rather than conform to institutions that were at odds with his convictions, he severed his connection with the Second Church and cast off the constraints of the ministry, though he still accepted invitations to preach to Unitarians from Bangor to Plymouth (where in 1834 he met Lydia Jackson, who would become his second wife the next year) and as far south as New York City.

The pulpit he really desired was the secular platform of the lyceum movement, where he was beginning to make his reputation. In the lecture room, he aspired to convey "the discoveries" and "stimulating thoughts" that were truly his own. As he began his new life in Concord, he looked forward to a speaking career that he could pursue with integrity and independence: "I design not to utter any speech, poem, or book that is not entirely & peculiarly my work. I will say at Public Lectures & the like, those things which I have meditated for their own sake & not for the first time with a view to that occasion." Like many other newcomers to the town, the would-be "oracle" of the lyceum movement was full of hopes for a fresh start.[2]

Emerson glimpsed that new beginning in the land of his ancestors. "Hail to the quiet fields of my fathers!" he exclaimed on November 15, 1834, as he sat in the manse built by his grandfather William in 1770. "Not wholly unattended by supernatural friendship & favor let me come hither. Bless my purposes as they are simple & virtuous." Yet Concord was hardly the best spot from which to launch a lecturing career. Given all the travel by stage he would have to undertake at a time when the railroad was just starting to link the principal towns of New England, Boston or Cambridge would have offered a more convenient base. Nor could the small town compete in cultural and intellectual resources; the modest collection of "useful" and "entertaining" books at the social library would never supply the learned works, many of them published abroad, that Emerson had regularly borrowed from the Boston Athenaeum and the Harvard College library. On the other hand, the rural landscape of Concord inspired his genius with prospects of the sublime seldom glimpsed on crowded city streets. One evening, not long after his move, he watched in wonder as a glorious sky radiated "a wreath of roses" from "every grey or slate coloured cloud." "I never see the dawn break or the sun set," he reflected the next day, "or look down the river with its tree planted banks . . . without a lively curiosity as to its reality & a self recollection that I am not in a dream." Such scenes entranced his eye and uplifted his spirit, as he began to compose the little volume *Nature* that would become in 1836 his first statement of Transcendentalism. Could he enjoy such daily contact with nature without sacrificing the advantages of the metropolis? The Boston-bred thinker strove to reconcile the competing pulls of country and city.[3]

If Emerson initially had no permanent plans to reside in Concord, he soon had incentives enough to settle down. Early in February 1835 his beloved brother Charles Chauncy Emerson, five years the junior, announced welcome news. A brilliant scholar at the top of his Harvard class (1828)—unlike Waldo, whose academic record was middling—Charles had gone on to train for the law and was struggling to establish a paying practice in Boston. Until that happened, he and his fiancée, Elizabeth Hoar, daughter of the squire, put off their nuptials. Then the newly elected congressman Hoar came up with an enticing plan. Since he would be away in the nation's capital for months at a time, he generously proposed to turn over his law office to his prospective son-in-law. The young man could take on whatever business was pending and use the opportunity to attract his own clientele. By that means the couple would finally possess the financial wherewithal to wed. Although the ambitious Charles preferred to succeed on his own and not through his father-in-law's patronage—it "in some sort hurts one's pride of independence," he admitted—this was an offer he could not refuse.

By early March 1835, Charles Emerson was hard at work in the squire's village office, "as black as [the] smoke & dirt of twenty years can smutch it." He joined a growing clan in town: his mother and Waldo at the manse, and Aunt Mary Moody Emerson boarding in the village. "The fiery and affectionate sibyl" of the family, Aunt Mary was custodian of the Emerson heritage, urging her nephews to live up to the example of piety and leadership set by their clerical forebears and challenging their intellects with her original religious and philosophical speculations. Famous for her bluntness and eccentricity—she would later become notorious for wearing her burial shroud as everyday garb just to be ready for her funeral—she circulated through the New England countryside, calling on the hospitality of relatives, clergymen, and friends. But she never abandoned her claims on Concord nor her "immeasurably high" expectations of her nephews. Her "devout genius," inspired by Puritan faith but impatient with Calvinist dogma and open to Romantic ideas, stood for Waldo as a model of spiritual striving, in sharp contrast to the stilted sermons and formal worship of Ezra Ripley. She was the unacknowledged muse of Transcendentalism.[4]

The turning point in Emerson's plans came in the spring of 1835. "Waldo thinks he shall settle himself as a citizen in this town," Charles informed their older brother William, a lawyer in New York City. That decision culminated two months of fraught discussions with his bride-to-be, Lydia Jackson, over where the couple would live. The future husband and wife were just getting to know one another after a brief acquaintance, which began with Emerson's visits to Plymouth as a guest lecturer and preacher the previous year. Born in 1802, nine months before Waldo, Jackson lived on the income from her late father's estate and was content with her independent existence as a single woman close to family and friends and active in charities and church. Her union with Waldo was founded on what both took to be shared ideals for a higher, spiritual life together; she looked upon her betrothed "with reverence as an angelic being." The thought of moving from Plymouth never entered her mind. But that relocation was precisely what Emerson proposed to the maiden he renamed "Lidian." Initially, he was open to various possibilities: "Concord is only one of a hundred towns" in which he could follow the calling of lecturer and poet. But Plymouth was out of the question. A crowded seaport hectic with trade, it lacked the privacy and peace of the countryside. "Plymouth is streets. I live in the wide champaign." That position quickly hardened. Concord became the only option. Nowhere else would he be able to write. His very "inkstand" dried up at the thought of relocation. "Inkstand says he will not budge one foot . . . his roots [are] in this paternal soil." Despite her attachment to Plymouth Rock, Lidian must "come & sit down by Concord Battle-Bridge." To abandon "my native quarters" for her hometown, he went on to explain, would "cripple me of some important resources." He got his way after the couple's wedding in September 1835.

Emerson did not specify what those "important resources" were. But his ultimatum came soon after brother Charles made his own decision to settle in "the land of their fathers." In anticipation of their marriages, the brothers evidently hoped to live together in a single, extended family, joined by their mother Ruth and perhaps Aunt Mary and other kin. In this setting they would raise their children, and all would flourish intellectually and spiritually. In the process, the Emersons, so long separated from one another in transient lodgings in Boston and beyond, would reestablish themselves and revive their standing in the town where the Patriot preacher William Emerson once inspired a people to Revolution.[5]

Happily, Waldo possessed the resources to make this possible, thanks to a legacy from his first wife Ellen's estate; in mid-1834 he received payment of $11,600, half of what he was ultimately due. With that sum he was able to purchase a two-story white house at the edge of the village, along with a barn, outhouses, and two and a half acres of land, at a bargain price of $3,500. Built by the Boston merchant John T. Coolidge in 1828 as "a gentleman's country seat," the spacious dwelling could accommodate the substantial domestic establishment its new owner had in mind. It had something of "a city air" in a country town. Standing at the head of the Cambridge Turnpike, it afforded a convenient route into the Hub; Emerson could virtually hail the stage from his front door. It was close to the center, alive with busy stores and shops, meetinghouses and courthouse, lyceum and social library, and simultaneously a comfortable walk to the Walden woods and pond. Most important of all, "Bush," the name the Emersons chose for their new home, planted the family in the "ancestral" town for the first time since 1776.

While such old clans as the Minotts and Prescotts were dying out, the Emerson men were returning to their origins and reclaiming their place on the land. But the grand plan was never achieved. Charles Emerson died of consumption in May 1836, and older brother William preferred to practice law in New York City, so Waldo was left to pursue the family dream on his own.[6]

No single place would bound Emerson's horizons or confine his search for purpose. Although he had relinquished a pastorate, he had not given up on preaching, and he continued to don the "robe" of eloquence and hold forth in the pulpit. No sooner had he dropped off his belongings at Ripley's manse than he was on his way to Manhattan for a four-week stint at a Unitarian church. (There he got word that another brother, Edward Bliss Emerson, had died in distant Puerto Rico at twenty-nine.) Return to Concord brought little rest. He was seldom in town on the Sabbath. During his first year of residence, Emerson delivered more than seventy sermons to congregations in various Middlesex towns, in Boston, and in Plymouth. When he wasn't preaching, he was giving lectures, in preparation for which he was often in the capital area to borrow books. He had few free moments to settle into Concord life. Sitting at his writing desk at the manse, with a view of the river, meadows, and battleground, he wrestled with new ideas stirring up intellectuals in Boston and beyond and tried out his thoughts in discourses designed for urban audiences. No pastoral retreat from the metropolis, his country home was a cosmopolitan outpost of the intellectual world of Cambridge and Boston.[7]

WHEN EMERSON TOOK UP LODGINGS IN CONCORD, HE WAS NOT YET KNOWN as a Transcendentalist. Nor were other Unitarian ministers and seekers in the Boston area—Elizabeth Palmer Peabody, Orestes Brownson, Frederic Henry Hedge, Theodore Parker, George Ripley, Margaret Fuller, most notably—with whom he would soon be associated. In the early 1830s the term enjoyed little currency; to the few in the know, chiefly in religious circles, it referred to the idealist philosophy of Immanuel Kant and his heirs, and that was not necessarily a good thing.

Owing to the abstraction and unfamiliar terminology of the German writers, *transcendental* became a byword for obscure, unintelligible, and useless speculation. Nonetheless, Continental thinkers had their champions, particularly the English poet Samuel Taylor Coleridge and the Scottish essayist Thomas Carlyle, and through their influence a rising generation of Unitarian clergymen, anxious to revive the spiritual fervor of their denomination, discovered a new way to think about faith. In the process, they took imported ideas in radical directions, exacerbated divisions on the religious landscape, and intensified the movement to expand individual freedom and achieve social equality in New England life.[8]

The main conduit of German idealism to Yankee readers was the Unitarian monthly the *Christian Examiner*, and with good reason. The new philosophy promised to inject vitality into liberal preaching. In reaction against the emotional excesses of evangelical revivals, ministers such as Ezra Ripley had taken a rationalist approach to religion. His discourses set forth reasoned arguments for the existence of God, the orderliness of Creation, the obligations of Christianity, the principles of morality, the duties of family and community, and the righteousness of divine judgment. Spare of metaphor, each sermon was a well-ordered statement, in which abstract nouns ruled like impersonal magistrates, defining and prescribing laws for rational minds. So constant was this refrain in Ripley's sermons that Mary Moody Emerson dubbed him "Dr. Reason."

These lessons were supplemented by appeals to Scripture and particularly to the life and mission of Christ. The miracles performed by Jesus served as compelling proof of his divine calling. No matter that such violations of natural law as walking on water and raising the dead were at odds with the regularity of physical existence that Ripley and his colleagues were otherwise at pains to point out. Most Unitarians managed to hold these opposing ideas without troubling over the contradictions. Their perspective, dubbed "supernatural rationalism," rested on seventeenth-century English philosopher John Locke's formulation that all our knowledge of the world, even of the divine plan for creation, derives from our senses. For just this reason, God sent his Son to preach his message to humanity and to prove his divine mission by working wonders. The New Testament was the record of such deeds. Its reports of miracles could be verified through the normal exercise of reason. Like testimony in a courtroom, the credibility of its accounts depended on their logical consistency, the strength of counterclaims, and the character of the witnesses. Nobody need take the truth of Christianity on faith.

Rehearsing these claims by expounding the Bible every Sabbath made for a conscientious course in the Christian walk. But formalistic preaching left many souls hungering for something more, and it could not stem the tide of defectors to the Calvinist and evangelical churches that were eager to take them in. On the eve of disestablishment, a famine of eloquence in the pulpit was starving Unitarian congregations of spiritual nourishment and abandoning them to torpor, indifference, and unbelief.[9]

That was the view of critics in the Unitarian ranks, who found in the new ideas from overseas a warrant for a different approach. Why labor so pedantically to argue people into faith and with so little profit? As the philosophers of idealism made plain, "men are not reasoned into good feelings." They obtain knowledge of God at birth; it is an endowment of every human soul, "coeval with existence." Formed in the divine image, each person desires instinctively to commune with the Creator and to realize "the great principles of religion." This spiritual yearning unites humankind, from savage to civilized, in all times and places. Transcendentalists called it "the sentiment of religion." Lodged in the heart, it was a faculty as intrinsic to living as breathing. Individuals came to it naturally, whenever they acknowledged the presence of God and aspired to realize the truths of religion and morality so perfectly modeled by Jesus. Too often, though, the sentiment was inchoate, dimly sensed but buried beneath the mundane concerns and selfish striving of everyday existence. It thus became the charge of the Transcendentally minded preacher to rouse that feeling, quicken it into consciousness, and make it the animating force of each listener's life.[10]

A liberal awakening was distinct from an evangelical revival. Trinitarian clergymen, such as Rev. Lyman Beecher, beat the pulpit drum to recruit soldiers for Christ. His sermons warned of the dire fate awaiting the unregenerate, and they aimed to provoke "sudden anxieties, and deep convictions of sin, and sudden joy in believing; followed by reformation and a holy life." Unitarians eschewed this "evangelical system." Not for them the Calvinist scheme with its unceasing talk of original sin and its exhortations to be born again in the Lord. Fearful of out-of-control emotions and social disorder, the liberals declined to separate humanity into saints and sinners and encouraged every individual to cultivate the divine potential within through a lifetime of moral and intellectual improvement. Unfortunately, this prospectus for Christian self-culture could fall short. Far from straining for perfection, some clerical advocates were prone to accommodate themselves to a world rife with injustice and to demand little more than respectable conduct from the faithful. Such religion could devolve into social conformity and spiritual death.[11]

The avant-garde of Unitarian thinkers transcended the orthodox-liberal divide. Unlike their denominational colleagues, they sided with revivalists and welcomed emotional expression in religion. But in contrast to the Calvinists, they trusted the sentiments of the heart. Human nature, in this view, was free of innate corruption; it did not require redemption through the experience of saving grace. Transcendentalist ministers did not rail against sin and invoke the terrors of hell in order to break the wills of the unregenerate and drive them, distraught and sobbing, into the arms of Jesus. Rather, they appealed to the better angels of parishioners, in the confidence that the "deep wants of our nature lead us to God." In like manner, they expounded on the principles of morality, to which every person, if true to eternal laws intrinsic to the self, would assent. The "Conscience" is "the voice of God in the Soul of Man." So completely did this faith rest on the inherent divinity of humankind that it dispensed with the familiar features of religion in the Western tradition: covenants and creeds, doctrines and discipline, sacred rituals and the officials to perform them. Preachers, in turn, were no longer tethered to Scripture and could explore nature and history, politics and society in sermons designed to engage the imagination and move the heart. Questioning even the indispensability of miracles to Christian faith, these clerical progressives pressed against the limits of liberalism in the Unitarian fold.[12]

In the forefront of religious reform were three ministers in the Boston area: Frederic Henry Hedge (1805–1890), George Ripley (1802–1880), and Orestes Brownson (1803–1876). Hedge and Ripley were children of privilege, one the son of a Harvard professor, the other of a wealthy merchant in western Massachusetts. Both attended college and divinity school in Cambridge; Hedge also enjoyed several years of schooling abroad to become expert in German language and learning. Each, upon finishing ministerial training, was called to a nearby church. Brownson, by contrast, was the self-educated son of a hardscrabble home in rural Vermont. A spiritual seeker, he migrated through Calvinism, Universalism, and skepticism in a roving career across northern New England and New York State before alighting on a Unitarian pulpit in the town of Canton, twenty miles south of Boston, in 1834. (George Ripley preached the sermon at his ordination.) Whatever their route, all three took the lead in introducing religious idealism to readers of the *Christian Examiner*. With an essay on Coleridge in March 1833, Hedge claimed priority in speaking "the *first word* . . . which any American had uttered in respectful recognition of the claims of Transcendentalism." These pioneering contributors took the Unitarian belief in every individual's "likeness to God" and, through the admixture of Continental philosophy, charged it with the emotional dynamism of the "religious sentiment."[13]

Waldo Emerson played no part in these efforts. In the fall of 1834, when he took up residence in Concord, he was unknown as an author and just embarking on a career as a public lecturer on such acceptable topics as biography, natural history, and his travels in Italy. While he avoided religious controversy, he was following his own path to the limits of Unitarian orthodoxy. As a ministerial student at Harvard's "theological institution" and then as a young pastor, Emerson had preached conventional sermons in defense of Unitarian doctrine, but on his own he was in search of deeper spiritual experience. Prodded by the "high counsels" of his Aunt Mary, he discovered Coleridge and the German idealists, and after assuming the helm of Boston's Second Church, he gradually worked his way toward a "new and strikingly modern theology." "Christianity is validated in each person's life and experience," he affirmed in 1830, "or not at all." On this principle of authenticity, the young minister declined to perform any ritual, such as the communion service, that was false to his feelings, and accordingly gave up his office. Unburdened by institutional responsibilities, he could explore the divine spirit within his deepest self and pursue a high calling in the pulpit, summoning others to do the same.[14]

The liberals of Concord's First Parish had ample opportunity to follow the religious evolution of Ezra Ripley's step-grandson. Between 1827 and 1830, he was guest preacher on eleven Sabbaths, delivering at least seventeen sermons. His performance in the spring of 1828 delighted Edward Jarvis. The sermons were "some of the purest & best I have ever heard in Concord," the medical student commented in his diary: "practical & instructive, not polemical nor vague but plain & applicable to our own business & life." But not everyone agreed: the discourses were "sometimes too refined & intellectual for a Concord audience."[15]

Emerson was gone from the Concord pulpit after April 1830 and did not return until mid-November 1834, a month after moving into Ripley's manse. His first sermon as a town resident revealed the expansive vision that had led him to resign the ministry. "God is within us," he proclaimed; "God is in our soul." To know God was to know ourselves, and that meant to delve into our minds and hearts, to probe our consciousness, rather than comply with outward rituals and formal prayers. Here Emerson conjured up the religious sentiment as the spring of faith, the feeling of communion by which "our whole soul becomes one refulgent mirror of the presence & power & love of God." Composed before his 1833 trip to Europe, the sermon testified to the influence of the German and British idealists; by the time he delivered it in Concord, he had met both

Coleridge and Carlyle in person and become the American agent of the latter. Emerson was thus in tune with the emerging faction of Transcendentalists in the Unitarian ranks. He read the *Christian Examiner* attentively, enthusing over Hedge's essay on Coleridge as "a living leaping Logos," and dreamed of launching a periodical of his own that would "speak truth without fear or favor to all who desire to hear it." But he held his fire for the time being. His affinity with the reformers was evident in the sermons he gave as a guest preacher and in his correspondence with intimates, but not in print. Concord got to follow the development of his religious convictions well before he expressed his Transcendentalist vision in *Nature* (1836) and shocked the Unitarian establishment with his iconoclasm at Harvard Divinity School in July 1838.[16]

The Transcendentalist focus on religious sentiment was well suited to a society in transition. For if the core of faith was an ineffable feeling of communion with the divine spirit, knowable only to the individual in the recesses of the soul, then the means of its expression were mere expedients, dependent on time and place. "Everything connected with [religion] is subject to change," George Ripley instructed the assembly at Brownson's ordination. All its "forms . . . may be varied." The place of worship may be "under the magnificent dome of a cathedral, or on the dreary hill-side with no canopy but the blue vault of Heaven." The rituals of one church can seem "deficient or superfluous" to another. So too with theology: "the speculative doctrines of religion . . . may assume new forms and be clothed in new language." Nothing was fixed but "the indestructible religious sentiment in the human heart . . . It is the same, today, that it always has been."

This very fluidity of faith—its multiplicity of forms—was key to the future of religion. For "great changes [were] taking place on every side," George Ripley observed, "old ideas, old institutions, old habits of thought" giving way to new conceptions "supposed to proceed more directly from reason, and the natural wants of man." Why cling to an outdated status quo? Nothing in nature was "still." The "material universe" was ruled by the "law of perpetual change." Likewise for human affairs: "our experience is diversified by a constant succession of changes." Under these shifting circumstances, organized religion—the institutions and practices of the Christian churches and of the Unitarians in particular—faced a fundamental challenge. "Will the progress of society . . . leave religion in the background," Ripley asked, "and reject it as an outworn and useless thing?"[17]

Not if these Transcendentalist ministers had their way. Their prospectus for change was framed for a democratic age. Religion, in this view, did not belong to the few; it was neither the property of priests nor the prerogative of an elect. The sentiment of faith inhered in every person, at once the foundation of human dignity and the spur to a virtuous life. It was thus crucial to awaken each individual to the divine potential within.

Brownson, the child of the laboring class, was acutely aware of the inequalities in American life and determined to overcome them in the name of faith. "The means of moral and intellectual growth, so far as society can furnish them," he wrote in the *Christian Examiner*, "should be within the reach of the humblest as well as the proudest member of the community." Free public education, overseen by an "aristocracy of real virtue," was indispensable to this end. With those "who best represent the spirit of Jesus" at the helm, "there would be no subordination of classes, no exclusive privileges, no monopoly of social advantages." All individuals would then exercise the opportunity to realize their highest selves. And in the process, government and society would embrace a "higher and purer principle of action." For "all social reforms must be the effect of individual reform." To encourage such personal transformation became the grand mission of the Transcendentalist clergy, Emerson included.[18]

The stirring of Transcendentalism quickened the currents of dissent in the Boston area. As the Standing Order was coming to an end, the bustling capital presented an unprecedented spectacle of religious pluralism. In 1833 over fifty congregations and chapels served some sixty thousand residents. While orthodox and liberal Congregationalists fought for control of a dying establishment, a variety of other Protestant faiths—Baptists, Methodists, Episcopalians, Quakers, and Universalists—took advantage of the disarray and found opportunities for growth among those who were disaffected from the mainline churches or flocking into the city from the countryside. Heterodoxy flourished. A Church of the New Jerusalem, founded on the teachings of the Swedish mystic Emanuel Swedenborg, promised to reveal the hidden spiritual meanings behind all living things—a doctrine with passing appeal to Emerson and other Transcendentalists. Also claiming a place in the City upon a Hill were two Roman Catholic houses of worship, serving a fast-growing population, overwhelmingly Irish immigrants, that would reach twenty thousand by 1835.[19]

A large body of citizens was unchurched, often by preference. Radical ideas were circulating in the Boston area during the early 1830s, as a Workingmen's

Party organized to protest harsh conditions of labor and inequalities of wealth and power in the industrializing economy. It denounced the capitalist class as furiously as the Anti-Masons assailed the secretive fraternity. The iconoclasm extended to religion. In 1830 an irreverent activist named Abner Kneeland (1774–1844) launched the *Boston Investigator* to foster "universal mental liberty" and to support the political program of Andrew Jackson. Once a Baptist layman and then a Universalist minister, the editor was now a freethinker who devoted himself to mocking the beliefs of faithful Christians and attacking the clergy for upholding an unjust social order. Twice a week he held forth to a Society of Free Enquirers with a thoroughgoing materialism that deemed the New Testament's account of Jesus's virgin birth, miracles, and resurrection to be utterly absurd. The "Temple of Reason" also hosted weekly dancing parties at which young men and women cultivated the "social affections." Adding to the scandal caused by the promiscuous assemblies was the open sale of a frank guide to birth control and sexuality, *Fruits of Philosophy*, written by a Massachusetts doctor named Charles Knowlton. Such concentration on physical existence, with no hint of religious sentiment, was antithetical to idealists like Emerson. "To be without God in the world," he reflected in April 1834, was to endure a "terrible solitude," void of hope and meaning. Yet Kneeland's convictions could easily be confused with Transcendentalism. "I believe that the whole universe is nature," the editor told readers, "and that God and Nature are perfectly synonymous terms."[20]

The growing openness and diversity of opinion in Boston provoked a backlash. State authorities took quick action to ban *Fruits of Philosophy* as an obscene book, charging its freethinking author with the intention to "debauch and corrupt, and to raise, excite and create . . . inordinate and lustful desires in the hearts of youth and other citizens." In December 1832 a court in Cambridge sentenced Knowlton to three months of hard labor in the Middlesex house of correction. Next it was Kneeland's turn to face the bar of public opinion and official judgment. Within a year of the skeptic's arrival on the Boston scene, Rev. Lyman Beecher ascended the pulpit of Park Street Church to rouse evangelicals against the "epidemic" of "political atheism" invading the capital. The social order was under siege, he warned; the enemies of faith meant to "turn the world up side down," set the poor against the rich, destroy private property, marriage, the family, and respect for the authority of "civil government." But Kneeland's popularity surged; he gathered a thousand dues-paying members in his society and twice as many listeners at his Sunday lectures.[21]

In the face of this growth, Boston's leaders lacked George Ripley's assurance that "the reign of unbelief is passing away"; nor did they share Emerson's view that "Good is promoted by the worst." "Don't despise the Kneelands & Andrew Jackson," he confided in his journal. Like insects fertilizing the soil with the dregs they leave behind, the demagogues "perform a beneficence they know not of, & cannot hinder if they would." But local authorities, determined to shield the newspaper-reading public from Kneeland's atheism, charged the editor with violating a 1782 state law and committing the crime of blasphemy. The case was filed in January 1834, a week after the separation of church and state went into effect. If government could no longer require citizens to attend public worship and support a Christian church, it could at least protect them from impiety. Despite the new regime of voluntary religion, the custodians of the Commonwealth continued to police the boundaries of public discourse.[22]

Popular pressure sustained and sometimes substituted for government in suppressing minorities. The social reformer Samuel Gridley Howe was outraged by the threat atheism posed to the sanctity of marriage and the harmony of society, but rather than prosecute Kneeland in court, he proposed a citizens' boycott of the freethinker and his supporters. "Let the merchants erase their names, from his books; let females close the doors of their drawing-rooms to them, as they would to blacklegs and swindlers." Accordingly, the Temple of Reason was booted from its headquarters at the Federal Street Theater and had to scramble for another venue.[23]

Far worse was the extralegal violence targeted at people of color and at Catholics. African Americans braved harassment by hostile whites whenever they ventured out of doors; in 1826, following a parade to celebrate the anniversary of U.S. withdrawal from the international slave trade, a mob invaded the African American neighborhood on Beacon Hill and destroyed several houses. The malefactors went unpunished.[24]

Catholics came under attack as their numbers soared. At the end of 1830, the tireless Reverend Beecher found time amid his campaigns against Unitarians and freethinkers to deliver a series of lectures branding Catholicism "incompatible" with republicanism. Shackled by loyalty to "a foreign Sovereign," the subjects of "the Pope of Rome" could not be trusted to uphold "civil and religious freedom." But they would surely be pliable tools in the hands of "Atheists and Infidels" for the purpose of "crushing Protestantism preparatory to the subversion of Christianity." Such fears gathered force in succeeding years and exploded in a night of violence on August 11, 1834, when a mob of Protestant workingmen vandalized and burned to the ground the Ursuline convent and boarding school atop "Mount Benedict" in Charlestown. Condemned by many in the Boston elite, the riot seared politics in the Bay State and furnished another wedge issue dividing the populists in the Democratic and Anti-Masonic parties from Whigs. The rights of individuals were at stake on numerous fronts.[25]

"The root & seed of democracy is the doctrine Judge for yourself," Emerson reflected early in his sojourn at the manse. "Reverence thyself." This confidence in the capacity of the individual extended the Transcendentalist faith in the soul to politics and society. It was also a product of the ongoing transformation of New England life: the advance of markets, the fraying bonds of interdependence, the spread of voluntary associations, the growing opportunities to exercise autonomy and choice. But the very forces allowing for greater personal freedom also threatened to curtail it and to impose new social controls. Emerson had glimpsed these possibilities and dangers in the mass society rapidly taking shape in Boston. Could the freedom of mind so essential to liberty and virtue be sustained when mass political parties, militant religious sects, intrusive moral crusades, angry mobs in the streets, and intolerant editors competed to harness and drive the citizenry to their own ends? Could the single individual exercise independent judgment and stay true to the voice of conscience? At this very moment, the French visitor Alexis de Tocqueville was highlighting two fundamental perils to "democracy in America": the "tyranny of the majority" over public opinion and the oppression of "Negro slavery" in the South.

Could Transcendentalism meet these challenges? The fields of Emerson's fathers would provide a crucial arena and test for his vision.[26]

No COMMUNITY IN THE BOSTON AREA WAS MORE IDENTIFIED WITH TRANscendentalism than Concord. That was due in large part to the promotional efforts of Emerson, whose home on the Cambridge Turnpike became a mecca for intellectuals, nonconformists, and oddballs, and whose personal efforts drew Amos Bronson Alcott, Nathaniel Hawthorne, and Margaret Fuller to the locale and publicized Thoreau as *the* man of Concord. So successful was this boosterism that the town eventually became a byword for the movement it hosted; to the teenage Henry Adams in the mid-1850s, New England idealism was enshrined in "the Concord Church." But twenty years earlier, as

Rev. William Emerson's grandson was returning to his roots, the social and political climate was quite different. With Doctor Ripley still in the pulpit, Concord was no temple of individualism, and although the inhabitants were seeking greater opportunities for personal choice, they continued to cherish the ties of interdependence and accept the claims of society on the self. Much work lay ahead for Emerson and his fellow seekers before Transcendentalism entered the mainstream of local thought.[27]

In this time of transition, Emerson found encouragement in social and cultural improvements. School reform was in high gear; in April 1835, with a substantial increase in its spending for education, the town ensured that pupils in the rural districts as well as the village could obtain instruction nearly all year long. Almost every child between four and sixteen was enrolled; even some three-year-olds were crowded into the schoolhouses, if only for day care. But the ambitious school committee was not satisfied. Troubled by irregular attendance, it groused about the waste of money on students whose frequent absences caused them to fall behind their classmates, lose motivation, and become "listless and idle." Some members contemplated drastic measures: "Ought there to be a Law compelling parents to send their children to school?" Committee secretary Edward Jarvis argued in favor of the proposition at a lyceum debate in December 1834. His was the losing position, well ahead of public opinion; Massachusetts would not adopt a mandatory attendance law until 1852.[28]

Though he was new to town and without children of his own, Emerson paid close attention to these debates. He had read Pestalozzi with enthusiasm and enlisted in the American Institute of Education, a Boston-based lobby for school reform, at its founding in 1830. His vision of education went beyond anything Concord had yet considered. The town, in Lemuel Shattuck's words, aimed to prepare the individual for "the greatest usefulness in the world." Emerson's ideal was far more expansive and individualistic. On December 27, 1834, he read an account of a lyceum lecture about education in the local press and responded in his journal. Every person, he reflected, has "a determination of character to a peculiar end"—a unique native "genius." No one can define or prescribe that intrinsic "Idea" for anyone else. Each of us must discover it "in those days or moments" when we enjoy "the sincerest satisfaction" from life. In this light, Emerson concluded, "the object of Education should be to remove all obstructions & let this natural force have free play & exhibit its peculiar product." Rather than drill knowledge into the child, the school should draw out the genius within and cultivate it for its own sake. Society would benefit in the process, though no one could say how in advance. Here was a message with which Emerson would challenge his neighbors.[29]

The Concord Lyceum welcomed the newcomer to its platform. The group thrived amid the Anti-Masonic conflict, continuing its program of adult education without a hitch. It sponsored twenty-two lectures in 1832–1833, as the insurgency was getting under way, and the same number in 1834–1835, when the protest movement peaked. Whatever their partisan differences, townspeople found common cause in the advancement of knowledge. Ezra Ripley— "our 'Corinthian Father'" to his enemies—discoursed about "the formation of character" and the "means of preserving health"; Trinitarian minister Wilder, a leader of the Anti-Masons, offered tips on the "means of personal improvement." The Masonic cotton manufacturer Ephraim Bellows discussed tariff laws; the carriage maker William Whiting, high priest of the Royal Arch Chapter, dilated on the qualities of "good working men" and of the worthy "man of business." Lyceum members continued to debate, too: "Does the solemnity of an oath increase the obligation to speak the truth?" Two weeks after Atwill began publishing Adams's denunciation of Masonic vows, the society considered the pros and cons of this question, though no decision was reported. The lyceum stayed true to its apolitical purpose by offering lectures on science (geology and meteors), history (Jesuits, Puritans, the Boston Tea Party, American history in general), and education. The four addresses Emerson gave in the 1834–1835 season easily fit the bill, and he gratified the members by providing free what he charged for in Boston. His discourse on "the character of Martin Luther," delivered on April 16, 1835, marked a red-letter day for the speaker and the town. It was his fifth appearance before the local audience. On those prior occasions, he had been identified in the lyceum records as a resident of Boston. Now, three days before the sixtieth anniversary of the glorious event in which his Patriot grandfather had played so notable a part, he came before the town and spoke as a man "of Concord," one of its own.[30]

While education united the townspeople in pursuit of individual improvement, politics confined their minds within partisan channels. Emerson arrived in Concord as National Republican fortunes were reviving, with Keyes and Barrett recovering their seats in the state legislature and Hoar en route to Congress. Three months later local power shifted back to the Anti-Masons, who swept the town elections in what the winners hailed as a "triumph of Demo-cratic principles over Masonic intolerance and Aristocratic insolence." Within a year the Anti-Masons merged with the Democrats to form a single party be-hind Jackson and Van Buren in a decade-long rivalry with the Whigs. Emerson was initially a bystander at this struggle for power, too new a resident to qualify for the vote. Even so, he had strong opinions about the candidates, the parties, and the democratic process.

Reared among the Federalist elite of Boston, Emerson had absorbed the view that republican government required the exercise of civic virtue and the cultivation of consensus. Who better to carry out those duties than the well-educated merchants, professionals, and gentlemen at the top of the social or-der? But that was not what the pastor of Boston's prestigious Second Church discerned during his three years (1829–1832) in the pulpit. Emerson lamented that "the ferocity of party spirit" divided citizens from one another and cor-rupted the conduct of government. No longer did the people follow "the best men"; nor did they subordinate private interests to the public good. To the ide-alistic young preacher, educated in the same elitist philosophy that his grand-sire Ripley expounded in Concord, selfishness was running rampant. Politicians treated power "as a prize instead of a trust," and in quest of that object, they appealed to the worst instincts of the crowd: ignorance and prejudice, self-interest and passion. Emerson pinned the blame for this sorry state of affairs on Jacksonian Democrats, "the Bad party in the country," whose "thoroughly selfish" leaders had but one aim in mind: to gain the spoils of office. In Novem-ber 1834, on a visit to Manhattan, he witnessed with rising anxiety the extrava-ganza of elections—"flags, boy processions, placards, badges, medals, bannered coaches, everything to *get the hurra on our side*." He could hardly bear the prospect of defeat. No sooner did he begin to speculate in his journal about what might happen "should the Whig party fail" than he immediately added "which god avert!"[31]

If Emerson expected small-town Concord to be an improvement over the city, he was quickly disabused of that notion. The newcomer beheld the conflict over Freemasonry while living in his embattled grandfather's manse. Not sur-prisingly, he had no sympathy for the populist insurgency, which he deemed a "disfigurement" of the landscape, unworthy of notice. The agitation, in his view, amounted to a self-serving bid by unscrupulous men to advance themselves at public expense. Just look at the editor of the *Boston Daily Advocate*: "Hallett feeds on the Masons." Anti-Masonry was another version of "the Bad party." Not that the Whigs were much better. While Emerson admired the character of Samuel Hoar—his "merits . . . seem pure & saintlike compared with practices & reputations of the mob"—he despaired of the low aims of his party. In late March 1835, on the verge of deciding to settle in Concord, the independent clergyman took the measure of the town's leading figures—Nathan Brooks, Abiel Heywood, Daniel Shattuck, among others—and found them wanting. These solid citizens were so mired in materialism that they could envision no higher goal than continued prosperity. They "have no theory of business that can stand scrutiny," Emerson judged, "but only bubble built on bubble without end." Eventually, the bubble would burst, leaving their reputation for "good sense" in ruins and exposing the utter inadequacy of their worldview.[32]

By the time he made his home in Concord, Emerson had shed the Federalist elitism of his youth in favor of an ideal of democracy more demanding than any contemporary politician espoused. Rather than elect the best men, as defined by education and social class, the citizens of his ideal republic would apply their "divine Reason"—the intuitive recognition of right and wrong—to public affairs, make up their minds on their own, without taking dictation from political parties or elites, and express their best judgment at the polls. This deliberative process would "insulate" the individual from "the partizan" and "make each man a state."[33]

By this exacting standard, Concord cried out for thoroughgoing reform, despite—or because of—the recent rise of political competition and the surge of voters to the polls. For the parties treated the citizenry not as thinking individuals with minds of their own but rather as obedient foot soldiers to be mobilized for victory by the rival campaigns. Every available weapon was put to use, from high-minded appeals to simplistic slogans, from personal insults to outright lies, and from door-to-door canvassing to stealing votes. No party was exempt from the shoddy tactics, though in Emerson's opinion, the Democrats were the worst offenders; a "Jackson Caucus" displayed "unmixed malignity, withering selfishness, [and] impudent vulgarity," the sight of which would "speedily cure me of my appetite for longevity."[34]

Whigs pretended to superior morality, but in the heat of battle they could play as fast and loose with the rules as their opponents. For all his rectitude, Samuel Hoar had no qualms about presiding over town meetings when he was on the ballot; nor did he rigorously enforce the rules. In December 1834 a second round of voting was necessary to choose a congressman for the district, since no one had gotten an absolute majority the month before. Hoar assumed the chair. With his own fate in the balance, the candidate looked on as the selectmen sorted and counted ballots before the polls closed—a clear violation of state law. Under his tolerant eye, party activists scanned the checklist of voters in search of potential supporters who had not yet shown up; runners were on hand to get the laggards to the polls. When voters' qualifications were challenged, the moderator ignored established procedures and referred the decision not to the selectmen, as the law prescribed, but to the entire house, in the apparent hope that the assembly would follow the recommendation of the town's leading men. Anti-Masons angrily objected to the irregularity. Who needed the opinion of Squire Keyes, Hoar, or "any other 'Squire' in Christendom"? Then again, the foes of the establishment were not above their own chicanery. As the selectmen flouted the rules and began counting votes, they discovered that one person had cast two ballots and not by accident. Then the same thing occurred again. In both cases, the double voting was to the advantage of the Anti-Masonic candidate. The selectmen stopped the counting and called for a fresh vote. By then some citizens—Whig voters—had already gone home. Emerson, in Boston for the day, missed the fireworks.[35]

None of the shenanigans put off voters. Party loyalty was intense and unwavering. The competing organizations printed up ballots with the names of their nominees and distributed them to supporters for use at the polls. The practice took off after 1830, when the state supreme court ruled in favor of Democratic politician David Henshaw, whose bid to submit a single sheet with the names of fifty-five candidates had been rebuffed by Boston officials. These paper strips, which could often be clipped from newspapers, made it easy to vote a straight party ticket. In the November 1834 election, Concord's partisans rallied behind the opposing slates almost to a man, with nearly as much cohesion as Federalists and Republicans had displayed two decades before. No level of government was exempt from the competition. Where Federalists and Republicans had cooperated to insulate local affairs from the political passions of the day, the new generation carried the fight for power into town meeting and voted along party lines for moderator, selectmen, and even overseers of the poor. So bitter was the contest that following Phineas Allen's defeat of long-serving Abiel Heywood for town clerk, the Whig elite pulled their sons and daughters out of the Concord Academy and recruited a new instructor.

The preceptor struggled on, and though he was reelected to a second term, he gave up the fight and departed the town. John Shepard Keyes, the twelve-year-old son of the imperious politician, was delighted by the closure; "the school had degenerated into a merely useless machine." Concord Academy reverted to the instability that had plagued it in its early years. Instead of educating the citizens in a deliberative process, as Emerson had hoped, town politics was clouding minds with partisan passions.[36]

No one was more unswerving in his partisanship than editor Herman Atwill. Having freed himself from the oversight of Shattuck and Keyes, he had defeated advertiser boycotts and subscription cancellations and prevailed over Wheildon's *Aurora*, which closed its Concord office in August 1833, after just seven months. The *Yeoman's Gazette* reclaimed the local field for itself, but now as an Anti-Masonic organ. The protracted struggle took its toll; after eight years of "unwearied application," the editor was eager for "less arduous" employment, perhaps a government job in reward for his political labors. In mid-June 1834 he sold the *Gazette* to George F. Bemis, a twenty-four-year-old printer raised in the adjacent town of Lincoln. The new owner pledged to continue on an Anti-Masonic course, in token of which he adopted the motto "Persevere." Soon he had a rival in the *Middlesex Whig*, an organ "of the same political stamp" as the *Aurora* and with no better hope of success. After the Anti-Masons forged an alliance with the Democrats for the November 1834 election, Bemis switched sides. Unable to stomach the "executive usurpation and misrule" of "King" Andrew Jackson, he merged with the competition; the result of this "singular match" was the *Yeoman's Gazette and Middlesex Whig*. With Keyes and Shattuck providing behind-the-scenes financing and editorial control, Concord was set to resume its status as a one-newspaper town, once more in service to the Whig elite.[37]

This alarming prospect brought Atwill back into the journalistic fray. His new medium was the *Concord Freeman*, which began publication in December 1834. The fiery printer assumed the helm as publisher and editor but, in fact, had "no pecuniary interest in the concern." The weekly was a local enterprise in name only. The actual owners were a consortium of Anti-Masonic politicians from Groton, Marlboro, South Reading, and Weston, whose identities were never publicly revealed. Just as the orthodox party at the Park Street Church in Boston surreptitiously lent crucial aid to the fledgling Trinitarian congregation and helped to bring religious diversity to Concord, so now out-of-town politicians took steps to ensure that an Anti-Masonic organ would be at the ready to wage a war of words in Concord and throughout Middlesex County against the Masonic and Whig establishment at the *Gazette*. Competing newspapers and parties, linked to wider political forces, were the new norm.³⁸

Under Atwill's management, the *Freeman* toiled tirelessly on "the side of the People manfully contending for Equal Rights and the Supremacy of the Laws—opposing Freemasonry, Aristocracy, Nullification, and every other noxious principle at war with the wholesome doctrines of pure Democracy." The newspaper aspired to be more than a party organ. It would be a forum for free speech, wherein every subject "interesting to the public" would be opened up to "free and fearless discussion." In this spirit, Atwill continued to assail the Masonic brotherhood for shackling minds and censoring opponents, and he added the Catholic Church to his list of enemies. Following the attack on the Ursuline convent, Atwill offered token disapproval of the violence—"the laws should rule, not mobs"—before heaping abuse on the alien institution and condemning proposals to compensate the religious establishment with public funds. The *Freeman* merged anti-Catholicism with Anti-Masonry into a conspiratorial worldview. In its pages the Church and the Fraternity, though sworn enemies in the Old World, shared the same authoritarian goal of "absolute and all-grasping power." Each constituted an elaborate hierarchy whose tentacles extended all over the globe through an army of agents bound by "dangerous" oaths to execute its commands. The victims were plunged into the darkness of mental "despotism," the "most cruel" of all. They had "no will of their own."³⁹

The *Freeman* was inconsistent, not to say insincere, in its commitment to freedom of expression. It endorsed limits on the right of assembly with a demand for a public registry of all secret society members. It inflamed anti-Catholicism by striking out against the wealthy Bostonians who sent their daughters to the Charlestown convent school for genteel education and strict supervision by the nuns. (Among those pupils were nieces of Concord's representative Joseph Barrett and of Emerson's fiancée Lydia Jackson.) Here was another weapon in the contest against the Whig elite, most of whom favored compensation. The editor denied any religious bigotry: "We feel conscious of no personal enmity towards the Catholics." Even so, one month after the convent burning, Atwill served on a committee of the state Anti-Masonic convention that expressed alarm at the speed with which immigrants were gaining access to the suffrage. Could newcomers from foreign lands, "whose habits and feelings have been fixed under monarchical and despotic forms of government," learn to appreciate "the value of equal rights and wholesome laws" in just five years' time? Let the waiting period be extended, so that the process could "operate as a primary school, to qualify those admitted to it to become free citizens."[40]

Whatever his stand on issues, Atwill pursued one unvarying line: his own advantage. Having jumped ship from the Masons to become their mortal enemy, he expected a reward. In the spring of 1835, the editor mounted a campaign to remove Keyes from his sinecure as postmaster. Surely it was time for the Jackson administration to follow through on its credo that to the victor belong the spoils and remove this Whig partisan from the lucrative post he had held for over three decades. And who better to replace him than Atwill? More than sixty "of the substantial true-hearted yeomanry" of the town got up a petition to this end. Grateful for the compliment to "our humble self," the self-important editor hastened to declare his availability. He could run the office as well as the incumbent, and he would be glad to receive the $200 annual income it was estimated to yield. With "hungry creditors" at his door "crying for pay," "we want it—we need it." These pleas were unavailing; Keyes stayed put. But the frank admission of pecuniary motives confirmed what the editor's opponents had always suspected. In Herman Atwill, Concord had its own personification of Jacksonian democracy: a political spoilsman unabashedly on the make, the epitome of Emerson's fears.[41]

In July 1835, with no advance warning, Atwill turned the *Freeman* over to Francis Richard Gourgas, a newcomer from the town of Weston, who had bought a half-share of the enterprise. Four months later he was rewarded for his partisan services with appointment as an inspector in the Boston Custom House. Ironically, this patronage plum was dispensed by Atwill's onetime nemesis at the Boston *Statesman*, David Henshaw, now collector of the port of Boston and indefatigable leader of Massachusetts Jacksonians. The editor bargained with the devil and got his price. He was soon gone from Concord for good.[42]

The new editor of the *Freeman*, twenty-four-year-old Gourgas, was as partisan as his predecessor, if not more so. The son of a Swiss immigrant father from Geneva and an English-born mother, the young man had started life in Dorchester, outside Boston, and spent his childhood in the Middlesex town of Weston. He grew up with money and privilege and early on cultivated an aristocratic hauteur in his manners and gait. Bright but willful and "not very studious," he attended the Concord Academy under Phineas Allen before going on to a short-lived college career. "Headstrong, ungovernable, and dissipated," he tangled with officials first at Amherst College, then at Harvard; the latter institution suspended him for vandalizing a faculty member's room. That was the end of his formal education. Back in Weston, he turned his attention to Freemasonry, perhaps in search of a steadying influence. The fraternity was a family tradition; his uncle had helped to found the Scottish Rite order in America. In the winter of 1833, when Anti-Masonry was at a peak, the young man took the three degrees of a master Mason in the Framingham-based Middlesex Lodge. It was another impetuous act that he would come to regret. Two years later, with $500 of his father's money, he became half-owner and editor of the *Concord Freeman* and enthusiastically (as well as belatedly) joined the fight against the secret society, which he now considered "at war with the principles of our free institutions, and the political and social rights of those living under them." Under Gourgas's guidance, the *Freeman* effected the union of Anti-Masons and Democrats that Atwill had begun.[43]

The *Gazette* returned to Whig control, its editor, Bemis, financially dependent on Shattuck and his associates, from whom he rented space in one of the new buildings on the milldam. His copy was often composed by subeditors, one of whom was evidently Charles Chauncy Emerson, now in charge of Samuel Hoar's law office.[44] By October 1835, the rising attorney was gaining notice at party conventions as a voice of Concord's "Young Whigs." The ambitious lawyer was drawn into the partisan fray that his brother shunned and enjoyed a ready outlet in the local press.[45]

The Transcendentalist maintained his intellectual independence. As he surveyed the political scene in 1835, he cherished the hope that as a lecturer, he could rise above the low debates of the day—"Antimasonry or Convent Riots or General Jackson & [his newspaper] the Globe"—and occupy higher ground. From that elevated stance, he hoped to discern "the principle out of which these [passing phenomena] proceed" and reveal the spirit of the age. Should that insight be lacking, he could always find refuge in nature: "In the hush of these woods I find no Jackson placards affixed to the trees."[46]

ONE ISSUE COULD NOT EASILY BE SET ASIDE: THE EVIL OF SLAVERY. AS EMERson was committing to Concord, William Lloyd Garrison's *Liberator*, based in Boston, was starting its fifth year of advocating for immediate emancipation and

for equal rights for all citizens regardless of color. The militant weekly spurred
the formation of antislavery societies by Black and white activists. Founded in
January 1832, the New England Anti-Slavery Society dispatched Garrison and
associates to lecture throughout the Bay State and instigate grassroots support
for the cause. Within two years, over two thousand individuals had put their
names on the rolls. Local auxiliaries of the parent society in Boston spread at a
quickening pace: 1832, two; 1833, six; 1834, twenty-three; 1835, twenty-one. In
Middlesex County, the citizens of Acton, Framingham, Groton, Littleton, Lowell, and Natick enlisted in the movement. Concord remained aloof. And so did
Emerson, notwithstanding his private acknowledgment that his core belief in
democracy was contradicted by the very existence of human bondage. "Because
every man has within him somewhat really divine," he averred in December
1834, "therefore is slavery the unpardonable outrage it is."[47]

Why the hands off? Not because Concord's leaders were indifferent to the
plight of the slave or the situation of the South. Just the opposite. With other
Northerners they recognized that the continuing expansion of slavery on cotton
plantations from South Carolina to Mississippi posed a threat to the well-being
and reputation of the republic. But what was to be done? A sudden end to slavery would burden American society with a "degraded" Black population who
were incapable of self-government and shunned by whites. This fear disposed
the elite of Concord, with its cautious counterparts across the nation, to favor
the gradualist program of the American Colonization Society (ACS). Before the
abolitionists entered the scene, the ACS set the agenda for putting slavery on the
road to extinction at some point in the distant future.

Launched in 1816 by prominent politicians and planters in the Upper South,
with Henry Clay in the forefront, the ACS aimed to eliminate slavery by getting
rid of the enslaved. It promoted emancipation with a program to remove Blacks,
freed from bondage, to the colony of Liberia that it was establishing on the West
African coast. No longer need whites fear the buildup of large communities of
color, as had already occurred in Richmond and Baltimore, Philadelphia, New
York, and Boston. By 1831, the free Black population numbered 300,000 people,
whom hostile whites deemed "indolent in their habits" and "vicious in their pro-
pensities." Colonization promised to remove these "unhappy" souls from the
land of their birth, where they would always be "strangers and aliens," and to re-
settle them in the land of their ancestors, where they could elevate themselves by
"industry and honesty," exercise "political rights and privileges," and feel pride

in a community of their own. These pioneers of a new society would, in turn, bring the benefits of civilization and Christianity to the natives of the area. Missionaries of America in Africa, they would bring the light of republicanism to a continent long lost in the darkness of slave trading and war.[48]

In the early 1830s, just as *The Liberator* was getting started, the ACS strengthened its presence in the Bay State with the organization of branches in several counties and the formation of a statewide body. Middlesex County was notably absent from the roster, along with neighboring Essex and Suffolk counties. Even so, both orthodox and liberal Protestants in Concord took up collections on behalf of the ACS during Sabbath worship. The rival churches cooperated in sending thirty dollars to the national organization in the fall of 1829, and the Trinitarians contributed again five years later. For the most part, this charity had special appeal to members of the First Parish. Year in, year out, from 1829 to 1835, the faithful generously pitched in as the collection plate went around.[49]

Giving to the ACS was touted as both a religious and a patriotic duty. The organization called on ministers all over America to preach on its behalf every Fourth of July. In 1830 the holiday fell on the Sabbath. Ezra Ripley answered the call in a sermon he titled "Love the most comprehensive and essential trait of the Christian character." On this day, when "we rejoice in our liberties and privileges," the parson reminded the congregation of "the enslaved and ignorant Africans in our own country." "Multitudes groan in slavery" in the South and the West, "held in bondage by masters boasting of their liberties as citizens of the United States." Who could deny that this "contradiction" between American ideals and practice was "a reproach to our country, which we ought to wipe away as soon as possible"?

But not immediately. Ripley appreciated the gradualist approach of the ACS. "The abolition of slavery in this country, however desirable, is a work of time and difficulty." Were Southern masters to free their slaves all at once, it would be "ruinous" for both. Provision had to be made so that owners could release their bondsmen "without extreme injury" to themselves and so that freed Blacks could be "conveyed away." Happily, the ACS was laboring to make this possible with financial assistance from people all over the republic. "Can we be deaf to the cries of the oppressed?" the minister asked before concluding that "patriotism and Christianity unite in calling upon us to do something for the relief of the enslaved in the United States."[50]

It is not surprising that Ripley sympathized with both the slaveholder and the slave. He had been a master himself in the years before the Massachusetts Supreme Court overturned the institution. Upon his marriage to his predecessor's widow in 1778, he had assumed control over the two servants for life in her household. A dozen years later one of those Black women, presumably now free, was still living in the manse. The parson's two sons gained firsthand acquaintance with the realities of human bondage on Southern plantations. The elder, Samuel (Harvard Class of 1804), spent close to three years (1804–1807) as a tutor on one of the grandest estates in Virginia, Mount Airy, the seventeen-hundred-acre plantation of John Tayloe III. Living in the heart of the aristocracy of the Old Dominion, the future minister witnessed the day-to-day labors of just over one hundred enslaved men and women in domestic duties and skilled crafts. The recent graduate was understandably impressed by the genteel style he enjoyed in one of the richest families of the Chesapeake. "Mr. Tayloe is a perfect gentleman," Samuel wrote to his father back in Concord, "above the common Virginians . . . Madam Tayloe is one of the finest ladies I ever knew; she is her husband's superior in every respect."

The younger Ripley, Daniel (Harvard Class of 1805), saw slavery in all its raw brutality as the Cotton Kingdom was being carved out of the wilds of Alabama during the second decade of the nineteenth century. Settling in the booming territorial capital of St. Stephens, the twenty-three-year-old lawyer looked to grow up with the country and command a five-hundred-acre estate, with its complement of slaves, within a few years; he never lived to reap that success. Periodic letters kept the family in Concord informed about his struggles to win entry into the local elite. The proud parson was taken aback to learn that Daniel's marriage to the daughter of a local judge was greeted with disdain by her kin. "My son does not merit [such] unworthy treatment," the upset father protested in a letter to his new daughter-in-law's uncle. "We look back upon our family for eight generations on the same farm—we see many branches in various professions—& we do not feel ashamed of . . . [our station], though we cannot boast of riches & high life . . . [This] is the first time I ever had occasion to vindicate in this manner the character of a son, or of my family."[51]

Despite occasional collisions, a fair number of Concord's sons and daughters sojourned below the Mason-Dixon line. Samuel Hoar preceded Samuel Ripley as a tutor at Mount Airy, and though he initially felt awkward in polite company, he gained an education in Southern manners that served him well on his return to the region as a congressman. Two of Edward Jarvis's brothers thrived as druggists in New Orleans; Tilly Merrick spent a decade in Charleston as a merchant and planter before his business failed and he was obliged to return home. Retaining his contacts in the Palmetto State, the storekeeper brokered the supply of cotton from the South Carolina Piedmont to the fledgling textile mill on the Assabet. Headed in the opposite direction, a long line of sickly townspeople trekked to the warmer climes of the South in hopes of restoring their health. Samuel Burr tried that remedy unsuccessfully at the mineral spa of St. Marys in Georgia; Ralph Waldo Emerson enjoyed better results from stays in Charleston and in St. Augustine, Florida, during the winter of 1827–1828. All of these contacts built friendships and business ties with white Southerners that helped to knit together the Union and sustain confidence in African colonization.[52]

Support for colonization transcended divisions of party and sect as well as region. On the national level, the political rivals Henry Clay, Andrew Jackson, and Daniel Webster joined in founding the ACS. In 1831 the Massachusetts branch chose for its first president Samuel Lathrop, the losing Anti-Masonic candidate for governor that year and the next. His fellow officers included well-known Jackson men and National Republicans. Congregationalists and Unitarians, Baptists, Episcopalians, and Quakers readily came together in this cause. In July 1831, when he was still a stalwart of the National Republican establishment, Atwill endorsed the fund drive of the ACS in the *Gazette*, and after he turned coat and took up Anti-Masonry, he reaffirmed his stance in the *Freeman*. So strong was interest in this subject that the Concord Lyceum brought a leading advocate of colonization, Benjamin B. Thatcher, to speak to the inhabitants twice in the same year. "Few, who heard him," Atwill exclaimed after the encore performance in October 1833, "could fail of becoming convinced of the benevolence of the scheme, whatever they may think, of the ultimate results."[53]

Many proponents of colonization stereotyped free people of color as a "reckless and abandoned people" who not only fell into vice and crime but also "corrupt[ed] and poison[ed] all around them." But not all ACS members blamed African Americans for this miserable condition. Black people were acknowledged by some, especially in the North, to be equal to whites in innate potential. Their progress was hindered by bigotry and hostility, which by excluding the oppressed from the community and denying them education and opportunity crushed their motivation for self-improvement, respectability, and material gain. The ACS decried this color line but saw no hope of eradicating white prejudice. Under the circumstances, the best prospect for men and women of African descent was relocation to a new environment, where they could take command of their future and better their lives.

The formula for progress rested on voluntary measures; no one would be forced to leave for Africa (though emancipation was often contingent on emigration). Indeed, promoters of the ACS plan in the Bay State were anxious to assist Black people at home as well as abroad. "The time has fully arrived," they urged in 1831, "when systematic and vigorous measures should be adopted to educate colored youth for school teachers, physicians, and ministers, *either to remain in this country, or to go out to Africa*. A fair experiment has never been made." The results would prove the capacity of Blacks to thrive in freedom and thereby win over skeptical whites "in due course of time" to the cause of total abolition.[54]

White do-gooders seldom sought out the intended beneficiaries of their benevolence and asked their opinion. Black Bostonians condemned the Massachusetts Colonization Society as "a clamorous, abusive and peace-destroying combination," whose plan to repatriate free people of color in Africa was really a plot to perpetuate slavery in the United States. "The whole spring of action," they declared, "seems to originate in the fear lest the free colored people may whisper liberty in the ears of the oppressed." The protesters insisted that the United States, *not* Africa, was their homeland, and they demanded equal rights as free citizens. Let the republic end slavery by releasing its victims from chains, and let them live wherever they pleased in the nation of their birth or in a foreign land of their own choosing—Africa, Haiti, or Upper Canada—"without asking the consent of a slaveholding party."[55]

These meetings in Boston and other major cities must have resonated in the countryside with Concord's Dugan, Garrison, Hutchinson, and Robbins families, striving industriously to acquire property, build prosperous farms, and participate in local churches and schools. What did Africa have to do with the descendants of Revolutionary War veteran Caesar Robbins, whose origins in Massachusetts went back to the 1740s, if not before? Why should Peter Hutchinson, who won prizes at the cattle show and added his name to an 1835 petition for a free bridge over the Charles River, or Susan Robbins Garrison, who joined the Trinitarian church in 1828, pull up their roots in the local community and transplant themselves to foreign soil?

These free Black citizens were undoubtedly conscious of the anticolonization sentiments of their fellows in the capital. They had strong connections to the First African Baptist Church, which two of Caesar Robbins's children—Obed and Susan—had joined in founding in 1806. Located on the west side of Beacon Hill, the church developed into a center of Black activism. Susan Robbins Garrison retained membership for two decades, until Concord's evangelicals afforded a new spiritual home. Peter Hutchinson worshiped in the African meetinghouse, too; his wedding took place there in 1828. About the same time, the son of Susan's first marriage, James Middleton, boarded in a lodging house owned by David Walker, who was a driving force in the Black rejection of colonization. His 1829 *Appeal . . . to the Coloured Citizens of the World, but in Particular, and Very Expressly, to Those of the United States of America* sent a blast of African American radicalism up and down the Eastern seaboard and probably out into Middlesex County. In Concord, the *Appeal* would bolster the claim of the town's free Black citizens to a heritage of liberty and a stake in the community equal to that of their white neighbors.[56]

Just as he had ignored criticism of Freemasonry as long as possible, so Atwill avoided the subject of abolitionism. Only when a local correspondent in June 1833 submitted a column in praise of a new periodical, *The Colonizationist and Journal of Freedom*, did the newspaper acknowledge with distaste the "inflammatory and incendiary publications" also coming off the presses of Boston. So unfriendly was local public opinion to the new mode of antislavery activism manifested by *The Liberator* that the founding meeting of the Middlesex County Anti-Slavery Society (MCASS) on October 1, 1834, was held not in Concord, the usual meeting place, but in Groton, not far from the New Hampshire border. Only one resident of Concord, the Trinitarian pastor John Wilder, just fourteen months into his job, turned up to become a charter member of the new voluntary association.[57]

Three months later abolitionism made a controversial debut in Concord. In January 1835 the MCASS advertised in the *Concord Freeman* its upcoming quarterly meeting, to be held at month's end in the Unitarian meetinghouse. The featured event was an appearance by the English abolitionist George Thompson, who was then on a well-publicized lecture tour of the Northeast. The notice provoked dismay in the rival *Gazette*: "We have seen nothing in any newspaper [over] the last year which has grieved us so much." Abolitionism, the paper editorialized, posed a clear and present danger to the nation. Its advocates presented themselves as champions of the oppressed; actually, through ignorance of the true facts, they "picture to us the horrors of slavery as they do not exist" and made the condition of the enslaved worse. Such agitation, playing on "feelings and sympathies" with wild "exaggerations," served only to endanger the "happiness-giving union of the States" and the safety of Southern whites. The *Gazette* conjured up a scenario as extreme as the imaginings of abolitionists. If the "friends of immediate emancipation" had their way, "they must break up this union; they must desolate and ravage with fire and sword this whole country; they must wade through seas of blood; they must succeed, if at all, at the expense of a civil, and perhaps a servile war."[58]

No more acceptable was the speaker the MCASS was bringing to Concord. The thirty-one-year-old Thompson had played a leading part in the successful campaign to end slavery in the British Empire, which culminated in the West Indian Emancipation Act of 1833. Arriving in the United States on the heels of that triumph, the antislavery radical looked forward to joining forces with Garrison in the fight against colonization. But many Yankees were loath to take the advice of a sanctimonious emissary from the former mother country. How dare this subject of "the land of titled aristocracy, of prejudice, and of white slavery," come to Concord, site of the "first organized resistance" to British "slavery," and presume to instruct the inhabitants about the "principles of government" and "civil or religious liberty"! Wherever he went, the *Gazette* noted, Thompson has "scandalized and vilified America and Americans." No wonder he had met with so hostile a reception. The previous December in Lowell, a "small company of low fellows" congregated outside the lecture hall where Thompson held forth and tried to drown him out with "loud stamping, vociferation, and hisses." When that got nowhere, the "disturbers" flung "missiles" at the building; one brickbat sailed through a window, whisked past the speaker, narrowly missing his head, and landed "harmless before the audience in front of the rostrum." Angry mobs would threaten worse as Thompson took to the stump over the next ten months.

Would something similar happen in Concord? Invoking the so-called "orderly proceedings" of Lowell, the *Gazette* seemed to raise a menacing prospect. Surely "the people of Concord will show as much Yankee blood as their neighbors." Were the publishers calling for a boycott or for a disruption of the event? The message remained ambiguous. But it was yet another bid by the real controllers of the press—notably, Keyes and Shattuck—to crack down on unwelcome dissent.[59]

Although Atwill sided with colonization, the editor hastened to uphold free speech. It was "exclusive, illiberal, [and] dogmatical" for the *Gazette* to disparage a speaker before he had been heard. A free people listened with an open mind. That was exactly what the inhabitants did on the appointed day. "The people came," the *Freeman* crowed, "true as you live, the people came!" Thompson made two presentations, first in the Unitarian, then in the Trinitarian meeting-house. In both performances he held a packed audience "spell-bound" with a complete command of fact, "a pure and lofty eloquence," and an "appeal to every man's understanding and conscience." At the close of the lecture, the "aged and venerable" Doctor Ripley rose to praise the speaker for "his eloquent discourse" and said "charity compelled him to acknowledge that he was engaged in a good cause." Yet the English abolitionist did not change many minds. Atwill remained a colonizationist "for the good of both the white man and the black man." So too did the editors of the *Gazette* dig into their entrenched position. "We have no right to meddle with slavery at all," the paper insisted. "We cannot legislate on the subject, either through our legislatures or through Congress." The best course of Northerners on the slavery question was silence.[60]

As the furor over Thompson erupted, Waldo Emerson wrestled with conflicting feelings. During the week of the Englishman's visit, Concord pulsated with fervent talk about abolitionism; on the next Sabbath, Rev. Hersey Goodwin preached a sermon in the colonizationist vein urging "a *kind* of toleration of slavery." Emerson was outraged, and he poured forth his anger in a long entry in his journal. He loathed slavery and would never say a word in its defense, not even in a dream. As a Christian, it was his duty to "speak ever for the poor & the low" and not for the planter, no matter the consequences: "If by opposing slavery I go to undermine institutions I confess I do not wish to live in a nation where slavery exists." Yet for all his radicalism, Emerson held back from Garrison's and Thompson's militant crusade. With many of his Concord neighbors, he was torn between antislavery principle and fear of slave rebellion, such as the bloody uprising of Nat Turner three and a half years earlier in Southampton County, Virginia. As a result, he would not denounce the slaveholder in public, lest his words reach the oppressed and stir them to "cut the planter's throat." The *Gazette*'s warnings had made an impact. Emerson kept his opinions to himself and his circle of family and friends.[61]

Other members of the Emerson family were quicker to embrace abolitionism. Aunt Mary thrilled to Thompson's lecture, and her commitment to the cause deepened during a visit to Concord by antislavery lecturer Charles C.

Burleigh two months later. Proselytizing for the New England Anti-Slavery Society, he sought out the eccentric old lady, noted for her intense piety and restless intellect, and pressed hard to recruit her into the movement. He soon ran up against a stumbling block: Miss Emerson had contracted "a strong dislike" for the editor of *The Liberator*. "Why do you have that Garrison engaged in your cause?" she demanded. The twenty-four-year-old lawyer with a "long, flowing beard" did not miss a beat. "You might as well ask me . . . why we permit the rivers to flow on in their channels, for the one could be prevented as easily as the other, while life remains and the physical power to labor [continues] in Garrison." The young man went on for a few minutes before striking the right chord when he dilated on the editor's "self denial, his sacrifices, his heart-&-soul devotion to the cause." It was just that selflessness in a divine calling that the "goodhearted" though "easily excited" woman deemed central to her own spiritual journey. Instantly her reservations vanished. "Her countenance brightened as I proceeded," Burleigh reported, "and before I could complete my narrative, she exclaimed, 'he ought to be *canonized*.'" She would soon be carrying the case to others, including Waldo's bride, Lydia Jackson, who shared her emotional response to "the subject [which] agitates the Country."[62]

Another receptive listener was Mary's nephew Charles Emerson, who accompanied her to Burleigh's lecture at the Trinitarian meetinghouse. The young lawyer was so inspired that he gave an address of his own on slavery the next month. Composed in Concord, the talk was delivered in the town of Duxbury on the Massachusetts South Shore, where the Emersons had kin, and it affirmed a commitment to emancipation and equal rights as radical as Garrison's or later Wendell Phillips's. "I am an abolitionist," he wrote to his brother William on the eve of the trip to Duxbury. "And give me an hour & a half of your company, & I'll undertake you shall be one too."[63]

Although it was given out of town, the lecture bore the imprint of the debates over abolitionism in the Concord press. It would certainly have outraged the managers of the *Gazette*, for which Charles Emerson was composing occasional editorials, and it went far beyond anything his brother Waldo said in public over the next few years. The speaker approached the subject as a lawyer and policy maker. He opened with a systematic review of the laws of slavery in the South, underscoring the total subordination of Black men and women. Stripped of all rights, subject to the arbitrary will of masters, and unable to do anything to control or improve their lives, the enslaved utterly lacked the individual freedom in which white Americans took such pride. So obvious was this oppression that Emerson decided to spare his audience the "unnecessary torture" of hearing about the "odious details of the slave market or the whipping post," to appeal to reason instead, and to focus on what Northerners could do to end the horrors. To that end, he challenged the unthinking identification of his listeners with Southern whites. "We know the men against whom this enormity is charged; they are our fellow citizens, some of them our personal friends[;] they live in the same light, stand on the same parallel of civilization as ourselves. Are we to believe them guilty of practices but one remove from those of cannibals?" And if we do so, as sadly we must, "why not put an end to this abomination? What hinders immediately to emancipate the slaves?"

The bulk of the lecture was devoted to refuting the fears of Southern whites and their Northern sympathizers. Would immediate emancipation "ruin" the slaveholders and reduce them to poverty? Not at all. Free Black workers, with the incentive of wages, would grow more productive than ever, as had supposedly proved to be the case elsewhere in the Americas. "The truth is Slave labor is a system of pauperism," which "puts a bounty on laziness, ignorance, &c." Even if economic decline ensued, that would be no excuse for perpetuating human bondage. It is "the plea of the thief" to say "I cannot give up my ill-gotten treasure, because I shall be beggared." The fear of "amalgamation"—interracial sex—was equally spurious. Intercourse between masters and slaves happened all the time; "the whole country south of Mason's and Dixon's line is a Nursery of the mixed breed." What greater "mischief" would issue from legal marriage (then against the law in Massachusetts as well as the South)? Emerson was untroubled by the prospect and optimistically forecast in the distant future the rise of a superior breed of men and women from the union of Black and white. Finally, the speaker dismissed fears of violence by vengeful ex-slaves against former masters. Unlike his brother Waldo and the publishers of the Concord *Gazette*, the lawyer saw no cause for concern. For all the cruelties and injustice of the slave system, its victims were not "ferocious or vindictive." Recalling his own observation of plantations in the South and the Caribbean, he reassured the audience that Blacks as a group were not simmering in a constant fury waiting to boil over when the time was right. With a liberal faith in the inner divinity of every human being, he was sure that "nothing, not even slavery, is able to transform man into beast . . . We see that the image of God in his human creature is ineffaceable. The slave is still open to the influence of kindness, still capable of the religious sentiment, & never wholly loses sight of the distinction between right & wrong."

That confidence in the inherent capacity of the individual to know and do good was of a piece with the progressive outlook of his better-known brother. It was more Christian than Transcendentalist and more lawyerly, too. But it spoke to the contradictions of slavery in a land of freedom with a directness and urgency that Waldo would not approach in public for another decade: "Nothing will prepare the slave for freedom, except freedom."

Charles Emerson was no more willing than William Lloyd Garrison to temper his message in hopes of accommodating the audience. As if in dialogue with the Concord *Gazette*, he acknowledged that Congress lacked the power to abolish slavery in the existing states (though, in his view, it did have jurisdiction over the territories and the District of Columbia), only to deny that this constitutional limitation mandated a rule of silence about the slave system. Likewise, he scorned the notion that to agitate against slavery was to "toss fire about in a magazine of powder." As for colonization, he indicted the plan of the ACS as a white racist scheme that would "accomplish directly almost nothing for the Blacks in this country." It would not end slavery in the South; if anything, it would benefit slaveholders financially by reducing the supply of bondsmen and thereby raising their price. Nor would it foster an egalitarian society in the North. Colonization derives "its root from a cruel prejudice against the blacks & fosters the spirit of alienation & caste. It exposes the colored people to great persecution in order to compel them to emigrate. It diverts the minds of men from the consideration of the wrong & sin of slavery." Emerson counted on the only power at his command—moral suasion—to concentrate his white listeners' minds. "So long as anywhere, the colored man, bond or free, [is] oppressed from ignorance or injustice in his white fellow man, our duty is simple . . . We owe it to our dear country to make an effort to expel this poison from her vitals . . . Let the negro be an object henceforth not of scorn, but of attentive charity. Let him be dear to you even for his sufferings."[64]

If Emerson's abolitionism was marred by paternalism in its view of free Blacks not as brothers in arms but as recipients of charity, it nonetheless stands as the most expansive vision of racial equality on record by a Concord speaker or writer in 1835 and for a long time thereafter. It clearly arose out of the intellectual ferment of a town and region reverberating with the political insurgency of Anti-Masonry and with idealistic movements for expanded and improved schooling and for an end to the plague of ardent spirits. Even so, it was a minority view, and it took time to spread.

This was one improvement that the Concord Lyceum was not eager to advance. No one lectured to the group in favor of abolitionism through the 1830s. In May 1833 the debaters examined the wisdom of immediate emancipation—was it an "act of humanity" or not?—with no decision. In October the question before them was whether an antislavery society should be encouraged; the negative side won. Fifteen months later, following Thompson's lecture, the lyceum considered again "whether the immediate abolition of slavery be expedient." On cold February nights for three weeks in a row, Charles B. Davis and Rev. Wilder pressed the case in favor, while Doctor Ripley, Edward Jarvis, and two others argued against. After President Hersey B. Goodwin ruled for the "cons," the participants appealed to the entire membership. The proposal was defeated by a vote of three in favor, thirteen opposed.[65]

No wonder, then, that Concord stood apart from the developing abolitionist movement. In the mid-1830s its citizens sent no petitions to Congress against slavery in the District of Columbia and in the federal territories; nor did they hurry to start an antislavery society of their own. Such activism was manifested by just four inhabitants, who followed Wilder's example and signed up with the MCASS during the two years after its founding: the Trinitarian merchant Charles B. Davis, the *Freeman* editor Gourgas, the farmer Samuel Barrett, and most notably, Mary Merrick Brooks, the thirty-three-year-old wife of lawyer and *Gazette* co-owner Nathan. The MCASS welcomed women from the start; of the 155 founding members, just over a quarter were female. Brooks was the first Concord woman to take up the invitation; she was soon participating in deliberations alongside men. Antislavery challenged gender norms as well as racial conventions—another reason many hesitated to join in.[66]

Although the local meetinghouses were the setting for abolitionist lectures, their congregations did not immediately bless the cause. John Wilder led the way in converting his parishioners to the antislavery creed. He was also said to be a frequent anonymous contributor to the *Concord Freeman* and occasionally its subeditor; on the topic of abolitionism, visiting lecturer Burleigh was told, the newspaper "bears the impress of his mind." Even so, it took several years of conscientious discussions before the church was prepared, in November 1836, to deny membership and withhold fellowship to any person "claiming property in human beings." Slaveholding, the church declared, was "palpably inconsistent with natural rights, and with the plainest teaching of the gospel." Ezra Ripley and the First Parish, by contrast, continued on a colonizationist course. The parson did not shut out opposing views; at Burleigh's lecture he took a prominent seat "in front of the pulpit," listened with "the most fixed attention," and sought out the speaker the next day for "an animated conversation." His only problem with abolitionism, he told Burleigh, was "what he could do—what . . . could any of us do to forward the liberation of the slaves."

The old man's imagination was limited by his enduring desire for consensus. Ripley felt as much responsibility for preserving the national Union as he had for holding his parish together. To his mind, colonization remained the antislavery measure best suited to keep the peace—in the republic, on the plantation, and in his flock. Thompson, Burleigh, and other abolitionist lecturers made no dent in this position. The First Parish continued to pass the collection plate for the ACS, while Congressman Samuel Hoar purchased a life membership with a donation of $100 in 1836.[67]

Ultimately, it was the freedom of whites, not Blacks, that took precedence in the politics of Concord and Massachusetts during Emerson's first year in Concord. The principal fights centered on freedom of speech and association. The *Freeman* reported various efforts all over the country to deny abolitionists a public hearing, while the *Gazette* allied with conservative voices in Boston and New York in calling for a halt to such discussions. In the face of mob assaults on antislavery lecturers and other attempts to shut down agitation, Gourgas ran an eloquent defense of free speech. The "champions of human bondage," he protested in late September 1835, were doomed to fail in their "foolish belief, that the human mind in its researches after truth and moral reformation can be stayed by terrors, and limited within the 'butts and bounds' which ridicule and contempt may in the hour of their short-lived supremacy build up around it."[68]

A month later in Boston a screaming mob of thousands set out to seize George Thompson, back in the capital attending a meeting of the local female antislavery society. Mistaking their man, the furious crowd grabbed Garrison instead, hung a noose around his neck, and marched him through the streets, until he was eventually rescued by the mayor and put in protective custody. Gourgas was appalled by the "scene of misrule and riot," which he blamed on the "depraved and corrupt minds" of the respectable men who had been rousing public sentiment against the agitators. If only the editor and his Concord readers had known the full story! That evening the Hon. John Keyes, then serving as speaker pro tempore of the Massachusetts House of Representatives, mounted the steps of an office building on Boston's Court Street and, with his fourteen-year-old son by his side, calmly observed the assault on Garrison. A half-century later John Shepard Keyes could still remember "the howls of the mob" and the "terrible" scene, which once "haunted [his] dreams," but with adult hindsight he had come to realize "where his [father's] feelings were." The "mob of gentlemen" unmistakably had the approval of the third-highest-ranking "officer of the State."[69]

The year 1835 was the year of the "antis," when all the hostilities provoked by a changing society surged together to produce a climate hostile to free speech. As Concord approached its two hundredth birthday as a town, the citizens argued furiously with one another about who belonged in the community and who had a right to be heard. Could abolitionists advocate their principles without fear of attack? Did free people of color have a stake in the society they had helped to build? Were Freemasons the natural fathers of the town or the evil agents of an international conspiracy? Could Catholics obtain a place as citizens of a secular republic? Could freethinkers mock religious beliefs without risking prosecution? Under siege in all these controversies, Charles Emerson recognized, was "Freedom of Opinion," the title of a lecture he presented to the Concord Lyceum in November. Although the talk was a historical survey of toleration and censorship since the Inquisition, nobody could miss the pertinence of the speaker's references to the press and "popular ignorance." "I fell foul of the mobs & convent rioters," Charles reported to a friend.[70]

Meanwhile Waldo held his fire, preferring to lecture on such timeless topics as biography and the lives of "great men," to the annoyance of his Aunt Mary. "All the lectures [which] Waldo gives on biography," she grumbled, "seemed like the fleeting flowers of a summer day compared to . . . [Burleigh's] zeal in humanity." Privately, in his journal, he appraised the possibilities for meaningful public speech. Abolitionism, he took heart, was unburdened by tradition and authority; its advocates spoke truth to power on behalf of the slave. How exciting to see "people just out of the village or the shop reason & plead like practised orators, such scope the subject gives them . . . This is one of those causes which will make a man." Yet Emerson was disappointed with professional agitators in the flesh; after a meeting with George Thompson over his breakfast table, ten days before the agitator would be mobbed in Boston, he sadly concluded that the Englishman belonged to the "great class of the Vanity-stricken." "If he gets a rotten egg or two," the man was unfazed, so long as "his name sounds through the world & he is praised & praised." Emerson's ideal speaker transcended all "mean egotism." As he surveyed the political scene, he cherished the hope that as a lecturer, he could rise above the low debates of the day and occupy higher ground. "What concerns me more than Orthodoxy, Antimasonry, Temperance, Workingmen's party, & the other Ideas of the time?" His goal was to keep his composure amid the hectic stream of events and to detect "the principle out of which these proceed." The Transcendentalist seer yearned to discover and disclose the spirit of the age.[71]

He soon had the opportunity to do just that.

10

A Little Democracy

As Waldo Emerson settled into the manse built by his minister-grandfather William before the Revolution and sat at his writing desk in an upstairs bedchamber overlooking the river and the battlefield, his mind turned understandably to the past. But it was neither the heritage of family nor the history of Concord that occupied his thinking in the winter of 1834–1835. A new lecture series was demanding attention. Under the auspices of the Boston Society for the Diffusion of Useful Knowledge, he had committed to deliver six addresses at the Masonic Temple from the last week of January to the first week of March. This would be the first course of lectures on a single theme that he had ever offered to the public. The topic was entirely new. Instead of natural history, he turned to human history, as embodied in the lives of great men. Biography, the title of the series, was a popular topic at lyceums, and Emerson would take advantage of that interest to give it his distinctive Transcendentalist twist.

Surprisingly, not a single American, not even Benjamin Franklin or George Washington, claimed a place in this pantheon. Emerson ignored notable men in the British colonies and in the struggle for American Independence. Instead, he cast his eyes across the Atlantic and back in time to the Renaissance, the Reformation, and the Enlightenment. The subjects he set forth before the Boston audience were five figures who had changed the world by the force of their minds and spirits: Michelangelo ("the artist"), Martin Luther ("the reformer"), John Milton (the poet of "the moral sentiment"), George Fox (a Quaker preacher of "the religious sentiment"), and Edmund Burke (a philosopher-statesman). Why single them out for special notice? Not because they were heroes, to be put up on a pedestal and admired from afar, nor because they bequeathed a legacy of words and deeds for which posterity should be forever grateful. Emerson did not hold them up as models for imitation. Their lives were not the stuff of ser-mons to berate the young for a lack of virtue or patriotism. Rather, the Tran-scendentalist had an altogether different purpose. In great men, he maintained, we can see not exceptions to human nature but representatives of its highest possibilities. "The office of every great man," Emerson learned from Milton, was "to raise the idea of Man in the minds of his contemporaries and of posterity." Luther demonstrated that "those talents and means which operate great results on society, are those which are common to all men." George Fox held up a mir-ror in which we saw reflected "the deepest secret of our capacity." Ultimately, Emerson was less interested in any "particular men" than in "Man" in general. The true service of his biographical quintet was to provoke by example. All peo-ple had the potential for greatness, if only they trusted to spiritual power and practiced self-reliance.[1]

Sitting in the manse, Emerson composed his iconoclastic message in an atmosphere of reverence for the ancestors. In September 1835 Concord was due to reach its two hundredth birthday as a town, the first inland settle-ment beyond tidewater, and neither Ezra Ripley nor his parishioners would let the occasion pass without reminding one and all of Concord's worthy past and the debt they owed to its forefathers. At a time when townsmen were rejecting the political and religious establishment, when people were aban-doning many inherited ways, the moment was not necessarily favorable for a celebration. How to commemorate a past whose hold was rapidly diminish-ing? Waldo Emerson, it turned out, had an eloquent answer.

WHILE EMERSON WAS COMPOSING HIS LECTURES IN THE WINTER OF 1835, Dr. Edward Jarvis was dreaming up yet another project of civic betterment. Nine days into the new year, he and Almira celebrated their first anniversary as a married couple on the same date he reached age thirty-two. Mindful of personal transitions, he took notice of collective milestones as well. Should Concord not commemorate its completion of two hundred years as a town on September 12? Plymouth had marked its bicentennial in 1820, with a memorable speech by Daniel Webster; Salem had followed suit with a celebration in 1828, and Boston in 1830. Why not Concord, the first inland settlement in Massachusetts? The earnest doctor took his idea to the Social Circle and won its endorsement. In short order, the proposal appeared on the warrant for the annual March town meeting; an eight-man committee—chaired, inevitably, by Daniel Shattuck and including Jarvis in its membership—was appointed to look into the matter; and the next month voters endorsed the plan for a celebration with a ringing statement of the town's historical significance.

"The history of Concord is the history of the trials, the sufferings, the energy of character, & love of liberty that gave to N. England a civilized population," reported Shattuck's committee. It was for the sake of "civil and religious freedom"—"man's highest privilege on earth"—that the forefathers of Concord had ventured into "this then savage wilderness" and suffered "perils, privations & disease." They had made these sacrifices not for themselves alone but also for those who came after them; the founders had been determined to establish principles of liberty in the new land and to pass them on to posterity. It was thus incumbent on their heirs, who "are enjoying to this day the fruits of all their labours & sufferings," to acknowledge that debt, to prove themselves worthy of the trust, and to transmit the "heritage" of freedom on to their children "as valuable" as ever. A day of commemoration would be at once an acknowledgment of the past and a commitment to the future.[2]

The townsmen affirmed a familiar understanding of the Yankee heritage. In the early nineteenth century, when they looked back to their colonial origins, people in Massachusetts took pride in the ideals animating the first settlers of New England. Unlike other adventurers to North America in the seventeenth century, their forefathers had not been driven by mercenary desires for wealth and empire. They had held higher aims: to practice their faith freely and to govern themselves under laws of their own making. In reality, the Puritans had not allowed the same religious freedom to dissenters, and many settlers had been more interested in trading goods and catching cod than in saving souls. Some were eager to acquire captive Indians and Africans as slaves and to profit from their labor and sale. In 1641 Massachusetts Bay was the first colony in British North America to legalize slavery in its "Body of Liberties." But in the mythology of New England, the true legacy of the founders lay in their principles.[3]

Ezra Ripley seldom missed an occasion to belabor this theme. During the jubilee of the Revolution, he had been assiduous in urging remembrance of the Patriot fathers and in promoting Concord's preeminence on the path to independence. In March 1826 he had persuaded the town to erect a monument to his clerical predecessor, William Emerson, who had died in service as an army chaplain during the 1776 expedition to Ticonderoga. Though his remains lay in an unmarked grave in Rutland, Vermont, Emerson's memory would be kept alive through a marble memorial in the burying ground across the road from the meetinghouse where he had once preached. "Enthusiastic, Eloquent, / Affectionate and Pious. / He loved his Family, his People / His God and his Country," proclaimed the testimonial, composed partly by his daughter Mary Moody Emerson.[4]

To Ripley's disappointment, the Emerson memorial had not inspired an immediate wave of patriotic remembrance. Following the jubilee, the anniversary of the Concord Fight had been intermittently observed with parades and speeches, and once Anti-Masonry rocked the town, the antagonists could no more come together amicably to observe the day than had Federalists and Republicans at the height of their partisan divide. The planned monument in the village languished, its damaged cornerstone a silent rebuke to the inhabitants. Nothing the parson said had any effect, not even the pointed reminder, in the sermon he delivered on his fiftieth anniversary in the pulpit, that "the fathers . . . have been too much overlooked and forgotten by their descendants."[5]

Meanwhile other communities tried to steal credit for igniting the Revolutionary War. In 1825 Lexington put forth its own history of events, tracing the first shots against the king's troops to the brave but outnumbered militiamen on its town common. Ripley challenged this "unjust claim upon the public faith" in his pseudonymous columns for the press.

In support of Concord's preeminence, the minister gathered up contemporary depositions, retrospective affidavits, and his own interviews with survivors of that fateful day. His account appeared in 1827 as *A History of the Fight at Concord, on the 19th of April, 1775 . . . Showing That Then and There the First Forcible Resistance Was Made to the British Soldiery, and the First British Blood Was Shed by Armed Americans, and the Revolutionary War Thus Commenced.* The printers, Atwill and Allen, took the copyright, and five years later Atwill alone issued a second edition. Commemorating the fifty-seventh anniversary of the Concord Fight, the pamphlet marked the last occasion when author and printer could cheerfully celebrate the Nineteenth of April together.[6]

At the height of the Anti-Masonic insurgency, Ripley took a decisive step to end the logjam over the "defaced granite" in the center. In February 1834 the pastor proposed to donate the land for the monument to "the Great Events at Concord North Bridge on the 19th of April 1775." Scuttling the "almost holy" ground where "Middlesex" had previously wanted the memorial, Ripley offered a still more sacred space: the land beside his manse, where the Redcoats had first felt the force of American resistance. There were just a few conditions. The town had to fence the site with "a good stone wall," and to keep up the path leading to it, all at its own expense. There was also a deadline: if the work wasn't completed in three years, the parson would take back the gift. At eighty-two, he was in no mood to wait.[7]

The minister's proposal came before the fateful town meeting of March 3, 1834, when Anti-Masons completed their ascendancy by capturing nearly all local offices and ousting Abiel Heywood as clerk. Following the voting, the male citizens turned to Ripley's plan. As ever, a special committee was delegated to look into the matter; with Daniel Shattuck as chair, joined by one Democrat and one Anti-Mason, it was carefully balanced to reflect all political factions. The body easily reached a nonpartisan consensus: the scheme was affordable and appropriate. The town agreed. But Atwill could not resist taking a last dig at his opponents. In his final issue as editor, he reprinted a column from the *Advocate* celebrating recent victories at the polls: "Now Middlesex is nearly regenerated and disenthralled, and the corner stone laid by masonic folly in Concord, has been dispersed to the four winds of heaven, so that no trace or remembrance of it will remain among men."[8]

Ripley's intervention was well timed. In the mid-1830s, Concord had good reasons to highlight its unique importance on the Massachusetts landscape, not all of them so high-minded as gratitude to the forefathers. Once again the town faced a challenge to its premier status as a shire town. To the north, Lowell was burgeoning into a major center of population, whose residents clamored for better access to the courts. Could not one judicial term—say, the June session of the court of common pleas—be relocated from Concord to the City of Looms? In January 1835 Lowell's citizens petitioned the General Court with that request. The town of Groton chimed in on Lowell's behalf and added a plea for a judicial term of its own, again at Concord's expense. The shire town took quick action to protect its interests. On February 1, 1835, a special town meeting declared that any removal of the courts to Lowell would be "greatly injurious" to the "welfare" of Concord and unhelpful to the county as a whole. A far better course was to eliminate the annual session in Cambridge and to hold all the courts in Concord, at the center of the county. Gearing up for a fight on Beacon Hill, the town took the unusual step of instructing Representatives Barrett and Keyes to argue its case, and it organized a petition drive to demonstrate popular backing for its goal to become the sole seat of courts in Middlesex County. The outpouring of support was unprecedented; a total of 354 men, just about every legal voter, signed the memorial. For the next two years, the rival towns contended for advantage in the capital. In this competition, Concord's geographical advantages were enhanced by its historical significance. A monument and a "second centennial" celebration would burnish its profile at a critical time.[9]

The anniversary gave promise of uniting all factions. Masons and Anti-Masons, Democrats and Whigs, abolitionists and colonizationists, Trinitarians, Unitarians, and "Nothingarians" sank their differences on the twelve-member committee of arrangements. The elite remained in charge, with eight members from the Social Circle. Keyes served as chair. Chosen for the post after lawyer Nathan Brooks stepped down, the forty-eight-year-old politician was back on top in local affairs.[10]

The committee's assignment was straightforward: to organize a "public procession" and to secure a speaker on a modest budget of seventy-five dollars. The task did not prove easy. The members broke up into subcommittees that met early and often, only to find themselves sharply divided. No records of their discussions survive, but according to Jarvis, the differences of opinion reflected a fundamental disagreement about "the object and character" of the event. Was this celebration to be a local party, "a love feast" for all the people of the town and its neighbors and for their numerous progeny? In this perspective, the commemoration was essentially a "domestic" affair, gathering the far-flung members of the Concord tribe for a family reunion in their original home. Alternatively, should the occasion serve to advance the town's standing in the wider world? The advocates of a "grand celebration" were eager to attract outsiders "of high degree" and thereby win for the town "a name and fame abroad." One side wanted an inclusive event, by and for the locals; the other urged a cosmopolitan approach, designed to appeal to elites within and beyond the town. The conflict symbolized the basic division in Concord over the previous two decades. Raising the specter of "another Lafayette celebration," it threatened to disrupt the bicentennial from the start.[11]

Initially, the cosmopolitans took charge, but their high-flying plans could not get off the ground. The first choice for speaker, Sen. Daniel Webster, declined the invitation; so did the next on the list, former Rep. Edward Everett.

There was some talk about recruiting the noted orator Rufus Choate, which came to nothing. By June the committee was getting worried. With three months to go, hopes for securing a "distinguished" figure were fading fast. What to do? Happily, in Jarvis's opinion, the committee turned at last to "the very man whom they should have first asked and who would better represent the hearts and history of Concord and be more an honor to the people and their principles." Ralph Waldo Emerson got the nod. Well regarded for his eloquent sermons and lectures at the meetinghouse and the lyceum, he combined the advantages of a cosmopolitan education with local residence and roots. This was an invitation he could not refuse, notwithstanding his skepticism about such anniversaries. "Why notice it?" he asked in his journal. "Centuries pass unnoticed." So fleeting is man's life that it resembles a "swallow that flew in at one window, fluttered around, and flew out at another." Likewise for "this population of the spot of God's earth called Concord. For a moment they fish in this river, plow furrows in the banks, build houses on the fields, mow the grass. But hold on to hill or tree never so fast they must disappear in a trice."[12]

The "ambitious party," as Jarvis dubbed it, hoped to compensate for the little-known speaker with a stellar guest list of state and national leaders and with a sumptuous banquet to cap the celebration for the male attendees. A separate "collation" would be organized for women and children at the courthouse. These plans too went awry. In late August and early September, the RSVPs to the committee's invitations began trickling into the post office, some as late as the day before the event. The regrets piled up: John Quincy Adams couldn't come; nor could Sen. John Davis, former governor Levi Lincoln, Supreme Court justice Joseph Story, state supreme court justices Lemuel Shaw and S. S. Wilde, state attorney general James T. Austin, and Harvard president Josiah Quincy. Acting governor Samuel T. Armstrong, who had ascended to the executive office following Davis's election to the Senate, did promise to attend if his schedule was clear. The elite of Concord would have to make do with the quantity, rather than the quality, of its guests.

Even the dinner the committee arranged was controversial. The caterer, William Shepherd, was "professionally ambitious" to show off "his skill and good taste." For so auspicious an occasion as the bicentennial celebration, he proposed a fine meal at the cost of $1.50 per person. That plan appealed to the fashionable members of the committee. If the price—more than a season's ticket at the lyceum or a year's borrowing privileges at the social library—was "a burden" for "very many" inhabitants and an "impossibility" for others, so be it. Not every member of the Concord family would enjoy a place at the table. The committee ignored the resentments of those excluded at its peril.[13]

CONCORD'S HISTORY OCCUPIED MANY MINDS IN 1835. EZRA RIPLEY COULD not let go of the running dispute with Lexington. The previous summer the parson read in the press that the Democratic politician and intellectual George Bancroft was launching a history of the United States. Immediately the old man sat down at his writing desk and penned a letter pressing the superiority of Concord's claim. Ripley never stopped collecting evidence to support his case. In the summer of 1835, Waldo Emerson was amused at the sight of his aged grandfather pestering eighty-year-old Thaddeus Blood, the last surviving local veteran of the Concord Fight, for his memories. Like a "keen hunter," the reverend doctor was "unrelenting" in pursuit of his prey. Yet Ripley "care[d] little for the facts the man can tell, but much for the confirmation" of his own long-held views.[14]

Occasionally, Lexington and Concord suspended their quarrel. On April 20, Lexington paid tribute to its martyrs for liberty by exhuming their remains and interring them in a place of honor next to its monument to the Revolution on the town common. Concord's citizens came forth in large numbers to witness the ceremony and hear yet another powerful oration by Edward Everett. Three months later another anniversary commanded attention: the centennial of the town of Acton, which had been carved out of Concord in 1735. Charles Emerson attended the proceedings and thrilled to the keynote speaker, a prominent lawyer named Josiah Adams, who evoked "the feeling of the Sublime" by reading aloud "the votes & resolutions of the town in Revolutionary times." "How wise & brave they were," he wrote brother William in New York. "This nation was then a genuine nation," expressing through its "organs" of government "a healthy Public Will." There was a lesson for Waldo in the orator's approach: "I hope [he] will search well the Concord Records for texts to his Commemorative talk in September. He says he shall."[15]

The most indefatigable student of Concord history no longer lived in the town. In June 1832 Lemuel Shattuck stepped away from the counter of his brother's store and, after a decade in Concord, took up a branch of trade more congenial to his intellectual interests. He became a principal in the Cambridge

firm of Brown, Shattuck, & Company, "Publishers, Booksellers, and Stationers" at the bookstore serving the faculty and students of Harvard. The move
came at an opportune moment. The reluctant storekeeper had just completed
a history of Concord, which he had researched during the previous four years,
and was now seeking to line up potential buyers. As soon as the manuscript
was ready for the press, Shattuck followed a standard practice in the early
nineteenth-century book business and printed up "proposals" to advertise the
work. This prospectus was designed to attract advance purchasers of the book,
sight unseen. A substantial subscription list with guaranteed sales usually reduced the risk to publishers.

Shattuck laid out his rationale succinctly. "Few places have so many interesting incidents associated with their history as Concord." The town was the
first inland settlement in Massachusetts; it cultivated peace with the Indians
and served as a military outpost in times of war; it played a "distinguished
part" in the Revolution and in "other peculiar eras" in state history. The proposed work would tell this story and incorporate other important topics, such
as religious history, "Natural History, Topography, Statistics," notices of college graduates, and accounts of "Early Families and Distinguished Men." The
local historian also looked for subscribers in neighboring towns by including
the history of those communities—Acton, Bedford, Carlisle, and Lincoln—that
were formerly within Concord's borders. Shattuck intimated that he would
disclose facts never known before: "He has spared no labor, nor left any source
of information within his reach unexplored, that he may be accurate, acceptable, and useful."[16]

The promotion paid off. Altogether, 160 people signed up for 220 copies of
a book running from three to four hundred "large octavo pages" and costing
$1.50, equal to the price of the dinner at the town's bicentennial celebration.
Of this number, 118 lived in the town; the rest resided in the vicinity or were
part of a Concord diaspora stretching from New York City to New Hampshire
and Maine. At the top of the subscription list stood Doctor Ripley with an
order of two copies, followed by Trinitarian minister Southmayd (four copies)
and by Unitarian pastor Hersey Goodwin (six), as if patronizing Shattuck's
History were a clerical duty. Members of the Social Circle came next: Samuel
Hoar (six), Nathan Brooks (four), John Keyes (six), and so forth, amounting
to twenty of the author's twenty-four associates in the exclusive coterie. Subscriptions were not confined to the elite. Seven years earlier John Thoreau had

urged the town to commemorate the jubilee of the Concord Fight; now he ordered a copy of the forthcoming *History* that in later years would be frequently
consulted by his writer son. Other manufacturers, mechanics, and farmers followed suit. Luckily for Shattuck, interest in Concord's past overcame internal
divisions; his Masonic affiliation did not hurt sales. Local history acted as a
unifying force.[17]

Shattuck's fascination with the New England past was of long standing.
Hardly had he arrived in town from Detroit than he composed a poetic saga
of the Bay State, from the Pilgrims' landing at Plymouth Rock to the first
act of the Revolution "in this ancient, memorable town," and read it aloud
to the Concord Debating Club. This engagement with history deepened with
his participation in the lyceum movement, which emphasized learning by doing through the firsthand collection and analysis of empirical "facts." Among
the activities that Josiah Holbrook had recommended for the branches of his
American Lyceum was the "compiling of town histories," especially the gathering of reminiscences from the dwindling corps of Revolutionary War veterans. Shattuck took up this charge and conducted firsthand interviews with
veterans of the glorious Nineteenth of April. With this research, he aimed to
contribute to the larger narrative of state and nation. He also had an iconoclastic purpose. He was skeptical of the various tales his neighbors told about
the past. "Traditions . . . are often contradictory," he observed, "tending to em-
barrass, rather than to elucidate." He would take those received opinions and
examine them against the original sources. Just as lyceum lecturers shed the
light of science on popular superstitions, so the local historian would replace
popular legends with "verified" facts.[18]

Shattuck entered a growing intellectual community. During the 1820s,
historical societies proliferated; seventeen state and county associations went
into operation from Maine to Tennessee. Not surprisingly, New England was
the vanguard of this movement. As Shattuck began his studies, he took care to
contact fellow antiquarians, sharing information and exchanging ideas about
how best to conduct their investigations. Quickly he built up a reputation in
the developing field. He was elected a member of the Massachusetts Historical
Society in 1830 and of the American Antiquarian Society the next year. He was
relentless in the pursuit of information. He pressed local officials for access
to town and church records. He scoured the files of Middlesex County and of
the Bay Colony. From deeds, wills, inventories of estates, and vital records, he

reconstructed the genealogies of Concord's founding families. He delved into diaries and letters in the collections of the MHS. And he compiled list after list, detailing the town's officers, its representatives to the legislature, its justices of the peace and lawyers, its succession of ministers and deacons, the changing value of property, the uses of land, the holdings of livestock, the productions from farm and shop, the numbers of births, marriages, and deaths year by year—the bedrock of data on which all later historians of Concord gratefully depend.[19]

His vision of the materials necessary for the study of history was capacious. In July 1831 he set forth the philosophy driving this quest: "How often little incidents, originating even in a comparatively obscure village or country town, and not considered, at the time, of great relative importance, have been the beginning of some mighty change, affecting the politics, the religion, or the improvements of a state, a nation, or the world." Without a record of these homely details, how could the historian ever fulfill his mission "to carry himself back to the times whose events he describes, and make himself, in imagination at least, a cotemporary [sic] with the feelings, the prejudices, the manners and customs, and the whole circumstances of the society which then existed"? To prevent the loss of such essential knowledge, Shattuck had an unusual suggestion. Every community could appoint "a suitable individual" to keep a running account of "the current events of the times." Annually, he would look over this memorandum book and extract therefrom a "retrospect" of the leading actions and developments—an assessment of social progress akin to the self-examination carried out at regular intervals, such as birthdays or new years, by conscientious men and women in the Puritan tradition. In some towns, the local lyceum might take on this project; elsewhere "a professional or other intelligent gentleman" would volunteer for the job.[20]

Shattuck became Concord's village historian, compiling the record and bringing it up to date. He made it his purpose to gather information as systematically as possible and to preserve it for posterity. Attentive to economics and demography, politics and religion, education and culture, he anticipated the concerns of the new social history of the later twentieth century, especially in his appreciation for tables and statistics. His *History of Concord* offered, in embryo, a social scientific approach to understanding past societies. He focused on institutions more than on individuals and looked for patterns and trends in collective action rather than in the minds of single persons.

This sensibility was not unique to Shattuck. It was shared by Edward Jarvis, ten years his junior, who felt a similar curiosity about the "minutiae of the past" and an equal passion for numbers to gauge "the life and manners of the people." Together, the two men would go on to play prominent roles in the American Statistical Association, founded in Boston in December 1839. (Jarvis would head the organization for three decades.) Their quantitative frame of mind was first cultivated in Concord in the school committee, the temperance campaign, the library and lyceum, and through the investigation of the past. Concerned with aggregates more than individuals, this line of inquiry gave rise to an intellectual tradition distinct from the Transcendentalism of Emerson and Thoreau. Concord was arguably a source of not one but two major currents of American thought. At one pole was Romantic individualism; at the other, social statistics. Seeming opposites, the two perspectives took shape in the same time and place and bore significant traces of their common origin. That would become evident at the 1835 bicentennial.[21]

Shattuck's *History* faithfully followed his detailed plan. The book's pages were so crowded with transcripts of noteworthy documents and with so many lists and tables that a reader could easily despair of finding a narrative thread and identifying the main themes. Shattuck added to the difficulty by eschewing explicit interpretation. "The object of local history," he explained, "is . . . to record facts rather than deductions from facts." One critic took a jaundiced view of the author's determination to pile up and display the many facts he had uncovered through so much "inveterate industry and unshrinking perseverance." "The years and years of dismal drudgery," he said a little unkindly, are evident "upon every page. No other literary labor . . . can convey so vivid a notion of a 'Slough of Despond.'"

Patience does yield rewards. Shattuck told a familiar story of the advance of Christianity and civilization in the wilderness. Nothing new there, nor in his emphasis on the principles of the founders. It was for religious freedom, not material gain, that the forefathers undertook "so hazardous and expensive an enterprise." The first settlers were united in this goal, as was signified in the name of the new community. They were guided as well by consistent regard for law and authority. The planting of the town was approved in advance by the Massachusetts General Court. The land was purchased in a free and fair bargain with the native people. Shattuck made a point of the amity between the English and the Musketaquids. He was at pains to describe the natives' way of life and to pay tribute to their "exemplary" leaders. He admired their conversion to Christianity and regretted the injustices done to them during King Philip's War.

The blemishes on the town's record were few. Under the steady hand of established leaders, the inhabitants overcame disappointments and divisions and rose to external challenges. In the face of British taxes and restrictions, they "took a rational but decided stand in favor of liberty." Their protests were well regulated; Concord marched into revolution at a prudent pace. "It is said to be characteristic of the people of Concord to act with great deliberation, but when they do act, to act effectually." That time came on the famous Nineteenth of April, "a day destined to live in the annals of Concord and the world, as long as freemen exist." Shattuck reaffirmed the local consensus.[22]

This narrative of elites and common people advancing together "in numbers, wealth, and intellectual improvement" culminated in a picture of a progressive community, thriving with farms and manufactures and forthcoming with funds for schools, the poor, roads and bridges, and other public purposes. Shattuck's *History* was clearly a tract for the times. It affirmed the conviction of the Whig establishment that community could be sustained in an age of advancing capitalism, political democracy, and religious pluralism. In 1835 that notion was very much in dispute. The local historian had to acknowledge periods of deep division in times past, particularly during the Great Awakening of the eighteenth century. After reviewing the bitter conflicts then splintering the church and the inability of various mediators to bring feuding factions together, Shattuck expressed confidence that Concord would no longer be torn apart by such struggles. With the separation of church and state, who needed official bodies to resolve disputes over religion? Let people "think and judge for themselves, and not . . . depend too exclusively on the opinions of the clergy." As in school reform, so in politics and religion: Shattuck put his faith in the individual.[23]

Although it quickly became a model for writing local history, the book arrived too late for Concord's bicentennial celebration. In his 1832 prospectus Shattuck had given assurances that the manuscript was just about ready for print. Over two years later, with yet another change of business—the move into Boston to start his own bookselling firm—the *History of Concord* remained unpublished. In the meantime, a number of subscribers had died or moved away. Others must have wondered when or whether their books would ever arrive. One resident in particular was anxious to read the text. As September 12, 1835, approached, Emerson turned to Shattuck and asked to consult the work for his upcoming address. Graciously, the historian passed along the page proofs. The result was an engagement between the two intellectuals—one now departed from town, the other just settling in—over the meaning of Concord's past and the direction of its future.[24]

IN THE DAYS LEADING UP TO THE BICENTENNIAL CELEBRATION, EXPECTA-tions were running high. Enough "distinguished men of the day" had accepted invitations to gladden the spirits of the "ambitious" faction. The committee of arrangements was hard at work planning the program for the day. It chose Chairman Keyes to do the honors of president and Deputy Sheriff Moses Prichard to serve as marshal for the grand parade. The Social Circle was fully in charge. Dr. Jarvis wrote the press releases. He promoted Emerson's oration as offering the "promise of eloquence and interest" and pitched the entire event as a family affair. "Concord invites her children home again."[25]

Entertaining all these guests posed a challenge. The expensive dinner for the gentlemen, catered by Shepherd, was already controversial. How would the town take care of the local ladies and women from out of town? A call went out for volunteers to host a "collation" at the courthouse. Would they con-tribute homemade treats, "both substantial and elegant," for the reception? The generosity was "almost universal." But the organizers stumbled when they recruited a young working woman to serve coffee. For her labor she was prom-ised "a large and satisfactory compensation." When word got around about the arrangement, some inhabitants professed outrage. "This was a menial ser-vice," the serving girl was told, "a humiliation that she ought not to submit to." She gave in to the pressure and withdrew. Rather than face the same situation again, the ladies' committee decided to do the work themselves. Ann Keyes, the politician's wife, and Almira Jarvis, the doctor's bride, poured the coffee.[26]

On Saturday morning, September 12, the *Yeoman's Gazette* and the *Concord Freeman* issued their weekly editions. The former observed the bicentennial by featuring the "order of exercises" for the day. The latter pointedly ignored the event, except for a communication from "a native-born citizen of Concord," which ran under the headline "Another 'Lafayette Celebration.'" Recalling the unfortunate reception for Washington's "adopted son" in 1824, the writer was certain that the "ARISTOCRATS" were once again intent on throwing a party at public expense for themselves and their self-important friends. Just look at who was coming: acting governor Armstrong and "other great Whigs." Consider, too, who were the officers of the day: all Whigs! This self-respecting citizen would not pay $1.50 for a "Whig glorification." Better to stay at home, "a place where every mechanic and farmer can feel his independence." Nor would he allow his wife and daughters to attend the reception at the courthouse. Class inequality threatened to spoil the party. So did the resentments of Concord's old families against the upstarts who had taken over the town. Not one of the men running the commemoration was a native. "Where are the Barretts, Buttricks, Melvins, Hunts, Wheelers, Haywards, Jones, and Lees? the original settlers—why, they are to follow the bidding of men whose very names were unknown in the town 20 years ago." The newcomer Francis Gourgas, resident for just a month, was pleased to publicize this protest for partisan advantage.[27]

Racial inequality intruded into the celebration, too. The official program assigned the town's children a prominent role. At the start of the day, all pupils in the public schools were expected to gather at the Trinitarian church, from which they would parade to the common and form "double lines," through which the adults would march to the First Parish meetinghouse. Were they all set to participate? Isaac N. Goodhue, master of the center school, asked his students a few days before. Everyone expressed enthusiasm but for one girl, who held back. Ellen Garrison, age twelve, was a child of color, whose mother, Susan Robbins Garrison, was determined to shield her from "ill treatment" by white racists. At an earlier public event, the girl had been "crowded out of the procession." That was never going to happen again! Besides, Ellen added, "no one would walk with her." Instantly nine-year-old Abba Maria Prescott rose to her feet and announced "she would walk with her,—she was as willing to walk with her as with any one." Would your mother approve? asked the teacher. "I know she will," Abba replied "with spirit." But Ellen was less confident of her mother's consent. Let me talk to her, the little white girl pleaded; I will persuade her. And she did. The two walked hand in hand throughout the day, braving "the gaze of curiosity, surprise, ridicule, and admiration." The incident had wider reverberations. It was soon popularized, in an oversimplified version, by an abolitionist magazine for children, *The Slave's Friend*. And it sealed the cooperation of the two mothers in the fight for equal rights.[28]

The protests against the celebration proved as fruitless as had the call for a boycott of George Thompson's antislavery lecture nine months earlier. The day opened to "calm and beautiful" weather, as if "the external world" itself smiled on the occasion. The town bell rang at precisely 10:30 a.m. to signal the start of the proceedings. Crowds filled the village streets to watch the Concord Light Infantry and Artillery companies, in "new and elegant uniforms," lead a procession, to the beat of the Concord Band, from Shepherd's Hotel down Main Street, onto the milldam, past the Middlesex Hotel, through the double row of five hundred schoolchildren assembled on the common, and over to the historic meetinghouse. The order of the march followed a design similar to the civic parade at the jubilee of the Concord Fight. President Keyes strutted at the front, momentarily preeminent over his rivals Everett and Hoar. The orator (Emerson), the chaplains (Ripley and Wilder), and the committee of arrangements came next, followed by invited guests and ten "surviving soldiers" of April 19, 1775, their numbers having dwindled from sixty a decade before. Although church and state were now formally separated, "Reverend Clergy" still claimed an honored place, just ahead of the selectmen of Concord's daughter towns and the general mass of citizens bringing up the rear. Unlike 1825, Masonic dignitaries were left out entirely. Nor were the tiers of civic and military officials given explicit recognition. This was a parade by and for the town in an assertion of local democracy.[29]

The commemoration was conducted in a spirit of religious reverence. The meetinghouse, it was said by the town's oldest residents, had never been so full; many people had to stand outside and peer through the windows to catch a glimpse. Others, "debarred of even that poor privilege," gave up and went home. In prayers and readings from Scripture, in odes, psalms, and hymns, the participants paid thanks to God and homage to the forefathers for the gift of civil and religious liberty. Almost every figure on the platform was a clergyman, including the speaker. Even the odes, a classical form, gave voice to the fervor of a Protestant faith that knew no sectarian borders. The congregation pretended for a moment to be back with the Pilgrims, following the lead of a deacon lining out a psalm (107) in a style of communal singing that Concord had long since abandoned for more fashionable and euphonious music. The words recalled the wandering of the Israelites in the desert before the Lord guided his "redeemed" to the Holy Land; the tune derived from mid-eighteenth-century England. This was followed, after a prayer by Doctor Ripley, himself a relic of the past, by the performance of "The Landing of the Pilgrim Fathers," an ode by the English poet Felicia Hemans, a favorite of Unitarians. Stirred to identify with the "band of exiles" on the *Mayflower* braving the ocean to seek "faith's pure shrine" on the wild New England coast, the assembly was led to conflate those hardy souls with the pious Puritans who had settled the first town above tidewater. Two hundred years later those gathered in the meetinghouse were heirs to a sacred trust:

> *Aye! call it holy ground,*
> *The spot where first they trod—*
> *They have left unstained what there they found*
> *Freedom to worship God!*

And then Emerson rose to speak.[30]

Would the orator say something fresh and fitting for the occasion? So many expectations already burdened the event, and so much of the ground had already been picked over by previous historians, including Ripley and Shattuck. But Emerson had bucked himself up for the challenge and spent the summer of 1835 delving into the same sources his predecessors had plumbed, one of which, the diary of the Patriot preacher William Emerson, would stay in his family until late in the twentieth century. He borrowed the town and church record books from their official custodians and took them home—a privilege not accorded to his successors—and from these and other original documents, he extracted a miscellany of facts about colonial government, the economy, Indians, and April 19 similar to Shattuck's compendium. His arrangement of the material followed a conventional division of Concord's history into three familiar phases: settlement, King Philip's War (1676), and the Revolution. Some of the leading actors in the narrative were his own kin, others the forebears of his neighbors sitting in the pews. This was hardly an occasion for fault-finding. Confined by older ways of seeing the past, dependent on the words and deeds of those who had come before him, and looking out at an audience anticipating a message of unity and uplift, Emerson faced much the same dilemma he would describe for "the American Scholar" two years later. Did he possess the "self trust"—the moral and intellectual independence—to find the truth and to assert it in an original voice for one and all?[31]

As he would do so many times in his career, Emerson turned to Nature. It furnished both his inspiration and his theme. Writers before him had fashioned a heroic saga of Puritan settlement. Emerson took the details, drawing on Shattuck alone some twenty times, and imbued them with new significance. His starting point was familiar. The founders of Concord were men and women of steadfast principle, armed by faith to endure the hardships of the wilderness in the quest for liberty. They dealt fairly with the natives to acquire the township; they cooperated effectively with one another to divide up the land and govern themselves. To what were these achievements due?

Surprisingly, the lecturer on biography did not look for representative men through whom to tell the story of Concord's founding (though he did mention his Bulkeley ancestors more than any other family). Man in general, rather than particular individuals, wrote a new chapter of human history in the wilderness. Emerson saw a force more powerful than custom, more elemental than visions of "a city upon a hill." Nothing was fixed by tradition or dictated by authority. It was Nature itself calling the shots as the first settlers re-created civilization in the tabula rasa of the woods: "The nature of man, and his condition in the world, for the first time within the period of certain [i.e., known] history, controlled the formation of the State."

Faced with unprecedented challenges, far from Boston and the General Court, the pioneers of a new society had no choice but to act on their own, take the initiative, and devise ways to meet their needs. Here was a model of innate "Reason" shaping the foundation of a new society—Transcendentalism in the wilderness. In the local church, the Puritan fathers joined together in "the ideal social compact." In the town meeting, they solved "the great secret of political science . . . how to give every individual his fair weight in the government, without any disorder from numbers." Every man, rich and poor, "just and unjust," could express his opinion in this forum; here "the roots of society were reached." "In every winding road, in every stone fence, in the smoke of the poor-house chimney, in the clock on the church," the people "read their own power . . . A general contentment is the result."

The community thus created was an original product of nature and culture. In Emerson's telling, it was on the frontier, where people were obliged to adapt to necessity, that the distinctive features of New England life—equality and democracy—were born. Seven decades later the historian Frederick Jackson Turner would turn this insight into the Frontier Thesis of American history.[32]

This original vision of a people acting in tune with nature and out of simple trust in God and man illuminated Emerson's survey of the past, lifting the assembly above Shattuck's "slough" of facts and revealing a celestial city of transcendent truths. The lecture, reported Hersey Goodwin, was "a beautiful and faithful abstract of the history of Concord." Although it lasted an hour and forty-five minutes, the audience hung on every word with "almost breathless attention." Thirteen-year-old John Shepard Keyes stationed himself "at the highest point in the meeting house," above the door to the upper gallery, and so caught up was he in the speech that "when the gallery cracked" under the weight of the crowd, he stayed put, while others fled for safety.

Who wouldn't have been captivated by the gems unearthed by Emerson from the dusty historical record and by the "passages of surpassing beauty and simplicity" with which he adorned them? The speaker carried his listeners back across the centuries to the early scenes of settlement. Imagine the "excitements" of the pilgrims, as they "beheld with curiosity all the pleasing features of the American forest." Witness the awakening of the native "man of the woods" to the preaching of the gospel, his "human heart" stirring to the "voice of love" and cherishing a "new hope" of equality with "his civilized brother." And sorrow over the betrayal of that hope during King Philip's War, when a small band of "praying Indians" was gathered into Concord for their protection, only to be seized by vigilantes in the grip of "envenomed prejudice" and driven into confinement, starvation, and death on Deer Island in Boston harbor.[33] Perhaps thinking of the impending removal of the Cherokee people from their homeland in Georgia, Emerson lamented the failure of human sympathy that allowed such injustice: "The worst feature in the history of those years is, that no man spake for the Indians . . . For them the heart of charity, of humanity, was stone."[34]

The biggest test of the speaker was yet to come. Passing quickly over the town's recovery from the war and participation in "the great growth of the country" and giving short shrift as well to the "ecclesiastical discords" of the Great Awakening, Emerson came to the subject closest to his neighbors' hearts and central to their pride of place. Here was the birthplace of the American Revolution; here at the North Bridge "the first organized resistance was made to British arms. There the Americans first shed British blood." The grandson of the Patriot preacher affirmed the local consensus. But he was not content just to rehearse twice-told tales about the Nineteenth of April and the War of Independence. As with his treatment of Puritan settlement, so with the Revolution: Emerson strove to unfold the deeper causes and larger meaning. The former was "the effect of religious principle," the latter "the fruit of another principle,—the devouring thirst for justice."

In upholding that principle and fighting for liberty, the townsmen were true to their origins. Town meeting democracy had begun, in Emerson's telling, when the first settlers came together and, in "the exercise of a sovereign power," voted to tax themselves. Their descendants were not about to yield that power to Crown and Parliament. From the start to the close of the quarrel with Great Britain, "the town records breathe a resolute and warlike spirit, so bold from the first as hardly to admit of increase." That was a considerable exaggeration; Concord lagged well behind nearby towns in its readiness to resist royal government. Such nuances did not enter Emerson's account. His gaze was fastened on the essential character of the people, as they rejected royal rule and "assumed sovereignty" over their own affairs. This was, in effect, a second founding, with the descendants of Puritan fathers insisting on a natural right to govern themselves. Propelled by "a religious sentiment that sanctified the thirst for liberty," the men in arms on April 19 went to war. Theirs was "the natural action" of farmers moved by "the simplest instincts" to defend their land. No one was dreaming of glory or striving for precedence. Like their forefathers, "they supposed they had a right to their corn and their cattle, without paying tribute to any but their own governors." The only authority they recognized and feared was their God.[35]

This sweep through two centuries of history culminated in praise for an "almost exclusively agricultural" community "of great simplicity of manners, and of a manifest love of justice." Emerson drew no explicit lessons from the past for the present. He did not liken the oppression of native people during King Philip's War to the contemporary plight of the Cherokee. He ignored slavery in New England altogether, despite its documentation in Shattuck's *History* and the presence of Black faces in the crowd. He overlooked the fashionable taste for fine fabrics, ribbons, and silks that kept business humming in the village stores. Remarkably, in a community so riven by political divisions and social conflict that one of the two newspapers refused even to cover the bicentennial celebration or to notice his speech, the orator judged that "for the most part, the town has deserved the name it wears." This was a day for unity.

Emerson's ideal of local democracy was a fantasy about the past. The town meeting of colonial times did not encourage freewheeling debate and dissent. It put no premium on majority rule. Its aim was to forge a binding consensus for a homogeneous community. Townsmen strove to think as their neighbors thought and conform to the prevailing view. Rev. William Emerson's world was not his grandson's. Projecting the more pluralistic and contentious circumstances of the Jacksonian age back onto the forefathers, the speaker was presenting a commentary on contemporary politics and a blueprint for reform.

At a moment when class antagonisms and party loyalties set neighbors apart from one another in mutual intolerance, Emerson troubled over the prospects of individual freedom. In his philosophy of self-government, the "crude remarks [of] a circle of people talking in a bar room" should not carry "equal weight with the sifted and chosen conclusions of experienced public men." But deep within every person, even the drunkard, lay a divinely given capacity to distinguish right from wrong. How to tap that inner "Reason" and mobilize it for the common good? With no awareness that colonial Concord was "a democracy without democrats," Emerson held up the town meeting as the model for public debate. "In this open democracy, every opinion had utterance," no matter how small-minded or self-interested; ignorance vied with wisdom, "petulance" with philanthropy. Concord was no "church of saints" nor "metropolis of patriots." But every townsman could truly have his say. As he scoured the volumes of town records, Emerson was pleased to note that "not a complaint occurs . . . of any inhabitant being hindered from speaking, or suffering from any violence or usurpation of any class." A similar spirit of toleration held sway in society at large. Concord never hunted witches, whipped Quakers, spied on households, or prosecuted "unnatural crimes." The inhabitants were thus free to advocate their opinions and interests in the open forum of the meeting, where every man had an equal voice and no one was shouted down. Here, Emerson implied, was a pattern for self-government as relevant in 1835 as two centuries earlier when it was born. No better institution could be devised for democratic deliberation than the town meeting.[36]

The speaker had a personal agenda as well. His family once occupied a central place in the town. His ministerial forebears—Peter Bulkeley and William Emerson—had played principal parts in the very episodes he was relating. But the war had severed that paternal link with the death of the Patriot chaplain on the expedition to Ticonderoga. His children dispersed from Concord and scattered from Boston and Newburyport on the Massachusetts coast to the interior of Maine. Only Aunt Mary Emerson, embittered by her "infant exile" from the manse, had returned for short sojourns. But now two Emerson men were back, and Waldo took the opportunity to remind listeners of his Concord blood. He was a Bulkeley and proud of it, and it was an "honor" to represent that ancient but long-absent family as the speaker of the day. Through William Emerson, he added, he could assert "a hereditary claim to the affection of the town." Concord history was thus family history, told through the words and deeds of his ancestors. Rootless for so long, the lecturer had only recently acquired a homestead in which to settle with his wife, Lidian, and to sink his roots into the "quiet fields of my fathers." Now, as the "organ" of the townspeople on a momentous anniversary, he was making sure to inscribe his ancestors—and himself—in the local history. He was coming home.[37]

That was a key objective of the commemoration: to bring the far-flung children of Concord home. For more than a century, the ancient town had been sending forth its sons and daughters to populate the great American interior, and despite the rising prosperity of the local economy in service to regional and national markets, it continued to shed its young to settlements ever farther away. Emerson took note of this constant exodus in his address. Concord's "sons have settled the region around us, and far from us. Their wagons have rattled down the remote western hills." Would the long-departed forget their forlorn mother? Was Concord destined to irrelevance in the expanding republic? The many former residents and their children at the anniversary celebration provided sorely needed reassurance.[38]

The bicentennial thus united families and generations, just as it overcame breaches in the community. The "elite of the town" could bask in the company of "men of distinction" in state and nation; even the mayor of New York, Philip Hone, spoke at the dinner under Shepherd's tent. Jarvis grumbled that few of the toasts and talks at that affair made "special reference to the town or to her two hundred years of experience." No matter. Despite the boycott by the *Freeman* and its supporters, the anniversary was a day for rejoicing, not resenting. Ward Safford, a New Hampshire–born laborer for Squire Abiel Heywood, was awed by the crowd ("the most people together . . . that ever I saw"), the parade, the music, the oration, and the dinner and toasts. Though he earned only $150 a year, the twenty-five-year-old paid his $1.50 for a ticket to the dinner without complaint and gladly took a place at the table. "I never sat down with so many before," he informed his parents, "some of the great men from Boston and New York and other places was there." For all the talk about elitism, he did not feel out of place.[39]

The Second Centennial Celebration was a triumph for both the orator and the town. Through his original appeal to the common nature, physical and human, shared by the founders of the town and the listeners in the meetinghouse, Emerson displayed his rhetorical power to overcome the differences among people and to weld them together in a higher union of sentiment and thought. The speech was a key step in the development of his career as a public lecturer. Concord had given him an important boost, and he had repaid his new hometown with a speech fostering the social harmony so lacking in public life.

But Emerson could not please everybody. Lemuel Shattuck was distressed that the speaker had borrowed and quoted so heavily from his forthcoming *History*. The bicentennial address had thereby stolen the author's thunder and likely hurt his future sales. So Shattuck complained in a testy note soon after the commemoration, to which Emerson replied with an extended self-defense. It was simply not true that he had harvested his material from Shattuck's well-tilled field. He had done his own digging in the original sources and from that common soil had extracted many of the same stories and facts. In only a few cases had he depended entirely on Shattuck for his information, and then he had taken care to acknowledge the debt. Would not such advance publicity be good for the book? To mollify the offended author, Emerson cited him repeatedly in the published *Discourse*.[40]

More important may have been his order of ten copies of the *History* from Shattuck, the biggest purchase by far, and his submission of a favorable review in the *Yeoman's Gazette*. In the October 3 issue, the reviewer, who signed his name as "E," praised the historian's exhaustive research, "great accuracy and completeness," and "plain style free from all affectations." "This is a work that, from its nature cannot be done in a hurry," the reviewer wrote in subtle reference to its belated appearance two weeks after the commemoration. Thanks to his "many years" of research, Shattuck had produced a work of "permanent value," which should be in every local home. That was just the first of the positive notices Shattuck's *History* received, the most notable of which was a long, appreciative essay in the nation's leading intellectual journal, the Boston-based *North American Review*. Written by Benjamin B. Thatcher, the tireless advocate for the American Colonization Society and frequent lecturer to the Concord Lyceum, the piece assayed the works of Emerson and Shattuck jointly but devoted most of its space to and bestowed nearly all its praise upon the latter. The industrious historian finally obtained his due. Thatcher offered an encomium to the patient investigator's "months of plodding toil and aching eyes." The *History* was exceptional in its "comprehensiveness of design," its "completeness of detail," and most important, its accuracy in all those "minute facts" Shattuck's years of labor had unearthed. Without the assurance of correctness in those details, the book would have been worthless. "Few town histories will ever be written a second time," he wrongly predicted. "The pains are too great, and the praise is too little." Fortunately, this example of the genre would long endure as "a good example" and "almost a model."[41]

And no town was more deserving of such attention than Concord! Thatcher's review more than satisfied the inhabitants' desire for recognition. "A history of the town of Concord, were it tolerably, nay, badly executed, could not well be an *obscure* one. It must be either famous or infamous." For "old Concord" was not just any town. Its history was intimately bound up with the origin and growth of the country and its leading incidents. Its "annals . . . are the pound of flesh nearest the heart of the Republic." Only a few communities, notably Boston and Plymouth, rivaled it in importance. "Concord has been not only a *town*, an American, New-England, Massachusetts town . . . but the first of all the inland class," nearly as old as its eminent predecessors on the coast and occupying "national and central ground; memorable now, and classical in all future time."[42]

With such tributes, who could complain that the bicentennial celebration ran well over its projected cost? Just to be sure there was no complaint, the leading gentlemen reached into their purses and made up the deficit. But they could not hold back the tides of conflict and the waves of change sweeping through the town. The reviewers of Shattuck's *History* were right. Concord was, in so many ways, an epitome of Massachusetts and New England, and it participated fully in the life of its turbulent times. It could celebrate the past, but it could not stop history from moving on.[43]

ON THE FOURTH OF JULY 1837, EZRA RIPLEY FINALLY GOT HIS WISH. THAT afternoon "a great concourse of people, old and young," assembled by the east bank of the Concord River and joined in a modest ceremony to dedicate the monument the town had finally raised in memory of the first battle of the Revolutionary War. The eighty-six-year-old minister's work was complete. He had broken the political paralysis that kept the project in limbo for a dozen years. Now a granite obelisk rose twenty-five feet high to consecrate this sacred site. The monument stood on land Ripley had donated for the purpose. It was his bequest to posterity, restoring public access to hallowed ground that had been lost four and a half decades earlier when, at Ripley's urging, the North Bridge was pulled down and the highway rerouted, its remnants quietly appropriated into the manse's domain. To the minister, the monument was to be a sermon in stone, reminding future generations of their debt to those who had risked their lives for liberty and inspiring them to sacrifice for the public good. If only that message of selflessness would get through! It had taken three years of skirmishing and infighting for the town to accept Ripley's gift, prepare the site, and raise the obelisk on its base, and by the time everything was ready for the opening ceremony, the conflicts in Concord had only gotten worse. The very tenor of local life belied the moral the monument was meant to convey.[44]

Initially, the plan for the monument had progressed smoothly. A committee of eight, headed by Daniel Shattuck, oversaw the project; five Anti-Masons worked together with two Whigs and one Democrat. But the next month a small band of inveterate opponents called on the town to reconsider the parson's gift. Why should a monument be located in "the backside of Dr. Ripley's house?" a writer styling himself "Old Concord" asked the readers of the *Freeman*. A better plan would be to erect a monument in the center, with a tablet directing visitors to the bridge site, "where rest the bones of the first victims of an indignant people." That idea was a last-ditch bid by village innkeepers to create a tourist attraction close by their places of business. The committee had no desire to revisit that issue. It moved ahead with the agreed-upon site.[45]

As the stonemasons went to work on the granite shaft, Shattuck's group put its mind to devising an appropriate inscription. That was no easy task; then as now, writing by committee is seldom efficient or elegant. Suggestions were solicited from "various leading men," and drafts were apparently vetted in the Social Circle. Everybody, it seems, had a favorite word or line to propose. Edward Jarvis hoped to conciliate people in Lexington by avoiding the formulation that Concord was the first site of "*forcible* resistance" to "British aggression." Why not say "*actual*" instead? Nobody seconded the idea. Concord would not back off its disputed claim. In the end the inscription was cobbled together from various sources, including Hoar, Ripley, and Emerson. The result drew mixed reviews. While many considered it "a masterpiece," others "severely criticized" the inscription, because at the last minute the words had been changed by Chairman Shattuck to suit the preferences of the Social Circle. The ensuing outrage intensified still more popular hostility to the local elite.[46]

The polarized politics belied Emerson's sunny view of town meeting democracy, where neighbors listened carefully to one another, weighed every opinion, and strove for the public good. As Anti-Masons merged with Democrats, the populist alliance carried Concord for Van Buren in November 1836, winning 60 percent of the ballots on a party-line vote. None of Concord's worthies escaped the popular tide. Samuel Hoar lost his bid for reelection to Congress.

In the anti-elitist mood, he was vulnerable to attack for his past support of the Standing Order, the Charles River Bridge Company, and property qualifications for suffrage. His wealth and education were held against him; an "aristocrat" was no man to represent "the HARD HANDS, but WARM HEARTS and CLEAR HEADS of the farmers and workingmen of old republican Middlesex." In his loss to Democratic businessman William Parmenter, the incumbent ran ahead of the Whig slate, but that was little solace, for he was rejected by the same margin in his hometown as in the district as a whole. Hoar was no favorite son.

Waldo Emerson was appalled at the result. How could his neighbors repudiate "their long honored townsman who had become a sort of second conscience to them, a Washington in his county," and put in his place "an obscure stranger whom they know not & have no right to trust"? He put the blame on *Freeman* editor Gourgas, "a young fellow with talents for intrigue" who came into the "peaceful town," "besot[ted] all the ignorant & simple farmers & laborers, and [rode] on their necks" to victory. The philosopher was obliged to acknowledge the sordid realities of popular democracy: "The low can best win the low and all men like to be made much of."[47]

Four months later John Keyes got his comeuppance. No longer a senator nor a representative, he now lost office as county treasurer after twenty-four years. Over that long period, amid all the ups and downs of politics, he had been able to count on steady support from his townsmen. All at once his base collapsed. In 1836 he made a strong showing with 130 votes; in 1837 the tally plummeted to 76, a mere 30 percent of the total and well below his share in the county as a whole. The winner was farmer Stedman Buttrick, grandson of the Revolutionary hero who gave the command to fire on British troops at the North Bridge. The Democrats were not yet finished with Keyes. At the start of 1838, he received word that President Martin Van Buren was removing him as postmaster. The lobbying of Middlesex Democrats had paid off.[48]

The defeats of Hoar and Keyes were not merely personal losses. They amounted to a rejection of the style of leadership and the vision of politics that had long held sway. The elite saw itself as stewards of the common good and not as spokesmen for special interests. Its agenda for economic progress and social improvement was meant to benefit everyone in town. In the fall of 1836, as voters prepared to choose new representatives to the state legislature, it appeared that Lowell would mount a renewed bid for the county courts. Concord's economic well-being and political standing were in jeopardy. Was this not the moment to take advantage of Keyes's experience, network of friends, mastery of parliamentary procedure, and talent for backroom deals? Let the two parties call a truce and send the veteran legislator and a Democratic colleague to Beacon Hill for the sake of the town. The opposition was unyielding. Better to risk the courts than return Keyes to power. The outcome was as the Whigs feared: Lowell would host two court terms, and Concord would be reduced in importance on the political map. Democrats had betrayed the town by declining to call on "men of tried experience" and "men of strength" in its time of need. The contrast with April 19, 1775, must have been in more than a few minds.[49]

The dispute opened up to debate the entire direction of the town. The Whig *Gazette* unleashed a no-holds-barred attack on the Democrats as "aliens to our best interest . . . who would rather the town should sink than lose their influence with their party." The paper had in mind the out-of-town politicians who owned the *Freeman* in partnership with Gourgas and who conducted its affairs to benefit their partisan coalition rather than the welfare of Concord.[50]

Gourgas rejected the charge and turned the table on his opponents. If they were such guardians of "the *town's* interests, the *town's* welfare, the *town's* growth, and the *town's* prospects," why had "Old Concord" fallen so far behind so many other communities in Middlesex? Why had its "monied men" done so little to encourage manufacturers and mechanics? For all their professions of public spirit, these capitalists preferred to speculate in real estate and get hold of "every inch of soil they could grasp in the village" rather than invest in productive enterprise.

The *Freeman* touched a sensitive nerve. Though Concord had prospered in the long commercial boom from the mid-1820s through the mid-1830s, the local economy was losing steam. Population was stagnating; the federal census counted 2,017 inhabitants in 1830, and seven years later, when the Commonwealth enumerated the population, it found just six more individuals in residence. For all the coming and going of transients through town, Concord was losing its young in an accelerating exodus from the mother town. And the local elite, charged Gourgas, was doing nothing to stem the loss.[51]

In April 1837 the dueling newspapers argued the pros and cons of the agenda for change that the business and political elite had been promoting over the last decade. The *Gazette* was not content to refute the charge that Concord's capitalists preferred the profits of land speculation over investment in local manufacturing. It raised the debate to a higher plane. "Who have been the leaders of every project for the benefit of the town?" asked the *Gazette*. "Whose names are at the head of every society for the promotion of philanthropy at home or abroad?" The answer was obvious: "Everybody knows and honors their names." Not Gourgas at the *Freeman*. He sneered at the self-appointed "benefactors of the town" and scoffed at their projects, such as "the Lafayette scrape" of 1824 and the more recent "centennial glorification." Such philanthropy was merely a cover for self-interest. "Who turns our Lyceum into a Whig caucus, puts down the discussion of all such questions and the attendance of all such lecturers as they do not like?" The *Gazette* resented the "slur" on the bicentennial celebration. Was the event not "honorable to our better feelings as a community?" The editor of the *Freeman* and his associates should be ashamed of their attempt to "mar the joyousness of the day." Happily, there was "too much good sense in our townsmen to permit them to succeed."[52]

The completion of the Concord monument was delayed by all the infighting. In December 1836 the cornerstone was laid in a simple ceremony, without any Masonic rigmarole. Beneath the stone were deposited a variety of pertinent documents: Shattuck's *History*, Ripley's *History of the Fight*, Emerson's Second Centennial address, one copy each of the *Freeman* and the *Gazette*. History was both the foundation and the focus of the memorial. Then the obelisk was raised on top. A formal dedication was the final step. But nothing happened. Contrary to expectations, the Nineteenth of April came and went with no notice of the monument, standing erect—and ignored—on the old battleground.[53]

No one was more upset than Ezra Ripley by the unending opposition to his benevolent schemes. One week before the sixty-second anniversary of the fight, the parson took to the lectern of the Concord Lyceum and administered a grim lecture on local history. He was distraught. He had suffered grievous losses, personal and institutional, over the last year. His twenty-seven-year-old step-grandson Charles Emerson had died the previous May, his assistant Hersey

Goodwin eight months earlier at age thirty. Though the First Parish soon hired Barzillai Frost to take Goodwin's place, the congregation was in trouble. Four years into disestablishment, little more than half (54 percent) of the townspeople were willing to pay for its support. Unitarianism was on its way to becoming a minority faith, claiming no more than a quarter of the town by the mid-1840s. Ripley's world no longer looked the same, and the parson could not summon up his customary optimism about the blessings of Providence.

This lecture was not an anticipatory celebration of April 19. Rather, the doctor of divinity presented a diagnosis of "the agitated and unsettled state of society." The symptoms were alarming: "bitter contention and discord among brethren . . . and the destruction of mutual confidence and harmony among the people." A house divided against itself could not stand. Consider what would happen when "jealousies and oppositions" divided "the centre and the remote inhabitants of a town." Everybody knew which town. It was inevitable, the parson observed, that in the course of time, "crooked roads must be straitened, narrow streets must [be] widened, new roads and bridges must be made, [and] public buildings must be erected and repaired." When improvements were brought forward, the only issue should be "the public good, that is, the good of the whole town." A gain for one section was a gain for all. Sometimes progress required personal sacrifices. Ripley pointed to the losses he had endured for the greater good. "Perhaps, no citizen has suffered more by the alteration of roads, than the present speaker," he claimed, "and yet he is convinced that those alterations were needful, and that the town is benefited." That statement must have astonished those in the audience who recalled the minister's part in the removal of the North Bridge and his enclosure of once-public land into his pasture. Ripley recalled a different instance, when the town laid out a bridle-way through his property, cutting off access to water; he was obliged to sell land at a loss in order to remedy the situation. He didn't like it, but that had been his public duty.[54]

The minister pressed the point. With the fight over the monument clearly in mind, he brought up the common impression that "one portion of the town is benefited by handsome alterations and not other sections" and branded it wrong. Whatever honor or advantages a town gained from a public improvement—say, a monument—"belong to the whole of the town in common. The citizen 3 miles from the centre shares in honor and dishonor equally with him who is a mile or half a mile of the church." By the same token, every inhabitant suffered directly from conflict. Ripley compared peaceful to contentious towns and guessed that real estate values were "12 to 20 per cent" higher in the former. Nobody of "a quiet and peaceable disposition" wanted to settle in a "contentious, divided, and quarrelsome town, and wealthy, respectable persons will leave such places even at a sacrifice."

Why, then, was there so much conflict in Concord? What had driven the inhabitants so far apart? Ripley intuited the significance of recent social changes. "With more than a few, it has been too much the practice of neighbors and fellow citizens to live like strangers, and to cherish little or no sympathy for one another. One class of citizens hold themselves at a distance from another class,—one individual from another." In what is still a common theme today, the patriarch who had presided over Concord for sixty years bewailed the loss of community. Neighbors used to know one another, share mutual interests, respect others' views. Now, with so little in common, they exaggerated "differences in opinion, on religion and politics," and polarized the community. Take politics, for example. "A thinks and says of B, he is a federalist, a whig, an opposer of government [that is, Jackson and Van Buren], and therefore ought to be opposed, though he professes to be a genuine Republican. B retorts and says of A that he is a tory, a friend of arbitrary government, and yet, a radical, a leveller." Similar enmities separate the classes.

> The professional man and the mechanic and manufacturer, the man of commerce and of civil office, should be sociable with the farmer, and the farmer, though he is acknowledged the nerve, the sinew, and the backbone of the country and the public welfare, should not pride himself in his importance and independence, and claim superiority to the mechanic, nor feel envy and unkindness towards men of profession, as though they were not working men and brothers.

This was a shrewd assessment of Concord in the 1830s, but with no acknowledgment that the inhabitants had been unraveling the threads of community for the last half-century in favor of greater individual freedom, and that the parson himself had contributed heavily to the withdrawal of the townspeople into separate enclaves of party and sect and into voluntary associations of the like-minded. But Ripley was right in one respect. Attending different churches or none at all, their loyalties captured by one party or another, separated by widening gulfs, the townspeople needed new bases of unity. The minister's ideology of interdependence no longer worked. Appeals to self-interest by the political parties could not lift up anyone's spirits. In history the "venerable" minister sought to reconnect his people. The monument for which he had labored so long was dedicated to this end.

THE FOURTH OF JULY TURNED OUT TO BE DEDICATION DAY, SOME THREE years since the town had accepted Ripley's gift. The ceremony was planned little more than a week before, and it was never advertised in the press. Local Democrats were, in fact, getting ready for a gala celebration with their partisan brethren at Bunker Hill and Faneuil Hall. Waldo Emerson had not much time to compose the hymn he was requested to provide for the occasion; he already had plans to be in Plymouth with Lidian that day. Even so, despite the "short notice," a "straggling" parade of citizens, escorted by the military companies, advanced "slowly" along the common and up the road to the former site of the North Bridge. It was a "very hot, sunny, July day"; at four o'clock, two to three hundred men, women, and children sat in the grass around the monument, enjoying the welcome shade of the same "stately elms" that six decades before had lent protection to the enemy from "the bullets of an oppressed people."

The exercises were conducted in a spirit of reverence, like a religious service. An opening prayer by new minister Frost, ordained just five months before, and another by his Trinitarian counterpart Wilder bracketed the main event, an address by Samuel Hoar. Neither local newspaper reported the politician's remarks. Fortunately, one participant sent off a lengthy summary to the *Boston Courier*. The speech was "full of truth and eloquence, and delighted all who heard it." If so, the listeners were politically inclined to the Whigs. For the "honorable" statesman took the occasion to present a partisan message, pointedly contrasting the Revolutionary fathers' "devotedness to country" and "pure and self-sacrificing efforts in the cause of freedom" with the "selfishness too frequent with men in office at the present day." Whigs looked to history as a guide; through commemorations and monuments, they hoped to purify politics and uphold authority. The best memorial "of our veneration for the fathers," Hoar told the assembly, was not a stone column, however "appropriate and beautiful," but a living display of "firm adherence to law, order, and good principles." Everyone knew he had brash, disorderly Democrats in his sights. Just to be certain that all were aware of "the dangers to which we were exposed, at the present day," the former congressman cited the case of the press. "Though an engine of great good, when well conducted," the news-papers of the day were far too ready to "spread before the people falsehood, instead of truth." Perhaps still smarting from his treatment by the *Freeman* in the recent election, Hoar was determined to counteract the vitriol and the lies with a proper appreciation of the past. As with the Second Centennial Celebra-tion, the sponsors of this ceremony had a distinctive viewpoint to project, one increasingly out of step with the majority of the town.[55]

Emerson's hymn struck a different note. Following the prayer offered up by Wilder, little slips of paper, six inches square, were handed out. They con-tained the words to an ode composed specifically for the ceremony by a citizen of Concord; Emerson's authorship remained anonymous. The tone was elegiac, detached from the passions and contests of the times. The poem certainly paid homage to the local patriotism with its now-famous opening lines about the "rude bridge," "the embattled farmers," and the "shot heard round the world." But the succeeding stanzas express a mood of meditation, not military bom-bast. The sounds of battle are long gone, the combatants in their graves. Nature has reclaimed the site. As in his "Historical Discourse," Emerson opposed the transitory works of men with the enduring force of nature. In a deft rewriting of history and landscape, the poet evoked the "ruined bridge" lost to "the dark stream" rather than the political initiative of his grandfather. For a rare moment, the Concord River was not sluggish. Through that theme of a natural world to which all things return in time, the work poses its central dilemma: how to "redeem" the Concord Fight from inevitable oblivion? That was the purpose of the "votive stone," funded by the Bunker Hill Memorial Association. Inscribed with a tribute to "heroes [who] dare[d] / To die, and leave their children free," the memorial would forge common bonds among a divided people. Its simple message was a reminder that both the combatants long gone (the "foe" and his "conqueror," now sleeping "in silence") and their descendants now and to come share a common nature, from which future acts of heroism could spring. That was unity enough and better suited to the occasion than Hoar's political pro-gram or Ripley's call to revive the traditional virtues of neighborliness.

This was a "hymn," not a secular ode. It was sung in unison by the patriotic worshipers, among whose voices could be heard that of Harvard College senior Henry David Thoreau, about to graduate in two months. Its religious faith was explicit; the piece addressed a Christian God in the words "O Thou." The tune was that of "Old Hundred," the Puritans' favorite hymn, dating back to the Geneva Psalter of 1551. Through words and music, the singers rose above the passing concerns of the present and united in spirit with the forefathers. Ripley concluded the service with a solemn benediction: "And let the people say, Amen."[56]

Gone for a brief afternoon were the confusions and conflicts of a splintered society struggling to find common purposes amid competing interests, ideologies, and identities. Standing together by the riverbank, the citizens were not only engaged in a patriotic ritual. They were also holding a requiem for a vanishing way of life.

The Philosopher of Modern History

The "Concord Hymn" was Ralph Waldo Emerson's last public utterance to enjoy universal acclaim for a long while. By the time he composed the poetic ode to the "embattled farmers," he had come under fire for his association with the nascent Transcendentalist movement. The year 1836 had seen the escalation of the reformers' attack on the Unitarian establishment, with both Orestes Brownson and George Ripley carrying the controversy beyond the pages of the Unitarian *Examiner* in separate publications addressed to the general public. Relocated to the outskirts of Boston, Brownson gathered a congregation of his own; breaking with conventional liberal practice, he appealed to the hearts, rather than the reason, of worshipers and drew as many as five hundred listeners weekly with a nonsectarian call for "Christian union and progress." Meanwhile the Connecticut-born educator Amos Bronson Alcott was raising concern with his School for Human Culture at the Masonic Temple facing Boston Common. In his third year of operation, aided by Elizabeth Peabody and then Margaret Fuller, Alcott strove to realize a child-centered pedagogy on Transcendentalist principles with the goal of awakening the inborn spirituality and intuitive morality of every girl and boy.[1]

This intellectual coterie was soon part of Emerson's expanding social network. He welcomed Alcott ("the most extraordinary man, and the highest genius of his time," according to his host) and Fuller ("an extraordinary person for her apprehensiveness, her acquisitions, and her power of conversation") to extended stays at his home "Bush," and he joined with the Transcendentalist ministers Hedge and Ripley in September 1836 to launch the informal association of like-minded thinkers that came to be known as the Transcendental Club.[2] At just this moment, his "prose poem" *Nature*, celebrating the spiritual connection between the natural world and the human soul, appeared in print, a couple months ahead of Brownson and Ripley. Almost a year to the day after his tribute to Concord's founders, Emerson bewailed his contemporaries' excessive veneration of the past. "Our age is retrospective," he began. "It builds the sepulchres of the fathers . . . The foregoing generations beheld God and nature face to face; we, through their eyes. Why should not we enjoy an original relation to the universe?" In this manifesto for a faith founded on experience of the divine in Nature, Emerson left behind the religion of his forebears, from his grandfather Ripley and his father William all the way back to Peter Bulkeley. The liberal clergyman eschewed polemics and shunned controversy. Rather than dispute the need for miracles to shore up Christian belief, Emerson simply beheld "the miraculous in the common" and invoked the "wonders" of a summer day.[3]

This affinity with the radical reformers in Boston was unmistakable to the reviewer of *Nature* in the *Christian Examiner*. Though it contained passages of "beautiful writing and sound philosophy," conceded Francis Bowen, the twenty-five-year-old tutor of philosophy at Harvard College, the book was marred by "occasional vagueness of expression, and by a vein of mysticism, that pervades the writer's whole course of thought." Not that the flaw was Emerson's alone. His volume was "the latest representative" of the "new school of philosophy" known as Transcendentalism, whose proponents refused to convey their ideas in language accessible to "the majority of educated and reflecting men" or to argue their case according to conventions of logic and usages of words well established in learned circles. The "deepest minds" wrote the clearest prose. In dismissing this standard and opting instead for "the heights of mystical speculation," the American acolytes of Coleridge and the German idealists displayed an insufferable "arrogance and self-sufficiency"—defects "no less absurd in philosophy, than criminal in morals." Withdrawing from the intellectual community of Boston Unitarianism, Emerson and his wayward colleagues willfully strode off on their own in a direction there was no good reason to follow.[4]

Ironically, while Emerson was accused of isolating himself in an intellectual cocoon, he was settling into Concord and cultivating ties with his Yankee neighbors. With the legacy from his late wife, Ellen, the newcomer assumed a place in the economic elite, the ninth-richest taxpayer in the spring of 1835. (Samuel Hoar ranked first.) His wealth differed from that of the gentleman farmers and real estate speculators of the town. It was concentrated not in land but in shares of banks and other corporations, valued at $13,000 when the bequest was complete. Emerson's income depended on the modern capitalist economy.[5]

As a man of means and a college-educated professional, he was welcomed into the local leadership. A veteran of the Boston School Committee, he was elected to its Concord counterpart in June 1835 and elevated to chairman the next year, only to resign "the vexatious office" after a few months.[6] More to his taste was service to the societies for social and cultural improvement. At the start of 1836, he bought a share in the social library and immediately joined the committee to choose new books and periodicals. It was during his tenure (1836–1841) that American-authored titles rose to a majority of new selections. He also subscribed to the ornamental tree society and to the lyceum, where he delivered the lectures for which he was gaining renown in Boston and beyond. In recognition of his civic-mindedness, he was nominated for the Social Circle in the fall of 1837, though he had to wait a couple more years to be admitted.[7]

Emerson's social world extended beyond the elite. As he and Lidian set up housekeeping following their marriage in September 1835, two days after the town bicentennial, and began raising a family—the firstborn, Waldo, arrived in October the next year—the newlyweds had to adapt to the customs of a country town unlike their respective birthplaces of Boston and Plymouth. A child of the city, accustomed to spending his days indoors, Emerson required assistance in establishing his garden. Luckily, an experienced husbandman was close at hand. Peter Howe, a man in his fifties, had worked the land in Vermont and New Hampshire before turning up in Concord about 1830 in a house opposite Emerson's. With a wife and two daughters to support, rent to pay, and a mere three-quarter-acre lot at his disposal, Howe was as much in need of employment as was Emerson of lessons in farming. For the next five years, the workingman manured, plowed, planted, hoed, and harvested in the scholar's garden, to the latter's complete satisfaction. "Peter Howe knows what to do in the garden," he reflected in his journal, as did Daniel Webster in the Senate and Emerson himself in the study. Why question this division of labor? "In my garden I find it best to pay a man's price or to buy good sense." In this way "I multiply myself." Even so, the literary man was anxious to contribute to the work, if only for the daily exercise and the connection with nature. Unfortunately, his enthusiasm exceeded his skill, as little Waldo, at four or five, readily discerned. "Papa," he worried aloud as he watched his father hard at work, "I am afraid you will dig your leg." Despite his deficiencies, Emerson was not ready to quit. After Howe moved away in 1840, the intellectual recruited his new friend Thoreau, whose handiness was legendary, to live in his household, tend the garden, and teach him a few tricks. His own expertise never got beyond pruning trees and "picking up pears and apples." With good reason, the Squire of Coolidge Castle never joined the agricultural society.[8]

Emerson paid greater heed to the symbolic uses of a garden than to its edible fruits. As he got to know other farmers in the vicinity—George Minott atop the ridge along the Bay Road, Edmund Hosmer on the way to the Walden woods—he admired their closeness to nature. Minott appeared to be a man of few words, but to his attentive neighbor, he "writes out his nature in a hundred works," from "drawing water" and "hewing wood" to building fences, feeding cows, and making hay. The land answered to his will, and he bore its impress on his character: "Thus his human spirit unites itself with nature." Emerson relished the homely metaphors and down-to-earth wisdom of such plainspoken men, as would his protégé Thoreau in later years. From Peter Howe, he picked up a "garden phrase" to describe activities of little use but to kill time—"puttering around"—and he recorded the laborer's dismay at a solar eclipse in September 1838. "He said 'the sun looked as if a nigger was putting his head into it.'" Emerson, who regularly employed the African American Jack Garrison to cut and stack wood, expressed no misgivings about Howe's casual white racism. The blunt speech, in his reckoning, provided a refreshing antidote to the stilted talk in Concord's parlors. He found in the manners of common folk a necessary tonic for social life. "The high people in the village are timid, the low people are bold & nonchalant." Speaking the truth as they knew it from their daily labors, the working people of Concord illustrated the varied uses of nature Emerson was conscientiously setting forth in his Transcendentalist manifesto.[9]

The longer he stayed in Concord, the more Emerson praised the country over the city. He congratulated himself on his choice of residence. Not only had he reclaimed roots in his ancestral town, but he had gained a crucial distance from the distractions of Boston and Cambridge. Sixteen miles from the capital, he was able to enjoy solitude in winter, when "the northwest wind with all his snows" kept company away, and likewise in summer, when "the hills & sand-banks" under a hot sun posed their own deterrent. In his rural setting he could draw inspiration from nature whenever he pleased, in contrast to city dwellers, shut out of the horizon by buildings without end and deprived of "the affecting spectacle of Day and Night." While writing *Nature* in the spring and summer of 1836, he often took walks to Walden to invigorate both body and soul. Just before sunset one August evening, he felt a sense of communion with the enchanting scene: "in the tranquil landscape I beheld somewhat as beautiful as my own nature." That epiphany, initially recorded in his journal, became the culminating sentence in *Nature*'s most famous passage, in which the author portrays himself in a state of "perfect exhilaration" on a "bare common" in winter, so open to "the currents of the Universal Being" that he merged with his surroundings, "a transparent eyeball" in harmony with all of creation, "part or particle of God."[10]

When he returned from the woods to the village, Emerson entered a community he considered superior to the city. A leading feature of the age, he declared in February 1837, was "the congregation of men into large masses." The onetime minister of the elite Second Church had decamped from Boston amid a surge of population from some 43,000 in 1820 to well over 85,000 two decades later. Crowded into dense urban space and separated by walls of class and race, the inhabitants of the capital seemed to its former resident an impersonal throng, their individuality lost in a sea of strangers on the streets. The poor struggled desperately for survival; the privileged selfishly competed for wealth and status. In contrast, small-town Concord, with its two thousand inhabitants, appeared a simpler place, where a person could stand out on his own and be appreciated for the content of his character rather than the weight of his purse or the glitter of his friends. Let "Boston dolls," as Emerson disdained them, live for show. In the countryside "our people are not crippled by family & official pride," and "the best man in town may steer his plough tail or may drive a milk cart."[11]

The learned observer delighted in daily contacts with the townsfolk. One November day in 1837, he conducted a mental survey of the town meeting in illustration of the theme that "perhaps in the village we have manners to paint which the city life does not know." First to mind came "Mr. S." (probably the butcher Cyrus Stow), "man enough" to fire an employee who "cheats in weights" and put an honest one in his place. Next up was an ungenerous spirit refusing to part with even a penny for a civic project, "though all say it is mean." He was followed by an open-handed philanthropist, who insisted on remaining anonymous when all the other donors wanted their names known. One citizen agreed with "what ever proposition you please to make"; another was sure to say "he will have nothing to do with the thing." And "Mr. H" (probably Samuel Hoar) retained his good cheer, though he lost the vote every time. Each vignette conjured up an ethical choice. In this portrait gallery of Concordians, Emerson witnessed the human comedy on a village scale and weighed each neighbor's character in the balance. A moral drama unfolded at every turn. "To show the force that is in you," Concord's Balzac concluded, "you need not go beyond the tinman's shop or the first corner; nay, the first man you meet who bows to you, may look you in the eye & call it out."[12]

Set against the divided city, Concord embodied norms of equality and inclusiveness with which Emerson gladly complied. His bride Lidian, raised in "aristocratic Plymouth," found it harder to adjust to country ways. Visitors to the new household were offended by her genteel style and "far-away manners," and they vowed never to come calling again. She, in turn, was ill at ease in social gatherings that, to her astonishment, included even the butcher. Nor did she see any reason to defer to sensitivities her husband felt obliged to honor. In 1837, as the economy was turning downward in the wake of the panic, the proud new mother wanted to outfit baby Waldo in a fashionable velvet cap. The head of household said no. In these hard times, the boy "would seem to the humbler people in town better dressed than their babies, [when] he ought to be dressed like the poorest." Rather than arouse class resentment with a conspicuous display of wealth, Emerson played down his privilege and conformed to community standards. He could not insulate himself from the trials of his neighbors even if he tried. Two hundred yards across the mill brook from Emerson's home stood the almshouse, where "poor Nancy Barron, the madwoman, scream[ed] herself hoarse" in the night until the town had her removed to the state hospital for the insane in Worcester. Emerson was personally involved in her care. For several years, he paid her bills at the institution, for which he was reimbursed by the overseers of the poor. Well after the middle-aged woman was out of earshot, Emerson could "still hear her whenever I open my window."[13]

So contented was Emerson with his country seat that at times he romanticized his rural neighbors and idealized their practical common sense. In 1838, when Transcendentalist George Ripley issued the latest volume of *Specimens of Foreign Standard Literature*, with excerpts from the "philosophical miscellanies" of leading French thinkers, his Concord colleague professed indifference. The work might win praise in Boston, Emerson conceded, but here "in the bushes we whistle at such matters" and "care little for Societies, systémes, or book-stores." Who needed the abstract musings of learned men? Give him "a genuine observation" of a brass knob or a button instead of "whole Encyclopædias."[14]

Anti-intellectualism was a fleeting pose. When Emerson dropped the urban gaze and trained his sights on Concord itself, he was quick to detect its defects and departures from democratic principles. He dismissed as naïve the claim by a foreign observer that no "selfish aristocracy" existed in the American republic. "I earnestly wish it could be proved . . . that no distinctions created by a con-temptible pride existed here & none but the natural ones of talent & virtue." But Emerson knew better and took note of the subtle signs of inequality in everyday life. The very coat a man wore advertised his standing in society: a "good coat" was welcomed on the stagecoach; a coat with a missing haunch button hinted at social decline; a "ragged coat" was a confession of defeat. Even the poorest peo-ple in Concord grasped at respectability. Emerson was told about a family "who were so poor, or so odd, that they had no table, & held their tea cups in their laps." The town was full of individuals so beaten down by the daily struggle for existence or so caught up in materialistic striving that they had no inkling of the "god within." Awakening such souls to their high destiny would be Emerson's self-appointed mission.[15]

While Emerson arrived in Concord as an urban transplant, he gradually rus-ticated himself and invested his new home with rich social significance. Close to nature, the country town sustained a simpler, healthier way of life than was possible in the dense and artificial city. It narrowed distances between classes and fostered contact across social ranks. On the Sabbath, men and women still gathered together, if not for stirring sermons from the pulpit, then for "the one opportunity of equal meeting with all citizens that is left." "I go to be of one counsel," Emerson admitted, "to own the sentiment of Holiness with Carr & Wright & Buttrick." The ideal of community retained a hold.[16]

At the same time, the rising generation was rejecting custom and con-straint and exercising greater independence and choice. In this setting, the individual could act and influence others rather than be absorbed in an urban mass. Here Emerson could observe, on a personal, human scale, the forces remaking the age and take lessons from the changing village scene. Concord did not make Emerson a Transcendentalist—he had already embraced the romantic idealism of Coleridge, Wordsworth, and Goethe before coming to town—but it afforded ample resources with which to illustrate and apply his observations of New England life. Like his farmer neighbors, Emerson took the yield of his work in the country town and carried it to market in Boston. There he won notice for his incisive reading of the times, built his reputation as a lecturer, and cultivated the Yankee audience for his Transcendentalist message.

IN THE FALL OF 1836, NEAR THE END OF A COMMERCIAL BOOM THAT WOULD collapse in financial panic and economic depression the following spring, the *Boston Courier* abounded with advertisements. The front and back sheets of the four-page semiweekly, aimed at merchants and tradesmen, were thick with notices of a vast array of imported goods from all over the globe. As in the Concord press, long lists of textiles dominated the columns. Jumbled with them was a miscellany of ads for new businesses, help wanted, houses and shops to buy or rent, recent publications at the bookstores, drugs to relieve headache and dyspepsia, and a reward for the recovery of a runaway inmate from the Cambridge House of Correction. It took a patient reader to scan them all, and one could easily miss an item sandwiched between the timetable for the Boston and Worcester Railroad on one side and an illustration on the other of Day and Martin's Real Japan Blacking Manufactory, whose casks of boot and shoe polish had just arrived from London.

"Mr. R. W. Emerson proposes to deliver a Course of Lectures on the PHILOS-OPHY OF MODERN HISTORY," the notice stated, covering the subjects of "Religion, Politics, Literature, Science, and Art." The scope would be as far-reaching as the global commerce reflected in the *Courier* and equally sweeping in its perspective from antiquity to the present. So ambitious was the scheme that it would take "at least twelve lectures"—one a week—to complete. Emerson planned to examine civilization—or more precisely, that of the Western world—as it arose "in the nature of things" and attained its "present condition and tendencies" from "general causes" operating over the ages. Lest anyone fear an abstruse or dry treatment, the lecturer planned to illustrate his themes with examples of "the popular Sciences" and "Men of genius." He also would show the relevance of his ideas to contemporary life by pointing up "the intellectual duties of the existing generation." In an era of rapid change, Emerson was offering to make sense of the complex world faced by his fellow New Englanders—the emerging world of railroads and steamships, of factory-made broadcloths and blacking polish, and of the expansive press that disseminated his prospectus. Such guidance in uncertain times came at a price: two dollars for the entire series, set to begin at the Masonic Temple (the place where Alcott kept school) on the first Thursday of December and to run into March—substantial intellectual fare for the winter ahead.[17]

The proposed series was a risky venture. Shedding his ministerial title, "Mr. Emerson" came before the public at his own initiative. His previous appearances had been sponsored by associations for intellectual improvement, such as the Boston Society for the Diffusion of Useful Knowledge (SDUK), under whose auspices he had recently delivered courses of lectures on "Biography" and "English Literature." The group had been founded in 1829 by prominent businessmen and politicians in Boston—the class that supported the *Boston Courier*—out of concern that young clerks and tradesmen in the vulnerable years from seventeen to the midtwenties, "when the mind is active and the passions urgent," were left to wander the city without supervision. There they encountered many "invitations to profitless amusements." How to keep them safe? Imbued with the same faith in workingmen's education that had inspired lyceum promoter Josiah Holbrook, the SDUK inaugurated a program of edifying lectures. Its speakers were carefully vetted to convey "useful information" in an "inviting form" and "at a cheap rate." Whatever the topic, the charge was to engage the restless young in their callings "more understandingly, with a deeper interest, and with better prospect of success." Emerson surely understood the agenda when he stepped up to the SDUK lectern. Speaking under the aegis of an organization whose president was Sen. Daniel Webster and whose vice-president was the next Massachusetts governor, Edward Everett, the lecturer from Concord carried a seal of approval from the Boston establishment, and he was assured a large audience, as many as seven or eight hundred, for his words. In October 1836, this was a status he no longer desired. Just as he had resigned from the ministry to carry on freelance preaching, so he now dropped the mantle of institutional authority and proceeded to lecture without encumbrance to anyone who cared to attend.[18]

Success was not guaranteed. "Private projects of this sort . . . are always attended with a degree of uncertainty," Emerson acknowledged. Competition was keen to fill seats in Boston's lecture halls. In the winter season of 1836–1837, seven different groups, including several lyceums, a debating club, and the SDUK itself, held their own programs, while the reformer Sylvester Graham discoursed three times a week on "Health, and Long Life," and Emerson's own brother-in-law, Dr. Charles T. Jackson, struggled to attract anyone to his discussions of geology. "A Prophet is not without honor except in his own country," the *Boston Courier* observed in sympathy with Jackson's plight.[19] These lectures vied with theaters, concert halls, and museums. As Emerson was launching his series at the Masonic Temple, the Anglo-Irish comedian Tyrone Power was starring in "Born to Good Luck; or, the Irishman's Fortune" at the Tremont Theater just down the street. The Boston Academy of Music opened its season shortly afterward with "the Oratorio of David." And in the first months of 1837, "The Philosophy of Modern History" contended against displays of "animal magnetism" (as hypnotism was known) and of "electro-magnetism." ("Animal magnetism is loathsome," Emerson would later grumble.) Thanks to this rich cultural calendar, along with its many schools and libraries, Boston boasted of being the Athens of America. But for a lecturer striving for the first time to attract an audience on his own, the outlook was not encouraging. Emerson could not avoid the fact that "the number of Lecturers" bore "a pretty large proportion to the number of ears in Boston." Scaling down his ambitions, he hoped simply to cover his costs.[20]

Despite the hurdles, Emerson was also drawn to freelance lecturing by its moneymaking potential. "If a man speaks well, he shall find this a well-rewarded work in New England," he informed Thomas Carlyle in a bid to recruit his intellectual hero for an American speaking tour. The German phrenologist Johann Spurzheim, to take one example, had earned as much as $3,000 over several months in Boston before typhoid canceled his engagements for good. In the winter of 1835, more than nine hundred people had followed scientist Benjamin Silliman's lectures on geology. Carlyle, a lion of British letters, was sure to outstrip them. The revenue would be huge, Emerson anticipated; at three dollars for a season ticket and sales equivalent to Silliman's, the Scotsman would bring in $2,700, far more than the $120 in expenses for renting a hall, advertising the program, selling tickets, hiring a doorman, and lighting the room. Carlyle resisted, in spite of the financial allure, so Emerson took the risk himself in hopes of realizing more than the "inconsiderable" fee of twenty dollars per lecture he had gotten from the SDUK.[21]

More than money, Emerson craved cultural influence, and the lecture room promised the best path to achieve it. It was his "secular pulpit," free from the constraints of a church. An ordained minister was presumed to be representative of an entire congregation and so could not speak the truth as he personally knew it. Subject to "the shackles of prescription," the clergyman halted in his delivery and emitted "an obstructed and uncertain sound." Put that same man in front of a lyceum audience, and he would find his voice. In Emerson's hopeful view, this forum had the power to liberate the New England mind. A new institution, it had no ancient usages or binding precedents: "Nothing is presupposed. The orator is only responsible for what his lips articulate." He could take up whatever topic he wished and say whatever he thought with all the verbal resources and emotional intensity at his command. "Here he may lay himself out utterly, large, enormous, prodigal, on the subject of the hour," he discovered. "Here he may dare to hope for ecstasy and eloquence." And here an audience of all classes in the community sat ready to take in the message and be converted to a new vision of life. Emerson may have dropped "Rev." before his name and shed the black gown of a minister, but in the novel setting of the lecture room he was still a preacher at heart.[22]

In the mid-1830s the lyceum was not yet "the great organ" of popular instruction Emerson envisaged. In too many towns, he told a young admirer in Concord, the programs were tedious affairs, with speakers often presenting "superficial" notions on the "easiest subjects" for no better reason than to fill up a season's schedule. (Perhaps he had Nehemiah Ball in mind.) Nor were all matters open to discussion. In August 1837 the Salem Lyceum invited Emerson to lecture on any subject he wished, "provided that no allusions are made to religious controversy, or other exciting topics on which the public mind is honestly divided." He declined to accept a request "so encumbered." In Boston, the Whig-dominated SDUK set its own limits of acceptable speech; Democrats were notably absent from its platform. Rather than conform to such tacit conditions, it seems likely, Emerson opted to go off on his own. As an independent lecturer, he pursued money, reputation, and most important of all, freedom to express his mind in his own distinctive way.[23]

As an entrepreneur, Emerson enjoyed modest success. The "Philosophy of Modern History" course drew an audience of 350 people, on average, over its twelve-week run, though a fair number consisted of friends and relatives, to whom the speaker gave free tickets, for fear of looking out on too many empty seats. His profit came to some thirty dollars per lecture—a tidy raise over the twenty dollars that the SDUK provided in compensation. From that auspicious beginning, Emerson proceeded to present a Boston lecture series in four of the next five years. Each course was universal in its reach, "a gay rag bag" into which the lecturer could stuff anything he wished: "Human Culture" (1837–1838), "Human Life" (1838–1839), "The Present Age" (1839–1840), and "The Times" (1841–1842). Attendance and profits peaked in 1837–1838; despite the hard times, Emerson pulled in 439 persons, on average, for his ten-week survey of "Human Culture" and netted fifty-seven dollars per talk. "We acquire courage by our success daily," he exulted. Thereafter his returns slumped. "The Times" was disappointing, yielding about forty dollars per lecture. Never did Emerson come close to the crowds that the SDUK regularly attracted and that he had predicted would fill the Masonic Temple were Carlyle to come to town.[24]

The benefits of these series went beyond direct contributions to Emerson's income. Success in the capital built his reputation elsewhere. Lyceums in Lowell and Salem, Cambridge and Framingham, and Providence, Rhode Island, among others, were eager to hear for themselves what the Transcendentalist had to say. Although these groups paid just ten to twenty dollars per lecture, without reimbursement of expenses, Emerson readily accepted. The bookings were a bonus for work already done. In one venue, there was never any charge. Emerson spoke in Concord for free and did so 126 times over five decades, more than anywhere else except Boston. In his home base, he appeared not as a professional lecturer but as a fellow member of the lyceum, one among equals participating in a forum full of volunteers. Emerson considered such talks to be acts of philanthropy. As a scholar, he felt duty bound to offer his thoughts to his countrymen, in hopes of raising "some counterweight" to the widespread materialism that left young people nearly "starving" for inspiration. The profits of lecturing in Boston underwrote this idealistic mission.[25]

The shift from pulpit to lectern called for a fresh approach to public speaking. As Emerson saw it, men of learning faced an unprecedented circumstance. Where scholars for centuries had courted the favor of nobles and kings, now "the democratic element" was ascendant, and it was imperative to write and speak to the people as a whole about what mattered to them here and now. Forget the fables and romances, the pastoral poems and apologetic sermons of yore. The current generation demanded to hear about "Texas [and] Oregon territory . . . , the abolition of Slavery & of Capital Punishment, [and] questions of Education" of importance to all. "The human race have got possession" of the forum and will not let go. But how to engage the vox populi? As Emerson was formulating his approach, he was constantly sizing up the competition for influence over the public mind. He had no patience for the dry preaching of his grandsire Ripley nor for the empty bellowing of assistant minister Frost. As much as Emerson respected the intellect and integrity of Samuel Hoar, the lawyer was, sadly, no orator but rather a "very slovenly speaker," whose addresses to judge and jury consisted of "interminable sentences . . . , clause growing out of clause 'like the prickly pear.'" As for the politicians, Emerson had only contempt for the demagoguery of Democrats and the artifice of Whigs, such as Edward Everett spouting "stereotyped phrases" and contriving "postures & sounds" in imitation of Daniel Webster. Time and again the Concord lecturer was advised to adapt his presentation to the limited intelligence of "the great mass." Emerson rejected that counsel of condescension and devised an approach through which speaker and listeners could meet on elevated ground.[26]

Emerson cut a figure of restraint at the podium. Six feet tall, "slender but bony," the lecturer looked like a Yankee schoolmaster in his frock coat and cravat. With his dark-blue eyes intent on the manuscript before him, he got right down to business, with no preliminary remarks to establish rapport and ease into the lecture. His posture was composed; he eschewed the "pathetic tones and gestures" so popular in the day. But as he proceeded, his "rich baritone" commanded the room; nearly four decades later the poet James Russell Lowell still recalled "that thrilling voice of his, so charged with subtle meaning and subtle music," that he had first heard as a Harvard student in the audience at the Masonic Temple. Over the course of fifty minutes, lecturer and listeners took an intellectual journey together. Emerson served as an impersonal medium of his text. He read the words as if discovering them for the first time and with the same feelings he had experienced in their composition. There were no spontaneous asides, no impromptu wit. The speaker stuck to the script, as he strove to enlist the aspiring men and women before him in his process of thought and awaken them to his insights and epiphanies as their own. For young Lowell, the experience was life-transforming. It was as if he and his contemporaries had been adrift on an uncharted sea; then Emerson came on the scene, and they responded like "shipwrecked men on a raft to the hail of a ship that came with unhoped for food and rescue." Not everyone felt that way. One listener in 1837 complained of his inability to comprehend much of what was said. There was no question-and-answer session at the end when such criticism could be voiced. Emerson gauged the response from the applause. "The orator's value," he reflected in September 1837, "might be measured by every additional round after the three first claps . . . , the first & second roll come very easily off, but it gets beyond the third very hardly."[27]

If lectures were to have "permanent value," Emerson considered in April 1836, men must "write upon such a subject as interests them—upon a subject that the time, the age, calls forth—upon a subject which has not been written upon before, or else they must treat it in a new way." The Concord sage found that subject in the series "The Philosophy of Modern History" that he inaugurated in December, and he elaborated on the theme in succeeding years. At the very moment that the French thinker Alexis de Tocqueville was popularizing the term *individualism* in the Western world, Emerson was putting the individual at the center of his own vision of democracy in America. What better topic for an entrepreneur of the lecture room coming before the public for the first time on his own? Emerson was a fit medium of his message.[28]

For the Transcendentalist, it was neither political liberty nor social equality that made the new republic unique. Rather, a distinct understanding of the individual, drawn from the German Romantics, provided the source and foundation for a democracy that was still a work in progress. Emerson proclaimed his ideal with the force of a religious revelation: "there is one Mind common to all individual men," a "Universal Soul" incarnated in each and every person, access to which could release all "the virtues and powers" intrinsic to humankind. Running throughout creation, that spirit united man and nature. "Every being in nature has its existence so connected with other beings," the lecturer declared—in language evocative of Ezra Ripley—"that if set apart from them, it would instantly perish." Unlike his grandfather, Emerson saw no need for hierarchy or institutions to bind them together. In his new philosophy, all people, past and present, shared a common divinity. This spiritual essence contained the potential for perfection that was embodied by Jesus, manifested by a few heroes across the ages, and inherent in every child born. "Every man is a new and incalculable power," he affirmed in December 1836; three years later he was repeating the point with the same fervor. "Every man and every woman in the planet [is] a new experiment, to be and exhibit the full and perfect soul."[29]

The implications of this outlook were radical. It called into question the wisdom of the ages, and it put all times and places on an equal plane. "What Plato has thought," you "may think. What a saint has felt [you] may feel," Emerson announced. Of the universal mind, "history is the record" in which we can see our own natures revealed. Why, then, conform to customs or profess beliefs that no longer carry conviction? "Incessant change is the condition of life and mind." By the same token, no one was entitled to legal privilege or to the right of ruling over others. Before the standard of human equality—the intuitive knowledge that we are common shareholders in a divine estate—"down topple . . . all the hierarchies, all the artificial ranks of the earth." Listen to the inner "voice of Reason" to "Reverence thyself," and be elevated from "a citizen" into a "state," for whose well-being the laws and government exist. So too would the "unpardonable outrage" of slavery meet an immediate end, once the principle took hold that "every man has within him somewhat really divine."[30]

It was the task of education, indeed, of "human culture" broadly, to draw out the "latent powers" within each person and develop them to the full. Unlike the school reformers of the day, Emerson put the development of the individual, rather than service to society, at the heart of his educational vision. "His own Culture,—the unfolding of his nature, is the chief end of man. A divine impulse at the core of his being, impels him to this." The inner capacities of every person—the unique mix of dispositions and talents, aptitudes and aversions that form each personality—should be cultivated for their own sake. "The world exists to instruct the private man."[31]

As Emerson exhorted his listeners to seek out the god within and cultivate their divine potential, he was also rethinking the relationship between individual and community. The right formulation came to him in December 1837. Opening his series "Human Culture," he announced a vast change had taken place in human affairs. Look at any period in the past—at the ancient Israelites, the Greeks, the Romans, or at the Protestant Reformation and the Elizabethan age—and compare its "institutions and books" with those of the present day, and what do you find? "The tone and aims are entirely changed." Previous generations had led a collective existence; theirs was the story of states and societies. No more: the individual was taking center stage and pronouncing "the awful words *I am*." "The former men," Emerson explained, "acted and spoke under the thought that a shining social prosperity was the aim of men, and compromised ever the individuals to the nation. The modern mind teaches (in extremes) that the nation exists for the individual; for the guardianship and education of every man." The insight stuck; though Emerson tinkered with the language, he repeated the point two years later at the start of his series "the Present Age," and made it central to his "Historic Notes on Life and Letters in New England" some four decades later. And with good reason: the statement captured the on-going revolution in values that was dissolving the bonds of interdependence and prompting individuals to withdraw from common institutions and pursue their own self-interest. "The social sentiments are weak," Emerson elaborated in December 1839. "The spirit of patriotism is weak. Veneration is low . . . There is an universal resistance to ties and ligaments once supposed essential to civil society." Put simply, America—or at least Emerson's New England—had entered a new era: "the age of the first person singular." It marked the passage from Ezra Ripley's world to Waldo Emerson's.[32]

The venue for these lectures was the Masonic Temple, where Emerson had given his previous talks under SDUK auspices. This imposing structure, facing Boston Common, had been built by the Grand Lodge of Massachusetts at the height of its power. Opened to public fanfare in May 1832, the building was the first in Boston to display the new Gothic style of architecture. In a city built of wood and brick, it was constructed of stone to symbolize permanence, with two towers rising nearly one hundred feet above ground. Its four stories had space for three schoolrooms (two in the basement, one on the third floor) and a lecture room, seating eight hundred, on the second floor. Winding staircases in the towers gave access to the interiors. The Gothic arches and rose window evoked the Middle Ages and associated Freemasonry with the authority and tra-dition of the Christian church. But hardly had the building been dedicated than it became a target of political attack. In the winter of 1833 the Anti-Masonic Party denounced the Grand Lodge for erecting a luxurious headquarters at a cost far in excess of the $20,000 in real estate it was authorized to hold by its legislative charter. To dodge criticism, the fraternity transferred ownership to a wealthy brother, who rented it out for public purposes. Bronson Alcott kept his experimental school there from 1834 to 1838; Orestes Brownson's Society for Christian Union and Progress assembled there on the Sabbath from 1836 to 1843. And almost every winter from 1836 to 1841, Waldo Emerson gave weekly lectures in a grand room (65 by 55 feet and 19 feet high) "with circular seats upon a spherical floor." In principle, the Masonic Temple stood for values an-tithetical to the individuality and equality prized by Transcendentalists. If any-one objected, there is no record.[33]

The lectures at the Masonic Temple heralded a new world in the making: a democracy of free and equal individuals, all striving to realize their highest selves. Emerson deployed his rhetorical gifts to inspire listeners with this vi-

This view of Concord center was engraved by Amos Doolittle a month or so after the clash of arms between British regulars and provincial forces on April 19, 1775. The Concord artist Timothy Martin Minot copied the engraving for this painting, made around the jubilee of that fight. The picture highlights the mill pond at the heart of the town. The painting was owned by the painter's niece, Mary Merrick Brooks, at whose home Henry D. Thoreau viewed it in 1855. (Painting attributed to Timothy Martin Minot, c. 1825. Courtesy Concord Museum)

Portrait of Reverend Ezra Ripley, D.D. (1751–1841), c. 1800. At the start of the nineteenth century, Ripley was in his third decade as pastor of the Concord church and geared up for the fight to defend the Federalist Party and the New England way. (Courtesy Trustees of Reservations)

Ezra Ripley in the early 1820s. One of the last ministers from the period of the Revolution to serve in the Congregationalist pulpit, Ezra Ripley was characteristically referred to as "venerable." In this portrait from 1823, he displays satisfaction that "his people" remained united. (Painting probably by James Frothingham. Courtesy First Parish Church, Concord)

Dubbed the "squire of the town" by later generations, the Honorable Samuel Hoar (1778–1856) was not always Concord's favorite son. A Federalist and Whig partisan, the attorney provoked opposition with his support for the Congregationalist religious establishment, chartered corporations, and the textile industry. (Courtesy Concord Free Public Library)

If anyone rivaled Samuel Hoar as "squire of the town," it was the Honorable John Keyes (1787–1844). At the peak of his power, he held office simultaneously as federal postmaster, state senator, county treasurer, adjutant of the Middlesex militia, justice of the peace, and moderator of town meetings. Starting out as a Jeffersonian Republican, he later joined Hoar among the Whigs. (Courtesy Corinthian Lodge of Freemasons)

The Federal-style house of worship erected by the Trinitarian parish in 1826 was modeled on the Boston meetinghouse of Reverend Lyman Beecher's Hanover Street church and financed with a loan from orthodox opponents of the Unitarians. (Courtesy Concord Free Public Library)

Maria Thoreau (1794–1881), one of the "little band" of dissenters who withdrew from Ezra Ripley's congregation and became a founder of the Trinitarian Church in 1826. (Mounted photographic portrait of Maria Thoreau, photographed by Alfred Winslow Hosmer from the original. Courtesy Concord Free Public Library)

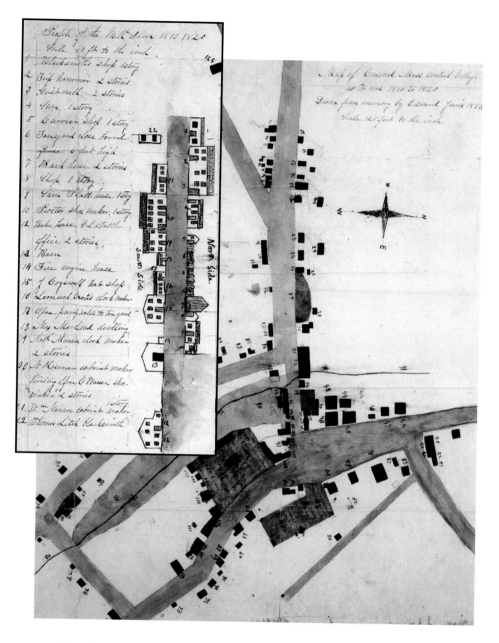

Map of Concord, "as it was 1810 to 1820, drawn from memory," and "Profile of the Milldam, 1810–1820" (*inset*), by Edward Jarvis. In his late sixties, Jarvis drew this map of the Concord center and its milldam as he remembered them from his childhood. The milldam developed into a little industrial district with a variety of craft shops, whose machine processes fascinated the boys of the village. (Courtesy Concord Free Public Library)

𝕿he one-and-a-half-story house (about 544 square feet) into which the Robbins and Garrison families moved in 1823 was a typical yeoman's dwelling. Built for their use and a half mile from any neighbor, it was the hub of Concord's small black community from the 1820s through the 1850s. The house was restored and relocated in 2007, as depicted in this contemporary photograph. (Courtesy Robbins House, Concord)

𝕵ack Garrison (1769–1860) in old age, depicted on a carte de visite produced by abolitionists in Concord. Born in New Jersey before the Revolution, Garrison escaped bondage and found a new home in Concord around 1810, where he wed Peter Robbins's daughter Susan. The Garrison family was active in the abolitionist movement. Daughter Ellen, who excelled in the local school, taught in Boston and Newport, and with the start of Reconstruction became an educator of free people in Maryland, Virginia, and North Carolina. (Courtesy Concord Museum)

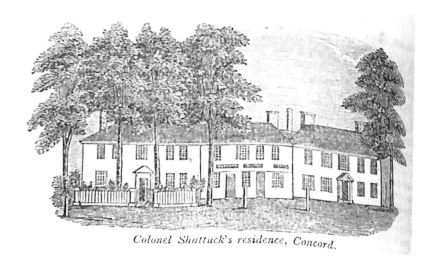

Colonel Shattuck's residence, Concord.

In a sign of Daniel Shattuck's prominence as a merchant and banker and one of Concord's richest men, his new "Mansion House" at the west end of the common (the dwelling on the left) was featured as an illustration in Barber's widely circulated *Historical Collections*. ("Colonel Shattuck's residence, Concord." Originally published in John Warner Barber, *Historical Collections: Being a General Collection of Interesting Facts, Traditions, Biographical Sketches, Anecdotes, &c., Relating to the History and Antiquities of Every Town in Massachusetts, with Geographical Descriptions* [Worcester, 1839]. Courtesy Concord Free Public Library)

The Jonas Minot farmhouse, Virginia Road. Henry D. Thoreau spent his first eight months of life in this eighteenth-century farmhouse built by his grandmother's second husband, Captain Jonas Minot, once a prominent figure in the local political elite. (Photograph by Alfred Winslow Hosmer. Courtesy Concord Free Public Library)

Certificate of Membership in the Society of Middlesex Husbandmen and Manufacturers, issued to Timothy Prescott, October 5, 1825. This membership certificate portrays the ideal of the agricultural society, with farming, commerce, and manufacturing bound together in peace and prosperity. (Courtesy Concord Free Public Library)

The Concord native Edward Jarvis (1803–1884) (*left*) and the New Hampshire-born Lemuel Shattuck (1793–1859) (*right*) promoted cultural improvements in the town during the 1820s and 1830s. Champions of school reform and devotees of local history, they pioneered the study of social statistics in Concord and would later play leading roles in the American Statistical Association. (Courtesy Concord Free Public Library)

Attendance Register for the Center Grammar School for the term ending November 25, 1834. This register of students in the grammar school, recording the attendance and absences of each child, was mandated by the Concord School Committee in the early 1830s. Note on the rolls the presence of eleven-year-old Ellen Garrison, the daughter of the formerly enslaved African American John ("Jack") Garrison. (Courtesy Concord Free Public Library)

Editorial cartoon, *Yeoman's Gazette*, November 9, 1833. Anti-Masonry spurred innovations in journalism as well as in political organization. To promote the party's cause in the upcoming November 1833 elections, the editor Herman Atwill took the unusual step of running this large-scale illustration of the Anti-Masonic ship of state sailing to victory on a tide of liberty and equal rights. (Courtesy Concord Free Public Library)

Portrait of Ralph Waldo Emerson (1803–1882) in 1829. In this miniature portrait, Emerson, at age twenty-five, newly appointed the junior minister of Boston's Second Church and engaged to marry Ellen Tucker later that year, looks out on the world with a considerable measure of self-satisfaction. Between 1827 and 1830 he was a frequent guest preacher in his step-grandfather Ezra Ripley's pulpit. (Courtesy Ralph Waldo Emerson Memorial Association and Houghton Library, MS Am 1280.235 [706.1], Harvard University, Cambridge, MA)

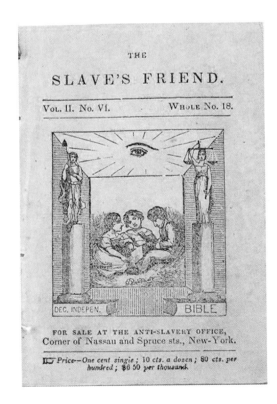

THE

SLAVE'S FRIEND.

VOL. II. No. VI.   WHOLE No. 18.

DEC. INDEPEN.   BIBLE

FOR SALE AT THE ANTI-SLAVERY OFFICE,
Corner of Nassau and Spruce sts., New-York.

☞ Price—One cent single; 10 cts. a dozen; 80 cts. per hundred; $6 50 per thousand.

Title page of the June 1837 issue of *The Slave's Friend*. The story of Ellen Garrison and Abigail Prescott marching hand-in-hand in Concord's 1835 bicentennial parade became well-known in antislavery circles. In this issue the New York–based periodical for children related the anecdote, somewhat inaccurately, as a case study in "New England Prejudice" and in the courage of the young girls who faced it down. (Courtesy Concord Museum)

"Central Part of Concord, Mass.," 1839. This image of Concord center looks out at the town common from the vantage of Daniel Shattuck's store. The common itself is ornamented only by a flagpole. The building to the left is the courthouse. To the right is the Middlesex Hotel, fronting on the milldam; it faces a dwelling that gained fame after April 19, 1775, as the Wright Tavern, beyond which stands the First Parish meetinghouse, rebuilt and enlarged in 1791. (Originally published in John Warner Barber, *Historical Collections: Being a General Collection of Interesting Facts, Traditions, Biographical Sketches, Anecdotes, &c., Relating to the History and Antiquities of Every Town in Massachusetts, with Geographical Descriptions* [Worcester, 1839]. Courtesy Concord Free Public Library)

Photograph of John Shepard Keyes (1821–1920) in 1860. At age thirty-nine, Keyes, the "Prince" of Concord, was thriving as his father's political heir. That year he was a delegate to the Republican convention that nominated Abraham Lincoln for president, after which he took charge of the new president's security at the 1861 inauguration. (Courtesy Concord Free Public Library)

Photograph of Lidian Jackson Emerson (1802–1892) with son Edward, c. 1850. The Plymouth native married Waldo Emerson in 1835, hopeful that the two would be soul mates in pursuit of moral and spiritual growth. Her sensitivity to suffering inspired deep identification with the plight of Native Americans and the enslaved. (Courtesy Concord Free Public Library)

LEFT: Silhouette of Cynthia Dunbar Thoreau (1787–1872), photographed by Alfred Winslow Hosmer (Courtesy Concord Museum). RIGHT: Photograph of John Thoreau (1787–1859) (Courtesy Concord Free Public Library). John and Cynthia Thoreau encouraged their four children's love of art and nature, and both lent their support to radical abolitionism.

Descendant of three generations of Massachusetts slaveholders dating back to the early 1730s, Mary Merrick Brooks (1801–1868) embraced Garrisonian abolitionism in the mid-1830s and was the driving force behind the Concord Female Antislavery Society from 1837 to the close of the Civil War. Her sympathies with the poor and the oppressed extended widely, including to struggling Irish immigrants. (Courtesy Concord Museum)

Portrait of Ephraim Wales Bull (1806–1895) with grapes. Trained as a goldbeater in Boston, Bull moved to Concord on doctor's orders to take the healthier country air. Failing in his craft, he turned his attention to domesticating the wild grapes he found growing in his backyard, and after a decade of patient development, he introduced the "Concord grape" to the world. The fruit proved wildly popular, and it helped spur Concord's growth as a center of dairy, fruit, and vegetable production for the Boston market. (Courtesy Concord Free Public Library)

State Petition.

Waldo and Lidian Emerson allowed their names to be placed at the head of this 1844 petition calling on Massachusetts to endorse an amendment to the U.S. Constitution ending slavery, to repeal all existing laws discriminating against citizens on the ground of race, and to protect the rights of people of color on the railroads. Note that Emerson declined to endorse the call for a law to bar the railroad companies from "insulting or assaulting" their black passengers. (Courtesy Massachusetts Archives)

Appointed junior minister to Ezra Ripley in 1837, the Harvard Divinity School graduate Barzillai Frost (1804–1858) was a conventional preacher whose dull sermons were taken by Waldo Emerson to represent a larger spiritual crisis in the Unitarian denomination. Frost also alienated local abolitionists with his inconsistent support for their cause. (Courtesy First Parish Church, Concord)

Henry David Thoreau (1817–1864), depicted in an 1854 portrait by Samuel Worcester Rowse. In Concord to paint a formal portrait of Emerson, the Boston artist Rowse boarded in the Thoreau household. Around the dining table he closely studied the features of his landlady's son and produced this chalk and charcoal sketch. The gentlemanly image of Thoreau contrasts sharply with the stereotype of the "hermit" of *Walden*. (Courtesy Concord Free Public Library)

Built by the Boston merchant John T. Coolidge in 1828 as "a gentleman's country seat," Ralph Waldo Emerson's house was named "Bush" by the Emerson family. Located at the head of the Cambridge Turnpike, it allowed easy access by stage to Boston for Waldo to deliver his lectures. At the same time, it was within convenient walking distance of Concord village in one direction and the Walden woods in another. (From *Homes of American Authors* [New York, 1853]. Courtesy Concord Free Public Library)

Miniature of Ralph Waldo Emerson, painted by Caroline Neagus Hildreth in 1844. Though he considered himself old after his thirties, Waldo Emerson, husband and father of two children, appears in this image as a dreamy young man whose lectures expressed the yearning and discontent of his contemporaries. Within a couple of years he would acquire a national reputation as "the Sage of Concord." (Reproduced by permission of the Ralph Waldo Emerson Memorial Association)

The view from Emerson's bedchamber in the Old Manse, looking out on the Concord River and the remains of the North Bridge, the very scene that evoked both the legacy of the Revolutionary fathers and the perennial cycles of nature. (Photograph by Christie Jackson, Trustees of Reservations)

sion. He was a masterful motivational speaker. He was also a forerunner of the public intellectual. Like his hero Carlyle, Emerson took a philosophical view of history; he looked for "the signs of the times" and identified "the tendencies" of the age. Combining the scholar with the social critic, he offered guidance in uncertain times. What forces propelled the rise of the individual? What obstacles stood in the way? Of all the times and places in history, why should now be the American moment for the "Universal Mind"? The "Philosophy of Modern History" series and its sequels took up these questions in a searching inquiry into the new conditions of life in modern democracy. One lecture, in particular, set forward the defining features of "the Present Age." This was a view from Concord as well as Boston, informed by Emerson's observations and experiences both in his ancestral home and in his birthplace. Although he rarely, if ever, referenced Concord directly in his lectures, the Transcendentalist put the social and political transformation of the small town at the center of his understanding of the American experience.[34]

Consider his picture of economic life. From his perch at the head of the Cambridge Turnpike, Emerson witnessed firsthand the worldwide expansion of trade and the penetration of the New England countryside by international markets. An "endless procession of wagons" lumbered out from Boston past his gate, carrying "the wealth of all regions of England, of China, of Turkey, of the Indies" deep into the interior of New Hampshire and Vermont. The traffic was nonstop; it pressed forward in every season, even in January, when "huge sledges" carried the "cargo" over the snow and bestowed "inexhaustible comfort & luxury" on "every cabin in the hills." Through the advance of commerce, diverse peoples were brought into contact; even Concord acquired a trace of diversity. Two centuries of slavery in the Americas had left their mark: Jack Garrison split wood for the Emerson family; Susan Robbins Garrison did their laundry. Dispossessed and distant from Concord, Algonquin Indians paid summer visits to the land they once knew as Musketaquid. A delegation of Western Natives—Sacs, Foxes, Sioux, and Ioways—came to the capital in November 1837 and performed a war dance for the largest crowd ever assembled on Boston Common, including an unimpressed Emerson. "Certainly it is right & natural that the Indian should come & see the civil White man," he groused in his journal, "but this was hardly genuine but [merely] a show so we were not parties but spectators." Just a year earlier he had encountered in the city an equally unlikely spectacle: "a Grand Hindoo Exhibition," displaying "seventy-eight figures as large as life! representing with perfect accuracy, the PEOPLE OF ASIA" and perhaps a few living examples as well.[35]

These varied experiences formed the view of the world from Concord. "The Present Age" is "the Age of Trade," Emerson declared in late February 1837, and at first sight the new era promised immense benefits for humankind. It had generated a vast "creation of property" that had not only uplifted the material condition of millions in Europe and the United States but had also raised their social standing. (Africans, bought and sold as property and degraded in status, were left out of the equation.) Fired with enthusiasm for science and technology, Emerson credited the industrial revolution to men of superior "intellect and organization" discovering the secrets of nature and applying them for human betterment. These agents of change—the rising capitalist class—soon demanded political rights in recognition of their "practical power." The ensuing upheaval toppled old orders of nobles and kings, broke "the chains of caste" and "monopoly," and liberated individuals to pursue their own ideas and interests. The release of energy quickened the momentum of change, for "the first effect of external freedom is . . . to open a market." Indeed, commerce and industry proved to be a revolutionary force, whose unprecedented consequences Emerson seemed to welcome with the fervor of a twentieth-century champion of globalization: "The old bonds of language, country, and king give way to the new connexions of trade. It destroys patriotism and substitutes cosmopolitanism." The world shrank; citizens of one nation owned property in another. Commerce "mingles all nations in its marts . . . What picturesque contrasts are crowded on us! We have the beautiful costume of the Hindoo, the Chinese, and the Turk in our streets. Our domestic labor is done by the African. Our trench dug by the Irish. The South Sea Islander is on the wharf. The Indian squaw sells mats at our doors." Who could complain? The individual now enjoyed greater latitude than ever to make choices, exercise autonomy, and explore the infinite resources of the self.[36]

If only all were as it seemed! Trade unleashed a wave of materialism that threatened to inundate Emerson's world. The prospect of riches—"the bribe which commerce holds out"—converted laudable ambition into mindless mania. In the "headlong" and "desperate" race for wealth, people became "unscrupulous," forgot their limitations, and lost all sense of morality. Government no longer served the public good; it had become a marketplace for the buying and selling of favors. The citizens who still harbored "sentiments of loyalty and patriotism" were "outraged by seeing power and law at auction." Even "men of genius" were corrupted by the atmosphere of greed. Too many thinkers were deserting their high calling for "the more gainful office of gratifying the popular taste." Both lecturer and audience were presumably exceptions in the dismaying trend.[37]

The message was much the same as Emerson examined other defining features of the age. Time and again positive developments were undercut by the very forces they set in motion, and the individual, for all his infinite potential, was the loser. The lecturer discerned this dialectic at work in the churches, the benevolent societies, the reform crusades, the caucuses and conventions, and the communications media he had contact with in daily affairs. Concord was always in the background, its people serving as touchstones of change.

A second characteristic of the age, Emerson proclaimed, was urbanization, the aforementioned "congregation of men into large masses"—hardly a circumstance in the small town of two thousand. Yet as city and country became more tightly integrated through transportation and trade and through "the universal facility of communication," the emerging suburbs came under the sway of "metropolitan refinement and opinion." The result was a profound alteration of manners. In crowded cities, strangers of diverse backgrounds had to get along, and without an aristocracy to dictate the rules of engagement, they looked to the "leading class in the capital" for a code of conduct. "Decorum" now set the standard by which everyone was judged, Emerson observed. "This is productive of much comfort": conventions of politeness and self-restraint certified character and kept the peace. But they exacted a stiff price. At social gatherings people conformed to norms of "propriety" and concealed honest sentiments. The "asperities of individual character" wore off; no one said what he really felt. Where were the singular individuals, ready and willing to violate etiquette and speak unpleasant truths? Emerson had a few examples in mind: one was the independent-minded yeoman George Minott; another Doctor Ripley, whose prayers during a pastoral visit to a bereaved parishioner expressed a living faith seldom seen among the decorous ministers of Boston. In his journal, the grandson penned an idealized portrait of the "old semi-savage," who spent his days in "Homeric simplicity," safe from city ways and close to nature. The aged man, who could not "eat sponge cake without a ramrod," was the implicit point of comparison in the public lecture. Would such exemplars of "plain dealing and high thinking" disappear in the modern world?[38]

Such questions were not easily answered. The new mass society dealt in quantities rather than qualities. It was "an age of facts and not of principles." The trend among scholars was to analyze aggregates rather than individuals, and to search for regularities rather than exceptions. That agenda had little appeal to Emerson, who as chairman of the Concord School Committee found someone else to prepare the annual report, with all its numbers on enrollment and attendance. Nor did he share Lemuel Shattuck's and Edward Jarvis's love of "Finance Reports, Statistical Estimates; all that may be counted and measured." These compendia were the characteristic genre of the age, putting "contemplative tastes and tendencies in proportionate disrepute."[39]

Emerson was still more scathing in his assessment of the project to diffuse knowledge among the people rather than concentrate it in a privileged elite. The formation of libraries and lyceums and the proliferation of newspapers, magazines, and cheap books were other distinguishing marks of the age. The lectures at the Masonic Temple participated in the cultural impulse. Far from praising the democratization of knowledge, Emerson had qualms. Drawing on a critique of popular culture held by Federalist intellectuals of his father's generation, the Harvard graduate, who spent his days among books, complained about a declining reverence for learning. Once gentlemen of erudition, steeped in the classics, sat in the councils of state. They no longer did. Who needed expertise on ancient Greece and Rome? Neither government nor business required the service of scholars. So men of learning, inspired by "the spirit of Trade," turned to the people for patronage and found an audience with neither time for nor interest in "laborious study." The reading public desired works that were easy to read and appealed to "vanity." The publishing world responded with gusto for the profits to be made from cheap works of all sorts, whose dissemination was promoted by the lyceums and societies for the diffusion of useful knowledge. Extensive reading—the quick "reading of many books" for transient gratification—drove an expansive literary marketplace. "The world is full of books," Emerson sighed, and there seemed no way to cut through the morass and discover the few gems within. The president of the Concord Social Library and regular lecturer at the Concord Lyceum could not restrain his disappointment at these institutions' slight results. "Every village has its social library, and the Lyceum reads everywhere its pleasant and superficial lecture which we may hear without weariness and forget without loss." More people read than ever before, but what they read was of passing significance. Acquiring information was not the same as achieving wisdom.[40]

Shallow and amiable, status conscious and money mad, the characteristic individual of the democratic age was no admirable figure. Even the virtues he embraced, such as temperance, did not always reveal strength of character. Emerson revived his quarrel with moral reformers (though he said nothing about abolitionism). He applauded the goal of the temperance crusade but despised its methods. Temperance advocates were so bent on "material growth"—raising money, collecting pledges, circulating petitions—that they suffered "spiritual decay." Let them focus on winning converts one by one. Each new recruit to the cause would become "a Temperance Agent, a Temperance Institution" by his—or more likely, her—own example. Unfortunately, the campaign against drinking had turned from persuasion to pressure in its drive for ever more members. Anyone declining to take a pledge of abstinence from intoxicating beverages risked the disapproval of "Public Opinion." Better to go along with the crowd than get an undeserved reputation as a drunkard. Emerson had rejected that demand for conformity in Concord, and now he generalized from the experience. Should he comply, "I degrade myself and have only exchanged one vice for another, self-indulgence for fear." The one true path to reform was self-reform, a principle that benevolent associations ignored at their peril: "Never let a man be addressed by any motive that is unworthy of a man." To "treat men as pawns and ninepins" in a greater cause was to propagate the very errors of the society reformers wished to redeem.[41]

Nowhere were those failings more visible than in the raucous politics of the day. Emerson had gone to Concord with a well-developed animus against the reckless partisanship he had observed in Boston and Manhattan, and the longer he lived there, the more alienated he became, his bicentennial speech celebrating town meeting democracy notwithstanding. In his republican ideal, thinking citizens concerned for the common good entrusted gentlemen of character and principle with office. That illusion was shattered by Samuel Hoar's defeat for reelection to Congress just a month before the "Philosophy of Modern History" series opened. Emerson channeled his dismay into his lectures, excoriating party as "that bellowing hound that barks or fawns, that defamer and bargainer and unreasoning self-lover," which "distorts all facts and blinds all eyes." Disgust over Hoar's loss would inform his discourses on politics in the years to come. As the party battles intensified, with Democrats taking the local majority and "King" Keyes dethroned, there would be no shortage of causes for complaint.[42]

One day in October 1838, as he walked into the village, Emerson eaves-dropped on Democratic selectman Cyrus Stow, the butcher, giving a pep talk to the party faithful. The little bit he heard was something of a shock. Evidently "the dictator of our rural Jacobins" was urging his "little circle" of followers to get out the vote in the upcoming election and firing up their enthusiasm with personal attacks on the opposition. "Here thought I," the onlooker recorded in his journal, "is one who loves what I hate . . . I hate persons who are nothing but persons. I hate numbers. [Stow] cares for nothing but numbers & persons." This remark made it into the lecture "Comedy" in late January 1839, in which Emerson underscored the pettiness of Stow's calculations. The politician, who went unnamed, was so caught up in electioneering that he could not behold the grandeur of nature all around him—"those mighty mountain chains, those vast fruitful champaigns . . . What an existence this is to have no home, no heart, but to feed on the very refuse and old straw and chaff of man, numbers, and names of towns and voters." There was nothing Romantic about American elections.[43]

These strictures on democracy applied the classical republicanism of the Revolutionary generation to Transcendentalist ends. Emerson was at pains to assure the audience at a lecture on "Literature" that when he spoke of the "democratic element," he had in mind a "spirit of love for the General good" and *not* "that ill thing vain & loud which writes lying newspapers, spouts at caucuses & sells its lies for gold." Like his grandfather Ripley, he recognized the vulnerability of republics to "ambitious and designing men." Demagogues were always on the lookout for dupes to manipulate; time and again in history, they had hijacked popular uprisings, betrayed their ideals, and installed themselves in power. Just look at the "abominable" record of the French Revolution. New England in the 1830s faced its own dangers. "Society always consists of a vast proportion of young, ignorant, and foolish persons capable of being deceived," Emerson warned. Here was a constituency ready made for "modern Jacobins" like Gourgas and Stow. Democrats posed as the champion of the many against the few and voiced their class resentments. These "innovators" promising change were actually driving "a private trade on the march of a principle." The conservative opposition was little better. Outnumbered by the masses, it em-ployed all its "wiles" to "resist indiscriminately the good and the evil measures of . . . antagonists." Its motives were no less materialistic. In the age of trade, government was for sale. "It is sought as property, administered as property, and handed down as property." As the parties fought over the spoils of office, what choice lay between them?[44]

It was an ignoble scene that Emerson exposed to his listeners in Boston and Concord during the second half of the 1830s. He held up a mirror to the rampant materialism pervading every sphere of life, the corruption in government, the conformity in society, the "profound unbelief" in the churches. Against this sorry spectacle, who could put faith in the Transcendentalist vision of a democracy of free and equal men and women, each "a new experiment, to be and exhibit the full and perfect soul"? Emerson saw no reason for doubt. "No greater men are now than ever were," nor were the challenges they faced unprecedented. Throughout history religions had ossified, governments grown oppressive. Means supplanted ends; forms confined the spirit. Yet the soul remained irrepressible, and the laws of nature were on its side. The "errors" of politics, "like the errors of the planets," were "periodic" and self-correcting. "There are limitations beyond which the folly or ambition of governors cannot go." Social distinctions were ineradicable, no matter what politicians said or did. To resent the greater fortune of a neighbor was fruitless; "the superiority in him is an inferiority in me." No law, no party, no mob would ever eliminate "the offence of superiority in persons." Character, in this view, was key, not the wealth or power with which it was rewarded. The office did not make the man; "it is the man makes the place."[45]

Paradoxically, the 1837 financial crash gave further grounds for optimism. Two years earlier, when the economy was booming, Emerson had complained of "hard times." When commerce flourished, the spirit slumbered, and preachers and lecturers found it tough to rouse individuals enjoying "sleep, full[-]eating, plenty of money, care of it, & leisure." Prosperity dulled the conscience and stagnated the soul. But the economic crisis caused confidence in material progress to collapse. In May the Concord Bank followed the lead of its counterparts in Boston and suspended payment of its notes in specie, lest it suffer a run on the vault and the exhaustion of its reserves. The merchant Josiah Davis was caught short in his real estate speculations, went under, and left town; rival storekeeper Phineas Howe survived by taking advantage of bankruptcy law and cutting his losses. Even Emerson's own brother William, overextended in his obligations for land purchases on Staten Island, importuned Waldo for a loan. The lecturer found a silver lining in the calamity: men were awakened to their folly of living for "Pride, and Thrift, and Expediency." "The present generation is bankrupt of principles & hope, as of property." It was impossible to ignore the emptiness of their lives without and within. Emerson saw in the crisis additional confirmation of his belief that common sense and virtue were rewarded in the market. The big losers in the panic were those who, eager to get rich quick, threw caution to the winds and contracted "land-fever." By contrast, the businessman who kept his head and "bought no acre in Maine or Michigan" had no trouble staying afloat. His reputation passed, like his notes, without question.[46]

Launched at the tail end of the boom and continuing through the panic and ensuing depression, the lectures at the Masonic Temple propelled Emerson to the forefront of the Transcendentalist movement. The winter series, running from 1836 to 1841, marked "an era in the social and literary history of Boston, as well as in the life and culture of many individuals," George Ripley recalled decades later. Expressing "the fermentation of thought and feeling" stirred by the Transcendentalists, Emerson opened "a new world" in "literature, Nature, and in thought." The lecturer gave voice to a rising generation. Crystallizing the inchoate sentiments of his listeners, he revealed to them "their own minds, souls, and being" and exposed their dissent from "the dogmatic formulas and conventional statements" of the authorities in church and state. At a time when freedom of mind was under attack in the streets and in the courts, the nascent challenge to orthodoxy needed a champion and a rationale. Emerson supplied both with an eloquent defense of the "absolute independence and right" of every soul to "interpret for itself the meaning of life, untrammeled by tradition and conventions." And he did so with a sincerity, cheerfulness, creativity, and idealism that "lifted his hearers into a loftier sphere" and gave them the confidence, upon leaving the lecture hall, to pursue their own paths of self-trust. Here unfolded a declaration of intellectual independence that outstripped in its immediate reach the more famous statements Emerson made to Harvard's Phi Beta Kappa society and its divinity school during these same years.[47]

In Concord as well as Boston, Emerson found his constituency among the young. Between 1837 and 1841, the townspeople got to hear nearly all the lectures their learned neighbor delivered at the Masonic Temple. This was a privilege few others outside the metropolis enjoyed, and none as fully or as cheaply, since Emerson spoke at the lyceum for free.[48] The discourses, taken together, offered a timely course on the transformation of the era, at the very moment Concord was experiencing its exhilarating and unsettling effects. As he laid out the new world in the making, Emerson highlighted the distinctive dilemmas faced by youth coming of age under unique circumstances. In previous eras, a boy went from home to school to be trained for an assigned role in a settled institution (the church, the state, the feudal lord). Always under authority, he "never came out of pupilage." (The perpetual subjection of girls to patriarchal supervision went unmentioned.) But that template no longer sufficed in a fluid society with multiple choices: "We have great contempt for the superstitions and nonsense which blinded the eyes of all foregoing generations." That disdain was accompanied by self-doubt. With the "moral power" to act on their own, young people had become acutely conscious of the gap between what was and what could be. No decision could be made without second-guessing. Freed from direction by elders, a young man now bore "the burdensome possession of himself."

What to do in this new age of "introversion"? Emerson sympathized with the trials of youth struggling with their new freedom, some so self-conscious of their uncharted way that they could barely take a step forward in life: "We pay a great price for this freedom. The old faith is gone; the new loiters on the way. The world looks very bare and cold. We have lost our Hope, we have lost our spring." But not for long. Characteristically, Emerson resisted that "gloomy view." The anxiety and "despondency" were, in his opinion, "temporary symptoms of the transition state, whilst the man sees the hollowness of traditions and does not yet know the resources of his soul." With Emerson's help, they would not be ignorant of those resources for long.[49]

SINCE THE OPENING OF THE NINETEENTH CENTURY, AS CONCORD QUICKened to the rising currents of trade and attracted a steady stream of workers to its homes and farms, stores and shops, local authorities had worried about the young, both natives and strangers. With ever more sons and daughters leaving for opportunities abroad, how to prepare them for adult lives? And how to integrate and discipline the newcomers who filled their places, sojourning for a few years and then moving on? The Masonic lodge provided temporary mooring for those men on the make willing to serve the hierarchy, perform the rituals, and bear the expense of belonging to the "ancient" fraternity. The Trinitarian church competed for the devotion of youth; in its embrace, born-again men and women could enjoy Christian fellowship, stay on the straight and narrow path, and look forward to an eternal home in heaven. The debating club and the lyceum offered rational recreation to young men desiring the skills and knowledge thought to be requisite for upward mobility. All these enterprises aimed to structure the lives of youth and mold their character. Transcendentalism was different. It urged self-direction and encouraged individuals to venture forth into the unknown. It spurned authority and established institutions. It measured success not by the number of adherents but by the loftiness of aims and the originality of results. It inspired young women to break from tradition, assert their own minds, and join their brothers in claiming independence. It cared little for interdependence. It favored the individual over the group.

Would this new "Saturnalia" of "Faith" win over the neighbors? No better gauge of Transcendentalism's appeal could be found than in Emerson's adopted town.[50]

Young Men and Women
of Fairest Promise

R alph Waldo Emerson was a champion of new beginnings. At twenty-nine, unhappy with his first choice of profession, he had resigned from the well-paid pulpit of Boston's Second Church and started over. Despite his advancing age, he took the risk of seeking his own way and, in the process, invented a new career as a public lecturer. Change proved exhilarating, and Emerson recommended it to others. "Man was made for conflict, not for rest," he told an assembly at the Masonic Temple. "In action is his power. Not in his goals but in his transition man is great." That advice spoke directly to the young, for "after thirty," he confessed in 1835, "a man wakes up sad every morning." In middle age, "a man begins to feel the walls of his condition which before the soul did overflow." "All that has been done in the planet was done by young men." Who better, then, to hear the summons to self-renewal than the rising generation, as it embarked on higher education or paused at the threshold of careers?[1]

Fittingly, Emerson sounded his call for individual growth in educational settings. Over the course of four decades as an itinerant lecturer, from 1837 to 1879, he became a popular speaker at academies, colleges, and universities. His addresses to Harvard's Phi Beta Kappa society (1837) and to the graduates of the Harvard Divinity School (1838) are only the best known of the nearly three dozen discourses he delivered for convocations, commencements, and other literary anniversaries at liberal arts institutions extending from New England to the Midwest. These lectures targeted the young people he embraced as his special constituency. In these talks, Emerson used the platform to speak for alienated youth, upholding their ideals and sympathizing with their discontent in far-ranging criticism of the adult world they hesitated to join.[2]

Emerson got on the academic speaking circuit by happenstance. In the spring of 1837, the innovative Boston school run by his close friend Bronson Alcott was stirring outrage, owing to the recent publication of the schoolmaster's *Conversations with Children on the Gospels*. Designed to showcase Alcott's use of Socratic dialogue to stimulate critical thinking and draw out the moral intuitions of the young, the volume included frank discussions of the New Testament, including such delicate matters as pregnancy and virgin birth. These passages, innocent in themselves, aroused suspicion that Alcott talked explicitly about sex with children as young as six. Reviewers excoriated the work as obscene and immoral and advised criminal prosecution of the author. In the face of these charges and threats of mob violence, most parents withdrew their children from the school. Yet Alcott had his admirers. In Providence, an instructor named Hiram Fuller was about to open an academy on Transcendentalist principles. Fuller was so enthusiastic about Alcott's ideas that he sometimes began classes by reading aloud from *Conversations*; he also recruited another of Emerson's intimates, Margaret Fuller (no relation to the headmaster), to the teaching staff. It was not long before Emerson, too, was associated with the Greene Street School.[3]

The Concord lecturer, fresh from the success of the "Philosophy of Modern History" series, was one of Alcott's few public defenders. He took up his friend's case in a letter to the *Boston Courier* hailing the educator's noble purpose: "He aims to make children think, and, in every question of a moral nature, to send them back on themselves for an answer." But Emerson was not willing to risk his reputation in the controversy—his letter to the editor was signed simply "R." Within Concord, he used his position as chairman of the social library's standing committee to acquire *Conversations* for the collection, and in an anonymous communication to the *Concord Freeman*, he recommended the "new experiment in education" to the "candid attention" of the townspeople. Having offered such moral support, he could hardly turn down an invitation to attend the dedication of the Greene Street School in June 1837, at which Alcott was scheduled to speak. But the next thing he knew, Alcott withdrew from the program, lest his notoriety injure the fledgling institution, and without asking permission, Fuller substituted Emerson as the orator. Touted as "a gentleman distinguished for his literary taste and classic attainments," the lecturer was boxed into the commitment.[4]

Nor did Emerson seek out his most famous speaking engagement, the Phi Beta Kappa address at Harvard on August 31, 1837. As was the case with his discourse at Concord's bicentennial commemoration, he was not the favorite for the assignment. Some two weeks after the Providence dedication, he received a surprise request from the committee in charge of the annual festival in Cambridge. Its planned speaker had suddenly pulled out, and with just two months to go, the organization was in a bind. Would he be willing to fill in? Despite his second-choice status and the limited time to prepare, Emerson unhesitatingly accepted.

The selection was an honor typically conferred on such Massachusetts dignitaries as Rep. Edward Everett and Supreme Court justice Joseph Story. Nothing Emerson had done during his brief tenure at Boston's Second Church or in the years since as an ad hoc preacher and freelance lecturer could compare to the accomplishments of his predecessors. Perhaps the most daunting precursor, in his mind, was the orator for the 1789 anniversary: his own father, William, chosen at twenty, just two months after graduating from Harvard, in recognition of his eloquence and scholarly accomplishments. Waldo had not even been selected for the elite academic fraternity during his time in college; his consolation prize was honorary membership, awarded in 1836, for which he paid the hefty fee of ten dollars.[5]

Yet Emerson struck a chord with his critical remarks on the philosophy and practice of education at all levels from the district and grammar schools to the academies and colleges. In his Transcendentalist manifesto *Nature* and in the "Philosophy of Modern History" lectures, he made plain his conviction that "the world exists to instruct the private man." Its lessons lay everywhere in waiting: nature and society furnished unlimited resources to draw out the intrinsic powers of the individual and reveal "the riches of his nature . . . embody his thoughts [and] . . . fulfill the predictions of his spirit." But Emerson had not yet applied this perspective to existing modes of instruction, public or private. Now, in the talks at Providence and Cambridge, he set forth a powerful indictment of how New England prepared its young for adult life.[6]

The lecturer drew on wide-ranging experience. As a boy, he had progressed through the town schools of Boston and Concord and on to Harvard, where he'd been a middling student. After graduation, he had been, in his own judgment, a "hopeless schoolmaster" at a private school for young ladies. He was a veteran of school committees in Boston and Concord, and while he was serving as a minister in the capital, he became a founding member of the American Institute of Instruction, a lobby for common school reform. He had also read Pestalozzi and talked at length with Alcott. From these readings, conversations, and experiences emerged a coherent view, in which Emerson took the side of a younger generation that shared his restlessness with the status quo. The Providence and Cambridge addresses aimed to expose the miseducation of Americans and to inspire a new vision of self-culture. Despite his "old" age at thirty-four, he linked his ambitions as a lecturer to the unmet aspirations of youth. Together they would form the party of the future.[7]

There could be no better time, as Emerson saw it, for a new departure. His talks on education took place in the wake of the 1837 financial crisis, which punctured the bubble of prosperity and revealed the hollowness of the commercial system. Like an earthquake to a geologist, the economic upheaval opened a rich vein of insight to the philosopher. "If one would know somewhat of the ground plan and interior architecture of Society," he told his audience in Providence, "let him study it when a commercial or political revolution has shattered its frame." The inquiry confirmed what he already knew: materialism was the "disease of which the world lies sick." The desire for gratification infected all; it drove the boundless demand for consumer goods available in ever-greater profusion through international trade and the accelerating industrial revolution. No area of life was immune, certainly not education. Schools had the noble purpose of encouraging boys "to aspire to be all they can." Instead, they betrayed their mission by taking an instrumental view of learning as merely a route to status, office, and wealth. In tune with parents' wishes, "we aim to make accountants, attornies, [and] engineers" but not "able, earnest, greathearted men." Surely it was not "the chief end of man that he should make a fortune and beget children whose end is likewise to make fortunes." In an uncertain world, where good times could suddenly vanish in an economic crash, was not the wiser, more meaningful course to "teach self-trust" and assist the individual in exploring the "inexhaustible mine" of the self? Anticipating centuries of argument about the value of a liberal arts education, Emerson steered the young away from practical preparation for jobs and urged the pursuit of knowledge for its own sake, in confidence that independent minds and spirits would achieve greatness in the end.[8]

If the lecturer was aware that the Greene Street School admitted girls as well as boys, he gave no indication, despite the fact that Margaret Fuller was teaching there. In principle, since every person shared in the universal mind, education for self-trust should take no heed of gender. Emerson's rhetoric remained emphatically masculine, perhaps because he identified so strongly with the male youths before him, whose prospects in life hinged on the mental stimulus and encouragement they received. In the troubled circumstances of the spring of 1837, the outlook was not promising: "At times the land smells with suicide. Young men have no hope. The educated class stand idle in the streets. No man calleth them to labor." It was thus imperative for the new school to guide its charges away from this dismal fate. "I think it the most deplorable failure . . . ," Emerson opined, "when the teachers . . . of a land, whether in the pulpit or in the Academy, lose sight of the capital secret of their profession, namely, to convert life into truth, or to show the meaning of events."[9]

Nearly three months later Emerson ascended the pulpit of Cambridge's First Church, "thronged (almost to suffocation)" by friends, relatives, Concord neighbors, Harvard alumni, faculty, students, and public officials, and took aim at his alma mater for betraying this sacred trust. His Phi Beta Kappa address was unlike any ever presented in the previous half-century. Ever since its inauguration in 1783, the annual ceremony had provided an occasion to praise the ancient seat of learning for its contributions to New England and American culture. The institution, which had observed its bicentennial in 1836, was acclaimed as the training ground of an intellectual elite necessary to sustain authority, hierarchy, and morality in a popular republic. Men of letters, schooled in Christianity and the classics, were to raise a bulwark against the onslaught of the "vulgar" masses opposed to established standards of language and taste.

But Harvard was also changing in ways that added to Emerson's concern. As it enlisted in the Unitarian camp, the school played a diminishing role as a nursery of Congregationalist clergy and hived off the education of liberal ministers to its new divinity school. More secular in emphasis, it created separate law and medical faculties and aligned its instructional program with the priorities of the metropolitan business class. The traditional college was gradually becoming a modern university, and though it remained a public agency of the Commonwealth of Massachusetts, it grew increasingly dependent on private endowments for new professorships and curricular initiatives. Under President Josiah Quincy, Harvard turned its back on the citizenry as a whole to focus on the sons of the Hub's wealthy merchants and financiers. The goal was to take these privileged teenagers, subject them to exacting standards in classroom and parlor alike, and transform them into gentlemen and scholars— refined ornaments of a new upper class, with the skills to preserve and expand their families' fortunes and the style and savvy to play notable parts in the wider world.[10]

Emerson was having none of this, and he did nothing to conceal his views from his distinguished audience, including Governor Everett, Justice Story, and President Quincy. Taking an uncharacteristic oppositional stance from the very start, he opened with the suggestion that there was little cause for celebration. "Our anniversary is one of hope, and perhaps, not enough of la-bor." It offered a mere token of regard for letters "amongst a people too busy to give to letters any more." But what could be expected in a society and at an institution with such narrow ambitions for the young? Ideally, the scholar was "Man Thinking," an expression of the "Universal Mind" in the creative effort to comprehend the laws of nature and the works of humankind for the better-ment of all. (Emerson did not shy away from alluding to the Transcendentalist philosophy animating his vision.) In practice, though, the man of letters was a drone, reproducing conventional wisdom without adding anything new. In this "degenerate state," he was a "victim of society"—"a mere thinker, or still worse, the parrot of other men's thinking."

This profile of the Harvard-trained scholar was unsparing. Emerson traced the process by which the schoolboy, overflowing with energy and curiosity, was beaten down. Instead of articulating his own thoughts and exploring his ge-nius, he wasted precious hours on the texts of men long dead. Such pedagogy, founded on authority and routine, drilled the student into submission. It cut him off from the vast world of nature in which he could discover himself. And it isolated him in an enclave of class and privilege, through which he came to view the great body of fellow citizens with condescension and disdain. That was exactly what the college, in its alliance with moneyed men, meant to ac-complish. Out of such training, men of learning became "bookworms" with-out backbones, "decent, indolent, complaisant." Why challenge conventional standards of propriety and taste, when conformity brought material reward?

Emerson sensed a profound unease in the graduates before him, members of the Class of 1837 with diplomas in hand and futures uncertain as the econ-omy sank into a prolonged depression. They were, in his view, "young men of the fairest promise," the best and brightest of their time. Such golden youth, stirred by the grandeur inherent in the American land, should have been impatient to enter the lists of society and compete for the prizes of their time. But they were held back by a paralysis of will stemming from their unique moment in time. "They find themselves not in the state of mind of their fathers, and regret the coming state as untried." Worse still, as they looked out upon a self-seeking society, they felt only revulsion at "the principles on which business is managed." In despair at the gap between the vital promise and the sordid reality of the republic, these idealists abandoned hope, "turn[ed] drudges, or die[d] of disgust, some of them suicides."

What was to be done? Emerson saw no reason for pessimism. For all the obstacles "in the way of the self-relying and self-directed," the present was a time of transition, open to any who dared to seize the moment. In language that evoked memories of the men who had broken with the past and waged a war of independence, the grandson of Concord's Patriot pastor asked:

> If there is any period one would desire to be born in, is it not the age of Revolution; when the old and the new stand side by side and admit of being compared; when the energies of all men are searched by fear and by hope; when the historic glories of the old can be compensated by the rich possibilities of the new era? This time, like all times, is a very good one, if we but know what to do with it.

This formulation captured the essence of the social transformation remaking his corner of New England. One order of society, which once seemed fixed, now appeared in flux; its successor had not yet hardened in place. In the interval lay unprecedented opportunities for the young to define their goals and chart their own way. The spirit of the age was democratic: a new importance was being accorded to the individual, and every aspect of life, even "the lowest class in the state," was claiming its due in the poetry and prose of the day, the snobbery of Harvard's self-satisfied elite notwithstanding. Let the rising American scholars attend to these "signs of the times." All they required was self-trust: to keep faith with their convictions, "plant [themselves] indomitably on [their] instincts," and carve out an independent, original place in the world. "A nation of men will for the first time exist, because each believes himself inspired by the Divine Soul which also inspires all men."[11]

The "American Scholar" address has long been considered a signal moment in U.S. cultural history—"our intellectual Declaration of Independence," in the words of the senior Oliver Wendell Holmes. On that hot August morning, in just one hour and fifteen minutes, Emerson took an aristocratic model of intellectual life borrowed from the Old World, blithely cast it aside, and embraced a democratic future for a distinctive American literature. His iconoclasm won recognition mainly in retrospect. At the time the discourse received a mixed reception. Emerson thrilled his Transcendentalist friends, including the beleaguered Bronson Alcott, with his forthright statement; building on the success of the Masonic Temple lectures, the speech lifted him to a place alongside Ripley and Brownson at the head of the intellectual movement. But the oration lost or offended those already ill-disposed to German idealism. Amid his enthusiasm, Alcott detected "mixed confusion, consternation, surprise and wonder" in the audience, one of whom, a conservative Unitarian minister, finding the talk "incoherent" and "unintelligible," counted the minutes until it was over. Nor did all young men of "fairest promise" salute Emerson as their spokesman. "It was not very good," judged seventeen-year-old Edward Everett Hale, the future editor and writer, "but very transcendental." With such a range of opinion, the toast to the speaker at the dinner following the ceremony was notable both for its cleverness and for its tact. "Mr. President, I suppose you all know where the orator came from, and I suppose all know what he said," proposed Charles Henry Warren of Plymouth, a man famous for bons mots. "I give you—The Spirit of Concord—it makes us all of one mind."[12]

Whatever disturbance Emerson set off in Cambridge made no ripples in Concord. Although various townspeople were in the audience for the speech, no record survives of their responses. Neither the Democratic *Freeman* nor the Whig *Yeoman's Gazette* mentioned a word about the affair. The local elite was untroubled. Six weeks after the address, the lecturer was nominated for the Social Circle; two years later, when a place opened up, the Transcendentalist was ushered into the exclusive club.[13]

The paradox of respectability and rebellion in Emerson runs deep. If the businessmen and politicians of Concord had no problem admitting into their midst so vocal a critic of the ways they made their money and claimed the spoils of office, perhaps he was expressing misgivings they all shared. Or maybe Emerson's status as one of Concord's wealthiest men supplied reassurance that he was no threat to their property and the social order. But what to make of his defense of the alienated "young men of fairest promise" who were no longer "in the state of mind of their fathers" but uncertain what paths to follow of their own? Did the lecturer have any of his young neighbors in mind when he evoked conscientious souls refusing to give up their infinite promise and accept the harness of convention and routine—a spiritual, if not literal, suicide? Were his lectures a bugle call to generational protest? Or did they provoke a wider range of responses, winning favor beyond a small circle of college graduates and among those who seemingly settled into families and occupations without a hitch?

It is time to meet this rising generation circa 1837 and explore what they took from the local philosopher's words.

TRANSCENDENTALISM HAD ITS ORIGINS IN A MOVEMENT TO REVITALIZE UNItarian piety, and if it had any chance of success, it would have to reach young men like George Moore. In the mid-1830s, as Emerson embarked on his lecturing career, Moore wrestled with a vocational dilemma of his own. Torn between the law and the ministry, the Concord resident and Harvard graduate (Class of 1834) was in search of a calling that would let him "go on improving both in mind and heart" all his days. "I am . . . resolved to make myself . . . a man," he vowed, "to cultivate and develope [sic] all my faculties . . . to study men and things as well as books—to seek to do good, whenever an opportunity offers . . . and most of all *to know myself*." With such aspirations the high-minded youth was drawn into Emerson's orbit. He attended his lectures, listened to his sermons, and visited in his parlor, conscientiously recording the great man's words in his diary—the fullest record of anyone's response to the Transcendentalist's public utterances during the formative decade of his freelance career. But did Emerson voice the young man's discontent or influence his life? The answer is surprisingly elusive.[14]

Born in 1811, Moore grew up in the seat of Concord's establishment. His father was the deputy sheriff and jail keeper Abel Moore, who raised his family in the county house on the common, just a stone's throw from the lockup and the Middlesex Hotel. Where other families ran farms or shops, Moore's tended to the jail, whose two dozen inmates required diligent scrutiny and care. The eight children, of whom George was the fifth, were enlisted in this household enterprise. The eldest, Harriet (born in 1802), helped out with the record-keeping while devoting most of her energies to the prisoners' material and spiritual needs. She visited the sick, read to the men in their cells, and gave religious instruction on the Sabbath. On Thanksgiving Day, she baked pies for the in-mates: one apple, one squash, and one mince for each and every person behind bars; one year, sixty-nine pies came from the oven. George too played useful roles. Skilled at penmanship, he drew up lists of inmates and other documents in a "magnificent" script, "both clerkly and elegant." No task, however custo-dial, was off-limits, including the irksome night duty to admit prisoners arriv-ing after dark. Worse still were the escapes and the tragedies that kept everyone on edge. In July 1834, during the wee hours of the morning, the twenty-three-year-old was jolted from sleep by an alarm at the jail. There he was horrified to discover that "an accused murderer" awaiting trial had cut his throat with a razor. "I never before witnessed so horrid a scene." The jail taught lessons in hu-man frailty and in the collective effort necessary to keep the community safe.[15]

A studious boy, nearsighted and socially awkward, Moore preferred to be at home with his books rather than outdoors with classmates at play. As he grew, he cherished ambitions for a liberal education. That was not Captain Moore's plan for his third son. In the late 1820s, the lawman faced competing claims on his purse. His oldest surviving son was already enrolled at Harvard Law School; the next was just coming of age and expecting his "portion" in or-der to start out in business. Beyond these expenses, Moore was pouring all his surplus funds into the model farm he was building along the Lexington Road. Under these tight circumstances, George would have to set aside his "deep, in-nate love of improvement" and forget about college. The boy had always been "obedient to his parents, and easily governed"; his teachers praised his docility. So the father must have been taken aback after George absorbed the disap-pointing news and "calmly" replied, "I shall comply with your wishes until I come of age, but then I shall certainly go [to college]." It was the first sign of an independent will that would carry the idealistic youth far from the deputy sheriff's world.[16]

In the face of such determination, the patriarch relented. George was al-lowed to pursue his educational goals with parental support, on condition that he drop everything and help out in the jail when needed. As much as possible, the young man paid his own way. With earnings from keeping school in nearby Acton, he entered Concord Academy in June 1829 and prepared for college under Phineas Allen; fifteen months later he began his freshman year at Har-vard. A latecomer to liberal studies, several years older than his peers, Moore was intent on making up for lost time, and he pursued self-improvement with as much zeal as had Edward Jarvis and Lemuel Shattuck. While attending the academy in Concord, he seized every opportunity to add to his stock of knowledge. He joined the lyceum and faithfully attended the lectures. He participated in the forensic contests of the young men's debating club. ("Do people generally improve *well* one *half* of their time?" Moore argued the affirmative, "much against my own opinion.") He signed up to teach a Sunday school class at the First Parish. His schedule was so packed that he rose at four in the morning and skipped dinners at noon in order to make more time for study. And just about every day he took stock of his progress. "Have I employed my time as I ought," he asked in his diary, "or have I wasted a good deal of it?" He was seldom satisfied with the answer. "I will improve my time and talents to the best advantage," he vowed after several months at the academy. "Let [my] motto be improvement." That pledge was the pole star of his educational journey for the next eight years.[17]

Self-improvement was not just a means to a vocation or a route to upward mobility. To seek wealth and popularity as ends in themselves, as did Moore's father and brothers, was "too sordid" an objective. "Was I sent here, merely to gratify worldly and sensual desires . . . ?" The teenager longed for a higher purpose and found it in the noble project of character building. This was a lifelong labor of controlling passions, refining manners, strengthening moral and intellectual faculties, and conducting a Christian life. Unitarians were assiduous promoters of such "self-culture"; the influential Boston minister William Ellery Channing treated it as tantamount to spiritual conversion: "Perfection [is] the end of our Being."[18]

Inspired by this rhetoric, Moore took advantage of opportunities to widen his horizons. He went beyond the official curriculum and followed contemporary literature, both English (Byron, Wordsworth, Dickens) and American (Irving, Cooper, Catherine Sedgwick). He frequented the Boston theater, especially when Fanny Kemble, the celebrated British actress, was on stage. He enjoyed outings in nature with friends and toured the Connecticut River Valley (where he ran into Orestes Brownson, "an interesting, eloquent man in conversation, though rather stern in his manners") and the White Mountains. He was welcomed into Harvard's Hasty Pudding, then an eating club intended to "cultivate the social affections and cherish the feelings of friendship and patriotism," and was elected to Phi Beta Kappa. He occasionally partook of a companionable drink. And when he was not socializing or studying, he put his penmanship skills to good use by transcribing documents for historian Jared Sparks, then engaged in writing his *Life of George Washington*.[19]

While he once sided reflexively with authority, Moore gradually came to share his classmates' disaffection with Harvard's "government." Subject to a relentless grading system that assigned points daily for academic performance and personal conduct (with demerits for such offenses as missing chapel or whispering in class) and that cumulated by the semester to determine each undergraduate's rank in class, the students seethed with resentment. Moore found the system oppressive—"we have no time to think but must study all the time," he complained soon after enrolling—and in his senior year signed a petition against it. Not long afterward a student's dispute with a tutor escalated into the great "Harvard College rebellion of 1834," as the future "American scholars" set off fireworks in chapel and vandalized a classroom, and then, in the face of harsh measures to crush the protests, rallied on the quad to "flaming rebellious speeches" about "liberty—rights—oppression &c.," and hanged President Quincy in effigy. Moore kept his distance from the uprising; "the Government are generally right in their decisions," he opined. But then the administration threatened to take the affair into the criminal courts. Outraged by this unprecedented step, he switched sides and joined his fellows in issuing a public indictment of Quincy's actions. But as the controversy wore on through the summer, the graduating senior was unwilling to jeopardize his hard-earned degree. A week before commencement, the Class of 1834 took a vote on whether to boycott the ceremony, in protest against the expulsion of seven members; Moore was in the minority voting no. On graduation day, in recognition of his academic achievement, the young man from Concord participated in a "Deliberative Discussion" of a topic well suited to the moment: the "Tendency of Free Institutions to bring First Principles into question." He was relieved to get through the exercise with "no blunders or stumbles." No one would mistake him for a rebel.[20]

Moore remained open to new influences. He spent the year after graduation in the town of Plymouth, where he took charge of a school for young ladies and participated in a lively intellectual circle gathered around the Unitarian minister James Kendall, a liberal preacher of Ezra Ripley's sort. There he met Lydia Jackson, "a religious seeker" who had withdrawn from Kendall's congregation to start an independent Plymouth Religious Society. The future Mrs. Ralph Waldo Emerson impressed him as "truly an original genius—one who thinks and reasons for herself, but whose peculiar notions about human nature often seem to lead her into error." On another occasion, he ran into Mary Moody Emerson, whose reputation as "very intellectual, & very eccentric" had preceded her. "We had quite a confab together." Plymouth's lyceum hosted both Waldo Emerson and his brother Charles that year. The former made no impact on Moore; the latter gave a lecture about "Modern Society" on which the schoolmaster took copious notes. The most important relationship Moore forged was with Elizabeth Russell, the twenty-year-old daughter of a ship captain whose siblings would form deep connections with the Concord Transcendentalists. In the summer of 1836, the two became engaged to marry.[21]

One year later Moore was back in Cambridge, still undecided about a career. He was registered for classes at Harvard Law School, at the same time as he resided in Divinity Hall. And his opinions were changing in significant ways. As he studied law, his interest in politics quickened. In 1832, having turned twenty-one, "an honorable citizen of this honorable Commonwealth," he had exercised the right to vote for the first time and cast his ballot for Henry Clay for president. In law school he remained a Whig, with a bent for social reform. In February 1836 he read Channing's systematic brief against slavery and found it "most convincing" and "unanswerable." That same month, in Simon Greenleaf's class on evidence, the professor departed from the textbook and went off on a stout defense of Freemasonry. The organization had done a great deal of good, he argued, and if it restricted its benefits to members, this bias was no different from Americans favoring fellow citizens over foreigners. The attacks by Anti-Masons displayed "a great deal of fanaticism—of party spirit." Moore was unconvinced. Despite his father's service as master of the Corinthian Lodge and membership in the Royal Arch Chapter, he dismissed this rationale and took satisfaction in the "death-blow" the fraternity had seemingly suffered—irrefutable proof of "the unsuitableness of the Institution for the present time."

The law student was going his own way, and a month later, in March, this earnest son of a man well known to enjoy a drink or two—or more—at the Middlesex Hotel took a pledge of total abstinence from all intoxicating beverages. Although Moore had no objection to an occasional glass of wine, he chose to stand up and be counted among the teetotalers in hope of influencing others to do the same. So too did he take up the cause of peace. That same month Moore attended a meeting in Boston of a "young men's peace society," at which his neighbor in Divinity Hall gave a speech portraying "the horrors of war" and staking out an uncompromising pacifist position. Impressed by the presentation, the law student wrote a report of the event and successfully submitted it for publication in the *Christian Watchman*, a Baptist-sponsored newspaper. Moore had grown up with a militia captain for a father. But the speaker persuaded him that war could never be justified, even in self-defense. "We wish most heartily to see such principles . . . spread abroad . . . ," recommended the author, under the pseudonym "M," "and to see people in all parts of our beloved country . . . enlightened by such evangelical truths." Back in Concord, the Moore family embraced Freemasonry, militia service, and social drinking with gusto. In Cambridge, the once-obedient son repudiated them all.[22]

As he endorsed these reforms, Moore followed Emerson's lectures with remarkable assiduity. From November 1835 through February 1836, he took breaks from his legal studies and attended four of his townsman's lectures on English literature and three on biography. When the next academic year opened in September 1836, the idealistic young man began training for the ministry, and in the winter of 1836–1837, amid the demands of his courses, he crossed the Charles River eight times and took a seat in the Masonic Temple for most of the series "The Philosophy of Modern History." During these years, on visits home, he also had opportunities to hear Emerson preach, and he became personally acquainted with the master of "Bush." One evening in the Emerson parlor, he listened with "much pleasure" to his host and Margaret Fuller discussing Goethe's ideas about architecture; on another occasion he was privileged to hear Emerson read aloud from some "entertaining, witty, [and] instructive" letters that had recently arrived from Thomas Carlyle. A couple years later he gained an intimate glimpse of Transcendentalist child rearing when little Waldo, a toddler of some twenty months, interrupted tea with his crying. The father calmly lifted up the child and "carried him out of doors to look upon the face of nature and the sky." He soon returned with "a happy boy." Here was a practical demonstration of Emerson's philosophy at work.[23]

Moore thus came to the Masonic Temple series with a favorable opinion of the speaker and an openness to new views. The record of his attendance is faithfully inscribed in his diary, sometimes in brief notes, often in extensive summaries and appraisals.[24] Yet it is not easy to say what Moore derived from the experience. He was definitely not there for Transcendentalism. The student of law and religion had no interest in speculative philosophy. In a lecture on the "genius" of Shakespeare, Emerson portrayed the Bard as superior to all other poets in his "Imaginative Power." To explain the point, he digressed into an account of the relation between mind and matter. "Every natural fact is a symbol of some spiritual fact"—a proposition that in these exact words would be central to the book he was composing, *Nature*. Emerson feared that this exposition would "tax the patience" of his audience. He was correct. Moore was bored by the "considerable metaphysics" and put off as well by excessive quoting from Shakespeare. The lecture thus "did not succeed so well" as many before or after. But the young man kept coming, even though he tuned out the religious mysticism. In the "Philosophy of Modern History" series, Emerson treated listeners time and again to his revelation of the "Universal Mind" incarnated in every individual. Moore largely ignored this Transcendentalist gospel; the divine soul may have been everywhere, but it seldom appeared in the ministerial student's notes. Moore might have welcomed the Spirit had he grasped what Emerson was saying. "What I understood of [Emerson's lecture "Religion"] I liked very much," he remarked in mid-January 1837, "but there was a good deal I could not understand."[25]

If the central theme of "The Philosophy of Modern History" was celebration of the individual, with an examination of the hindrances and helps to self-realization, it went over Moore's head. The young man was not particularly introspective; nothing Emerson said inspired him to look within and explore his deeper self. Instead, he incorporated the various addresses into his ongoing quest for self-improvement. For the inquisitive youth, the Transcendentalist's discourses served the same purpose as any other lyceum lecture: they disseminated information, expanded horizons, urged experiment and change, and furnished moral instruction. From Emerson the diarist learned about the lives and works of major writers (Chaucer, Shakespeare), artists (Michelangelo), reformers (Martin Luther), and statesmen (Edmund Burke). He gained perspective on the democratization of literature and the changing relation of scholars to the public—a matter of significance to a would-be minister and novice lecturer. (Moore debuted at the Concord Lyceum in April 1836 with a talk about Isaac Newton, on which he had "worked like a slave, manufacturing thoughts, collecting and arranging facts.") Undoubtedly, Emerson provided a model on the platform, in both his language and his delivery. Moore prized him as a historian and social critic.

Why did so few people read history, and why was it "generally considered dull"? In that concise formulation, the student distilled the guiding question of "The Philosophy of Modern History," and he took down the lecturer's reply with precision—that conventional history featured kings and courts, wars and battles, rather than common people. He admired Emerson's portrait of the farmer ("full of beauty & naturalness") and the gentleman ("a citizen of the world"). He attended carefully to his delineation of "the Present Age." Newly engaged to marry, he deemed Emerson's remarks on the innate differences between men and women "just and eloquent . . . Man's sphere is out of doors and among men—woman's is in the house—Man seeks for power and influence—woman for order and beauty—Man is just—woman is kind." But when the lecturer condemned temperance pledges as "degrading," the young man demurred. "Here probably his audience differed from him." Characteristically, he said nothing about his own vow of total abstinence a year before. Moore rarely made connections to his personal circumstances. His diary was not a journal of the self.[26]

Following the "Philosophy of Modern History" series, Emerson's influence on Moore waned. In late July 1837, the divinity student had to suspend his ministerial training and travel out to Chicago, where his brother Henry, plagued by illness and ridden by debt, needed care. George was thus far from Cambridge when Emerson delivered the Phi Beta Kappa address. He returned home three months later, only to sail to Cuba at year's end and meet up with Henry, convalescing in the tropical climate. He was not back in Divinity Hall until mid-April 1838, and so he missed Emerson's lecture series "Human Culture." Thereafter, busy with classes and then on the road as a guest preacher in various churches, he was able to hear just two more lectures by his townsman, in the 1838–1839 series "Human Life."

Absence was not the key reason for the Transcendentalist's diminishing role in Moore's life. As the young man prepared for the clergy, he found a new mentor, Henry Ware, Jr., "Professor of Pulpit Eloquence and Pastoral Care" at the divinity school. Ironically, Ware had been senior pastor at Boston's Second Church when Waldo was hired as his assistant and then successor. The two men of the cloth had remained on good terms, even as Emerson turned away from Bible-based religion and Ware became an influential advocate for Unitarianism. Under the professor's tutelage, Moore stayed safely within the denominational fold. Professing his faith, he underwent baptism and joined the college church. His view of religion as a means of self-improvement was in keeping with Ware's. "The great object of my life," he pledged in 1838, was "the formation of the truly Christian character," invoking the title of the Unitarian thinker's most influential book. Ware's counsel for aspiring ministers now filled the pages of Moore's diary.[27]

The transition from Emerson to Ware was seamless. The divinity student manifested no awareness of divergence, not to mention discord, between his two mentors, and it is easy to see why. Ware urged preachers to speak from their hearts, to throw away prepared texts, and to convey their lived experience of faith in extemporaneous words right for the occasion. "The success of preaching," he observed in September 1836, "lies, in great measure, in the unaffected earnestness and zeal of the minister, in the fact that he feels what he is saying is eternal truth." Emerson shared this ideal; his famous address to the divinity school in July 1838 drew heavily on Ware's ideas, even as it outraged many with its heterodox views of Christ. Surprisingly, Moore never mentioned that controversial speech. The Transcendentalist controversy that rocked the Unitarian denomination was never engaged in the privacy of his diary.[28]

Perhaps Moore was conflict averse and ignored clashes of opinion wherever possible. Or maybe Emerson did not stand out from the liberal clergy as sharply as he now appears to have done. His diagnosis of the Panic of 1837 as a case of materialism gone mad was not unique. At about the same time, the eminent William Ellery Channing was blaming the financial crisis on the "mania" among all social classes to get rich quick, and divinity school dean John G. Palfrey was attributing it to "the gambling spirit of trade, and the profuse manner of living." On the pages of Moore's diary, these assessments were of a piece. To the consensus-minded student, the authorities he respected—from Ezra Ripley back in Concord to the clergy in Cambridge and Emerson on the lecture platform, at the meetinghouse, and in the parlor—conveyed compatible views. From this perspective, the Concord Transcendentalist neither unsettled Moore's faith nor inspired a departure from familiar ways. Arguably, Emerson contributed to the young man's decision to pursue the ministry, but Moore later gave the credit to Ware for having been "as a father to me. He has done more for me, as a Christian, than perhaps any other man."[29]

To his contemporaries in Concord, George Moore was a well-meaning but prosaic figure, incapable of a spontaneous gesture or an original thought. "He is a slave to propriety," Fanny Prichard observed, "and has swallowed all ministerial formulas, he will never see anything in a new light, nor strike off in any untrodden path." That judgment was unfair. The young man was more

open-minded and intellectually curious than his peers realized. Before entering the divinity school and after, he sought out various modes of Christian
worship. He attended Baptist, Methodist, and orthodox Congregationalist
services as well as Unitarian; he visited the Shaker community in the Middlesex County town of Harvard; he explored the mystical faith of Swedenborg;
and he enjoyed the Episcopalian rites most of all. As a divinity student, he
threw himself into benevolent causes; appropriately for one who had grown
up around a jail, he participated in a program of outreach to inmates at the
Cambridge House of Correction and the state penitentiary in Charlestown.

Nor was he narrow-minded in his social and political outlook, as his classmates recognized in electing him president of the Philanthropic Society, a student group that organized discussions of politics and reform at the divinity
school. Initially opposed to Garrison's militant abolitionism, he came around
to support immediate emancipation and equal rights, and he preached a distinctively Unitarian brand of antislavery. "We believe in the infinite worth of
every human Soul—that the Soul of the poor African is possessed of godlike
powers—that his colour is but an accident—and consequently we must regard
every attempt to enslave and degrade this soul as a sin against God." He even
sympathized with the radicals who withdrew from the American Peace Society
in 1838 to form a voluntary association opposed not only to war but to every
measure of coercion by the state. This philosophical "anarchism" was an unlikely stance for a jail keeper's son.[30]

So caught up in his studies and in his extracurricular activities was Moore
that he seems to have neglected his fiancée, Elizabeth Russell, back in Plymouth, and after his trips out west and to Cuba, she broke off the engagement,
to his astonishment. Typically, he strove to overcome despondency over the
rejection with intense self-scrutiny and prayer; here was another opportunity
to make "rapid advances in the Christian life." But he never got over the heart-
break; five years later he was still nursing hurt feelings and unable to move on.
He never married; neither did Russell. With no prospect of marriage, he signed
up as an "Evangelist" in the Unitarian campaign to plant liberal Protestantism
in the Western territories and eventually became pastor of a small congregation in Quincy, Illinois, on the Mississippi River.[31]

The persona of an unhappy lover, forever alone in devotion to an unat-
tainable ideal, appealed to Moore's romantic sensibility, and it resonated with
themes in Emerson's picture of the alienated young man of fairest promise. A

devotee of Wordsworth's poetry, Moore delighted in "studying God's book of nature, wh[ich] is ever open to the thoughtful man." He preferred the silence of the woods to the "vain, frivolous, nonsensical chit-chat of a tea-party." "Solitude has charms for me," he wrote. "I do love to be alone—to meditate—and muse the hours away with no mortal near." On another occasion, he revealed a relish for paradox reminiscent of Thoreau: "Solitude is my best friend." Such inclinations were born of philosophy as well as temperament. One "all-glorious" spring morning in 1838, Moore's spirit soared to the song of the birds, as he made his way to teach a Sunday school class for young children. The experience moved him to preach a lesson in natural religion, to "look through nature up to Nature's God." Just as the birds expressed the instinct of their nature, so human beings had a force within them—"a soul, an immortal spirit"—implanted by God. "The course of that soul is ever onward—improvement is part of its nature." Be true to the voice of that spirit, he advised; it represented the law of God within.[32]

For all these affinities with Emersonian themes, Moore would never stray from the Unitarian fold. On one occasion, as a guest preacher in the Essex County town of Lynn, he encountered a woman who was pleased to learn that he was from Concord, the home of Emerson and Transcendentalism. She "undertook to question me pretty closely" about "the new views" of religion. Displeased by this turn in the conversation, Moore must have given an unsatisfactory response: "I say, give me good sound common sense—faith in the gospel, in truth, and in man, and a living out of the truth—and such a person I can fully sympathize with. But this blue-light, flashy, cloudy, misty talk is to me all moon-shine."[33]

IN THE SECOND QUARTER OF THE NINETEENTH CENTURY, THE CONCORD elite was having trouble controlling the young. As the parents ushered in a world of unprecedented opportunities and risks, the children asserted the freedom to make their own decisions and chart their own way. In the tug-of-war between generations, the elders were at a disadvantage. Having relaxed the grip of patriarchy in the Revolutionary era, they now strove to rear citizens capable of self-government, both in the public arena and in the domestic sphere. To this end, the families of the commercial and professional classes, in particular, grew more child-centered, intent on nurturing the autonomy of every girl and boy. Or so they said. But not every father or mother could abandon so easily the desire to steer the life choices of their offspring. The resulting clash between parental expectations and filial inclinations resonated in Emerson's summons to self-reliance.

The new norms were evident in the town clerk's register of births. In the patriarchal world of eighteenth-century Concord, parents customarily named children for themselves. Some 80 percent did so, and they were also likely to confer grandparents' names, in a practice designed to sustain a family line across the generations. Children, in this view, were *not* unique. In the colonial era, when an infant died, the parents grieved, then recycled his or her name at the earliest opportunity. Frequently that name had its source in Scripture: John, Joseph, and Samuel for boys, Mary, Elizabeth, and Sarah for girls. But in the new republic, with its premium on individual autonomy, naming practices changed decisively and dramatically. By the second decade of the nineteenth century (1811–1820), a mere 10 to 15 percent of parents named children for themselves, and fewer still opted to honor grandparents. The young were also freed from the burden of carrying deceased siblings' names. Instead, they were frequently flattered or perhaps cursed with names chosen to express the patriotism or the whimsy of their parents. As biblical names lost popularity, Concord gained numerous Franklins, George Washingtons, and occasional Thomas Jeffersons among its boys and Mirandas, Augustas, and Alma Americas among its girls. One little boy, whose father Franklin was born in 1812, would eventually go to school with the imposing name Albert Butler Curling Dakin. Little "ABC" would surely learn his letters.[34]

John Keyes bucked this trend. In 1816 the ambitious lawyer wed the well-connected stepdaughter of the late sheriff of Middlesex County, and over the next decade and a half the couple celebrated the births of five children. These were the very years when the preference for names to signify individuality was gaining sway. Not so in the Keyes household, which opted to honor kin and perpetuate a family line. The eldest son, John Shepard, epitomized the parental union: his first name came from his father, followed by the surname of his mother. Two daughters, neither of whom survived beyond age eight, were named for maternal relatives, one son for a paternal uncle who had died in childhood. Only the youngest, George, received a classic English name with no familial antecedents. By such choices, John and Ann (Shepard) Keyes cherished and bequeathed a pride in ancestry to the next generation. Genealogy helped to forge elite identity and instill a sense of continuity in an uncertain world. Even the local philosopher of individualism acknowledged the family claim. When his first child was born in October 1836, the choice of name was preordained. "Waldo," pronounced Emerson, "the oldest son should always be named for his Father."[35]

The burden of family expectations weighed on the politician's eldest son. Born in 1821, John Shepard Keyes was a boy at the height of his father's power and entered adolescence as the "King" was being dethroned. The youth was well aware of his privileged position. The Keyes home, next door to the court-house, where the county treasurer had his office, was one of the grandest in town; its large northwest parlor was notable for the thick carpets on the floor and the oil paintings on the walls, and through its prominent windows, pass-ersby could glimpse the select parties at which the squire cultivated political allies and hosted his peers with a well-stocked liquor cabinet. The boy found his companions in the village elite, whose children were his classmates at the academy. But he preferred sports and games to books and delighted in sail-ing on the river, skating on the ponds, and tramping in the woods, with his fowling piece at the ready to shoot a bird for dinner—a practice he later came to regret as he learned to appreciate "the beautiful creatures" and study their habits with a naturalist's curiosity similar to Thoreau's.[36]

Fearless and high-spirited, young Keyes was always up for an adventure or a fight. In one unfortunate incident, he amused himself by "plaguing" George Frisbie Hoar, the squire's son, nearly five years his junior, until the victim tired of the abuse and threw a rock at his tormentor. The stone broke Keyes's two front teeth. The bully went home in acute pain, which the dentist alleviated at a severe cost. The treatment—an application of nitric oxide—deadened the nerves but "killed" the teeth, which ultimately had to be removed, in an age before novocaine, with "old-fashioned twisters." Not only was Keyes without his two front teeth, but he also had to endure a lifetime of dental misery, from which he obtained relief only by smoking cigars. The missing teeth were a per-manent reminder of another Hoar family triumph over the Keyeses.[37]

The boy also threw himself into the political contests of the day, eager to advance his father's cause. During the struggle over Freemasonry, his daring and agility were put to advantage. Every Saturday morning Atwill's *Gazette* ap-peared with outrageous attacks on the fraternity, and every Saturday evening Wheildon's *Aurora* came to the defense. With little time to spare, the latter got the eleven-year-old son of the Masonic king to crawl through a broken window into the *Gazette* office, when no one was around, and snatch an advance copy of the forthcoming issue. By this means the *Aurora* could answer charges within hours of their circulation. "I must have been an ardent 'jack mason' to have gone through so small a hole for so little use," Keyes recollected a half-century later. The "escapade" won him the nickname "Prince John" and earned cheers from the crowd at the post office when he arrived with his much-awaited prize.[38]

With his love of adventure and zest for competition, the junior Keyes yearned for a life of action rather than study. He thrilled to tales of military glory from grizzled veterans of the Revolution and delighted in militia musters on the common. Envisioning himself as "a dashing cavalry officer . . . displaying a bright uniform [and] mounted on a black horse," he had his heart set on a military career. Without telling his father, he sent off to Washington for an application to West Point. When a response arrived on official stationery from the adjutant general of the army, it caught the notice of Concord's postmaster. John Keyes sat his son down for a serious talk about the future. The army was a terrible choice, he informed the boy. It offered a one-way ticket to nowhere, "there being only frontier Indian wars on hand." Although the politician had the clout to swing an appointment to the nation's military academy, the boy would have to give up his dream. He was to go to college in Cambridge, after which he would study law and enter his father's office.[39]

The teenager complied "unwillingly," with an ill-concealed resentment that long troubled relations with his patriarch. Under Phineas Allen's indifferent instruction, he made little progress in his studies, and though he enjoyed an intellectual awakening under a new teacher, Keyes barely scraped by the entrance examination into Harvard's Class of 1841. College proved no more inspiring. The lessons were boring, the recitations tedious; no professor or tutor ever offered an encouraging word. Students and faculty confronted each other as "foes" in unremitting "battle." His four years in Cambridge conferred little benefit beyond the stimulus of smart classmates and the reading he did on his own. Years later he reflected that "I ought not to have gone to college but have been put to some practical business for which I was much better suited." That insight was available to neither the domineering father nor the immature son.[40]

The reluctant student did not rebel against his father's grand plan. He misbehaved. College life held temptations and perils for those determined to escape adult supervision. Keyes won the admiration of classmates for his boldness in breaking the rules. He set bonfires in Harvard Yard, slipped off campus to the racetrack in Cambridge and the billiard room in Boston, and was always game for a drinking "spree." Then there was the allure of girls: he danced and partied in the parlors and ballrooms of Boston and Cambridge, Waltham, and Concord. So thoroughly did he neglect his lessons that he nearly flunked out after a semester. He was spared only by his father's unwelcome intercession with President Quincy.[41]

College afforded no sanctuary from paternal supervision. Time and again the wayward son was startled by the father's arrival at his dormitory room for an on-the-spot check. On one occasion, when the boy was absent, the squire snooped in his desk, and he was not above peeking into the diary therein. A steady stream of hectoring letters flowed from Concord to Cambridge. What are your latest grades? How do you spend every hour, from getting up in the morning to going to bed at night? John Keyes demanded regular reports. College was an unprecedented opportunity, he urged; don't waste it. "If you duly appreciate the advantages given you, and consider that an education will or may be the means of gaining a livelihood, and that it will add to your happiness and enjoyment in life, I am sure you will be disposed to do what you can to obtain one," the struggling freshman was counseled in January 1838. A letter the next month was more encouraging: "You have talents and now is your time to improve them." The message was the same twenty months later, when the recipient was a junior. "Do you attend, like a good young man, wishing to make the most of his time & talents, to the studies required? Do you appreciate the advantages put into your hands to get wisdom? . . . Study then to be wise—study then to be happy—study then to be useful to your self & the community." And if you won't study for your own sake or for the benefit of others, then consider the feelings of your dear father and mother. "Children never can know the anxious thoughts of parents on their behalf—They can never pay for the sleepless nights—the watchings—the prayers—the toil and labor in their cause but . . . by being good & doing good." Should gratitude and guilt not be motivation enough, there were also material inducements to academic success. The wealthy lawyer looked for signs that his firstborn son would not "squander away his inheritance, if he had it at his command." His future depended on passing grades.[42]

For all his dislike of school, the younger Keyes never went as far in his resistance to patriarchy as did another undergraduate from Concord. In March 1840 Edward Sherman ("Ned") Hoar was in his freshman year at Harvard, following his father Samuel and older brother Rockwood in a family tradition dating back to the Puritans. Then, to everyone's astonishment, the seventeen-year-old took a different path. Impulsively, he "ran away" from college and headed west, intending to "traverse the continent, mostly on foot." All he carried with him were a rifle and ammunition, a "little clothing, and hardly any money." For more than a week nobody knew his whereabouts.

The troubles in the Hoar family alarmed John Keyes, who dashed off a series of anxious letters to his own difficult son. What had gotten into Ned Hoar? "Is the boy crazy?" he asked. "How and wherefore does he reason? Can he expect to work his way at his age in this wide world . . . before he is fitted for active life?" Between the lines, John Shepard read a warning against Ned's example. Look how much "pain" a "wayward child [can] inflict!" The father predicted that the "prodigal son" would soon be back, begging "pardon and forgiveness," and he proved correct. Young Hoar made it as far as Lexington, Kentucky, before his westering impulse and resources gave out. On his return, he re-enrolled in Harvard College, went on to law school, and entered the family profession. But he continued to harbor the dream of striking out on his own in a place where the Hoar family was unknown. In 1849 he joined the forty-niners in the Gold Rush to California and eventually settled in Santa Barbara, where he practiced law and farmed. He would not return to the Bay State until after his father's death.[43]

John Shepard Keyes lacked the strength to make a new beginning. "I am free and alone," he exulted on the eve of commencement. But after graduating with an academic standing surprisingly strong enough to earn a speaking part in the ceremony ("the proudest day of my life"), he returned home to wrestle with the same unresolved emotional issues. Living under the paternal roof, reading law in his father's office and "at [his] instigation," the young man outwardly complied with expectations while flouting them at every turn. He plodded his way through Blackstone at a pace the squire considered "poor," even as he devoured such novels as Cooper's *Deerslayer* at a rapid clip. Romances and sprees took precedence over professional training.[44]

In contrast to the earnest George Moore, whom he deemed "too formal and prosy," Keyes did little to improve his time. The lyceum was as much an opportunity to meet girls as to acquire useful information. Bored at a lecture on education, "that trite and worn-out subject," the young man amused himself by joking with the lively wife of banker John Cheney. "[We] had a little private fun during the feast of reason and the flow of Soul."[45] Likewise for Sunday meeting, where he often ignored the sermon to make eyes with female favorites and indulge in "luscious reveries." Benevolent societies held no interest for him; nor did crusades for reform. But these causes drew young women, so he occasionally showed up, if only to mock the proceedings. At a temperance picnic, he tricked an earnest young woman into taking the pledge by asking her "if she would sign if I would, and she not understanding rushed up and signed. But I had no idea of signing such a foolish thing, and refused entirely." An outright racist, he had no sympathy for the slave and dismissed the abolitionist talk of such women as Cynthia Thoreau as "niggering." Nonresistance struck him as equally absurd. In January 1841 he witnessed a lyceum debate on the issue between Bronson Alcott and Henry Thoreau and dismissed the event as a farce. "The most foolish as well as amusing I ever heard, it amounted to plain common nonsense and awfully highflown in the bargain."[46]

While Keyes knew what he disliked, he had no plan of his own. Despite his college degree, he remained stuck in an adolescent drama all too familiar today. On his twentieth birthday he skipped the annual ritual of reviewing his conduct and renewing the resolutions that framed his diary. (The list included promises "to study faithfully," "to attend to prayers in chapel and out," and "to obey the requests of my Parents." He invariably came up short.) He was surprised to discover on his desk a gift from his father: a bank book in his name, recording $250 in deposits and interest. "I am much obliged, as it makes me more independent and gives me the wherewithal to seek my fortune with." But gratitude did not change his conduct. He came and went as he pleased, heading out to dances and sprees without permission and returning home well after midnight. After one such escapade in late December 1841, he suffered "a tremendous scolding about Temperance" from a red-faced father; it was "equal in fury to . . . last Sunday's [lecture] on Extravagance. Then however it was my 'foolish abominable INFERNAL habits' which were blasted and why? Because I drank a mug of flip at the ball here. I shall drink when and what I please while I can get it. Hon. John Keyes," he fumed, "for all your blasting.—Sir, Shut up." Prudently, he kept these opinions to himself.[47]

Caught in a cultural limbo, distant from his father's viewpoint but with no direction of his own, the young man should have been ripe for Emerson's call to self-reliance. As a boy of fourteen, he had been mesmerized by the orator at the Concord bicentennial, and before entering college, he had also enjoyed various lectures and sermons by Emerson—"with pleasure if not profit." He had thus been eager to hear the Phi Beta Kappa address. A few days before that event, he was scheduled to take the Harvard entrance examination. If he did well enough on the test, John Keyes had promised, the lad could go to the literary festival with a female companion—and without any adult supervision. His date was to be a fellow student at the academy who had stolen his heart: seventeen-year-old Caroline Brooks, daughter of lawyer Nathan. What a fine impression the couple would make as they rode into Cambridge in a white chaise with yellow wheels pulled by a bobtailed horse! The expectant freshman could hardly wait. But on second thought, the parents concluded that the teenagers were too young for such an adventure. Caroline Brooks attended the speech with others from Concord, including Rockwood Hoar, whom she would wed several years later in yet another victory of Hoar over Keyes. John Shepard stayed home and sulked as his initial year of college was about to begin.[48]

The first opportunity that Keyes, as a Harvard student, got to hear Emerson lecture—or at least the first record of his attending such an event—came in late July 1838, when the spokesman for "the American Scholar" was invited to address the literary societies of Dartmouth College during its commencement week. So pleased was John Keyes, an 1809 graduate of the small New Hampshire school, with the honor being bestowed on his Concord neighbor that he decided to gather up his entire family and accompany the lecturer to his alma mater. He may also have been thinking about taking his wayward son out of Cambridge, where there were so many distractions, and transferring him to the orthodox Congregationalist institution deep in the New England countryside. It was the freshman's first trip outside Massachusetts, and while he was exposed to new scenes, he considered the small college inferior to "my Cambridge." His father's school looked "tame and poor beside the rich and dashing Harvard." While Dartmouth was disappointing, not so Emerson's address. Entitled "Literary Ethics," it reprised the themes of the Phi Beta Kappa address but without the biting attack on educational malpractice at the institution hosting him.

To the young man from Concord, the speech was "a revelation." Reading the text a half-century later, Keyes, a man in his seventies, felt once more "the stir to . . . life and spirit" evoked by the orator's "power and eloquence." Forthright in Transcendentalist rhetoric about the "Universal Soul" common to all men, the speech looked forward to a new chapter in the American mind. "Now our day is come," Emerson proclaimed, "and now will we live,—live for ourselves . . . we will put our own interpretation on things, and . . . our own things for interpretation." This "assertion of spiritual independence" inspired Keyes with its idealism; "it roused the new aspirations then just beginning to be felt all over New England." It also appealed to his iconoclasm, for it "shocked the Orthodoxy and old-fashioned notions" at Dartmouth. The irreverent student, engaged in his own struggle against authority, had found an intellectual hero.[49]

For the next two years, Keyes welcomed chances to hear Emerson speak. He was in the audience at the Masonic Temple for at least one lecture ("Genius") in the "Human Life" series and at the Concord Lyceum eleven months later for another, "Philosophy of Labor," which was "one of his best." In January 1839, back home in Concord for the Sabbath, he sat in the family pew at the First Parish meetinghouse as Emerson held forth from the pulpit for the very last time. On this morning, the young man was not distracted by pretty girls. He was rapt by the poetry of the sermon. In "the most beautiful illustration" of his theme, Emerson described the humble blackberry growing in sandy soil just inches above ground, yet extracting "spices and sweetness" from that bare existence. It was a metaphor of "the whole creation" providing for the "birth and nurture" of every living being. In Keyes's view, the discourse was "well worth the money." For Emerson, it marked the close of a clerical career and a commitment to letters—to lecturing and writing—as a full-time profession.[50]

John Keyes was skeptical of his son's engagement with Transcendentalism. In December 1839, now a junior at Harvard, John Shepard was planning to attend Emerson's new lecture series "The Present Age." His father threw cold water on the plan: "Will you be the wiser for them, do you think? Or do you consider the attendance upon them in the light of recreation?" The patriarch knew his namesake. The young man gave up on the series after just two lectures, the second of which, "Politics," was "not over and above interesting" for this fierce partisan of the Whigs. Thereafter his presence at Emerson's lectures in Boston and Concord tapered off. He did continue to frequent the intellectual's parlor, in part to hear the discussions with Margaret Fuller, Bronson Alcott, and others of their ilk, and even more to spend time with the young woman employed as a child minder in the Emersons' growing family.[51]

Born in 1820, Mary Russell, a friend of Lidian Emerson from Plymouth, won the devotion of Keyes as completely as her sister Elizabeth had claimed the affections of George Moore. Having gotten over his disappointment at the hands of Caroline Brooks and cultivated various dalliances and infatuations thereafter, the romantic young man adored "Saint Mary." She "inspired me with something of the worship devout catholics have for their saints, and drew me" to Emerson's parlor "oftener than philosophy would." In the fall of 1841, the two went for walks in the woods and rowed on the river. Just to see his "Angel," Keyes feigned interest in abolitionism and showed up at an antislavery meeting. But he had a rival for her affections in Henry Thoreau. One afternoon Keyes was chatting up "Sanctissima Maria" at a tea party when Thoreau arrived to take her sailing. It was proposed that Keyes join the group; Thoreau "flatly refused." Keyes was annoyed but impressed by his challenger's aplomb: "Cool— Transcendental—Independence now and forever." He managed to get even. A couple of months later, after a "swarry" in the village, he beat Thoreau to the punch and escorted "the Saint" home. "Completely cut out 'Henry David,'" he reported in his diary, "and made another 'vain striving' to be added to his list."[52]

Keyes and Russell were hardly soul mates. After one summer's walk, the suitor acknowledged their opposing temperaments—"she is entirely transcendental in her thoughts and I am just the reverse"—but waved away those differences. "We get along quite finely together and I like her." As it turned out, she wanted neither admirer from Concord and married Benjamin Marston Watson, a like-minded nature lover and horticulturalist in her hometown of Plymouth. Her rejection of Keyes was understandable. Hard as he tried, he could no longer summon up enthusiasm for Emerson and his followers. In November 1841, as the courtship was foundering, Keyes sat through Emerson's lecture "The Poet" at the Concord Lyceum in uncomprehending despair. The talk "disappointed me excessively, and made me feel so utterly and completely untranscendental." By contrast, the discourse excited the sensibilities of Russell and Elizabeth Hoar. He was obliged to sit glumly as the women shared the "longings, aspirations, and exstacies [sic]" Emerson had inspired. The following summer, when Charles Stearns Wheeler, his former Harvard tutor and Thoreau's close friend, preached on Transcendentalism at Sunday worship, Keyes was similarly unresponsive. Although he liked the presentation, he did "not quite understand" it, and it "did me but little good."[53]

Emerson's school of thought, it turned out, held only passing appeal for Keyes. It gave voice to the young man's yearning for independence. While his resistance to patriarchal direction held firm and his dreams of going his own way (whatever that was) still blazed, he was inspired by the champion of youth just down the road from his home. But Keyes could not bring himself to break with his father and make a fresh start. He toyed with various possibilities: a post as tutor on a Virginia plantation; an opening in India as an agent for a Boston trading firm ("I should like to go out there and acquire say $10,000 in two or three years"); a job as schoolmaster in Louisville, Kentucky, where Dr. Edward Jarvis, now settled in the rising city on the Ohio River, promised to promote his interest. In the end, Keyes could not abandon Concord. "I that is my Father have decided not to go to Louisville this fall," he reported on November 30, 1841, "and I won't go in the spring after getting through all the dull stupid winter & summer coming on in all its glory. No I shant go at all now." At twenty-one, with Mary Russell out of reach and no better prospects for employment, he accepted defeat, adjusted his sights, and buckled down to fulfill his father's plan.[54]

For all the talk of independence, Keyes could not give up the status and wealth to which he would become heir. The young man was a snob. He took pride in belonging to the "bon ton upper crust" of Concord and socializing with leading families: the Bartletts, Brookses, Hoars, Moores, Munroes, Prichards, and Shattucks, even the Thoreaus. His coterie at the academy considered itself "an uncommon lot." In college he relished invitations to parties in Waltham, where "there never was quite so much aristocracy any where in America," and he complained when a ball he attended there admitted "greasy factory girls" to dance with gentlemen. Such elitist disdain for common folk was hardly compatible with the democratic vision of Emerson, proclaiming the divine potential of every human being, rich or poor, Black or white, beautiful or not.[55]

Even more challenging to Keyes's sensibility was the Transcendentalist premium on solitude in nature. Young Keyes loved the outdoors as much as anyone of his class in Concord except for Thoreau. He fished, hunted, sailed, and swam in all the scenic locations his generation was exploring in a new embrace of nature as a source of recreation and a balm for the soul. Sometimes he simply stood in awe of the beauty all around him, particularly at Walden Pond ("the 'purest of the pure' waters"). One day he went gunning for birds in Sleepy Hollow, the rocky land to the north of the village, but the "woods were so calm, gentle, and beautiful that I could not bear to disturb them with my vain firing, and amused myself rather by lying still and watching the various birds or choosing out the finest paths to ramble."

But Keyes was no loner. Most of the time, when he went for a walk or a sail, he preferred company and not just female. At Dartmouth College he had thrilled to Emerson's summons to young men in quest of originality and in-dependence: "go cherish your soul; expel companions; set your habits to a life of solitude." Two summers later he forgot those stirring words and threw himself with abandon into a raucous, two-day chowder party with a dozen or so friends at Flint's Pond in nearby Lincoln—an adventure that profaned the natural setting and outraged their elders. So too did he fail to heed Emerson's warning against "the lust of display" as "fatal to man." In November 1841, as he thrashed about in indecision over what to do and where to live, he tried to "drive away . . . the blues" by dressing up in a new coat and vest and showing off at church. The truth was, as Keyes admitted to himself on occasion, he found solitude "gloomy," and "I can't live alone."[56]

Abandoning the self-reliance of the Transcendentalist individual, Keyes conformed to his parents' expectations, turned away from the reforming en-thusiasms of his contemporaries, and became something of a young fogy. He also found the emotional support he craved in the love of a young woman he had known for years. Martha Prescott, whom he married in 1844, was the daughter of the gentleman politician Timothy Prescott, the onetime friend turned Anti-Masonic antagonist of "King" Keyes. From Caroline Brooks to Mary Russell to Martha Prescott, "Prince John" kept falling for principled young women who were disposed to abolitionism and Transcendentalism. In his choice of a partner for life, he revealed the residual sentiments that had inspired the abortive quest for independence shaping his college years and that he now permanently left behind.[57]

EMERSON LARGELY OVERLOOKED THE "AMERICAN SCHOLAR'S" SISTERS IN his lectures. His aim was to cheer on the young men of fairest promise in their refusal of conventional ways. Yet the daughters of New England had far more to complain about than did the sons. If college graduates were unhappy with the paths open to them, at least they had options. The vast majority of white women led preordained lives. Marriage and family formed their fate, and to this end, girls grew up acquiring the skills of housewifery by their mother's sides, with little time in school to progress beyond the three Rs. The big de-cision before them was the choice of a husband. The typical bride was in her early twenties, the groom four or five years older, and the union they forged was as much a practical arrangement for mutual aid as an outgrowth of ro-mantic love.

In entering wedlock, a woman claimed the prerogatives of adulthood at a heavy cost. Under the rules of Anglo-American patriarchy, two parties became one in marriage, and that one was the husband, legally empowered to rule his domain. Subject to male authority, a wife had no independent standing. Whatever property she brought to the marriage as a dowry became the man's (unless protected by a prenuptial agreement). She could not earn money of her own, enter contracts, or execute a will. Nor did she enjoy access to the privileges of white male citizenship. She cast no ballot at the polls, held no public office, took no seat on a trial jury, and had no say in any public forum. It was assumed that men represented their households. The home was truly their castle: men led family prayers, inflicted discipline (on wives as well as children), picked callings for sons, and pressed marriages on daughters. In the rare cases of divorce, fathers normally got custody of minors. Under these circumstances, dependent and subordinate throughout their lives, could most women ever be individuals? That question posed a fundamental challenge to Emerson's vision.[58]

It was a challenge he largely ignored. During his formative years as a lecturer, Emerson had little to say about women's lives. And when he did offer comments, it was to highlight the pettiness of female concerns and to decry their impact on men. In the early republic, young people enjoyed greater freedom in courtship than had previous generations. Women now chose their mates, subject to their fathers' veto, rather than the other way around. But these unions, in Emerson's view, were too often founded on "frivolous [and] superficial fancies." Sadly, physical beauty counted for more than inner virtue. In a society that prized "seeming" over "being," young women were taught "most unhappily" to play up their "appearance," in the mistaken belief that "it is . . . the form or the face," enhanced by "the skill of dress," that "conquers opinion and hearts." These short-lived features could never sustain a true "bond of souls." Beauty faded after age thirty, as did "the celestial rapture" of love, Emerson opined after three years with Lidian; only character endured.[59]

Few unions approached this lofty ideal. For all the talk of romantic love, most couples came together for reasons of "prudence" as much as affection. Emerson once again blamed women for a disheartening practice. Girls were educated to believe that "marriage is nothing but housekeeping and that woman's life has no other aim." A good wife thus devoted herself to domestic duties, but in too many cases, Emerson feared, she lost sight of any higher purpose than the day-to-day labors of managing a home. So exacting could be her standard of "taste," so rigid her "love of order," that her separate sphere, sentimentalized as a refuge from the crass world of business and politics, could degenerate into "a trivial tyranny." The philosopher was evidently speaking from experience. Exasperated by the anguish Lidian suffered over "the little difficulties & failures of a housekeeper," he took to calling her "Asia," in mockery of the "depth of feeling" she expended for so little cause. (She hated the Orientalist nickname.) Publicly, he counseled husbands to be tolerant of the "superfluous, supererogatory order and nicety of the housewife."[60]

Emerson was even more critical of the woman's role as hostess. With the economic boom in trade and industry from the 1820s on, an expanding middle class aspired to the style of gentility that had once distinguished the narrow colonial elite from the rest of the population. A hallmark of this cultural trend was a novel use of domestic space. Where Yankee families had been accustomed to carry on diverse activities in multipurpose rooms, now they remodeled their houses to create a fashionable area specifically designed for the entertainment of guests, as John and Ann Keyes had done. The parlor was a site of leisure, to which a select company came to take tea, chat about art, literature, and other uplifting topics, perhaps enjoy a piano performance, and contribute to one another's improvement. Like the academy, it excluded the common sort; like the lyceum, it eschewed local gossip in favor of cosmopolitan knowledge.

The parlor epitomized the ongoing changes in economy and society. As household production waned, business and politics relocated to cities and towns, and the dwellings left behind gained new significance as centers of domestic life. Among the privileged classes, who led the way, the home was idealized as woman's sphere, and no part of that realm more so than the parlor. Here a genteel lady presided over a refined gathering. Following norms of politeness tracing back to the aristocratic courts of early modern Europe, host and guests enacted, in their deportment, manners, and conversation, a code of courtesy and self-restraint. Free from worldly cares—even the labor of servants to prepare food and drink was kept out of view—the select coterie pretended to be at ease and enjoying one another's company.[61]

It was an illusion, Emerson was quick to point out. The parlor was touted as a venue for open and sincere conversation, without affectation. In practice, the guests often felt false and artificial for fear of offending with a spontaneous remark. In this woman-controlled setting, the "most cultivated" men held their tongues and shrank into "timorous, desponding whimperers." Who dared raise his voice at a polite party and bellow out an unvarnished truth? "We are afraid of reality, afraid of truth, afraid of fortune, afraid of death, afraid of each other," the lecturer told audiences in Boston and Concord. "We are parlour soldiers." But the "rage of the cultivated classes" was no cause for alarm. Expressed in "sour faces" and disapproving eyes, it amounted merely to a "feminine rage."

In this dismissal Emerson associated femininity with weakness; manliness was imperiled by too much time in the parlor. Indeed, a man could lose the respect of his peers through excessive engagement with the ladies. In his Phi Beta Kappa address at Harvard, Emerson famously jibed at the liberal clergy, emasculated by identification with the female majorities in the churches. These unhappy ministers were "addressed as women," the speaker bluntly declared. In the parlors of the pious, they never heard "the rough, spontaneous conversation of men . . . but only a mincing and diluted speech. They are often virtually disfranchised; and . . . there are advocates for their celibacy." In his own home Emerson strove to set a different tone. The young people who flocked to the elegant house at the head of Cambridge Turnpike recalled the lively gatherings at which Alcott, Fuller, and other Transcendentalist friends of the host held forth as taking place in *Mr.* Emerson's parlor and not his wife's. No matter that Lidian bore the burden of these affairs. So self-absorbed were the guests in their abstract discussions that they barely noticed who furnished the refreshments.[62]

For all his talk about the universal soul, Emerson saw men and women as fundamentally different in nature. Each sex was endowed with innate "tastes and genius," which, not surprisingly, conformed to conventional gender roles. Emerson was no radical in this matter; he simply put his own idealistic stamp on the stereotypes of the day. In his scheme, man stood for "intellect," woman for "affection." The one was driven to pursue "Truth, whose effect is Power"; the other, "delights in Goodness, whose effect is Love." These principles gave rise to separate spheres of action well suited to the new capitalist society: "The man goes abroad, and works in the world. The woman stays at home, and draws him to his place." In this division of responsibilities, men took charge of economics and politics, education and the professions; women found their outlets in art, religion, benevolence, and concern for others. Together the sexes were not opposed but complementary. An enduring union was founded on the "heroic qualities, which reside in each."[63]

In actuality, the feminine got short shrift. Emerson's discourses were devoid of the emotional appeals that mobilized women in the temperance and antislavery causes. Irritated by what he considered Lidian's excessive grief over "the wretched negro in the horrors of the middle passage"—and perhaps a little guilt-ridden over his own detachment from the abolitionist crusade—he generalized his complaint: woman is "keenly alive to suffering; tears are always near her eye; anguish near her heart." The lecturer's strictures on parlor and church challenged key sources of female power in a society that afforded very few. Ultimately, no institution met his standard, not even marriage and the family.

For the test of every association, from the political party to the wedded couple, was its benefit to the individual. In this view, marriage formed a school for lifelong instruction in character and ethics; "by strictest dependence" husband and wife "rear each other to independence." The value of the union was measured in personal growth. As for the home the two made together, it served as a platform for launching the young into the wider world. His character formed in the "sacred relations" of the family, the single person ideally went forth with the flexibility and the confidence to make his own place. "Where I am well, there I am at home," Emerson declared. Inhabiting a world "in perpetual flux," no one could expect a permanent residence. The wise man thus carried "his household god with him" and "finds a home wherever truth, love, and justice and the symbolic laws of nature are found." The ancient homestead, with the aging parents, "once so familiar as to seem part and parcel of himself," would in time seem "strange and foreign." The "citizen of the world" had to be able to abandon old attachments and thrive on his own. In Emerson's plan for the self-reliant individual, there was no assisted living.[64]

This philosophy of separation was at odds with most women's lives, enmeshed in household labors and family ties. The mistress of a home rarely enjoyed the luxury of solitude, and the few women who lived alone were aging widows, sunk in poverty, without children at hand to support them. It was an exceptional person who preferred to be on her own, such as Mary Moody Emerson, who led a peripatetic existence from Concord and Boston to the Maine woods, thereby sustaining the independence that enabled her lifelong spiritual journey. Even so, she frequently answered the call of family duty and assisted in rearing nephews Waldo and his brothers. Self-culture thus appeared to be a masculine prerogative, as Emerson privately admitted. "In conversing with a lady," he wrote in his journal late in October 1837, two months after delivering the Phi Beta Kappa address, "it sometimes seems a bitterness & unnecessary wound to insist . . . on this self sufficiency of man . . . To women my paths are shut up."[65]

Even the women in Emerson's circle rejected his individualism. At thirty-two, Lidian Emerson had given up a comfortable spinsterhood in Plymouth for marriage in Concord, in the optimism that she and Waldo were on the same spiritual quest. "I respect Unitarianism," she reportedly said early in 1835, "for without it we should never have had Transcendentalism." But her version of that faith led outward from self to society. A devotee of the Swedish mystic Swedenborg, she envisioned every human soul as "part of a great whole," with "its own relation to the universe." Each discovered its purpose through engagement with others—and not apart, as her husband insisted. "This doctrine that 'none liveth to himself'—none can nor should—is universally true." Elizabeth Palmer Peabody, to whom Lidian confided this belief a couple months before her wedding, wholeheartedly agreed. A Transcendentalist long before Emerson—she was probably the first New Englander to employ that term, in an essay of 1826—Peabody was inspired by German idealism and the British Romantics to develop her own theory of "the unfolding of the human soul." In her view, a "social principle" lay at the core of every being, animating our spirits in contact with others. The "more man has learned of his nature, the more he has felt there is no solitary enjoyment." The old New England ideal of interdependence, so antithetical to Emerson, was revitalized in this female model of Transcendentalism.[66]

Despite all the unflattering remarks, the gender stereotypes, and the uncongenial philosophy, Emerson attracted a female audience. It would have been surprising had he not. Women had long dominated the membership of the Congregationalist churches, the liberal bodies even more than the orthodox, and as an erstwhile Unitarian minister, Emerson was accustomed to addressing the sisterhood in the pews. From that experience, he concluded that women were innately religious, "somewhat sacred and oracular" in their constitution and "nearer to the Divinity." He respected their minds, morality, and idealism. His aunt Mary had been his first model of spiritual intensity and intellectual restlessness, and he surrounded himself in adulthood with female friends of a similarly strong-minded character, including Peabody, Margaret Fuller, Elizabeth Hoar, and Sarah Alden Bradford Ripley (wife of Doctor Ripley's minister son Samuel), all of whom he welcomed into the Transcendental Club.

These intellectuals, well read in the Greek and Latin classics and in Continental philosophy, were part of an ever-expanding procession of educated women emerging from the numerous private academies, both single-sex and coeducational, multiplying across the extensive republic. From their ranks arose a legion of Yankee schoolmistresses in charge of both public and private schools from the Bay State to the Western frontier; roughly one out of every four women born in Massachusetts in these years taught at some point in their lives. Thanks to their education, they were able to leave home, support themselves, and enjoy a taste of independence before most eventually married and concentrated on their families. They were the counterpart of the army of farm girls departing the countryside for the textile factories of Waltham, Lowell, and lesser mill towns; some were even attracted by higher wages to give up blackboard and chalk for loom and spindle. Whatever work they performed in the variety of fields opening up to women, New England's daughters increasingly faced futures of opportunity and uncertainty, and like their brothers, they were anxious for advice about how to make new lives as individuals in unsettled times. Perhaps Emerson had an answer.[67]

Although the lecturer did not devote an entire discourse to the subject of "Woman" until 1855, he occasionally revealed his agreement with the Transcendentalist view that there is "no sex in souls." Whatever the inherent dispositions of male and female, every individual could call on the infinite potential of the God within. In December 1837, as he was launching his series "Human Culture," Emerson encountered a "fair girl" in Boston who embodied his ideal of individuality. A friend of Margaret Fuller, eighteen-year-old Caroline Sturgis displayed an independence of mind, a freedom of will, and a natural expression "so careless of pleasing" that he was irresistibly drawn into her orbit. In her "nobleness" he longed to "be ennobled," and in gratitude for this elevating influence, he cheered her on. "Never strike sail to any," he exclaimed in his journal. "Come into port greatly, or sail with God the seas."

But the voyage of life was strewn with obstacles; as Elizabeth Hoar sadly informed him, no "idealizing girl" in her experience had ever fulfilled her early promise after coming of age and marrying. To warn against that shipwreck of hopes, Emerson incorporated Sturgis's example into the lecture "Heroism" two months later. This virtue, commonly associated with men in arms, expressed a "military attitude of the soul." Its essence was "self-trust," for it grew out of an inner faith so unshakable that a patriot could be inspired to risk his life for his country as naturally as he breathed: "It is the state of the soul at war." Could a woman be a hero? Emerson took a gender-neutral stance: heroism was necessary to man and woman alike. For in the everyday battle of life, the young had to muster the strength to follow their dreams in the face of a hostile world. A "forming Colossus" was in danger of shrinking "to the common size of man." A woman with aspirations might stumble on an uncharted path. But there was no cause for despair. Consider the obstacles "a new and unattempted problem to solve," he advised, and in that effort, "let the maiden, with erect soul, walk serenely on her way, accept the hint of each new experience, try, in turn, all the gifts God offers her, that she may learn the power and the charm . . . her new-born being is." Was such independence possible? Emerson took heart from the example of Sturgis, whose exemplary qualities he evoked in the language of his journal: "Not in vain you live, for every passing eye is cheered and refined by the vision."[68]

During the 1830s, a joke made the rounds in Boston that a gentleman distinguished for "learning and ability" was at a loss to comprehend Emerson's lectures. But, the gentleman added with chagrin, "his daughters could." Not everyone did. Caroline Healey, the daughter of a wealthy merchant, was often in the audience at the Masonic Temple, despite the fact that the teenager found the speaker's philosophy "incomprehensible," considered his view of self-reliance "extravagant and unsafe," and deplored "his selfish abstraction from society." Yet she kept coming back and in middle age became an acolyte of the great man. In Concord too the local sage claimed a female following, who not only took in his performances at the lyceum but also traveled into Cambridge and Boston for his talks. Unfortunately, the record of their reactions is sparse. From the scattered letters and diaries that survive, it is evident that the young women of Concord were in search of a message that spoke to their idealism, their intellects, and their souls and that offered an escape from lifelong domestic drudgery. Whether and how Emerson answered that need are matters of speculation.[69]

Martha Prescott, for one, aspired to a life of the mind. In 1833 the fifteen-year-old enrolled in Concord Academy not long after her parents moved to town from Littleton, where her father had flourished as a storekeeper. Retiring from business in middle age, Timothy Prescott settled his small family, including Martha and two younger siblings, on a farm just down the road from Ripley's parsonage. A native of Westford, the ex-merchant was a childhood friend of John Keyes, and thanks to that connection, he was welcomed into town government and onto the board of the Concord Bank. But after embracing Anti-Masonry, he became unacceptable to the Social Circle. Even so, intent on overcoming "an imperfect education" and "little refinement of manners," he seized on the cultural opportunities of his new home. The "self-relying" Prescott participated actively in the social library and the lyceum, and he sent his firstborn child, Martha, to Phineas Allen's academy. (The younger daughter, Abba, went to the grammar school and marched in the bicentennial parade with Ellen Garrison.) There she would study and socialize with the sons and daughters of the establishment that had spurned her father.[70]

Martha Prescott attended the academy in a turbulent time. Following Allen's enlistment in the Anti-Masonic movement, angry parents abandoned the preceptor en masse. Amid the turmoil, the school faltered, running through four instructors in a row from 1833 to 1836. For a student to prosper under these circumstances required dedication and discipline. Martha Prescott took after her father and persevered. In April 1834 she had started to keep a diary, only to give it up after a few entries; two years later, from March to May 1836, she returned to the mostly blank book and poured into it her thoughts about the purposes of education. At eighteen, approaching adulthood, she took stock of herself and her classmates and, like the young men addressed by Emerson, recoiled from the unsatisfying options she faced. Her private criticisms anticipated the gendered concerns the Transcendentalist would soon lay out in his public lectures.[71]

A bookish girl, full of intellectual ambition, Prescott was excited by her studies, including the same Latin lessons afforded to college-bound boys. Her diary contains précis of lyceum lectures, Sabbath sermons, assigned readings, and such contemporary works as George Combe's *Constitution of Man* (1828), a study of phrenology popular among Transcendentalists. Her object was plainly to develop her capacity to think and judge for herself. "I would be a learned woman," she pledged, and "have much treasure in my own mind." It proved difficult to pursue this objective. At times her schooling was interrupted by the claims of family. At four, she had lost her mother, and now in her teenage years, she bristled at the demands of her stepmother. In March 1836, with both parents away from home, she was responsible for the housekeeping for almost three straight weeks. It was a drudgery she detested. "Who can be contented to be a mere housekeeper . . . ?" she wondered. "Of all the things in the world, may I be delivered from that." She preferred "a Life of single blessedness, if I may only have time to read & study & can escape cooking & all other 'about house' horrors."[72]

Shy and "nervous," acutely self-conscious, Prescott suffered miserably whenever she was required to make social calls in local parlors. At times she was too tongue-tied to say a word, her unhappiness hidden behind a false smile. Nor could she tolerate the discomfort of fashionable clothes. An aspiring "belle" of her acquaintance, "gay, dressy . . . & fond of company," was an example to shun. Shortly after her eighteenth birthday, she stopped wearing corsets and avoided the "silly things" for the next three decades. If only she could escape so easily the strictures of her elders and the pressure of her peers! Her stepmother bluntly told the sensitive girl she was "growing very odd &c." How would she ever find a husband?[73]

Friendships and flirtations preoccupied her social circle. In an enduring teenage ritual, the classmates gossiped about one another's romances and infatuations. Prescott dismissed such talk and took a clear-sighted view of courtship and marriage. When a young man complimented her singing, she was unimpressed: "I despise flattery as much as any one." She was as appalled as Emerson by the superficiality of contemporary relationships. Detecting "little love" in a newlywed couple, she wondered how the pair could live together without a true union of souls. "Matrimony seems to be a matter of fact business now-a-days," she grumbled, more "an expediency than any thing else." Rather than submit to a loveless marriage, she envisioned a happy future as an "old maid." Perhaps she would share life with the one close friend who embodied her ideal of female independence: "unchanging, firm as a rock," and unaffected by others, reminiscent of Emerson's favorite, Caroline Sturgis. But it was one thing to be "an intelligent, learned, wise lady," quite another to constitute a bluestocking, that is, "a female pedant" intent on showing off her knowledge for the sake of praise, but possessing little "actual wisdom . . . If there is any thing on earth I detest it is a genuine 'blue.'"[74]

Amid the ups and downs of her personal life, the introspective teenager wrestled with large issues of philosophy and religion. John Locke's *Essay on Human Understanding* (1690) was required reading at Harvard College; supplemented by eighteenth-century Scottish thinkers, it furnished the epistemological foundation of Unitarian belief. In the spring of 1836, the classic work was also assigned at Concord Academy. Prescott dug into the book with tenacity and mounting skepticism. Its "lengthy & subtile [subtle] speculations" made her brain ache; its arguments for Christianity only weakened her faith. "The more I study [the work], the more I doubt." Locke's empiricism, she feared, led directly to atheism. In her uncertainty, she cast about for religious counsel.

Reverend Goodwin, junior minister of the First Parish, frequently visited the Prescott home and debated orthodoxy with her father; Martha listened attentively and clarified her thinking: "I have erred by taking opinions on trust." Sabbath sermons were often wanting, at times so "monotonous" they put her to sleep, on other occasions unacceptable in doctrine, as when a visiting preacher maintained that the best-educated were the most moral (and implicitly, best suited to rule). "This I think is false," she retorted. " . . . We often see the best & most humble Christians among ignorant men, or those having but little capacity." No more satisfying was the routine conduct of public worship; even the ceremony of baptism appeared pro forma. Instead of dedicating children to Christ, parents too often disregarded the "spiritual education" of the young. As a novice teacher in the Unitarian Sunday school, Prescott was well aware of the neglect. One Sabbath morning, she strove to evoke in the young scholars a sense of "the omnipresence of God &c." but to little effect. "It is discouraging. Where are their feelings? by the most solemn truths you can engage their attention but for a moment."[75]

Martha Prescott was in search of a more strenuous spiritual life than that on offer at Doctor Ripley's church. But she kept her doubts and dissatisfactions to herself. Who cared what she thought? "People stare if anything is said by one so young about religion." At the First Parish, one had no choice but "to work out our own salvation" alone. The young woman granted the necessity of organized religion, without which "there is no permanent happiness." But why confine true faith to the meetinghouse? "The woods, the fields, are God's fittest temples."[76]

The earnest seeker thus inclined to Unitarian reform or even Transcendentalist dissent, though she never said so directly. She shared Emerson's faith in the perfectibility of every soul. But after reading the phrenologist Combe's *Constitution of Man,* she conceded that individuals have inborn aptitudes and limitations. Even so, everyone "should improve his one talent. Any mind can advance and advance forever." In one area—racial egalitarianism—Martha was well ahead of Emerson. In April 1836, she paid a call on Mrs. Susan Garrison at the farmhouse on the edge of the Great Field and Great Meadow and found the mother of her sister's classmate Ellen to be superior "in sound sense" to "many of our aristocratic dames." Martha's religion was a democratic faith.[77]

Emerson is a distant figure in Prescott's diary. The teenager admired his family and sympathized with its trials. Accompanying her stepmother on a visit to the Emerson home, she felt a mix of disappointment and relief on learning that the lady of the house was regrettably "engaged." "I really wanted to see her & hear her converse," she sighed, but "I dreaded to have her speak to me. If there is any thing which makes us feel our *littleness*, it is seeing those so far superior." She followed closely the reports of Charles Chauncy Emerson's final illness and death in New York City that spring. The grief experienced by his fiancée Elizabeth Hoar was unimaginable: "How can she bear this sudden and dreadful affliction?" Waldo himself was a model of stoicism. But would his philosophy hold up under the loss? "Is his negative goodness?" she asked in the only intimation of a response to his ideas. The young woman had clearly been attending to Emerson's sermons, as she sat alongside her father in the family pew. His brother's death would surely put the preacher's characteristic optimism to the test.[78]

Whatever sympathy Prescott felt for the Transcendentalist did not extend to her beliefs. In the absence of any further diaries, letters, or memoirs, it is impossible to know her reactions to Emerson's lectures. Even so, despite her early doubts about John Locke, she never went so far as Emerson to question the foundations of her faith. In March 1839, a month before her twenty-first birthday, Prescott affirmed her Christian beliefs and entered the covenant of the First Parish Church. This was a family commitment: her father did the same that day, as had her stepmother some two years before. She continued her mission as a Sunday school teacher for "the immortal beings under my care." For a time she also left home for a teaching job in Brighton, next door to Cambridge. She was back by 1841, when she discovered a new outlet for her evangelical aspirations. John Shepard Keyes, her old academy chum, became her special project.[79]

During his years at Harvard, the irrepressible Keyes had lived up to the prediction of his female friends that during his time in Cambridge he would be "dashing for a while" and "fickle in his first loves." He continued on that wild course after graduation, when he returned home reluctantly to study law in his father's office. The spoiled "Prince" shocked and outraged many in town with his dalliances at "swarreys" and balls, toying with the affections of diverse young ladies and "stealing" as many kisses as he could. (He even kept a record of his conquests.) Occasionally, as with the tutor of the Emerson children, Mary Russell, he showed a deeper interest, only to experience the sting of rejection. In the riot of his passions, Keyes imagined himself a Byronic hero in the model of the popular novels he devoured. He identified in particular with Festus, the namesake of a narrative poem, published in 1839, that put a new twist on the myth of Faust. In this version, composed by a twenty-three-year-old English Romantic, Philip James Bailey, the title figure is in the thrall of Lucifer from the start but comes to repent and gain salvation at the end. The poem, with its echoes of Goethe, Coleridge, and Wordsworth, enjoyed a brief popularity among the Transcendentalists, for it put a "passionate, disillusioned youth," asserting an unbounded "freedom of himself," at the heart of the narrative. A devotee of the work, many of whose verses he spouted from memory, Keyes was still affecting this exaggerated pose when he renewed his friendship with "Matty" Prescott.[80]

To judge by the many references in Keyes's diary, the young woman treated the frustrated rebel, three and a half years her junior, with kindness, hearing out the stories of his heartthrobs and extending a nonjudgmental sympathy. For months the two maintained a Platonic friendship. They studied Greek together (Martha still aspired to be "a learned woman"). They rowed on the river, hiked in the woods, and were "enraptured" at Walden Pond ("a perfect mirror, a silver lake"). Gradually, they unburdened themselves to one another. John rose to the occasion of Timothy Prescott's sudden death in February 1842 and provided Martha welcome support. "What would I not give for her religious faith!" he exclaimed. "She is almost a Saint." She embarked on his religious reclamation. At her urging, the irreverent law student took on a Sunday school class. She pressed him to pray at bedtime, even composed an essay about prayer "for my own good." She gave him a copy of Henry Ware, Jr.'s, *Formation of the Christian Character*. As he warmed to her encouragement, he felt the stirring of moral progress. "I think I am growing better day by day and feel I shall while I have Martha's gentle teachings to make me improve. How much she is to me!" Love of God and woman flowed together.

Steadily, the connection deepened. From regarding one another as brother and sister, the two crossed a threshold of feeling before they noticed. The turning point came when they exchanged diaries, exposing to one another their innermost thoughts. ("Four years—The record of a woman's heart from twenty to twenty four. What a prize!" Keyes exclaimed. "What a treasure!") With their marriage in 1844, John subdued his rebelliousness and, inheriting his father's mantle, served the cause of established authority. Martha, his "Angel, of purity, truth, and light," devoted herself to a domestic congregation. "Let the world think me a fool," she once mused in her diary. "Can that change me? I can still think my own thoughts, enjoy my own opinions, and make myself worthy the love of those few who know and understand me." Preserving the traces of her mind in diaries that have been lost or destroyed, she retreated within the home, an early paragon of Victorian domesticity. In nineteenth-century marriage, two became one, and the one was *his* documentary record.[81]

EMERSON COULD NO MORE DIVERT GEORGE MOORE FROM THE UNITARIAN ministry than he could draw Martha Prescott from the Unitarian fold or extract John Shepard Keyes from his hectic social round. The lecturer spoke to recurring themes in their experience: disquiet at the practices of commerce; disdain for the dictates of fashion and the conventions of the parlor; appreciation of nature; yearning for an authentic life of the spirit; determination to forge independent paths for themselves. But on one crucial matter, they resisted the Transcendentalist. "According to the spirit of the Christian religion," Hersey Goodwin instructed the Unitarian congregation in April 1836, "no man may live for himself alone." Martha Prescott recorded those words in an epitome of the ancient social ethic of New England dating back to John Winthrop's "Model of Christian Charity." They were the staple of the Concord pulpit. The message still spoke to the rising generation, even as the young pressed for greater autonomy and choice. Emerson's call for self-reliance helped identify the numerous obstacles in the way of the individual. But it offered little guidance on the ties that bound, the satisfactions and support to be enjoyed with others, and the enduring power of community in human lives.[82]

Only one native son of Concord fully appreciated Emerson's ideal of the soul. Coming of age with Keyes, Moore, and Prescott, he took Transcendentalism more seriously, enacted its logic more rigorously, and gave literary expression to its vision more powerfully than even the lecturer himself. Henry David Thoreau marched to a different drummer from his contemporaries. But he too traced a route through the familiar village scenes and the well-known streets of Boston and Cambridge.

The Man of Concord

No young man appeared more promising to Emerson than Henry Thoreau. Even before they became acquainted, the youth had caught his notice, and the Harvard alumnus went out of his way to promote the undergraduate's cause, even interceding with President Quincy to secure a cash award for the college senior in recognition of his academic merit. About the same time, the restless student, who spent many hours in his Cambridge dormitory daydreaming about the woods and rivers of Concord, discovered his townsman's book, *Nature*, and recognized a kindred spirit. It would have made a fitting start to their connection had they first met at Harvard's 1837 commencement, when Thoreau spoke at his graduation ceremony and Emerson delivered the Phi Beta Kappa address the next day. But they never crossed paths there. The friendship developed later back in Concord, where Emerson welcomed the young man into his home, hiked with him to Walden, and delighted in the intellectual irreverence of "my good Henry Thoreau." "Every thing that boy says makes merry with society," judged the erstwhile clergyman, "though nothing could be graver than his meaning." Thoreau astounded with original insights and fresh turns of phrase that paid no heed to the cant of polite society. His was "as free & erect a mind as any" Emerson had ever encountered. Who better to represent his native land? "When Mr. Carlyle comes to America," the proud citizen anticipated, "I expect to introduce Thoreau to him as *the* man of Concord."[1]

Such admiration would have surprised Thoreau's contemporaries, many of whom considered his gregarious, fun-loving brother John to be "the star of the family." Three years junior, Henry was as withdrawn as John was outgoing. The older boy was a natural athlete, bursting with high spirits; when he was not exciting his classmates with such feats as jumping somersaults and walking on his hands, he was entertaining them with anecdotes that made their "sides ache with laughter" and their "eyes flood with tears." The younger, by contrast, declined to join in the play. Content to stand on the sidelines and watch, he aroused resentment with his seeming "indifference." He was mocked as an "old maid" and bombarded with snowballs. Yet nobody could deny his intellectual superiority. When the short, "fine scholar with a big nose"—as "curved" as a parrot's beak—rose to recite, recalled one classmate a half-century later, he displayed "a better understanding . . . of the books at twelve than most of the class at sixteen." It was the same story at Harvard College. His classmates found him "cold and unimpressible" and made him the "butt for jokes." Even his handshake, "moist and indifferent," was objectionable. But when he cared to compete for honors, he excelled, and he gathered a small circle of friends, who penetrated his mien of "mystic egotism."

He returned to Concord after graduation and, with only a brief interruption, stayed for good. Yet after a few years, he was largely disengaged from the commitments of his neighbors, who still could not abide his idiosyncrasies. How dare he pass acquaintances in the village without saying "Hello"! By what right did he presume to change the name he was given at birth? "His name ain't no more Henry D. Thoreau than my name is Henry D. Thoreau," one man said in disgust. "And everybody knows it, and he knows it. His name's Da-a-vid Henry and it ain't never been nothing but Da-a-vid Henry. And he knows it!" One thing he knew for sure was the low regard in which he was held. "There is some advantage in being the humblest cheapest least dignified man in the village," he would say in 1851, "so that the very stable boys shall damn you. Methinks I enjoy that advantage to an unusual extent."[2]

For all his difficulties with the neighbors, Thoreau was inextricably bound to them by a thousand imperceptible ties. He was as characteristic of the town as wild grapes, rye-and-injun, and English hay. Far from being indifferent to his townsmen, he was observing them closely and taking the measure of their way of life. Raised in a family at the heart of the village, he grew up in a community undergoing rapid change, and from his perch in the family's succession of homes in the center and its involvement in local life, he had a front seat at Concord's "age of Revolution." If he was typically in dissent from the hectic striving of the townspeople, he shared their zeal for improvement and surpassed their quest for knowledge. No one outdid this lover of solitude in going his own way except for a few alienated old-timers like George Minott, and his declaration of independence had a modern philosophical rationale akin to Emerson's. An exacting critic of the community, he gauged its dominant currents even when he sailed against the winds. Through such immersion, the only native son among the famous Concord writers became the town's representative man.

"I HAVE NEVER GOT OVER BEING A BOY": GEORGE FRISBIE HOAR'S SUNNY remembrance of his childhood in Concord could have been his older companion Thoreau's as well. Residing in the town center, the pencil maker's son grew up in the mainstream of local life. The busy shops and stores, hotels and taverns of a thriving business district were close at hand, while only a few minutes away, beyond the milldam and the town common, the woods and rivers invited exploration. John and Cynthia Thoreau cultivated a love of nature in their young. The family's initial trip to Walden in 1822 was followed by many return visits; the future writer took pride at age seven in helping to boil a kettle of chowder on a sandbar at the pond and stored the memory for later use. Once they were old enough to be on their own, the boys ranged freely across the landscape. Henry might have shunned schoolyard games, but he was always ready to join his brother and pals on forays to Walden, Fairhaven Cliffs, Egg Rock, and other favored sites. He acquired a knowledge of the landscape—with "the best places to find huckleberries and blackberries and chestnuts and lilies and cardinal and other rare flowers"—that dazzled Frisbie Hoar. The Thoreau children were also exposed to agricultural pursuits. Each had a little garden to tend; the younger son drove the family cow to pasture—presumably one unlike the ill-tempered beast that kicked his father in "the muns" and broke his nose. So familiar did the budding naturalist become with the local surroundings that Sarah Sherman Hoar, the squire's wife (and Frisbie's mother), quipped that "Henry talks about Nature just as if she'd been born and brought up in Concord."[3]

The social world of the Thoreau sons was as varied as their physical environment. It was a mixed lot in attendance at the brick grammar school, and among their closest friends were the Hosmer brothers, Joe and Ben, scions of an old Concord family fallen on hard times. Their father was a landless laborer all his life. The boys didn't care. When the Hosmers arrived, John and Henry would race into the house, "slamming the doors, or leaving them open," in haste to pack lunch and be off for the day. The Hosmer clan had slipped a lot farther down the social ladder than the Thoreaus. The pencil maker and his wife were determined to recover the wealth and status their parents had once enjoyed, and to this end they staked out a place on the Main Street, albeit a rented one, where they could socialize with such notable neighbors as the Hoar family and Nathan and Mary Brooks. A village residence allowed easy access to the library and the lyceum and to Sunday worship at the First Parish meetinghouse.

Like many middle-class families then and now, John and Cynthia Thoreau pitched their hopes and ambitions on their children and sacrificed for their education at the uninspiring Phineas Allen's academy, where Henry learned just enough to scrape by the entrance examinations into Harvard College. (Had he failed "one branch more," President Quincy informed the incoming freshman, "you had been turned by entirely. You have barely got in.") Whatever the defects of this education, the Thoreaus obtained the necessary training to preside over classrooms of their own. Teaching was the profession of last resort; it had been a refuge for John Thoreau after his business ventures failed, and it would be a source of support for all his children in turn. The academy also conferred social credentials. Parting ways with the laboring class at the brick grammar school, the rising generation of the Thoreau family cast its lot with the educated elite.[4]

Cynthia Thoreau took inordinate pride in her children. To anyone who cared to listen, along with those who did not, the talkative mother boasted about their accomplishments, especially those of "my David Henry." She boosted his prospects with more than words. While her quiet husband attended to the pencil shop, she took in boarders and helped pay for her children's schooling. The practice was common in Concord; even John Keyes opened his house to boys from the out-districts, who needed a place to stay while attending the winter session of the village grammar school. The burden of these lodgers fell on women, adding to the work of cooking and serving, washing and cleaning that constituted the domestic duties of a housekeeper. Cynthia Thoreau was accustomed to the role. In 1798, when she was a girl of twelve, her widowed mother had made ends meet by keeping a boardinghouse in Boston. A quarter-century later the pencil maker's wife converted her labors at home into a paying proposition. The table she furnished earned tributes to its "abundance of fruit and vegetables, puddings and pies, and . . . delicious brown and white bread. There was an absence of heat, noise, fat greasy meat, of everything unpleasant." The boarders contributed more than money. Among the lodgers were the Trinitarian pastor Southmayd and his bride; Emerson's sister-in-law Lucy Jackson Brown, who may have been the first to inform him about her landlady's talented son at

Harvard; and a variety of visiting lecturers and reformers. A few long-term residents, such as the widow Prudence Bird Ward and her maiden daughter, also named Prudence, became close family friends. Enlivening the conversations at the Thoreau dining table, the boarders carried the wider world into the home. The passing parade expanded the future writer's view of American life.[5]

Caught up in making and selling pencils and shy by nature, John Thoreau had little time for civic affairs. His brash wife, half a head taller than her husband, and his maiden sisters represented the family in the public sphere. Eliza, Jane, and Maria Thoreau were among the "little band" of dissenters who split off from the First Parish in the fall of 1825 and founded the Trinitarian congregation nine months later. Drawn to the intense spirituality of the new religious body, Cynthia Thoreau vacillated over doubts about Calvinist orthodoxy and ultimately stuck with Doctor Ripley's church, where she had been a member since 1811. Her siblings and in-laws took the opposite side in the sectarian divide. Discussions of faith must have been at times a topic of intense conversation in the family parlor.[6]

Cynthia Thoreau also contributed her time and talents to others. In September 1825, two and a half years after returning to town, she joined the Concord Female Charitable Society and entered its leadership as one of nine "managers," serving four annual terms over the next decade. Founded in 1814, the group was the first voluntary association of women in town and just the tenth such organization in the Commonwealth.[7] Established for the purposes of "relieving distress, encouraging industry, and promoting virtue and happiness among the female part of the community," it was a bold and innovative bid by women to step outside the traditional domain of the home and act independently to address social problems. In keeping with Ezra Ripley's ethic of interdependence, the founders affirmed that it is "the duty of every one, as far as in his [sic] power, to relieve the wants of the indigent and distressed." This obligation entailed more than doling out food and clothing to penurious women. It directed particular attention to needy children— understandably so, since the majority of members were middle-aged mothers themselves.[8] Unlike their own offspring, the sons and daughters of the poor often went without necessary "instruction in religion and morality" for lack of "decent" clothing to wear to school or to Sunday meeting. Rather than suffer the ridicule of peers on account of their shabby dress, these little boys and girls chose to stay home—or were made to do so by protective parents.

The charitable society aimed to eliminate this obstacle. It would supply the material means to a moral and religious end.[9]

By 1825, when Cynthia Thoreau paid her one-dollar annual dues, the charitable society was in its second decade and as active as ever. Once a month the managers gathered in one another's homes to discuss the cases of need, and as they deliberated, they took up needle, yarn, cloth, and thread and labored together to knit stockings and caps, sew shirts, and make bed quilts. (All that talk prompted a local wag to dub the group "the chattable society"—a sexist pun that Henry Thoreau relished.) The handiwork went to clothe "suffering fellow creatures," as did donations to an open "sack" into which members could deposit old clothes for recycling to the poor. The meetings thus perpetuated cooperative labor at a time when men were abandoning such practices on the farm. But as the industrial revolution accelerated, the charitable ladies adapted and began buying factory-made goods for direct distribution to those in need. In keeping with the larger capitalist transformation of the economy, the group shifted from giving charity in kind to dispensing charity in cash.

The charitable society also moved beyond the limited goal of outfitting ragamuffins in respectable clothes. It hired a woman to keep a "dame school" for children unable to afford a private instructor. This charge became the society's single largest expense, for which the ladies raised funds not only by collecting donations but also by lending out money at interest to local businessmen. Conducting all these operations—ordering supplies, negotiating loans, hiring teachers, interviewing candidates for relief, balancing the books, composing and presenting semiannual reports—took charitable women out of the house and exposed them to the imperatives of conducting a business. As a manager of the society, Cynthia Thoreau built on the practical experience of running a boardinghouse. The society schooled its members in the ways of the world.[10]

The generosity was circumscribed. Although it was inspired by examples elsewhere, the charitable society followed the maxim that "charity begins at home." In some communities, such as Andover and Williamstown, women dedicated funds for the support of Protestant missionaries to "the destitute" on the nation's borders and to "the heathen" in other lands. Not so in Concord, where assistance was bestowed on deserving neighbors. Those who gave and those who received were personally known to one another.[11] In any given year, two dozen or more individuals got help, with married women the main beneficiaries, followed by children and widows. Local African Americans—the Dugan,

Garrison, and Robbins families, among others—struggling to keep their fragile foothold in town, were regular recipients, but so too were aged whites down on their luck, like the spinster sisters Nabby and Sally Brown, eking out existence on the run-down farm of their late father David, who had commanded a company of Minutemen at the North Bridge. In reaching out to these fellow inhabitants in distress, Cynthia Thoreau and her colleagues personally crossed the gaps of race and class that increasingly distanced the townspeople from one another. However top-down and paternalistic its ethos, the charitable society resisted the trend of the times and strove to sustain the traditional ideal of an interdependent community.[12]

Whatever it did for the poor, the society rewarded benevolence. Cynthia Thoreau had good reasons to join. She knew what it was like to suffer a reversal of fortune and to need a helping hand—the unhappy fate of her mother following Jonas Minot's death.[13] In like manner, the charitable society functioned as a mutual insurance policy for members in case they ever endured hardship. It enlisted women of every rank and order, from Daniel Shattuck's spouse Sarah all the way down to Miss Mary Minott, the hardworking tailoress clinging to threadbare gentility. The leadership came chiefly from the elite. In 1825, when Cynthia Thoreau assumed her duties, over half of the officers—president, vice-president, secretary, treasurer, and nine managers—were married to members of the Social Circle. While John Thoreau was never invited into the exclusive coterie of Concord's businessmen, politicians, and professionals, his socially ambitious spouse entered the genteel company of their wives. Participation in the charitable society made for upward mobility and helped to raise the Thoreau family's status in the town.[14]

Henry Thoreau was a bit of a charity case himself when he (age sixteen) matriculated at Harvard College on August 30, 1833. It cost $200 a year for tuition, room and board, and other expenses at the Cambridge school, and to cover the bills, his mother contributed savings from the boardinghouse and his sister Helen's earnings from teaching. The family economized by forgoing tea, coffee, sugar, and other "luxuries" and by moving in with the aunts to save on rent. Additional funds derived from the undergraduate's own efforts. Each year he received twenty-five dollars from a trust established on behalf of worthy students of limited means. The money came from the rents on real estate in the town of Chelsea, which Thoreau had to collect by taking a ferry across the Mystic River and calling personally on the tenants. He also won cash prizes for his academic performance, and in his junior year he took advantage of a Harvard policy that granted leaves of absence to students wishing to earn money by teaching school. By all these means, he paid the bills, but as "a scholarship boy" at a college where the sons of Boston's elite set the tone, he surely obtained lessons in social class as well as in the classics.[15]

In 1833 the incoming freshman from Concord was a loyal son of his family and town. He followed his father in politics and supported the anti-Jackson Whigs. But if he was a partisan in any cause, it was that of his birthplace. He wore pride in its Revolutionary heritage like a badge of honor, boasting of his origin in "Concord North Bridge." His "Concord self conceit" was a standing joke among his classmates, and after four years of college, it blazed more intensely than ever. "If I forget thee, O Concord," he pledged in mock-serious allusion to Psalm 137, "let my right hand forget her cunning." On the Fourth of July 1837 he joined the chorus that sang Emerson's "Concord Hymn" at the dedication of the battlefield monument.[16]

For most of his undergraduate career, Thoreau showed no signs of a desire to question authority. Like George Moore, he steered clear of the student rebellion that disrupted the campus during the spring of his freshman year, and he belonged to the well-behaved minority of the Class of 1837—just nineteen out of sixty-three members—who never got in trouble for breaking the rules.[17] The Harvard curriculum was designed to train an intellectual elite capable of guiding the American republic, and to judge by the compositions he submitted to his English professor, Edward Tyrrel Channing, Thoreau went along with that agenda until nearly the end of his studies. Channing was an arch-conservative with a deep distrust of democracy. His assignments obliged students to think within his tight intellectual framework. The youth from Concord complied in essays that disdained the pursuit of money and power as life goals. "He is a true patriot," Thoreau maintained in his sophomore year, who "[casts] aside all selfish thoughts" and labors selflessly for the public good. To fulfill that mission, he elaborated the next month, took mental independence and moral strength. "The majority of mankind are too easily induced to follow any course which accords with the opinion of the world." By deferring to friends or giving way to "the tide of Popular feeling," they risked becoming "all things to all men" and "mere tools in the hands of others." The nonconformist was forming the rationale for going his own way. But he had yet to question "the organic interdependence of men in society," the governing idea behind the Harvard curriculum, or to put in writing his reaction to Channing's warning against isolation from others. Beware the temptation to withdraw from your fellows in search of truth, urged the professor. That way lay the intellectual cul-de-sac of the hermit, "forever . . . musing upon himself, revolving a few favorite opinions, and buried in speculations all of one character."[18]

The break with orthodoxy began when Thoreau took time off from his studies to teach in the town of Canton, fifteen miles southwest of Boston. There for six weeks, from December 1835 to mid-January 1836, the visiting schoolmaster discharged his duties, while boarding in the household of the Unitarian minister Orestes Brownson, then gaining notice as a leader of the fledgling Transcendentalist movement. The two men studied German together and talked into the nights about the exhilarating "new views" of Christianity and society that Brownson was introducing not only to elite readers of the *Christian Examiner* but to the common people of his vicinity. A self-educated son of the laboring class, the pastor infused his Transcendentalist outlook with a social awareness that appealed to the "charity scholar" from Concord. The message was compelling. "We have equality in scarcely any sense worth naming," Brownson had declared in a controversial Fourth of July speech in 1834. "Will you say that we are equal while all our higher seminaries of learning are virtually closed to all except the rich? Equal while we have those who are born with the right to live in luxury and idleness, while there are others who are born with only the right to starve if they do not work?" Let nothing stand in the way of "human improvement" and the "indefinite perfectibility" of every soul. Here was a chanticleer to wake Thoreau up. The sojourn in Canton, he later told Brownson, was "an era in my life," inaugurating a moral and intellectual rebirth.[19]

The junior returned to Cambridge with an appetite for the avant-garde and a reading list of European Romantics, which he devoured with enthusiasm, even as he did his coursework with diminishing interest in the academic competition for points and prizes. By his final term, he was taking Channing's prompts for essays and turning them to his own ends, as he worked out an increasingly critical stance on contemporary society. Called on to appraise "methods of gaining or exercising public Influence," Thoreau compared the pulpit unfavorably to the press. The youth who had grown up under Ezra Ripley's watch presented a vivid portrait of a country parson as the undisputed monarch of a petty domain. "His parish is his kingdom, where he rules with an almost despotic sway; the young, even from the cradle, are taught to value his approving smile, and tremble at his frown," while their elders listen respectfully to his teachings. But the minister is a minor figure on the Massachusetts map, his reach "comparatively narrow and circumscribed." By contrast, the press addresses a "mass" of strangers; its "field of labor is the universe." Its value is vitiated, in turn, by ill-conceived editorials and excessive partisanship. What path, then, to "public influence"? The aspiring author came to no conclusion. But he was not headed for the ministry.[20]

Thoreau was gravitating toward Transcendentalism and reshaping his sense of self. The second term of his senior year coincided with Emerson's lecture series "The Philosophy of Modern History," but there is no evidence that Thoreau crossed the Charles to join the audience at the Masonic Temple. (He had not yet begun to keep a diary.) Obliged to make up for time lost during his stint in Canton and a subsequent sick leave at home the following spring, he piled up courses to accumulate credits and likely could not afford to spend the evenings in Boston. In April 1837 he borrowed Emerson's *Nature* from the library and renewed it two months later; he also bought a copy as a farewell gift to a classmate. The impact was immediate. His final compositions invoked "the religious sentiment" as the key to "moral excellence," and he set that intuitive sense of divinity against the conventional practice of the churches, which served to "contract" people's views and make them "illiberal." A week later, asked to discuss "the mark or standard by which a nation is judged to be barbarous or civilized," he argued, in the spirit of Emerson, that "the end of life is education." Did it foster "the religious sentiment" and "continually . . . remind man of his mysterious relation to God and Nature, and exalt him above the toil and drudgery of this matter-of-fact world?" For Thoreau, the answer was obvious. Nature was superior to civilization. "The civilized man is the slave of matter. Art paves the earth, lest he may soil the soles of his feet; it builds walls, that he may not see the heavens; year in, year out, the sun rises in vain to him." The so-called savage enjoyed the better deal; his life was "practical poetry—a perfect epic . . . —the sun is his time-piece, he journeys to its rising or its setting." So what if he was bereft of books and libraries! "A nation may be ever so civilized and yet lack wisdom."[21]

As Thoreau planted his standard in nature, he began to carve out a new identity as a Romantic individualist, at odds with the mainstream. His nonconformity grew more strident, at least on paper: "the fear of displeasing the world ought not, in the least, to influence my actions," he vowed. This defiant stance shaped his brief autobiography in the Class of 1837 yearbook. The piece traced his descent from French Protestants who fled the oppression of Louis XIV for religious freedom on the Isle of Jersey, and from that sturdy stock came his grandfather Jean, arriving in Massachusetts just in time "to take an active part in the Revolution, as a sailor before the mast." In this telling, the Loyalist relatives on his mother's side were forgotten, despite their refusal to bow to the Patriot mob. Better to move on to his birth in "Concord North Bridge": "may she never have cause to be ashamed of her sons." Thoreau thus claimed a heritage of freedom, and his self-image was as a protester for principle.[22]

He gave public voice to this new sensibility at the Harvard commencement. Ranking in the top half of his class, he was awarded a speaking part in the ceremony. The assignment was to participate with two classmates in a "conference" on "the commercial spirit of modern times" and its "influence" on the "Political, Moral, and Literary Character of a Nation." To each speaker went one aspect of the subject; fittingly, the Concordian got the "moral" dimension. The topic invited close scrutiny of personal sins and social evils, but Thoreau resisted the temptation to itemize the flaws of his countrymen. Instead, he stepped back and set the "commercial spirit" in the wider context of the times.

The dominant feature of the epoch, he declared, was "a perfect freedom— freedom of thought and action," which expressed itself, first and foremost, in the pursuit of economic gain. To this end, "man thinks faster and freer than ever before," remaking the world to serve his will. If only the goals were as worthy as the means! But no, Thoreau noted ruefully, the American aimed too low; his "ruling principle" was "a blind and unmanly love of wealth." Selfishness infected "our patriotism," "our domestic relations," even "our religion." Were "buying and selling, money-changing and speech-making" the best uses of our "entire and universal freedom"?

Imagining himself in "an observatory among the stars," Thoreau viewed "this beehive of ours" from the heavens. In this lofty perspective, nature beckoned "more to be admired and enjoyed" than to be "used." "This curious world which we inhabit is more wonderful than it is convenient, more beautiful than it is useful," he declared in language reminiscent of Emerson's *Nature*. Thoreau doubted that morals necessarily advanced with commerce. But he held out the promise of progress. Even as Americans threw their energies into the quest for wealth, they were unconsciously preparing themselves for a higher destiny. Eventually, he predicted, they would see that spirit is superior to matter, that material goods are meant to serve moral and intellectual growth, that individuals are not to be tools of their tools but "Lords of Creation." From the standpoint of nature, it was the human spirit, not the "commercial spirit," that counted.[23]

Thoreau took for granted "perfect freedom" as the hallmark of the age. He had grown up among townspeople casting off the hold of custom and constraint and opting to choose their own ways. Little did he appreciate the interior struggle so many experienced between the old and the new. But he would soon discover the clash between his ideas and his neighbors'. Packing up his belongings, he skipped Emerson's Phi Beta Kappa address and returned home.[24]

EIGHTEEN THIRTY-SEVEN WAS NOT A GOOD YEAR TO GRADUATE FROM COL-lege. Following the financial panic that spring, banks contracted credit and the economy shrank. By October, the Concord Bank had reduced its lending by more than $20,000, on a downward course to a four-year low six months later. By this "careful business," the institution remained solvent, never missing a semiannual dividend of 3 percent, but the cost was paid in "general distress in the community."

Members of the Harvard Class of 1837 faced a shortage of opportunities to employ their education. But Henry Thoreau had no reason to complain. A week after commencement, he became master of the brick grammar school on the common—yet another in a long line of recent Harvard graduates to rotate through that post. The salary was $500 for the year, a substantial and steady income at a time when many Americans were out of work. A decade earlier Edward Jarvis had faced opposition to his appointment to the school, owing to doubts that he could ever command the respect of students who had known him as a boy. Thoreau, who had studied under Jarvis in this very school, met with no such objection. The twenty-year-old's ability to maintain discipline went unquestioned.[25]

The new master looked forward to running his school on an innovative plan. He hoped to eliminate corporal punishment entirely and to "make educa-tion a pleasant thing both to the teacher and the scholar." That intention was in tune with the prevailing mood. Progressives dominated the school commit-tee. Once a fifteen-man body representing seven districts, it had recently been streamlined to facilitate centralized management.[26] The board that oversaw the hiring of Thoreau consisted of just three members: Rev. Barzillai Frost, then in his first year as Ezra Ripley's assistant, as chair; the trader Nehemiah Ball, a deacon of the Unitarian church; and Sherman Barrett, scion of the distinguished farming family. Ball was charged with overseeing the grammar school. This reform-minded group, elected in April 1837, presided over the biggest school budget ever: an appropriation of $2,000, up by 25 percent. Its outlook was entirely in line with the policies promoted by Horace Mann, appointed that very year as secretary of the newly established state board of education. Indeed, in 1838 Concord would bid unsuccessfully to be the home of the first "normal" school in Massachusetts for training teachers. Thoreau had good grounds for anticipating approval of his educational experiment.[27]

Ten days into the term, Deacon Ball made a surprise visit to Thoreau's classroom to see how the new master was working out.[28] It was his obligation to do so under the committee's rules, and as he entered his sixth year of service on the board, he enjoyed a reputation for being "very punctual in visiting the schools." He cared deeply about education, as his frequent lectures to the lyceum made plain, and he "spared nothing" in the schooling of his own eight children. In the fall of 1837, four of them, from Caroline, age thirteen, down to Ephraim, age eight, were among the ninety pupils in Thoreau's charge. The deacon thus had a strong personal as well as official interest in the pedagogical abilities of the novice teacher. "Precise, prosy, and pompous," he also had great confidence in his own judgment. Many years earlier the middle-aged leather dealer had kept a district school, and on that basis he presumed to know something about managing the young.

The pupils in the grammar school were apparently too noisy or unruly to suit Ball, as he hastened to inform the instructor. In his opinion, Thoreau needed to crack down right away on the disobedient and disruptive. Otherwise, "the school [would] spoil" entirely. The advice was unwelcome. But instead of protesting or ignoring the officious counsel, Thoreau seethed silently. That afternoon, after the committeeman was gone, he did as he was told. At least two students and perhaps half a dozen, including a thirteen-year-old girl working as a maid in his parents' home, suffered the sting of the ferule. The reluctant disciplinarian felt a different kind of pain. Applying the rod in violation of his beliefs, he did violence to his conscience, and that was intolerable. Hours later Thoreau sought out the deacon and resigned.[29]

It was a bold stand in defense of his principles, the first of many to come. It was also a risky step in the midst of a deepening depression, comparable in its imprudence to his father's opening a store amid an embargo on trade. Was it necessary? School reformers in Concord and beyond were anxious to reduce, if not entirely eliminate, the use of corporal punishment. Horace Mann himself was urging teachers to "supersede the necessity of violence by moral means" and to rely upon "the power of conscience and the love of knowledge" to ensure discipline. But the uncompromising instructor said nothing. Uncomfortable with the committee's oversight and doubtful that he could ever keep it happy, he preferred to follow his own conscience. Consistent with his college essays, this would be his characteristic gesture in the ensuing years.[30]

In his parents' latest residence on the Main Street, the so-called Parkman House, the unemployed schoolmaster took refuge in his "upper empire"—the third-floor attic—and regrouped. With older siblings Helen and John away teaching, he was left to cope with his situation largely by himself. His immediate prospects were thin, since the school year had already begun. To keep busy and pay his board, he put his hands and mind to work in the pencil factory and devised a superior product. By year's end, he renewed the search for employment, seeking help from classmates, relatives, and mentors, including Orestes Brownson. His reputation remained solid; leading figures in Concord—the esquires Brooks, Hoar, and Keyes—were still prepared to vouch for him, and Ezra Ripley recommended him as "well disposed and well qualified to instruct the rising generation." In principle, he was open to relocating far from Concord. He scouted out positions in different parts of the country, from Maine to New York State to Virginia. In mid-March 1838 he and brother John decided to head for Louisville, Kentucky, twelve hundred miles southwest, where teaching jobs supposedly abounded, according to Concord transplant Edward Jarvis, who had settled there eleven months earlier. "Go *I* must at all events," Henry vowed. The event never came. He reversed course after Harvard president Quincy put him on to an opening in Alexandria, the Potomac River town bordering the nation's capital. He did not get an offer, but in all likelihood he did not want one. Thoreau was as reluctant as John Shepard Keyes to leave home. Rather than move, he opened a school in the Parkman House and attracted a handful of "well advanced" student boarders.[31]

The more Thoreau clung to his roots, the deeper his discontent. Stuck in his birthplace, he watched the world go by at an ever-quickening pace. Let steamships speed across the Atlantic, let Nantucket whalers go "afishing" the seas, let Yankees scour the earth in search of new "fields for speculation." Thoreau stayed put in his native soil, like the "plants [that] spring silently by the brook sides," and as "indifferent" to human affairs as the woods. Not entirely: in his debut before the lyceum that April, he decried the artificiality of society. Even in the small town of Concord, men and women did not meet "as gods." They kept one another at a distance with "excessive ceremony" and much "shaking of hands and rubbing of noses." The situation was even worse when people congregated in cities or gathered in crowds. In large assemblies—parades and rallies, commencements and cattle shows—men were absorbed into the mass, "another name for the mob," and were reduced to the lowest level. Individuality dissolved. Thoreau yearned for authentic contact, what he would call in *Walden* "simple and sincere" communication. But to whom could he reveal himself in this superficial, workaday world?[32]

Emerson, for one. The friendship between the two congenial spirits began in the fall of 1837 and deepened during their walks to Walden over the next year. At Emerson's suggestion, the graduate started keeping a journal, initially as a commonplace book in which to store extracts from his reading and observations about various subjects, later as a "literary workbook" containing drafts of future lectures and publications. The influence was reciprocal. In the older man's lectures, the younger heard his own thoughts about nature and culture; in turn, he provided a living demonstration of Transcendentalist self-reliance. Emerson admired "brave Henry" for his refusal to conform to conventional ways: "he does not postpone his life, but lives already." He welcomed "my protestor" into the Transcendental Club and never lost an opportunity to promote his protégé. The support was at once valuable and restricting.

Hardly had this close association formed than Thoreau was mocked for copying his master's voice and looks. On a visit to Concord in the spring of 1838, David Greene Haskins was astonished by the transformation of his Harvard classmate in the months since graduation: "In his manners, in the tones and inflections of his voice, in his modes of expression, even in the hesitations and pauses of his speech, he had become the counterpart of Mr. Emerson." Haskins closed his eyes while the two Concordians talked and could not tell "with certainty" who was speaking. The future poet James Russell Lowell, rusticated from Harvard under Barzillai Frost's care that summer, had the same impression: "with my eyes shut I shouldn't kn[ow] them apart." In later years he would deride Thoreau in print as an Emerson wannabe, stealing the apples from his neighbor's orchard. So long as the two writers remained close, Thoreau would struggle to separate inspiration from imitation.[33]

In September 1838 Thoreau got a second chance to prove his talents as an educator when a vacancy opened up at the Concord Academy. The private school had lost its hard-won stability with Phineas Allen's enlistment in Anti-Masonry and had run through four instructors in as many years. For a time it suspended operations.[34] The new instructor, now an adult of twenty-one, embarked on his duties with a blank slate. Here was the chance to create the ideal school he had dreamed of, where the love of learning, rather than fear of "the cowhide," made each day a joy. On the principles of Pestalozzi, the teacher was to be a "fellow-student" with the pupils; together they would share the excitement of discovery not just in books but in the wider world, making weekly field trips to village craft shops to see how things were made and expeditions to Sleepy Hollow, Walden, and along the Concord River for lessons in natural history. The town school could not compete, even with progressive texts. Its enrollment was too big, its confinement to the brick structure on the common too narrow. Most important, it lacked the prerequisite of Thoreau's scheme: "a degree of freedom which rarely exists . . . —a freedom proportionate to the dignity of [the child's] nature—a freedom that shall make him feel that he is a man among men, and responsible only to that Reason of which he is a particle, for his thoughts and actions."[35]

This Transcendentalist experiment in education gradually gained enough students that John Thoreau, Jr., was able to join Henry when a new term opened in March 1839. The older brother took charge of the "English branches," the younger the "classical department." Support for the enterprise cut a broad swath through the town. The elite put its confidence in the Thoreau boys; so did Cynthia's co-workers in the female charitable society. A number of students came from middling farms and shops in Concord and vicinity. A few had to scrape together the tuition, including Ben and Joe Hosmer's younger brother Horace and the eldest daughter, Anna, of Bronson and Abigail Alcott, new to town in April 1840. Nearly all their families were active in the campaign for cultural improvement.[36]

This mix of young people gained an unusual education for the day. Within the school, John won their hearts with his wit and warmth, Henry their respect and resentment for being "merciless" and "rigidly exacting." In the woods and along the river, each of the instructors had his following. Joseph Boyden Keyes, the politician's son, spoke for most in recalling John as "one of the most kind and indulgent masters," who "rendered the road to learning easy and pleasant." The skilled naturalist delighted in pointing out the various birds and occasionally shooting them to obtain specimens for study. Keyes was forever grateful for the exposure to "the beauties of nature." For his part, Henry dazzled with his uncanny ability to find Indian relics and his vast knowledge of ornithology. "He knew birds and beasts as one boy knows another," recalled Frisbie Hoar. For student Horace Hosmer, who came from a dirt-poor farm to attend the school and board in the Parkman House, the entire Thoreau family was an education. In the parents' love of nature and art and in their shared ideals, he glimpsed a vision of a higher, purer life. John Jr. embodied that spirit: he made "all things [seem] possible[,] in school life at least." To ten-year-old Hosmer, Henry, by comparison, was a forbidding figure, though he would later come to view him as "the realization of the hopes and aspirations of the Thoreau family."[37]

The success of the school drew Thoreau more deeply into local life. Overcoming his distaste for the formalities of society, he frequented parties, participated in the rituals of courtship, served two terms as secretary of the lyceum, and tried his hand at journalism with an obituary of Miss Anna Jones, an eighty-six-year-old pauper who had died in the almshouse. Thoreau sought out the aged woman as she lay dying and was impressed by "the religious sentiment that was strongly developed in her." This "bright sample of the Revolutionary woman" stirred his reverence for the "days which the man and patriot would not willingly forget." Like Thoreau's maternal grandmother, Jones actually came of a family with divided loyalties in the War of Independence. Uninformed by this history, Thoreau's tribute was an implicit rebuke of his neighbors for allowing so pious and virtuous a woman to spend her last days alone in the poorhouse: "Poverty was her lot," he wrote, "but she possessed those virtues without which the rich are but poor." Appearing anonymously, the piece attested to Thoreau's engagement with his countrymen in the aftermath of graduation and during the two and a half years that he and John conducted their academy—a venture that came to an end in April 1841, owing to the older brother's failing health. Thoreau once again faced a vocational choice.[38]

WHEN HENRY THOREAU WENT OFF TO COLLEGE AT THE END OF AUGUST 1833, Anti-Masonry was on the rise in Concord, shattering the long political calm with the insurgency against "King John" Keyes and his National Republican friends. By the time the graduate returned exactly four years later, partisan battles were the norm in the ferocious contest between Democrats and Whigs

that ousted Keyes from his several seats of power and installed antiestablish-
ment populists in the local majority. The fierce competition transformed the
conduct of politics, as the rivals threw themselves into mobilizing the grass
roots with popular conventions, massive rallies and parades, a blizzard of
newspapers and broadsides, and intense get-out-the-vote efforts on Election
Day. Turnout surged to unprecedented heights, with nearly every man in town
casting a ballot. For a time, politics became all-absorbing, not just a fight over
candidates and issues but also a fund of entertainment, a form of civic participation, and an affirmation of social identity. Thoreau got home just in time to
witness the integration of "Concord North Bridge" into the mass democracy
of the era. Reaching voting age during this critical passage of the republic, he
had little sympathy with the new politics and was never at a loss to indict its
selfishness and corruption and its betrayal of America's promise.

The unemployed schoolmaster was still too young to vote in November
1837, when partisan hostilities incited an angry showdown at town meeting.
Hardly had the opening prayer been offered and the warrant for the meeting
read aloud than John Keyes, "the most obnoxious man" of his party, rose to
electioneer on behalf of the Whig ticket. Such a "caucus speech" produced
immediate calls for order. Keyes plunged ahead, ignoring the moderator and
insisting that "he had been in town twenty years and had a right to speak."
The "King," who had been voted out of the treasurer's office just eight months
before, droned on, to growing restlessness in the room. Finally the Democratic leader Gourgas could bear "his insolence and abuse" no longer. At the
Freeman editor's direction, the Democrats en masse "hooted and hissed him
down." "It was the kind of treatment which he richly merited," Gourgas exclaimed. The Whig *Gazette* saw things differently. Gourgas and his flunkies, in
its telling, had acted without cause to shut down "free discussion." Instead of
treating his neighbors with respect, the Democrat had imitated his partisan
mentors in Boston and given lessons "in viper hissing . . . He was guilty of
conduct that would disgrace even the drunken brawlers in Boston with whom
he associates."[39]

Partisanship strained neighborly ties. Even in local elections, Democrats
urged supporters to ignore personal sentiments and vote the party line. A Whig
candidate "may be your townsman, and a very good, fair, clever sort of man,"
Gourgas once acknowledged; "he may be your father or your brother." But forget
these bonds; set aside those affections. Democrats must act for a higher good:

"When you vote, let it be not for men but for the cause, the principles you hold to be right." Whigs grudgingly followed suit. While their preference was to exempt town government from the relentless struggle for power, what alternative was there? "A disposition to conciliate" could prevail only "where it is honestly and frankly met by a corresponding disposition."[40]

The new ethos of party violated the convictions Thoreau had absorbed at Harvard. In Cambridge, he had professed an antipathy to Jacksonian democracy. His essays for Channing had paid tribute to the eighteenth-century ideal of the disinterested statesman, who deliberated rationally and acted impartially for the public good, with no thought of gain to himself.[41] Back in Concord, Thoreau watched as his townsmen rejected that vision. In the fall of 1838, the Whigs looked forward to taking back the congressional seat that Samuel Hoar had lost to William Parmenter two years earlier. Their candidate this time was the genial lawyer Nathan Brooks, the next-door neighbor and landlord of the Thoreau family in the Parkman House.[42] A former supporter of Jefferson and Madison, he carried none of the Federalist baggage that had weighed Hoar down. Brooks was "exemplary and estimable in private life," admitted opponents. But his personal qualities mattered less than his public views. The people demanded a representative whose opinions coincided with their own. The Whig candidate declined to meet that test. He aspired to be an independent and impartial leader or none at all. The contemporary of John Thoreau spoke the language of the pencil maker's younger son.

In the 1838 campaign, local abolitionists took the unusual step of quizzing the candidates about their views of the right of Congress to bar slavery in the nation's capital and the federal territories. During his one term in the House of Representatives, Samuel Hoar had defended the constitutionality of this exercise of congressional power.[43] Would not Brooks, whose wife Mary was already well known in antislavery circles, do the same? Surprisingly, the Whig candidate declined to answer on principle. His explanation was forthright. If he were to address the abolitionists' concerns and take a public stand, there would be no point in sending him to Washington. The duty of a representative was to deliberate with his colleagues, "to listen to every argument and fact that might bear upon [a] question," and to accept the most persuasive case. How could he do so if he pledged himself in advance to a specific position? Should he change his mind, his constituents would rightly feel betrayed; should he refuse to entertain the ideas of fellow legislators, he might as well stay home and communicate his thoughts by mail. Better to remain silent and keep an open mind. The Whig candidate affirmed his loyalty not to a party but to an ideal: the republican model of the disinterested representative, acting in concert with his colleagues to make laws for the public good.

Brooks earned no more credit for his reticence than for his amiability and integrity. It took four rounds of voting, extending from November 1838 to April 1839, before a winner was declared in the race to represent the fourth district of Massachusetts in the Twenty-sixth Congress. This was the most hotly contested seat in the Union, for which Brooks fought tenaciously, denying an absolute majority to his opponent three times in a row before conceding defeat. His admirable qualities proved insufficient to get him first past the post. It was the same story in 1840, when Brooks tried again and lost in a single vote. In 1842, when Samuel Hoar mounted a final challenge to Parmenter, the Whig did worse than ever. Time and again party lines held firm and determined the results.[44]

If Henry Thoreau had any reaction to these defeats, he left no record. His father was a stalwart of the party of Daniel Webster and Henry Clay. The son affected indifference to the sound and fury of the constant campaigns. In November 1837 Whigs celebrated their statewide victory with a hundred-gun salute; standing atop Punkatasset Hill, the schoolmaster heard the distant report from the village and dismissed it as "a puff of smoke" fading into the horizon. Thoreau's aloofness from current affairs frustrated correspondents, who pestered him to say "something of the Yeoman's Gazette[,] of the politics of the town and county, of the events, that are daily transpiring there"—to no avail. The schoolboy who had stayed on the sidelines while his classmates played was no more disposed as a young adult to join in the contests of his contemporaries.[45]

Thoreau did not just disdain the game of politics. He also had no interest in the economic policy debates that divided the major parties during the presidencies of Jackson and Van Buren. Northern Whigs were the party of big government, whose support of banks, tariffs, and internal improvements appealed strongly to the manufacturer John Thoreau and his fellow entrepreneurs in Concord village. The Thoreau firm depended on commercial credit, benefited from duties on imported pencils, and welcomed better access to markets. With good reason, the pencil maker was an "ardent Whig."[46] His college-educated son paid no mind to such mundane matters; he deemed himself superior to the pursuit of gain. But father and son, not to say the entire family, could rally with the Whigs in opposing the dispossession of the Cherokee Indians from their ancient homelands in Georgia and adjacent states and urging Congress to abolish slavery in the District of Columbia and the federal territories. Henry joined his parents and siblings in signing petitions to Congress for these ends. In his first years back in Concord, the idealistic schoolmaster was willing to participate in a political effort for a moral goal.[47]

Thoreau was not a lost cause for Democrats. The party championed principles with potential appeal to the young Transcendentalist. Its opposition to the Whigs' high-flying schemes was driven by a determination to keep government small and taxes low and to curb the influence of banks and corporations over public policy. This stance, dubbed "Loco Focoism"[48] by critics, advocated the economic interests of the small farmers, mechanics, and laborers composing the Jacksonian base in Concord and the Bay State. But it also upheld a positive vision of a society in which individuals could lead their own lives free from interference by the state. The outlook was succinctly summarized in the motto of the *United States Magazine, and Democratic Review*, launched in October 1837 with the backing of Van Buren: "the best government is that which governs least." The slogan caught Thoreau's notice; it would serve as the jumping-off point for his essay "Resistance to Civil Government" a dozen years later. (Thoreau would also become a contributor to the magazine.) In this statement, the recent graduate could read a commitment to the "perfect freedom" of the individual coincident with the view he had expressed at his Harvard commencement.

While the Whigs preferred wealthy, college-educated professionals as candidates for major offices, the Democrats were surprisingly successful in recruiting literary men and intellectuals to their cause. In Massachusetts, the Romantic historian George Bancroft, a Harvard graduate with a German doctorate, led the way into the party of the common man. In 1838, when Bancroft was named collector of the port of Boston, he used his patronage power to bring Orestes Brownson into the fold. With a sinecure on the federal payroll, the Transcendentalist thinker turned his new periodical, the *Boston Quarterly Review*, into an influential voice of Massachusetts Democracy. In its pages, Henry Thoreau could follow his old friend's odyssey to the radical extreme.

With Brownson, spiritual idealism turned political and partisan. The editor derided the Whigs as a mere lobby for "commercial capital," advocating for merchants, banks, corporations, and "the credit system" at the expense of their fellow citizens. How dare that party call its program "the American system"! It took direction from the Bank of England, the citadel of international finance, and subordinated American interests to those of the former mother country, "the ruling commercial nation." It was "a foreign party, and anti-American in its principles." But what could be expected of men with no higher purposes than money and profits?

Brownson imbued the party of Van Buren with his grandest hopes for humanity. It was "the American party," standing for "the supremacy of Man." It was "the patriotic party," putting "national honor" above "the facilities of trade or commerce." It was the "party of liberty," of "freedom of mind and conscience, the basis of all freedom." It upheld the American idea that "things are subordinate, and subservient to Humanity," and it enacted that principle by supporting universal suffrage. In this faith, it affirmed the revolutionary insight of the age: that in every human soul resides the "religious sentiment, the strongest sentiment of our nature." Possessing this spiritual endowment, we are all equal to one another and "in the sight of God," apart from all "accidents of birth." To be a Democrat was thus to be a Transcendentalist, albeit without the German baggage or the off-putting name.[49]

The intellectual carried his radicalism into practical politics. Thanks to Bancroft, he held a lucrative post as steward of the U.S. naval hospital in Boston harbor, and he soon rose to prominence in his party's affairs. In October 1839, Brownson crafted the official resolutions of the state Democratic convention, elevating the party's message to voters with an impassioned idealism. "Democracy is the recognition of the supremacy of Man over his Accidents [of birth, status, or wealth]," the delegates affirmed unanimously in language straight from the pages of the *Boston Quarterly Review*; "it founds government on the broad basis of humanity, for the freedom and growth of universal man." Opponents were quick to denounce the author of that platform. In Brownson, charged the Whig *Boston Atlas*, the Democrats had found their "philosopher and metaphysician . . . who transcendentalises Loco Focoism, at a salary of $1,200 a year." In Concord, where Brownson had lectured to the lyceum on "Social Progress" three years earlier, the press took notice. The *Freeman* publicized the proceedings of the party convention; the *Gazette* ridiculed the talk of man and his "accidents," scorned Brownson as a "renegade Whig," and professed outage at a reputed remark by the "reverend politician" that "the Almighty was the first Democrat." "What will our Christian voters say of a cause," the paper asked rhetorically, "which is supported by such fearful blasphemy in its clergyman?" In effect, Brownson was another Abner Kneeland, his Transcendentalism an assault on the social order and religious faith. The preceptor of the Concord Academy would surely have recoiled at this attack on a mentor he admired and on ideas he shared.[50]

Whatever Thoreau's leanings, Concord was a Democratic town in a Whig state. Once Anti-Masonry shattered the political calm, there was no returning to a nonpartisan era of good feelings. For more than a decade, from the mid-1830s to the eve of the Mexican War, elections were sharply contested for nearly every office, from overseer of the poor to president of the United States. Later generations would remember the town as a Whig bastion, whose people "had been instructed from the cradle to the grave to fear God and the Hoar family" and to vote as the Social Circle prescribed. In fact, at the height of the two-party struggle, the majority asserted its will, without any hint of deference, and decisively chose the Democracy, even when the county and the state went the other way. The common folk and not the well educated held sway in hostility to special privilege and demand for equal rights.[51]

As Concord entered the age of popular democracy, Thoreau remained a critical bystander. The two parties seized upon the ongoing communications revolution to promote candidates, to push issues, to coordinate national, state, county, and local efforts, and to mobilize voters in unprecedented numbers. For all their differences, the rivals adopted similar practices. At the center of the electioneering were the dueling newspapers, the Democratic *Freeman* and the Whig *Gazette*, which kept up the fight for close to a decade (1835–1842).[52] Politics crowded out other news during campaign seasons, as the editors labored to rouse enthusiasm and get out the vote. Each organ was devoted to the party faithful; in the polarized atmosphere, few swing voters were to be had. Starting in 1839, the regular weeklies were supplemented by special campaign vehicles, the *Sunbeam* for Democrats, the *Hornet* for Whigs, both free of advertising and carrying only "matters of general public interest." These were available along with periodicals from all over the country at the "reading rooms" that both Gourgas and his rival William S. Robinson (Thoreau's schoolmate) opened in their respective offices. It is unlikely that Thoreau ever entered the premises. Despite his obituary of Anna Jones for the *Gazette*, he had a low regard for the press as a medium of ideas and information. A partisan editor, he opined in a March 1837 essay for Professor Channing, was "very much in the situation of one who looks through a microscope, and thus obtains a correct idea of the minute parts of an object; but is apt to lose sight of its outward bulk and more obvious qualities."[53]

Even those dismayed by political conflict wore partisan blinders. On November 14, 1838, two days after a rancorous election, eighty-seven-year-old Doctor Ripley took the podium at the lyceum to offer his thoughts on "Patriotism." Only a one-page outline survives. Invoking the ideal of the disinterested citizen, Ripley briefly noted the moral and intellectual requirements of a patriot. He must be both knowledgeable about government and principled in upholding "truth, honesty, [and] virtue." The parson then went on to apply this standard to the contemporary scene. Was it true that "one half of our people are Tories [i.e., Democrats]?" Not at all, he replied. "The people mean well; but are some times deceived, and made to destroy their own freedom." As ever, the minister equated his views with the general good; those who disagreed were either misguided or self-serving. That analysis was unlikely to go down well with citizens who had just turned out en masse to give the Democrats another majority. One man's independence was another's party line.[54]

Competition between the parties was as powerful a force for integrating the far-flung republic as were railroads and canals, banks and factories, and the ascendant financial market with its locus on Wall Street. And no political event proved more crucial to this nationalizing process than the presidential election of 1840. In this contest, the Whigs, determined to oust Van Buren from the White House after twelve years of Democratic rule, overcame their lingering qualms about popular politics. The challengers took their candidate, William Henry Harrison, scion of the Virginia gentry and owner of a large estate on the Ohio River, and rebranded him as a frontier farmer enjoying the simple life in a log cabin, with a barrel of hard cider by his side. With a folksy nickname, "Old Tip" (the hero of the Battle of Tippecanoe) became the people's choice: a respectable workingman equal to anyone in the land. To sell this public image, his party built on Jacksonian precedents and transformed the presidential campaign into a national extravaganza combining the enthusiasm of a religious revival with the pleasures of popular entertainment. Mass rallies and parades, accompanied by music and song and featuring floats with log cabins and barrels of cider, propelled the electioneering forward.[55]

As Thoreau watched, his hometown played a notable part in the Whig campaign. On the Fourth of July, it was the host of a great Harrison rally and barbecue. The event was sponsored by the Middlesex County Whigs, with a "Committee of 76," chaired by Daniel Shattuck, overseeing the arrangements, and a "Concord Young Men's Tippecanoe Club" supplying manpower. After decades of exhortation to shun the tide of westward migration and remain in New England, the proper Whigs of the ancient town embraced the frontiersman from Ohio and flaunted the symbols of primitive life in the woods.[56]

Concord had never experienced anything like Independence Day in 1840. Somewhere between eight and ten thousand Whigs streamed into town from every Middlesex village and farm in a popular rising not seen in the county since April 19, 1775. Twice as many people turned out for the rally as had taken up arms against the king's troops; Concord's population swelled four- or five-fold on this sixty-fourth anniversary of American independence. The bicentennial of 1835 had been a modest affair by comparison.

People came from every direction on foot, by horse and carriage, "in every variety of vehicle," and in a "large boat" on the Concord River, all headed for the festivities at the site of the historic battleground. The Lowell delegation, twelve hundred strong, drew cheers for the "immense Log Cabin" that it brought to the parade. So many large wagons arrived from the City of Looms that "it seemed as if the whole of the great manufacturing city of New England" had picked up and moved to Concord. From Boston, the "great Whig ball," an immense paper contraption twelve or thirteen feet in diameter, "striped with red and white" and "covered with mottoes," came rolling into town, thanks to the hard labor of the Cambridge Tippecanoe Club, pulling the ropes attached to the sphere. This ingenious invention by Ohio Whigs "kept the ball rolling" all over the land. It was "both empty and hollow," jibed Gourgas, "like the heads of those who were harnessed to it."

All the participants from every direction were in their places when the signal gun fired at ten that morning to begin the march into the town center and up the road past the manse to the scene of the historic battle. Along Main Street, the boys in the Thoreau brothers' academy reveled in the jamboree. Thanks to their instructors' father, they were well furnished with campaign paraphernalia—Log Cabin hats, breast pins, medals, and canes "with small hard-cider barrels for heads"—and as the Great Ball passed by, they shouted themselves hoarse with enthusiasm. The procession from Lexington to Concord alone was ten miles long. So numerous were the ranks that it took about half an hour to pass any point. The signs on display were well calculated to reinforce Concord's view of itself as the heart of Middlesex. At the head of the line the committee of arrangements hoisted a blue-and-white silk banner offering tribute to "Middlesex County: As in 1775, her people meet in Concord" and noting "There stand Concord, Lexington and Bunker Hill." On its own placard, Concord stood alone. One side read "Concord, 19th of April, 1775"; the other explained, "The people take their own cause into their own hands."[57]

When all arrived at the battlefield, the crowd occupied nearly two acres. Close to the monument stood a platform for the speaker and honored guests, including Doctor Ripley, who must have taken satisfaction at the sight of so many thousands of patriotic citizens assembled on the sacred ground he had labored so long and hard to memorialize. At least they could hear the orator, state senate president Myron Lawrence, who had recovered sufficiently from an overnight asthma attack as a guest in the Keyes home to hold forth for nearly two hours under a hot July sun without any amplification. Undoubtedly, everybody cheered when the speaker concluded and it was time to proceed to nearby Sleepy Hollow, where a huge tent had been set up to accommodate 6,300 men for a dinner of ham, corned beef, tongue, bread and cheese, lemonade, and cold water. Mindful of the class resentments provoked by the Lafayette celebration and the Concord bicentennial, the organizers of the Whig gala collected donations and furnished the dinner free for all. Not everyone was attracted by the "plain, substantial fare." After watching the parade from the cupola of the courthouse with "a bevy of girls of my own selection" and a handful of male friends, Harvard senior John Shepard Keyes opted to skip "the coarse Harrison fare" and enjoy "some good eatables and a glass of wine at home." Here was one young Whig unwilling to give up the prerogatives of "aristocracy" and play democrat for a day.[58]

Even Henry Thoreau was drawn to the hoopla. His curiosity aroused, the schoolmaster visited an encampment of militiamen in Sleepy Hollow and admired the "lofty emotions" they exhibited in hopes of performing "some heroic deed." Later he beheld the Great Ball as it rolled "majestically along," its curve an emblem of beauty. If only people could live up to nature's model! Still preferring a mental observatory in the sky, he remained a detached spectator of his neighbors' enthusiasms.[59]

The election campaign of 1840 completed Concord's transition to the modern regime of popular politics. Whigs finally accepted the necessity of courting votes and flattering the people if they were ever to pose a serious challenge to the

Democratic Party. In August 1840 the *Republican*, the Whig successor to the *Gazette*, noticed a new development on the political scene. The "stumping system," popular in the West, was now spreading to the East. Even in Massachusetts, candidates for Congress in Essex and Worcester counties were now going out on "the stump" to speak with voters and address their questions. Was it not time for the office seekers of Middlesex to put aside "false delicacy" and do the same? Editor Robinson clearly had in mind Nathan Brooks, then making his second bid for Congress. Rejecting the lawyer's refusal to commit himself to specific positions in 1838, the young Whig endorsed a new approach to electoral competition. Candidates should always be willing to come before the voters, "whenever they desire it," and to state "what policy they deem to be the right one, and which they will pursue if elected." The citizens had every right to demand such responses from those who would represent them. "A mighty revolution has been commenced among the PEOPLE," Robinson pronounced, "and its progress CANNOT and WILL NOT be stayed."[60]

Election Day was the first Monday in November, and on that day "a terrible rainstorm" poured down on the voters, who trudged through wet leaves piled up on the common and made their way into the courthouse to cast ballots. No one was deterred by the weather. The turnout was astounding, as the parties strained to round up every last vote, registering supporters and challenging the eligibility of opponents on the very morning before the polls opened.[61] The list of voters drawn up by the selectmen the previous March numbered 355 male citizens. By November, some were gone, but their places were taken by the last-minute additions to the rolls. When the ballots were counted, the selectmen reported a remarkable result: for every office from presidential electors and congressman to governor, state senators, and town representative to the legislature, the total number of votes cast was almost identical: 356 or 357. Just about everyone eligible to vote had performed his civic duty.[62] The universal turnout was unprecedented in the town's history; it outstripped even the bitter contests between Federalists and Republicans, when the selectmen had manipulated the voter lists to benefit their side and a sick man had been dragged in from his bed to break a tie. Through 1850, no election before or after brought as many voters to the polls.[63]

The surge of voters statewide mainly benefited the Whigs. The party recaptured the governorship, lost for the first time to Democrats in 1839, and added the state's electoral votes to the Harrison-Tyler column. Middlesex County, too, went Whig in every race but for Congress, where Parmenter squeaked out a victory over Brooks. But Concord itself held firm for the Loco-Focos. Although local Whigs raised their vote by over 30 percent, the Democratic ship of state maintained a steady course and even added a half-dozen or so members to the crew. In the face of the most powerful challenge they had faced to date, Gourgas and his associates prevailed by solid margins. The *Freeman* editor consoled readers over the party's losses by highlighting the returns from Lexington, Concord, and Charlestown: "These old battlefields of the Revolution are yet pure in the faith which brought victory to the arms of the patriot fathers."[64]

Four decades later the younger Keyes, now a veteran politician in his fifties, looked back at the excitement of 1840 and reflected that the campaign had "opened a new vein" in the "body politic" and launched "a new era in political management." The election was the coming of age for modern political parties. For all their policy differences and antagonistic stances, Democrats and Whigs came to resemble one another in their organizational structure, their techniques of electioneering, their populist rhetoric, their enjoyment of the political game, and their sheer relish of the competition. Partisanship became an accepted feature of American democracy, with townspeople choosing their parties as they did their churches and passing the affiliations on from generation to generation. No one expected to eliminate the opposition any more than they hoped to gather all religious sects under one roof. On Election Day, the townsmen would turn out to vote at rates unmatched today, compete furiously with one another, and then go back to being neighbors, if not always friends.[65]

THE ELECTION OF 1840 PUT HENRY THOREAU IN A BIND. AT TWENTY-THREE, he was qualified to vote, and this was his first opportunity ever to participate in the choice of the president of the United States. A canvasser for the Whigs would have considered him a sure vote. His father was an enthusiast of the party, whose policies aligned with the pencil maker's economic interests. His Main Street neighbors were party leaders; congressional candidate Brooks, family friend and landlord, lived next door, while Hoar lived across the road. The Thoreau brothers' academy drew its pupils from Whig families and depended on the patronage of trustees Brooks, Hoar, and Keyes. These prominent figures had overlooked Henry's quixotic departure from the grammar school and endorsed him as a teacher. Would he not express his gratitude or, more broadly, signify his affiliation with Whig culture by voting for the party ticket?[66]

Benefactors, no matter how generous, can breed resentments. The independent Thoreau grew up in a family that had slipped downward on the social scale and now resided in houses rented from men of means who had once been their peers. Henry attended Harvard on scholarship, obliged to scrimp and save, at a time of sharpening social distinction among the students, and he came away from the experience with a lasting preference for the company of workingmen over the genteel. The Democratic message, as crafted by Brownson, was well designed to appeal to the young man's egalitarianism with its stirring call to pursue ideals, rather than interests, and to elevate the progress of humanity over the protection of property. Was not Democracy his rightful home?[67]

The stumbling block was the dislike of parties and the political process that lingered with Thoreau long after he had left Edward Channing's classes. "The ringleader of the mob will soonest be admitted into the councils of state," he observed in February 1840. By the time the presidential campaign was in full swing, Whigs had stooped to the Democrats' level, with their sloganeering and rallies and their parade of numbers, in place of arguments addressed to individual minds. The "tide of Popular feeling" had drowned out rational discourse.[68]

Had Thoreau been following his former mentor Brownson, he would have found answers to his objections in the *Boston Quarterly Review*. The Transcendentalist politician was well aware of the "repugnance to party, and party action," felt by "many excellent men." For he had once shared this sentiment himself. He was no longer so naïve. After gaining experience in the world and observing how society works, he had come to the conclusion that "parties are inevitable, and will be till all men become perfect, or until a uniformity of opinion is brought about by means of absolute despotism." In this light, Brownson urged the true "friends of progress" to act on their faith in "the power of human nature to advance" and enlist in the "party of the future." The Democrats embraced "movement" and marched forward, in contrast to the Whigs, who clung to the status quo. "Destitute of faith in man's power of progress," the opposition was "the party of yesterday," "the stationary or stand-still party." Let young America hop aboard the train of progress and speed ahead into better times.[69]

By 1840 Thoreau had found a very different mentor in Emerson. For a time, he too appeared to be drifting in a Democratic direction. A couple months after Brownson put a Transcendentalist spin on his party's platform, Concord's resident philosopher stepped onto the platform of the Masonic Temple and opened his latest lecture series, "The Present Age." "What is the soul of the age?" he began. How do we choose among the "many activities" and "many unlike purposes" of people in a particular time and place, so as to characterize an era? The lecturer took a dialectical approach. He proposed to identify the "new and operative" forces in "the present epoch" that were "detaching the future from the past." From this perspective, the defining terms seemed obvious—and surprisingly familiar: "There are two parties to one of which all men belong. The party of the Past and the party of the Future." Or put differently, men aligned themselves either "with the Movement Party or with the Establishment." The rift ran through every major field of endeavor: "in Literature, in Philosophy, in Church, in State, in Social Customs." It splintered churches and sects; it separated philosophers into materialists and spiritualists. In politics it divided America "into Whig and Democrat." Emerson had clearly been reading the latest issue of the *Boston Quarterly Review*.[70]

Emerson appropriated and polished Brownson's language without any acknowledgment of his source.[71] But his central theme was very much his own: the rise of the sovereign individual as the central actor on the social stage. Brownson had affirmed, "Here man is not made for the state, but the state is instituted for man." That formulation resembled a point Emerson first made in 1837 and reasserted once again: where previous generations "sacrificed uniformly individuals to the nation," contemporary America operated on the principle that "the nation exists for the Individual;—for the guardianship and education of every man."

The series "The Present Age" elaborated on this insight. In the fourth lecture, "Politics," Emerson voiced a preference for limited government in keeping with the motto of the *Democratic Review*. "The less government we have," he declared, "the better; the fewer laws, the less confided power." Like the advocates of nonresistance, Emerson inclined to a philosophical anarchism. In his ideal world, government took its character from the individual and not the other way around. Thus the purpose of the state was to "educate the wise man," and once that was done, it could wither away. Let the individual be a law unto himself.

Emerson never took an explicit political stand in these lectures; nor did he identify either party with liberty, democracy, or the American idea. But his libertarian outlook and his vivid evocation of "the new race"—the advance guard of the coming age—as "fanatics in freedom," who "hate tolls, taxes, turnpikes, banks, hierarchies, yes, almost laws," could easily create the impression that the gentleman from Concord was aligning himself with Brownson and the most radical faction of the Democratic Party.[72]

That was exactly what the scholar-politician George Bancroft thought. The collector of the port of Boston was "in extasies," reported the Transcendentalist minister Theodore Parker; "he was rapt beyond vision at the loco-focoism of the ["Present Age"] lecture." Parker had the same reaction. "It was democratic-loco-foco throughout, and very much in the spirit" of Brownson. One Whig gentleman wondered aloud what had gotten into Emerson. The only explanation he could come up with for the speaker's radical turn was that he "wished to get a place in the Custom House." A "good lady" regretted that Emerson had not been a passenger on the steamboat *Lexington*, recently consumed by fire on Long Island Sound at the cost of over one hundred lives.[73]

Still, Emerson would disappoint the enthusiasts. His patrician dislike for electoral politics was as strong as ever. Even as he envisioned a future governed by wise men, he decried a present in which popularity-seeking politicians courted the favor of voters rather than deliberate measures for the good of all: "The people are feared and flattered. They are not reprimanded. The country is governed in bar-rooms." As the presidential campaign wore on, his feelings went up and down, like the great Whig ball bobbing along the road. In July 1840, the inaugural issue of the Transcendentalist journal *The Dial*, edited by Margaret Fuller, came before the public, and the rumor circulated in Boston that an editor of the periodical, "though not an active politician, is a friend of the Administration party." Back in Concord, Gourgas hastened to correct that impression. "This is untrue," the *Freeman* stated. "Mr. Emerson is a whig and votes with the whig party."

But the lecturer's sentiments were lukewarm. In mid-September, following a Whig rally in Boston that brought out some forty to fifty thousand cheering Whigs, Emerson professed confidence in the popular judgment. "The people do not wish to be represented or ruled by the ignorant & base," he observed, sounding like his grandfather. "They only vote for these to be sure that they are free: they will not vote for them long: they inevitably prefer wit & probity." The more he witnessed and considered the Whig reliance on the extravaganza of conventions and parades, the greater were his doubts. The purpose of these vast assemblies was to put on view hundreds and thousands of people all joined together in a common cause. It was a show of strength for its own sake—a "cheap sublime of magnitude and number." The mass of men on parade embodied and celebrated "THE PEOPLE." Into its maw the individual was ineluctably drawn, his sense of self inflated by its power. "The young patriot feels himself greater, stronger than before, by a new thousand of eyes & arms." But that was an illusion: "It is only as a man detaches himself from all support & stands alone, that I see him to be strong and to prevail. He is weaker by every recruit to his banner. Is not a man better than a town?"[74]

No party, it appeared, was truly the agent of the individual. Americans were casting off older hierarchies and traditional constraints in pursuit of greater autonomy and choice. Would they now forfeit those possibilities in new modes of subordination? By Election Day, Emerson could summon little enthusiasm for the victory of "Old Tip." "Let whosoever will, rejoice," he told Lidian. "I confine my satisfaction to the fact of the ejectment of Mr Van Buren & his company at Washington." As for the new administration, he saw no reason for optimism: "I hardly dare hope that his successors will behave better. They come in a little too strong to be on their good behavior."[75]

Thoreau evidently felt some guilt over his detachment from the passions of his countrymen. "If want of patriotism be objected to us, because we hold ourselves aloof from the din of politics," he mused a few weeks after the great Harrison rally, just remember what the Greek philosopher Anaxagoras replied to a similar rebuke from the Athenians. It was not true that he was "indifferent to his country because he had withdrawn from it" in order to dedicate himself "to the search for truth." "On the contrary," he declared, "pointing to the heavens, 'I esteem it infinitely.'" But he could never esteem men in the mass, their individuality absorbed into the vast crowds cheering for "Tippecanoe and Tyler Too." "The mass never comes up to the standard of its best member," he had told the lyceum in April 1838, "but on the contrary degrades itself to a level with the lowest." The 1840 campaign surely strengthened this view.[76]

Did Thoreau forgo his first opportunity to vote for president? The name of "David H. Thoreau" was on the list of qualified voters, right after his father and brother, that the selectmen drew up on February 17, 1840. Whether he went to the polls is unknown. But since exactly as many ballots were cast as men were eligible to vote, it seems likely that Henry Thoreau overcame his scruples and joined his townsmen in performing his civic duty.

If so, it was a decision he quickly came to regret. The next November 377 men were on the list of voters, and as they arrived at the courthouse to declare their preferences for state offices, the selectmen checked them off on a document preserved in the town archives. An *x* appears next to the names of 339. That was the case for the two John Thoreaus, father and son, and for Emerson as well. But Henry D. Thoreau—he now insisted on the name change—was one of the thirty-eight men who were not checked in. Divorced from the ardent political spirits of his neighbors, he evidently opted to abstain. That same year he withdrew from the First Parish, stopped signing antislavery petitions, declined reelection as lyceum curator, and closed his school.[77]

Torn between the Whig culture of his family and sponsors, on the one hand, and the opposing loyalties of Brownson and the misgivings of Emerson, on the other, Thoreau must have felt a good deal of ambivalence. Under such conflicting circumstances, he may have compromised his beliefs in 1840 and cast a ballot for the Whig ticket, only to feel disgust over that choice. He did not make the same mistake again. At the close of 1841 he rationalized the decision: "The merely political aspect of the land is never very cheering—Men are degraded when considered as the members of a political organization." Thoreau thus began to draw apart from his townsmen, even as he was pulled to participate in their common life. There was undoubtedly considerable strain in maintaining such independence. But in Transcendentalism he found the strength to resist the pressure and follow his own truth.[78]

Famine in the Churches

When Emerson came to Concord in late 1834, he was returning to the fields of his fathers and *not* to their faith. Unlike his Aunt Mary and his brother Edward, he never sought full admission to the First Parish church, not even after his remarriage. Nor did he join Lidian or brother Charles in teaching Sunday school. But the erstwhile clergyman was quick to rent a pew in the meetinghouse and to attend public worship on the Sabbath whenever he was not engaged to preach out of town. When the tax collector came by, he readily paid his dues as a member of the parish. No one in Concord could have predicted that in the summer of 1838, the latest in a long line of Congregationalist clergymen would become notorious as the scourge of the New England Protestant tradition. But just as Doctor Ripley's church was adjusting to a new world of religious diversity and voluntary choice, his grandson was growing ever more impatient with the dull preaching and conformist theology he endured on too many Sundays in Concord. His dissatisfaction erupted into a screed against "the famine of our churches" that he delivered at Harvard Divinity School on July 15, 1838, the second of the two addresses that made him for a time persona non grata at the university and that secured his place at the forefront of the Transcendentalist movement. In Concord, the speech had its own reverberations, for the disaffection to which Emerson gave voice added to the forces of change creating a new religious landscape and intensified the sorrows of his elderly grandsire's last years. Ironically, in the very campaign to revitalize New England religion, Emerson helped to diminish the role of the churches in sustaining personal piety and to curtail their influence over society as a whole.[1]

The First Parish entered an uncertain era with the separation of church and state. At first glance, the congregation was in a strong position to compete for adherents and sustain the flock. In 1834 it claimed the support of some 85 percent of taxpayers, who now paid willingly what had once been their due. The ancient meetinghouse, built in 1712 and renovated in 1792, was theirs, as was the historical legitimacy associated with it. So too were the endowed funds bequeathed by past generations for the support of religion. Local authorities even continued to issue warrants for parish meetings and to collect funds for parochial expenses, as if nothing had changed. To be sure, no one was legally required to pay a ministerial rate; a person needed only to "sign off" the parish to be free of the demand. But that required an active decision to withdraw. Most residents went along with membership by default.[2]

The First Parish had to share the Sabbath with a chorus of rivals. The Trinitarian challenge was more vigorous than ever as the orthodox church entered its second decade. In 1838 Methodists began Sabbath services, initially in the brick schoolhouse, then in the hall of the Concord Academy on an annual lease. Universalists rented the quarters of the Corinthian Lodge, now largely unused, and offered their version of Christian brotherhood. The new options were regularly advertised in the press.[3] In this contest, the First Parish could appear out of date. In contrast to the new Federal-style meetinghouse of the Trinitarians, Doctor Ripley's house of worship was as ancient and worn down as the minister. The "quaint queer old church" left an indelible impression on young John Shepard Keyes, who never shook the memory of climbing the long, narrow staircases on the exterior of the building to reach the upper galleries. The passage through "creaks and cobwebs and dust" was "dark and weird and strange" even to "the bravest of us boys." A town committee in 1836 found the building "fast going to decay," with the roof leaking in many places. The parishioners dithered about whether to undertake short-term repairs or a massive rebuilding, and when the economy turned down, they could not justify a huge expense. The "shattered, weatherbeaten, and mouldering" structure remained as a relic of times past down to 1841, when it was entirely remade in the popular Greek Revival style.[4]

The antiquated church was no match for the competition. In 1834 the Trinitarians counted seventy-five members in full communion, the Unitarians 125. Ripley had lowered the bar for admission to full membership, in hopes of widening participation in baptism and communion. By contrast, the orthodox body narrowed the gate into the fold. It required applicants to testify to saving grace, assent to a Calvinist creed, embrace its covenant, and accept church discipline. Even so, in the five years after the Standing Order was dismantled (1834–1838), the evangelical church took in forty-two new members, double the number of recruits into the liberal ranks. While many converts were transients, the upstart outpaced its rival and by the early 1840s was nearly equal in size. For all their disagreements, the two churches were alike in one crucial respect: the over-whelming majority of members were women, as they had been before the split. In the Trinitarian congregation, the "Misses Thoreau," along with Henry's Aunt Louisa Dunbar, formed the core of a conscientious sisterhood.[5]

The orthodox gains were achieved despite financial problems and internal conflicts. Cut off from the trust funds that shored up the First Parish, the Trin-itarians struggled to pay the bills not only for the minister's salary and the up-keep of the meetinghouse but also for the large debt they owed to their Boston financiers. The revenue from annual dues, the sale of pews, and a few legacies from church founders fell short of expenses; the congregation got by thanks to grants from the Massachusetts Missionary Society. One minister after another departed after finding it impossible to support a family on the paltry sum of $600 to $700 a year, which was often in arrears. Key donors failed to fulfill their pledges. No one was more responsible for the plight of the church than parish treasurer Josiah Davis, whose early accession to the Trinitarian ranks had been hailed as the financial salvation of the fledgling enterprise. Instead of adding to the church coffers, the self-important merchant borrowed heavily from the ministerial fund to keep his store and land speculations afloat. Falling behind on his bills, Davis was caught short by the financial panic, and his situation quickly went from precarious to irretrievable. Bankrupt and humiliated, he slipped out of town to take up residence in Boston, where he ran a boarding-house for the rest of his days. Left behind with an unpaid debt, the parish periodically dispatched plaintive letters urging redemption of their faith with his works. The loan was never repaid.[6]

Adding to Trinitarian woes was the incessant squabbling among members. The disputes turned not on doctrine—the underlying reason for the excommu-nication of church founder Joseph Green—but on the administration of church discipline. While the Unitarians exhorted parishioners to be good Christians, the orthodox went beyond words in the determination to steer one another on the straight and narrow path. A folder in the Trinitarian archives labeled "Grievances" overflows with complaints about members' behavior. Women were scrutinized for their sexual conduct. Committees looked into unfounded rumors of adultery by one female member and excommunicated another on more solid evidence. No man was exempt from the church's demand for ethics in the marketplace. The wheelwright George Hunstable was called to account in 1834 for creating "a public scandal" by laboring in his shop on the Sabbath. The struggling mechanic freely acknowledged his error, but what alternative was there? "He had had hard fortune & must work to get out of debt," he pleaded; "his employers were particular, would have their work done when they wanted it done, or would withhold their custom." The sinner was suspended from communion until he "confessed his wrong." No sooner was Hunstable restored to good graces than he turned around and accused Josiah Davis of "falsifying" and "dishonest dealing," perhaps in retaliation for the merchant's role in exposing his Sabbath breaking. Such accusations kept the church in a state of perpetual unrest. In April 1840 the deacons went so far as to visit every member's home and conduct a discussion of "personal godliness." The privacy so treasured by Unitarians gave way before the orthodox crusade against sin.[7]

The arrival of itinerant Universalist preachers in Concord, beginning in the fall of 1837, generated a rare consensus among the feuding factions. Both sides loathed the new sect. Universalism offended the orthodox with its denial of the Calvinist scheme of salvation and upset liberals with its promise of a heavenly reward to every human soul, saint and sinner alike. To Ezra Ripley, this hetero-dox faith was the most dangerous denomination in the land, threatening "more injury . . . to the peace and order of Congregational societies" than any other religious movement. Writing as an "aged clergyman" in the *Unitarian Advocate*, the doctor of divinity dismissed the doctrine of universal salvation as the flip side of Calvinism. "The less intelligent and discriminating classes of people," he opined, "with great facility, run from the gloomy extreme of Calvinism to the other of denying all future consequences of sin." While some followers of this sect may be "sincere and pious," Ripley worried that "others [will] feel a release from moral obligations and christian duties, in consequence of having lost sight of the necessary connection between sin and society." If Ripley and his Trinitarian colleagues had their way, Universalism would remain "as bad as atheism."[8]

The danger of "infidelity" was all too real in Boston. There the former Uni-versalist minister Abner Kneeland continued to assail organized religion for upholding an unjust social order. His freethinking newspaper, the *Boston Inves-*

tigator, delighted in mocking essential articles of Protestant belief. A December 20, 1833, piece denied the existence of God, spurned the biblical account of Jesus as a "fable and fiction" on par with the Greek myth of Prometheus, dismissed Christ's miracles as "mere trick and imposture," and repudiated belief in life after death and a heavenly reward. His was a materialist worldview, in which "God and Nature were perfectly synonymous terms"—an outlook superficially bordering on Transcendentalism.

Published just as the separation of church and state was about to go into effect, Kneeland's forthright attack on Christian faith disturbed officials responsible for law and order in the fast-growing city. To question "the government of God" was to undermine the authority of the state, unleash a tidal wave of immorality, and deny the poor "the consolations of religion." In the face of this threat, prosecutors took the radical editor to court in January 1834 and charged him with violating the 1782 Act Against Blasphemy. In a case reminiscent of the charges against David Lee Child for criminal libel, Kneeland was obliged to defend his statements before tribunals from the Boston municipal court to the highest bench in the Commonwealth. By the spring of 1838, his appeals had been exhausted, and with the state supreme court upholding his conviction and sentence to sixty days in jail, the editor awaited incarceration.[9]

With so many challengers on the religious scene, the leaders of the First Parish Church were ill suited to defend their domain. The octogenarian Ripley was something of a natural phenomenon, whose remarkable vigor drew frequent comment by parishioners and the press. In 1838, his sixtieth year in office, he gave an anniversary address, lectured to the lyceum about patriotism, published an article on "the morality of the Sabbath," recommended Thoreau "as a teacher in the higher branches of useful literature," and endorsed the use of cast-iron combs as beneficial to health. (They alleviated headaches and promoted the circulation of blood.) A visitor to Concord praised "the aged minister" in the *Gazette* as a living "monument of former men and former times to remind us that we are the descendants of the pilgrims." At eighty-eight, the parson's "natural force" in the pulpit was barely "abated," as he preached with "an almost youthful fervor of feeling." That was on a good day; the gout-ridden minister suffered a good many ups and downs and false alarms. In late May 1838, he was said to be on his deathbed; the next day the doctor reported, "with joy sparkling in his eyes," that the patient had presented "the most correct apoplexy" he had ever seen, "the symptoms perfect." Ripley soon resumed his active life. But nobody expected him to change his ideas or his peremptory ways. His sermons could still be dull as ever.[10]

The preaching was no more inspiring when Ripley turned over the pulpit to his new assistant minister, Barzillai Frost. The replacement for the beloved Rev. Hersey Goodwin, who died at thirty in July 1836, Frost was the unanimous choice of a committee headed by John Keyes. Born in 1804 on a rock-strewn farm on New Hampshire's eastern border with Maine, he had pulled himself out of a marginal existence with granite resolve, laboring strenuously for the support of his widowed mother and siblings until he accumulated the means to strike out for an education. Paying his costs by school keeping and aided by scholarships, he made his way to Phillips Academy in Exeter and then to Harvard College, from which he graduated in 1830 at the mature age of twenty-six. After two years of teaching at Framingham Academy, he was called back to Cambridge to serve as a proctor (in charge of enforcing discipline on the obstreperous undergraduates) and instructor, first of mathematics and natural philosophy, then of history. Amid these responsibilities, he completed training for the ministry at the divinity school. In the fall of 1836, the aspiring clergyman was much in demand. Churches in Barnstable on Cape Cod and Northfield in the Connecticut River Valley wanted his services. But the Concord pulpit was a plum position, well paid at $1,000 per year, close to Boston and Cambridge, and with a designation as Ripley's successor. Frost was not without competition; Theodore Parker, fresh from the divinity school and soon to emerge as a leading Transcendentalist, craved the appointment, chiefly because Emerson was there. But after giving one guest sermon in Concord, he fell out of contention. Frost became the prime candidate with a four-week tryout in the pulpit. The church and parish liked what they heard. Ironically, Parker would go on to become one of the great preachers of the age. Frost suffered a different fate.[11]

Installed in February 1837, Frost was a fitting colleague and heir apparent of Ripley. He espoused Christianity as a "divinely inspired religion," whose truths had been revealed in the Bible and confirmed by Christ's miracles. Its core message was the gospel of Jesus: the "few and simple" moral truths proclaimed in words "suited to the comprehension and the wants of such imperfect beings as are we." Like the senior pastor, Frost pledged to avoid theological speculation and sectarian controversy. The congregation would never hear him dispute about "the sublime mysteries of the Trinity" nor about how much water should be sprinkled in baptism. But from time to time, he proved as fallible as Ripley in succumbing to temptation and asserting the superiority of liberal religion: "Those who have gone back to Calvinism have changed much more, than those who have gone forward to Unitarianism." Claiming the mantle of Peter Bulkeley for Concord's First Parish Church, the new minister promised continuity in an era of unsettling change.[12]

Frost was not an eighteenth-century parson without knee breeches and high stockings. He brought to Concord the distinctive outlook of a liberal clergyman trained at the quarter-century-old Harvard Divinity School. His intellectual framework rested on the epistemology of Locke, "the greatest Englishman that ever lived," in his opinion, and on the moral philosophy of Scottish Common Sense. Whatever the subject—religion or science, history or ethics—Frost tested every proposition by the application of reason to the evidence of the senses, and he was sure to relate his conclusions to the "broad principles of moral duty" and the great "principles of action," the constant refrain of his conversation.

In Cambridge, the aspiring cleric absorbed an exalted view of his calling, and in the first sermon he delivered in Concord following his ordination, "the most interesting & solemn moment of all my life," he told the congregation how he expected to perform his duties. As a preacher of the gospel, he would need to spend many of his days in "private study." Expounding Scripture was no easy matter. It called for facility in ancient languages (Hebrew, Greek, Latin, Coptic) to uncover the truths buried beneath the mistranslations and corruptions of the ages. It demanded a vast knowledge of the peoples and customs of antiquity, in order to grasp biblical passages in the context of their times, and it required familiarity with the history of Christianity as well. If that agenda was not capacious enough, then consider the burden on the minister to reconcile nature and revelation—to take "all men's discoveries in the outward world and in their own souls" and to find in them "illustrations, analogies, and arguments for Christianity." He must become a "general scholar," "acquainted in some degree with all branches of knowledge." So much for the plain and simple truths of the gospel! Frost's clerical model was a walking encyclopedia.[13]

When the scholar emerged from the closet with written sermons in hand, he would find much else to do. In the expanded view promoted at Harvard, it was the clergyman's responsibility to encourage benevolent societies. Ezra Ripley had done so in Concord, and Frost promised to follow suit. True to his word, the new parson took an active part in the lyceum and the library, the school committee and the temperance society. The Sunday school came under his particular care. His weekly schedule was crowded with meetings and not just with organizations to do good. He held many appointments with individuals as part of his pastoral role. He felt a responsibility to step down from the pulpit and minister to parishioners one on one. In their homes people might feel free to express to "a spiritual guide" feelings they could not say aloud in public, even to intimate friends. It was the parson's duty to seek out "the poor, the friendless, the bereaved, [and] the heart-broken" and extend his "sympathy and counsel." No one deserved to be known and respected as a member of the Christian clergy who preferred "scenes of social enjoyment and ease" over the sickroom, the deathbed, and situations of "moral and bodily distress."

Amid this litany of details, Frost never lost sight of his central purpose. Whatever he did in the ways of "private study, public ministration, and personal intercourse" was designed to further the highest calling of the servant of God. On his administration of the gospel, "the moral regeneration of those around him mainly depends." And through his faithful performance of this duty "the moral condition of society and the present happiness & future salvation of individuals" would be set.[14]

The stakes of Frost's ministry were limitless, the demands on his time unrelenting. But the Yankee parson was not the man to realize his lofty ideal. For all his earnestness, the new clergyman was a pedant, whose ideas were derivative and bound by convention. In the summer of 1838, Harvard senior James Russell Lowell was exiled to Concord for an infraction of college discipline and required to live and study under Frost's supervision. The thirty-three-year-old minister and his wife Elmira, married for just over a year and with a newborn to care for, proved to be kindly and "good-natured" hosts. That was the best the future American poet could say about the tutor whose measure he took around the dining table and in the study, where the two argued vociferously about Locke's *Essay on Human Understanding*. Frost had a "railroadlike" mind, in Lowell's opinion, that went up and down the same track "over and over . . . again & again." Worse still, he lacked any self-awareness but made up for this defect with an abundance of vanity. "The man's cardinal fault is that he delights to hear the sound of his own voice." Lowell satirized him in verse as a man

Who, born for the universe, narrowed his mind
And to Concord gave up what was meant for mankind.

The parson would probably have missed the joke. He took whatever he read literally and reduced each author to "views" he would judge unambiguously to be correct or not. His life was "one stretched syllogism." The nineteen-year-old houseguest was unsparing. Frost was "one of those men . . . who walk through this world with a cursed ragged under-suit of natural capacity entirely concealed in a handsome borrowed surtout of other men's ideas buttoned up to his chin."[15]

The minister's faults as a thinker were compounded by his flaws as a preacher. Frost was a plodder in the pulpit. His dreary style usually defeated his optimistic message. A college classmate gently acknowledged his rhetorical faults: no "flexibility of voice," no "play of imagination," no "gush of emotion." The irreverent teenager John Shepard Keyes painstakingly took note of one "prosing dull sermon" after another: "if he only knew how to deliver them, they would be very fine." During one discourse, a worshiper suddenly stood up in his pew "to avoid going to sleep"—a disruption the preacher naïvely attributed to the man's weariness after a hard week of work. Even Frost's officiating at weddings cast a gloom. He "blundered through" the nuptials of one couple "in the clumsiest manner," even forgetting the name of the bride, and made "all angry with his awkwardness &c. &c." Intent on explicating Scripture, the parson was not one to seek inspiration in nature and unfold the divine mind behind the glories of creation. As Lowell discerned, the literal-minded parson was fearful of the imagination. On one Sabbath, he launched into a stirring evocation of Niagara Falls as a "mighty flood discharging the waters of the vast lake in a torrent so broad and grand," only to lose hold of the soaring metaphor and plunge down into the humdrum world of fact. Lowell chuckled as Frost concluded the passage with a petty detail: the water was "several feet deep."[16]

One unhappy man in the pews regularly panned both preachers. As Frost was taking up his new office at the First Parish and working out his style and message in the pulpit, Waldo Emerson was steadily cutting his ties to a ministry in which he no longer felt comfortable. Breaking with a profession so deeply rooted in his family history and in which he had invested such immense hopes was a painful process, and in the course of doing so, he contemplated the examples of Concord's senior and junior pastors. Ripley served as a model of the country parson, who assiduously ministered to the wants of his rural parishioners without ever igniting their religious sentiments. The old man possessed a deep knowledge of every family reaching back several generations. When he offered prayers on behalf of "sick or bereaved persons," he was at pains to set forth "all the degrees" of kinship on their family trees "with botanical precision," as if the Lord cared about pedigrees. Such familiarity enabled the minister to maintain the support of most townspeople for over a half-century, but at what a cost! So accustomed was Ripley to his way of life that he equated its "homely & dry" traditions with the natural order of things. "He idealize[d] nothing" and so was at a loss to cheer and inspire the congregation. One Sunday in mid-June 1838, the parson threatened his listeners that when the Savior finally "cometh in clouds" on judgment day, He would be "ashamed" of "A. & B." for never having joined the Concord church. His grandson could bear such prating no longer. It was "the foolishest preaching—which bayed at the moon. Go, hush, old man, whom years have taught no truth."[17]

At least Ripley was authentic. His language could smack of the woods and fields he knew so well, and he did not shrink from telling plain truths to sinners. By contrast, the young men coming out of Harvard Divinity School could not fathom "the depth of the religious sentiment," the piety that had once animated their Puritan forebears. Emerson took an early dislike to Barzillai Frost.[18] In May 1837 he and Lidian brought their six-month-old baby, Waldo, to church for baptism, and on that happy occasion he longed to be uplifted by the new preacher. He was bitterly disappointed. "I could ill dissemble my impatience at the show of instruction without one single real & penetrating word," Emerson fumed in his diary. The sermon amounted to "page after page" of clichés—"a houseful of words" not worth the time or "pew tax." Six months later Frost was still clueless. "The young preacher"—actually just a year behind his critic—spoke "from his ears & his memory, & never from his soul. His sermon was loud & hollow." By March 1838 the Sabbath service proved so uninspiring that Emerson "was almost tempted to say I would go no more." There was little chance of improvement. Frost evidently "thought himself a faithful, searching preacher" and in fact said so "several times." He pressed on with his labored discourses, oblivious to the boredom and despair in the pews. "He grinds & grinds in the mill of a truism & nothing comes up but what was put in." He had yet to realize "the capital secret of his profession . . . to convert life into truth."[19]

Emerson correctly gauged the worsening plight of the church. Worshipers were deserting in droves. In 1836 the First Parish was supported by 379 polls;

in 1838, by just 206. Not even half the taxpayers—just 44 percent—were willing to pay a parish tax. No end to the hemorrhaging lay in sight. The ministers had no answer. The old and the new—the country parson and the recent divinity school graduate—stood side by side to be compared, and neither pointed a way forward. Here was an opening for the Transcendentalist doctrine of the universal soul.

AT JUST THIS MOMENT, WITH HIS DISCONTENT WITH CONCORD'S PREACHers at a peak, Emerson got the chance to make his case against conventional worship at Unitarianism's most influential forum. In late March 1838 a letter addressed to "Rev. R. W. Emerson" arrived at the post office with an unexpected invitation from the seniors at Harvard Divinity School. Would he be willing to deliver "the customary discourse" to mark the "occasion of their entering upon the active Christian ministry"? Emerson readily consented; for this ceremony, he was the first choice, unlike his appearances at the Concord bicentennial and the Phi Beta Kappa anniversary. How could he turn down the opportunity to address another group of promising young men at the threshold of their careers and, in the process, justify, if only to himself, the decision to disavow the very profession on which those graduates were embarking? The event would be a turning point for speaker and audience alike.[20]

In the weeks leading up to the address, Emerson could barely suppress his "murmur" of protest against the inadequacy of the First Parish. The Sabbath services numbed the mind and killed the spirit. It was difficult to breathe the stagnant air of the meetinghouse: "in the dead pond which our church is, no life appears." He could barely contain the demand for change: "Let the new generation speak the truth, & let our grandfathers die." Sadly, in the gathering crisis, the clergy went about their usual routine. One day Waldo ran into Frost as "the young preacher" was engaged in the home visits he considered central to the work of the ministry. The former pastor of Boston's Second Church had disliked this chore; he excelled in the pulpit, not by the bedside. On this afternoon, he could summon up no fellow feeling for his erstwhile colleague. There was nothing fresh about him, no vitality at all as he trudged about town with "tablebook" in hand to record each of his calls. Rather than chart his own way, Frost asked what his "venerable predecessor" would do and followed that example. Let him be a man, not a clergyman, and convey "the bread of life" to hungry souls. Alas, that was seldom possible while men of the cloth droned on about resurrection, the last judgment, and an afterlife in heaven. Emerson shocked a meeting of Sunday school teachers by repudiating these articles of Christian belief. "Eternal law" is "now & not hereafter," Emerson insisted; "I proceed from God now & ever shall so proceed." He was ready to discard the label "Unitarian" altogether. One Sunday evening in his parlor, he told George Moore that "he hated the name." Let him be known as a "Realist" or "still better" as a "Seeker."[21]

Such impiety was dangerous. With his denial of Christian supernaturalism and his exaltation of the divine spirit in nature, the Transcendentalist could appear to be a fellow traveler of the atheist Abner Kneeland. In July 1838 the editor was set to begin a sixty-day prison sentence for blasphemy. As the date of incarceration neared, a coalition of liberal ministers and radical reformers petitioned Gov. Edward Everett to pardon the notorious freethinker. Not that they approved of his doctrines, "as pernicious and degrading as they are false." But jailing a man for his opinions was unacceptable. The group, headed by Unitarian luminary William Ellery Channing, denounced the state's action as a violation of "those civil and religious rights"—the freedom of speech and press—that are "at once founded in our nature" and guaranteed by the U.S. and Massachusetts constitutions. To silence the press was to block "the chief instrument of the progress of truth and social improvements." Where would such censorship end? "There [are] few or no opinions, in which an adverse party may not see threatenings to the state." Religion did not require government protection. It was capable of its own self-defense. Let faith in God face the "severest and most unfettered examination"; if its truths were "essential to the existence of society," they would win the day. Criminal prosecution would serve only to make a "martyr" of Kneeland, drive dissent underground, and pervert it into "fanaticism."

The petition obtained just eighty-four signatures during the several weeks it circulated in Boston. But the subscribers included major figures at the forefront of religious thought and social reform. The leaders of abolitionism—William Lloyd Garrison and Wendell Phillips, most notably—who faced their own fights for freedom of expression, signed the plea. So did a dozen participants in the Transcendental Club, including Bronson Alcott, Orestes Brownson, Theodore Parker, and George Ripley. Emerson took time off from drafting the divinity school address to travel into the city and add his name. Though he had no sympathy with the "miserable babble of Kneeland & his crew," he found orthodoxies of all sorts anathema. The gentleman from Concord was about to "shock the religious ear of the people" with a public challenge to the widespread "reverence for Jesus" and His miracles. How could he condemn the workingman's advocate Kneeland for doing the same? Governor Everett disagreed and denied the prayer. When Emerson took the podium at Divinity Hall, Kneeland was securely behind bars on the other side of the Charles River.[22]

Unlike the "literary festival" of Phi Beta Kappa, the divinity school exercises were a small-scale affair. The graduates numbered half a dozen young men, in what was perhaps a token of the Unitarian ministry's decline. Together the aspiring clerics sat with their parents and friends, the dean and faculty of the school, and a few of Emerson's invited guests. The audience of about sixty people "very much crowded" the chapel.[23]

The modest audience did not deter Emerson from delivering a speech meant to shake the foundations of Unitarianism. His ideas were not new. The opening paean to the "refulgent summer" that New Englanders were enjoying on this mid-July day was a prose-poem to nature in the spirit of his little book of that name. Then the speaker proceeded to show that a universal soul lay within nature corresponding to the intuitions of the individual mind. Every person, he declared, was part and parcel of the divine. No one should have been surprised by this proclamation. At the Masonic Temple, Emerson had been preaching his gospel of the soul for two seasons. "Nature is an Eternal Now," he had declared in the most recent series, "Human Culture." It instructs us that miracles have never ceased, indeed, that they are ongoing in a pinecone, a leaf, the turpentine flowing from a tree, the bright light penetrating into the woods.[24]

Did Christianity celebrate that miracle of life? Did it devote itself to helping each soul realize the perfection within? Far from doing so, "historical Christianity" had committed two fundamental missteps. Instead of recognizing that Jesus came to reveal the divinity within every human being, it wrongly made him into a god to be worshiped from afar. So too did the church miss the purpose of his miracles. Faith did not require a show of supernatural power, as when Jesus turned water into wine or raised Lazarus from the dead. It drew sustenance from the revelation that "man's life was a miracle," at one with "the blowing clover and the falling rain." The results of this misreading had been profoundly damaging to the human spirit. Religion came to be rooted in ancient texts, presided over by educated clerics lacking in the "sentiment of virtue," the very essence of faith. Worship ossified into hollow formulas, remote from the richness of interior life.

By this route, Emerson arrived at the heart of the matter: "the famine of our churches." Combing through his journal, the onetime minister drew on the case of Concord to illustrate the devastating consequences of uninspired preaching, though he discreetly spoke in general terms. Barzillai Frost served as a monitory example of what could go wrong. The unnamed parson put nothing of himself into his sermons. His wooden performances gave no hint that he had ever lived and struggled, "laughed or wept," "ploughed, and planted," sorrowed and grieved. In reality, the New Hampshire farm boy had endured a great deal of pain and tragedy in the course of his arduous journey to the Concord pulpit, but he kept his feelings to himself. He stood before the congregation a formal figure of authority, his individuality subsumed in a black robe and empty words. One stormy day in March 1838, as Frost droned on in the high pulpit of the decaying meetinghouse, a bored Emerson looked past the preacher to the window behind him and admired the snow falling outside. "The snowstorm was real; the preacher merely spectral; and the eye felt the sad contrast in looking at him, and then out of the window behind him, into the beautiful meteor of the snow. He had lived in vain." So useless was this spiritual counselor, so devoid of true faith, that Emerson said aloud what he had previously admitted in his diary: he had been "sorely tempted . . . to say, I would go to church no more." He persevered, but a good many of his soul mates did not. In the countryside, he reported, "half parishes are *signing off*." The estimate was generous, a little higher than the 44 percent figure on the latest town assessment. For those who still attended public worship, the gathering had become as much social as religious. It had once been "mere circumstance, that the best and the worst men in the parish, the poor and the rich, the learned and the ignorant, young and old, should meet one day [a week] as fellows in one house." But now to see the neighbors in their Sunday best had become "a paramount motive" for showing up—no small matter in a community fracturing into enclaves of neighborhood and class. Emerson's critique was well grounded. In the failings of Concord's ministers, the Transcendentalist found the materials for an indictment of the Unitarian clergy as a whole.

Once again Emerson had spoiled a party. At the very moment the graduates were observing the completion of their ministerial preparation and looking forward to pulpits of their own, the divinity school alumnus bluntly informed them that their clerical training had been useless, indeed, that it would likely disable them in the pursuit of their high calling. This address, like the Phi Beta Kappa discourse, was a severe commentary on miseducation at Harvard: of the American scholar in the one case, of the American cleric in the other. In Emerson's unsparing view, the nation's finest academic institution engaged in pedagogical malpractice.[25]

The backlash was swift and harsh. Andrews Norton, recently retired from the divinity school faculty, had sat unhappily through his former student's address, and as soon as it became available in print, he fired off a letter to the *Boston Daily Advertiser* to denounce Emerson's role in the commencement program and to warn against his work. The newspaper, aimed at Boston's business community, was an unlikely outlet for a theological debate, but Norton was less interested in Transcendentalist ideas than in erecting barriers against their influence. The "new school in literature and religion," to which Emerson belonged, would have been laughable, were it not so threatening to religion and social order. Who could make sense of these self-appointed prophets of "transcendental truths by immediate vision"? Their writings were impenetrable, their reasoning impossible to follow. Yet somehow these religious visionaries managed to woo "silly young men" and "silly women" away from Christian faith and thereby satisfy their own "restless craving for notoriety and excitement."

Norton could not remain silent while "the principles which are the foundation of human society and human happiness" came under attack. Emerson's speech was not only an "insult to religion" in general but also "a personal insult" to the divinity school faculty in particular, whose conscientious efforts to train faithful ministers of the gospel had been dismissed as useless. The professor hastened to assure the public that the "highly respectable officers" of the Cambridge seminary had nothing to do with the invitation. The blame lay with the graduating class, who, innocently or not, had made themselves "accessories to the commission of a great offence" by choosing a speaker who did not deserve the name of a "Christian Teacher."

The brief letter sparked an extended controversy in print, with Norton and his colleague Henry Ware, Jr., squaring off against George Ripley, Orestes Brownson, and Theodore Parker. Back in Concord, Emerson remained above the fray. But he could not escape the opprobrium of being classed by Norton as a spokesman for "the latest form of infidelity." To the upholder of Unitarian orthodoxy, he was not much better than Abner Kneeland, now out of jail and glad to defend the heresy of Transcendentalism. For his part, Emerson considered conventional divinity school graduates to be incapable of refuting "the bold village blasphemer."[26]

In Concord, the controversy made no public stir. Neither the *Freeman* nor the *Gazette* noticed Emerson's speech or the ensuing debate. If Ripley or Frost weighed in on the matter, nobody left a record. Divinity student George Moore was in Cambridge for the graduation festivities, but the faithful diarist passed over his townsman's speech in silence. By contrast, the next fall he took careful notes on Henry Ware, Jr.'s, argument for "the personality of the Deity" without ever acknowledging the target of the professor's critique.[27] But the scandal could not be ignored, at least in the household of Concord's junior pastor. Emerson, it turned out, had not been altogether discreet in sharing his opinions of Frost's preaching. Word had gotten around, and the minister took offense, as his boarder Lowell discerned. Frost "dislikes Emerson because E. invariably rows him up." Following the divinity school address, he had a lot more to complain about, though it is unlikely the vain parson recognized himself in the "spectral" figure Emerson conjured up.

One person who was ready to stand up on behalf of revealed religion was Lowell. Though he had enjoyed Emerson's hospitality and found him "a pleasant man," the Harvard student was no acolyte. He was irked by the lecturer's affected manner of speaking, even in private conversation. "He seemed to try after effect &—fail." Frustrated by his distance from Cambridge, Lowell begged his friends for gossip about the divinity school address. "I hear it was an abomination," he wrote in hope of getting a straight answer. For just that reason, he anticipated the publication of the address with spite. "If it excites any notice (which I very much doubt)," he predicted, "it will put the man down." The irreverent youth toyed with the idea of sending a critical "snub" to the press but opted instead to satirize the entire affair in the poem he composed for the Class of 1838 graduation. In witty verse he called out Emerson in terms Boston's authorities would surely have approved:

> *Woe for Religion, too, when men, who claim*
> *To place a "Reverend" before their name,*
> *Ascend the Lord's own holy place to preach*
> *In strains that Kneeland had been proud to reach.*

Nor did he let the divinity school graduates off the hook; like Andrews Norton, he scolded those "men just girding for the holy strife, / Their hands just cleansed to break the bread of life," who "Invite a man their Christian zeal to crown / By preaching earnestly the gospel down." For all his flouting of college rules, the poet took the side of the establishment.[28]

Nowhere did the divinity school address create greater turmoil and distress than in the extended Emerson family. Lidian rallied in defense of her husband's "bold speech" and marveled at his grace under pressure. The attacks upset him not a bit; his course remained as "uniformly true and bright" as "the daily path of the sun in the sky." His only regret was over the distortion of his message by unfair critics, who scared off potential followers. Lidian admired his "moral courage" in the face of "so much obloquy." If only she could be "worthy of him"! Once the criticism died down, the episode exposed the fundamental rift between husband and wife. Lidian had agreed to the marriage in the conviction that the two were on the same spiritual journey. Waldo's repudiation of "historical Christianity" shattered that hope. The realization that "he was not a Christian in her sense of the word" came as "a most bitter discovery." She continued to go to church and teach "large classes" in the Sunday school; he gave up on public worship, delivered his final sermon in January 1839, and sought inspiration in solitude.

The older generation of Emersons and Ripleys was similarly torn between family loyalty and religious principle. Aunt Mary had originally introduced her nephew to the intuitive nature of religious faith, but she never gave up on the need for a Savior nor doubted the scriptural account of Christ's miracles. Even as she "valued" his speech, she disagreed with Waldo's theological unorthodoxy and lamented his indifference to the church as an institution. Without organized religion, who would care for the poor and the oppressed? Uncle Samuel Ripley took a more practical approach. Fearful that Waldo's reputation would suffer from association with the atheist Kneeland, he urged him not to publish the address. Not that the "furious and bigoted notices" of the speech were justified. "Oh, he is a dangerous man," the critics shouted. "The church is in danger; Unitarianism is disgraced." Ripley had no truck with these objections, even though he admitted to not understanding everything Emerson said. He knew his nephew to be a "mild, lofty-souled, independent, true man." Who would not gain from his influence? Ripley put his own standing on the line by inviting the Transcendentalist to come to Waltham and preach from his pulpit. But the patriarch of the family, Doctor Ripley, was adamant in his disapproval. "Father is a good deal disturbed at Waldo's sentiments," Samuel reported, "and thinks his example is a hindrance to the progress of professed religion in Concord." The controversy over Emerson's address was a family fight.[29]

As the split in Unitarianism deepened, the First Parish suffered yet another blow. In December 1838 an unlikely notice appeared at the post office and the village inns: "all those in favor of the Universal Salvation of Mankind" were invited to gather at Hartwell Bigelow's tavern on the last Sunday evening of the year. With that announcement, the Universalists undertook to raise their status from an itinerant ministry to an organized church with a meetinghouse and pastor of their own.[30] Seventy-three men answered the call and "in the most perfect unanimity and purpose" established the First Universalist Society. The denomination had broad appeal to supporters of both political parties and to the great body of mechanics, small retailers, and farmers outside the economic elite. Its theology claimed a wide range of detractors among the orthodox and liberal alike. But it was the Unitarians who suffered from the competition. Trinitarians shed just one soul to the upstart, with no regret, whereas a dozen of the new church founders had been members of the First Parish.[31] Theirs was a loss the once-prosperous body could ill afford. Between 1837 and 1839, some 116 ratepayers dropped off the parish roll, a massive decline of 43 percent. Reverend Frost struggled to stem the exodus with what he considered "very useful—unanswerable" arguments," but to no avail. Not even the replacement of the church covenant in May 1841 with a simple admission form, transforming the body into a voluntary association of Christians "united in a social capacity," made a difference. The flight continued; by 1840, the First Parish could count on financial support from just one-third of the town.[32]

The Transcendentalist challenge could not have come at a worse time. Emerson's salvo spurred young people to decamp from the First Parish one by one, in personal quests for deeper spiritual experience. Thoreau's schoolmate William S. Robinson, the bookish boy whose mechanic father would not let him attend Harvard as a charity scholar, accompanied his family in defecting from Ripley to the Universalists as soon as the sect showed up in town. But after discovering Transcendentalism, he lost all interest in the sectarian squabbles of the ancestral faith. Emerson's *Nature* opened the young printer up to new possibilities; then the divinity school address transformed his thinking. "Faith makes us, and not we it, and faith makes its own forms": reading those inspirational words in his fellow Concordian's speech, Robinson brimmed with confidence that a man could build his own world. In that hope, he aspired to create a new form of journalism, free of "cant and personal abuse" and addressed to the reason rather than to "the passions and prejudices" of readers. The *Republican*, launched in 1840, was his first foray in this line. The paper had literary ambitions, and it occasionally featured notices of Emerson and Hawthorne. But in the heat of elections, the weekly devolved into a Whig campaign organ. After the *Republican* ceded the field to the Democratic *Freeman* at the close of 1841, Robinson would soldier on in Massachusetts journalism for the next four decades, a fiercely independent figure in the fight against slavery who quit one post after another rather than compromise his principles for partisan gain. His credo, as relayed by his widow, evoked the idealism that was quickened in Concord. "It was not to live for ourselves alone, or for those we love," she wrote, "but to forget ourselves, to aim at a higher life, and to do some one thing to make the world better, wiser, and happier for our having lived in it."[33]

So too did Frances Jane Prichard, the eldest daughter of the former partner in the green store, seek an alternative to Ripley and Frost. Her father, Moses, was unbending in his Unitarian orthodoxy; at his insistence, the social library had excised from its copy of Thomas Jefferson's *Works* skeptical remarks about Jesus's virgin birth. Her mother, Jane, admired Ezra Ripley as a touchstone of character, whose "goodness of purpose" set the standard for judging others. But the former classmate of the Thoreau siblings chafed under "our good ministers." In the summer of 1841, twenty-four-year-old "Fanny" ran into George Moore, on a visit home after nine months in the West, and was sadly disappointed. The new minister in Quincy, Illinois, "will do good," she thought, "because he tries so hard." But what did he really have to offer? "He is a good deal like our good ministers" Ripley and Frost, "contented with teaching as he was taught" and "fearing lest evil should come to the people from these new [Transcendentalist] teachers." A few years later, in a defense of abolitionism, she expanded on her faith: "I cannot reverence men who are so wholly conservative that they will worship existing institutions merely as such & will hold them immaculate because they have been the means of great good." With a principled self-reliance, she evidently agreed with Emerson that "an institution is the lengthened shadow of one man."[34]

And then there was Henry Thoreau. A fierce piety ran through his family line. The church schism of 1825–1826 had divided his parents from their kin.

His aunts Eliza, Jane, and Maria led the way out of Ripley's congregation in quest of a stricter Calvinist faith; they were soon joined in the communion by sister Sarah Thoreau and by Louisa Dunbar, Henry's maternal aunt. But Cynthia Thoreau could not accompany her relatives in dissent and stayed with her husband in the family pew in the First Parish meetinghouse. Theirs was a religious household, observant not only of the Sabbath but, unusually for the time, of Christmas. As John Thoreau, Jr., later remembered, on the night before the holiday, the children were encouraged to hang their stockings above the fireplace, in anticipation of a visit from Santa Claus, "a very good sort of sprite," who flew through the air on a broomstick, came down the chimney while they slept, and left a token of his regard. "If we had been good children," they would find "doughnuts, sugar plums, and all sorts of nice things" in their stockings, but if they had been "naughty," they were in for an unpleasant surprise: a rotten potato, a letter detailing their faults, and a wooden rod, too short to be applied but warning of punishment in store for the unreformed. In keeping with their Huguenot heritage, John and Cynthia Thoreau made Christmas a child-centered festival long before their neighbors did the same.[35]

BY THE TIME THOREAU LEFT COLLEGE, HE HAD PUT HIS CHILDHOOD RELI-gion behind and embraced the Transcendentalist "religious sentiment." But he said little about this intuitive faith until after Emerson's divinity school address. In mid-August 1838 he was marking the Sabbath at the Fairhaven cliffs, when the meetinghouse bell penetrated the temple of nature with its insistent call to public worship.

"The sound . . . does not awaken pleasant associations alone," Thoreau inveighed in his journal. "It is as the sound of many catechisms and religious books twanging a canting peal round the world." Every aspect of organized religion now provoked his ire. Like his mother, he had conscientious objections to written articles of belief; the only "true creed," in his opinion, was the principles "we unconsciously live by." His brother John shared these unconventional views. But the two schoolmasters were in no hurry to break free of their parents' church. In January 1840 their names appeared on a list of residents who had agreed to be taxed for support of the First Parish. Just one year later Henry changed his mind. Five days into 1841 he sent a matter-of-fact note to "Mr. [Town] Clerk," Cyrus Stow: "I do not wish to be considered a member." The withdrawal was routine and free from publicity; it lacked the drama with which

Thoreau later reported the incident in his essay "Resistance to Civil Government": "Know all men by these presents, that I, Henry Thoreau, do not wish to be regarded as a member of any incorporated society which I have not joined." Even so, the spirit was the same. In church and state, he was declaring independence from the commitments that entangled his neighbors.[36]

Thoreau's decision to sign off the parish liberated him to pursue his religious iconoclasm wherever it led. He set forth his convictions in a letter to a spiritual seeker who had found a home in the mystical "new church" founded on the principles of the theologian Emanuel Swedenborg. Why turn to social institutions—the "paltry expedients" devised by "other men like ourselves"—as the pathway to faith? No soul needed to "look abroad" for instruction. The New Testament, Thoreau acknowledged, could provide inspiration; likewise the Hindu scriptures. But no text, however ancient or approved, could take the place of personal experience. Ezra Ripley's sermons slipped away during a walk in the woods. "The strains of a more heroic faith vibrate through the week days and the fields than through the sabbath and the church. To shut the ears to the immediate voice of God, and to prefer to know him by report will be the only sin." Ultimately, the purpose of religion was not to uphold authority and enforce convention but to inspire and elevate the individual: "Our religion is where our love is." The dictate of such a faith was simple: "For my part if I have any creed it is so to live as to preserve and increase the susceptibleness of my nature to noble impulses—first to observe if any light shine on me and then faithfully to follow it."[37]

The religious upheaval in Concord—the multiplication of sects, the defections from the First Parish, the conflict within Unitarianism—added to the miseries of Ezra Ripley's old age. The patriarch was pained by his grandson's notorious outburst in Cambridge. In November 1838, as he made notes for the sermon he would deliver on his sixtieth anniversary in office, the parson jotted down the following point: "Give counsel against erroneous doctrines." He then listed various versions of strict Calvinism before noticing "the singular opinions recently published among us, which are now undergoing the ordeal of private and public scrutiny, of friendly and unfriendly criticism." He was loath to discuss these notions, despite the expressed desire of some parishioners to learn his views. "I do not myself understand them," he added, "and feel unqualified to speak of them in public." This was clearly a sore subject: Ripley could not bring himself to state his grandson's name or to specify the recent divinity school address. Better to ignore the entire debate and count on "truth" to "eventually prevail." Silence was the best course, as the lines Ripley drew through the passage made plain.[38]

Waldo Emerson was not the only cause for concern. Wherever Ripley turned, he ran into advocates of the "newness." George Ripley, the early champion of German idealism, was his first cousin once removed. As a boy of sixteen, he had come from Greenfield in the Connecticut River Valley to prepare for college under Rev. Samuel and Sarah Alden Bradford Ripley in Waltham. He received a warm welcome at the Concord parsonage. In the Ripleys' school, the youth from western Massachusetts met Sarah's twelve-year-old brother, George Partridge Bradford, who would attend Harvard and then the divinity school, become a close friend of Emerson, and embrace Transcendentalist ideas of reform. A frequent visitor to Concord, he was a familiar figure at the manse before enlisting in George Ripley's experimental community, Brook Farm. The Transcendentalist heresy thus infected Ezra Ripley's family circle, and his manse provided a setting not only for Emerson's composition of *Nature* but also for numerous conversations about the most advanced thought of the age.[39]

While the Concord parson kept silent in public, he poured out his distress over "the present state of Christianity" in a February 1839 letter to Unitarian elder statesman William Ellery Channing. "Broken down with the infirmities of age, and subject to fits that deprive me of reason and the use of my limbs," the old man was nevertheless mentally sharp and well informed. "My mind labors and is oppressed" by "the various speculations, opinions, and practices" of the day," he confided. Ripley was particularly troubled by "our modern speculators, Transcendentalists, or, as they prefer to be called, Realists." These thinkers claimed to "follow Reason in her purest dictates, her sublime and unfrequented regions," and by that means to perceive and judge religious truth. The man whom Mary Moody Emerson once called "Dr. Reason" did not recognize this way of thinking. When he examined "moral questions," he applied a simple standard: "whatever is unreasonable, self-contradictory, and destitute of common sense, is erroneous." Transcendentalism failed this test, for it was lacking in the "common sense, by which mankind are generally governed."

Ripley's objection was not merely philosophical. Transcendentalism offended him with its single-minded focus on individual growth. The new movement was, at heart, selfish; instead of fostering charity and benevolence, it neglected each man's "power of doing good to his fellow-men . . . I honor most the man who transcends [i.e., exceeds] others in capacity and disposition to do good, and whose daily practice corresponds with his profession." As ever, the parson invoked the ideal of interdependence. He even had a name for the disposition that Emerson articulated and that Alexis de Tocqueville's *Democracy in America* was popularizing as *individualism*. In the summer of 1840, George Ripley and Theodore Parker were en route to a conference of religious radicals in the town of Groton, when they made a stop in Concord and called at the manse. The minister welcomed the younger men and advised them not to elevate their own opinions over the settled wisdom of Christendom. He "charged us to keep the true faith," Parker recorded in his diary, "and admonished us of the evils of becoming *Egomites*," his term, derived from Latin, for those who "claimed a divine mission" on which they "sent themselves."[40]

On Sunday, May 2, 1841, the day after his ninetieth birthday, a "very feeble" Ezra Ripley climbed the steps of his high pulpit, "with difficulty" but "without assistance," and preached one last time to the congregation he had served for sixty-two years. His sight nearly gone, the pastor who had composed close to three thousand sermons was forced to speak without notes and extemporize his remarks. The text from Ecclesiastes 12:13—"Fear God and keep his commandments: for this is the whole duty of man"—epitomized his career. He had grown "worn out and worthless" in its service. But on this Sabbath, as he warmed to his theme, "his mind kindled," his "youthful vigor" returned, and he commanded "profound attention." With "mournful pleasure" his people took in a familiar injunction to unity, followed by an affectionate farewell. In Frost's opinion, this was "the most impressive and eloquent" sermon Ripley had ever preached. Four and a half months later, on September 21, the ancient parson, the oldest minister in Massachusetts, was gone, the victim of a stroke. The Lord had called him back, and an era of Concord history came to an end.[41]

"The fall of this oak makes some sensation in the forest, old & doomed as it was," Waldo Emerson remarked within hours of the death. As he gazed at the body laid out on the large sofa of the manse, he searched for the wider historical significance of his grandfather's long and vigorous life, and after reviewing his journals and letters, he penned a tribute for the *Republican*. Appearing a week after the funeral over the signature "E.," the piece portrayed Ripley as the vicar of Concord, whose innate social sympathies and public spirit made him the natural shepherd of his flock. The patriarch's virtues were plain to see: simplicity and sincerity, honesty and generosity, native dignity, and natural eloquence. His speech was pungent with the sights and sounds of the countryside, his mental horizon bounded by village and farm. Ripley knew his parishioners intimately; he "seemed to talk with each person, rather as the representative of his house and name than as an individual."

Emerson praised his grandfather's sociable nature only to underscore its limitations. Ripley derived knowledge not from books but from "external experience"; his was "an Indian wisdom," which accrued over the decades, as he went about the clerical duties—pastoral visits, prayers, and personal counseling—in which his eulogist was unsuccessful and his assistant performed so well. His uninspired preaching was quickly passed over. While he was in tune with the ordinary range of human life, "the common temptations, the common ambitions," he had no sympathy "with extraordinary states of mind," with "enthusiasm," or with "enlarged speculation." The parson was too attached to the forms and institutions of his church and his society for the congregation's good, not to mention his own.

To his kinsman, Ripley embodied the ancient heritage of the New England clergy. "Eminently loyal in his nature" and averse to "adventure or innovation," he upheld "the creed and catechisms of the fathers," albeit "in the mildest forms." His type had once been central to the social order, but no more. His passing marked a changing of the guard, with the last custodians of inherited authority and tradition stepping from the stage and a new cast of characters bidding to shape a more open, uncertain, and individualistic future. "In his constitutional leaning to their religion" Ripley appeared "one of the rear-guard of the great camp and army of the Puritans; and now, when all the old platforms and customs of the Church were losing their hold on the affections of men, it was fit that, in the fall of laws, a loyal man should die."[42]

The obituary proved surprisingly controversial. The leaders of Boston Unitarianism were not willing to concede that the heroic age of the clergy was over and that the pulpit would never see Ripley's like again. Reluctantly, the editors of the *Christian Register*, the official organ of the liberal establishment, reprinted "E's" appraisal of Ripley's ministry. "It falls far short of giving such a view of Dr. Ripley's character and services as the Christian part of the community ought to desire," they apologized. Two sentences of the original were deliberately omitted—those consigning not only Ripley but the tradition he represented to the grave—"because we do not like them." And with good reason: the memorial written by Emerson was not a disinterested assessment of a historical transition long since complete. It constituted a new salvo in the bitter war of words he had provoked at the divinity school. The party of the past was not ceding its ground without a fight, so the Transcendentalist subtly, but unmistakably, crafted the eulogy to do more than pay respects to a revered figure. He was also aiming to speed the exit of the old-time religion from the contemporary scene. In his view, the future lay with the religious sentiment.[43]

The religious conflicts had weakened and worn out the churches of every denomination. But contrary to Emerson, the spirit of the Puritans was not gone for good. It was at that very moment finding new avenues for expression in movements for reform.

The Spirit of Reform

A few days after Emerson's Phi Beta Kappa address and while Thoreau was still settling in as master of the brick grammar school, Concord once again faced a test of its commitment to free expression. In the first full week of September 1837, the Grimké sisters, Angelina and Sarah, came to town to lecture on slavery and abolitionism. The white South Carolina natives were on a speaking tour of Massachusetts in a bid to witness against the horrors of slavery and to drum up support for their cause. Their presentations violated two norms at once: they defied Northern desires to avoid controversy about Southern slavery, and they flouted the custom barring women from speaking in public to audiences of both sexes. Two and a half years earlier local leaders had strongly condemned Scottish abolitionist George Thompson's appearance in town and had urged a boycott of his talk, albeit to little effect. This time was different, and no one issued calls to stay away.

Angelina Grimké delivered three well-received lectures to "crowded and deeply attentive audiences" in the Trinitarian meetinghouse. According to Gourgas's *Freeman*, the talks were "masterly"; with a power of "utterance at once strong, fluent, distinct, and eloquent," this white daughter of the South "drew a picture of slavery—its injustice—its moral enormities, and its wide and evil influence" that ought to move any listener to work for its "steady and utter annihilation." Beyond the meetinghouse, the sisters were a social success. They lodged in the home of Nathan and Mary Merrick Brooks, chatted with the Thoreaus in local parlors, and dined with Lidian Emerson, who was so moved by these "angel strangers" that she vowed "not [to] turn away my attention from the abolition cause till I have found whether there is not something for me personally to do and bear [in order] to forward it." The "exceedingly attractive" Angelina, thirty-two, "perfectly charmed" Squire Hoar, who drew her out in private gatherings to discuss not only abolition but also education, corporal punishment, and the legal rights of married women. The Southern ladies also took tea with Susan Garrison, daughter and wife of former slaves, in a commitment to racial equality not often manifested by the Garrisons' Yankee neighbors.[1]

Surprisingly, there was no cry of outrage at the breach of female decorum. The promoters of the sisters' lectures had done their job well, disarming criticism in advance with the explanation that public speaking by women was a customary practice among Quakers, the denomination to which the visiting abolitionists belonged. But in the wider world of the Bay State, these "ladies of character and standing" aroused controversy for stepping beyond their proper sphere. In the summer of 1837, the official body of the Congregationalist clergy had ruled the public arena off-limits for Christian women. To take on "the obtrusive and ostentatious part" of a reformer was to assume an "unnatural" character and forgo masculine "care and protection." In God's design, women were made to be soft vines clinging to a trellis for support, *not* hard elms towering imperiously into the sky. Through dependence, the vine acquired "strength and beauty"; on its own, it would "cease to bear fruit" and "fall in shame and dishonour into the dust."[2]

The Grimké sisters took the opposition as a spur to reflect on the injustices suffered by American women in tandem with slaves. During their week in Concord, while Angelina was dominating platforms and parlors, forty-five-year-old Sarah employed her time to take stock of the many "legal disabilities" that restricted female lives. Denied any voice in government, women had to submit to laws they had no part in making, and should they own property in their own names, it was subject to "taxation without representation"—the very "cause of our Revolutionary war." Within wedlock, wives had no separate legal standing; under the English rule of coverture that held sway in the new republic, "the very being of a woman, like that of a slave, is absorbed in her master." Whatever goods she owned, whatever pin money she accrued, whatever wages she earned became his to dispose of at will, "in the ale house, the gaming table, or in any other way he pleases." There was little point to objecting: a wife had few rights a husband was bound to respect—if she even knew them. Women were "kept in ignorance" of the laws "as profound" as that of slaves. This subordination was calculated to "destroy [their] independence" and "crush [their] individuality." To be sure, white women did not endure "suffering" as severe or "degradation" as complete as the enslaved. But they felt the misery of dependence on a superior with few checks to his arbitrary will.

Sarah Grimké thus linked the restrictions on women to the antislavery crusade. Who better to appreciate the sufferings of Blacks in bondage than the "daughters of New England" chafing against the "slavery" of sex? This was the message of the "Letters on the Equality of the Sexes, and the Condition of Women," that the elder sister had been publishing since July in the *New England Spectator*, a reform-minded Boston periodical—eleven in print by her arrival in Concord. The next in the series, the indictment of "legal disabilities," carried the dateline "Concord, 9th Mo., 6th, 1837," in keeping with Quaker style. Collected into a volume published in 1838, the incisive analysis of gender inequality made a powerful case for female participation in the abolitionist movement. Its message was soon felt in Concord.[3]

The lecture tour set in motion a renewed drive by the Massachusetts Anti-Slavery Society (MASS) to expand membership. Launched on New Year's Day 1832, the organization counted around 120 affiliates four years later.[4] It relied on county associations to coordinate activities within their respective spheres; it was under the aegis of the Middlesex group (MCASS) that the Grimké sisters made their appearance in Concord.[5] The climate looked favorable for the abolitionist initiative. While only a handful of residents, notably Mary Brooks, Gourgas, and Reverend Wilder, had joined MCASS,[6] the Trinitarian parish was a hotbed of antislavery sentiment. It denied membership to anyone "claiming property in human beings," closed its pulpit to defenders of slavery, and supported its own activist group. In 1836 the orthodox church welcomed its liberal neighbors to a joint "Religious and Anti-Slavery" celebration of the Fourth of July, with Ezra Ripley offering an opening prayer and Acton's orthodox minister James Woodbury delivering a two-hour oration on "the wrong and impolicy, and cruelty of Slavery." It was fitting that Angelina Grimké lectured at the Trinitarian meetinghouse, the disapproval of the statewide Congregationalist clergy notwithstanding. In September 1837 local abolitionists were straining to break out of the parish limits. Partisan sentiment was changing, too. In the run-up to the fall elections, Democrats and Whigs competed to be known as opponents of Texas annexation, which was then rumored to be in the works, and as supporters of antislavery measures. It was time to organize the entire town in an inclusive effort from the bottom up.[7]

The opportunity arrived some two weeks after the Grimkés left. In late

September townspeople assembled in the Trinitarian meetinghouse to discuss whether Concord should start its own antislavery society. An ad hoc committee was set to report on its canvass of local opinion. Waldo Emerson agreed to deliver an address. Expectations ran high. The lecturer was well known as an advocate of freedom, but did he approve of antislavery societies, and would he ever join one? No one could say. The widow Prudence Ward, who had come to board in the Thoreau household in the spring of 1837, "rejoiced" that Emerson was going to take a public stand. But rather than wait for the event, she called on his wife for reassurance. Burning with antislavery zeal, Lidian Emerson anticipated similar sentiments from her husband: "She didn't think he would be lukewarm."

Alas for Lidian and her friends, Emerson was tepid, if not downright cold. No copy of his speech has survived, but to judge from the outline and notes he made, plus a fragmentary account printed a half-century later, he was more concerned to uphold freedom of discussion about slavery than to take action against it. As ever, the speaker made plain his hatred of human bondage as "wholly iniquitous" and his conviction that every individual had an inherent right to freedom. But he expressed no urgency to get involved in a social movement. Once we had made up our minds about "the right and wrong of this question," he advised, "I think we have done all that is incumbent on most of us to do." Mindful perhaps that his own grandfather, the Patriot minister of Concord, had held slaves, as had Lidian's Plymouth forebears, Emerson also urged listeners to reject the vituperation that abolitionists heaped upon the slaveholder and to put themselves in the planter's place: "His misfortune is at least as great as his sin."

This plea for a disinterested view, free from emotion and moral superiority, amounted to a rationale for inaction: "Sorely as we may feel the wrongs of the poor slave in Carolina or in Cuba, we have each of us our hands full of much nearer duties." Coming just weeks after his bold summons to "the American scholar," Emerson's remarks surely disappointed his admirers. On the subject of abolitionism, he was no more than a sympathetic observer, in contrast to his late brother Charles, his Aunt Mary, and his wife Lidian. By the time he stepped away from the podium, enthusiasm must have drained from the room. The meeting broke up without any plan to move forward. Transcendentalism would remain on the sidelines of antislavery activity in Concord well into the next decade.[8]

What was to be done? Concord was at an impasse, with local men hesitant or opposed to antislavery activism. If anything was to happen, the women would have to take the lead. The Grimké sisters pointed the way with their compelling rationale for female abolitionism and their principled defiance of masculine disapproval. And so, some sixty women overcame their trepidation and gathered in November 1837 to form the Concord Female Anti-Slavery Society (CFASS). Theirs was one of eight such groups founded that year in the Grimkés' wake. The Concord association belonged to a select minority in the Bay State. The great majority of antislavery societies were dominated by men; just a fifth—40 out of 221—were run by women.[9]

Far from being shamed by their wives and daughters, Concord's male leaders paid the new organization no mind. Its founding went unmentioned in the press; informally, it was "noticed but to be ridiculed," charter member Mary Brooks later recalled. The men did nothing on their own. They could establish one voluntary association after another to promote temperance, advance knowledge, and foster economic and social improvements, but no town-wide antislavery society ever sprang into action. Democrats and Whigs preferred to compete over economic issues and ignore the subject of slavery as much as possible, and when that proved impossible, they contended over whether and how to remove the scourge of human bondage from the nation's capital, restrict its expansion into the Western territories, and curb its reach in the supposedly free North. Abolitionism was not on their agenda; nor was it a top priority for any of the religious sects or even for the Transcendentalists. It was left to Concord's women and a minority of men to push for immediate emancipation in the South and equal rights for all citizens, regardless of race, right at home in Massachusetts.

And so it was with other social movements. Although men dominated the official leadership and controlled the public proceedings, women were the foot soldiers of reform. They signed temperance pledges in huge numbers; they contributed funds to women and children in need and to organizations aiding fugitive slaves; they pressed antislavery principles on lawmakers in massive petition campaigns to state and federal governments. Such action marked a bold declaration of the right of women to act on their own to promote religion, aid the poor and oppressed, and serve the Lord—even to shake up the social order. Ultimately, they would demand equal rights for themselves. In the 1830s and early 1840s social reform was a job not for the famous Transcendentalists of Concord but for their female kin—their mothers and aunts, sisters and wives.[10]

THE FEMALE ANTISLAVERY SOCIETY HAD PRECEDENT IN CONCORD. IT DREW on the model and experience of the Concord Female Charitable Society, itself an innovative assertion of women's leadership at its founding in 1814. For more than two decades the "benevolent fair" of the town, led by wives of Social Circle members, had been assisting needy women and children. These errands of mercy were regarded as an extension of maternal care beyond the home. In reality, they expanded women's presence in the civic arena. The charitable society had given its members practical experience in running a voluntary association. It had adopted a formal constitution and bylaws, raised and spent funds, made investments, elected officers, and met annually in a public space to hear their reports. It was no stretch to apply this mode of action to the cause of the slave.

But that was to enter a realm fraught with politics and controversy. In Boston, New York, and Philadelphia, it was a step too far for the elite women at the helm of the leading charities. Not in Concord, where twenty-three founders of the antislavery society were alumnae of the charitable society and fifteen of the Trinitarian Ladies Sewing Society. These activists were no longer content to dispense alms to the Black and white poor; they aspired to strike at the roots of degradation and misery among African Americans close to home and on Southern plantations far away. If this effort required them to challenge existing ways, such as speaking and acting in public, so be it. As they saw it, this was their moral and religious duty, free of partisan taint.[11]

For all their challenge to convention, the charter members of the female antislavery society resembled their charitable predecessors.[12] The typical founder was a wife and mother in her mid- to late thirties, approaching the end of her childbearing years. No longer caring for infants and toddlers, she could set aside an occasional afternoon and labor on behalf of the suffering slave. The cause was inclusive; the abolitionist sisterhood came from families prominent and obscure. Lidian Emerson was on the rolls, as was the sizable Thoreau clan: the matriarch Cynthia (whose mother had grown up in a slaveholding household before the Revolution), her sisters Sophia and Louisa Dunbar, her older daughter Helen, her sisters-in-law Elizabeth, Jane, and Maria Thoreau, and the two Prudence Wards boarding in her household. Mary Brooks and her daughter Caroline came from the heart of the Whig establishment, Maria Prescott from its Democratic counterpart. But elite support for abolitionism was thin. Only five members of the Social Circle had wives or daughters in the antislavery society; by contrast, nearly every married man in that exclusive club was united in wedlock to a "chattable." The rank and file of the antislavery society belonged to the middling and laboring classes. The self-supporting tailoress Mary Minott, sister of the reclusive farmer George, joined in the founding. So did Susan Robbins Garrison, the only woman of color in the group. A sharp gap of class and race separated her from Maria Prescott, in whose fields Jack Garrison and his sons could often be seen laboring for a living. The antislavery society strove to blur, if not erase, that line. Soon after its debut, the group convened in the Garrisons' new home in the onetime windmill off the river road.[13]

Religious faith lay at the core of antislavery activism. Abolitionist women were churchgoers, with orthodox Congregationalists narrowly outnumbering Unitarians. Ignoring the strictures of the Congregationalist clergy, the Christian idealists of Concord overcame the sectarian divide. The female members of Wilder's congregation could nonetheless congratulate themselves on supporting the cause with even greater enthusiasm than their liberal sisters.[14]

Mary Merrick Brooks was the heart and soul of the antislavery enterprise. Born to privilege in the home of merchant Tilly Merrick, she learned early on to cultivate piety and practice "self-denial." At fourteen, she had grieved over her mother's death and absorbed the lessons preached by Ripley. In a world full of "sorrow and suffering and sin," happiness resided not "in terrestrial objects" but in the love of God. In this spirit she set out on a path of religious duty and social usefulness. In 1823, at twenty-two, she wed Nathan Brooks, a widower fifteen years her senior, and assumed care of his strong-willed three-year-old daughter Caroline. Seven months later the young wife and expectant mother professed her faith and joined the First Parish Church; she stuck with it through the Trinitarian schism, renewed the covenant in 1832, and sought solace within the sanctuary after losing her second child the next year. The female charitable society welcomed her and employed her abilities as secretary and treasurer. The Unitarian Sunday school too benefited from her intelligence and generosity. One former student remembered her as "a lady born," looking "like a porcelain miniature" in her black lace dress, "high lace ruff" around her neck, and yellow bow "above the puff of her beautiful hair." Seated in the library of her home, she gathered the children about her and "in beautiful, loving, quiet tones" communicated "the God-love surrounding us all" and "placed us in God's arms, making us feel safe throughout the week."[15]

Mary Brooks was not always a soft and gentle soul. She had a fierce determination that could occasionally ignite in passion and scorch the targets of her fury. Once when her nineteen-year-old son George, then a Harvard senior (Class of 1844), embarrassed himself by drinking too much, his angry parent was not satisfied to deliver a lecture on temperance. If only she had "strangled" him in the cradle, the distraught mother scolded, or "some kind fortune had taken [him] away in . . . infancy, rather than have reserved [him] to be such a trial to [his] mother"! The abject son threw himself on her mercy, offering as evidence of true "penitence" that he had taken a temperance pledge and, more important, that he was terrified of incurring her wrath ever again.[16]

The teachings of Christianity aroused Brooks's passions, especially when it came to matters of inequality and injustice. To her sorrow, she descended from three generations of slaveholders dating back to the first decades of the eighteenth century. One Tilly Merrick after another had exploited human "property." Her great-grandfather, a farmer and tanner in the central Massachusetts town of Brookfield, bequeathed a "Negro boy" named Coffee, valued at £70, to his heirs in 1732. His namesake moved to Concord, entered trade, and accumulated riches. At his death in 1768, his substantial estate was valued at £3,464, including a "Female Mulatto Slave for Life," priced at £40 but not worth naming. His widow, left with four boys aged six to thirteen, remarried several years later; her new husband, the sea captain Duncan Ingraham, had retired from the East Indies trade to conduct business in Boston. His mercantile firm was built on "slave dealing." The last Tilly Merrick to own slaves was Mary's father, the morose storekeeper, who had grown up with "servants for life" in the home and evidently saw no contradiction between the ideals of the republic, which he had advanced as a diplomat during the War of Independence, and the perpetuation of human bondage. As a merchant in Charleston, South Carolina, in the first decades of the new nation, he traded in slaves and invested the earnings from his store in a plantation worked by African labor. The record of his intimate involvement with Southern slavery was inscribed in the several leather-bound ledgers among his belongings in the family home on Main Street. It was probably no coincidence that his daughter, confronted with this damning evidence of her forebears' complicity in slaveholding, joined the county antislavery society in July 1836, shortly after her father's death. She was the first woman in Concord to do so.[17]

Mary Brooks spent the rest of her life atoning for her family history. She did everything possible to separate herself from slavery. Her chemises and gowns were devoid of cotton; likewise her bedding. Her principled choice of textiles caused a problem for husband Nathan, who could not bear to sleep on linen. Fortunately, the couple enjoyed an affectionate marriage—he was "Ma chere Hus," she his "petkin"—so they devised a compromise. He rested his head on a cotton pillowcase, she on a linen one, and they slept as best they could on one sheet of each. The Whig lawyer-politician declined to follow his wife into radical abolitionism, and they agreed to disagree. She would not spend a penny of his money on antislavery activities, unless he explicitly designated funds for that purpose. Instead, she earned her own income by baking her famous "Brooks cake"—what today would be called a pound cake—not just for charitable events but for weddings and other parties. Coming up with the sweetener proved as challenging as picking out sheets, for Brooks would use no sugar raised by slaves. At the village store, she always opted for the bin advertising "free-labour" sugar, though the local wags scoffed at her naïveté. "All the free-labour given to any sugar," they insisted, "was scooping it from one barrel to another in some back grocery." To the conscientious Brooks, these consumer decisions were no laughing matter. They constituted religious duties, as imperative to fulfill in the bedroom and kitchen as in the public arena. Following those dictates took her ever more often out of the home and eventually out of the church. In abolitionism she found a vehicle to leave behind the chastened expectations of her youth and to strive for perfection in this life, rather than always be preparing for heaven. Steeped in piety, her antislavery activism aimed "to turn our world of sin and misery into a world of purity, holiness, and happiness."[18]

Mary Brooks bonded with her stepdaughter Caroline in the cause of the slave. An attractive and indomitable schoolgirl at the Concord Academy, the teenager reigned as the belle of the town, attracting the interest of John Shepard Keyes and James Russell Lowell before agreeing to marry Rockwood Hoar. But she had more serious concerns than romance in May 1838, when mother and daughter traveled to Philadelphia to represent Concord at the second annual meeting of the Anti-Slavery Convention of American Women. Theirs was just one of eight delegations from the Bay State in a gathering of 208 reform-minded women from New England, New York, and Pennsylvania.

The convention marked the grand opening of Pennsylvania Hall, built at a cost of $40,000 to serve as a temple of freedom in a city whose meeting-houses were closed to abolitionists. The imposing structure, completed "in the most beautiful manner," impressed the two women from small-town Concord with its large lecture rooms, "Grand Saloon," and spaces for a "free produce" store, an antislavery reading room, and the printing office of the *Pennsylvania Freeman*. But there was little opportunity to admire "the splendid building" or to reflect on its motto, "Virtue, Liberty, and Independence," inscribed in large letters on an arch over the speaker's platform. Hardly had the speeches be-gun than they were forced to compete with the noise of a boisterous mob sur-rounding the hall. Soon "brickbats, clubs, and stones" came crashing through the windows. "Sashes broke in, and glass came rattling down in all directions," yet the ladies at the lectern kept their composure and the audience its seats.

Then the scene grew even more menacing, as Caroline Brooks described for her friend Lizzy Prichard back in Concord. The "well-dressed" gentlemen in the mob pressed against the entrance, and with the rioters on the verge of breaking into the room, convention participants, "frightened almost to death," got ready to flee. "You know what a rushing sound this makes in a crowded building," the teenager observed; "this, with the howling, screeching and screaming, oaths and yells without, carriages rolled around the building to make a noise, the [false] alarm of fire screamed in every direction, glass rattling, etc., made a most terrific scene." But the women inside would not be moved. The crowd had done its worst for the night. "I never saw women behave so well as this audience," Brooks exulted.

Caroline Brooks showed her own mettle the next evening, as she and her mother walked unescorted through the crowded streets to the meeting hall, only to find it shut up by order of the mayor, anxious about the prospect of violence. Turning back toward their boardinghouse, they stared at a thicket of bodies blocking the way. Mary Brooks proposed walking on until a space opened up to cross the street. But Caroline braved the crowd. "Will you please to let me pass?" she requested. The mass of men politely made way, even as they muttered, "Oh, she's an Abolitionist, she's an Abolitionist." And so mother and daughter returned to their lodgings "in all the dignity of our womanhood."

Pennsylvania Hall suffered far greater damage. The building finally fell to its assailants, whose numbers had swelled beyond the so-called gentlemen's mob at the start of the convention, and they burned the "splendid" structure to the ground, with all its contents, "lamps, chandeliers . . . books, carpets, everything." The Brooks women witnessed the destruction from the roof of their boardinghouse. The blaze "looked beautifully" from that safe height. The convention completed its work in various private locales, and after a trip to Washington, the Concord travelers returned home with their thrilling stories and with a deeper commitment than ever to the abolitionist cause.[19]

There was much to be done. Abolitionists labored to shape public opinion by sponsoring lectures, proselytizing in churches, and publicizing their proceedings in the press. The next step was to mobilize popular sentiment in a bid to influence lawmakers in the nation's capital. From the earliest days of the republic, citizens had been calling on Congress to put an end to slavery and the slave trade in the District of Columbia; with the founding of the American Anti-Slavery Society (AASS) in 1833, the push for such measures steadily expanded into a massive petition campaign. The Twenty-fifth Congress, which met in three sessions from September 1837 to March 1839, was the primary target. From its headquarters in Manhattan, fast growing into America's communications hub, the AASS launched an all-out crusade in the Northern states to inundate the people's representatives in Washington with a flood of anti-slavery memorials. It was soon joined in the field by the Anti-Slavery Convention of American Women.

The abolitionist agitators took advantage of the ongoing communications revolution to integrate communities all over the North into a single, coordinated effort. From their headquarters in New York, they composed a medley of texts, employing the latest innovation in printing, the steam-powered press, to generate copies by the thousands, and shipped them through the mail to the many auxiliaries proliferating across the country. All a local chapter had to do was to pick a petition and carry it from door to door for signing by local citizens. MCASS supervised the effort in its area, assigning members responsibility for specific towns. Concord and nine other communities were assigned to Acton's Reverend Woodbury. A separate, ad hoc network was established to solicit the signatures of women; CFASS undoubtedly led the way. "Leave not a person unvisited," canvassers were advised. "Neglect no one. Follow the farmer to his field, the wood-chopper to the forest. Hail the shop-keeper behind his counter; call the clerk from his desk; stop the waggoner with his team; forget not the matron; ask for her daughter. Let no frown deter, no repulses baffle. Explain, discuss, argue, persuade."

The circulation of petitions went forward, despite the fact that both the House and the Senate adopted "gag rules" barring notice, let alone discussion, of antislavery pleas—yet another in the series of attacks on freedom of expression by mobs in the streets and by officials in statehouses and courts. Abolitionists were infuriated by the congressional refusal to consider their memorials; this "trampling . . . upon one of the dearest rights of the people," this "usurpation and tyranny," broadened the struggle against slavery into a fight for the right of petition. "The time to exercise [the right] most effectually is when it is endangered." So AASS leaders urged grassroots activists, who proved their devotion by amassing some 425,000 subscriptions to the immense pile of petitions that arrived by the "wagon loads" at the Capitol and threatened to rise into "a pyramid that shall vie with the proudest on the plains of Egypt as a great moral monument to the expressed will of a free people." The most popular petition railed against the rumored annexation of Texas by the Van Buren administration; it garnered over 180,000 signatures nationally. Calls for an end to slavery in the District of Columbia came in second, with more than 130,000 endorsers.[20]

The people of Concord, long absent from the field, enlisted in the new campaigns and favored the most popular petitions. But there was a striking gender gap in their responses. Men and women subscribed to the memorials in very different numbers and with divergent outlooks. In keeping with the conventions of the day, the sexes were as segregated in the appeals for government action as they were in other civic affairs. More than half of Concord's women penned their signatures on at least one of four memorials opposing Texas annexation and urging abolition of slavery and the slave trade in the nation's capital. That was a remarkable outpouring of antislavery sentiment. By contrast, only a fifth of the men were willing to come forward and endorse a petition for the same goals or against the admission of any new slave states into the Union. Female signers outpaced them by two and a half times, 340 to 130.[21]

Women took up the petition campaigns a little later than men, but they persisted with them much longer. The townsmen submitted memorials to the House of Representatives between October 1837 and January 1838 and then dropped the effort. Their female counterparts entered the arena in February 1838 and continued during the January 1839 lame-duck session. For most men, signing a petition was a familiar act; for women, excluded from the franchise, it offered an unprecedented opportunity to contribute their voices and influence government. Conservative writers were appalled; educator Catherine Beecher, the minister's daughter, counseled women to take their concerns to male "friends," who were "the proper persons to make appeals to the rulers whom they appoint." By acting on their own, they were "surely . . . out of their place." That advice carried little weight in Concord, where enhanced freedom for individuals was altering the social relation of the sexes. The petitions were not just statements about public policy on behalf of the oppressed; they were also memorials to the agency of the signers themselves, "that in the holy cause of Human Freedom, 'We have done what we could.'"[22]

The starkest contrast between the male and female petitioners lay in their arguments and rhetoric. Men invoked the secular terms of politics, women the language of faith. The long statement drafted by the AASS and signed by 128 men forcefully objected to acquiring Texas on the grounds that it would risk war with Mexico, extend the realm of slavery, and give slave states "predominant power in our national councils," thereby portending the "dissolution of the Union—an event we sincerely deprecate." This litany of complaints repeated arguments made by Concord's Whigs and did not necessarily signify abolitionist sentiment; even John Keyes, who had watched approvingly the mobbing of William Lloyd Garrison, added his name. By contrast, the women of Concord eschewed an elaborate statement of the anti-Texas case in 1838. Their brief protest stressed the "sinfulness of Slavery" as the fatal flaw from which followed "the consequent impolicy and disastrous tendency of its extension in our country." The 203 subscribers denounced the measure "with all our souls."

The men's petition reflected the calculating ethos of the caucus, the women's the selfless spirit of the church.[23] It is thus fitting that seven out of every ten antislavery petitioners were women, exactly their proportion in the two main congregations. And just as they often professed faith in concert with their kin, so these women committed to the memorials. Clusters of mothers and daughters, aunts and nieces, and sisters fill the rolls. Mary Brooks was euphoric over "the friendship and love" women displayed in the cause, as they rose above sectarian differences. "They stood hand in hand upon the broad platform of humanity, united against a common foe." The antislavery crusade of 1837–1839 had the spiritual fervor of a female revival.[24]

All these family and neighborly influences ultimately faded in the face of larger social forces coursing through the community. In a remarkably fluid society, where people were constantly on the move, the old lines between natives and newcomers, stay-puts and transients, dissolved in the antislavery endeavor. One out of seven newcomers on the tax rolls signed the memorial against Texas annexation—almost exactly the same ratio among native sons and longtime residents. The antislavery culture of Concord reflected the wider ethos in the Bay State. Instead of shaping local opinion, the town was losing its distinctive hold and devolving into a setting for contests originating in the wider world.[25]

As much as he hated slavery, Waldo Emerson tried to maintain distance from the abolitionist movement. That was no easy matter when Lidian could not stop crying over the miseries of Africans in the Middle Passage. She had been quick to join the CFASS and, in tandem with her mother-in-law, to endorse the antislavery petitions. His new protégé, Henry Thoreau, came from Concord's first family of antislavery activists. Nine members of the extended clan put their names on the memorials; Cynthia Thoreau headed up the campaign to end slavery and the slave trade in federal territory. The petitions against Texas annexation circulated as the new grammar master assumed and then abandoned his post. Amid personal turmoil, he did not neglect to join his father and brother and sign the plea; in fact, "D. H. Thoreau," as he then styled himself, was the eighth man in town to do so. Surrounded by all these activists, Emerson set aside his compunctions about efforts to accumulate numbers, rather than foster independent thought, and inscribed his signature on the lengthening list. But he was slow to do so; of 123 endorsements, his was number 118, a reflection perhaps of his ambivalence.[26]

The detached observer of the times did not like to be pressured. Just as he resisted temperance crusaders importuning him to take the pledge, so he resented moral bullying by abolitionists. One day in late March 1838, he rode into Acton and ran into a "stiff, hard, proud, clenched Calvinist"—probably Rev. Woodbury—who insisted on inflicting his abolitionist views upon the unenthusiastic visitor from Concord. Overwrought with self-righteous anger, the minister just had to tell Emerson the "last news from Montserrat." It never occurred to him that his interlocutor did not share his "incredible tenderness for black folks a thousand miles off." Such "fierce" philanthropy, in Emerson's opinion, masked a "hard uncharitable ambition." Forget about these faraway ills, he was tempted to exclaim. "Out upon this nonsense; hush. Go learn to love your infant, your wood-cutter; [and] be good natured & modest." Instead, he held his tongue and recycled this journal passage in his famous 1841 essay "Self-Reliance."[27]

Emerson could not remain in a philosopher's camp. Concord was caught up in the conflicts and tensions of a tumultuous age, and his neighbors were determined to pull him into the public arena and draw on his intellectual powers and moral force. At the start of April 1838, his composure was shaken by news of a tragedy unfolding a thousand miles south in north-central Georgia, not far from the Tennessee border. "The Plunder of the Cherokee" was about to take place, as a column in the Boston *Atlas*, the leading Whig newspaper in the state, announced. After a decade of struggle to hold off assaults on their sovereignty and land, the "civilized" tribes of the Southeast, who had adopted settled agriculture, constitutional governance, and Christian religion, faced an imminent deadline to decamp for "Indian territory" beyond the Mississippi River. In a last-ditch attempt to avoid that fate, the natives appealed to the American people, and Northern Whigs took up their cause. The outrages were many; Andrew Jackson's administration had broken faith with the Cherokees and driven them into an impossible situation: either submit to rule by hostile authorities in Georgia or move west with federal assistance. Seeing no hope, a rump faction of the Cherokee Nation had given in and agreed to leave. It fell to the Van Buren administration to enforce the resulting Treaty of New Echota. The clock was ticking down. After May 23 the U.S. Army would begin rounding up the remaining natives in Georgia and neighboring states and force them onto the "Trail of Tears."[28]

The *Atlas* story, reprinted by the abolitionist *Liberator*, stirred alarm in Concord, where Mary Brooks, feeling "great trouble about the Indians," sprang into action. She dispatched a note to Angelina Grimké, then lecturing in Boston, and urged her to speak out against the injustice. She consulted her associates in the antislavery society, fresh from their extensive petition campaigns. Accompanied by the younger Prudence Ward, she called on Emerson and, despite his disappointing speech about abolitionism the previous September, pressed him "to set the men to work." If nothing was done to stop "the new outrages" against the "poor Cherokees," "one almost dispairs [*sic*] for the slave." How could Americans do nothing and "profess to be republicans & christians"? The cries of protest had already entered Emerson's study. Lidian urged her husband to speak out against this "outrage on humanity"; to remain silent was to "share the disgrace and the blame of its perpetration."[29]

The high-minded lecturer did not require much priming. Seven years earlier he had joined in protests against the Indian Removal Act, preaching from Boston's Second Church against the nation's "bad heart," as seen in the "barefaced trespass of power upon weakness" amid "the general indifference" of the public. He had also listened with rapt attention to emissaries of the Cherokee Nation, whose eloquence "put to shame" the white notables with whom they shared a platform and attested to what he viewed as their capacity for civilization. The Cherokees' plight claimed his notice, despite their being a thousand miles away. Now, as their fate hung in the balance, he answered his friends' appeals and took a leading part in organizing a protest meeting.[30]

On Saturday, April 22, the Whig *Gazette* prepared the ground with a reprint of the Boston *Atlas* column and an editorial summons to readers to rise up and stop "an act of the vilest injustice . . . against an unoffending and most injured race." "The wrongs which these poor people have received at the hands of our Government are already enough to rouse the indignation of every man of common feeling," fumed the *Gazette*, "but it makes the blood boil to hear of atrocities such as those which are now meditated. They MUST NOT be executed. As Men and Christians, we cannot allow them in silence. We must protest and remonstrate against it." (The Democratic *Freeman* said nothing.) The meeting was scheduled for the next day following the close of public worship. Arguably, such a gathering was inappropriate for the Sabbath, since it dealt with a political matter. But the organizers dismissed that objection. The assembly, as they saw it, possessed "moral and religious bearings."

Townspeople of all sects, if not parties, assembled in the Trinitarian meetinghouse and listened with mounting anger to accounts of the American government's bad faith and unjust conduct. The speakers were all Whigs, including Emerson. Taking an uncharacteristic leadership role, he opened the session with an explanation of its purpose and then read aloud the Remonstrance of the Cherokee Nation. Later in the program Rev. Emerson—the *Gazette* insisted on using his title—expanded on his views as one of the featured speakers. After all the orators, including Squire Hoar and his son Rockwood, had been heard, the meeting proceeded to a vote. The "misnamed treaty" with the Cherokees violated "the principles of humanity, justice, and religion," the participants declared with one voice, and was therefore utterly invalid.

A petition to Congress circulated among the citizens. Unlike the antislavery memorials, this Concord "remonstrance" was not composed by a distant committee in New York City. It was a homegrown product of Rockwood Hoar's pen. The handwritten statement condemned the seizure of the Cherokees' lands "without their consent" as "an outrage upon justice and humanity, a violation of all the principles of free government, and of the solemn obligations of the U[nited] States to this dependent people." Altogether, 173 men endorsed the document; the signature of Ezra Ripley, still strong and legible in his eighties, headed the list; Emerson's came next. At the same time, 316 women signed separate petitions with the same text, with Mary Wilder, the Trinitarian minister's wife, in the forefront, followed by Cynthia Thoreau. The concerned citizens raised their voices both in a collective declaration of sentiments and in their own individual names.[31]

There was nothing special about either Emerson's or Concord's opposition to Indian removal. A good many communities in the Bay State did the same things. But the Transcendentalist thinker took one further step to publicize his distress at the disturbing course of events. At the urging of his neighbors, he sat down after the public meeting and composed an open letter of protest to President Martin Van Buren. The statement was then dispatched to Washington and submitted to an outlet the chief executive and other policy makers were likely to see: the *National Intelligencer*, the voice of the Whig establishment in Jacksonian Washington. It appeared in print on May 14, just as the petitions from Concord were being presented to the U.S. Senate. Headed "Communication," the letter carried the dateline, "Concord, Massachusetts, April 23, 1838," and the byline of Ralph Waldo Emerson, "fellow citizen" of the president. No further information about the author was supplied. Little known beyond New England, the writer could not depend on his reputation to attract readers. He had to rely on the power of his words.[32]

A public message to the president from a private citizen was rare, if not unprecedented, in American politics during the first half-century of government under the Constitution. No one imitated Emerson's example at the time, and few commented on it. Just seven newspapers, all in Massachusetts and New Hampshire, reprinted the letter. One was his hometown weekly, the *Gazette* (to which he supplied a copy), another the *Boston Courier*, full of praise for the "boldness and independence" of the statement and relieved that it partook "not in the remotest degree of transcendentalism," and a third Garrison's *Liberator*. The letter traveled in narrow circles geographically and politically.

Nonetheless, it marked an unusual intervention by Emerson in the political arena, and one with a rhetorical extravagance uncharacteristic of the man. This plea for justice did not simply rehearse objections to the dispossession of the Cherokees and their forced relocation to the new "Indian Territory" beyond the Mississippi. It also personalized the dispute in an emotional appeal to a president about to commit "an act of fraud and robbery" in the name of the American people—a "crime" certain to "bring down the renowned chair in which you sit into infamy," he warned Van Buren, and to ruin the reputation of the republic as "the sweet omen of religion and liberty." Let the "instrument of perfidy"—the Treaty of New Echota—be executed, and "the name of this nation . . . will stink to the world." Could anything stop this headlong descent into evil? Rather than give in to the general sense of "despondency" among "a great part of the northern people," Emerson summoned all his rhetorical powers to awaken the "moral sentiment" in the chief executive's breast and spur him to do the right thing. The letter overflowed with anguish and outrage in an outpouring of hurt feelings seldom seen in his prose.[33]

For the Natives were not the only victims of the federal government. So were the upstanding citizens of Concord and New England, who had watched in distress as their "agents" in Washington committed illegal and immoral acts. Emerson framed his statement as a narrative of alienated affections, recounting how his neighbors, once confident of the honor and good intentions of the national government, had steadily lost faith in their leaders. Step by step, the chief magistrates—first Jackson, then his successor—had betrayed the trust of both white citizens and Indian subjects. Everywhere "the men and the matrons sitting in the thriving independent families all over the land" had welcomed the advancement of the Cherokees in civilization. But instead of "tast[ing] justice and love" from federal authorities, the Natives were "abandoned to their enemies." The "sham treaty" was signed against "the will of the [Cherokee] nation," and despite the Cherokees' overwhelming repudiation of the agreement, it was being enforced mercilessly.

The people of Concord could hardly believe what they read in the press. "Men and women with pale and perplexed faces meet one another in streets and churches here, and ask if this be so." Sadly, it was. "Such a dereliction of all faith and virtue, such a denial of justice and such deafness to screams of misery" were without precedent in a time of peace. "Sir, does the Government think that the people of the United States are become savage and mad? . . . The soul of man, the justice, the mercy, that is the heart's heart in all men from Maine to Georgia, does abhor this business."

This was strong language, meant to speak truth to power without inhibition or fear of affront. Emerson acknowledged going beyond "the bounds of decorum," only to throw the charge back at potential critics. "Would it not be a higher indecorum, coldly to argue a matter like this?" How could he not speak as bluntly and forcefully as possible when "a crime is projected that confounds our understandings by its magnitude"? So immense was this wrong that it injured all people of principle and piety throughout the United States. It "really deprives us as well as the Cherokees of a country, for how could we call the conspiracy that should crush these poor Indians, our Government, or the land that was cursed by their parting and dying imprecations, our country, any more?" Emerson and his neighbors were being dispossessed of a republic in which they could no longer believe.

Was there no hope of justice? Many people had advised Emerson not to waste his breath; a plea to Van Buren would fall on deaf ears. But the Concord citizen would not affect "the contumely of this distrust." Nor would he give up on the chief executive. "A man with your experience in affairs," he appealed, "must have seen cause to appreciate the futility of opposition to the moral sentiment. However feeble the sufferer, and however great the oppressor, it is in the nature of things that the blow should recoil on its aggressor. For God is in the sentiment, and it cannot be withstood." The faith of the Transcendentalist animated the protest, even if the editor of the *Boston Courier*, not to mention the president, failed to notice.[34]

Emerson won praise for the letter from his Concord friends, but he took no pride of authorship. The protest was, in his view, a "shriek" as shrill as the "howl" from the Cherokees shortly to be dragged along the Trail of Tears. Emerson "hated" the address; it was "a deliverance that does not deliver the soul." This foray into the public arena filled him with remorse.

Why this about-face? For one thing, the statement was pointless. The fate of the Cherokees was fixed; nothing he said was going to prevent the impending disaster: "Why strike ineffectual blows?" Then again, something had to be done, if only to release pent-up anger. "Sometimes a scream is better than a thesis." Emerson was loath to engage in a moral protest—what he called a "holy hurrah"—for its own sake, as if to put his superior sensibility on parade.

Yankees were far too prone to making such displays, which hung "like dead cats around one's neck." His regrets went deeper still. He had broken his long-standing resolution to give voice only to those thoughts that were truly his own. Writing an open letter to Van Buren was not the result of his own inspiration. It came from his neighbors, and he took on the assignment out of a sense of duty. "It is not my impulse to say it & therefore my genius deserts me, no muse befriends, no music of thought or of word accompanies. Bah!" He had consented to be an amanuensis of outrage, channeling the passions of others through the tip of his quill pen. The result, in his opinion, was a superficial piece, full of wrought-up emotions and calculated for effect. Emerson vowed never to repeat the experience.[35]

In effect, the philosopher of originality and self-reliance had betrayed himself. His protest, serving the machinations of the Whigs, appeared a calculated, partisan act. At the same time, the letter reflected the influence of the women who had pressed him to speak out on their behalf. Its sentiments were "put into his heart by the women . . . He was only the pen in their fingers." Yielding to the supplications of reform-minded women, he reluctantly became the medium of feminine feelings he barely recognized as his own—hardly a route to "manly power." Though Emerson did seek to reach Van Buren's better self by appealing to moral sentiment, the letter spoke chiefly to politicians and reformers and not to the universal mind. Transcendentalism was at a disadvantage when it entered the political arena.[36]

Emerson's was not the only letter about Cherokee removal from a citizen of Concord to a distinguished figure in the nation's capital. Mary Brooks composed a message to John Quincy Adams, then in his third term as a member of the House of Representatives and a leading opponent of Cherokee removal. She did not write for herself alone. The communication was on behalf of "a band of women, emphatically women," who turned "instinctively" to the former president with their "hearts . . . bleeding for the woes and distresses of their suffering brethren in this most guilty land"—the CFASS. Would he not be "our Moses" in the defense of the "poor Indians"?

Confident of a positive reception, Brooks combined apocalyptic rhetoric with an emotional appeal for empathy. Consider the oppressed natives, she urged Adams; they were about to be dragged from their "dear homes to a far-off land, with little or no prospect before them, but death by weariness, famine or disease." Put yourself in their place: "See that aged man whose only earthly desire is that he may lay his bones in the sepulcher of his fathers; see him trembling with age and decrepitude stretching out his withered hands to you and feebly, but earnestly [crying], 'Save me, O save me, from the dreadful fate that awaits us.'" "See that sick husband and wife," behold "the concentration of agony in their looks," and heed their "speechless sorrow." With infants in their arms they "entreat you to seize yonder trumpet and blow such blasts as you alone can blow and cry."

It was not the Cherokees alone who were in danger of destruction. Adopting a prophetic mode, Brooks anticipated the "magnetic bolts of God's direst wrath about to descend upon this nation." Could the "awful judgments" of an "offended" Lord be averted? There was yet time for America to repent its sins and change its ways. Fearful that the congressman might give way to despair, Brooks offered encouragement from Concord. "A ray of hope from the throne of God has visited our souls," she affirmed, "and we could not rest until we had unfurled it to you." With Adams pleading for mercy before "the footstool of divine mercy," the republic could still, at the last minute, escape the punishment it so richly deserved.

The appeal to Adams was steeped in a language of Christian piety utterly lacking in Emerson's letter to Van Buren. But the statements from Concord were alike in giving vent to cries and howls from the depths of the protesters' souls. Playing on the passions, they were designed to "harrow up" the "feelings" of the recipients. Much as he regretted his "shriek," Emerson could not match the emotional intensity of his female neighbors; nor could his impersonal abstractions about the soul mobilize their protest. Brooks was well aware of the difference. While she was careful to observe the proprieties of gender, she hinted that women would not always be so contained. "We could almost be willing to peril our own souls by the temptations of worldly greatness, that we might from some commanding station, under the influence of present feelings, plead the cause of those who have none to help them."[37]

THE UNITY OF WOMEN IN A MORAL CAUSE FRACTURED AT THE MOMENT OF ITS greatest success. The orthodox ministers, who dominated MCASS at the start, had never accepted women on the lecture platform or as equal participants with men in antislavery organizations. They also objected to the religious iconoclasm and social radicalism of William Lloyd Garrison, who filled *The Liberator* with inflammatory articles questioning the sanctity of the Sabbath, the truth of the Bible, and the legitimacy of government. To critics, the editor was not only spreading false ideas but also ruining the reputation of their movement, and in August 1838 they pushed a resolution through MCASS calling on abolitionists to stick to their common cause, free from taint by any extraneous subject. Eight months later the friends of Garrison countered with a statement that "the anti-slavery enterprize has incomparably more to fear from the lukewarmness, timidity, and sectarian and party spirit of its professed friends, than from the violence, misrepresentation and malignity of its avowed enemies." The two sides were at war, and in July 1839, at a session in Acton, the clerical faction lost a bid to bar women from speaking or voting at the group's meetings. As the minority left the hall to start a competing society in line with orthodox convictions, MCASS reaffirmed the right of members to participate in all its proceedings, "without reference to age, sex, clime, color or condition." Mary Brooks likely cast a vote in favor; in ensuing years, she took an active part in the conventions as a frequent member of the business committees that were charged with drawing up resolutions for the delegates' consideration. The rift in the Middlesex group paralleled similar divisions in state and national organizations. By 1840, the American Anti-Slavery Society no longer spoke for a united movement.[38]

The infighting shattered the alliance between liberal and orthodox women in Concord. "Sectarianism," Brooks remarked a few years later, "that fell destroyer of all that is lovely and of good report," invaded the CFASS and dispersed "the armies of freedom." Undoubtedly under the prodding of their new minister, James Means, who succeeded Wilder at the start of 1840, the Trinitarian congregants cut ties to their freethinking sisters, lest they be infected with dangerous ideas. They eventually founded the Ladies' Emancipation Society, whose gatherings were devoted to "prayer, discussion, and work," particularly sewing clothes to be sold for relief of fugitive slaves in Canada. Maria Thoreau, one of the original band of dissenters who had deserted Ripley to launch the new church, could not abide Garrison's heresies. "I can no longer follow such a leader," the devout woman explained. "He has mixed up everything with it, even the doing away of the *Sabbath*."[39]

The secession "thinned" the ranks of the antislavery society, drained the enthusiasm of activists, and weakened support in the wider community. *Freeman* editor Gourgas, though an early member of MCASS, was disgusted by the politicking. "The Abolitionists in their scramble for personal aggrandizement, for rule and mastery, have well nigh forgotten slavery and the slave," he grumbled. "Their efforts seem now to be principally directed to abolishing each other." For a change, his Whig rival at the *Gazette* agreed, excoriating abolitionist leaders as "miserable demagogues and hypocrites . . . a contemptible set of scoundrels." In the winter of 1840 Concord abolitionists responded to a request from MASS leaders in Boston and dutifully went door to door with petitions calling on the state legislature to denounce the Gag Rule in Congress and to oppose the admission of Florida into the Union as a slave state. In a sign of changing gender norms, men and women no longer submitted separate pleas; the latest memorials had separate columns for "males" and "females." The CFASS succeeded in securing only ninety-four signatures, in contrast to its record of 304 names a year before. The results among men were far worse: just thirty-three. Among the stalwarts were all the Emersons and the Thoreaus. Despite his dislike for these campaigns, Waldo went along with his wife and mother. Henry Thoreau joined all his kin. But he evidently had mixed feelings too, for these were the last antislavery memorials he would sign. If he was going to be in the minority, it would be "a minority of one."[40]

Abolitionists pinned the blame for their lagging support on the churches. Instead of fulfilling their solemn calling and directing the "moral energies" of the people, ministers and parish committees sacrificed the "claims of justice and humanity" to "sectarian interests." Not surprisingly, the targets of these attacks returned the hostility. In the fall of 1841, MCASS asked its members to assess the antislavery views of the clergy and churches in their areas. From Concord arrived a damning indictment, probably written by Brooks. "The ministers are not abolitionists," it flatly declared. Unlike his predecessor, Trinitarian pastor Means did not encourage outside speakers, and no one could address the congregation without his approval. As for the First Parish meetinghouse, it was closed for renovations, and word was that upon reopening, it would be "too clean to admit [lecturers on such] impure subjects."[41] The rumor proved correct; the new rules reserved the chapel exclusively for religious activities and made the vestry available only to those groups the parish committee permitted. Even handbills for antislavery meetings were barred from the meetinghouse door. On the first Sunday of 1843, John Shepard Keyes arrived early for public worship, only to confront "a flaming abolition notice" posted at the entrance. It had been "stuck up" there by Dr. Josiah Bartlett. Enraged at the sight, the twenty-one-year-old immediately tore the sheet down and prepared himself to face the doctor's fury.

"If I cannot and don't give him as good as he sends," the young man told a friend, "I will be contented to get worsted, though I have all 'the respectable men in the parish' on my side!"[42]

Mary Brooks was no more accepting of Barzillai Frost than was Waldo Emerson. Sometime in the early 1840s, she became a "come-outer," no longer resigned to suffering through the Unitarian service for the sake of community. The same was the case for Helen Thoreau, the older sister of the budding writer. She was said to have abandoned the Unitarian church in despair over its complicity with slaveholding. The congregation included men from all political parties, pledged to uphold the Constitution and hence "the accursed institution" of human bondage. "Almost universally," in her opinion, it extended the right hand of fellowship to slaveholders; it allowed pro-slavery divines to occupy the pulpit. To confront these facts, as Helen did, was to be cast into "darkness and gloom." How could she listen to the sermon or be uplifted by the psalms when thoughts of the "wrongfulness" of the church's conduct weighed on her mind? "The call to her was imperative— 'Come out [of the church], that ye be not partaker of her plagues,' and she obeyed."

That account was provided by Mary Brooks in an anonymous obituary at Helen Thoreau's death in 1849. It purported to be an authentic account of the spiritual struggles of the young woman with whom she had collaborated closely in the CFASS. If nothing else, it was her own story, and it attested to her affinity with the sensibility famously identified with Helen's brother and with Emerson. "I never saw a woman more truly independent and conscientious," a visiting abolitionist said in praise of Brooks. "She is very lively and very good tempered and perfectly fearless—what the transcendentalists might hail as the truest of women." To preserve her faith, she had to be true to her self—and leave the church.[43]

With meetinghouses unavailable and ministers disengaged if not hostile, abolitionists turned to the lyceum for a forum. Concord's pioneering venture in adult education was flourishing in its second decade of operation, with full seasons of weekly lectures from October to April on a wide range of topics from science and technology to biography, history, literature, politics, law, and contemporary affairs. The Concord Lyceum was a crossroads of community. With some eighty dues-paying members in the mid-1840s, it brought together Democrats and Whigs, advocates and adversaries of temperance, pastors and parishioners of the three churches, and their family members. Everyone in town was welcome to attend at no charge.[44]

One subject remained off-limits: slavery and abolition. While the lyceum had discussed and debated African colonization several times during the 1830s, it had never invited William Lloyd Garrison or any other abolitionist to its dais. Concord was not unique in declining to give its imprimatur to antislavery addresses. Waldo Emerson, building a career on the lecture circuit, lamented that such censorship was all too common. "The platform of the lyceum, hitherto the freest of all organs, is so bandaged and muffled that it threatens to be silent." There was no reason to expect the situation to change anytime soon in Concord; the president of the lyceum in 1842 was none other than Barzillai Frost, just elected to his fifth consecutive term.[45]

The lecture season of 1842–1843 was notable for its ambition. It comprised twenty-five talks, more than half of them by gentlemen recruited from the Boston area, New York City, even England and Ireland; as elsewhere, the lyceum was shedding its original character as a site for self-improving amateurs like Nehemiah Ball and becoming part of a new "culture industry" featuring well-paid professional lecturers like Emerson. The series was the responsibility of the lyceum's three curators, but the bulk of the work was apparently done by a newcomer to the office, Henry Thoreau. The lineup of lecturers included some of the most advanced thinkers of the age: Thoreau's former mentor Orestes Brownson; George Bancroft, the historian and rising Jacksonian politician; Transcendentalist clergymen James Freeman Clarke and Theodore Parker; Whig journalist Horace Greeley, founding editor of the year-old *New York Tribune*; Charles T. Jackson, official geologist for the state of New Hampshire and brother of Lidian Emerson; and Charles Lane, an English newcomer planning a utopian community with Bronson Alcott. Emerson and Thoreau were on the list, too, along with a few locals. This collection of iconoclasts and idealists exposed Concord to the avant-garde ideas of reform stirring and unsettling culture, society, and politics on both sides of the Atlantic.[46]

One speaker was added to the roster on short notice. On December 9, 1842, the *Freeman* carried an advertisement of the upcoming month's talks; scheduled for the twenty-first was Wendell Phillips, scion of a distinguished Boston family who had scorned respectability and a legal career to become a leading spokesman for the Garrisonian wing of abolitionism. Seven weeks earlier the thirty-one-year-old radical had gained added notoriety with his furious remarks at a public meeting in Faneuil Hall to rally support for an escaped slave from Virginia. The man, George Latimer, had been taken into custody and was in danger of being returned to his aggrieved enslaver in Norfolk under the Fugitive Slave Law of 1793. In a dramatic display of outrage that such an unjust proceeding could take place under the cover of federal law, Phillips thundered in judgment and pronounced a "CURSE [upon] THE CONSTITUTION OF THE UNITED STATES." His comments were greeted with "overwhelming hisses." In Concord such extremism was equally incendiary.

Two evenings before Phillips was to speak, the lyceum held an "extra" session to hear the visiting newspaperman Greeley. At the close of the talk, the audience was reminded of the next event on the calendar. John Keyes immediately rose to make a motion. "As this Lyceum is established for Social and Mutual Improvement," the lawyer maintained, "the introduction of the vexed and disorganizing question of Abolitionism or Slavery should be kept out of it." Once again, as in his bouts with the seceding Trinitarians in 1826, with David Lee Child in 1828, and with the Anti-Masons in 1833, Keyes appointed himself the protector of the public against undesirable opinions. But his intervention was shot down right away. Another member successfully moved to cut off debate. Phillips's lecture went forward as planned. The embargo on antislavery lectures at the lyceum came to an end.[47]

It is tempting to credit Thoreau for breaking the silence on slavery at the lyceum. But the instigators of the change were Mary Brooks and the CFASS, working behind the scenes to bring Phillips to the town. In the cash books of the lyceum for 1842 are recorded the receipts for dues, the payments to lecturers—ten dollars each to George Bancroft and Charles T. Jackson, a mere three dollars to Theodore Parker—and a contribution of $13.76 on November 21 "by the Ladies." That terse record does not indicate the purpose, but coming a month before the abolitionist's appearance, it was likely a donation to fund the speech. Brooks served as a broker of the lyceum's invitation. A month after the lecture, the group got around to debating Keyes's motion to bar abolitionists from the platform. The lawyer branded Phillips "a traitor" to his country, who merited "a traitor's fate." No such man should ever disgrace the Concord Lyceum again. Brooks listened to these remarks with rising anger. Keyes "made the most gross barefaced malignant representations of your lecture I have ever heard," the CFASS firebrand informed Phillips. But the "King" of Concord no longer ruled over his neighbors. The lyceum declined to vote on his resolution and put it back on the table.

Far from realizing Keyes's goal, the controversy had the opposite effect. So much "curiosity" did it provoke among those who had missed the original performance that Brooks was commissioned to seek Phillips out for a return engagement at the end of March 1843. That proved impossible, but in the next year's season he was back, over the protests of Keyes, who exhorted the members to deny a hearing to such a "vile, pernicious and abominable" harangue. It was to no avail; a "large majority" endorsed the decision by the new curators— Chairman Samuel Hoar along with Emerson and a local educator—to renew the invitation. Mary Brooks once again served as the intermediary. A "crowded audience" was riveted by Phillips's ninety-minute address, which, true to form, "charged the sin of slavery upon the religion of the country" and brought down "the curse of every honest man" upon the Constitution. "Concord stirred by the Spirit of Liberty" was the headline of a report in *The Liberator* by a local resident with the pseudonym "H.M." Once blasted by Garrison as one of the "three hardest towns in the Commonwealth," along with Charlestown and Lexington, for abolitionists to crack, Concord was at last redeeming its reputation. "The old spirit of liberty is not yet quite extinct in our ancient town."[48]

The furor continued over the next two weeks. The next Wednesday evening the lyceum had no scheduled speaker, so the members assembled to discuss Phillips's address. Rumor had it that a resolution would be introduced to condemn his extreme remarks. Phillips was alerted, and he made his way back to Concord and quietly took a seat, unnoticed, at the back of the Unitarian vestry and listened intently to the proceedings. One gentleman, the sponsor of the resolution, spoke for an hour, and in the course of his remarks, he derided the female supporters of the abolitionist, in the words of St. Paul, as "captive silly women" easily seduced by false teachers. "With equal severity," the second speaker dismissed the thirty-two-year-old Phillips as a "stripling" carried away by the "arrogance" of youth "to assert such monstrous doctrines." The first was clearly Keyes, recycling the insult he had cast upon the female dissidents at the core of the Trinitarian schism back in 1825–1826; his comment caused "a buzzing like a hornet's nest." The second was Hoar, sounding a familiar call for deference to age and experience.

Much to their surprise, the target of the attack suddenly rose from a rear pew and took on his critics in words that "H.M." considered "perfectly electrical."

Phillips readily admitted his youth, only to claim that "I but echo the voices of ages, of our venerated fathers, of statesman, poet, philosopher." And it was true, as Hoar argued, that the abolitionist's curse on the Constitution endangered the Union. But, he pointed out, the "life, liberty, and happiness" enjoyed by whites was founded upon the oppression of Blacks. "My liberty has been bought at too dear a price. If I cannot have it, except by sin, I reject it." As for the prominent role of women and youth in the abolitionist cause, Phillips had no apologies. "Our pulpits are silent"; it was thanks to "silly women and striplings" that protest against slavery was being heard at all. The speaker summoned the young to set aside "selfish ease," take up the charge, and "throw yourselves upon the altar of some noble cause." "Enthusiasm," he concluded in an Emersonian vein, "is the life of the soul."[49]

These stirring words won the crowd, who cheered so wildly that President Frost struggled to restore "order and propriety." Yet a motion to thank Phillips for his lecture faced opposition, and the meeting had to reconvene the following week. In the end, no vote of appreciation was approved, and the contest over abolitionism continued at the lyceum. The episode highlighted the fundamental role of women in forcing moral issues into public life and turning the antislavery movement into a religious crusade. Reverend Frost could not fathom the universal support for Phillips by his female parishioners; it is as if they were "bewitched," he told Brooks. And Squire Hoar was puzzled that the women "are in favor of such *stuff*, and he thinks it augurs badly for Concord people."[50]

Mary Brooks was in a state of religious excitement in June 1843, when, in her role as CFASS secretary, she took stock of the previous year's activities and penned an "annual report" for *The Liberator*. Never before had the group done so much. It had sponsored a dozen lectures, in addition to Phillips's talk; it had held a successful fundraising fair; and it had collected signatures from as many as 146 women on petitions to the General Court urging repeal of the state's longtime ban on interracial marriage and passage of a law prohibiting racial discrimination on the new railroads running across the Bay State. A still bigger campaign, arising out of the successful effort to secure liberty for George Latimer, pressed for a statute to bar Massachusetts officials from cooperating in any way with the return of fugitive slaves to the South—a sanctuary law for refugees from oppression. The "grand Latimer petition" amassed over 64,000 subscribers from 205 towns; Concord's was signed by 385 inhabitants, the seventh-highest total in Middlesex County—a remarkable achievement given its modest population.[51]

These accomplishments attested to the staying power of clear-sighted, brave, and principled women, who had held fast to "the rock of truth," stuck with the CFASS in the face of attacks and defections, and trusted in "the living God." Having "breasted the storm," they were now "comparatively few in number, but invincible" in the faith.[52] Under the influence of the Grimké sisters and through the lessons of experience, they had broken with inherited ideas about ladylike conduct and intervened with increasing confidence in the public arena. In December 1838, when she dispatched the Concord women's remonstrance against Texas annexation to John Quincy Adams for presentation to the House, Brooks took pains to answer objections in advance. "I herewith send you the prayers of a small company of *unsphered* women," she informed the congressional champion of women's right to petition. Implicitly, she acknowledged the violation of decorum: the petitioners had strayed from their assigned sphere, but only out of necessity: "Were we permitted, we would humbly inform the honourable body of which you are a member, how ardently we long to return to those simple but delightful duties of which God and Nature so evidently designed us, viz., those of knitting, spinning, mending hose, making puddings &c. &c." But that would not happen "until our prayers are heard and answered." Brooks's remark was sarcastic; its tone suggests that she was in no hurry to return to the kitchen.[53]

In June 1843 Brooks embraced a public calling and summoned her sisters to rededicate themselves in a religious movement to redeem America from sin. It was their special mission, conferred by the Lord. Men, absorbed in economic striving and partisan calculations, had abdicated responsibility to the "fair sex": "God in his providence has placed this cause, in a great and unusual manner, in the hands of women." Let them answer the divine call and sacrifice everything—"our time, our money, our reputation"—on the altar of freedom. "Blessed is he that considereth the poor; the Lord will deliver him in time of trouble." Mary Brooks may have come out of the church, but the church had not come out of her.[54]

RALPH WALDO EMERSON RESISTED ANTISLAVERY ACTIVISM AS LONG AS HE could. Much as he hated slavery as an affront to his democratic faith, he had mixed feelings about the rhetoric and tactics of the abolitionists. On the one hand, he hailed the rising debate over slavery as a positive stimulus to the American mind. Here was a question untrammeled by "traditions & usages"; unlike age-old controversies in religion and philosophy, it could be argued freely, with "no check from authority" and no ingrained sensitivities to avoid. To make the case for freedom enlarged the heart and expanded the mind. "This is one of those causes which will make a man." On the other hand, the antislavery campaign fell far short of the scholar's ideal. Emerson was disgusted when MCASS activists declined to support Nathan Brooks for Congress after the Whig candidate would not commit to their program; as a result, the election went to the unworthy Democrat, Parmenter. Far from being ennobled by agitation of a moral question, the disputants confined themselves to petty calculations of short-term advantage: "Thus you cease to be a man that you may be an Abolitionist."[55]

No more effective in drawing Emerson to abolitionism were Christian piety and feminine tears. He felt more sympathy for Lidian, as she grieved over the victims of the Middle Passage, than for the objects of her pity, the captive Africans themselves. "The obtuse & barbarous" of the world were bound to suffer in one way or another; "they exchange a cannibal war for a stinking hold" of a slave ship. White racism narrowed his sights and blinded him to the latent divinity of every human soul. At times he seemed to resent the claims of Black people on his compassion. What was the point? he asked in 1840: "It is plain that so inferior a race must perish shortly like the poor Indians." Then again, antislavery activism would benefit whites, for the extension of philanthropy to a "somewhat foreign & monstrous" people would provide an "education . . . in ethics." Still, he did little but sign a few petitions and utter occasional animadversions on slavery. To his female friends in Concord's abolitionist community, he was missing in action, and he was disturbed at the thought—although not enough to commit himself publicly to the cause.[56]

What was he waiting for? Emerson temporized for fear of the price to be paid for engagement in the abolitionist agitation. Would he devolve into a crass politician in the ranks of reform? Would he succumb to "enmity & fault-finding" and grow hateful? Or would he forgo "manly action" for female sentimentalism and tears? Rejecting all those routes, he held back, championed freedom of thought, and urged self-reform as the best route to improving the condition of humankind. What he craved was a fighting faith akin to the Puritanism of his ancestors. That spirit no longer animated the church, as he acknowledged in the divinity school address. It had deserted its old haunts and obtained new quarters in the social movements of the day. "What is this abolition and Nonresistance & Temperance," he asked his Aunt Mary after Ezra Ripley's death, "but the continuance of Puritanism, though it operate inevitably the destruction of the Church in which it grew, as the new is always making the old superfluous."[57]

The Iron Horse

On a winter's day in January 1842, when the ground was so clear of snow that the "wheeling" of horse-drawn vehicles on the highways was "like unto a rail road," the political adversaries John Keyes and Francis Gourgas drove the nine miles southeast from Concord to Waltham to join in a rare bipartisan act. The partisan rivals were among one hundred delegates from Middlesex and Worcester counties assembling to deal with a pressing economic challenge. Massachusetts was teeming with railroad projects; trains ran regularly from the capital west to Worcester, Springfield, and Pittsfield on the New York border and northeast to the textile mills along the Merrimack River and deep into the New Hampshire hills. These "great railroad thoroughfares" brought "increasing wealth and prosperity" to Boston and the towns they traversed. But northern Massachusetts had been left out, as had been Concord, whose importance as a market center stood in peril. Its prospects depended on this convention.

The delegates met in response to a call from citizens of Fitchburg, close to forty miles away. That town's entrepreneurs, led by ambitious paper manufacturer Alvah Crocker, had been pursuing a rail link to Boston for five years without success. As they saw it, the broad swath of territory, midway between the Lowell and Worcester lines, was ordained by "the God of Nature" as a pathway into the interior. Fitchburg itself would be only a way station in the advance. In this visionary scheme, the railroad would extend west to the Connecticut River, then turn north to Brattleboro, Vermont, and hug the valley all the way up to the St. Lawrence River in the Canadian province of Quebec. By this means, steamships would be able to cross the Atlantic, dock in Montreal, and unload passengers and freight onto cars headed south for destinations in New

England all the way back to the coast. New England's hinterland would belong to Boston, *not* to the "Empire City" of New York. And the trade it carried would benefit every community along the route.[1]

The initiative was a wake-up call for Concord. In the early 1840s the town was stagnating. Having lost more than 10 percent of its population during the economic turndown, it was recovering at a snail's pace. Too few newcomers arrived to replace the young men and women departing for opportunities elsewhere. In July 1841 *Republican* editor Robinson came across the record book of the young men's debating club to which he had belonged as a schoolboy between 1827 and 1831. As he looked over the fifty-one members' names, he made note of their current whereabouts and pursuits. The vast majority of the "little circle," he informed readers, had scattered to the winds. Four out of five were gone, a couple to sea, some to the Western country, others to the Cotton Kingdom, most elsewhere in the Northeast. Just ten of their number remained in Concord. Robinson himself would soon join the exodus. "Alas for Concord!" he sighed, as he closed down the newspaper and packed up for Lowell. "It has been going down hill pretty fast in these latter days, and we fear the Railroad will not save it." John Shepard Keyes agreed; on returning home from college, he found business "if anything . . . duller" than ever. To outsiders, the town looked stuck in the mud. An observer from Lowell looked down on the ancient community as having been mired "in status quo" for many years.[2]

Politically, the town's influence was diminishing. Under an amendment to the Massachusetts Constitution adopted in 1840, Concord no longer qualified for two seats in the state legislature, and it faced a renewed bid by Lowell to pick off yet another session of the county courts. Economically, its role as a center of commerce was in jeopardy. Off the grid of the expanding railroad network, it had already lost business to venues with quicker and cheaper access to the Boston market. The Fitchburg proposal could reverse the slide or make it worse. On the one hand, a direct line through Concord "would be of great and apparent benefit to the town," Gourgas opined. On the other hand, Fitchburg could opt for a connection to the Boston and Lowell Railroad and bypass Concord entirely. Should that happen, the town would be "almost or quite cut off from the benefit of the traditional travel which it now enjoys, and must become no inconsiderable sufferer."[3]

Happily for Concord, the direct Fitchburg-Boston route won out, and the convention took quick steps to realize Crocker's plan. Although the inspiration came from Fitchburg, Concord's representatives made it their own. *Freeman* editor Gourgas was a driving force behind the scheme. The Democrat promoted it in his newspaper, became one of three petitioners for a corporate charter, and joined with Fitchburg representative Crocker in pushing the measure through over vociferous objections by spokesmen for the rival Western Railroad.[4]

Concord was quick to rally behind him. Ten days after the Waltham session, a citizens' meeting gathered at the Middlesex Hotel to discuss the plan, and conversations continued over the next two weeks. In a burst of enthusiasm, $48,000 was pledged in stock subscriptions by early February, with Keyes, Samuel Hoar, and Daniel Shattuck among the first takers. "Well Done Old Concord," saluted the *Fitchburg Sentinel*. Eventually, thirty-two residents bought shares for $115 each; in their number were not only stalwarts of the local elite like Daniel Shattuck, who laid out $5,750 for fifty shares, but also a good many farmers and workingmen, including Daniel Hunt, little known for risk-taking and progressive ideas. Even local literary men—Ralph Waldo Emerson and the Transcendentalist poet Ellery Channing—signed on, as did Henry Thoreau's father. Not since the campaign to erect a toll-free bridge over the Charles River into Boston rocked Middlesex County in the late 1820s had a transportation plan generated so much enthusiasm. By 1845, a total of $63,565, well over the original pledges, had been subscribed from Concord alone. Far from being invaded by the iron horse, the enterprising citizens were part of the conquering horde.[5]

The Fitchburg Railroad went from an idea in Alvah Crocker's head to a chartered company with a plan in little more than two months. Thanks to its strong show of support, Concord gained mightily. It acquired two stops on the route authorized by the legislature in early March 1842: one south of "Walden's Pond [*sic*] to a point of Concord plain" a half-mile southwest of the village, where a depot would shortly be constructed, and a second "near Loring's Lead Factory" in West Concord.

Financing and constructing the railroad took more time. Unlike its predecessors, the new line neither sought nor received state aid; it depended entirely on voluntary purchases of stock. Despite early success in selling shares, the company could not begin construction until it had $600,000 in hand, the capital requirement set by the state. It was well short of that amount in 1843 until Sewell F. Belknap, a Vermont railroad builder, came up with a creative arrangement. He would take the final fifteen hundred shares, valued at $150,000, in exchange for the contract to construct the first twenty-seven miles. That speculative agreement sufficed to get the work going, though it is doubtful that Belknap ever fulfilled his pledge to buy all that stock.[6]

Securing labor proved a different challenge. To build the road quickly and cheaply, the company required large numbers of men with strong backs and willing hands, prepared to toil with pick and shovel for as many as sixteen hours daily, week after week, at meager wages. Few natives of Massachusetts, constantly on the move in quest of better prospects, would take the offer. So Crocker, as president of the railroad, looked elsewhere. In 1843 he spent days "haunting the wharves" in Boston harbor, where Cunard packets steamed into port after crossing the Atlantic, their decks crowded with Irish Catholic immigrants looking to escape the harsh conditions and limited opportunities of their homeland. These newcomers, about four thousand arriving in Boston annually during the early 1840s, were, for the most part, "neither destitute nor desperate." It would be several years before the potato crop failed completely across the emerald isle and the Great Famine of 1845–1851 sent hundreds of thousands of their countrymen into flight. The young men whom Crocker encountered on the docks were the working poor, from the homes of smallholders, tenants, and laborers. What they lacked in capital they made up in willingness to toil. The railroad president snapped them up. By August 1843 Belknap, aided by Crocker, had an army of 700 Irishmen in the field, digging, hammering, and blasting their way through the woods. Four months later the number had risen to 1,100.[7]

The coming of the Irish introduced a foreign element into a community grown up almost entirely from native Yankee stock. Although the population was constantly on the move, although farmers relied ever more on transient laborers and servants to do chores once carried out by sons and daughters, the strangers who regularly passed through town were nonetheless familiar products of New England. Even the small minority of African Americans—the Garrison, Hutchinson, and Robbins families—were Black Yankees, with deep roots in the soil. A few immigrants, to be sure, had come from afar to make new lives in Concord during the early republic: the ingenious London-trained tailor James Weir, a veteran of the British Navy, who brought state-of-the-art methods of taking a man's measure to the local clothing trade; the Italian confectioner Lazzaro Montefiore ("old 'Montefury'"), who ran a candy store conveniently located between the stone jail and the brick schoolhouse; and Hugh Quoyle, the hard-drinking Irish veteran of Waterloo, who went from defeating Napoleon to ditching wet meadows on Concord farms before losing his own battle with the bottle and dying on the road to Walden at sixty-one. These scattered souls were mere exotics adding to the local color. The Irish workers who suddenly showed up in the woods in the late spring of 1843 were something else entirely: the advance front of a wave soon to sweep over the Boston area. In its wake, Concord would no longer be the same.[8]

The first arrivals received a positive reception. In late July two Irish settlements were alive with activity in the Walden woods, one named Dublin, the other Cork, out of "love to their fatherland." Their shanties quickly became objects of fascination; built of rough boards, they were covered with earth, heaped up to the roof for insulation. "They live very comfortably," reported Charles C. Hazewell, the new editor of the *Freeman*, "and their abodes are neat and cheerful." The sight of laundry strung between the trees "fluttering and gamboling in the breeze" and the "shouts and laughter" of children lent a pleasant domestic character to the scene. These Irish folk actually defied the usual stereotypes. Hazewell disclosed that a liquor dealer had recently attempted to set up shop among them, only to be greeted with hostility. The denizens of the woods called a meeting and gave the rum seller twenty-four hours to settle his affairs and "decamp." Let no one "seek to make them slaves to intemperance." These foreigners were as committed to "total abstinence principles" as Concord natives and as capable of governing themselves. The *Freeman* congratulated them on being "very apt scholars in learning the duties of citizens."[9]

Nothing shocked the townspeople more than the cruel exploitation the railroad workers endured. Ward Safford, a New Hampshire native still performing day labor at thirty-three, considered himself "well off" compared to the "poor Irish." They were paid sixty cents a day, the same wage he earned, but where the Yankee was furnished room and board as part of his compensation, the immigrants had to "find themselves." Rising before dawn, they were "on the road" before morning light and toiling on the tracks until after dark. "I hardly knew what work was until I saw them," he reflected. "It is slavery indeed." Peter Hutchinson, widely admired for his prodigious labors at hog butchering and sheep shearing, was relieved that he did not have to work like an Irishman. He "had never seen men perform so much," he told Emerson. Never again would he complain if an employer kept him busy after sundown.

The punishing work reminded Emerson of "negro driving": "The humanity of the town suffers with the poor Irish." And then there was the ever-present danger from "the blowing of rocks, explosions all day," resulting "now & then" in "a painful accident." But what could be done about their plight, the scholar mused in his study, when so many "new applicants for the same labor are coming in every day"? The iron laws of the capitalist market pushed wages down to mere subsistence; only a bachelor could survive on that compensation. What a comfortable Emerson attributed to the workings of supply and demand, the day laborer Safford blamed on stark oppression. Hearing rumors that the Fitchburg Railroad was going to be extended into Vermont, the laborer sympathized with the men and beasts who would carry out that work: "The poor paddys have to make it and the rich receive the money; it makes the rich richer and the poor poorer, and so it is now a days."[10]

The demand for Irish labor extended to Concord's farms. Even as railroad crews were setting up camp in the woods, the laborers James Conlon, David Dole, and Michael Kelly were getting work on Abel Moore's model farm. These hands were put to tasks that Yankee help had customarily done, such as reaping and threshing rye and piling manure; other stints drew on long experience in the old country. A crew of three spent the last days of November in their boss's boggy meadows, cutting peat for fuel and fertilizer. These illiterate laborers had considerable advantages: they were cheap, and they were tractable. The calculating Moore had once used prisoners in the county jail to ditch and drain his wetlands. Immigrants cost little more. One hired man received just six dollars a month or twenty cents a day, plus room and board. That was no better than railroad work, and the hours could be just as long. On Elijah Wood's farm a few years later, an immigrant named Michael Flannery was required to rise every morning at 4:30 a.m. and milk a total of twenty-eight cows; his pay was just $6.50 a month for the heroic effort. To add insult to injury, Wood would not spare even a drop of milk for his employees' tea and coffee. Yankee farmers would never have treated so badly the "ruffians, rum-drinkers, and half-breeds" from New Hampshire and Vermont they once had no choice but to hire. The "poor Irish" had to take such abuse or else. Abel Moore set severe terms for Barney Kelly's service. To earn his meager pay, the man agreed to labor "well and faithfully" at "any kind of work" he was asked to do, "and not to murmur about said work nor to scold" the other help and "to work his time out." The penalty for violating this pledge was an entire loss of wages.[11]

The immigrants' suffering did not pass unnoticed. *Freeman* editor Hazewell sympathized with the centuries-old struggle of the Irish people to free themselves from English oppression and particularly with the contemporary nationalist movement led by Daniel O'Connell for separation from Great Britain. Ireland, the *Freeman* instructed, was now "the scene of a contest the most singular ever waged between a numerous and brave people on the one hand, and an oppressive aristocracy of foreign descent on the other." Like the Patriots of 1776, the Irish were engaged in a struggle for national liberation. The implication was obvious: Erin's sons and daughters—"brave, ingenious, quick in perception, and patient of toil"—should be received in Concord with open arms.[12]

Such sentiments were widespread among Garrisonian abolitionists. Dr. Bartlett freely treated Irish patients without any hope of payment, and he went out of his way to assist them with "food, clothing, and fuel" and with loans to buy a house or satisfy a debt. Mary Brooks could not ignore the needs of the shanty dwellers living behind her house on the Sudbury Road. "If [she] had cloth for *one* good chemise, she would cut two skimpy ones and give one away." So too did members of the Concord Female Charitable Society act quickly to meet the immigrants' needs. Hardly had the work crews set up housekeeping in the Walden woods than the benevolent ladies were making shirts, aprons, and other items of apparel for the young. Cynthia Thoreau took special responsibility for a newcomer named Michael O'Brien; through her intervention, he periodically received provisions of tea and sugar, a dress for his wife, and pantaloons for his "little boy." This avant-garde of Irish settlers was incorporated into local life with surprising speed, their births, marriages, and deaths registered with the town clerk soon after the events. The weddings themselves took place at St. Mary's Church in Waltham, whose priest ministered to the faithful in Concord on circuit. In 1844 Catholic Mass was celebrated for the first time in the town founded by Peter Bulkeley as a Puritan city upon a hill. The ceremony took place in the "long yellow block" of tenements right next to the First Parish meetinghouse.[13]

When railroad construction was over, the shanties gradually disappeared from the Walden woods, their boards sold by the departing owners to frugal Yankees and recycled for such uses as Thoreau's house by the pond. In their wake, desperate refugees from famine-ravaged Ireland began pouring in, nearly 250 individuals by 1850; they were joined by some thirty migrants from hard-pressed rural Nova Scotia and Quebec.

Nationally, the influx of immigrants from 1845 to 1854 raised the foreign-born share of the total population to an all-time high (14.5 percent), close to its peak in 1910 (14.7 percent) and unsurpassed even today. Within Massachusetts, newcomers flocked to the Boston area and to the leading manufacturing cities. In 1850 one out of every three people in the state capital was foreign-born, as was a fifth of Middlesex County. Concord, in comparison, drew 12 percent of its residents from abroad. But the Irish share was gaining rapidly. In 1850 such immigrants and their children made up 15 percent of the town; five years later, a quarter. So frequently did Irish births match or even exceed those in native families that one year when the gap narrowed, town clerk George Heywood announced that "America will have cause to be hopeful."[14]

The foreign-born inhabitants were not distant "others" set apart in an isolated enclave. Just over half of the Irish immigrants (124) lived and labored in a Yankee household, almost the same number (122) as shared quarters with their countrymen. And the Catholic children were nearly as likely to attend Concord's schools as their Protestant counterparts. In a community that was too small for segregation, the townspeople experienced ethnic diversity face to face. Thanks to this firsthand knowledge, they opened their hearts and purses to the plight of the newcomers' countrymen across the sea; in 1847 Concord contributed $382 to the New England Committee for the Relief of Ireland and Scotland.[15]

THE FIRST LOCOMOTIVE STEAMED INTO CONCORD ON THURSDAY, JUNE 6, 1844, its "shrill" whistle shattering "the repose of that quiet venerable town"; soon afterward the trains began running back and forth to Charlestown four times a day. Four years later the route was extended into Boston. The Fitchburg Railroad proved an immediate success. It cut travel time into the city from four hours by stage to one in the cars, and the cost of the twenty-mile trip fell from seventy-five to fifty cents. "The cars are large, roomy, and handsome," the *Freeman* enthused, and the conductors "gentlemen of great politeness and intelligence." For all his skepticism of statistics, Emerson was so impressed by the speed that he calculated its remarkable rate: one mile for every minute and forty-five seconds. Older modes of transportation could not compete. As he took to the road to deliver his lectures, Concord's leading intellectual noticed protests from the losing side. "No monopoly!" teamsters scribbled on their wagons; "free trade and teamsters' rights," they painted on guideboards along the highways. Emerson discerned the signs of the times and bought railroad stock. Patronage of this "most picturesque route" answered the "most sanguine hopes." By 1847–1848 the Concord station was earning $5,745 in ticket sales and nearly $6,000 for freight. The shareholders did very well on their investment; dividends ranged from 8 to 10 percent annually. As the railroad network spread, every town demanded connections. At least three new lines were projected to link up with the Fitchburg trains in Concord but were never built. Meanwhile "the fertile vallies of Vermont, the ore beds of the lake and the capital of Canada" awaited the locomotive. "We have constructed a fate, an Atropos, that never turns aside," Thoreau complained of the iron horse. His neighbors gladly rode the rails to their rendezvous with destiny.[16]

Even before the first train pulled into the station, Concord was enjoying an economic boost from the improved means of transportation. In October 1843 the *New York Herald*, the sensational penny paper published in Manhattan, carried a surprising item: a detailed description of Concord, full of statistics about population, agriculture, and manufactures. The piece was written by the newspaper's managing editor, Frederick Hudson, who had grown up in the small Massachusetts town and evidently absorbed the same fascination with facts that had mesmerized Jarvis and Shattuck. On a visit to his hometown, the twenty-four-year-old journalist surveyed "the progress of the village" from 1820 to 1840, as documented by the changing valuation of property at the start of each decade. Hudson was dismayed by the various signs of stagnation: declining population, few new houses; diminishing textile production; loss of woodland and growing acreage left unimproved: "All these speak unfavorably for the village." But hope was on the horizon. "It is expected, and certainly to be hoped, that the Fitchburg Railroad, now building, will give an impulse to the enterprize and energy of the place." The prediction was sound. The real estate market boomed as the opening of the railroad drew near. A "large depot" rose to accommodate travelers; the area in its vicinity, nicknamed "Texas," saw a spate of new houses, including the first home to be owned by John and Cynthia Thoreau. "We never saw Concord so busy as at the present time," observed the *Lowell Journal*.[17]

Back in 1825 the town was described as situated "almost in the suburbs of the city." Now it was being touted as a bedroom community, from which businessmen could commute to State Street and Beacon Hill. Within four years of the railroad's opening, three dozen passengers, on average, were traveling daily from Concord into the metropolis. One such commuter was William W. Wheildon, who relocated himself, but not the *Bunker-Hill Aurora*, to the country town; he became a familiar sight on the cars, entirely absorbed in writing as the landscape passed by unnoticed. Undoubtedly, Henry Thoreau paid closer attention, especially on the way past Walden. In 1849 he persuaded the president of Harvard to revise the rules limiting library privileges to graduates living within ten miles of Cambridge. The railroad, he protested, had "destroyed the old scale of distances." That was likewise its crucial advantage for Emerson. From Concord, he could easily ride the lecture circuit not just in the Northeast but to points ever farther west. Without the Fitchburg Railroad, he could not have remained the Concord Sage.[18]

Just as the workdays of many villagers revolved around the trains, so local businesses became satellites of the city. No longer did "great baggage-wagons" drawn by six or even eight horses—the "freight-cars of their day"—"lumber" into town with loads of country produce for exchange at Shattuck's store on the common or Phineas How's establishment on Main Street. Why make a long, laborious journey to Concord center, when the iron horse could carry passengers and goods to market in Boston at far greater speed and much lower cost? As village merchants, once vital intermediaries in the flow of goods between country and city, lost bargaining power, their stores were reduced to showrooms of items from "the most celebrated manufactories" in the land and of imports from abroad. Seldom did retailers advertise the products of nearby farms—butter and cheese, pork and lard—alongside flour from the West and sugar from the West Indies. Such "country pay" steadily fell out of favor; storekeepers preferred to make sales in cash and at fixed prices. Shopping, in turn, shed much of its sociable character. Merchants had no incentive to haggle with customers over prices or means of payment. Nor could buyers look forward to "treats" of rum at the conclusion of a sale; the temperance movement had killed that practice. Economically and socially, Concord's stores came to play a less prominent part on the local stage.[19]

The eclipse of the village had its beginnings in the late 1830s, but that fate was sealed by the Fitchburg Railroad. Trade contracted severely in size and scale. In 1835 the stores and shops were at the peak of prosperity, with thirty-five businesses reporting nearly $50,000 in goods for sale. The Panic of 1837 swept through the countinghouses and thinned the ranks in trade. The surviving enterprises curtailed outlays on goods. In the summer of 1837, inventories were down by more than a quarter, and by the time they began to recover, the railroad transformed the local scene. A year after the trains began running to and from Concord, businesses sharply reduced their stockpiles to $23,000. The retrenchment continued through 1850, when the typical establishment was less than half the size of its counterpart fifteen years before.

Retailers catered primarily to a local clientele. But they could not take those customers for granted. Competing strenuously for that trade were out-of-town stores, many based in Boston, whose notices filled the columns of the *Freeman*. Local merchants fought back by promoting their up-to-date supplies of dry goods, domestic and imported, and by guaranteeing prices as low as anywhere. One village trader illustrated his ads with icons of the latest technology: a steamship in one case, a locomotive in another. The latter was labeled "Fitchburg Railroad," and it ran early in June 1843, just as the Irish workers were setting up camp and starting to prepare the track. Concord, the ad suggested, would not be left behind in the march of progress. But the town was soon relegated to the rear of the train. In March 1847 the *Freeman* surprised subscribers by closing up shop and moving to Charlestown. Whatever advantages it once enjoyed from being at the heart of Middlesex, the final editor, Henry S. Warren, explained, were lost with the coming of the railroad. "Those who have job work to execute or advertisements to insert in our paper . . . complain of the inconvenience and expense they are subjected to in order to communicate with us." Charlestown, the terminus of the Fitchburg Railroad at the eastern edge of the county, was now a superior base of operations to "old Concord" at its center.[20]

The status of merchants diminished with the reach of their trade. Daniel Shattuck, the Davis brothers, Burr and Prichard had been village nabobs, with their fingers in every pie. Not so their successors. In the mid-1840s, Shattuck turned over the store on the common to his twenty-one-year-old son Henry and a partner and was now free to concentrate on running the Mill Dam Company and the Concord Bank and on buying and selling land in the town center and near the railroad station. Into his hands gravitated the property of rivals. He should have kept a closer watch over the store. Lacking his father's talent for business, Henry Shattuck could not make a profit; the fixture on the common closed in 1848. The store's debts lingered on; at his death in 1867, the claims of creditors in Boston ate up a good deal of Daniel Shattuck's estate. In the end, Concord's richest man proved to be as insolvent as Samuel Burr; even his Mansion House went up for auction, like so many of the properties he had frequently bought up.[21]

As Concord ceased to be a magnet for trade, it was also becoming a less hospitable place to run a tavern. Through 1840 the townspeople had resisted strict laws to curtail access to intoxicating beverages; three inns and three retail stores continued to furnish drinks, to the dismay of the Concord Total

Abstinence Society, a new organization founded in 1840 to eliminate the sale and consumption of all alcoholic beverages.[22] Then in March 1842 temperance advocates won a surprise victory. Under Massachusetts law, liquor licenses were awarded annually by elected county commissioners, who normally followed the recommendations of local selectmen in certifying retailers and tavern keepers. But what if town authorities refused to approve any applicants? Following that strategy, moral reformers could skip the arduous work of collecting temperance pledges. Rather than engage in voluntary suasion, they would impose prohibition by public demand, one town at a time. To this end, the warrant for the March 7 town meeting asked whether "the public good" required the issuance of any liquor licenses and, if not, whether the selectmen should be instructed to "withhold their certificates to the falsehood."

No one expected the controversial article to pass. But with a crowded agenda, the meeting dragged on, and attendance dwindled. When the anti-license proposal finally came up, Samuel Hoar, a temperance crusader since 1814, led the charge. In a "feeling and eloquent" speech, the squire set forth "the awful consequences of the traffic in strong drink" and then "urged the duties of all good citizens" to terminate it. As he warmed to the subject, an impatient inhabitant interrupted with a complaint. He had not come for a temperance lecture; "he could hear enough of them elsewhere." Moreover, "the gentleman" had talked long enough. It was time to call the question, "as he and his friends were rather dry" and wanted to get the discussion over with and "adjourn to the tavern." Graciously, Hoar said "he would not keep" his neighbors "in distress any longer."

By then, a meeting that had begun with 290 men had devolved into a rump of the town. A mere ninety-seven citizens were on hand to decide the crucial question: whether the selectmen should decline to certify rum sellers. The measure carried with fifty-seven in favor, forty against. A small fraction of legal voters—one out of every seven men on the rolls—weighed in personally to stop the sale of ardent spirits. Yet the vote stuck. In 1844 and again in 1846, the town "unanimously" rejected motions to rescind the ban on licensing innkeepers, and it affirmed its view that the sale and use of hard liquor "greatly tends to pauperism, crime, human degradation and suffering." In this conviction, Concord dropped its traditional practice of "warning" town meetings by posting notices at the taverns. The public house, once the crossroads of community, would no longer be a vital center for news.[23]

What Concord lost in commerce, it regained in other arenas. The railroad was a boon to agriculture—or at least to those farmers prepared to enlist their land and labor in service to the advancing industrial revolution. Construction of the Fitchburg line immediately spurred demand for wood to fuel the locomotives and to furnish the "sleepers" supporting the rails on which the trains ran. In 1844 one canny speculator moved quickly to tap this market. Joel Britton, a forty-three-year-old yeoman, arrived from nearby Littleton and began buying land and lumber from local property holders. He was soon the preeminent wood dealer in town. Employing ten men to wield axes and saws on his behalf, he accumulated a staggering 372,000 feet of lumber and 2,023 cords of firewood. Britton nearly monopolized the timber business and dominated the supply of firewood, evidently acting as a middleman for the Fitchburg Railroad. But his business deals got ahead of him, and he eventually went bust, though "the woods continue[d] to fall before the axes of other men," as Henry Thoreau was quick to notice. The inexhaustible hunger of the iron horse generated a speculative boom in woodlots that steadily hacked away at the town, including the stands of oak and pine surrounding Walden Pond. Over the 1840s, loggers reduced the woodlands so relentlessly that by 1850 just one acre in ten lay in forest.[24]

Britton and Belknap, the railroad contractor, hoped to profit still more from the new means for converting the natural growth of local woodlands into raw materials for construction and transportation. In the winter of 1846, they joined with thirty-five mechanics and merchants to address a gap in the local economy. Ever since the Mill Dam Company had taken down the ancient establishment in the center, Concord village had lacked a convenient facility to grind grain and saw wood. The result was a serious detriment to local growth. "From the want of water power . . . many branches of mechanical pursuits cannot be carried on"; the residents incur "much inconvenience and expense" in getting to distant mills; and "the prosperity" of the center is "much diminished," notwithstanding the great improvement of communications effected by the railroad.

Britton, Belknap, and associates laid out these complaints in a plea to the state legislature setting forward a remedy. With the Concord River too sluggish to drive a mill wheel, the petitioners would take up state-of-the-art technology and employ a steam engine for "sawing lumber, planing boards, grinding grain, and . . . other mechanical purposes." All they asked of the General Court was a corporate charter. One obstacle stood in their way: a counterpetition from sixty-three inhabitants of Acton objecting that the Concord area already had enough mills for the existing business and nothing more was required. Fortunately, with Rockwood Hoar in the Massachusetts Senate, Concord's entrepreneurs had an influential voice on their behalf. The Concord Steam Mill Company was approved with an authorized capital of $50,000. The economic revival of the village appeared at hand.[25]

The scheme was troubled from the start. The company erected its structure and installed its steam-powered machinery at a cost of $11,000, but a year and a half after the launch, the directors were looking for somebody else to run the enterprise. Fittingly, they fastened on Abel Moore, the man most responsible for removing the old mill from the center of town and a member of the company's board. Together with Britton and two associates, he leased the operation, then immediately turned around and subcontracted it to a veteran miller from New Hampshire. The ultimate goal was to divest entirely, but before a public auction could be held, mill and machinery fell victim to a common accident involving steam power. They were consumed in yet another disastrous fire. The insurance did not fully cover the loss, and nobody took steps to rebuild. The economic prospects of Concord kept going up in smoke.[26]

Another manufacturing project existed in name only; the Concord Steam Power Company, incorporated in February 1845, never got around to its declared purpose of "manufacturing and printing cotton and woollen goods and furnishing and letting steam power . . . for manufacturing and the mechanic arts." Textile manufacturing remained confined to factory village in the west part of town, where under the ownership of Calvin C. Damon, the enterprise finally enjoyed prosperity, turning out a staple cloth known as "domet," woven from a cotton warp with a woolen filling. Light, warm, and resistant to shrinkage, the flannel fabric provided a popular substitute for the linsey-woolsey undergarments regularly worn by women and children in the "age of homespun." Like the original manufactory begun by Brown and Hartwell in 1807, the Damon mill depended on the waterpower of the Assabet River; it employed sixty operatives—thirty men, thirty women—many of whom lived in a company boardinghouse; and it loosened Concord's link to the cotton plantations of the South. The Damon mill was the largest industrial enterprise in town. Like Whiting's carriage company, Loring's lead factory, and the competing Munroe and Thoreau pencil-making concerns, it benefited from the arrival of the railroad. But in its own operations, it had not yet entered the age of steam.[27]

The clearing of forests was part of a larger reorganization of farming in

Concord. Why tie up so much acreage in woodlots, when coal from Pennsylvania and lumber from Maine could be readily imported on the freight cars? Progressive farmers accepted the capitalist logic of specialization in cash crops for the changing market. Since the mid-1820s they had ceased to raise flax and wool, the raw materials of everyday clothes, in favor of factory-made garments, and they steadily cut back on "rye and Injun" from their fields in favor of cheap Western flour at the stores. So, too, were wetlands and forests being cleared to create meadows for English hay, the fodder crop so much in demand in area stables and barns.

With the arrival of the Fitchburg Railroad, Concord entered still more deeply into the regional division of labor. The Society of Middlesex Husbandmen and Manufacturers had long been promoting the cultivation of fruits and vegetables for sale. Now this produce became practical and profitable on a large scale. Within a year of the trains chugging into the station, nearly a quarter of local growers were giving up "the old corn-and-pumpkin farming" for "modern 'sauce-gardening'" with carrots and beets, onions and turnips, and a new vegetable known as asparagus that became so identified with the town that it was nicknamed "Concord grass." At the same time, more than a third were supplying perishable apples, peaches, and pears to urban dining tables; strawberries would soon join the mix. Even more notably, the railroad enabled the shipment of fresh milk into the city. Twenty-one men—10 percent of all farmers—were already engaged in this venture by the summer of 1845. Just two years after its completion, the Fitchburg Railroad was delivering nine hundred cans—3,600 gallons—of milk daily to Charlestown and Boston, and it would soon introduce a special night train for the purpose. In short, the steady chopping of the ax; the bustle of men spading up meadows, hauling gravel, and raking hay; the clanging of milk pails and the lowing of milch cows—these were the dominant sounds on Concord's farms in the 1840s, and they were orchestrated to the movements of the locomotive whose piercing whistle as it swept through town announced the ascendancy of a new order of things.[28]

Nathan Barrett led the way into the future. On his scenic 229 acres atop Punkatasset Hill overlooking the river, he planted thriving orchards of apples and peaches that frequently won premiums at the annual cattle show from the 1820s on. With the arrival of the railroad, in which he held three shares of stock, this "clever, honest Yankee farmer" redoubled his efforts and branched out into new ventures. In 1845 he raised 500 bushels of fruit, the highest total in town, and 450 bushels of vegetables, perhaps including the beets, carrots, and tomatoes for which he had earned a prize two years earlier. He was among the first to carry milk to the depot, making a twice-daily trip into town that was "as regular as old 'Deacon Brown's accommodation stage.'" En route the companionable Barrett welcomed passengers, carried messages, gave rides to schoolboys, and paused to hear the latest gossip on the milldam before delivering the fluid product of his twenty-five milch cows at the station. On virtually every count he deserved recognition as the most up-to-date agriculturalist in Concord. He was tops in hay (90 tons) and garden seeds (700 bushels, sold to the Boston firm of Ruggles, Nourse & Mason), as well as in fruit. No one else, not even Abel Moore, outdid him in so many areas, although the former deputy sheriff still harvested more vegetables (800 bushels) than anyone else and ranked second in hay (60 tons).

What made this superior achievement possible? Like the other elite farmers in the forefront of change, Barrett amassed the capital and labor to carry out production on a large scale. He belonged to the investing class, with shares in the Concord Bank as well as the railroad. Though he had four boys, they were too young to provide much help until the 1850s, by which time the eldest was at Harvard and the next in a clerkship. The ambitious farmer had to rely on others to get the chores done. One clever idea was to allow two young idealists, the brothers George William and Burrill Curtis, to board in his household for $1.50 a week, plus five hours' unpaid labor a day. The "thoroughly skilled practical farmer" took one look at "the refined gentlemen" with shoulder-length hair parted at the middle and dispatched them to shovel manure, just to "test their metal." They passed with flying colors and soon moved on to the potato patch, the apple orchard, and the hayfield. So captivated was the future literary editor George Curtis by the sublime view from the farm that he never noticed his employer's daily trips with the milk pails into the village. After cutting his hand on a scythe, he was soon of little use. Barrett found more reliable help in hired labor. By 1850 four men—two Yankees, two Irish immigrants—lived and worked on the farm, along with an Irish woman in domestic service. Without the emigrants from the famine, Concord's entrepreneurial farmers would never have been able to carry on such intensive production of milk, vegetables, and fruit.[29]

One newcomer labored in obscurity for years to develop a single specialty crop. Born and bred in Boston, Ephraim Wales Bull was trained in the craft of gold beating, spending his days in the shop pounding precious yellow metal into the thinnest of sheets for use by gilders and bookbinders. But confinement in the crowded city was not good for his health, so in 1836, on doctor's orders, the thirty-year-old mechanic moved with his wife to seven acres along the Bay Road, reestablished his business, and threw himself into Whig politics. By 1843, the skilled craftsman was at a low point in his fortunes. That year he declared bankruptcy and determined to make a new start.

Nobody mistook the clean-shaven and impeccably dressed Bull for a working farmer. For nearly a decade, he kept no livestock, raised no hay, and grew just five bushels of corn on a single acre of tillage. He was overlooked in the 1845 state survey of agriculture and industry and in its federal counterpart five years later. Even George Minott, his independent neighbor just down the road, ran a bigger operation. But Bull loved to be outside in his garden, and after acquiring an adjacent piece of land, he invested "almost childish enthusiasm" in setting out trees, shrubs, and vines on his ten acres. The grape was his special "passion."

Although Bull did not join the agricultural society until December 1844, he was well aware of the competition in Middlesex and beyond to develop the fruit of the vine. European grapes did not flourish in the eastern part of the United States, no matter how hard such optimists as Thomas Jefferson had tried to cultivate them, and by the 1830s the race was on to find a native substitute. Many temperance advocates cheered them on; as John M. Cheney, the bank cashier, had reminded the audience at the 1831 cattle show, Concord abounded in wild grapes ripe for conversion into a flavorful, healthy drink. Local vineyards could be the answer to ardent spirits. Perhaps that goal inspired Bull, an activist in the total abstinence campaign. Or maybe he relished the challenge of taking his wide reading of European horticulture and applying it with the patient, methodical approach of a gold beater to accomplish what no one else had done before. It was not for lack of trying that Nathan Barrett's prizewinning "native purple Fox Grapes" with "very large berries," exhibited in 1832, did not become a big seller, nor that the specimens of mixed parentage from the Old and New Worlds submitted by others did little better in the marketplace.

Bull kept his experiments to himself. In October 1843 an apt candidate for development caught his eye: a volunteer creeping up a stone wall in his backyard, whose fruit tokened sweetness and hardihood. Bull transplanted the vine to the center of his garden and carefully nurtured its growth over several seasons. Six years later the grape was ready to try out on a neighbor, who tasted the fruit and immediately exclaimed, "Why, this is better than the Isabella," then the reigning queen of the agricultural fair. Even then Bull bided his time to perfect the product. "In no department . . . has there been so much improvement as in the cultivation of fruit," Moses Prichard, secretary of the agricultural society, remarked in 1845, and "it is by far the easiest and most profitable part of farming." The painstaking grape grower would surely have scoffed. Not until 1853 was Bull ready to display his achievement.

Rather than introduce the fruit to the world in its local habitat, Bull opted for the prestigious annual exhibition of the Massachusetts Horticultural Society in Boston. Illness kept him from attending the event, so he sent the grapes ahead to the exhibition hall, where they were misplaced. A committee came out to Concord to inquire what had happened. Assured that the fruit had been sent, they headed back to the city, located the missing display, then on tasting the fruit were so astonished by the flavor, they made another trip back to Concord, where they grilled Bull about his methods. Convinced by his account, the judges hailed the grower's accomplishment. The Concord grape rode to triumph in the metropolis on the iron horse.[30]

On the eve of the railroad age, most farms in Concord preserved as much of the old agrarian regime as they could. A bare majority (53 percent) stuck with familiar crops and eschewed the new commodities in demand by urban consumers. Even those adapting to change aimed to do as much as possible for themselves. On Daniel Hunt's farm opposite the Nathan Barrett place, "the old style of farming" provided for a family of eleven straining at the seams. Brown bread from the rye and corn fields was on the daily board, and it was spread with butter from the six cows in the barn. Virtually everything on the table—beef and pork, chicken and eggs, beans, applesauce and "green" sauce— was homegrown. But it took the all-out effort of everyone in the household to obtain a "competency" and to earn the money needed for goods at the store, including the cotton and woolen cloth that now came from the mills instead of the farm.

The Hunt operation was not self-sufficient; nor did it resist production for market. The proprietor had, after all, bought stock in the railroad, on which he could have shipped the fifty bushels of fruit he raised in 1845: apples and peaches from the orchard, cranberries from the river bogs. The main cash crop came from the dairy: five hundred pounds of butter annually, twice the town average. To sustain this output, Daniel Hunt arduously converted his wet meadows into arable fields capable of producing immense supplies of English hay. His wife and six daughters bore the heavier burden. Day in, day out, when the cows were "fresh," the women milked, strained, churned, preserved, and packed butter for delivery to customers in town. "My mother prided herself on the quality of her butter," recalled her youngest son, "and spared no pains to keep up that quality."[31]

When Frederick Hudson of the *New York Herald* returned to his hometown in October 1843 and witnessed the ongoing construction of the Fitchburg line, he worried about what lay ahead. The railroad would undoubtedly provide a boost to local manufactures, but would it benefit farmers? The journalist feared "they may be injured." Once suppliers close to Boston had the market for grains and other bulky commodities to themselves. Let the trains in, and that advantage would disappear. Farms in the interior, where land was both cheaper and more fertile, would easily outsell the produce of "old Concord" and make its agriculture unprofitable. These concerns proved exaggerated. Barretts, Bulls, and Hunts survived and often thrived by adapting to the new circumstances, laboring more intensively (thanks to Irish immigrants), and concentrating on high-value perishable goods. Concord's dairies, orchards, and market gardens helped to feed the rapidly growing city.[32]

But a good many yeomen were lost in the transition. In the fall of 1842, on a hike into the backcountry, Emerson was startled by the contrast between the attractive landscape, "very cultivated," and the dreary farms and houses along the way. Hardly anyone was in evidence, even in distant fields. This was a depressed countryside seldom seen by those who stayed on the main-traveled roads. Emerson attributed the decay to a relentless process by which ancient homesteads were stripped of their most talented and ambitious young men. Whenever "any large brain is born in these towns," he departed by age sixteen or twenty to seek his fortune in the city. The farm fell to "the inferior class of the people," from whose incompetent management resulted "all these shiftless, poverty-struck pig-farms." Depopulation and degeneration went together. The railroad accelerated the exodus from the land, as beleaguered inhabitants gave up the struggle to carry on the old ways and lacked the will and/or resources to adopt new ones. In his daily walks in the woods, by the river, and past meadows and fields, Thoreau was struck by the thin traces of habitation: "There are square miles in my vicinity which have no inhabitant." He was drawn to neighborhoods emptying out and reverting to the wild, such as the Old

Marlborough Road, where the Black man Elisha Dugan scrabbled a marginal existence. His father, Thomas, had escaped slavery in Virginia and built a new life as a small farmer and householder in the southern part of town. Elisha followed a different course; in 1850 the forty-three-year-old landless laborer, solitary and independent on the edge of the woods, struck Thoreau as a kindred spirit. Thanks to the writer, he would be remembered as

> *The man of wild habits*
> *Partridges & Rabbits*
> *Who has no cares*
> *Only to set snares*
> *Who liv'st all alone*
> *Close to the bone—*
> *And where life is sweetest*
> *constantly eatest.*

A scattering of souls was dispersed in such thinly settled districts. "We walk," Thoreau concluded, "in a deserted country."[33]

As old-timers moved out, their farms fell into other and fewer hands. Thanks to the short-term impetus given to the economy by the railroad, Concord's population rebounded; by 1850, it numbered 2,249, the highest figure yet reported by the federal census. The growth was owing to the influx of immigrants from abroad, few of whom had the means to replace the natives on the land. Economic inequality, rising since the early 1820s, reached new heights. In the mid-eighteenth century, as Concord was beginning to cope with population pressure on land, seven out of ten taxpayers had possessed farms of their own. A century later, as newcomers from Ireland, Nova Scotia, and Quebec were pouring in, seven out of ten taxpayers had no land at all. Structurally, the community was becoming more stratified than ever, its wealth consolidated at the top, its residents divided by class, ethnicity, and religion, even as egalitarian rhetoric swirled in popular politics and, perhaps with more serious purpose, in the abolitionist movement.[34]

IRONICALLY, THE VERY ECONOMIC CHANGES ACCELERATED BY THE RAILROAD— the outflow of people from the out-districts, the receding of trade and traffic in the center, the concentration of industry in factory villages—fostered a new view of Concord as the pastoral setting for a Transcendentalist counterculture. Well before the locomotive intruded into its garden, the town was already emerging as a literary center, thanks to Emerson's growing stature and its own natural attractions. Though he was still a provincial figure, best known in the environs of Boston, the lecturer began to draw like-minded thinkers to his home, and he was eager to see them settle nearby. Margaret Fuller and George Bradford came for extended stays; Bronson Alcott arrived in the spring of 1840, his controversial school at an end, and embraced a new way of life as a Transcendental farmer with wife Abigail and three "little women" (and a fourth on the way)—"Orpheus at the plough." Emerson's circle expanded with idealistic artists and poets—Jones Very, Ellery Channing, Caroline Sturgis—in whom he glimpsed new hopes for American culture. A village of intellectuals, he dreamed, was taking shape in Concord. (Unfortunately, he could never persuade his Scottish friend Carlyle to cross the Atlantic and take up residence.) The Transcendental Club periodically gathered in his parlor; *The Dial*, the organ of the movement, was produced after April 1842 in his study. Thoreau boarded in his home. This literary coterie enlivened local life, though its participants were too peripatetic and too intent on their own pursuits ever to form a community.[35]

For just this reason, Emerson had declined to join Brook Farm. Launched by Transcendentalist minister George Ripley in the spring of 1841, the experiment in cooperative living was founded on principles of individual liberty, social equality, and shared devotion to higher ideals. It addressed social ills that had long concerned Emerson: selfishness and materialism, the overspecialization of labor, dishonest competition, widening gaps between classes, separation from nature, and the sacrifice of individual potential to the necessity of earning a living. But much as he admired Ripley's plan "to combine the thinker and the worker, as far as possible, in the same individual" and to foster "a more simple and wholesome life" on the land, Emerson was unwilling to give up his study and leave behind his garden for the collective endeavor in West Roxbury. Far from inspiring him with a new vision of human possibility, the scheme depressed his spirits with its detailed blueprint for working and living in common. It was all "arithmetic & comfort" for the sake of providing rooms in a Transcendentalist hotel. The philosopher of self-reliance saw no reason to exchange "my present prison" for a "little larger" one, when the change would do nothing to fire up and free his soul. Just as he had eschewed affiliation with organized abolitionism, so he now steered clear of institutionalized utopia. To join the community would violate his bedrock principle: "one man is a counterpoise to a city," and he must find salvation on his own. Thoreau expressed this objection more bluntly: "I think I had rather keep batchelor's hall in hell than go to board in heaven."[36]

While Emerson stayed put, Brook Farm came to him—or more precisely, defectors from that colony, as it struggled with financial problems and internal conflicts. Concord was a magnet for the disappointed and disillusioned denizens of utopia; in 1844–1845 a dozen found refuge in the town and consoled themselves with the beauty of the landscape and the intellectual culture of the village. To twenty-year-old George William Curtis, the banker's son from Providence, Rhode Island, whose boyish enthusiasm for Emerson had led him and his brother first to Brook Farm and then to Nathan Barrett's Concord farm, the country town offered a welcome alternative to crowded habitations. "It is so still a life after the city," the fledgling writer and future editor of *Harper's Weekly* rhapsodized. "I am glad to be thrown so directly and almost alone into nature." Concord "hides under a quiet surface most precious scenes."[37]

No one did more to fashion the image of Concord as a bucolic retreat from an age of upheaval than did Nathaniel Hawthorne. In July 1842 the newlywed author of *Twice-Told Tales* and other short fiction moved with his bride, Sophia Peabody, into the forlorn manse that had sat empty since Ezra Ripley's death close to nine months earlier. Despite his rising reputation "at the head of American literature," the thirty-eight-year-old Salem native still struggled to earn a living by his pen. He had briefly held a patronage job in the Boston Custom House, only to find that the duties of inspecting shipments of salt and coal stifled his imagination. He had then enlisted as a charter member of Brook Farm, drawn by its egalitarian promise and by the hope that through the cooperative scheme for labor and leisure, he would not only earn a subsistence but also gain the freedom to write. He soon soured on that plan. Farming proved exhausting; his thoughts turned "cloddish" with the soil. "Intellectual activity is incompatible with any large amount of bodily exercise," he concluded. Back in Boston, at loose ends, and eager for nuptials after a three-year engagement, he was glad for the opportunity of a fresh start in Concord. Thanks to Sophia's Transcendentalist convictions and connections—her sister Elizabeth was a key figure in the intellectual avant-garde—the Hawthornes were welcomed by Emerson as tenants in the reverend family seat. Here the spinner of tales looked forward to communing with nature and cultivating his muse for a receptive periodical press.[38]

The new accessions quickly claimed public notice. William S. Robinson heralded the Hawthornes' arrival in the *Lowell Journal*. "Concord is becoming more literary every year," he said with pride, as the town became home to "one of the most delightful of American writers." The newcomers were soon "quite the rage among our literaries," reported John Shepard Keyes, among the earliest to pay a call at the manse. Although Hawthorne had a reputation for being solitary, he enjoyed an active social life. He hiked with Emerson, rowed on the river with Thoreau, fished with Channing, chatted with Alcott and Fuller, and enjoyed the hospitality of John Keyes. He made daily stops at the post office and regularly checked out the newspapers and periodicals at the Concord Atheneum, founded a few weeks after he moved in. The summer of 1842 was a honeymoon for the newlyweds, whom the writer fancied as Adam and Eve relocated to paradise along the Concord River. By fall he was hard at work on stories for the press, which he turned out steadily in the very room where Emerson had composed *Nature*. As one after another appeared in the *United States Magazine, and Democratic Review*, perhaps the most influential journal of the time, the *Concord Freeman* reprinted them in swift succession. Its new editor, Charles C. Hazewell, who had replaced Gourgas in February 1843, was a would-be man of letters himself, so enamored of Hawthorne's fiction that in later years he was said to have memorized every sentence of *The Scarlet Letter*. Altogether, the *Freeman* reprinted no fewer than fifteen of Hawthorne's tales during Hazewell's twenty-two-month editorship. If Emerson was available to the townspeople at the lyceum, the storyteller at the manse was on display in the local press. The American Renaissance was a town as well as a national achievement.[39]

Hawthorne witnessed the absurdities and the tragedies of Concord life. He found Barzillai Frost "a good sort of hum-drum parson . . . and well fitted to increase the stock of manuscript sermons," and he kept his distance from the many "queer and clever young men" who beat a path to Emerson's gate. When a crisis occurred in the neighborhood, he rose to the occasion. On the night of July 9, 1845, their third wedding anniversary, the Hawthornes were startled by a sudden knocking at their door. The poet Ellery Channing had come with news that Daniel Hunt's eldest child, nineteen-year-old schoolmistress Martha, had gone missing, after having last been seen descending the steep hill from the homestead to the banks of the river. A search party was being assembled, and Hawthorne's boat was urgently needed. The two men soon rowed downstream to the probable site of her disappearance, where Gen. Joshua Buttrick and a local youth got on board and under "the most lustrous moon" fished for the body. Eventually, the long poles they plunged into the dark waters hit something solid, and up came the body of the young woman, her arms fixed and hands clenched in the act of struggling against an inescapable fate. "I never saw nor imagined a spectacle of such horror," Hawthorne confided in his literary notebook. "The rigidity . . . was dreadful to behold." The shock was not merely physical. To a writer ever on the alert for moral lessons, the rigor mortis served as "an emblem of inflexible judgment pronounced upon her." It signified a clash between aspirations and reality that sealed the young woman's doom.[40]

Martha Hunt had fallen into a cultural trap awaiting many young women of her time. Born in 1826 soon after her parents' wedding, the eldest of Daniel and Clarissa Hunt's nine children and six daughters attracted attention early on for her precocious mind. The village grammar school, at which she excelled, could not satisfy her thirst for knowledge, so the parents determined to sacrifice, spared her from the dairy, and sent the sixteen-year-old to Groton Academy, some twenty miles from home. It was her first time away, and the sophisticated society of cultivated young women turned her head. Her classmates were charmed by her wholesome "grace suggestive of the woods and fields" and by her lively contributions to their lessons and games. "She admired and was admired. She was surrounded by gratifications of taste, by the stimulants and rewards of ambition. The world was happy, and she was worthy to live in it."

Martha returned home with academic honors and elevated aspirations, and she attracted the interest of the village intellectuals. Emerson, Channing, and Margaret Fuller encouraged her ambitions and lent her books. Excited by the Transcendentalists' idealized vision of life, she found the farm "repulsive" and resented her duties in the dairy. A summer job as a schoolmistress offered a respite, but managing sixty children in a cramped schoolhouse on a hot July day overwhelmed her. Unable to win over the young, she also felt patronized and out of place among the elite. To the farmers in her neighborhood, she was simply unfathomable: "a strange girl" who was not content "to milk cows and churn butter, and fry pork, without further hope or thought." But the young woman could not find the internal fortitude Emerson promised to those who would go their own way. In her melancholy, she retreated into self-obsession. "Am I indeed so selfish," she plaintively asked, "that I think only of self?" Cut off from others, Martha

Hunt spent the last weeks of her short existence in a cultural limbo, at odds with the rural family and society that had shaped her and with seemingly nowhere to go but the grave. As Hawthorne heard the story, Martha Hunt "died for want of sympathy—a severe penalty for having cultivated and refined herself out of the sphere of her natural connections."[41]

The tragedy of Martha Hunt was a perfect subject for a Hawthorne story. It told of the mismatch between individual and society; it exposed the false promises of Transcendentalism; it manifested the costs of social isolation. But Hawthorne waited to turn life into art. Not until *The Blithedale Romance* (1852) did he reuse this episode, chiefly to describe the rigid corpse of the character Zenobia, a "high-spirited Woman" whose protest "against the narrow limitations of her sex" ended in suicide by drowning.[42]

While he resided at the manse, Hawthorne incorporated other local characters and scenes into his fiction. As nature came back to life in the spring of 1843, the writer surveyed the debris of branches and leaves and the detritus of his garden suddenly visible after the snowmelt, and he took heart in the ongoing regeneration. "Each human soul is the first created inhabitant of its own Eden," he asserted in the spirit of Emerson. "We dwell in an old moss-covered mansion, and tread in the worn foot-prints of the past . . . yet all these outward circumstances are made less than visionary, by the renewing power of the spirit." But he also liked to poke fun at his Transcendentalist neighbors' penchant for vague and opaque statements. A sketch in a new Boston magazine, *The Pioneer*, placed Emerson in "The Hall of Fantasy," where he was surrounded by disciples eager to enlist in his search for truth, "although, sometimes, the truth assumes a mystic unreality and shadowyness in his grasp." So, too, did "The Celestial Railroad," a satirical updating of John Bunyan's Protestant classic, *The Pilgrim's Progress*, find room for a potshot at the town's resident philosopher. In this retelling of Christian's arduous journey to the Celestial City, the "two cruel giants, Pope and Pagan," who once stood in the way of the hero's advance, have been replaced by "a giant Transcendentalist," a German by birth, whose defining feature is indistinctness. No one had ever succeeded in describing him. He appeared "more like a heap of fog and duskiness" than a physical being, and his words were indecipherable.[43]

No aspect of Concord life struck Hawthorne more concretely than the coming of the railroad. In the fall of 1843, he took a solitary walk to Walden Pond and paid a visit to the encampment of Irish laborers in the woods. Their rough shanties, piled high with earth for insulation, made an unfamiliar sight, yet these structures did not "break or disturb the seclusion of the place." The "poor people" adapted to the forest as "natural inhabitants," unlike the iron horse, whose advent was signaled by a "great, high, ugly embankment"—"a torment to see." The following summer Hawthorne took to Sleepy Hollow on a quiet Saturday morning, with a view to noticing and recording all the sights, sounds, and scents that he could take in. Birds twittered overhead; flies buzzed about his head; a catbird mewed; an angry red squirrel emitted "a sharp, shrill chirrup": and a mosquito hummed in his ear. The village clock struck noon in the distance. But nothing could match the sudden intrusion of the locomotive, with its "long shriek, harsh, above all other harshness," bringing "the noisy world into the midst of our slumbrous peace" and leaving in its wake "the shattered ruins of a dreamer's Utopia."

On such skepticism of technological change, Hawthorne had constructed his "Celestial Railroad." The Fitchburg line had promised to ease Concord's path into the modern age; the town would not be left behind in a forsaken "Valley of Humiliation." The fabulist raised the ante. Did the embrace of progress ensure spiritual rewards? "Mr. Smooth-it-away," the railroad official, waved aside all reservations. The journey would be free of obstacles and require no effort on the passengers' part to reach the Celestial City. Yet with Hawthorne's irony, his reminders of Christian's worthy struggles, and his jibes at the "flimsy faiths" of the day, there was good reason to suspect that sin and guilt could not be shed from the traveler's knapsack and that the train would never reach its heavenly destination.[44]

The economic disruption wrought by the railroad was neither seen nor heard in the Hawthornes' residence by the Concord River. For all his disquiet with the extravagances of the age, when it came time to gather together his short stories into a new volume for the press, the author set them within a frame designed to evoke nostalgia for a time long gone. *Mosses from an Old Manse*, published in June 1846, nine months after his departure from Concord, conjures up in its title and preface a secluded parsonage, lost in the mists of time, overlooking a sluggish river incapable of turning a mill wheel. Although it had not been even a year since Ezra Ripley was laid to rest when Hawthorne penned that description, the property had already faded into the past. The entrance gate of the Old Manse is unhinged, the passage "almost overgrown with grass," the house shingles covered with "mosses of ancient growth." Set back from the highway, the dwelling appears in shadows, as if no longer "belonging to the material world." To step inside is to enter another century, the atmosphere made otherworldly by the "holy men" who lived there, one of whom haunts the premises. "Houses of any antiquity in New England," the narrator assures readers, "are so invariably possessed with spirits, that the matter seems hardly worth alluding to."[45]

The landscape is as steeped in history as the manse. From the window of the study, where Emerson composed *Nature* and Hawthorne penned the very same preface, the battlefield is visible where "a long and deadly struggle between two nations" broke out over control of a bridge long since abandoned and reduced to stone abutments. Rather than brood over "the shot heard round the world," the narrator casts a glance at the granite obelisk Ezra Ripley labored so long and hard to erect, then pauses at the nearby grave of two British soldiers, calling to mind the "tradition" that one of the Redcoats was felled by an ax wielded by a terrified youth passing by. Was the boy's "soul . . . tortured by the blood stain"? The Revolutionary scene proves too recent for Hawthorne's muse. The narrator is drawn by "a wilder interest" in a tract of land behind the manse, where once an Indian village stood, evidence of which abounds in the form of stone arrowheads in the soil, each exhibiting "an individuality . . . so different from the productions of civilized machinery." In Hawthorne's telling, the setting embodies virtues at odds with the standardized, mass society taking shape in the new industrial age. Even the apple trees in Ripley's orchard possess "individuality of character." With its "grey, homely" mien, the manse "rebuke[s] the speculative extravagances of the day."[46]

The preface to *Mosses* presents an alternative world to the present. The Old Manse serves as a foil to the stories that follow, its virtues of modesty and restraint, rooted in recognition of human fallibility and in reverence for God, offering a stark contrast to the misbegotten schemes of the crazed souls of Hawthorne's invention. But the portrait went beyond the printed page to reshape the image of Concord in the wider world. Hawthorne was well aware that the town was already a destination for patriotic tourists eager to see the opening scene of the Revolution. The "poor little country village" was also a magnet for a motley crew of "queer, strangely dressed, oddly behaved mortals" drawn to Emerson's orbit. In *Mosses*, past and present came together to refashion Concord into a place apart from the hustle and bustle of the times, where visitors could pay tribute to the past, enjoy the serenity of nature, and perhaps run into a great thinker.

For all their philosophical differences, here Hawthorne and the Transcendentalists were at one. Concord could stand as a living critique of the railroad age.[47]

In this reinvention, Concord's long history of economic striving and political ambition was conveniently forgotten; the town was being written out of the industrial revolution just as the Steam Mill Company was getting started. As it turned out, this image of a pastoral refuge from the stresses and strains of modern living had its own economic uses; it helped to build up a tourist trade in the years to come. The impact of the railroad was thus double-edged. On the one hand, it reduced the independence of the town, sapped its commercial vitality, and tied its fortunes to the rhythms of the ascendant urban-industrial world. On the other hand, it furnished a new blueprint for agriculture, gave rise to a suburb, and brought numerous visitors to the local attractions. Concord had long claimed a central place in the American heritage as the birthplace of the Revolution. Now, thanks to the presence of major writers and reformers, it would be a nursery of great ideas and a crucible of American identity.

Walden and Beyond

In the early 1840s, Emerson and Thoreau were provincial figures in a republic rooted in regions. The lecturer spoke to audiences primarily in Boston and Cambridge (though no longer at Harvard College), in Concord and nearby towns, along the Massachusetts and Rhode Island coasts, and at colleges in northern New England, while his youthful protégé was still finding his voice. As the young man gave up school-keeping to chart his own way as poet, essayist, and observer of nature, Emerson hailed "my good Henry Thoreau" as a conscientious objector to a society unworthy of his talents and at odds with his ideals. The two men bonded still more over the shared experience of loss: the deaths of Thoreau's older brother John and of Emerson's five-year-old son Waldo some two weeks apart in January 1842. But the larger environment for their work appeared unfavorable. The intellectual movement of which they were a part was shedding whatever unity it once possessed. Christian believers, such as Frederic Henry Hedge, declined to follow the heterodox Emerson out of the church, and while Brook Farm beckoned to those seeking collective arrangements to release individual potential, the Concord Transcendentalists clung to individual self-reform as the one true route to social progress. The Transcendental Club held its final meeting in September 1840, a few months after *The Dial*, the aspiring voice of "the newness," came into being for a creative but unprofitable four-year career. New England resonated with calls for change from activists divided from one another in enclaves of mutual suspicion, especially in the ranks of abolitionism.[1]

Yet these parochial circumstances stirred the Transcendentalists' muse and prompted their enduring achievements. Emerson embraced his origins and carried them to wider settings in a bid to form American identity on a New England model, based on Boston and Concord. Thoreau burrowed ever more deeply into Concord itself, and the more he probed its inhabitants, natural and human alike, the more he discovered universal truths. The two men acted locally but thought globally, and they inscribed their hometown into their ideal visions of America. Their works would fire a second "shot heard round the world"—a call to make America "the country of the future" on a Yankee design of liberty and equality that for all its idealism would ultimately clash with other versions of the nation in a coming Civil War.[2]

AS THE 1842–1843 LECTURE SEASON APPROACHED, EMERSON HAD FEW COM-mitments on his schedule. For a second time in the new decade, he was entirely absent from the Masonic Temple. His last series, "The Times," undertaken in 1841–1842 to fill a gap in the household budget, had been a succès d'estime— "the peculiarity of his views and language and his deserved reputation as an agreeable speaker, draw good audiences," observed the *Concord Freeman*—but the financial returns proved disappointing. With the Boston market shrinking, it became imperative to extend the geographical reach of his secular ministry. In 1840 and 1842 he found appreciative audiences in Providence and successfully tested the waters in Manhattan and Staten Island, where his brother William practiced law and made his home.[3]

His reputation as an author was gaining, too. His collected *Essays*, published in 1841, received mixed reviews: as many readers were mystified by his prose as auditors had been by his lectures, while others objected to his Germanic jargon and religious iconoclasm. But a few critics, such as Horace Greeley's *New-Yorker* magazine, hailed the Concord writer as "one of the profoundest thinkers and loftiest spirits in the land" and predicted that "the world will soon recognize [him] as one of the most spiritual and wisest of its teachers." The *Essays* gained wide notice in Britain, thanks to Thomas Carlyle's promotion of his friend's work—a mixed blessing, since reviewers inclined to dismiss the American as a poor imitation of his Scottish publicist. Even so, one critic felt compelled to admit that for all his detestable doctrines, Emerson was something new un-der the sun: "Nothing like, or second to it has hitherto appeared in Ameri-can literature." With his "new thoughts and exquisite illustrations," Emerson wrote "like a man who had received his culture in the woods, and then came forth full of genius, power, and originality." Despite his condemnation of his countrymen's Anglophilia, such endorsements in the former mother country enhanced the value of Emerson's stock at home. Within the United States, he remained closely associated with his native region—a representative of the "fanaticism" that had taken over the Boston area "under the name of transcendentalism." His audiences consisted mainly of New Englanders, and his books barely circulated south of Philadelphia. The cosmopolitan thinker was still a provincial Yankee.[4]

That regional identity turned out to be a professional asset. Early in the fall of 1842, Emerson had no plans for a new lecture series, until disappointing dividends from bank stocks drove him back to peddling his "literary pack of Notions." His calendar was open, and he could presumably have filled it with invitations from lyceums in the area. Instead, he eschewed these low-paying engagements and struck out for new territory four hundred miles to the south in the thriving port city of Baltimore, where the following January he delivered two lectures to the Mercantile Library Association, a three-year-old institution that catered to the intellectual interests of merchants' clerks—yet another audience of young men preparing for adulthood. From there he steered his course northward with no firm commitments in hand. In Philadelphia and New York City, Brooklyn and Newark, he arranged sponsors and venues on the go, trusting that the returns would be worth the expense of being away from home for the winter. In a fluid society, he would be as mobile as his countrymen, experiencing the uncertainties of life on the road and relishing the greater exposure he gained to the variegated American scene.[5]

This foray into new markets was motivated by more than money. It was a bid for a wider stage on which to pursue his ideal of the American lecturer as man speaking to and for his fellow citizens about the possibilities of a democratic culture. Yet Emerson chose a seemingly parochial subject for this purpose. Instead of following his usual practice and exploring a universal theme, such as "Human Culture" or "The Times," the itinerant intellectual focused on the subject he knew best: his native region of New England. That fall he was in a retrospective mood, mining his memories of boyhood in Boston and his Aunt Mary's stories about the Emerson family and the heroic age of Puritan preaching to furnish anecdotes for his lectures. With these materials, he combined more recent observations of life in Concord and critical assessments of contemporary efforts for cultural improvement and social reform. His vast reading supplied contexts for these developments; he reached back to Greek and Roman classics and ancient Saxon laws and forward to Renaissance thinkers, Puritan preachers, Napoleonic dicta, and the bracing influences of German idealism and British Romanticism (including, of course, Carlyle).

All of these sources of information and inspiration were deployed in a dazzling display of intellectual virtuosity, as if to show that no matter how fast things were changing and how overwhelming and unfathomable the world appeared, nothing was beyond the capacity of a single human mind to put in order and employ for the benefit of all. The New Englander, as Emerson demonstrated with his wide-ranging knowledge, was no narrow provincial. Although his account evoked unfavorable images of the Yankee as Puritan bigot, backcountry rube, calculating merchant, and fanatical reformer, none of those labels stuck. The characteristic figure of the region was a representative man of the North. In the forefront of social and economic change, he embodied the exhilarating possibilities and the unsettling risks of the modern American age.[6]

In Baltimore, Emerson examined his subject in two talks; in Philadelphia and Manhattan, the survey of New England grew into a five-part series. In either version, the discourses would have been familiar to the lecturer's faithful followers in Boston and Concord. At the heart of this story was a continuing tension between "conscience" and "commerce." The Puritans, "the most religious in a religious era," had planted a *New* England in America on a foundation of "passionate piety" and austere morality, examples of which were drawn from such revered ancestors as Peter Bulkeley. "The history of what is best in New England is the unfolding of this [religious] sentiment." But the age of faith had given way to the reign of trade. Through the "great enterprize and acuteness" bred into their character, Yankee traders set in motion a radical transformation of the region, integrating town and country in the pursuit of wealth, unleashing the prodigious energies of men and women with a staunch work ethic, displacing the simple ways of the past with an insatiable appetite for worldly goods, and reducing social relations to matters of calculation and profit: "Trade is the God and walks supreme in his streets and wharves."[7]

For his audiences of merchants and clerks in the leading seaports of the Middle Atlantic region, Emerson set forth the costs and benefits of globalization, as he had done six years earlier at the Masonic Temple and in many of the same words. This was the view from his doorstep in Concord and from the docks in Boston, to which he appended a glimpse of the dreary "pig farms," mired in poverty and ignorance, that he had seen in the backcountry of Concord just a few months before. To their ranks he added a new, even more degraded element: Irish laborers, "a low and semi-barbarous legion, who can subsist almost on offal, and be clothed almost by rags." The influx of the foreigners, driving wages below subsistence, gave "the proud Caucasian race" no option but to flee. Still, Emerson found reason for hope in the progressive farmers, who stirred to calls for reform and took advantage of expanding markets. In several lengthy paragraphs, he conjured up an anonymous master of the arts of managing men, livestock, and land; drawn from life, that model farmer was Abel Moore, charting the region's agricultural future.[8]

By the 1840s, Massachusetts was well known—and often notorious—as the nursery of cultural innovations and the hothouse of radical reforms. Emerson took up these developments in Philadelphia and New York. One lecture treated the rise of lyceums, the popularity of public speaking, and the proliferation of libraries as "moral agents" to check the aggressive "spirit of economy and commerce." Lyceums were few and far between in the Middle Atlantic states, so the professional lecturer discoursed at length on this "organ of unparalleled power for the elevation of sentiment and enlargement of knowledge." Here lay "the true church of the coming time," offering "a pulpit that makes the other chairs of instruction cold and ineffectual." Unfortunately, its influence was imperiled by competition from hypnotists, magicians, phrenologists, and cheap entertainments of all sorts. Even in Concord the mountebanks drew crowds; one self-proclaimed expert in reading character from the contours of the head had recently disturbed the grave of a British soldier killed at the North Bridge and removed the skull for a phrenological reading. Such impiety and hocus-pocus made a mockery of the lyceum's mission to diffuse scientific knowledge, not to mention Emerson's lofty ambition to touch souls.[9]

A similar conflict was manifest in "recent literary and spiritual influences." In his fourth lecture, Emerson took heart from the welcome that "all the youth" of his home region had given to the works of Coleridge, Wordsworth, and especially Carlyle, whose "words spake to their condition." But it was not easy for these demanding Romantic seers to gain an audience; the literary marketplace was deluged by "wretched swarms of novels" pouring from "the new cheap press" and glamorizing "purely external success," so unlike the "moral sentiment" and "reverence for a virtuous action" upheld by Carlyle. The craze for sensational fiction had swept through Concord itself and spawned profit-making alternatives to the sober social library, still devoted to "solid instruction" and "rational amusement." The erudite lecturer decried the spread of a commercial mass culture serving up superficial knowledge and transient entertainment to easily distracted and satisfied consumers. "Is not this tragic in so far as it is true," he asked, "that this great country, hospitable to all nations, opened for the experiment of new ideas . . . , should be a country of dwarfs; cities and nations of democrats, and never an upright man?"[10]

The final lecture scrutinized the "results" of the social changes transforming New England and inquired into the "tendencies" of the times. A critical spirit was abroad in the land, Emerson declared, calling every institution and practice before the bar of judgment. Religious seekers no longer found inspiration in the church; in quest of "other and better means of spiritual regeneration," they turned to projects of reform. Diverse schemes of "restoring the world to innocence and happiness" abounded. No aspect of life—not government and taxes, not trade and money, not diet or dress—went unexamined: "The land is full of rebellion, the country is full of kings. Men say, Stand off—let me alone; leave me to follow my own course." The advocate of self-reliance sympathized with this "growing desire to cast away whatever is superfluous" in the "belief that the human soul is sufficient for itself." Emerson painstakingly described the schemes of the "Communitists" to separate from society and form alternative associations, where they would live and work together on the basis of equality. These experiments would undoubtedly "do good," he predicted, then rehearsed the objections that had kept him from joining Brook Farm. Far from freeing participants to lead "a nobler and better life," the cooperative enterprises diminished them, allowing the weak to live off the strong, and confining the aspirations of all "to a limited circle." The truth is that "no community or institution is so great as a *single man*."

That was Emerson's bedrock principle, and to the businessmen in his audiences, more interested in practical information than in dreams of utopian reform, it must have been reassuring. For so ridden with "evil" and "falsehood" was the entire "system" of society that no single measure was adequate to its reform. "Why, my friend, parade your non-resistance, and your temperance, and your abolition, and your vegetable diet, with so much ostentation? Why make so much noise and bluster about them, when your whole life is full of falseness and wrong?" No one need feel guilty about abstaining from good causes. Collective efforts would inevitably fall short. The real answer to America's ills lay not in blueprints for social reorganization but in individual striving for "a nobler life." And where else to pursue this agenda for self-realization other than New England? The region was so favored by nature and history, so free and prosperous that it enjoyed "a boundless, unlimited opportunity. Here may the human soul give free expansion to its wondrous powers and develope [*sic*] its diviner life." Here might a land of "sublime landscapes," of "majestic mountains and towering forests," inspire its inhabitants to seek grandeur in their lives, to be fit "companions of Nature," and to take the lead in fulfilling the promise of American freedom.[11]

The lectures on New England were both personal and professional milestones. Gathering up the strands of familial and local pasts, private experiences, and contemporary observations, Emerson crafted autobiography in the form of regional history. If the *Historical Discourse* of 1835 rooted him in the home of his ancestors, the 1843 series took his Concord heritage and asserted its meanings and significance to fellow citizens, near and far, in the quest for a shared national identity. Transcendentalism—all that language of the soul—receded in his rhetoric, though it still set an ideal standard by which to judge the shortcomings of his countrymen. Carving out the new role of public intellectual, he impressed with keen observations of the American scene and optimistic forecasts of the future. He was a Yankee Tocqueville (he carried *Democracy in America* in his baggage), making "free with the errors of his own countrymen in a style that would have brought a tempest of indignation around the ears of a foreigner." Partiality to New England raised no objections, according to a correspondent of the Baltimore *Sun*; his was an "unprejudiced and reflecting mind," telling "wholesome truths" in a frank, "reasonable" manner. No one commented on his all-white story, the erasure of Indians and Africans from the narrative, and the omission of the looms and spindles of Lowell—agents of the industrial revolution—from the present-day landscape.[12]

The Yankee philosopher was altered by the trip. Life on the road exposed him to new people and places. A year and a half before the Fitchburg Railroad steamed into Concord, he took the train with a sense of wonder. The railroad, he marveled, is "highly poetic, this strong shuttle which shoots across the forests, swamp, rivers & arms of the sea, binding city to city." Mingling and chatting easily with his fellow travelers proved an unexpected pleasure. The restrained Yankee particularly enjoyed the company of merchants. In his lectures, he warned about excessive devotion to trade; away from the podium he admired the energy and competence of the businessmen he met. They showed "more manly power of all kinds than scholars." But there were also the shocking sights of urban squalor, especially in New York: the desperate souls reduced to picking rags, sifting cinders from coal bins, scavenging cigar butts, even collecting "dog and hog manure" on the streets. Emerson returned home with an enlarged sense of the republic—its dynamism, its diversity, its extremes of wealth and poverty—and of his own potential place in it.

IRONICALLY, THE TOUR WAS A FINANCIAL FLOP. TRAVEL EXPENSES ATE UP ticket sales; Emerson's earnings fell short of nine dollars per lecture, just about the worst pay he had ever received. But he found ample compensation in an expanded sense of mission. Peddling his "notions" of New England, of Boston and Concord, he broke out of regional confines and launched a national career.[13]

Close to a year later Emerson signaled his widening sense of nationality. Rather than offer a new series of his own, Emerson accepted an invitation from the Boston Mercantile Library Association to join a dozen or so "gentlemen of established reputation" in a new course of lectures for its audience of traders and clerks. The roster of speakers included statesmen, ministers, and a few professional orators like Emerson in a respectable forum reminiscent of the Society for the Diffusion of Useful Knowledge.[14] Emerson was scheduled for February 7, 1844. In the months leading up to this engagement, he made repeated visits to the Walden construction site where the Irish laborers were laying track for the Fitchburg Railroad, and while he deplored the long hours, the "pitiful wages," and the physical risks the men suffered, he was awed by their heroic energy and force. "How grand they are," he exclaimed. "*They* are men, manlike employed." He felt a growing excitement at the transportation revolution unfolding before his eyes: "It will be American power & beauty, when it is done."[15]

Although the "bold mole" would not burrow its way into Concord until June, the lecturer speculated about the immense changes the railroad would set in motion, not only in the economy and society but in the realm of thought. For one thing, it would open up the vast interior of the continent to rapid settlement and reorient American culture from the Atlantic seaboard to "the nervous rocky West." A "new & continental element" was about to invigorate "our national mind" and inspire "an American genius." At the same time Emerson feared that the westward rush would accelerate the depopulation of long-settled towns and the degradation of the local backcountry. His lecture would pull together these twin concerns in a Concord-centric vision of a "bountiful" agrarian republic from the shores of the Atlantic to the "waves of the Pacific sea."[16]

Emerson titled the lecture "The Young American" in a gesture to a contemporary literary-political movement to rejuvenate national life and letters on democratic principles. The name also saluted the demographic cohort the speaker took as his special constituency. To the aspiring teenagers and twenty-year-olds clerking in Boston's mercantile houses, the discourse opened a broad vista on the immense field of action awaiting those youths with the imagination and initiative to embrace the spirit of liberty and aid in the fulfillment of America's destiny.[17]

The starting point of the lecture was Emerson's familiar refrain. Americans were still a neocolonial people, importing their "intellectual culture" from an aristocratic Old World while striving to build a democracy in the New. But change was in the air, and Emerson came to herald the fresh winds from the West, breaking up the stagnant atmosphere on the seaboard and stimulating new appreciation of the American land. No force was more crucial to this development than the rapid extension of railroads into the interior. Boston itself was the hub of iron highways to Providence, Albany, and Portland, Maine; a new route—the Fitchburg line—was "shooting northwest towards the Connecticut and Montreal." The "rage for road building" was annihilating distance and accelerating time. It was bringing far-flung places together, eroding "local peculiarities," and tightening the bonds of Union. From his visits to the Walden woods, the lecturer conjured up "a multitude of picturesque traits" introduced by the iron horse into "our pastoral scene," among which was "the village of shanties, at the edge of beautiful lakes." The progress of the railroad unleashed an assault on the natural order. It "violates and revolutionizes the primal and immemorial forms of nature."[18]

Emerson was not an environmentalist before his time. He was exhilarated by the speed with which the vast domain of the West was being converted into farms: "This great savage country should be furrowed by the plough, and combed by the harrow . . . ; these wild prairies should be loaded with wheat; the swamps with rice; the hill-tops should pasture innumerable sheep and cattle; the interminable forest should become graceful parks, for use and for delight." The gardener of Cambridge Turnpike spared not a thought for the dispossession of native peoples nor for the disappearance of wildness in nature that Thoreau would so compellingly indict. The spread of slavery and the Cotton Kingdom never came up.[19]

Just as Emerson verged on the rhetoric of "manifest destiny"—a doctrine that would be proclaimed the next year during the fight over Texas annexation—his thoughts migrated back to Boston and Concord. If a soul wished to enjoy the "tranquillizing" and "sanative influences" of the land, the lecturer advised, he could find opportunities everywhere. No one had to go to Niagara Falls or the White Mountains, much less pioneer in the West, to benefit from nature. A small farm, even a garden, "makes it indifferent where you live." A "well-laid garden" adorned the landscape and beautified a home; along with orchards and woodlands, it attached the owner to the soil and instilled patriotism. That pleasant scenario was meant to appeal to the aspiring merchants in the audience, to draw them into the back-to-the-land movement, if not now, then once they earned enough to acquire land in the suburbs, from which they could commute by train into the city. Such recruits would reverse the decline of the countryside, as "the flower of the youth, of both sexes," headed to the cities and relegated "poverty-stricken" homesteads to a "much inferior class" incapable of halting the decay. Under the newcomers' management, agricultural science would increase returns from the land, instruct the neighbors, and lift the burden of "debt and bankruptcy": "Whatever . . . shall go to disgust men with cities, and infuse into them the passion for country-life . . . will render a prodigious service to the whole face of the continent."[20]

"The Young American" was more than a paean about farming to a roomful of merchants. Reflecting his new appreciation of businessmen, Emerson downplayed his familiar criticisms of the marketplace and paid tribute to commerce as a liberating force in the history of humankind. In his perspective, trade was as natural as the invisible hand it obeyed. In accord with Adam Smith, he championed free trade and laissez-faire, and he accepted Thomas Malthus's gloomy prediction that the growth of population would always drive down wages to bare subsistence, the sufferings of Irish laborers notwithstanding. Such miseries were transient; ever the optimist, Emerson had no doubt that "love and good are inevitable, and in the course of things," and that the fit instrument of that progress was the production and exchange of commodities for profit.[21]

Of goods and the man the philosopher of modern history sang. Trade flourished with liberty; it spurred initiative and rewarded intelligence and merit. It had broken the power of feudalism in Europe and "planted America" on principles of equality and freedom. It promoted and preserved peace. Nothing could resist its ever-expanding reach: "This is the good, and this the evil of trade, that it goes to put everything *into market*, talent, beauty, virtue, and man himself." So dynamic was commerce, so at odds with aristocracy and privilege, that Emerson predicted, against all evidence, "it will abolish slavery." Under its aegis, government would gradually wither away, as "private adventurers" came to provide public services at lower cost and self-reliant individuals took care of themselves. Who needed Brook Farm, with its scheme of equal wages for all, so at odds with nature? Let the members of the Boston Mercantile Library Association and their counterparts employ their talents and energy for higher purposes than social esteem or material gain. In them lay the potential for an American "nobility," whose personal virtues—deliberation, "elegant" learning, "perseverance," "self-devotion," and loyalty to "humble" friends—would "guide and adorn life for the multitude."[22]

By this route Emerson brought together country and city, agriculture and commerce, in a plan to reform New England and fulfill the promise of America. For all the praise of trade, he still envisioned grander uses of nature than convenience and profit. "In America, out of doors all seems a market," he lamented; "in doors, an air-tight stove of conventionalism." Why capitulate to that dreary scene? The exciting prospects in the West, thanks to the railroad, evoked Emerson's own utopian dreams of a nation emancipated from the Old World heritage of inequality and oppression and ambitious to write a new script for humankind. With enlightened gentlemen on the land and in the countinghouse, Concord would have nothing to fear from the westward movement. The town would retain and recruit men and women with the ability to sustain progressive farms and thriving villages and with the determination to strive for noble ideals. So reformed, it could serve as a model for the agricultural communities to be planted in the interior by a "heterogeneous population" streaming into America from "all corners of the world . . . How much better when the whole land is a garden, and the people have grown up in the bowers of a paradise"!

"In every age of the world," Emerson exhorted, there was one "leading nation," whose "eminent citizens" were moved by "a more generous sentiment" to step up for "the interests of justice and humanity." Now, in 1844, it was the time for America, "the country of the future." And "which [states] should lead that movement, if not New England?" "Who should lead the leaders, but the Young American?" Even as he rejected the burden of the past, the descendant of Peter Bulkeley was still seeking to erect a City upon a Hill. It was an idealized Concord writ large, with Emerson as its prophet.[23]

BACK IN CONCORD, EMERSON ENJOYED THE ESTEEM OF HIS NEIGHBORS AND the natural advantages of the place. The divinity school address had not harmed his reputation; in 1839 the local elite welcomed him into the Social Circle, and he delighted in their company, "much the best society I have ever known." The gatherings drew him out of the study and into contact with an interesting mix of successful figures in the trades and professions—"solidest of men, who yield the solidest of gossip," and far superior to any Harvard had to offer. The lecturer won regard for his generosity; in the spring of 1839 the Concord Lyceum heard his series "Human Life" free of charge, and in token of their appreciation, some twenty gentlemen presented him with several expensive sets of scholarly books imported from Paris and London.[24] In his comfortable situation, the father of a growing family, with three children under age six in 1844, Emerson was taken aback when Margaret Fuller and her friend Caroline Sturgis, the "maiden, with erect soul" he had admired years before, separately accused him of settling for a placid suburban existence. A noble soul required a sublime setting, such as ocean beaches and mountain peaks. How could the "poor cold low life in Concord" ever measure up? Somewhat defensively, the country gentleman counted his blessings. Lacking "the thickets of the forest and the fatigues of mountains," Concord was easy to reach and travel through. It was close enough to the city to attract notable lecturers and performers and far enough away to possess "the grand features of nature . . . The great sun equalizes all places,—the sun and the stars . . . Niagara is in every glance at the heavens & earth." Rejecting his friends' challenges, the proud citizen rededicated himself to his adopted home and made it famous as a center of Transcendentalism. "Concord is a little town," he allowed, "and yet has its honors."[25]

Not everyone was so enamored of Emerson or his influence over youth. In July 1840 the long-suffering Parson Frost delivered an unusually "animated" sermon against such "humbugs" as abolitionism and "Emersonianism." Then on April 19, 1843, the minister renewed the attack in a lecture, "The True Principles of Reform." Speaking near the end of the series that had featured so many calls for root-and-branch change, Frost charted a middle way between the poles of conservatism and radicalism. Both positions, in his opinion, fell victim to the same error of clinging rigidly to abstractions. The "ultra conservative" equated the "imperfect institutions" of the present with "immutable truth & justice & love" and would not alter them one whit; the "ultra reformer" held current arrangements up against the ideal model in his head and would accept nothing less than a perfect fit. Each perspective purported to be the only solution to the world's ills. Frost wrestled with the dilemma of choice. He was "afraid to oppose the ultra reformer, lest he should oppose all reforms," and "slow to oppose the ultra conservative lest he should encourage the revolutionary spirit of the radicals." What was this anxious moderate to do? Triangulating between extremes, the minister discovered "the true principle of reform" in "improvement": "It is not casting away the past, but proved by experience, matured wisdom, and adding our experience to it."[26]

Despite his claim to be evenhanded, Frost skipped over the conservatives and trained his sights on reformers of all sorts, past and present, in church, society, and state. From the early Christians to the Protestant Reformation, and thence through the English, American, and French revolutions down to his own time, the advocates of change were prone to "separate [and] shut themselves up in their peculiar ideas, & deny all truth in others." The president of Concord's Total Abstinence Society was well aware of the intolerance and infighting in the "great Benevolent enterprises of the day." He was especially disturbed by the do-gooders who declined to engage with their neighbors and withdrew into enclaves of the like-minded. Come-outers deserted the churches, particularly Frost's own; nonresisters refused allegiance—and taxes—to government; the "community people" at Brook Farm turned their backs on a corrupt world to create their own Eden.

Then, Frost continued, there were the alienated young for whom Waldo Emerson advocated. In the January 1843 issue of *The Dial*, the Concord author had published his lecture "The Transcendentalist," which had debuted in his 1841–1842 series "The Times." The piece presented a sympathetic portrait of youthful idealists so put off by the shallowness and selfishness, the dishonesty and insincerity of everyday life that they could not bring themselves to join in the work of the world. Conventional callings were beneath them. Better to retreat into solitude, "ramble in the country," and wait for something worthy of their talents and ambitions. If these dissidents were neither "good citizens" nor "good members of society," if they declined to vote, if they did not "willingly" contribute to charities and aid benevolent causes, so be it. Emerson held out hope that one day "the good and wise" would realize their genius and "carry salvation to the combatants and demagogues in the dusty arena" of daily existence. This prophetic minority would, in the end, serve society "by speaking for thoughts and principles not marketable or perishable." They were the caretakers of the highest ideals.[27]

Frost could hardly believe what he read. Here was "something new under the sun": a select society of superior souls deliberately withholding their contributions to "the cause of improvement" and doing so "out of a misguided principle." To his astonishment, such self-indulgence was being defended in print by a fellow minister whose name he did not deign to mention. Having long suffered the criticisms of Emerson and his supporters, Frost struck back, and he did so donning the mantle of Ezra Ripley. Everyone, he insisted, belonged to the community, with an obligation to the collective good. Nobody lived alone. That was as true for the Transcendentalists as for everyone else. Far from waiting for the world to come around to them, these "men of purer fire" had a duty "to convey the Heavenly spark" they alone apprehended "to the cold & inert bodies around them." The field of labor was immense, the need nearly inexhaustible: "Can it be possible that any can want work in a world like this, where the drunkard lies weltering in the gutter, the poor stretching out their hand at the corner of every street? where Education, government, religion all call for reform & new life?" Surely the rarefied spirits Emerson admired would not be so selfish as to turn away from their neighbors in need.[28]

The Transcendentalist's aloofness from the moral causes of the day was as troubling to Mary Merrick Brooks as it had been to her former pastor. In her tireless efforts for abolitionism, she would not leave Emerson alone. His friendly sentiments did not suffice; it was imperative to enlist him publicly in the work of reform. In the fall of 1843 she scored one success when Waldo and Lidian Emerson allowed their names to head a memorial to the Massachusetts legislature seeking an end to racial oppression by law. If the petitioners had their way, the General Court would endorse an amendment to the U.S. Constitution outlawing slavery and would eliminate all state laws "making any distinction among citizens on account of color." A third demand was for the passage of a statute barring railroad conductors from "the right of insulting or assaulting" passengers because of their race. This bold statement, drawn up by the Massachusetts Anti-Slavery Society, was signed by 263 of the Emersons' neighbors. Mingled with their signatures and those of the Thoreau family were the names of John Garrison, father and son, and of Peter Hutchinson, in disregard for invidious distinctions of color. Men and women mixed together on the document in violation of the ordinary rules of gender. The memorial put the Emersons in the forefront of the crusade for equality—a position with which they were uneasy. Next to their signatures was an explicit caveat: husband and wife did not endorse state action to end segregation and mistreatment of African Americans on the trains.[29]

Conversion to abolitionism was a work in progress. Even as he edged into a deeper commitment, Emerson protested against the distraction of causes that were not truly his own. "More than our good will we may not be able to give," he conceded in "The Young American." "We have our own affairs, our own genius, which chains us to our proper work." The only obligation he recognized was negative: "not to blaspheme" the good deeds of others in aid of "the debtor," "the slave," or "the pauper," nor to "throw stumbling blocks in the way of the abolitionist, [or] the philanthropist." As he told a convention of social activists a month later in March 1844, he feared the loss of individuality in the pursuit of reform. Like political parties and business corporations, benevolent societies were large-scale organizations dedicated to amassing numbers and dollars for the achievement of specialized goals. He refused to become a cog in the machinery of philanthropy. Nor would he distort his personality by obsessing over a single wrong. "Society gains nothing" when a man became "tediously good in some particular, but negligent or narrow in the rest . . . Hypocrisy and vanity are often the disgusting result." Emerson kept up an internal debate over activism through the spring of 1844: "Does not he do more to abolish Slavery who works all day steadily in his garden, than he who goes to the abolition meeting & makes a speech?" But he could not escape a guilty conscience. Intent on avoiding the self-righteousness he associated with abolitionists, Emerson finally gave in to the importuning of Mary Brooks and agreed to be the featured speaker at the Middlesex County Anti-Slavery Society's (MCASS) commemoration of the tenth anniversary of the British emancipation of slaves in the West Indies, to be held in Concord on the first of August 1844. He vowed to adopt a stance of "lowliness" and to "free the slave by love in the heart."[30]

True to his word, Emerson assumed the abolitionist platform without succumbing to the rhetorical excesses he feared. Not for him the vituperation against slave owners to which Garrison and his followers were prone. Emerson appreciated that the case for freedom appeared indisputable to its advocates. In their eyes, opponents were either "stupid" or "malignant." But so "overbearing and defying" an approach only defeated the purpose. The newcomer to the antislavery campaign took a different tack: "The dictates of humanity make us tender of such as are not yet persuaded." He was prepared to put up with "the hardest selfishness" and to refrain from "every reproachful" and "every indignant remark." Then again, so had the leaders of the English campaign against the slave trade and slavery whose victory was being celebrated. Emerson traced the long struggle by antislavery activists to win support through rational arguments, based on facts and attentive to economic interests, and through high-minded appeals to "the moral sense." The matter was debated "with a rare independence and magnanimity." Here was one large-scale collective enterprise, combining the power of numbers with the voice of conscience, to which the Transcendentalist did not object. Its success constituted a "signal" event "in the history of civilization"; it amounted to a "moral revolution."[31]

Yet the abuses and vices of slavery could not be set forth without heated language and intense emotions. The speaker, who had once trivialized his wife's tears over the suffering of slaves in the Middle Passage, was now "heart-sick" when he considered the torments to which Africans were subjected in "the filthy hold" of the "slave-ship." Emerson painted a vivid picture of the unabated violence and lust of the planter's regime, "an ominous state of cruel and licentious society," where "every house had a dungeon" and "every slave was worked by the whip." Who would not be outraged by the images of pregnant women "set in the treadmill for refusing to work," of "men's backs flayed with cowhides" and salt rubbed into the wounds; of "run-aways hunted with blood-hounds into swamps and hills" and captives thrown into vats of "boiling cane-juice"? "The more this business was looked into," the more apparent that "the crimes and cruelties of the slave-traders and slave-owners could not be overstated."[32]

Responsibility for slavery was not restricted to man sellers and planters. Emerson extended the blame to consumers of tropical commodities and the shop-keepers who sold them. No one wished to know how their "excellent" sugar was raised; "nobody tasted blood in it . . . The coffee was fragrant; the tobacco was incense; the brandy made nations happy; the cotton clothed the world." Why inquire into the sordid circumstances that made these everyday pleasures so readily available? The critic of materialism seized the opportunity to rehearse a familiar theme and took consolation in the knowledge that "man is born with intellect, as well as with a love of sugar, and with a sense of justice, as well as a taste for strong drink."[33]

While the indictment of slavery and materialism gave voice to long-held beliefs, Emerson took the occasion to endorse for the first time the abolitionist crusade for equal rights. Gone was his talk about an "inferior" race doomed to extinction. Instead of disparaging men of African descent as insensate barbarians, he praised their skill and prudence in economic affairs following emancipation in the British West Indies. "It now appears, that the negro race is, more than any other, susceptible of rapid civilization." To be sure, he had moved from ostracizing Africans from the human family to admitting them on condition of conformity to white standards. But he was open to novel displays of accomplishment. "The black race," he proclaimed, "can contend with the white." After having played "a very low and subdued accompaniment" in "the great anthem" of history, people of color were ready to "take a master's part in the music."

In this new spirit of equality, Emerson called attention to racism and injustice not in the faraway Caribbean but closer to home. He singled out the injuries suffered by "the poor black men" employed as "mariners, cooks, or stewards" on Massachusetts vessels, "freeborn as we," who were seized and sequestered in the jails of Charleston, Savannah, and New Orleans when their ships docked in port. This outrageous violation of the seamen's rights was also an assault on the sovereignty of the Commonwealth: "I thought the deck of a Massachusetts ship was as much the territory of Massachusetts, as the floor on which we stand. It should be as sacred as the temple of God." Emerson called on the state's representatives in Congress to take up the issue and, if necessary, bring the federal government to a halt, until Southerners agreed to respect the "privileges and immunities" of Massachusetts citizens and release them from illegal arrest. The speaker, who only months before had objected to state-enforced integration of railroad cars, was now ready to put the republic at risk. "The Union is already at an end, when the first citizen of Massachusetts is thus outraged," he fumed. In the heat of the moment, Emerson rivaled Garrison and Phillips as a firebrand. In the months to come, he would be heartened when the governor of the Commonwealth dispatched Samuel Hoar to Charleston for the purpose of challenging South Carolina's unjust law, and he would be provoked to new heights of anger when his distinguished townsman was forced by mobs to depart that state with his mission unaccomplished. In disgust he wanted nothing to do with a place "where the people are degraded, for they go with padlocked lips & with seared consciences." Why remain in a Union with a state that "treats us like a footpad"?[34]

Emerson did not change in a day and become a one-idea man. Though now publicly identified with the radical wing of abolitionism, he remained a fellow traveler of the movement, *not* a professional agitator. His next lecture series in 1845–1846 would, in fact, lead away from contemporary affairs and into the lives and "uses" of "great men" from the past: Plato and Montaigne, Shakespeare and Goethe, Napoleon and Swedenborg. Nonetheless, his two-hour address on August 1, 1844, proved a turning point, for it infused his vision of the American republic with a new commitment to racial equality. "The civility of no race can be perfect," he affirmed that day, "whilst another race is degraded . . . Man is one, and . . . you cannot injure any member, without a sympathetic injury to all the members. America is not civil, whilst Africa is barbarous." To one person in the audience, the former Brook Farmer George William Curtis, it was a new Emerson on the stage, "ardent and strong," with no trace of "that cold, clear, intellectual character which so many dislike." As Texas and the Mexican War inflamed the body politic, Emerson manifested the symptoms in militant opposition to the South. At Mary Brooks's urging, he backed a successful move to bring Wendell Phillips to the Concord Lyceum again, while he refused an invitation from a segregated lyceum in New Bedford.[35]

On August 1, 1845, abolitionists met in Waltham to celebrate another West Indian anniversary, and Emerson showed up to make brief remarks. In just a few sentences, he laid bare the crux of the slavery issue in New England. In his telling, Northerners did not question "the equity of the Negro's cause" nor doubt the sincerity of reformers. Economic interest prompted few farmers and mechanics to side with the slaveholders. Why, then, object to emancipation? The answer was simple: white racism. The cry of "the Niggers," he said bluntly, "blows away with a jeer all the efforts of philanthropy . . . [and] the cries of millions, now for hundreds of years." No longer tolerant of the dehumanizing language his white neighbors applied to Blacks without a second thought, Emerson repudiated the damaging slur in the name of the "moral sentiment." Transcendentalism was turning political in a Concord-centric blueprint of a republic based on free soil, free labor, and free men. At forty-three, on the verge of a national career, the man whom Margaret Fuller would soon dub "the Sage of Concord"[36] pledged himself to the fight. "All just men, all intelligent agents, must take the part of the black man against the white man."[37]

WHILE EMERSON WAS EXPANDING HIS AUDIENCE AND STEPPING ONTO A NA-tional stage, Henry Thoreau was pulling back from worldly affairs and disengaging from his neighbors. In April 1841, with his brother John's health under siege from the consumption that plagued the family, the pair shuttered their academy after two successful years. Out of a job, the Harvard graduate, now twenty-three, once again faced an uncertain future. He had solid credentials as a schoolmaster but made little effort to find another situation. One option for a reform-minded young man with scarce resources was to join Brook Farm, but communal living had no appeal to this veteran of the family boardinghouse. If he was going to farm, he would do so on his own. After scouting out various properties, he arranged to purchase the Hollowell place, a run-down farm along the Sudbury River, only to see the bargain dissolve when the seller changed his mind.

Far from being disappointed, Thoreau expressed relief at having escaped the fate of becoming a land owner. In his survey of properties, he had been shocked to see the depressed condition of the countryside; "wherever I go, the farms are run out, and there they lie, and the youth must buy old land and bring it to." Did he really want to harness himself to that yoke? "I must not lose any of my freedom by being a farmer and land holder." Better to earn his living as a day laborer for seventy-five cents a day. As he "heaved manure out of a pen" a few weeks after leaving the schoolroom behind, he had no complaints. While his hands were hired out, his thoughts were his own, and he was free to muse about "how he may live uprightly."[38]

Instead of striking out on his own, Thoreau moved into the Emerson home, where he boarded rent free in exchange for helping out in the garden and around the house and for looking after the children, four-year-old Waldo and two-year-old Ellen. In return, he enjoyed access to his mentor's library and counsel, contact with a fascinating array of visitors, and most of all, the leisure time to read, write, and develop as an author. He was a man with a purpose but no recognized vocation. A college graduate without any property to his name, he was indistinguishable on the annual list of polls and estates from the host of landless laborers passing through town.[39]

Subsumed in the Emerson household, Thoreau rejected the trappings of conventional adulthood. Marriage was not on the horizon; in 1840 both Henry and John had courted Ellen Quincy Sewall without success, and the writer never sought anyone else's hand. While some bachelors, such as eight-term selectmen Jonathan Hildreth and Cyrus Stow, were devoted to the town,[40] Thoreau kept his distance from church and state. He did not vote, never held office, and paid not a penny to a parish. His only contribution to government was the obligatory $1.50 poll tax, which he stopped paying in 1843 in a personal declaration of independence from an institution whose protection he spurned.[41] His parents and sisters regularly signed antislavery petitions; his name was absent from nearly all memorials after 1840. Only the Concord Lyceum enlisted his services; he put in two terms as secretary and curator (1838–1840) before declining reelection. (He reluctantly came back as curator in 1842–1843.)[42]

With no visible vocation and hardly any institutional ties, the Harvard graduate resembled the alienated young men whose case Emerson had pleaded in "The Transcendentalist," to Rev. Frost's chagrin. Shunning "the common labors and competitions of the market and the caucus," these "intelligent and religious persons . . . betake themselves to a certain solitary and critical way of living . . . They hold themselves aloof . . . they prefer to ramble in the country . . . They are striking work, and crying out for somewhat worthy to do!" But in Emerson's eyes, "my brave Henry" had not put his life on pause. He "is content to live now, & feels no shame in not studying any profession, for he does not postpone his life but lives already." Little did he realize how restless was the new inmate of his household. After eight months under Emerson's roof, Thoreau sat in his chamber on Christmas Eve and recorded the desire "to go soon and live away by the pond where I shall hear only the wind whispering among the reeds." His friends, including Emerson, were skeptical: what would he do there? "Will it not be employment enough," the future naturalist mused, "to watch the progress of the seasons?" "I don't want to feel as if my life were a sojourn any longer," he vowed the next day. "It is time now that I begin to live." But he stayed put for another year and a half.[43]

At the very start of his literary apprenticeship, Thoreau took nature as his special subject. As summer was giving way to fall in 1841, he conceived a project about his native town. "I think I could write a poem to be called Concord," he wrote in his journal. "For argument I should have the River—the Woods—the Ponds—the Hills—the Fields—the Swamps and Meadows." And then there were "the Streets and Buildings—and the Villagers. Then Morning—

Noon—and Evening—Spring Summer—Autumn and Winter—Night—Indian Summer—and the Mountains in the Horizon." What better terrain to explore as he imagined living by a pond?[44]

Instead, with Emerson's encouragement, the young man followed a different course. He spent more time editing and translating the works of others than in composing his own. Through his efforts the Transcendentalist house organ, *The Dial*, acquainted readers with select Greek and Roman poets from antiquity and "ethnical scriptures" from India and China. Another project was handed down by his mentor: an anthology of English poetry, over which Thoreau labored intermittently for several years, with little tangible result. His own productions were copious, but only a few poems saw print in *The Dial* while Margaret Fuller was editor. A frustrated author trashed over one thousand pages of his journal and started over. When Emerson took the helm of the magazine, Thoreau became his deputy. The new regime featured more of his pieces and opened the way to his future as a nature writer. In a review entitled "The Natural History of Massachusetts," and in a "Winter's Walk" through the woods after the first snow of the season, Thoreau displayed his remarkable ability to evoke "the wonderful purity" and simplicity of nature in fine detail. Both essays ran despite Emerson's objections to the author's contrarian style. The patron, with his effusions about the natural world, did not appreciate the satirical bite of his protégé's prose.[45]

Dependence on Emerson was a mixed blessing. Subtle forms of hierarchy and dependence linked the two men in ways that neither could acknowledge, given their fierce insistence upon independence and self-reliance. Even as Thoreau "consolidated a sense of himself as above all a writer," he relied on his mentor for professional opportunities. It became difficult to emerge from the great man's shadow. As a lecturer at the Concord Lyceum, he struck an unsympathetic John Shepard Keyes as "a coarse imitation of [Emerson] . . . so badly done as to make it painful to listen to him."

The close connection between host and guest gradually strained. In January 1843 Thoreau was dejected as he took stock of his situation. "What am I at present? A diseased bundle of nerves standing between time and eternity like a withered leaf that still hangs shivering on its stem. A more miserable object one could not well imagine." He desperately needed to get away, and ironically, it was Emerson who devised an escape. Thoreau would move into the household of Waldo's brother William in Staten Island and earn his keep as a tutor of the family's seven-year-old son. From that base the aspiring writer, who had finally broken out of *The Dial* and sold an article to a Boston magazine, could take the ferry to Manhattan and pitch ideas to publishers and editors in Gotham, fast becoming the nation's publishing capital. Nathaniel Hawthorne, who had become friends with both Emerson and Thoreau after taking up residence in the Old Manse, thought the change would be good for both men. In his view, Thoreau was at sea; "morally and intellectually," he "seems not to have found exactly the guiding clue." It was time for him to stake out "a circumstantial position in the world." Emerson, in turn, would be rid of "the inconveniency" he experienced from Thoreau's everyday presence as a lodger. "It may well be that such a sturdy and uncompromising person is fitter to meet occasionally in the open air, than to have as a permanent guest at table and fireside."[46]

The foray into New York was a bust. The rural scenery of Staten Island proved captivating, but not the hosts. The Emersons were a stuffy, middle-class couple without the intellectual interests or the Transcendentalist sentiments of their Concord kinsman. The tutor did not hit it off with his charge. But Manhattan beckoned, and Thoreau went "up to the city" in hopes of making his name as an author. He did not take publishers' row by storm. Though he was warmly welcomed by *New York Tribune* editor Horace Greeley, who had lectured in Concord the previous December, and by various acquaintances of Emerson, he failed to excite interest among the many editors he called on. At one point, in need of cash, he took to selling magazine subscriptions door to door.[47]

Hawthorne's friend, *Democratic Review* editor John O'Sullivan, was initially encouraging. The editor snapped up an unusual piece by Thoreau: a genial sketch of the country innkeeper as a distinctive character type. Composed in a style reminiscent of Hawthorne, "The Landlord" portrays a quintessentially public man, extending hospitality to one and all, catering to every opinion with none of his own, and content to spend his every waking hour in the company of others. Such a figure, utterly devoid of individuality, should have provoked outrage in the author. But Thoreau withheld judgment. At a time when Concord was refusing to issue liquor licenses, he approved the tavern for its democratic inclusiveness—an outlook welcome in the *Democratic Review*. Not so the next piece Thoreau submitted: a review-essay of a German engineer's blueprint for a technological utopia in which machines would control nature, eliminate labor, and create abundance for all. Thoreau scoffed at the very idea as "transcendentalism in mechanics." Its fundamental flaw was to start with society, rather than the individual, on the route to reform. This scathing critique contradicted the editorial line of the *Democratic Review*, so O'Sullivan turned it down, then changed his mind after the author held his ground.[48]

By November 1843, when the review appeared, Thoreau had gotten his fill of New York and its publishing scene. Although he enjoyed the cultural attractions—canoe races, museums, and fairs—and took advantage of the Mercantile Library, under whose auspices Emerson spoke, he loathed the ubiquitous crowds. It was impossible to sustain individuality in the big city. "The pigs in the street are the most respectable portion of the population," he groused. Lonely and homesick, he lapsed into nostalgia. When he was in Concord, Thoreau piled up criticisms of the neighbors. Out of town, he idealized them. In April, as he anticipated the departure from home, he had saluted Concord as "my Rome" and "its people . . . my Romans." He had barely unpacked his bags before reaffirming loyalty to his birthplace: "I carry Concord ground in my boots and in my hat—," he wrote to Lidian Emerson, "and am I not made of Concord dust?" In the end, he sojourned in Staten Island for just seven months. It was the longest time he would ever be away.[49]

In the face of the many forces threatening to engulf the individual—the mass society taking shape in New York and Boston, the conformity of the small New England town, the constraints of hierarchy inherited from the past, and the new fetters imposed by the markets, caucuses, and benevolent organizations of the present—Thoreau was adamant. The more uncertain his prospects, the more fiercely he celebrated the power of the self. Back in Concord, he returned to his room in the Parkman House, employed his ingenuity in the pencil factory, and felt the fervor of abolitionism in his family. Sister Helen was now vice president of the Concord Female Anti-Slavery Society and frequent participant in meetings of MCASS, where she struck up a friendship with the noted African American abolitionist Frederick Douglass. In May 1844 Cynthia Thoreau and her two daughters joined Mary Brooks at a convention of the statewide abolitionist body and publicly endorsed a call for "no union with slaveholders." But Henry did not budge from his insistence on individual action. Although the petition for a constitutional amendment to end slavery in the nation and racial discrimination in Massachusetts law was still circulating when he arrived home, he abstained from joining his family and adding his signature. He bided his time and awaited the right occasion to take a stand.[50]

Two figures served as his models for action on principle. One was the antislavery editor Nathaniel Peabody Rogers of Concord, New Hampshire, whose *Herald of Freedom* was a favorite of the Thoreau family. An "ultra" among the abolitionists, Rogers won the Transcendentalist's admiration for the fearlessness and independence of his judgment. For the final issue of *The Dial* in April 1844, Thoreau penned a tribute to the journalist as a force of nature, whose principles were as solid as rock and whose prose flowed "like his own mountain torrents." Here was a spirit truly "free and uncalculating," in sharp contrast to the "fraternity" of do-gooders Thoreau detested. Such sickly souls "mistake their private ail for an infected atmosphere." If they suffer a stomach ache, they think all of society has indigestion. Instead of prescribing for others, let them cure themselves first. Only healthy individuals could be trusted to address the needs of humankind.[51]

The other hero was the great abolitionist crusader Wendell Phillips, whose lecture to the Concord Lyceum in March 1845 once again bitterly divided the townspeople. As before, Mary Brooks and the CFASS issued the invitation behind the scenes, with Emerson, senior curator for the season, acting as their front man. The proposal was quickly shot down by the other curators. Rev. Frost could not forgive Phillips's attacks on the clergy, while John Shepard Keyes, newly risen to prominence by his father's death, would not countenance an enemy of the Constitution and Union. The twenty-three-year-old lawyer was as much a young fogy as his father had been an old one. The advocates of Phillips successfully appealed to the lyceum membership; Frost and Keyes quit in protest, with Henry Thoreau filling one of their seats; and the lecture went forward little more than a week after outgoing President John Tyler signed a hotly contested bill annexing Texas into the Union.[52]

Amid the controversy Phillips was imperturbable, his performance so compelling that Thoreau composed an admiring review for *The Liberator*. The abolitionist came before the audience as a lone figure speaking with "unquestionable earnestness and integrity." His words were not designed for the occasion or calculated for effect. They gave voice to convictions at the core of his being. Phillips sought no one's approval before expressing his views. He required no "alliance" with any party or sect. To be sure, as the abolitionist reminded the audience, he came forward as the representative of "the American [Anti-Slavery] Society." In Thoreau's eyes, Phillips transcended that role so completely that he stood "distinctly," "firmly," and "effectively alone"—living proof that "one honest man is so much more than a host." So fit was his discourse, so sincere his manner that "he unconsciously tells his biography as he proceeds . . . Here is one, who is at the same time an eloquent speaker and a righteous man." His words *were* his deeds.[53]

Would Thoreau be as true to his self when conscience called? On the first of August 1844, he had shown his mettle. As the day began, people were streaming into town for the tenth anniversary of West Indian emancipation. The program, overseen by Mary Brooks, had been in the works since late June. Emerson's keynote speech, along with talks by such abolitionist luminaries as Frederick Douglass, had been well advertised. But on the morning of the festivities, there was one hitch: no venue had been secured. The local ministers had declined to make available their meetinghouses, and town officials had refused use of the brick schoolhouse and the courthouse. Why furnish public space for attacks on church and state? A fiasco loomed, and with a sudden rain coming down, the gathering crowd in front of the courthouse forced the issue, pushing its way into the building and occupying the premises. How to spread the news to the visitors from out of town arriving on the newly opened Fitchburg Railroad? The usual method was to ring the meetinghouse bell, but could anyone do that on his own? Five or six individuals declined the duty; one young man raced off in search of the parish committee to obtain permission.

Thoreau saved the day. Just an hour earlier he had returned home from a two-week hike as far as the Catskills and across the breadth of Massachusetts. Without hesitation, he stepped forward into the belfry, grabbed the rope, and sounded the alarm. "The ringing of the church bell is a much more melodious sound than any that is heard within the church," he once quipped—and all the more so in a righteous cause. In a moment of crisis he had consulted no one and acted decisively on his own.[54]

In that independent course lay a solution to Thoreau's vocational crisis and the path to literary achievement. The opportunity came from Emerson once again. In September 1844, as the writer took his regular "solitary" walk by Walden Pond, he happened upon a court-ordered auction of a piece of land once belonging to an impecunious yeoman named Tommy Wyman, who had died insolvent the year before. With no bidders, it was selling for a song, so on a whim, Emerson staked his claim. A few days later he acquired a neighboring "pine grove." Altogether, he was now landlord and "waterlord" of eleven acres, on which he invited Thoreau to fulfill his long-held dream of living by the shores of a pond and observing the progress of the seasons.[55]

Here was the chance for the nonconformist to dispel the lull in which his life was becalmed, to revitalize his spirit and inspire his writing. "Go . . . build yourself a hut," his friend Ellery Channing urged, "& there begin the grand process of devouring yourself alive. I see no alternative, no other hope for you." By March 1845, amid the fight over Wendell Phillips, Thoreau was getting ready for the dramatic change in his life. He was once again a recipient of Emerson's favor, carrying out an experiment in independence on land he obtained rent free. No matter: just as Hawthorne succeeded in identifying himself with Ezra Ripley's forlorn manse, so Thoreau would occupy Emerson's snap purchase and make it his own. The elements of *Walden* were at hand: woods and pond as setting, Transcendentalism as philosophy, the changing world of Concord a central subject, and the quest for personal renewal a driving force. Abolitionism, plus self-reliance, inspired Thoreau to go it alone, and his own inclinations took him to Walden's shores. After two years, two months, and two days of residence, he would emerge with the draft of a manuscript that was simultaneously the record of one man's rebirth and the story of an American town. It was the core of the volume he would publish seven years later. Emerson generalized Concord into New England and New England into America. Thoreau planted himself in a specific social and physical landscape and made that site an enduring place on the literary map.[56]

HENRY THOREAU DID NOT GO TO WALDEN TO LAUNCH A PUBLIC PROTEST. His purpose was to "transact some private business with the fewest obstacles." That business was writing, the profession to which he had committed himself, so far with limited success. At Walden he would be apart from family and friends, with all their distractions, and obtain the time and space to concentrate on literary projects. At the top of his agenda was a long-planned memoir of the boating trip on the Concord and Merrimack rivers that he had taken with his brother John back in 1839. It was meant to be an "elegy" for a friendship cut short and a contemplative narrative through nature and time. As Thoreau sat at his green writing desk and penned that work, a second venture took shape in his mind and his journals: a first-person account of his very life in the woods. Once he had envisioned himself in "an observatory among the stars" viewing "this beehive of ours" from the heavens and taking its measure. Now, living on the edge of town a mile from any neighbors, he could actually secure that critical distance. "I imagine it to be some advantage to live a primitive and frontier life—though in the midst of an outward civilization," he wrote two weeks into his stay. From that vantage he could shed the everyday assumptions and practices of Concord and get back to basics, to what was truly necessary for a fulfilling existence, physical, intellectual, and spiritual. "I wish to meet the facts of life—the vital facts . . . face to face. And so I came down here. Life! Who knows what it is—what it does?"[57]

That existential question infused every aspect of his activities, his surroundings, and his experience with potential significance. On the surface his daily affairs were mundane. He built a house, laid a chimney, gathered firewood, and tended a hearth. He supplied his meals with the bread he baked, the potatoes he grew, and the fish he caught in the pond. He cultivated beans and sold the harvest for cash. He regularly walked into town to catch up with friends and welcomed visitors, in turn, to his "hermitage." As for the immediate neighborhood, he acquainted himself with the ice cutters and woodchoppers, railroad men and farm laborers who flocked to the woods, and he explored the cellar holes and legends of "former inhabitants." The creatures of "the wild"—the flora and fauna, the woods and the pond itself—became his intimates, as he acclimated himself to a world following rhythms of its own. Most of all, he kept to his schoolmaster's pine desk and filled the pages of his notebooks with observations and reflections that steadily turned his narrative into a searching work of personal exploration and social criticism. By the time he returned to "civilized life" in September 1847, he had compiled the first draft of a book that would take his hometown, expose its flaws and contradictions, and make it an exemplar of America's failure to realize its own promise and possibilities of freedom. Like Emerson's New England, Thoreau's Concord stood in for a republic gone off course and in need of spiritual renewal.

For all its personal origins, Thoreau's experiment at Walden could not avoid public notice. It was not just that his bean field abutted the old highway south to Wayland, where it connected with the main route from Boston to Hartford and New Haven; nor that his well-built house was readily visible to passersby on the carriage road farmers had been using for generations to get to their woodlots bordering the pond and to fish in the nearby marsh known as Pout's Nest; nor that it stood below the tracks of the new Fitchburg Railroad, along which he could conveniently walk the mile to his parents' new home in "Texas" and into the village. Rather, the writer's retreat attracted curiosity for its defiance of a fundamental rule of social life in Concord. Nobody lived alone—nobody, that is, with any choice in the matter.

In 1837, the year Thoreau graduated from college and returned home, only a dozen individuals in a town of two thousand lived alone. Nearly all of them were widows, without children at hand to care for them, such as Sarah Hollowell, sixty-five, eking out a scanty existence on the worn-out land Thoreau was all set to buy, and Eunice P. Wyman, an intrepid woman who had farmed successfully for several decades with the aid of two sons and a daughter until they scattered to the winds—and even she had brothers down the road. Just one man was in the same situation: Tommy Wyman (no kin to Eunice), whom the literary "hermit" of Walden was glad to succeed on the land. Had Thoreau stayed on that lot long enough to be enumerated on the 1850 federal census, he would have raised the roster of solitary souls in Concord that year to four. Undoubtedly to his satisfaction, he would have been in the same company as Elisha Dugan, the "man of wild habits" the writer had memorialized in "The Old Marlborough Road."

But Thoreau, the Harvard graduate, was different. He had opted to set up housekeeping deep in the woods, far from any neighbors, thereby putting himself in the very "wilderness" Parson Ripley had once advised Mary Moody Emerson to shun. "Surely, it cannot add to your happiness or improvement," the patriarch had advised his stepdaughter, "to hear the screaming of loons, the hooting of owls, and the howling of wolves." Thoreau thus separated himself from a community that was supposedly in need of his talents for education and reform. Approaching thirty and still without a clear social role, the Transcendentalist epitomized the selfish, antisocial outlook Barzillai Frost had decried at the lyceum two years before—or so it looked to the neighbors. The unemployed schoolmaster, whose college education had been obtained at such sacrifice by his family, was a conundrum.[58]

No wonder, then, that when Thoreau emerged from the woods on a cold Wednesday evening in January 1846, nearly eight months after taking up residence at Walden, and stood at the podium to address the lyceum, many in the audience were disappointed. The discourse dealt with "the writings and style" of Emerson's friend, the Scottish author Thomas Carlyle, whose hard-driving, colloquial prose, with its extravagant humor and fertility of expression, furnished a model for Thoreau's own. But that was not what the listeners had come to hear. What was he doing by the pond, they inquired, and how was he getting by? The queries were practical, not philosophical; they cut to the quick and demanded the details of a woodland way of life: "Some wished to know what I got to eat—If I didn't feel lonesome—If I wasn't afraid—What I should do if I were taken sick—and the like." Others asked what Thoreau had done for the poor and how much of his income had gone to charity. These questions followed a familiar logic: no one is an island, sufficient unto himself; each of us needs others to get by; even more, every person has a duty to contribute to the collective well-being. Without the support of our fellows, we are subject to loneliness, vulnerability, and fear. The interrogators had absorbed the ideology of interdependence, as preached by Ripley and Frost, and from that perspective, they could not fathom why anyone would forfeit the mutual insurance policy afforded by membership in the community. Thoreau understood their concerns; he had, after all, heard the same sermons over the years. The questions were "very natural and pertinent," he conceded, "considering the circumstances," and they set the agenda for the lectures he would deliver to the lyceum almost exactly one year later. Fittingly, the initial manuscript of *Walden* was "Addressed to my Townsmen." Through their questions, the neighbors focused Thoreau's thinking. Far from originating as an artifact of individualism, the work was from the start a social text.[59]

Walden took shape as a lecture beyond the subtitle. In February 1847, one year after his unpopular discourse on Carlyle, Thoreau returned to the lyceum and for two consecutive weeks presented a "History of Himself." This time the lecturer addressed the issue on everyone's minds. Why was he living in the woods? A fair question, he acknowledged, only to throw the challenge back at the audience. Why did they maintain *their* "mode of life"?

As he surveyed the local scene, having "travelled a good deal in Concord," the prospect was uninviting. "Everywhere, in shops and offices and fields, the inhabitants have seemed to me to be doing penance in a thousand curious ways." In a display of the classical learning he had acquired at Harvard, he likened his townsmen's travails to "the twelve labors of Hercules," only to suggest that his contemporaries' suffering was worse, for it was not mythical but actual—self-imposed and without end. Just look at the young men with the "misfortune" to inherit the homestead. Far from enjoying an easy path in life, these unlucky heirs staggered under the load of "farms, houses, barns, cattle, and farming tools." Burdened with debts and care, they began "digging their graves as soon as they are born," and with every furrow they plowed their manhood into the soil. Did the farmers in Lyceum Hall—perhaps, Daniel Hunt—recognize the portrait?

Other listeners may have seen themselves in the grim gallery of debtors, laborers, and tradesmen the lecturer brought forth. Would Peter Hutchinson or

Ward Safford (the longtime employee of Abiel Heywood) have nodded in agreement that "the laboring man has not leisure for a lofty integrity day by day," for were he to take time off to cultivate "the finer fruits" of life, "his labor would depreciate in the market"? Would the multitude of inhabitants owing bills at the stores, loans at the Concord Bank, and mortgage payments to Daniel Shattuck, Samuel Hoar, and other wealthy lenders have been at once shocked and embarrassed by Thoreau's harsh assessment of their lives? "Some of you who hear me . . . are poor, find it hard to live . . . I have no doubt that some of you who are here tonight are unable to pay for all the dinners you have actually eaten, or for the coats and shoes which are fast wearing or already worn out, and have come here to spend borrowed time, robbing your creditors of an hour." The speaker's grasp of detail was exact; no one could doubt his appreciation of the neighbors' struggles. The Thoreau family's slow climb back up the economic ladder had left its mark.[60]

Why did they live this way? Thoreau was well aware of the abuses of industrial capitalism; he observed in passing that "our factory system is not the best mode by which men may be clothed," for it degraded the operatives who tended the spindles and looms, and its ruling principle was not that "mankind may be well and worthily clad, but unquestionably that the corporation may be enriched." But unlike the Loco-Focos in town, the pencil manufacturer's son did not blame the few for exploiting the many. The problem ran deeper, and it affected nearly everyone. Its origins lay in human consciousness—or more precisely, false consciousness. People pretended that they had "deliberately chosen" a way of life that was anxious and unfulfilling. Thoreau refused to believe it. To his eyes, the neighbors accepted their miserable condition because "they really think that there is no choice left." Never doubting that "the whole ground of human life . . . [has] been gone over before us by our predecessors, both the heights and the valleys," they trudged along in the well-worn path of tradition and adapted to whatever came their way. This blinkered perspective— surrendering to circumstances without a fight—was what Thoreau would later call "quiet desperation," but not yet. Instead, he hastened to remind the audience that they lived in an era of rapid change and that "no way of doing or thinking, however ancient," was fixed. The proof was all about them in the reforms of the day: "Men have left off rum safely and imprisoning for debt, and chattel slavery in some places." Those advances, so evident in Concord life, hinted at the untold possibilities of the human spirit: "Man's capacities have never been measured, nor are we to judge of what he can do by any precedent, so little has been tried." Why not put this to the test and explore our true nature? "All change is a miracle to contemplate, but it is a miracle which is taking place every instant." The lecturer shared in the perfectionist spirit of the age.[61]

Thoreau's voice in the early pages of *Walden* is often taken as hectoring. But the townspeople assembled in the vestry of the Unitarian meetinghouse on those February evenings did not necessarily take offense. The lecturer had reason to expect a positive reception. In his view, "the mass of men . . . are discontented and idly complaining of the hardness of their lot and of the times, when they might improve them." This was the target audience, to whom he would dispense the lessons of his experience. His message was also directed to those who performed their duty to society, day in and day out, with no satisfaction from following the rules, and to "that seemingly wealthy, but most terribly impoverished class of all," the idle rich, "who have accumulated dross but know not how to spend it, and thus have forged their own golden or silver fetters."[62]

These restless souls were a constituency open to change, if only the speaker hit the right notes to win them over. There was nothing untoward in Thoreau's assault on custom and convention. Lyceum lecturers regularly inveighed against the dead hand of the past holding the current generation in its grip. Educators urged parents to welcome new schoolbooks rather than cling to the outmoded texts on which they had learned the ABCs. Scientists called on mechanics to jettison the time-honored secrets of their craft and put new methods and machines to work. Agricultural reformers urged farmers to break with custom, test new techniques, and report their experiences to the agricultural society. Thoreau rose to the occasion with his forthright challenge to the neighbors, even if his rhetoric was more hyperbolic, more strident, than usual at the lyceum. "What old people say you can't do, you try and find that you can," he opined. "Age seems no better[,] hardly so well qualified for an instructor as youth, for it has not profited so much as it has lost." The listeners could appreciate the lecturer's satirical hits without taking everything literally. Prudence Ward, the longtime boarder in the Thoreau household, considered the lectures "much needed," even if few individuals would ever imitate the Transcendentalist's example.[63]

Walden thus began as a lyceum lecture, and the opening chapters— "Economy" and "Where I Lived and What I Lived For"—reflect the themes and form of the genre. Except, of course, that most such discourses urged listeners to jettison tradition and adopt improvements for the sake of operating more efficiently and profitably in the marketplace. Thoreau's purpose was just the opposite. He meant to show that the so-called wisdom of the past was wrong, that people did not need to reduce their lives to constant work and worry and to the endless accumulation of goods. Let them pare their needs, curb their wants, and follow nature's way. That was the path to freedom and serenity.

When Emerson had assayed the state of New England in his 1843 lecture series, he took a long, historical view of the contending forces—commerce and conscience—shaping society and culture over the centuries. Thoreau ignored the past in his lyceum lectures and chose instead to set his personal example of "economy"—of obtaining the "necessaries of life"—against the practices of his contemporaries. Undoubtedly, some in the audience recalled Ezra Ripley's lecture on the same topic, "Economy," a decade earlier—one of the few of the parson's voluminous manuscripts that no longer survives. Thoreau's approach owed little to his predecessors. "I went down to the pond," he explained, "because I wished to live deliberately, and front only the essential facts of life, and see if I could not learn what it had to teach, and not when I came to die discover that I had not lived." In an age of proliferating choices of goods to buy, places to reside, and callings to follow—so many, in fact, that some felt overwhelmed by the immense array and went along with whatever the neighbors were doing—Thoreau was intent on exercising his personal autonomy to the fullest. He would live "deliberately," not desperately; instead of bending to the winds of custom and conformity, he would stand erect and stride forth purposefully, his every act authentically his own. His life at Walden was an experiment in determining what was truly necessary and what was not.[64]

In this spirit, Thoreau related how he obtained the means of existence—"food, shelter, clothing, and fuel"—while living in the woods. Each rubric afforded ample opportunity for his satire, as he contrasted his simple, utilitarian choices with the expensive and unnecessary preferences of others. His clothing was unfashionable and cheap; eschewing a taste for the new, he wore old coats and shirts and hand-me-downs so long they became part of his being, bearing the impress of his character. "Beware of all enterprises that require new clothes," he advised, "and not rather a new wearer of clothes." His tidy, well-constructed house, made of "tall, arrowy pines" cut from his Walden woodlot and of boards recycled from a shanty he purchased from an Irish laborer, kept him at once warm and close to nature. He had built cheaply, gotten firsthand experience, and was not obliged to toil "for 10—20—or 30 years" to pay off a mortgage, unlike his parents, who had grown weary of paying rent to landlords and acquired a house near the railroad depot in 1844 with a loan from the ubiquitous Daniel Shattuck. As for food, the lecturer gave a brief accounting of his venture in raising beans, along with potatoes, turnips, and corn. He itemized the expenses of the small farm, added the costs of food from the store, and triumphantly announced that his simple vegetarian diet, with just "a very little salt pork," cost a mere twenty-seven cents a week. He reserved a fuller discussion for "Bean Field," a separate chapter of the manuscript, wherein he displayed his deep immersion in local life and his determination to explore a new, more natural way of living on the land.[65]

On the two and a half acres of sandy upland fronting the Wayland road, Thoreau finally realized his long-held ambition to be a farmer. His was a small effort, to be sure, conducted on terms unlike any other site of husbandry in Concord. A child of the central village, the college graduate had little experience of practical farming, though he took pride in growing "the biggest and juiciest melons" in his parents' backyard garden and had seen to the family cow and pig. Nonetheless, he held strong opinions about agriculture, based on the depressing conditions he had observed as he scouted out potential properties to buy. On the other hand, the "model farmers" of the agricultural society—men like Abel Moore—offered no alternative. Thoreau was disgusted by the "extremely artificial and unclean methods of cultivation" recommended by reformers. Their emphasis on manures had turned local fields "into pens or hot beds" for "the fattening of swine and cattle—and the pampering of depraved tastes and appetites." The air of New England had once been sweet with the scent of fragrant native plants, but no more: "Our offence is rank; it smells to heaven"—an unnatural act he denounced in echo of Shakespeare. Thoreau was determined to find another way, in keeping with his philosophy of deliberate living.[66]

The novice farmer staged the account of his "Bean Field" as a satire of the literature of agricultural reform. The report was presented with mathematical exactitude and a straight face. The author calculated that he planted seven miles of beans in all. With each row precisely fifteen rods long and spaced three feet apart, the field comprised 110,632.5 square feet—equivalent to 2.5 acres. The other vegetables he grew—potatoes, turnips, and corn—were overshadowed by the massive commitment to the leguminous plant. Why beans? Arguably, the pulse was well suited to the light, sandy soil. But Thoreau could have opted for other crops, such as rye and corn, whose neglect by Yankee farmers he bewailed in the lyceum lecture. "Every New Englander might easily raise all his bread stuffs in this land of Rye & Indian corn," rather than resort to the bake house for the flour processed from wheat grown on distant Western lands. As it happened, Tommy Wyman had furnished himself with the staff of life from the very fields Thoreau converted to beans.[67]

Despite his preference for johnnycake, Thoreau eschewed Wyman's example. Not because he looked forward to eating vegetables. Baked beans—the edible product of all that effort—might have been a staple in Yankee households, but the nonconformist shunned them on principle. "I am by nature a Pythagorean." Any way he looked at them, beans were unappealing. As counters in a ballot—the ancient Greeks had voted by putting white or black beans in a box, a tradition kept up in the Social Circle—or as the mainstay of noontime dinners, beans unsettled mind and body alike. Upsetting the stomach and stirring up the bowels, they disturbed the serenity Thoreau craved. Appropriately, beans caused gas—exactly what was emitted, in its cultivator's view, whenever politicians spoke.[68]

Thoreau grew beans not to eat but to carry to market. They constituted his cash crop, and with the earnings from their sale, he planned to purchase more suitable sustenance: "It was fit that I should live on rice, mainly, who loved so well the philosophy of India." As a moneymaker, the legumes were an unlikely choice. A standby in local homes, they sat in a pot, flavored with a piece of pork, and simmered for hours, allowing women to direct their attention to other tasks; they were ready to eat whenever the men came in from the fields. Everybody raised beans, including John Thoreau, whose backyard crop was delayed in the summer of 1836, according to the gossipy boarder Prudence Ward, by unusually cold weather. So commonplace were beans in local gardens and fields that hardly anyone raised them for sale. In 1850, when the federal government conducted a census of agriculture, asking farmers what crops they grew, what animals they raised, and how much money they earned, half of the yeomen reported no beans at all. Of the sixty who did, only four surpassed Thoreau's harvest of twelve bushels four years before. The literary cultivator was in the running for "bean king" of Concord. The eccentric choice of crop led local farmers to christen Thoreau's field "the Paradise of Beans," and passersby could not resist the urge to offer the lessons of experience: "Corn, my boy, for fodder, corn for fodder."[69]

Why, then, did Thoreau invest so heavily in a crop with so limited a market? The answer lay in the larger objectives of the Walden experiment: every activity in which Thoreau engaged was purposeful, at once material and spiritual, practical and symbolic. In the writer's vision, "husbandry was anciently a sacred art, but it is pursued with heedlessness and haste by us. Our object is to have large farms and large crops." It was imperative to recover a reverent posture toward the land. At Walden, he would create a practical demonstration of how to do so. He meant "to know beans" as fully as possible. They provided a medium for his philosophy of nature.

Beans carried symbolic advantages for Thoreau's experiment. They were not an import from the Old World but a crop native to the New, whose cultivation the English settlers had adopted from the Indians along with corn. Thoreau imaginatively identified with the indigenous inhabitants, and he was delighted to discover, by the arrowheads he turned up in the course of hoeing, "that an extinct nation had dwelt here and planted beans ere white men came to cut & clear the land." Beans thus smacked of the wilderness. At the same time, the pulse was a national symbol of the Yankee. Thoreau's common white bush bean was the source of Boston's minor claim to culinary distinction. "This is the happy land of baked beans and pure religion," one humorist quipped; another wit, Josh Billings, developed a considerable monologue on the subject:

> Next to rhy bread, beans hav been called by the poets, and philosphers the cumfort, and staff ov life . . . Beans are az old as Esau, he sold out for bean porridge . . . I luv beans, but don't hanker for them. But beans, and me wont quarrel. Baked beans are a grate necessity in Nu England, and not to hav a platter ov them for Sunday dinner, iz lookt upon thare az being stuck-up to the neighbors. One ov the old blue laws ov Massachusetts waz, "thou shalt eat baked beans on Sunday." I kan remember now ov eating baked beans, and rhy, and injun bread every Sunday, when I waz a boy, and luving it, bekauze I was obliged to.[70]

Beans thus partook of both wildness and civilization. Unlike the cinquefoil, johnswort, and blackberries uprooted by Thoreau's diligent hoe, they required human assistance to reach fruition. But the helping hand was modest, in contrast to the massive intervention necessary to bring forth English hay, the epitome of the cash crop, scientifically produced for profit—"carefully weighed, the moisture calculated, the silicates, and the potash." In beans, despite his distaste, Thoreau cultivated a fitting emblem of his project. The pulse was, he said, "the connecting link between wild and cultivated fields; as some states are civilized, and others half-civilized, and others savage or barbarous, so my field was, though not in a bad sense, a half-cultivated field."

Thoreau slyly presented the account of his bean field as an unassuming contribution to the literature of agricultural improvement, deserving a place in Rev. Henry Colman's official *Report on the Agriculture of Massachusetts*—the very volume that celebrated Abel Moore's "magic power" in ditching and draining wet meadows and converting them to the production of prodigious amounts of English hay. Thoreau's recitation was a subversive document. It mimicked the submissions that farmers like Moore sent to the agricultural societies, only to reject the counsel of improvement those groups were established to promote. The literary farmer did not merely defy the wisdom of his elders by specializing in beans. He happily ignored advice on other matters as well. He planted late. He did nothing to improve the thin soil, which one observer deemed incapable of sustaining anything but chipmunks. No foul manures, no commercial, chemical fertilizers for this field. He left three feet between rows and eighteen inches between plants; the *New England Farmer* that same year recommended around two feet and six inches, respectively. Thoreau's beans needed room to grow. He hoed them while they were still wet with morning dew: "I would advise you to do all your work if possible, while the dew is on," he would later add. He claimed to have spent numerous hours cultivating them, from five in the morning to noon, day in and day out, yet somehow never managed to finish the task. Nor was he any more industrious in dealing with pests. He asked one old woodsman: "Mr. W., is there any way to get woodchucks without trapping them—" "Yes, shoot 'em, you damn fool." He declined the advice until there was no choice: it was either him or the woodchucks. Supposedly, Thoreau laid a successful trap, but rather than end the creature's career of pillaging, he carried it two miles away, administered a schoolmasterly beating with a stick, then let the rogue go in peace. Later on he would devour its kinsman.[71]

By the time he totaled up the results of his labors with pulses, the joke was out. This experiment in agriculture was guaranteed to disappoint. Compared to other producers of legumes, Thoreau achieved only paltry returns. Among Thoreau's co-workers in the bean fields of Massachusetts in the late 1840s and early 1850s, the "brag" crop was thirty-five bushels per acre, and the normal yield was around twenty. The willful scholar could boast at best seven or eight. Of the twelve bushels he did harvest, Thoreau was able to sell just nine. That shortfall did not trouble him. He had become attached to his beans: after all the "planting, and hoeing, and harvesting, and threshing, and picking over," he found "the selling . . . the hardest of all."[72]

Thoreau lost all interest in beans as a commercial enterprise. His point in the "Bean Field" chapter, which he altered little from its first draft at the pond to its final appearance in print eight years later, was to turn the sober literature of agricultural improvement, with its spiritually deadening obsession with crop rotations, manures, turnips, and tools, upside down. The conventional agricultural report would proudly testify that the farmer had taken a run-down field or swamp, fit only for crickets and frogs, and—by dint of heroic labor, rational planning, large doses of money, and not uncommonly, exploitation of Irish laborers—"raised [the land] from the dead and adorned [it] with life and beauty," as was said of Abel Moore.

By contrast, Thoreau started with exhausted, barren land, did nothing to improve it, obtained little from it, and announced himself quite content. His inspiration was not the model farmer Moore but the "most poetical farmer" George Minott. The reclusive bachelor represented the old-style husbandry to the writer and his friends. "He reminds me of *beans*, plow-fields, deep grass, hoeing, and corncake," the Transcendentalist poet Ellery Channing once observed. Minott treated the land with respect; he regarded the plants he grew, the cow he kept, even the chickens in his dooryard, not as sources of profit but almost as members of his household and vital to its well-being. Yet in the end, for Thoreau, the bean field was too demanding. Even before he harvested his meager crop, he had decided not to repeat the effort. "I will not plant beans and corn with so much industry another summer," he vowed in mid-August 1845, "but such seeds . . . as sincerity—truth—simplicity—. . . —innocence—and see if they will not grow in this soil even with less toil & manurance and sustain me."[73]

The true harvest of the bean field was spiritual. Thoreau planted himself in nature and opened up to all its influences. He wanted not just to "hoe" beans but to "know" them, and he succeeded in making an intimate acquaintance. He protected the green shoots from invading armies of wormwood, pigweed, and piper grass. He stood in the furrows beneath the bright sun, absorbing the rays equally with the growing legumes. He put his confidence in nature. A brown thrasher on the branch of a nearby birch sounded a chorus to the tinkling of the hoe on the stones in the soil; a nighthawk wheeled overhead. The cultivator paused often to admire the birds in flight and to wonder at the salamander, "a trace of Egypt and the Nile," in a rotten stump at his feet. He merged unconsciously into the natural scene: "it was no longer beans that I hoed, nor I that hoed beans." Thoreau thereby realized his Transcendentalist ideal: his labor had become an end in itself and not merely a "degraded" means of robbing nature for profit. In the very course of making a living, he cultivated his higher self. Man and nature joined together in a sacred calling.[74]

The bean field served as a metaphor for human relations. While Thoreau took time with cultivation, coming to know his beans as fully as possible, most farmers raced through their work, intent on getting the biggest result in the shortest time. Sadly, the same haste governed contacts among neighbors. "We should not meet them in haste," he advised. "Most men I do not meet at all, for they seem not to have time—they are busy about their beans." What if they paused and took stock of their lives? Would they continue on the same heedless course? Let them attend to Thoreau's example. Having absorbed the lessons of growing beans, he moved on to new fields of experience: "Why should not the New Englander try new adventures—& not lay so much stress on his grain, his potato and grass crop, and his orchards!—raise other crops than these?"[75]

Despite his reputation as the "hermit of Walden," Thoreau never lost sight of the "outward civilization" from which he had taken temporary leave. All of the manuscript he drafted at his "inkwell" in the woods is as steeped in the details, large and small, of local life as is "Bean Field." Thoreau captured the driving forces of the day—the coming of the iron horse, the waves of Irish and French-Canadian immigrants, the advance—and inadequacy—of modern communications, the remaking of farming in response to changing markets, the struggles of the library, lyceum, and schools to uphold a worthy culture, the moral and spiritual failures of church and state, the problematic programs of the reformers, and the loss of wildness in nature—and provided a compelling reflection on the transformation of an entire way of life.

The Mexican War disrupted his woodland retreat. One day in mid-July 1846, on a trip into town to get a shoe repaired, he ran into Sam Staples, the constable and jail keeper, who pressed the delinquent taxpayer to pay his overdue bill. Thoreau seized on the demand to stage a protest against a government engaged in an immoral war to extend the empire of slavery. No matter that the poll tax was irrelevant to the issue. The dissenter meant to dramatize his opposition to an unjust state. Once again he acted on his own, without consulting anyone, and took a stand on principle. The penalty, as it turned out, was slight: a single night in jail, after his aunt interfered and settled his debt. Even so, the protest put the position he had advocated at the Concord Lyceum—"resistance to civil government"—into practice. Thoreau refused "blind reverence" for authority and institutions. His neighbors could do so as well and decline to be agents of state-sanctioned "villainy." His was an act of social withdrawal more extreme than his fellow Concordians, even those opposed to the Mexican War, had contemplated. And it was made possible by the "sincere and simple" way of life the writer was then conducting at Walden and that he would one day reveal to his neighbors.[76]

The remaking of Concord gathered force during his childhood and youth and culminated during his stay at Walden. Thoreau witnessed and criticized the changes from both the center and the margin. He never lost sight of the interconnection of all the parts. Luxuries for the few, he inveighed, were obtained through the degradation of the many. The railroad ran not just on steam but on the sacrifices of the anonymous men who built it: "Did you ever think what those sleepers are that underlie the rail-road? Each one is a man—an Irish-man, or a Yankee-man—The rails are laid on them . . . and the cars run smoothly over them!"[77]

Thoreau never sloughed off the heritage of Ezra Ripley and the message of community. As he approached the first anniversary of his move to Walden, he troubled over criticism that he had already spent too long in the woods: "My friends reprove me for not devoting myself to some trade, or profession, and acquiring property." He acquitted himself of that fault but could not deny the charge that he had neglected "the advantages of society [and] of worthy and earnest helpful relations to people . . . I am convicted—and yet not I only but they also." What alternative was there but to be himself? "I am useless for keeping flocks & herds, for I am on the trail of a rarer game." In his mind he was never alone. The community came with him, whether he was recounting his activities at Walden in the language of civic duty—he was the "self-appointed inspector of snow storms and rain storms, and did my duty faithfully"—or business enterprise (Walden was "a good place for business," particularly, to trade with "the Celestial Empire"). He repopulated his woodland neighbor-hood with "former inhabitants," and he tested his ability to overcome class divides in conversations with the Irish laborer John Field and the French-Canadian woodchopper Alex Therien. And he creatively extended the ideas of social obligation he had heard in the meetinghouse and schools of his youth in ways that nobody had anticipated. In the fields and woods, rivers and ponds, Thoreau discerned an interdependent community in which humans were truly neighbors and not masters of all other living things. The civic spirit and reli-gious vision that Puritans had bequeathed to the Minutemen and thence to the leaders of Concord in the new republic were the seedbed in which the na-tive son's vision of ecology germinated.

"I have never got over my surprise," Thoreau once reflected, "that I should have been born into the most estimable place in all the world, and in the very nick of time, too." In tribute to that origin, he composed a quintessential Concord—American—book.[78]

Notes

List of Abbreviations

AAS American Antiquarian Society

BL Baker Library, Harvard Business School

BPL Boston Public Library

CAS Concord Antiquarian Society

CF *Concord Freeman*

CFPL Concord Free Public Library, Special Collections

CGMY *Concord Gazette and Middlesex Yeoman*

CTMM Concord Town Meeting Minutes

EL *The Early Lectures of Ralph Waldo Emerson*, ed. Stephen E. Whicher, Robert E. Spiller, and Wallace E. Williams, 3 vols. Cambridge, Mass., 1966–1972.

EMP *Ralph Waldo Emerson: The Major Prose*, ed. Ronald A Bosco and Joel Myerson, Cambridge, Mass., 2015.

ETR Early Town Records, Town of Concord Archives, at CFPL

Gross, *Minutemen* Robert A. Gross, *The Minutemen and Their World* (New York, 1976)

H&P Jarvis, "Houses and People," CFPL

HDS Harvard Divinity School

Houghton Houghton Library, Harvard University

J *The Journal of Henry David Thoreau*, ed. Bradford Torrey and Francis Allen, 14 vols. Boston: Houghton Mifflin, 1906; New York: Dover, 1962.

JMN *The Journals and Miscellaneous Notebooks of Ralph Waldo Emerson*, ed. William H. Gilman et al., 16 vols. Cambridge: Harvard University Press, 1960–82

Keyes, Autobiography John Shepard Keyes, Autobiography (1866), in Series 1, John Shepard Keyes Papers, 1837–1908, CFPL

Keyes, Diary John Shepard Keyes, Diary, vols. 2–5 (1839–1842), in Series 1, John Shepard Keyes Papers, 1837–1908, CFPL

MA Massachusetts Archives, Boston

MCPR Middlesex County Probate Records, East Cambridge, Mass.

MCRD Middlesex County Registry of Deeds, East Cambridge, Mass.

MG *Middlesex Gazette*

MHS Massachusetts Historical Society

MO *Middlesex Observer*

MSA Massachusetts Archives, Boston

NEHGS New England Historic Genealogical Society Research Library, Boston

PEJ *The Journal of Henry D. Thoreau* (Princeton ed.), 8 vols. to date (Princeton University Press, 1981–)

R *The Republican*

SCM *Social Circle Memoirs*

Shattuck, *History* Lemuel Shattuck, *History of Concord*

T&R Edward Jarvis, *Traditions and Reminiscences of Concord, Massachusetts 1779–1878*, ed. Sarah Chapin (Amherst, Mass., 1993)

TJHM Thoreau Journal, Houghton Mifflin ed.

Walden Henry D. Thoreau, *Walden*, ed. J. Lyndon Shanley (Princeton, N.J., 1971)

YG *Yeoman's Gazette*

Preface

1. Emerson, "Self-Reliance," in *EMP*, 128; Barbara L. Packer, *The Transcendentalists* (Athens, Ga., 2007), 1.
2. Philip F. Gura, *American Transcendentalism: A History* (New York, 2007), 69–97.
3. *Walden*, 3; Henry Adams, *The Education of Henry Adams* (Washington, D.C., 1907), 51.
4. For a classic statement of the "two revolutions" thesis, see Ralph Henry Gabriel, *The Course of American Democratic Thought: An Intellectual History Since 1815* (New York, 1940), 51. Emerson and Thoreau, he writes, were "carrying on the fight which had been started by the farmers at the bridge."
5. George Kateb, *The Inner Ocean: Individualism and Democratic Culture* (Ithaca, N.Y., 1992); Emerson, "Self-Reliance," 135; Emerson, "Introductory" lecture to series "The Present Age," December 4, 1839, *EL* 3:188 (compare to his first formulation of this idea in the "Introductory" lecture to the series "Human Culture," December 6, 1837, in *EL* 2:213); Henry D. Thoreau, "Resistance to Civil Government," in Wendell Glick, ed., *Reform Papers* (Princeton, N.J., 1973), 81; *PEJ* 2:262.
6. For the sources of this view of Concord as a pastoral place, see Robert A. Gross, "The Celestial Village: Transcendentalism and Tourism in Concord," in Conrad E. Wright and Charles Capper, eds., *Transient and Permanent: The Transcendentalist Movement and Its Contexts* (Boston, 1999), 251–57.
7. The picture of Concord as a quiet, pastoral place, set apart from an urban-industrial nation, no longer holds sway in scholarship on Transcendentalism. But the "new views" articulated by such Unitarian thinkers as Orestes Brownson, Frederic Henry Hedge, Elizabeth Palmer Peabody, and George Ripley, as well as Emerson, have only loosely been connected to the social settings in which they took shape. Concord is irrelevant in such accounts. It serves at best as a stage on which the Transcendentalists enacted their principled commitments, taking abolitionist stands under the prodding of local female activists or ignoring the pervasive white racism and the active Black community in their midst. Only in the works of eco-critics and environmental historians do local developments, such as the loss of woods and "wild" lands to the plow, bear directly on Thoreau's vision in *Walden*. See Gura, *American Transcendentalism*; Packer, *Transcendentalists*; Sandra Harbert Petrulionis, *To Set This World Right: The Antislavery Movement in Thoreau's Concord* (Ithaca, N.Y., 2006); Elise Lemire, *Black Walden: Slavery and Its Aftermath in Concord, Massachusetts* (Philadelphia, 2009); Lawrence Buell, *The Environmental Imagination: Thoreau, Nature Writing, and the Formation of American Culture* (Cambridge, Mass., 1995); Brian Donahue, "Henry David Thoreau and the Environment of Concord," in Edmund A. Schofield and Robert C. Baron, eds., *Thoreau's World and Ours: A Natural Legacy* (Golden, Colo., 1993), 181–89; Robert M. Thorson, *The Boatman: Henry David Thoreau's River Years* (Cambridge, Mass., 2017). But recent biographies of key figures in the Transcendentalist circle—Mary Moody Emerson, Margaret Fuller, Theodore Parker, the Peabody sisters, and Thoreau himself—are notable for treating their subjects in social context.

Prologue: A New Beginning

1. *The Boston Directory; Containing Names of the Inhabitants; Their Occupations, Places of Business and Dwelling Houses* (Boston, 1822), 229; *Independent Chronicle and Boston Patriot*, August 10, 1822; *MO*, August 10, 1822; Walter Muir Whitehill, *Boston: A Topographical History*, 2nd ed., enlarged (Cambridge, Mass., 1968), 60–62; *PEJ* 2:173–74.

2. Laura Dassow Walls, *Henry David Thoreau: A Life* (Chicago, 2017), 23–26; *The Boston Directory, Containing the Names of the Inhabitants; Their Occupations, Places of Business, and Dwelling Houses* (Boston, 1798), 112.

3. Walls, *Henry David Thoreau*, 31–37.

4. Edmund Hudson, "The Wide Spreading Jones Family," *Boston Evening Transcript*, June 27, 1917, Concord Pamphlet 21, Item 19, CFPL; Daniel S. Lamson, *History of the Town of Weston, Massachusetts, 1630–1890* (Boston, 1913), 72–73; Doris Whipple Jones-Baker, "Colonel Elisha Jones of Weston and the Crisis of Colonial Government in Massachusetts 1773–1776" (Ph.D. thesis, University College, University of London, 1978); Elva Richards McGaughey, "JONES, EPHRAIM," in *Dictionary of Canadian Biography*, vol. 5, University of Toronto/Université Laval, 2003–, accessed January 25, 2021, http://www.biographi.ca/en/bio/jones_ephraim_5E.html; Clifford K. Shipton, "Asa Dunbar," in Shipton, *Sibley's Harvard Graduates*, 16 vols. (Boston, 1873–1972), 16:457–63; Gross, *Minutemen*, 59, 63; Walls, *Henry David Thoreau*, 28–30; administration of the estate of Jonas Minot, 1813, File no. 15242, MCPR; F. B. Sanborn, *Henry D. Thoreau* (Boston, 1882), 13–14. Mary Dunbar was listed in the 1798 *Boston Directory*, published by John West, as keeping a boardinghouse at 15 Marlborough Street. Her second husband, whom she married in June of that year, had tried to keep his militia company in check amid the rising passions of the Revolutionary movement; he soon lost his captaincy. Minot held eighty-six acres of land in 1801; his estate ranked in the middle of the assessment list, valued at $66.72, close to the average of $74.80 for all property holders. In 1811, a year or so before his death, Minot's relative position had improved; he now stood below the top tenth of taxpayers. Of the four Dunbar children to reach adulthood, two—Charles and Louisa—never wed; a third, Sophia, born in 1781, married Luther Lapham, a Boston tailor, in 1805; after his death in 1818, she returned to her maiden name and moved with her only child, Charles Howard, to the town of Haverhill in northeastern Massachusetts, some forty-two miles from Concord. She died there on July 6, 1868, just twelve days from her eighty-seventh birthday. *List of Persons Whose Names Have Been Changed in Massachusetts, 1780–1892* (Boston, 1893), 41 (law enacted February 18, 1822); File no. 13603, MCPR; 1806 *Boston Directory*, 79.

5. J 8:245–46, 12:38; John Farmer and Jacob Bailey Moore, *A Gazetteer of the State of New Hampshire* (Concord, N.H., 1823), 86–87; *MO*, November 9, 1822; *Independent Chronicle and Boston Patriot*, November 13, 1822; *Columbian Centinel*, November 9, 16, and 23, 1822; Walls, *Henry David Thoreau*, 38.

6. *Independent Chronicle and Boston Patriot*, October 8 and 25, 1823.

7. Concord's population grew from 1,590 to 1,679 between 1790 and 1800, a gain of 5.6 percent; it then fell by 2.7 percent to 1,633 in 1810; rebounded to 1,788 (a 9.5 percent increase) in 1820; and rose again to 2,017 in 1830 (a 13 percent rise). There is an inconsistency in the tally of Concord's population on the 1830 federal census. The assistant marshal who enumerated the population reported a total of 2,017. Shattuck, *History*, p. 211, recalculated the figures to come up with a total of 2,021. Since the marshal's report is used in later compendia, I have used the smaller number. Even in Middlesex County, which increased in numbers from 42,737 to 61,472 in the period 1790–1820—a rise of 43.8 percent—Concord was a laggard. See Oliver Warner, Secretary of the Commonwealth, *Abstract of the Census of Massachusetts, 1865* (Boston, 1867), 192–93. The drop from 1800 to 1810 came after 1807. Each year the town levied taxes on the property and polls of the inhabitants to pay for the public schools. Every man sixteen and over—i.e., in the working years—was assessed for the poll tax, and on the tally sheets for the "school

money," local officials recorded the number of "ratable" polls for each district. "Unratable" polls consisted of paupers and of men well beyond their productive years. The number of ratable polls on these sheets went from 325 in 1800 to 364½ in 1805 and to 368½ in 1807; then in the wake of the embargo, young men began an exodus. Polls numbered 343½ in 1808, 341 in 1809, 322 in 1810, and 329 in 1811. Population growth, as measured by polls, resumed thereafter, reaching 358 in 1815, 376 in 1819, 388 in 1820. See Assessors' Records, Box A3, 1800–24 folders, ETR. On the cotton factory, see the comments of Ephraim H. Bellows in "Schedule of the 1820 Census of Manufacturing for Maine, Massachusetts, New Hampshire and Rhode Island," Records of the Bureau of the Census, Record Group no. 29, Microcopy no. 279, Roll 15, National Archives.

8. *MO*, January 4, March 15, 1823; *YG*, December 16 (Adams), December 23 (Whiting), 1826.

9. A. Bradford Smith, "The Concord Turnpike," *Lexington Historical Society Proceedings* 3 (1905): 11; Frederic J. Wood, *The Turnpikes of New England and Evolution of the Same Through England, Virginia, and Maryland* (Boston, 1909); H&P, 120–21; Shattuck, *History*, 204–5; letters of Dick Roby, *MO*, February 1, 1823. The Middlesex County commissioners took over the Cambridge Turnpike in 1829 and converted it to "a public highway and free road." See *YG*, May 16, 1829.

10. Christopher Roberts, *The Middlesex Canal 1793–1860* (Cambridge, Mass., 1938); H&P, 47–48; *T&R*, 20; Henry D. Thoreau, *A Week on the Concord and Merrimack Rivers*, ed. Carl F. Hovde (Princeton, N.J., 1980), 211–12.

11. *MO*, January 4, 1823, September 21, 1822; *Independent Chronicle and Boston Patriot*, October 8, 1823.

12. *MO*, June 29, 1822 ("A Middlesex Rustic"), January 4 ("A Mechanic") and March 29 ("W.A."), 1823.

13. Rev. Charles Brooks, *Memoir of John Brooks* (Boston, 1865); Francis R. Gourgas, "Memoir of Abiel Heywood," *SCM* 2:232.

14. Keyes, Autobiography, 69; *CGMY*, April 24, 1824; *MO*, June 22 and 29, 1822, June 7, 1823; *Independent Chronicle and Boston Patriot*, June 28, July 4 and 9, 1823; John Shepard Keyes, "The Second Great North Bridge Battle," CFPL.

15. *MO*, February 8 and 15, March 1, April 21, 1823; Ronald P. Formisano, *The Transformation of Political Culture: Massachusetts Parties, 1790s–1840s* (New York, 1983), 63–65, 79–81, 120–23.

16. *T&R*, 145–47. Fourteen-year-old Joseph Merriam looked forward to election day with anticipation. "I should like to have you come home at election and go a gunning with me," he wrote his absent brother Charles in April 1819, "and then ... it will seem a little like old times." John M. Merriam, *The Family Name Merriam: Its Origin and a Sample Record* (Framingham, Mass., 1935), quoted in genealogy of Abner Wheeler Merriam. My reading of the bird hunt has been inspired by Robert Darnton's imaginative interpretation of a very different outburst of cruelty to animals: the slaughter of cats by journeymen printers in Paris during the late 1730s. See Robert Darnton, *The Great Cat Massacre and Other Episodes in French Cultural History* (New York, 1984), 75–104.

17. *MO*, May 10, 17, and 31, 1823.

18. *MO*, June 7 and 14, 1823; *Independent Chronicle and Boston Patriot*, June 28, July 4 and 9, 1823.

1. A Day of Good Feelings

1. Andrew Burstein, *America's Jubilee: How in 1826 a Generation Remembered Fifty Years of Independence* (New York, 2001), 8–9; *Inaugural Addresses of the Presidents of the United*

States from George Washington 1789 to George Bush 1989 (Washington, D.C., 1989), 54; *CGMY*, April 17 and 24, September 4, 1824; meeting of March 7, 1825, CTMM 7:237, CFPL; Town resolution to celebrate fiftieth anniversary of the Concord Fight, Committee of Arrangements for the 50th Anniversary Celebration in Concord of the Battle of Concord, Records, 1825, CFPL; *CGMY*, April 23, 1825.

2. F. B. Sanborn, *Henry D. Thoreau*, rev. ed. (Boston, 1882), 46; David Henry Thoreau, "Class Book Autobiography," ca. June 1837, in Henry D. Thoreau, *Early Essays and Miscellanies*, ed. Joseph J. Moldenhauer and Edwin Moser, with Alexander C. Kern (Princeton, N.J., 1975), 114. According to Sanborn, Thoreau "could remember the visit of Lafayette to Concord in 1824, and the semi-centennial celebration of the Concord Fight in 1825."

3. I have been able to identify only three Fourth of July celebrations in Concord, all sponsored by Federalists, during the early republic. See William Jones, A.B., *An Oration Pronounced at CONCORD. July 4th, 1794. Being the Anniversary of the American Independence* (Concord, Mass., 1794); Samuel P. P. Fay, *An Oration, Delivered at Concord, on the Anniversary of American Independence, July 4th, 1801* (Boston, 1801); "Concordia," *Hampshire Gazette*, July 26, 1815. For an in-depth account of partisan festivities on Independence Day, see David Waldstreicher, *In the Midst of Perpetual Fetes: The Making of American Nationalism, 1776–1820* (Chapel Hill, N.C., 1997), 26, 219–21.

4. Susan Kurland, "'A Political Progress': Processes of Democratization in Concord, Massachusetts, 1750–1850" (senior honors thesis, Brandeis University, 1973), 15; Formisano, *Transformation of Political Culture*, 33–35; Paul Goodman, *The Democratic-Republicans of Massachusetts: Politics in a Young Republic* (Cambridge, Mass., 1964), 137. Voter participation in Concord peaked at 72 percent of adult males in the elections of 1812 to 1814; in Massachusetts as a whole, turnout reached roughly 67 percent in 1812.

5. James M. Banner, *To the Hartford Convention: The Federalists and the Origins of Party Politics in Massachusetts, 1789–1815* (New York: Knopf, 1970), 204–6, appendix 2, 357–62; Goodman, *Democratic-Republicans of Massachusetts*, 82–85; Kurland, "'A Political Progress,'" 212–50. Concord supported the successful Republican candidates in every congressional race from 1800 to 1816 except for 1812 and 1814, when the town turned Federalist as a way of expressing opposition to war with Great Britain. In the two elections in which the Massachusetts General Court allowed the people to choose presidential electors (1804, 1812), the voters of Concord endorsed Jefferson for a second term and repudiated Madison. On the state level, Concord went for the Federalist candidate for governor eight times and eight times for the Republican nominee between 1800 and 1816; the 1815 result was a dead tie, with Caleb Strong (F) and Samuel Dexter (R) receiving 145 votes each. Finally, Republican Joseph Chandler gained solid majorities in eight of ten consecutive victories for representative to the Massachusetts House, peaking at 58.6 percent in 1808. Thereafter (1809–1817) the seat shifted back and forth between parties, until the issues of the embargo and war died out; then Concord reverted to the Republican camp (1818–1823). Compared to neighboring Bedford and Lincoln, both of which had split off from Concord to become separate towns in the eighteenth century, the mother town was niggling in its support for Republicans. Lincoln gave overwhelming majorities to the Republican candidate for governor from 1801 on; the Republican vote averaged 67 percent in 1806–1810 and 85 percent in 1811–1815. Bedford was somewhat less enthusiastic: its average Republican vote was 57 percent in 1806–1810, 66 percent in 1811–1815. See Richard John Holmes, "Communities

in Transition: Social Change in Bedford and Lincoln, Massachusetts, 1729–1850"
(Ph.D. diss., State University of New York, Binghamton, 1979), 312–13, 351. Middlesex County overall was a bulwark of Democratic-Republicanism, supplying an
"abundance" of party leaders. Goodman, *Democratic-Republicans of Massachusetts*, 83.

6. Formisano, *Transformation of Political Culture*, 57–106 (quoting Elbridge Gerry on
   "house divided, 74); Jonathan J. Den Hartog, *Patriotism and Piety: Federalist Politics and
   Religious Struggle in the New American Nation* (Charlottesville, N.C., 2015), 78–89; Ezra
   Ripley, annual Thanksgiving sermon, November 19, 1795, bMS 490/1, HDS; "On
   gratitude to God and man," annual Thanksgiving sermon, November 29, 1798, and
   annual Fast Day sermon, April 9, 1801, bMS AM 1835 (1), Houghton.

7. Clarence Winthrop Bowen, *The History of Woodstock, Connecticut: Genealogies of Woodstock Families*, 8 vols. (Norwood, Mass., 1926–1943), 8:216–18; Barzillai Frost, "Ezra
   Ripley," in William Ware, ed., *American Unitarian Biography. Memoirs of Individuals
   Who Have Been Distinguished by Their Writings, Character, and Efforts in the Cause of Liberal Christianity*, 2 vols. (Boston, 1850), 1:119, 122–23; Gross, *Minutemen*, 134–35.

8. Ezra Ripley, "The duty of parents to restrain children from vice," February 17,
   1799, bMS AM 1835 (11), Houghton; Ezra Ripley, Concord, to George Thatcher,
   New York City, March 30, 1789, BPL; Ezra Ripley, "The duties of magistrates and
   rulers," March 10, 1799 [no. 1028], bMS 490/1, HDS; Ripley, "The duties of subjects," March 3, 1799, Houghton.

9. The first six sermons in the series, plus the fourteenth and the sixteenth, are not
   extant. The surviving manuscripts are as follows:

—7th sermon: "The duty of candour in judging the character and conduct of others," November 18, 1798, bMS 490/1, HDS.

—8th sermon: "Forgiveness of injuries," November 18, 1798, bMS 490/1, HDS:

—9th sermon: "On gratitude to God and man," November 29, 1798, annual Thanksgiving sermon, bMs AM 1835 (11), Houghton.

—10th sermon: "On friendship," [November 29,] 1798, bMS 490/1, Andover-Harvard Theological Library.

—11th sermon: "Peaceableness," December 2, 1798, bMS 490/1, HDS.

—12th sermon: "On civility and condescension," December 16, 1798, bMS 490/1, HDS.

—13th sermon: "On public spirit," December 16, 1798, bMS 490/1, HDS.

—15th sermon: "Domestic peace explained and recommended," February 3, 1799, bMS AM 1835 (11), Houghton.

—17th sermon: "The duty of parents to restrain children from vice," February 17, 1799, bMS AM 1835 (11), Houghton.

—18th sermon: "The duty of children to honor their parents," February 24, 1799, bMS AM 1835 (11), Houghton.

—19th sermon: "The duties of servants, and briefly of masters," February 24, 1799, bMS AM 1835 (11), Houghton.

—20th sermon: "The duties of subjects," March 3, 1799, bMS AM 1835 (11), Houghton.

—21st sermon: "The duties of magistrates and rulers," March 10, 1799, bMS 490/1, HDS.

If Ripley launched the series by delivering two sermons each Sabbath, he must
have begun on October 28, 1798.

10. Ezra Ripley, "Redemption and pardon through Jesus Christ," May 4, 1806, deliv-
    ered as a sermon in 1812 and a lecture in 1820, Houghton; Ripley, "On gratitude to

God and man," 6–7; annual Thanksgiving sermon, November 28, 1799, bMS Am 1835 (11), Houghton; Middlesex County, Mass., Convention, *Address to the Friends of Independence, Peace, and Union in the County of Middlesex* (n.p., 1812); *Pittsfield Sun*, September 17, 1840, reprinting a piece from the *Boston Post* recalling Ripley's part in the 1812 convention and condemning him as "one of the political preachers against the government in the war, and a uniform Federalist"; Waldstreicher, *In the Midst of Perpetual Fetes*, 203–4. The 1812 Concord convention, which opened on July 15 and adjourned to August 10, came two days after a mass protest in Boston. The August session drew more than seven hundred participants, who listened reverently to the "very solemn and pertinent" address Ripley made in his opening prayer for the convention's success. Similar conclaves were held in Barnstable, Plymouth, and Worcester counties and in western Massachusetts. See Richard Buel, Jr., *America on the Brink: How the Political Struggle over the War of 1812 Almost Destroyed the Young Republic* (New York, 2005), 160.

11. Ralph L. Rusk, *The Life of Ralph Waldo Emerson* (New York, 1949), 50–53; Alan Taylor, *The Civil War of 1812: American Citizens, British Subjects, Irish Rebels, and Indian Allies* (New York, 2010), 414–15; Ripley, annual Thanksgiving sermon, December 1, 1814, bMS Am 1835, Houghton.

12. Ripley, annual Thanksgiving sermon, December 1, 1814; Taylor, *Civil War of 1812*, 8–9, 88–87, 118.

13. Republican leader John L. Tuttle, a Harvard graduate and lawyer, left his post in the state senate to enlist as a lieutenant colonel in the U.S. Army (Ninth Regiment, Infantry). In late May 1812, even before the formal declaration of war, Concord's town meeting approved a payment of three dollars for each private and noncommissioned officer called out for military training and a sum of ten dollars per month in the event the men were actually mobilized for service. See meeting of May 26, 1812, CTMM 6:394–95, CFPL; *Independent Chronicle* (Boston), August 27, 1812; Samuel Hoar, "Memoir of John L. Tuttle," SCM 2:72.

14. *Independent Chronicle* (Boston), October 27, 1814; Taylor, *Civil War of 1812*, 414–16; Buel, *America on the Brink*. The Middlesex Republicans met in Concord on October 21, 1814, five days after the state legislature called for a convention of New England states to discuss their "public grievances and concerns" and what could be done about them through amendments to the U.S. Constitution. See Theodore Dwight, *History of the Hartford Convention: with a Review of the Policy of the United States Government, Which Led to the War of 1812* (New York, 1833), 341–43.

15. Ezra Ripley, National Thanksgiving sermon, April 13, 1815, bMS Am 1835, Houghton; *Hampshire Gazette*, July 26, 1815.

16. *Columbian Centinel*, July 5 and 12, 1817; Daniel Walker Howe, *What Hath God Wrought: The Transformation of America, 1815–1848* (New York, 2007), 91–95; Shaw Livermore, Jr., *The Twilight of Federalism: The Disintegration of the Federalist Party 1815–1830* (Princeton, N.J., 1962), 47–68, 81–82, 117–19. Middlesex County Republicans were loath to abandon the fight. In March 1817 a party convention in Concord warned voters not to be fooled by the moderate rhetoric of politicians who had betrayed the republic at the Hartford Convention. "These things should ever keep alive that pure republican principle so congenial to every American heart," the assembly resolved. In their view, the time was not right for an era of good feelings. See *American Advocate and Kennebec Advertiser* (Hallowell, Me.), March 29, 1817. Likewise, when Federalists nominated Harrison Gray Otis for governor in 1823, Republicans returned to battle in force. Turnout at the polls rose to 250 voters, fewer than at the height of the party conflict but well above the previous year's low of 171.

17. *T&R,* 148–49; Kurland, "'A Political Progress,'" 97–98, 100–1. Twenty-eight men held the selectman's post between 1750 and 1780, for an average of 4.45 terms each; only fourteen men did so during the next forty years, serving eight terms each. The rise in political inequality was owing primarily to the town's decision in 1771 to reduce the number of selectmen from five to three—one for each section (East, North, South)—in an attempt to mute geographical rivalry for power. With fewer offices available, it is not surprising that officeholding became more concentrated. See Gross, *Minutemen,* 17. Heywood's endurance in office from 1796 to 1838 raises the typical selectman's tenure to eight terms. In the text, I prefer the median number of terms, 5.5, to the average inflated by Heywood's marathon service.

18. Harlow W. Sheidley, "Preserving the 'Old Fabrick': The Massachusetts Conservative Elite and the Constitutional Convention of 1820–1821," *Proceedings of the MHS* 103 (1991): 114–37, and Sheidley, *Sectional Nationalism: Massachusetts Conservative Leaders and the Transformation of America, 1815–1836* (Boston, 1998), 33–61; John D. Cushing, "Notes on Disestablishment in Massachusetts, 1780–1833," *William and Mary Quarterly* 26 (April 1969): 169–90; Johann N. Neem, *Creating a Nation of Joiners: Democracy and Civil Society in Early National Massachusetts* (Cambridge, Mass., 2008), 21–23; Merrill D. Peterson, ed., *Democracy, Liberty, and Property: The State Constitutional Conventions of the 1820s* (Indianapolis, 1966).

19. E. R. Hoar, "Samuel Hoar," *SCM* 3:30–53; George F. Hoar, *Memoir of Samuel Hoar of Concord* (Cambridge, Mass., 1882); William Minot, *Memoir of the Hon. Samuel Hoar; Prepared Agreeably to a Resolution of the MHS* (Boston, 1862); John S. Keyes, "Memoir of John Keyes," *SCM* 2:161–67; Asa Keyes, *Genealogy of Robert Keyes of Watertown, Mass., 1633. Solomon Keyes of Newbury and Chelmsford, Mass., 1653. And Their Descendants: Also Others of the Name* (Brattleboro, Vt., 1880), 150–52. John Shepard Keyes claims that his grandfather Joseph had twenty children. This seems unlikely; the Westford, Massachusetts, records and the Keyes genealogy indicate that Joseph Keyes fathered thirteen children, of whom nine reached adulthood. John Keyes of Concord was the firstborn child of his father's second marriage to the widow Sarah Boyden Dalrymple of Groton, Massachusetts.

20. Hoar, *Memoir of Samuel Hoar,* 22; John A. Andrew, *Boston Atlas,* November 10, 1856, in scrapbook of newspaper clippings entitled "The Death of Samuel Hoar," George Frisbie Hoar Papers, MHS; Keyes, "Memoir of John Keyes," 167; Samuel Hoar (Washington City) to John Farrar (Cambridge), February 12, 1803, George Frisbie Hoar Papers, Correspondence, Box 2 (1802–52), MHS; Keyes, Autobiography, 151–53.

21. *TJHM* 7:445–46; Hoar, "Samuel Hoar," *SCM* 3:34–35; Robert A. Gross, "Squire Dickinson and Squire Hoar," *Proceedings of MHS* 101 (1989): 11.

22. Dwight, *History of the Hartford Convention; Pittsfield Sun,* September 17, 1840, reprinting from the *Boston Post; T&R,* 149–50. Samuel Hoar's father was one of the dissenting members of the state senate who issued a public protest against the legislature's decision to send delegates to the Hartford Convention. See "Protest of the Minority of the Senate of Massachusetts, against the Report of the joint Committee of the Legislature, on the Governor's Message," October 15, 1814, *Columbian* (New York), October 25, 1814.

23. Samuel Hoar, "Memoir of John L. Tuttle," *SCM* 2:71–74; Keyes, "Memoir of John Keyes," 163; 1826 assessment list, CFPL; report of Middlesex County convention of Republicans, submitted by John Keyes, Esq., secretary, *Independent Chronicle* (Boston), October 27, 1814.

24. Hoar, "Memoir of Samuel Hoar," 49; Sheidley, "Preserving the 'Old Fabrick'"; *Jour-*

nal of Debates and Proceedings of the Convention of Delegates, Chosen to Revise the Constitution of Massachusetts, Begun and Holden at Boston, November 15, 1820, and Continued by Adjournment to January 9, 1821 (Boston, 1821), 162–63.

25. Goodman, *Democratic-Republicans of Massachusetts*, 136–41; *Journal of Debates and Proceedings of the Convention*, 115–22, 125, 186–87, 281; Richard P. McCormick, *The Second American Party System: Party Formation in the Jacksonian Era* (Chapel Hill, N.C., 1966), 29; Alexander Keyssar, *The Right to Vote: The Contested History of Democracy in the United States*, rev. ed. (New York, 2009), 24–25, and tables A.2, A.3, A.4. The constitutional amendment (Article 6) expanded the electorate for offices in state government (governor, lieutenant governor, senators, and representatives). A separate statute, enacted in February 1823, confirmed the extension of the ballot for town and county elections. See *MO*, March 1, 1823.

26. *Journal of Debates and Proceedings of the Convention*, 60–63, 91, 252; Keyes, "Memoir of John Keyes," 167.

27. Gross, *Minutemen*, 156–57; meeting of April 9, 1821, CTMM 7:156, CFPL. The list of fourteen amendments submitted to the voters for ratification appears in *Journal of Debates and Proceedings of the Convention*, 274–79. Concord was in the mainstream of the state in its rejection of Articles 1, 2, 5, 9, and 10 of the proposed amendments and in its endorsement of taxpayer suffrage and the right of militia companies to elect their officers. Likewise, it joined the majority of voters in approving an amendment giving the governor a "pocket veto" of bills passed in the waning days of a legislature (Article 3); another empowering the governor and council to appoint notaries public for fixed terms and to fill vacancies in the offices of Commonwealth treasurer and secretary when the General Court was not in session (Article 7); a third eliminating a profession of Christian faith from the oath required of all individuals assuming public office in the Commonwealth (Articles 11 and 12), and a fourth barring multiple officeholding by state officials (Article 13). With the rest of the state, Concord also rejected a change in the governance of Harvard College. The townsmen showed their conservatism by rejecting a successful amendment empowering the legislature to charter city governments (Article 4) and by declining to go along with a lowering of the threshold for the passage of future constitutional amendments from two-thirds of the voters to a majority. It is worth noting that Concord favored taxpayer suffrage by a margin similar to that in the state as a whole (61 percent yes, 39 percent no in the town, 65 to 35 percent overall); by contrast, 81 percent of Middlesex County voters ratified the change. To judge by these votes, Concord was reluctant to democratize or modernize state government in substantial ways, but it was not opposed to modest change. For the county and statewide returns on the amendments, see *Columbian Centinel*, May 26, 1821.

28. *MO*, April 12, 1823; *MG*, April 17, 1819; Kurland, "'A Political Progress,'" 234. On Keyes's elevation to the state senate, the *Middlesex Observer* enthused that "no one can more universally meet the wishes of the people, or discharge the duties of the office with greater attention and fidelity than the late incumbent [Keyes], who is now transferred to a higher sphere of influence." *MO*, May 3, 1823.

29. CGMY, April 17 and 24, 1824. The organizers of the event chose not to hold a reenactment of the famous shots at the North Bridge site. Such a "sham battle," they explained, would be "altogether unworthy of the dignity of the occasion," since men who had participated in the actual exchange of fire would be present. That decision was well considered. The last time a reenactment was held, back in October 1812, the participants got so carried away that the "sham-fight" became

all too real, and twenty-eight fighters were wounded. See *New England Palladium*, October 13, 1812.

30. Burstein, *American Jubilee*, 11–13; Rusk, *Life of Emerson*, 102; Edward Everett, *An Oration Pronounced at Cambridge, before the Society of Phi Beta Kappa. August 26, 1824* (Boston, 1825).

31. Keyes's son, not yet three years old, was so fascinated by the "pageant" that he was nearly trampled by the horses pulling Lafayette's coach. Luckily his alert older sister pulled little John Shepard Keyes out of harm's way. See Keyes, Autobiography, 2.

32. This account of the Lafayette reception is drawn from the following sources: *CGMY*, September 4, 1824; *CF*, September 12, 1834; Edward Jarvis, manuscript notes on Shattuck's *History of Concord*, CFPL; A. Levasseur, *Lafayette in America in 1824 and 1825; Journal of a Voyage to the United States*, trans. John D. Godman, 2 vols. (Philadelphia, 1829), 1:71; Gross, *Minutemen*, 188; "To the Inhabitants of Concord," broadside (Concord, Mass., 1824), CFPL; meeting of November 1, 1824, CTMM 7:231, CFPL. What caught the notice of Lafayette's party was a scene on the burial hill across the town common, where a woman "clad in black" and two children were grieving by a recent grave. In the "sorrowing attitudes" of the mourners, Lafayette's secretary, August Levasseur, discerned a melancholy lesson: they "seemed to say that festival days are not days of repose for death; but not one of the gay party [in the bower] appeared to regard this; all were too happy to remark the narrowness of the space by which they were separated from the spot where all sink into oblivion."

33. Elias Phinney, *History of the Battle at Lexington, on the Morning of the 19th April, 1775* (Boston, 1825), 6; "Middlesex," *Boston Patriot*, December 3, 1824; "A Young Soldier," *Boston Patriot*, December 4, 1824; *CGMY*, December 11, 1824, January 1, 1825.

34. "To the Inhabitants of Concord," *Boston Patriot*, October 2, 1824; Charles Cowley, *History of Lowell*, 2nd rev. ed. (Boston, 1868), 127; John Shepard Keyes, "Reminiscences" (ca. 1903), 1, Keyes Papers, CFPL.

35. Paul Revere Frothingham, *Edward Everett: Orator and Statesman* (Boston, 1925), 86–89; George Washington Warren, *The History of the Bunker Hill Monument Association During the First Century of the United States of America* (Boston, 1877), 125; *Boston Patriot*, October 26 and 29, November 3, 1824; *CGMY*, September 18, October 23, 1824; Marshall Foletta, *Coming to Terms with Democracy: Federalist Intellectuals and the Shaping of an American Culture, 1800–1828* (Charlottesville, N.C., 2001), 47, 50, 53, 59; Michael J. Dubin, *United States Congressional Elections, 1788–1997: The Official Results of the Elections of the 1st Through 105th Congresses* (Jefferson, N.C., 1998), 58, 64, 69, 75.

36. *Address of the Bunker Hill Monument Association to the Selectmen in the Several Towns in Massachusetts* (Boston, 1824), reprinted in *CGMY*, October 23, 1824; "A Young Soldier," *Boston Patriot*, December 3 and 11, 1824; *CGMY*, December 11, 1824. Concord's leaders tried unsuccessfully to obtain state aid for a monument first in 1792 and then in the legislative session of 1813–1814.

37. Notices of public meetings, *CGMY*, January 1 and 19, 1825; Reuben Brown and nine others (including John Thoreau), petition, February 12, 1825, ETR; town vote to celebrate the fiftieth anniversary of the Concord Fight, Committee of Arrangements for the 50th Anniversary Celebration, Records, CFPL.

38. Committee of Arrangements for the 50th Anniversary Celebration, Records, CFPL; "The Old Farmer," *CGMY*, March 5, 1825; "Concord Celebration," *CGMY*, April 16, 1825. Of the fifteen members on the arrangements committee, four were in their twenties, seven in their thirties, one forty-six, one fifty-five, and the senior member, Daniel Wood, the son of Ephraim Wood, was sixty-four.

The most unlikely member was Lt. Stedman Buttrick, the great-grandson of Maj. John Buttrick, the officer who gave the order to fire at the North Bridge. At twenty-eight, Buttrick was still working on the family farm, without any property of his own; nonetheless, as his military title attests, he was gaining influence among the young men. I suspect he carried the Buttrick firelock to Boston and displayed it to Lafayette. The committee reached more deeply into the economic ranks than was usual. Of the fourteen members on the 1826 assessment, half were in the economic elite (top 20 percent), four in the next quintile, two in the middle fifth, and one (Buttrick) without property. Lawyer Elisha Fuller contested the election for county treasurer at the same March town meeting that authorized the committee of arrangements for the jubilee. He garnered 21 votes to the incumbent Keyes's 132.

39. Meeting of April 4, 1825, CTMM 7:244, CFPL; Sheidley, *Sectional Nationalism*, 134–35; John D. Seelye, *Memory's Nation: The Place of Plymouth Rock* (Chapel Hill, N.C., 1998); "Bunker Hill," *CGMY*, December 25, 1824. The median age of the twenty-six men added by the town to the monument committee (whose original members were Keyes, Barrett, Brooks, and Thomas Hubbard) was 67.5; nineteen were sixty or over. At least five of these men had been in arms at the Concord Fight. Of the thirty members as a whole, eighteen were in the top 20 percent in assessed wealth (ten in the top tenth); one, Rev. Ripley, was exempt from taxes by law. Finally, eight of the committee had been representatives, five selectmen, and eight justices of the peace (of course, some had been all three).

40. I have reconstructed the fight over the North Bridge from the following sources: John Shepard Keyes, "The Second Great North Bridge Battle" and "The Old Roads of Concord" (paper read before the Concord Antiquarian Society, February 4, 1889), both at CFPL; meetings of December 5, 1791, January 2, 5, and March 26, April 2, May 7, and September 3, 1792, May 13 and July 1, 1793, in CTMM, vol. 6, CFPL; Middlesex County Court of General Sessions of the Peace Records Book, September 1790–March 1801: Book 1 of 2, September 1790–March 1796, pp. 77, 105–6, MSA; and Elisha Jones and others, petition, September 7, 1792, and memorial of David Brown and others, September 13, 1792, in file papers for March 1793 session of Middlesex County Court of General Sessions, MSA. The journalist George William Curtis heard the anecdote about Ripley's vanity at owning the "battlefield" and passed it along in *Homes of American Authors; Comprising Anecdotical, Personal, and Descriptive Sketches, by Various Writers* (New York, 1853), 297–98. Part of the text draws on Gross, "Celestial Village."

41. Warren, *History of Bunker Hill*, 125; meetings of April 4, 8, and 11, 1825, CTMM 7:244–46, CFPL; Kurland, "'Political Progress,'" 201–6.

42. *CGMY*, April 23, 1825; Shattuck, *History*, 207; Neil Harris, *Building Lives: Constructing Rites and Passages* (New Haven, Conn., 1999), 7–27; Len Travers, "'In the Greatest Solemn Dignity': The Capitol Cornerstone and Ceremony in the Early Republic," in Donald R. Kenyon, ed., *A Republic for the Ages: The United States Capitol and the Political Culture of the Early Republic* (Charlottesville, Va, 1999), 163–70; Steven C. Bullock, *Revolutionary Brotherhood: Freemasonry and the Transformation of the American Social Order, 1730–1840* (Chapel Hill, N.C., 1996), 137–38, 150–53; *The Order of Proceedings, at the Celebration on the Nineteenth of April 1825 of the Fiftieth Anniversary of Concord & Lexington Battles* (Concord, Mass., 1825); meeting of April 11, 1825, CTMM 7:245–46, CFPL.

43. Travers, "'In the Greatest Solemn Dignity,'" 168–70; *Order of Proceedings*; Edgar Wesley Tucker, "The Meeting Houses of the First Parish," in John Whittemore

Teele, ed., *The Meeting House on the Green: A History of the First Parish in Concord and Its Church* (Concord, Mass., 1985), 316; *CGMY*, April 16 and 23, 1825.

44. *Order of Proceedings*; *CGMY*, April 23, 1825.

45. *CGMY* was loosely quoting the Queen of Sheba's awe at the "wisdom and prosperity" of King Solomon's reign (1 Kings 10:7).

46. *CGMY*, April 23, 1825; George B. Forgie, *Patricide in the House Divided: A Psychological Interpretation of Lincoln and His Age* (New York, 1979), 165; Edward Everett, *An Oration Delivered at Concord, April the Nineteenth, 1825* (Boston, 1825); Edward Everett, Diary, entries for April 11, 1825–August 9, 1827, entry for April 19, 1825, MHS; *Order of Proceedings*.

47. Waldstreicher, *In the Midst of Perpetual Fetes*, 26, 219–21; toasts for April 19, 1825, celebration prepared by committee of arrangements, Records, CFPL; *CGMY*, April 23, 1825; Rusk, *Life of Emerson*, 109–13.

48. *Inaugural Addresses of the Presidents*, 56–57; Formisano, *Transformation of Political Culture*, 81–83; *CGMY*, April 9, 1825. As it turned out, Samuel Hoar, Jr., failed to win a majority of the vote in the senate election; neither did candidate John Wade. As a result, when the General Court convened in May, one seat in the Middlesex delegation was vacant. In accord with the state constitution, the two houses of the legislature, meeting in convention, filled the office by choosing between Hoar and Wade, the two highest vote-getters among the also-rans. Hoar was, in effect, an appointed senator and *not* the popular choice. See *Columbian Centinel*, April 13, 1825; *Boston Patriot*, May 31, 1825; *Boston Commercial Gazette*, June 2, 1825.

49. Keyes, Autobiography, 7; *T&R*, 222–23; Louis A. Surette, *By-Laws of Corinthian Lodge of Ancient, Free and Accepted Masons of Concord, Mass.* (Concord, Mass., 1859), 132–33; column by "Massachusetts," *Daily American Statesman* (Boston), March 17, 1826.

2. *Community and Conscience*

1. Cynthia Dunbar was admitted to membership in Concord's First Parish Church by "confession" on July 7, 1811; she and John Thoreau married ten months later, on May 11, 1812. Their first child, Helen Louisa, was born on October 22, 1812, five months after the wedding. See First Parish Church Record Book, original at Houghton, transcript at CFPL. The birth of Helen L. Thoreau was not registered with the Concord town clerk; the exact date appears on her gravestone in Sleepy Hollow Cemetery.

2. On March 10, 1792, the Massachusetts General Court implemented article three of the constitution's declaration of rights and enacted a statute "providing for the due observance of the Lord's Day." Any able-bodied person absent from public worship on the Sabbath for the space of three months was liable to a fine of ten shillings. However, the law exempted from its sanctions anyone who could not "conscientiously or conveniently" attend the nearest house of worship. The measure was laxly enforced, but it remained on the books until disestablishment in 1834. The duty of enforcing attendance fell to the local tythingmen. See chap. 58, 1791–92 session, *Acts and Laws of the Commonwealth of Massachusetts*, 13 vols. (Boston, 1890–1898), 6:351–55, and John Bacon, *The town officer's guide, containing a compilation of the general laws of Massachusetts, relating to the whole power and duty of towns, districts, and parishes* (Haverhill, Mass., 1825), 254.

3. Shattuck, *History*, 191; John Wood Sweet, "The Liberal Dilemma and the Demise of the Town Church: Ezra Ripley's Pastorate in Concord, 1778–1841," *Proceedings of the MHS* 104 (1992): 83–84; Mary Babson Fuhrer, *A Crisis of Community: The Trials and Transformation of a New England Town, 1815–1848* (Chapel Hill, N.C., 2014), 29, 32–34. Elizabeth Orrock Thoreau joined the First Parish Church on

December 27, 1801, at nineteen; Jane Thoreau on April 25, 1802, at eighteen; Maria Thoreau on January 4, 1818, at twenty-three. A fourth Thoreau sister, Mary, had entered the fold on October 25, 1807, at twenty-one; she died on July 24, 1812, six weeks after John Thoreau and Cynthia Dunbar wed. From 1810 to 1818, the church attracted eighty-six new members by confession, a quarter of them men. Altogether, 38 percent of the women were single (*n* = 23) and 42 percent of the men (*n* = 11). The average age of the single women was 22.8, of the men 28.1. At twenty-four, Cynthia Dunbar was a little older than her female counterparts entering the church. Over the entire period from 1778 to 1857, 74 percent of the 529 church members were women. The female share of 233 new members in the era when Cynthia Dunbar joined the church (1800-1825) was 76 percent.

4. Gross, *Minutemen*, 18-29; Shattuck, *History*, 166-86; Ezra Ripley, D.D., *Half Century Discourse, Delivered November 16, 1828, at Concord, Massachusetts* (Concord, Mass., 1829), 6.

5. Barzillai Frost, "Ezra Ripley," in William Ware, ed., *American Unitarian Biography. Memoirs of Individuals Who Have Been Distinguished by Their Writings, Character, and Efforts in the Cause of Liberal Christianity*, 2 vols. (Boston, 1850), 1:119-23; Ripley, Autobiographical sketch, in Journal and notebook, bMS AM 1280.235 (513), Houghton; Steven J. Novak, *The Rights of Youth: American Colleges and Student Revolt, 1798-1815* (Cambridge, Mass., 1977), 4-5; Harvard College Faculty and Student Records, University Archives, Harvard University; Gross, *Minutemen*, 134-35.

6. H&P, 192-93.

7. Ezra Ripley, "The duties of magistrates and rulers," March 10, 1799, HDS; Ripley, Record of Marriages, 1778-1840, and Record of Deaths in Concord, 1778-1830, CFPL; Ripley, *Half Century Discourse*, 7-9, 38-40; Ripley, annual Thanksgiving sermon, November 19, 1795, HDS; epitaphs of Humphrey Barrett, Letter file 9, B-1cd, B-2, and of Col. John Buttrick, Letter file 3 R-1, CFPL; G. W. Hosmer, Letter regarding Ezra Ripley, March 14, 1861, in William B. Sprague, ed., *Annals of the American Pulpit; or Commemorative Notices of Distinguished American Clergymen of the Various Denominations* (New York, 1865): 8:120-21; Edward Jarvis, Diary 1827-42, 1:11-15, CFPL; Ripley to Rev. and Hon. Trustees of Phillips Academy in Andover, September 24, 1805, Ripley to Nathan Brooks, June 22, 1809, Ripley to Sally Chandler, June 6, 1816, Ripley to Gov. John Brooks and Council, January 16, 1822, all in Ripley Correspondence, 1805-1838, Series I, Ezra Ripley Papers, 1784-1838, Folder 1, CFPL.

8. Hosmer, Letter regarding Ezra Ripley, 119-20; Phyllis Cole, *Mary Moody Emerson and the Origins of Transcendentalism: A Family History* (New York, 1998), 92. The reference to Ichabod is to 1 Samuel 4:21. Ripley held his old friends to the same exacting standards he demanded of his parishioners. In March 1789 he warned his Harvard classmate George Thatcher, a representative to the first U.S. Congress, that as a result of his "free conversation," he was getting a reputation as "a deist," with "no regard to religion." "Whether you will thank me or conjure me, I leave [to you]," Ripley proposed; "but I undertook to clear you of the charge of infidelity, and to maintain, that you were not only a believer in religion, but in revealed religion." Ripley to Thatcher, March 30, 1789, BPL.

9. Conrad Wright, "Institutional Reconstruction in the Unitarian Controversy," in Conrad Edick Wright, *American Unitarianism 1805-1865* (Boston, 1989), 23-24.

10. Ezra Ripley, *The Obligations of Parents to Give Their Children a Virtuous Education, and*

to Provide Schools for This Purpose (Cambridge, Mass., 1820), 9; Ripley, Half Century Discourse, 41; "Importance of Religion in Early Life," "Aged People Exhorted to Practical Goodness," "The Covenant of Grace Explained and a Pious Walk in It Recommended and Urged," and "The Faults of Christians Exposed and Guarded Against," bMS AM 1835 (11), all at Houghton.

11. Ripley, "On gratitude to God and man," November 29, 1798, annual Thanksgiving sermon, bMs AM 1835 (11), Houghton; Ripley, "Domestic peace explained and recommended," February 3, 1799, bMS AM 1835 (11), Houghton; and Ripley, "Duty of parents to restrain children from vice," February 17, 1799, bMS AM 1835 (11), Houghton.

12. Shattuck, History, 186. On July 11, 1776, the First Parish Church renewed its covenant and welcomed back into communion its no-longer-aggrieved brothers and sisters. Its statement of the convictions and obligations of members was similar to that adopted in 1749 and to earlier versions going back to founding minister Peter Bulkeley. The religious creed incorporated into the 1776 covenant was taken from the catechism endorsed by the Westminster Assembly of Divines in 1647—an "excellent compendium" of the Bible, according to the subscribers to the Concord covenant in 1776. In summarizing the Calvinist scheme of salvation, I have relied on and quoted from The Shorter Catechism of the Westminster Assembly of Divines (London, 1897).

13. Ripley, Half Century Discourse, 32–38; E.R. [Ezra Ripley], "Recollections and Remarks of an Aged Clergyman, Now Living, Respecting the Changes That Have Taken Place in Religious Opinions, and in the Character of Preaching, in New England, for the Last Fifty Years," Unitarian Advocate, and Religious Miscellany, n.s., 3 (1831): 129–32. For good accounts of the theological issues at stake in the fight over Calvinism, see Joseph Haroutunian, Piety Versus Moralism: The Passing of the New England Theology (New York, 1932), and Conrad Wright, The Beginnings of Unitarianism in America (Boston, 1955), 259–69, quotation at 259.

14. Ezra Ripley, "On proving doctrines, institutions, and customs in religion and adhering to the best," February 12, 1826, bMS AM 1835 (11), Houghton.

15. Ripley, Half Century Discourse, 32–5; E.R., "Recollections," 130; Sweet, "Liberal Dilemma," 84–85.

16. Ezra Ripley, A.M., A Sermon Preached on the Completion of a General Repair of the Meeting House in Concord, January 24, 1792 (Boston, 1792), 15, 47–48; Ripley, "The love of God & waiting for Christ explained & recommended," rescript from no. 1211 in 1804, preached July 6, 1817, Box 1, bMS AM 1835 (11), Houghton; Ripley, Obligations of Parents, 16; Ripley, Half Century Discourse, 39.

17. Shattuck, History, 150–51; Gross, Minutemen, 160; Covenants of Concord Church, 1646 and 1776, and "Report of EZRA RIPLEY and BARZILLAI FROST and Deacons Reuben Brown, Nehemiah Ball, and Elisha Tolman, Adopted unanimously March 4, 1841," in John Whittemore Teele, ed., The Meeting House on the Green: A History of the First Parish in Concord and Its Church (Concord, Mass., 1985), 72–77; Wright, Beginnings of Unitarianism, 9. The classic account of the Puritan venture in building churches of the elect is Edmund S. Morgan, Visible Saints: The History of a Puritan Idea (New York, 1963). For a more recent interpretation, see David D. Hall, Worlds of Wonder, Days of Judgment: Popular Religious Belief in Early New England (New York, 1989), 117–65.

18. First Church Record Book (transcript), 201–2, 206–12, CFPL; Ripley to Church in Concord, March 10, 1795, and Ripley, "Sketch of Report" [report of committee to revise the church covenant, March 12, 1795], Series 4. Reports, 1795–1831, Folder 4, Ezra Ripley Papers, 1784–1838, CFPL.

19. Meetings of May 19, June 2 and 9, 1793, First Church Record Book (transcript), 204–5, CFPL; "The Form of Church Covenant Accepted by the Church 1795," in Teele, *Meeting House on the Green*, 78–79; "Report of RIPLEY and FROST," 240–42. For a more extended account of these reforms and of Ripley's ministry, see Robert A. Gross, "'Doctor Ripley's Church': Congregational Life in Concord, Massachusetts, 1778–1841," *Journal of Unitarian Universalist History* 33 (2009–2010): 1–37.

20. Wright, *Beginnings of Unitarianism*, 229–37; Ripley to Church in Concord, March 10, 1795. Ripley's program of church reform, rooted in the eighteenth-century reaction against the Great Awakening, could be dubbed an Arminian Reformation.

21. Shattuck, *History*, 156, 191; Sweet, "Liberal Dilemma," 83–84; meetings of November 17 and December 8, 1816, September 1, October 9, and December 4, 1825, First Parish Church Record Book (transcript), 235–36, 245–47, CFPL. At Ripley's recommendation, the church made regular donations to the Evangelical Missionary Society, of which he was a founding member, and in 1822 to the Board of Commissioners for Foreign Missions, "to be applied to the civilization and christianizing the Indians in the Western parts of this country." See meetings of September 27, 1809; April 26, 1813; October 2, 1814; October 1, 1815; September 29, 1816; and January 6, 1822, First Parish Church Record Book (transcript), 224–25, 231, 233–35, 242–43, CFPL. About the same time as the Concord church was steering clear of discipline cases, "genteel" Vermonters in towns in the Connecticut River Valley were resisting moral oversight by their Congregationalist brothers and sisters. Such "intrusions into the personal lives of members" had become "distasteful." See Randolph A. Roth, *The Democratic Dilemma: Religion, Reform, and the Social Order in the Connecticut River Valley of Vermont, 1791–1850* (New York, 1987), 61.

22. Robert A. Gross, *Much Instruction from Little Reading: Books and Libraries in Thoreau's Concord* (Worcester, Mass., 1987), 156–57; Ezra Ripley, "The care of heaven for widows and fatherless children," March 15, 1801, sermon delivered the Sabbath following the death of John Thoreau, Ezra Ripley, Writings, Box 1, Folder 27–34, Trustees Archives and Research Center, Sharon, Mass. Between 1790 and 1820, 154 women entered the First Parish Church in full communion; the marital status of 128 is known. Well over half (56 percent) were married; more than a third (36 percent) were single; and 8 percent were widows. The average age of the wives was thirty-eight, the single women twenty-five, and the widows fifty-seven. ($N = 114$). For the Thoreau family genealogy, see *Bangor Historical Magazine* 11 (July 1886–June 1887): 164. It was undoubtedly the presence of siblings that drew John and Rebecca Kettell Thoreau to Concord: sisters Esther White (1746–1804), married to the merchant John White, and Abigail Kettell (1744–1842), and bachelor brothers John (1742–1823) and Thomas Kettell (1754–1833). See Charles Collyer Whittier, *Genealogy of the Stimpson Family of Charlestown, Mass.: and Allied Lines* (Boston, 1907), 22–26.

23. "Sketches of the Life of Mrs. Rebecca Thoreau," *Christian Disciple* 3 (October 1815): 289–94; *List of Members in Full Communion with the Church in Charlestown, on the 30th of April 1789*, the day of Jedidiah Morse's installation, in *Records of the First Church of Charlestown, Massachusetts, 1632–1789*, accessed on Ancestry.com. This piece was published anonymously, but it bears the hallmarks of Ripley's style and values. In a telling indication of Ripley's authorship, Rebecca Thoreau won praise for "declining to read controversial publications on religious subjects, lest her mind should be perplexed more than edified" (p. 292). The Concord parson was constantly reminding his congregation to avoid unnecessary debate about things "not essential" to true faith.

24. Ripley, Memorandum of conferences, January 1810, in Ripley, Other Material, Box 5, Folder 16, Series 2, Old Manse Manuscripts, 1755–1938, Trustees Archives and Research Center, Sharon, Mass.; Jonathan D. Sassi, *A Republic of Righteousness: The Public Christianity of the Post-Revolutionary New England Clergy* (New York, 2001), 123–26; Robert A. Gross, "Faith in the Boardinghouse: New Views of Thoreau Family Religion," *Thoreau Society Bulletin* 250 (Winter 2005): 1–5. If Rebecca Thoreau was disappointed by Ripley's crackdown on the "religious conferences," she got over that feeling by the time of her death. Her last will and testament named "my worthy friend" Ripley as the first beneficiary of her estate; he received a gift of one hundred dollars, equal to the bequests to her five siblings and the only award to a person not kin. With good reason, the parson praised "her benevolence and largeness of heart" in charitable causes, which "far exceeded her ability." That was a prescient remark; as it turned out, there was not enough money in the estate to fund all the legacies. Ripley's share came to seventy-one dollars. See Rebecca Thoreau, Last Will and Testament, June 3, 1814, and order for the disbursement of bequests, February 11, 1819, File no. 22536, MCPR; "Sketches of the Life of Mrs. Rebecca Thoreau."

25. Ripley, Memorandum of conferences, January 1810.

26. Clifford K. Shipton, "Asa Dunbar," in Shipton, *Sibley's Harvard Graduates,* 16 vols. (Boston, 1873–1972), 16:457–63; Anne S. Brown and David D. Hall, "Family Strategies and Religious Practice: Baptism and the Lord's Supper in Early New England," in David D. Hall, ed., *Lived Religion in America: Toward a History of Practice* (Princeton, N.J., 1997), 41–68; Gross, *Minutemen,* 100, 106, 181–82, 184–85.

27. Ripley, *Sermon Preached on the Completion of a General Repair,* 43–44.

28. George M. Brooks, "Memoir of Tilly Merrick," *SCM* 2:59–62; letters from Mary Merrick (Concord) to Maria Parker (Billerica), 1819–1836, Brooks Family Papers, CFPL. The specific letters cited in the text are dated September 16, 1819 (stargazing), March 16, 1820 (moonlight walks), June 1820 ("tame housewife"), November 1820 ("think of eternity"). The young woman not only attended worship regularly but went to special lectures Ripley gave for young people: "I have heard two fine sermons," she wrote on January 1, 1821, "and after meeting went to a schoolhouse where Dr. Ripley delivers lectures to young people every Sunday when he is in town. I think this will be very profitable to me."

29. Merrick to Parker, September 16, 1819 ("vanity"); March 27, 1820 ("egotism," "comparative nothingness"); July 10, 1820 ("dearest friends," "self-denial"); November 22, 1820 ("fleeting time," "piety to God"); November 26, 1820 ("evil passion," "I sometimes despair"); December 15, 1820 ("prepare for Heaven"); January 6, 1821 ("sorrow and suffering," "moralizing," "make our peace"). In a sermon delivered on November 4, 1792, and repeated on November 25, 1821, Ripley urged his listeners not to expect "uninterrupted happiness" in this world. "This is not . . . the condition or the lot of humanity. We are instructed that in the world we shall have tribulation." "The benefit of affliction, and especially to young people," bMS AM 1835 (11), Houghton.

30. Merrick to Parker, March 27, 1820 ("how much do we feel"), and January 6, 1821 ("importance of religion"). Mary Merrick Brooks followed her mother's example in linking motherhood and church membership. Sally Minot Merrick had joined the Concord church in 1800, one month after the birth of her first child. She was quick to obtain baptism for her infants, usually by the first or second Sabbath after their births. The following are the available dates of birth and of baptism for her young: Mary Merrick, born April 5, 1801, baptized April 12, 1801; Sarah, born May

17, 1805, baptized May 26, 1805; Augustus, born November 11, 1810, baptized November 18, 1810. There is no record of baptism for Sally Minot Merrick's first child Francis-John, born December 26, 1799, twelve months after the wedding. Given her promptness in baptizing the other children, it is likely that Parson Ripley, less regular than usual, unwittingly omitted the record. As for Mary Merrick Brooks, her firstborn George Merrick Brooks was born July 26, 1824, and baptized August 29, 1824; her second child Charles Augustus was born April 18, 1832, and baptized May 18, 1832; he died before his first year on March 31, 1833. See First Parish Church Record Book (transcript), CFPL, and *Concord Births, Marriages, and Deaths.*

31. Cole, *Mary Emerson and Transcendentalism*, 78 ("orphanship"), 84 ("God's electing love"), 98 ("Alive with God"), 101 ("at the throne"), 102 ("danced to the music"), 164–65 ("Dr. Reason," "bone of metaphysics"); Ripley (Concord) to "my dear daughter M.M.E." (Augusta, Me.), December 18, 1827, bMS AM 1280.226 (3970), Houghton; Phyllis Cole, "The Advantage of Loneliness: Mary Moody Emerson's Almanacks, 1802–1855," in Joel Porte, ed., *Emerson: Prospect and Retrospect* (Cambridge, Mass., 1982), 7–8; *JMN* 16:175. Though she declined to be confined to Concord, Mary Moody Emerson was among the subscribers to the renewed covenant of the First Parish Church in 1815 and 1832.

32. Ezra Ripley, "Showing why some people, who believe in Christ, do not confess him," rescript from no. 1201, March 24, 1816, bMS 1835 (11), Houghton; Ripley, Journal and notebook, entry for November 16, 1823; Teele, *Meeting House on the Green*, 75. From his ordination in 1778 through the jubilee of 1825, a total of 337 individuals—248 women, 89 men—entered the fold by "confession," just seven a year. By decade, average annual admissions were as follows: 1778–1784: 3.5; 1785–1794: 5.0; 1795–1804: 8.8; 1805–1814: 9.2; 1815–1824: 6.8. The average age of new church members in Concord was as follows:

PERIOD	MEN	WOMEN
1778–1795	42.4	40.0
1796–1805	41.9	34.5
1806–1815	37.9	32.5
1816–1825	49.0	43.2
1826–1835	36.8	36.2

In 1776, when the First Parish Church renewed its covenant, 61 men subscribed; women were apparently not invited to sign. Four decades later, in 1815, the church repeated the exercise; this time, 50 men put down their names, as did 104 women. In 1832 the same ritual drew 38 men and 87 women. Considering that the town's population had grown from some 1,700 in 1776 to 2,017 in the early 1830s, the fall-off of male members is notable. The 50 male subscribers in 1815 constituted 15 percent of the 333 adult males on that year's tax list; their 38 counterparts in 1832 included just 10 percent of that year's 400 taxable adult males. Another way to gauge the reach of the church is to estimate the percentage of households with a church member. The 1810 federal census of Concord enumerated 288 households, the 1820 census 328. Interpolating between these figures, I estimate 310 households in 1815. The subscribers to the 1815 covenant represented 116 households, roughly 37 percent of all homes.

33. Rev. Henry M. Grout, *Trinitarian Congregationalism in Concord. An Historical Discourse, Delivered at Concord, Mass., June 4, 1876* (Boston, 1876), 18, 22–23; Samuel B. Simonds (Lowell) to Rev. George Tewksbury (Concord), August 27, 1892, file of letters related to the manual of the Trinitarian Congregational Church, Trinitarian

Congregational Church Records, Box 1, CFPL; "A Cry from the North West" by "A Hopkinsian," in *Cry from the Four Winds, in the Cause of Religious Liberty, and Against Clerical Intrigue and Ecclesiastical Oppression* 1, no. 5 (December 15, 1827): 38–39; Constitution of the Second Congregational Society and the first Calvinistic Religious Society in the Town of Concord, April 27, 1826, folder labeled "Letters and papers to form church, 1826–1836," Trinitarian Congregational Church Historical Materials 1826–1900, CFPL; First Parish Church Record Book (transcript), May 7, 1826, p. 248, CFPL.

34. Conrad Wright, "The Election of Henry Ware" and "The Controversial Career of Jedidiah Morse," in Wright, *The Unitarian Controversy: Essays on American Unitarian History* (Boston, 1994), 1–16, 59–82; Peter S. Field, *The Crisis of the Standing Order: Clerical Intellectuals and Cultural Authority in Massachusetts, 1780–1833* (Amherst, Mass., 1998), 141–72; Joseph W. Phillips, *Jedidiah Morse and New England Congregationalism* (New Brunswick, N.J., 1983), 129–42; Daniel Walker Howe, *What Hath God Wrought: The Transformation of America, 1815–1848* (New York, 2007), 164–88; *Walden*, 134; Anne C. Rose, *Transcendentalism as a Social Movement, 1830–1850* (New Haven, Conn., 1981), 28–37.

35. Wright, "Institutional Reconstruction," 6–17; Richard Holmes, *Communities in Transition: Bedford and Lincoln, Massachusetts 1729–1840* (Ann Arbor, Mich., 1980), 136–38; Ripley, Journal and Notebook, entry for May 1, 1821; Ripley, "On the superior excellence of charity," rescript from no. 1212 in 1804 and delivered March 14, 1819, Houghton; Ripley, "On proving doctrines"; and Ripley, "On Conscience, Its Design, Use, and Obligations," May 11, 1823, bMS Am 1835 (11), Houghton. On the manuscript of the sermon, Ripley noted its delivery in the following places: Chelmsford, Acton, Burlington, Waltham, Marlboro, East Dedham, Weston, East Sudbury, Stow, Bedford, Charlestown, Lincoln, New Bedford, Littleton. Typically, if a sermon was given in a year after its composition, Ripley indicated the date. Hence I have assumed that he delivered "On Conscience" in all these towns (and in the order of listing) during 1823.

36. Joseph S. Clark, *A Historical Sketch of the Congregational Churches in Massachusetts, from 1620 to 1858* (Boston, 1858), 255–60; "Cry from the North West," 38; Holmes, *Communities in Transition*, 136–38; Richard Eddy Sykes, "Massachusetts Unitarianism and Social Change: A Religious Social System in Transition, 1780–1870" (Ph.D. diss., University of Minnesota, 1966), 100–102.

37. It has long been thought that the First Parish Church precipitated the split by opting in 1826 to drop the Trinity from its covenant, but that is unlikely. No such decision is recorded in the minutes of church meetings kept by Ripley, a man so assiduous in his habits that he once boasted of hanging his hat every day for forty years on the same large nail outside his study door "and on no other." By contrast, the covenant of 1776, adopted under William Emerson, is carefully inscribed in the old volume, as are the landmark changes of 1795 and later innovations in 1832 and 1841. Why would the parson omit so controversial a decision from the official record? Actually, why make it in the first place? At a time when churches were fracturing all around him, it seems doubtful that Ripley, a man determined to keep his people under one roof, would have pressed for a change certain to drive them apart. Most tellingly, no one involved in these consequential choices ever pointed to the revision of the First Parish Church covenant as the impetus to the formation of an orthodox church. They were not suddenly pushed out of Ripley's church. They chose to leave on their own. Edward Jarvis, Letter regarding Ezra

Ripley, in Sprague, *Annals of the American Pulpit*, 8:123; Shattuck, *History*, 150–51; Gross, *Minutemen*, 160; First Parish Church Record Book, Houghton.

The suggestion that the split in the First Parish was provoked by the decision to omit reference to "the Father, the Son, and the Holy Ghost" in the covenant was first made by Trinitarian pastor Henry M. Grout. In 1876 the minister set out to prepare an address for the jubilee of the orthodox congregation. Born in 1831 and raised in Vermont, Grout had come to Concord only a few years before, and he knew about the origins of his church only from the stories handed down from its founders. In an effort to determine the precise reasons for the separation, he sought out Rev. Grindall Reynolds, the Unitarian pastor of the congregation that had once been "Doctor Ripley's church," and got permission to consult the original records. There in the worn leather-bound volume kept successively by Bliss, Emerson, and Ripley, the inquisitive minister uncovered his answer. It lay buried in a committee report of 1841 reviewing the two-hundred-year history of the church covenant.

> The Covenant of this church was formerly a Creed. It included all the doctrines of the Assembly's Shorter Catechism. In 1795 these were all left out, except the Trinity. In 1826 the Trinity was left out.

In that "last mentioned act"—the deletion of the Trinity—Grout saw the light of truth, illuminating what "moved a company of good and true men and women to separate themselves from a church, pastor, and place of worship to which they were tenderly bound." The secession, he reported in a "historical discourse" for the anniversary, was a reluctant response to a sudden innovation. The founders of the Trinitarian church had no desire "to introduce any new form of faith or new order of worship. It was to rescue and perpetuate that form of doctrine which, in the old church itself, they and their fathers had been taught, and taught to cherish; and from which, after nearly two hundred years, that church had now deliberately and formally turned away." By dropping the Trinity, the First Parish Church was betraying its heritage. In reaction, the dissenters felt compelled to act, in order to keep faith with the fathers. The Trinitarians did not choose to leave; they were pushed out. For the above-mentioned reasons, I find this origin story implausible. See Grout, *Trinitarian Congregationalism*, 12–13; "Report of EZRA RIPLEY and BARZILLAI FROST," in Teele, *Meeting House on the Green*, 242, reprinted from First Parish Record Book (transcript), CFPL; Elizabeth E. Boice Jones, comp., *Captain John Grout of Watertown and Sudbury, Massachusetts and Some of His Descendants* (Waterloo, Ia., 1922), 25; Rev. George A. Tewksbury, *Manual of the Trinitarian Congregational Church of Concord, Concord, Mass.* (Boston, 1895), 76.

38. Stephen Nissenbaum, *The Battle for Christmas* (New York, 1996), 45, 47; Vincent Harding, *A Certain Magnificence: Lyman Beecher and the Transformation of American Protestantism, 1775–1868* (Brooklyn, N.Y., 1991), 213–15, 221, 223; Lyman Beecher, *The Faith Once Delivered to the Saints: A Sermon, Delivered at Worcester, Mass., Oct. 15, 1823* (Boston, 1823), 17–19, 43.

39. "Cry from the North West," 38–39. Although the series of articles in *Cry from the Four Winds* does not identify the town or the author by name, it is unmistakably a behind-the-scenes account of the Concord separation, written by an early participant who came to feel manipulated and betrayed by the orthodox party in Boston and its henchmen in his native town. A founder of the Trinitarian church, Joseph C. Green, admitted circulating the periodical in Concord, and from the various

initials he uses—"Deacon P." for Deacon John Proctor of Park Street Church; "the Rev. D.S." for Daniel Southmayd; "J.D." for the wealthy Concord merchant Josiah Davis—and from his description of the town as a place "of considerable size, not more than twenty miles from the city of Boston," the author and his community can be securely attributed. In May 1819 John C. Proctor was elected, along with Jeremiah Evarts, a deacon of Park Street Church. See H. Crosby Englizian, *Brimstone Corner: Park Street Church, Boston* (Chicago, 1968), 75, 92. Green's exposé unfolded in three consecutive issues of volume 1 of *Cry from the Four Winds*: no. 5 (December 15, 1827): 38–39, no. 6 (December 22, 1827): 47–48; and no. 7 (December 29, 1827): 54–55.

40. "Cry from the North West," 47.

41. First Parish Church Record Book (transcript), meeting of May 7, 1826, 248, CFPL.

42. Ibid., meeting of May 21, 1826, 248–50; *Journal of Debates and Proceedings of the Convention of Delegates, Chosen to Revise the Constitution of Massachusetts, Begun and Holden at Boston, November 15, 1820, and Continued by Adjournment to January 9, 1821. Reported for the Boston Daily Advertiser* (Boston, 1821), 260–61, 269. Jeremiah Evarts married the sister of Hoar's wife, Sarah Sherman. As the Unitarians were organizing as a denomination in 1824–1825, they sought to enlist the involvement of Hoar, a man known for his "deep interest in religion." See Henry Ware, Alden Bradford, and R. O. Sullivan to Samuel Hoar, December 29, 1824, Miscellaneous Hoar Family Papers, 1817–93, CFPL.

43. First Parish Church Record Book (transcript), meeting of May 21, 1826, 248–50, CFPL.

44. *YG*, May 27 and June 10, 1826; John Wood Sweet, "'Churches Gathered Out of Churches': The Divergence of Liberal and Orthodox Congregationalists in Concord, Massachusetts, 1800–1850" (senior honors thesis, Amherst College, 1988), 73–75.

45. *Boston Recorder and Telegraph*, June 9, 1826; Record of meetings, March 23–April 28, 1826, regarding the organization of the new church, Folder 1, Loose papers, Trinitarian Congregational Church Records, Box 1, CFPL; *Boston Recorder*, June 23, 1826; Samuel B. Simonds (Lowell) to Rev. George Tewksbury (Concord), August 27, 1892, file of letters in reply to questions of Tewksbury for his manual of the Trinitarian Congregational Church, Trinitarian Congregational Church Records, Box 1; Sweet, "Liberal Dilemma," 91. Thomas Todd, printer of the *Manual of the Trinitarian Congregational Church of Concord* (Boston, 1895) and member of the congregation, identified Keyes as the party responsible for "nailing up" the doors of the brick schoolhouse in a note he penciled on the back of a typewritten copy of the *Boston Recorder*'s June 1826 report of the incident. Todd evidently came across this account in the church archives, and he observed that he had been told the same story "some years before" by Deacon Samuel B. Simonds of Lowell, an early member of Concord's Trinitarian church, who named "Mr. Keyes, father of Judge John S. Keyes of the Criminal court in Concord." See Todd's note, dated February 24, 1896, on the back of the typescript in a folder labeled "Encouraging Prospects, Boston *Recorder and Telegraph* 1826," Trinitarian Congregational Church Records, Box 1, CFPL. Rand became co-editor and co-owner of the *Boston Recorder* in July 1826. Gaylord P. Albaugh, *History and Annotated Bibliography of American Religious Periodicals and Newspapers Established from 1740 Through 1830*, 2 vols. (Worcester, Mass., 1994), 1:3–4.

46. *YG*, June 17, 1826; *Boston Recorder*, June 23, 1826. The calculations of pews and population were pretty accurate. With about 2,000 inhabitants and 400 households in the mid-1820s, Concord provided places in the meetinghouse for 30 percent of its population and a quarter of its families.

47. "No Friend to Hypocrisy," *YG*, June 17 and 24, 1826; Sweet, "'Churches Gathered Out of Churches,'" 76; "Observer," *Boston Recorder*, June 23, 1826. In February 1844 Keyes stood up at a meeting in the First Parish meetinghouse to denounce an incendiary lecture given the week before by the radical abolitionist Wendell Phillips. Keyes was outraged by Phillips's insistence that "the curse of every honest man should be upon" the nation's pro-slavery Constitution. According to a local witness to Keyes's performance, the magistrate "talked an hour, quoting St. Paul, about leading captive silly women," in what was clearly a slur on abolitionists for depending, like the Congregationalist and Unitarian churches, so heavily on female support. That is one clue to Keyes's authorship. Another is the offense that "No Friend to Hypocrisy" took at "Observer's" emphasis upon the use of "hammers and nails" to keep the Trinitarians from gathering in the brick schoolhouse for Sunday worship. See communication by "H.M." to *Liberator*, February 16, 1844.

48. Bible Society in the County of Middlesex, Minutes of annual meetings, 1814–34, CFPL; *The Constitution of the Middlesex County Bible Society, Auxiliary to the American Bible Society* (Concord, Mass., 1826); Ripley to James Walker, July 26, 1826, bMS 478/2 (17), HDS.

49. Nathaniel Hawthorne, *Mosses from an Old Manse* (New York, 1846), 7; Ripley, "Things essential to christianity and salvation"; Ripley, "On proving doctrines"; and Ripley, "Temptations to sin distinguished from trials and God not the author of the former, but are the fruit of our lusts," January 15, 1826, bMS 64/1, HDS; Joseph A. Conforti, *Samuel Hopkins and the New Divinity Movement: Calvinism, the Congregational Ministry, and Reform in New England Between the Great Awakenings* (Grand Rapids, Mich., 1981); Hannah Adams, *A View of Religions, in Two Parts . . .* (Boston, 1791); Michael W. Vella, "Theology, Genre, and Gender: The Precarious Place of Hannah Adams in American Literary History," *Early American Literature* 28 (1993): 21–41.

50. Ripley, journal and notebook, entries for November 2 and 27, 1826; John Hay Farnham (Harvard College) to Mary B. Farnham (Newburyport), March 29, 1810, Farnham folder C, Farnham Family Papers, MHS; William H. Brantley, *Three Capitals: A Book About the First Three Capitals of Alabama: St. Stephens, Huntsville and Cahawba* (privately printed, 1947), 25–26. Ripley was spared the knowledge that Phebe, his partner of forty-four years, still harbored a preference for her first husband, the late Revolutionary chaplain William Emerson. "Don't call Dr. Ripley," she instructed. "His boots squeak so; Mr. Emerson used to step so softly, his boots never squeaked." See Cole, *Mary Emerson and Transcendentalism*, 71.

51. "A Dialogue on Persecution," *Boston Recorder*, January 25, 1828. This piece reports on a conversation that Asa Rand had with Ripley back in May 1827, while the Trinitarians' request for dismission was hanging fire. The orthodox minister was serving temporarily as pastor to the "little band." In hopes of winning Ripley's consent to the separation, he introduced himself to the old man and asked permission to explain "the principles on which I act." Ripley reciprocated with a friendly greeting but declined to say anything about the pending case. The two men agreed on the general "right of Christians to form societies separate from others," but Ripley took a narrow view of when such actions were justified. As Concord's settled minister saw it, separation was called for only if a minority in a church was "deprived of some of their privileges and rights" and subjected to "some kind of persecution." But that would never happen so long as ministers freely exchanged with one another, as they had once done, and exposed their parishioners to diverse views of the gospel. Rand begged to differ. Surely an incumbent could not be required

to violate his conscience and open up his pulpit to someone whose opinions he condemned. On that same principle, individuals who considered Unitarianism "a false gospel" should not be expected to put up quietly with such preaching: "They do not demand that their Unitarian ministers shall renounce the right to judge for themselves. They simply bear their protest and withdraw." It was all too much for the exasperated Ripley.

52. First Parish Church Record Book (transcript), 250–53, CFPL; Mary Moody Emerson ("M.M.E.") to Ripley (Concord), July 25, 1826, in Nancy Craig Simmons, ed., *The Selected Letters of Mary Moody Emerson* (Athens, Ga., 1993), 218–19, 220n10. The First Parish Church admitted thirteen members in 1828 and sixteen in 1830; by 1833, the new accessions, amounting to sixty, more than compensated for the losses.

53. First Parish Church Record Book (transcript), 257–62, CFPL; Albert J. von Frank, *An Emerson Chronology*, 2 vols., 2nd ed., rev. and enlarged (Albuquerque, N.M., 2016), 1:22–23, 25–26, 35, 38, 40, 43, 47, 57; Jarvis, Diary, 1:222–23, CFPL; Ripley, "On the Bible Method of Becoming Religious," *Liberal Preacher*, no. 5 (November 1827): 63–72; E.R. [Ripley], "Recollections and Remarks of an Aged Clergyman"; "Hersey Bradford Goodwin," in Sprague, *Annals of the American Pulpit*, 8:548–52; subscription list, Society Auxiliary to the American Unitarian Association, May 24, 1828, CFPL. Ripley also joined in deliberations of the Unitarian clergy at the annual Berry Street conference, held in the vestry of William Ellery Channing's Federal Street Church in Boston; served as a delegate to the ordination of a new pastor for the Unitarian church in distant Baltimore, Maryland; and assumed the presidency of the Middlesex (County) Unitarian Association. See *YG*, May 24, 1834.

54. Meetings of June 28 and August 31, 1832, First Parish Church Record Book (transcript), 272–77, CFPL; E.R., "Recollections and Remarks of an Aged Clergyman," 213.

55. *YG*, December 9, 1826, and April 28, 1827; Tewksbury, *Manual*, 80–82. A dozen converts were added in the church's third year (June 1828–May 1829), five in the fourth (June 1829–May 1830), eight in the fifth (June 1830–May 1831). Of the initial twenty-two members admitted in the calendar year 1826, eighteen were transfers from the First Parish and other congregations; in 1827, fifteen out of thirty-one; and in 1828, six of fourteen. From 1830 on growth was propelled by individuals giving original testimony of being born again.

56. Tewksbury, *Manual*, 83; list of members of Second Congregational Society Parish, Box 1, CFPL. Sarah Thoreau presented a reference from the Hanover Street Church, Beecher's original outpost in Boston. Louisa Dunbar transferred her membership from the Bowdoin Street Church, the second congregation over which Beecher presided. Charles Dunbar did not enter the communion but did provide financial support for the "society."

57. Joanna Kent Southmayd (Concord) to Betsey Kent (Benson, Vt.), September 24 and October 30, 1827, transcripts of Southmayd family letters, 1826 to 1829, made by Margery Norris (1917–2008) of Lakeway, Texas, and now in the private collection of attorney Jeffrey D. Southmayd of Palm Coast, Florida, and shared with the author in January 2002 and January 2021); entry for April 22, 1827, First Parish Church Record Book (transcript), 253, CFPL. Maria Thoreau felt especially close to the Southmayds, and long after they had left New England for Texas, she was still recalling them with affection. In 1876, living in Bangor, Maine, she received a letter from a friend, Harriet Lincoln Wheeler, in which Joanna Kent Southmayd's name came up. "This reminds me of your mention of Mrs. Southmayd," she re-

plied, "how delighted I should be to hear from her." Maria Thoreau to Harriet Lincoln Wheeler, December 5, 1876, in Thoreau Family Correspondence, CFPL. I am grateful to Sandy Petrulionis for providing me with a transcription of this letter. *The Self-Interpreting Bible . . . [with] Explanatory Notes and Evangelical Reflections,* compiled by the Reverend John Brown, a self-taught Scottish weaver who became a Presbyterian minister in his native land, was first reprinted in the United States in 1792. President George Washington headed the list of subscribers. It was reissued in 1820, 1822, and apparently 1826 in a folio edition of 1,223 pages. In its appeal to self-trust, both on the author's and the reader's part, the volume was a fitting gift from a Thoreau. See Margaret T. Hills, *The English Bible in America: A Bibliography of Editions of the Bible and the New Testament Published in America 1777–1957* (New York, 1961), 8–9, 63, 67, 85.

58. Of the ninety-one members of the society from 1826 to 1829, eighty (88 percent) were male, eleven (12 percent) female.

59. M. M. Cushman (Litchfield, Pa.) to Rev. H. M. Grout (Concord), September 3, 1876, and Nathan Robbins (Boston) to Mary Munroe (Concord), July 31, 1876, semi-centennial folder, Trinitarian Congregational Church Records, Box 1, CFPL; John Sweet analyzed the origins of 231 men and women who joined either the Trinitarian society or church. Only thirty were born in Concord. See Sweet, "'Churches Gathered out of Churches,'" 61; Grout, *Trinitarian Congregationalism,* 22. Mary Cayton finds a similar appeal of Calvinist orthodoxy to young, mobile newcomers to Boston in the 1820s. See Cayton, "Who Were the Evangelicals? Conservative and Liberal Identity in the Unitarian Controversy in Boston, 1804–1833," *Journal of Social History* 31 (Fall 1997): 89–90, 94–100. Since the publication of Tewksbury's *Manual* in 1895 (p. 19), it has been thought that sixty-nine individuals joined the Trinitarian society at its formation in April 1826. That impression derives from a manuscript copy of the Trinitarian constitution, followed by the names of sixty-nine subscribers. The entire document is inscribed in the same handwriting. A second manuscript in the Trinitarian archives sets forward the constitution, to which is appended separate sheets pasted together; these were signed by subscribers as they enlisted in the society. Each signature is unique, and the signers are grouped into blocks according to the year of subscription. This document clearly gives the running tally of Trinitarian subscribers over time: 20 in 1826, 16 in 1827, 36 in 1828, and 18 in 1829 (one name was not matched on the two lists). Church membership grew at a different pace: 22 in 1826, 31 in 1827, 14 in 1828, 4 in 1829. See Loose papers to form church, Trinitarian Congregational Church Records, Box 1, CFPL; Tewksbury, *Manual,* 81–82. Thirty members of the Trinitarian society had died or moved away by 1832; see list in CA, Reel 2, CFPL. The enfranchisement of women in the Trinitarian church is revealed in Joseph C. Green, *An Appeal to the Christian Public: Containing the Discipline of the Trinitarian Church in Concord, Mass.* (Boston, 1828), 13.

60. "Cry from the North West," 38–39, 47; Green, *Appeal to the Christian Public,* 22, 26–27, 29, 61; Richard Rabinowitz, *The Spiritual Self in Everyday Life: The Transformation of Personal Religious Experience in Nineteenth-Century New England* (Boston, 1989), 85–96.

61. Green's charges against Hannah Hunstable, July 2, 1827, file on grievances, Trinitarian Congregational Church Records, Box 1, CFPL; Nathan Robbins, Boston, to Mary Munroe, Concord, July 31, 1876, Box I, Historical materials 1826–1900, Semi-centennial file, Trinitarian Congregational Church Records, CFPL; Green, *Appeal to the Christian Public,* 10.

62. Green, *Appeal Appeal to the Christian Public*, 12, 33–34; "Cry from the North West," 55; Albaugh, *American Religious Periodicals*, 1:306–8; Trinitarian Congregational Church Record Book, 25–31, CFPL; "A Cry from 'Limbo,'" in *A Cry from the Four Winds* 1, no. 15 (February 23, 1828): 117–19; "Orthodox Church in Concord," *Trumpet and Universalist Magazine* 2 (May 8, 1830); Joel Dakin (clerk of the First Baptist Society of Sudbury) to town clerk of Concord, March 17, 1831, certifying that Joseph C. Green is a member of his society, ETR; Joanna Southmayd (Concord) to Betsy Griswold Kent (Benson, Vt.), February 7, 1828 [this letter is dated 1827 on the typewritten transcript, but this has to be a misreading, since the events described therein, including Green's excommunication, took place from November 1827 through January 1828]. The periodical *A Cry from the Four Winds* ran from November 1827 through September 1828. In the appendix to his *Appeal*, Green says he was expelled by seventeen votes, half of which came from women.

63. Samuel Green, *The Grand Theme of the Gospel Ministry. A Sermon Preached at the Dedication of the Trinitarian Church in Concord, Massachusetts, December 6, 1826* (Concord, Mass., 1827), 26–31.

64. Sweet, "Liberal Dilemma," 103–4; Lucinda Steven Duncan, "Young People and the Sabbath School," in Teele, *Meeting House on the Green*, 210–12; Daniel S. Southmayd, *The Sure Advancement of Gospel Truth: A Sermon Preached on the Day of the Annual Thanksgiving, November 26, 1829* (Boston, 1830), 18, 24.

65. Sweet, "'Churches Gathered out of Churches,'" 74–75, 86–87; meetings of September 4, 1826, and March 5, 1827, CTMM 7:275–77, 282–83, 288–89, CFPL; J. K. Hosmer et al., *Memorial of George Washington Hosmer, D.D.* (n.p., 1882), 18.

66. Joanna Southmayd (Concord) to Betsey Griswold Kent (Benson, Vt.), April 20, 1827; meetings of June 2 and October 15, 1832, February 15 and May 11, 1833, Trinitarian Congregational Church Record Book, 37–43, CFPL; Daniel S. Southmayd (grantor) to John Vose and Moses Davis, trustees of the Trinitarian Congregational Church (grantees), September 26, 1831, MCRD 310:207 (the mortgage was foreclosed on December 20, 1834; see MCRD 480:490); D. S. Southmayd (Lowell) to Nathan Brooks, January 28, 1833, Nathan Brooks Papers, 1832–33 folder, CFPL.

67. Sweet, "'Churches Gathered Out of Churches,'" 60, 69–78; Robbins to Munroe, July 31, 1876; Tewksbury, *Manual*, 82; Louis P. Mazur, *1831: Year of Eclipse* (New York, 2001), 63–72. In 1827 the Trinitarian Congregational Church admitted sixteen new members "by confession," one more than in 1831. The peak year for new admissions was 1842, when twenty-three individuals were accepted into communion, nineteen by testifying to their experiences of saving grace.

68. Southmayd, *The Sure Advancement of Gospel Truth*, 18, 24, 5, 7–8, 10–11, 18–20.

69. Joanna Kent Southmayd (Concord) to Betsey Griswold Kent (Benson, Vt.), July 23, 1828; Ezra Ripley (Concord) to Ruth Haskins Emerson (Brookline), May 30, 1830, bMS AM 1280.226 (3964), Houghton.

70. William G. McLoughlin, *New England Dissent, 1630–1833: The Baptists and the Separation of Church and State*, 2 vols. (Cambridge, Mass., 1971): 2:1245–62; meeting of November 11, 1833, CTMM 7:443, CFPL.

71. Ezra Ripley (Concord) to Edward Bliss Emerson (St. John's, Porto Rico), August 23, 1831, bMS 1280.226 (3968), Houghton; "The duty of candour in judging the character and conduct of others," November 18, 1798, bMS 490/1, HDS; Denny R. Bowden, "Sermons, Debates, and the Environmental Essay: Conflicting Discourses in Nineteenth-Century America and the Emergence of Print Culture in

Ezra Ripley, Alexander Campbell, and Henry David Thoreau" (Ph.D. diss., Indiana University of Pennsylvania, 2001), 167.

3. The White Village

1. Wayne T. Dilts, "Henry's Houses: The Houses in Concord That Henry Called Home," *Thoreau Society Bulletin*, no. 263 (Summer 2008): 6; Brian Donahue, *The Great Meadow: Farmers and the Land in Colonial Concord* (New Haven, Conn., 2004), 5–6, 48, 184–85; Shattuck, *History*, 202; William Jones, "A Topographical Description of Concord," *Collections of the MHS* 1 (Boston, 1792): 238. Joshua Jones died at fifty-one on January 9, 1820, leaving a substantial estate worth $7,246.55, but debts, medical and funeral expenses, and the cost of administration came to $4,659.93, more than double the value of the personal property. It thus proved necessary to sell Jones's real estate at public auction to raise sufficient cash for all the claims. John Stacy, the husband of Jones's only child—daughter Eliza from his first marriage to Betsy Barrett—obtained ownership of half the dwelling house and land for $1,010; Daniel Brooks secured the "reversion of the dower right"—the widow's third—for $150. It is unclear from whom John Thoreau rented. See estate of Joshua Jones, File no. 12880, MCPR; advertisement for sale of the late Joshua Jones's real estate, *MG*, March 4, 1820.

2. Gross, *Minutemen*, 4–7.

3. Joseph S. Wood, *The New England Village* (Baltimore, 1997), 43–48, 119, 139; Jack Larkin, *The Reshaping of Everyday Life 1790–1840* (New York, 1988), 7–8; Donahue, *Great Meadow*, 186; Shattuck, *History*, 206–8; Frederic J. Wood, *The Turnpikes of New England and Evolution of the Same Through England, Virginia, and Maryland* (Boston, 1909), 119–23, 133–36; Roger N. Parks, "Roads in New England, 1790–1840," Old Sturbridge Village Research Report, Sturbridge, Mass., 1965, 55–57, appendix; Grindall Reynolds, "Memoir of William Parkman," *SCM* 2:23–24. Since the Middle Ages, the word *shop* has designated an enterprise "where goods are made or prepared for sale and sold." In early nineteenth-century Concord, establishments for selling, but not making, consumer goods were commonly called stores; businesses that conducted both activities were shops, typically mechanics' shops. I follow this distinction throughout the text. See *Oxford English Dictionary*.

4. H&P, 345–89; David F. Wood, ed., *The Concord Museum: Decorative Arts from a New England Collection* (Concord, Mass., 1996), 96–109; Wood, "Concord, Massachusetts, Clockmakers, 1789–1817" and "Concord, Massachusetts, Clockmakers, 1811–1831," *Antiques* (May 2000): 760–69 and (May 2001): 762–69; Edwin B. Burt and Fraser R. Forgie, "Clockmakers of the Concord, Massachusetts Community," *Bulletin of the National Association of Watch and Clock Collectors*, supp. (Summer 1967): 1–37; Philip Zea and Robert C. Cheney, *Clock Making in New England, 1725–1825: An Interpretation of the Old Sturbridge Village Collection*, ed. Caroline F. Sloat (Sturbridge, Mass., 1992), 29–55; Paul J. Foley, *Willard's Patent Time Pieces: A History of the Weight-Driven Banjo Clock 1800–1900* (Norwell, Mass., 2002), 75–82, quotation at 82. I am grateful to David Wood of the Concord Museum for suggesting the comparison to the Boston and Roxbury Mill Dam.

5. H&P, 350, 353–54, 360–61. For another reminiscence of the shops on the dam and in the village, see Keyes, Autobiography, 22–25.

6. H&P, 401–403; Rose Hawthorne Lathrop, *Memories of Hawthorne* (Boston, 1897), 53. The newlywed Sophia Hawthorne considered Thoreau's antics on the ice "very remarkable, but [also] very ugly."

7. Clyde A. Haulman, *Virginia and the Panic of 1819: The First Great Depression and the Commonwealth* (London, 2008), 3–37; Wood, "Concord Clockmakers," 765–68; David F. Wood, *An Observant Eye: The Thoreau Collection at the Concord Museum* (Concord, Mass., 2006), 118–19; assessment of Samuel Whiting for three ratable polls in 1826 (Whiting had married in 1819, so two of those polls, taxable males over the age of sixteen, must have been his employees); Nathan Warren (administrator) to Samuel Barrett, John Buttrick, and Jonas Buttrick, April 30, 1820, MCRD 234:1, 349:364; advertisement of gristmill for sale or rent, *CGMY*, April 9, 1825; advertisement of tanyard in Concord for sale, *Columbian Centinel*, January 15, 1825. The winning bid on Jones's real estate was made by Samuel Barrett and the brothers John and Jonas Buttrick; the first two ranked in the top tenth of taxpayers in 1820, Jonas Buttrick in the top fifth. The two brothers were sons of Concord's Revolutionary hero Maj. John Buttrick, who ordered the provincial forces to fire on the king's troops in the fateful encounter at the old North Bridge.

8. Donahue, *Great Meadow*, 186; *J* 7:445–46; Samuel Hoar, John Keyes, Nathan Brooks, and Joseph Barrett, report, committee on the sluiceway, March 3, 1823, ETR; Reuben Brown, Daniel Shattuck, and Ebenezer Hubbard, report, new committee on the sluiceway, November 11, 1825, ETR; John M. Cheney, "Memoir of Abel Moore," *SCM* 2:290; *T&R*, 15. Thoreau heard the story about the bullfrogs from Samuel Hoar and recorded the anecdote in his journal on July 31, 1855. The event took place around 1807. Ironically, the trip-hammer Jones installed soon after proved so noisy that it drove the few remaining bullfrogs away and caused a tenant in the blacksmith's brick house to seek quieter quarters.

9. Isaac Hurd and forty-four others of Concord, petition, January 1, 1826, ETR; submitted to January 7, 1826, session of Middlesex County Court of General Sessions of the Peace Record Books, January 1809–May 1831, Microfilm Reel 4, 1972, MSA; H&P, 346, 396–97. Interestingly, John Thoreau did not sign the petition, and that spring the family moved two blocks west into a house owned by Josiah Davis. The new quarters were not only roomier, they also distanced the Thoreaus from the noise and inconvenience of the several-year construction project on the milldam. See Dilts, "Henry's Houses," 6.

10. Advertisement for Daniel Shattuck & Co., *CGMY*, June 26, 1824; John S. Keyes, "Memoir of Daniel Shattuck" and "Memoir of Samuel Burr," *SCM* 2:134–40 and 209–13; E. R. Hoar, "Memoir of Isaac Hurd, M.D.," *SCM* 1:165–67; Cheney, "Memoir of Abel Moore," 287–89. Of the seven stores operating in 1826, Daniel Shattuck & Co. held the largest inventory of goods, valued at $6,500; Burr came next, with $6,000. Altogether forty-three taxpayers—storekeepers, craftsmen, and manufacturers—were assessed that year for stock in trade. Hurd's ownership of the "hotel tavern" is documented in MCRD 236:168, mortgaging several properties, including his residence and the tavern, in 1820; his title to the green and yellow stores, acquired in 1807 and 1808, was conveyed to Abel Moore and Nathan Brooks in 1829 and from them to Daniel Shattuck and John Keyes; see MCRD 289:1, 292:301. For Hurd's ownership of the Bigelow tavern, see MCRD 288:141. Politically, Burr, Keyes, and Moore had been Republicans, Hurd, Shattuck, and Whiting Federalists. Cyrus Stow entered politics in 1831 as a Jacksonian Democrat. All were loyal supporters of the First Parish, though by the mid-1820s only Hurd had formally joined the church. Whiting affiliated in 1830. The associates in the milldam project could be seen as representative figures of the "first generation of Americans" born after the Revolution, as portrayed by Joyce O. Appleby, *Inheriting the Revolution: The First Generation of Americans* (Cambridge, Mass., 2000).

11. The sales of the gristmill, blacksmith shop, and water privilege are documented in deeds dated March 11 and 13, 1826 (MCRD 349:364, 365); the two lists of subscribers to the fund for purchasing the gristmill and water privileges from Samuel Burr and others are dated March 13 and 15, 1826, Winnifred Sturdy Collection of papers and records connected primarily with Concord, Mass., 1663–1951, Box 2, Folder 56, CFPL. The replacement of the sluiceway can be followed through the reports of the 1823 and 1825 sluiceway committees (see note 8); minutes of town meetings in 1823 and 1825, CTMM 7:185, 189, 245, 274, CFPL; and the "memorandum of an agreement" made between Abel Moore of Concord and Jesse Stone of Stow, dated September 7, 1826, for opening a sluiceway across the milldam, Josiah Davis estate, Nathan Brooks Papers, Estate files, Box 9, Folder 5, CFPL. For the transfer of the water right by the milldam associates, see the deed dated August 14, 1826, MCRD 349:370, and the contract for executing that instrument made twelve days later, August 26, 1826, CFPL. Originally twenty-seven persons pledged $425 to acquire and extinguish "the right of flowing." Included in that group were Moore, Shattuck, and the Stow brothers. But apparently not everyone fulfilled his subscription, since only thirteen individuals were grantees of the water right. Or the milldam associates decided to act philanthropically and abandon their title for a token sum. See the two lists of subscribers to the fund for purchasing the water privilege in the Winnifred Sturdy Collection, CFPL.

12. Report of Middlesex County commissioners' decision to widen the "mill dam street," YG, May 26, 1827; "Hats! Hats!," advertisement of Comfort Foster, YG, November 12, 1831; advertisement of Emerson Melven, YG, June 16, 1827; Daniel Shattuck and Abel Moore, report, committee to erect block of buildings on south side of milldam, April 10, 1837, Concord Mill Dam Co. Records, 1826–1854 ("industrious mechanic"); Concord Historical Commission, Survey of Historical and Architectural Resources, Concord, Mass., 4 vols. (Concord, Mass., 2002), entries for buildings at 42–44, 36–40, 29, and 23–25 Main Street. For the restrictions of manufacturing on the milldam, see the deeds from Daniel and Sarah Shattuck to the Middlesex Institute for Savings and Concord Bank, December 8, 1836, MCRD 348:424; and from Mill Dam Company to Daniel Shattuck, January 12, 1844, Winnifred Sturdy Collection, CFPL. The widening of the road across the milldam necessitated taking the old gristmill by eminent domain. In compensation, the proprietors received $200 in damages from the county commissioners. In his recollections of life in Concord during the early republic, Jarvis surmised that the spur to the milldam project was the 1827 decision to widen the road on the north side by twenty-six feet—an action requiring the removal of the structures along the route. But that decision, made in response to a petition from Concord merchant Josiah Davis and other inhabitants (unfortunately, the document no longer survives, so we don't know their names), was announced in May 1827, more than a year after Hurd and associates made the agreement to transfer the water right to their neighbors, and the actual work of extending the highway did not begin until the spring of 1828. See H&P, 396–97; Middlesex County Court of General Sessions of the Peace Record Books, January 1809–May 1831, Microfilm Reel 4, MSA.

13. Burr and Moore took the lead in buying up the land and shops along the milldam. Heywood ran the insurance company from its organization in 1826 until shortly before his death thirteen years later. Shattuck served as president of the bank for its first two decades from 1832 to 1852, Brooks as head of the Middlesex Institution for Savings at its incorporation in 1835. Keyes sat on nearly every board.

14. Concord Historical Commission, Survey, entry for 46/48 Main Street; YG, July 21,

1832; Abiel Heywood, Nathan Brooks, William Munroe, Abel Moore, Lemuel Shattuck, and Rufus Hosmer, petition for a bank in Concord, January 17, 1832, file papers for chap. 82, 1831–1832 legislative session, Massachusetts General Court, MSA; Naomi R. Lamoreaux, *Insider Lending: Banks, Personal Connections, and Economic Development in Industrial New England* (New York, 1994), 80–83; *YG*, June 9, 1827, June 27, 1829; "An Act to Incorporate the Middlesex Mutual Fire Insurance Company," *Private and Special Statutes of the Commonwealth of Massachusetts, From May 1822, to March 1830* (Boston, 1837), 6:419–23; "An Act to Incorporate the Concord Mill Dam Company," February 28, 1829, chap. 105, *Laws of the Commonwealth of Massachusetts, Passed at the Several Sessions of the General Court, Beginning May, 1828, and Ending March, 1831* (Boston, 1831), 11:1743–75; "An Act to Incorporate the President, Directors, and Company of the Concord Bank," *Private and Special Statutes of the Commonwealth of Massachusetts, From May 1830, to April 1837* (Boston, 1837), 7:218–19; "An Act to Establish an Institution for Savings in Concord," *Private and Special Statutes*, 7:497. Keyes did not join the board of the savings bank. The original stockholders in the Mill Dam Company were Shattuck, Keyes, Brooks, Moore, and Cyrus Stow, each investor paying $1,000 for ten shares in the firm. By the time the company was organized in August 1835, two of the initial participants (Burr and Nathan Stow) were dead, and two (Hurd and Whiting) had dropped out. See Agreement to purchase shares in the Concord Mill Dam Company, undated document signed between January 1832 and August 1835, CAS Papers, D-2068.19, CFPL. For a view of the merchant class in Northampton, a county seat similar to Concord, see Gregory Nobles, "The Rise of Merchants in Rural Market Towns: A Case Study of Eighteenth-Century Northampton, Massachusetts," *Journal of Social History* 24 (Autumn 1990): 5–23.

15. H&P, 260–61; Shattuck, *History*, 92, 104; Woden Teachout, *Capture the Flag: A Political History of American Patriotism* (New York, 2009), 26.

16. H&P, 292–93; *YG*, June 6, 1829; Ornamental Tree Society Records, 1833–37 (typescript), CFPL; graveyard committee (Atwill, Shattuck, and Dr. Josiah Bartlett), report, March 5, 1832, CTMM 7:416, 421–23, CFPL; Leslie Perrin Wilson, *In History's Embrace: Past and Present in Concord, Massachusetts* (Hollis, N.H., 2007), 33–37. According to John S. Keyes, shade trees were not planted around the village square until 1851, when he became superintendent of public grounds. But the records of the ornamental tree society indicate that in March 1834 Cyrus Warren was directed by the group to "procure and set out a sufficient number of elms, and sycamore trees, in the public Square in the centre of the town." See Keyes, Autobiography, 119; meeting of March 1834, Ornamental Tree Society Records, CFPL.

17. "Ornamental Tree Society," *New-Bedford Mercury*, October 24, 1834 (reprinting account in the *Boston Advertiser*); "Shade Trees," *Bunker-Hill Aurora*, April 23, 1836; Wood, *New England Village*, 119–47; Joseph A. Conforti, *Imagining New England: Explorations of Regional Identity from the Pilgrims to the Mid-Twentieth Century* (Chapel Hill, N.C., 2001), 124–50; Ornamental Tree Society, report of October 13, 1836, Ornamental Tree Society Records (typescript), CFPL.

18. Robert A. Gross, "The Celestial Village: Transcendentalism and Tourism in Concord," in Conrad E. Wright and Charles Capper, eds., *Transient and Permanent: The Transcendentalist Movement and Its Contexts* (Boston, 1999), 251–81; Middlesex, "Monument at Concord," no. 3, *YG*, March 18, 1826.

19. Middlesex, "Monument at Concord," *YG*, March 18, 1826.

20. Ibid., March 25, 1826.

21. See the wonderfully titled *A History of the Fight at Concord, on the 19th of April, 1775, with a Particular Account of the Military Operations and Interesting Events of That Ever Memorable Day; Showing that Then and There the First Regular and Forcible Resistance Was Made to the British Soldiery, and the First British Blood Was Shed by Armed Americans, and the Revolutionary War Thus Commenced. By Ezra Ripley, with Other Citizens of Concord* (Concord, Mass., 1827). Ripley had good reason to hide behind a pseudonym. The Trinitarian separation was under way, and it made sense to be discreet. Besides, he was vulnerable to the charge of bad faith. For who had urged the abandonment of the North Bridge so many years before? Who had cut off public access to the site where the Redcoats met their match? And who was now urging the erection of a monument conveniently across the river, on land owned by somebody else? The parson wisely conformed to the conventions of newspaper discourse and kept his name out of print.

22. John Shepard Keyes, "Reminiscences," 2, CFPL; *YG*, May 7, 1831.

23. Shattuck, *History*, 211, 217–18; John G. Hales, surveyor, *Plan of the Town of Concord, Mass. In the County of Massachusetts* (Boston, 1830); *Documents relative to the Manufactures in the United States, Collected and Transmitted to the House of Representatives*, 2 vols. (1833; rpt. New York, 1969), 1:308; Elijah Wood, Jr., "Memoir of Elijah Wood," *SCM* 2:194–200. The 1820 census reported the number of persons in each household employed in Concord's three main branches of economic activity: 262 in agriculture, 16 in commerce, 140 in manufactures. It is evident from the manuscript returns that for the assistant marshal enumerating Concord's population, only male "persons" counted. Ephraim H. Bellows, who operated the cotton factory, was listed as heading two separate households, one with 26 inmates, 15 of whom were women between sixteen and twenty-five. They were clearly laboring in the factory. Only two persons in this household were said to be engaged in manufactures. On this reading, the census reports a male labor force of 418. This number appears consistent with the evidence of the 1820 town tax list, which encompassed 347 individuals. Few men under eighteen ever paid taxes in their own name; they were charged as ratable polls to the account of their father or employer. In 1850, in the federal census for Concord, 118 men were between sixteen and twenty; they accounted for nearly 15 percent (14.8) of all males sixteen and over. Applying that proportion to the number of male taxpayers in 1820 yields an estimate of 52 men ages sixteen to twenty omitted from the list. The result gives an estimate of 399 males, close to the 418 men in the 1820 labor force.

24. Laurence Eaton Richardson, *Concord River* (Barre, Mass., 1964), 38–39, 41, 74; Shattuck, *History*, 197–201; Nathan M. Whitney, Jr.'s, account of the cotton factory in Concord, based on report by Ephraim Bellows, agent, "Schedule of the 1820 Census of Manufacturing for Maine, Massachusetts, New Hampshire and Rhode Island," Records of the Bureau of the Census, Record Group no. 29, National Archives; William R. Bagnall, *The Textile Industries of the United States Including Sketches and Notices of Cotton, Woolen, Silk, and Linen Manufactures in the Colonial Period*, vol. 1, *1639–1810* (Cambridge, Mass., 1893), 552–56; Ephraim Hartwell and John Brown, petition, Senate Unpassed Legislation 1809, no. 3922, MSA. Hartwell and Brown proclaimed their public-spirited purpose in a petition to the Massachusetts legislature seeking a tax exemption for their infant enterprise. They were unsuccessful.

25. Advertisement for "Cotton Factory at Auction," *MO*, June 14, 1823, and *Columbian Centinel*, June 21, 1823; Charles Hammond, "Concord's 'Factory Village': 1776–1862," *Old-Time New England* 66 (Summer-Fall 1975): 32–33; inventory of "the

property of the late firm of Hartwell Brown & Co.," September 4, 1816, Ephraim Hartwell estate, Nathan Brooks Papers, Series 1 (Estate Papers), Box 10, Folder 7, CFPL; "Schedule of the 1820 Census of Manufacturing"; Caroline F. Ware, *The Early New England Cotton Manufacture: A Study in Industrial Beginnings* (1931; rpt. New York, 1966), 22–28. The $25,000 investment in 1820 was equivalent to well over half a million dollars ($553,000) in 2019 values. I am grateful to Andrian Paquette, curator at the Slater Mill in Pawtucket, R.I., for his guidance in understanding the organization of the Concord mill and of the process of cotton manufacturing more generally. Based on an 1834 survey of the "Cotton Factory establishment situated in the westerly part of Concord" (38n7), which is no longer available to researchers, Hammond describes the cotton factory as a five-story building (including the basement). This account is at odds with the details set forth when the factory was put up for auction in the spring of 1823. It is possible that the structure gained an additional story when the power looms were installed or when James Derby carried out a massive renovation in 1834, in preparation for converting the factory into an enterprise for producing *not* textiles themselves but rather the machines necessary for spinning and weaving cotton and woolen cloth.

26. Ware, *Early New England Cotton Manufacture*, 29–30, 60–66; Jonathan Prude, *The Coming of Industrial Order: Town and Factory Life in Rural Massachusetts, 1810–1860* (New York, 1983), 35–37, 84–89; J. W. Lozier, "The Forgotten Industry: Small and Medium Sized Cotton Mills South of Boston," *Working Papers from the Regional Economic History Research Center* 2, no. 4 (1979): 112–18; federal census of Concord, 1810 (households of "Hartwell & Brown" and of Roger Brown); "Schedule of the 1820 Census of Manufacturing"; 1820 federal census of population for Concord (household of Ephraim H. Bellows). The new superintendent of the works, Bellows, told the assistant marshal of the U.S. census that the factory relied chiefly on child labor for its operations. Of its twenty-eight employees, six were men, two women; "boys and girls" made up the rest. Such a labor force was characteristic of a yarn mill. But the actual enumeration of inhabitants on the 1820 population census offers a more complicated picture. In that year Bellows was listed as the head of two households, one consisting of his immediate family (wife Sarah and ten-month-old son Benjamin Franklin Bellows), along with one male and one female between ages sixteen and twenty-five, and a second embracing the employees of the cotton factory. Twenty-six people lived in this boardinghouse: four males, twenty-two females. One male was a youth between ages sixteen and twenty-five; three ranged from twenty-six to forty-four. Of the females, six were girls between ten and fifteen; fifteen were young women between sixteen and twenty-five, and one a woman between twenty-six and forty-four. H&P, 35–39. If the laborers for Hartwell & Brown were anything like those at Slater's factories in Dudley and Oxford, Mass., they stuck around for no more than twelve or eighteen months. No payroll books or other records exist to identify the youthful operatives of Concord and chart their movements in and out of town. From 1816 to the mid-1830s, the cotton factory was noticed in the local press only when it was advertised for sale in the legal notices.

27. Mrs. Emily R. Barnes, *Narratives, Traditions, and Personal Reminiscences Connected with the Early History of the Bellows Family and of the Village of Walpole, New Hampshire* (Boston, 1888); John Brown and Ephraim Hartwell to Ephraim Hartwell Bellows, February 19, 1813, MCRD 208:211; notice of dissolution of Hartwell, Brown & Co. and of succeeding business, Eph. H. Bellows & Co., *MG*, July 19, 1817; announcement of co-partnership of Lord and Parks in *Boston Commercial Gazette*, March 11, 1824, in which they advertise for sale "unbleached Shirtings and Sheetings," ginghams,

stripes, checks, tickings, yarns, and threads—all goods manufactured by Bellows; S.V.S. Wilder to James C. Dunn, Esq. (treasurer), Ware, Mass., July 26, 1827, Ware Manufacturing Company Letterbook, American Textile History Museum, Lowell, Mass., quoted in Hammond,"Concord's 'Factory Village,'" 35; "An Act to Incorporate the Concord Manufacturing Company," chap. 7, *Laws of the Commonwealth of Massachusetts, Passed at the Several Sessions of the General Court, At their Session Which Commenced on Wednesday, the Fourth of January, and Ended on Saturday, the Twenty-Fourth of March, One Thousand Eight Hundred and Thirty-Two* (Boston, 1832), 179–80.

28. *Documents relative to the Manufactures in the United States*, 1:328; Advertisement for "3 or 4 good weavers," YG, May 30, 1829; Ephraim H. Bellows to Parks and Lord, April 14, 1831, MCRD 306:289; Shattuck, *History*, 217; list of goods attached by Abel Moore according to writ issued April 1826, in *Lord and Parks v. Bellows*, Middlesex County Court of Common Pleas, File Papers—October 1826, Continued Actions, no. 569, MSA. Of the textiles in the cotton factory attached by Lord and Parks in April 1826, shirting made up the single largest category, accounting for more than half (2,027 out of 3,694 yards). Common gingham ranked second (441 yards), followed by stripes (315 yards).

29. Robert A. Gross, "Culture and Cultivation: Agriculture and Society in Thoreau's Concord," *Journal of American History* 69 (June 1982): 42–61; Stephen F. Ells, "Henry Thoreau and the Estabrook Country: A Historic and Personal Landscape," *Concord Saunterer*, n.s., 4 (Fall 1996): 73–150; John Hanson Mitchell, *Walking Towards Walden: A Pilgrimage in Search of Place* (Reading, Mass., 1995), 200 ("five to ten square miles depending on who makes the depiction"); Edmund A. Schofield, "The Ecology of Walden Woods," in Edmund A. Schofield and Robert C. Baron, eds., *Thoreau's World and Ours: A Natural Legacy* (Golden, Colo., 1993), 155–71; Elise Lemire, *Black Walden: Slavery and Its Aftermath in Concord, Massachusetts* (Philadelphia, 2009). On the eve of the Revolution, 80 percent of Concord's improved land was in meadow and pastures; by 1821 that figure had risen to 87 percent. Woodland slowly declined to a quarter and then a fifth of all acreage, before plummeting over the decade of the 1820s to just 13.6 percent, in a continuing retreat to a mere 10 percent by 1850.

30. Schofield, "Ecology of Walden Woods," 158–59, 162–63.

31. Joanne Pope Melish, *Disowning Slavery: Gradual Emancipation and "Race" in New England, 1780–1860* (Ithaca, N.Y., 1998), 17–21; Shattuck, *History*, 211; Jackson Turner Main, *Society and Economy in Colonial Connecticut* (Princeton, N.J., 1985), 130. The 1749 valuation of Concord lists nineteen slave owners holding twenty-three "Indian, negro and molatto servants, whether for life or for a term of years." Two decades later the province ordered a new valuation of property in the towns. By then Concord had lost both territory and prominent citizens, including the royal judge Chambers Russell, to the new town of Lincoln. Not surprisingly, then, the figures are lower for 1771: twelve slave owners and fifteen slaves. But these reports require corrections to come up with reliable estimates. For one thing, ministers were exempt from taxation, so the slaveholdings of Rev. Daniel Bliss in 1749 and his successor William Emerson in 1771 need to be added to the totals. More important, the valuation law for 1749 called for the listing of "*all* Indian, negro, and molatto servants" for life; the 1771 law restricted the count to "all Indian, negro or molatto servants for life" in the prime ages for productive labor (fourteen to forty-five years old). Supplementing the information in the valuation lists with evidence from the record of births, marriages, and deaths in Concord, Elise Lemire estimates that thirty-two persons were held in slavery on the eve of the war. For various reasons— duplication of names, a couple oversights, and inclusion of several decedents—I

have adjusted Lemire's figures and come up with twenty-five or twenty-six slaves in Concord in the early 1770s. This number accords with the reported Black population on the 1765 colonial census: 27; see Oliver Warner, *Abstract of the Census of Massachusetts, 1865* (Boston, 1867), 228. On these bases, I conclude that slavery was essentially stagnant in Concord and environs in the generation before the Revolution (1750–1775). This finding squares with what we know about the Black population of Boston: in 1742, about 1,500 Blacks lived in the capital; twelve years later officials counted some 1,350 Black adults in Boston and surrounding Suffolk County. By 1775 that number had dwindled to fewer than 700. For the valuation laws, see Ellis Ames et al., *The Acts and Resolves, Public and Private, of the Province of the Massachusetts Bay*, 21 vols. (Boston, 1869–1922), 3:425–26 (1749 act); 5:156–59 (1771 act). Lemire's enumeration of enslaved individuals in Concord is set forth in *Black Walden*, 9, 185–86n13. The stagnation of Boston's Black population can be traced in William D. Piersen, *Black Yankees: The Development of an Afro-American Subculture in Eighteenth-Century New England* (Amherst, Mass., 1988), 15, and James Oliver Horton and Lois E. Horton, *Black Bostonians: Family Life and Community Struggle in the Antebellum North*, rev. ed. (1979; rpt. New York, 1999), xiv, xvii.

32. Melish, *Disowning Slavery*, 95–96; Gross, *Minutemen*, 94–98, 151–52; Lemire, *Black Walden*, 98–99, 103; John D. Cushing, "The Cushing Court and the Abolition of Slavery in Massachusetts: More Notes on the 'Quock Walker Case,'" *American Journal of Legal History* 5 (April 1961): 118–44, quotation at 133; Thomas J. Davis, "Emancipation Rhetoric, Natural Rights, and Revolutionary New England: A Note on Four Black Petitions in Massachusetts, 1773–1777," *New England Quarterly* 62 (June 1989): 248–63. Information about Black soldiers enlisting from Concord can be found in George Quintal, Jr., *Patriots of Color: "A Peculiar Beauty and Merit"* (Boston, 2004).

33. Melish, *Disowning Slavery*, 53, 80–83; "An Act for the Orderly Solemnization of Marriages," 1786, chap. 3; "An Act to Prevent the Slave Trade, and for Granting Relief to the Families of Such Unhappy Persons as May Be Kidnapped or Decoyed Away from This Commonwealth," 1787, chap. 48; and "An Act for Suppressing and Punishing of Rogues, Vagabonds, Common Beggars, and Other Idle, Disorderly and Lewd Persons," 1787, chap. 54, all in *Acts and Laws of the Commonwealth of Massachusetts*, 13 vols. (Boston, 1890–1898), 4:7–11, 5:615–17, 623–26; George Henry Moore, *Notes on the History of Slavery in Massachusetts* (New York, 1866), 246. The ban against foreigners of color exempted subjects of the Kingdom of Morocco from its restrictions. In September 1800 the town of Boston set out to enforce the law against undocumented Black immigrants. On September 16, 1800, the *Massachusetts Mercury* published a long list of allegedly illegal inhabitants from up and down the Atlantic coast, starting in Halifax, stopping in New York, Philadelphia, and Baltimore, going down to the Carolinas, then into the Caribbean, across the ocean to England and France, and ending in the Ile de France (now Mauritius) and Africa, and warned them to depart or suffer the consequences of the law. The "Notice to Blacks" appeared over the signature of Charles Bulfinch, the noted architect who was also superintendent of Boston's House of Correction. See Moore, *Notes on Slavery in Massachusetts*, 231.

34. Lemire, *Black Walden*, 118–19, 122–27, 148–49, 151–52; administration of estate of Charles Russell, physician, 1777, File no. 19593, MCPR; Last will and testament of John Cuming, January 10, 1782, File no. 5430, MCPR. According to Lemire, two former slaves of the Russell estate—Zilpah and her supposed brother

Bristo (i.e., Brister Freeman)—took up residence in the Walden woods. But this supposed kinship is implausible. Zilpah White, who lived on her own along the Great County Road, came to Concord from the Worcester County town of Spencer, as Ezra Ripley noted in the church record of her death at age eighty-two on April 16, 1820; see *CBMD*, 336. This origin was independently confirmed in 1860 by a local historian of Spencer who remarked that "a female slave, named Zilpah," was once owned by John White, Sr., of that town. James Draper, *History of Spencer, Massachusetts, from Its Earliest Settlement to the Year 1860* (Leicester, Mass., 1860), 131. If Zilpah had not grown up on the Russell estate in Lincoln, there is no reason to think that Brister Freeman was her brother. In 1777, after the Loyalist doctor Charles Russell fled Lincoln for safety on the island of Antigua, legal measures were taken to confiscate his estate. A committee made an extensive inventory of his property in March 1778; it listed no slaves. But Black dependents were evidently still on the place, since in July of that year the committee spent £5.8.0 for two yards of linen to clothe a "Negro."

35. Lorenzo Johnston Greene, *The Negro in Colonial New England* (1942; rpt. New York., 1974), 192–95; Melish, *Disowning Slavery*, 129; Jack Larkin, "Counting People of Color: Worcester County, Massachusetts 1790–1860. A Preliminary Report" for Old Sturbridge Village (2002), accessible at resources.osv.org/explore_learn/document _viewer.php?Action=View&DocID=1943; Lemire, *Black Walden*, 3, 153–57; Gross, *Minutemen*, 187; *MG*, April 22, 1820 (obituary of Zilpah White); *Walden*, 256–58. The proportion of Blacks living in households headed by an African American went from 65 percent (19 out of 29) in 1790 and 60 percent (23 out of 38) in 1800 to 68 percent (19 out of 28) in 1810, 70 percent (24 out of 34) in 1820, and 76 percent (22 out of 29) in 1830. Concord was at the forefront of the movement to independent Black households in rural communities. In 1830 only one in four townspeople of color lived with a white "family"; in Worcester County, one in three. The 1820 census of Concord shows eight out of nine "free colored" males under age fourteen living in a Black-headed household, but only two out of five such males between fourteen and fifteen doing the same; the two young women of color (14 to 25) remained in Black families. Altogether, two-thirds (12 out of 18) of Concord's African American youths resided in households headed by a racial compatriot. By contrast, in Worcester County "through 1830 well over half of all older girls and boys, young men and women of color, were living as dependents in households not their own, under the economic and social control of whites." Larkin, "Counting People of Color," 12.

36. *MG*, April 22, 1820; Lemire, *Black Walden*, 156–71; *Walden*, 264.

37. In 1800 the Black population of Concord peaked at 2.3 percent (38 out of 1,679), fell to 1.9 percent in 1820 (34 out of 1,788), then slipped to 1.3–1.4 percent in the next three censuses (1830: 28 out of 2,017; 1840: 23 out of 1,785; 1850: 33 out of 2,249). For the state as a whole, the comparable figures are 1830: 1.2 percent; 1840: 1.2 percent; 1850: 1.0 percent.

38. Horton and Horton, *Black Bostonians*, 2–4; George A. Levesque, *Black Boston: African American Life and Culture in Urban America, 1750–1860* (New York, 1994), 23–34. The figures reported in *Black Bostonians* do not all square with the tabulation made in 1865 "under the direction" of the secretary of the Commonwealth Oliver Warner (*Abstract of the Census*, 198, 231). I have recalculated the Black proportions of Boston's population from Warner's summaries. The results are as follows: 1790: 4.2 percent (766 out of 18,320); 1800: 4.7 percent (1,174 out of 24,937); 1810: 4.3 percent (1,468 out of 33,787); 1820: 3.9 percent (1,690 out of 43,298); 1830: 3.0 percent (1,875 out

of 61,392); 1840: 2.6 percent (2,427 out of 93,383); 1850: 1.5 percent (1,999 out of 136,881).

39. *MG*, April 18, 1818, 4. Of the ten white households with Black inmates in 1790, six were headed by men who had held slaves before 1783: Timothy Hoar, Duncan Ingraham, Dr. Joseph Lee, Capt. George Minott, Samuel Potter, and Rev. Ezra Ripley. In 1800 and 1810, Blacks were recorded in the households of innkeeper Phineas Paine and of Tilly Buttrick and Thomas Murphy, respectively. Ten years later young men of color inhabited the households of blacksmith James Jones, machinist Jesse Willis, and farmers Tilly Holden and Benjamin Hollowell (in the south quarter not too far from Thomas Dugan); in 1830 the carriage builder Isaac Thayer, blacksmith Henry H. Merrill, and clockmaker Samuel Whiting, along with Jones, included Black inmates in their homes.

40. *MG*, April 18, 1818; obituary of Thomas Dugan, *YG*, May 12, 1827; inventory of the real and personal estate of Thomas Dugan, December 3, 1827, File no. 6495, MCPR; Robert A. Gross, "From Southern Slave to Yankee Farmer," *Concord Journal*, June 11, 2015.

41. *J* 9:213 (entry for January 11, 1857); Sidney Perley, *Historic Storms of New England* (Salem, Mass., 1891), 180. On the 1810 federal census of Concord, eight people were recorded in the household of Jonas Minot. The census gives the name of the head of household; all other "inmates" are recorded only by sex and age. But it is easy to figure out that Jonas and his wife Mary Jones Dunbar Minot were there, along with Cynthia and Louisa Dunbar. One boy under age nine was in the household— probably Jonas's grandson, orphaned the year before by the death of his father, Jonas, Jr. Another youth, between ages ten and fifteen, was there, but it is unclear who he might have been. The other two unnamed individuals in the household were counted in the category "the number of all other free persons." I infer that Jack Garrison was one, perhaps the Esther whom Cynthia Thoreau recalled the other. New Jersey's 1804 gradual emancipation law applied to children born after its passage and did not release them from bondage until after long terms of service. It did nothing for enslaved men like Jack Garrison, who was thirty-five years old when the statute was passed. (At his death in September 1860 Garrison was said to be ninety-one and hence born in 1769. The 1850 census confirms this; on that record, his age is given as eighty-two, hence he was born in 1768, though his birthplace was stated incorrectly as Virginia.) See Melish, *Disowning Slavery*, 224–25.

42. 1798 Direct Tax of Massachusetts and Maine, NEHGS database; Nathan Brooks, "Memoir of Humphrey Barrett," *SCM* 1:64. John Hannigan, Curator at MSA, found the name of "Cezar, a Negro," on the roll of a company of volunteers raised by Capt. Thomas Penniman for service in the French and Indian War. Dated February 7, 1761, the document gives the residence of Cezar as Chelmsford; under the column for "parents or masters of servants," the name "John Robings, master," appears. Caesar would be associated with this Robbins family for several decades. His enslaver, John Robbins, was born in Chelmsford in 1710, the son of John and Dorothy (Hildreth) Robbins. He wed Susannah Harwood of Chelmsford in 1736, and among their children was Susannah, born on December 30, 1760, not long after sixteen-year-old Caesar returned from six months at war. Susannah Robbins, in turn, married Israel Heald of Acton, in whose militia company Caesar served for six days in March 1776, participating in the maneuvers in Roxbury that drove the king's troops from Boston. These connections allow the identification of Caesar as the bondsman of John Robbins and the estimation of his year of birth as 1745. (He died on May 19, 1822, at seventy-six; *CBMD*, 340.) He was one of the few soldiers of African de-

scent to serve both in the French and Indian War and in the War of Independence. Following his brief service in Roxbury, he went on to serve in a company led by Capt. Zechariah Fitch (a native of Bedford) that marched to Bennington, Vermont, in late August 1776, only to find that a rumored attack by British regulars was not happening; the Middlesex company arrived ten months too soon. By September 30, the troops were back home, and Caesar's enlistment was over. Among his fellow soldiers in Fitch's company was "Bristol Cummings," the former bondsman of John Cuming, who would later change his name to Brister Freeman. See 1760 muster and pay roll of Captain Thomas Penniman's company, v. 98, 292, Massachusetts Archives Collection, MSA; *Massachusetts Soldiers and Sailors of the Revolutionary War: A Compilation from the Archives* 17 vols. (Boston, 1896–1908), 3: 218; 13: 373; Samuel A. Green, *Groton During the Revolution* (Groton, Mass., 1900), 61–63.

With his military service at an end, Caesar moved to Concord by 1779; he married Catherine Boaz on December 16 of that year, with Ezra Ripley officiating. Twenty years later he appeared on the 1798 Direct Tax as the owner of a house and two acres of land. His property was not far from a ninety-eight-acre plot owned by George Robbins and a thirty-two-acre piece owned by Dorothy Robbins, both of Acton. George was the younger brother of Acton's Capt. Joseph Robbins, and Dorothy their widowed mother. Their father, Nathan Robbins, and Caesar's master, John Robbins, were cousins. It seems likely that Caesar obtained his acreage in Concord with assistance from the Robbins family. He was, after all, a newcomer, without established connections. In time, Humphrey Barrett would become a patron of the Robbins family, but probably not right away. I am grateful to John Hannigan for sharing his ingenious tracking of Caesar Robbins's paper trail.

43. *JMN* 4:363; Nathan Barrett (grantor) to Martha Keyes (grantee), deed, March 4, 1863, transferring eight acres of meadowland bounded by "a lane leading to Caesar's Woods so called," in Keyes Family Deeds, CFPL; Humphrey Barrett, yeoman of Concord, to Peter Robbins, laborer of Concord, April 16, 1823, MCRD 248:376. The reservation of the easterly half of the house for Susan Garrison and her family was later recorded by Nathan Brooks as he worked on the Peter Robbins estate; see Nathan Brooks Papers, Series 1 (Estate Papers, 1666–1864), Box 17, Folder 9, CFPL.

44. Lawrence Sorli, "Description of Robbins-Hutchinson House," a 2013 report on the architectural restoration of the property for the Drinking Gourd Project, Concord, Mass.; inventory of the Real and Personal Estate of Thomas Dugan, December 3, 1827, File no. 6495, MCPR. Peter Robbins was assessed for a house, barn, and six acres of improved land, valued at $333, and eight acres of unimproved land, worth $64 on the 1827 assessment list.

45. H&P, 188–90; John Shepard Keyes, "Houses and Owners or Occupants in Concord 1885," 54–55, CFPL; Nathan Brooks, Household account book, 1836–63, entries for April 26, June 18, 1836, and June 9, September 18, 1846, Nathan Brooks Papers, CFPL; Ralph Waldo Emerson, Account Book, 1836–40, entries throughout 1836 and 1837, in collection of Emerson's Journals and Notebooks, 1820–1880, bMs Am 1280H, Houghton. I am grateful to Joel Myerson for providing his transcriptions of the Emerson account books.

46. Meetings of October 24, November 2, 1828, Trinitarian Congregational Church Records, 1826–67; Brooks, Household account book, entries for January 18, 1839, October 1, 1840, September 21–22, 1841, October 12, 1848; Timothy Prescott, Diary, April 1, 1830, to April 12, 1840, Houghton; Leslie Perrin Wilson, ed., "'Treasure in My Own Mind': The Diary of Martha Lawrence Prescott, 1834–1836," *Concord*

Saunterer, n.s., 11 (2003): 127. Two days after that visit, Martha Prescott would celebrate her eighteenth birthday.

47. Gross, *Minutemen*, 95–98, 187; George Tolman, *John Jack, the Slave, and Daniel Bliss, the Tory* (Concord, Mass., 1902); *CF*, June 20, 1835; Melish, *Disowning Slavery*, 210–37. For reprints of the epitaph for John Jack, see *Herald of Freedom*, August 14, 1789; *Independent Chronicle* (Boston), May 19, 1791; *Rural Repository*, September 15, 1796 ("Ingenious Epitaph"); *Philadelphia Minerva*, September 17, 1796; *Weekly Visitant: Moral, Poetical, Humorous, &c.*, August 2, 1806; *American Citizen*, March 25, 1807; *Boston Intelligencer*, June 20, 1818; *Berks and Schuylkill Journal*, July 18, 1818; *American* (New York), June 30, 1819, reprinting the item from *MG*; *New-York Commercial Advertiser*, July 27, 1819; *Rhode-Island American*, August 13, 1819; *Centinel of Freedom*, July 4, 1820; *Saratoga Sentinel*, October 7, 1823.

48. Gross, "Culture and Cultivation," 44, 56.

49. Wood, *New England Village*, 119–34; Robert A. Gross, "Transcendentalism and Urbanism: Concord, Boston, and the Wider World," *Journal of American Studies* 18 (1984): 369–71; *YG*, December 30, 1826; Shattuck, *History*, 218. My estimate of the share of the population encompassed within the center school district is based on an analysis of the 1830 federal census of Concord. The assistant marshal who enumerated the population clearly went door to door in the different neighborhoods of the town, and it is possible to discern the various districts in his manuscript return. Unfortunately, he was not as systematic as a later historian would wish, particularly with regard to the inhabitants of the village, some of whom are intermingled with townspeople in other sections. Using additional sources, such as the unpublished 1830 directory, I have been successful in assigning most heads of household to their appropriate school district. My calculation is confirmed by "Concord Directory, containing the names of the legal voters and householders in town with the occupations, offices, etc. for the year 1830," NEHGS. This listing shows 152 out of 321 people living in the town center—47 percent of the whole. Nineteen of the top twenty estate holders on the 1826 assessment list had homes within a mile of the meetinghouse. A different gauge of the distribution of wealth by section of town comes from the report of the town school committee in May 1831. It reported that the center school district paid 54 percent of the town tax. See school committee report, May 11, 1831, CTMM 7:397, 405–10, CFPL.

50. Gay Wilson Allen, *Waldo Emerson: A Biography* (New York, 1981), 250–51; Raymond R. Borst, *The Thoreau Log: A Documentary Life of Henry David Thoreau, 1817–1862* (New York, 1992), 108–9, 514; *TJHM* 11:436–37.

51. Gross, "Transcendentalism and Urbanism," 361–81. In 1815 more than half of 328 male taxpayers (56.4 percent) were Concord natives; the comparable figure in 1826 was 43 percent (395 taxpayers) and 35.5 percent in 1835 (470 taxpayers). I have treated all taxpayers whose origins are unknown as newcomers to the town. The turnover of the laboring class is evident from the low persistence rate of men in the bottom fifth of taxpayers: only three out of ten (31.7 percent) persisted between 1826 and 1835 (N = 82). By contrast, 85 percent of men in the top fifth of taxpayers stayed put. The richer the taxpayer, the higher the persistence rate. It appears that most of the transients came and went within five years. Between 1835 and 1840 it was again the case that only three out of ten men (30.8 percent) in the bottom quintile of taxpayers remained in town; nine out of ten men in the top fifth remained in place. (The relation between wealth and mobility is statistically significant; p = .000.)

52. Shattuck, *History*, 205; waybills for the Concord Mail Stage and other stage lines, 1823–1843, CFPL; *The Boston Directory; Containing Names of the Inhabitants; Their Occu-*

pations, Places of Business and Dwelling Houses (Boston, 1825), 18–23; *The Massachusetts Register, and United States Calendar, for the Year of Our Lord 1826* (Boston, 1825), 238–39; John S. Keyes, "Memoir of William Shepherd," *SCM* 2:356–63, quotation at 360.

53. *CGMY*, May 14, 1825; William S. Robinson (Concord) to Jeremiah A. Robinson (Lowell), April 28, 1833, Robinson Shattuck Papers, Reel 2, Schlesinger Library, Harvard University; entry for Sleepy Hollow Cemetery, Concord Historical Commission, *Survey*, 3; reports of Middlesex cattle fair in *YG*; *Massachusetts Register, and United States Calendar, for the Year of Our Lord 1830* (Boston, 1829), 33–35; Joseph Hosmer, "Concord in Ye Olden Time," Adams Tolman Newspaper Scrapbook Collection, CFPL; J. K. Hosmer et al., *Memorial of George Washington Hosmer, D.D., edited by his Children* (n.p., 1882), 34; Keyes, "Middlesex Hotel," 10–11; *YG*, April 28, 1827; *Ninth Annual Report of the Board of Managers of the Prison Discipline Society, Boston, May 27, 1834* (Boston, 1834), 34; "Rogues" [report of three thieves in Concord], *YG*, July 4, 1829, July 3, 1830.

54. Gross, *Minutemen*, 7, 39–40, 175–76; Shattuck, *History*, 144–47; various Middlesex towns, petitions regarding the location of county courts, Senate Unpassed Legislation, February 1813–January 1814, File nos. 4777, 4998, 4999, MSA. In January 1812 the town chose Federalists Samuel Hoar, Jr., and Joseph Barrett, along with Republican Jonas Lee, to draft a petition to the legislature. After that petition was approved, Federalists Tilly Merrick, Isaac Hurd, and Francis Jarvis and Republicans Jonas Buttrick and Benjamin Prescott, Jr., were added to the committee, which went off with the document to Boston.

55. "Resolves for ascertaining the sense of the inhabitants of the several towns in the Counties of Worcester and Middlesex, for a new County, as prayed for in the petition of Ivers Jewett and others," approved by the governor, March 8, 1828, in *Massachusetts Spy*, March 19, 1828; vote of town meeting, April 7, 1828, CTMM 7:314, CFPL; results of 1828 vote on proposed new county, *Newburyport Herald*, June 13, 1828 (1,350 in favor, 5,953 against); *YG*, July 24, 1830, March 8, 1834; *Lowell Journal*, July 21, 1830.

56. E. R. Hoar, "Memoir of Isaac Hurd, M.D.," *SCM* 1:166–67; Isaac Hurd to Nathan Brooks and Abel Moore, March 28 and 31, 1829, MCRD 288:141 and 289:1.

4. The Curse of Trade

1. *Walden*, 70; Ralph Waldo Emerson, "Man the Reformer" (1841), in Emerson, *Nature, Addresses, and Lectures*, ed. Robert E. Spiller and Alfred R. Ferguson (Cambridge, Mass., 1979), 147; Michael T. Gilmore, *American Romanticism and the Marketplace* (Chicago, 1985), 35–51.

2. Gordon S. Wood, *Empire of Liberty: A History of the Early Republic* (New York, 2009), 649–58, 664–70; Anne Bezanson, Robert D. Gray, and Miriam Hussey, *Wholesale Prices in Philadelphia, 1784–1861*, 2 vols. (Philadelphia, 1936–1937), 1:142–46. Concord's population fell by 2.7 percent between 1800 and 1810; comparable declines were registered by its neighbors: Acton, –1.8 percent; Lincoln, –5.7 percent; Sudbury, –1.2 percent. Two adjacent towns resisted the trend: Bedford's population rose by 10 percent, Carlisle's by 6 percent. For Middlesex County as a whole, the population grew from 46,928 to 52,789, an increase of 12.5 percent. See Oliver Warner, secretary of the Commonwealth, *Abstract of the Census of Massachusetts, 1865* (Boston, 1867), 192–94.

3. *TJHM* 11:436–37; H&P, 261–62; Grindall Reynolds, "Memoir of Isaac Hurd, Jr.," *SCM* 2:110–11; "Abstract of Merchandise entered since our Last," *Ming's New-York Price-Current*, June 13, 1807. Not only did Hurd have a father for a landlord, but he

was also able to obtain his stock of goods on the cheap. The previous occupants of the green store, Francis Jarvis and Charles Hammond, were eager to get out of business, so in April 1807 they offered their inventory "at reduced prices" and with "generous credit." *Columbian Centinel*, April 8, 1807; *Independent Chronicle* (Boston), April 13, 1807. Hurd gave up the store sometime in 1811 to take over a large farm in Billerica, which he had recently inherited from his maternal grandfather.

4. According to Franklin Sanborn, who got to see the Thoreau family account books, John Thoreau opened the yellow store in 1809. He was in court at least twice that year to collect debts. He won a suit against Concord farmers Tarrant P. Meriam and Ralph Hill for an unpaid note for $45.47 and took a two-acre house lot from farmer Stephen Jones, Jr., in execution of a court judgment on his behalf. F. B. Sanborn, *The Life of Henry David Thoreau, Including Many Essays Hitherto Unpublished and Some Account of His Family and Friends* (Boston, 1917), 29–31, 35; *John Thoreau vs. Tarrant P. Meriam and Ralph Hill*, Middlesex County Inferior Court of Common Pleas Record Book, December 1809 term, 440, MSA; judgment for John Thoreau against Stephen Jones, Jr., December 13, 1809, MCRD 183:188.

5. Naomi R. Lamoreaux, "The Partnership Form of Organization: Its Popularity in Early-Nineteenth-Century Boston," in Conrad Edick Wright and Katheryn P. Viens, eds., *Entrepreneurs: The Boston Business Community, 1700–1850* (Boston, 1997), 269–95; *John Thoreau vs. Isaac Hurd, Jr.*, Middlesex County Inferior Court of Common Pleas Record Books, v, September–December 1811, December term, 305, and File Papers, December 1811, Continued Actions, no. 191, MSA. As Henry Thoreau heard the story, his father "did so well" in the yellow store that Isaac Hurd, Jr., "went into partnership with him, to his injury." *TJHM* 11:436. That seems unlikely. No advertisement of the purported partnership of Hurd & Thoreau ever appeared in the Boston press, nor any notice of its dissolution. The archives of the Middlesex County Inferior Court of Common Pleas and of the Massachusetts Supreme Court on its Middlesex circuit lack any record of a suit over the termination of the supposed partnership. What does appear in the record book and file papers of the court of common pleas are the sparse details of the suit that Thoreau initiated against Hurd in May 1811. Already resident in Bangor, the plaintiff made the following argument. On April 16, 1810, Hurd gave a note of hand for $130.32, with payment due in thirty days; should that sum remain unpaid, interest would start to accrue, and the debt could be called at any time. The file papers do not reveal the details of the agreement; Hurd merely acknowledged the debt in exchange for "value received." That amount seems too low for a stake in a store. My guess is that the two men joined together not in a store but in a specific trading venture, for which Thoreau obtained the goods; when the plan went south, Hurd failed to pay his share, and one year later, Thoreau went to court. Filing his case for hearing at the June 1811 session of the court of common pleas in Concord, Thoreau claimed $200 in damages. The case was continued to the September session of the court, at which Hurd defaulted—that is, failed to appear; Thoreau was awarded $143.15 in damages and $19.26 in court costs. It is doubtful that Thoreau had to close the yellow store because of the failure of his deal with Hurd. A more plausible speculation is that Dr. Hurd declined to renew John Thoreau's lease in order to spare his son the competition. This is the only suit between Hurd and Thoreau on record. (I am grateful to John Hannigan, curator of the Massachusetts Archives, for finding the records of this case and furnishing me with copies of the documents.) John Thoreau's early miscalculations in trade were apparently evident to his kin, upon whose memories Franklin Sanborn relied in his account in *Henry D. Thoreau* (Bos-

ton, 1882). Sanborn notes that "the small estate" the young merchant inherited from his father was "lost in trade, or by some youthful indiscretions" (25).

6. Laura Dassow Walls, *Henry David Thoreau: A Life* (Chicago, 2017), 31–35; *The Boston Directory; Containing Names of the Inhabitants, Their Occupations, Their Places of Business and Dwelling Houses* (Boston, 1813), 243 (John Thoreau, "merchant," living at 22 Pinckney Street); administration of the estate of Rebecca Thoreau, 1814, File no. 22536, MCPR; third account of estate of late John Thoreau, submitted by Joseph Hurd, May 29, 1816, MCPR.

7. *Walden*, 32–33.

8. Of the storekeepers in Concord from 1808 to 1835, fourteen were broadly from the central Massachusetts–New Hampshire border (Ashby, Ashburnham, Winchendon, Mass., and New Ipswich, Amherst, Nelson, and Mont Vernon, N.H.); six from Acton and Lincoln (John Adams and John White; Charles and George Fiske, Albert A. and William Cole, respectively), another from Boxborough (Amos F. Pollard), next door to Acton, and an eighth (Ebenezer Woodward) from Canterbury, Connecticut, by way of marriage to a Lincoln woman; one from Groton (Daniel Shattuck's original partner Bela Hemenway); two from Methuen in Essex County (John Currier and his partner Phineas How), five from Concord (Jonathan and George W. Hildreth, Isaac Hurd, Jr., Ephraim Meriam, and Stephen Wood), and three from Boston and Concord (Jonathan P. Hayward, Reuben Rice, and John Thoreau). Rice and Thoreau apprenticed and clerked in Concord. I was unable to discover the origins of Stephen G. Hidden and Aaron Thompson.

9. Bascom's vicissitudes can be traced through the following advertisements in *YG*: November 24 and December 23, 1826, March 24, May 19, July 30, December 8, 1827, January 5, February 9, March 13 and 29, and October 18, 1828, April 11, 1829; Lysander Bascom to Nathan Brooks, summer 1829, Nathan Brooks Papers, Box 2, Folder 1826–29, CFPL. Bascom had already suffered a good deal of misfortune in his life; his father died when he was two, his widowed mother committed suicide two years later, and the boy, the youngest of eleven children, was raised by his aunt, the itinerant portraitist Ruth Henshaw Bascom, and her husband, Rev. Ezekiel Bascom, in Phillipston and Ashby. (See the entry for the Rush Henshaw Bascom Papers, 1789–1848, in AAS catalog.) William Cole was twenty-two when he entered into partnership with Bascom in February 1828; Albert A. Cole was only eighteen in March 1828. For Hurd, see Reynolds, "Memoir of Isaac Hurd, Jr." For an engaging view of the young men deserting farms for positions in trade and the professions, see J. M. Opal, *Beyond the Farm: National Ambitions in Rural New England* (Philadelphia, 2008) and Brian P. Luskey, "'What Is My Prospects?': The Contours of Mercantile Apprenticeship, Ambition and Advancement in the Early American Economy," *Business History Review* 8 (Winter 2004): 665–86. Shattuck was hardly alone in bewailing the hastiness with which young men abandoned the farm for the countinghouse. For similar criticisms in the years 1817 to 1821, see Christopher Clark, *The Roots of Rural Capitalism: Western Massachusetts, 1780–1860* (Ithaca, N.Y., 1990), 162–64.

10. Daniel Shattuck, "Memoir of John White," *SCM* 1:145–47; John S. Keyes, "Memoir of Daniel Shattuck," *SCM* 2:134–35; bill of sale for White's stock in trade and indenture between Deacon John White, on one part, and Bela Hemenway and Daniel Shattuck, traders of Concord, on the other part, both dated November 3, 1812, Daniel Shattuck estate, Nathan Brooks Papers, Series 1 (Estate Papers), CFPL; advertisement of "Goods Cheap at *Concord*, (Mass)," *Columbian Centinel*, November 14, 1812.

11. Shattuck, *History*, 205, 237–38; Keyes, "Memoir of Samuel Burr," *SCM* 2:209–212; Grindall Reynolds, "Memoir of Moses Prichard," *SCM* 2:116–18; T&R, 132–33; Richard R. John, *Spreading the News: The American Postal System from Franklin to Morse* (Cambridge, Mass., 1995), 112–15, 122–24; E. R. Hoar, "Reuben Nathaniel Rice," *SCM* 3:144; Samuel Burr Daybooks, 1812–13, CFPL. In 1810 the annual flow of mail exceeded one letter per inhabitant, almost twice the national average. I have estimated the volume of mail from a quarterly report submitted by Postmaster William Parkman, entitled "Post-office at Concord in account with the general post office from October 1 to December 31, 1810," Concord Post Office Records from the Tenure of Postmaster William Parkman, Concord, Mass., CFPL. That account indicates a quarterly revenue of $49.49 from postage on letters received in Concord or, by extrapolation, $197.96 for the year. Under the rates prevailing from 1799 to 1814, a single letter from Boston, sixteen miles away, cost eight cents; one from New York City, covering 250 miles, seventeen cents. Assuming a normal distance of ninety miles, I estimate the average postage per letter at ten cents. On that basis, Parkman was paid for 1,980 letters at his store. Since Concord's population was recorded as 1,633 in the 1810 census, the ratio of letters to inhabitants was 1.21 (1980/1633), surpassing the national average of 0.7 reported by John, *Spreading the News*, 4. That volume had swollen since 1799, when Parkman reported a total revenue of $112.16 from letter postage. According to my estimate, that figure increased by 60 to 70 percent over a decade. I am grateful to Robert Dalton Harris, coeditor of *Postal History Journal*, for supplying me with the 1799 account (found in the Post Master General's Account Current for 1799, National Archives) and for valuable advice on interpreting these data.

12. For a view of the goods for sale at Concord's stores and of the reliability of their supply, see the daybook of Burr & Prichard for the period December 1811–October 1813, Safe Shelf 14, Item 5, CFPL; account of Samuel Burr with John Thoreau, 1828–29, CAS Collection, Box 1, Folder 34, CFPL; advertisement of Genesee wheat flour for sale by Daniel Shattuck, *YG*, June 17 and July 1, 1826.

13. Clark, *Roots of Rural Capitalism*, 170; Diane E. Wenger, *A Country Storekeeper in Pennsylvania: Creating Economic Networks in Early America, 1790–1807* (University Park, Pa., 2008), 55–57; Ann Smart Martin, *Buying into the World of Goods: Early Consumers in Backcountry Virginia* (Baltimore, 2008), 75–83; Thomas M. Doerflinger, "Farmers and Dry Goods in the Philadelphia Market Area, 1750–1800," in Ronald Hoffman et al., eds., *The Economy of Early America: The Revolutionary Period, 1763–1790* (Charlottesville, Va., 1988), 166–95. After Jonathan H. Davis, the storekeeper with whom Shattuck served his apprenticeship, died suddenly at thirty-eight in March 1815, his entire stock of goods was appraised for probate by fellow traders Francis Jarvis, Moses Prichard, and Stephen Wood. The inventory was valued at $2,035.75. All the textiles, haberdashery (gloves), sewing notions (thread), buttons, ribbons, and other items of apparel (shawls, bonnets, some shoes) are grouped together, amounting to roughly $675. So cloth and apparel accounted for a third (33.2 percent) of the value of goods on sale in 1815. Five years later Stephen Wood died, leaving behind a much smaller stock of goods, valued at $691, little more than what Davis had invested in the materials for making clothes. Even so and despite his reputation for running a drinking shop, where men stopped by mainly to consume rum by the glass, yard goods, sewing supplies, and items of apparel made up close to half of Wood's inventory, approximately 47 percent ($325 out of a total $691). These proportions correspond to the findings of Martin and Wenger cited above. See inventories of the estates of Jonathan H. Davis, 1815, Administration no. 6041, and

of Stephen Wood, 1820, Administration no. 25543, Middlesex County Court of Probate Records, MSA.

14. Carole Shammas, "How Self-Sufficient Was Early America?" *Journal of Interdisciplinary History* 13 (Autumn 1982): 247–72; Daniel Shattuck, advertisements in *MG*, October 17, 1818, and *YG*, November 10, 1827; Florence M. Montgomery, *Textiles in America 1650–1870* (New York, 1984); Lynne Zacek Bassett, *Textiles for Clothing of the Early Republic, 1800–1850* (Arlington, Va., 2001); Ann Buermann Wass and Michelle Webb Fandrich, *Clothing Through American History: The Federal Era Through Antebellum, 1786–1860* (Santa Barbara, Calif., 2010); *T&R*, 76–85; *YG*, August 25, 1827. In a January 1828 advertisement for "CHEAP CLOTHS" for the new year, Josiah Davis offered "Homespun Cloths, for common wear" alongside more fashionable items from mills both foreign and domestic. *YG*, January 5, 1828.

15. "W.A.," *MO*, March 29, 1823. Another so-called workingman critic complained that marriage was a constant struggle to rein in his wife's expenses. It was bad enough that he had to furnish their home with "carpets, looking glasses, cabinet furniture, &c.," so that it was fit to receive polite company. Once the "throng" of visitors departed, the demands on his purse mounted. "My dear," his wife appealed, "did you not observe what a beautiful Nankeen Crape Gown Mrs. Chalkline had on; you will certainly allow me to purchase one off the same piece." It did no good to protest lack of funds. "Mr. Yardstick," the merchant, she pointed out, would gladly provide credit, and it was imperative to keep up with the neighbors. "Do you think that I will wear my old clothes forever" and endure the shame of appearing at "Mrs. Pimp's party dressed in the old-fashioned style, just like yourself"? Beseeched with words and tears, the economical husband gave in to the demands time and again to keep the peace. See "Q," *CGMY*, June 25, 1825.

16. *MO*, January 4, 1823; R. S. Sharpe, *Old Friends in a New Dress*, 5th ed., enlarged and corrected (London, 1837), 48–49.

17. Shattuck, "Memoir of John White," 145–46, 150.

18. Keyes, "Memoir of Daniel Shattuck," 136–38.

19. Keyes, "Memoir of Samuel Burr," 213; Reynolds, "Memoir of Moses Prichard," 119–20, 123.

20. Between 1804 and 1810, three out of every four accounts at Stephen Wood's stand on the milldam were being settled, in part or full, in cash—in sharp contrast to the conduct of commerce in western Massachusetts, where currency was far more scarce. Nonetheless, so plentiful were payments in kind that cash accounted for little more than a quarter of total receipts. Although the record of Wood's store extends over two decades, the business was at its peak in these years. Fifty-eight separate customers paid a total of $3,974 for goods, of which $1,100 (27.6 percent) was in cash. Thereafter the store contracted; over the next decade, from 1811 to 1820, only twenty-one individuals appeared on the books, an average of two a year. The store took in just $2,146 in this period, only $359 (16.7 percent) in cash. Of the fifty-eight customers in the store's heyday, forty-three (74 percent) settled their bills, in full or part, with cash—a far greater proportion than Christopher Clark found at stores in Amherst and Northampton around the same time. Cash payments figured in only 7.5 percent of accounts at William Boltwood's Amherst store between 1800 and 1805, and 44 percent at Asa Dickinson's Northampton establishment in 1804–1805. In Concord, goods earned credits for over half (57 percent) of customers, labor for another 21 percent. Nearly one out of every four account holders (24 percent) settled bills with IOUs. The contrast between Wood's store in Concord and Boltwood's in Amherst appears less stark when we consider

the proportion of total transactions accounted for by goods and labor: 60 percent in the former, 88 percent in the latter. Measured by value, cash accounted for 28 percent of all payments at Wood's store between 1804 and 1810, goods and services 40 percent, notes and bills due 15 percent. "Balancing accounts"—with the parties comparing credits and debits on each other's books—represented 24 percent. Cash payments fell sharply during Wood's second decade in business, when they accounted for just under 10 percent of all transactions and 17 percent of total receipts. For the Amherst and Concord figures, see Stephen Wood, Account Book, 1799–1820, CFPL, and Clark, *Roots of Rural Capitalism*, 55–67, 69. Thomas S. Wermuth finds similar low rates of cash payment in the mid-Hudson River Valley of New York before the 1820s; see *Rip Van Winkle's Neighbors: The Transformation of Rural Society in the Hudson River Valley, 1720–1850* (Albany, N.Y., 2001), 91–113. I am indebted to Laurie Butters and Michael Goddard for research assistance with the Wood store records and to William Mathews for assistance in analyzing the Excel database of the store credits.

21. Shattuck's annual statements of financial condition begin in March 1814 and continue to April 1836; he started categorizing debts according to their prospects for collection in 1827. I infer the merchants' practice of converting book debts, which carried no interest, into promissory notes, which did, from the tallies in Shattuck's annual accounts and from the many IOUs due to Burr's estate at his death in 1831. See Daniel Shattuck accounts and list of "notes of hand with interest to July 1, 1831," due to the estate of Samuel Burr, late of Concord in the County of Middlesex, Esquire, intestate, Nathan Brooks Papers, Box 7, Folder 6, CFPL. For evidence of Burr's successful prosecution of debt cases against various customers and the seizure of their property, see the executions in the Burr & Prichard accounts, Folder 3, BL.

22. Wayne T. Dilts, "Henry's Houses: The Houses in Concord That Henry Called Home," *Thoreau Society Bulletin*, no. 263 (Summer 2008): 6; MCRD 588:301. In 1830 the proportion of adult male taxpayers without a house was 47 percent, the same as four years before. The real percentage was somewhat higher, since some individuals, such as John Thoreau, were assessed and taxed for the dwellings they rented.

23. Peter Robbins, promissory note to Cyrus and Nathan Stow and Ephraim Meriam, March 14, 1827; Daniel Shattuck, agreement to pay Robbins's debt to Stows and Meriam, July 9, 1831, and Stows and Meriam, receipt for Daniel Shattuck's payment of the Robbins debt, October 8, 1831; and Peter Robbins, authorization of Shattuck to cut wood in his lot, November 14, 1832, all in Peter Robbins estate, Nathan Brooks Papers, Series 1 (Estate Papers, 1666–1864), Box 17, Folder 9, CFPL; Memorandum, April 20, 1832, of Daniel Shattuck's foreclosure of Robbins's land, accompanied by a promissory note, Peter Robbins to Daniel Shattuck, November 10, 1830, Miscellaneous Property Documents relating mainly to Concord, 1673–1925, CFPL; *Shattuck v. Robbins*, Middlesex County Court of Common Pleas Record Books, March–June 1833, 270–71, and file papers for June 1833, Continued Actions, no. 44, MSA; writ of execution against Peter Robbins, June 25, 1833, in *Daniel and Lemuel Shattuck v. Robbins*, Box 1, Moses Prichard Papers, 1815–60, Folder 6, writs, 1829–34, CFPL; Moses Prichard, deputy sheriff of Middlesex County, deed to Daniel Shattuck, August 20, 1833, and Patrick Byrne, executor of the last will and testament of David Wilson, conveyance to Daniel Shattuck, April 13, 1835, both in Peter Robbins estate, Box 17, Folder 9, CFPL.

24. When Shattuck embarked on trade in 1812, his stock of goods was worth $5,000; three years later, following his partner Hemenway's death in January 1816, it was up 50 percent to more than $7,500 and then hovered around $7,000 through the mid-1820s. The inventory jumped again to $10,000 and more after brother Lemuel joined the firm, then fell back to $7,500 in 1834. In the bookkeeping of the day, Shattuck deemed his business profitable if the value of inventory rose from one year to the next; but at any one time many of those goods might simply have been gathering dust on the shelf. Shattuck & Company undeniably gained over the years, as did the entire commercial sector of Concord. Between 1801 and 1831, the real value of inventory in the town's stores and shops rose by 40 percent, from $7.15 to $10.02 per capita. Concord's consumers had access to a larger and more valuable supply of goods than a generation before. But that increase is visible only in hindsight, which enables us to adjust contemporary figures for changes in the cost of living. To Shattuck and his colleagues, the actual situation of trade might have offered less assurance. To judge by the assessors' estimates, Concord businesses had on hand a richer stock of goods to offer the inhabitants in 1801 ($10.51 per capita) than they did three decades later ($10.02). For the changing value of his trading stock, see Shattuck's annual statements of financial condition, Nathan Brooks Papers, CFPL. His method of gauging profits by the increase in the value of inventory was followed by the booksellers of his day, as described by James N. Green, "The Rise of Book Publishing," in Robert A. Gross and Mary Kelley, eds., *An Extensive Republic: Print, Culture, and Society in the New Nation, 1790–1840* (Chapel Hill, N.C., 2010), 94–95.

In 1831 Concord ranked well behind Northampton as a market center, with half the value of stock in trade per capita ($10.02) held in the more populous western Massachusetts town ($20.33). Even so, Concord had actually outpaced Northampton in its growth between 1801 and 1831: the value of inventory per capita rose by 84.5 percent in Concord and 77 percent in Northampton. See Clark, *Rise of Rural Capitalism*, 158–59. Figures on stock in trade for Concord are taken from: Massachusetts General Court Valuation Committee, 1791, Aggregates of Valuation, showing polls ratable and not ratable, and the estates real and personal in the towns of Massachusetts, vol. 1, MSA (£1,898), converted in $8,635.90 according to Lawrence H. Officer, "Dollar-Pound Exchange Rate from 1791," Measuring Worth, 2010, www.measuringworth.org/exchangepound; 1801 Valuations (microfilm), 34, MSA ($17,644); Massachusetts General Court Valuation Committee, 1831, Valuation of Massachusetts, MSA ($29,950).

25. Abiel Heywood and others, petition seeking incorporation of a bank in Concord, submitted to Massachusetts House of Representatives, January 10, 1822, file papers, Acts 1821, chap. 44, "Act to Incorporate the President, Directors and Company of the Middlesex Bank," approved January 29, 1822, MSA. Shattuck's directorships of banks and insurance companies outside Concord are documented in *Salem Gazette*, October 14, 1828 (Lowell Bank), *Laws of the Commonwealth of Massachusetts, Passed at the Several Sessions of the General Court, Beginning May, 1831, and Ending March, 1833* (Boston, 1833), 12:336–38 (chap. 96 incorporating the Lowell Mutual Fire Insurance Company), and *Massachusetts Register and United States Calendar* for 1829, 183. On Burr & Prichard's banking activities, see H&P, 265–70.

26. Burr's shipments of onions and cranberries are documented in Burr & Prichard accounts, Folder 8, BL; the estimate of his loss was given by John Richardson in Samuel Burr estate, Nathan Brooks Papers, CFPL; advertisements for workers to braid palm leaf hats, *YG*, January 29 (Shattuck) and March 26, 1831 (Davis); Thomas

Dublin, "Women's Work and the Family Economy: Textiles and Palm Leaf Hat-making in New England, 1830–1850," *Tocqueville Review* 5 (1983): 297–316; Clark, *Roots of Rural Capitalism*, 181–90; "An Act to Establish the Lead Pipe Manufacturing Company" of Concord, June 11, 1828, chap. 16, *Laws of the Commonwealth of Massachusetts Passed at the Several Sessions of the General Court Beginning May, 1828, and Ending March, 1831* (Boston, 1831), 22.

27. Joanna Cohen, "'The Right to Purchase Is as Free as the Right to Sell': Defining Consumers as Citizens in the Auction-House Conflicts of the Early Republic," *Journal of the Early Republic* 30 (Spring 2010): 25–62; Michael Zakim, *Ready-Made Democracy: A History of Men's Dress in the American Republic, 1760–1860* (Chicago, 2003), 37–46; advertisements in *CGMY*, March 30, 1822 (Adams & Potter's "Cheap Store"), November 2 and December 28, 1822 (Charles B. Davis), December 13, 1823 (Shattuck), June 19, 1824 (Davis); *YG*, November 1827 (Shattuck), May 30, 1829 (Shattuck), April 24, 1830 (Davis). Another "cheap store" in Concord was Abraham G. Beard's short-lived venture of 1823; see *CGMY*, April 5, 1823.

28. Stephen Mihm, *A Nation of Counterfeiters: Capitalists, Con Men, and the Making of the United States* (Cambridge, Mass., 2007), 1–15.

29. Louis A. Surette, *By-Laws of Corinthian Lodge of Ancient, Free and Accepted Masons of Concord, Mass.* (Concord, Mass., 1859), 69–70, 125; H&P, 261–62; *MG*, August 15, December 5 and 12, 1818. Three years into the counterfeiter's prison sentence, the ever-charitable Doctor Ripley took up Smith's cause. In January 1822 the parson got behind his bid for early release and petitioned Gov. John Brooks and his council to let the repentant wrongdoer back into society. "He has been long in the first class of criminals," Ripley conceded, but after enduring incarceration "with becoming humility," Smith was a changed man. "His spirits are broken down, and the frustration of his schemes of avarice and ambition has deeply convinced him that 'the way of transgressors is hard' and that honesty is the best policy." The authorities were not convinced; Smith served out his term, and after leaving prison, he settled first in Manhattan, where he sold groceries on Hudson Street, and then in New Orleans. For this episode and the connections between Ripley and Smith, see Ezra Ripley, "doctor of divinity," deed conveying land to Daniel Smith, gentleman, for $2,000, October 7, 1816, Daniel Shattuck estate, Nathan Brooks Papers, Box 17a, Folder 8, CFPL; Massachusetts Supreme Judicial Court, Middlesex County, Record Books, 1817–18, 1819, 419–22, MA; *Commonwealth vs. Daniel Smith*, file papers, Massachusetts Supreme Judicial Court, Middlesex County, March 1819 term, MSA; Abiel Heywood, criminal case records for Middlesex County, 1798–1823, CFPL; Ezra Ripley, petition to Gov. John Brooks on behalf of prisoner Daniel Smith, January 15, 1822, Series I. Correspondence, 1805–1838, Folder 1, Ezra Ripley Papers, CFPL.

The original letter is housed with two petitions from Smith himself and another from various inhabitants of Mont Vernon, N.H., Smith's hometown, and several neighboring communities, in GC3/Series 771, Files of Inactive Pardons and Pardons Not Granted, Daniel Smith file, January 22, 1822, MSA. The roster of inmates committed to the Massachusetts State Prison in Charlestown indicates that Smith, age forty-five, a native of Mont Vernon, N.H., began serving his five-year sentence on April 1, 1819. See Charlestown State Prison, Commitment Register, April 1, 1819, HS9.01/Series 289, MSA.

30. Burr & Prichard Daybooks, 1823–24, 1828–29, CFPL; Keyes, "Memoir of Samuel Burr," 212; *YG*, March 21, 1829.

31. Clark, *Roots of Rural Capitalism*, 223–25; Wermuth, *Rip Van Winkle's Neighbors*, 131–34; Burr & Prichard accounts (MSS 77 1813–1855–1), Folder 5, BL; list of claims

on the late firm of Samuel Burr, commissioners' report, Samuel Burr estate, Nathan Brooks Papers, Series 1 (Estate Papers, 1666-1864), Box 8, Folder 2, CFPL. The following Boston merchant houses held notes against Burr: Daniel Denny (dry goods), Samuel B. Doane (sugar), M. S. Lincoln (dry goods), S. Pierce & Co. (crockery), Pickens & Littlehale (hardware and groceries), Gilman Prichard (cloth), Townshend & Dunbar (flour), Ezra Trull (distillery). These firms were identified in *The Boston Directory, Containing Names of the Inhabitants, Their Occupations, Places of Business, and Dwelling Houses* (Boston, 1830). From mid-October 1828 to late May 1829, Burr accepted cords of firewood and planks of lumber from various customers; the latter may have been used for local construction projects. On October 31, 1827, Burr & Prichard agreed to build a barn for Samuel Hoar; see CAS Collection, Box 1, Folder 32, CFPL. The storekeepers evidently had a strong need for such supplies; on October 30, 1828, Jack Barrett earned $3.75 in Burr's daybook for "transporting 1,400 feet Boards from Boston" to Concord. It is possible that Burr & Prichard were shipping butter in substantial amounts to Boston wholesalers; the farmer Abel B. Heywood sold 69 pounds of butter to the firm in 1827, 58 pounds on October 2, 1828, and 86 pounds on October 21, 1829. See Heywood's account over the years from 1827 to 1830, Burr & Prichard accounts, Folder 1, BL. Butter was "the most frequently traded" item at Samuel Rex's Schaefferstown, Pennsylvania, establishment between 1789 and 1807. As it came in, the butter was stored in a firkin or keg, and once the container was full, Rex sealed it up for shipment to Philadelphia. See Wenger, *Country Storekeeper*, 76.

32. Samuel Burr and John Thoreau, memorandum of contract for 100 gross of red pencils, late 1820s, Burr & Prichard accounts, Folder 7, BL; account of Samuel Burr with John Thoreau, September 24, 1830, CAS Collection, Box 1, Folder 34, CFPL; entries for John Thoreau, October 23, 1823 (6 gross of pencils), and January 17, 1829 (11 8/12 gross red pencils), in Burr & Prichard Daybooks, CFPL. On September 10, 1819, Munroe was credited for 20 gross of pencils, worth fifty dollars, in Burr & Prichard's accounts, Folder 6, BL. No other credits for pencils appear in statements covering 1819 to 1823 and 1828-1829, nor in the Burr & Prichard Daybooks for 1823-1824 and 1828-1829.

33. Keyes, "Memoir of Samuel Burr"; *YG*, March 21, 1829, September 4, 1830; *Boston Courier*, February 22, 1830; guardianship of John Burr, 1813, Worcester County Probate Records, no. 9301; trial of John Burr, June 5, 1830, in Abiel Heywood, Criminal docket for Middlesex County, 1823-38, Special Collections, Harvard Law Library; mortgages and sales of Burr's real estate in October 1830 recorded in MCRD 298:534-35, 301:23537, 349:370; Ephraim B. Patch (principal) and Stephen Patch (surety), four notes to Samuel Burr, September 2, 1830, for total amount of $2,588.62, Samuel Burr estate, Nathan Brooks Papers, Box 8, Folder 1, CFPL; Samuel Burr (St. Marys, Ga.) to Nathan Brooks (Concord), January 13, 1831, Samuel Burr estate.

34. *YG*, April 23 and 30, 1831; "An Inventory of the Estate of Samuel Burr late of Concord in the County of Middlesex, Esquire, intestate, taken on oath by us the subscribers" (Daniel Shattuck, Reuben Brown, Jr., and Ephraim Meriam), September 2, 1831, Samuel Burr estate, Nathan Brooks Papers, Series 1 (Estate Papers), Box 7, Folder 6, and list of claims made and allowed, Commissioners' report on Samuel Burr's estate, Box 8, Folder 2, CFPL; H&P, 265-70. A document in the same folder of the Burr estate papers, signed by Ephraim Meriam, Nathan Barrett, Reuben Brown, Jr., John Keyes, James Rogers, and Thomas Tarbell on April 17, 1832, notes that the administrator Nathan Brooks held "sundry notes of hand

and accounts" that could not be collected at present, among which are four notes signed by Ephraim B. and Stephen Patch. In the July 16, 1831, issue of the *Yeoman's Gazette*, Jonathan P. Hayward announced that he had bought the general store of E. B. Patch and was now selling dry goods, groceries, and West Indian goods. One of the smallest claims on the Burr estate was for $1.53, owed to "C&G Waters." These were Cornelius and George, the brothers of Phila Waters Burr. See Hugh D. McLellan, *History of Gorham, Me.*, compiled and edited by his daughter, Katherine B. Lewis (Portland, 1903), 806-7.

35. Notice of co-partnership under name of Daniel Shattuck & Company, *CGMY*, April 3, 1824; Lemuel Shattuck, Autobiography, MHS; statements of assets and liabilities, April 1, 1824, and April 1, 1832, Daniel Shattuck accounts, Nathan Brooks Papers, Box 17a, Folder 1a, CFPL; notice of co-partnership with William Rogers, YG, April 2, 1836; John Warner Barber, *Historical Collections, Being a General Collection of Interesting Facts, Traditions, Biographical Sketches, Anecdotes, &c., Relating to the History and Antiquities of Every Town in Massachusetts* (Worcester, Mass., 1839), 380; Concord Historical Commission, *Survey of Historical and Architectural Resources, Concord, Mass.*, 4 vols. (Concord, Mass., 2002), entries for buildings 48 Monument Square; Abner Forbes and J. W. Greene, *The Rich Men of Massachusetts: Containing a Statement of the Reputed Wealth of About Fifteen Hundred Persons* (Boston, 1851), 101-3.

36. Henry Petroski, *The Pencil: A History of Design and Circumstances* (New York, 1992), 47-66.

37. William Munroe, "Autobiography" (1839), Concord Museum; William Munroe, Jr., "Memoir of William Munroe," *SCM* 2:145-52.

38. Munroe, "Autobiography." Munroe summed up the results of his year and a half of pencil making as follows. The shop produced a total of 1,202 gross of pencils, earning revenues of $5,946.81. His costs included $980 for labor; $350 for materials (black lead, cedar, and other items); travel expenses for sales trips to Boston and Salem; and the loss of $511 he incurred from Andrews's bad debt, for a total of $1,841. Net profits were thus $4,105.81.

39. Munroe, "Autobiography"; advertisement for Massachusetts Lead Pencil Manufactory, *Columbian Centinel*, November 9, 16, and 23, December 7, 1822 ("perfection of their goodness"); William Munroe, Account Book no. 2, entries for 1817 and 1818 (coffin for Jonathan Hildreth, crib for Moses Prichard), Concord Museum. In his autobiography Munroe reported the price paid per gross and the annual revenue earned by his pencils; from these figures I calculated his output. As production rose, prices dropped: $3 per gross in 1819, $2.50 in 1821, $1.50 in 1825.

40. William Munroe, "Autobiography"; H&P, 223-24; Charles Hudson, *History of the Town of Lexington, Middlesex County, Massachusetts from Its First Settlement to 1868. Revised and Continued to 1912*, vol. 1, *History* (Boston and New York, 1913), 151. Two years after arriving in Concord, Munroe was appraised on the 1801 assessment list for a mere six dollars in personal estate and nothing in real property; the same was the case four years later in 1805. This small holding put him in the third decile of taxpayers. By 1811 Munroe stood smack in the middle of the wealth distribution; with $107.40 in real estate, he now placed in the fifth decile. The next fifteen years saw Munroe's ascent to the top, as documented on the 1826 assessment, where his estate was more than triple the size of the average holding ($4,287, compared to $1,363). His local offices included a seat on the school committee in 1824 and 1827-1829, membership on a committee to determine the best way of providing aid to the

poor (an ironic assignment given town officials' early fear that he would someday be among those in need of assistance), and service on committees to repair the First Parish meetinghouse and to find a pastoral colleague to assist the aging Doctor Ripley.

41. Munroe, "Autobiography."

42. Clark, *Roots of Rural Capitalism*, 176–90; Munroe, "Autobiography"; Munroe, "Memoir of William Munroe," 153–54. In his autobiography, Munroe pointedly noted the date, around June 10, 1824, when he gave up the remaining physical task he carried out in the shop—applying veneers to the pencils—and hired Ebenezer Wood to do the work in his stead.

43. Munroe, "Autobiography"; W. J. Rorabaugh, *The Craft Apprentice: From Franklin to the Machine Age in America* (New York, 1986), 32–56.

44. Munroe, "Autobiography"; Munroe, "Memoir of William Munroe," 148.

45. Munroe, "Autobiography."

46. Of known pencil makers in Concord and beyond, Joshua Melvin was working for Munroe in 1823, but there is no evidence of his independent activity in the field until the fall of 1826, when he and the miller Beriah Blood put specimens of their work on display at the Brighton fair of the Massachusetts Agricultural Society. Blood later paired up with Reuben Farrar of Concord in pencil making; see their conveyance of land to James Wilson of Keene, N.H., in a mortgage deed dated September 21, 1829, MCRD 292:261. Beyond the local limits, Concord native Benjamin Ball was recruited about 1831 to manage a pencil factory in the town of Harvard. Joseph Dixon, who went on to become a leading manufacturer of pencils in the 1840s, did not inaugurate his pencil-making efforts until 1827. Thoreau biographer Walter Harding speculated that John Thoreau learned pencil making during his stay in Salem as a store clerk. If so, he did not get any lessons from Dixon, who was born in 1799 and would have been a boy of six or seven when Thoreau was in Salem. See William Munroe, Account Book no. 2, 1816 to 1825, Concord Museum; *YG*, December 16, 1826; Henry S. Nourse, *History of the Town of Harvard, Massachusetts, 1732–1893* (Harvard, Mass., 1894), 459; Walls, *Henry David Thoreau*, 516n43; Elbert Hubbard, *Joseph Dixon, One of the World-Makers* (East Aurora, N.Y., 1912), 14; Walter Harding, *The Days of Henry Thoreau: A Biography*, rev. ed. (New York, 1982), 16–17.

47. Munroe, "Autobiography"; *Columbian Centinel*, November 9, 1822; *MO*, November 9, 1822; *Independent Chronicle* (Boston), October 25, 1823; *Massachusetts Agricultural Repository and Journal* 8, no. 1 (January 1824): 14, and no. 3 (January 1825): 235; Burr & Prichard Daybook, 1823–24, entry for October 23, 1823, CFPL; Edward Waldo Emerson, *Henry Thoreau, as Remembered by a Young Friend* (Boston, 1917), 32. Dunbar's discovery of the black lead mine was incorrectly dated "about 1821" in Grindall Reynolds's "Memoir of Cyrus Stow" in *SCM* 2:297–98.

48. Munroe, "Autobiography." One likely collaborator with Thoreau was Joseph C. Green, who shared the dissatisfactions of the "Misses Thoreau" with Ezra Ripley's policies and preaching at the First Parish and was with them in the little band who seceded in the fall of 1825.

49. Munroe, "Autobiography"; *YG*, November 25, December 9 and 16, 1826. No record of a loan to Green appears in Shattuck's annual financial statements. It is likely that the merchant listened politely to Green's plans and never came through with any money.

50. Munroe, "Autobiography"; *Village Register and Norfolk County Advertiser*, October 26, 1826; *YG*, November 25, December 9 and 16, 1826; *Boston Commercial Gazette*,

November 27, December 18 and 25, 1826; Munroe pencil labels, Collection of materials generated by pencil manufacturing, CFPL.

51. Wood, "Autobiography."

52. Ibid.; Munroe, Account Book no. 2, entries for Ebenezer Wood on February 22, 1819, June 22, 1819, March 12 and April 19, 1823, among others, Concord Museum; *YG*, June 7, 1823.

53. Surette, *By-Laws*, 76–77, 155–57; Rev. Edwin R. Hodgman, *History of the Town of Westford* (Lowell, Mass., 1883), 318; Munroe, "Autobiography."

54. Munroe, "Autobiography"; advertisement in *Washington Globe*, November 16, 1836, including a statement, dated February 1829, by five Boston artists endorsing the "very superior quality" of Munroe's pencils "for the purposes of drawing." By 1830, the "best pencils" accounted for one-third of Munroe's sales ($377 out of $1,550). Starting in October 1825, Munroe began organizing his account book by the merchant houses with which he did business; each firm had its separate pages for debits and credits. See William Munroe, Account Book no. 3, October 11, 1825, to December 1834, Concord Museum. Munroe usually spelled his surname with a *u*, but it not infrequently appears with two *o*'s.

55. Munroe, "Autobiography"; Harding, *Days of Thoreau*, 17; Shattuck, *History*, 218. My interpretation of Munroe's conduct is admittedly speculative. The anecdote about Munroe's bid to prevent the Thoreau firm from getting its black lead ground at Wood's mill was told to Edward Waldo Emerson in the late nineteenth century, apparently by someone who had worked in the pencil manufacture. Assuming the story is accurate, why would Munroe, having shared the territory of pencil making with the Thoreau firm for close to a decade, suddenly try to cut off his competitor's ability to obtain raw materials? The market was actually expanding, and neither firm had the capacity to satisfy the demand all on its own. My guess is that Munroe was worried about overproduction, although it's possible that he was having his own troubles getting sufficient supplies and so needed to gain an advantage over Thoreau. Munroe himself makes no reference to this incident either in his autobiography or in his account books.

56. Shattuck, *History*, 216; E. R. Hoar, "Memoir of William Whiting," *SCM* 2:252–62; *Documents Relative to the Manufactures in the United States, Collected and Transmitted to the House of Representatives*, 2 vols. (1833; rpt. New York, 1969), 1:308. The 1832 survey of manufactures in Concord reported production of riding vehicles worth $10,830. Whiting harbored no nostalgia for the artisanal world of his youth. In 1803, at fifteen, he came to Concord from central Massachusetts for an apprenticeship with a harness maker and carriage trimmer. His six-year indenture to a harsh master who flogged him "severely" for dereliction of duty but failed to live up to his own responsibilities—the youth lacked proper clothes to go to Sunday meeting and was cheated out of his pay—left bitter memories similar to Munroe's. "If ever I should have apprentices," Whiting vowed, "I never would deceive or wrong them."

57. Surette, *By-Laws*, 91–94; Elizabeth Willis, advertisements in *Yeoman's Gazette*, May 20, 1826, December 6, 1828, May 31, 1834; Marla R. Miller, *The Needle's Eye: Women and Work in the Age of Revolution* (Amherst, Mass., 2006), 185–210; Mary Minott, Account Book, June 1, 1825, to September 1, 1839, CAS Collection, CFPL (for transactions with the Thoreau men, see entries for April 11, 1825, September 23 and October 2, 1828, October 27, 1830, July to December 1831, and October 29, 1838 [coat for Henry Thoreau, $2]); George Hendrick, ed., *Remembrances of Concord and the Thoreaus: Letters of Horace Hosmer to Dr. S. A. Jones* (Urbana, Ill., 1977), 113; *Walden*, 25. Fourteen women advertised their dressmaking and millinery busi-

nesses in the Concord press between 1823 and 1837; only a couple were ever active at one time.

58. Zakim, *Ready-Made Democracy*, 69–95; Surette, *By-Laws*, 94.

59. The sad career of John C. Newell can be traced in the following sources: *CGMY*, May 24 and December 27, 1823; *YG*, October 30, 1824; *J* II:20; *Evangelical Magazine and Gospel Advocate*, July 1831; "Communications" from John C. Newell, *The Gospel Anchor* (Troy, N.Y.), March 17, 1832; Lilley Eaton, *Genealogical History of the Town of Reading, Mass., Including the Present Towns of Wakefield, Reading, and North Reading, with Chronological and Historical Sketches, from 1639 to 1874* (Boston, 1874), 210; Overseers of Poor in Wrentham to Selectmen of Concord, December 22, 1836, ETR; *YG*, March 3, 1832, September 1, 1833.

60. Hendrick, *Remembrances of Concord and Thoreaus*, 23–25; Munroe, "Autobiography." Munroe earned revenues of $5,947 from his first foray into pencil making. From those returns, $980 went for journeymen's wages (16.5 percent), $350 for supplies and transportation (5.9 percent), and $350 for Andrews's bad debt (5.9 percent). The remaining $4,106 remained for profit (and to repay whatever loans Munroe had contracted to begin production). See Munroe, Account Book no. 1, Concord Museum.

61. Munroe, "Autobiography"; William Munroe, Book of Stocks, Concord Museum; "An Act to Incorporate the President, Directors and Company of the Concord Bank," *Laws of the Commonwealth of Massachusetts, Passed at the Several Sessions of the General Court* (Boston, 1832), chap. 82, 306–7; List of Subscribers to Concord Bank, 1832, and Directors' Discount Sheet (1965.29.6), entry for October 16, 1843, Concord Bank Records, Old Sturbridge Village Research Library, Sturbridge, Mass. In 1835 Munroe ranked among the top 10 percent of taxpayers, number fourteen in assessed wealth; in 1850 he was the second-richest taxpayer on the assessment list, just below Samuel Hoar. At the close of his autobiography Munroe set his net worth on January 1, 1839, at $24,470, equivalent to $694,000 in 2019 dollars.

62. William Munroe, Memorandum Book no. 1, 1819 to 1829, entries for July 2 to 24, 1821, and Account Book no. 3, October 11, 1825, to end of 1834, entry for August 29, 1826, Concord Museum; Munroe's account with Samuel Burr, 1828–1829, Burr & Prichard accounts, Folder 7, BL; Munroe, "Autobiography." The Boston merchant was Elijah S. Curtis, whose hardware store was at 9 Dock Square. See *Stimpson's Boston Directory* (Boston, 1832), 122. Nathan Munroe the shoemaker, born in Lexington in 1780, held no property on the 1826 and 1835 assessment lists.

63. Munroe, "Autobiography"; *Boston Courier*, January 13 to April 13, 1838.

64. Robert A. Gross, "The Nick of Time': Coming of Age in Thoreau's Concord," in Kevin Van Anglen and Kristen Case, eds., *Thoreau at 200: Essays and Reassessments* (New York, 2017), 102–17.

5. Husbandmen and Manufacturers

1. Walter Harding, *The Days of Henry Thoreau: A Biography*, rev. ed. (New York, 1982), 12–13, 20; Laura Dassow Walls, *Henry David Thoreau: A Life* (Chicago, 2017), 32–35; Leslie Perrin Wilson, *In History's Embrace: Past and Present in Concord, Massachusetts* (Hollis, N.H., 2007), 39–42; administration of estate of Capt. Jonas Minot, 1813, File no. 15242, MCPR; F. B. Sanborn, *Henry D. Thoreau*, rev. ed. (Boston, 1882), 49–53. The 1826 list of polls and estates in Concord assesses John Thoreau for a cow and a pig, valued together at twenty-one dollars. Three decades later Henry Thoreau penned a hilarious account of the pig that got loose and led him on a wild chase through the village. See *J* 8:451–57.

2. Brian Donahue, *The Great Meadow: Farmers and the Land in Colonial Concord* (New Haven, Conn., 2004), 54–78, 155–96, 199, 203–8; Robert A. Gross, "Culture and Cultivation: Agriculture and Society in Thoreau's Concord," *Journal of American History* 69 (June 1982): 44–49; *J* 14:329–30; administration of estate of Jonas Minot. The output and land use on the Minot farm are reported on the 1801 valuation of the town. In that year he held 6 acres of tillage, 37 acres of mowing (8 of English meadow, 29 of fresh meadow), 20 acres of pasture, and 23 acres of woods and unimproved land. Minot ranked in the seventh decile, with an assessed worth of $66.72, below the average property holding of $75.56. That was owing to his division of property with son Jonas Jr. Upon the son's death in 1809, the father assumed control of the farm and ascended to the top fifth of property owners. Further details on the farm are in the inventory of Minot's estate; among the tools in the household were a flax break and an "old" spinning wheel. No sheep were listed among the livestock, so the aging Minots may have ceased to raise their own supply of wool. By the second decade of the nineteenth century, the cotton and woolen mills on the Assabet may have been a convenient source of yarn.

3. Administration of estate of Jonas Minot; Gross, *Minutemen*, 59, 63, 68–108; *Boston Gazette*, September 5, 1774.

4. Gross, "Culture and Cultivation"; Michael Rawson, *Eden on the Charles: The Making of Boston* (Cambridge, Mass., 2010), 31–32, 132; George Rogers Taylor, *The Transportation Revolution, 1815–1860* (New York, 1968).

5. Thomas B. Wyman, Jr., comp., *Genealogy of the Name and Family of Hunt* (Boston, 1862–1863), 74–75, 89–91; Adams Tolman, *Indian Relics in Concord* (Concord, Mass., 1902), 10; Ruth R. Wheeler, "North Bridge Neighbors: A History of Area B, Minute Man National Park," 127, 153–54, typescript (Concord, Mass., 1964), CFPL; Donahue, *Great Meadow*, 88, 272n34; William Henry Hunt, "Reminiscences of the Old Hunt House on Monument Street and of Life in Concord in the Mid-19th Century" (1926), ed. Leslie Perrin Wilson, in *Concord Saunterer*, n.s., 10 (2002): 87–89.

6. William Hunt to Nehemiah Hunt, June 16, 1744, and February 19, 1749, MCRD 51:587–88; William Hunt to William Hunt, Jr., June 16, 1744, MCRD 51:575–77; inventory of estate of Nehemiah Hunt, 1786, File no. 12275, MCPR (quotation is from report of a committee, made up of Ephraim Wood, David Brown, and John Buttrick, recommending the distribution of the widow's third of the estate to Nehemiah Hunt, April 5, 1792); Gross, *Minutemen*, 74–89; Nehemiah Hunt to Daniel Hunt, January 8 and 15, 1827, MCRD 280:5–6; Alfred Sereno Hudson, *The History of Concord, Massachusetts*, vol. 1, *Colonial Concord* (Concord, Mass., 1904), 211. In 1785 the Hunt farm consisted of 130 acres, organized in six parcels. The bulk of the land was inherited by Nehemiah Hunt (1764–1846); the remainder, the widow's third, went to him exclusively in 1792. In 1798 Nehemiah Hunt was credited with six parcels of land totaling 76 acres (Federal Direct Tax, 1798); the 1801 state valuation reported his holdings at 66 acres; and by 1826, when he was transferring the property to Daniel, the estate comprised 54 acres of improved land. The deed apparently omitted the eight acres of woods and unimproved land for which Daniel Hunt was credited on the tax rolls in 1829. Five years later the assessment was 61 acres in all. The landholding is larger still on the 1840 valuation: 66 acres, exactly what Nehemiah Hunt held on the 1801 valuation. To compare the farms under father and son, I use the 1801 and 1840 figures.

7. Hunt, "Reminiscences," 89; Nehemiah Hunt to Daniel Hunt, January 8 and 15, 1827, MCRD 280:5–6; Concord town assessment for 1827, which values the house,

barn, shed, and fifty-two acres at $1,542; Benjamin Floyd, *Lowell Directory: Containing the Names of the Inhabitants, Their Occupations, Places of Business, and Dwelling Houses* (Lowell, Mass., 1833), 71; Concord Directory (1830), NEHGS; Gross, *Minutemen,* 74–89; Hal S. Barron, *Those Who Stayed Behind: Rural Society in Nineteenth-Century New England* (New York, 1984), 93–97. Francis Hunt was approaching his twentieth birthday when Daniel purchased the homestead; Augustus was eighteen.

8. Col. John Flint, Clarissa's grandfather, married the widow Submit (Bateman) Hunt, Daniel's grandmother, on July 23, 1787. It was a second marriage for both. The union was cut short by Submit's death at age forty-nine on October 11, 1791. Colonel Flint, twenty years older, died several months later. I have inferred Clarissa (Flint) Cutter's pregnancy before her marriage to Daniel Hunt from the following circumstance: when Martha Hunt died on July 19, 1845, her age was given as nineteen. Assuming that figure is accurate, she would have been born within seven months of her parents' wedding. Her arrival was never registered with the town clerk. Finally, the 1830 federal census of Concord shows that Nehemiah Hunt kept a separate household from that of his son Daniel, even though they shared the same dwelling. Daniel's family numbered six, whose ages and sexes match those of Daniel, Clarissa, and their children. Of the four people in the elder Hunt's household, Nehemiah and Mary (Edes) Hunt were undoubtedly the two individuals in their sixties; I am guessing that the white female between thirty and thirty-nine was Daniel's widowed sister, Catherine Benjamin, age thirty-one, who had a five-year-old son, exactly the age and sex of the fourth member of the family. For premarital pregnancies in eighteenth-century New England, see Gross, *Minutemen,* 100–1, 181–82, 184–85. On the new white house with the "green blinds," see Hunt, "Reminiscences," 95, and Howard S. Russell, *A Long, Deep Furrow: Three Centuries of Farming in New England* (Hanover, N.H., 1976), 410.

9. John Shepard Keyes, "Houses & Owners or Occupants in Concord 1885" (1885), 21, CFPL; Nora Pat Small, "The Search for a New Rural Order: Farmhouses in Sutton, Massachusetts, 1790–1830," *William and Mary Quarterly,* 3rd ser., 53 (January 1996): 68; Jack Larkin, "From 'Country Mediocrity' to 'Rural Improvement': Transforming the Slovenly Countryside in Central Massachusetts, 1775–1840," in Catherine E. Hutchins, ed., *Everyday Life in the Early Republic* (Winterthur, Del., 1994), 175–200; Hunt, "Reminiscences," 90–91, 95–103; Gross, *Minutemen,* 85–86; *T&R,* 57–69; Samuel Burr Daybook, 1823–24, entries for Nehemiah Hunt, October 1, 23, and 27, 1823, and Account Book for 1828, entries for Daniel Hunt, November 3 and 13, December 1, 2, 3, and 23, 1828, CFPL; Concord Directory (1830), showing younger brothers Francis, a carpenter, and Thomas F., a stonemason, living in the village close to the common. The reminiscences of William Henry Hunt, born in 1839, date back to the mid-1840s at the earliest. By then the family was not raising its own beef. In the winter it did without; in the summer it was glad to patronize the weekly butcher's cart. It is not clear whether this practice went back to the previous decades. I have assumed the Hunts were slaughtering a cow annually before the 1840s. Since the Hunt farm was producing seventy bushels of corn and twenty bushels of rye in 1840—exactly the average for farmers in the town that year—it is likely that in the 1820s and 1830s, it was furnishing its own breadstuff and rarely purchasing wheat flour for pies, as William Henry Hunt recalled the family doing occasionally in the 1840s and 1850s. See Gross, "Culture and Cultivation," 60 (table 7).

10. See Edward Jarvis, *Supposed Decay of Families in New England Disproved by the Experience of the People of Concord, Mass.* (Boston, 1884), which documents the diminishing

presence of Concord's founding families on the land, even as it seeks to counter the notion that Yankee families were going to seed.

11. Shattuck, *History*, 227, 235; Hunt, "Reminiscences," 89. Nehemiah Hunt, Sr. (1764–1846), Daniel's father, served seven terms on the Concord School Committee from 1815 through 1821.

12. Gross, "Culture and Cultivation," 44, 58. At the start of the nineteenth century, the Hunt farm consisted of 66 acres, and even then it was more intensively cultivated than the average Concord farm. In 1801, fifty-six acres (78 percent) were improved for tillage, pasture, and meadow, compared to 68 percent for the typical operation. Four decades later the valuation list recorded the same acreage for Daniel Hunt: 88 percent of the farm was improved, compared to 73 percent for the average farm. See listing of Nehemiah Hunt on 1801 valuation list, CFPL. There was a close balance between the consumption needs of the Hunt household and the land and livestock required to meet them.

Six acres of tillage yielded just enough brown bread and johnnycake, baked beans, and corn pudding to satisfy the growing family. Six cows were needed for milk, butter, and meat—exactly the herd Hunt was keeping by the late 1830s, along with a yoke of oxen. To sustain the cattle during the winter months, when each beast devoured one and a half to two tons of hay in the barn, sixteen acres of meadow were required; the farm reported seventeen in 1840. It took even more land to put the animals out to pasture in warm weather. Usually the Yankee cow, the hardy red Devon carried by the Pilgrims to Massachusetts, survived on two and a half acres of grassland annually, but so run-down were Hunt's pastures from overgrazing and undermanuring that four acres were needed per head. In 1840 a total of thirty-six acres, capable of supporting nine cows, lay in pasture. In short, the livestock dictated land use on the Hunt farm. Like Jonas Minot's homestead, it was a veritable sea of grass, extending over 90 percent of the improved land. For a broader view of the "self-provisioning" of colonial farms, see Richard Lyman Bushman, *The American Farmer in the Eighteenth Century: A Social and Cultural History* (New Haven, Conn., 2018).

13. Hunt, "Reminiscences," 89.

14. Ibid. Brother Francis was a housewright, Thomas Ford a bricklayer, Augustus a stonemason.

15. Eunice P. Wyman Account Book, 1820–40, Special Collections and Archives, W. E. B. Du Bois Library, University of Massachusetts, Amherst. On the exchanges of goods and services among neighbors, see Susan Geib, "'Changing Works': Agriculture and Society in Brookfield, Massachusetts, 1785-1820" (Ph.D. diss., Boston University, 1981); Christopher Clark, *The Roots of Rural Capitalism: Western Massachusetts, 1780–1860* (Ithaca, N.Y., 1990), 72–74; Bushman, *American Farmer*, 11–17, 103–4. Wyman, born in Littleton, Massachusetts, in 1781, came from a prosperous family of merchants. One brother, George, kept a store in "the Plains." Another, Jonathan, ran a farm with brother Andrew. Jonathan served as a selectman from 1822 to 1827. By 1837, Eunice Wyman was living alone, her children long since gone. See Shattuck, *History*, 235, and census for Concord, May 1, 1837, ETR.

16. In 1807 Thomas Hubbard, one of Concord's wealthiest farmers, estimated the manpower requirements for raising the staple crops of the area. An acre of corn demanded fifteen days' labor from plowing to husking; an acre of potatoes eighteen days from planting to harvest. Haying was less onerous: it took two or three days to mow, cure, and stack a ton of meadow hay, two and a half for the same quantity of cultivated grasses. Hubbard was famous for his attentiveness to the best practices

of the day; "whatever is worth doing," he would often say, "is worth doing well." Others, less well endowed with money and time, might have rushed through their chores less carefully. Massachusetts Society for Promoting Agriculture, *Papers for 1807* (Boston, 1807), 234–26, 29–30; Samuel Hoar, "Memoir of Thomas Hubbard," *SCM* 1:121.

17. Clarence H. Danhof, *Change in Agriculture: The Northern United States, 1820–1870* (Cambridge, Mass., 1969), 126–28. Applying Hubbard's manpower estimates to Hunt's reported output in 1840, I calculate that Hunt's 70 bushels of corn consumed thirty-five days' labor (at a yield of 30 bushels per acre), his 3 tons of meadow hay seven and a half days, his 14 tons of English hay thirty-five days. Hunt reported similar figures to the 1845 state census of agriculture and industry: 70 bushels of corn, 13 tons of hay, and 100 bushels of potatoes. I have assumed that he was regularly raising all those potatoes in previous years on roughly a single acre. These estimates omit consideration of the labor required to produce the 20 bushels of rye and 15 of oats Hunt reported in 1840 and the 10 bushels of beans he noted in 1845.

18. Donahue, *Great Meadow*, 92–97, 168–76; Brian Donahue, "Henry David Thoreau and the Environment of Concord," in Edmund A. Schofield and Robert C. Baron, eds., *Thoreau's World and Ours: A Natural Legacy* (Golden, Colo., 1993), 181–89; Gross, "Culture and Cultivation," 48–49, 59–60; Darwin Kelsey, "New England Field Crops, 1790–1840" (unpublished manuscript), 16–22, Old Sturbridge Village Research Library, Sturbridge, Mass.; *YG*, July 29, 1826. Thanks to the greater productivity of English hay, Concord's farmers got in nearly as many tons from their uplands in 1840 (eight on average) as from their river meadows (8.5).

19. Donahue, "Thoreau and Environment of Concord," 185–87; Concord assessors, reply to Ephraim Meriam regarding their return on the 1840 state valuation, November 12, 1840, ETR; Brian Donahue, "'Dammed at Both Ends and Cursed in the Middle': The 'Flowage' of the Concord River Meadows, 1798–1862," *Environmental Review* 13, no. 3–4 (Autumn–Winter 1989): 46–67; Robert M. Thorson, *The Boatman: Henry David Thoreau's River Years* (Cambridge, Mass., 2017), 30–32. On the 1840 state valuation, Daniel Hunt was credited with 66 acres of land, the same amount as his father held in 1801. At the beginning of the century, Nehemiah Hunt reported 5 acres of tillage, 16 of mowing (4 of English meadow, 12 of fresh meadow), 31 acres of pasture, 10 acres of woodland, and 4 acres of unimproved. By 1840 the pasture had increased to 35 acres, apparently absorbing the 4 acres of unimproved, which disappeared from Daniel Hunt's holdings. Woodland fell by 2 acres, and compensating for this loss, tillage rose by 1 acre to 6 and mowing to 17. It thus appears that Daniel Hunt expanded his acreage of English meadow chiefly by converting his river meadows to this use. It is likely that Nehemiah and Daniel Hunt used the same tract of land for growing hay. In 1786 Nehemiah Hunt inherited a "piece of Mowing and Pasture Land below the Dwelling house" comprising eighteen acres. It was bounded "northerly on the road [river road to Carlisle], easterly on Barrett's Land, southerly on the river, and westerly on Wid° Flint's thirds." On June 15, 1827, Daniel Hunt purchased this same eighteen-acre tract from his father; the boundaries were the same (with Nathan Barrett, Esq., having taken possession of his father's property and Capt. Nehemiah Flint succeeding to his mother's). See inventory of estate of Nehemiah Hunt, 1786, and Nehemiah Hunt to Daniel Hunt, January 15, 1827, MCRD 280:5.

20. Hunt, "Reminiscences," 89–90, 98; Elinor F. Oakes, "A Ticklish Business: Dairying in New England and Pennsylvania, 1750–1812," *Pennsylvania History* 47, no. 3 (July

1980): 208; Joan M. Jensen, *Loosening the Bonds: Mid-Atlantic Farm Women, 1750–1850* (New Haven, Conn., 1986), 83–98. Daniel Hunt reported producing 500 pounds of butter annually on the 1845 state census of agriculture and industry and on the 1850 federal census of agriculture. His household in 1840 consisted of ten people. The family would thus have consumed 150 pounds of the supply, leaving 350 pounds for sale. Of the ninety-nine farmers reporting butter production in 1845, the average output was 253 pounds, half of that on the Hunt farm. Son William Henry recalled making daily deliveries of butter to customers in the village, including "Judge Hoar, Mr. Bigelow, Mrs. Nathan Brooks, Dr. Bartlett." This was probably in the 1850s, when he would have been a teenager. I have assumed that such sales began in the 1830s; by 1840, the herd of cows numbered six, the same size as in 1845 and 1850, when the family clearly was engaged in the production of butter for sale. Certainly, Concord's farmers were satisfying the local demand for butter by the mid-1840s. The population was around 2,020 in 1835. If average butter consumption was thirteen pounds per person (or, in today's measures, 1.1 tablespoons a day, a figure suggested by Billy G. Smith for Philadelphia consumers in 1771), then the townspeople required 26,260 pounds to spread on their bread and use for their pies—almost exactly the production reported on the 1845 agricultural census (26,330 pounds, worth $4,345). See John G. Palfrey, *Statistics of the Condition and Products of Certain Branches of Industry in Massachusetts, For the Year Ending April 1, 1845* (Boston, 1848), 50. The Hunts' dairy herd of six cows in 1840 was the same size as that kept by a typical farm family in northern Delaware that year; Jensen, *Loosening the Bonds*, 96–98. In the spring of 1835, to save money for David Henry's tuition and expenses at Harvard, the Thoreau family moved into the aunts' house on the common, where there was no barn to keep a cow. On that year's assessment list, John Thoreau possessed neither cow nor pig. See Wayne T. Dilts, "Henry's Houses: The Houses in Concord That Henry Called Home," *Thoreau Society Bulletin*, no. 263 (Summer 2008): 6.

21. Hunt, "Reminiscences," 89–90; Leslie Perrin Wilson, ed., "Mrs. Woodward Hudson's Memoir of Mrs. Ebenezer Rockwood Hoar," *Concord Saunterer*, n.s., 9 (2001): 100–3. Of the six Hunt daughters, only two wed: Louisa, born in 1834, and Emma, born in 1843. Louisa moved as far away from Concord as possible; Emma, joined in wedlock to Lewis Flint, made her life in her hometown. For all their faithful attendance at Sunday meeting, Daniel and Clarissa never became full members of the First Parish Church, nor did Clarissa ever join the female charitable society. Daniel served just one term in public office, as a highway surveyor in 1828–1829. He never joined the agricultural society.

22. Ethel Stanwood Bolton, "Some Descendants of John Moore of Sudbury," *New-England Historical and Genealogical Register* 57 (July 1903): 369; John M. Cheney, "Memoir of Abel Moore," *SCM* 2:286–89; Samuel Freeman, Esq., *The Town Officer* (Boston, 1802), 112–13.

23. The canny Moore got hold of the Prescott farm by a roundabout route. In the summer of 1824, seventy-nine-year-old Benjamin Prescott, aging alone on the farm with his wife Dorothy and strapped for money, mortgaged the estate to Samuel Burr for $480. The cash was not enough to save him. The butchers Cyrus and Nathan Stow successfully sued the doctor for an unpaid bill, and to satisfy the judgment, Prescott was obliged to surrender his right to redeem the mortgage. Sold at public auction for $160, that privilege was transferred to Dr. Hurd in November 1825; ten months later the veteran real estate speculator purchased the mortgage from Burr for $539. He foreclosed and two months later, in December 1826, turned

over the place to Moore for $613, at a loss of $80. See Benjamin Prescott to Samuel Burr, August 16, 1824, MCRD 257:94; advertisement of sheriff's sale of Prescott's right to redeem his mortgaged real estate, *CGMY*, October 22, 1825; Abel Moore to Isaac Hurd, November 14, 1825, MCRD 270:45; Samuel Burr to Isaac Hurd, August 4, 1826, MCRD 270:49; Benjamin Prescott to Abel Moore, October 21, 1826, and Isaac Hurd to Abel Moore, December 2, 1826, Abel Moore file, Nathan Brooks Papers, Box 40, Folder 3A, CFPL; Cyrus Hubbard, Plan of a part of the Prescott Farm belonging to Capt. Abel Moore, surveyed December 1825, Nathan Brooks Papers, CFPL. On December 1, 1827, the Concord assessors valued the "Prescot place" in Abel Moore's holdings as follows: house, barn, and seventy acres improved land, $1,765, and thirty acres unimproved land, $220. As for Benjamin Prescott, the 1820 census shows him as the head of a household consisting of two free white persons, one male and one female in the category forty-five years and over.

24. Cheney, "Memoir of Abel Moore," 287–88; "Notice of Farms—Minutes by the Way, &c.," *New England Farmer, and Horticultural Register,* August 28, 1839; "The Answers of Abel Moore, of Concord, to the questions proposed by the Massachusetts Society for the Promotion of Agriculture," *New England Farmer* 19 (February 17, 1841), 260–61.

25. Cheney, "Memoir of Abel Moore," 289–90; "Answers of Abel Moore," 260.

26. "Answers of Abel Moore," 260–61.

27. Freeman, *Town Officer,* 112. For evidence of the fees Moore received in the performance of his official duties, see the folder of bills and receipts for 1830, Abel Moore files, Nathan Brooks Papers, Box 42, Folder 1, CFPL; for Brooks's payments to Moore, see Box 42, Folder 1; for Keyes's payments to Moore, see Box 42, Folder 2; for his shoemaking, see Box 41, Folder 13; for his sales of pork products, see Capt. John Adams's (of Lowell) account with Moore, from June 1822 to February 15, 1831, Box 42, Folder 1, Bills & Receipts 1830, all in Nathan Brooks Papers, CFPL.

28. Cheney, "Memoir of Abel Moore," 286; George Moore, "Diary 1828–44," in Kenneth Walter Cameron, comp., *Transcendental Epilogue: Primary Materials for Research in Emerson, Thoreau, Literary New England, the Influence of German Theology, and Higher Biblical Criticism,* 3 vols. (Hartford, Conn., 1965–1982), 1:38–40; George W. Hosmer, obituary of Harriet Moore, *Christian Register,* November 30, 1878.

29. John Shepard Keyes, "Houses and Owners or Occupants in Concord 1885," 225, CFPL; "Answers of Abel Moore," 261; "Notices of Farms—Minutes by the Way, &c.," *New England Farmer, and Horticultural Register,* August 28, 1839.

30. Middlesex Agricultural Society, "Report on Farms &c.," *New England Farmer,* December 25, 1833; Middlesex Cattle Show, "Report on Farms &c.," ibid., November 5, 1834.

31. "Answers of Abel Moore," 261; "Notices of Farms—Minutes by the Way, &c."; Small, "Search for a New Rural Order," 68–71; Jeanne Ellen Whitney, "'An Art That Requires Capital': Agriculture and Mortgages in Worcester County, Massachusetts, 1790–1850" (Ph. D. diss., University of Delaware, 1991), 44; Russell, *Long, Deep Furrow,* 360–61. Both the Berkshire and Mackay breeds were introduced into New England in the 1830s. Moore was an early adopter, displaying his eagerness for agricultural innovations.

32. "Notices of Farms—Minutes by the Way, &c."; "Answers of Abel Moore," 261; John Welles, chairman, "Report on Farms," *New England Farmer,* February 17, 1841; Henry Colman, *The Fourth Report of the Agriculture of Massachusetts, embracing the Counties of Franklin and Middlesex* (Boston, 1841), 360–62, 408; *JMN* 10:101.

33. *Walden*, 157–58; Robert A. Gross, "The Great Bean Field Hoax: Thoreau and the Agricultural Reformers," *Virginia Quarterly Review* 61 (Summer 1985): 483–97.

34. Tamara Plakins Thornton, *Cultivating Gentlemen: The Meaning of Country Life Among the Boston Elite, 1785–1860* (New Haven, Conn., 1989), 57–77; Samuel Abbot Green, "The Western Society of Middlesex Husbandmen," in Green, *Groton Historical Series*, no. 5 (Groton, Mass., 1885), 1–4; Mark Anthony Mastromarino, "Fair Visions: Elkanah Watson (1758–1842) and the Modern American Agricultural Fair" (Ph.D. diss., College of William and Mary, 2002); "Concord Cattle Show, and Exhibition," *Boston Patriot and Daily Mercantile Advertiser*, October 17, 1820.

35. Thornton, *Cultivating Gentlemen*, 63 ("spirit of emulation"), 85–105; "An Act for the Encouragement of Agriculture and Manufactures," 1818, chap. 0114, State Library of Massachusetts, archives.lib.state.ma.us/handle/2452/110060?show=full; Simon Brown, "Origins, and Brief History, of the Middlesex Agricultural Society," in *Transactions of the Middlesex Agricultural Society, for the Year 1856* (Concord, Mass., 1856), 1–14; Shattuck, *History*, 231; *MG*, October 21, 1819, September 23 and 30, October 7, 1820; "Middlesex Cattle Show &c.," *Independent Chronicle and Boston Patriot*, October 10, 1821.

36. John R. Stilgoe, *Common Landscape of America, 1580 to 1845* (New Haven, Conn., 1982), 137–38. For the classic analysis of this ideology, see Leo Marx, *The Machine in the Garden: Technology and the Pastoral Ideal in America* (New York, 1964).

37. *MG*, November 11, 1819; *CGMY*, October 2 and 16, 1824. Of 353 male taxpayers in 1826, 98 (27.5 percent) belonged to the agricultural society. Six out of ten members ranked in the top 20 percent of wealth holders (as measured by value of total estate); almost all the others (38 percent) fell in the next highest quintile. "Elite" farmers in the top fifth of the wealth distribution were especially enthusiastic: more than half of them (25 out of 49 individuals, or 51 percent) joined the group, at a far greater rate than nonelite farmers (17 out of 61 individuals, or 28 percent). The average age of a member was 39.5, the median 37 ($N = 89$); the average landholding 41 acres. Of the 97 members on the 1826 assessment list, 60 were farmers (owners of land and livestock), and 23 were farmer-tradesmen (owners of commercial property, e.g., a store or shop, along with land and livestock). Eleven laborers, one craftsman, and one plowboy made up the remainder. Of Concord's founding families, the Barretts, Buttricks, Hubbards, Wheelers, Woods, and Wrights were well represented, but not the Minotts. While Daniel Hunt declined to join, his brothers Nehemiah and Thomas were quick to affiliate.

38. Keyes, "Memoir of Daniel Shattuck," *SCM* 2:39–40; *MG*, October 17, 1818. *CGMY* reported on October 9, 1824, that over one hundred persons had joined the agricultural society on the previous day; the record books show that seventy-nine were inhabitants of Concord. The foregoing analysis is based on the two-volume records of membership in the Society of Middlesex Husbandmen and Manufacturers, one covering 1820–1861, the other 1820–1888, CFPL. By October 1830, dissatisfaction was growing with Concord as the exclusive location of the cattle show. A committee appointed that year recommended the annual event rotate among Concord, Lowell, Groton, and Framingham. The report, presented at the 1831 annual meeting, provoked "considerable debate." In the end the proposal was rejected by "an almost unanimous vote, thus putting an end," observed *YG*, October 8, 1831, "to a project of dangerous tendency towards the future harmony and stability of the Society." Middle-class merchants and professionals dominated the Hampshire and Worcester county agricultural societies as fully as they did the Middlesex associa-

tion. See Catherine E. Kelly, "'The Consummation of Rural Prosperity and Happiness': New England Agricultural Fairs and the Construction of Class and Gender, 1810–1860," *American Quarterly* 49 (September 1997): 580, and Whitney, "'Art That Requires Capital,'" 221–58.

39. *Independent Chronicle and Boston Patriot*, October 8, 1823, reprinting account of Middlesex Cattle Show in *MO*, October 4, 1823 (no longer extant); Edward Waldo Emerson, *Emerson in Concord: A Memoir; Written for the "Social Circle" in Concord, Massachusetts* (Boston, 1890), 129–30; *CF*, October 7, 1842; *J* 1:490 (entry for November 20, 1843), 2:80–83.

40. Henry D. Thoreau, *A Week on the Concord and Merrimack Rivers*, ed. Carl F. Hovde (Princeton, N.J., 1980), 337; *Columbian Centinel*, October 11, 1823; *New England Farmer*, October 12, 1822, October 5, 1827, October 9, 1834; *CGMY*, October 8, 1825; *YG*, October 14, 1826; Kelly, "'Consummation of Rural Prosperity,'" 583–84. Thoreau wasn't exaggerating; at the 1834 cattle show, a single team "comprising *one hundred and seventy-six* yoke . . . paraded through the streets in a discipline as useful, if not as exact as the military." George M. Brooks, "Memoir of Nathan Brooks," *SCM* 2:207.

41. Shattuck, *History*, 231–32, lists the annual speakers. The lawyers were Rufus Hosmer (Abel Moore's benefactor), Thomas G. Fessenden (editor of the *New England Farmer*, founded in Boston in 1822), Josiah Adams, Luke Fiske, John P. Robinson, Elias Phinney, and John M. Cheney; the ministers Charles Briggs, Ezekiel L. Bascom, Edward Everett (congressman from Middlesex County), and Bernard Whitman. I identified the Harvard graduates in Harvard University, *Quinquennial Catalogue of the Officers and Graduates of Harvard University* (Cambridge, Mass., 1890), 115. See Whitney, "'Art That Requires Capital,'" 221–58, for an analysis of agricultural reformers in Worcester County.

42. Charles Briggs, *A Discourse Delivered at Concord, October the Fifth, 1825* (Concord, Mass., 1825), 6; Josiah Adams, Esq., "An Address delivered before the Society of Middlesex Husbandmen and Manufacturers, on their Anniversary at Concord, October 2, 1823," *CGMY*, November 29, 1823; Thomas G. Fessenden, Esq., "Address delivered at the Middlesex Cattle Show and Exhibition of Manufactures, at Concord, October 3, 1822," *MO*, October 26, 1822.

43. Arthur H. Cole, "Agricultural Crazes, A Neglected Chapter in American Economic History," *American Economic Review* 16 (December 1926): 622–39; Danhof, *Change in Agriculture*, 164–66; Shattuck, *History*, 217; J. Fay Barrett, "Memoir of Joseph Barrett," *SCM* 2:92–94; *CGMY*, October 9, 1824, October 8 and 22, 1825; *YG*, October 14, 1826; C. Benton and S. F. Barry, comps., *A Statistical View of the Number of Sheep in the Several Towns and Counties in Maine, New Hampshire, Vermont, Massachusetts, Rhode Island, Connecticut, New York, Pennsylvania, and Ohio . . . in 1836* (Cambridge, Mass., 1837), 41. The 1831 valuation of Concord recorded 881 sheep; a year later Shattuck counted over 1,000. By the 1840 valuation of the town, only 69 sheep remained.

44. William Cornelius Wyckoff, *Report on the Silk Manufacturing Industry of the United States* (Washington, D.C., 1884), 13–14; *YG*, March 31, 1827, June 21 and 28, July 12 and 19, 1828.

45. Cole, "Agricultural Crazes"; 627–32; *YG*, June 28, 1828; John M. Cheney, *An Address Delivered before the Society of Middlesex Husbandmen and Manufacturers, at Concord, Mass., Oct. 5, 1831* (Concord, Mass., 1831), 17–19; Christopher Clark, *The Communitarian Moment: The Radical Challenge of the Northampton Association* (Ithaca, N.Y., 1995), 31–32, 140–49. The thirty-four-year-old lawyer Cheney was well connected to the leaders of agricultural reform. Within a few months of speaking at the cattle show, he

would take up the position of cashier at the new Concord Bank, where his father-in-law, Rufus Hosmer, past president of the Middlesex Agricultural Society, sat on the board with Brooks, Shattuck, and Moore. See R. W. Emerson, "Memoir of John M. Cheney," *SCM* 2:310–16. The Concord Bank elected seven residents of the town to its initial board of directors; all were members of the Society of Middlesex Husbandmen and Manufacturers. Cheney served as secretary pro tempore. See minutes of stockholders' meeting, March 20, 1832, Concord Bank, Directors' Records, Old Sturbridge Village Research Library, Sturbridge, Mass.

46. Gross, "Culture and Cultivation," tables 5 and 6, 59 (showing that oats production rose by 82 percent between 1821 and 1831 and 68 percent between 1831 and 1840 and that woodlands fell by 37 percent between 1821 and 1831); Clay McShane and Joel A. Tarr, *The Horse in the City: Living Machines in the Nineteenth Century* (Baltimore, 2007), 57–63, 136–48. In 1826 and 1835, 18 percent of Concord's adult male taxpayers were assessed for ownership of a riding vehicle. Eighty-three farmers produced an average of 17.4 bushels of oats in 1801; by 1840, the number of producers had risen to 118 and average output to 67.6. In 1840 Daniel Hunt grew only 15 bushels of oats, and in what may be a sign of his traditionalism or of the constraints on his farm's possibilities, he abandoned the crop soon after. (He reported no oats on the 1845 and 1850 agricultural censuses.)

47. H&P, 165–67; *T&R*, 192–93; John S. Keyes, "Memoir of Nathan Barrett, Jr.," *SCM* 2:266–72; *MG*, September 23 and 30, October 7, 1820; *YG*, October 21, 1826; *New England Farmer*, October 9, 1833. See premiums for fruit at the 1832 cattle show, *YG*, October 13, 1832.

48. Cheney, *Address*, 16–17; Edmund A. Schofield, "'He Sowed; Others Reaped': Ephraim Wales Bull and the Origins of the 'Concord' Grape," *Arnoldia* 48 (1988): 4–16; Philip J. Pauley, *Fruits and Plains: The Horticultural Transformation of America* (Cambridge, Mass., 2007), 73–78. For premiums on grapes, see *YG*, October 16, 1830, October 8, 1831, October 13, 1832 (none of these contestants were from Concord); and *New England Farmer*, October 21, 1833 (Nathan Barrett received 50 cents for native grapes).

49. *YG*, March 31, 1827; Briggs, *Discourse*, 18–19 (calomel); *MG*, August 1, 1818; Gross, "Culture and Cultivation," 52–53; Gross, "Great Bean Field Hoax," 483–97; Whitney, "'Art That Requires Capital,'" 221–58; Thornton, *Cultivating Gentlemen*, 125–31; David Jaffee, "The Village Enlightenment in New England, 1760–1820," *William and Mary Quarterly*, 3rd. ser., 47 (July 1990): 329–33.

50. Adams, "Address," *CGMY*, November 29, 1823, reprint from *Connecticut Courant* in *MG*, May 30, 1818; *MO*, October 19, 1822; Stilgoe, *Common Landscape*, 138–40; Albert H. Nelson, "Address Before the Middlesex Agricultural Society, October 5, 1836," *New England Farmer, and Gardener's Journal*, November 16, 1836; John S. Keyes, "Memoir of Albert H. Nelson," *SCM* 2:382–83; Briggs, *Discourse*, 14.

51. Briggs, *Discourse*, 14–16; *YG*, March 25, 1826; "Domestic Economy," *CGMY*, March 27, 1824; "Neat Farms, &c.," *YG*, August 20, 1831.

52. Gross, "Culture and Cultivation," 51–52; George Lyman Kittredge, *The Old Farmer and His Almanack* (New York, 1904), 179; "A Husking as It Is," *YG*, November 15, 1828; *CGMY*, December 31, 1825, January 28, 1826.

53. Briggs, *Discourse*, 4–6, 18–19.

54. *MO*, September 21, November 16, 1822; Cheney, *Address*, 4, 11–14; John P. Robinson, "Extracts from Mr. Robinson's Address to the Late Cattle Show in Concord," *YG*, October 24, 1829; Gross, "Great Bean Field Hoax," 11–14; Thornton, *Cultivating Gentlemen*, 130–34.

55. F. B. Sanborn, "Ellery Channing in New Hampshire," *Granite Monthly* 32, no. 3 (March 1903): 158–59.

56. Shattuck, *History*, 379–83; administration of estate of James Minott, 1759, File no. 15233, MCPR.

57. *Massachusetts Soldiers and Sailors of the Revolutionary War: A Compilation from the Archives*, 17 vols. (Boston, 1896–1908), 10:816–17; Keyes, "Houses and Owners or Occupants in Concord 1885," 244, CFPL; Ezra Ripley, Record of Deaths in Concord, 1778–1830, CFPL. Ephraim Minott and Jonas Minot were first cousins, so George was Jonas's first cousin once removed. Jonas spelled his name with one *t*, George with two. As Henry Thoreau heard the story, "[George] Minott's father was rich and died early in the army." The misdating of Ephraim Minott's death, which occurred a decade after he had returned to Concord, suggests that the veteran suffered from battlefield wounds for the rest of his life. It was thus easy for those who didn't know him to garble the story and imagine Minott had died in the war. Ripley was well aware of the deeper tragedy in the family; it was he who attributed Ephraim Minott's death to intemperance. See *J* 9:273.

58. Administration of estate of Dr. Abel Prescott, 1805, File no. 18041 MCPR, and of Abigail Minott, File no. 15226, MCPR; Abigail Minott estate, Nathan Brooks Papers, Series 1 (Estate Papers), Box 16, Folder 1, CFPL; *J* 9:131. Abel Prescott's estate was valued at $24,807 in January 1806. Abigail Minott received real estate in Lincoln and Concord, valued at $3,509, and $2,620 in personal property. In the initial inventory of Abigail Minott's estate, dated April 26, 1825, the total assets, consisting of personal property ($723.27) and real estate ($2,043), amounted to $2,766.24. The debts were calculated at $3,116. Included in the papers for the Abigail Minott estate is a formal note made out to George Minott by his mother: "For value received I promise George Minott, to pay him by the first day of April next two hundred dollars with interest." I have assumed that the interest rate was 6 percent, the going charge.

59. Administration of estate of Abigail Minott, File no. 15226, MCPR; Abigail Minott estate, Nathan Brooks Papers, CFPL; advertisement of sale of estate of late widow Abigail Minott, *CGMY*, April 30, 1825; John Adams (administrator of the estate of Abigail Minott) to Abel Moore (gentleman), June 26, 1826, MCRD 272:51. Initially George Minott submitted a claim of $720, representing unpaid wages for six years from 1820 to 1825; the commissioners discounted it by half. The final settlement records the debt as $1,100 and allows $740. The arbitrator in this process was the lawyer Nathan Brooks. Among the creditors of the estate was Middlesex Probate Court justice Samuel P. P. Fay, who claimed payment of $796.46. Despite what would appear today to be an obvious conflict of interest, Fay did not recuse himself from the case. He must have been pleased that the commissioners of the Minott estate recommended that he be paid his full claim.

60. Henry David Thoreau and his brother John paid frequent calls on Mary Minott for her services as a tailor. Her account book records making "spencers" (short jackets), coats, and pantaloons for the brothers from April 11, 1827, to October 29, 1838. See Mary Minott, Account Book, June 1, 1825, to September 1, 1829, CAS Collection, CFPL. Horace Hosmer recalled his boyhood trips to the Minott house to get his clothes made, in George Hendrick, ed., *Remembrances of Concord and the Thoreaus: Letters of Horace Hosmer to Dr. S. A. Jones* (Urbana, Ill., 1977), 113–14. The Minott siblings and the Thoreau clan maintained close relations over the years. Mary Minott made pantaloons for Charles Dunbar, Thoreau's uncle, sold a 151-pound shoat to father John Thoreau, and made room for Louisa Dunbar,

Thoreau's aunt, in her home in 1850. See the federal census return for Concord in that year. The census taker listed George Minott as head of the household, but according to Horace Hosmer, Mary "ruled" the domestic domain.

61. *PEJ* 1:172 (entry for August 14, 1840); *J* 7:154–55, 169 (entries for January 30 and February 3, 1855, on foxes and rabbits); 8:150–51 (entry for January 30, 1856, on the "great September gale" of 1815); 9:177–78 (entry for December 11, 1856, on Minott's woodlot), 273–74 (entry for February 20, 1857, on "cat in his lap"); 10:51–54 (entry for September 30, 1857, on clock); 11:128–29 (entry for August 26, 1858, on haying in Great Meadow); *PEJ* 4:142 (entry for October 12, 1851, "world turned upside down"); Sanborn, "Channing in New Hampshire," 158–59, 162.

62. Sanborn, "Channing in New Hampshire," 158–59; Susan Sutton Smith, ed., *The Topical Notebooks of Ralph Waldo Emerson* (Columbia, Mo., 1990), 1:73 ("balloting," ca. 1851); "Speech of Edward Waldo Emerson," *The Centenary of the Birth of Ralph Waldo Emerson as Observed in Concord, May 25, 1903* (Cambridge, Mass., 1903), 124; *J* 9:131; charges to Mary Minott's account, July 16 and 24, August 7, 1823, Burr & Prichard Daybooks, 1823–24, CFPL; Samuel Burr, bill submitted to Abigail Minott estate, Nathan Brooks Papers, Series 1 (Estate Papers), Box 16, Folder 1: Abigail Minott, 1807–26, CFPL; *PEJ* 4:116–18 (entry for October 4, 1851).

63. *PEJ* 4:116–118. Emerson lived across the Bay Road from Minott, and for all his praise of Abel Moore, he preferred his neighbor's approach to the land. "We go to Captain M[oore].'s farm, and say, Selfishness plants best, & prunes best; Selfishness makes the best citizen and the state," Emerson remarked in 1847. But Minott's operation revealed another truth: "we look into George Minott's field and resolve to plough & hoe by old Cause & Effect henceforward. Life is a puzzle & a whirl & the cards beat the best players." *JMN* 10:84.

64. "Hints to Young Farmers," *YG*, February 28, 1829; *PEJ* 4:179 (entry for November 12, 1851, on "partridge by the wing"); William Cronon, *Changes in the Land: Indians, Colonists, and the Ecology of New England* (New York, 1983), 3–15.

65. *J* 10:168 (entry for November 7, 1857); Sanborn, "Channing in New Hampshire," 158–59.

6. Knowledge Is Power

1. Though he was formally known as "David Henry" until he reversed the order of his first and middle names around 1842, the future writer was familiarly known as "Henry" to his family and friends. Hereafter I will refer to him by that name.

2. Laura Dassow Walls, *Henry David Thoreau: A Life* (Chicago, 2017), 45; F. B. Sanborn, *The Life of Henry David Thoreau, Including Many Essays Hitherto Unpublished and Some Account of His Family and Friends* (Boston, 1917), 39; Keyes, Autobiography, 5; Keyes, "Reminiscences," 3, and Keyes, "Houses & Owners or Occupants in Concord 1885," 294, both at Keyes Papers, CFPL; School Regulations adopted May 6, 1811, CTMM 6:358b, 371–77, CFPL; Report of the Committee to Revise School Regulations, December 28, 1826, Ezra Ripley Papers, CFPL; E. Jennifer Monaghan, *Learning to Read and Write in Colonial America* (Amherst, Mass., 2005), 386–87. Born in 1792, Phoebe Wheeler spent most of her adult life with her widowed mother in the house on Walden Street, where she kept her infant school. Her father, Peter, who died in 1813, operated a slaughterhouse on the property, and it was into his barn that Brister Freeman was lured to confront a raging bull. See Chapter 3.

3. "J. H.," "A Rare Reminiscence of Thoreau as a Child," *Thoreau Society Bulletin* 246 (Fall 2003): 1–2; Shattuck, *History*, 240–53. Sixty-six sons of Concord graduated from college from 1642 to 1833, all but three from Harvard (the exceptions went

to Dartmouth and Williams). In September 1833, when Thoreau was admitted to Harvard, three of his townsmen were already enrolled; two others were attending Yale, and one was at Union College in New York.

4. Ralph L. Rusk, *The Life of Ralph Waldo Emerson* (New York, 1949), 50–52. The village schoolhouse attended by the Emerson boys was a wooden structure that burned to the ground on the New Year's eve ushering in 1820. It was replaced by the brick grammar school where Thoreau was a pupil.

5. *T&R*, 118–25; Report of Committee, headed by Ezra Ripley, on School Regulations for 1799, May 6, 1799, CTMM 6:148a–b, 157b–160a, 166a–b, and ETR; School Regulations adopted May 6, 1811, CTMM 6:358b, 371–77, CFPL; Report of the Committee to Revise School Regulations, December 28, 1826, ETR. The primary purposes of the town schools, according to Ripley, were to inculcate religion and instill morality. Educating citizens capable of participating in self-government had no place in his scheme. See Ezra Ripley, *The Obligations of Parents to Give Their Children a Virtuous Education, and to Provide Schools for This Purpose, with Advice to Scholars, Illustrated and Urged in a Sermon Delivered, September 7, 1820, at the Opening of Three New School Houses, Which Were Religiously Appropriated to the Interests of Learning and Virtue, and Directed to the Honour of God; and Which Sermon Is Now Affectionately Inscribed to the Children and Youth in Concord, Who Usually Attend the Schools,* "Published at the request of the Committee for building the school houses, and many others who heard it" (Cambridge, Mass., 1820).

6. *JMN* 5:452–53 (entry for February 11, 1838). Thoreau related the anecdote of the disobedient school chum on a walk with Emerson. "I delight much in my young friend," the mentor wrote in his journal, "who seems to have as free & erect a mind as any I have ever met."

7. JoAnn Early Levin, "Schools and Schooling in Concord: A Cultural History," in David Hackett Fischer, ed., *Concord: The Social History of a New England Town 1750–1850* (Waltham, Mass., 1983), 384–85; *T&R*, 125–27; Records of the Grammar School in Concord, 1834–1835, CFPL. The roster of enrollment and attendance kept by the master of the grammar school records anywhere from 78 to 129 on the rolls each quarter of the 1834–1835 year. Attendance averaged 55 to 65 students per day.

8. *T&R*, 115–16.

9. Shattuck, *History*, 222, 244–45; "Timothy Minott," in John Langdon Sibley and Clifford K. Shipton, *Sibley's Harvard Graduates: Biographical Sketches of Those Who Attended Harvard College in the Classes*, 17 vols. (Boston, 1873–1975), 6:257–59; Harvard University, *Quinquennial Catalogue of the Officers and Graduates 1636–1925* (Cambridge, Mass., 1925); "J. H.," "Recollections and Incidents of School Days in Old Concord Fifty Years Ago, Number One," *Shrewsbury News*, June 29, 1877. Son of Capt. James and Rebecca (Wheeler) Minott, the grammar schoolmaster was the uncle of Capt. Jonas Minot (Cynthia Dunbar's stepfather) and of Lt. Ephraim Minott (father of the "poetical farmer" George). Thirty men served as masters of the grammar school from 1785 through 1827. All but three graduated from Harvard; the exceptions attended Dartmouth (Chase and Temple) and Williams (Forbes). Through the center school passed a promenade of future ministers, professors, doctors, and lawyers, even a Federalist partisan accused and acquitted of murdering the son of a Republican political enemy. See "The Trial of Thomas O. Selfridge, for the Killing of Charles Austin, Boston, Massachusetts, 1806," in John Davison Lawson, ed., *American State Trials: A Collection of the Important and Interesting Criminal Trials Which Have Taken Place in the United States*, 17 vols. (St. Louis, 1914–1936), 2:544–702.

10. Report of Committee on School Regulations for 1799; *T&R*, 110–16; Harriet H. Robinson, ed., *"Warrington" Pen-Portraits: A Collection of Personal and Political Reminiscences from 1848 to 1876, from the Writings of William S. Robinson* (Boston, 1877), 9. Whatever his difficulties in Concord, Furbish made education his profession, teaching at academies in Maine and at Bowdoin College. He took pride in "having Thoreau and [Ebenezer Rockwood] Hoar among his pupils." See George Addison Emery, "The Old Thornton Academy," in *Collections and Proceedings of the Maine Historical Society*, 2nd ser., 10 (1899): 26–27.

11. Joel Perlmann, Silvana R. Siddali, and Keith Whitescarver, "Literacy, Schooling, and Teaching Among New England Women, 1730–1820," *History of Education Quarterly* 37 (Summer, 1997): 128–32; Jo Anne Preston, "Feminization of an Occupation: Teaching Becomes Women's Work in Nineteenth-Century New England" (Ph.D. diss., Brandeis University, 1982), 23–28. Of fourteen female teachers in the Concord schools from 1827 to 1830, seven were born in the town, another in Lincoln. All were unmarried. The median age of the dozen women whose year of birth is known was twenty-one.

12. Shattuck, *History*, 211–22; Levin, "Schools and Schooling in Concord," 352, 355, 362–65, 382–84; Record of School Committee meeting, October 15, 1801, Letter file 9, S-2, CFPL; School Regulations adopted May 6, 1811; Mary McDougall Gordon, "Union with the Virtuous Past: The Development of School Reform in Massachusetts, 1789–1837" (Ph.D. diss., University of Pittsburgh, 1974), 23–30, 143, 160–64, 208–10; Walter Herbert Small, *Early New England Schools* (Boston, 1914), 333.

13. Gordon, "Union with the Virtuous Past," 23–30, 143–57.

14. Ibid., 143–60 (quotation at 160), 208–10, 213–26; William J. Reese, *The Origins of the American High School* (New Haven, Conn., 1995), 22–24; James G. Carter, *Letters to the Hon. William Prescott, LL.D., on the Free Schools of New England, with Remarks upon the Principles of Instruction* (Boston, 1824), 40–46; Thomas Gray, "Elegy Written in a Country Churchyard" (1751).

15. "An Act further to provide for the Instruction of Youth," March 4, 1826, chap. 170, *Laws of the Commonwealth, Passed at the Several Sessions of the General Court, Beginning May, 1824, and Ending March, 1828* (Boston, 1828), 10:299–303; Gordon, "Union with the Virtuous Past," 246–53. Defenders of the educational status quo mounted a campaign to overturn the school law in the 1827 legislature, but they succeeded in extracting only minor concessions, including a guarantee of the right of districts to hire teachers, subject to vetting by the general school committee. Far from backing away from reform, the General Court reaffirmed its commitment to change in a comprehensive law spelling out the responsibilities of towns for local schools. Among other things, it took the responsibility of filing annual reports away from selectmen and laid the burden on school committees. See "An Act to Provide for the Instruction of Youth," March 10, 1827, chap. 143, *Laws of the Commonwealth of Massachusetts, Passed by the General Court, at Their Session . . .* (Boston, 1827), 557–72.

16. *YG*, March 11, 1826.

17. Septentrion, Review of *American Journal of Education*, in *YG*, February 18, 1826; "Public Schools," *CGMY*, December 3, 1825.

18. *YG*, March 11, 1826; Gibraltar, "Education," *YG*, January 27, 1827.

19. School Regulations adopted May 6, 1811; Report of the Committee to Revise School Regulations, December 28, 1826. The schoolhouse had seats and desks for eighty pupils; if more than forty boys were enrolled in the winter session, they would need to sit in the girls' section. So the threshold for barring girls over ten from the winter school was forty. The 1826 regulations also sought to insulate the schools from the

rising sectarian conflict in Congregationalism. Religious and moral instruction, long required on Saturday mornings in preparation for the Sabbath, was dropped. And textbooks with an orthodox or liberal bias were banned. Deferring to the Sunday schools of the competing churches, public education made do with daily prayers and Bible readings.

20. Edward Jarvis, "Memoir of Francis Jarvis," *SCM* 2:30–39.

21. Edward Jarvis, "Autobiography" (1873), 2–4, Houghton; Jarvis, Diary, 1827–42, 1:7–19, Edward Jarvis Papers, CFPL.

22. Jarvis, "Memoir of Francis Jarvis," *SCM* 2:35–36, 44–45; *T&R*, 51, 71–72, 91.

23. Jarvis, Diary, 1:32–33, 41–51. As a young man, Jarvis repeatedly violated the norms of community. When his mother died in the spring of 1826, the college senior insisted that the family drop the practice of treating the pallbearers with rum and wine. Soon after graduation, with his future still uncertain, Jarvis ignored his father's objections and took the rash step of becoming engaged to Almira Hunt, the daughter of a local farmer. To celebrate, he organized a cotillion ball and caused hurt feelings by being too tight with the invitations. Nor was he any more inclusive as master of ceremonies at the wedding of a kinsman. On that occasion he eliminated the customary public procession to the home of the betrothed, lest it attract "the gaze of boys, young women, and gossips." The Harvard student was something of a snob. Jarvis, Diary, 1:32–33, 41–51, 129–30, 336–38.

24. *T&R*, 76, 79; Jarvis, Diary, 1:99–102. Jarvis initially shared the doubts about the appointment; when his father first brought it up, he dismissed the idea out of hand: "I had not courage then even to think of teaching those with whom I had been to school." But he relented to satisfy the parent. Half a dozen Concord natives kept the center school soon after graduating from Harvard, including John Brown in 1813–1814 and Benjamin Barrett in 1819–1820. See Shattuck, *History*, 222. Moses Prichard, incidentally, never did reconcile himself to Jarvis as schoolmaster. The two men disagreed about the schoolmaster's right to vacation time, and as Jarvis's year of service was approaching an end, the school committeeman never proposed to renew the contract. Jarvis meanwhile resented the fact that Prichard never complimented him on the success of the school. See Jarvis, Diary, 1:120–25, 141–43.

25. "Thoughts on Schools," *YG*, October 28, December 2 and 23, 1826; Jarvis, Diary, 1:132–33. In a diary entry sometime around February 1827, Jarvis claimed to have submitted three essays to the *YG* reviewing the *Scientific Class Book*; only two were published. The schoolmaster was so upset that he vowed never to submit anything to the newspaper again.

26. Jarvis, Diary, 1:32–33, 43–51, 120–25, 127–29, 135,141–43, 151, 154–56, 160–61.

27. Jarvis, Diary, 1:137–39, 151, and Jarvis, "Autobiography," 28–31; H&P, 250–51; Robert A. Gross, "'The Most Estimable Place in All the World': A Debate on Progress in Nineteenth-Century Concord," *Studies in the American Renaissance* 2 (1978): 6–7. According to one of his former students at the grammar school, Jarvis was "liked very well." Robinson, *"Warrington" Pen-Portraits*, 9.

28. Meeting of December 12, 1832, CTMM 7:432, CFPL. This special town meeting replaced two departing school committeemen, Rev. Daniel Southmayd and Lemuel Shattuck, with merchant Phineas How and Jarvis, respectively.

29. Lemuel Shattuck, *Memorials of the Descendants of William Shattuck, the Progenitor of the Families in America that Have Borne His Name* (Boston, 1855), 300–302, and Lemuel Shattuck, "Autobiography" (1844), 15–17, Lemuel Shattuck Papers, MHS. My account of Shattuck is indebted to a paper written for the course "Culture and Com-

munity: The Worlds of Emerson, Dickinson, and Thoreau," History 55, offered at Amherst College in the fall semester of 1985. Entitled "Lemuel Shattuck, Statist: A Puritan in a Transcendental Age," it was submitted by Maria Farland, now associate professor of English at Fordham University.

30. Shattuck, "Autobiography," 27–32, 35.

31. Ibid., 35–49; Lemuel Shattuck (Detroit) to Daniel Shattuck (Concord), November 5, 1819, included with "Autobiography." Shattuck earned fifteen dollars per month keeping schools in Mason and New Ipswich and fourteen dollars per month as a farm laborer.

32. Carl F. Kaestle, ed., *Joseph Lancaster and the Monitorial School Movement: A Documentary History* (New York, 1973) 1–49; David Hogan, "The Market Revolution and Disciplinary Power: Joseph Lancaster and the Psychology of the Early Classroom System," *History of Education Quarterly* 29 (Autumn 1989): 381–417; Shattuck, "Autobiography."

33. Shattuck, "Autobiography"; Benjamin F. Butler, "Discourse delivered before the Albany Institute, at its First Anniversary after its Incorporation by the Legislature, April 23d, 1830," *Transactions of the Albany Institute* 1 (1828–1830): 223–24; Claude Eggertsen, "The Primary School of the University of Michigania," *Michigan Alumni Quarterly Review* 55 (December 4, 1948): 37–44. Shattuck's instructor in the Lancasterian method, William A. Tweed Dale, published a *Manual of the Albany Lancaster School: or the System of Mutual Instruction Simplified, Improved and Adapted to the United States* (Albany, N.Y., 1820).

34. Shattuck, "Autobiography"; Eggertsen, "Primary School," 40; B. O. Williams, "Sketch of the Life of Oliver Williams and Family" and "My Recollections of the Early Schools of Detroit That I Attended from the Year 1816 to 1819," in *Pioneer Collections: Report of the Pioneer Society of the State of Michigan*, 9 vols. (Lansing, 1874/1876–1886), 2:36–40 and 5:547–50, reprinted in Kaestle, *Joseph Lancaster*, 167–69. The fierce competition among the students did have a downside. Shattuck devised a currency for the school, consisting of tin coins in the same denominations of mills, cents, half dimes, dimes, dollars, and eagles used in the wider economy. (Mills were stamped "L.S." for the creator.) It was the medium for the rewards and fines used to spur on the scholars. Unfortunately, so popular were the tokens that some students, out of "cupidity, or the temptation to do wrong," got a local blacksmith to counterfeit them, and they were put in circulation. The fraud was soon detected. The scandal exposed an unfortunate flaw in the Lancasterian system: it could encourage "undesirable passions and genius."

35. Lemuel Shattuck to Daniel Shattuck, November 5, 1819, included in Shattuck, "Autobiography."

36. Shattuck, "Autobiography"; Eggertsen, "Primary School," 40–42. Shattuck concluded the narrative of his life with his arrival in Concord.

37. *Boston Recorder*, January 25, 1823.

38. George Keyes, "Memoir of Lemuel Shattuck," SCM 2, 224–27; Maria Thoreau (Concord) to Prudence Ward, September 8, 1821, Papers of Thoreau and Sewall Families, Huntington Library, San Marino, Calif.; "W. Daniel Baxter, Sr.," in John T. Heard, *A Historical Account of Columbian Lodge of Free and Accepted Masons of Boston, Mass.* (Boston, 1856), 493–96; William T. Davis, *Professional and Industrial History of Suffolk County, Massachusetts*, 3 vols. (Boston, 1894), 2:238, 266. Shattuck's third term on the school committee (1832–1833) was cut short by his relocation to Cambridge, where he went into the publishing business. In November 1832 his seat was filled by Jarvis.

39. *Regulations of the School Committee of the Town of Concord. Revised and adopted March, 1830* (Concord, Mass., 1830), printed in *YG*, May 15, 1830; "Report of the Concord School Committee for 1829–30," *YG*, April 17, 1830; Lemuel Shattuck, *Memorials of the Descendants of William Shattuck, the Progenitor of the Families in America that Have Borne His Name* (Boston, 1855), 300–2.

40. Carl F. Kaestle, *Pillars of the Republic: Common Schools and American Society, 1780–1860* (New York, 1983), 67, 87–88, 142–43; Johann N. Neem, *Democracy's Schools: The Rise of Public Education in America* (Baltimore, 2017), 52–53, 102–3.

41. Charles Monaghan and E. Jennifer Monaghan, "Schoolbooks," in Robert A. Gross and Mary Kelley, eds., *An Extensive Republic: Print, Culture, and Society in the New Nation, 1790–1840* (Chapel Hill, N.C., 2010), 312–18; *T&R*, 118–24; *Regulations of the School Committee . . . adopted March, 1830*; "Report of the Concord School Committee for 1829–1830." The 1826 school regulations did not prescribe any books, so I am assuming the titles set in the 1811 rules—Webster, Morse, et al.—still held good. Of the twenty-one titles prescribed or allowed in the 1830 school regulations, fifteen had been published within the previous five years. Some of the titles advertise their affiliations with Pestalozzi's "inductive" approach: W. B. Fowle, *The Child's Arithmetic or the Elements of Calculation: In the Spirit of Pestalozzi's Method* (Boston, 1826); Roswell Chamberlain Smith, *Intellectual and Practical Grammar, in a Series of Inductive Questions, Connected with Exercises in Composition* (Boston, 1830); Warren Colburn, *An Introduction to Algebra upon the Inductive Method of Instruction* (Boston, 1825). Other Pestalozzian texts used in Concord were Samuel Worcester's *Primer of the English Language for the Use of Families and Schools* (Boston, 1826), John Pierpont's *First Class Book; or Exercises in Reading and Recitation* (Boston, 1823), and Pierpont's *National Reader: A Selection of Exercises in Reading and Speaking* (Boston, 1827). In 1830–1831 the committee added S. Griswold Goodrich's *A System of School Geography; Chiefly Derived from Malte-Brun, and Arranged According to the Inductive Plan of Instruction* (Hartford, Conn., 1830). School reformers urged teachers to imitate the example of agricultural societies and share accounts of their classroom methods and results with one another in such periodicals as the *American Journal of Education*, launched in January 1826. Under the 1830 Concord school regulations, they were also encouraged to take a day off, with permission of their district committee, and visit other schools in town, in order "to witness the mode of government and instruction." Monthly teachers' meetings were also advised. See Septentrion, Review of *American Journal of Education*, in *YG*, February 18, 1826.

42. Set immediately above the place of publication on the title page, the phrase "Knowledge Is Power" may have been inserted by printer Herman Atwill rather than by Shattuck. See *Regulations of the School Committee . . . adopted March, 1830*.

43. Shattuck repeatedly tinkered with his statement of "the great object of education." He incorporated the language of his "Resolutions of a Teacher of Youth" with little change into the "Lecture on Education" he delivered to the Concord Lyceum on December 30, 1829. See Lemuel Shattuck Papers, Box 7, Folder 161, NEHGS. Several months later the passage became the preamble to the school regulations. This version introduced the mission of education to prepare the individual for "the greatest usefulness in the world." The wording was more economical, the rhetoric less pious. In June 1830 Shattuck took a final stab at the subject. As chairman of a committee appointed by the Middlesex Lyceum to consider "Improvements in Our Common Schools," he put a new twist on the purpose of education. Why cultivate "all our physical, intellectual, and moral powers" to their "highest perfection"? The answer was made explicit in the following words: "to develop those powers *so as to*

make every individual educate himself." See *American Annals of Education and Instruction* 1, no. 3 (October–November 1830): 133. His colleagues on the Concord School Committee liked the formulation in the school regulations so much that they reprinted it in their second annual report. See *YG,* May 7, 1831.

44. *Boston Daily Advertiser,* June 23, 1832, July 31, 1834; meeting of November 12, 1832, CTMM 7:432, CFPL; Max Hall, "Cambridge as Printer and Publisher: Fame, Oblivion, and Fame Again," *Proceedings of the Cambridge Historical Society* 44 (1977): 63–85. The partnership with James Brown, who would go on to found the great Boston publishing house Little, Brown & Co., lasted only two years. Shattuck moved into Boston, where he became junior partner in the firm Russell, Shattuck & Co., whose interests suited him well. The business specialized in "the publication of valuable books for the use of common schools, high schools and academies." Shattuck was now turning out some of the very titles he had chosen for the Concord schools. See advertisement in the *Christian Register,* December 5, 1835.

45. Kenneth Walter Cameron, "Young Henry Thoreau in the Annals of the Concord Academy (1829-1833)," *Emerson Society Quarterly* 9 (1957): 3, 16; Reese, *Origins of the American High School,* 31–34; Wayne T. Dilts, "Henry's Houses: The Houses in Concord That Henry Called Home," *Thoreau Society Bulletin,* no. 263 (Summer 2008): 6; Hubert H. Hoeltje, "Thoreau and the Concord Academy," *New England Quarterly* 21 (March 1948): 104; Gladys Hosmer, "Phineas Allen, Thoreau's Preceptor," *Thoreau Society Bulletin,* no. 59 (Spring 1957): 1–3; Thoreau (Concord) to Henry Williams, Jr. (Boston), September 30, 1847, in Robert N. Hudspeth, ed., *The Correspondence of Henry D. Thoreau,* vol. 1, *1834–1848* (Princeton, N.J., 2013), 307–9. Walter Harding, *The Days of Henry Thoreau: A Biography,* rev. ed. (New York, 1982), 25–26, suggests that John and Henry Thoreau attended the academy together in the fall of 1828. The available evidence indicates they were enrolled for different terms, John for the quarter ending in early September 1828, Henry for the succeeding quarter ending in February 1829.

46. E. R. Hoar, "Memoir of William Whiting," SCM 2:258; Shattuck, *History,* 222; *MO,* July 27, 1822. Abner Forbes was beginning his second year as master when Willy Whiting entered his school. Despite the bullying, the boy stayed long enough to forge a relationship with Forbes that would benefit the schoolmaster in later years. Forbes eventually settled in Boston, where he became the master of the all-Black Smith School and came under fire for mismanagement and ill treatment of the African American students. His lawyer in the public inquiry conducted by the Boston School Committee was William Whiting. See Stephen Kendrick and Paul Kendrick, *Sarah's Long Walk: The Free Blacks of Boston and How Their Struggle for Equality Changed America* (Boston, 2004), 80–84; obituary of Abner Forbes, *Boston Daily Journal,* October 26, 1877.

47. Hoar, "Memoir of William Whiting," 248, 251, 258–59, and "Memoir of Josiah Davis," SCM 2:99; advertising notice for Concord Academy, *MO,* July 27, September 7, 1822; Shattuck, *History,* 222–23; Mary Larsen, "The Concord Academy 1822–1862: Another Look at Private Education" (paper for Boston University seminar on "Concord in the Era of Emerson and Thoreau," December 13, 1973, on deposit at CFPL), 2–3. Of the academy's five founders, the three wealthiest—Davis, Heywood, and Hoar—agreed to pay a quarter of the expenses; Whiting and Brooks split the remaining share. In 1820 Davis, Heywood, and Hoar ranked in the top tenth of taxpayers, Brooks and Whiting in the next highest decile; six years later all but Brooks were at the top. In the winter of 1822, Brooks, thirty-six, was a widower caring for a twenty-two-month-old toddler; Hoar, forty-three, had three

children at home, ranging from four to eight; Davis, forty-eight, had one son and four daughters, from six on down, and Whiting, forty-three, and wife Hannah were raising eight-year-old Willy, seven-year-old Anna Maria, and six-month-old Louisa Jane.

48. "Academies and Other Public Schools," *Quarterly Register and Journal of the American Education Society* 2, no. 4 (May 1830): 231–33; Kaestle, *Pillars of the Republic*, 51–52, 118–20; Mary Kelley, *Learning to Stand and Speak: Women, Education, and Public Life in America's Republic* (Chapel Hill, N.C., 2012), 67–68; J. M. Opal, *Beyond the Farm: National Ambitions in Rural New England* (Philadelphia, 2008), 103–17. From 1780 to the 1820s, the Massachusetts legislature granted corporate charters to academies one by one, employing much the same language in the acts of incorporation to designate the public purposes these institutions served. See, for example, the charters granted to Deerfield Academy and Milton Academy in "Acts and Resolves of Massachusetts, 1796–97," *Acts and Laws of the Commonwealth of Massachusetts*, 13 vols. (Boston, 1890–1898), 6:125–27 (Deerfield Academy, chap. 62) and 6:476–77 (Milton Academy, chap. 78), and to Lexington Academy (1822, chap. 80), *Laws of the Commonwealth of Massachusetts, Passed at the Several Sessions of the General Court, Beginning May, 1818, and Ending February, 1822* (Boston, 1822), 676–68. By 1822 the legislature dropped the cultivation of "piety" from the purposes of chartered academies and restricted itself to favoring "religion and morality." On the Middlesex Female Academy, see "An Act to Establish an Academy at Concord, in the County of Middlesex," March 14, 1806, chap. 118, Acts 1805, in *Laws of the Commonwealth of Massachusetts, Passed at Several Sessions of the General Court, Holden in Boston* (Boston, 1806), 153–54; John Vose, Ezra Ripley, and twenty-three others, petition for a charter of incorporation, included in the file papers for this passed legislation; subscription list for Middlesex Female Academy, January 9, 1806, Tilly Merrick Papers, CFPL. Among the trustees of the new institution were Artemas Ward of Charlestown, Timothy Bigelow of Groton, the ministers of Lincoln and Acton, and Rev. William Emerson, Ripley's step-grandson and father of the Concord Sage. Two-thirds (17 out of 25) of Social Circle members in 1805 subscribed to the fund for the Middlesex Female Academy.

49. "Academies and Other Public Schools," 231–33; John S. Keyes, "Memoir of John Keyes," SCM 2:161–62; Jarvis, Diary, 1:24–31; *Catalogue of the Officers and Students of Lawrence Academy, From the Time of Its Incorporation* (Groton, Mass., 1855); Ruth F. Hatch, "A Study of the History of the Development of Coeducation in Massachusetts (M.A. thesis, University of Massachusetts at Amherst, 1933), 40. The other Middlesex County academies within roughly twenty miles of Concord were located in Billerica (nine miles away) and Framingham (twenty-one miles). For these calculations, I have used current driving distances between town centers.

50. CGMY, December 6, 1823, August 19, 1824, September 10, 1825.

51. CGMY, December 6, 1823, August 21, 1824; Nancy Beadie, "Academy Students in the Mid-Nineteenth Century: Social Geography, Demography, and the Culture of Academy Attendance," *History of Education Quarterly* 41, no. 2 (Summer 2001): 255; Elizabeth Hoar (Concord) to Marianne Cornelia Giles (St. Johnsbury, Vt.), October 1, 1828, in Elizabeth Maxfield-Miller, ed., "Elizabeth of Concord: Selected Letters of Elizabeth Sherman Hoar (1814–1878) to the Emersons, Family, and the Emerson Circle (Part Two)," *Studies in the American Renaissance* (1985): 97–103; Leslie Perrin Wilson, ed., "Mrs. Woodward Hudson's Memoir of Mrs. Ebenezer Rockwood Hoar," *Concord Saunterer*, n.s., 9 (2001): 93–95; Kelley, *Learning to Stand and Speak*, 86–92.

52. MO, July 27, 1822; CGMY, August 21, 1824; Shattuck, *History*, 222–23; Cameron, "Young Thoreau in the Concord Academy," 2–3, 7, 16–17.

53. Josiah Davis represented the center district on the school committee from 1811 through 1821; Nathan Brooks and Samuel Hoar were elected to that body the very year the academy opened its doors.

54. Reese, *Origins of the American High School*, 30–37; "Academies and Other Public Schools," 231–33. Of the thirty-five academies in Massachusetts receiving charters of incorporation from the General Court between 1780 and 1821, only twelve—roughly a third—survived to appear in the list of such institutions reported in the *Massachusetts Register* for 1821. Elected to the school committee in 1822, Samuel Hoar put in three terms as a representative of the center district; Nathan Brooks joined him on that body in 1822 and continued through 1828. Besides his long-term service on the school committee, Josiah Davis served on the three-man committee that supervised construction of the new schoolhouses in 1820. Whiting himself eschewed such duty, but in 1820 he helped to arrange a donation of land for a schoolhouse to serve village children living west of the mill brook. See Tilly Merrick (grantor), deed to William Whiting, Nathan Brooks, and Cyrus Stow (grantees), April 22, 1820, in Tilly Merrick estate, Nathan Brooks Papers, CFPL.

55. To replace Folsom, the academy recruited Josiah Barnes, fresh out of Yale College, who moved on after a year. His successor, Richard Hildreth, a Harvard classmate of Edward Jarvis, would in later life gain renown as a journalist, historian, and reformer, but he proved a disaster in the classroom. He had no time for "dull scholars" and little more for the rest; some days he sat behind his desk in silence for as long as two hours, without calling on anyone to recite. The only student who commanded his notice was a pretty sixteen-year-old, whom he courted in secret. Discipline broke down; "a considerable number" withdrew; and a few parents declined to pay a single penny for the haphazard instruction. Hildreth had been guaranteed a salary of $500 for the year, with the trustees promising to pay out of pocket if tuition revenue fell short. But the young man had driven so many pupils away that the deficit ballooned and his employers reneged. Never again would the proprietors make such a pledge. Lynn Gordon Hughes, "Richard Hildreth," in *American National Biography Online* (April 2002 update), www.anb.org/articles/16/16-03462 .html (accessed October 14, 2015); Jarvis, Diary, 1:162–64; Richard Hildreth (Newburyport) to Edward Jarvis (Concord), May 29, 1828, Edward Jarvis Papers, Box 1, Folder 4, CFPL; Hosea Hildreth (Gloucester) to Samuel Hoar (Concord), October 10, 1827, Miscellaneous Hoar Family Papers, CFPL.

56. Altogether, fifteen sons of Concord went on to gain bachelor's degrees, mostly from Harvard, in the two decades after the academy was founded in 1822. A dozen of them prepared for college admission under George Folsom, Richard Hildreth, or Phineas Allen. Three others took Jarvis's route to Westford Academy or went to its counterpart in Groton. Perhaps the other two acquired the necessary training at the village grammar school, but that is unknown.

57. *YG*, August 30, 1828, July 17, August 14, 1830, February 27, September 3, 1831, May 26, 1832; Frank Allen Hutchinson, comp., *Genealogical and Historical Sketches of the Allen Family of Dedham and Medfield, Mass., 1637–1890* (Lowell, Mass., 1896), 42–43; Mary Anne Greene, *Nathaniel T. Allen: Teacher, Reformer, Philanthropist* (privately printed, 1906), 66–67; Hosmer, "Phineas Allen, Thoreau's Preceptor." In the fall of 1828, fourteen out of thirty-two students were from out of town; four years later eighteen out of fifty-six, or one-third, were sojourners. Local enrollment doubled over that time, far outpacing the small growth in the number of outsiders. The student from Claiborne, Alabama, Susan C. Colburn, was returning to her ancestral

home. Her grandfather, James Smith Colburn (1780–1859), was a Concord native who, after failing as a merchant in Boston, moved to Charleston, South Carolina, around 1819 in hopes of recouping his fortunes. His son, James B. Colburn, born in 1801, remained in Boston and conducted trade before moving to Alabama, marrying, and fathering the future student of Phineas Allen. See *Colburn v. Holland* in J. S. G. Richardson, *Reports of Cases in Equity Argued and Determined in the Court of Appeals and Court of Errors of South Carolina*, vol. 14, *From January, 1868, to May, 1868, Inclusive* (1869; rpt. St. Paul, Minn., 1916), 176–244, and *Columbian Centinel*, May 19, 1824.

58. Concord Directory (1830), NEHGS; "Early Records of the Concord Lyceum," in Kenneth Walter Cameron, comp., *Transcendental Epilogue: Primary Materials for Research in Emerson, Thoreau, Literary New England, the Influence of German Theology, and Higher Biblical Criticism*, 3 vols. (Hartford, Conn., 1965–1982), 117–18, 121, 125; *YG*, May 26, 1832.

59. *Regulations of the School Committee . . . adopted March, 1830*; Cameron, "Young Thoreau in the Concord Academy," 5, 9, 10, 14, 16–17; Robinson, *"Warrington" Pen-Portraits*, 9; "Old School Fellows," *R*, July 19, 1841; Dorothy Nyren, "The Concord Academic Debating Society," *Massachusetts Review* 4 (Autumn 1962): 81–84; Walls, *Henry David Thoreau*, 54.

60. The grammar school ran through several masters in 1830, regained its "general discipline and good order" under "a faithful and skillful instructor," then suffered still more disruption with a series of unsatisfactory teachers. In April 1833 the school committee blamed the troubles on the need to make last-minute hires of inexperienced and unsuitable men. See "Third Annual Report of the Concord School Committee, for the year ending March 5, 1832," *YG*, March 17, 1832, and "Fourth Annual Report of the School Committee for the town of Concord, for the year ending March 4, 1833," *YG*, April 6, 1833.

61. Hutchinson, *Sketches of the Allen Family*, 42–43; Keyes, Autobiography, 8, 10, 14, 29–30; Wilson, "Mrs. Woodward Hudson's Memoir," 93–95; Edward W. Emerson, "Ebenezer Rockwood Hoar," *SCM* 4:10–11. The "big boy" from Weston, who fought with Allen, was Isaac Lamson Fiske, nineteen-year-old son of the longtime Middlesex County register of probate Isaac Fiske. See Joseph Palmer, *Necrology of Alumni of Harvard College, 1851–52 to 1862–63* (Boston, 1864), 340–42.

62. Keyes, Autobiography, 34; Edward Waldo Emerson, *Henry Thoreau, As Remembered by a Young Friend* (Boston, 1917), 14. On academies as staging grounds for personal and social class distinction, see Catherine E. Kelly, *In the New England Fashion: Reshaping Women's Lives in the Nineteenth Century* (Ithaca, N.Y., 1999), 70–92; Opal, *Beyond the Farm*, 96–125.

63. Robinson, *"Warrington" Pen-Portraits*, 7–11. Robinson remembered Jarvis's instruction favorably; the onetime schoolmaster, in turn, paid tribute to the boy "who always knew his lessons," "always stood at the head of his class, and . . . never gave me any trouble in his life" (p. 11). For more on Robinson, see Robert A. Gross, "'That Terrible Thoreau': Concord and Its Hermit," in William E. Cain, ed., *A Historical Guide to Henry David Thoreau* (New York, 2000), 220–25.

64. Walls, *Henry David Thoreau*, 44–45, 59–60, 62; Gross, "'Terrible Thoreau,'" 183, 232; Stanley K. Schultz, *The Culture Factory: Boston's Public Schools, 1789–1860* (New York, 1973), 9; Richard D. Brown, *The Strength of a People: The Idea of an Informed Citizenry in America, 1650–1870* (Chapel Hill, N.C., 1996), 100–1; "Winter Schools," *YG*, December 6, 1828; Records of the Grammar School for the term ending November 25, 1834 (entries for William B. Barrett; Horace Brown, Jr.; Abby, Mary, and Sarah Carr; Ellen Garrison; George Heywood; Dolly, Edmund, and John Hosmer),

CFPL; Mary Merrick Brooks (Concord) to Maria Weston Chapman (Boston), October 10, 1841, Anti-Slavery Collection, Ms. A.9.2.15, p. 76, BPL. It is noteworthy that Henry Vose and Stearns Wheeler, the two close friends Thoreau made at the academy, who accompanied him to Harvard, were not citizens of Concord.

65. The school committee reported enrollments at the public school as follows: 779 (1829–1830), 660 (1830–1831), 785 (1832–1833), 772 (1833–1834), 749 (1834–1835). According to the 1837 census of Concord, 596 inhabitants, out of a total population of 2,023, were between ages four and sixteen. Applying that fraction to the population enumerated on the federal census of 1830, 2,017, yields 595. Clearly, enrollment exceeded the pool of typical school-age children. Since most students left the public schools by sixteen, the additional students on the books were likely below age four. On the fad for infant education, see Dean May and Maris A. Vinovskis, "A Ray of Millennial Light: Early Education and Social Reform in the Infant School Movement in Massachusetts, 1826–1840," in Tamara K. Hareven, ed., *Family and Kin in Urban Communities, 1700–1930* (New York, 1977), 91. A different measure was used by Carl F. Kaestle and Maris A. Vinovskis to gauge enrollment rates. For the year 1826, when Massachusetts first required townships and cities to report educational statistics annually to the secretary of the Commonwealth, they computed the ratio of enrollment in the public schools to the population under age twenty in each town. The average for communities with 1,250 to 2,499 inhabitants was 72 percent. The comparable figure for enrollment in all schools, public and private, was 82 percent. Concord's enrollment rate in public schools was 74.5 percent and in all schools 83 percent. It appears from the more detailed evidence from Concord that small towns were enrolling nearly all eligible children in school. Attendance was another matter. See Kaestle and Vinovskis, *Education and Social Change in Nineteenth-Century Massachusetts* (New York, 1980), 21 (table 2.7). For additional evidence of near-universal enrollment of school-age children in Concord, see Levin, "Schools and Schooling in Concord," 369.

66. In 1830–1831 Concord's seven districts held school sessions for a total of 75 months. The school week was 5½ days; at four weeks per month, that comes to 22 days per month, yielding an aggregate of 1,650 school days for the year. Concord had seven school districts; the average length of school sessions per district comes to 236. That is well above the figure that Kaestle and Vinovskis report for cities with five thousand or more people, 204, and 1.6 times the average of 143 for towns of Concord's size. Then again the ratio is somewhat misleading, since the center district supported the grammar school and three primary schools. See their *Education and Social Change*, 24–25, and "Second Annual Report of the School Committee for the year ending May 1, 1831," YG, May 7, 1831.

67. "Second Annual Report of the School Committee of the Town of Concord for the Year Ending May 1, 1831," YG, May 7, 1831; CTMM 7:44, 48 (meetings of April 7, May 5, 1817), and 397, 405–10 (meetings of May 11, November 14, 1831), CFPL; Robert A. Gross and John Esty, "The Spirit of Concord," *Education Week* 14 (October 5, 1994): 44–45. In 1833 the appropriation briefly rose to $1,500 before dropping back to $1,400 the next year. In his unpublished autobiography, Jarvis pointedly noted Daniel Shattuck's "sharp trading." In *Traditions and Reminiscences* he softened that judgment and called Shattuck "a trader of great sagacity in purchasing." For Jarvis's account, see his "Autobiography" (1873), 2–4, Houghton, and *T&R*, 221.

68. Boarding in the district was ending as a common practice by 1833. The fourth annual school report, submitted on April 6, 1833, noted that "most of the Districts

pay their instructors in money, and they board themselves. The female teachers generally board at home." *YG*, April 6, 1832.

7. Internal Improvements

1. Ralph Waldo Emerson, "Introductory" lecture to series "The Present Age," *EL* 3:187 ("party of the Future"); Edward Waldo Emerson, "Remains of Thoreau," lecture in his manuscript notes on Thoreau, n.d., CFPL.

2. *CGMY*, May 14, 1825.

3. George Hendrick, ed., *Remembrances of Concord and the Thoreaus: Letters of Horace Hosmer to Dr. S. A. Jones* (Urbana, Ill., 1977), 22, 74–75, 84, 91, 93; F. B. Sanborn, *The Life of Henry David Thoreau Including Many Essays Hitherto Unpublished and Some Account of His Family and Friends* (Boston, 1917), 33; Laura Dassow Walls, *Henry David Thoreau: A Life* (Chicago, 2017), 29. Hosmer was a boy of nine when he boarded in the Thoreau household in 1839–1840 and attended the Concord Academy under John and Henry Thoreau. His reminiscences were penned in old age, starting in February 1891 and ending in December 1893, a few days before his death.

4. Johann N. Neem, *Creating a Nation of Joiners: Democracy and Civil Society in Early National Massachusetts* (Cambridge, Mass., 2008), 18–20; "An Act to Enable the Proprietors of Social Libraries to Manage the Same," March 3, 1798, and its replacement of the same name, March 8, 1806, reprinted in Henry Stedman Nourse, *Ninth Report of the Free Public Library Commission of Massachusetts, 1899: The Free Public Libraries of Massachusetts* (Boston, 1899), 433–35; Constitution and bylaws, list of shareholders, and meeting of January 4, 1830, Concord Social Library Records, CFPL; Robert A. Gross, *Books and Libraries in Thoreau's Concord: Two Essays* (Worcester, Mass., 1988). The quotation in the text is from the January 4, 1830, report of the standing committee. The constitution and bylaws of the library had no preamble declaring the group's purposes.

5. For the full story of the Charitable Library Society, see Gross, *Books and Libraries*. The charitable library succeeded an earlier effort to sustain a proprietary library in Concord. Back in 1784, leading figures in the Revolutionary elite founded the Library Company of Concord for "the diffusion of entertaining and useful knowledge." The venture was short-lived, but it left behind scattered traces of the varied tastes it served. Among the donations on the shelves were Jonathan Edwards's evangelical *Treatise Concerning the Religious Affections* (1746)—an unlikely gift from Ripley—resting uneasily alongside the ribald novels of Tobias Smollett and Laurence Sterne. See Library Company of Concord, Constitution and Record Book (1784), CFPL. Initially, the successor to the library company was known simply as the Charitable Society, in token of its benevolent purpose. With its restricted membership and philanthropic mission, it was unlike the many voluntary libraries established elsewhere in New England from the 1790s to the 1820s. See Charitable Library Society, Constitution and Records, CFPL; Jesse H. Shera, *Foundations of the Public Library: The Origins of the Public Library Movement in New England, 1629–1855* (Chicago, 1949), 54–126; Lynda K. Yankaskas, "Borrowing Culture: Social Libraries and American Civic Life, 1731–1854" (Ph.D. diss., Brandeis University, 2009), 9–10, 37–46.

6. Gross, *Books and Libraries*, 142–43, 154–55. The "Record of Books Lent by the Charitable Library Society, 1795–1800," CFPL, lists 110 borrowers, in addition to the prisoners in the Concord jail. There were fifty works of biography, history, and politics in the Charitable collection between 1795 and 1820; religious titles numbered ninety-nine. Jonas Minot, who married the widow Rebecca Thoreau in 1798, was president of the Charitable Library Society from 1797 to 1800.

7. Gross, *Books and Libraries*, 141, 152–56; Charitable Library Society, Constitution and Records, CFPL.

8. Gross, *Books and Libraries*, 158n29, 164. During its first decade of existence (1795–1804), the charitable library added an annual average of thirteen books from purchases and gifts; thereafter, it took in just five a year.

9. *T&R*, 129. Burgh's *Dignity of Human Nature* was also staple reading for Cynthia Dunbar Thoreau. See Henry Thoreau (Staten Island) to Cynthia Dunbar Thoreau (Concord), August 6, 1843, in Robert N. Hudspeth, ed., *The Correspondence of Henry D. Thoreau*, vol. 1, *1834–1848* (Princeton, N.J., 2013), 218–19.

10. Meetings of January 1 and 11, February 8, 1821, Charitable Library Society, Constitution and Records, 1:69–76; Concord Social Library Records, 1–13; Gross, *Books and Libraries*, 158–60. Josiah Davis, still a faithful follower of the minister in both library and parish, became the treasurer of the social library. He was joined by Daniel Shattuck as clerk and John Stacy as librarian.

11. List of shareholders, Concord Social Library Records; Shera, *Foundations*, 69. Of the 40 founding shareholders in 1821–1822, the economic standing of 36 could be identified on the 1826 assessment list of the town. Twenty-two (65 percent) were in the top 20 percent of property holders; 6 (18 percent) in the upper middle; 3 (9 percent) in the middle fifth; 2 (6 percent) in the lower middle; and 1 (3 percent) in the bottom fifth. The median age of the 40 founders was thirty-eight. Other charter members not mentioned in the text were Daniel Hunt's brother Nehemiah, the sensitive wool grower Joseph Barrett, the silk producer Anthony Wright, the cotton manufacturers Ephraim H. Bellows and sometime partner Eli Brown, the inventive pencil manufacturer Ebenezer Wood, and the shoe manufacturer Elijah Wood.

12. By-laws, and meeting of January 6, 1824, Concord Social Library Record Book, 11–13, 33–34; James N. Green, "The Rise of Book Publishing," in Robert A. Gross and Mary Kelley, eds., *An Extensive Republic: Print, Culture, and Society in the New Nation, 1790–1840* (Chapel Hill, N.C., 2010), 118–19. In the 1820s a new English novel would typically be reprinted in two volumes. Each would sell for one dollar.

13. Green, "Rise of Book Publishing," 126–27; Robert A. Gross, "Introduction," in Gross and Kelley, *Extensive Republic*, 1–50; CGMY, December 25, 1824. See, for example, the advertisements placed by the Cambridge firm Hilliard & Brown and its successor, Brown, Shattuck, & Co., YG, December 2, 1827, January 22, September 24, 1831, June 23, 1832, May 25, 1833, and by Richardson, Lord, and Holbrook of Boston in YG, January 15, 1831.

14. Concord Social Library Record Book, 33–34 (January 6, 1824), 36–38 (January 3, 1825), 41–44 (January 2, 1826), 45–48 (January 3, 1827), 63–64 (January 4, 1830). Ironically, borrowing by proprietors was more closely correlated with new acquisitions than were withdrawals by others. The sponsors of the library were misled by their own rhetoric. In fact, they were more eager than anyone to read the latest publications. Gross, *Books and Libraries*, 164.

15. Gross, *Books and Libraries*, 162–63; MG, July 18, 1821; YG, April 29, 1826; Shattuck, *Memorials*, 300–2.

16. Gross, *Books and Libraries*, 142–43, 163, 415. The drop-off of religious titles in the switch from the charitable to the social library was dramatic. Half of the twenty-two works acquired by the former institution between 1815 and 1819 dealt with religion and moral philosophy; only two of the forty-seven titles obtained by the latter between 1821 and 1824 did the same. Over the entire history of the social library from 1821 to 1850, only 4 percent of the 491 titles dealt with religion. As for politics, the library did admit the occasional publication by prominent Whigs.

It purchased a volume of speeches made in Congress against the removal of the Cherokee Indians from Georgia (1830) and accepted the gift of former Middlesex congressman Edward Everett's *Orations and Speeches* (1836).

17. Gross, *Books and Libraries*, 174–75; Thomas Jefferson Randolph, ed., *Memoir, Correspondence, and Miscellanies, From the Papers of Thomas Jefferson*, 4 vols., 2nd ed. (Boston, 1830), 4:320–23, 363–65; Concord Social Library Record Book, 70–73 (January 2, 1831). The missing pages in the Concord library's edition are pp. 321–22, 364–65. Actually, the committee understated the damage it inflicted on the text. The mutilated volume still survives in the collection of the Concord Free Public Library, mute testimony to the industry of the local censors. Not one but two of Jefferson's letters were expurgated. The "obnoxious" passages were what the committee said: rude dismissals of the authenticity of the Gospels. One letter brands Saint Paul "the first corrupter of the doctrines of Jesus"; the second, written to John Adams in 1823, derides the doctrines of Calvinism. "The day will come," the freethinking Virginian predicted, "when the mystical generation of Jesus, by the Supreme Being as his father, in the womb of a virgin, will be classed with the fable of the generation of Minerva in the brain of Jupiter." The volume also reveals which member of the committee initiated the destruction. On the page facing the irreverent letter to John Adams, a question is penciled in the margin: "Does [Moses] Prichard want to tear out 3 or 4 leaves out of this Book?" Though a loyalist to the First Parish, the junior partner of Samuel Burr, then struggling with the collapse of their business, was no more sympathetic to Enlightenment deism than were his charitable library predecessors to the radicalism of Thomas Paine. The incident passed quickly without stirring any interest in Jefferson's *Works*. Two years later a new selection committee, including Lemuel Shattuck, proposed selling off several books in the collection that "are of little use," and it singled out the Jefferson edition, "an interesting and valuable work for a private Library, but not sufficiently popular to be of much use where it now is, having been loaned out but once during the past year." Fortunately for the historian, this early venture in deaccessioning went nowhere.

18. Gross, *Books and Libraries*, 142–43, 164–66, 390, 412, 415; Concord Social Library Record Book, 45–48 (January 7, 1827). Books devoted to "matters of fact" comprised 40 to 45 percent of new purchases in the 1820s and 1830s.

19. Gross, *Books and Libraries*, 152–53, 167–69; George F. Hoar, *Autobiography of Seventy Years*, 2 vols. (New York, 1903), 1:58. The incident must have occurred in 1832, when the future U.S. senator from Massachusetts was six years old. That was the publication date of "Parker's Revised Edition" of Scott's *Redgauntlet*, which had originally appeared from the Boston publisher in 1824. The youngest child in the family, the boy was unaware that his sister Elizabeth, a dozen years his senior, ignored their father's prohibition and happily read Scott's *Chronicles of Cannongate* and *St. Valentine's Day* upon their publication in 1828. See Elizabeth Sherman Hoar to Marianne Cornelia Giles, October 1–2, 1828, in Elizabeth Maxfield-Miller, ed., "Elizabeth of Concord: Selected Letters of Elizabeth Sherman Hoar (1814–1878) to the Emersons, Family, and the Emerson Circle (Part Two)," *Studies in the American Renaissance* 9 (1985): 99. In its inaugural year the social library acquired eight titles; six were novels by Scott. The next year, 1822, brought three more, and they kept on coming for the rest of the decade.

20. Gross, *Books and Libraries*, 168–69. Works by American authors constituted an amazing 70 percent of all novels ordered by the social library during the late 1830s.

21. Jarvis, Diary, 1:136, 185, 188, 201–2, 226–27.

22. Ibid., 2:134–35; Gross, *Books and Libraries*, 168.

23. Gross, *Books and Libraries*, 160–62; Concord Social Library Record Book, 99–103 (January 5, 1835). The *Catalogue of Concord Social Library* (Concord, Mass., 1836) lists 587 titles and 926 volumes in the collection. In 1837 Concord possessed nearly six hundred books, two and a half times the size of the average library.

24. "Concord," *YG*, April 29, 1826.

25. The earliest meeting of the Concord Debating Club of which there is a record took place on November 21, 1822. But since this was an "adjourned meeting," the group had clearly been in existence longer. See *MO*, November 16, 1822. The Boston Debating Society was launched in January–February 1821, apparently the first in the Bay State; see *Boston Commercial Gazette*, February 1, 1821; *Columbian Centinel*, February 3, 1821. It was followed by Newburyport (*Newburyport Herald*, June 26, 1821), New Bedford (*New-Bedford Mercury*, September 21, 1821), Concord, Salem (*Salem Gazette*, October 12, 1824), Haverhill (*Haverhill Gazette and Patriot*, February 12, 1825), Hingham ("Jefferson Debating Society of Hingham," *Salem Gazette*, January 30, 1827), Fall River (*Massachusetts Spy*, March 7, 1827), Gardner (*National Aegis*, July 18, 1827), and Worcester (*Massachusetts Spy*, September 15, 1830). Massachusetts lagged behind New York, Philadelphia, and Baltimore in forming these societies. See "Debating Society," *Boston Commercial Gazette*, December 11, 1820.

26. "Debating Society," *Boston Commercial Gazette*, March 1, 1821; "Debating Society," *Independent Chronicle and Boston Patriot*, March 21, 1821; "Communication," *New-Bedford Mercury*, September 21, 1821; Angela G. Ray, "The Permeable Public: Rituals of Citizenship in Antebellum Men's Debating Clubs," *Argumentation and Advocacy* 41 (Summer 2004): 1–16; Carolyn Eastman, *A Nation of Speechifiers: Making an American Public After the Revolution* (Chicago, 2009), 118–23.

27. *Boston Commercial Gazette*, March 7, 1827. The only record of membership in the Concord Debating Club is a list of the fourteen individuals belonging to the group at its merger with the Concord Lyceum on March 11, 1829. See "Early Records of the Concord Lyceum," in Kenneth Walter Cameron, comp., *The Massachusetts Lyceum During the American Renaissance; Materials for the Study of the Oral Tradition in American Letters: Emerson, Thoreau, Hawthorne, and Other New-England Lecturers* (Hartford, Conn., 1969), 114. Of the thirteen members whose ages are known, close to a third (31 percent) were ages twenty-three to twenty-five; well over half (54 percent) were in their thirties; and the remaining two were ages forty-one and fifty-four. Seven were single, six married, though two would wed not long after the debating club gave up its separate existence. Four of the entire fourteen in 1829 were members of the Social Circle: Josiah Davis, Ephraim Meriam, Lemuel Shattuck, and William Whiting; Phineas Howe would enter the elite club in 1831.

28. *MO*, November 16, 1822; "An Act to Incorporate the President, Directors and Company of the Middlesex Bank," January 29, 1822, *Private and Special Statutes of the Commonwealth of Massachusetts from June 1814 to February 1822* (Boston, 1823), 5:451–53; *YG*, November 4, 1826, February 16, 1828. For debates over the establishment of religion and the usefulness of religious controversies, see *CGMY*, December 3, 1825, March 25, 1826; *YG*, December 2, 1826, February 17, 1827, March 29, 1828; on political parties and instructions, *CGMY*, November 13, 1824, January 14, 1826; *YG*, March 22, 1828. Economic policies on state and federal levels—protective tariffs for the benefit of manufacturing, the banking system, the regulation of interest rates, the proposal for a railroad from Boston to Albany—were regular items on the club's agenda.

29. *CGMY*, January 21, 1826 (female education), December 10, 1825 (relative influence

of "ladies" and "gentlemen"), January 3, 1824 (Napoleon); *YG* (February 9, 1828 (intellectual abilities of whites and Blacks), December 16, 1826 (dispossession of "savages"), April 12, 1828 (French Revolution), February 2, 1828 (progress of morals), November 17, 1827 (debating clubs).

30. Jarvis, Diary, 1:127-28, 132-33, 205-206, 211, and Autobiography, 33-34.

31. [William S. Robinson], "Old School Fellows," *R*, July 19, 1841; Harriet H. Robinson, ed., *"Warrington" Pen-Portraits: A Collection of Personal and Political Reminiscences from 1848 to 1876, from the Writings of William S. Robinson* (Boston, 1877), 9-10; Dorothy Nyren, ""The Concord Academic Debating Society," *Massachusetts Review* 4 (Autumn 1962): 81-84; *Walden*, 102.

32. *CGMY*, December 17, 1825 (South America), January 17, 1824 (manners and morals).

33. Franklin Dexter Bowditch, *Biographical Sketches of the Graduates of Yale College with Annals of the College History*, vol. 6, *September, 1805-September, 1815* (New Haven, Conn., 1912), 334-38.

34. [Josiah Holbrook], "Associations of Adults for Mutual Education," *American Journal of Education* 1 (October 1826): 594-97; Carl Bode, *American Lyceum: Town Meeting of the Mind* (New York, 1956), 10-12.

35. Chandos Michael Brown, *Benjamin Silliman: A Life in the Young Republic* (Princeton, N.J., 1989), 57, 115, 117-18, 147, 220; Cecil B. Hayes, *The American Lyceum: Its History and Contribution to Education* (Washington, D.C., 1932), viii; Bode, *American Lyceum*, 13-19, 101-10; Josiah Holbrook, *American Lyceum, or Society for the Improvement of Schools, and Diffusion of Useful Knowledge* (Boston, 1829).

36. John L. Brooke, *The Heart of the Commonwealth: Society and Political Culture in Worcester County, Massachusetts, 1713-1861* (New York, 1989), 283-303; Bode, *American Lyceum*, 13-14; "American Lyceum," *YG*, August 23, 1828.

37. *YG*, August 23, November 8 and 29, 1828; "Early Records of the Concord Lyceum," 109.

38. "Early Records of the Concord Lyceum," 109-10, 115-16.

39. *YG*, January 17, 1829; "Boston Lyceum," *Boston Recorder*, May 28, 1829. Of the fifty-seven charter members of the Concord Lyceum, the ages of fifty-three are known. Their average age in January 1829 was thirty-five, median age thirty-four. One fifth were between ten and nineteen years old; 13 percent in their twenties; just about one-third in their thirties; 14 percent in their forties; 13 percent in their fifties; 6 percent were in their sixties and older. The twelve-year-old charter member was Ebenezer Rockwood Hoar, a future attorney general of the United States. Of the twenty officers of the social library between 1821 and 1835, all but three (85 percent) helped to found or were officers of the lyceum. In Worcester as in Concord, members of the commercial and professional elite, notably the law partners Emory Washburn and John Davis, controlled the top offices in the lyceum. See Christopher Young-Min Chi, "Diffusing Useful Knowledge in Worcester and Concord: The Early Lyceum Movement in Two Massachusetts Towns" (senior honors thesis, Harvard College, 1993; on deposit at AAS), chap. 1.

40. "Early Records of the Concord Lyceum," 110-11, 113-14, 116; *YG*, February 21, March 7, 1829. The lyceum sponsored 143 lectures between 1829 and 1834 and 118 over the ensuing five years. There were two and a half times as many lectures as debates between 1829 and 1834.

41. *CGMY*, January 8 (advertisement for "Lectures on Astronomy") and May 14, 1825; November 7, 1830; "Early Records of the Concord Lyceum," 116. For other examples of lectures and exhibitions, see the favorable comment on the "Astro-

nomical Lectures" given by Rev. Hervey Wilbur, author of *Elements of Astronomy, Descriptive and Physical* (New Haven, Conn., 1830), in *YG*, March 17, 1832, and the description of Howe's Menagerie, exhibited at the Middlesex Hotel, in early June 1834, in *YG*, May 31, 1834.

42. "Early Records of the Concord Lyceum," 116, 124, 126, 136, 139; Donald M. Scott, "The Popular Lecture and the Creation of a Public in Mid-Nineteenth-Century America," *Journal of American History* 66 (March 1980): 792. For the lecturers, in order of appearance in the text, see "Early Records," 130 (Bellows), 123–24 (Wright), 120 (Cyrus Hosmer), 114 (G. W. Hosmer), 116 and 126 (Southmayd), 117 (Bartlett), 125 (Moore), 121, 125 (Allen), 121 (Goodwin), 122 (Shattuck). Eight of the eighty-two lectures in the period 1829–1834 could not be classified by subject area. Of the remaining seventy-four, over half (52 percent) dealt with science (31), technology (4), and agriculture (4). Manuals on agriculture aimed to transmit scientific knowledge to farmers. The Salem Lyceum did much better than Concord in recruiting local speakers; on its early programs, residents made up three out of every four lecturers.

43. John S. Keyes, "Memoir of Nehemiah Ball," *SCM* 2:234–40. Ball lectured a dozen times between 1829 and 1834, more than anyone else. Ebenezer Rockwood Hoar remembered Ball's presentation more generously. In his recollection, the youthful listeners experienced "delight" at the illustrations of apes, monkeys, and baboons that Ball projected with the use of a magic lantern. See Hoar, "Introductory Address," *Proceedings on the Fiftieth Anniversary of the Organization of the Concord Lyceum, Tuesday, Jan. 7, 1879* (Concord, Mass., 1879), reprinted in Cameron, comp., *The Massachusetts Lyceum During the American Renaissance*, 27.

44. Eleven clergymen addressed the lyceum between 1829 and 1834, the years when the orthodox-liberal contest ended with the separation of church and state: six were Unitarians, five Trinitarian Congregationalists. Over the next five years, even as more ministers took the platform, they reflected the growing religious diversity in the Bay State: Unitarians, Congregationalists, Baptists, and a single Universalist.

45. "Early Records of the Concord Lyceum," 116, 120, 133; Prudence Ward (Concord) to Dennis Ward (Spencer), December 7, 1833, Ward Papers, Thoreau Society Archive at Thoreau Institute, Concord. For other talks in which lecturers revealed their biases against Jacksonian populism and workingmen's radicalism, see Edward Everett, *A Lecture on the Working Men's Party, First Delivered October Sixth, before the Charlestown Lyceum* (Boston, 1830), 25, and Cornelius C. Felton, *An Address Pronounced on the Anniversary of the Concord Lyceum, November 4, 1829* (Cambridge, Mass., 1829), 32; Chi, "Diffusing Useful Knowledge," introduction. See also Rev. Warren Burton's pronouncement that subordination to political party was a form of "white slavery" and hence "a new emancipation cause." Burton developed this view in two lectures of 1839, one recorded as "Citizen Slave," the other on "Responsibilities of Suffrage." See Burton, *White Slavery: A New Emancipation Cause, Presented to the People of the United States* (Worcester, Mass., 1839), and *YG*, March 2, 1839. In 1831 Emory Washburn, a future governor of Massachusetts, gave a lecture at the Worcester Lyceum in which he leveled the same charge as Everett, denouncing the Workingmen's Party for "artfully fomenting" divisions in the manufacturing town and "striking at the very foundations of civil society." See Chi, "Diffusing Useful Knowledge," 27.

46. *YG*, September 15, 1832; Whitman, *Lecture*, 9; Chi, "Diffusing Useful Knowl-

edge," 6–7. For similar sentiments regarding the contribution of lyceums to local unity, see the responses to a survey conducted by the Middlesex County Lyceum in *YG*, February 11, 1832.

47. "Early Records of the Concord Lyceum," 125–26.

48. Jonathan T. Davis, Class of 1829, Class Book, Harvard University Archives, 317–20; "Early Records of the Concord Lyceum," 127. From 1829 to 1841, the Concord Lyceum hosted eighty-nine debates, in which a total of fifty-one members took part. The average age of the forty-three participants at their first appearance on the platform was thirty-four; the median age thirty-three. But a dozen men dominated the stage. Some debates enlisted as many as six participants, others as few as two or three. Altogether, 335 slots were available over the years. A dozen men spoke more than ten times, a few more than thirty. Daniel Shattuck was the most frequent debater with thirty-five appearances; he was followed by Edward Jarvis with thirty-two. Other prominent debaters were Lemuel Shattuck and Nehemiah Ball. The twelve most active debaters accounted for 63 percent of all speaking slots. The median age of these speakers was nearly thirty-nine; that of the thirty-one less active debaters whose ages are known was twenty-eight. Young men still in school had ample opportunities to participate in debates. A "Young Men's Debating and Declaiming Society" was founded in December 1827 by grammar schoolmaster Horatio Wood for the boys under his charge, and it lasted until March 1831. Students at the Concord Academy started a similar society to which they gave the name "the young men's Society for mutual improvement." See *CR*, July 19, 1841, for records of the first group, and George Moore, "The Diary of George Moore," in Kenneth Walter Cameron, comp., *Transcendental Epilogue: Primary Materials for Research in Emerson, Thoreau, Literary New England, the Influence of German Theology, and Higher Biblical Criticism*, 3 vols. (Hartford, Conn., 1965–1982), 1:25–27, for the second.

49. E. R. Hoar, "Memoir of Josiah Davis," *SCM* 2:100; "Early Records of the Concord Lyceum," 128–29. The debate over the relationship between the soil of a country and the energy of the inhabitants, held on November 21, 1832, seems the most likely occasion for Davis's memorable remark. Rockwood Hoar, who recalled the incident, was sixteen at the time.

50. "Early Records of the Concord Lyceum," 123–24, 127–28, 141; *YG*, February 11, 1832; survey of lyceums in Massachusetts for the year leading up to July 1, 1840, in Horace Mann, secretary of the Massachusetts Board of Education, *Third Annual Report* (Boston, 1840), 74–77. The Middlesex Lyceum surveyed the lyceums in the county at the end of 1831. It received replies from sixteen towns, one more than were represented at the founding of the Middlesex association in November 1829 and that were in existence the following year. According to the committee in charge of the survey, an additional nine lyceums failed to respond. Twenty-four lyceums thus were operating in the thirty-five Middlesex towns in 1832—the same numbers as in 1840. Boston was, truly, a hub of lyceums, with one for every 3,684 Suffolk inhabitants. Middlesex supported one lyceum for every 4,442 inhabitants. Norfolk County, with thirteen lyceums in twenty-two towns, came close to Middlesex. Elsewhere, only 43 percent of Essex County towns (12 of 28) had lyceums; roughly, a third of the towns in Bristol (6 of 19), Plymouth (7 of 21), Barnstable (5 of 14), and Worcester (18 of 57) counties could say the same. Lyceums were few and far between in the western hinterland of the Commonwealth, in Hampshire (3 of 23 towns), Hampden (1 of 18), and Franklin (5 of 26) counties. Middlesex had the

same number of lyceums in 1840 as in 1832; thus, the movement seems to have hit a plateau in the early 1830s and was working hard to sustain numbers and enthusiasm by the end of the decade. In its response to the Middlesex Lyceum survey, Concord's reported a membership of "about 100." By September 1832 the number had risen to 118.

51. "Early Records of the Concord Lyceum," 124, 142, 146; *YG*, January 17, November 28, 1829, September 17, 1831; Whitman, *Lecture*, 9. See Ripley, "On the government of the temper," a lecture delivered at Concord Lyceum, December 29, 1830, CFPL.

52. "Early Records of the Concord Lyceum," 113–14, 118, 121, 129, 133, 136–37.

53. *EL* 1:5–26 (quotations at 7, 10–11, 18, 23), 87–88.

54. Holbrook, *American Lyceum*, 6; E. R. Hoar, "Memoir of William Whiting," *SCM* 2:260, 262.

55. *YG*, April 19, December 20, 1828; "Early Records of the Concord Lyceum," 126, 130.

56. W. J. Rorabaugh, *The Alcoholic Republic: An American Tradition* (New York, 1979), 5–11, 225–33, estimates the national consumption of spirits per capita as 5.0 gallons in 1825 and 5.2 in 1830; wine was 0.2 gallons in the first year, 0.3 in the second. It is hard to gauge whether these estimates are appropriate to Concord, since they register the heavy use of whiskey, derived from corn and rye, in the country at large, whereas Yankees were still wedded to rum. The figures for Concord come from "Traditions and Reminiscences of Concord, Massachusetts, 1779–1878, or a Contribution to the Social and Domestic History of the Town, 1779 to 1878," at CFPL, which was later published by the University of Massachusetts Press (Amherst, 1993); they were put into print by Jarvis as *Financial Connection of the Use of Spirits and Wine with the People of Concord, Massachusetts* (Boston, 1883). Jarvis's tables are riddled with errors of calculation and transcription. With the mistakes corrected, consumption of spirits of all kinds in Concord seems to have come to 5.4 gallons per capita in 1828 (9,675 gallons of spirits at the stores, 823 gallons at the taverns, with population estimated at 1,960); wine consumption in 1828 averaged 0.6 per capita (939 gallons at the stores, 210 at the taverns), two to three times the national figure. One contemporary estimate put consumption of ardent spirits at four gallons per capita; see "Intemperance" in *CGMY*, March 6, 1824, reprinting from the *Boston Telegraph*. These numbers can create a misleading impression. Five gallons annually translates into 640 fluid ounces; a shot of whiskey or rum is typically 1.5 ounces. In other words, the average American consumed a little over one shot per day (640 fluid ounces = 427 shots, equivalent to 1.2 shots a day). But children should be omitted from the calculation. Omitting children fifteen and under roughly doubles the estimate to 2.4 shots a day or 3.6 ounces. The daily rum ration of a Continental Army soldier was 4 ounces. Rorabaugh, *Alcoholic Republic*, 65. In 1828 liquor sales at the village stores earned three times as much revenue ($3,564) as did wine purchases ($1,130). At the taverns that year the ratio was 3.8 ($4,534/$1,197). *T&R*, 177, 179, and Jarvis, *Financial Connection*, 7.

57. *CGMY*, July 17, 1824; "Dr. Josiah Bartlett," *Boston Medical and Surgical Journal* 98 (January 17, 1878): 88–89; *T&R*, 155.

58. *T&R*, 164–66; Daniel Shattuck, "Memoir of Jonathan Davis," and John Shepard Keyes, "Memoir of Daniel Shattuck," in *SCM* 2:106–7, 137–39. Under Massachusetts law, minors (individuals under 21) were barred from drinking in public houses unless they had permission from their parents, masters, or guardians. "An

Act for the Due Regulation of Licensed Houses," 1786, chap. 68, in *Acts and Laws of the Commonwealth of Massachusetts*, 13 vols. (Boston, 1890–1898), 5:210.

59. Entries for March 17 and 23, April 27, 1812, in Tilly Merrick Account Book, CFPL; for May 13, June 4, August 6, November 6, 1812, in Stephen Wood Account Book; and May 13, June 21, 1812, in Samuel Burr Daybooks, CFPL; *T&R*, 12; Ezra Ripley, "On the duty & advantages of temperance," rewritten with alterations, December 17, 1826, 6–8, Ezra Ripley sermons, bMS 64/2, Folder 5, HDS.

60. David W. Conroy, *In Public Houses: Drink and the Revolution of Authority in Colonial Massachusetts* (Chapel Hill, N.C., 1995), 37; "Act for the Due Regulation of Licensed Houses," 206–16; *T&R*, 155–59; Keyes, "Memoir of Daniel Shattuck," *SCM* 2:138. Alcoholic beverages—chiefly West Indian rum, followed by Lisbon wine, brandy, and gin—accounted for 6 to 7 percent of the value of Jonathan H. Davis's inventory when his stock of goods was appraised in March 1815; that is close to the 8.6 percent share that such goods comprised of Samuel Rex's stock in trade when he set up his store in Schaefferstown, Pennsylvania, in 1790. Diane E. Wenger, *A Country Storekeeper in Pennsylvania: Creating Economic Networks in Early America, 1790–1807* (University Park, Pa., 2008), 124.

61. Votes of the town to post notices of future meetings at the public houses in the center, CTMM 7:433 (meeting of March 4, 1833), 8:12 (meeting of April 8, 1834), CFPL; Fay & Wesson, landlords of the Middlesex Hotel, account with the Town of Concord, March 5, 1827, ETR; John S. Keyes, "Memoir of William Shepherd," *SCM* 2:130–31, 357; Jack Larkin, *The Reshaping of Everyday Life 1790–1840* (New York, 1988), 281–86.

62. John S. Keyes, "The Middlesex Hotel" (unpublished manuscript dated April 2, 1900), 3–4, 9–10, in Keyes Papers, CFPL; Keyes, "Memoir of William Shepherd," 356–63; *T&R*, 159–61; Larkin, *Reshaping of Everyday Life*, 282. On the role of taverns in congregating and segregating social classes in big cities, see Peter Thompson, *Rum Punch and Revolution: Taverngoing and Public Life in Eighteenth-Century Philadelphia* (Philadelphia, 1998).

63. Sanborn, *Life of Thoreau*, 33; Records of Middlesex County criminal cases kept by Justice of the Peace Abiel Heywood of Concord, 1798–1823, CFPL, and Abiel Heywood, Criminal Docket for the County of Middlesex, 1823–38, Special Collections, Harvard Law School. Cases of assault (53) and theft (51) abounded on Heywood's docket, intermixed with charges of destroying property, disorderly conduct, and profanity. Just two men were brought before the justice's court at the Middlesex Hotel to answer complaints of public drunkenness; both were acquitted.

64. John M. Cheney, "Memoir of Abel Moore," *SCM* 2:291–92; Keyes, "Middlesex Hotel," unpublished manuscript, 11–12. Patch operated what became known as the Bigelow tavern, and when he abandoned that enterprise to keep bar for Tom Wesson at the Middlesex Hotel, the deal with Moore went with him, to the amusement of the new employer.

65. Ezra Ripley, manuscript record of deaths in Concord, 1778–1841, CFPL; *T&R*, 204–19; Ripley, "The inattention of man to divine operations considered and reproved, the contrary urged," an "occasional" sermon delivered December 24, 1814, Box 3 of 13, Houghton. The accidental deaths Ripley had in mind were evidently those of Jonas Blood on January 13, 1814, which the parson attributed to "a fit of drunkenness, falling, bruised, bleeding, cold, suffocation, death," and of Capt. Nathan Brown in December of that year, owing to a fall "from the pole of a waggon [*sic*] under ye wheels."

66. Joel Charles Bernard, "From Theodicy to Ideology: The Origins of the American Temperance Movement" (Ph.D. diss., Yale University, 1983), 187–92; *Constitution of the Massachusetts Society, for the Suppression of Intemperance, and Report of the Board of Counsel* (Boston, 1813), 3; Concord Auxiliary Society for the Suppression of Intemperance, resolutions adopted by the board of officers, January 17, 1814, and first annual report (written by Ripley), December 5, 1814, Record Book, CAS Collection D-2076, CFPL; Robert L. Hampel, *Temperance and Prohibition in Massachusetts, 1813–1852* (Ann Arbor, 1982), 19–22.

67. George M. Brooks, "Memoir of Nathan Brooks," *SCM* 2:62; Concord Auxiliary Society, annual report at December 5, 1814, and December 2, 1815, meetings, and entry for meetings of January 16 and 30, 1817, Record Book, CFPL; Ripley, "On the duty & advantages of temperance."

68. *YG*, May 12, October 13, December 8, 1827, January 3 (Fiske brothers), May 2, 1829 (Moses Davis), September 1 (Middlesex Mutual Fire Insurance Co.), September 8, 1832; *T&R*, 172 (Charles B. Davis); J. Fay Barrett, "George Minot Barrett," *SCM* 3:100; Nehemiah Ball, "Memoir of Samuel Buttrick," *SCM* 2:157–58; *YG*, March 31, 1827 (Middlesex Husbandmen).

69. *YG*, April 14, June 15, July 28, 1827, September 21, 1833; *T&R*, 172–83, 185; Rorabaugh, *Alcoholic Republic*, 228, 293n8, citing Jarvis, *Financial Connection of the Use of Spirits and Wine with the People of Concord, Massachusetts* (Boston, 1883). Jarvis's statistics, compiled and analyzed when he was in his late seventies, are something of a mess, and the published version of *Traditions and Reminiscences* adds to the errors. In several places he made shrewd adjustments to the numbers, estimating, for example, that only half of the sales of ardent spirits at taverns were to local inhabitants, but then he forgot to carry the revised figure over to the table of "total spirits and wines sold to people of Concord at stores and taverns" (p. 179). The published version of his manuscript confuses matters still more with inaccurate headings for the columns in that table (p. 179). After correcting these errors, I find that per capita consumption of spirits was 5.4 gallons in 1828, a little above Rorabaugh's estimate of 5 gallons in 1825 and 5.1 in 1830. Drinking in Concord was typical of the nation as a whole. But the town's turn away from strong drink was much faster. Per capita consumption in Concord was 3.5 gallons in 1833 and 4.2 overall. In sum, drinking of ardent spirits per person declined by 35 percent between 1828 and 1833.

An earlier survey of liquor sales in Concord is consistent with these results. In 1827 printers John C. Allen and Herman Atwill moved beyond running pro-temperance pieces in the *Yeoman's Gazette*. In January of that year the partners engaged in a rare act of journalistic initiative; they visited the village stores and asked the owners how much "New England rum," the product of Massachusetts distilleries, they had sold in the previous year. Each merchant readily complied with this unusual request, and after checking over their account books, they reported the results. Total sales came to more than twelve thousand gallons, two-thirds of which was consumed locally; that was the equivalent of over four gallons for every man, woman, and child in town. Altogether, the stores took in $2,800 from the rum, about half of all the taxes collected in Concord over the same period. The figures were considerable; if other spirits had been counted, per capita consumption would unquestionably have exceeded five gallons. "New England Rum," *YG*, January 13, 1827.

70. Rev. William A. Hallock, *"Light and Love" A Sketch of the Life and Labors of the Rev. Justin Edwards, D.D., the Evangelical Pastor: the Advocate of Temperance, the Sabbath, and the Bible* (New York, 1855); *YG*, November 14, 1829; *Boston Recorder*, February 24, 1830; Ian R. Tyrrell, *Sobering Up: From Temperance to Prohibition in America, 1800–1860* (West-

port, Conn., 1979), 58–70; Hampel, *Temperance and Prohibition*, 25–26; Joel Charles Bernard, "From Theodicy to Ideology: The Origins of the American Temperance Movement" (Ph.D. diss., Yale University, 1983), 324–32, 387–88.

71. *CGMY*, March 6, May 1, 1824; "The Proser No. V," *CGMY*, January 24, 1824.

72. *CGMY*, November 27, 1824; *YG*, June 1, February 18, 1832, February 3, 1827; December 3, 10, 24, 31, 1831; May 19, June 2, 1832; January 23, 1830; *CGMY*, May 8, 1824; "New England Rum," *YG*, January 13, 1827.

73. Rod Phillips, *Alcohol: A History* (Chapel Hill, N.C., 2014), 103–5, 112–13; *YG*, June 18, 1827; *New England Journal of Medicine* 1 (February 1828 to February 1829): 720; Matthew Warner Osborn, *Rum Maniacs: Alcoholic Insanity in the Early American Republic* (Chicago, 2014), 108–13; Bernard, "From Theodicy to Ideology," 351–61; Grindall Reynolds, "Memoir of Dr. Josiah Bartlett," *SCM* 2:172–75, 184–85, Franklin B. Sanborn, "Dr. Bartlett of Concord," *Springfield Daily Republican*, January 8, 1878.

74. Rorabaugh, *Alcoholic Republic*, 39–45; Joel Bernard, "Between Religion and Reform: American Moral Societies, 1811–1821," *Proceedings of the MHS*, 3rd ser., 105 (1993): 26–32; "X.Y.Z.," *YG*, February 22, 1834 (citing the opinions of physicians in Boston, Albany, and Cincinnati), and March 22, 1834 (quoting Benjamin Rush as "the highest medical authority"). Given the emphasis on medical arguments against the consumption of alcohol, I have attributed the authorship of the "X.Y.Z." essays to the three physicians in town, all of whom were active in the Middlesex County Temperance Society in 1834, Bartlett as treasurer, Jarvis as secretary. At the end of 1834, Bartlett was also elected president of the Concord Temperance Society (*CF*, January 3, 1835). Prescott moved from Meredith Bridge, N.H., to Concord during the winter of 1832–1833, and despite his brief residence, was elected vice president of the Concord Temperance Society at its formation in October 1833 (*YG*, October 19, 1833). Prescott joined the Trinitarian church and served as the physician to the orthodox Congregationalists, before returning to New Hampshire in the winter of 1835. See William Prescott, *The Prescott Memorial: or a Genealogical Memoir of the Prescott Families in America* (Boston, 1870), 323–24.

75. "Early Records of the Concord Lyceum," 126; *YG*, March 17, September 15, 1832; *Spirit of the Age and Journal of Humanity*, June 13, 1833; *YG*, October 19, 1833; Report of the Concord Temperance Society at the quarterly meeting of the Middlesex County Temperance Society (MCTS), January 28, 1834, CFPL. Harvard faculty sat on the executive board of the MCTS with bitter enemies of their school. What made this collaboration possible was an ingenious compromise. The MCTS began as an independent organization, unaffiliated with either the ATS or the MSSI. Moreover, its statement of purpose skirted potentially divisive issues. The constitution of the Concord Temperance Society (CTS) was nearly word for word the same as that of the MCTS. Its initial slate of officers was divided between Unitarians (Ripley as president, John Stacy as treasurer) and Trinitarians (Dr. Prescott as vice-president, Josiah Davis as secretary).

76. Report of the CTS at the quarterly meeting of the MCTS, January 28, 1834; report of the officers of the CTS, February 25, 1834, printed in *YG*, March 15, 1834; William Munroe, Jr., "Memoir of William Munroe," *SCM* 2:155; Mary Babson Fuhrer, *A Crisis of Community: The Trials and Transformation of a New England Town, 1815–1848* (Chapel Hill, N.C., 2014), 152–70. The federal census of 1830 counted 1,993 white inhabitants of Concord, of whom 1,073 were age twenty and over. (The Black population numbered 28, lumped together without respect to age.) The 550 subscribers to the CTS constitution by the end of 1834 thus comprised 51 percent of the adult white

population. The 1837 census of the town found 2,023 residents, nearly the same as seven years before. Shattuck, *History*, 211.

77. Bernard, "From Theodicy to Ideology," 388–93; George Faber Clark, *History of the Temperance Reform in Massachusetts, 1813–1883* (Boston, 1888), 12; First Parish Record Book (transcript), July 1, 1832, 272–73, CFPL; Mary Munroe, "Historical Sketch of the Second Congregational Church and Society, Concord, Mass., 1826–1876," 14, Trinitarian Congregational Church Records, Box 1, CFPL; December 27, 1833, resolution to require total abstinence from ardent spirits as a condition of church membership, Second Congregational Church Record Book, 1826–67, 48, CFPL; Barzillai Frost, "Memoir of Hersey B. Goodwin," *SCM* 2:282–83.

78. *T&R*, 172–74. Between 1828 and 1833, sales of wine rose from 150 to 225 gallons at Phineas How's store and from 500 to 542 gallons at the green store, remained flat at Shattuck's establishment (200 gallons), and fell slightly at Hildreth's (from 25 to 20 gallons). Wine sales showed no change at the Middlesex Hotel and at Shepherd's inn. (Bigelow's provided no figures.) In short, sales of rum and brandy may have been falling off, as a result of the temperance movement, but wine was as popular as ever. When Jarvis looked over the reports he and Bartlett had collected from the village merchants, he was so taken by the sharp decline in liquor sales that he overlooked the steady consumption of the fruit of the vine.

79. "Read! And Reflect!" by "A," *YG*, March 8, 1834; Timothy Prescott, Diary, entries for January 28, 1834, February 23, 1835, bMS AM 2312, Houghton. The likely author of the *YG* article was Squire Abiel Heywood. It was common for anonymous contributors to the *Gazette* to identify themselves by the initial of their first or last names; for example, Jarvis signed his articles "J" and Lemuel Shattuck "S." My surmise that "A" was Abiel Heywood is based on several considerations. First, few inhabitants had surnames beginning with "A," and those who did, such as the merchant John Adams and the cabinetmaker James Adams, either were not present in Concord from 1824 through 1834 or were unlikely to express the point of view in his communications to the newspaper. Second, that perspective was that of a public servant, arguing for heavy taxes on distilled liquor to reduce consumption or better enforcement of the license laws to stop sales of rum by the glass in stores. Third and most crucially, "A" wrote in his communication of March 8, 1834, that critics of his refusal to make a public statement in favor of total abstinence implied "that I was a time-server, and preferred the applause of the people, to the approval of conscience." Squire Heywood had served as selectman and town clerk since 1796; he would be ousted from office in the spring of 1835. Given his long tenure in elective office, is there any better example of a "time-server"? The conflicts in the ranks of temperance reformers can be followed through state and county conventions. See *Proceedings of the Convention of the Young Men of Massachusetts, Friendly to the Cause of Temperance, Held at Worcester; July 1 & 2, 1834* (Boston, 1834), 24; *YG*, June 14, 1834; *CF*, June 6, October 24, 1835; *Lowell Patriot*, June 12, 1835.

80. Middlesex County Temperance Society, 1834 Circular, CFPL. The MCTS circular reports the number of temperance societies and the size of membership in forty-three towns. Not all communities apparently responded to its survey, so in those cases (e.g., Acton, Groton, and Tyngsboro) the number of members is not stated. In other instances several societies were operating in a town (e.g., Framingham, Newton, and Lowell), and it is uncertain whether the combined membership should be compared directly to the population. After omitting towns with missing or unclear data, thirty-eight towns remained. The average proportion of members to population was 29.4 percent; Concord, at 27.2 percent, was not far behind.

81. *Boston Courier*, October 25, 1832 (calling for first national temperance day), *YG*, February 22, November 29, 1834; MCTS circular, sent over the signature of Edward Jarvis, chairman of the finance committee, 1834, CFPL. It is uncertain whether the CTS amended its constitution to require a pledge of total abstinence of would-be members.

8. *Privilege and Conspiracy*

1. Entry for John Thoreau, October 8, 1824, Membership records of the Society of Middlesex Husbandmen and Manufacturers, 1820–61, CFPL; entries for John Thoreau, 1836, 1838, and 1843, Membership Roll and Cash Book, Concord Lyceum Records, 1828–1928, CFPL; entry for John Thoreau, 1825, in Book of Regulations, Concord Fire Society, CFPL; meetings of February 21, 1839 (election of John Thoreau as secretary and John Keyes as president), September 7, 1840 (appointment of Keyes and Thoreau as committee to provide supper for annual meeting), Concord Fire Society Records, CAS Collection, B1889, covering 1821–1849, CFPL; advertisements for meetings of Concord Fire Society, signed by John Thoreau, secretary, *R*, August 21, September 4, December 25, 1840, January 8, 1841.

2. F. B. Sanborn, *Henry D. Thoreau* (Boston, 1882), 27; *J* 11:436–37, entry for February 3, 1859, the day of John Thoreau's death.

3. The Adams ticket took 157 out of 159 votes in 1824 and followed up with 155 out of 159 in the president's losing campaign for reelection four years later. Edward Everett easily defeated John Keyes for Congress in 1824 with 58 percent of the vote, but in Concord, the result was a tie, each candidate receiving 90 ballots. Thereafter the incumbent had no serious competition in Concord or the entire district. In 1832, his final campaign for Congress, Everett garnered 102 votes, against his Jacksonian opponent's 12. Gov. Levi Lincoln won six terms in a row (1825–1830) with little or no contest. As late as 1832, he captured a commanding 82 percent of the Concord vote against the perpetual Democratic also-ran Marcus Morton. Resolve [of the General Court] Directing the mode of choosing Electors of President and Vice President of the United States, printed circular approved by the governor, June 8, 1824, with results of Concord's vote on November 1, 1824, written thereon, ETR; *YG*, November 8, 1828; Ronald P. Formisano, *The Transformation of Political Culture: Massachusetts Parties, 1790s–1840s* (New York, 1983), 81–83; Susan Kurland, "'A Political Progress': Processes of Democratization in Concord, Massachusetts, 1750–1850" (senior thesis, Brandeis University, 1973), 206–7, 216–17, 235–37, 249; Michael J. Dubin, *United States Congressional Elections, 1788–1997: The Official Results of the Elections of the 1st Through 105th Congresses* (Jefferson, N.C., 1998), 81, 86, 92, 97, 105.

4. Formisano, *Transformation of Political Culture*, 173–96; F. B. Sanborn, *The Life of Henry David Thoreau Including Many Essays Hitherto Unpublished and Some Account of His Family and Friends* (Boston, 1917), speculates that when he entered Harvard in September 1833, the future writer was "an anti-Jackson Whig" (468). I am assuming that he had imbibed his partisan sentiments from his father, who was later an enthusiast for the Whigs.

5. The 1830 federal census of Concord counted 2,017 inhabitants; that figure was virtually the same, 2,023, on the state census of 1837. There were 324 households in 1830 (including the almshouse, jail, and several hotels), 346 in 1837.

6. The county courts maintained a heavy schedule in Concord during the 1820s. Each year's calendar was reported in the *Massachusetts Register, and United States Calendar*, issued by Richardson & Lord and James Loring in Boston. The court of common pleas convened three times a year, in March, June, and September;

the supreme judicial court of Massachusetts tried cases annually at the end of March; the probate court oversaw the administration of estates in five separate sessions, held every ten weeks in February, April, June, September, and November. The court of general sessions, which administered the county, met twice a year in Concord (May and September) and once in Cambridge (January). The Middlesex County commissioners, who replaced the court of general sessions in 1831, followed the same timetable. Altogether, county courts were in session during seven or eight months of the year, depending on the calendar. Only in winter (December and January) and summer (July and August) were the justices absent from town. Then the local justices of the peace were the only officials to hold court.

7. The first newspaper to appear in Concord was the *Middlesex Gazette*, inaugurated by Joseph Peters in April 1816. It was succeeded by weeklies with varying names—the *Middlesex Observer* (1822–1823), the *Concord Gazette and Middlesex Yeoman* (1823–1826), and the *Yeoman's Gazette* (1826–1840). See Louis A. Surette, *By-Laws of Corinthian Lodge of Ancient, Free and Accepted Masons of Concord, Mass.* (Concord, Mass., 1859), 144–45, for the record of newspapers published in Concord during the first half of the nineteenth century. From 1816 to 1825, the Concord press claimed the Middlesex journalistic field for itself, with the exception of short-lived competitors in Charlestown in 1819–1820 (the *Franklin Monitor and Middlesex Republican*, followed by the *Bunker-Hill Sentinel and Middlesex Republican*). As textile manufacturing took off at the confluence of the Concord and Merrimack rivers, a series of newspapers arose to meet the needs of the growing population in what was first the town of Chelmsford and then the rising city of Lowell. The *Chelmsford Courier* launched in June 1824 and, following the destruction of its office by fire in 1825, was reborn as the *Phoenix*, only to become the *Merrimack Journal* and then the *Lowell Journal* over the next two years. The latter title stuck. A Democratic newspaper, the *Lowell Mercury*, began publication in 1830; it was absorbed into the *Journal* three years later. Meanwhile journalism revived in Charlestown at the eastern corner of Middlesex, where the *Bunker-Hill Aurora* was introduced in 1827. The *Yeoman's Gazette* bested these rivals. In August 1831 it claimed the biggest circulation in the county, with 1,300 copies weekly. The *Lowell Journal* supposedly reached 800 readers, the *Mercury* 1,000, and the *Bunker-Hill Aurora* was estimated to have 400 subscribers, though Concord editor Herman Atwill considered this figure too low. See *Lowell Mercury*, September 17, 1831; *YG*, November 22, 1828, August 13, 1831; Charles C. Chase, "Lowell," in D. Hamilton Hurd, comp., *History of Middlesex County, Massachusetts, with Biographical Sketches of Many of Its Pioneers and Prominent Men*, 3 vols. (Philadelphia, 1890), 2:188–92. For publication details of these newspapers, see the online catalog of the AAS. Through the 1820s, Concord had a larger population than the average Middlesex town. It was 1,788 in 1820, compared to a Middlesex mean of 1,421 ($n = 44$), and 2,017 in 1830, compared to an average 1,695 ($n = 46$).

8. Charles Cowley, *History of Lowell*, 2nd rev. ed. (Boston, 1868), 127; Formisano, *Transformation of Political Culture*, 151–52. In the thirteen elections from 1823 to 1835, Concordians were on the ballot for Middlesex senator and gained office eleven times. Samuel Hoar was a candidate for the state senate six times from 1822 to 1833; he held office in 1825–1826 (when annual terms started in May), 1832, and 1833. Keyes served continuously in the senate from May 1823 to May 1829. In 1825–1826, he and Hoar were colleagues in the senate. No one from Concord sat in the Middlesex delegation between May 1829 and May 1831. Then Nathan Brooks joined the body for a short term running from May 1831 to the year's end, after which the political year coincided with the calendar year. Hoar took a seat in

1832 and 1833, followed by Daniel Shattuck in 1834 and 1835. Shattuck defeated William Munroe, running as an Anti-Mason, for the seat in 1834. The annual *Massachusetts Register and United States Calendar* provides a yearly record of membership in the General Court. Hoar's unsuccessful runs for the senate are documented in *Columbian Centinel*, March 20, 1822, March 19, 1823, and *YG*, March 31, April 7, 1827. For Nathan Brooks's election as state senator in May 1831, see *YG*, April 2, May 14, 1831.

9. Keyes was a director of the Concord Bank, who held twenty shares worth $2,000 in 1832; by 1838 that investment had risen to $2,700. He was also a director of the Middlesex Institution for Savings and a shareholder in the Mill Dam Company. Hoar held $6,000 of Concord Bank stock in 1835; at the same time he amassed a fortune through lending money on mortgages. His financial investments rose from $8,000 in 1826 to $18,000 in 1835 and then to $20,000 in 1838. Both men were active in the debating club, the social library, and the lyceum.

10. *The Journal of the Free Trade Convention, Held in Philadelphia, from September 30 to October 7, 1831: and Their Address to the People of the United States* (Philadelphia, 1831), 15–16, 34 ("odious"); *Address of the Friends of Domestic Industry, Assembled in Convention, at New-York, October 26, 1831, to the People of the United States* (Baltimore, 1831), 3 (quoting the Philadelphia convention's characterization of protective duties as a species of "tyranny"), 39–44; "The Tariff," *YG*, June 9, 1832; "Voice of Industry," reporting the meeting of "Farmers, Manufacturers, Mechanics, and others, interested in the Protection of American Industry," *YG*, June 16, 1832; Daniel Walker Howe, *What Hath God Wrought: The Transformation of America, 1815–1848* (New York, 2007), 270–75. A debate over the scale of manufacturing in Middlesex County took place in the *Boston Courier* in response to the *Gazette*'s report on the Concord convention. No one doubted the primacy of Middlesex in American manufacturing; disagreement centered on the estimates of output, capital investment, employment, and wages. See *Boston Courier*, June 21 ("largest manufacturing county") and 25, 1832.

11. *YG*, June 15, 1832; Daniel Walker Howe, *The Political Culture of the American Whigs* (Chicago, 1979), 101–2.

12. *Boston Courier*, January 19, 1832; *YG*, June 9 and 16, 1832. The Concord *Gazette*'s account of this convention gained national circulation when it was reprinted by *Niles' Weekly Register*, July 7, 1832.

13. *YG*, April 8, November 11, 1826; Alexander Keyssar, *The Right to Vote: The Contested History of Democracy in the United States*, rev. ed. (New York, 2009), 309; Formisano, *Transformation of Political Culture*, 81–83; Kurland, "'Political Progress.'" Concord's turnout in the election for governor peaked at 291 in 1814; it steadily dwindled to 214 in 1818, 205 in 1819, 183 in 1820, and 176 in 1823. Then, with the dissolution of the old parties, it plummeted to 126–27 in the second half of the decade. In the presidential election of 1832, the Democratic share of the vote in Concord (18 percent) for Jackson's reelection was below that (25 percent) in Middlesex County. The National Republican candidate for presidential elector in Middlesex, Nathan Brooks, received 134 votes (68 percent) in Concord to support Henry Clay; the new Anti-Masonic ticket ran third with 27 votes (14 percent). Return of Concord Vote for Presidential Electors, 1832, Records and Archives Committee Roll 001, CFPL.

14. One dissenter lambasted the "fiend of improvement" for uprooting "the good old customs of the countryside," including the practice of bundling by courting couples; he was roundly denounced for peddling immorality in the press. See *CGMY*, December 31, 1825, and January 28, 1826.

15. Daniel Shattuck Estate Papers, Series I, Nathan Brooks Papers, Box 17a, Folder 1a, CFPL; assessment list for June 30, 1828, Treasurer's Department, Roll T-1, CFPL. Allen's taxable property on the 1828 assessment list included a house and garden valued at $550, the same amount as his debt to Shattuck. Moreover, the assessors called this "the Shattuck house." Either Allen was renting from Shattuck and, as part of his lease, agreed to pay the property tax, or he had purchased the real estate with a mortgage from Shattuck. Among the scores of legal instruments at the Middlesex County Registry of Deeds in which Shattuck appears as a grantor or grantee, no transaction with John C. Allen appears. Nonetheless, the available documentation points to a mortgage.

16. Edward Everett (Washington) to Lemuel Shattuck (Concord), April 8, 1826, and Shattuck (Concord) to Everett (Cambridge), November 6, 1826, Papers of Lemuel Shattuck, 1637–1850, Huntington Library, San Marino, Calif. Daniel Shattuck's patronage of the Concord newspaper is confirmed by a casual comment in Lemuel's November 9, 1826, letter to Everett. During the election campaign of that year, the *Gazette* published a communication critical of Everett's conduct in office. Though the piece was mean-spirited, the editors could not refuse to run it, since the pseudonymous author, "Looker On," was none other than Keyes. To answer the politician's charges, Allen called on "the other patron" of the *Gazette* with a request. Would Lemuel "write something in [Everett's] favour"? It appears that Allen was going through the senior partner at Shattuck & Co. to get to the junior one. See *YG*, October 28, November 4, 1826. The reference to the "other patron" raises the possibility that both Keyes and Daniel Shattuck were financial backers of the local press.

17. Everett to Shattuck, April 20 and 28, November 30, 1826; Shattuck to Everett, November 6, 1826; *YG*, November 4, 1826. For Everett's speeches, see *YG*, March 25, May 13, 1826, and January 27, 1827. The columns on "Affairs at Washington" ran during the second session of the Nineteenth Congress. See *YG*, December 9, 1826, January 6, 13, 20, 27, February 10, 17, 24, and March 10, 1827.

18. Stanley I. Kutler, *Privilege and Creative Destruction: The Charles River Bridge Case* (1971; rpt. Baltimore, 1990).

19. Ibid., 18–20; Formisano, *Transformation of Political Culture*, 190–96; *Review of the Case of the Free Bridge between Boston and Charlestown: In Which the Expediency and Constitutionality of That Measure Are Considered* (Boston, 1827), 84–87.

20. *Columbian Centinel*, March 20, 1822; *MO*, April 21, 1823; *Boston Patriot*, April 2, May 31, 1825; *Columbian Centinel*, April 13, 1825; *Boston Commercial Gazette*, June 2, 1825.

21. "Report of the Committee upon the Petition of John Skinner and others for a free bridge, January session, 1826," in *Review of the Case*, 84–87; George F. Hoar, *Autobiography of Seventy Years*, 2 vols. (New York, 1903), 1:37; Kutler, *Privilege and Creative Destruction*, 21. I am assuming here that as chair of the committee, Hoar either composed or oversaw the writing of its report.

22. See *Decision of the Supreme Judicial Court of Massachusetts, in a Case Relating to the Sacramental Furniture of a Church in Brookfield; with the Entire Arguments of Hon. Samuel Hoar, Jun. for the Plaintiff, and of Hon. Lewis Strong for the Defendant* (Boston, 1832).

23. "Report of the Committee upon Petition of Skinner for free bridge," 88–89; Kutler, *Privilege and Creative Destruction*, 18–22.

24. Formisano, *Transformation of Political Culture*, 194–95; Kutler, *Privilege and Creative Destruction*, 26–28. Under the Massachusetts Constitution of 1780, it took a two-thirds vote of both houses to override a gubernatorial veto. The Senate vote was 15 in favor, 12 against.

25. Nathaniel Austin, John Skinner, and Thomas Goodwin, committee appointed to act "in behalf of the town of Charlestown," printed circular letter, October 13, 1824, ETR; CTMM, manuscript volume from March 1815 to November 1833, 227, 231, CFPL; *YG*, February 24, March 17, 1827. Perhaps owing to division over the bridge issue, Concord sent no representative to the legislature for the 1826–1827 session. The following year the town meeting made up for its neglect and, in an election marked by "an unusual degree of interest," chose two delegates, to which it was entitled by population size. Both Reuben Brown, Jr., and Samuel Burr voted against a charter for the Warren Bridge. The vote was close: 133 in favor, 127 against. *YG*, May 12, 1827.

26. I infer John Thoreau's support for a free bridge from his signature on a petition to the state assembly in March 1835 calling for the elimination of tolls on the Warren Bridge. Endorsed by fifty-five townsmen, mostly tradesmen and mechanics in the village, the memorial offered a critical account of the efforts by the Charles River Bridge Corporation to prevent the chartering and construction of a toll-free alternative crossing. The company's claim to an exclusive right to maintain a bridge over the Charles River was rightly rejected, the petitioners affirmed. "The public voice . . . imperiously demanded" an alternative, and so the Warren Bridge got its charter. It took only a couple of years for the company to recoup its costs from tolls. Nonetheless, the charges remained in force, and after the legislature voted in 1833 that the bridge should become free, the revenue went into the state treasury. Fed up with the delay, the Concord petitioners were part of an area-wide campaign to get the tolls eliminated once and for all. See Kutler, *Privilege and Creative Destruction*, 103–7; Josiah Davis and fifty-four others of the town of Concord, petition praying that Warren Bridge may be made free, House Unpassed Legislation, 1835, MSA. (I am grateful to John Hannigan for providing me with copies of this petition in the state archives.)

27. Hoar's opposition to the Warren Bridge was held against him in subsequent years. In November 1832 the squire was again a nominee for the state senate, at a time when the status of the Warren Bridge was at issue. Would this thoroughfare become a free route, as originally contemplated, or would it continue to charge tolls and generate revenue for the state treasury? Advocates of the Warren Bridge pressed to elect a sympathetic legislature. The *Lowell Mercury* took particular exception to the candidacy of Samuel Hoar, who used his position as chair of the committee on bridges in 1825–1826 to stab "his constituents under the fifth rib, by his *cunning*, lawyer-like Report in favor of the *monopolies* of the *old bridge* proprietors." See *Lowell Mercury*, November 9, 1832.

28. *American Traveller*, April 3, 1827; *Columbian Centinel*, April 5, 1828. In the April 1827 election for governor, Lincoln lost Middlesex County, with the nominee of the free bridge party receiving 57 percent of the vote; by contrast, roughly nine out of ten voters in Concord chose the incumbent. Formisano observes that turnout in this contest "rose to its highest level of the period." Not in Concord, where participation in state elections had fallen steadily following the amalgamation of parties. Turnout was 142 in 1825, 126 in 1826, then revived to 146 in 1827. In the senate elections of these years, Keyes either topped the ticket in Concord or came close to his running mates. See Formisano, *Transformation of Political Culture*, 194–95; Kurland, "'Political Progress,'" 235–36.

29. Formisano, *Transformation of Political Culture*, 192–93, 195, 247–49; Mason A. Green, *Springfield, 1636–1886: History of Town and City* (Springfield, Mass., 1888), 394, 439, 453, 486; Arthur B. Darling, *Political Changes in Massachusetts, 1824–1848: A Study of Liberal Movements in Politics* (New Haven, Conn., 1925), 53–54; *Boston Patriot*, April 1,

1828; *Massachusetts Journal*, March 18, 1828; Carolyn L. Karcher, *The First Woman in the Republic: A Cultural Biography of Lydia Maria Child* (Durham, N.C., 1994), 47; "Protest of the Minority in the House of Representatives against the law authorizing the free bridge," in *Review of the Case*, 94–95. Keyes's friends disputed these accusations of false dealing. There was nothing exceptionable about his early backing of John Mills over Webster for the U.S. Senate, they said; virtually all of Keyes's colleagues in the state senate did the same. As for delaying a vote on a general ticket for presidential electors, this was merely a courtesy to the next legislature. Nobody should doubt Keyes's commitment to the National Republican cause. The self-restrained lawyer might not make as much "bustle and pretensions" as some "over-zealous friends" of the president, but he followed "a higher, more dignified course." See *Boston Patriot*, April 2, 1828; "Republican Administration Ticket," *YG*, March 15, 1828, and the letter from "A Republican," *YG*, March 29, 1828. Another communication, from "Truth" (March 22, 1828), was probably written by Keyes himself, since it suggests an insider's knowledge of state senate deliberations.

30. *Boston Intelligencer*, June 2, 1827; *Boston Statesman*, June 7, 1828; *Massachusetts Register* for 1826 and 1827; "The New Nomination in Middlesex," *Massachusetts Journal*, March 29, 1828, reprinted in *Trial of the Case of the Commonwealth versus David Lee Child, for Publishing in the Massachusetts Journal a Libel of the Honorable John Keyes, before the Supreme Judicial Court, Holden at Cambridge, in the County of Middlesex* (Boston, 1829), 5–7.

31. *Trial of the Case*, 51–52, 57. The storekeeper Moses Prichard accompanied Keyes on this trip, so that there would be a witness of the meeting between the politician and the editor. He became the source for the account in the text.

32. Ibid., 114.

33. *YG*, April 5, 1828

34. *YG*, April 4, 1827, April 12, 1828; *Columbian Centinel*, May 14, 1828. Turnout increased by 39 percent from 145 to 202. Keyes received 131 votes to Timothy Fuller's 71.

35. *Trial of the Case*, 3–4, 54, 114.

36. Norman L. Rosenberg, *Protecting the Best Men: An Interpretive History of the Law of Libel* (Chapel Hill, N.C., 1986), 105–20; Clyde Augustus Duniway, *The Development of Freedom of the Press in Massachusetts* (Cambridge, Mass., 1906), 147–58; Karcher, *First Woman*, 82–85, 97, 126; Josiah H. Benton, Jr., *A Notable Libel Case: The Criminal Prosecution of Theodore Lyman, Jr. by Daniel Webster in the Supreme Judicial Court of Massachusetts* (Boston, 1904); Elizabeth Bussiere, "Trial by Jury as 'Mockery of Justice': Party Contention, Courtroom Corruption, and the Ironic Judicial Legacy of Antimasonry," *Law and History Review* 34 (February 2016): 155–98; *Trial of the Case*, 4–5; "An Act relating to Prosecutions for Libel, and to Pleadings in Actions for Libel and Slander," *Boston Patriot*, March 10, 1827. In mid-December 1828, a few weeks before Child's trial was set to be heard by the Massachusetts Supreme Court, a Federalist-turned-Jacksonian named Theodore Lyman, Jr., faced charges in Boston of libeling the newly elected senator Daniel Webster. The jury proved unable to reach a verdict.

37. *YG*, April 12, 1828, January 17, 1829; Jonathan H. Earle, *Jacksonian Antislavery and the Politics of Free Soil, 1824–1854* (Chapel Hill, N.C., 2004), 103–22; William Thomas Davis, *Bench and Bar of the Commonwealth of Massachusetts*, 2 vols. (Boston, 1895), 1:239, 426; Alden Bradford, "Juridical Statistics of the County of Suffolk," *American Quarterly Review* 13 (May 1841): 426, 453.

38. Child had evidently garbled information about the sequence of events leading to the award of the printing contract to the *Statesman*. Keyes had actually been on

leave from his senate duties when the committee on accounts advertised for and received sealed bids for the state printing. He arrived back at the statehouse as the committee was starting to review the competing proposals and took the chair only upon request. Did he then suggest the plan to retain the printers of the *Statesman* in violation of the stated rules? The witnesses disagreed about what Keyes said and when he said it.

39. *Trial of the Case*, 102–3.

40. Ibid., 38–39, 50–51.

41. *Review of the Report of the Case of the Commonwealth Versus David Lee Child, for Publishing in the Massachusetts Journal a Libel on the Honorable John Keyes* (Boston, 1829), 6–13; reprint of review from *Yankee*, in *YG*, March 21, 1829.

42. *Review of the Report*, 5–6; *YG*, November 29, 1828; January 10 and 17, March 7 and 21, May 16, 1829.

43. *Review of the Report*, 8–9; John Keyes to the convention assembled at Concord, March 27, 1828, Concord Free Public Library Letter File, 1755–1995, Box 2, J. Keyes, 1, CFPL.

44. *YG*, October 22, November 19, 1831, November 17, 1832; *Boston Courier*, January 7, 1833; *Weekly Messenger*, October 4, 1832; *YG*, October 20, 1832, noting activities of Hoar and Keyes at a statewide convention of National Republicans held at Worcester. The wealthy farmer Joseph Barrett was Keyes's colleague in the state house of representatives. In his November 1832 bid for reelection to the senate, Hoar ran behind his ticket and fell short of an absolute majority. Once again he was chosen as a senator by the legislature meeting in convention. The drop in Hoar's vote was due to a renewed push for a free bridge across the Charles River. By 1832 the Warren Bridge had recouped its costs, but the tollgates had not yet been taken down. As popular agitation revived, the *Boston Statesman* reminded voters in Middlesex of Hoar's role in blocking the Warren Bridge back in 1825. If the "great enemy" of a free bridge were not defeated, he would do so again. The prediction was correct. In March 1833 Hoar engaged in legislative maneuvering to kill the effort to make the Warren Bridge free. See *Lowell Mercury*, reprinting from *Boston Statesman*, November 9, 1832, *Boston Daily Advocate*, March 20, 1833.

45. Wayne T. Dilts, "Henry's Houses: The Houses in Concord That Henry Called Home," *Thoreau Society Bulletin*, no. 263 (Summer 2008): 6–7; John Thoreau and Maria Thoreau (grantors) to Daniel Shattuck (grantee), September 29, 1849, MCRD 588:301; Elizabeth Hoar (Concord) to Marianne Cornelia Giles (St. Johnsbury, Vt.), November 2, 1829, in Elizabeth Maxfield-Miller, "Elizabeth of Concord: Selected Letters of Elizabeth Sherman Hoar (1814–78) to the Emersons, Family, and the Emerson Circle (Part Two)," *Studies in the American Renaissance* (1985): 103–109; Keyes, Diary, vol. 2, entry for August 15, 1839; Keyes, Diary, vol. 4, entry for September 15, 1841.

46. Gross, *Minutemen*, 174–75; *SCM* 1:2, 49–50, 55–62, reproducing the manuscript history of the Social Circle in Concord in Ripley Family Papers, Notebook no. 1, Houghton.

47. John Adams, Diary, entry for July 21, 1786, in Adams Family Papers: An Electronic Archive, www.masshist.org/digitaladams/archive/doc?id=D44 (accessed July 25, 2014); Gross, *Minutemen*, 174–75.

48. In June 1798 some seventy-one citizens of Concord signed a public letter in support of beleaguered President Adams. This statement was evidently initiated by the Social Circle, twenty of whom (80 percent of the entire membership) subscribed. *A Selection of the Patriotic Addresses, to the President of the United States, Together with the President's Answers* (Boston, 1798), 48–52. The manuscript address to Adams

is in Adams Family Papers, MHS: see the file Letters Received and Other Loose Papers, 1638–1889, Section 4, Chronological Papers, 1638–1889, June 1798, Reel 389, www.masshist.org/adams/catalog/view_slip.php?id=091037. I am grateful to Sara Martin, editor-in-chief of the Adams Papers at MHS, for providing me a copy of the Concord address to the beleaguered chief executive.

49. Of the ten citizens who petitioned the town to organize a celebration of the jubilee of the Concord Fight, eight were current, former, or future members of the circle: Humphrey Barrett (member 1782–1822), Nathan Barrett (current member), Reuben Brown (current), Dr. Isaac Hurd (current), Francis Jarvis (current), Tilly Merrick (member 1801–1821), and John Vose. An eighth petitioner, Ephraim Meriam, was elected to the circle in 1828. See Committee of Arrangements for the 50th Anniversary Celebration, Records, CFPL.

50. Of the twenty-five members of the Social Circle in 1819–1825, seventeen (68 percent) joined the Society of Middlesex Husbandmen and Manufacturers, and twenty (80 percent) subscribed to the Concord Social Library. In January 1829, when the Concord Lyceum was launched, sixteen (64 percent) of the current Social Circle members subscribed. When the Massachusetts legislature voted a charter to the Concord Bank in 1832, six men were named incorporators. Five (Nathan Brooks, Abiel Heywood, William Munroe, Abel Moore, and Lemuel Shattuck) lived in Concord; the other, Rufus Hosmer, a Concord native, was an inhabitant of Stow. Six Concord residents were on the original board of directors; all belonged to the circle (Brooks, Heywood, merchant Phineas How, John Keyes, Abel Moore, and Daniel Shattuck). The president, Daniel Shattuck, came from the circle, as did cashier John M. Cheney. Of the twenty-five members in 1832, twenty (80 percent) subscribed to the bank stock. See Concord Bank records, Old Sturbridge Village Research Library, Sturbridge, Mass.

51. *SCM* 1:49–50; Social Circle Record Book, CFPL.

52. The average age of the 23 founders of the Social Circle at election between 1782 and 1794 was thirty-six, the median age thirty-four—virtually the same for the 27 new members between 1795 and 1814 and the 28 between 1815 and 1834. Of 22 members of the Social Circle on the 1795 town assessment list, 16 (73 percent) ranked in the top fifth of property holders; of 21 members on the 1826 assessment list, 16 (76 percent) had the same standing. Close to 40 percent of the circle served as selectman, town clerk, or representative to the General Court between 1816 and 1835. As for nativity, of the 27 new members between 1816 and 1834, nearly 60 percent were born outside Concord: 11 percent in adjacent towns, 11 percent in other Middlesex towns, and a third from elsewhere in Massachusetts.

53. Surprisingly, Samuel Hoar did not apply for membership in the club during the years when he was rising in stature as a lawyer and public servant, even after election to the senate. Nor did the members honor him with election until 1848, when he was sixty years old and in the twilight of his career.

54. List of applicants at the end of the original record book, January 30, 1804, to December 1868, entry for March 1829, CFPL. In 1826 Charles B. Davis, age twenty-nine, ranked in the top tenth of property holders with $4,623 in assessed wealth. In early 1829, when he was nominated for the Social Circle, the storekeeper lacked any record of public service. He had not yet held a town office nor served on any committee appointed by the town meeting. His active engagement in local government began after 1835.

55. Margaret C. Jacob, *The Origins of Freemasonry: Facts and Fictions* (Philadelphia, 2006), 1–19; Steven C. Bullock, *Revolutionary Brotherhood: Freemasonry and the Transforma-*

tion of the American Social Order, 1730–1840 (Chapel Hill, N.C., 1996), 10–16; David G. Hackett, *That Religion in Which All Men Agree: Freemasonry in American Culture* (Berkeley, Calif., 2014), 32.

56. For a comprehensive chronology of Masonic lodges chartered in Massachusetts from 1733 to 1856, see Charles W. Moore, *The Constitutions of the Grand Lodge of Massachusetts: and General Regulations for the Government of the Craft under Its Jurisdiction* (Boston, 1857). Counting only lodges chartered within the Bay Colony and then the Commonwealth, the surge in the popularity of Freemasonry is readily apparent in the first two decades of the American republic: 1733–1772, eleven; 1777–1779, nine; 1780–1789, four; 1790–1799, thirty-nine; 1800–1809, forty-nine; 1810–1819, twenty-four; 1820–1829, twenty-six. Issuance of charters for new lodges came to an abrupt halt from 1830 to 1843. The Massachusetts Grand Lodge chartered thirteen lodges in 1797, a record number up to that time; four years later, in 1801, that achievement was repeated, but it was never surpassed. Of the Corinthian Lodge's twenty-five charter members in 1797, seventeen (68 percent) lived in Concord; of the seventy-four individuals enlisting in the lodge during 1797–1798, forty (54 percent) lived in Concord. The residence of one member is unknown.

57. Bullock, *Revolutionary Brotherhood*, 242–51; Moore, *Constitutions*; Surette, *By-Laws*.

58. *The By-Laws of Corinthian Lodge, As Revised, Corrected, and Adopted 5820* (Concord, Mass., 1822), 10–11; Surette, *By-Laws*, 110–11, 117; Bullock, *Revolutionary Brotherhood*, 10–16; Hackett, *That Religion*, 32.

59. Quotation from Entered Apprentice's Oath, *YG*, June 29, 1833.

60. Ezra Ripley, *A Masonic Sermon, Preached at Greenfield, Massachusetts, on 24th June, A. D. 1802—and A. L. 5802, before the Members of the Republican, Harmony and Pacific Lodges* (Greenfield, Mass., 1802), 16; Benjamin Gleason, *An Address, Pronounced at the Dedication of the New Masonic Hall, in Concord, Ms. November 13, A.L. 5820* (Concord, Mass., 1820), 14–17.

61. Bullock, *Revolutionary Brotherhood*, 188, 222–25; John L. Brooke, "Ancient Lodges and Self-Created Societies: Voluntary Association and the Public Sphere in the Early Republic," in Ronald Hoffman and Peter J. Albert, eds., *Launching the "Extended Republic": The Federalist Era* (Charlottesville, Va., 1996), 328–29; Hackett, *That Religion*, 63–73; Gerald E. Kahler, *The Long Farewell: Americans Mourn the Death of George Washington* (Charlottesville, Va., 2008), 86–99; A. Levasseur, *Lafayette in America in 1824 and 1825; Journal of a Voyage to the United States*, trans. John D. Godman, 2 vols. (Philadelphia, 1829), 1:208–10.

62. Ezra Ripley, *The Obligations of Parents to Give Their Children a Virtuous Education, and to Provide Schools for This Purpose, with Advice to Scholars, Illustrated and Urged in a Sermon Delivered, September 7, 1820, at the Opening of Three New School Houses, Which Were Religiously Appropriated to the Interests of Learning and Virtue, and Directed to the Honour of God; and Which Sermon Is Now Affectionately Inscribed to the Children and Youth in Concord, Who Usually Attend the Schools*, "Published at the request of the Committee for building the school houses, and many others who heard it" (Cambridge, Mass., 1820), 9, 27; Surette, *By-Laws*, 127; Gleason, *Address*, 10–11; Harriet H. Robinson, ed., *"Warrington" Pen-Portraits: A Collection of Personal and Political Reminiscences from 1847 to 1876, from the Writings of William S. Robinson* (Boston, 1877), 14. The collaboration between lodge and town in building the new schoolhouse was not uncommon. See Paul Goodman, *Towards a Christian Republic: Antimasonry and the Great Transition in New England 1826–1836* (New York, 1988), 17.

63. *CGMY*, June 26, 1824; *YG*, August 19, 1826; Surette, *By-Laws*, 45, 126, 131–32.

64. Bullock, *Revolutionary Brotherhood*, 175–77; Hackett, *That Religion*, 74–76; Ezra

Ripley, *The Design and Utility of Free-Masonry Considered in a Discourse, Delivered at Haverhill, (Massachusetts) at the Consecration of Merrimack Lodge, June 9th, 1803 . . . A.L. 5803* (Newburyport, Mass., 1803), 3–4. In the 1825–1826 legislature, three of the Middlesex senators (Keyes, Seth Knowles of Charlestown, and Micah M. Rutter of Sudbury) were Masons; their colleagues (Hoar and Abel Jewett of Pepperell) were not. Of the six appointive officials of county government at that time, three (Samuel P. P. Fay, judge of probate; Isaac Fiske, register of probate; and William F. Stone, register of deeds) belonged to the fraternity. For lists of Middlesex senators and county officials, see *Massachusetts Register* for 1826 and 1827; for membership in the fraternity, I drew on the records in the database Massachusetts Mason Membership Cards, 1733–1990, at Ancestry.com.

65. For contrasts with Concord, see Bullock, *Revolutionary Brotherhood*, 215; Kathleen Smith Kutolowski, "Freemasonry Revisited: Another Look at the Grass-Roots Bases of Antimasonic Anxieties," in R. William Weisberger, Wallace McLeod, and S. Brent Morris, eds., *Freemasonry on Both Sides of the Atlantic: Essays Concerning the Craft in the British Isles, Europe, the United States, and Mexico* (Boulder, Colo., 2002), 587–93; Shattuck, *History*, 235–36. The clothier Roger Brown, a charter member of the Corinthian Lodge, served as selectman between 1795 and 1800. Deacon Jarvis was a representative from Concord to the legislature in 1817, Keyes in 1821 and 1822, then again in 1832, 1833, and 1835. Abel Moore, deputy sheriff and county jailer, was a brother in the fraternity chapter, whose formation was spearheaded by Dr. Isaac Hurd. Republican politician and state senator John L. Tuttle provided a model for Keyes in using the lodge as a base for his political career.

66. *By-Laws of Corinthian Lodge*, 10–11; Ripley, *Masonic Sermon*, 15–16. Altogether, between 1797 and 1828, 156 residents went through the rituals to obtain the three degrees necessary to become master Masons; more than 70 percent of them were newcomers to Concord, and about the same proportion (69 percent) would soon be elsewhere. The mean age for new members between 1797 and 1828 was 28.9, the median 27 ($N = 127$, with 29 missing cases). The median age fluctuated by decade between 25 and 27. Concord's recruits were a little older than those in Windham County, Connecticut, where roughly 80 percent of new members were under thirty, and in Danvers, Massachusetts, where the comparable figure was 75 percent. See Bullock, *Revolutionary Brotherhood*, 207–9, and Dorothy Ann Lipson, *Freemasonry in Federalist Connecticut* (Princeton, N.J., 1977), 143–44. Lipson estimates that 43 percent of the members of Putnam Lodge in Connecticut were on the move, shuttling among towns or flowing into and out of the vicinity (139). By this measure, Concord's Freemasons were considerably more mobile, with six out of ten (61 percent) eventually settling and dying elsewhere. Concord natives comprised a declining share of lodge membership over time: 36 percent at its founding in 1797–1798, 38 percent in 1798–1808, 22 percent in 1809–1818, 20 percent in 1819–1828—striking testimony to the accelerating movement in and out of the town.

67. Clifford K. Shipton, "Asa Dunbar," in Shipton, *Sibley's Harvard Graduates*, 16 vols. (Boston, 1873–1972), 16:457–63; Sanborn, *Life of Thoreau*, 49; Leslie Perrin Wilson, *In History's Embrace: Past and Present in Concord, Massachusetts* (Concord, Mass., 2007), 42.

68. *By-Laws of Corinthian Lodge*, 10–11; Surette, *By-Laws*, 110–11; Kutolowski, "Freemasonry Revisited," 590. At its organization in 1797, the Corinthian Lodge required candidates to deposit three dollars with their applications. Initiation cost $10.50, raising to master Mason four dollars, and admission to lodge membership an-

other four. Two years later the required deposit was dropped to ten dollars, while the charge for raising went up to five. The membership fee for individuals initiated in the Corinthian Lodge remained at four dollars. I have used the 1799 fee schedule in the text. For a fuller account of Freemasonry in the Concord context, see Robert A. Gross, "Lodges and Lyceums, Freemasonry and Free Grace," *Massachusetts Historical Review* 19 (2017): 1–22.

69. *The By-Laws of Concord Chapter of Royal Arch Masons. Adopted July, A. L. 5826* (Concord, Mass., 1826), 4–6; Bullock, *Revolutionary Brotherhood*, 252–72; transcribed list of members of Concord Royal Arch Chapter from bylaws book re-created in 1905, Corinthian Lodge of Freemasons archive, Concord, Mass. Of the twenty-five subscribers to the 1820 bylaws of the Corinthian Lodge still in Concord in 1826–1827, sixteen (64 percent) became companions of the Royal Arch Chapter.

70. Whitney R. Cross, *The Burned-Over District: The Social and Intellectual History of Enthusiastic Religion in Western New York, 1800–1850* (1950; rpt. New York, 1965), 3–4, 113–20; Ronald P. Formisano and Kathleen Smith Kutolowski, "Antimasonry and Masonry: The Genesis of Protest, 1826–1827," *American Quarterly* 29 (Summer 1977): 139–65; Bullock, *Revolutionary Brotherhood*, 282–85. Between 1831 and 1834, Anti-Masons held the governorship of Vermont.

71. Testimony of Herman Atwill, *Report of Joint Committee of the Legislature of Massachusetts on Freemasonry*, March 1834, House Doc. no. 73, 31–36; *YG*, November 25, 1826, January 6, March 24 ("diabolical") and 31, June 30, September 8, October 6, November 3 and 10, 1827, June 28, July 19, 1828 ("contemptible Morgan fever"), January 16, 1830, November 12, 1831 ("friends of good order"), September 1, 1832 ("A.S.S.").

72. Surette, *By-Laws*, 146, 152–53, 162–65; Corinthian Lodge, Record of Proceedings 3:234–72, Corinthian Lodge archive, Concord, Mass.; Bullock, *Revolutionary Brotherhood*, 312–13. From 1820 to 1828, four or five inhabitants entered the Corinthian Lodge annually; hardly anyone—just three townsmen—joined over the next five years. Before the Morgan scandal, half of the fifty-person membership or more was present for the monthly sessions, along with ten or eleven visitors. By mid-1827, no more than ten were showing up. Two years later the sessions were often pro forma.

73. *Boston Masonic Mirror*, December 31, 1831; *YG*, January 14, 1832; Bullock, *Revolutionary Brotherhood*, 299, 314–15. Nearly all of the twenty-seven men who had ascended to the Royal Arch Chapter came forth to defend the order. By contrast, more than half (57 percent) of the men on the rolls of the Corinthian Lodge were nowhere to be found when the declaration was being circulated for signatures. Perhaps they had already dropped out in the face of hostile public opinion. From the membership lists of the Corinthian Lodge, I estimate that forty-four men were in town and eligible to sign. Sixteen of them had gained membership in the Royal Arch Chapter; thirteen subscribed to the public statement. By contrast, six of twenty-eight men belonging only to the Corinthian Lodge associated themselves with the declaration. (The finding is statistically significant at the .000 level.) According to Lodge records, thirty-four men were members in October 1830. So ten men had either quietly withdrawn from the lodge or moved out of town by the turn of 1831. Using a base of thirty-four members and eliminating two signers who were not residents of Concord produces a subscription rate of nearly two-thirds (65 percent). See Surette, *By-Laws*, 146.

74. *Boston Daily Advertiser and Patriot*, November 20, 1832; *YG*, December 1, 1832; Howe, *What Hath God Wrought*, 384–85; Atwill testimony. Everett's remarks on the election first appeared in the *Boston Daily Advertiser*, November 14, 1832; Atwill

took two weeks to consider them before putting his call for the "great reform" of Freemasonry into print.

75. *YG*, December 8, 15, and 22, 1832 (history of "Masonic Outrages"), December 29 (calls for lodges to give up charters), 1832, December 5, 12 ("I am neither a Mason nor an Antimason"), 19, and 26 ("our columns are free," "I, H—A—"), January 1833 ("brief history").

76. Bullock, *Revolutionary Brotherhood*, 282–88; *YG*, February 16, March 30, 1833.

77. *YG*, December 1 and 8, 1832 (testimonials to Child), February 16, March 9 (Keyes) and 30 (Shattuck and Moore), 1833; *Boston Daily Advocate*, March 14, 1833. The real estate transactions in which Atwill became financially obligated to Keyes can be followed in MCRD 292:535, 298:18; 306:248; 334:124; 360:46. Atwill's debt was finally discharged on August 4, 1834.

78. Subscription paper, announcing the publication of the *Bunker-Hill Aurora and Middlesex County Advertiser*, William Wheildon Scrapbooks, H80.257, BPL; *Bunker-Hill Aurora*, February 9, 1833; *YG*, October 29, 1831, February 16 (subscription terms), March 9, 1833; *New-Bedford Courier*, March 5, 1833; Charles Cowley and Jonathan Johnson, *Middlesex County Manual* (Lowell, Mass., 1878), 105; membership record for Samuel P. P. Fay, Grand Lodge of Massachusetts, NEHGS database. See *YG*, April 13 and 20, 1833, for allegations that at the recent session of the state supreme court in Concord, Keyes advised the presiding justice that the *Aurora* was the local paper of record, *not* the *Yeoman's Gazette*. For evidence of the close political friendship between Keyes and Wheildon, see John Keyes (postmaster, Concord) to William W. Wheildon (editor), *Bunker-Hill Aurora*, Charlestown, Mass., February 25, 1831, Concord Free Public Library Letter File, 1755–1995, Box 2, J. Keyes, 2, CFPL.

79. *YG*, March 9 ("tottering"), 30 ("palpable combination," "Press Gang"), January 26 ("All-Seeing Eye"), 1833.

80. *YG*, April 20, 1833; William S. Robinson (Concord) to Jeremiah A. Robinson (Lowell), April 28, 1833, Robinson-Shattuck Papers, Reel 2, Schlesinger Library, Harvard University; *Bunker-Hill Aurora*, April 27, 1833; *CF*, December 20, 1834; Surette, *By-Laws*, 151–53; meeting of April 1, 1833, Corinthian Lodge Proceedings 3:276. The last straw in Atwill's journalistic assault on his former brethren was his exposé of the proceedings of a lodge meeting, held on April Fool's Day. Supposedly derived from an anonymous source, the report gave a step-by-step account of the elaborate rituals for opening and closing the lodge. Presented as the script of a play, it reproduces the formulaic language and the clandestine passwords and signs used by each officer in the proceedings, from "worshipful master" William Whiting through junior warden Ephraim H. Bellows down to treasurer Abel Moore. See *YG*, April 6, 1833.

81. "The Yeoman's Gazette vs. Masonry," reprinted from *Boston Daily Advocate* by *New-Bedford Courier*, March 5, 1833; *YG*, February 16, March 2 ("open and palpable attack"), 9, and 23 ("our press is our own"), 1833; *Boston Daily Advocate*, February 27, March 14, 1833; *New-Bedford Courier*, March 5, 1833; *Bunker-Hill Aurora*, March 16, 1833. From the winter of 1833 to the end of 1834, Atwill was a fixture of the Anti-Masonic leadership: he was Concord's representative on the Middlesex committee, secretary of county and state conventions, and star witness before the joint committee of the state legislature assigned to investigate Freemasonry. See *YG*, March 2, July 6 and 13, October 26, 1833, August 23, October 8, 1834; *Antimasonic Republican Convention of Massachusetts, Held at Boston, September 11, 12, & 13, 1833, For the Nomination of Candidates for Governor and Lt. Governor of the Commonwealth, and For the Purpose of "Consulting upon the Common Good, by Seeking*

Redress of Wrongs and Grievances Suffered" from Secret Societies (Boston, 1833), 44; *Antimasonic Republican Convention, for Massachusetts, Held at Boston, September 10 and 11, 1834, for the Nomination of Candidates for Governor and Lieutenant Governor, and to Advance the Cause of Equal Rights, by the Suppression of Secret Societies* (Boston, 1834), 3, 28; Atwill testimony, 31–35.

82. *YG*, March 2, 1833; Susan Kurland, "Democratization in Concord: A Political History, 1750–1850," in David Hackett Fischer, ed., *Concord: The Social History of a New England Town, 1750–1850* (Waltham, Mass., 1984), 271. Kurland shows that voter participation ranged from a quarter to a third of eligible adult men from 1825 to 1832, then jumped to 52 percent in 1833, 59 percent in 1834, slipped a bit for the next two years, then jumped to 66 percent in 1838 and 71 percent in 1840. I used two methods to estimate the proportion of adult males, ages twenty-one and over, turning out to vote. The 1850 federal census of Concord indicates that 632 men were twenty-one and older. They constituted 81.6 percent of all males sixteen and above, the legal definition of polls. I applied this percentage to the number of polls reported on assessment lists for select years. Voting participation in 1834 peaked at 288 to 292 votes; with an estimated 405 men twenty-one and over, the participation rate was 72 percent. An alternative method was to take the extant voters' list of 1838, which enumerated 436 voters, and to compare it with the number of reported voters that year. The 332 men who voted for governor constituted 72 percent of eligible men. The figures fluctuate in the 1830s and early 1840s in the range of 67 to 70 percent. Donald J. Ratcliffe disputes the notion that Anti-Masonry galvanized a new popular politics in state and nation, spurring broader participation in elections and invigorating the Whig challenge to Jacksonian Democrats with a crusading, evangelical spirit. Contrary to Ratcliffe, the evidence from Concord supports that case. The elections of 1833–1834 spurred the rise of voting rates to the high levels characteristic of the second party system in its heyday. Democrats claimed a marginal presence before and during the Anti-Masonic uprising; it was only when the two parties merged in 1836 that Democrats gained a regular majority in the town. See Ratcliffe, "Antimasonry and Partisanship in Greater New England, 1826–1836," *Journal of the Early Republic* 14 (Summer 1995): 197–237.

83. Gordon S. Wood, *The Creation of the American Republic, 1776–1787* (Chapel Hill, N.C., 1969), 189; Richard R. John, *Spreading the News: The American Postal System from Franklin to Morse* (Cambridge, Mass., 1995), 185–93; Francis Paul Prucha, "Protest by Petition: Jeremiah Evarts and the Cherokee Indians," *Proceedings of the MHS* 97 (1985): 50–52.

84. Herman Atwill and fifty-three other inhabitants of the town of Concord, Memorial to the Honorable Senate and House of Representatives in General Court assembled, House Unpassed Legislation, no. 12324 (presented March 14, 1833, by Joseph Barrett of Concord), MSA; Memorial, Commonwealth of Massachusetts, For an act to render Masonic and extrajudicial Oaths penal, and in aid of the Memorial for a full investigation into Freemasonry, and the repeal of the Charter granted to the Grand Lodge, House Unpassed Legislation, no. 13904A (submitted January 29, 1834), MSA; Charles B. Davis and sundry other citizens of Concord, petition for the passage of a law against Free Masonry, House Unpassed Legislation, no. 13028, Item 283 (presented by Mr. Everett, March 5, 1835), MSA; *Massachusetts Spy*, March 20, 1833; *Boston Weekly Messenger*, February 6, 1834; *Boston Daily Advertiser and Patriot*, March 6, 1835; *YG*, April 19, 1834 ("equal rights," "supremacy of the laws"); Bullock, *Revolutionary Brotherhood*, 294–302.

85. The National Republican candidate for governor, John Davis, received 85 ballots

(33 percent of the vote) and Democrat Marcus Morton a mere 26 (10 percent). *YG*, November 16, 1833; Formisano, *Transformation of Political Culture*, 213.

86. *YG*, November 16, 1833; Formisano, *Transformation of Political Culture*, 213. Barrett was brother-in-law of the prominent Mason Samuel P. P. Fay.

87. Meeting of March 3, 1834, CTMM 8:5, CFPL; *YG*, March 8, May 17, 1834; Keyes, Autobiography, 29–30. Keyes triumphed with 115 votes, compared to the Anti-Masonic challenger's 98 and 3 for "others." Atwill speculated that had the balloting been held later in the meeting, when all the voters had arrived, the Antis would probably have won. Keyes returned to the treasurer's office in 1834 with 54 percent of the Concord vote and 60 percent of the Middlesex County total.

88. Surette, *By-Laws*, 127; *Columbian Centinel*, October 16, 1830; *YG*, June 30, 1832, June 15 and 29, July 6, 1833; "Masonic Celebration at Concord, Ms.," *Boston Masonic Mirror*, July 6, 1833. The Corinthian Lodge awarded honorary memberships to Dr. Isaac Hurd, Roger Brown, and Reuben Brown along with Ripley on February 12, 1821.

89. *YG*, June 25, 1831, January 21 ("perpetual theme"), February 18, 1832; meeting of November 11, 1833, CTMM 7:443, CFPL. Disestablishment won 57 percent of the vote in Concord.

90. Daniel Southmayd, the first Trinitarian minister, was himself a master Mason, having taken the three degrees in St. Matthew's Lodge in Andover soon after graduating from the orthodox divinity school in 1825. But on coming to Concord in 1827, he never joined the Corinthian Lodge. Still, word somehow got around about his previous affiliation; soon he was being called on to "publicly renounce Masonry." Southmayd resisted the demand. In his defense, he claimed that he had visited a lodge "but four times" in his life—actually, just enough occasions to go through the necessary rituals—before deciding never to do so again. This weak excuse upset "two or three" Anti-Masonic parishioners, whose voluble complaints made the pastor's unhappy situation still more miserable and contributed to his request for "dismission." Southmayd gave up his ministry in the summer of 1832, well before Anti-Masonry became an active force in the town. See entry for June 8, 1832, Second Congregational Church Records 1826–67, 37–41, CFPL; Daniel S. Southmayd, membership card in the Massachusetts Grand Lodge, NEHGS database.

91. While they constituted just one out of every eight male residents in the mid-1830s, Trinitarians made up a quarter of the Anti-Masonic rank and file.

92. Of the 377 men recorded on the First Parish rolls in 1835, 97 (26 percent) signed an Anti-Masonic memorial. Trinitarian petitioners numbered 32. The contrast between the readiness of Trinitarians to sign Anti-Masonic petitions (65 percent) and the indisposition of First Parish supporters to do so (25 percent) is statistically significant at the .000 level. Of the 31 male church members embracing the 1832 covenant of the First Parish Church, only 6 (19 percent) subscribed to an Anti-Masonic memorial. On Reuben Brown, Jr., see William Whiting, "Memoir of Reuben Brown, Jr.," *SCM* 2:168–71. Brown was an early adopter of Anti-Masonry; in the closing days of 1829, he attended the first state convention of the new political movement. His embrace of this cause must have put him at odds with his eighty-one-year-old father, who joined the Corinthian Lodge in 1802 and became an honorary member twenty years later. See *An Abstract of the Proceedings of the Anti-Masonic State Convention of Massachusetts, Held in Faneuil Hall, Boston, Dec. 30 and 31, 1829, and Jan. 1, 1830* (Boston, 1830), 26.

93. The average age (mean and median) of new selectmen in this period was forty-two;

the Anti-Masonic delegates had a mean age of forty-four and a median of forty-seven. Of the dozen Anti-Masonic delegates from the out-districts, 60 percent were Concord natives; by contrast, 70 percent of the ten delegates in the center village were newcomers. Sixty percent of the Anti-Masonic delegates ranked in the top fifth of property holders on both the 1830 and 1835 assessment lists; another fifth were in the upper-middle quintile in 1830; a third in 1835. Thirteen of the 22 served as surveyor, school committeeman, or both.

94. Ralph Waldo Emerson (Boston) to William Emerson (New York), January 18, 1834, in Ralph L. Rusk, ed., *The Letters of Ralph Waldo Emerson*, 6 vols. (New York, 1939), 1:404.

95. George F. Hoar, *Autobiography of Seventy Years*, 2 vols. (New York, 1903), 1:38–39.

96. *YG*, November 2, 1833; Hoar, *Autobiography*, 38; *CF*, December 11 and 20, 1834; Formisano, *Transformation of Political Culture*, 158. Interestingly, about the same number of men (128) took no public stand on Freemasonry as voted for Hoar in November 1834 (129), suggesting that they shared his view that the only thing sillier than the fraternity was the movement to suppress it. The figure for nonsubscribers takes in all men in their thirties, forties, fifties, and sixties on the 1835 tax list, whose names are absent on Anti-Masonic petitions in 1834 and 1835. This suggests that nonsigning is a fair proxy for rejection of Anti-Masonry.

97. *YG*, March 8, 1834; List of applicants for membership, Social Circle Record Book, CFPL. During the Anti-Masonic fight, Representatives Barrett and Keyes vied with Reuben Brown, Jr., for spots on Beacon Hill. John Cheney ran for town treasurer on the Anti-Masonic slate and ousted the incumbent, Daniel Shattuck, in March 1834. But the wealthy merchant survived a challenge in 1833 for a seat in the state senate by William Munroe, still smarting over what he took to be Masonic bias in the arbitration of his financial dispute with Ebenezer Wood a half-dozen years earlier.

Of the twenty-five members of the Social Circle in 1833–1835, 20 percent were Anti-Masons, another 20 percent Masons, and the remaining 60 percent independent of the contending blocs; for the town as a whole in 1835, the distribution was as follows: Anti-Masons, 27 percent, Masons, nearly 9 percent, and unaffiliated 64 percent (N = 414). There was one turncoat, Herman Atwill, who signed the 1831 pro-Masonic declaration and then headed up the Anti-Masonic petitions. In October 1832, J. P. Heywood, who succeeded to the green store, lost his bid for membership; that was before Atwill unleashed Anti-Masonry in Concord. But the next three candidates to be rejected were all Anti-Masons: Joshua Buttrick (December 1832), Timothy Prescott (April 1833), and Isaac Cutler (January 1834). It was from Cutler that Atwill bought his house, barn, and garden. A key figure in the local elite, Nathan Brooks, briefly flirted with Anti-Masonry, accompanying Brown to the Boston convention at the close of 1829. That was the end of Brooks's association with the movement. See *An Abstract of the Proceedings of the Anti-Masonic State Convention of Massachusetts*, 26. As for John M. Cheney, he accepted the Anti-Masonic nomination for treasurer but did not sign any of the party's memorials. Both his father, Hezekiah, and his father-in-law, Rufus Hosmer, were stalwarts of the Corinthian Lodge. See Surette, *By-Laws*, 176–77.

98. As in all other aspects of local life, the young, the newly arrived, and the transient were disengaged from the conflicts absorbing their elders and employers. Few belonged to the Corinthian Lodge; not many more were asked or volunteered to sign Anti-Masonic memorials. These inhabitants, on the margins of the community, inflated the number of residents who appeared to take an independent

stance, neither for nor against the Masons; in reality, they were simply not involved. But the conflict polarized the middle-aged men, both natives and long-term transplants, long accustomed to running the town. The older a resident, the more likely he was to take sides. Among those in their twenties, one out of six signed a petition, while 80 percent were silent; a third of thirty-year-olds endorsed Anti-Masonry, with just over half (54 percent) refraining, and by the fifties, close to half (49 percent) enlisted in the insurgency, nearly a fifth rose to Freemasonry's defense, and just a third were truly independent.

To carry out this analysis, I identified the ages of most male inhabitants and then explored the relationship between age and position on Anti-Masonry. Approximately a quarter of men on the 1835 assessment list were of indeterminate ages. In my experience, these unknowns were nearly all men under thirty; taken together with their contemporaries whose years of birth could be ascertained yields an age distribution of male taxpayers (men over 21) consistent with the pattern revealed on the 1850 federal census. On similar reasoning, I considered all men whose place of birth could not be identified to be newcomers to Concord, and those who disappeared from the assessment lists, leaving no trace of their deaths, as emigrants. Very few men born and bred in Concord escaped the notice of the town clerk. The connections between positions on Anti-Masonry and such factors as age, residency, mobility, and wealth are all statistically significant at the 0.000 level.

99. Gross, "Lodges and Lyceums"; *YG*, February 8, 1834.

100. It is sometimes suggested that the Anti-Masons were anxious about "the commercialization of society" and projected their fears of social change onto an institution that seemed to extend its tentacles wherever stores and shops, taverns and hotels, lawyers and courts were found. Not in Concord. Anti-Masonic leaders looked outward to the wider world and actively contributed to economic, social, and cultural improvement. Atwill's *Gazette* thrived on the connections it forged between local readers and the markets of the metropolis and beyond. William Munroe started the manufacture of pencils from scratch, built a national business shipping his product to Kentucky in the West and New Orleans in the South, and invested his profits in corporate stocks. Nor were most of the farmers in the movement old-style husbandmen stuck in customary ways. In its heyday, twenty-two men represented Concord at Anti-Masonic conventions; a dozen belonged to the Society of Middlesex Husbandmen and Manufacturers and eleven to the Concord Lyceum. Goodman, *Towards a Christian Republic*, 37–38, stresses social anxiety as central to Anti-Masonry. The evidence from Concord supports Ronald Formisano's argument that Massachusetts Anti-Masons were progressive in outlook and "fully attuned to the spirit of 'improvement.'" See Ronald P. Formisano, *For the People: American Populist Movements from the Revolution to the 1850s* (Chapel Hill, N.C., 2008), 91–95.

101. Whiting, "Memoir of Reuben Brown, Jr.," 168–70.

102. Surette, *By-Laws*, 153–65.

103. Ralph Waldo Emerson, "Self-Reliance," in *EMP*, 135; Gross, "Lodges and Lyceums," 4–5.

9. *Freedom of Mind*

1. Ronald A. Bosco and Joel Myerson, *The Emerson Brothers: A Fraternal Biography in Letters* (New York, 2006), 19–20, 359n5; Ralph L. Rusk, *The Life of Ralph Waldo Emerson* (New York, 1949), 89, 198, 208–9; Gay Wilson Allen, *Waldo Emerson: A Biography* (New York, 1981), 9; Albert J. von Frank, *An Emerson Chronology*, 2 vols., 2nd ed.,

rev. and enlarged (Albuquerque, N.M., 2016), 4–15; Mary Kupiec Cayton, *Emerson's Emergence: Self and Society in the Transformation of New England, 1800–1845* (Chapel Hill, N.C., 1989), 15–17; *JMN* 4:xiv. William and Ruth Emerson were living in the parsonage of Boston's First Church in 1803 when Waldo was born; four years later they moved briefly into a house on Atkinson Street, while a new manse was being prepared on Chauncy Street. That became their home in September 1808. After her husband's death in 1811, the widow Ruth Emerson was allowed to remain in the parsonage until a new minister made it his own. She relocated to lodgings on Bennet Street (April 1813), Hancock Street (August 1816), Essex Street (October 1817), Franklin Place (January 1821), and Federal Street (August 1822). Thereafter she set up housekeeping in Roxbury, Newton, Cambridge, Newton again, and Concord.

2. Rusk, *Life of Emerson*, 128–30, 159–63; Robert D. Richardson, Jr., *Emerson: The Mind on Fire* (Berkeley, Calif., 1995), 97; *JMN* 4:335, 372; Peter S. Field, *Ralph Waldo Emerson: The Making of a Democratic Intellectual* (Lanham, Md., 2002), 131–66; Lawrence Buell, *Emerson* (Cambridge, Mass., 2003), 13–31.

3. *JMN* 4:335, 345; for Emerson's use of the Athenaeum and the Harvard College library, see von Frank, *Emerson Chronology, passim*; Robert A. Gross, "Transcendentalism and Urbanism: Concord, Boston, and the Wider World," *Journal of American Studies* 18 (December 1984): 361–81.

4. Charles Chauncy Emerson (Boston) to Elizabeth Hoar (Concord), January 29, 1835, bMS AM 1280.220 (52), Folder 28, Houghton; Charles Chauncy Emerson (n.p.) to William Emerson (New York), February 12, 1835, Ms N-251 (355), MHS (I thank Joel Myerson for sharing with me his transcripts of these Emerson letters); Edward Waldo Emerson, *Emerson in Concord: A Memoir Written for the "Social Circle" in Concord* (Cambridge, Mass., 1888), 52; Phyllis Cole, *Mary Moody Emerson and the Origins of Transcendentalism: A Family History* (New York, 1998), 4, 10–12, 164–70; Ralph Waldo Emerson (Concord) to William Emerson (New York), November 23, 1834, in Ralph L. Rusk, ed., *The Letters of Ralph Waldo Emerson*, 6 vols. (New York, 1939), I:423–24. For more on Mary Moody Emerson's life in Concord, see Chapter 2.

5. Charles Chauncy Emerson (Concord) to William Emerson (New York), April 7, 1835, Emerson Family Papers, N-251 (359), MHS; Ellen Tucker Emerson, *The Life of Lidian Jackson Emerson* (Boston, 1980), 47; Ralph Waldo Emerson (Concord) to Lydia Jackson (Plymouth), February 1 and 15, c. March 4, 1835, in Rusk, *Letters of Emerson*, 1:434–35, 437–38, 440; Bosco and Myerson, *Emerson Brothers*, 172–73.

6. Rusk, *Life of Emerson*, 223–24; *YG*, March 5, 1831; George William Curtis, "Emerson," in *Homes of American Authors; Comprising Anecdotical, Personal, and Descriptive Sketches* (New York, 1853), 244; Gross, "Transcendentalism and Urbanism," 172; Bosco and Myerson, *Emerson Brothers*, 174–76. Ripley's assistant minister, Hersey B. Goodwin, offered $3,000 for the Coolidge property in March 1831, but the seller would not take less than $3,500—the price that Emerson paid four years later. See Lucretia A. Goodwin (Concord) to Mrs. B. M. Watson, March 28, 1831, Watson-Goodwin Papers, Box 1, January–April 1831 folder, MHS.

7. *JMN* 2:242; Wesley T. Mott, *Ralph Waldo Emerson in Context* (New York, 2014), xxviii–xxix; William R. Hutchison, *The Transcendentalist Ministers: Church Reform in the New England Renaissance* (New Haven, Conn., 1959), 38. Emerson delivered 71 to 73 sermons annually from 1834 to 1837 and 23 to 29 lectures a year from 1835 to 1837. Thereafter he cut back sharply on preaching—13 sermons in 1838, 3 in 1839, and none from 1840 on—while committing himself to public speaking on the lecture platform. The turning point came in 1838, when he gave 44 lectures, triple the number of sermons. Hutchison calculates that from 1834 to 1837 Emerson

preached on the Sabbath an average of 41 times a year—three out of every four Sundays.

8. James Elliot Cabot, *A Memoir of Ralph Waldo Emerson*, 2 vols. (Boston, 1887), 1:248–53; Octavius Brooks Frothingham, *Transcendentalism in New England: A History* (New York, 1880), 115–22; Philip F. Gura, *American Transcendentalism: A History* (New York, 2007), 46–68. A search of Boston newspapers, 1830 to 1835, in the Early American Newspapers database yielded just seventeen articles containing the term *transcendental*. Most appeared in the religious press: the orthodox *Boston Recorder*, the Baptist *Christian Watchman*, the Unitarian *Christian Register*. Several pieces used the word to mean "transcendent," e.g., to suggest the supreme power of a government (speech of Senator John Rowan of Kentucky, *Boston Statesman*, May 1, 1830; speech of Rep. Horace Binney, *Boston Courier*, January 18, 1834). The Unitarian minister Orville Dewey, a kinsman of Emerson, complained about the obscurity of Transcendentalist writing in an 1830 Phi Beta Kappa address at Harvard. "I should be glad, at least, to *understand* Kant and Coleridge, before I can agree to [Transcendentalist philosophy]," he grumbled. If only the message were not "clothed" in such "absurd language"! Then Dewey would have been drawn to the doctrine. By 1837 German writers were assumed to be "given to useless and transcendental speculations." See *Boston Recorder*, September 1, 1830, reviewing Dewey's *Oration Delivered at Cambridge before the Society of the Phi Beta Kappa, August 26, 1830* (Boston, 1830), 17; extract from *Eclectic Review* praising Wolfgang Menzel as "thoroughly practical," hence not transcendental, in *Christian Watchman*, July 7, 1837.

9. Gura, *American Transcendentalism*, 64–68; Conrad Wright, *The Beginnings of Unitarianism in America* (Boston, 1955), 135–60; Cole, *Mary Emerson and Transcendentalism*, 165.

10. Gura, *American Transcendentalism*, 51–53; Orestes A. Brownson, "Benjamin Constant," and George Ripley, "Jesus Christ, the Same Yesterday, Today, and Tomorrow," in Perry Miller, ed., *The Transcendentalists* (Cambridge, Mass., 1950), 86–88, 285–89.

11. Lyman Beecher, *The Faith once delivered to the Saints: A Sermon, Delivered at Worcester, Mass., October 15, 1823, at the Ordination of the Rev. Loammi Ives Hoadley, to the Pastoral Office over the Calvinistic Church and Society in That Place* (Boston, 1823), 17–19, 43; Anne C. Rose, *Transcendentalism as a Social Movement, 1830–1850* (New Haven, Conn., 1981), 11–13.

12. Hutchison, *Transcendentalist Ministers*, 40–41, 44; George Ripley, "Jesus Christ," 289, 292, 293; [Frederic Henry Hedge], "Coleridge's Literary Character," *Christian Examiner* 14 (March 1833): 124.

13. Hutchison, *Transcendentalist Ministers*, 46–47; Gura, *American Transcendentalism*, 46–79; Caroline H. Dall, *Transcendentalism in New England: A Lecture Delivered before the Society of Philosophical Enquiry, Washington, D.C., May 7, 1895* (Boston, 1897), 15; Christopher Grasso, *Skepticism and American Faith from the Revolution to the Civil War* (New York, 2018), 323–56; William Ellery Channing, "Discourse at the Ordination of the Rev. F. A. Farley, Providence, R.I. 1828," in Channing, *Discourses, Reviews, and Miscellanies* (Boston, 1830), 455–82. Ripley was ordained over Boston's new Purchase Street Church in 1826; Hedge became minister of the West Cambridge Congregational Church in 1829. George Ripley was the first cousin once removed of Concord's Ezra Ripley; he prepared for the admissions test into Harvard College with his second cousin, Rev. Samuel Ripley (Ezra's son). See H. W. Ripley, comp., *Genealogy of a Part of the Ripley Family* (Newark, N.J., 1867), 32–33, and Octavius Brooks Frothingham, *George Ripley* (Boston, 1882), 6–7. Brownson came to Can-

ton in May 1834 after serving as pastor of a Unitarian congregation in Walpole, New Hampshire.

14. Richardson, *Emerson*, 72, 79–83, 93–94, 97; Cole, *Mary Emerson and Transcendentalism*, 4, 202, 209–10; Ralph Waldo Emerson, Sermon 162 ("The Lord's Supper"), September 9, 1832, in Joel Myerson, ed., *Transcendentalism: A Reader* (New York, 2000), 75. Up to 1835, Emerson's record of publications was slight: a few anonymous pieces in Boston periodicals and a couple of appearances in pamphlets commemorating the ordination of clerical colleagues. See Joel Myerson, *Ralph Waldo Emerson, A Descriptive Bibliography* (Pittsburgh, 1982), 2–5, 599, 661.

15. Edward Jarvis, Diary 1827–42, entry for May 1, 1828 ("practical & instructive," "sometimes too refined"), 1:222–23, CFPL. George Moore, the eighteen-year-old son of Abel, heard Emerson preach "two excellent sermons" on October 4, 1829. See "The Diary of George Moore," in Kenneth Walter Cameron, comp., *Transcendental Epilogue: Primary Materials for Research in Emerson, Thoreau, Literary New England, the Influence of German Theology, and Higher Biblical Criticism*, 3 vols. (Hartford, Conn., 1965–1982), 1:17.

16. Wesley T. Mott, *"The Strains of Eloquence": Emerson and His Sermons* (University Park, Pa., 1989), 102–8; Kenneth S. Sacks, *Understanding Emerson: The American Scholar and His Struggle for Self-Reliance* (Princeton, N.J., 2003), 72–83; Ralph Waldo Emerson (Boston) to Edward Bliss Emerson (Porto Rico), December 22, 1833, in Rusk, *Letters of Emerson*, 1:401–2; Richardson, *Emerson*, 146; Leon Jackson, "The Social Construction of Thomas Carlyle's New England Reputation, 1834–36," *Proceedings of the AAS* 106 (1996): 165–89. Between mid-November 1834 and February 1838, Emerson delivered thirty sermons in Concord. See von Frank, *Emerson Chronology*, 1:173–263.

17. Ripley, "Jesus Christ," 284–92. Hedge also viewed the forms of religion as transient, in contrast to the eternal principles of faith. Institutions, he remarked, are "the creations of the day, they can vouch only for the passing generation." See Hedge, "Progress of Society," in Miller, *Transcendentalists*, 73–74.

18. Ripley, "Jesus Christ," 289; Brownson, review of *An Essay on the Moral Constitution and History of Man* [Edinburgh, 1834], *Christian Examiner* 18 (July 1835): 353–64. Hedge also invoked trust in the infinite resources of the individual self. "Let us ground it [the call for reform] on universal Man," he vowed, "on the might of the human will, and on the boundless resources of the human mind." Hedge, "Progress of Society," 74.

19. Rose, *Transcendentalism as Social Movement*, 14–16; Grasso, *Skepticism and American Faith*, 337; Gura, *American Transcendentalism*, 59–64. The *Massachusetts Register* for 1833 listed in Boston twenty-two Congregational churches (12 Unitarian, 10 orthodox), six Baptist, five each of Episcopalian and Methodist; four Universalist, two Roman Catholic, one Society of Friends, one Church of the New Jerusalem, one unspecified (Mariner's). I followed Rose's characterization of the orthodox-liberal divide in the Congregational churches, updating it with one additional orthodox church in 1833. I did not include chapels in the tabulation, since the denominations of some (Buttolph, Commercial, and Sea Street chapels) were not specified. The orthodox had one chapel, likewise for the liberals and the Episcopalians. See *Massachusetts Register, and United States Calendar for 1833* (Boston, 1833), 121–22.

20. Grasso, *Skepticism and American Faith*, 334–40; Henry Steele Commager, "The Blasphemy of Abner Kneeland," *New England Quarterly* 8 (March 1935): 29–41; Roderick S. French, "Liberation from Man and God in Boston: Abner Kneeland's Free-Thought Campaign, 1830–1839," *American Quarterly* 32 (Summer 1980):

202-21; Robert E. Burkholder, "Emerson, Kneeland, and the Divinity School Address," *American Literature* 58 (March 1986): 1-14; Robert E. Riegel, "The American Father of Birth Control," *New England Quarterly* 6 (September 1933): 470-90; *JMN* 4:280-81.

21. Michael Sappol, "The Odd Case of Charles Knowlton: Anatomical Performance, Medical Narrative, and Identity in Antebellum America," *Bulletin of the History of Medicine* 83, no. 3 (Fall 2009): 461-62; Grasso, *Skepticism and American Faith*, 338-39; Lyman Beecher, *Lectures on Scepticism: Delivered in Park Street Church, Boston, and in the Second Presbyterian Church, Cincinnati* (Cincinnati, 1835), 58-59.

22. Ripley, "Jesus Christ," 290; *JMN* 4:281; French, "Liberation from Man and God."

23. S.G.H., "Atheism in New England," *New-England Magazine* 8 (January 1835): 61; French, "Liberation from Man and God," 218.

24. Shane White, "'It Was a Proud Day': African Americans, Festivals, and Parades in the North, 1741-1834," *Journal of American History* 81 (June 1994): 35-38; *Boston Patriot*, July 14, 1826; Leonard P. Curry, *The Free Black in Urban America, 1800-1850: The Shadow of the Dream* (Chicago, 1981), 100.

25. "Dr. Beecher's Lectures," *Boston Recorder*, January 5, 1831; Daniel A. Cohen, "The Respectability of Rebecca Reed: Genteel Womanhood and Sectarian Conflict in Antebellum America," *Journal of the Early Republic* 16 (Fall 1996): 419-61; Cohen, "Alvah Kelley's Cow: Household Feuds, Proprietary Rights, and the Charlestown Convent Riot," *New England Quarterly* 74 (December 2001): 531-79.

26. *JMN* 4:342.

27. David Greene Haskins, *Ralph Waldo Emerson, His Maternal Ancestors, with Some Reminiscences of Him* (Boston, 1887), 119; Henry Adams, *Education of Henry Adams* (Boston, 1922), 62-63.

28. CTMM 7:441, 8:12, 37, CFPL; "Third Annual Report of the School Committee of the Town of Concord, for the year ending March 5, 1832," *YG*, March 17, 1832; "Early Records of the Concord Lyceum," in Kenneth Walter Cameron, comp., *The Massachusetts Lyceum During the American Renaissance; Materials for the Study of the Oral Tradition in American Letters: Emerson, Thoreau, Hawthorne, and Other New-England Lecturers* (Hartford, Conn., 1969), 137; *CF*, December 27, 1834. On school enrollment, see Chapter 6n66. The annual budget for the schools was $1,500 in 1833, dropped to the usual $1,400 in 1834, then rose to $1,800 in 1835.

29. Richardson, *Emerson*, 121; Mary McDougall Gordon, "Union with the Virtuous Past: The Development of School Reform in Massachusetts, 1789-1837" (Ph.D. diss., University of Pittsburgh, 1974), 263-69, 289-91; *JMN* 4:326, 378. The lawyer and litterateur Benjamin Bussey Thatcher, familiar to Concord audiences for his advocacy of African colonization, addressed the lyceum "on Self-Education" in December 1834. Going against the grain, the speaker decried the excesses to which popular enthusiasm for education had gone. Parents were pushing their children too soon and too hard to excel in school, at the cost of mental well-being and physical health. The consequences, he complained, were "an unnatural stimulating of the youthful mind, an overtaxing of its energies in a particular direction, to the great detriment of a full, and proportionate, and natural development of its powers." His concerns were well received. The *Concord Freeman* gave a favorable account of his lecture in its issue of December 27, 1834, praising the speaker for treating an "extremely interesting and delicate subject" with "a power of just and tasteful discrimination, and an elegance and forcibleness of manner, which held the attention of the audience for nearly two hours." That same day Emerson recorded his thoughts

on the "object of Education." Thatcher evidently spoke from experience; he would die five years later, at age thirty, supposedly from overwork. See "Early Records of the Concord Lyceum," 137; Martha L. Prescott, Diary, entry for December 10, 1834, CFPL; Nehemiah Cleaveland, *History of Bowdoin College. With Biographical Sketches of Its Graduates, from 1806 to 1879, Inclusive*, edited and completed by Alpheus Spring Packard (Boston, 1882), 356–58.

30. *YG*, July 27, 1833 ("Corinthian Father"); "Early Records of the Concord Lyceum," 129, 130, 134–39. The lyceum hosted twenty-six lectures in the 1831–1832 season, twenty-two in 1832–1833, twenty-one in 1833–1834, and twenty-two in 1834–1835; it held five debates in 1831–1832, twenty in 1832–1803, eleven in 1833–1834, thirteen in 1834–1835. Emerson also participated in lyceum debates. He argued against the proposition that immigration into the United States should be limited by law and in favor of the question, Was the French Revolution "the cause of more good than evil"? In both debates Emerson's side won. "Early Records of the Concord Lyceum," 138–39.

31. Daniel S. Malachuk, "The Republican Philosophy of Emerson's Early Lectures," *New England Quarterly* 71 (September 1998): 404–28; Cayton, *Emerson's Emergence*, 49–52; *JMN* 4:332–33.

32. *JMN* 5:22–24, 29. In his shortlist of "the most powerful men in our community," Emerson also included the hotel owner William Shepherd.

33. *JMN* 4:342; Malachuk, "Republican Philosophy," 413, 415.

34. *JMN* 4:369.

35. *CF*, December 20, 1834; *Boston Courier*, December 22, 1834, quoting from the *Middlesex Whig*. On election day, December 15, 1834, Emerson was in Boston visiting with his brother Charles and with his Transcendentalist colleague Hedge. (See *JMN* 4:360.) In his outrage at Whig attempts to manipulate the election, editor Herman Atwill revealed an ugly side to his populism. "A 'Squire's opinion," he jibed, "is no more to be asked than Jack the wood-sawyer's, and is worth no more." Everyone would have gotten the reference to Jack Garrison, the industrious workingman well-known around town "with his saw-horse over his shoulder and his saw on his arm." See John Shepard Keyes, "Houses and Owners or Occupants in Concord 1885," 54–55, CFPL.

36. Richard Franklin Bensel, *The American Ballot Box in the Mid-Nineteenth Century* (New York, 2004), 14–17; Jill Lepore, "Rock, Paper, Scissors: How We Used to Vote," *New Yorker*, October 13, 2008; Susan Kurland, "Democratization in Concord: A Political History, 1750–1850," in David Hackett Fischer, ed., *Concord: The Social History of a New England Town, 1750–1850* (Waltham, Mass., 1984), 274–75; meeting of March 3, 1834, CTMM 8:5, CFPL; *YG*, March 8, 1834; Keyes, Autobiography, 29–30, 32–33. If all of a party's nominees received the same number of votes, its measure of party cohesion would be 100. In November 1834, the index for the populist coalition (Anti-Masons and Democrats cooperated on a slate) was 90, and it was 91 for the Whigs. As the Democratic-Whig rivalry solidified in succeeding years, the measure approached 100 for both parties.

37. *Bunker-Hill Aurora*, February 9, August 10, 1833; *YG*, March 8, November 8, 1834; *American Traveller*, July 29, 1834; Louis A. Surette, *By-Laws of Corinthian Lodge, of Ancient, Free and Accepted Masons, of Concord, Mass.* (Concord, Mass., 1859), 145; D. Hamilton Hurd, comp., *History of Middlesex County, Massachusetts, with Biographical Sketches of Many of Its Pioneers and Prominent Men*, 3 vols. (Philadelphia, 1890), 1:637; *CF*, December 11, 1834. No copies of the *Middlesex Whig* are extant. Its existence is

documented by references and reprints in other contemporary newspapers. Bemis apprenticed to the printer's trade in Amherst, then operated the *Nantucket Inquirer*, from which he came to Concord. According to the printers' files at AAS, Bemis was with the Amherst firm of J. S. and C. Adams & Co. in July 1829. *Nantucket Inquirer*, October 6, 1832, January 16, 1833, July 2, 1834.

38. *CF*, December 11 and 20, 1834, July 18 ("no pecuniary interest"), 1835. For documentation of the changing ownership of the press, see notes 43 and 45.

39. *CF*, December 11, 1834, July 18, 1835.

40. Cohen, "Respectability of Rebecca Reed," 419-61; Cohen, "Alvah Kelley's Cow," 531-79; *CF*, March 14, April 11, 1835; *Antimasonic Republican Convention, for Massachusetts, Held at Boston, September 10 and 11, 1834, for the Nomination of Candidates for Governor and Lieutenant Governor, and to Advance the Cause of Equal Rights, by the Suppression of Secret Societies* (Boston, 1834), 19-21.

41. Shattuck, *History*, 205; Richard R. John *Spreading the News: The American Postal System from Franklin to Morse* (Cambridge, Mass., 1995), 121-35, 206-42; *CF*, June 27, 1835; *YG*, June 20, 1835; *Lowell Mercury*, August 2, 1833; Marvin Meyers, *The Jacksonian Persuasion: Politics and Belief* (Stanford, Calif., 1960).

42. *CF*, July 18, August 15, 1835; *Columbian Centinel*, December 12, 1835; *Massachusetts Register and United States Calendar* for 1836 (Boston, 1836), 229; Ronald P. Formisano, The *Transformation of Political Culture: Massachusetts Parties, 1790s-1840s* (New York, 1983), 246-64. Over the course of a decade, from 1826 to 1835, Atwill and Keyes traded places on the Massachusetts political map. Concord's cagey "fence man," once a favorite of the *Statesman*, was considered by many to be a closet Jacksonian. But the Anti-Masonic insurgency pushed him into the Whig camp. Atwill, in turn, moved from antagonist to political bedfellow of Henshaw and the Jacksonians. In his movement from National Republican to Anti-Mason to Democrat, he consistently took the opposite side from Keyes.

43. E. R. Hoar, "Francis Richard Gourgas," *SCM* 3:25-29; W. L. Montague, ed., *Biographical Record of the Alumni of Amherst College, During Its First Half-Century, 1821-1871*, 2 vols. (Amherst, Mass., 1883-1901), 1:22, 165; G. Washington Warren, "The Class of 1830," *Harvard Register* 1, no. 6 (May 1880): 127; Surette, *By-Laws*, 44; "Reminiscences of Middlesex Lodge, Framingham," *Freemason's Monthly Magazine* 26 (1867): 149-50; Robert N. Hudspeth, ed., *The Correspondence of Henry D. Thoreau*, vol. 1, *1834-1848* (Princeton, N.J., 2013), 54; *CF*, August 15, 1835. The memoir of Gourgas was written by his Whig political antagonist, Ebenezer Rockwood Hoar. Gourgas's investment in the *Concord Freeman* was recorded, along with the names of the other shareholders, in the account book of his father, who supplied the funds. See John M. Gourgas, Notes, Book no. 3, January 1, 1834, to July 23, 1838, entry for August 7, 1835, Gourgas Family Papers, CFPL. The partners in the newspaper were: Stephen Pope of Marlboro and Burrage Yale of South Reading, both past nominees of the Middlesex Anti-Masons for state senator; Alpheus Bigelow of Weston, who served as president of the party's county convention in August 1834; and Dr. Amos Farnsworth of Groton, a leading figure in the MCASS. See *YG*, November 19, 1831, August 23, November 8, 1834; *CF*, October 31, 1835; Samuel A. Green, *An Account of the Physicians and Dentists of Groton, Massachusetts* (Groton, Mass., 1890), 25-26.

44. One political insider claimed in mid-June 1835 that "a young man (or young men) in the office of Hon. Samuel Hoar (one of them recently with Mr. Keyes), furnish most of the editorial matter." The former lawyer with experience in Keyes's office was probably Albert H. Nelson, then completing his legal studies and an aspiring

Whig politician. The other was Charles C. Emerson. See *CF*, June 27, 1835, and John S. Keyes, "Memoir of Albert H. Nelson," *SCM* 2:382–83.

45. Daniel Shattuck and Abel Moore, report of committee to erect block of buildings on south side of Mill Dam, April 10, 1837, Mill Dam Company Papers, CFPL; *Boston Daily Advertiser*, October 10, 1835; Ralph Waldo Emerson (Boston) to William Emerson (New York), January 18, 1834, in Rusk, *Letters of Emerson*, 1:404. According to Harriet Hanson Robinson, the editor William S. Robinson purchased the *Gazette* in 1840 from a consortium including Nathan Brooks, Daniel Shattuck, and unnamed others. It seems likely that these were the men who started the *Middlesex Whig* back in 1834 and merged it with the *Gazette* in November of that year. Since Bemis is recorded on assessment lists and Mill Dam Company records as renting his printing office from Shattuck and others, I assume that they were the proprietors of the newspaper continuously until the sale to Robinson. Keyes was surely among them. See Harriet H. Robinson, ed., *"Warrington" Pen-Portraits: A Collection of Personal and Political Reminiscences from 1848 to 1876, from the Writings of William S. Robinson* (Boston, 1877), 20–21. No copies of the *Yeoman's Gazette* survive in the CFPL collection from June 21, 1834, until November 14, 1835; scattered issues are available at AAS and MHS.

46. *JMN* 4:369, 5:28–29.

47. Roman J. Zorn, "The New England Anti-Slavery Society: Pioneer Abolition Organization," *Journal of Negro History* 42 (July 1957): 172; *Proceedings of the Anti-Slavery Convention Assembled at Philadelphia, December 4, 5, and 6, 1833* (New York, 1833), 10; "List of anti-slavery societies," *Sixth Annual Report of the Board of Managers of the Massachusetts Anti-Slavery Society. Presented January 24, 1838* (Boston, 1838), xxxviii–xlv; *JMN* 4:356–57.

48. Matthew Spooner, "'I Know This Scheme Is from God': Toward a Reconsideration of the Origins of the American Colonization Society," *Slavery and Abolition* 35 (2014): 559–75; *American Colonization Society, and the Colony at Liberia* (Boston, 1831), 12; *Report Made at an Adjourned Meeting of the Friends of the American Colonization Society, in Worcester County, Held in Worcester, December 8, 1830, by a Committee Appointed for That Purpose* (Worcester, Mass., 1831), 11–15; Manisha Sinha, *The Slave's Cause: A History of Abolition* (New Haven, Conn., 2016), 161–68.

49. *Proceedings of the Massachusetts Colonization, Held in Park Street Church, February 7, 1833, Together with the Speeches Delivered on That Occasion* (Boston, 1833), 3, 8; *American Colonization Society, and the Colony at Liberia*. Donations to the ACS were regularly listed in the official publication of the group, *African Repository and Colonial Journal* 5 (October 1829): 255; 6 (October 1830): 250; 7 (January 1832): 348; 9 (April 1833): 64; 10 (July 1834): 160; 11 (March 1835): 95. See also *Colonizationist and Journal of Freedom* (Boston, 1834), 32. Trinitarians made contributions only in 1829 and 1834; in the first instance, the funds provided by the two religious societies in Concord amounted jointly to $30 ($850 in 2019 purchasing power). In 1834, under Rev. John Wilder, the Trinitarian society gave $11, well below the First Parish Church's $19. Ripley's congregation never missed an annual contribution to the fund drive. Its largest collection, $24 in 1833, is the equivalent in purchasing power of $754 in 2019.

50. For Ripley's sermon, see "Love the most comprehensive and essential trait of the Christian character," bMS 64, Box 2, Folder 7, HDS.

51. Elise Lemire, *Black Walden: Slavery and Its Aftermath in Concord, Massachusetts* (Philadelphia, 2009), 178–79; Richard S. Dunn, *A Tale of Two Plantations: Slave Life in Jamaica and Virginia* (Cambridge, Mass., 2014), 182, 187; Adam Rothman,

Slave Country: American Expansion and the Origins of the Deep South (Cambridge, Mass., 2005), 180–81; Ezra Ripley (Concord) to Rev. Henry Fitts (Warren County, N.C.), July 22, 1818, Trustees of Reservations Archives Center, Sharon, Mass. (I am grateful to Lynn Hyde for providing me access to her research into Daniel B. Ripley's experiences in Alabama and to Tom Beardsley for furnishing a transcript of Ripley's letter to Rev. Henry Fitts.) At Mount Airy, Ripley resided on the "home place," surrounded by somewhat over one hundred enslaved domestic servants and craftsmen; on the eight farm quarters of the plantation, 276 slaves made up the workforce in the fields. Each winter he moved with his employers and young charges to the elegant townhouse, the famous Octagon, which the Federalist Tayloe, a friend of ex-president Washington, built in the rising national capital. See Orlando Ridout V, *Building the Octagon* (Washington, D.C., 1989), 105–6.

52. Ridout, *Building the Octagon*, 105; Samuel Hoar (Washington City) to John Farrar (Cambridge), February 12, 1803, George Frisbie Hoar Papers, Correspondence, Box 2: 1802–52, MHS; Paula Ivaska Robbins, *The Royal Family of Concord: Samuel, Elizabeth, and Rockwood Hoar and Their Friendship with Ralph Waldo Emerson* ([Philadelphia], 2003), 27–29; George A. Jarvis et al., *The Jarvis Family: or, The Descendants of the First Settlers of the Name in Massachusetts and Long Island, and Those Who Have More Recently Settled in Other Parts of the United States and British America* (Hartford, Conn., 1879), 238; Samuel Maverick to Tilly Merrick, March 3, November 18, 1808, and John Harth to Merrick, January 10, 1807, Tilly Merrick Papers, Boxes 59/16 and 60/19, CFPL; Richard Lowitt, "Tilly Merrick, Merchant in a Turbulent Atlantic World," *Atlantic Studies* 11 (2014): 236, 251; von Frank, *Emerson Chronology*, 1:20–24. For Burr, see Chapter 4.

53. "Early Records of the Concord Lyceum," 130, 132; *YG*, July 9 and 16, 1831, June 1, October 12, 1833; *CF*, January 31, 1835; *American Colonization Society, and the Colony at Liberia*, 12. The initial secretary of the Massachusetts Colonization Society was the physician-politician Jerome van Crowninshield Smith, coeditor with John Eaton of Andrew Jackson's *Memoirs* (1828). Other notable political figures on the first board of managers were the National Republican collector of customs in Boston, Henry A. S. Dearborn, who notoriously was removed from office by the Jacksonians, and Samuel T. Armstrong, who would be elected lieutenant governor of the state on the National Republican ticket in November 1833. The Baptist minister Charles Train, a Democrat from Framingham, served on the board of managers with the Unitarian Ezra Stiles Gannett, the orthodox Congregationalist Samuel M. Worcester, a professor at Amherst College, the Hicksite Quaker Thomas A. Greene of New Bedford, and the Episcopalian Alonzo Potter, rector of St. Paul's Church in Boston.

54. *Report Made at an Adjourned Meeting of the Friends of the American Colonization Society*, 11; *American Colonization Society, and the Colony at Liberia*, 12–13 (emphasis added); *YG*, June 1, 1833.

55. William Lloyd Garrison, *Thoughts on African Colonization: or An Impartial Exhibition of the Doctrines, Principles, and Purposes of the American Colonization Society*, part 2, *Sentiments of the People of Color* (Boston, 1832), 17–21; Sinha, *Slave's Cause*, 196–214.

56. The 1830 *Boston Directory* places James Middleton, mariner, on Bridge Street (p. 329). A year and a half later he died a pauper under the care of the Boston overseers of the poor, who sought repayment of their costs from Concord. See *YG*, August 13, 1831, and Boston overseers of the poor to Concord selectmen and overseers, January 22, 1831, ETR.

57. Zorn, "New England Anti-Slavery Society," 172; *Proceedings of the Anti-Slavery Convention Assembled at Philadelphia, December 4, 5, and 6, 1833* (New York, 1833), 10; "List of anti-slavery societies," xxxviii–xlv; *YG*, June 1, 1833; meeting of October 1, 1834, and list of members following the Constitution (Wilder's is the lone Concord name among the original 155 subscribers), MCASS Record Book, 1834–51, CFPL; Sandra Harbert Petrulionis, *To Set This World Right: The Antislavery Movement in Thoreau's Concord* (Ithaca, N.Y., 2006), 12–13; Leonard L. Richards, *"Gentlemen of Property and Standing": Anti-Abolition Mobs in Jacksonian America* (New York, 1970), 37. Of the 221 local antislavery societies recorded in the survey published in 1838, the founding years for 142 could be determined. The banner year for antislavery organization was 1837, when fifty groups were started.

58. *CF*, January 10 and 17, 1835.

59. Richards, *"Gentlemen of Property and Standing,"* 63–70; *Letters and Addresses by George Thompson: During His Mission in the United States, from October 1st, 1834, to Nov. 27, 1835* (Boston, 1837), 30–32; *YG*, January 17 and 24, 1835, AAS; C. Duncan Rice, "The Anti-Slavery Mission of George Thompson to the United States, 1834–1835," *Journal of American Studies* 2 (April 1968): 13–31.

60. *CF*, January 24 and 31, February 7, 1835; *YG*, January 31, 1835, reprinted in *CF*, November 11, 1837.

61. *JMN* 5:15; Mary Moody Emerson (Concord) to unknown recipient, February 1, 1835, in Nancy Craig Simmons, ed., *The Selected Letters of Mary Moody Emerson* (Athens, Ga., 1993), 115–16 (identifying Goodwin as the preacher who set off Emerson's tirade). Thompson arrived in Concord on January 27, 1835, two evenings before Emerson launched a new lecture series on biography at the Masonic Temple in Boston.

62. *CF*, March 21 and 28, April 4 ("long, flowing beard"); C. C. Burleigh to S. J. May, April 3, 1835, Anti-Slavery Collection, Ms. A.1.2.V.5, 23, BPL; Mary Moody Emerson (Concord) to unknown recipient, February 1, 1835, and to Lidian Jackson Emerson (Concord), October 9, 1835, in Simmons, *Selected Letters*, 355–56, 364; Cole, *Mary Emerson and Transcendentalism*, 233–36.

63. Charles C. Emerson (Concord) to William Emerson (New York), April 29, 1835, Ms N-251 (361), MHS; Charles C. Emerson, Lecture on Slavery, composed in Concord, April 29, 1835, MS AM 82.6, Houghton, reprinted in *Emerson Society Quarterly* 16 (1959): 12–26. There is no evidence that Emerson gave this address in Concord. It was not a lyceum lecture, and it was not advertised in the press by any other group. Charles's letter to William, dated April 29, makes plain that it was composed for delivery in Duxbury, where Sarah Alden Bradford, one of Mary Moody Emerson's circle of friends and later the wife of Rev. Samuel Ripley, spent much of her childhood. It is tempting to imagine that the Bradfords of Duxbury arranged the speaking invitation to Charles Emerson through Aunt Mary. I thank Carolyn Ravenscroft of the Duxbury Rural and Historical Society for information about the town's antislavery activists.

64. C. Emerson, Lecture on Slavery.

65. "Early Records of the Concord Lyceum," 132, 138. The lyceum twice debated the issue of racial difference, asking in April 1833, "Are the intellectual qualities of the whites naturally superior to those of the negro race?" and ten months later examining whether "the difference of Colour in the human species [is] the effect of Climate or other causes?" No decision was reported in either case. See "Early Records," 130, 134.

66. List of subscribers to the Constitution, MCASS Record Book. The names of Davis,

Gourgas, Barrett, and Brooks appear in a cluster of subscribers after the date July 22, 1836. I presume that the initial set of 155 signatories recorded their assent to the group's plan of operation in 1834–1835. Gourgas may well have joined the group before the summer of 1836; he and Wilder served as delegates in January to the quarterly meeting of the MCASS, held in Woburn. See *Liberator*, January 23, 1836.

67. C. C. Burleigh to S. J. May, April 3, 1835, Anti-Slavery Collection, Ms. A.1.2.V.5, 23, BPL; Second Congregational Church of Concord Records 1826–67, 60, CFPL; *African Repository and Colonial Journal* 12 (August 1836): 264 and (October 1836): 326. The Trinitarian congregation made its last contribution to the ACS in 1834. Three years later the members donated $21.33 to the abolitionist cause. See *Sixth Annual Report of the Board of Managers of the Massachusetts Anti-Slavery Society* (Boston, 1838), xxxiii.

68. *CF*, May 23 and 30, July 18, September 26 ("foolish belief"), October 31 ("scene of misrule"), 1835; *YG*, August 15, September 5, 1835; Sinha, *Slave's Cause*, 233–34.

69. Keyes, Autobiography, 41–42.

70. Charles Emerson quoted in Cole, *Mary Emerson and Transcendentalism*, 236.

71. Ibid., 233–34; *JMN* 4:342, 5:28–29, 32, 71, 73, 90–91.

10. A Little Democracy

1. *EL* 1:95, 149, 119, 165; Scott E. Casper, *Constructing American Lives: Biography and Culture in Nineteenth-Century America* (Chapel Hill, N.C., 1999), 89–90, 213–15. Emerson touched off a vogue for biography at the Concord Lyceum. Between 1835 and 1860, at least twenty-one lectures on biographical subjects were presented to the group.

2. John Seelye, *Memory's Nation: The Place of Plymouth Rock* (Chapel Hill, N.C., 1998), 73–85; CTMM 8:27, 37–38, CFPL.

3. Wendy Warren, *New England Bound: Slavery and Colonization in Early America* (New York, 2016), 30–36; Mark Peterson, *The City-State of Boston: The Rise and Fall of an Atlantic Power, 1630–1865* (Princeton, N.J., 2019), 61–66.

4. Ezra Ripley and twelve others, petition, September 20, 1825, ETR; meetings of March 6, April 3, 1826, CTMM 7:259, 265, CFPL; Nancy Craig Simmons, ed., *The Selected Letters of Mary Moody Emerson* (Athens, Ga., 1993), 209–10; Phyllis Cole, *Mary Moody Emerson and the Origins of Transcendentalism: A Family History* (New York, 1998), 184–86; Kristi Lynn Martin, "Creating 'Concord': Making a Literary Tourist Town, 1825–1910" (Ph.D. diss., Boston University, 2019), 48–58. The erection of the memorial to William Emerson was discussed and endorsed by the Social Circle in September 1825; the thirteen subscribers were all members of the exclusive group, including Lemuel Shattuck.

5. *YG*, April 26, 1828, April 23, 1831, April 21, 1832, April 26, 1834; *CF*, April 18, 1835; *Bunker-Hill Aurora*, April 20 and 27, 1833; Ezra Ripley, D.D., *Half Century Discourse, Delivered November 16, 1828, at Concord, Massachusetts* (Concord, Mass., 1829), 16–19. The *Gazette* snubbed the 1833 commemoration; it is evident from the names of participants that Anti-Masons boycotted the 1834 event.

6. Robert A. Gross, "The Celestial Village: Transcendentalism and Tourism in Concord," in Conrad E. Wright and Charles Capper, eds., *Transient and Permanent: The Transcendentalist Movement and Its Contexts* (Boston, 1999), 259–69; "Middlesex," "The Monument at Concord," no. 4, *YG*, March 25, 1826; Ezra Ripley, *History of the Fight at Concord* (Concord, Mass., 1827), v, 60. For the controversy sparked by the Lafayette reception and the jubilee of the Concord Fight, see Chapter 1.

7. *YG*, June 22, 1833; Gross, "Celestial Village."

8. CTMM 8:2, 4, 10–12, 39, CFPL; report of committee chaired by Daniel Shattuck on Ezra Ripley's proposed gift to the town for a monument, April 7, 1834, ETR; *YG*, June 14, 1834. The committee argued that Ripley's proposal was a good deal for the town. It was economical. Building a monument by the riverside would cost no more than at any other location. The expenses of the stone wall for which Ripley called would be covered by private donations. And the $600 in the hands of the trustees of the monument fund would go entirely for the granite obelisk long in the works.

9. Abiel Heywood and seventeen others, petition for town meeting, January 1835, ETR; meeting of February 1, 1835, CTMM 8:53–55, CFPL; "Removal of the Courts," *CF*, February 28, 1835; Elijah Wood and fifty others, Citizens of Middlesex, petition praying for the removal of all the Courts in said County to Concord; Isaac Hurd and thirty-nine others, petition; Phineas How and forty-six others, petition; Abiel Heywood and 117 others, petition; and Heartwill Bigelow and ninety-seven others, petition for same, Senate Unpassed Legislation 1835, 9673/8, 11, 12, 14, and 16, respectively, MSA. For earlier contests over the county courts, see Chapters 1 and 3.

10. CTMM 37–38, 43, CFPL. It should come as no surprise that Daniel Shattuck served on the committee of arrangements, along with such other village worthies as Dr. Bartlett, Phineas How, and Reuben Brown; from the out-districts came pencil maker William Munroe, textile manufacturer Ephraim Bellows, and farmers Nathan Barrett, Eleazer Brooks, and James Wood. Of the twelve men on the committee, five were Anti-Masons (Brooks, Brown, Munroe, Wheeler, and Wood), three were Masons (Bellows, Keyes, and Whiting), and four were independents (Barrett, Bartlett, How, and Shattuck). Two Trinitarians (Brooks and Bellows) joined with nine Unitarians on the committee; one member (Elisha Wheeler) signed off the parish and paid for the support of no church. At least seven were Whigs (Barrett, Bartlett, Bellows, How, Keyes, and Shattuck). Selectman Cyrus Stow was a Democrat; his colleagues on the board (Daniel Clark and Isaac Lee) were Anti-Masons, giving that faction nearly half (7) of all seats (15). Abolitionists included Bartlett and Whiting.

11. CTMM 8:37–38, CFPL; *T&R*, 33–37. Decades after the bicentennial, Jarvis recalled the debates over the celebration—or, more precisely, what he had heard about them from others. Despite his role in instigating the commemoration, he was left off the committee of arrangements. It is likely that he got his information through the Social Circle.

12. *T&R*, 34–35; *JMN* 5:54.

13. *T&R*, 36; letters to and from the committee of arrangements for the second centennial celebration of the incorporation of Concord, August 20 to September 11, 1835, Records, CFPL.

14. Ezra Ripley (Concord) to George Bancroft (Northampton), July 23, 1834, George Bancroft Papers, 1827–34 box, MHS; *JMN* 5:71. George Bancroft would not reveal his judgment about Lexington and Concord until 1858, when he deemed the skirmish at the North Bridge "more eventful" in world history than the battles of Agincourt and Blenheim. See Bancroft, *History of the United States, from the Discovery of the American Continent*, 10 vols. (Boston, 1834–1874), 7:303.

15. "Nineteenth of April," *CF*, April 18, 1835; Charles C. Emerson (Concord) to William Emerson (New York), July 25, 1835, Emerson Family Papers, Box 2, Ms N-251, MHS. The first Patriots to fall in battle at the North Bridge were Minutemen from Acton, as the inhabitants of that town never ceased to boast. Charles Emerson was

amused at the neighboring town's exaggerated sense of its own importance. Had he been called on to speak at Acton's Centennial Celebration in 1835, he was prepared to offer the following toast: to "the blessed Memory of the Pilgrim Fathers, who first landed at Acton." See George F. Hoar, *Autobiography of Seventy Years*, 2 vols. (New York, 1903), 1:63.

16. *Boston Daily Advertiser*, June 23, 1832; *Proposals for Publishing by Subscription The History of the Town of Concord* (Concord, Mass., 1832), with subscription list, CFPL; *Boston Courier*, May 24, 1832; James N. Green, "The Rise of Book Publishing," in Robert A. Gross and Mary Kelley, eds., *An Extensive Republic: Print, Culture, and Society in the New Nation, 1790–1840* (Chapel Hill, N.C., 2010), 82–83, 89. In May 1832 Shattuck's project won a strong endorsement from Herman Atwill, who got an advance look at the manuscript. The editor echoed the claims of his former master at the Corinthian Lodge and onetime assistant at the *Gazette*: "Every source of information seems to have been sought after, discovered and explored," the details "compared, digested, and arranged with great fidelity and care." Every reader would find something of value in the book, as potential buyers could see in the extracts from Shattuck's manuscript, dealing with the events leading up to the Concord Fight, that were published in the newspaper. See *YG*, May 19 and 26, 1832.

17. Of 115 male residents of Concord subscribing to the *History*, 16 percent were Masons, 36 percent Anti-Masons, and 47 percent independents. Producers of all sorts—pencil maker Munroe, his difficult employee Ebenezer Wood, boot- and shoemaker Elijah Wood, the farmers Abel B. Heywood and Nathan Barrett, silk grower Anthony Wright, cotton manufacturer Bellows—were glad to patronize local history. Considering the stiff price, it is not surprising that no laborers signed up, nor did any free people of color. Two women, Lydia Hosmer and Mary Heywood, ordered copies. For Henry D. Thoreau's use of Shattuck's *History* as a reference work, see *J* 9:255–56, 264, and William Brennan, "An Index to Quotations in Thoreau's 'A Week on the Concord and Merrimack Rivers,'" *Studies in the American Renaissance* (1980): 260, 262, 267, 273, 289.

18. Among the short pieces Shattuck wrote on Concord history during the 1820s were an account of the "Concord Light Infantry" by "S," *YG*, October 3 and 10, 1829, and an inquiry into the origins of the Social Circle (*SCM* 1:55–62). As he got involved in school reform, he also became a pioneer of educational history. See Lemuel Shattuck, "Lecture on Education" (undated), Lemuel Shattuck Papers, Box 7, Folder 161, NEHGS Research Library, Boston; Josiah Holbrook, *American Lyceum, or Society for the Improvement of Schools, and Diffusion of Useful Knowledge* (Boston, 1829), 9; Shattuck, *History*, iv. Shattuck grounded his argument for school reform on a pathbreaking survey of the laws and practices of Massachusetts from Puritan settlement to his own time. It was never published in his lifetime.

19. Alea Henle, "Preserving the Past, Making History: Historical Societies in the Early United States" (Ph.D. diss., University of Connecticut, 2012), app. 2, "Historical and Related Societies Established in the United States, by Date, 1791–1850"; John Ward Dean, "Lemuel Shattuck," *Memorial Biographies of the New England Historic Genealogical Society*, vol. 3, *1856–1859* (Boston, 1883), 296–99; John Farmer (New Hampshire Historical Society), Christopher C. Baldwin (Worcester, AAS), and John G. Palfrey (MHS) to Lemuel Shattuck, Box 1 of 2, 1827 and July–December 1831 folders, Lemuel Shattuck Papers, MHS.

20. Lemuel Shattuck, "A Plan for Providing Materials for History," *Collections of the New Hampshire Historical Society* 3 (1832): 234–37.

21. *T&R*, 6; Walter F. Willcox, "Lemuel Shattuck, Statist Founder of the American

Statistical Association," *American Statistician* 1 (August 1947): 11–13; Gerald N. Grob, *Edward Jarvis and the Medical World of Nineteenth-Century America* (Knoxville, Tenn., 1978), 36–39; Robert A. Gross, "A Majority of One: Counting Consciences in Concord," in Loretta Valtz Mannucci, ed., *Making, Unmaking and Remaking America: Popular Ideology Before the Civil War* (Milan, Italy, 1988), 51–62. A good many official documents ended up in Shattuck's personal papers at NEHGS and MHS.

22. B. B. Thatcher, "History of Concord," *North American Review* 42 (April 1836): 451; Shattuck, *History*, v, 10, 28 ("exemplary"), 91. Shattuck challenged the tradition that Concord was taken as the name of the town in tribute to the "peaceable manner in which . . . [the land] was obtained from the Indians." He establishes that the name was adopted before then to signify "the Christian union and concord, subsisting among the first company, at the commencement of the settlement" (4–5).

23. Shattuck, *History*, 66, 180.

24. For the correspondence between Emerson and Shattuck, see Ralph L. Rusk, ed., *The Letters of Ralph Waldo Emerson*, 6 vols. (New York, 1939), 1:452–56. The partnership of Brown, Shattuck, & Co. was announced in the *Boston Daily Advertiser* on June 23, 1832; it was dissolved on July 1, 1834—see *Advertiser*, July 31, 1834. Sometime in 1834 the bookish merchant started his own company, Shattuck & Co., at 8 School Street in Boston. See *Stimpson's Boston Directory* (Boston, 1834), 312, and (Boston, 1835), 326. For the influence of Shattuck's book on other local histories, see William Lincoln, *History of Worcester, Massachusetts, from Its Earliest Settlement to September, 1836* (Worcester, Mass., 1837), vi: "The general plan of arrangement has been imitated from Mr. Shattuck's *History of Concord*."

25. *YG*, August 15, 1835; undated clipping from *YG*, either August 15 or 22, 1835, Jarvis's interleaved copy of Shattuck's *History*, following p. 392, CFPL. Four members of the Social Circle were vice-presidents of the celebration: Dr. Bartlett, John Stacy, Phineas How, and William Munroe.

26. *YG*, August 22, September 19, 1835, clippings in Jarvis's interleaved copy of Shattuck's *History*; *T&R*, 38.

27. *CF*, September 12, 1835; *T&R*, 37. Of the officers of the day, William Munroe had been an Anti-Mason, but unlike most members of that party, he came to affiliate with the Whigs.

28. Obituary of Abba M. Brooks, *Christian Register*, Obituary Scrapbooks, 1:4, CFPL; *Slave's Friend* 2, no. 6 (June 1837): 9–10.

29. *YG*, September 5 and 19, 1835 (the latter in Jarvis's interleaved copy of Shattuck, *History*); report on Concord bicentennial included in Ralph Waldo Emerson, *A Historical Discourse, Delivered before the Citizens of Concord, 12th September, 1835, on the Second Centennial Anniversary of the Incorporation of the Town* (Concord, Mass., 1835), 48. Ward D. Safford (Concord) to Mark Safford (Washington, N.H.), September 20, 1835, CFPL. See Chapter 1 for an account of the April 19, 1825, parade. On the Safford family, see John B. Hill, *History of the Town of Mason, N.H., from the First Grant in 1749, to the Year 1858* (Boston, 1858), 61, 266–67. Safford's grandparents, Joseph Barrett and Sarah Brooks, were Concord natives who moved to Mason before the Revolution.

30. *Order of Exercises, at the Second Centennial Celebration of the Settlement of Concord* (Concord, Mass., 1835); *YG*, September 19, 1835, clipping in Jarvis's interleaved copy of Shattuck, *History*; Seelye, *Memory's Nation*, 93–97. The initial ode on the program was written by Unitarian minister John Pierpont for the Second Centennial Celebration of Boston in 1830. The final hymn, composed for the occasion by

twenty-year-old Benjamin D. Winslow, a recent Harvard graduate and a convert to the Episcopal Church, avoided the theme of religious persecution as the force driving the Puritan settlers from England; he celebrated the peaceful acquisition of the land from "the red-men" and the transformation of the "uncultured homestead" into productive farms. See William B. Sprague, D.D., ed., *Annals of the American Pulpit; or Commemorative Notices of Distinguished American Clergymen of the Various Denominations*, vol. 5, *Episcopalian* (New York, 1859): 750–53.

31. *JMN* 4:335, 12:3–32; Emerson to Shattuck, September 27, 1835, in Rusk, *Letters of Emerson*, 1:455–56.

32. Emerson, *Historical Discourse*, 12–16.

33. For a modern account of this sorry episode, see Jenny Hale Pulsipher, "Massacre at Hurtleberry Hill: Christian Indians and English Authority in Metacom's War," *William and Mary Quarterly* 53 (July 1996): 459–86.

34. *YG*, September 19, November 28, 1835; John Shepard Keyes, "Reminiscences," manuscript written ca. 1903, Keyes Papers, CFPL; Charles Chauncy Emerson (Concord) to William Emerson (New York), September 14, 1835, Ms N-251 (371) [timing the lecture at an hour and forty-five minutes], MHS; Emerson, *Historical Discourse*, 9–10, 18–19, 20, 25–26. In his copy of Shattuck's *History*, Jarvis revealed that the *YG* report on the September 12 commemoration was co-written by Rev. Goodwin, Charles C. Emerson, and himself. He also included a clipping of the story with the interleaved pages. This is the only copy of that account extant—no issue of the *YG* for September 19, 1835, survives. Jarvis made plain that he wrote the first section of the report on the procession to the meetinghouse; Goodwin described the program and the oration; and Emerson took responsibility for the dinner, with speeches, toasts, and the "Ladies' Collation."

35. Emerson, *Historical Discourse*, 26, 29, 30, 32–37; Gross, *Minutemen*, 30–41; Mary Babson Fuhrer, "The Revolutionary Worlds of Lexington and Concord Compared," *New England Quarterly* 85 (March 2012): 78–118.

36. Emerson, *Historical Discourse*, 16–17, 41; *JMN* 4:342, 356–57; Gross, *Minutemen*, 10–15; Michael Zuckerman, *Peaceable Kingdoms: New England Towns in the Eighteenth Century* (New York, 1970), and for a recent restatement of his views, Zuckerman, "Mirage of Democracy: The Town Meeting in America," *Journal of Public Deliberation* 15, no. 2 (2019). For other reflections by Emerson on the conditions essential to intellectual independence and free expression, see *JMN* 4:354, 367, 384; 5:22.

37. Emerson, *Historical Discourse*, 4, 36–37; Cole, *Mary Emerson and Transcendentalism*, 71, 79.

38. Emerson, *Historical Discourse*, 41; *YG*, September 19, 1835. Looking over the assembly in the meetinghouse, Rev. Hersey Goodwin exulted at the sight of "the children of the ancient family, some separated by many generations, gathered home again." Even those gone for more than a century had bequeathed "the affection for their first home as an heirloom for their posterity." Many were now back to see firsthand the source of that inheritance and "to greet their old mother once more." See *YG*, September 19, 1835.

39. *T&R*, 36–37; *YG*, September 19, 1835; Ward D. Safford to Mark Safford, September 20, 1835. Charles Chauncy Emerson was delighted by his brother's address. See his deft summary of the main points of the discourse in his letter to William Emerson, September 14, 1835, cited in note 34. The farm laborer Safford was not the only member of the laboring class to enjoy the bicentennial celebration. Praise for the event also came from the "wife of a Middlesex farmer," who described her happy experience in a communication to the *Concord Freeman*. She

had originally been reluctant to attend the festivities for fear that it would be another "Lafayette scrape," designed to show off the local elite. Fortunately, she ignored the warnings and decided to join in. The entire affair was joyous, especially, the "Ladies' Collation" at the courthouse. She was warmly welcomed into the room and invited to partake of the rich spread. And though the space was decorated "with a display of the most elegant and refined taste," there was not a hint of "aristocracy" or condescension at the reception. "Those who in independence might leisurely recline on a hair-cloth sofa with a volume of the Illiad [sic], or ride in a splendid carriage," mixed easily with women in "the humbler walks of life," whose days were normally spent plying needles and churning butter. Class consciousness gave way to a "reciprocity of entire good feeling between the citizens." The farmer's wife took a cautionary lesson from the experience. Maybe, she suggested, working people could be too proud and prickly for their own good: "Jealousy does not always emanate in good feelings, and its effects less often produce them; let us then lay aside all animosity, cultivate and reciprocate kinder feelings." This conservative moral, aimed at diminishing class antagonisms in Concord, raises doubts about the actual social status of the author. So does the literary style of the letter, along with its references to the *Iliad* on the couch. Intended to counteract the populism of the *Freeman*, the communication was as likely the product of a gentleman's pen as the handiwork of a farmer's wife. *CF*, September 19, 1835.

40. Emerson to Shattuck, September 27, 1835, in Rusk, *Letters of Emerson*, 1:455–56.

41. Ibid.; subscription list for Shattuck's *History of Concord*, CFPL (Emerson's is the final order on the list and the biggest; Hersey Goodwin and Samuel Hoar come next with six copies each); "E," "Review of Shattuck's *History of Concord*," YG, October 3, 1835; Thatcher, "History of Concord," 448–50, 454.

42. Thatcher, "History of Concord," 453–54. For another review of Shattuck, *History*, see *American Traveller*, October 16, 1835. Upon hearing that Thatcher had been commissioned to produce a review-essay of Emerson's *Historical Discourse* and Shattuck's *History of Concord*, Ezra Ripley hastened to write the author and lobby him to examine the debate over which town—Acton, Concord, or Lexington—deserved the most credit for instigating the military resistance to the king's troops. "An enlightened and impartial review" of the controversy was imperative, in Ripley's opinion. Would Thatcher undertake the task on his own? Or perhaps he could collaborate with another gentleman on the work? Ripley suggested the names of his step-grandson Charles C. Emerson and of Boston lawyer and historian William Sullivan, whose *Public Men of the Revolution. Including Events from the Peace of 1783 to the Peace of 1815* had recently been published (Boston, 1834). The parson was anxious to see the "matter settled" as soon as possible, "because I am old, & I am tired of controversy, & because I find that time sharpens the memory of some people, & there is no knowing what new claims to honor, & courage, & patriotism may yet be made, as time progresses." The resulting essay, composed by Thatcher alone, provided a measure of satisfaction. Declining to enter into "controversy upon minutiæ," the author allowed that Concord was "partially . . . the scene of the *first military action of the Revolution*." And although Shattuck's account of events contained "slight inaccuracies," he unhesitatingly agreed that "here was the first regular resistance to British troops by Americans." Ripley would have to be content with that verdict. See Ezra Ripley (Concord) to B. B. Thatcher, Esq. (Boston), March 25, 1836, Morgan Library (I thank Christine Nelson for steering me to this document); Thatcher, "History of Concord," 466.

43. Subscription to defray expenses of September 12, 1835, celebration, September 7, 1835, Letter file 8, S-2, CFPL. Samuel Hoar's pledge of ten dollars topped the list; he was followed by Nathan Brooks, John Keyes, and Daniel Shattuck with five dollars each. Altogether, twenty-three men, fifteen of them members of the Social Circle, contributed $65.50 to match the $75 the town had allocated for the event. Neither Emerson nor John Thoreau paid in.

44. Robert A. Gross, "Celestial Village," 266–74; *YG*, December 10, 1836; "The Monument at Concord," *Boston Courier*, July 5, 1837.

45. Among the petitioners were "Uncle Tom" Wesson, keeper of the Middlesex Hotel, and Heartwill Bigelow, proprietor of his namesake tavern. Joseph Meriam and nine others, petition asking the town to reconsider its votes of April 1834 and 1835 on the monument, ETR; *CF*, May 2, 1835; meeting of May 4, 1835, CTMM 8:43, CFPL.

46. *T&R*, 223; Keyes, Autobiography, 47–48. One piece of evidence in support of Keyes's version is his statement that the monument committee cobbled together the inscription during a meeting at Timothy Prescott's house. The rising Anti-Masonic politician Prescott, the father of Keyes's future bride, Martha, was an active member of the committee. In his diary, Prescott noted his attendance at the meetings of that body but said nothing about the inscription. Prescott died in 1842, two years before his bereaved daughter wed the younger Keyes. It is likely that the Hon. John Keyes, with his fingers in so many Concord pies, was his son's source. See Timothy Prescott, Diary, April 1, 1830–April 12, 1840, entries for January 9, April 24, June 5 and 24, July 9, August 6, October 8, 1836, Houghton.

47. "Lawyer Hoar, the Tithingman and the Lawyer," *CF*, November 12 and 19, 1836; *YG*, November 5, 1836; Michael J. Dubin, *United States Congressional Elections, 1788–1997: The Official Results of the Elections of the 1st through 105th Congresses* (Jefferson, N.C., 1998), 115; Arthur B. Darling, *Political Changes in Massachusetts 1824–1848: A Study of Liberal Movements in Politics* (New Haven, Conn., 1925), 235, 249; *JMN* 5:247. The margin in Concord was virtually the same as in Middlesex County as a whole: 56 percent for Parmenter, 43 percent for Hoar.

48. *YG*, March 11, 1837; *CF*, March 11, May 13, June 17, 1837, January 13, 1838; *Boston Courier*, June 15, 1838. Stedman Buttrick received 179 votes in Concord to Keyes's 76; for the county, the division was 3,907 to 3,501, with 35 scattered among others. The combative butcher Orville Tyler, who once threatened to "slap" the "chops" of Herman Atwill for mocking him in the *Gazette*, was now the "trusty friend" who carried out the orders of Gourgas and Buttrick at town meeting.

49. *YG*, April 1 and 15, 1837. The Massachusetts General Court passed two acts authorizing the shift of court sessions from Concord to Lowell. The first was "An Act relating to certain courts in the County of Middlesex," April 16, 1836, chap. 275, *Laws of the Commonwealth of Massachusetts, Passed at the Several Sessions of the General Court, Beginning January, 1834, and Ending April, 1836* (Boston, 1836), 13:1002. This was followed by "An Act in Addition to an Act relating to certain courts in the County of Middlesex," March 24, 1837, chap. 89, Theron Metcalf and Luther S. Cushing, eds., *Laws of the Constitution of Massachusetts, Passed Subsequently to the Revised Statutes* (Boston, 1844), 21. The split between Whigs and Democrats over the best strategy for keeping the courts crystallized in the winter of 1836, when the *Gazette* pushed for the hiring of a special counsel to assist the town's two representatives in making its case before the legislature. Evidently, Whigs hoped to hire Keyes, defeated for representative in the November 1835 election, for the job. Such an appointment was taken by Democrats as an insult to "the abilities" of Stedman Buttrick and

Cyrus Stow and to "the feelings" of those who voted for them. See *YG* and *CF*, January 30, February 6 and 13, 1836.

50. *YG*, April 1, 1837; *CF*, April 8, 1837. Neither newspaper noted that the issue had essentially been decided in the winter 1836 session of the General Court, following the submission of petitions to the legislature by the various Middlesex towns. Thirty-four petitions from twenty-five towns favored Lowell; six urged the holding of all courts in Concord; twenty-three protested against any change in the existing arrangements. The weight of public opinion appeared to be in support of Lowell's bid, particularly in the towns to the west and north of Concord. Crucially, the Democratic stronghold of Charlestown, at the eastern edge of the county, backed the change. This seems to confirm the *Gazette*'s charge that the Democrats in the legislature went for Lowell rather than Concord for partisan advantage. See Petitions to General Court for and against request of George F. Farley and others to hold Middlesex court sessions in Lowell, File papers for chap. 275, "An Act relating to certain courts in the County of Middlesex," April 16, 1836, MSA.

51. *CF*, April 8, 1837; Shattuck, *History*, 211; Census of population of the Town of Concord with the number of each Family as existed on the first day of May, A.D., 1837, ETR. One sign of the stagnant times was the departure of Edward Jarvis. The return of the native in 1832 had received a mixed reception. On the surface all looked good. He was finally able to marry and start a household; he was admitted into the Social Circle and chosen for leadership positions at the library, lyceum, and school committee. But his medical practice was going nowhere. "I had come to a stand," he reflected in the winter of 1836; "I was able to get a bare living," but "no more"; he and Almira managed only "with the greatest economy." The problem was that Josiah Bartlett remained the senior physician in town, and nobody was prepared to desert him for the newcomer. Even "my best friends did not employ me." The situation grew ever more frustrating. "I began to distrust myself—to feel that I would not & perhaps ought not to command men's confidence." The difficulty was structural, *not* personal. No new doctor, however talented, could build much of a clientele in a town barely holding its own. With his local prospects so discouraging, Jarvis listened with rising interest to reports of great opportunities in the West. Then in the fall of 1836, as the monument committee squabbled over the inscription, he received a visit from Unitarian minister James Freeman Clarke, who had recently settled in the boomtown of Louisville on the Ohio River. His congregation was looking for a physician trained in the East, and Jarvis was just the man: "He painted in glowing colors the growth, prosperity, and capacity of Louisville." The thirty-three-year-old physician took the chance, though with considerable trepidation. In late March 1837 he was on his way to Kentucky, where he would soon be founding libraries and lyceums, campaigning for temperance, promoting local history, and composing accounts of the West for the *Yeoman's Gazette*. The change was not for the better. After five years he wearied of Kentucky and returned to Massachusetts. He never again resided in Concord, though to the benefit of future scholars, he would devote the last decades of his life to writing the history of his native town. See Jarvis, Diary, 2:142–47; Rosalba Davico, ed., *The Autobiography of Edward Jarvis* (London, 1992), 56–57; Gerald N. Grob, *Edward Jarvis and the Medical World of Nineteenth-Century America* (Knoxville, Tenn., 1978), 43–48, 53–56; Bridget Ford, *Bonds of Union: Religion, Race, and Politics in a Civil War Borderland* (Chapel Hill, N.C., 2016), 5–6.

52. *CF*, April 8 and 22, 1837; *YG*, April 15 and 29, 1837.

53. *YG*, December 10, 1836; *CF*, December 10, 1836. The author of the column on the cornerstone-laying ceremony expressed hope that a formal dedication of the monument would be held the next April 19. This was probably the general expectation.

54. Ezra Ripley, lecture at Concord Lyceum, written March 1837, delivered April 12, 1837, in Ezra Ripley (1751–1841), Writings, Box 1, Folder 15, Old Manse Manuscripts, 1755–1938, Series 2, Ripley Family Papers, Trustees of Reservations Archives and Research Center, Sharon, Mass. This section is taken from Gross, "Celestial Village." In 1837 the assessors counted 493 polls within their jurisdiction; 267, or 54 percent, contributed to the support of the First Parish Church. At disestablishment this ratio was 86 percent (430/497); it fell to 80 percent in 1836 (279/475), 44 percent in 1838 (206/463), and was down to 28 percent in 1845 (129/467). In 1843 Massachusetts eliminated the tax on polls under the age of twenty, reducing the tax base of the parish from 162 to 132 or by 18 percent.

55. Rusk, *Letters of Emerson*, 2:85n121; *CF*, July 8, 1837; *YG*, July 8, 1837; "The Monument at Concord," *Boston Courier*, July 5, 1837; Keyes, Autobiography, 48–49.

56. *CF* and *YG*, July 8, 1837 (the same account ran in both newspapers); *Boston Courier*, July 5, 1837; Gross, "Celestial Village," 273–74; Walter Harding, *The Days of Henry Thoreau: A Biography* (1962; rpt. New York, 1982), 48.

11. The Philosopher of Modern History

1. Perry Miller, ed., *The Transcendentalists* (Cambridge, Mass., 1950), 106–7; Philip F. Gura, *American Transcendentalism: A History* (New York, 2007), 69–97.

2. *JMN* 5:293, 328; James Elliot Cabot, *A Memoir of Ralph Waldo Emerson*, 2 vols. (Boston, 1888), 1:274–75; Gura, *American Transcendentalism*, 5, 69–71.

3. Oliver Wendell Holmes, *Ralph Waldo Emerson* (Boston, 1884), 93; Emerson, *Nature* (Boston, 1836), reprinted in *EMP*, 34, 68.

4. Miller, *Transcendentalists*, 173–76; Bowen, review of *Nature*, *Christian Examiner* 21 (January 1837): 371, 377–81, 385.

5. Ronald A. Bosco and Joel Myerson, *The Emerson Brothers: A Fraternal Biography in Letters* (New York, 2006), 319–20. The 1835 assessment list of Concord, drawn up in the spring of 1835, credits Emerson with $11,500 in financial assets; he had not yet purchased his house and land. Three years later, his holdings were set at $16,300, including his homestead ($3,300) and personal estate ($13,000). See Concord assessment lists, Town Treasurer's Records, CFPL.

6. R. W. Emerson (Salem) to William Emerson, May 3, 1836, in Ralph L. Rusk, ed., *The Letters of Ralph Waldo Emerson*, 6 vols. (New York, 1939), 2:15–16. Emerson clearly resented the claims of the school committee on his time. Responsible as chairman for overseeing the annual report on the town schools, he delegated the job to the young lawyer Albert H. Nelson and paid him five dollars out of pocket for the service. See entry for November 7, 1836, in Emerson account books, 1836–39 (transcript), Ms AM 1280H (112a), Houghton (Joel Myerson transcription).

7. Ralph L. Rusk, *The Life of Ralph Waldo Emerson* (New York, 1949), 152–53; meeting of June 1, 1835, CTMM 8:44, CFPL; Edward Waldo Emerson, *Emerson in Concord. A Memoir Written for the "Social Circle" in Concord, Massachusetts* (Boston, 1890), 142–43; Robert A. Gross, *Much Instruction from Little Reading: Books and Libraries in Thoreau's Concord* (Worcester, Mass., 1988), 166; entry for June 18, 1836, Emerson account books, 1836–39 (transcript); Social Circle Record Book, CFPL. Emerson was serving as president of the social library in 1837, when he delivered the Phi Beta Kappa

address at Harvard and decried the excessive deference of American scholars to "the courtly muses" of Europe. A month or so after that event, he was nominated for membership in the Social Circle by his Harvard classmate John M. Cheney, cashier of the Concord Bank.

8. Seventeen payments to Howe, starting on April 29, 1836, and continuing to October 16, 1840, in Emerson account books (transcript); *JMN* 5:177, 240–41, 296; Emerson, *Emerson in Concord*, 59, 124–27, 129; Cabot, *Memoir*, 2:447–50. Peter Howe (1785–1869) was born in the central Massachusetts town of Hubbardston to parents who hailed from Sudbury, next door to Concord. He lived with his first wife, Elizabeth Haynes, and their seven children in Stratton, Vermont, and Rindge, New Hampshire. The union ended sometime after September 1826, and on December 20, 1829, Howe remarried to Sarah Whitney of Lunenberg in Worcester County and settled in Concord soon thereafter. Howe was widowed again in December 1834 but not for long; nine months later the farm laborer wed Dorcas Deeth of Fitzwilliam, New Hampshire. Renting half a house, first from Abel Moore, then from Charles B. Davis, he somehow acquired the "heater piece," the triangular plot opposite Emerson's house on which the Concord Museum now stands, and sold it to his employer before moving away. His final destination was the town of Westfield, in Hampden County, Massachusetts, where he labored in a shop making whips. Howe's itinerant existence, moving from town to town in search of land and work, could have modeled for Emerson the descent of the Yankee yeoman into the industrial working class. See D. K. Young, *Echoes in the Forest: The Family History Supplement to the History of Stratton, Vermont* (n.p., 2000), 236–38; 1830, 1835, and 1838 assessment lists of Concord; 1830 federal census and 1837 town census of Concord; 1840 and 1850 federal censuses of Westfield, the latter of which records Howe's occupation as "whips." Emerson hastened to purchase Howe's lot after hearing that a blacksmith was about to buy up the property. "It would not do to have a smithy" right across the road from his home, Emerson declared, so he paid $200 to obtain the land at public auction. See R. W. Emerson (Concord) to William Emerson (Staten Island), December 25, 1838, in Rusk, *Letters of Emerson*, 2:176–77. The deed for the lot, dated December 17, 1838, records the grantor not as Peter Howe but as his yeoman son Emerson; the grantee was Ralph Waldo Emerson, "gentleman." MCRD 377:414.

9. *JMN* 5:296, 422–23, 7:10–11, 79. Emerson also employed Garrison's sons John Jr. and William for day labor and his wife Susan Robbins Garrison for "washing."

10. Robert A. Gross, "Transcendentalism and Urbanism: Concord, Boston and the Wider World," *Journal of American Studies* 18 (December 1984): 361–68; *JMN* 5:283, 189; Emerson, "The Eye and the Ear," delivered December 27, 1837, as the fourth lecture in the "Human Culture" series, *EL* 2:272; W. Barksdale Maynard, "Emerson's 'Wyman Lot': Forgotten Context for Thoreau's House at Walden," *Concord Saunterer*, n.s., 12–13 (2004–5): 68–69; *EMP*, 36–37.

11. Gross, "Transcendentalism and Urbanism," 366–67; Emerson, "The Present Age," lecture read February 23, 1837, *EL* 2:161–62; Oscar Handlin, *Boston's Immigrants: A Study in Acculturation*, rev. and enlarged ed. (New York, 1972), table 2, 239; *JMN* 5:317–18, 7:201, 219.

12. *JMN* 5:422–23.

13. Ellen Tucker Emerson, *The Life of Lidian Jackson Emerson*, ed. Delores Bird Carpenter (Boston, 1980), 50, 63–64, 76; entries from April 20, 1837, to December 21, 1839, in Emerson account books (transcript); *JMN* 7:376; Gross, "Transcendentalism

and Urbanism," 368–69, 373. Barron was removed from Concord in the spring of 1837, possibly at Emerson's instigation. Nancy Barron, age forty-six, died on March 29, 1843, the cause attributed to "insanity."

14. *JMN* 5:455–56. In a May 1838 entry in his journal, Emerson imagined himself in conversation with a critic, who accused him of "egotism & presumption." Not at all, he replied. Just look at his relations with the common people of Concord: "I see with awe the attributes of the farmers & villagers whom you despise. A man saluted me today in a manner which at once stamped him for a theist, a selfrespecting gentleman, a lover of truth & virtue. How venerable are the manners often of the poor." *JMN* 5:493.

15. *JMN* 5:63, 390, 289, 395. The foreign observer was the Frenchman Gustave de Beaumont, the traveling companion of Alexis de Tocqueville on their 1831 tour of the United States. Beaumont's novel, *Marie, or Slavery in the United States* (1835), was a travel narrative purporting to be fiction, but it struck at the heart of American democracy with its exposure of the brutal oppression of African Americans by the white majority. The novel was reviewed in the April 1835 issue of the British *Quarterly Review*. In his response to that article, Emerson ignored entirely its theme of racial injustice and focused instead on Beaumont's idealized view of social equality in everyday life. See review of *Marie, or Slavery in the United* States, in *Quarterly Review* 53 (April 1835): 296–97. Emerson was told by Edward Jarvis about the impecunious family with no table on which to take tea. Supposedly, Francis Jarvis, the doctor's brother, witnessed the situation firsthand when he paid a visit to "Mrs. G." I suspect that he was referring to Susan Robbins Garrison, the wife of the wood sawyer Jack. In 1837 only ten families bore a surname beginning with G, and of these, the free family of color is the likeliest candidate.

16. *JMN* 5:456. Emerson incorporated this observation into his Harvard Divinity School address five months later. See Emerson, "The Divinity School Address," in *EMP*, 121.

17. Daniel Walker Howe, *What Hath God Wrought: The Transformation of America, 1815–1848* (New York, 2007), 502–3. The initial advertisement of "Mr. Emerson's Lectures" ran in the October 18, 1836, issue of the *Boston Courier*. It continued to appear twice weekly in the newspaper down to December 8. The other ads referred to in the text were in the October 18 number. Emerson limited his advertising to the Whig *Courier*. A search of America's Historical Newspapers finds no advance notices of the upcoming lecture series in any other Boston newspaper.

18. Proposal for *Society for the Diffusion of Useful Knowledge* (Boston, 1829), broadside, available in the "America's Historical Imprints" database from Readex, Inc.; SDUK officers listed in *Massachusetts Register* for 1834 to 1836; Helen R. Deese and Guy R. Woodall, "A Calendar of Lectures Presented by the Boston Society for the Diffusion of Useful Knowledge (1829–1847)," *Studies in the American Renaissance* (1986): 17–47; Carl Bode, *The American Lyceum: Town Meeting of the Mind* (Carbondale, Ill., 1968), 17. The publisher of the *Boston Daily Advertiser*, Nathan Hale, served as vice-president along with Everett. In November and December 1836, as Emerson was launching his series "The Philosophy of Modern History," the SDUK featured Daniel Webster, Harvard law professor Theophilus Parsons, Jr., and the distinguished lawyer and orator Rufus Choate on its platform. See *Boston Courier*, November 2, 18, 25, December 8, 15, 23, 30, 1836. Emerson's first foray into lecturing was sponsored by Boston's Natural History Society; it was followed by appearances at the Concord Lyceum.

19. R. Waldo Emerson (Concord) to Thomas Carlyle (London), April 8, 1836, in

Joseph Slater, ed., *The Correspondence of Emerson and Carlyle* (New York, 1964), 122–27; *Saturday Morning Transcript*, November 19, 1836; Charles T. Jackson in *Boston Courier*, October 4, November 25, 1836; SDUK series in *Boston Courier*, November 18, December 8, 15, 23, 30, 1836; Sylvester Graham in *BC*, December 19, 1836; *Boston Recorder*, January 13, 1837. To make matters still more challenging, Emerson's proposed series resembled a course on "The Civilization and Social State of Modern Christendom" given from October 1834 to January 1835 by Whig congressman Caleb Cushing under SDUK sponsorship. Deese and Woodall, "Calendar of Lectures," 41–42.

20. *Boston Courier*, December 16 ("Born to Good Luck") and 19 ("Oratorio of David"), 1836, February 15 ("animal magnetism"), March 10 ("galvanism and electromagnetism"), 1837; Emerson, "Present Age," *EL* 2:166–67; R. W. Emerson (Concord) to William Emerson (New York), November 29, 1836, in Rusk, *Letters of Emerson*, 2:47. Tyrone Power was a major figure on the transatlantic stage. See Montrose J. Moses, *Famous Actor Families in America* (New York, 1906), 283–308.

21. Emerson to Carlyle, April 20, 1835, April 8, 1836, in Slater, *Correspondence of Emerson and Carlyle*, 122–27, 142–44.

22. *EL* 3:xvii; Emerson to Carlyle, April 8, 1836; George Moore, "The Diary of George Moore," entry for April 8, 1836, in Kenneth Walter Cameron, comp., *Transcendental Epilogue: Primary Materials for Research in Emerson, Thoreau, Literary New England, the Influence of German Theology, and Higher Biblical Criticism*, 3 vols. (Hartford, Conn., 1965–1982), 1:184; *JMN* 7:265 (entry for October 1839); Peter S. Field, *Ralph Waldo Emerson: The Making of a Democratic Intellectual* (Lanham, Md., 2002), 134.

23. Moore, "Diary," 1:184; *JMN* 5:376; Robert A. Gross, "Talk of the Town," *American Scholar* 84, no. 3 (Summer 2015): 31–43; Field, *Ralph Waldo Emerson*, 131–66.

24. Rusk, *Life of Emerson*, 261–62; *JMN* 5:286, 450–51, 459; R. W. Emerson (Concord) to Frederic Henry Hedge (Bangor, Me.), March 27, 1838, in Rusk, *Letters of Emerson*, 2:121; R. W. Emerson (Concord) to William Emerson (Staten Island), January 24, 1842, in Rusk, *Letters of Emerson*, 3:5.

25. William Charvat, "A Chronological List of Emerson's American Lecture Engagements," *Bulletin of the New York Public Library* 64 (1960): 495–96; Gross, "Talk of the Town"; R. Waldo Emerson (Concord) to Thomas Carlyle (London), September 13, 1837, in Slater, *Correspondence of Emerson and Carlyle*, 166–69. The Emerson account books show that between January and March 1838, Emerson received $200 for ten lectures in Lowell and $70 for seven lectures in Framingham. The lyceums of Cambridge and Salem paid better: thirty dollars for a lecture at the former on March 22, 1836, twenty-five at the latter on March 2, 1836. See Charvat, "Chronological List," 501. Field reports that Emerson delivered thirty-eight lectures in 1838; half of these were presented in Boston and Concord. Field, *Ralph Waldo Emerson*, 137; Charvat, "Chronological List," 502.

26. Emerson, *JMN* 5:31–33, 91–93 (Hoar and Everett), 201–3 (the "democratic element"), 241 ("great mass"), 380 (Frost), 407 ("adapting your word"). Emerson incorporated his account of the democratization of literature into his lecture "Literature" in the "Philosophy of Modern History" series, delivered January 5, 1837; see *EL* 2:66–67. On Emerson as a "connected critic" of his time, see Richard F. Teichgraeber III, *Sublime Thoughts/Penny Wisdom: Situating Emerson and Thoreau in the American Market* (Baltimore, 1995).

27. Gura, *American Transcendentalism*, 131–33; Willard Thorp, "Emerson on Tour," *Quarterly Journal of Speech* 16 (1930): 25–27; James Russell Lowell, *My Study Windows* (Boston, 1874), 379–83; Emerson, "Present Age," *EL* 2:162–63; Lawrence Buell,

Emerson (Cambridge, Mass., 2003), 27–31; Cabot, *Memoir*, 248–53; Emerson, *JMN* 5:296 (fifty minutes), 376 ("orator's value").

28. Moore, "Diary," 1:184; Rusk, *Life of Emerson*, 261–62; Steven Lukes, "The Meanings of 'Individualism,'" *Journal of the History of Ideas* 32 (January–March 1971): 45–53.

29. Emerson, "Introductory" lecture to "Philosophy of Modern History," *EL* 2:9, 11–12, 15, 17; Emerson, "The Individual," *EL* 2:181; Emerson, "The Protest," sixth lecture in the series "Human Life," delivered in Boston, January 16, 1839, *EL* 3:85–86; Rusk, *Life of Emerson*, 246–48. See also this formulation in the lecture "Reforms," first read in Boston January 15, 1840: "There is a new possibility in every man that is born." *EL* 3:269–70.

30. Emerson, "Introductory" lecture, *EL* 2:12; "Present Age," *EL* 2:159, 167; Emerson, "Politics," read in Boston January 12, 1837, *EL* 2:70–71; *JMN* 4:356–57. Emerson explored the antislavery implications of the universal mind in his journals, not in his public lectures in the 1830s. "In the light of Christianity," he remarked on February 2, 1835, "there is no such thing as slavery." *JMN* 5:15.

31. Emerson, "Introductory" lecture to series "Human Culture," delivered in Boston December 6, 1837, *EL* 2:215–216; Emerson, "The Individual," *EL* 2:185. On school reform, see Chapter 6.

32. Emerson, "Introductory" lecture to "Human Culture," *EL* 2:213–14; Emerson, "Introductory" lecture to series "The Present Age," delivered December 6, 1839, *EL* 3:188–89; Emerson, "Historic Notes on Life and Letters in New England," *Atlantic Monthly* 52 (October 1883): 529.

33. Charles A. Cummings, "Architecture in Boston," in Justin Winsor, *Memorial History of Boston, Including Suffolk County, Massachusetts, 1630–1880*, 4 vols. (Boston, 1880–1881), 4:479–80; Deese and Woodall, "Calendar of Lectures," 24; *Bowen's Picture of Boston, or, The Citizen's and Stranger's Guide to the Metropolis of Massachusetts, and Its Environs*, 2nd ed. (Boston, 1833), 87–89; *Columbian Centinel*, June 2, 1832; Bridget Ford, *Bonds of Union: Religion, Race, and Politics in a Civil War Borderland* (Chapel Hill, N.C., 2016), 49–50; Herman Atwill and fifty-three other inhabitants of the town of Concord, Memorial to the Honorable Senate and House of Representatives in General Court assembled, House Unpassed Legislation, 1833, no. 12324, MSA; John Matteson, *Eden's Outcasts: The Story of Louisa May Alcott and Her Father* (New York, 2007), 57–58, 83–84; Henry F. Brownson, *Orestes A. Brownson's Early Life: From 1803 to 1844* (Detroit, 1898), 137–40. Upon its completion, the Masonic Temple, along with the ground on which it stood, was valued at $50,000—two and a half times the amount of real estate the fraternity was allowed to hold by its charter. See *Bowen's Picture of Boston*, 89.

34. Gura, *American Transcendentalism*, 10; Emerson, "Present Age," *EL* 2:160–61; Emerson, "Address on Education," *EL* 2:194–95; Spiller and Williams, "Introduction," *EL* 3:xv; Emerson, "Tendencies," tenth lecture in the series "The Present Age," delivered in Boston, February 12, 1840, *EL* 3:302–15. Emerson was inspired by two important essays by Carlyle in the *Edinburgh Review*: "Signs of the Times" (1829) and "Characteristics"(1831), both in Carlyle, *Critical and Miscellaneous Essays* (Philadelphia, 1852). Emerson joked that the topics covered in the "Philosophy of Modern History" series arose out of his personal interests—"whatsoever elements of humanity have been the subjects of my studies." Actually, his approach was systematic, taking in politics, society, religion, voluntary associations, literature, art, and science. See R. W. Emerson (Concord) to William Emerson (New York), October 23, 1836, in Rusk, *Letters of Emerson*, 2:41–43. On Emerson as public intellectual, see Teichgraeber, *Sublime Thoughts/Penny Wisdom*.

35. *JMN* 5:296–97 ("endless procession of wagons"), 417–18 (Western natives on Boston common); Laura Dassow Walls, *Henry David Thoreau: A Life* (Chicago, 2017), 5. The "Grand Hindoo Exhibition" at Amory Hall ran from October to December 1836. See advertisements in the *Boston Courier*, October 1, November 30, 1836. John Brown, Jr., son of the former partner in the Concord textile factory, was clerking in a Boston store at the time of the Western natives' visit to the capital. He estimated that a quarter of the city's "enlightened population" crowded onto the common to watch the warriors as if they were "fresh imported baboons." See John Brown, Jr., Diary, entry for October 29, 1837 (in possession of the late Roger Brown, professor of history emeritus at American University, who graciously allowed me to read and quote from his ancestor's journal).

36. Emerson, "Present Age," *EL* 2:160–61; Emerson, "Politics," *EL* 2:80–81; *JMN* 5:237.

37. Emerson, "Present Age," *EL* 2:161–62.

38. Ibid., 2:161–63; *JMN* 5:21, 96. "Father" Samuel Moody of York, Maine, Emerson's great-great-grandfather, furnished another stark contrast to the "decorous" ministers of Boston. Through Aunt Mary Moody Emerson, Waldo absorbed the stories of his charismatic ancestor's fearlessness in the pulpit. Moody did not merely denounce sin; he named the sinners. On one occasion an offended parishioner rose from his seat and started to leave. "Come back, you graceless sinner," the pastor demanded, "come back!" See Phyllis Cole, *Mary Moody Emerson and the Origins of Transcendentalism: A Family History* (New York, 1998), 10–11, 19–20.

39. Emerson, "Present Age," *EL* 2:166–67.

40. Ibid., 2:164–66; Gross, *Much Instruction from Little Reading*, 136–37; Catherine O'Donnell Kaplan, *Men of Letters in the Early Republic: Cultivating Forums of Citizenship* (Chapel Hill, N.C., 2008). Emerson doubted the worth of the typical lyceum lecture or social library book to the workingman. "If any man thinks that a woodsawyer or canal-digger is to be made a good citizen by reading and spelling an account of Stonehenge or the order and superposition of the strata of Mount Blanc, he thinks amiss." Did he have Jack Garrison, the well-known sawyer who chopped his wood, in mind? Emerson, "Present Age," *EL* 2:166.

41. Emerson, "Society," delivered in Boston January 26, 1837, *EL* 2:107. Emerson reiterated his criticism of temperance pledges in "Duty," the ninth lecture in his series "Human Life," delivered only in Boston, February 6, 1839, *EL* 3:140–44, and in "Reforms," the sixth lecture in the series "The Present Age," delivered in Boston, January 15, 1840, *EL* 3:256–57.

42. Emerson, "Politics," *EL* 2:80–81.

43. Emerson, "Comedy," eighth lecture in "Human Life" series, delivered in Boston, January 30, 1839, *EL* 3:135; *JMN* 7:99–100.

44. Ezra Ripley, Annual Thanksgiving sermon, November 19, 1795 [no. 890], 12–13, bMS 490/1, HDS; *JMN* 5:201–203; Emerson, "Literature," *EL* 2:66–67; Emerson, "Politics," *EL* 2:75, 80–81; Emerson, "Comedy," *EL* 2:100; Emerson, "Present Age," *EL* 2:160–61.

45. Emerson, "Protest," *EL* 3:85; "Individual," *EL* 2:175; "Religion," *EL* 2:83–97; "Politics," *EL* 2:75–76, 79–80, 81–82; "Comedy," *EL* 2:100.

46. *JMN* 5:37 (entry for May 10 or 12, 1835), 308–309 (entry for April 29, 1837), 331 (entry for May 21, 1837); Concord Bank Records, entry for May 12, 1837, Series 1, Directors' Books, 1965.29.1.1 BV, Old Sturbridge Village Research Library, Sturbridge, Mass.; E. R. Hoar, "Memoir of Josiah Davis" and "Memoir of Phineas How," *SCM* 2:100–1, 274; Bosco and Myerson, *Emerson Brothers*, 328–29; William Charvat, *The Profession of Authorship in America, 1800–1870*, ed. Matthew J. Bruccoli

(Columbus, Ohio, 1968), 49–67. Emerson poured his reactions to the Panic into "Address on Education" at the opening of the Greene Street School in Providence, Rhode Island. See *EL* 2:194–97.

47. Gura, *American Transcendentalism*, 131–33; George Ripley and George P. Bradford, "Philosophic Thought in Boston," in Winsor, *Memorial History of Boston*, 4:304–5. According to Rev. Samuel Ripley, the step-uncle of Emerson, the audience at the Masonic Temple was "composed mostly of young men and women of the higher and more intelligent classes." Samuel Ripley (Waltham) to Mary Moody Emerson, January 1, 1839, in James B. Thayer, *Rev. Samuel Ripley* (n.p., ca. 1897), 46–47.

48. Of the twelve lectures in the "Philosophy of Modern History" series, Emerson gave three in Concord (one each in 1837, 1838, and 1839). Thereafter the neighbors heard nearly all the lectures soon after their delivery in Boston (8 of 10 in the "Human Culture" series, 7 of 10 in "Human Life," 9 of 10 in "The Present Age"). Few other towns enjoyed such access: Emerson tried out the "Human Culture" course in Lowell in November–December 1837 and repeated it in Framingham in February–March 1838. Providence, Rhode Island, heard the "Human Life" series in March–April 1840. See Charvat, "Chronological List," 501–4.

49. Emerson, "Present Age," *EL* 2:167–70; Emerson, "Protest" *EL* 3:89. Emerson never presented his 1837 lecture "The Present Age" in Concord. This brief for alienated youth was a precursor of his lecture on education at the opening of the Greene Street School and of "The American Scholar." It led up to "The Protest," which adopts the perspective of the "young soul" full of hope and ideals, looking out on a society demanding that he follow the old way and think obsolete thoughts. I assume in the text that Emerson's encouragement of the young was evident in his earlier lectures in Concord. "The Protest" was read only in Boston (January 16, 1839) and Concord (April 3, 1839).

50. Emerson, "The Transcendentalist," in *EMP*, 168.

12. *Young Men and Women of Fairest Promise*

1. R. W. Emerson, "The Present Age," lecture read February 23, 1837, *EL* 2:158; *JMN* 5:77; Emerson, "The Protest," lecture read January 16, 1839, *EL* 3:88.

2. William Charvat, "A Chronological List of Emerson's American Lecture Engagements," *Bulletin of the New York Public Library* 64 (1960): 492–507, 551–59, 606–10, 657–63; 65 (1961): 40–46. Unwelcome at Harvard for several decades following the divinity school address, Emerson found receptive audiences at Tufts, Amherst, and Williams College in Massachusetts; Wesleyan University in Connecticut; Dartmouth College in New Hampshire; Bowdoin and Waterville [now Colby] College in Maine; Middlebury College in Vermont; Genesee, Hamilton, Union, and Vassar colleges in New York State; and Antioch, Miami, and Oberlin College in Ohio. He spoke at only two institutions below the Mason-Dixon line and then only after the Civil War: Howard University in 1872 and the University of Virginia in 1876.

3. Frederick C. Dahlstrand, *Amos Bronson Alcott: An Intellectual Biography* (East Brunswick, N.J., 1982), 139–42; John Matteson, *Eden's Outcasts: The Story of Louisa May Alcott and Her Father* (New York, 2007), 75–81; Judith Strong Albert, "Transition in Transcendental Education: The Schools of Bronson Alcott and Hiram Fuller," *Educational Studies* 11 (1980): 209–19; Kenneth S. Sacks, *Understanding Emerson: "The American Scholar" and His Struggle for Self-Reliance* (Princeton, N.J., 2003), 98–120.

4. Sacks, *Understanding Emerson*, 112; "R." to *Boston Courier*, April 4, 1837; "Additions to Concord Library," *CF*, April 15, 1837; Concord Social Library Records, 1821–51, 95, 103, 118, CFPL; editors' notes, *EL* 2:189–93. Emerson's anonymous endorse-

ment of *Conversations* has gone undetected until now. There are a couple reasons to credit Emerson with the authorship. For one thing, he was chairman of the standing committee of the social library in 1837, and it had been the practice of his predecessor, the late Rev. Hersey B. Goodwin, to submit to the local press "brief accounts of the principal books" added to the collection. That Emerson did so in this instance is clear from the similarity of the *CF* notice to his letter printed in the *Courier*. After noting the divided opinions of *Conversations*—it is "warmly praised by some, and by others bitterly condemned"—the notice described Alcott's work as "an account of a new experiment in education . . . to see how far children may be taught to think for themselves on moral questions, and the New Testament made a living book to them by the habit of exercising their conscience." The letter to the *Boston Courier* makes the same points in slightly different language: "He [Alcott] aims to make children think, and, in every question of a moral nature, to send them back on themselves for an answer. He aims to show children something holy in their own consciousness, thereby to make them really reverent, and to make the New Testament a living book to them."

5. Ralph L. Rusk, ed., *The Letters of Ralph Waldo Emerson*, 6 vols. (New York, 1939), 2:94n150; Sacks, *Understanding Emerson*, 5–6, 10–12, 151n12; Phyllis Cole, "Emerson Father and Son: A Precedent for 'The American Scholar,'" *New England Quarterly* 78 (March 2005): 101–11; entry for August 20, 1836, Emerson account book, 1836–39 (Joel Myerson transcription). The very man Emerson was replacing as the 1837 Phi Beta Kappa speaker, Jonathan M. Wainwright, was the Episcopalian rector of Boston's Trinity Church. Awarded an honorary doctorate by Harvard two years before, he had preached an election sermon to the Massachusetts General Court on the theme "inequality of individual wealth the ordinance of Providence and essential to civilization." See "A Sketch, in Outline, of the Late, Loved, and Lamented Bishop [Jonathan Mayhew] Wainwright," in *A Memorial Volume: Thirty-Four Sermons by the Rt. Rev. Jonathan Mayhew Wainwright*, ed. Mrs. A. M. Wainwright (New York, 1856), 23–35.

6. Emerson, "The Individual," *EL* 2:177, 185.

7. Ralph L. Rusk, *The Life of Ralph Waldo Emerson* (New York, 1949), 89–91; Mary McDougall Gordon, "Union with the Virtuous Past: The Development of School Reform in Massachusetts, 1789–1837" (Ph.D. diss., University of Pittsburgh, 1974), 263–69; George Moore, "The Diary of George Moore," in Kenneth Walter Cameron, comp., *Transcendental Epilogue: Primary Materials for Research in Emerson, Thoreau, Literary New England, the Influence of German Theology, and Higher Biblical Criticism*, 3 vols. (Hartford, Conn., 1965–1982), 1:191.

8. Emerson, "Address on Education (Providence, R.I., June 10, 1837)," *EL* 2:195–96, 199.

9. Ibid., 2:198, 202.

10. *Boston Courier*, September 2, 1837; Sacks, *Understanding Emerson*, 13–17, 24–27; Ronald Story, *The Forging of an Aristocracy: Harvard and the Boston Upper Class, 1800–1870* (Middletown, Conn., 1980).

11. Sacks, *Understanding Emerson*, esp. 121–28; Emerson, "The American Scholar," *EMP*, 91–92, 95, 104–105, 107–108.

12. Oliver Wendell Holmes, *Ralph Waldo Emerson* (Boston, 1885), 115; Sacks, *Understanding Emerson*, 17–19; Rusk, *Life of Emerson*, 262–66; Winslow Warren, "Memoir of the Hon. Charles H. Warren, A.M.," *Proceedings of the MHS* 19 (1881–1882): 424–28. Emerson's speech made his wife, Lidian, proud; his "noble doctrine," she enthused, was "God's truth." But to her eyes, the bulk of the audience did not look

"particularly edified." One member of the audience, the scholarly Sarah Alden Bradford Ripley (and Emerson's kinswoman by virtue of her marriage to Ezra Ripley's son Samuel), enthused that the address "fully answered the hopes of his most devoted literary friends." See Lidian Jackson Emerson (Concord) to Lucy Jackson Brown, September 2, 1837, in Delores Bird Carpenter, ed., *The Selected Letters of Lidian Jackson Emerson* (Columbia, Mo., 1987), 58–59, and Joan W. Goodwin, *The Remarkable Mrs. Ripley: The Life of Sarah Alden Bradford Ripley* (Boston, 1998), 151.

13. Entry for October 10, 1837, Social Circle Record Book, list of candidates and elected members by year, CFPL; Rusk, *Life of Emerson*, 429. In his diary for August 31, 1837, the wealthy land owner and Democratic politician Timothy Prescott noted his attendance at the Phi Beta Kappa ceremony. "Mr. Emerson delivers the Oration," he added laconically, in contrast to the previous year's anniversary, when he pronounced the "Oration good and Poem excellent." See Timothy Prescott, Diary, 1830–40, Houghton. Members of the Social Circle had ample opportunity to learn about Emerson's heterodox opinions before they voted on his admission. His Phi Beta Kappa address had been printed in one thousand copies and excerpted in the Unitarian newspaper, the *Christian Register*, September 30, 1837. Likewise the divinity school address, delivered on July 15, 1838, aroused a storm of controversy in the Boston press and was available in print. Neither of these discourses stood in the way of Emerson's accession into the local elite, whose membership formed the counterpart of the Boston and Cambridge worthies, who were said to have been furious over Emerson's controversial speeches.

14. Moore, "Diary," entry for September 6, 1836, 191.

15. John H. Moore, Genealogical Information about the Moore Family, Moore Family Papers, AAS; "G.W.H." [George Washington Hosmer], obituary of Harriet Moore, *Christian Register*, November 30, 1878, typewritten transcript in Moore Papers, CAS Collection, 1422–1957, CFPL; Ruth R. Wheeler, *Concord: Climate for Freedom* (Concord, Mass., 1967), 172; Thomas Cushing, "George Moore," in *Memorials of the Class of 1834 of Harvard College* (Boston, 1884), 8; Moore, "Diary," 39, 149–50.

16. "F" [Barzillai Frost], obituary of George Moore, *Christian Examiner* 42 (May 1847): 467–68; Rev. B. Frost, "The Christian Missionary: A Sermon on the Life and Character of Rev. George Moore of Quincy, Illinois," *Monthly Religious Magazine* 4 (June 1847): 255–65. Abel Moore's first son, Daniel, died in 1819 at age fifteen. The first boy to reach adulthood was Henry, born in 1806, who became a lawyer and entrepreneur in Chicago; the next in line was Reuben, born in 1808, who went into the lumber business in Lowell in partnership with Concord's Ephraim Meriam. Two other children—John Brooks (born in 1817) and Mary Augusta (born in 1820)—had to be provided for after George. Meanwhile Harriet, who never married, remained at home to assist in the jail. Barzillai Frost's memorials of George Moore incorrectly state his birthplace. The son was born in Sudbury, not in Concord; the Moore family did not move to the shire town until 1815. Moore, "Genealogical Information about the Moore Family."

17. Moore, "Diary," 19–24. Before debating how well young men used their time, Moore had already found himself wanting. "I have not accomplished one half as much as I might have done, no, not *one half*," he confessed in his diary. In 1828 eleven boys were enrolled at Concord Academy; of the ten whose years of birth are known, the median age was fourteen. Moore was eighteen when he entered the school in 1829.

18. Moore, "Diary," 20, 65; Daniel Walker Howe, *Making the American Self: Jonathan Ed-*

wards to Abraham Lincoln (1997; rpt. New York, 2009), 107–35, quotation at 132. Moore's initial reflection on the purpose of his life was prompted by reading the evangelical Congregationalist minister Joel Hawes's *Lectures to Young Men, on the Formation of Character &c., Originally Addressed to the Young Men of Hartford and New-Haven* (Hartford, Conn., 1829). He would soon be framing the challenge of character development in Unitarian terms.

19. Moore, "Diary," 98–103 (Connecticut River Valley, Brownson), 111 (Hasty Pudding), 122–23 (Kemble), 124–34 (White Mountains), 139 (Phi Beta Kappa), 96, 122, 129 (drinking); "The Hasty Pudding Club's Centennial," *Harvard Graduates' Magazine* 4 (March 1896): 379; Cushing, "George Moore," 8–9; Jared Sparks, ed., *The Writings of George Washington: Being His Correspondence, Addresses, Messages, and Other Papers Official and Private*, 12 vols. (Boston, 1834–1837). Moore was also invited to join a student group known as "Med. Facs.," whose members got together for the convivial purpose of satirizing the Harvard authorities. It was too irreverent for his taste. "I could not conscientiously witness and assent to what I hear is done at their meetings," he explained. "I cannot bear to see a mockery made of sacred things." The College government shut the society down not long after. Moore, "Diary," 112; Henry Winthrop Sargent, "College Recollections and Stories," *Harvard Register* 3 (January–July 1881): 119–20.

20. Moore, "Diary," 140–43, 152–53; Robert A. McCaughey, "The Usable Past: A Study of the Harvard College Rebellion of 1834," *William and Mary Law Review* 11 (1970): 587–610; *Saturday Morning Transcript* (Boston), August 30, 1834. In the spring of 1832, Josiah Quincy headed off a student rebellion by sending the entire freshman class away from Cambridge for a week. Moore approved of this measure to calm the situation. "I think the government have proceeded perfectly right," he commented, "and done no more than their duty." Two years later he took the other side. See Moore, "Diary," 83.

21. Moore, "Diary," 154–58 ("original genius," 155), 161–63 ("very intellectual," 161), 179, 199; L. D. Geller, *Between Concord and Plymouth: The Transcendentalists and the Watsons with the Hillside Collection of Manuscripts* (Concord, Mass., 1973), 13–16, 82, 86–87; William T. Davis, *Plymouth Memories of an Octogenarian* (Plymouth, Mass., 1906),123, 287–88. Elizabeth Russell, born in 1815, was the first child of ship captain Thomas Russell and Mary Ann (Goodwin). Her sister Lydia married William Whiting of Concord, who preceded Moore as instructor of the Plymouth girls' school. Another sister, Mary Russell, wed the horticulturist Benjamin Marston Watson, a good friend of Emerson, Thoreau, Alcott, and Channing. As it turned out, Elizabeth broke the engagement with Moore and never married. The first mention of the engagement in Moore's diary appears on January 21, 1837; evidently, the alliance was contracted in late August of the previous year. See Moore, "Diary," 190, 199.

22. Moore, "Diary," 114 ("honorable citizen"), 147 (Whig Fourth of July celebration), 150 (contribution to *Middlesex Whig*), 163 (Divinity Hall, law school), 178 (Freemasonry), 181 (antislavery), 182 (total abstinence pledge), 179–80 (peace lecture); "The Anniversary of the Bowdoin St. Yong Men's Peace Society," *Christian Watchman*, February 12, 1836; Peter Brock, *Radical Pacifists in Antebellum America* (Princeton, N.J., 1968), 36–76. The speaker, Rufus Phineas Stebbins, was an Amherst College graduate (Class of 1834) who broke with orthodox Congregationalism and went on to train as a Unitarian minister at Harvard Divinity School. His dorm room was next door to Moore's. He would go on to serve as president of the Meadville (Pennsylvania) Theological School, an outpost of liberal Protestantism in the West. See *Quinquennial Catalogue of the Officers and Graduates of Harvard University, 1636–1905*

(Cambridge, Mass., 1905), 494; Francis Albert Christie, *The Makers of the Meadville Theological School, 1844–1894* (Boston, 1927), 26–40.

23. Moore, "Diary," 176 (sermons of "a high literary order"), 189–90 (Goethe, "most excellent sermons"), 203 (Carlyle's letters), 224 (little Waldo). Altogether Moore attended fifteen of Emerson's lectures between November 1835 and March 1837. Moore heard Emerson preach on four separate Sabbaths in 1836. For additional visits to Emerson's parlor, see "Diary," 184, 221.

24. Back in October 1829, Moore had admired Emerson's preaching at the First Parish meetinghouse, and his esteem had risen still more following the oration at the Concord Second Centennial. The address presented "great historical research" in simple and elegant prose, with "many passages shewing great beauty," and despite the two-hour length, it was delivered in "Rev. Mr. Emerson's usual easy & simple style." Moore was also impressed by Emerson's performance at the February 1830 ordination of Rev. Hersey B. Goodwin as junior minister of Concord's First Parish Church. The pastor of Boston's Second Church offered the right hand of fellowship in a "very solemn and affecting" manner. But Moore was disappointed in the poem Emerson read at the 1834 Phi Beta Kappa gathering. The graduating senior deemed the composition to be lacking in the necessary ingredient of humor. In the winter of 1835, while living in Plymouth, Moore attended a lecture by Emerson on the life of Martin Luther. See Moore, "Diary," 17 (two "excellent" sermons), 164 (bicentennial). 27 (right hand of fellowship), 153 (1834 poem), 179 (Martin Luther).

25. Emerson, "Shakspear," *EL* 1:288–91, quotation at 289; Emerson, *Nature* (Boston, 1836), 33; Moore, "Diary," 175 ("considerable metaphysics"), 198 (lecture on religion). For a rare reference to the universal mind in Moore's diary, see his summary of the lecture "Society," in which a superior speaker or conversationalist is said to possess "a greater share of the universal mind, of the common nature of his race, than most men." "Diary," 200. In the lecture on religion, Emerson set forth the Transcendentalist distinction between "the reason" and "the understanding," a division of intellectual labor that Moore described precisely.

26. Moore, "Diary," 173–74 (poets and "popular taste"), 179 (Luther), 180 (Burke), 184–85 ("worked like a slave"), 196 ("dull"), 200 ("differences of the sexes," "degrading" temperance pledges), 202 (the farmer), 203 ("citizen of the world"); Emerson, Lecture on "Society," *EL* 2:102. Why is history so dull? Emerson's point was that our histories concentrate on the few, on kings and courts, at the expense of the many and are preoccupied with wars and battles, rather than with the ways of life of common people, the ideas they hold, and the forces making for revolutions in government and religion. The record of history reveals the infinite potential of humankind. Moore summarized this theme accurately. Emerson anticipated the "new social history."

27. Moore, "Diary," 212–13 (joins church, goes West), 219 (Cuba), 251 (introduction to "Human Life"), 252 ("great object"), 253 (lecture "Genius"); George Moore, biographical notice of Henry Moore, in Diary, December 27, 1840, to May 12, 1845 (typescript), Moore Family Papers, AAS; Daniel Walker Howe, *The Unitarian Conscience: Harvard Moral Philosophy, 1805–1861* (Cambridge, Mass., 1970) 14–15, 106–8, 112–13; Henry Ware, Jr., *Formation of the Christian Character, Addressed to Those Who Are Seeking to Lead a Religious Life* (Cambridge, Mass., 1832).

28. While Moore took no note of Emerson's divinity school address, he conscientiously recorded Ware's response to his former colleague two months later. God is "a *conscious, intelligent agent*," Ware preached, and *not*, as some would claim, "a principle,

like Electricity, or Gravitation." Politely, the critic did not mention Emerson by name, though everybody knew whom he had in mind. In his notes Moore followed suit. Moore, "Diary," 192–93 ("success of preaching"), 242 ("conscious, intelligent agent"); William R. Hutchison, *The Transcendentalist Ministers: Church Reform in the New England Renaissance* (New Haven, Conn., 1959), 76–80; Tim Jensen, "'Their own thought in motley . . .': Emerson's Divinity School Address and Henry Ware, Jr.'s Hints on Extemporaneous Preaching," *Journal of Unitarian Universalist History* 24 (1997): 17–18. Ware recommended "the earnestness of spontaneous speech" in *Hints on Extemporaneous Preaching* (Boston, 1824), 41.

29. Moore, "Diary," 207 ("mania"), 209 ("gambling spirit"), 221 ("seeker"); Moore, Diary [at AAS], December 27, 1840, to May 12, 1845, 220 ("father to me"), 226 ("forming my character").

30. Frances [Fanny] Jane Prichard (Concord) to Elizabeth ("Lizzie") Prichard, August 22, 1841, Prichard, Hoar, and Related Family Papers, Box 7, Folder 1, CFPL; Moore, "Diary," 160, 232 (Baptist), 181, 281 (Episcopalian), 77 (Methodist), 68, 128, 255, 280 (Orthodox), 72–73 (Shakers), 230 (Swedenborg), 222 (New-England Anti-Slavery Society meeting, "the most spirited meeting that I attended"), 264 and 295 (Non-Resistance Society); Moore, Diary [at AAS], December 27, 1840, to May 12, 1845, 249–50; Gary L. Collison, "'A True Toleration': Harvard Divinity School Students and Unitarianism, 1830–1859," in Conrad Edick Wright, ed., *American Unitarianism 1805–1865* (Boston, 1989), 209–37; Peter Brock, *Radical Pacifists in Antebellum America* (Princeton, N.J., 1968), 113–38; Lewis Perry, *Radical Abolitionism: Anarchy and the Government of God in Antislavery Thought* (Ithaca, N.Y., 1973), 55–73, 81–89. In June 1834, as a Harvard senior, Moore attended an early meeting of the Cambridge Anti-Slavery Society, an organization spearheaded by Henry Ware, Jr., to provide a moderate alternative to Garrisonian abolitionism. Ware favored a well-ordered program of gradual emancipation, with financial compensation to slaveholders. His antislavery campaign was to be conducted in a "tone of Christian kindness and meekness." It was the "institutional representation" of Channing's approach to the issue, which Moore found "most convincing, and . . . unanswerable." Even this cautious approach to ending slavery was too much for the Harvard authorities, who closed it down. By May 1838 it no longer suited Moore, whose sentiments were now represented in the New-England Anti-Slavery Convention, "perhaps the most spirited meeting" he attended during the "Anniversary Week" of the benevolent societies. See Moore, "Diary," 144–45 (Cambridge Anti-Slavery Society), 181 (Channing), 221 (antislavery debate at Philanthropic Society); Howe, *Unitarian Conscience*, 281–82; Douglas C. Stange, *Patterns of Antislavery Among American Unitarians, 1831–1860* (Cranbury, N.J., 1977), 30, 84–86.

31. Moore, "Diary," 219–20, 226–28, 252 ("rapid advances"), 263–64 (all dealing with Russell), and Moore, Diary [at AAS], December 27, 1840, to May 12, 1845, 226–27, 236–39; *Christian Register*, November 14, 1840, September 19, 1841; Frost, "Christian Missionary," 260–62.

32. Moore, "Diary," 32 ("Nature's God"), 46 ("chit-chat"), 121 ("love to be alone," "solitude has charms"), 203–4, 221–22 ("all-glorious"), 224 ("works of nature"), 257 ("my best friend"), 297–98 (Wordsworth).

33. Ibid., 273.

34. David Hackett Fischer, "Forenames and the Family in New England: An Exercise in Historical Onomastics," *Chronos: A Journal of Social History* 1 (Fall 1981): 88–92.

35. Ibid., 94–95; Asa Keyes, *Genealogy of Robert Keyes of Watertown, Mass., 1633, Solomon Keyes of Newbury and Chelmsford, Mass., 1653, and Their Descendants: Also Others of the*

Name (Brattleboro, Vt., 1880), 150–52; Ellen Tucker Emerson, *The Life of Lidian Jackson Emerson*, ed. Delores Bird Carpenter (Boston, 1980), 70. The firstborn child in the Keyes family was named Ann-Alicia for her mother (Ann) and her maternal aunt (Alicia); the second daughter, Mary, bore her maternal grandmother's name. Joseph Boyden Keyes got his names from his paternal grandfather (Joseph) and paternal grandmother (née Sarah Boyden). As Fischer notes, middle names were introduced by elite families in the late eighteenth century as a means of strengthening kin ties. The middle name mediated between the demands of family and the desire for individuality.

36. Keyes, Autobiography, 45, 85½, 86–87; Keyes, Diary, vol. 2, entries for July 24 to 26, 1839, January 4, July 25, 1840. According to Keyes, Colonel Isaac Hurd, the doctor's son, acquired the paintings in China, where he was engaged in trade, and brought them home to Concord. At the time it was thought that the works were copies of European originals; in Keyes's opinion, the landscapes, including "an old mill on the Tiber, a grotto near Naples, and a ruined castle," were probably painted on the shores of the Mediterranean. The dozen canvases that Colonel Hurd carried home were given to his physician father, to merchant Daniel Shattuck, and to Keyes. In the 1820s and early 1930s "they were the only oil paintings in Concord."

37. Keyes, Autobiography, 34½.

38. Ibid., 29–30.

39. Ibid., 45½.

40. Ibid., 32–33, 59, 82.

41. Ibid., 56–57, 66; Keyes, Diary, vol. 3, entry for August 12–13, 1840; Keyes, Diary, vol. 5, entry for June 12, 1842; John Keyes (Cambridge) to John Shepard Keyes (Concord), December 20, 1837, Keyes Family Correspondence, 1837–61, CFPL.

42. John Keyes (Concord) to John Shepard Keyes (Cambridge), January 31, February 15, 1838, October 7, November 22, 1839, April 15, 1840, Keyes Family Correspondence; Keyes, Diary, vol. 4, entry for December 21, 1841.

43. Edward Wheelwright, *The Class of 1844, Harvard College, Fifty Years after Graduation. Prepared by the Class Secretary, Edward Wheelwright* (Cambridge, Mass., 1896), 127–29; John Keyes (Concord) to John Shepard Keyes (Cambridge), March 30, April 2 and 15, 1840.

44. Keyes, Autobiography, 83; Keyes, Diary, vol. 4, entries for August 24–26, September 19–20 (*Deerslayer*), October 25 ("pretty poor"), 1841; account of Harvard commencement, *Christian Watchman*, August 27, 1841.

45. In his reference to "feast of reason and flow of soul," Keyes was showing off his literary knowledge. The phrase comes from Alexander Pope's *First Satire of the Second Book of Horace, Imitated* (1733).

46. Keyes, Diary, vol. 4, entries for August 2, 1840 ("luscious reveries"), February 10, 1841 ("feast of reason"), August 1, 1841 (temperance pledge), January 25, 1839 ("niggering"), January 27, 1841 (Non-Resistance). On another occasion, after enduring a temperance lecture from his father, young Keyes derided the entire enterprise of reform. "By the bye, what good people will inhabit this world when all these reformers have accomplished their work! What a pity I was not born one century later, I might have been the Lord knows what." Diary, vol. 4, entry for September 29, 1841. While George Moore's company was not to Keyes's taste, he earned respect for his "talents and integrity." Keyes especially admired the young minister's performance in the pulpit. On the Sabbath of February 16, 1840, Moore "astonished our weak nerves . . . by a brilliant display of his oratorical powers. He

is a real good preacher." Keyes, Diary, vol. 2, entries for February 2 and 16, 1840, and vol. 4, entry for September 17, 1841.

47. Keyes, Diary, vol. 2, resolutions dated January 1, 1839, renewed January 1, 1840 and 1841, and Diary, vol. 4, entries for September 19, December 13 and 21, 1841.

48. Keyes, Autobiography, 52–53; John Shepard Keyes, "Ralph Waldo Emerson," manuscript from first decade of twentieth century, Keyes Papers, Series 2, Box 1, Folder 3, CFPL; Leslie Perrin Wilson, "Mrs. Woodward Hudson's Memoir of Mrs. Ebenezer Rockwood Hoar," *Concord Saunterer*, n.s., 9 (2001): 99. Hudson says that Brooks went to the ceremony with Martha Prescott; Keyes thought she attended with Rockwood Hoar.

49. Keyes, Autobiography, 59–61; *Triennial Catalogue of Dartmouth College: Including the Officers of Government and Instruction, the Graduates of the Several Departments, and All Others Who Have Received Honorary Degrees* (Hanover, N.H., 1873), 18; Ralph Waldo Emerson, "Literary Ethics," in *Nature, Addresses, and Lectures*, ed. Robert Spiller and Alfred R. Ferguson (Cambridge, Mass., 1971), 101–2. Unfortunately, the first volume of Keyes's diary, covering 1837–1838, has been lost, so it is impossible to know whether as a college student he heard any Emerson lectures before the Dartmouth talk.

50. Keyes, Diary, vol. 2, entries for January 9 and 20, November 27, 1839; Emerson, Sermon 164, in Albert J. von Frank and Wesley T. Mott, eds., *The Complete Sermons of Ralph Waldo Emerson*, 4 vols. (Columbia, Mo., 1989–1992), 4:234; Rusk, *Life of Emerson*, 273.

51. John Keyes (Concord) to John Shepard Keyes (Cambridge), December 8, 1839, Keyes Family Correspondence; Keyes, Diary, vol. 2, entries for January 1 and 8, 1840; Keyes, Autobiography, 85. It is not surprising that Emerson's lecture on politics did not engage Keyes. The college student had spent New Year's Eve at a ball in Concord and gotten only a couple hours' sleep before returning to his dormitory in Harvard Yard. Later that day he crossed the Charles to hear the second installment of Emerson's series "The Present Age." After all that partying, he was hardly in a state to take in the lecture's challenging discourse. The following week he was present—and doubtless more alert—at Emerson's "very fine lecture," "Private Life." "His domestic policy," Keyes thought, was "very good if practicable." Nearly two years passed before Keyes attended another Emerson lecture. For visits to Emerson's parlor, see Keyes, Diary, vol. 2, entries for March 1, 1839.

52. Keyes, Diary, vol. 3, entry for July 28, 1841, and Diary, vol. 4, entries for September 10, 15, 17, 19, October 13, 1841; Geller, *Between Concord and Plymouth*, 16–22; Davis, *Plymouth Memories of an Octogenarian*, 123.

53. Keyes, Diary, vol. 3, entry for July 20, 1841 ("entirely transcendental"), Diary, vol. 4, entry for November 3, 1841 (lecture on the Poet), and Diary, vol. 5, entry for July 31, 1842 (Stearns Wheeler).

54. Keyes, Diary, vol. 3, entry for February 21, 1841, and Diary, vol. 4, entries for September 7 and 16, November 7 and 30, December 6, 1841; Keyes, Autobiography, 84. The mercantile firm with which Keyes hoped to secure a position, Augustine Heard & Co., was just getting started in "the East." It would soon become one of the two leading American merchant houses in China. See Stephen Chapman Lockwood, *Augustine Heard and Company, 1858–1862: American Merchants in China* (Cambridge, Mass., 1971).

55. Keyes, Diary, vol. 2, entries for January 5 ("aristocracy"), August 7, November 29 ("upper crust") and 30, 1839, January 1, 1840 ("bon ton upper crust"); Keyes, Diary, vol. 3, entry for February 3, 1841 ("greasy factory girl"); Keyes, Autobiography,

34. In retrospect, Keyes considered the elitism of the representatives of the "old Boston families" he met at Harvard to be insufferable. Autobiography, 65–66.

56. Keyes, Diary, vol. 3, entries for July 25 ("'purest of the pure' waters"), July 28–30 ("chowder party"), August 6 ("gloomy"), 1840, July 9, 1841 ("I can't live alone"); Keyes, Diary, vol. 4, entry for September 17, 1841 (Sleepy Hollow); Emerson, "Literary Ethics," 109.

57. Keyes, Autobiography, 90–93. His descendants had a similar view of Keyes to the one presented in the text. "Above all, he was intensely sociable," observed Amelia F. Emerson. "He was dependent on companionship, and hated to be alone." Amelia Forbes married Raymond Emerson, the grandson of J. S. Keyes, in 1913, several years after the older man's death at eighty-nine. Though neither lived to see the day, Ralph Waldo Emerson and John Shepard Keyes were grandfathers-in-law. See Amelia F. Emerson, "John Shepard Keyes," in Memoirs of Members of the Social Circle in Concord. Fifth Series: From 1909 to 1939 (Cambridge, Mass, 1940), 92–93.

58. Jonathan Bishop, Emerson on the Soul (Cambridge, Mass., 1964), 145–50; Nancy F. Cott, The Bonds of Womanhood: "Woman's Sphere" in New England, 1780–1835 (New Haven, Conn., 1977), 19–22, 43–44, 77–80; Michael Grossberg, Governing the Hearth: Law and the Family in Nineteenth-Century America (Chapel Hill, N.C., 1985), 235–47; Linda K. Kerber, "Can a Woman Be an Individual? The Discourse of Self-Reliance," in Kerber, Toward an Intellectual History of Women (Chapel Hill, N.C., 1997), 200–23.

59. Gross, Minutemen, 184–85; Emerson, "Society," EL 2:102–103; Emerson, "Being and Seeming," EL 2:302; Emerson, "Love," EL 3:56.

60. Emerson, "Love," EL 3:62–63; Emerson, Life of Lidian Jackson Emerson, 68–69, 87. When his second daughter was born in 1841, Waldo proposed to name her Asia; Lidian said no.

61. Cott, Bonds of Womanhood; Richard L. Bushman, The Refinement of America: Persons, Houses, Cities (New York, 1992), 36–37, 120–22, 250–79, 440–46; Karen Halttunen, Confidence Men and Painted Women: A Study of Middle-Class Culture in America, 1830–1870 (New Haven, Conn., 1982), 59–61, 104–5; Marla R. Miller, Entangled Lives: Labor, Livelihood, and Landscapes of Change in Rural Massachusetts (Baltimore, 2019), chap. 8.

62. Emerson, "Reforms," EL 3:264; JMN 7:201–2; Emerson, "Self-Reliance," EMP, 141–42; Emerson, "The American Scholar," EMP, 97–98; Keyes, Autobiography, 85; Emerson, Life of Lidian Jackson Emerson, 82–83. On Emerson's masculine version of individualism, see David Leverenz, Manhood and the American Renaissance (Ithaca, N.Y., 1989), chap. 2. Even the great Unitarian leader William Ellery Channing suffered from his closeness to women, in Emerson's view. His preaching was "feminine or receptive & not masculine or creative." JMN 5:195.

63. Emerson, "Society," EL 2:102–3, and "Love," EL 3:62; Armida Gilbert, "'Pierced by the Thorns of Reform': Emerson on Womanhood," in T. Gregory Garvey, ed., The Emerson Dilemma: Essays on Emerson and Social Reform (Athens, Ga., 2001), 93–97.

64. Emerson, "Love," EL 3:62–63, 67; JMN 5:382, 410 (October 1 and 23, 1837); Emerson, "Love," EL 3:66–67; Emerson, "Home," EL 3:27–29, 31–33.

65. Phyllis Cole, Mary Moody Emerson and the Origins of Transcendentalism: A Family History (New York, 1998); JMN 5:410.

66. Emerson, Life of Lidian Jackson Emerson, 49–50, 79, 84; Lydia Jackson (Plymouth) to Elizabeth Peabody (Lowell), July 28, 1835, in Delores Bird Carpenter, Selected Letters of Lidian Emerson, 29–30; Phyllis Cole, "'Men and Women Conversing': The Emersons in 1837," in Wesley T. Mott and Robert E. Burkholder, eds., Emersonian Circles: Essays in Honor of Joel Myerson (Rochester, N.Y., 1997), 130–33; Megan

Marshall, "Elizabeth Palmer Peabody: The First Transcendentalist?" *Massachusetts Historical Review* 8 (2006): 4–9.

67. Emerson, "Love," *EL* 3:62; Cole, *Mary Emerson and Transcendentalism*; Caroline Wells Healey Dall, *Transcendentalism in New England: A Lecture Delivered before the Society for Philosophical Enquiry, Washington, D.C., May 7, 1895* (Boston, 1897), 16; Goodwin, *Remarkable Mrs. Ripley*, 150–55; Mary Kelley, *Learning to Stand and Speak: Women, Education, and Public Life in America's Republic* (Chapel Hill, N.C., 2006), 34–36, 67–68; Richard M. Bernard and Maris A. Vinovskis, "The Female School Teacher in Ante-Bellum Massachusetts," *Journal of Social History* 10 (Spring 1977): 332–45; Thomas Dublin, *Women at Work: The Transformation of Work and Community in Lowell, Massachusetts, 1826–1860* (New York, 1979).

68. Len Gougeon, "Emerson and the Woman Question: The Evolution of His Thought," *New England Quarterly* 71 (December 1998): 570–92; Dall, *Transcendentalism in New England*, 23–24; *JMN* 5:407, 410, 443–44; Kathleen Lawrence, "The 'Dry-Lighted Soul' Ignites: Emerson and His Soul-Mate Caroline Sturgis as Seen in Her Houghton Manuscripts," *Harvard Library Bulletin* 16, no. 3 (Fall 2005): 43–44; Emerson, "Heroism," *EL* 2:331, 335, 336. For brief remarks on Emerson's equal-opportunity view of self-culture, see Lawrence Buell, *Emerson* (Cambridge, Mass., 2003), 343n10.

69. George Ripley and George P. Bradford, "Philosophic Thought in Boston," in Justin Winsor, ed., *The Memorial History of Boston, Including Suffolk County, Massachusetts, 1630–1880*, 4 vols. (Boston, 1880–1881), 4:304–5; Helen Deese, "'A Liberal Education': Caroline Healey Dall and Emerson," in Mott and Burkholder, eds., *Emersonian Circles*, 237–44. The befuddled father in the anecdote was probably the "distinguished jurist" Jeremiah Mason (1768–1848), whose remark was later recalled by Julia Ward Howe. See her memoir, "Ralph Waldo Emerson as I Knew Him," *Critic* 42 (May 1903): 411.

70. Obituary of Timothy Prescott, *CF*, March 4, 1842; Kenneth Walter Cameron, "Young Henry Thoreau in the Annals of the Concord Academy (1829–1833)," *Emerson Society Quarterly* 9 (1957): 16–17. Prescott ranked in the top tenth of property holders on the 1835 Concord assessment list, with $2,700 in real estate and $4,434 in personal estate (including $3,800 in stocks). He bought a share in the social library in November 1833 and served as treasurer of the institution in 1835; upon joining the lyceum in 1833, he put in a term as secretary. He acted twice as moderator (1835, 1840), chaired the body that came up with the inscription for the battlefield monument, and served two terms as selectman (1840–1841). In March 1836 the Anti-Masons put up Prescott for moderator of town meeting, in an unprecedented partisan contest for the post. Keyes prevailed after four ballots. That same meeting witnessed a contest between Keyes and Prescott for Middlesex County treasurer; the challenger came close with 102 votes to the incumbent's 130. In the county as a whole, Keyes prevailed with a narrow majority for his final term in office. *YG*, March 12 and 19, 1836; *CF*, March 12 and 19, 1836.

71. Leslie Perrin Wilson, "'Treasure in My Own Mind': The Diary of Martha Lawrence Prescott, 1834–1836," *Concord Saunterer*, n.s., 11 (2003): 101–4; report of election returns for county treasurer, *CF*, March 19, 1836. Before coming to Concord, Martha Prescott had been a student at Westford Academy; see Wilson, "'Treasure in My Own Mind,'" 98. Timothy Prescott was nominated for Social Circle membership in April 1833, but the vote on his candidacy was not taken until November 8, 1836. On that evening, Prescott noted in his diary, "the Club met at the house of Mr. Keyes and rejected 3 Gentlemen who were considered for admission." The Social Circle records make plain that he was one of those three.

72. Wilson, "'Treasure in My Own Mind,'" 126 ("mere housekeeper," "single blessedness"), 131 (Combe), 135 ("treasure in my own mind").

73. Ibid., 128 ("talked with no one"), 133 (corsets), 135 (forced smiles), 133 ("very odd").

74. Ibid., 138–39 (gossip), 141 ("flattery"), 136 ("little love," "matrimony"), 136 ("matter of fact business"), 139 ("old maid"), 127 ("unchanging"), 133, 137 (pedantry, "intelligent, learned," "female pedant"). One afternoon in May 1836, Prescott and five academy friends gathered at Boiling Spring in the watershed of Walden Woods and idled their time by predicting one another's future. John Shepard Keyes was the only male in the group. The fourteen-year-old was confidently pronounced to be headed for college, where he would be "dashing for a while" and "fickle in his first loves" before buckling down to the law and politics and marrying "a handsome & excellent woman." As for Martha Prescott, everyone expected her to wed a "clever man" who shared her love of books and nature. She doubted her worthiness: who "that I could love & respect would marry poor inferior me?" Nobody suspected that the two would eventually marry in 1844. Ibid., 138.

75. Philip F. Gura, *American Transcendentalism: A History* (New York, 2007), 24–26; Daniel Walker Howe, *The Unitarian Conscience: Harvard Moral Philosophy, 1805–1861* (Cambridge, Mass., 1970), 27–40; Wilson, "'Treasure in My Own Mind,'" 128 ("lengthy & subtile," "infidelity"), 130 (taking "opinions on trust"), 131 ("monotonous"), 137 ("false"), 139 (baptism and "spiritual education"), 141 ("omnipresence").

76. Wilson, "'Treasure in My Own Mind,'" 141 ("people stare," "our own salvation," "no permanent happiness"), 137 ("God's fittest temples").

77. Tiffany K. Wayne, "Phrenology," in her *Encyclopedia of Transcendentalism* (New York, 2006), 217–18; Wilson, "'Treasure in My Own Mind,'" 113 (phrenology), 127 (Mrs. Garrison).

78. Wilson, "'Treasure in My Own Mind,'" 130–31 ("hear her converse"), 139 ("sudden and dreadful"), 141 ("negative goodness"); Timothy Prescott, Diary, notes seven occasions between November 16, 1834, and July 10, 1836, when Emerson was the guest preacher. The Emerson and Prescott families did exchange social calls; see entries in Prescott's diary for January 16, October 11, 1836, and October 30, 1838.

79. First Parish Church Record Book (transcript), entries for September 4, 1836, March 3, 1839, CFPL; Wilson, "'Treasure in My Own Mind,'" 137 ("immortal beings").

80. Wilson, "'Treasure in My Own Mind,'" 138 ("fickle"); Keyes, Diary, vol. 3, entries for July 1, 1840 (Byron), May 10–16, 1842 (references to Festus), May 17 ("Matty"), 1842; Philip James Bailey, *Festus: A Poem* (London, 1839); Alan D. McKillop, "A Victorian Faust," *PMLA* 40 (September 1925): 747–63. Margaret Fuller reviewed *Festus* in *The Dial* of October 1841 (2:231). Emerson later dismissed the work: "Festus and Shelley have both this merit of timeliness; that is the only account we can give of their imposing on such good heads." See McKillop, "Victorian Faust," 62–63.

81. Keyes, Diary, vol. 5, entries for May 21 ("perfect mirror"), June 1 ("growing better"), May 18 ("Four years!"), June 20 ("essay on prayer"), June 12 (*Formation of Christian Character*), March 3, 1842 ("almost a Saint"); Wilson, "'Treasure in My Own Mind,'" 133 ("think me a fool").

82. Wilson, "'Treasure in My Own Mind,'" 127 ("no man may live").

13. *The Man of Concord*

1. Walter Harding, *The Days of Henry Thoreau: A Biography*, rev. ed. (New York, 1982), 46–47; David Henry Thoreau, "Class Book Autobiography," ca. June 1837, in

Henry D. Thoreau, *Early Essays and Miscellanies*, ed. Joseph J. Moldenhauer and Edwin Moser, with Alexander C. Kern (Princeton, N.J., 1975), 113; *JMN* 5:452–53; David Greene Haskins, *Ralph Waldo Emerson, His Maternal Ancestors, with Some Reminiscences of Him* (Boston, 1887), 119. In February 1835 Emerson served on a committee of the Harvard Board of Overseers that examined the members of the sophomore class, Thoreau included, on Whately's *Rhetoric*. See Raymond R. Borst, comp., *The Thoreau Log: A Documentary Life of Henry David Thoreau, 1817–1862* (New York, 1992), 16; Harding, *Days of Thoreau*, 60-61. For an up-to-date review of the Emerson-Thoreau friendship, see Jeffrey S. Cramer, *Solid Seasons: The Friendship of Henry David Thoreau and Ralph Waldo Emerson* (Berkeley, Calif., 2019).

2. Laura Dassow Walls, *Henry David Thoreau: A Life* (Chicago, 2017), 42; Walter Harding, ed., *Thoreau as Seen by His Contemporaries* (New York, 1989), 9; "A Rare Reminiscence of Thoreau as a Child," *Thoreau Society Bulletin* 245 (Fall 2003): 1–2; George F. Hoar, *Autobiography of Seventy Years*, 2 vols. (New York, 1903), 1:70; [John Weiss,] "Thoreau," *Christian Examiner* 79 (July 1865): 97–98; Edward W. Emerson, "Remains of Thoreau," undated lecture in his manuscript notes on Thoreau, CFPL; Harding, *Days of Thoreau*, 54; *PEJ* 3:287 (thanks to David Wood for alerting me to this passage). For all Thoreau's supposed detachment from his fellows in the Harvard Class of 1837, it is noteworthy that the first volume of his collected *Correspondence: 1834 to 1848*, ed. Robert N. Hudspeth (Princeton, N.J., 2013) contains letters or warm references to and from nine of his forty-six classmates: David Greene Haskins, Charles Hayward, Augustus Goddard Peabody, Charles Wyatt Rice, James Richardson (sophomore roommate), Henry Vose, John Weiss, Charles Stearns Wheeler (freshman roommate), and Henry Williams. See *Memorials of the Class of 1837 of Harvard University. Prepared for the Fiftieth Anniversary of Their Graduation, by the Class Secretary, Henry Williams* (Boston, 1887).

3. Hoar, *Autobiography* 1:40; Harding, *Days of Thoreau*, 19–20; *Walden*, 180; William Ellery Channing, *Thoreau: The Poet-Naturalist. With Memorial Verses* (Boston, 1873), 3; *TJHM* 8:93–94 (entry for January 7, 1856); F. B. Sanborn, *Henry D. Thoreau* (Boston, 1882), 96.

4. George Hendrick, ed., *Remembrances of Concord and the Thoreaus* (Urbana, Ill., 1977), 92–93; Thoreau, "Class Book Autobiography," 112–13; Sanborn, *Henry Thoreau*, 29.

5. Priscilla Rice Edes, *Some Reminiscences of Old Concord* (Gouverneur, N.Y., 1903); Elizabeth Hoar to Marianne Cornelia Giles (St. Johnsbury, Vt.), October 1, 1828, and November 2, 1829, in Elizabeth Maxfield-Miller, "Elizabeth of Concord: Selected Letters of Elizabeth Sherman Hoar (1814–1878) to the Emersons, Family, and the Emerson Circle (Part Two)," *Studies in the American Renaissance* (1985): 100, 107; Sarah Sherman Hoar (Concord) to Frances J. H. Prichard (New Haven), October 18, 1836, in Prichard, Hoar, and Related Family Papers, Box 5, Folder 1, CFPL; Keyes, Diary, vol. 2, entry for January 25, 1839; Wendy Gamber, *The Boardinghouse in Nineteenth-Century America* (Baltimore, 2007), 2–10; Keyes, Autobiography, 3; *Boston Directory, Containing the Names of the Inhabitants, Their Occupations, Places of Business, and Dwelling Houses* (Boston, 1798), 43; Harding, *Days of Thoreau*, 60; Hendrick, *Remembrances of Concord and Thoreaus*, 74–75. Mary Dunbar's boardinghouse was at 15 Marlborough Street.

6. Sanborn, *Henry Thoreau*, 25; Rev. Henry M. Grout, *Trinitarian Congregationalism in Concord* (Boston, 1876), 80 (Elizabeth, Jane, Maria, and Sarah Thoreau), 83 (Louisa Dunbar). Charles J. Dunbar affiliated with the Trinitarian parish in 1829. For more on the church split, see Chapter 2.

7. The earliest and most active female charitable society was founded in Salem in

1801; it spurred similar groups in Newburyport (1803) and Northampton (1803) and then five more in Berkshire County (Becket, Great Barrington, Pittsfield, Sheffield, and Williamstown) between 1812 and 1814. The Concord society was at the head of a new wave (1814 to 1820) of such organizations; founded in January 1814, it was the first in Middlesex County, ahead of Groton by several months. See Daniel Chaplin, *A Discourse Delivered before the Charitable Female Society in Groton October 19, 1814* (Andover, Mass., 1814), 13. Another twenty-six female charitable societies went into operation between 1812 and 1817. Boston alone boasted eighteen such groups between 1800 and 1830, a figure that nearly doubled over the next decade. Eventually, hundreds of women would be assisting their unfortunate sisters in similar associations throughout the Commonwealth. For a census of charitable organizations in the Bay State, I relied on Conrad Edick Wright, *The Transformation of Charity in Postrevolutionary New England* (Boston, 1992), app. 3. See also Anne M. Boylan, *The Origins of Women's Activism: New York and Boston, 1797–1840* (Chapel Hill, N.C., 2002), 223–26.

8. Of the eighty-six founders of the Concord Female Charitable Society in 1814, the marital status of seventy-three is known: 47 were married, 17 single, and 9 widows. (For comparisons, see Boylan, *Origins*, 55 and table A.5.) The median age of the forty-two wives among the founders was forty-two (almost the same as the mean).

9. *Constitution of the Concord Female Charitable Society, 1814* (n.p., 1815), CFPL. The spread of female charitable societies was not a response to the actual toll of poverty in the state. The movement began in good times, when business was booming in such seaports as Salem and Newburyport, and it temporarily stalled during the hardship of Jefferson's embargo on trade. Only during the last years of the War of 1812 and its aftermath did female charitable societies multiply across the land. Even then, the organizational growth was independent of wartime distress. Under Massachusetts law, each town collected taxes for assistance to inhabitants in need, and the state furnished funds for newcomers and transients in dire straits. Concord fulfilled its duty every year at May town meeting, when the voters approved a budget for poor relief. From the start of the century to 1820, public aid to the needy rose, from $1,000 in 1801 to $1,139 in 1814, and then soared to $1,600 in 1820. But the real burden of such spending on taxpayers varied, owing to the ups and downs of prices. In 1801, when farming and commerce were flourishing on transatlantic trade, support for the poor cost each taxpayer $2.59 (the equivalent to $53.70 in 2019); in 1814, as the CFCS was being organized, the real burden fell (nominally $3.09 per taxpayer, but $46.50 in constant dollars); five years later, following the financial panic of 1819, the charge had nearly doubled ($3.95 per taxpayer or $81.90 in 2019 dollars). By then, enthusiasm for the women's cause was well past its peak. Yet the CFCS persevered through prosperity and privation for reasons that had less to do with the prevalence of poverty than with the motivations of the earnest women seeking to help the female poor and with the inclusive vision of community driving them on.

On Concord's appropriations for the poor, see CTMM 1790 to 1814, town meetings of May 4, 1801 (p. 203), May 2, 1814 (p. 424); for the meeting of May 1, 1820, CTMM 7:132, CFPL. From 1800 to 1819 the town lumped together appropriations for the poor with other "town charges" (that is, other financial obligations). In 1820 the town treasurer started separating out these expenses. The cost of poor relief was $1,600, double that for "town charges." I applied this ratio to the budget for 1801 and 1814 to estimate spending on the poor in each year, then divided by the number of taxpayers to estimate the per capita burden. I adjusted for inflation and deflation by applying the relative cost of living calculator on the website Measuring Worth. The CFCS enrolled eighty-six members in 1814, nine in 1815, and seven in 1816. Thereafter new accessions slowed: none in 1817, four in 1818, two in 1819, three in 1820. On the Massachusetts laws governing poor relief, see Cornelia H. Dayton and Sharon V. Salinger, *Robert Love's Warnings: Searching for Strangers in Colonial Boston* (Philadelphia, 2014), 44-50.

10. *TJHM* 12:38 (entry for March 11, 1859); Report of expenses, July 1, 1824 ("suffering fellow creature"), meetings of June 1826, May 1827, June 1828 (payment of $19 to M. Parker for keeping "charity school"), Concord Female Charitable Society Records, 1814-48, vol. 1, CFPL; Janet Granger and Margaret Andrews, "The Concord Female Charitable Society and the Ladies' Sewing Society, 1814-1840," paper submitted for "Culture and Community: The Worlds of Emerson, Dickinson, and Thoreau," Amherst College, May 23, 1982, on deposit at CFPL; Lori D. Ginzberg, *Women and the Work of Benevolence: Morality, Politics, and Class in the Nineteenth-Century United States* (New Haven, Conn., 1990), 36-66.

11. In October 1828, forty women in the new Trinitarian congregation organized a Ladies' Sewing Society (LSS) on very different principles from the CFCS. Membership was fifty cents a year, half the fee of its counterpart, and if a woman could not pay in cash, she could donate her labor. Like the liberal women's group, the LSS devoted its energy to the traditional products of women's work. But the clothing its members donated and made was not given away to needy inhabitants of Concord. It was sold for cash, and the proceeds were transmitted to worthy causes beyond the town. The evangelical women bought Rev. Southmayd a life membership in the American Bible Society, and they contributed to a campaign to reclaim prostitutes in distant New York City. The money was sent by Maria Thoreau. As for the local poor, they would have to find aid elsewhere. Ladies' Sewing Society Records, Trinitarian Congregational Church Records, Box 1, CFPL; *McDowall's Journal* 1 (August 1, 1833).

12. *Proceedings in Commemoration of the One Hundred and Fiftieth Anniversary of the First Congregational Church, Williamstown, Massachusetts* (Pittsfield, Mass., 1916), 133-34; *Constitution of the Andover South Parish Female Charitable Society, May, 1815* (Newburyport, Mass., 1815); Granger and Andrews, "Concord Female Charitable Society and Ladies' Sewing Society." The localism of the CFCS won praise from the *YG*, July 29, 1826. Instead of vainly pursuing "foreign" projects "beyond their reach," the paper editorialized, the CFCS prudently attended to "the wants of our people . . . The maxim that charity begins at home, should first be observed . . . The poor we shall always have, but still those who are crowned with abundance are bound to consider them, and to lend a helping hand." For similar charitable practices in the Worcester County town of Shrewsbury, see Jack Larkin, "'An Extended Link in the Great Chain of Benevolence': The Shrewsbury Charitable Society, 1832-1842," paper delivered at meeting of New England Historical Association, April 19, 1980, Old Sturbridge Village Research Library, Sturbridge, Mass.

13. Sanborn, *Henry Thoreau*, 10-11. In 1815 Ezra Ripley composed and endorsed Mary Jones Dunbar Minot's appeal for charity from the Massachusetts Grand Lodge.

14. Sixty-eight of the founders of the CFCS in 1814 were wives and widows; fifty-six of them could be linked through husbands or in their own right to the 1815 tax list. One out of three ranked in the top tenth, over half (31) in the top fifth, and three-quarters (42) in the top two quintiles. Sixteen of the eighty-six founders (18.6 percent) were married to members of the Social Circle; that proportion rose to over half (53 percent) of the top officers of the group (president, vice-president, secre-

tary, and treasurer) between 1814 and 1824 (N = 15) and nearly half (49) of the CFCS board of directors. In 1825, when Cynthia Thoreau joined the leadership, eight of the thirteen officers were wives of Social Circle members. In the ensuing decade (1825–1834) three out of four held that distinction. The male elite supported the charitable society as strongly as it backed the Concord Bank and the Society of Middlesex Husbandmen and Manufacturers. In 1814 nineteen members of the Social Circle were married; sixteen had wives in the charitable society. That proportion remained steady over the following decade. Cynthia Thoreau's colleagues included Mrs. Nathan Brooks, Mrs. Samuel Hoar, and Mrs. Isaac Hurd, as they were designated in the records; in subsequent years she would serve alongside Mrs. William Munroe, her husband's pencil-making rival. Each year a few less-privileged women penetrated the in-group; Cynthia's sister Louisa Dunbar was a manager in 1825 with her.

15. Walls, *Henry David Thoreau*, 59; Emerson, "Remains of Thoreau," 10–11; F. B. Sanborn, *The Life of Henry David Thoreau, Including Many Essays Hitherto Unpublished, and Some Account of His Family and Friends* (Boston, 1917), 153; Edmund A. Schofield, "Further Particulars on Thoreau's Harvard Scholarship Awards," *Thoreau Society Bulletin* 264 (Fall 2008): 4–6.

16. Sanborn, *Life of Thoreau*, 468; Thoreau, "Class Book Autobiography," 113–14; Keyes, Autobiography, 50. Thoreau was playing on the famous vow of the Psalmist: "If I forget thee, O Jerusalem, let my right hand forget her cunning."

17. Walls, *Henry David Thoreau*, 63–65; Frederick T. McGill, "Thoreau and College Discipline," *New England Quarterly* 15 (June 1942): 352. According to classmate John Weiss, Thoreau uttered a memorable line during a student meeting in the spring of 1834 to protest arbitrary grading by Greek instructor Christopher Dunkin. "Our offence was rank," he quipped. Thoreau put his convictions into practice by signing a petition urging the faculty to abolish the point system for determining class rank; he was one of thirty-eight members of the Class of 1837 to do so. Weiss, "Thoreau," 96; Harding, *Days of Thoreau*, 33.

18. Daniel Walker Howe, *The Unitarian Conscience: Harvard Moral Philosophy, 1805–1861* (Cambridge, Mass., 1970), 123–24, 185–87, 206, 310–11; Henry D. Thoreau, *Early Essays and Miscellanies*, ed. Joseph J. Moldenhauer and Edwin Moser, with Alexander C. Kern (Princeton, N.J., 1975), 7, 9–11, 23–24; Edward T. Channing, "A Writer's Preparation," in his *Lectures Read to the Seniors in Harvard College* (Boston, 1856), 195–96.

19. Walls, *Henry David Thoreau*, 73–76; O. A. Brownson, *An Address, Delivered at Dedham, on the Fifty-Eighth Anniversary of American Independence, July 4, 1834* (Dedham, Mass., 1834), 9–10, 12; Thoreau (Concord) to Orestes Brownson (Boston), December 30, 1837, in Hudspeth, *Correspondence of Thoreau*, 1:30–32.

20. Walls, *Henry David Thoreau*, 70–72, 76–78; Thoreau, *Early Essays*, 86–88.

21. Borst, *Thoreau Log*, 25–26; Thoreau, *Early Essays*, 106–7, 108–10. Besides the references to "the religious sentiment," Thoreau also shows the influence of Emerson's *Nature* in his statement that a proper education draws out "that which is in a man, by contact with the Not Me."

22. Thoreau, "Class Book Autobiography," 106, 113–14 .

23. Walls, *Henry David Thoreau*, 79–81; Henry D. Thoreau, "The Commercial Spirit of Modern Times," in *Early Essays*, 115–18.

24. Walls, *Henry David Thoreau*, 82–83.

25. Reports of October 2, 1837, March 30, 1838, Concord Bank Records, Series 1, Directors' Books, 1965.29.1.1 BV, Old Sturbridge Village Research Library, Stur-

bridge, Mass. Daniel Walker Howe, *What Hath God Wrought: The Transformation of America, 1815–1848* (New York, 2007), 501–5. The value of notes discounted, the Concord Bank reported in March 1838, was $146,962.70, the lowest sum since 1834. In 2019 values, the reduction of loans amounted to $567,000.

26. In "Thoreau in the Town School, 1837," *Concord Saunterer*, n.s., 4 (Fall 1996): 150–72, Dick O'Connor mistakenly interprets the shrinking of the school committee as a sign of declining support for education in Concord. The board had fifteen members from 1820 to 1825, fell to ten in 1826–1827, oscillated between seven and eight over the years 1826–1836 and then plunged to three in 1837. The shifting numbers reflect the struggle between reformers and traditionalists for control. The reformers pushed to eliminate the decentralized management of schools through large committees made up of district representatives. Their preference was to choose a small body on an at-large basis and empower it to hire and fire the teachers in line with the latest ideas of the experts. Shattuck and Jarvis had long supported this design, and in 1837 the reformers got their way with the choice of a three-man committee and a substantial increase in the "school money." In April 1838, the town reelected Frost, Ball, and Barrett and added two more members—Albert H. Nelson and Elisha Wheeler—to their ranks. Power continued thereafter to seesaw back and forth. For the broader history of school reform in Massachusetts, see Carl F. Kaestle, *Pillars of the Republic: Common Schools and American Society, 1780–1860* (New York, 1983), 111–15.

27. Thoreau to Brownson, December 30, 1837, in Hudspeth, *Correspondence of Thoreau* 1:31; Annual Report of the School Committee for 1837–38, *YG*, April 14, 1838; meeting of September 17, 1838, CTMM, 8:129, CFPL; John Keyes, Barzillai Frost, and John Wilder to Horace Mann, secretary of Massachusetts Board of Education, September 18, 1838, Horace Mann Papers, Box 5 (1838–40), MHS. The 1837 board that approved the hiring of Thoreau was bipartisan, with two Whigs (Frost and Ball) and one Democrat (Barrett). Residents of the central village, Ball and Frost, could command a majority. The sizable increase in the school budget was voted in early March 1837, before the financial crash, and it was continued over the next two years, despite the economic depression. See CTMM 8:89, 94, 108, 113, 143, 150, CFPL.

28. William Ellery Channing identified the official who visited Thoreau's school as "a knowing deacon." That could only have been Nehemiah Ball, who assumed the office in the First Parish Church on September 7, 1834. Channing, *Thoreau: Poet-Naturalist*, 24; First Parish Church Record Book (transcript), entries for September 4 and 7, 1834, CFPL.

29. Walls, *Henry David Thoreau*, 84–86; Channing, *Thoreau: Poet-Naturalist*, 24; Prudence Ward (Concord) to Caroline Ward Sewall (Scituate), September 25, 1837, Prudence Ward and Anne J. Ward Correspondence, Huntington Library, San Marino, Calif.; John S. Keyes, "Memoir of Nehemiah Ball," *SCM* 2:234–40; Records of the Grammar School in the term ending November 24, 1837, CFPL.

30. Horace Mann, "Lecture on School Punishments" (1839), in Felix Pécant, George Combe Mann, and Mary Tyler Peabody Mann, eds., *Life and Works of Horace Mann*, 5 vols. (Boston, 1891), 2:348. Thoreau's brief tenure as master of the grammar school was alluded to in the annual report of the school committee for 1837–1838, submitted by Barzillai Frost: there was "an interruption in the Fall term of the centre grammar school." *YG*, April 14, 1838. Emerson resigned from the school committee in November 1836; had he completed his term and been reelected in March 1837, he would have been on the body that supervised the employment of Thoreau.

31. Wayne T. Dilts, "Henry's Houses: The Houses in Concord That Henry Called Home," *Thoreau Society Bulletin* 263 (Summer 2008): 6–7; *PEJ* 1:73–74 (entry for June 4, 1839); Harding, *Days of Thoreau*, 58; Prudence Ward (Concord) to Prudence Bird Ward (Scituate), April 13, 1838, Abernethy Collection, Middlebury College Library (I am grateful to Tom Blanding for sharing with me his transcripts of these letters); *The Autobiography of Edward Jarvis*, ed. Rosalba Davico (London, 1992), 39; Walls, *Henry David Thoreau*, 96. Thoreau's search for teaching jobs can be traced in letters to classmates David Greene Haskins and Henry Vose, February 9, May 28, 1838, to Orestes Brownson, December 30, 1837, from Josiah Quincy, April 12, 1838, and to brother John Thoreau, Jr., February 10 and 17, 1838, all in Hudspeth, *Correspondence of Thoreau*, 1:30–44.

32. *PEJ* 1:42 (entry for April 24, 1838), 44 (entry for May 3–4, 1838), 35–39 ("Scraps from a Lecture on 'Society' written March 14th 1838. delivered before our Lyceum April 11th").

33. Robert Sattelmeyer, "Historical Introduction," *PEJ* 2:2:446–47; Walls, *Henry David Thoreau*, 89–90, 119–23; Cramer, *Solid Seasons*, 13–15; David Greene Haskins, *Ralph Waldo Emerson, His Maternal Ancestors, with Some Reminiscences of Him* (Boston, 1887), 122; Joel Myerson, "Eight Lowell Letters from Concord in 1838," *Illinois Quarterly* 38 (Winter 1975): 28. Late in life John Shepard Keyes told an interviewer that after he came home from college, Thoreau became "a thorough-going imitator of Emerson, whose manner, speech, and ideas he copied with great fidelity and success." Harding, *Thoreau Seen by Contemporaries*, 81–83, reprinting an interview conducted by George W. Cooke for the *Independent* in 1896.

34. It has been assumed that Thoreau was able to take over the Concord Academy because the incumbent instructor suddenly resigned. That appears incorrect. Following his election as town clerk on the Anti-Masonic ticket, Phineas Allen lost the support of the proprietors, and they brought in a competing instructor, William Whiting, Jr., to win over his students. Allen left Concord in 1836, and Whiting went on to practice law. An orthodox Calvinist, Williams College and Andover Theological Seminary graduate Levi Brigham then took over the school. He left to assume a pulpit in Dunstable. Josiah G. Davis, the Yale-educated son of merchant Josiah, came next. He moved on after the summer term 1837, and no one seems to have taken his place. Thoreau's Harvard classmate James Richardson, Jr., heard about the vacancy by early September. No advertisement for Concord Academy ran in the Concord or Boston press from the summer of 1837 through the following summer, until Thoreau announced that his school would open on September 10, 1838. It was the customary practice for preceptors of academies to advertise for students in advance of an upcoming term. In June 1838, for example, the instructors of academies in Marlborough, Stow, and Westford placed notices in the *YG*; none appeared for Concord. As soon as Thoreau got up an academy, he advertised. See *Boston Recorder*, April 15, 1836; *YG*, November 26, 1836, June 17, 1837, June 2, September 15, 1838; Melvin Ticknor Stone, *Historical Sketch of the Town of Troy, New Hampshire, 1764–1897* (Keene, N.H., 1897), 139; James Richardson, Jr. (Dedham) to Thoreau (Concord), September 7, 1837, in Hudspeth, *Correspondence of Thoreau*, 1:16–17.

35. *YG*, September 15, 1838; Walls, *Henry David Thoreau*, 96–101; Thoreau to Brownson, December 30, 1837, in Hudspeth, *Correspondence of Thoreau*, 1:31–32.

36. *YG*, February 9, 1839; Hendrick, *Remembrances of Concord and Thoreaus*, 72. Of the thirty-five students at the Thoreau brothers' academy listed by Harding, *Days of Thoreau*, 76–77, seven had fathers in the Social Circle (Gorham and Martha Bartlett, children of Dr. Josiah; George Brooks, son of Nathan; Frisbie Hoar, son of Samuel;

Joseph Boyden Keyes, son of John; George Loring, son of David; Cyrus Thompson Warren, son of Cyrus; and Elijah Wood, Jr., son of the shoe and boot manufacturer). Nine pupils had mothers in the CFCS: Mary Merrick Brooks (mother of George), Sarah Sherman Hoar (mother of Frisbie), Sally Hosmer (mother of Sarah), Susan Loring (mother of George), Margaret Rice (mother of Sidney), Almira Tuttle (mother of Sherman and Almira), Betsy Wood (mother of Elijah Wood, Jr.), and Rizpah Wood (mother of James Barrett Wood).

37. Harding, *Days of Thoreau*, 75–88; Walls, *Henry David Thoreau*, 96–101, 345; Gregory Nobles, "'One of his Ideas was that Everyone Should Think for Themselves,'" in Giorgio Mariani et al., ed., *Emerson at 200* (Rome, 2004), 239–46; Joseph B. Keyes, entry in Class of 1849, Harvard Class Book, 335–37, Harvard University Archives, Cambridge, Mass.; Hoar, *Autobiography*, 70–72; Hendrick, *Remembrances of Concord and Thoreaus*, 9, 21, 35; Emerson, "Remains of Thoreau," 14; Robert A. Gross, "'That Terrible Thoreau': Concord and Its Hermit," in William E. Cain, *A Historical Guide to Henry David Thoreau* (New York, 2000), 225–29.

38. *YG*, November 25, 1837; Thoreau, obituary of Anna Jones, in *Early Essays*, 121; Kenneth Walter Cameron, *Thoreau and His Harvard Classmates* (Hartford, Conn., 1965), 91–93; Roger Nason, "Jones, John (d. 1823)," in *Dictionary of Canadian Biography*, vol. 6 (1987), University of Toronto/Université Laval, 2003, accessed January 19, 2021, http://www.biographi.ca/en/bio/jones_john_1823_6E.html. Anna Jones was born in Concord on July 28, 1751, the daughter of John and Anna (Brooks) Jones and one of at least seven children to reach adulthood. The firstborn in this long-established Concord family, John, Jr. (1743–1823), surveyed land for the Plymouth Company in Maine during the years before the Revolution. When war broke out in April 1775, he sided with the king, was seized at his home in Hallowell, and was imprisoned in Boston. He escaped from jail in the spring of 1779 and found his way to Lake Champlain, where he enlisted with a Loyalist regiment under Capt. Robert Rogers. His wife was Ruth Lee, daughter of Dr. Joseph Lee, one of Concord's most outspoken opponents of resistance to British policies. The couple wed on January 24, 1775, and settled in Maine. His brother Stephen (1746–1811) served in Capt. David Brown's Minuteman Company; brother Timothy (1748–1804) served in a Bedford company. See Gross, *Minutemen*, 55–56, 58–59, 61–62, 131, 134, 137–38. Anna Jones at sixty joined the First Parish of Concord on New Year's Day, 1815. She had evidently moved from Concord, her birthplace, to Walpole, New Hampshire, at some point in her life, since she presented a letter of dismission from the church of that town as proof of her visible faith. See First Parish Church Record Book (transcript), CFPL.

39. *YG*, November 11, December 2, 1837; *CF*, November 25, 1837.

40. *YG*, March 3, 1838; *CF*, November 6, 1840.

41. Thoreau, *Early Essays*, 5–7, 23–24.

42. William Parkman died at ninety-one on February 5, 1832; fourteen months later (April 27, 1833), his heirs, scattered from Camden, Maine, to Concord and Charlestown to Baltimore, Maryland, sold the property in the middle of town for $1,365 to Nathan Brooks and John Keyes. In turn, Keyes sold title to the house and lot to Brooks in two separate transactions, the first on April 24, 1834, the second on July 15, 1835. MCRD 335:172, 562; 342:510. Brooks was thus sole owner and landlord when the Thoreau family moved into the Parkman place in the spring of 1837.

43. *Remarks by Samuel Hoar, of Massachusetts, on the Resolutions Introduced by Mr. Jarvis, of Maine, and Mr. Wise, of Virginia, Delivered in the House of Representatives, Thursday, January 21, 1836* (Washington, D.C., 1836).

44. "The Federal candidate for Congress," *CF*, December 14, 1838; Nathan Brooks to

Amos Farnsworth, public letter, October 25, 1837, *CF*, November 11, 1837; Richard Buel, Jr., "Democracy and the American Revolution: A Frame of Reference," *William and Mary Quarterly* 21 (April 1964): 165–90; Michael J. Dubin, *United States Congressional Elections, 1788–1997: The Official Results of the Elections of the 1st Through 105th Congresses* (Jefferson, N.C., 1998), 121, 124, 126, 136; Susan Kurland, "'A Political Progress': Processes of Democratization in Concord, Massachusetts, 1750–1850" (senior honors thesis, Brandeis University, 1973), 49. In the election of the twenty-sixth Congress, only two districts in the Union were forced to hold runoffs. The Vermont fourth filled its seat in two trials. The Massachusetts fourth was the last to be decided in the country. Brooks held on to his base throughout the contest and inched up from 141 votes in November 1838 to 158 or 159 in February and April 1839. His support in Concord was below his share of the county vote on the first trial (46.5 to 48.2 percent), essentially the same the second time (45.9 to 45.6 percent), and higher on the third (48.9 to 42.1 percent) and last ballots (47.7 to 45.8 percent). Parmenter eventually prevailed both in Concord and in the district thanks to a surge of new votes, raising his total by 11 percent. In 1840 Brooks's proportion of the Concord vote (48.2 percent) matched that of the county (48.4 percent). Two years later, when the Liberty Party fielded a candidate to challenge the Democratic and Whig nominees, the race was forced into a runoff. In the first round Hoar fared worse in Concord (41 percent) than in Middlesex (43.7 percent); on the second ballot his share fell to 38.5 percent, compared to 39.6 percent in the district overall. In the fevered elections of the second American party system, there was no hometown advantage.

45. *PEJ* 1:13 (entry for November 16, 1837); Henry Vose (Butternuts, N. Y.) to Thoreau (Concord), October 22, 1837, in Hudspeth, *Correspondence of Thoreau*, 1:22–23.

46. Hendrick, *Remembrances of Concord and Thoreaus*, 72. American-made pencils enjoyed tariff protection against foreign competition. In 1824, not long after John Thoreau took up the manufacture, Congress imposed a 40 percent *ad valorem* duty on imports of black lead pencils carried on U.S. and foreign vessels enjoying equal access to American ports. (Goods imported on other foreign vessels suffered a higher duty—44 percent in the case of black lead pencils.) The rates remained unchanged under the Act of 1828, the so-called Tariff of Abominations. This charge was reduced to 25 percent in 1832, then to 23 percent in 1840 and 21½ percent in 1842. *Collection of U.S. Documents relating Chiefly to the Tariff* (Washington, D.C., 1831–1832), 40, 85; Hunt's *Merchants' Magazine, and Commercial Review* 7 (1832): 483, 494; *Tariff, or, Rates of Duties Payable on Goods, Wares and Merchandise, Imported into the United States of America: On and after the First Day of January, 1840, Until the Thirtieth day of June, 1842, Inclusive, in Conformity with the Compromise Act: Also, the Rates of Duties Imposed by the Tariff Law of 1832, Together with Many Important Laws, Circulars, and Decisions of the Treasury Department, Relating to Commerce and the Revenue, and Much Useful Information to Merchants, Masters of Vessels, and Others* (New York, 1842), 48. As for access to credit, John Thoreau likely discounted notes at the Concord Bank during the 1830s, but the loan records do not survive for those years. Sometime in 1842 or 1843, if not before, the manufacturer borrowed $800 from that institution, for which he gave a promissory note. To secure the loan, he put up a supply of pencils equivalent in value. By October 1843, the pencil maker evidently lacked the cash to pay off his debt. Rather than forfeit the pencils, he enlisted the help of Daniel Shattuck. The bank president agreed to guarantee the loan for another year. The outstanding sum ($800) was due at the bank in October 1844; crucially, it was free from interest. The bank agreed

that as soon as Shattuck presented his guarantee of the loan, the pencils would be turned over to the merchant. He was likely planning to sell them at his store, obtaining the revenue right away, in case Thoreau was unable to pay off the loan in October 1844. See Directors Discount Sheet, October 16, 1843, Concord Bank Records, 1965.29.6, Old Sturbridge Village Research Library, Sturbridge, Mass.

47. Howe, *What Hath God Wrought*, 270–75, 346–56. The Indian Removal Act of 1830 was the defining issue in crystallizing pro- and anti-Jackson parties in the nation. For Thoreau's participation in petition campaigns, see Chapter 15.

48. *Loco Focos* was an epithet for the radical faction of Jacksonians associated with the fledgling labor movement in New York and other northern cities. The label was coined in October 1835, when dissident Democrats in Manhattan rebelled against the rule of Tammany Hall. In a bid to quash the uprising at a party gathering, the bosses employed a familiar tactic and shut down the gaslights in the meeting hall. But the "insurgents" defeated this maneuver by taking from their pockets a new implement—the friction match, known as a "loco foco"—and lighting candles to illuminate the room. The faction was thereafter known by this name. Arthur M. Schlesinger, Jr., *The Age of Jackson* (Boston, 1945), 191–92.

49. Ibid., 254–55; Sean Wilentz, *The Rise of American Democracy: Jefferson to Lincoln* (New York, 2005), 499–501; [Orestes A. Brownson], Article 4, a review-essay of four pamphlets on politics and social reform, *Boston Quarterly Review* 2 (October 1839): 485–516. *Massachusetts Register, and United States Calendar for 1839* (Boston, 1839), 163, and *for 1840* (Boston, 1840), 204.

50. *Massachusetts Register, and United States Calendar for 1839*, 163, and *for 1840*, 204; *New-Bedford Mercury*, quoting the *Boston Atlas* on the "late Loco-Foco Convention in Boston," October 11, 1839; *CF*, October 18, 1839; *YG*, October 19, 1839.

51. Hendrick, *Remembrances of Concord and Thoreaus*, 3; Ronald P. Formisano, *The Transformation of Political Culture: Massachusetts Parties, 1790s–1840s* (New York, 1983), 268–83; Susan Kurland, "'A Political Progress': Processes of Democratization in Concord, Massachusetts, 1750–1850" (senior honors thesis, Brandeis University, 1973), appendixes. In elections for governor from 1837 to 1844, for example, Democrats prevailed with anywhere from 54 percent to 60 percent of the votes. Democrats captured the town seat in the state House of Representatives by similar margins until 1842, when the rise of an antislavery Liberty Party reduced the Democrats to a slender majority.

52. In the state as a whole, Whigs held a commanding journalistic advantage, with three times as many newspapers as the Democrats. Not so in Middlesex County. Gourgas took over the *Freeman* in 1838 and ran it successfully to advance his party's interests and his own. His local opponents fared no better in the quest for readers than for votes. Controlled by the Whig inner circle of Brooks, Keyes, and Shattuck, the *Gazette* wore out one editor after another, until William S. Robinson, the school chum of Thoreau, initiated the *Republican* in 1840 at his own risk. It lasted in Concord for just two years. Thereafter the *Freeman* had the field to itself. See *CF*, January 14, 1837 (24 Democratic newspapers); *Sunbeam*, September 27, 1839 (60 Whig organs, fewer than 20 Democratic in November 1838); Formisano, *Transformation of Political Culture*, 263. In November 1836 the *Yeoman's Gazette and Middlesex Whig* boasted a circulation of twelve hundred, up 20 percent over two and a half years; *YG*, November 26, 1836. More than six years later, in the spring of 1843, the *Freeman* claimed a circulation of two thousand; *CF*, April 14, 1843. In July 1838 Gourgas bought out his partners and became sole proprietor of the *Freeman*, thanks to a timely gift of $500

from his generous father. From 1835 on, Daniel Shattuck and associates owned the printing office in which George F. Bemis, Elbridge G. Jefts, Thomas L. Scates, and William S. Robinson in succession turned out the *Yeoman's Gazette*. In 1839 Robinson, "a minor," was assessed for the "printing shop of D. Shattuck and others"; it was valued at $250. In July 1840 Daniel Shattuck, Nathan Brooks, and others "relinquished" to Robinson ownership of "the property and appurtenances of the 'Yeoman's Gazette.'" It thus appears that the Mill Dam Company rented quarters to the *Gazette*, the consortium headed by Shattuck and Brooks owned the printing equipment, and the various "publishers" controlled the business that produced the newspaper and did job printing. The local elite was clearly the power behind the press. See John M. Gourgas, Notes, Book no. 3, January 1, 1834, to July 23, 1838, entries for June 26, 1837, January 26, July 11 and 18, 1838, CFPL; Concord assessment list for 1840; Harriet H. Robinson, ed., *"Warrington" Pen Portraits: A Collection of Personal and Political Reminiscences from 1848 to 1876, from the Writings of William S. Robinson* (Boston, 1877), 20.

53. *CF*, March 1, 1839; *YG*, March 7, 1840; *R*, March 12, 1841; Formisano, *Transformation of Political Culture*, 261; *Sunbeam*, September 27, 1839; *CF*, August 18, November 17, 1843, May 31, 1844, August 5 and 29, 1845; Ronald G. Shafer, *The Carnival Campaign: How the Rollicking 1840 Campaign of "Tippecanoe and Tyler Too" Changed Presidential Politics Forever* (Chicago, 2016), 98–104; Thoreau, essay on "Methods of gaining or exercising public Influence," in *Early Essays*, 86–88. William S. Robinson promised that *The Hornet* would "be active in the good cause of Whigism [*sic*], and make stinging work with the whole troop of tories, loco focos, levellers, disorganizers, sham patriots and public plunderers, who, under the mask of democracy, have been cajoling, humbugging and cheating the honest yeomanry of the country." Only a single issue of this campaign newspaper is known to exist. Identified as volume 1, number 9, it was advertised for sale on eBay in January 2020; the successful bidder is unknown, and the notice has disappeared from the eBay website.

54. Outline of a lecture on patriotism at the lyceum, November 14, 1838, Ripley Family Papers, Notebook 1, Houghton; "Early Records of the Concord Lyceum," in Kenneth Walter Cameron, comp., *The Massachusetts Lyceum During the American Renaissance; Materials for the Study of the Oral Tradition in American Letters: Emerson, Thoreau, Hawthorne, and Other New-England Lecturers* (Hartford, Conn., 1969), 151.

55. Harry L. Watson, *Liberty and Power: The Politics of Jacksonian America*, rev. ed. (New York, 2006), 198–230; Shafer, *Carnival Campaign*, 77–83; Howe, *What Hath God Wrought*, 572–73.

56. For articles arguing against emigration to the West, see *YG*, November 29, 1834, April 30, June 11, 1836.

57. Not all the slogans were in harmony: Lexington revived its claim to be "the birthplace of American Liberty," while Acton boasted of being the home of "the first martyrs" in the fight. "We dispute any other right" to that distinction.

58. Gross, *Minutemen*, 130; *YG*, June 20 and 27, July 4 and 11, 1840; Shafer, *Carnival Campaign*, 23–24; Hosmer, *Remembrances of Concord and Thoreaus*, 72; Keyes, Autobiography, 70, 72; *CF*, July 17, 1840; Keyes, Diary, vol. 3, entry for July 4, 1840; Keyes, Autobiography, 69–70; John Brown, Jr., Private journal, September 1, 1839–July 8, 1843, entry for July 4, 1840, manuscript owned by the late Roger Brown, American University.

59. *PEJ* 1:149–50.

60. *R*, August 21, 1840; *YG*, June 6 and 20 ("the PEOPLE"), 1840. Older Whigs found it hard to adjust to the new expectations. In December 1839, upon returning from

the Harrisburg convention, Samuel Hoar appeared before a large meeting of Whigs in Faneuil Hall to explain why he had switched his vote from Clay to Harrison. Laboriously, he took his listeners through the steps by which "he had been induced to change his views from the conviction that by adhering to such a course, he would be but endangering the success of the cause we all had at heart." Whatever the reasonableness of that decision, the Concord gentleman did not win over the crowd. John Brown, Jr., then clerking for a Boston merchant, was disappointed by his townsman's presentation. "Mr. Hoar is out of his line in addressing promiscuous audiences, he is too deliberate, too serious to suit such appetites." Brown, Private journal, entry for December 13, 1839; *Boston Atlas*, December 14, 1839.

61. See the bulging file of applicants for the voters' list, November 7 and 9, 1840, ETR.

62. Keyes, Autobiography, 70, 72, 74; Formisano, *Transformation of Political Culture*, 264–67; Kurland, "'Political Progress,'" 27. In the runup to the election, Concord's Whigs participated in a massive rally held in Boston that dwarfed their "great Harrison" barbecue. In September as many as fifty thousand impassioned Whigs assembled on Boston Common and paraded across the Warren Bridge to Charlestown and up to the top of Bunker Hill. Amid the mass of humanity were the young Whigs of Concord, including John Shepard Keyes, pulling strenuously on drag ropes to keep the ball rolling to the pinnacle. *R*, September 4, 1840; Brown, Private journal, entry for September 10, 1840; Keyes, Autobiography, 70, 72, 74; Anthony Banning Norton, *The Great Revolution of 1840: Reminiscences of the Log Cabin and Hard Cider Campaign* (Mount Vernon, Ohio, and Dallas, Tex., 1888), 301, 304.

63. Richard P. McCormick, *The Second American Party System: Party Formation in the Jacksonian Era* (Chapel Hill, N.C., 1966), 41–49, 341–42. Turnout for the 1838 state elections had already reached a new high. The list of voters drawn up by the selectmen in March of that year recorded the names of 395 legal voters; in November 332 votes were cast for governor, for a participation rate of 84 percent. Two years later virtually every registered voter turned out. Concord was hardly unique; participation in the 1840 election broke all previous records in most of the country. Overall close to 80 percent of all eligible white men are estimated to have come out to vote. With a turnout of approximately two-thirds, Massachusetts lagged considerably behind. If those figures are correct, then Concord stood at the head of the class.

McCormick's *Second American Party System* is the standard source for figures on state-by-state voting in presidential elections. The author did not indicate how he came up with his estimates of eligible voters. Presumably, he took the population of white males reported by the federal census every ten years and estimated the proportion of men twenty-one and over. A parallel method is to take the number of polls (men 16 and over) enumerated by the assessors and to reduce that figure by the proportion aged twenty-one and above (.815). On that basis I estimate that 377 men were of legal voting age in 1840; the turnout rate was thus 94 percent (356/377). This is a much higher rate than Kurland calculated from her method of using the federal census and estimating therefrom the population of men twenty-one and over. Her figure is 70–71 percent. Kurland, "'Political Progress,'" 27.

64. *CF*, November 13, 1840. The Democrats won 195 votes for governor in 1840, compared to 187 in both 1838 and 1839; Whigs obtained 145 in 1838, slumped to 122 in 1839, then rebounded to 160 in 1840. In the face of the Whig sweep of the state, the Democratic margin—55 percent to 45 percent—was an impressive victory. The presidential contest was a little closer: 53 to 46 percent; and Parmenter received only 51.6 to Brooks's 48.4 percent.

65. Keyes, Autobiography, 74.

66. Hosmer, *Remembrances of Concord and Thoreaus*, 72; George Ward to Prudence Ward, July 29, [1840], Abernethy Collection, Middlebury College Library. The Thoreaus had previously rented houses owned by Daniel Shattuck, "a uniform and consistent whig," and by Josiah Davis, who moved from Concord to Boston by 1840, following his financial failure in the Panic. See Lemuel Shattuck, *Memorials of the Descendants of William Shattuck, the Progenitor of the Families in America That Have Born His Name* (Boston, 1855), 300–302.

67. "Proceedings of the Massachusetts Democratic Convention," *CF*, October 18, 1839.

68. *PEJ* 1:108.

69. [Orestes A. Brownson], Article IV, a review-essay of four pamphlets on politics and social reform, *Boston Quarterly Review* 2 (October 1839): 485–516.

70. Emerson, "Introductory" lecture to series "The Present Age," delivered December 4,1839, *EL* 3:187–88. Compare Brownson's statement that "philosophy, literature, art, religion . . . are enlisting in the service of the democracy." Brownson, Article IV, 486.

71. A critical Theodore Parker detected the influences on Emerson's "Present Age" series. The lectures were "splendid," he allowed, but derivative, consisting of "the 1/8 of Brownson, the 1/10 of Alcott, the 1/1,000,000 of Dwight, and the ½ of Miss Fuller." See Joan W. Goodwin, *The Remarkable Mrs. Ripley: The Life of Sarah Alden Bradford Ripley* (Boston, 1998), 174.

72. Emerson, "Introductory" lecture, *EL* 3:187–89, and "Politics," *EL* 3:242. Emerson turned this lecture into the piece "Politics" in *Essays: Second Series* (Boston, 1844), 235, for passages quoted in the text.

73. Ralph L. Rusk, *The Life of Ralph Waldo Emerson* (New York, 1949), 258–59; Goodwin, *Remarkable Mrs. Ripley*, 174. In the April 1840 issue of *Boston Quarterly Review*, Brownson adopted Emerson's wording and described the opposition between "the party of the past" and "the party of the future." See his review of Michel Chevalier's *Society, Manners, and Politics in the United States, Boston Quarterly Review* 3 (April 1840): 210. A search of America's Historical Newspapers (ProQuest) and of the AAS's Historical Periodicals Collection (EbscoHost) for the period October 1839 through December 1840 finds that only Brownson and Emerson used the terms "party of the past" and "party of the future." With good reason, Emerson could be suspected of seeking a patronage job in the Boston Custom House under Bancroft. On the tragedy that befell the steamship *Lexington* on the night of January 13, 1840, see John A. Buehrens, *Conflagration: How the Transcendentalists Sparked the American Struggle for Racial, Gender, and Social Justice* (Boston, 2020), 15–19. The explosion killed 150 passengers, including the Transcendentalist Karl Follen, a key figure in the transmission of German idealism to the United States, who was about to assume the pulpit of a new liberal congregation in East Lexington, Massachusetts.

74. *CF*, August 7, 1840; Emerson, *JMN* 7:395, 403. In "Man the Reformer," delivered several months after the presidential election, Emerson put the point differently. "The people do not wish to be represented or ruled by the ignorant and base. They only vote for these, because they were asked with the voice and semblance of kindness. They will not vote for them long." "Man the Reformer," Emerson, *Nature, Addresses, and Lectures*, ed. Robert E. Spiller and Alfred R. Ferguson (Cambridge, Mass., 1971), 158.

75. Ralph Waldo Emerson (Concord) to Lidian Emerson (Plymouth), November 10, 1840, in Ralph L. Rusk, ed., *The Letters of Ralph Waldo Emerson*, 6 vols. (New York, 1939), 2:358–59.

76. *PEJ* 1:164.

77. List of Voters in the Town of Concord as made out by the selectmen, February 17, 1840, and checklist of voters for town meeting, prepared by the selectmen, November 8, 1841, ETR; Walls, *Henry David Thoreau*, 118.

78. *PEJ* 1:353–54. Thoreau indited his scorn for political parties on the last day of 1841; seven months later the statement reappeared in his "Natural History of Massachusetts," *Dial* 3 (July 1842): 20.

14. *Famine in the Churches*

1. Entries for November 28, 1794 (Mary Moody Emerson), and July 6, 1828 (Edward Bliss Emerson), List of members admitted to full communion, April 19, 1776, to September 6, 1857, First Parish Church Record Book (transcript), CFPL; entries for payment of parish taxes for 1837 and 1838, Emerson Account Book 1836–38, Houghton (Joel Myerson transcription), 69–70, 98, and for rental of pew from Maj. James Barrett, October 1, 1835, to September 30, 1836 (paid on November 2, 1836), and same, October 1836 to September 1837 (paid on October 4, 1837), 29, 59; Edward W. Emerson, "Emerson in Concord," *SCM* 2:70; Ralph Waldo Emerson, "An Address Delivered before the Senior Class in Divinity College, Cambridge, Sunday Evening, 15 July, 1838," *EMP*, 118.

2. John Wood Sweet, "'Churches Gathered Out of Churches': The Divergence of Liberal and Orthodox Congregationalists in Concord, Massachusetts, 1800–1850" (senior honors thesis, Amherst College, 1988), 69–73. Starting in 1834, the assessors distinguished between polls (men sixteen and older) liable for town and county taxes and "ministerial polls," men in the same age group subject to the parish rate. In 1834, 430 out of 497 polls (86.5 percent) funded the First Parish Church.

3. *YG*, March 3, May 26, 1838; *Trumpet and Universalist Magazine*, October 7 and 21, November 25, December 2, 1837, April 28, May 19, June 2 and 16, 1838.

4. Sweet, "'Churches Gathered Out of Churches,'" 90–91; Edgar Wesley Tucker, "The Meeting Houses of the First Parish," in John Whittemore Teele, ed., *Meeting House on the Green: A History of the First Parish in Concord and Its Church* (Concord, Mass., 1986), 317–19; Keyes, Autobiography, 19–21; CTMM 8:70 (meeting of September 10, 1836), 118 (January 6, 1838), 186–91 (January 21, 1841), CFPL; Barzillai Frost, *The Church. A Discourse Delivered at the Dedication of the New Church of the First Parish in Concord, Mass., December 29, 1841* (Boston, 1842), 25.

5. In the period 1834–1838 the Unitarian congregation admitted twenty-one members in full communion, the Trinitarian forty-two; in both denominations, eight out of ten new communicants were female. First Parish Church Record Book (transcript), CFPL; *Minutes of the General Association of Massachusetts, at Their Meeting in Dorchester, June, 1833* (Boston, 1833), 38; *Minutes of the General Association of Massachusetts, at Their Meeting at Framingham, June, 1835* (Boston, 1835), 29; *Minutes of the General Association of Massachusetts, at Their Session in Westboro', June, 1841* (Boston, 1842), 16; *Forty-Fifth Annual Report of the Massachusetts Home Missionary Society, Presented by the Executive Committee, at the Anniversary Meeting in Boston, May 28, 1844* (Boston, 1844), 10. Between 1826 and 1833, the Trinitarian church admitted a median of 11.5 new members annually; the figure for the period 1834–1844 was 8. By 1840, total membership was 90, and it surged to 110 in 1842. Of the fifteen converts to the Trinitarian church in the great revival year of 1831, twelve moved away; of the twenty-two new members in 1842, a dozen emigrated. The Unitarian church took in fifty-five new members between 1834 and 1844: thirty-nine women, sixteen men. The Trinitarians enrolled eighty women out of ninety-five new communicants during the same period.

6. Sweet, "'Churches Gathered out of Churches,'" 73–79; E. R. Hoar, "Memoir

of Josiah Davis," *SCM* 2:98-101; *Fiftieth Annual Report of the Massachusetts Home Missionary Society, Presented by the Executive Committee, at the Anniversary Meeting in Boston, May 29, 1844* (Boston, 1849), 17-18.

7. Case of Mrs. R. Oliver, October 9 to December 6, 1840; report of committee on Mrs. Cash's case, November 12, 1847; case of George Hunstable, June 17 to July 11, 1834, Box 1, File on "grievances," and meeting of April 17, 1840, Second Congregational Church Records, 1826-67, CFPL.

8. *Trumpet and Universalist Magazine* 10 (October 7, 1837): 63; 10 (October 21, 1837): 71; 10 (November 25, 1837): 91; 10 (December 2, 1837): 95; 10 (April 28, 1838): 179; 10 (May 19, 1838): 191; 10 (June 2, 1838): 199; 10 (June 16, 1838): 207; [Ezra Ripley], "Recollections of an Aged Clergyman," *Unitarian Advocate* 3 (1831): 167. In 1843 a Trinitarian church committee was dismayed to learn that Mrs. Abel B. Heywood had withdrawn from communion and was attending a Universalist church, where "error is taught." Rather than excommunicate the apostate, the committee attributed her defection to mental illness: "She has in former times been disordered in intellect and is thought by some to be now suffering from that cause." See meetings of October 14, November 18, 1842, February 3, 1843, Second Congregational Church Records, 1826-67, CFPL.

9. Henry Steele Commager, "The Blasphemy of Abner Kneeland," *New England Quarterly* 8 (March 1935): 32, 35; Roderick S. French, "Liberation from Man and God in Boston: Abner Kneeland's Free-Thought Campaign, 1830-1839," *American Quarterly* 32 (Summer 1980): 202-21; Robert E. Burkholder, "Emerson, Kneeland, and the Divinity School Address," *American Literature* 58 (March 1986): 1-14; John D. Lawson, ed., *American State Trials: A Collection of the Important and Interesting Criminal Trials Which Have Taken Place in the United States from the Beginning of Our Government to the Present Day*, 17 vols. (St. Louis, 1914-1921), 13:575. Kneeland's conviction was appealed to the Massachusetts Supreme Court on March 8, 1836, and the judgment was reaffirmed by Chief Justice Lemuel Shaw on April 2, 1836. Neither the *Freeman* nor the *Yeoman's Gazette* (either in its Anti-Masonic or Whig phase) commented on the Kneeland case.

10. "The Aged Minister," *YG*, November 17, 1838; Ezra Ripley, outline of a lecture at the lyceum, November 14, 1838, on patriotism, Ripley Family Papers, Notebook 1, Houghton; "The Morality of the Sabbath," *Christian Register*, July 8, 1838; Ripley, "To the Friends of Education," May 1, 1838, in F. B. Sanborn, *Henry D. Thoreau* (Boston, 1882), 57-58; Ripley to Capt. Nathan Barrett, recommending Martha T. Meriam for a teaching position, February 22, 1838, Series I. Correspondence, 1805-1838, Folder 1, Ezra Ripley Papers, CFPL; letter from "R" about iron combs, *Christian Register*, January 21, 1838; *JMN* 5:503 (entry for May 22, 1838); Keyes, Diary, vol. 2, entry for January 27, 1839. For other accounts of Ripley in the press, see *Norfolk Advertiser*, June 16 ("Rev. Dr. Ripley"), September 22, 1838 ("An Aged Teacher"). These tributes were undoubtedly composed by Dedham editor Elbridge G. Robinson, the older brother (born in 1805) of William S. Robinson, printer and proprietor of the *Yeoman's Gazette* and then *The Republican* from 1838 through 1841.

11. Henry Frost, "Barzillai Frost," *SCM* 3:52-59; Dean Grodzins, *American Heretic: Theodore Parker and Transcendentalism* (Chapel Hill, N.C., 2002), 75-77; *Massachusetts Register and United States Calendar for 1834* (Boston, 1834), 142, and *for 1835*, 144; meetings of December 20, 1836, and January 3, 1837, CTMM 8:82-86, CFPL. Frost was just two years old when his father died, and he grew up in a household headed by an older brother with no sympathy for his educational aspirations. He married Elvira Stone of Framingham in June 1837, five months after his ordination.

12. Barzillai Frost, Sermon delivered on February 11, 1837, in First Parish, Concord Records, 1695-2014, Series 6, Ministers, visiting ministers, and sermons, 1735-2013, CFPL; Frost, *The Church. A Discourse*, 20-23.

13. Horace Elisha Scudder, *James Russell Lowell: A Biography*, 2 vols. (Boston, 1901), 1:48; Philip Graham, "Some Lowell Letters," *Texas Studies in Literature and Language* 3 (Winter 1962): 561; Frost, Sermon delivered February 11, 1837; Daniel Walker Howe, *The Unitarian Conscience: Harvard Moral Philosophy, 1805-1861* (Cambridge, Mass., 1970), 90-92.

14. Frost, Sermon delivered February 11, 1837; Howe, *Unitarian Conscience*, 134-35.

15. Joel Myerson, "Lowell on Emerson: A New Letter from Concord in 1838," *New England Quarterly* 44 (December 1971): 651; Graham, "Some Lowell Letters," 561-62.

16. Frost, "Barzillai Frost," 59; Keyes, Diary, vol. 2, entries for January 27, July 14, 1839, February 16, 1840; Keyes, Diary, vol. 3, entry for February 25, 1841; Keyes, Diary, vol. 4, entry for December 30, 1840; Keyes, Diary, vol. 5, entry for August 14, 1842; Myerson, "Lowell on Emerson," 651; Edward Everett Hale, *James Russell Lowell and His Friends* (Boston, 1899), 45. The Concord minister did not always disappoint his listeners. His sermon at the dedication of the meetinghouse won high praise from the younger Keyes. The pastor was "in his happiest mood and really outdid himself." Diary, vol. 4, entry for December 30, 1841.

17. Conrad Wright, "Emerson, Barzillai Frost, and the Divinity School Address," *Harvard Theological Review* 49 (January 1956): 19-23; *JMN* 5:326 (idealizes nothing"), 7:20-22 ("botanical precision," "foolishest preaching"). Emerson acquired an early "suspicion & dislike" of Ripley from his aunt, Mary Moody Emerson, who spurned her stepfather's rationalist approach to religion; in later years he came to rethink this bias and conclude that Ripley was "a worthy, honorable, & generous man." See *JMN* 16:175.

18. Emerson attended Frost's ordination but took no part in the ceremony. At one point during the day he sat next to Rev. Caleb Stetson, a fellow member of the Transcendentalist Club, whose witty commentary on the proceedings proved so amusing that Waldo was hard-pressed to maintain proper decorum. See *JMN* 5:285.

19. *JMN* 5:323 ("depth of the religious sentiment"), 324-25 ("ill dissemble," "mouth-filling," "capital secret"), 380 ("preached from his ears"), 463-64 ("go no more"), 481 ("grinds & grinds"). Emerson credited his Aunt Mary for showing him what genuine piety was like. Through the family stories she told and her own personal example he was exposed to "the influences of ancestral religion." *JMN* 5:323.

20. Ralph L. Rusk, ed., *The Letters of Ralph Waldo Emerson*, 6 vols. (New York, 1939), 2:147; Wright, "Emerson, Barzillai Frost, and the Divinity School Address," 27-31.

21. *JMN* 5:491 ("dead pond"), 499 (Sunday school teachers' meeting), 500-1(Frost on his pastoral calls), 502 ("wretched" preaching about resurrection), 7:21 ("bread of life"), 39 ("let the new generation"); George Moore, "The Diary of George Moore," in Kenneth Walter Cameron, comp., *Transcendental Epilogue: Primary Materials for Research in Emerson, Thoreau, Literary New England, the Influence of German Theology, and Higher Biblical Criticism*, 3 vols. (Hartford, Conn., 1965-1982), 1:203-4. The day after his conversation with Moore, Emerson remarked in his journal that "Realist seems the true name for the movement party among our scholars here." *JMN* 5:503.

22. William Ellery Channing and others, petition, Abner Kneeland Pardon File, 1838, Files of Inactive Pardons and Pardons Not Granted, 1785-2001 (GC3/series 771), MSA; *Salem Gazette*, June 1, 1838; *Liberator*, July 6, 1838; *JMN* 5:71 ("miserable

babble"), 7:41–42 ("shocks the religious ear"); Burkholder, "Emerson, Kneeland, and Divinity School Address," 1–14. In addition to the Transcendentalists named in the text, other participants in the club signing the pardon petition were Cyrus A. Bartol, George N. Briggs, John Sullivan Dwight, Charles Follen, Chandler Robbins, Caleb Stetson, and Jones Very. Other abolitionists among the signatories were Ellis Gray Loring, a founder of the New England Anti-Slavery Society, who actually composed the petition and set the campaign in motion; Francis Jackson; Samuel E. Sewall; Edmund Quincy; and Thomas Wentworth Higginson. Others in Emerson's circle endorsing the plea were his half-uncle (and Ezra Ripley's son) Rev. Samuel Ripley, and Gamaliel Bradford, to whose sister the Waltham minister was married. An antipardon petition, headed by former Boston mayor Samuel T. Armstrong, garnered 261 signatures. See Abner Kneeland Pardon File, 1838.

23. Ralph L. Rusk, *The Life of Ralph Waldo Emerson* (New York, 1949), 267–68; Conrad Wright, "Soul Is Good, but Body Is Good Too," *Journal of Unitarian and Universalist History* 37 (2013): 10. *General Catalogue of the Divinity School of Harvard University, 1915* (Cambridge, Mass., 1915), 52–53, lists seven graduates in the Class of 1838. Among them were George F. Simmons, the future son-in-law of Rev. Samuel Ripley and occasional resident of Concord, and Harrison Gray Otis Blake, who would become a close friend of Thoreau. See Samuel A. Eliot, ed., *Heralds of a Liberal Faith*, 4 vols. (Boston, 1910–1952), 2:173–74. The divinity school enrolled thirteen to fifteen students in the Classes of 1830 to 1835 (with the exception of just ten in 1834), then declined to ten in 1836, nine in 1837, eight in 1838, a brief resurgence to eleven in 1839, then a return to the downward course of seven in 1840 and six in 1841. Enrollment waxed and waned over subsequent years. See *General Catalogue*.

24. Emerson, "The Eye and the Ear," lecture given December 27, 1837, as the fourth in the "Human Culture" series, *EL* 2:274.

25. Wright, "Emerson, Barzillai Frost, and the Divinity School Address," 30–37; William R. Hutchison, *The Transcendentalist Ministers: Church Reform in the New England Renaissance* (New Haven, Conn., 1959), 55–68; Philip F. Gura, *American Transcendentalism: A History* (New York, 2007), 98–106; Emerson, "An Address Delivered before the Senior Class in Divinity College, Cambridge," *EMP*, 111, 115, 119, 121; *JMN* 5:324–25, 463–64.

26. Andrews Norton, "The New School in Literature and Religion," reprinted from *Boston Daily Advertiser*, August 27, 1838, in Lawrence Buell, ed., *The American Transcendentalists: Essential Writings* (New York, 2006), 146–49; Gura, *American Transcendentalism*, 106–22; Hutchison, *Transcendentalist Ministers*, 68–97; Wright, "Soul Is Good," 10–12, 15–18; French, "Liberation from Man and God," 220–21; *JMN* 7:20–22.

27. Moore, "Diary," 1:224–25.

28. Graham, "Some Lowell Letters," 561, 564; Myerson, "Lowell on Emerson," 650; Scudder, *James Russell Lowell*, 57–60.

29. Edward W. Emerson, "Emerson in Concord," *SCM* 2:66, 70–72; Rusk, *Life of Emerson*, 270–73; Keyes, Diary, vol. 2, entry for January 20, 1839; Phyllis Cole, *Mary Moody Emerson and the Origins of Transcendentalism: A Family History* (New York 1998), 201–6, 253–54; James B. Thayer, *Rev. Samuel Ripley* (n.p., ca. 1897), 45–47. Mary Emerson accused Samuel Ripley's wife Sarah of "infecting" Waldo with "infidelity" and faulted her and Lidian for doing nothing to stop the publication of his essay "Self-Reliance," that "strange medly [sic] of atheism and false independence." See Joan W. Goodwin, *The Remarkable Mrs. Ripley: The Life of Sarah Alden Bradford Ripley* (Boston, 1998), 181.

30. By the late 1830s, Universalism had spread beyond its original home on the northern margins of New England and in a scattering of Massachusetts towns and had planted churches in the heart of the Commonwealth. From a mere 20 in 1820, the denomination grew to over 130 two decades later. Concord's congregation was established near the close of this wave of expansion. It was one of twenty-six such bodies in Middlesex, second only to Worcester's twenty-nine. See William G. McLoughlin, *New England Dissent, 1630–1833: The Baptists and the Separation of Church and State*, 2 vols. (Cambridge, Mass., 1971), 2:1234; Ronald P. Formisano, *The Transformation of Political Culture: Massachusetts Parties, 1790s-1840s* (New York, 1983), 292. The *Massachusetts Register* for 1840 furnishes a roster of Universalist churches in the Commonwealth. Middlesex had 18, plus 8 without a settled minister; Essex 17, with an additional 4; Worcester 16, with another 13 lacking ministers. Universalist congregations were rare in western Massachusetts: three in Berkshire, plus one without a minister; none in Hampshire; three in Franklin, plus three without ministers; and two in Hampden County. For the rural origins of Universalism in the post-Revolutionary backcountry, see Stephen A. Marini, *Radical Sects of Revolutionary New England* (Cambridge, Mass., 1982) and his further reflections in "The Origins of New England Universalism: Daughter of the New Light," *Journal of Unitarian Universalist History* 24 (1997): 64–75. Historians of Universalism stress its eighteenth-century origins in evangelical fervor and social disorder spawned by the Great Awakening. Concord's mid-nineteenth-century Universalists, by contrast, were defectors from the liberal preaching of Ripley and Frost.

31. *Trumpet and Universalist Magazine* 11 (January 12, 1839): 119; List of subscribers, Records of the First Universalist Society in Concord, begun December 1838 by James Giles, CFPL; petition from members of the First Parish for a new meetinghouse, December 23, 1837, ETR; meeting of February 3, 1843, Second Congregational Church Records, 1826–67, CFPL. Seventy-three men put their names on an agreement creating "the First Universalist Society in Concord." It begins at the end of December 1838 and adds names without indicating the date of subscription. A dozen of the men did not live in Concord until after 1840. The remaining sixty-one can be treated as the original founders of the society from 1838 to October 1, 1840. A dozen of them had signed a petition just the year before calling on the town to build a new meetinghouse. In October 1840, when the society dedicated its new meetinghouse, eighty communicants from Concord and vicinity were present, according to the *Universalist Palladium* (October 24, 1840). The estimated sixty-one founders of the Universalist Society represent 52 percent of the 116 polls lost by the First Parish between 1837 and 1839.

32. Moore, "Diary," 310–12; "Report of Ezra Ripley and Barzillai Frost and Deacons Reuben Brown, Nehemiah Ball, and Elisha Tolman, Adopted unanimously March 4, 1841," in Teele, *Meeting House on the Green*, 236–43, reprinted from First Parish Church Record Book (transcript), CFPL. In 1839 only a third of polls (151/462) was assessed for the First Parish rate. That figure rose to 35 percent (175/494) in 1841, perhaps as a result of the elimination of the covenant, only to resume the downward slide the next year; by 1845, just 27 percent of polls (129/469) supported the First Parish.

33. Harriet H. Robinson, ed., *"Warrington" Pen Portraits: A Collection of Personal and Political Reminiscences from 1848 to 1876, from the Writings of William S. Robinson* (Boston, 1877), 15–20, 49–50; Emerson, "An Address," *EMP*, 125; *R*, July 24, 1840; Robert A. Gross, "'That Terrible Thoreau': Concord and Its Hermit," in *A Historical Guide to Henry David Thoreau*, ed. William E. Cain (New York, 2000), 221–25.

34. Jane Hallett Prichard (Boston) to Frances J. H. Prichard (Concord), March 8, 1836, Box 5, Folder 1, and Frances J. T. Prichard (Concord) to Mrs. Jane T. Prichard (New York), August 22, 1841, Box 7, Folder 1, and March 1844, Box 2, Folder 4, all in Hoar, Prichard, and Related Family Papers, CFPL; Emerson, "Self-Reliance," *EMP*, 135.

35. John Thoreau, Jr. (Concord) to George Sewall (Scituate), December 31, 1839, Sewall Family Collection, Huntington Library, San Marino, Calif.; Stephen Nissenbaum, *The Battle for Christmas* (New York, 1996), 45–47. It is possible that the Christmas celebrations the Thoreau family observed took place in the years 1817–1819, when a campaign was conducted in Boston to promote religious services and a suspension of business on December 25. But John Thoreau's recollection includes details, such as Santa's provision of sugar plums to good boys and girls, that come from Clement Clark Moore's December 1823 poem "The Night Before Christmas." His reminiscence attests to the development of the commercial, child-centered holiday that took shape in the 1820s and 1830s.

36. *PEJ* 1:51, 55; Thoreau to "Mr. Clerk," January 6, 1841, Box IV.6, Folder 1: Membership requests and withdrawals, 1840–48, First Parish Church Records, CFPL; Joel Myerson, "Barzillai Frost's Funeral Sermon on the Death of John Thoreau, Jr.," *Huntington Library Quarterly* 57 (Autumn 1994): 373; Henry D. Thoreau, "Resistance to Civil Government," in Wendell Glick, ed., *Reform Papers* (Princeton, N.J., 1973), 78.

37. Thoreau (Concord) to Isaiah Thornton Williams (Buffalo), October 8, 1841, in Robert N. Hudspeth, ed., *The Correspondence of Henry D. Thoreau*, vol. 1, *1834–1848* (Princeton, N.J., 2013), 88–90.

38. Ezra Ripley, "Anniversary sermon sixty years," November 1838, Ezra Ripley Sermons, bMS 64/3, HDS. Barzillai Frost was more willing to take on the critics in the Unitarian house. In July 1840 the parson surprised John Shepard Keyes by "preaching right at the prevailing doctrines and humbugs of the day such as Abolitionism, Emersonianism, &c." He was "quite alive to the importance of his sermon and quite animated for him." See Keyes, Diary, vol. 3, entry for July 19, 1840.

39. H. W. Ripley, comp., *Genealogy of a Part of the Ripley Family* (Newark, N.J., 1867), 32–33; Octavius Brooks Frothingham, *George Ripley* (Boston, 1882), 6–7; James W. Mathews, "George Partridge Bradford: Friend of Transcendentalists," *Studies in the American Renaissance* (1981): 133–56; Goodwin, *Remarkable Mrs. Ripley*, 84–87. Following her marriage to Samuel Ripley in October 1818, Sarah Alden Bradford moved to Lincoln with her husband; younger brother George came with her. He thus would have been living in Lincoln in June 1819, when George Ripley came to study. In July 1838 George Bradford was in the audience for Emerson's divinity school address, to which he listened with mixed feelings. "George says his intellect approves the doctrine of the Cambridge Address," Emerson noted in his journal, "but his affections do not." *JMN* 7:64.

40. F. B. Sanborn, *Henry D. Thoreau*, rev. ed. (Boston, 1882), 81, 143–46; John Weiss, *Life and Correspondence of Theodore Parker*, 2 vols. (New York, 1864), 1:125; Carol Johnson, "The Journals of Theodore Parker: July–December 1840" (Ph.D. diss., University of South Carolina, 1980), 34. In a different incident related by Sanborn, Emerson once took Bronson Alcott to meet Ripley at the Manse. The parson advised his guest to beware of "his brilliant young kinsman, who was not quite sound in the faith" and who might lead him into a "sect of his [Ripley's] own naming, called 'Egomites' (from *ego* and *mitto*), who 'sent themselves' on the Lord's errands without any due call thereto." Sanborn, *Henry Thoreau*, 80.

41. [Barzillai Frost], "A Venerable Minister," *R*, May 7, 1841; *Two Sermons on the Death of Rev. Ezra Ripley, D.D.: One Preached at the Funeral by Rev. Barzillai Frost, of Concord,*

the Other on the Following Sabbath by Rev. Convers Francis (Boston, 1841), 19–20; *CF* and *R*, both on September 24, 1841. At his fiftieth anniversary in the pulpit, Ripley estimated that he had written some 2,500 sermons. By 1842, when Nathaniel and Sophia Hawthorne settled into the "Old" Manse, that number was approaching three thousand. A comparison between the *Republican*'s May 1841 account of Ripley's farewell sermon and the memorials delivered at his funeral makes plain that Barzillai Frost was the author of the newspaper report.

42. Ralph Waldo Emerson to Mary Moody Emerson and to William Emerson, both on September 21, 1841, in Rusk, *Letters of Ralph Waldo Emerson*, 2:450–53; "The Late Rev. Dr. Ripley," *R*, October 1, 1841. Emerson's memorial of Ripley was appended to *Two Sermons on the Death of Rev. Ezra Ripley, D.D.*, 41–43.

43. "Rev. Dr. Ripley," *Christian Register and Boston Observer* 20 (October 9, 1841): 163; Robert A. Gross, "Doctor Ripley's Church: Congregational Life in Concord, Massachusetts, 1778–1841," *Journal of Unitarian Universalist History* 33 (2009–10): 1–3. The theological debate over the character of Jesus—his divinity and his prophetic words and mission—was at a new fervor in the fall of 1841, following Theodore Parker's *Discourse on the Transient and Permanent in Christianity* in June of that year. Two weeks after Ripley was laid to rest, Parker inaugurated a series of five lectures on religion at the Masonic Temple. See Grodzins, *American Heretic*, 248–67.

15. The Spirit of Reform

1. *CF*, September 2, 9, and 16, 1837; *YG*, September 2, 1837; Timothy Prescott, Diary, entries for September 4–8, 1837, Houghton; Prudence Ward (Concord) to Caroline Sewall (Scituate), September 25, 1837, Prudence Ward and Anne J. Ward Correspondence, Huntington Library, San Marino, Calif.; Lydia Jackson Emerson (Concord) to Sophia Brown (Stow), September 9, 1837, in Delores Bird Carpenter, ed., *The Selected Letters of Lidian Jackson Emerson* (Columbia, Mo., 1987), 60–61; Gerda Lerner, *The Grimké Sisters from South Carolina: Rebels Against Slavery* (Boston, 1967), 183–204.

2. Notice for "Anti-Slavery Meeting" and letter by "Z," *CF*, September 2, 1837; *YG*, September 9, 1837; *CF*, September 30, 1837; *Minutes of the General Association of Massachusetts, at Their Meeting at North Brookfield, June 26, 1837* (Boston, 1837), 10, 12, 19–22. The "Quaker argument" gave the American Anti-Slavery Society (AASS) a pretext to deny that it was encouraging the Grimké sisters to lecture to mixed audiences of men and women in public. In actuality, Angelina and Sarah had been trained as its first female agents. See Lerner, *Grimké Sisters*, 197–200.

3. "Legal Disabilities," *New England Spectator* 151 (October 4, 1837): 153; Sarah M. Grimké, *Letters on the Equality of the Sexes, and the Condition of Woman: Addressed to Mary S. Parker* (Boston, 1838), 74–83; Larry Ceplair, ed., *The Public Years of Sarah and Angelina Grimké: Selected Writings 1835–1839* (New York, 1989), 135–41, 231–37. Based on its dateline, Letter 12 was evidently composed in Mary and Nathan Brooks's Concord home, perhaps with the aid of her lawyer host's multivolume set of William Blackstone's *Commentaries on the Laws of England*, from which Grimké extracted numerous quotations. At the same time as Sarah's fifteen pieces were appearing in the *New England Spectator*, Angelina was answering Catherine Beecher's criticisms of female abolitionism in thirteen columns published in the *Liberator*, the *Emancipator*, and the *Friend of Man* from late June to December 1837. Ceplair, *Public Years*, 146.

4. "List of anti-slavery societies," *Sixth Annual Report of the Board of Managers of the Massachusetts Anti-Slavery Society Presented January 24, 1838* (Boston, 1838), xxxviii–xlv. A

survey sponsored by the MASS recorded 215 groups in existence as of mid-January 1838. The founding year was given for 132; of these two dated from 1832, 5 from 1833, 21 from 1834, 18 from 1835, 28 from 1836, 48 from 1837, and 9 from 1838. Well over half (57 percent) were inaugurated through 1836. Applying this proportion to the 83 chapters whose founding year is unknown yields an additional 47 started before 1837 for a total of 122.

5. The Grimké sisters began their Massachusetts antislavery mission in late May 1837. Their first speaking engagements were in the Boston area, after which they expanded into Essex County. Then in August they barnstormed in Middlesex County. The sisters had already spoken to "full houses" in Groton, Littleton, Boxboro, and Harvard before coming to Concord, which then served as a base for expeditions to Acton and Lowell. I am presuming that the tour in Middlesex County was facilitated by members of the MCASS. See *Liberator*, July 25, 1837; Lerner, *Grimké Sisters*, 183–204.

6. The other Concord members of the MCASS by 1837 were Dr. Josiah Bartlett, the farmer Samuel Barrett, and the merchant Charles B. Davis. See list of subscribers to constitution following the date of July 22, 1836, MCASS Record Book, 1834–51, CFPL.

7. *CF*, July 16, 1836, August 26, September 2 and 16, November 11, 1837; *YG*, August 12 and 26, 1837. *The Liberator* reported on January 23, 1836, that a "Concord A[nti-] S[lavery] S[ociety]" had sent two delegates to the fourth anniversary meeting of MASS in Boston. They were Gourgas and Wilder, both from the Trinitarian parish. Apart from this one mention, the group left no other trace of its existence. In mid-April 1837 the Trinitarian meetinghouse was also the venue for a talk by AASS agent Henry B. Stanton, "the able and eloquent defender of the slave." *CF*, April 15, 1837.

8. *CF*, September 23, 1837; *YG*, September 23, 1837; Ward to Sewall, September 25, 1837; James Elliot Cabot, *A Memoir of Ralph Waldo Emerson*, 2 vols. (Boston, 1888), 2:425–26, 733; *JMN* 5:281–82; 12:151–57; Len Gougeon, "Abolition, the Emersons, and 1837," *New England Quarterly* 54 (September 1981): 345–64; Sandra Harbert Petrulionis, *To Set This World Right: The Antislavery Movement in Thoreau's Concord* (Ithaca, N.Y., 2006), 17–19. My account of Emerson's 1837 speech and its impact differs from Gougeon's. Cabot, *Memoir of Emerson*, dates the speech about slavery to a Tuesday in November 1837; this was evidently what Emerson wrote on the manuscript, now lost. The only speech Emerson was advertised to give on the subject in Concord during the fall and early winter of 1837 was scheduled for Monday, September 25. It was actually presented the next evening, as Ward's letter indicates. No evidence documents an antislavery meeting in November 1837 at which Emerson spoke. Gougeon builds on Cabot's account and argues that Emerson was spurred by the early November 1837 murder of abolitionist Elijah Lovejoy to speak out in defense of free speech. But Emerson does not allude to that episode in the extant text. His concern to sustain free discussion of slavery and abolition is not tied to any specific event. Emerson did not need the outrage in Alton to speak out. In 1835–1837 there were numerous attempts to silence antislavery activists—the Gag Rule, interference with the mails, mob assaults, and exclusion of abolitionist speakers from churches and lyceums. For these reasons, I conclude that at the September 25 citizens' meeting, Emerson played a key part in discouraging the formation of an antislavery association.

9. "List of Anti-Slavery Societies in Massachusetts," *Liberator*, April 20, 1838; "Annual Report of the Concord Female A.S. Society," *Liberator*, June 23, 1843; Gerda Lerner,

"The Political Activities of Antislavery Women," in Lerner, *The Majority Finds Its Past: Placing Women in History* (New York, 1979), 123; Petrulionis, *To Set This World Right*. Of the 215 antislavery societies active in 1838, 38 were "female" associations, 8 juvenile female associations, and 1 a ladies' association.

10. "List of Anti-Slavery Societies in Massachusetts"; "Annual Report of the Concord Female A.S. Society," *Liberator*, June 23, 1843; Lerner, "Political Activities of Anti-slavery Women," 123; Petrulionis, *To Set This World Right*.

11. Of the sixty-three members of the CFASS, twenty-three (36 percent) had connections to the CFCS, fifteen to the Ladies' Sewing Society, and twenty-eight were not on the books of either charitable group. By contrast, Anne Boylan observes that "only an occasional woman . . . with experience serving in a benevolent organization became active in the new reform groups that emerged" in the 1830s. Boylan, *The Origins of Women's Activism: New York and Boston, 1797–1840* (Chapel Hill, N.C., 2002), 44. See also Mary B. Fuhrer, *A Crisis of Community: The Trials and Transformation of a New England Town, 1815–1848* (Chapel Hill, N.C., 2014), 223–33. Only a minority of charitable women in Concord joined the antislavery society. Of 52 current members of the CFCS in 1838, a little over a quarter (14) joined the CFASS; the remaining three-quarters (38) stayed aloof.

12. No list of the original members of the CFASS in 1837–1838 is extant. I estimate the original membership as follows. In the winters of 1838 and 1839, 326 women in Concord circulated and signed three petitions to Congress on issues involving slavery (opposition to slavery and the slave trade in the District of Columbia and to the annexation of Texas). I hypothesize that only the most committed antislavery activists signed all three, but it turned out that sixty-three women did so—just two more than the reported membership of the CFASS in the January 1838 report of the MCASS. In June 1843 Mary Brooks recalled that the CFASS had seventy members at its start. *Liberator*, June 23, 1843. I supplemented the numbers with a few individuals—Susan Garrison, Lidian Emerson—known from other evidence to have been members. Using the sixty-three petitioners as a proxy for the original CFASS membership, I found that the mean age of these subscribers was forty-two, the median thirty-eight—exactly the same ages as were the founders of the CFCS in 1814. Sixteen (21 percent) were in their teens and twenties, fifteen (25 percent) in their thirties, and six (10 percent) in their forties. This group was a little older than the members of the Boylston Female Antislavery Society. See Mary B. Fuhrer, "'We have all something to do in the cause of freeing the slave': The Abolition Work of Mary White," in Peter Benes, ed., *Women's Work in New England, 1620–1920* (Boston, 2001), 114; Fuhrer, *Crisis of Community*, 313n28.

13. Over half the members of the female antislavery society were married, more than a quarter single, the rest widows. In 1837 five members of the Social Circle had wives and/or daughters in the CFASS: Nathan Brooks (Mary and Caroline), William Munroe (Martha and daughter Martha S.), Alvan Pratt (Sarah), Cyrus Warren (Nancy), William Whiting (Anna Maria and Louisa Jane). From 1814 to 1834, nearly every married man in the circle was united in wedlock to a woman in the charitable society. On the history of slaveholding in the family of Cynthia Dunbar Thoreau's grandfather, Col. Elisha Jones of Weston, see Doris Whipple Jones-Baker, "Colonel Elisha Jones of Weston and the Crisis of Colonial Government in Massachusetts 1773–1776" (Ph.D. thesis, University College, University of London, 1978), 310–18, and the advertisement for the capture of a runaway slave that was placed in the *Connecticut Courant*, May 8, 1775, by Elisha Jones, Jr., who had relocated to the western Massachusetts frontier town of Pittsfield, in which his father had been a prominent

investor. See Grace Greylock Niles, *The Hoosac Valley: Its Legends and Its History* (New York, 1912), 187–93.

14. Of the charter members of the CFASS, more than eight out of ten affiliated with the Unitarian or Trinitarian church. (Just one joined the Universalists.) Trinitarians outnumbered liberals 28 to 23. Reflecting the close split, the founding president was Mary Wilder, the Trinitarian pastor's thirty-five-year-old wife; the secretary was seventeen-year-old Caroline D. Brooks, who joined her parents, Nathan and Mary, in the family pew at Doctor Ripley's church.

15. Mary Merrick (Concord) to Maria Parker (Billerica), November 1820, Brooks Family Papers, CFPL; Covenant of First Parish Church (Concord), August 31, 1832, First Parish Church Records, CFPL; Priscilla Rice Edes, *Some Reminiscences of Old Concord* (Gouverneur, N.Y., 1903). Brooks served as secretary of the Concord Female Charitable Society from 1824 through 1827, vice-president in 1834, and treasurer from 1835 through 1847.

16. George M. Brooks (Cambridge) to Mrs. Mary M. Brooks (Concord), March 1, 1844, Brooks Family Papers, CFPL; J. S. Keyes, "George Merrick Brooks," *SCM* 3:219–39; Sandra Harbert Petrulionis, "Selective Sympathy: The Public and Private Mary Merrick Brooks," *Thoreau Society Bulletin* no. 226 (Winter 1999): 1–3, 5.

17. Inventory of the estate of Tilly Merrick, late of Brookfield, August 11, 1732, case no. 41121, Worcester County Probate File Papers, 1731–1881, NEHGS database; inventory of the estate of Tilly Merrick, late of Concord, April 26, 1768, case no. 15123, Middlesex County Probate File Papers, 1648–1871, NEHGS database; Josiah Bartlett, "Duncan Ingraham," *SCM* 1:127–30; Elise Lemire, *Black Walden: Slavery and Its Aftermath in Concord, Massachusetts* (Philadelphia, 2009), 110–11, 148–49; Robert A. Gross, "Helen Thoreau's Antislavery Scrapbook," *Yale Review* 100, no. 1 (January 2012): 105; Middlesex County Anti-Slavery Society Record Book, 1834–51, list of subscribers to constitution following the date of July 22, 1836, CFPL. Tilly Merrick died at eighty-one on June 8, 1836.

18. Edes, *Some Reminiscences*; Mary M. Brooks (Boston) to Nathan Brooks (Boston), February 10, 1833, Nathan Brooks Papers, 1830–38 Letters, 1832–33 file, CFPL; Ann W. Weston (Boston) to Deborah Weston (Weymouth), September 16, 1841, Ms. A.9.2.15, 67, BPL; Leslie Perrin Wilson, "Mrs. Woodward Hudson's Memoir of Mrs. Ebenezer Rockwood Hoar," *Concord Saunterer*, n.s., 9 (2001): 97–99; Harriet H. Robinson, ed., *"Warrington" Pen Portraits: A Collection of Personal and Political Reminiscences from 1848 to 1876, from the Writings of William S. Robinson* (Boston, 1877), 73–74; "Annual Report of the Concord Female A.S. Society," *Liberator*, June 23, 1843. (Brooks was secretary of the group that year, and it was her responsibility to compose and submit the report.) Her recipe for two loaves of cake has been preserved for posterity. Use "one pound flour, one pound sugar, half-pound butter, four eggs, one cup milk, one teaspoonful [baking] soda, half-teaspoonful cream of tartar, [and] half-pound currants (in half of it)." Robinson, *"Warrington" Pen Portraits*, 73–74. On Brooks as a pious young woman, see Chapter 2.

19. Caroline D. Brooks (Philadelphia) to Lizzy Prichard (Boston), May 13, 1838, in Wilson, "Mrs. Hudson's Memoir of Mrs. Hoar," 99–100; *Proceedings of the Anti-Slavery Convention of American Women, Held in Philadelphia. May 15th, 16th, 17th and 18th, 1838* (Philadelphia, 1838), 12; Manisha Sinha, *The Slave's Cause: A History of Abolition* (New Haven, Conn., 2016), 282–84; Beverly C. Tomek, *Pennsylvania Hall: A "Legal Lynching" in the Shadow of the Liberty Bell* (New York, 2013).

20. Gilbert Hobbs Barnes, *The Anti-Slavery Impulse, 1830–1844* (New York, 1964), 130–45, quotations at 136, 144; *CF*, January 28 ("trampling," "usurpation"), August 19,

1837; "Petitions! Petitions!" *Liberator*, June 23, 1837; William Lee Miller, *Arguing About Slavery: The Great Battle in the United States Congress* (New York, 1996), 27–33, 108, 277–79, 305–6; Julie Roy Jeffrey, *The Great Silent Army of Abolitionism: Ordinary Women in the Antislavery Movement* (Chapel Hill, N.C., 1998), 87–88; Beth A. Salerno, *Sister Societies: Women's Antislavery Organizations in Antebellum America* (DeKalb, Ill., 2005), chap. 3.

21. Female subscribers to the petitions made up more than half (56 percent) of the adult women in town. By contrast, the 130 male signers represented a fifth of all men over age twenty and a third of legal voters.

22. Catherine E. Beecher, *An Essay on Slavery and Abolitionism, With Reference to the Duty of American Females* (Boston, 1837), 105; Mary F. W. Wilder and 192 others of Concord, Massachusetts, petition for the abolition of slavery in the District of Columbia and of the slave trade in the United States, submitted February 13, 1838, Senate Petitions and Memorials on Slavery, Tabled (25A-H5: Tray 2), 25th Congress, 2nd sess., Record Group 46, National Archives. There were 123 men and 313 women who subscribed to anti-Texas petitions; 70 men and 306 women urged an end to slavery and the slave trade in the capital city. I estimate the participation rates in the petition campaigns by the following method. First, the population of Concord, according to the 1837 state census, was 2,017; the number of male polls—taxable males ages sixteen and over—was simultaneously reported to be 486. The ratio of male signers of the anti–Texas annexation petition is 120/486 or 25 percent. An alternative estimate was derived from the 1850 federal census of Concord, which shows the distribution of the population by age and sex. In 1850 males over twenty accounted for 29.6 percent of the population, females over twenty for 30.2 percent. I applied these proportions to the total population in 1837 to produce estimates of 598 adult men and 611 adult women in 1837. The results are as follows: 130 out of 598 men or 22 percent signed one of the three petitions in 1837–1838; 340 out of 611 women or 56 percent signed one of the four petitions submitted in 1837–1838. The selectmen registered 395 voters in 1838, one-third of whom signed a petition.

23. The opposing emphases of the petitions are all the more noteworthy, since the men's declaration against annexation was headed by the "venerable" Ripley, followed by his rival Wilder and by his assistant Frost farther down the column of names; the women's by the Trinitarian minister's wife and CFASS president Brooks. Despite the ministerial leadership, the men's memorial was secular in its argument, the women's religious.

24. *YG*, August 12 and 26, 1837; *Boston Courier*, October 5, 1837; Joel H. Silbey, *Storm over Texas: The Annexation Controversy and the Road to Civil War* (New York, 2005), 6–27; Mary W. F. Wilder and a number of other women of Concord, petition against the annexation of Texas to the United States, submitted February 12, 1838, Senate Petitions and Memorials on Annexation of Texas (25A-G1: Tray 2), 25th Congress, 2nd sess., Record Group 46, National Archives; Ezra Ripley and 127 others of Concord, Massachusetts, petition against the annexation of Texas into the Union, Petitions and Memorials of the House of Representatives: Annexation of Texas (25A-H1.1), 25th Congress, 1st sess., Record Group 233, National Archives; "Annual Report of the Concord Female A.S. Society," prepared by the secretary Mary M. Brooks, *Liberator*, June 23, 1843; Deborah Bingham van Broekhoven, "'Let Your Names Be Enrolled': Method and Ideology in Women's Antislavery Petitioning," in Jean Fagan Yellin and John C. van Horne, eds., *The Abolitionist Sisterhood: Women's Political Culture in Antebellum America* (Ithaca, N.Y., 1994), 182–83. At least a third of female petitioners against slavery and the slave trade in federal territory were related

to others on the memorials, a proportion similar to that on petitions from up-state New York and rural Ohio. Lerner, "Political Activities of Antislavery Women," 126–27; Judith Wellman, *Grass Roots Reform in the Burned-Over District of Upstate New York* (New York, 2000), 194–95, which estimates that 54 percent of adult women in Paris, N.Y., signed petitions in 1837, almost exactly the same figure as in Concord. Of the 190 households in which I could group signers of the two antislavery petitions of 1837–1838, 32 had two or more members, and they accounted for 80 signers out of a total 238; hence, my estimate of one-third of signers having a close relative on the petitions. This estimate omits the pairs of aunts and nieces, mothers and daughters-in-law, and mothers and daughters in separate households I know to be on these lists.

25. Cynthia D. Thoreau and other women of Concord, petition praying for the abolition of slavery and the slave trade in the District of Columbia and the territories of the United States, submitted January 7, 1839, Library of Congress Collection of Records of the House of Representatives: Massachusetts Anti-slavery Petitions (25A-H1.8: N.A. Box 33 of L.C. Box 122, Folder 2), 25th Congress, 3rd sess., Record Group 233, National Archives.

26. The "petition of Ezra Ripley and 127 others of Concord, Massachusetts, against the annexation of Texas into the Union" actually has only 123 subscribers. D. H. Thoreau ranks eighth on the list, his brother John ninth, his father tenth.

27. *JMN* 5:437 (entry for November 24, 1837), 470 (entry for March 27, 1838); Emerson, "Self-Reliance," *EMP*, 130. Emerson took his private eruption at Woodbury's intrusive moralism and reworked it for "Self-Reliance," changing the Acton minister's source of distressing news from Montserrat to "Barbadoes."

28. "The Plunder of the Cherokees," first published in *Boston Atlas*, reprinted in the *Liberator*, April 6, 1838; Daniel Walker Howe, *What Hath God Wrought: The Transformation of America, 1815–1848* (New York, 2007), 415–23; Theda Perdue and Michael D. Green, *The Cherokee Nation and the Trail of Tears* (New York, 2007), 69–115.

29. Prudence Ward (Concord) to Prudence Bird Ward (Scituate), April 13, 1838, and Prudence Ward (Concord) to Dennis Ward (Spencer), May 2, 1838, Abernethy Collection, Middlebury College Library; Lydia Jackson Emerson (Concord) to Lucy Jackson Brown (Plymouth), April 23, 1838, in Carpenter, *Selected Letters*, 74–75; Lerner, *Grimké Sisters*, 230–38.

30. Ralph Waldo Emerson (Boston) to Edward Bliss Emerson (Santa Cruz, Puerto Rico), January 24, 26, and 29, 1831, and to Charles Chauncy Emerson (Cambridge), March 5, 1832, in Rusk, *Letters of Emerson*, 1:316, 345–46; Nancy Craig Simmons, ed., *The Selected Letters of Mary Moody Emerson* (Athens, Ga., 1993), 302n4; Ronald A. Bosco and Joel Myerson, *The Emerson Brothers: A Fraternal Biography in Letters* (New York, 2006), 132–33; Susan L. Roberson, "Reform and the Interior Landscape: Mapping Emerson's Political Sermons," in T. Gregory Garvey, ed., *The Emerson Dilemma: Essays on Emerson and Social Reform* (Athens, Ga., 2001), 11–12.

31. *YG*, April 21 and 28, 1838; *CF*, April 28, 1838; A number of citizens of Concord, Mass.: a memorial praying that the treaty made with the Cherokees at New Echota, may not be enforced, May 28, laid on the table, Senate 25A-H6, Petitions and Memorials Tabled, Treaty with Cherokee Indians, Tray 1 of 1; Mary W. F. Wilder and 202 other women of Concord, memorial praying that the treaty made with the Cherokees at New Echota may not be enforced; Hannah Hunstable and 107 other women of Concord, memorial to the same end, Senate Petitions and Memorials, Tabled, Regarding treaty with Cherokee Indians (25A-G21), 25th

Congress, 2nd sess., Record Group 46, National Archives; *Journal of the United States House of Representatives* 32:720–21, 912, 986, 1027; *Journal of the United States Senate* 28:393 (recording receipt of three memorials from citizens of Concord, Massachusetts).

32. Since Concord was represented in Congress by Democrat William Parmenter, Emerson dispatched his communication to the Whig member from Cape Cod, John Reed, Jr. See Emerson (Concord) to John Reed (Washington), April 25, 1838, in Rusk, *Letters of Emerson*, 2:127; "John Reed (1781–1860)," *Biographical Directory of the United States Congress* (bioguide.congress.gov/scripts/biodisplay.pl?index=R00012); *Daily National Intelligencer*, May 14, 1838, 2; *National Intelligencer*, May 14, 1838; Andie Tucher, "Newspapers and Periodicals," in Robert A. Gross and Mary Kelley, eds., *An Extensive Republic: Print, Culture, and Society in the New Nation, 1790–1840* (Chapel Hill, N.C., 2010), 402. The remonstrances from Concord were submitted to the Senate on May 11, 1838.

33. Massachusetts papers: *YG*, May 19, 1838; *New Bedford Mercury*, May 25, 1838; *Christian Register* (Boston), June 2, 1838; *Boston Courier*, June 18, 1838; *Liberator*, June 22, 1838. New Hampshire papers: *Portsmouth Journal of Literature and Politics*, June 9, 1838; *New-Hampshire Sentinel*, June 14, 1838.

34. *YG*, May 19, 1838. For another interpretation of the letter to Van Buren, see Bethany Schneider, "Boudinot's Change: Boudinot, Emerson, and Ross on Cherokee Removal," *ELH* 75, no. 1 (Spring 2008): 151–56.

35. Emerson, *JMN* 4:335; 5:475, 477, 479–80.

36. George Moore, Diary 1828–44, in Kenneth Walter Cameron, comp., *Transcendental Epilogue: Primary Materials for Research in Emerson, Thoreau, Literary New England, the Influence of German Theology, and Higher Biblical Criticism*, 3 vols. (Hartford, Conn., 1965–1982), 1:221.

37. M. M. Brooks (Concord) to John Quincy Adams (Washington), April 23, 1838, Reel 509, Adams Papers, MHS; Leonard L. Richards, *The Life and Times of Congressman John Quincy Adams* (New York, 1986), 146–49; Lynn Hudson Parsons, "'A Perpetual Harrow upon My Feelings': John Quincy Adams and the American Indian," *New England Quarterly* 46 (September 1973): 339–79. Brooks's letter left a deep impression on the former president. She wrote that only "a ray of hope from the throne of God" would induce the women of Concord to "harrow up your feelings" for the sake of the Cherokee people. Several years later Adams took the metaphor and employed it to explain why he was turning down the chairmanship of the Committee on Indian Affairs: "Its only result would be to keep a perpetual harrow upon my feelings."

38. *Liberator*, August 31, 1838, May 3, July 26, 1839; *Massachusetts Abolitionist*, August 1, 1839; Sinha, *Slave's Cause*, 285–91. Interestingly, voting was not restricted to members of the MCASS or its auxiliaries; anyone in favor of "immediate emancipation without expatriation" was officially approved. Garrison himself attended the convention, made motions from the floor, and voted on resolutions. Residence thus took second place to sentiment; this was a meeting *in* but not necessarily *of* Middlesex County. For Brooks's offices in the MCASS, see *Liberator*, September 17, 1841, October 21, 1842, May 5, 1843, June 21, 1844.

39. "Annual Report of the Concord Female A.S. Society"; Maria Thoreau (Concord) to Mary Wilder (Marshall, Calhoun County, Mich.), March 20, 1841, Yale University Library, New Haven, Conn.; Mary Munroe, "Historical Sketch of the Second Congregational Church and Society Concord, Mass., 1826–1876," Trinitarian Congregational

Church Records, Box 1, CFPL; Henry M. Grout, *An Historical Discourse, Delivered at Concord, Mass., June 4, 1876, on Occasion of the Completion of the First Half-Century of the Trinitarian Congregational Church* (Boston, 1876), 76.

40. *CF*, August 2, 1839; *YG*, August 10, 1839; William Gallup and 113 other male and female citizens of Concord, petition calling on legislature to protest against the admission of Florida as a slave state, House Unpassed Legislation 1840, MSA; William Gallup and 112 others of Concord, petition calling on legislature to protest against Gag Rule of U.S. House of Representatives, House Unpassed Legislation 1840, MSA. Despite his opposition to the Garrisonians, Trinitarian minister Means subscribed to the 1840 memorials, both of which were headed by a member of his congregation, Dr. William Gallup. Barzillai Frost withheld his signature. A total of 127 individuals signed the two antislavery petitions in 1840: thirty-four men (26 percent), ninety-three women (74 percent), once again mirroring the gendered composition of church membership.

41. *Liberator*, October 8, 22, and 29, 1841; meetings of March 3, April 4, 1842, CTMM 8:219, 221, 229, CFPL. Brooks's condemnation of Frost would have been even stronger had she known that he was a colonizationist, who would become a life member of the ACS in 1845. See *African Repository and Colonial Journal* 22 (February 1846): 70. Samuel Hoar chaired the ten-man committee that recommended the new policies for use of the meetinghouse; predictably, among the other members were John Keyes and Daniel Shattuck. Surprisingly, Brooks said nothing in praise of the Universalists, in whose meetinghouse the MCASS met in October 1841 to hear her report.

42. John Shepard Keyes (Concord) to Christopher Gore Ripley, January 1, 1843, bMS AM 2178 (58)–(66), Houghton. The incident at the start of 1843 was not the first time Keyes tore down notices of abolitionist meetings. See his Diary, vol. 5, 65–69, 70–73.

43. Edes, *Some Reminiscences*; obituary of Helen Thoreau, *Liberator*, June 22, 1849; Ann M. Weston (Concord) to Deborah Weston (Weymouth), September 16, 1841, Ms. A.9.2.15, 67, BPL. The anonymous tribute to Helen Thoreau in *The Liberator* evidently came from the pen of a woman, who claimed intimate knowledge of Helen Thoreau's journey into abolitionism and out of the "pro-slavery" churches. Brooks and Thoreau worked together closely as officers of the CFASS; for seven years they were next-door neighbors. The telltale evidence of Brooks's authorship is the passage from Psalms 41, "Blessed is he that considereth the poor," that was quoted both in the June 1843 "Annual Report of the Concord Female A. S. Society," printed in *The Liberator*, June 23, 1843, and in the obituary of Helen Thoreau six years later. According to Edes, the admiring Sunday school pupil of Brooks, her teacher gave up on the Unitarian church "with many others" sometime in the early 1840s. Before then, she would attend divine worship with others but leave before the communion service; the dissenters would then regroup at her home or that of Emerson or Rockwood Hoar for "Silent Introspection." Edes was seventy-three when she published her reminiscences, and she had long since left Concord for a new home in Vermont. Her account of Brooks's disenchantment with the Unitarian church recalls events in the early 1840s, when she was growing into her early teens, old enough to notice what the adults were doing but too young (and too distant in time when she penned her recollections) to know all the details. It is highly unlikely that the unhappy worshipers in Barzillai Frost's congregation took refuge, as Edes recalled, in Doctor

Ripley's home, unless this happened during the years of Nathaniel and Sophia Hawthorne's residence (1842–1845) or that of Samuel and Sarah Alden Bradford Ripley thereafter.

44. "Early Records of the Concord Lyceum," in Kenneth Walter Cameron, comp., *The Massachusetts Lyceum during the American Renaissance; Materials for the Study of the Oral Tradition in American Letters: Emerson, Thoreau, Hawthorne, and Other New-England Lecturers* (Hartford, Conn., 1969), 156. The cashbooks of the Lyceum, CFPL, show eighty-five men and one woman (a Mrs. Hosmer) as dues-paying members for the 1843–1844 season. Members included such Democratic leaders as Stedman Buttrick, Daniel Clark, Charles B. Davis, Colburn Hadlock, Samuel Staples, and Anthony Wright and such Whigs as Rockwood and Samuel Hoar, John Keyes, Daniel Shattuck, and John Stacy. Temperance advocates Josiah Bartlett and William Whiting collaborated with opponents Hartwell Bigelow and Carlos Tewksbury. The pastors of the three churches—Fay, Frost, and Means—gave their blessing.

45. Cabot, *Memoir of Emerson*, 2:425; Vern Wagner, "The Lecture Lyceum and the Problem of Controversy," *Journal of the History of Ideas* 15 (January 1954): 119–35. One of the two vice-presidents of the Lyceum in 1842 was James Means, who had served in that office since settling into the Trinitarian pulpit.

46. The 1842–1843 season in Concord was as impressive as the better-known series of lectures at Amory Hall in Boston, which showcased the leading progressive thinkers in the Boston area. See Linck Johnson, "Reforming the Reformers: Emerson, Thoreau, and the Society Lectures at Amory Hall, Boston," *ESQ: A Journal of the American Renaissance* 37 (1991): 245–89. The local speakers on the program included Edward Jarvis (back from Kentucky for good) and John Shepard Keyes, in his first year at Harvard Law School.

47. *CF*, December 9, 1842, April 21, 1843; *Liberator*, November 4, 1842; "Early Records of the Concord Lyceum," 156–57; Bruce Laurie, *Beyond Garrison: Antislavery and Social Reform* (Cambridge, Mass., 2005), 78–79.

48. Concord Lyceum, Membership Roll and Cash Book, entry for November 21, 1842, Concord Lyceum Records, 1828–1928, CFPL; Mary Brooks to Wendell Phillips, February 21, 1843, quoted in Petrulionis, *To Set This World Right*, 31–32, 36–38; *Liberator*, February 16, 1844; "Early Records of Concord Lyceum," 158.

49. *Liberator*, February 16, 1844; Keyes, Autobiography, 110; Petrulionis, *To Set This World Right*, 36–37. The passage about "captive, silly women" comes from 2 Timothy 3:6. See Chapter 2 for Keyes's previous invocation of this biblical text to write off women with whom he was at odds.

50. Mary M. Brooks to Wendell Phillips, March 17, 1844, quoted in Petrulionis, *To Set This World Right*, 37–38.

51. "Annual Report of the Concord Female A.S. Society"; *CF*, December 23, 1842; *Liberator*, July 29, 1842, January 6, March 17, 1843; broadside announcement of Anti-Slavery Fair, to be held Wednesday, August 3, [1842,] at Shepherd's Hotel, Concord Anti-Slavery Society, Notices of Meetings, C. Pam. Organizations—Reform, Item 62, CFPL; Table of Signers of the Petition of George Latimer and others, Massachusetts Anti-Slavery and Anti-Segregation Petitions, Passed Acts, St. 1843, c. 69, SC1/ series 229, MSA; Josiah Bartlett and 132 others, inhabitants of Concord, petition for the repeal of the intermarriage Law, submitted January 19, 1843, Passed Acts, chap. 5, Acts 1843, MSA; Josiah Bartlett and 145 others, inhabitants of Concord, petition for equal rights of Coloured people on Railroads, submitted January 19,

1843, House Unpassed Legislation, SC1/Series 230, MSA. The biblical quotation is from Psalm 41; Brooks also drew on Isaiah 30:21 and 58 in this report. Earlier in 1843 Brooks submitted a report, "Good Meetings in Concord, Massachusetts," to the *Liberator* (March 17, 1843); another account, with similar religious fervor, described a "Meeting at Concord, Mass.," two weeks later (March 31).

52. Brooks did regret the all-female membership of organized abolitionism in Concord. "Alas, men there are none" in the CFASS ranks, she lamented in the June 1843 report. Following the 1839–1840 schism in the abolitionist ranks, female antislavery societies considered their future. Should they disband and become mixed-sex organizations, where men and women would act on an equal basis? That was the decision by Garrisonian women in Nantucket. By contrast, the Dedham Female Anti-Slavery Society, which was loyal to Garrison, declined to open up its ranks. To judge by Brooks's comment, the Concord group remained all-female as much by necessity—the lack of response from men—as by choice. See Salerno, *Sister Societies*, 110–11.

53. "Annual Report of the Concord Female A.S. Society"; Amy Dunham Strand, *Language, Gender, and Citizenship in American Literature, 1789–1919* (New York, 2009), 56–58; Richards, *Life and Times of John Quincy Adams*, 126–30; Mary M. Brooks (Concord) to John Quincy Adams (Washington), December 26, 1838, Reel 512, Adams Papers, MHS; Elizabeth Barrett and 182 other women, petition against the annexation of Texas, presented to the House January 7, 1839, Library of Congress Collection of Records of the House of Representatives: Annexation of Texas (25A-H1.1: N.A. Box 35 of L.C. Box 126), 25th Congress, 3rd sess., Record Group 233, National Archives; *Journal of the House of Representatives of the United States: Being the Third Session of the Twenty-Fifth Congress* (Washington, D.C., 1839), 228 (documenting Adams's presentation of a petition "from 183 females of Concord in the State of Massachusetts").

54. "Annual Report of the Concord Female A.S. Society."

55. *JMN* 5:32 ("no check from authority"), 7:226 ("drunk by party," "cease to be a man").

56. *JMN* 5:382 ("obtuse & barbarous", "stinking hold"), 437, 440, 7:393 ("so inferior a race," "education of this generation in ethics," "foreign & monstrous"). Emerson vacillated between an exclusionary racism that consigned Africans to permanent inferiority and an assimilating racism that approved of those complying with white norms. In December 1836 he was impressed to learn that in the African Colonization Society's settlement in Liberia, Blacks preferred to engage in trade rather than serve in public office—not unlike a good many merchants in Boston. "They dislike the trouble of it," he commented. "Civilized arts are found to be as attractive to the wild negro, as they are disagreeable to the wild Indian." *JMN* 5:261–62; Ibram X. Kendi, *Stamped from the Beginning: The Definitive History of Racist Ideas in America* (New York, 2016), 2–4.

57. *JMN* 7:200 ("enmity & fault-finding"); Ralph Waldo Emerson to Mary Moody Emerson, September 21, 1841, in Rusk, *Letters of Emerson*, 2:450–51; Kenyon Gradert, "Swept into Puritanism: Emerson, Wendell Phillips, and the Roots of Radicalism," *New England Quarterly* 90, no. 1 (March 2017): 103–18. For another account of Emerson's "silent years" (1838–1844), see Gougeon, *Virtue's Hero*, 41–85. Emerson reused this formulation of the relations between the old religion and the new reform in his 1844 lecture "New England Reformers." "The Church, or religious party," he observed, "is falling from the church nominal, and is appearing in temperance and non-resistance societies, in movements of abolition-

ists and socialists," and in numerous other utopian efforts to build a new heaven on earth. "What a fertility of projects for the salvation of the world!" See *Essays: Second Series* (Boston, 1844), reprinted in Joel Porte, ed., *Ralph Waldo Emerson: Essays and Lectures* (New York, 1983), 591.

16. The Iron Horse

1. Ward D. Safford (Concord) to Mark and Mercy Safford (Washington, N.H.), January 12, 1842, Folder 2, Safford Family Papers, CFPL; Henry A. Willis, "The Early Days of Railroads in Fitchburg," *Proceedings of the Fitchburg Historical Society and Papers Relating to the History of the Town* 1 (1895): 1–49; Cliff Schexnayder, *Builders of the Hoosac Tunnel* (Portsmouth, N.H., 2015), 100–10; "Railroad Meeting at Waltham," *CF*, December 31, 1841; "Proceedings of the Railroad Meeting at Waltham," *Boston Courier*, January 20, 1842, and *CF*, January 21, 1842; John Warner Barber, "Waltham," in his *Massachusetts Historical Collections* (Worcester, Mass., 1839), 433.

2. *R*, July 19, December 31, 1841; Keyes, Autobiography, 89; *Lowell Journal*, April 20, 1844. The state census of 1837 reported a Concord population of 2,023, much the same as in 1830 (2,017); the federal census of 1840 showed a loss of 229 inhabitants (11 percent) over the next three years. The drop in population was matched by a drop in the number of legal voters, from 395 in 1838 to 355 in 1840, a 10 percent decline. The labor force in 1842, numbering 484 polls, was still below the 500 polls assessed in 1835.

3. "Contemplated Railroad from Fitchburg to Boston," *CF*, December 17, 1841; *CF*, February 18, 1842. Concord qualified to send two representatives to the state legislature in the 1820s and 1830s; and it filled its quota in all but two years (1831 and 1837). In 1840 state voters approved a new system, granting one seat in the House to every town with 1,200 inhabitants and additional seats with each increment of 2,400 people. Struggling to get back to 2,000, Concord was far below the threshold for two representatives on Beacon Hill. Not surprisingly, both Democrats and Whigs in Concord had opposed the change, and Concord voters rejected it at the polls by an overwhelming margin of 24 in favor, 117 against. *CF*, April 3 and 10, 1840, *YG*, April 4 and 11, 1840.

4. Keyes presided over the railroad convention, Gourgas served as one of two secretaries. Concord's delegation to the convention also included Whig manufacturer David Loring and Democratic selectman Cyrus Stow, who served on two key committees.

5. *CF*, December 17 and 31, 1841, January 21 and 28, February 4, 1842; *Act of Incorporation, Together with the Additional Acts and By-Laws, of the Fitchburg Railroad Company* (Charlestown, Mass., 1854); *National Ægis*, February 16, 1842 (reprinting from *Fitchburg Sentinel*); Concord town assessment lists, July 26, 1842, and August 16, 1845, Town Treasurer's Records, CFPL. The other petitioners with Gourgas were Nathaniel Fellows Cunningham, a Boston merchant and banker with family roots in Fitchburg, and Abner Phelps, a Boston banker, merchant, and recent representative on Beacon Hill. See Henry Winchester Cunningham, "Andrew Cunningham of Boston, and Some of His Descendants," *New-England Historic Genealogical Register* 55 (October 1901): 419, and *Massachusetts Register and United States Calendar for 1840–42*. Thirty-two taxpayers (out of 523) were assessed for shares of Fitchburg Railroad stock, valued at $63,565, in 1845, 29 out of 652 taxpayers in 1850. Interestingly, the railroad was not a pet project of the Social Circle, over half of whom (13 of 24) did not subscribe. The single biggest investors were not individuals but

other companies: the Concord Bank, with nearly $35,000 worth of stock, and the Middlesex Institution for Savings, with $8,165. I assume that most of the investors made their pledges in 1842 but had not actually paid for their shares when the assessment was taken that July. Crocker took pride in the many investors of moderate means his project attracted. See Schexnayder, *Builders of the Hoosac Tunnel*, 106–7.

6. In 1845 Belknap was a new resident of Concord; his substantial estate, valued at over $8,000, placed him in the top tenth of taxpayers, but it included not a single share of stock. See 1845 Concord Assessment List.

7. Schexnayder, *Builders of the Hoosac Tunnel*, 108; Willis, "Early Days," 43; Oscar Handlin, *Boston's Immigrants*, rev. and enlarged ed. (New York, 1972), 51–52; Kerby A. Miller, *Emigrants and Exiles: Ireland and the Irish Exodus to North America* (New York, 1985), 193–279, quotations at 200; "Second Annual Report of the Fitchburg Rail-Road Company," in *Annual Reports of the Rail-Road Corporations in the State of Massachusetts for 1843* (Boston, 1844), 87.

8. Keyes, Autobiography, 9; *Walden*, 261–62; Emerson (Concord) to Thoreau (Staten Island), June 10, 1843, in Robert N. Hudspeth, ed., *The Correspondence of Henry D. Thoreau*, vol. 1, *1834–1848* (Princeton, N.J., 2013), 191. On Weir, see Chapter 4.

9. *CF*, July 21, 1843; Claude M. Simpson, ed., *The American Notebooks*, vol. 8 of *The Centenary Edition of the Works of Nathaniel Hawthorne* (Columbus, Ohio, 1972), 394–96.

10. Ward D. Safford (Concord) to Mark and Mercy Safford (Washington, N.H.), December 28, 1843, Safford Family Papers, CFPL; Emerson (Concord) to Thoreau (Staten Island), September 8, 1843, in Hudspeth, *Correspondence*, 1:228–29; *JMN* 9:7, 23.

11. Receipts for payment to various Irish immigrant workers, including Bartley and James Conlon, David Dole, Bernard ("Barney") Kelly, and Owen Rooney, July to November 1843, and contract between Abel Moore and Barney Kelly, December 9, 1843, in Abel Moore estate, 1801–57, Series 4, Nathan Brooks Papers, Box 42, Folder 25, CFPL; Leslie Perrin Wilson, "Cutting Peat in Concord" [(2016), manuscript shared by the author]; Bradley P. Dean, "Thoreau and Michael Flannery," *Concord Saunterer* 17 (December 1984): 27–33; J. Fay Barrett, "Memoir of Joseph Barrett," *SCM* 2:93; Laura Dassow Walls, "'As You Are Brothers of Mine': Thoreau and the Irish," *New England Quarterly* 88 (March 2015): 5–36. See also Sherman Barrett's account of hiring Irishmen in 1843 to reclaim two acres of peat meadow. "Sketches of Middlesex Husbandry," *Massachusetts Ploughman*, October 23, 1847.

12. "The Wrongs of Ireland," *CF*, December 22 and 29, 1843, January 5, 1844; Miller, *Emigrants and Exiles*, 241, 249.

13. Manisha Sinha, *The Slave's Cause: A History of Abolition* (New Haven, Conn., 2016), 359–63; Grindall Reynolds, "Memoir of Josiah Bartlett," *SCM* 2:179; Leslie Perrin Wilson, "Mrs. Woodward Hudson's Memoir of Mrs. Ebenezer Rockwood Hoar," *Concord Saunterer*, n.s., 9 (2001): 98–99; entries for July 1843, January, March, and June 1844, and December 2, 1845, in Concord Female Charitable Society Records, 1814–1943, Series 1, vol. 5, 1843–68, CFPL; David Britton Little, "Concord and Its Churches," in John Whittemore Teele, ed., *The Meeting House on the Green: A History of the First Parish in Concord and Its Church* (Concord, Mass., 1985), 119; William M. Bailey, Janet M. Beyer, and Anna M. Manion, *A History of St. Bernard's Parish* (Concord, Mass., 1986).

14. Jason Lange and Yeganeh Torbati, "U.S. Foreign-Born Population Swells to Highest in over a Century," Reuters, September 13, 2018; Campbell Gibson and Kay Jung,

"Historical Census Statistics on the Foreign-Born Population of the United States: 1850 to 2000," Working Paper no. 81 (February 2006), Population Division, U.S. Census Bureau; "Nativity of the Population for the 25 Largest Urban Places and for Selected Counties: 1850," table 21, March 9, 1999, U.S. Census Bureau, www.census .gov/population/www/documentation/twps0029/tab21.html; Bailey et al., *History of St. Bernard's Parish*, 7.

15. *Boston Evening Transcript*, June 7, 1844; *New England Puritan*, June 14, 1844; *CF*, June 21, 1844; Walls, "'As You Are Brothers,'" 5–7; *Walden*, 42–44; Tyler Anbinder, *Nativism and Slavery: The Northern Know-Nothings and the Politics of the 1850s* (New York, 1992), 3; Handlin, *Boston's Immigrants*, 51–52; *Boston Semi-Weekly Atlas*, February 27, 1847. The official opening of the railroad in Concord was on June 17, 1844. The number of immigrants who arrived in the United States between 1845 and 1854 constituted 14.5 percent of the 1845 population, the highest share of foreign-born ever reached within a single decade. In 1850 Concord's Irish-born population numbered 246; I added the 89 Massachusetts-born children living within Irish-headed households to estimate the total population of Irish descent (335, or 15 percent of the town). In 1855 Irish natives made up a fifth of the town, and on the same reasoning the population of Irish descent was at least a quarter. The 1850 census asked of each family whether the children in the household had attended school during the previous year. Of the children, ages five to nineteen, in Yankee families ($N = 308$), 91 percent were enrolled; of those in Irish families ($N = 146$), 88 percent.

16. *CF*, June 21, 1844; *JMN* 7:241, 9:119; *Boston Evening Transcript*, June 7, 1844; Willis, "Early Days," 43; "An Act to authorize the Fitchburg Rail-road Company to extend their Road to the City of Boston," April 20, 1847; Income of Concord Station, Fitchburg Railroad, from October 31, 1847, to November 1, 1848, William Wheildon Scrapbooks, H80 257, BPL; "An Act to Incorporate the Concord and Chelmsford Rail-Road Company," March 14, 1845, in *Documents Printed by Order of the Senate of the Commonwealth of Massachusetts, During the Session of the General Court, A.D. 1845* (Boston, 1845), 96–97; T. J. Carter, petition for "Union Railroad" from Wilmington to Concord, submitted April 15, 1847, Senate Unpassed Legislation 1847, no. 12130, MSA; Alpheus Richardson and others, petition to build a railroad from South Reading to Concord, submitted March–April 1849, Senate Unpassed Legislation 1849, no. 12819, MSA; *Walden*, 118.

17. "Concord, Mass.," *New York Herald*, October 16, 1843; John Shepard Keyes, "Houses & Owners or Occupants in Concord 1885" (1885), 352, CFPL; *Lowell Journal*, April 20, 1844. The statistical portrait of Concord carried the byline "H." The *Herald* hoped to inspire readers in "the inland towns throughout the country" to pen similar accounts of their communities, but "H's" contribution appears to have been a one-off. Why such attention to Concord? The best bet is that Hudson was making good journalistic use of a recent visit to his old hometown. His father had died the previous July, and he was likely back in Concord to see his brother and deal with the disposition of their father's estate. Years later the editor retired to Concord. There he died in 1875, when a railroad car collided with his carriage. On Hudson, see the entry by David A. Copeland in *American National Biography Online*.

18. *G&Y*, May 14, 1825; *CF*, March 12, 1844; *New England Puritan*, June 21, 1844; Henry F. Smith, "William Willder Wheildon," *SCM* 3:199, 203; Robert A. Gross, "Transcendentalism and Urbanism: Concord, Boston, and the Wider World," *Journal of American Studies* 18 (1984): 378; Edward Waldo Emerson, *Emerson in Concord: A Memoir, Written for the "Social Circle" in Concord, Massachusetts* (Boston, 1890), 178;

Income of Concord Station, Fitchburg Railroad, from October 31, 1847, to November 1, 1848. I estimate the number of daily commuters into the city as follows: according to the record in the Wheildon scrapbooks, 11,490 tickets were sold for passage from Concord to Charlestown over the year from October 31, 1847, to November 1, 1848, for an average of 958 tickets per month; figuring a six-day work-week, that comes to 37 passengers per day. In the late 1870s Jarvis was told that fifty men and eighty boys commuted to work outside Concord each day. See *T&R*, 141–42, 199–200. Wheildon first rented and then purchased his home from the railroad contractor Belknap.

19. Grindall Reynolds, "Concord," in Samuel Adams Drake, ed., *History of Middlesex County, Massachusetts: Containing Carefully Prepared Histories of Every City and Town in the County by Well-Known Writers*, 2 vols. (Boston, 1880), 1:398–99; advertisements for R. N. Rice & Co., *CF*, May 13, 1842, October 20, 1843; for F. Potter's store, *CF*, February 11, 1842; and for J. W. Walcott's store, *CF*, April 17, 1846; Christopher Clark, *The Roots of Rural Capitalism: Western Massachusetts, 1780–1860* (Ithaca, N.Y., 1990), 220–27.

20. Reynolds, "Concord," 399; E. R. Hoar, "Memoir of Josiah Davis," *SCM* 2:99; *CF*, January 13, 1838, July 5, 1839; Charles B. Davis, mortgage to sundry merchants of Boston, July 11, 1837, Nathan Brooks Papers, Box 9, Folder 5, CFPL; advertisement of C. O. Wardwell's "Cheap Cash Store on the Mill Dam," *CF*, June 9, September 22, 1843, March 19, 1847. At the annual assessment of taxpayers, the owners of shops and stores were required to estimate the value of goods on their shelves. I computed the total value of stock in trade for the following years: 1826: $38,986 ($N$ = 43); 1835: $49,673 ($N$ = 35); 1837: $35,850 ($N$ = 30); 1840: $31,835 ($N$ = 42); 1842: $36,000 ($N$ = 33); 1845: $23,110 ($N$ = 27); 1850: $21,150 ($N$ = 36). Between 1835 and 1850, the average valuation of stock in trade at Concord's shops and stores went from $1,419 to $588—a decline of 58 percent. At the nine stores in 1842, the inventory of goods averaged $3,208; the comparable value for the seven stores in 1845 was $1,614. The median figures were $2,000 in 1842, $1,000 in 1845. Five years later, only five stores were operating in Concord. They held $6,900 in inventory; the median value was $1,000.

21. Lemuel Shattuck, *Memorials of the Descendants of William Shattuck, the Progenitor of the Families in America that Have Borne His Name* (Boston, 1855), 300–2; John S. Keyes, "Memoir of Daniel Shattuck," *SCM* 2:139–40; estate of Daniel Shattuck, 1867, File no. 41335, MCPR. When Phineas How declared bankruptcy in 1845, Shattuck picked up several prime pieces of real estate, and he presided over the disposition of his colleague's assets. How had overextended his business "imprudently" and borrowed heavily, and after his store was robbed and burned, he could not meet his obligations, even with the insurance money. To the resentment of creditors, the merchant was soon back behind the counter, having paid just twenty cents on the dollar. But this was a shrunken establishment, its stock of goods reduced from $5,000 to $500. Ironically, How outlasted Shattuck's son in trade. See E. R. Hoar, "Memoir of Phineas How," *SCM* 2:273; notice of bankruptcy of Phineas How, *Boston Courier*, May 19, 1845; "Fire," *CF*, July 29, 1842.

22. List of persons licensed to sell liquor in Concord during the last year, notice to selectmen from Middlesex court, March 1841, ETR, CFPL; meeting of December 21, 1840, Concord Total Abstinence Society Records, 1840–1852, CFPL. The three innholders were Hartwell Bigelow, Thomas D. Wesson, and Luther G. Whitcomb; the three retailers were the "Green Store" partners Reuben Rice and David Loring, Daniel Shattuck, and George W. Hildreth. Concord's politicians were, for the most part, opposed to temperance measures. Their indefatigable adversaries were long-

time Concord Total Abstinence Society president Barzillai Frost and Dr. Josiah Bartlett. In April 1838 the General Court barred the sale of brandy, rum, and other distilled spirits in quantities below fifteen gallons. The "Fifteen Gallon Law" was designed to eliminate the sale of liquor by the glass at the many "grog shops" and taverns in the state. If an individual craved ardent spirits, he would have to buy in bulk and haul his order home. A rich man could easily comply with this mandate and enjoy a drink at home, but people with limited means were out of luck. No longer could they stop at their favorite watering hole after a day of hard toil and relax over a comforting mug of toddy or new rum. Concord's representatives in the state legislature—Stedman Buttrick in the House, Nathan Brooks in the Senate— voted against the law. In the Middlesex County delegation, Concord was in the minority as an antitemperance town. The "Fifteen Gallon Law" was unpopular, and its enforcement a nightmare. The act was repealed in 1840 with Concord's representatives in the house, Gourgas and Ephraim Meriam, consistently support- ing the change. (No one from Concord was in the senate that year.) See Robert L. Hampel, *Temperance and Prohibition in Massachusetts, 1813–1852* (Ann Arbor, 1982), 61–69, 79–85; "An Act to regulate the sale of Spirituous Liquors," April 19, 1838, chap. 157, *Laws of the Commonwealth of Massachusetts, Passed by the General Court, in the Years 1837 and 1838* 14 (Boston, 1839), 442–43; *CF*, April 7, May 12, 1838; *YG*, March 31, April 12, June 23, 1838; *CF*, January 31, February 7, 1840.

23. *CF*, March 18, 1842; CTMM 8:219–21, 280, 302, 322, 325, CFPL; Keyes, Auto- biography, 74; *Lowell Journal*, March 11, 1842. A checklist of legal voters, drawn up by the selectmen in November 1841, lists 375 names. So just 15 percent of them (57/375) voted against awarding licenses. See Selectmen's checklist of vot- ers, November 8, 1841, ETR. At the March 7 meeting, only the first item on the warrant, the vote for county treasurer, drew a full attendance. After that poll was taken, some forty townsmen departed. Close to 250 stayed to ballot for se- lectmen and town clerk. By the time article 9 on the licenses came up, only 147 men were left in the room. That number slipped to 143 by the time the question was called on a motion to "dismiss" the article. It failed by a margin of 54 to 89. With the writing on the wall, still more people went home, and each successive motion drew fewer voters until the final motion on instructing the selectmen passed with just 97 men in the room.

24. "Wood for Sale," ad placed by Joel Britton, *CF*, October 13, 1843; Memo of the conveyances to and from Joel Britton since January 1, 1843, prepared by MCRD Office, Cambridge, January 19, 1848, Abel Moore estate, Nathan Brooks Pa- pers, CFPL; Manuscript survey of agriculture and industry in Concord, 1845, ETR; John Gorham Palfrey, comp., *Statistics of the Condition and Products of Certain Branches of Industry in Massachusetts, for the Year Ending April 1, 1845* (Boston, 1846), 50; Thoreau (Concord) to Emerson (Manchester, England), February 23, 1848, in Hudspeth, *Correspondence of Thoreau* 1:347; Thomas Blanding, "Historic Walden Woods," *Concord Saunterer* 20 (1988): 41–44; Robert A. Gross, "Culture and Culti- vation: Agriculture and Society in Thoreau's Concord," *Journal of American History* 69 (June 1982): 53, 59; Brian Donahue, "Henry David Thoreau and the Environ- ment of Concord," in Edmund A. Schofield and Robert C. Baron, eds., *Thoreau's World and Ours: A Natural Legacy* (Golden, Colo., 1993), 181–82, 186; Howard S. Russell, *A Long, Deep Furrow: Three Centuries of Farming in New England* (Hanover, N.H., 1976), 384–93. Of the 213 farmers and manufacturers included in the 1845 state survey, just two others prepared timber for sale, and another thirty-one sold firewood. The collective result of their labors amounted to nearly 3,800 cords, over

half of it attributable to Britton alone. The typical producer operated on a modest scale, bringing thirty-two cords to market (median is 31.5; N = 32). The clearing of woodlands proceeded even more rapidly in the 1820s, when farmers were busily opening up land for meadows and pastures. Over that decade the acreage of woodland fell by 37 percent, compared to a decline of 23 percent over the 1840s. Britton was conveniently located to carry on this lumber trade with the Fitchburg line. His house stood at one end of a new road called Railroad Lane; the car house at which the locomotives stopped for fuel lay at the other. See "Cottage Lane," architectural and historical description in the Massachusetts Cultural Resource Information System, Massachusetts Historical Commission.

25. Joel Britton and thirty-seven others, petition to be incorporated as the Concord Steam Mill Company, January 10, 1846, and Daniel Harris and others, petition, both in File Papers for the Acts of 1846, chap. 225, MSA; "An Act to Incorporate the Concord Steam Mill Company," April 15, 1846, chap. 225, *General Acts and Resolves Passed by the General Court of Massachusetts in the Year 1846* (Boston, 1846), 154; *CF*, May 5, 1846. Reuben Rice, proprietor of the Green Store, became the first president; the innovation-minded farmers Abel Moore and Anthony Wright joined the board of directors; a dozen yeomen bought stock (at $50 a share) in the corporation.

26. Concord Steam Mill Company Records, 1846–48, CFPL. Before the fire the machinery belonging to Moore, Britton, and others was used to saw logs, grind grain, and crush graphite for lead pencils (probably for the Thoreau family, whose shop was close by). Rice was an appropriate choice to head a company that expected to make money from sawing logs. In mid-February 1840 the operator of the green store sought wood choppers to cut three hundred cords of wood for him. *CF*, February 15, 1840.

27. *Boston Recorder*, May 26, 1848; *New York Herald*, February 16, 1845; "An Act to Incorporate the Concord Steam Power Company," February 26, 1845, chap. 74, *General Acts and Resolves Passed by the General Court of Massachusetts in the Year 1845* (Boston, 1845), 426; *CF*, July 21, 1843; *New York Herald*, October 30, 1843; Palfrey, *Statistics of the Condition and Products of Certain Branches of Industry*, 50; Henry F. Smith, "Edward Carver Damon," *SCM* 4:178–80.

28. Sean Patrick Adams, *Home Fires: How Americans Kept Warm in the Nineteenth Century* (Baltimore, 2014), 81; Richard Judd, *Second Nature: An Environmental History of New England* (Amherst, Mass., 2014), 108–9; Donahue, "Thoreau and Environment of Concord," 185–89; Gross, "Culture and Cultivation," 53–54; Emerson, "Emerson in Concord," *SCM* 2:135–37; *T&R*, 192–98; "Milk in Boston," *Farmers' Cabinet, & American Herd-book* 12 (January 15, 1848): 198. The original return of the 1845 survey of the "condition and products of certain branches of industry" and agriculture in Concord, taken in compliance with state law, is in ETR. The aggregate report for all the towns in the Commonwealth was Palfrey, *Statistics of the Condition and Products of Certain Branches of Industry*. Of the 213 producers enumerated by the assessors, 21 reported sales of milk, 48 produced vegetables, and 76 carried fruits to market. According to an article in a revived edition of *CF*, June 17, 1878, which Jarvis pasted into the manuscript of *T&R*, 194–95, a farmer named Charles Bartlett planted an acre of strawberries and another of asparagus in 1842; he was alone in this effort for almost eight years. The production of both took off after 1850. The 1845 agricultural census credited Bartlett with $300 in vegetable sales, the ninth biggest producer, but with no fruit. For the wide range of vegetables on offer at Quincy Market in Boston, see *Massachusetts Ploughman*, May 3, 1845.

29. John S. Keyes, "Memoir of Nathan Barrett, Jr.," *SCM* 2:266–72; *New England Farmer*, October 21, 1843; Robert A. Gross, "The Celestial Village: Transcendentalism and Tourism in Concord," in Charles Capper and Conrad Edick Wright, eds., *Transient and Permanent: The Transcendentalist Movement and Its Contexts* (Boston, 1999), 256–57; George Willis Cooke, ed., *Early Letters from George William Curtis to John S. Dwight* (New York, 1898), 68–73, 183–84. In October 1845 Moore won first prize at the cattle show for "the best apple orchard, set out since 1835"; Barrett took third place. See John G. Palfrey, comp., *Abstract from the Returns of Agricultural Societies in Massachusetts, for the Year 1845* (Boston, 1846), 44.

30. William Barrett, "Ephraim Wales Bull," *SCM* 4:146–52; *A Letter [from] Ephraim Wales Bull of Concord, February 12, 1843, to Henry Moore* (Champlain, N.Y., 1932); bankruptcy file of Ephraim W. Bull, Case No. 2941, The U.S. District Court for the District of Massachusetts, Bankruptcy Act of 1841 Case Files, National Archives depository, Kansas City, Missouri (thanks to Nathaniel Wiltzen of the National Archives in Boston for guiding me to this material); Edmund A. Schofield, "'He Sowed, Others Reaped': Ephraim Wales Bull and the Origins of the 'Concord' Grape," *Arnoldia* (Fall 1988): 4–15; Philip J. Pauly, *Fruits and Plains: The Horticultural Transformation of America* (Cambridge, Mass., 2007), 25–26, 65–67, 73–78; *New England Farmer*, October 13, 1832 (Nathan Barrett's "Fox Grapes"); *New England Farmer*, October 21, 1843 (13 contestants for premiums for grapes); *Boston Courier*, October 6, 1845 ("Isabella Grapes were abundant, well ripened, and of high flavor"); *Massachusetts Ploughman*, October 23, 1847 (premiums for grapes to Joseph Merriam, John B. Moore, Micajah Rice, and Cyrus Wheeler); John G. Palfrey, *Abstract from the Returns of the Agricultural Societies in Massachusetts, for the Year 1845, with Selections from Addresses at Cattle Shows and Fairs* (Boston, 1846), 39. The 1860 federal census of agriculture credited Bull with producing 150 gallons of wine. On the Massachusetts Horticultural Society, see Tamara Plakans Thornton, *Cultivating Gentlemen: The Meaning of Country Life Among the Boston Elite, 1785–1860* (New Haven, Conn., 1989), 147–72.

31. On the Hunt farm, see Chapter 5. William Henry Hunt, "Reminiscences of the Old Hunt House on Monument Street and of Life in Concord in the Mid-19th Century" (1926), ed. Leslie Perrin Wilson, *Concord Saunterer*, n.s., 10 (2002): 89–90, 97–103. Of the 213 individuals included in the 1845 census of agriculture and industry, 111 reported no fruit, vegetables, or milk for sale. I take this group to be the traditionalists among Concord's farmers. In 1845 Daniel Hunt was one of seventy-two farmers (out of 213 individuals surveyed) still raising both rye and corn. The typical producer in this group raised 79 bushels of corn, 25 of rye. Hunt reported 70 bushels of corn, 30 of rye; five years later he was credited with 80 bushels of corn and 30 bushels of rye on the federal census of agriculture. He was thus typical of those husbandmen who continued to grow their own breadstuffs. Likewise, his herd of cattle was representative. On the 1840 and 1850 assessments and the 1845 agricultural census, he reported six cows. The average dairy herd consisted of five cows in 1840 and six in 1850. Hunt had one yoke of oxen; the typical farmer had two. See Gross, "Culture and Cultivation," 57. Hunt's 1845 production of butter (500 pounds) was twice the average of 251 ($N = 100$); the same ratio held for the small sample in 1850: 500 pounds for Hunt, an average of 249 for all producers ($N = 42$). Hunt added the provision of fruit, 50 bushels in 1845 and $75 worth in 1850; in the latter year he also slaughtered $30 worth of meat. Of the 76 producers of fruit in 1845, the average output was 66 bushels and the median 38. The Hunt orchard had a fairly typical yield.

32. *New York Herald*, October 16, 1843.

33. *JMN* 8:271–73; *PEJ* 3:102–4, 4:196; Judd, *Second Nature*, 137–40; Elise C. Lemire,

"Repeopling the Woods: Thoreau, Memory, and Concord's Black History," in Kristen Case and K. P. Van Anglen, eds., *Thoreau at Two Hundred: Essays and Reassessments* (New York, 2016), 66–68. On Thomas Dugan, see Chapter 3.

34. Gross, "Culture and Cultivation," 56; Robert A. Gross, "Thoreau and the Laborers of Concord," *Raritan* 33, no. 1 (Summer 2013): 56–58. The landless share of the population rose sharply between 1840 and 1845, from 59 to 69 percent of all male taxpayers. In 1850 the fraction was the same: 69 percent. Thoreau noticed the trend to consolidation: "One man now often holds 2 or 3 old farms," he observed after a walk in sparsely settled areas. *J* 4:196.

35. Leo Marx, *The Machine in the Garden: Technology and the Pastoral Ideal in America* (New York, 1964); John Matteson, *Eden's Outcasts: The Story of Louisa May Alcott and Her Father* (New York, 2007), 84–85, 91.

36. Sterling F. Delano, *Brook Farm: The Dark Side of Utopia* (Cambridge, Mass., 2004), 34–38; *JMN* 7:407–8; *PEJ* 1:277.

37. Delano, *Brook Farm*, 316–17; Cooke, *Early Letters from Curtis to Dwight*, 185–86, 196–97. The following ex–Brook Farmers were assessed for taxes in Concord for the year 1845: George Bradford, James Burrill Curtis and George William Curtis, Nathaniel Hawthorne, and Minot Pratt. Other sojourners included Marianne Ripley, sister of Brook Farm founder George Ripley, and Almira Barlow, and her three sons.

38. Brenda Wineapple, *Hawthorne: A Life* (New York, 2003), 132–60 ("at the head of American Literature"), 155; Nathaniel Hawthorne, *The Blithedale Romance* (Boston, 1852), 79.

39. Harriet H. Robinson, ed., *"Warrington" Pen-Portraits: A Collection of Personal and Political Reminiscences from 1848 to 1876, from the Writings of William S. Robinson* (Boston, 1877), 20–21; *Lowell Journal*, July 7, 1842; John Shepard Keyes (Concord) to Christopher Gore Ripley (Fort Monroe, Va.), Houghton; Keyes, Autobiography, 92½; Wineapple, *Nathaniel Hawthorne*, 163–72; Monica Elbert, "Nathaniel Hawthorne, the Concord Freeman, and the Irish 'Other,'" *Éire-Ireland* 29 (Fómhar/Fall 1994): 61n4; obituary of Charles C. Hazewell, *Boston Evening Traveller*, October 6, 1883. Elbert discovered "no fewer than eleven" reprints of Hawthorne's stories in the *Concord Freeman*; I found four others, all from the *Democratic Review*: "The New Adam and Eve," *CF*, February 10, 1843; "The Celestial Railroad," *CF*, May 5, 1843; "Buds and Bird-Voices," *CF*, July 9, 1843; and "Air-Tight Stoves," *CF*, December 29, 1843. Enthusiasm for Hawthorne was bipartisan; Whig editor Robinson reprinted "A Rill from the Town Pump," a popular short piece included in *Twice-Told Tales* (Boston, 1837), 148–55, in *R*, July 9, 1841.

40. Simpson, *American Notebooks*, 261–67; F. B. Sanborn, "A Concord Note-Book: Ellery Channing and his Table-Talk," *Critic* 47 (July 1905): 79.

41. Simpson, *American Notebooks*, 261–67; *Homes of American Authors; Comprising Anecdotical, Personal, and Descriptive Sketches, by Various Writers* (New York, 1853), 309–13, reprinted in George William Curtis, *Literary and Social Essays* (New York, 1894), 55–60; Randall James Fuller, "Reviving Zenobia: The Last Days and Forgotten Life of Martha E. Hunt, Transcendentalist," *New England Quarterly* 93 (June 2020): 161–87. (I am grateful to Professor Fuller for sharing his article with me before publication.) Having resided across the road from the Hunt farm, George William Curtis must have known the family and/or learned the details of the tragedy from Nathan Barrett.

42. Hawthorne, *Blithedale Romance*, v. In his preface to the novel, Hawthorne denied that any of the characters were based on anyone he met at Brook Farm. But he was silent about the models he might have found in Concord.

43. Nathaniel Hawthorne, "Buds and Bird-Voices," *Democratic Review* 12 (June 1843): 605–8, reprinted in *CF*, July 9, 1843; "The Hall of Fantasy," *Pioneer* 1 (February 1843): 52–53; "The Celestial Railroad," *Democratic Review* 12 (May 1843): 515–23, reprinted in *CF*, May 5, 1843. All of the stories discussed in the text were gathered into *Mosses from an Old Manse* (Boston, 1846). The editor of *The Pioneer*, James Russell Lowell, must have enjoyed the satirical thrusts at Emerson. These references were deleted in the version appearing in *Mosses*. *Concord Freeman* editor Hazewell defended Emerson against Hawthorne's strictures in "The Celestial Railroad." The giant who took over the cave once guarded by Pope and Pagan should have been named "Fanaticism" and *not* Transcendentalist. "Seeing how [Transcendentalist] . . . is shunned and denounced by the world," Hazewell would have placed him in "the House Beautiful" with the ladies "Prudent, Piety, and Charity." *CF*, May 5, 1843. Larry Reynolds suggests that the tour guide for the Celestial Railroad, Mr. Smooth-it-away, is a thinly veiled stand-in for Emerson. See Larry J. Reynolds, "Hawthorne's Labors in Concord," in Richard H. Millington, ed., *The Cambridge Companion to Nathaniel Hawthorne* (New York, 2004), 16–18.

44. Simpson, *American Notebooks*, 245–48, 395–96; Hawthorne, "Celestial Railroad," in *Mosses*, 173–92 ("flimsy-faith," 189). See Leo Marx's classic treatment of Hawthorne's literary experiment in Sleepy Hollow as the formulation of a complex "pastoral design" that became "a new, distinctively American, post-romantic, industrial" sensibility. Marx, *Machine in the Garden*, 3–33 (quotation at 32).

45. Hawthorne, *Mosses*, 1 ("almost overgrown," "belonging to the material world"), 13 ("mosses of ancient growth"), 15 ("houses of any antiquity"). On Hawthorne's role in constructing Concord as a tourist town, see Kristi Lynn Martin, "Creating 'Concord': Making a Literary Tourist Town, 1825–1910" (Ph.D. diss., Boston University, 2019), 126–76.

46. Hawthorne, *Mosses*, 4 ("long and deadly"), 7 (tradition," "blood stain"), 8 ("wilder interest," "civilized machinery"), 9 ("individuality of character"), 22 ("grey, homely").

47. Ibid., 28 ("queer, strangely dressed").

17. Walden and Beyond

1. William Charvat, "A Chronological List of Emerson's American Lecture Engagements," *Bulletin of the New York Public Library* 64 (1960): 503–5; Laura Dassow Walls, *Henry David Thoreau: A Life* (Chicago, 2017), 122–31; *JMN* 5:453 (entry for February 17, 1838); Philip F. Gura, *American Transcendentalism: A History* (New York, 2007), 120–22, 136–49; Joel Myerson, "A History of the Transcendental Club," *ESQ: A Journal of the American Renaissance* 23 (1977): 32–33.

2. Ralph Waldo Emerson, "The Young American," in *Nature, Addresses, and Lectures*, ed. Robert E. Spiller and Alfred R. Ferguson (Cambridge, Mass., 1971), 230.

3. Charvat, "Chronological List," 503–4; *CF*, January 14, 1842; Ralph L. Rusk, *The Life of Ralph Waldo Emerson* (New York, 1949), 285–87. Emerson's series "The Times" earned just forty dollars per lecture, well below his previous high of fifty-seven dollars.

4. *New-Yorker*, April 3, 1841; *New York Review* 8 (April 1841), 509–12, reprinted in Joel Myerson, ed., *Emerson and Thoreau: The Contemporary Reviews* (New York, 1992), 77; *Eclectic Review* 76 (December 1842): 667–87, reprinted in part in *Pioneer* 1 (February 1843): 93–95. James Russell Lowell's new periodical quoted from the *Eclectic Review* in a roundup of "Foreign Literary Intelligence"; this same issue carried Hawthorne's

satire of Emerson in the sketch, "The Hall of Fantasy." For other British reviews dismissing Emerson as an acolyte of Carlyle, see Myerson, *Emerson and Thoreau*, 95-107. He "out-Carlyles Carlyle himself," jibed the *Literary Gazette* (95). As for the circulation of the 1841 *Essays*, a search of America's Historical Newspapers found no advertisements south of Philadelphia (see *National Gazette*, May 27 and 29, 1841) and an extract of the "Gems from Emerson's Essays" in the Washington, D.C., newspaper *The Madisonian* (April 20, 1841); the latter was a reprint from Greeley's *New-Yorker*. Emerson chose to publish his books by a method that restricted their sales and circulation. He funded the costs of production and paid the publisher, James Munroe, a fixed commission for selling the works. The author did better financially than if he had traded the copyright for a royalty on each book sold. But Munroe had little incentive to market Emerson's publications aggressively, and so the books found buyers chiefly in New England. In 1845 Hawthorne attributed Emerson's "provincial" reputation to the "defects of the New England system of publication." See Joel Myerson, "Ralph Waldo Emerson's Income from His Books," in Richard Layman and Joel Myerson, eds., *The Professions of Authorship: Essays in Honor of Matthew J. Bruccoli* (Columbia, S.C., 1996), 135-49, and Edward L. Widmer, *Young America: The Flowering of Democracy in New York City* (New York, 1999), 107.

5. Ralph L. Rusk, ed., *The Letters of Ralph Waldo Emerson*, 6 vols. (New York, 1939), 3:87, 99; Nancy Craig Simmons, "Emerson and His Audience: The New England Lectures, 1843-1844," in Ronald A. Bosco and Joel Myerson, eds., *Emerson Bicentennial Essays* (Boston, 2006), 54-56; *Constitution, Rules and Regulations of the Mercantile Library Association of Baltimore, As Amended October 11, 1841. Established November 14, 1839* (Baltimore, 1841). The Baltimore commitment was firm by November 1842, when the Mercantile Library Association listed Emerson in its schedule of speakers for the coming season. See *Baltimore Sun*, November 18, 1842.

6. Simmons, "Emerson and His Audience," 53-55, 60-63; *JMN* 8:295-96; Ronald A. Bosco and Joel Myerson, eds., *The Later Lectures of Ralph Waldo Emerson, 1843-1871*, 2 vols. (Athens, Ga., 2001), 1:8, 20.

7. Bosco and Myerson, *Later Lectures*, 1:9, 11, 14, 32, 40. For his lecture "The Trade of New England," Emerson borrowed heavily from his 1836-1837 series "The Philosophy of Modern History." Compare the following passages in *EL* 2:116-17 ("pensioner of the wind"), 160-61 ("old bonds of language"), and 455 ("commerce subdues the world") with those in *Later Lectures*, 1:31, 32-33, 36-37.

8. Bosco and Myerson, *Later Lectures*, 1:22-26; F. B. Sanborn, *Henry D. Thoreau*, rev. ed. (Boston, 1910), 120-22; *JMN* 8:271-73, 10:101.

9. Carl Bode, *The American Lyceum: Town Meeting of the Mind* (New York, 1956), 60-74; Bosco and Myerson, *Later Lectures*, 1:42 ("moral agents"), 48 ("organ," "true Church," "pulpit"); *JMN* 7:277 ("true church of today"); *YG*, April 18, May 15, 1840; *CF*, January 21, July 29, October 28, 1842; *Lowell Journal*, July 7, 1842; *Proceedings of the Worcester Society of Antiquities* (1905): 140-41 (skull of British soldier). The phrenologist departed Concord with the skull, which was not returned until forty years later.

10. Bosco and Myerson, *Later Lectures*, 1:57 ("recent literary"), 62 ("reverence"), 65 ("spake," "wretched swarms"), 56 ("country of dwarfs"); Robert A. Gross, *Books and Libraries in Thoreau's Concord: Two Essays* (Worcester, Mass., 1988), 168-69, 177-78.

11. "Literary and Spiritual Influences: Ralph Waldo Emerson Lecture in Providence," in Kenneth Walter Cameron, comp., *The New England Writers and the Press: Evaluations in Contemporary Journalism of Emerson, Hawthorne, Thoreau, Alcott, Longfellow, and Others: New Dimensions for Transcendentalism and the American Renaissance* (Hartford,

Conn., 1980), 13–15; Simmons, "Emerson and His Audiences," 76–79. The text of Emerson's final lecture does not survive; I draw here on the transcript of the address recorded by a reporter for the *Providence Daily Journal*, January 29, 1844. Emerson had offered similar critiques of projects for social reform in his January 1840 lecture, "Reforms," the sixth in his Masonic Temple series "The Present Age," and in "Man the Reformer," presented one year later to the Mechanics' Apprentices' Library Association in Boston. See *EL* 3:256–70, and "Man the Reformer," *Nature, Addresses, and Lectures*, 141–60.

12. Simmons, "Emerson and His Audience," 51–53, 63, 68; "Lecture of Ralph Waldo Emerson, Esq., before the Mercantile Library Association," *Baltimore Sun*, January 19, 1843. Emerson quoted Tocqueville on several points: the eagerness of Americans to get rich quick, their readiness to take risks, ignore rules, and suffer disaster for the sake of competitive gain, the anxiety they constantly betray in fear of failure, and their intellectual conformity to the demands of the majority, owing to a "lack of masculine independence of opinion." See Bosco and Myerson, *Later Lectures*, 1:21, 27, 36, 55–56.

13. Simmons, "Emerson and His Audiences," 55–58; Ralph Waldo Emerson (New York) to Margaret Fuller (Cambridge), and Emerson (Staten Island) to Lidian Emerson (Concord), February 2 and 26, 1843, in Rusk, *Letters of Emerson*, 3:137, 150; *JMN* 8:330, 335, 338.

14. *Daily Evening Transcript* (Boston), September 4, 1843; "Mercantile Library Association of Boston," *Hunt's Merchants' Magazine* 11, no. 6 (December 1844): 572–73. The Mercantile Library Association inaugurated its lecture series in the fall and winter of 1843–1844, with a view to raising money and enhancing the organization's "usefulness." Among the speakers were New York mayor Philip Hone, Boston city councilman and soon-to-be mayor Josiah Quincy, Jr., U.S. senator Levi Woodbury of New Hampshire, Unitarian minister Henry Bellows, the "learned blacksmith" Elihu Burritt (a self-improving workingman favored by the Whigs), Wendell Phillips (speaking on a topic other than abolitionism), and "others no less distinguished in the walks of public usefulness." Some of Boston's leading merchants funded the series; the Boston SDUK, through its president, Daniel Webster, added a $500 contribution.

15. *JMN* 9:13 ("pitiful wages"), 19 ("they are men" [emphasis added], "how grand they are"), 23 ("American power & beauty").

16. *JMN* 9:7 ("bold mole"), 51 ("nervous rocky West," "American genius"); Emerson, "The Young American," *Nature, Addresses, and Lectures*, 226. Emerson drew on the following journal entries for his comments on the railroad in "The Young American": *JMN* 9:7, 13, 19, 23, 51, 62.

17. Widmer, *Young America*, 59–60.

18. Emerson, "The Young American," 222–26.

19. Ibid., 227.

20. Ibid., 226–29; Lawrence Buell, *Emerson* (Cambridge, Mass., 2003), 250. In its summer 1845 issue the *United States Magazine and Democratic Review*, edited by John L. O'Sullivan, first affirmed the "manifest destiny" of the United States "to overspread the continent allotted by Providence for the free development of our yearly multiplying millions." *Democratic Review* 17 (July–August 1845): 5. O'Sullivan, a protégé of President Martin Van Buren and a strong advocate of Jacksonian Democracy, regularly published Hawthorne's short fiction along with a review by Emerson of Ellery Channing's poems and two pieces by Thoreau: a sketch of an

innkeeper, entitled "The Landlord," and an essay-review, "Paradise (to be) Regained." See Widmer, *Young America*, 68–70.

21. Emerson, "Young American," 230–31 ("love and good"); John C. Gerber, "Emerson and the Political Economists," *New England Quarterly* 22 (September 1949): 338–39.

22. Emerson, "Young American," 233–34 ("this is the good," "it will abolish"), 237 ("private adventurers"), 238–39 ("nobility," "guide and adorn life").

23. Ibid., 229 ("heterogeneous," "how much better," "country of the future"), 239 ("out of doors," "in every age"). Emerson's lecture shared in a northern agrarian myth of the West as "the garden of the world" with the independent yeoman "as its focal point." For the classic account of this myth and symbol, see Henry Nash Smith, *Virgin Land: The American West as Symbol and Myth* (1950; rpt. Cambridge, Mass., 1978), quotation at 133.

24. Edward Waldo Emerson, *Emerson in Concord: A Memoir, Written for the "Social Circle" in Concord, Massachusetts* (Boston, 1890), 146; Rusk, *Letters of Emerson*, 2:207n103. The imported works were Victor Cousin's twelve-volume French translation of Plato (Paris, 1822–1839), a four-volume set of Thomas Browne's *Works* (London, 1835–1836), and the three-volume *Letters of Horace Walpole* (London, 1833). The "Human Life" course consisted of eight lectures at the Masonic Temple; Emerson read seven of them in Concord. Charvat, "Chronological List," 502–3. Of the twenty donors, fourteen were members of the Social Circle in 1838. The contributors included Nathan Brooks, Samuel Hoar, John Keyes, Abel Moore, and Daniel Shattuck. In his role as one of the Lyceum's three curators in 1839, Barzillai Frost was charged with obtaining the books and arranging for their delivery to Emerson.

25. Emerson, *Emerson in Concord*, 103–4; *JMN* 8:xii–xiii ("Concord is a little town") and 9:19–20 ("poor cold low life," "grand features," "great sun"). For Emerson's suburban vision, see Robert A. Gross, "Transcendentalism and Urbanism: Concord, Boston and the Wider World," *Journal of American Studies* 18 (December 1984): 361–81. On Sturgis, see Chapter 12.

26. Barzillai Frost, "The True Principle of Reform," 1, 6–8, 20–21, lecture to the Concord Lyceum, April 19, 1843, in the collection of John Gately, Marlborough, Mass. I thank Professor Gately for permission to cite this and other Frost manuscripts.

27. R. W. Emerson, "Lectures on the Times. Lecture III. The Transcendentalist," *Dial* 3 (January 1843): 303–8.

28. Frost, "True Principle of Reform," 21–22. Frost also quoted from Emerson's essay, "Man the Reformer," *Dial* 3 (April 1841): 525. The minister implied that the alienated youth whom Emerson championed were, in essence, selfish brats. "Are those children in a family most amiable, or most likely to make good men & women, 'who do nothing but make immense demands on others'? Would not the opposite be nearer the truth, to ask nothing of others, but to make immense demands on themselves?"

29. *Liberator*, August 11, 1843; Ralph Waldo Emerson and 264 other inhabitants of Concord, petition for a proposed amendment to the Constitution of the United States, February 6, 1844, chap. 87, Resolves 1844, MSA. The Middlesex County Anti-Slavery Society endorsed this petition campaign on August 1, 1843; the document was submitted to the General Court on February 6, 1844. As with previous petitions, twice as many women (171) signed as did men (88). (Some names are illegible, making it impossible to determine the gender of all 265 subscribers.) The document included a dozen or so children as young as eight, whose names on the document, inscribed by parents or older siblings, would surely have surprised the legislators to whom it was addressed. Only three subscribers declined to endorse a

ban on racial discrimination on the railroad: Waldo and Lidian Emerson, plus the philosopher's mother Ruth. The Emersons' discomfort with racial integration was evident in the winter of 1842–1843, when no member of their household signed the petitions circulating in town for a repeal of the state ban on intermarriage across racial lines and for a statute barring discrimination on the railroads on the basis of color. (Emerson left Concord early in January 1843 to lecture in Baltimore on the tenth of the month. The petitions were submitted to the legislature in mid-January. I'm assuming that the memorials were circulating in Concord during December 1842, giving Waldo and Lidian ample time to add their signatures.) By contrast, the Thoreau connection was well represented on all these petitions by John and Cynthia Thoreau, daughter Helen, Aunt Louisa Dunbar, Aunts Jane and Maria Thoreau, and the two Prudence Wards. Henry was probably living in Staten Island when the petition for a constitutional amendment ending slavery was being circulated in town. See Josiah Bartlett and 145 other inhabitants of Concord, petition "for equal rights of Coloured people on Railroads, " SC1/Series 230, House Unpassed Legislation, MSA; Bartlett and 132 others of Concord, petition "for the repeal of the intermarriage Law," SC1/Series 229, Passed Acts, chap. 5, Acts 1843, MSA.

30. Emerson, "Young American," 241; Emerson, "New England Reformers. A Lecture Read Before the Society in Amory Hall, on Sunday, March 3, 1844," in *Essays: Second Series* (Boston, 1844), 286; *JMN* 9:126–27; Sandra Harbert Petrulionis, *To Set This World Right: The Antislavery Movement in Thoreau's Concord* (Ithaca, N.Y., 2006), 41–46.

31. Emerson, "An Address . . . on . . . the Emancipation of the Negroes in the British West Indies," August 1, 1844, in Len Gougeon and Joel Myerson, eds., *Emerson's Antislavery Writings* (New Haven, Conn., 1995), 8 ("overbearing," "dictates of humanity"), 22 ("whole transaction"), 19 ("history of civilization"), 26 ("moral revolution").

32. Ibid., 9 ("heart-sick"), 10 ("crimes and cruelties," pregnant women, "men's backs," "boiling cane-juice"), 13 ("ominous state," "dungeon").

33. Ibid., 20–21.

34. Ibid., 23–26, 30-31; *JMN* 9:173-74; Petrulionis, *To Set This World Right*, 49–50; Philip M. Hamer, "Great Britain, the United States, and the Negro Seamen Acts, 1822–1848," *Journal of Southern History* 1, no. 1 (February 1935): 3–28; Buell, *Emerson*, 252–55. See the various messages, resolutions, and reports concerning the Hoar mission in "Samuel Hoar's Expulsion from Charleston," *Old South Leaflets*, no. 140, *The World Which Emerson Knew* (Boston, 1903).

35. Emerson, "Address," 32–33; George Willis Cooke, ed., *Early Letters of George Wm. Curtis to John S. Dwight: Brook Farm and Concord* (New York, 1898), 193. In another sign of Emerson's deepening involvement in the antislavery movement, he subscribed to a little-known petition to the Massachusetts House of Representatives "against the illegal detention of men." The memorial, which evidently circulated in Concord during December 1844 and January 1845, argued that "many thousand" people in federal jurisdictions were unconstitutionally deprived of liberty, and, consequently, that it is "no offence against law (more than against morals)" to aid in their escape from illegal bondage. The petitioners urged passage of a law authorizing the governor of Massachusetts to provide legal counsel to any citizen of the Commonwealth arrested in a slave state for assisting fugitives' flight to freedom. Of the sixty-five subscribers to this petition, only eighteen, including Emerson, were men. William L. Mather and sixty-four others, petition against illegal detention of men as slaves in territories of the United States and in the District of Columbia, introduced February 11, 1845, Passed Acts, chap. 39, Acts 1845, MSA.

36. S. Margaret Fuller, *Papers on Literature and Art* (New York, 1846), 128. A reviewer for *Graham's American Monthly Magazine* scoffed at Fuller's designation of Emerson as "the Sage of Concord." The partiality for her Transcendentalist friend at the expense of the poets Longfellow and Lowell was not a considered literary judgment. It merely expressed "favoritism" for a fellow member of her literary "clique." See *Graham's American Monthly Magazine of Literature, Art, and Fashion* 29 (November 1846): 262. The sobriquet did not gain wide acceptance until the 1850s.

37. Louis Ruchames, "Emerson's Second West India Emancipation Address," *New England Quarterly* 28 (September 1955): 383–88; Petrulionis, *To Set This World Right*, 51–55. Sadly, Emerson was inconsistent in his vision of racial equality. In 1853 he advanced the view that each race has its own intrinsic characteristics. "The sad side of the Negro question," he commented, is that the abolitionists have misunderstood the origins of slavery. In their minds, "it is violence, brute force," that gives rise to "property in Man." But the propensity to violence, exemplified by such figures as Harriet Beecher Stowe's fictional character Simon Legree, has its origins in Africa. "It is the negro in the white man which holds slaves," according to Emerson. If southern slavery were abolished, that would not put an end to the war of man against man that is the essence of human bondage. For "the brute instinct rallies & centres in the black man. He is created on a lower plane than the white, & eats men & kidnaps & tortures, if he can. The Negro is . . . imitative, secondary, in short, reactionary merely in his successes, & there is no origination with him in mental & moral sphere." This derogatory statement recalls his dismissal in 1837 of the torments suffered by captives on slave ships as not much worse than the horrors of "cannibal" conflicts on the African continent. *JMN* 13:198 (entry for July 20 1853). I thank Ken Sacks for calling my attention to this and similar passages in Emerson's journals.

38. Walls, *Henry David Thoreau*, 118–19; *PEJ* 1:263, 265, 291, 301, 302; *Walden*, 82. As Thoreau lightheartedly recounted the incident in *Walden*, the deal collapsed after the seller's wife had second thoughts. "Every man has such a wife," the disappointed—and somewhat sexist—buyer grumbled. Actually, the situation was more complicated than Thoreau realized. The owner of the twenty-two-acre farm was Samuel Green Hollowell, who had bought the property from his aging father for $500 in July 1829. The arrangement was clearly meant to provide for the sixty-six-year-old Benjamin Hollowell and his wife Sarah, fifty-seven (who was guaranteed life occupancy of the house on the property). At the time of the purchase Samuel, twenty-eight, was living in Lowell with his new bride and earning a living as a farmer. He remained an absentee proprietor, while his parents stayed on the farm. Benjamin Hollowell died in October 1836; the next year the assessors listed Samuel, now a resident of Dracut, next door to Lowell, among the nonresident owners of Concord land. His estate was the same twenty-two acres, with a house and barn. Widow Sarah Hollowell was now subject to taxes; though she owned no real estate, her personal property consisted of money at interest: $500 in 1840, $550 in 1842. By the latter date, Samuel Hollowell no longer appears on the assessors' list of nonresident landholders. It is likely that widow Sarah inherited from her late husband the note for $500 that Samuel had given to his father back in 1829. To redeem that pledge, Samuel must have decided to put the property on the market. Why, then, back out of the agreement with Thoreau? One possibility is that his stepmother Sarah, now sixty-nine, was unwilling to move from her home; another is that Samuel regretted accepting too low an offer

for the property and decided to wait for a higher bid, using his wife's supposed change of mind as an excuse. As it happened, Sarah Hollowell died in 1844, and the farm must have been sold thereafter. Meanwhile Samuel Hollowell presided over a downwardly mobile household. In 1850 he was a gardener in Dracut, his sons operatives in the textile mills. Ten years later the sons had moved out of the household, and he had relocated to Lowell, where he worked as a laborer. Had Thoreau been looking for a family to embody the plight of hardscrabble farmers, he needed to look no further than the struggling Hollowells. See Benjamin Hollowell and Samuel C. Lee to Samuel Green Hollowell, July 9, 1829, MCRD 291:171; 1826, 1835, 1840, 1842, and 1845 Assessment Lists; 1850 census of Dracut, 1860 census of Lowell.

39. Walls, *Henry David Thoreau*, 119–23. The 1842 and 1845 assessment lists record Henry D. Thoreau immediately after his father John and charge him for a single poll, taxable at $1.50.

40. The lifelong bachelor Jonathan Hildreth served eight terms as selectman (1822–29); Cyrus Stow remained unmarried during his tenure as selectman and town clerk from 1835 to 1843. At fifty-six he finally wed, but his new status did not interrupt his public service, which continued to 1847. See Grindall Reynolds, "Memoir of Cyrus Stow," *SCM* 2:295–301.

41. The two Thoreau brothers settled their tax bill in 1842. See List of persons who have paid taxes, prepared in early 1842, ETR.

42. Robert A. Gross, "Quiet War with the State: Henry David Thoreau and Civil Disobedience," *Yale Review* 91 (October 2005): 4–5; "Early Records of the Concord Lyceum," in Kenneth Walter Cameron, comp., *The Massachusetts Lyceum During the American Renaissance; Materials for the Study of the Oral Tradition in American Letters: Emerson, Thoreau, Hawthorne, and Other New-England Lecturers* (Hartford, Conn., 1969), 148, 152, 155–56. Starting on January 13, 1841, and continuing in the meetings of January 27 and February 5, the members of the Lyceum discussed the question, "Is it ever proper to offer forcible resistance" to authority? On the twenty-seventh the Thoreau brothers took the affirmative position, Bronson Alcott the negative. The nonresistance movement was clearly gaining a hearing in Concord. John Shepard Keyes was not impressed. "Mr. Alcott, Henry Thoreau &c carried on a nonresistance discussion," he wrote in his diary, "which was the most foolish as well as amusing that I ever heard, it amounted to plain common nonsense and awfully highflown into the bargain." "See "Early Records of the Concord Lyceum," 155, and Keyes, Diary, vol. 3, entry for January 27, 1841. In addition to the lyceum, Thoreau joined the Concord Atheneum, an association that provided a reading room for contemporary magazines, at its formation in August 1842. There is no evidence that he ever held office in the group. See Concord Atheneum Record Book, CFPL.

43. Emerson, "The Transcendentalist," in *Nature, Addresses, and Lectures*, 207; *JMN* 7:201–2 (entry for May 27, 1839); *PEJ* 1:347–48 (entry for December 24, 1841). In the summer of 1837, before graduation from Harvard, Thoreau and his classmate Charles Stearns Wheeler camped out for six weeks in a hut along the shore of Flint's Pond in Lincoln. It was back to this site he was hoping to return when he made his Christmas Eve journal entry. See Harding, *Days of Thoreau*, 49. As for Emerson, in May 1839 he took his young friend as a model of self-reliance and used his admiring description of Thoreau in the January 15, 1840, lecture, "Reforms," in the series "The Present Age." This language then went into the essay "Self-Reliance." But to judge by Emerson's portrait of "The Transcendentalist,"

Thoreau was clearly not always so resourceful or self-confident. See "Reforms," *EL* 3:264–65, and "Self-Reliance," *EMP*, 142.

44. *PEJ* 1:330 (entry for September 4, 1841).

45. Walls, *Henry David Thoreau*, 122–23, 131–33, 143–46; Robert Sattelmeyer, "Thoreau's Projected Work on the English Poets," *Studies in the American Renaissance* (1980): 239–57; Thoreau, "A Winter Walk," *Dial* 4 (October 1843): 211–26, quotation at 214.

46. Walls, *Henry David Thoreau*, 122, 137, 148–49; Walter Harding, ed., *Thoreau as Seen by His Contemporaries* (New York, 1989), 81–83, reprinting an interview conducted by George W. Cooke for the *Independent* in 1896; *PEJ* 1:447 (entry of January 16, 1843); Claude M. Simpson, ed., *The American Notebooks*, vol. 8 of *The Centenary Edition of the Works of Nathaniel Hawthorne* (Columbus, Ohio, 1972), 369, 371.

47. Walls, *Henry David Thoreau*, 149–55.

48. Ibid., 155–57; Thoreau, "The Landlord," *United States Magazine and Democratic Review* 13 (October 1843): 427–30; J. A. Etzler, *The Paradise within the Reach of All Men Without Labor, by Powers of Nature and Machenery* [sic], *An Address to All Intelligent Men* (Pittsburgh, 1833); Thoreau, "Paradise (To Be) Regained," in Wendell Glick, ed., *Reform Papers* (Princeton, N.J., 1973), 20; Steven Stoll, *The Great Delusion: A Mad Inventor, Death in the Tropics, and the Utopian Origins of Economic Growth* (New York, 2008).

49. Thoreau (Staten Island) to Emerson (Concord), June 8, 1843; Thoreau (Concord) to Richard Frederick Fuller (Cambridge), April 2, 1843, and Thoreau (Staten Island) to Lidian Jackson Emerson (Concord), May 22, 1843, in Hudspeth, *Correspondence of Thoreau*, 1:179–82, 152, 166–68; Robert A. Gross, "Transcendentalism and Urbanism: Concord, Boston, and the Wider World," *Journal of American Studies* 18 (December 1984): 361–81.

50. Walls, *Henry David Thoreau*, 163–67; *Liberator*, June 23, 1843 ("Annual Report of the Concord Female A.S. Society"), June 21 ("Middlesex County A.S. Society"), and June 14, 1844 ("No Union with Slaveholders!"); Frederick Douglass to "my kind Friend Helen," n.d. [ca. March 15, 1844], CAS Collection, CFPL. Douglass used the same language in a public letter to the *Liberator* (March 15, 1844) about "Conventions in Middlesex County" as he did in the private letter to Helen Thoreau.

51. Thoreau, "Herald of Freedom," in Glick, *Reform Papers*, 49–57, quotation at 49; Thoreau (Staten Island) to Helen Louisa Thoreau (Concord), October 18, 1843, in Hudspeth, *Correspondence of Thoreau*, 1:250–51. In a lecture delivered at Boston's Amory Hall on March 10, 1843, Thoreau threw this negative view in the reformers' faces. His talk, with its strictures on reform, is the companion piece to his appreciative account of Nathaniel Rogers, written about the same time. See Linck C. Johnson, "Reforming the Reformers: Emerson, Thoreau, and the Sunday Lectures at Amory Hall, Boston," *ESQ: A Journal of the American Renaissance* 37 (1991): 235–89.

52. Petrulionis, *To Set This World Right*, 51–53; Len Gougeon, *Virtue's Hero: Emerson, Antislavery, and Reform* (Athens, Ga., 1990), 95–96; "Early Records of the Concord Lyceum," 159–60; *JMN* 9:102; Keyes, Autobiography, 102–3, 110. Keyes later regretted his position in the lyceum dispute: "It was the only difference I ever had for a moment with Mr. Emerson and I have often regretted that I let Mr. Frost put me up to that disagreement." But he never forgave Mary Brooks for publicly impugning his honesty. When she stood up in the open meeting and disputed a statement—"That's false, Mr. Keyes"—he kept his cool and, making "a low bow," offered a barbed riposte: "I had it, Madam, from your own husband." The lawyer thought he had "the better" of the exchange, but a half-century later he was still smarting over the female reformer's challenge.

53. "To the Friends of Freedom in Middlesex and neighboring Counties," *Liberator*, July 5, 1844; *J* 2:120–24; "Wendell Phillips Before Concord Lyceum," *Liberator*, March 28, 1845, reprinted in Glick, *Reform Papers*, 60–62. For Thoreau's critical view of reform, which he put forward in March 1844 to "the Society" in Amory Hall, see Johnson, "Reforming the Reformers," 235–89.

54. Petrulionis, *To Set This World Right*, 42–44; Walls, *Henry David Thoreau*, 174–76; *CF*, July 19 and 26, 1844; *Liberator*, August 9, 1844; *PEJ* 1:355.

55. W. Barksdale Maynard, "Emerson's 'Wyman Lot': Forgotten Context for Thoreau's House at Walden," *Concord Saunterer*, n.s., 12–13 (2004–5): 59–84; Emerson (Concord) to William Emerson (Staten Island), October 4, 1844, in Rusk, *Letters of Emerson*, 3:262–63; Walls, *Henry David Thoreau*, 182–84; Cyrus Stow to Emerson, October 3, 1844, MCRD 449:515; administration of the estate of Thomas Wyman, 1843, File no. 45338, MCPR. Wyman's assets consisted of the eleven acres, appraised at $80, and a motley personal estate valued at $29.06. It included foodstuffs (bushel of rye, a "lot" of potatoes), farming tools (hoe, shovel, rake, scythe, and sneath), furniture (bed and bedding, three chests), and clothes. At sixty-nine, Wyman—born in Townsend in 1774, married in Concord in 1813, and a widower since 1837—barely scraped by. The claims on the estate included $131 in principal and interest owed to James Barrett for part of the tract, grocery bills from Reuben Rice's green store, a $2.57 debt to tavern keeper Bigelow, back taxes, and $1.50 to the African American laborer Jack Garrison, among others. A kinswoman named Almira Wyman—perhaps a daughter whose birth was not registered—put in for $76.89. The administrator of the estate, Cyrus Stow, requested a huge fee, $40, for his services. Those included posting a notice of the auction at public places in Concord and two neighboring towns, but in contrast to the usual practice, the sale was not advertised in the press. Perhaps the estate was considered too low in value to bear the charge of newspaper advertisements.

56. Walls, *Henry David Thoreau*, 181–84.

57. Ibid., 196–97; *PEJ* 2:156, 161.

58. Walls, *Henry David Thoreau*, 192–94; Bradley P. Dean, "Rediscovery at Walden: The History of Thoreau's Bean-Field," *Concord Saunterer*, n.s., 12–13 (2004–5): 87–137. In 1837 the state-authorized census of Concord counted 346 households, of which twelve (3.5 percent) consisted of a single person. The results were nearly identical for 1850. Of 401 households in that year, again twelve (3 percent) had but one inmate, and only three of them resided in a separate dwelling. In both years "solitaries" represented less than 1 percent of the total population (0.6 percent of 2,023 in 1837, 0.5 percent of 2,249 in 1850).

59. Thoreau, "Thomas Carlyle and His Works," in Thoreau, *Early Essays and Miscellanies*, ed. Joseph J. Moldenhauer and Edwin Moser, with Alexander C. Kern (Princeton, N.J., 1975), 219–67; J. Lyndon Shanley, *The Making of Walden with the Text of the First Edition* (Chicago, 1957), 105–6; Walls, *Henry David Thoreau*, 244. Since my emphasis is on the manuscript Thoreau composed during his sojourn in the woods, I cite the first version of *Walden*, edited by Shanley, and not the authoritative Princeton edition.

60. "Early Records of the Concord Lyceum," 162; Shanley, *Making of Walden*, 106–8.

61. Shanley, *Making of Walden*, 108–10, 118. Thoreau's famous remark that "the mass of men lead lives of quiet desperation" initially appeared in a draft of *A Week on the Concord and Merrimack Rivers*. It was prompted by an encounter that the Thoreau brothers had with an organ-grinder, who had traveled 250 miles from New York City to New Hampshire in search of work. Thoreau eventually dropped the passage

from his memoir of the boating trip and moved it to *Walden* as a commentary on the resignation of Concord farmers to their fate. See Shanley, *Making of Walden*, 52–53.

62. Shanley, *Making of Walden*, 112.

63. Walls, *Henry David Thoreau*, 245; Shanley, *Making of Walden*, 109.

64. "Early Records of the Concord Lyceum," 119, 142; Shanley, *Making of Walden*, 141.

65. Shanley, *Making of Walden*, 117, 121, 123, 131; Walls, *Henry David Thoreau*, 18.

66. Harding, *Days of Thoreau*, 89; *PEJ* 1:301, 2:125; inventory of estate of Thomas Wyman, 1843, File no. 45338, MCPR. Thoreau's indictment of the stench of manure emanating from Concord's fields was borrowed from Claudius's confession of his brother's murder in *Hamlet*, Act 3, scene 3. On the 1826 list of polls and estates, John Thoreau possessed one cow and one pig, valued together at twenty-one dollars; on successive assessments (1830, 1835, 1837) he held no livestock at all. Then in 1840 he once again kept a pig, undoubtedly to be fattened and slaughtered for pork in the fall. On the same 1840 valuation list Tommy Wyman was credited with three acres of tillage, on which he had grown fourteen bushels of rye and five of corn. Three years later, following his death, the appraisers of his estate found some eleven bushels of rye and "lots of potatoes" in storage. He also regularly kept a cow on five acres of pasture and cultivated a hayfield, for whose standing grass Emerson was obliged to pay extra.

67. Robert A. Gross, "The Great Bean Field Hoax: Thoreau and the Agricultural Reformers," *Virginia Quarterly Review* 61 (Summer 1985): 483–97; Shanley, *Making of Walden*, 132.

68. Shanley, *Making of Walden*, 128–32, 181.

69. Shanley, *Making of Walden*, 179, supplemented by "Fluid Edition" of *Walden* created by a team of Thoreau scholars directed by Paul Schacht of the State University of New York at Geneseo. See Version A, paragraph 82, at https://digitalthoreau .org/walden/fluid/text/07.html. Of the 108 farmers surveyed in the 1850 federal census of agriculture, 48 (44 percent) reported no peas and beans. Only four men raised more than 12 bushels; ironically, the "bean king," with 60 bushels, was the progressive agriculturalist John B. Moore, son and heir of Captain Abel, who died in 1848. In 1845 the Commonwealth of Massachusetts conducted a census of agriculture and industry. The Concord return enumerated 213 individuals, 166 of whom provided readable responses regarding their production of beans. Just 7 percent reported a crop; only one of these 12 individuals, Thomas H. Davis, exceeded Thoreau's harvest with a total of 25 bushels.

70. Shanley, *Making of Walden*, 182, 178; Don C. Seitz, *Artemus Ward (Charles Farrar Browne): A Biography and Bibliography* (New York, 1919), 297; *Josh Billings' Old Farmer's Allminax, 1870–1879, with Comic Illustrations* (New York, 1902). Born in 1818, Billings gained popularity as a humorist in the Civil War era.

71. Shanley, *Making of Walden*, 179; *Walden*, 156; Henry Colman, *Report on the Agriculture of Massachusetts*, 4 vols. (Boston, 1838–1841), 4:360–62; Maynard, "Emerson's 'Wyman Lot,'" 63.

72. Shanley, *Making of Walden*, 181, supplemented by "Fluid Edition" of *Walden*, Version A, paragraph 10.

73. Colman, *Report*, 361; F. B. Sanborn, "Ellery Channing in New Hampshire," *Granite Monthly* 32 (March 1903): 158–59 (emphasis added); Shanley, *Making of Walden*, 182; *PEJ* 2:175, 4:116–18. On Minott, see Chapter 5. During his sojourn in Staten Island, Thoreau was frequently homesick for his native town, and whenever he thought about Concord, "Geo. Minott loom[ed] up considerably" in his mind. See

Thoreau (Staten Island) to Ralph Waldo and Lidian J. Emerson (Concord), July 8, 1843, in Hudspeth, *Correspondence of Thoreau,* 1:201–3.

74. Shanley, *Making of Walden,* 180–81, 184.

75. Ibid., 182.

76. Robert A. Gross, "Quiet War with the State: Henry David Thoreau and Civil Disobedience," *Yale Review* 91 (October 2005): 1–17; *PEJ* 2:262–64; Walls, *Henry David Thoreau,* 208–13. In the published version of "Resistance to Civil Government," Thoreau alludes to Samuel Hoar's ill-fated mission to South Carolina, only to suggest perversely that his distinguished townsman could have done more to end slavery by staying at home. "If my esteemed neighbor, the State's ambassador . . . , instead of being threatened with the prisons of Carolina, were to sit down the prisoner of Massachusetts, that State which is so anxious to foist the sin of slavery upon her sister,—though at present she can discover only an act of inhospitality to be the ground of a quarrel with her"—the legislature would have been compelled to take strong action on the subject. See "Resistance to Civil Government," in Glick, *Reform Papers,* 75–76.

77. Shanley, *Making of Walden,* 119–21, 142.

78. *J* 2:248–49, 9:160; Robert A. Gross, "Thoreau and the Laborers of Concord," *Raritan* 33, no. 1 (Summer 2013): 50–66.

Acknowledgments

This inquiry into individualism was not done alone. Emerson pressed against the claims of friends and the demands of associations. I could not have carried out this project over four decades without the help of many individuals and institutions. To acknowledge their contributions amounts to a retrospect of my academic career. It has taken a village to bring forth this study of a single community in changing times.

The study traces its origins back to the introductory course in the History of American Civilization at the University of Pennsylvania in fall 1964, when James J. Flink posed a question that stayed with me over the years: how did Puritan communalism give way to Yankee individualism? At Penn, Flink excited my interest in American studies, the late Lee Benson encouraged me to become a historian, and Mike Zuckerman provided a model of intellectual playfulness and democratic teaching. Everyone who has studied with Mike knows how exhilarating and daunting it is to receive his comments on a manuscript. This work has benefited immensely from his incisive reading of several chapters and its author has gained even more from our long friendship.

Graduate school at Columbia University allowed its students to pursue whatever interested them in the American past, and I am grateful to Alden Vaughan for introducing me to the study of early America and to the late Stuart Bruchey for being a supportive dissertation advisor. My training as a historian was interrupted and enhanced by a two-year stint as a writer for *Newsweek*, where, under the guidance of senior editors Edwin Diamond and Jack Kroll, I learned the craft of writing for a general audience. The *Newsweek* experience has shaped my approach to presenting the results of historical investigation as accessibly as possible, with a focus on narrative, human agency, and lived experience.

When I moved to Concord in 1972, my purpose was to contribute to the growing genre of community studies and research a dissertation on "population, land, and society" in the first half-century of the new nation, 1790–1840. In the spirit of the new social history, I planned to treat Concord as a case study of social and economic processes representative of New England. Happily, the late David B. Little, a Concord native who was then directing the Essex Institute in Salem, steered me in a different direction. Highlighting his hometown's role at the start of the Revolution and its significance as a seedbed of Transcendentalism, he provoked the obvious question, "Why Concord?" Rather than look for a typical community, I embraced a distinctive one and explored how Concord was like other places, how it differed, and, most important, how and why it came to be in the forefront of important episodes in our national history. As the Bicentennial of the American Revolution approached, I took up these questions and set out to write a quick book for the occasion that would place the events of April 19, 1775, in the context of Concord's own history and would show how individuals from all ranks of the social order participated in the coming of revolution and war. *The Minutemen and Their World* was the result, and it became the dissertation that set me on my way.

Amherst College provided the setting and support for returning to Concord in the era of Emerson and Thoreau. As a new faculty member in the Department of American Studies (with a joint appointment in History), I was incredibly fortunate in my colleagues, who trusted a newcomer with little teaching experience to offer the junior seminar required of all majors on the topic "Culture and Community: The Worlds of Emerson, Dickinson, and Thoreau." The course delved deeply into the lives and works of these major literary figures and set them in the context of the communities in which they lived and wrote. It also jump-started this project, allowed me to combine teaching and research, and, in its most powerful impact, engaged me with the most extraordinary students in probing the relevance of Concord's writers and Amherst's poet to our own lives, to our sense of the relation between individual and community, and to our critical understanding of culture and society. Offered first in American Studies and then as a History course from 1977 to 1988, it also generated a remarkable body of research papers, some of which are cited in my endnotes. The course was a concrete demonstration of the continuing appeal of Emerson and Thoreau to young people, who, at a key moment in their coming of age, were wrestling with fundamental ideas about individual and society, community and conformity, self-fulfillment and careers. It was exhilarating to join with them in these conversations.

This book thus reflects the formative influence of American Studies at Amherst College during the 1970s and 1980s. I was incredibly lucky in the colleagues who shaped the early versions of this project with their interest and insights and who inspired me with their strenuous intellectual lives. Our gatherings in Morgan Hall, in which we developed and taught collaborative courses in American Studies, provided an ideal introduction to college teaching. Amherst College proved to be my second liberal arts education. I regret that Ted Greene and Hugh Hawkins will never get to read this work, but hope that Allen Guttmann, Gordie Levin, Barry O'Connell, and Laura Wexler will discern their influence in its pages. Beyond the Amherst campus, three faculty members at the Five Colleges were important interlocutors: Jack Wilson at Smith, Joe Ellis at Mount Holyoke, and, most of all, Steve Nissenbaum at UMass–Amherst, not only a close friend but something of an intellectual alter ego. Time and again we have found ourselves independently pursuing similar paths in our interests and careers and deepening our connection in the process.

The Trustees of Amherst College furnished crucial financial support for this project with a faculty fellowship, sabbatical funding, and salary supplements that enabled me to accept several external awards. During my time at Amherst, I received a summer stipend from the National Endowment for the Humanities and fellowships from Harvard University's Charles Warren Center for Studies in American History, the John Simon Guggenheim Foundation, and the George A. and Eliza Gardner Howard Foundation.

When I assumed the directorship of the new American Studies program at the College of William and Mary in 1988, I had to continue this project outside New England and in a new intellectual environment. Williamsburg, not Boston or Concord, was the center of intense social-historical inquiry, and I was challenged to situate my project in a broader geography, to question the relevance of Transcendentalism to Tidewater Virginia, and to address skeptical questions from scholars deeply invested in research and graduate education. At the same time, I enjoyed the camaraderie and intellectual fellowship of new colleagues in developing an innovative doctoral program in American Studies. In these years the interdisciplinary field was altered by new emphases on multiculturalism and transnationalism, and as I incorporated these approaches into my teaching, my research expanded in turn. So, too, did another emerging field of inquiry, the history of the book, capture my interest and prompt new questions about Emerson and Thoreau as public intellectuals seeking an audience in an expansive literary marketplace. As I proceeded in these directions, many of the outstanding students we recruited in American Studies gladly came along for the ride, wrestling, like their counterparts in New England, with the questions raised by the Transcendentalists about how to lead intellectual lives of integrity in a society riven by inequalities and insistent upon convention and conformity. Among the colleagues in Williamsburg who left their marks on this project, I want to thank Bob Scholnick, who as graduate dean in the College of Arts and Sciences brought me to William and Mary, where I found key collaborators and friends in building American Studies, notably, Chandos Brown, Margaretta Lovell, Rich Lowry, and Alan Wallach. The Omohundro Institute of Early American History and Culture, where I spent two years as book review editor of the *William and Mary Quarterly*, also made its mark in the stimulating conversations I had with Chris Grasso, Phil Morgan, the late Mike McGiffert, and the late Ron Hoffman, whose warm friendship, shrewd questions, and intellectual comradeship I will always treasure.

The College of William and Mary was generous in its provision of leaves and financial support of this project. Dean of Arts and Sciences David Lutzer supplemented the Howard Foundation fellowship in 1988–1989 before I even arrived in Williamsburg, and he made it possible for me to take up a National Endowment for the Humanities Faculty Fellowship in 1994 and extend it for an additional semester with a sabbatical leave. I was able to spend these three semesters as an associate of the Charles Warren Center, thanks to sponsorship by the late Bernard Bailyn, and to enjoy residence in Cabot House on the Radcliffe campus. A month's stay at the Rockefeller Foundation's Study and Conference Center in Bellagio, Italy, furnished a sublime setting in which to think and write about Concord in the early nineteenth century and to culminate my leave. This was the first of several occasions in which I was able to take my study of Concord and Transcendentalism abroad and discover the strong international interest in Emerson and Thoreau. Dean Geoffrey Feiss of William and Mary enabled me to take up an appointment as Fulbright Chair of American Studies at Odense University (now Southern Denmark University) during the 1998–1999 academic year. I am grateful to the Fulbright Commission for Denmark and its executive director, Marie Mønsted, for their support, and to David Nye and Stuart Ward for their friendship during that year and since.

My final year at William and Mary, as it turned out, was spent as Mellon Distinguished Scholar in Residence at the American Antiquarian Society in Worcester, Massachusetts. Once again William and Mary deserves thanks for supplementing this award. The AAS has been a second intellectual home throughout my career, and I am grateful to two past presidents, the late Marcus McCorison and his successor, Ellen Dunlap, for their continuing support. John B. Hench, then director of academic programs, oversaw the arrangements for this fellowship and extended a warm welcome to AAS. The year in Worcester proved to be a turning point for my project; thanks to the richness of the library's collections, I was able to situate Concord developments within larger contexts and to identify the arenas in which it was in advance of other communities and those in which it lagged behind, or was simply average. Key sources at AAS revealed the influence of outside groups in stirring up the sectarian split and partisan divides in the town. It was fitting that in the setting of a national research library I should come to realize that a central theme of this project was the waning of local autonomy and the accelerating integration of the town into the wider world. For their intellectual companionship and assistance during this fellowship year, I thank AAS staff members Hench, Joanne Chaison, Vince Golden, Tom Knoles, Marie Lamoureux, Jim Moran, and Caroline Sloat and AAS fellows Bridget Ford, Jim Sidbury, and Nick Yablon. Since completing that fellowship year in Worcester, I have returned often, benefiting from the generosity and skill of such new staff members as Ashley Cataldo and Jaclyn Penny and from the unsurpassed knowledge of Vince Golden.

My final academic appointment at the University of Connecticut proved to be a most congenial and productive setting for teaching and research. It seemed fitting to be back in my native Connecticut, some ninety miles from Concord, as I moved to bring years of research together into a book. The James L. and Shirley A. Draper Chair in Early American History furnished funds to hire research assistants and database consultants. The History Department afforded a one-semester sabbatical. And the University of Connecticut Humanities Institute, directed by Sharon Harris, awarded a fellowship for the 2013–2014 academic year, and in the final stages of publication, the Institute, under director Michael Lynch, provided a Humanities Book Award to support the costs of preparing the index. The most unexpected boon to this project came in the classroom. Through the Honors Program, headed by the late Lynne Goodstein, I collaborated with the geologist Robert Thorson and the photographer Janet Pritchard to develop an interdisciplinary course for first- and second-year students. "Walden and the American Landscape" explored the making of Walden—the pond and the book—in the contexts of the various communities, biotic and human, that made and remade the local environment from the Ice Age (the Pleistocene) to the industrial revolution and the dawn of the Anthropocene, our current epoch of human-driven climate change. The course adapted the model of American Studies at Amherst to the setting of a large public research university; it engaged students with science, history, literary study, and artistic representation in a single syllabus; and, most of all, it immersed them in *Walden* and the works it inspired. Thoreau and Transcendentalism evoked a similar combination of excitement and exasperation from UConn millennials as it had for the tail-end Baby Boomers and emerging Gen Xers I had taught at Amherst. It is, in part, a reflection of my teaching experience over the years that *The Transcendentalists and Their World* gives so much attention to youthful rebellion and generational change. I was fortunate to find such committed teachers and expansive thinkers as Pritchard, Thorson (a noted Thoreau scholar in his own right), Chris Clark, and Wayne Franklin with whom to create and offer this course.

The University of Connecticut History Department was—and remains—a lively intellectual home, whose productive scholars take a strong interest in one another's work. Dick Brown, a friend since the 1970s, has set a high bar for intellectual colleagueship and personal friendship. His example has been matched by Irene Q. Brown, Chris Clark, Frank Costigliola, John Davis, Nina Dayton, Michael Dintenfass, Ken Gouwens, Brendan Kane, Sylvia Schafer, Altina Waller, and Walt Woodward, along with Lynn Bloom and Wayne Franklin in English, Robert Thorson in Geology, and Kathryn Myers and Janet Pritchard in Art and Art History. (Janet deserves thanks as well for taking the photograph of the author on the book jacket.) I hope they will see the reflections of conversations with each of them in this work.

Central to this project was a reconstruction of the economy, politics, and society of Concord over the decades from 1790 to 1850. Following the model I had used in *The Minutemen and Their World,* I set about assembling databases from such sources familiar to social historians as town assessments, census rolls, and lists of elected officials. Little did I realize how massive a task this would become even for so small a community as Concord, whose population never reached 2,500, the census definition of an urban place, through 1860. My databases of taxpayers from 1825 to 1850 and of petitioners to Congress and to the Massachusetts General Court on such issues as slavery and Freemasonry numbered from 1,400 to 1,600 individuals. This was just the beginning. In the era of Emerson and Thoreau, it was not individuals alone who became conscious of themselves, but so, too, did society. It was a "calculating age," to use Patricia Cline Cohen's well-chosen term, and a wide range of agencies, from state and federal governments to banks and corporations, from churches and denominations to benevolent associations, produced a profusion of records. Here lay opportunities to make connections among the several realms of local life, to see, for example, how church membership was linked to support for abolitionism or how wealth and elite affiliations affected participation in the movements for social and cultural improvement. Meanwhile, sources kept expanding, especially the genealogical databases made available by Ancestry and the New England Historic Genealogical Society, so I kept adding new details to individual records.

I began gathering such information back in the now-forgotten world of punch cards and mainframe computers and migrated the databases to tapes, floppy disks, CD-ROMs, and online storage in the cloud. More precisely, a platoon of research assistants did so on my behalf and under my direction. Their labors have ranged from coding data and abstracting deeds to scouring archives for documents, indexing newspapers, and hunting for pertinent items in the microfilmed copies of the Concord press. Back in the mid-1970s Brandeis University undergraduates Debby London, Michael Baumrin, and Alisa Belinkoff (now Katz) launched the database of assessment lists. At Amherst College I was aided by Debby Applegate, Gloria Brackman, the late David Bryan, Brad Campbell, Maria Farland, Stuart Goldberg, Janet Granger, Katherine M. Grant, Jim Kobe, Catherine O'Donnell, Mark Rennella, Noel Selegzi, John Sweet, and David Zonderman. I also drew on the technical expertise of individuals at the Amherst Computer Center: Duane Bailey, Mike Friedman, Ted Romer, and Jonathan Welch. During my fellowship year at the Charles Warren Center, I drew on the assiduous labors of Harvard undergraduate Cheryl Green and doctoral student Alex Von Hoffman at the East Cambridge Registry of Deeds.

William and Mary students picked up where their Amherst counterparts left off. American Studies doctoral students Phyllis Hunter, Joe Rainer, and James Spady added sources and expanded the database, while Augustine Sedgewick, a major in American Studies and enthusiast of the Transcendentalists, kept my ballooning files in order. Na'ama Ely, a computer programmer and friend, took my historical databases and upgraded them to a format on which subsequent specialists at UConn built. The move to Connecticut propelled this work to completion. Thanks to the labor and talents of History major Elizabeth Kelly and of graduate students Michael Goddard, Adam Jacobs, Amy Sopcak-Joseph, Justin Spitzer, and Will Mathews, key gaps in my compendium of assessment lists and censuses were filled in and my survey of business records and newspapers was made more systematic. But I would not have been able to make sense of all these data without the crucial assistance of Brian Urlacher, a doctoral candidate in political science, who put his expertise at SPSS, sophistication in quantitative methods, and interests in political behavior to work in merging files and enabling me to carry out multivariate analyses. His contributions were supplemented by those of Andres Pletch, a master's student in History with experience in database management.

As I carried the Concord project with me to different schools, at home and abroad, I canvassed an ever-wider geography in the location of sources. Concord was a fluid place in the first half of the nineteenth century, with many newcomers flowing in and out and a majority of native sons and daughters departing for the expanding cities and mill towns of the East and the agricultural frontiers of the West. As they moved, these ex-Concordians carried documents about life in their former residence, especially letters from folks back home, across the republic. And so, I found myself calling on the assistance of librarians and archivists in likely depositories in New England and unexpected ones in North Carolina, Texas, and California. Starting farthest from Concord, I have consulted the Thoreau and Sewall families' papers, 1790–1917, at the Huntington Library in San Marino, California, and am grateful to Olga Tsapina, curator of historical manuscripts, for providing me with digital scans of letters in the Lemuel Shattuck collection at that institution. A Google search for materials regarding Daniel Southmayd, the first pastor of Concord's Trinitarian Church, turned up an important set of letters in Texas. In 1836 the parson emigrated to the then-Mexican territory with his wife Joanna; he died within a year or so, but the widow stayed, and her correspondence with family back in Vermont, including letters sent from Concord, were passed along to descendants, transcribed, and preserved on a website by attorney Jeffrey Southmayd of Palm Coast, Florida, who kindly sent me copies. The David M. Rubenstein Rare Book and Manuscript Library of Duke University holds the diary kept by Elizabeth Hoar when she accompanied her father, Samuel, on his ill-fated embassy to Charleston, South Carolina, to litigate on behalf of Massachusetts seamen of color in that Southern port. Matt Cohen, then a faculty member in the Duke English Department, obtained a copy for me. The National Archives in Washington is the repository of the vast corpus of antislavery memorials and petitions in defense of the Cherokee Indians on which I drew. I am indebted to Rodney Ross, now retired specialist in these congressional documents, for guiding me to the Concord materials and sending me copies. (Brad Campbell and Alan Wallach helped in these searches.) Moving back to New England, I am grateful to Yale's Sterling Library for access to the commonplace book of the second Trinitarian minister, John Wilder, and to letters of Maria Thoreau, the writer's aunt, in the Loomis-Wilder Family Papers; to the Middlebury College Library for Thoreau documents in its Abernethy Collection; and to the Maine Historical Society for the Brown Family correspondence.

Not surprisingly, the bulk of the materials for this study resides in Massachusetts. The Boston Athenaeum's curator of manuscripts, Stephen Nonack, made available the diary of John Brown, Jr., a Concord native clerking in Boston before returning to his hometown. (An earlier volume of the diary was graciously shared with me by the late Professor Roger Brown of American University, a descendant.) Roberta Zonghi, former curator of rare books and manuscripts at the Boston Public Library, guided me through that institution's antislavery collections. The Massachusetts Historical Society holds a miscellany of sources, including papers of the Ripley-Emerson and Hoar families, pertinent to this investigation; I also want to acknowledge the assistance of two staff members of the Adams Papers Project at MHS, Sara Martin and Karen Northrop Barzilay (my former doctoral student at William and Mary), for retrieving and scanning significant documents. The Massachusetts Archives presides over a vast trove of government documents, encompassing legislative files, petitions for corporate charters, memorials on controversial issues, records of the county courts, probate files, and archives of the state judiciary, among other materials. Fortunately, the staff has expertly guided me through the labyrinth and has efficiently and cheerfully answered my many requests. I want to single out former librarians Jennifer Fauxsmith, Autumn Haag, and William Milhomme, and especially former head of reader services and current curator John Hannigan, researcher extraordinaire, who has helped me gain access to a wealth of materials in the collection. I am indebted as well to Elizabeth Bouvier, head of archives for the Massachusetts Supreme Judicial Court, for facilitating my research into several crucial court cases involving

Concordians, and to Silvia Mejia for providing access to sources at the State Library of Massachusetts.

Given the many connections between Concord and Harvard College, it is understandable that I spent a great deal of time in the university's libraries. Houghton Library was indispensable for its Emerson and Ripley collections, John Shepard Keyes letters, and Timothy Prescott diary. Timothy Mahoney provided access to the Baker Business Library's collection of records pertaining to Burr and Prichard's "green store." The Andover-Harvard Theological Library offered an abundance of Ezra Ripley sermons to supplement the great many held at Houghton and others at the Trustees of Reservations Archives Center in Sharon, Massachusetts, where Alison Bassett, Sarah Hayes, and Christie Jackson have been quite helpful. The Harvard Law School Library, then overseen by David Warrington, afforded insights into the work of a justice of the peace by making available the record book of Esquire Abiel Heywood, documenting petty offenses and serious crimes in town. And the Harvard University Archives was a cornucopia of unexpected finds in the files of Concord alumni, some of whom, far from entering into the Yankee elite, confessed to lives of disappointment and failure.

Concord, of course, has been the center of my research over the years. As this book recounts, its citizens have cherished their town's signal role in the New England and American past, and since the second quarter of the nineteenth century, they have taken steps to preserve the records of that history in local libraries. Key figures in my narrative—Edward Jarvis and Lemuel Shattuck, Waldo Emerson, Samuel Hoar, and John Shepard Keyes—have pioneered in the writing of local history, led in the creation of municipal archives, and joined in support of a public collection of artifacts from attics and estate sales to evoke the ways of life in generations past. Their legacy flourishes in the William Munroe Special Collections of the Concord Free Public Library (CFPL) and in the Concord Museum. Once known as the Concord Antiquarian Society, the museum under directors Dennis Fiori, Peggy Burke, and now Tom Putnam has welcomed me into its fold, given me unparalleled access to its collections (including the manuscript autobiography and account books of William Munroe), enlisted me in the organization of exhibits, and shaped my understanding of everyday life in Concord during the eighteenth and nineteenth centuries, thanks in large part to decades-long conversations with curator David Wood. I am also grateful to Jessica Desany for assistance with the illustrations.

More than any other archive, the CFPL has made possible this book. Established in 1873 as a public-private partnership by William Munroe, Jr., the successful merchant son of the pencil manufacturer, the Special Collections document the activities and associations, the ideas and writings of the townspeople with astonishing richness and scope. The collection is a regular destination for literary scholars wishing to consult its Alcott, Emerson, and Thoreau materials. It beckons to the social historian for its records of the Main Street elite, of Ezra Ripley and his fellow pastors, of the storekeepers and mechanics in the village, of the farmers in the out-districts, of laborers and African Americans. The lawyer Nathan Brooks handled his neighbors' estates for over a half-century, and all his files are open to study, attorney-client privilege long gone. The principal churches and the many voluntary societies have deposited their records; all the newspapers from 1816 to the early 1850s are available on the library website. Also housed in Special Collections are the minutes of town meetings and the archives of local government dating back to the early eighteenth century and forward to the Civil War. I could and did get lost in the abundance of materials—especially, the diaries, letters, and memoirs—over the many years of research. And I could not have done so in a better place, so well served by Marcia Moss, the late curator who tended Special Collections when I first came to Concord, and then by her successor, Leslie Perrin Wilson, who transformed the archive into a remarkable research center with exceptional finding aids, brilliant exhibitions in the library's gallery and online, valuable books and articles of her own, and a capacious vision of collections, which she realized in acquisitions of works documenting the lives of women, workers, and others on the margins of the town. It was always a delight to be greeted by Leslie when I visited Special Collections and to learn about her latest acquisitions and discoveries. She became a valuable guide, critic, and interlocutor, and a good friend. Her assistants, the late Joyce Woodman and late Connie Manoli-Skocay, did much to enhance my visits with their helpfulness, interest, and grace. Special Collections became perhaps the best small-town research center in the nation under Leslie's guiding hand, with the support of CFPL directors Barbara Powell and Kerry Cronin, and her successor, Anke Voss, who became curator in 2019, is building on Leslie's achievement with admirable professionalism and with exciting ideas and initiatives of her own. Her assistant, Jessie Hopper, lent valuable assistance in my selection of illustrations for this book. The new municipal archivist, Nathanial Smith, has gone out of his way to provide generous access to government documents during the final stages of this work.

Concord abounds in institutions charged with maintaining the cultural heritage of the town and with communicating the life and legacies of its prominent authors. All have welcomed my inquiries, facilitated my research, invited me to speak to their constituencies, and given unflagging support for this project. I thank the Minute Man National Historical Park and its longtime superintendent Nancy Nelson and staff members Jim Hollister and Leslie Obleschuk; the Old Manse, maintained by the Trustees of Reservations, and former executives Laurie Butters (who also did research for me), Tom Beardsley, Guy Hermann, and Sara Varrelli; Orchard House, overseen by the Louisa May Alcott Memorial Association, and its ebullient executive director, Jan Turnquist; the Ralph Waldo Emerson House and board chair Margaret Emerson Bancroft; the Thoreau Farm, birthplace of the writer, and its executive director, Margaret Carroll-Bergman; the Thoreau Society of America and executive director Mike Frederick; the First Parish (Unitarian) Church (whose head sexton, Bruce Davidson, photographed the portraits of Ezra Ripley and Barzillai Frost for the illustrations) and the Trinitarian Congregational Church; the Social Circle and former members John Esty and Tim Warren; and the Corinthian Lodge of Ancient, Free and Accepted Masons, of Concord, whose late secretary James Parker and past master and historian Doug Ellis allowed me to read the record books of the fraternity from the days when John Keyes was honored and then excoriated as the would-be "King" of Concord and Herman Atwill turned his back on the brethren and exposed their secrets.

The most recent addition to this panoply of institutions is the Robbins House, a center for the interpretation of African American history in slavery and freedom in Concord and New England. Spearheaded by Maria Madison and Liz Clayton, the Robbins House has been a dynamic force in sponsoring research into Concord's Black history, and through my association with the group, I was spurred to look more deeply into the lives of the Dugan, Garrison, Hutchinson, and Robinson families and to highlight their stories in this book. Concord's history has never been all white nor unvaryingly progressive. Its past and present take on a greater complexity when we come to terms with this reality. My research and my life in Concord have been enriched by members of the Robbins House circle: Clayton and Madison, Anne Forbes, Rob Morison, and Ronni Olitsky.

Jayne Gordon deserves separate notice and thanks; she has held positions as executive director of Orchard House and the Thoreau Society and as director of education at the Concord Museum and the Massachusetts Historical

Society. Her enthusiasm, intellectual curiosity, and savvy judgment of individuals in the Transcendentalist circle, past and present, have been an inspiration.

A good many townspeople have welcomed me into their homes, shared documents they have inherited or acquired, and attended my talks over the years. My hosts have included Peggy and Bill Brace, Claiborne Dawes, Michael and Nancy Ehrlich, John and Catherine Esty, Jayne Gordon, David and Margery Little, John and Lorna Mack, Ronni Olitsky and Jeff Young, and Rick and Betty Ann Wheeler. It was always a joy to stay at the Hawthorne Inn when it was in the care of the inimitable innkeepers Gregory Burch and Marilyn Mudry, who shared not only their rooms but their friendship and who, as real estate agents, found us an ideal historic house in town. Gregory also obtained and shared records of the Burr & Prichard store.

Pursuing this project since the mid-1970s, I am beholden to a long list of colleagues and friends (overlapping groups). Tom Blanding, Joel Myerson, Michael Meyer, and the late Ed Schofield welcomed me into the community of Thoreauvians; Blanding generously shared his transcriptions of the Davenport-Sewall letters. Old Sturbridge Village, the outdoor historical museum in Massachusetts, was another important influence. Early on, intrigued by the ways OSV re-created life in early nineteenth-century Massachusetts, I spent a week in costume on the Pliny Freeman farm and began lifelong conversations with the late Jack Larkin, Richard Rabinowitz, and Caroline Sloat. All three commented on chapters of this work; OSV supported my research with a fellowship in the summer of 1991. I hope my picture of Concord rings true to veterans of OSV.

As the writing of this work unfolded, I benefited from the comments of Chris Grasso, Ron Hoffman, and Richard John at William and Mary and from the assistance of John L. Brooke, Dean Grodzins, Len Gougeon, Elise Lemire, Sandy Petrulionis, and Bob Sattelmeyer, all of whom shared sources they had found and/or transcribed. Former students, many now accomplished academics in their own right, have contributed ideas and read chapters with unflagging interest: Steve Aron, Debby Applegate, Tom Chambers, Dan Cohen, Tom Ferraro, Dave Gellman, Andrea Greenwood (and her husband, Mark Harris), Jessica Linker, Norma Moruzzi, Catherine O'Donnell, Joel Paul, Jan Saragoni, Renee Sentilles, and John Wood Sweet.

The bulk of this book was drafted between 2015 and 2020. As I composed, I sought out the expertise of specialists in particular areas: Brian Donahue on farming; Chris Clark, Woody Holton, Stephen Mihm, and Robert E. Wright on the history of banks, money, corporations, and capitalism; David Hall on New England churches and religious history; Johann Neem and Richard D. Brown on schools, lyceums, and the advancement of knowledge; Jeffrey Pasley on the press; Ted Widmer on Jacksonian politics and radical reform; Dan Carpenter on antislavery petitioning; Henrik Otterberg on the Fitchburg Railroad; Albert von Frank on Emerson; Beth Witherell, Audrey Raden, and Laura Dassow Walls on Thoreau; Leon Jackson and Eric Slauter on the literary marketplace; Mary Kelley and Linda Kerber on intellectual history and women's history; Nina Dayton on Boston and social reform. Phyllis Cole, a friend since we met in Concord and discovered that our lives and scholarship were moving on parallel tracks, has been reading and improving my work for decades. With Phyllis as the audience, I took care to engage the history of New England religion, take a broad but critical view of Emerson, and to think hard about women and Transcendentalism.

A half-dozen friends stuck with me and read the work in progress, chapter by chapter, as I turned out a very long first draft and then revised, rewrote, and restructured to produce the final version. Joel Myerson, the noted scholar of Transcendentalism, whom I have known since we met at the Concord Free Public Library in the early 1970s, kept reminding me not to lose the Transcendentalists in the exploration of their world and attended meticulously not only to the text but to the endnotes. Larry Buell brought his deep knowledge of Emerson and Thoreau and his keen editorial eye to the project and challenged me to resist easy dismissals of the Concord Sage. Ken Sacks, another knowledgeable Emersonian, buoyed me with his enthusiasm and deepened my understanding of what I had drafted with his close readings and sophistication about the history of ideas and social thought. I took it as a triumph whenever he confessed to finding little to edit. Joanne Pope Melish, historian of race, slavery, and social history, would never let me off the hook in dealing with issues of inequality and democracy. And how can I ever thank Mary Babson Fuhrer and Matt Cohen enough? A fellow historian of small-town New England in an "age of Revolution," Mary repaid my reader's reports for her book, *A Crisis of Community: The Trials and Transformation of a New England Town, 1815–1848* (2014), with amazingly fast and in-depth readings of my drafts. Her grasp of my arguments was acute, her exhortations to prune details and reserve them for the endnotes on point. Matt Cohen, who received a Ph.D. in American Studies at William and Mary, outdid my comments on his graduate student essays. His explications of the draft chapters opened up the wider implications of what I had written for literary history and for social and cultural theory. An expert on Walt Whitman, the history of the book, and digital humanities, Matt bridges the "old" and "new" American Studies better than anyone I know. In his comments on my manuscript, the student educated the teacher.

Sadly, neither Arthur Wang, my publisher and editor, nor Wendy Weil, my agent, lived to see the completion of a manuscript they had unfailingly championed over the years. Arthur, cofounder of Hill and Wang, took a bet on a doctoral candidate with a proposal for a bicentennial book and signed him up right away. *The Minutemen and Their World* flourished, and so did Hill and Wang, as it was becoming a division of Farrar, Straus and Giroux. Arthur made decisions quickly and well, so it surely pained him to wait so long for this book; even so, he remained enthusiastic about the project, and I am so grateful to have enjoyed his friendship. I have been lucky, too, to have Alex Star, my editor at FSG, shepherd this work to publication with keen editing and unflagging support. His assistant, Ian Van Wye, improved the manuscript by attending astutely to both style and structure, as well as the choice of illustrations. Wendy Weil was justly famous for her talents as an agent and for her unhesitating loyalty to clients, no matter how long they took to finish their books. Her sudden death in 2012 was a severe blow to the New York literary community and to her many devoted friends. Happily, Wendy delighted in taking on and training aspiring agents, and I was fortunate to secure one of her much-loved assistants, Emily Forland, as my representative. Emily has taken up where Wendy left off in sustaining this project to publication.

When I wrote *The Minutemen and Their World*, Matt Gross was a toddler and an only child, and in my acknowledgments, with the enthusiasm of a still-new father, I remarked that he had led me "to realize what was truly important and what was not"—perhaps the most frequently quoted line from the book. In the ensuing years Matt was joined by brother Steve and sister Nell, and together they filled our home with energy and curiosity, with love and joy. There has never been a time in their lives when I wasn't working on this book, and as they have grown from childhood to adolescence, then graduated from college, embarked upon families and careers, and now approach middle age, there were surely many times when they doubted that it would ever be done. Happily, they usually kept these misgivings to themselves. I'm grateful for that reticence and for so much more. In their intellectual openness and freethinking, their ethical consciousness and social conscience, in their devotion to one another, their families, and their friends, they inspire with admiration for lives well led. Granddaughters Sasha, Sandy, and Camille do the same as active, growing souls, living proof of the Transcendentalist faith that every child creates the world anew.

Ann Gross has been on this journey with me for more than half a century. She has been my partner and best friend, editor, muse, support, and love over the many years of the project. It was she who first proposed that I study Concord, after we spent a beautiful Columbus Day there in 1971, with the skies a brilliant blue, the autumn air crisp, tourists (like us) crowding the center, and the Boy Scouts selling steamer clams; within nine months we had moved to the town. Time and again in later years, to accommodate my research, she relocated our household and endured my absences during summers and sabbaticals. All the while she retained her confidence in the work and never once asked aloud when I would ever be done. She has listened to and/or heard every word of this book as it has gone through several drafts, and her skill as an editor, wordsmith, and standard-setter has left its mark on every page. I took it as a challenge to produce chapters that would escape her red pencil and never once succeeded. Now, as this project reaches completion, it is intertwined with our lives, and it has brought us ever closer together. "Joy is the condition of life," Thoreau once exulted. And so it has been of our union. Ann has made this long trip worthwhile, and to her in gratitude and love this book is dedicated.

Index

Page numbers in *italics* refer to illustrations.

AASS, *see* American Anti-Slavery Society

Abbot, John, 138

abolitionism and abolitionists, xvii, 329–30, 494, 569; Atwill on, 334; Brooks, M. M., on, 467, 515–19, 534, 582–83, 591; in Concord, 334–42, 467, 509–12, 520–22, 531–38; Concord Lyceum and, 340, 532–36, 586, 592; Emerson, M. M., on, 336–37; Emerson, R. W., on, 342, 438, 512, 522–23, 537–38, 582–87, 760n8; of Emerson, C. C., 337–40; First Parish Church and, 531–32; *Gazette* on, 334–39; Gourgas on, 530–31; Grimké sisters on, 509–11, 513, 537; Hoar, S., on, 535–36; militant, 422; of Phillips, 533–36, 586, 592; Prichard, F. J., on, 501; Ripley, E., on slavery and, 99, 330–31, 341; *The Slave's Friend* magazine on, 359; Thompson, G., on, 334–37, 340–41, 359, 509; Thoreau, H. D., on antislavery and, 468–69, 522, 531, 591–93; of Thoreau, C., 429, 764n25; women on, 438, 510, 513–21, 536–37, 759n3; *see also* antislavery; antislavery societies

ACS, *see* American Colonization Society

Acton, 69, 131–32, 137, 139, 352

Adams, Hannah, 70

Adams, Henry, xiv, 319

Adams, James, 7, 137–38

Adams, John, 11, 23, 279, 681n17, 691n3, 697n48

Adams, John Quincy, 110, 271; as Anti-Masonic nominee for governor, 294; Brooks, M. M., letter to, 528–29, 537, 765n37; Concord for, 259; on fiftieth anniversary of American Revolution, 15; on Freemasons, 288, 298; Hoar,

S., and, 298; Jackson, A., and, 259, 264–65, 277, 283; on partisanship, 41

Adams, Josiah, 169, 352

Adams, Samuel, 23

Adams & Potter, 124

African American radicalism, 334

African Americans: Beaumont on, 726n15; CFCS and, 454–55, 514; segregation of, 583, 585; students, 674n46; violence against, 318; *see also* Black people

African Baptist Church, 105

African colonization, 533; ACS on, 329–30, 332–34, 339, 341, 768n56; Atwill on, 335–36; Emerson, C. C., on, 339; Liberia, 329–30, 768n56; Ripley, E., on, 341

Age of Reason (Paine), 221–22

agricultural capitalism, 150, 175, 183

agricultural reform and reformers: in Concord, 165, 171, 173, 175–77, 179, 183, 204, 225; Thoreau, H. D., on, 599, 601

agricultural technology, 174

agriculture and farmers, in Concord. *See* farmers and agriculture, in Concord

alcohol and drinking, 244–56, 417, 429, 516, 551–52; Jarvis, E., on, 686n56, 688n69, 690n78; minors and, 686n58; Ripley, E., on, 246–47, 249–51, 255, 687n65; *see also* temperance movement

Alcott, Amos Bronson, 387, 394, 412, 429, 561, 730n4; Fuller, M., and, 379, 406, 431; Ripley, E., and, 758n40; on school and education, 379, 408; at School for Human Culture, 379

Alcotts, the, xiv

Algonquin, 395

Allen, John C., 67, 265–66, 688n69, 694nn15–16
Allen, Phineas, 295, 297–98, 676nn56–57; in Anti-Masonic movement, 442, 464; at Concord Academy, 212–15, 238, 324, 327–28, 426, 442, 464, 746n34
American Antiquarian Society, 354
American Anti-Slavery Society (AASS), 519–21, 530, 592, 759n2
American Colonization Society (ACS), 329–30, 332–34, 339, 341, 713n49, 716n67, 768n56
American exceptionalism, 20
American individualism, xiii
American Institute of Education, 320
American Institute of Instruction, 408
American Journal of Education, 673n41
American Lyceum, 235, 354
American Peace Society, 422
American Renaissance, in Concord, xiv, 563
American Revolution, 229; alcohol use and, 244; Black veterans of, 333; Concord and, xvii–xviii, 15–16, 18, 30–42, 348, 353, 361, 568; Concord North Bridge in, xiv, 9–10, 24, 32, 35–36, 40, 42, 93–94, 348–49, 363, 370; Emerson, William, and, 309; fiftieth anniversary of, 15; generation, xiv–xv, 9–10; Harvard College in, 18; Hunt, N., in, 154; Lexington in, 348, 352, 369, 753n57; Minott, E., and 178; Ripley, E., and, 18–19, 30, 36, 45, 348–49; slavery and, 99; Thoreau, Jean, in, 458–59
American Scholar, the, 361, 409–12, 430, 434, 512
American Statistical Association, 356
American Temperance Society (ATS), 252
American Unitarian Association, 72
Anaxagoras, 480
Andover Divinity School, 62, 68
Andrews, Benjamin, 130, 135
anti-Catholicism, 326
Anti-Masonic movement and party: Adams, J. Q., in, 294; age and, 705n98; Allen, P., in, 442, 464; Atwill, on Freemasons and, 287–92, 294–95, 297–98, 321, 326–28, 334, 702n81, 705n97, 706n100; average age of

delegates, 704n93; Brooks, N., and, 705n97; Brown, Reuben, Jr., in, 704n92, 705n97; in Concord partisanship, 471; Democrats and, 328, 370, 703n82; Emerson, R. W., on Freemasons and, 298, 328; on Freemasonry, 261, 286–90, 292–301, 317, 321–28, 705n98; against Grand Lodge, 394; on Hoar, S., 324, 705n96; Hunt, D., in, 297–98; Jackson, A., and, 322; against Keyes, J., 294–95, 465, 704n87; Moore, G., on, 417; Prescott, T., in, 441, 739n70; Ripley, E., on, 295–96, 348–49; The Social Circle and, 705n97; on Southmayd, D., 704n90; Thoreau, J., and, 298; Whigs and, 298–99
antislavery: African Americans in, 334, 515, 583, 591; Brooks, M. M., on, 467, 515–19, 534, 582–83, 591; campaign, of Ware, 735n30; colonization and, 341; Emerson, L., on slavery and, 438, 512, 514–15, 522, 538, 582–84, 781n35; Garrison, W. L., on, 530; gender norms and, 340; journalism, of Robinson, 216; Liberty Party, 749n51; movement, in Concord, 106, 340, 511–13, 520–22; petition campaigns, 519–23, 531, 536–37, 582–83, 591, 763nn21–24, 780n29; religious faith and, 515; Thoreau, C., on, 103, 429, 522, 591; Unitarian, 422; Wilder, J., on, 340; women and, 340, 437–38, 511–21, 536–37, 759n3
Anti-Slavery Convention of American Women, 517–19
antislavery societies, 715n57; AASS, 519–21, 530, 592, 759n2; Cambridge Anti-Slavery Society, 735n30; CFASS, 513–15, 519, 522, 528, 530–32, 534–37, 591–92, 761nn11–13; MASS, 511, 531, 582–83, 759n4; MCASS, 334–35, 340, 511, 519, 529–31, 538, 583–85, 591, 593, 765n38; New England Anti-Slavery Society, 329, 337
Appeal . . . to the Coloured Citizens of the World, but in Particular, and Very Expressly, to Those of the United States of America (Walker, D.), 334
Aristotle, 235
Arminianism, 49–50, 63, 70, 623n20
Armstrong, Samuel T., 714n53

Assabet River, 6–7, 95, 123, 554
Atlas, 523–24
ATS, *see* American Temperance Society
Atwill, Herman, 67, 92, 265–66, 276;
 on abolitionism, 334; on ACS,
 332; against Catholicism, 326; on
 colonization, 335–36; on Concord
 Fight monument, 349; at *Concord
 Freeman*, 325–28, 332; on Corinthian
 Lodge, 289, 702n80, 718n16; on
 Freemasons and Anti-Masonry,
 287–92, 294–95, 297–98, 321, 326–28,
 334, 702n81, 705n97, 706n100;
 on Garrison, J., 711n35; Keyes, J.,
 and, 327, 702n77, 704n87, 712n42;
 partisanship of, 292, 325; populism
 of, 711n35; Ripley, E., and, 297, 348;
 on Shattuck, L., 718n16; Tyler, O.,
 on, 722n48; on Whigs, 711n35; at
 Yeoman's Gazette, 283, 287–92, 325,
 332, 425, 688n69, 706n100, 718n16,
 722n48

Bailey, Philip James, 446, 740n80
Ball, Benjamin, 655n46
Ball, Nehemiah, 238–39, 242–43, 389,
 460–61, 533, 684n43, 685n48
Bancroft, George, 352, 469–70, 479, 534,
 717n14
banks, nineteenth century growth of,
 124–25
baptism, 51–53
Barber, John Warner, 129
Barnes, Josiah, 676n55
Barrett, Humphrey, 103–104, 642n42
Barrett, Jack, 652n31
Barrett, Joseph, 170, 294, 296, 298,
 349–50, 680n11, 697n44
Barrett, Nathan, 172, 555–58, 562,
 776n41
Barrett, Samuel, 340, 634n7
Barrett, Sherman, 460–61
Barrett's mill, 95, 104, 131–32, 143
Barron, Nancy, 384, 725n13
Bartlett, Charles, 774n28
Bartlett, Josiah, 238, 245, 251, 253, 256,
 531, 689n74, 690n78, 723n51
Bascom, Ezekiel, 647n9
Bascom, Lysander, 116, 647n9
Bascom, Ruth Henshaw, 647n9
Bascom & Cole, 116
Bates, Hervey, 131, 134–35, 137, 142

Battle of Trenton, 178
Beaumont, Gustave de, 726n15
Bedford, 62–63, 67
Beecher, Catherine, 521, 630n56, 759n3
Beecher, Lyman, 63–64, 66–67, 73, 76,
 312, 317–18, 630n56
Belknap, Sewell F., 543–44, 553
Bellows, Ephraim H., 97, 237, 321,
 637n23, 638n26, 680n11, 702n80
Bemis, George F., 325, 328, 711n37
BHMA, *see* Bunker Hill Monument
 Association
Bigelow, Hartwell, 109–10, 500
Bigelow's Tavern, 248, 687n64
Biglow, Asa, 10, 12
Billings, Josh, 603
Black people: ACS, colonization and,
 332–34; in Boston, 102, 333, 640n33,
 641n38; in Concord, 101–107,
 333–34, 454–55, 641n35; at Concord
 bicentennial, 364; Emerson, R. W., on,
 585–87; in the Great Field, 103–105,
 122–23; in Walden woods, 99–102
Blackstone, William, 759n3
Black veterans, 99–100, 103–104, 333
Blake, Harrison Gray Otis, 756n23
Bliss, Daniel, 44–45, 49–50, 99, 106–107,
 639n31
Blithedale Romance, The (Hawthorne, N.),
 565
Blood, Beriah, 655n46
Blood, Jonas, 687n65
Blood, Thaddeus, 352
Boaz, Catherine, 103, 642n42
Boltwood, William, 649n20
Boston: Black people in, 102, 333,
 640n33, 641n38; Brownson in, 379;
 Concord and, 63–65, 67–69, 77,
 84, 109, 123–24, 131, 144, 223–24;
 Congregationalist churches in,
 709n19; constitutional convention,
 1820, 23–24, 27–30, 65; Emerson,
 R. W., and, xvii–xviii, 13, 383;
 Federalists, 27, 33, 35, 322; First
 Church, 305; Hanover Street Church,
 63, 66, 630n56; Irish immigrants
 to, 544–45, 548; Kneeland in, 487;
 lyceums in, 685n50; Monroe in,
 22; newspapers, 708n8; Park Street
 Church, 63–64, 317, 325–26, 627n39;
 pencils of Munroe, W., in, 143–44;
 radicalism in, 316–17, 380;

Boston (*cont.*)
religious pluralism in, 316; schools
in, 190–91, 216; Second Church,
305–306, 314, 322, 383, 405, 407,
420, 493; Thompson, G., and,
341–43; Thoreau, John, moving to,
220; Transcendentalism in, xvii;
Unitarianism, 380, 506; violence and
intolerance in, 318–19; Warren Bridge
to, 266–68, 270; Whigs rallying in,
751*n62*
Boston Atlas, 470
Boston Commons, 395
Boston Courier, 144, 375, 386–88, 406,
525, 527, 693*n10*, 726*n17*, 730*n4*
Boston Daily Advertiser, 497
Boston Daily Advocate, 289, 292, 294,
322–23, 349
Boston Investigator, 317–18, 486–87
Boston Masonic Temple, 345, 379, 388,
391, 728*n33*; Emerson, R. W., lectures
at, 387, 390, 394, 398, 402, 405, 412,
418–19, 431, 441, 458, 477–78, 495
Boston Mercantile Library Association,
579
Boston Quarterly Review, 469–70, 477,
726*n15*, 752*n73*
Boston Recorder, 63, 67–69, 202, 628*n45*
Boston Society for the Diffusion of
Useful Knowledge (SDUK), 345,
387–90, 394, 576, 726*nn18–19*
Boston Statesman, 290, 327, 696*n38*,
697*n44*, 712*n42*
Boston Tea Party, 132, 321
Bowdoin, James, 23
Boylan, Anne, 761*n11*
Bradford, George, 758*n39*
Bradford, George Partridge, 504, 561
Bradford, Sarah Alden, 715*n63*, 758*n39*
Briggs, Charles, 169, 176, 226
Brigham, Levi, 746*n34*
British idealists, 314–15
British Romantics, 439
Britton, Joel, 553–54, 773*n24*,
774*nn25–26*
Brook Farm, 776*n37*; Emerson, R. W.,
on, 561–62, 574; Frost on, 581;
Fuller, M., at, 561; Hawthorne,
N., at, 562, 776*n42*; of Ripley, G.,
504, 561; Thoreau, H. D., on, 587;
Transcendentalists at, 504,
561–62

Brooks, Caroline, 214–15, 430–32,
517–19
Brooks, Daniel, 633*n1*
Brooks, George, 516
Brooks, John, 7, 9–11
Brooks, Mary Merrick, 56–58, 71, 340,
521; abolitionism and antislavery
activism of, 467, 515–19, 534, 582–83,
591; Brooks, N., and, 58, 515, 517;
in CFASS, 513, 528, 530, 532, 534,
536–37, 592, 761*nn12–13*, 768*n52*;
on Cherokees and Indian removal,
523, 528–29; on Christianity, 516,
529; Emerson, R. W., and, 582–83,
586; First Parish Church and, 515;
on Frost, 532, 766*n41*; on Irish
immigrants, 547; Keyes, J. S., on,
784*n52*; letter to Adams, J. Q., 528–29,
537, 765*n37*; in MCASS, 530, 583,
593; Merrick, S. M., and, 624*n30*;
Phillips and, 534–36, 586, 592;
Thoreau, C., and, 591; on Thoreau, H.,
532, 766*n43*; Unitarians and, 515–16,
532
Brooks, Nathan, 42, 162, 169, 262,
643*n43*, 653*n34*; Anti-Masons and,
705*n97*; Bascom, L., and, 116; Brooks,
M. M., and, 58, 515, 517; Concord
Bank and, 91; in Concord elections,
692*n8*, 747*n44*; on Concord School
Committee, 676*nn53–54*; on Jarvis, E.,
195; MCASS and, 538; as Minott, A.,
estate arbitrator, 667*n59*; Southmayd,
D., and, 79; as Whig candidate,
467–68, 475–76, 538
Brown, David, 454–55
Brown, James, 674*n44*
Brown, John, 74–75, 630*n57*
Brown, John, Jr., 95–96, 179, 627*n24*,
729*n35*, 750*n60*
Brown, Leonard, 109
Brown, Lucy Jackson, 452–53
Brown, Nabby and Sally, 454–55
Brown, Nathan, 687*n65*
Brown, Reuben, 176, 280
Brown, Reuben, Jr., 297–98, 695*n25*,
704*n92*
Brown, Roger, 700*n65*
Brown, Shattuck, & Company, 352–53
Brown, Tilly, 176
Brownson, Orestes, xvii, 315–16, 394,
497, 708*n13*; in Boston, 379; on

Calvinism, 313; at Concord Lyceum, 470; on democracy, 470, 477; on Democrats, 469–71, 477–79; Emerson, R. W., and, 752n73; Ripley, G., and, 379–80; Thoreau, H. D., and, 457, 462, 469, 477, 481; in Transcendentalist movement, 457; on Whigs, 469–70

Bulfinch, Charles, 640n33

Bulkeley, Peter, 305, 380, 547, 622n12; on baptism, 51; Emerson, R. W., and, 365–66, 572, 580; Frost on, 489; on interdependence, 278; Puritan practices and mantle of, 76, 81

Bull, Ephraim Wales, 556–58

Bunker Hill, 35, 41, 94, 375, 474, 751n62

Bunker-Hill Aurora, 290, 292, 325, 425–26, 549, 692n7, 702n78

Bunker Hill Monument Association (BHMA), 33–35, 376

Bunyan, John, 565

Burgh, James, 222

Burke, Edmund, 345

Burleigh, Charles C., 336–37, 340–41

Burr, Samuel, 88–89, 91, 94, 116–18, 332; business and personal difficulties, 125–28; death of, 127; estate of, 653n34; Munroe, W., and, 143; Shattuck, D., and, 121, 123–24, 128–29, 132, 262; Smith, D., and, 125, 128–29; against Warren Bridge, 695n25

Burr & Prichard, 118–19, 121, 123, 126–28, 135, 153, 174, 181, 652n31

Burton, Warren, 684n45

Buttrick, John, 30–31, 634n7

Buttrick, Jonas, 634n7

Buttrick, Joshua, 563–64

Buttrick, Stedman, 370, 618n38, 722nn48–49

Cabot, James Elliot, 760n8

Calvinism, 60, 71, 502; Arminianism and, 49–50, 63, 70; Beecher, L., on, 63; Brownson on, 313; Emerson, M. M., on, 308; of Morse, 62, 65; Ripley, E., on, 48–51, 61, 70, 486, 503; of Southmayd, D., 76; Thoreau, C., on, 453; Trinitarians and, 74, 312, 484–85; Unitarians against, 312; Universalism against, 486

Cambridge, First Church of, 409

Cambridge Anti-Slavery Society, 735n30

Cambridge Turnpike, 108, 159–60, 309, 319, 395, 437, 577–78

capitalism, xvi–xviii, 87; agricultural, 150, 175, 183; banks and, 125; farmers on, 555; industrial, Thoreau, H. D., on, 598; industrial revolution and, 144, 396; Munroe, W., and, 142; railroad workers and, 546; wealth of Emerson, R. W., and, 381

Carlyle, Thomas, 310, 314–15; Emerson, R. W., and, 388, 390, 395, 418, 449, 570, 573, 596

Carter, James G., 190–91

Cass, Lewis, 200

Catholics and Catholicism: Atwill and *Concord Freeman* against, 326; Irish, 547–48; republicanism and, 318; violence against, 318–19

"Celestial Railroad, The" (Hawthorne, N.), 565–66, 777nn43–44

CFASS, *see* Concord Female Anti-Slavery Society

CFCS, *see* Concord Female Charitable Society

Channing, Edward Tyrrel, 456–57, 467, 477

Channing, William Ellery (poet), 180, 594, 745n28; Hawthorne, N., and, 563–64; on Minott, G., 605

Channing, William Ellery (reverend), 415, 494, 504; on Panic of 1837, 421; against slavery, 417

Charitable Library Society, 221–22, 679nn5–6, 680n8

Charles River Bridge, 266–67, 543; as Warren Bridge, 267–71, 290, 695nn25–27, 697n44

Charles River Bridge Company, 267–70, 370, 695n26

Charlestown, 33, 54–55, 62, 98–99, 267–68, 318–19

Chauncy, Charles, 49

Chelmsford Courier, 692n7

Cheney, John M., 171–73, 177, 179, 557, 665n45, 705n97

Cherokees, 293, 363–64, 468–69, 523–29, 764n31

Child, David Lee, 271–76, 289, 487, 534, 696n36, 696n38

Child, Lydia Maria, 227, 271

Chinese mulberry, 171

Choate, Rufus, 26, 351

Christian Examiner, 311, 313, 315–16,
  379–80, 457, 732*n13*
Christianity: Brooks, M. M., on, 516,
  529; Brownson on, 457; Charitable
  Library Society and, 221; Emerson,
  R. W., on, 306, 314, 494–95, 499;
  Freemasonry and, 283–84, 286, 300;
  Frost on, 488–89; Native Americans
  and, 357; Prescott, M., on, 443–46;
  rationality and, 311; republicanism
  and, 18; Ripley, E., on, 47–53, 311,
  330, 504; slavery and, 340–41;
  Transcendentalists and, 497
Christian Register, 506
Christian Watchman, 418
Church of Christ, Concord, 49–60
Church of the New Jerusalem, 316, 422,
  439, 503
civic republicanism, xv
Civil War, US, xvi, 570
Clark, Christopher, 649*n20*
classical republicanism, 28, 400
Clay, Henry, 260, 329, 332, 417, 693*n13*
clockmakers, in Concord, 85–87, 90
Colburn, James B., 676*n57*
Colburn, James Smith, 676*n57*
Colburn, Susan C., 676*n57*
Cole, William, 116, 647*n9*
Coleridge, Samuel Taylor, 310, 314–15,
  380, 446, 573
Colman, Henry, 164, 604
Colonizationist and Journal of Freedom, The,
  334
Columbian Centinel, 131
Combe, George, 442, 444
Commentaries on the Laws of England
  (Blackstone), 759*n3*
Commercial Gazette, 136
community: Concord Lyceum and, 239;
  the individual and, 393, 574; Ripley,
  E., on, 18–19, 47–48, 53, 82, 374,
  607; shifting form of, 1830s, 257–58;
  Thoreau, H. D., on, 607–608
Concord: abolitionism and abolitionists
  in, 334–42, 467, 509–12, 520–22,
  531–38; for Adams, J. Q., 259; agrarian
  landscape of, xvi; agricultural reform
  and reformers in, 165, 171, 173,
  175–77, 179, 183, 204, 225; alcohol
  and drinking in, 244–58; American
  Renaissance in, xiv, 563; American
  Revolution and, xvii–xviii, 9–10, 15–16,

18, 24, 30–42, 348–49, 353, 361, 363,
  370, 568; antislavery movement, 106,
  340, 511–13, 520–22; Black people
  in, 101–107, 333–34, 454–55, 641*n35*;
  Boston and, 63–65, 67–69, 77, 84,
  109, 123–24, 131, 144, 223–24; Burr
  & Prichard country store in, 118–19,
  126; business and trade in, 113–24,
  141–45, 395, 403, 550–53; Charitable
  Library Society in, 221–22; "Cheap
  Stores" in, 124; Church of Christ
  in, 49–60; clockmakers in, 85–87,
  90; Convention of 1812, 614*n10*;
  cotton mills in, 6–7, 97–98, 102;
  counterfeiting in, 125; Democrats and
  Whigs in, 465–72, 474–77; Democrats
  in, 400; diversity in, 395–96; Dunbars
  in, 4–5; economic downturn, in early
  1840s, 542; economic inequality in,
  560; elections in, 11–13, 17, 19, 22,
  29–30, 259–60, 264–65, 268, 273, 277,
  294–95, 298–99, 323–25, 349, 369–71,
  399–400, 465–68, 471, 474–75,
  480–81, 501, 691*n3*, 695*n28*, 751*n63*,
  773*n23*; elections in, Brooks, N., and,
  692*n8*, 693*n13*, 747*n44*; elections in,
  governors and, 693*n13*; elections in,
  state senate, 692*n8*; elections in, voter
  participation, 703*n82*; Everett in,
  36–37, 39–41; farms and homesteads,
  147–64, 178–83, 546, 556–59;
  Federalists and Republicans in, 11,
  16–17, 19–23, 26–30, 32–33, 35, 39,
  58, 82, 613*n5*; First Parish Church
  in, 65, 67, 71–74, 76, 78–80, 314,
  444; Fitchburg Railroad in, 541–51,
  553, 555–56, 559–61, 566, 575–77,
  595; forest clearing in, 554–55;
  Freemasons' Hall, 283, 287–88, 297;
  Freemasons in, 37–38, 280–93, 297,
  342, 700*n66*; geography of, 207;
  growth of village, 1820s–1830s,
  107–109, 112; Harrison rally, 1840,
  472–73, 480; Hawthorne, N., on,
  565–68; the Hawthornes in, 562–63;
  highways and roads connected to,
  7–8, 84–85, 88, 94, 98–99; Hudson
  on, 549, 559, 771*n17*; immigrants
  to, 544–45; Independence Day in,
  10, 13, 16–17, 21–22, 613*n3*; Irish
  immigrants in, 544–48; jail, 110–11,
  159, 161, 163, 221–22; Jim Crow

in, 110; Keyes, J., in, 23–33, 35, 37, 41–42, 68–69, 89; Lafayette in, 30–34; landscape and village center, 83–87, 89, 98–99, 108–109; Lexington and, 32, 34, 40–41, 352, 369, 717*n14*; as literary center, xiv, 561, 563, 568; map of town, *x–xi*; map of town plan, *ix*; as Middlesex County seat, 111; migrants to West from, 176–77; milldam in, 6–7, 83–92, 102, 108, 112, 137–38, 161, 194, 635*nn11–13*; milldam redevelopment, 88–91, 112; mills in, 553–54; Minutemen and, xvi–xvii, 35; Munroes in, 85–87; in National Republican era, 260–68; new business district in, 90; newspapers, of nineteenth century, 692*n7*; parents and young people in, 423–24; partisanship in, 17–19, 21–23, 41–42, 399, 471; pencil-making industry in, 5–7, 85, 108, 113, 129–31, 135–38, 141–44; political unity in, 1824, 30, 616*n17*; population growth and movement, xix–xx, 109; population of, 6–7, 261–62, 371–72, 611*n7*, 628*n46*, 637*n23*, 638*n26*, 644*n49*, 678*n65*, 689*n76*, 691*n5*, 769*nn2–3*, 776*n34*; private clubs and organizations in, 260–61; Puritans and, xvi–xviii, 22, 81, 153, 360–64; religious equality and, 82; school budget, 1833–1835, 710*n28*; school enrollment rate, 678*n65*; school reform in, 20, 186, 192–93, 217–18, 320, 462; schools and education in, 185–98, 200–202, 204–18, 227–28; Shattuck, L., on history of, 353–57, 361–62, 364, 367–68, 718*nn16–18*, 719*n22*, 720*n34*; slavery in, 99, 106–107, 395, 639*n31*, 640*n34*, 642*n39*; Sleepy Hollow area, 110; The Social Circle, 260–61, 277–82, 284, 299, 346, 358, 369, 412, 455, 580, 705*n97*, 739*n71*; Society of Middlesex Husbandmen and Manufacturers in, 110, 165–68, 170, 172; stage lines through, 109–12; storekeepers, 1808–1835, 647*n8*; stores and shops in, 633*n3*, 772*n20*; taverns, alcohol sales and, 246–51, 257, 551–52, 634*n10*, 688*n69*, 690*nn78–79*, 772*n22*; taxpayers, 644*n51*; taxpayers, in agricultural society, 664*n37*; textile mills and factories in, 7, 95–98, 262, 554; Thoreau, C., in, 43; Thoreau, H. D., and, xiv, xvi–xvii, 3, 16, 83–84, 86; Thoreau, John, in, 4, 6, 11, 15, 25, 34, 43, 114–15, 147; Thoreau, R., in, 54–55; Thoreau sisters in, 60–61, 63–65, 73–74, 77, 81; Transcendentalism and, xiv–xvii, 13, 319–20, 404, 417, 423, 560–61, 569–70, 580, 610*n7*; Unitarians in, 80, 373; water rights, 635*nn11–12*; Whigs, at Harrison rally, 472–74; woodland of, 639*n29*; wool farmers in, 170; *see also* Emerson, Ralph Waldo, in Concord; farmers and agriculture, in Concord; Ripley, Ezra, in Concord; Thoreau, Henry David, Concord and; *specific people; specific topics*

Concord Academy, 211, 325, 414–15; Allen, P., and, 212–15, 238, 324, 327–28, 426, 442, 464, 746*n34*; Brooks, C., at, 517; debating society, 685*n48*; founders, 674*n47*; Hosmer, H., at, 679*n3*; Moore, G., at, 732*n17*; Prescott, M., at, 441–43; The Social Circle and, 746*n36*; Thoreau, H. D., as student at, 208–209, 214, 216, 232–33, 452; Thoreau, H. D., as teacher at, 464–65, 746*n34*

Concord Atheneum, 563

Concord Band, 360

Concord Bank, 90–91, 124, 142, 460; Barrett, N., and, 556; Cheney at, 665*n45*, 698*n50*; in financial crash of 1837, 401; Fitchburg Railroad and, 769*n5*; Keyes, J., at, 693*n9*; Mill Dam Company and, 129, 167–68, 284, 551, 693*n9*; Shattuck, D., at, 698*n50*; The Social Circle and, 279, 698*n50*; Thoreau, John, and, 748*n46*

Concord bicentennial, 346–47, 350–52, 358–61, 717*nn10–12*, 719*n30*; Black people at, 364; *Concord Freeman* on, 358–59, 366; Emerson, R. W., address to, 351–52, 358, 360–67, 399, 407, 429, 720*n39*; *Gazette* on, 358, 372; Goodwin on, 362–63, 720*n38*; Jarvis, E., on, 346–47, 350–51, 358, 366, 717*n11*; Keyes, J., as committee chair, 350, 358, 360; racism and, 359; Ripley, E., on, 346, 349–50, 360; Shattuck, D., on, 346–47

Concord cattle shows, 166–67, 169–74, 176, 180, 230–31

Concord Debating Club, 229–32, 354, 404; Concord Lyceum and, 235–37, 240, 682n27, 685n48; earliest meeting of, 682n25; on economic policies, 682n28; membership of, 682n27

Concord Female Anti-Slavery Society (CFASS), 535, 761nn11–13; Brooks, M. M., in, 513, 528, 530, 532, 534, 536–37, 592, 761nn12–13, 768n52; charter members, church affiliations of, 762n14; and Concord Lyceum, 534–35, 586; Emerson, L., in, 522; MCASS and, 519; in petition campaign, 531; Thoreau, H., in, 591; Thoreau women in, 514–15; Trinitarian church on, 530

Concord Female Charitable Society (CFCS), 453–55, 464, 514, 547, 741n7, 742nn8–9, 743nn11–14, 761n11

Concord Fight, 21–22, 33, 348, 352, 617n29; see also Concord North Bridge

Concord Fight anniversary and monument, 15, 30, 109, 129, 230–31, 279; Atwill on, 349; committee, 34–37, 369, 619n39, 722n46, 723n51; Concord Freeman on, 369; cornerstone, 37, 42, 92–93, 107, 132, 283, 372, 384; Emerson, R. W., at dedication, 375–77; Freemasons at, 37–38; Hoar, S., on, 375–76; inscription on, 38, 369; location of, 93–94; parade for, 360; Ripley, E., on, 41, 348–49, 368–69, 372–73, 375–77, 717n8; Shattuck, D., and, 369; The Social Circle on, 369, 698n49; Thoreau, John, on, 353–54

Concord Fire Society, 259

Concord Freeman, 334–36, 340–41, 710n28; Atwill at, 325–28, 332; on Brownson, 470; on Concord bicentennial, 358–59, 366; on Concord Fight monument, 369; Emerson, R. W., and, 406, 570; on Fitchburg Railroad, 548, 551; Gazette versus, 470–71; Gourgas at, 371–72, 466, 471, 476, 479, 543, 712n43, 749n52; Hawthorne, N., in, 563; Hazewell at, 545–47, 563; on Irish immigrants, 545–47

Concord Free Public Library, 681n17

Concord grammar school: enrollment and attendance, 669n7, 678n65; Jarvis, E., at, 193–98, 227–28, 231–32, 460, 671n24, 676n55, 677n63; schoolhouse building, 669n4, 670n19; schoolmasters, 669n9, 677n60; Thoreau, H. D., as master, 460–62, 745n30; Thoreau, H. D., as student, 185–87, 189, 193, 197, 208, 214, 216

Concord grape, 173, 558

"Concord Hymn" (Emerson, R. W.), 375–77, 379, 456

Concord Light Infantry Company, 154, 247, 360

Concord Lyceum: abolitionism and, 340, 532–35, 586, 592; ACS and, 332; ages of charter members, 683n39; Ball, N., at, 238–39, 242–43; Brownson at, 470; clergymen addressing, 684n44; community and, 239; Concord Debating Club and, 235–37, 240, 682n27, 685n48; Davis, Josiah, at, 240–41, 685n49; debates at, 683n40, 685n48, 711n30, 715n65; dues-paying members, 1843–1844, 767n44; education and, 219; Emerson, C. C., at, 242, 342; Emerson, E. B., at, 242; Emerson, R. W., and, 242–43, 321, 342, 390, 398, 431–32, 533, 580, 710n29, 711n30; Freemasons and Anti-Masons at, 321; Frost at, 533, 536, 596; Goodwin at, 236, 238; Holbrook and, 235; Keyes, J., on Phillips lecture at, 534–35; lecture topics at, 237–42, 684n42; Moore, G., at, 419; Phillips at, 533–36, 586, 592; Ripley, E., and, 235–36, 239–42, 321, 472, 487, 600; social reform and, 220, 244; temperance movement and, 244; Thatcher, B. B., at, 710n29; Thoreau, H. D., and, 219, 463, 465, 533–34, 588–89, 592, 596–602, 607, 783n42

Concord Manufacturing Company, 97–98

Concord Mozart Society, 213

Concord North Bridge, 617n29, 717nn14–15; in American Revolution, xiv, 9–10, 24, 32, 35–36, 40, 42, 93–94, 348–49, 363, 370; Minutemen at, 93–94, 150, 454–55; Ripley, E., on, 368–69, 373; Thoreau, H. D., on, 16, 456, 459, 466

Concord Ornamental Tree Society, 91–92, 636n16

Concord River, 83–84, 103, 150, 157, 161, 368, 473, 553

Concord School Committee, 204–207, 381, 398, 676nn53–54, 678n65, 724n6, 745n26, 745n30

Concord Social Library, 220–29, 240, 307, 381, 398, 501; books on "matters of fact" at, 681n18; economic standing of shareholders, 680n11; expurgated letters of Jefferson at, 681n17; religious titles at, 680n16; The Social Circle, 698n50; total titles and volumes, 682n23; works by American authors at, 681n20

Concord Steam Mill Company, 554, 568, 774nn25–26

Concord Steam Power Company, 554

Concord Temperance Society (CTS), 254–55, 257–58, 689nn74–76

Concord Total Abstinence Society, 551–52, 557, 581, 772n22

Concord Turnpike, 7–8

Concord Young Men's Tippecanoe Club, 473

Congregationalism, 61, 81–82, 202, 670n19, 733n22

Congregationalist churches and ministers, 10, 50, 54, 61–63, 80, 231, 252; in Boston, 709n19; Emerson family and, 306, 483; on women in public arena, 510–11

Congregationalist Standing Order, 23, 27, 29, 65, 68, 75, 81, 269, 485

"Conscience, Its Design, Use, and Obligations" (Ripley, E.), 62

Constitution, Massachusetts, 38, 296, 494, 542

Constitution, U.S., 38, 269, 494, 532, 534–36, 582, 591

constitutional convention, in Boston, 1820, 23–24, 27–30, 65

Constitution of 1780, 23, 27, 29, 47, 694n24

Constitution of Man (Combe), 442, 444

consumerism, 9, 119–20

Continental philosophy, 310, 313, 439–40

Convention of 1812, Concord, 614n10

Conversations with Children on the Gospels (Alcott, A. B.), 406, 730n4

Coolidge, John T., 309

Cooper, James Fenimore, 227, 428

Corinthian Lodge, Concord, 37, 701n72, 704n88, 705n98; age of members, 700n66; Atwill on, 289, 702n80, 718n16; charter members, 700n65; at Freemason's Hall, 283, 287–88, 297; membership fee, 700n68; as refuge from partisanship, 285; Ripley, E., at, 283–84; Royal Arch Chapter of Freemasons and, 285, 300, 417, 701n73; The Social Circle and, 260–61, 280–81; St. John's Day parade, 295; Thoreau, John, and, 284–85; Wood, Ebenezer, in, 138

corporal punishment, in schools, 188–89, 460–62, 509–10

cosmopolitanism, 92, 111–12, 220, 226, 258, 396

cotton mills, 6–7, 26, 97–98, 637n25, 639n28

counterfeit banknotes, 125

Crocker, Alvah, 541–44

Cry from the Four Winds, 627n39, 632n62

CTS, see Concord Temperance Society

Cuming, John, 100

Curiosities of Literature (Disraeli), 228

Curtis, George William, 556, 562, 586, 776n41

Curtis, Lemuel, 87

Cushing, William, 99

Cushman, Marcus M., 75

Cutler, Isaac, 705n97

Cutter, Clarissa, 159, 659n8

Daily American Statesman, 271–72, 275

Damon, Calvin C., 554

Damon mill, 554

Dartmouth College, 24, 430–31, 433–34

Davis, Charles B., 251, 280, 297–99, 340, 698n54

Davis, Daniel, 274

Davis, John, 683n39

Davis, Jonathan H., 648n13, 687n60

Davis, Jonathan T., 240

Davis, Josiah, 115, 122–23, 129, 212, 280, 634n9, 635n12; at Concord Lyceum, 240–41, 685n49; on Concord School Committee, 676nn53–54; in financial crash of 1837, 401; First Parish Church and, 71; Trinitarian church and, 73, 485–86

Davis, Josiah G., 746*n34*, 752*n66*

Davis, Moses, 76–77, 251

Dawes, William, 40

Dearborn, Henry A. S., 714*n53*

Deerslayer, The (Cooper), 428

democracy: Brownson on, 470, 477; Channing, E. T., on, 456; Emerson, R. W., on, 319, 323, 329, 362, 364–65, 369–70, 392, 400; equality and, 362; the individual and, 392; local, 360, 364, 369–70; partisanship in, 476; popular, 370, 471; slavery against, 329

Democracy in America (Tocqueville), 505, 575

Democratic-Republicans, 11; *see also* Republicans, Federalists and

Democratic Review, 590–91

Democrats, 749*n51*; Anti-Masons and, 328, 370, 703*n82*; Brownson and, 469–71, 477–79; in Concord, 400; Emerson, R. W., and, 477–79; Gourgas and, 466–67; Hoar, S., on, 375–76; Jacksonian, 261, 288, 300, 322, 327, 467, 779*n20*; Transcendentalists and, 470, 477–78; Whigs and, 371, 465–72, 474–81, 513, 711*n36*, 722*n49*, 751*n64*

Derby, James, 637*n25*

Dewey, Orville, 708*n8*

Dial, The, 461, 581–82; Emerson, R. W., at, 589; Fuller, M., at, 479, 589, 740*n80*; Thoreau, H. D., in, 589–90, 592; in Transcendentalist movement, 561, 569, 589

Dickinson, Asa, 649*n20*

Dignity of Human Nature, The (Burgh), 222

Discourse on the Transient and Permanent in Christianity (Parker), 759*n43*

Disraeli, Isaac, 228

diversity, religious, 80, 325–26, 483

divine soul, xv, 411, 419

Dixon, Joseph, 655*n46*

Douglass, Frederick, 591, 593

Dugan, Elisha, 559–60, 596

Dugan, Thomas, 102, 560

Dunbar, Asa, 5, 285

Dunbar, Charles J., 5–6, 741*n6*

Dunbar, Cynthia, 4–5, 13, 54, 56, 58, 103, 642*n41*; *see also* Thoreau, Cynthia

Dunbar, Louisa, 5, 73, 485, 502, 642*n41*

Dunbar, Mary, 149, 611*n4*

Dunkin, Christopher, 744*n17*

economic individualism, 269

education, *see* school and education

Edwards, Jonathan, 679*n5*

Edwards, Justin, 252

egalitarianism, 76, 339, 444, 477, 560, 562

Emerson, Amelia F., 737*n57*

Emerson, Charles Chauncy, 309–10, 715*n63*, 717*n15*, 720*n34*; abolitionism of, 337–40; on Adams, Josiah, 352; at Concord Lyceum, 242, 342; death of, 372–73, 445; on Emerson, R. W., Concord bicentennial address, 720*n39*; Hoar, S., and, 307–308; Moore, G., on lecture by, 417; Whigs and, 328

Emerson, Edward Bliss, 72, 242

Emerson, Lidian, 431; in CFASS, 522; on Cherokees, 523; Emerson, R. W., and, 308–309, 366, 375, 381, 384, 435–39, 499, 512, 523, 582–84, 731*n12*; on Harvard Divinity School address, by Emerson, R. W., 499; on slavery and antislavery movement, 438, 512, 514–15, 522, 538, 582–84; Thoreau, H. D., to, 591; Unitarians and, 439

Emerson, Mary Moody, 58, 309, 348, 625*n31*; as abolitionist, 336–37; on Calvinism, 308; Emerson, R. W., and, 308, 311, 314, 365, 439, 499, 539, 596, 729*n38*, 755*n17*, 755*n19*; independence of, 438; Moore, G., and, 417; Ripley, E., and, 59, 71, 308, 504, 596, 755*n17*; on Ripley, Sarah, 756*n29*; on "Self-Reliance," 756*n29*; Transcendentalism and, 308

Emerson, Ralph Waldo, 709*n14*; on abolitionism and antislavery, 342, 438, 512, 522–23, 537–38, 582–87, 760*n8*, 781*n35*; on Alcott, A. B., 406, 412, 730*n4*; on American individualism, xiii; on the American Scholar, 361, 409–12, 430, 434, 512; assets and holdings, 724*n5*; on Black people, 585–87; Boston and, xvii–xviii, 13, 383; in *Boston Courier*, 726*n17*; at Boston Second Church, 305–306, 314, 383, 405, 407, 420, 493; on Brook Farm, 561–62, 574; Brooks, M. M., and, 582–83, 586; Brownson and, 752*n73*; on Bulkeley, 365–66, 572, 580; on business success,

113–14; Carlyle and, 388, 390, 395, 418, 449, 570, 573, 596; on Cherokees and Indian removal, 524–28; on Christianity, 306, 314, 494–95, 499; on commerce, 578–79; on commerce and trade, 396–97; *Concord Freeman* and, 406, 570; "Concord Hymn" by, 375–77, 379, 456; on democracy, 319, 323, 329, 362, 364–65, 369–70, 392, 400; Democrats and, 477–79; at *The Dial*, 589; Emerson, L., and, 308–309, 366, 375, 381, 384, 435–39, 499, 512, 523, 582–84, 731*n12*; Emerson, M. M., and, 308, 311, 314, 365, 439, 499, 539, 596, 729*n38*, 755*n17*, 755*n19*; Emerson, William (father), and, 364–66; *Essays* by, 570; on Everett, 391; on Federalists, 322–23; on "Festus," 740*n80*; on financial crash of 1837, 401–402; on Fitchburg Railroad, 548, 550, 575–77; on Freemasons and Anti-Masonry, 298, 328; Frost and, 491–93, 496, 498, 580–82, 588, 755*n18*, 780*n28*; Fuller, M., on, 580, 586–87, 782*n36*; on government, 401; in grammar school, 186; on the Great Awakening, 363; Greene Street School and, 406–407, 409; "Hamatreya" by, 147, 165; at Harvard, 305, 307, 314, 402, 407–408; Hawthorne, N., and, 562–63, 565, 777*n43*; on Hoar, S., 323, 370, 391, 399–400; on Howe, Peter, 381–82, 725*n8*; on idealism, 314–15, 317, 431; on the individual, xv–xvi, 319, 392–94, 397–99, 419, 438, 478, 480, 574; on individual freedom, 365; on individualism, xiii, 220, 439, 505; on industrial revolution, 396; on Jackson, A., 318, 328; Jackson, L., and, 306, 308–309, 326, 337; Jarvis, E., on, 314, 351, 726*n15*; on Kneeland, 317–18, 494–95; on local democracy, 364, 369–70; lyceum movement and, 306, 373; on *Marie, or Slavery in the United States*, 726*n15*; Massachusetts Horticultural Society and, 168–69; on mass society, 397–98; on materialism, 323, 385, 390, 396, 401, 408, 421, 561; Minott, G., and, 181, 397, 668*n63*; Moore, A., and, 164–65, 573, 668*n63*; Moore, G., and, 413, 417–23, 447, 494, 709*n15*, 734*nn24–26*, 755*n21*;

Munroe, J., and, 777*n4*; on names of children, 425; on nature, 361–62, 379–80, 383, 407, 418–19, 495; open letter to Van Buren, 525–29; on politics, 399–400, 477–79; Prescott, M., and, 444–45, 447; Prescott, T., and, 740*n78*; on public speaking, 390–92; on Puritans and Puritanism, 538–39, 572; on racial equality, 782*n37*; racism and, 538, 585–86; on railroad workers, 545–46; on reading, 398–99; on religious sentiment, 507; Ripley, E., and, xvii, 18–19, 41, 48, 71, 305, 314, 322, 352, 392, 394, 397, 499–500, 503–507; on school and education, 320–21, 381, 393, 398, 406–11, 710*n29*; on school reform, 218, 320, 393, 408; at SDUK, 345, 387–90; on self-government, 365; on self-reliance, 346, 424, 429, 438, 447, 501; "Self-Reliance" by, 522–23, 756*n29*, 764*n27*; on the sexes, 437–38; Shattuck, L., and, 208, 357–58, 361–62, 367; on slavery, 329, 336, 393, 512, 522, 537–38, 583–87, 760*n8*; in the South, 332; on statistics, xix, 398; on Sturgis, 440–41, 443, 580; on temperance movement, 399; Thompson, G., and, 342–43; Thoreau, H. D., and, xiii–xviii, xx, 108, 144, 165, 208, 218, 220, 301; on Tocqueville, 779*n12*; Transcendentalism of, 13, 307, 310, 315–16, 320, 343, 362, 385–86, 392; in Transcendentalist movement, xiii, 379, 402, 412, 483, 497; Unitarianism and, 310, 313–14, 380, 439, 494–96; on universal mind, 392–93, 395, 410, 419, 430; on universal soul, 495; Ware and, 420–21, 734*n28*; wealth of, 380–81, 412; on Western expansion, 576–79; Whigs and, 479–80, 528; women and, 434–42, 538; *see also Nature* (Emerson, R. W.); Thoreau, Henry David, Emerson, R. W., and

Emerson, Ralph Waldo, in Concord, xvii–xviii, 108, 305–15, 319–22, 328–29, 380–86, 726*n14*; at Concord bicentennial, 351–52, 358, 360–67, 399, 407, 429, 720*n39*; at Concord Fight memorial dedication, 375–77; at Concord Lyceum, 242–43, 321,

Emerson Ralph Waldo, in Concord
(*cont.*)
  342, 390, 398, 431–32, 533, 580,
  710*n29*, 711*n30*; on Concord School
  Committee, 381, 398, 724*n6*, 745*n30*;
  Concord Social Library and, 381, 398;
  on farms and homesteads, 559; at
  First Parish, 314, 431, 483–84, 488,
  491–93, 496; Fuller, M., and Sturgis
  on, 580; on history of, 361–67; lecture
  series and, 402–403, 572–73, 575–77,
  580; on partisanship, 399; The Social
  Circle, 412, 580; Thoreau, H. D., and,
  319, 449–51, 569–70; on town politics,
  325; Transcendental Club in, 561; on
  youth and young people, 580–82,
  588
Emerson, Ralph Waldo, lectures
  and addresses by, 780*nn23–24*; on
  abolitionism and slavery, 583–86,
  760*n8*; on academic speaking circuit,
  405–407; in Baltimore, 571–72, 575;
  on biographies of great men, 345–46,
  586; at Boston Masonic Temple, 387,
  390, 394, 398, 402, 405, 412, 418–19,
  431, 441, 458, 477–78, 495; Concord
  and, 402–403, 572–73, 575–77, 580;
  at Concord bicentennial, 351–52,
  358, 360–67, 399, 407, 429, 720*n39*; at
  Concord Fight monument dedication,
  375–77; at Concord Lyceum,
  242–43, 321, 342, 390, 398, 431–32;
  on education, 407–11; at Harvard
  Divinity School, 315, 402, 405, 483,
  493–500, 502–504, 538–39, 758*n39*;
  at Harvard Phi Beta Kappa society,
  404, 405, 407–12, 420, 429–30,
  437–38, 449, 460, 509, 708*n8*, 724*n7*,
  732*n13*; "Heroism," 440–41; "Human
  Culture," 393–94, 440, 495; "Human
  Life," 390, 420, 431, 580; Keyes,
  J. S., on, 363, 430–34, 447, 737*n51*;
  "Literary Ethics," 430–31; Lowell on,
  498–99; "Man the Reformer," 752*n74*;
  to MCASS, 583–85, 593; Moore, G.,
  on, 418–20, 709*n15*, 734*nn23–26*;
  on natural history, 242–43; on New
  England, 571–76, 594, 600; "New
  England Reformers," 768*n57*; in New
  York City, 571–73, 575–76; payment
  for, 727*n25*; in Philadelphia, 571–73;
  "Philosophy of Labor," 431; "The

Philosophy of Modern History,"
  386–87, 389–90, 392–99, 406–407,
  418–20, 458, 728*n34*; "The Poet," 432;
  "The Present Age," 393–97, 420, 431,
  477–78, 730*n49*; Ripley, G., on, 402;
  SDUK and, 726*nn18–19*; sermons,
  71–72, 310, 314–15, 351, 431, 445,
  707*n7*; on Shakespeare, 418–19; on
  social reform, 778*n11*; "The Times,"
  570, 581; "The Transcendentalist,"
  581–82, 588, 783*n43*; workingmen
  and, 729*n40*; "The Young American,"
  576–80, 583
Emerson, Ruth, 80, 305, 309, 706*n1*
Emerson, William: at First Parish
  Church, 626*n37*
Emerson, William (brother), 337,
  401–402, 589–90
Emerson, William (father), 18, 44,
  49–50, 99, 305–307, 309–10, 319–20;
  diary of, 361; Emerson, R. W., and,
  364–66; Harvard Phi Beta Kappa
  society address by, 407; memorial to,
  716*n4*; Ripley, E., on, 347–48
English hay, 165, 172, 604, 661*nn17–18*
English Reader, 207
equality: Brownson on, 457; democracy
  and, 362; racial, 339, 510, 586,
  782*n37*; religious, 82; social, 106,
  310–11, 392, 561
Erie Canal, 107, 171
Essay on Human Understanding (Locke),
  443, 490
Essays (Emerson, R. W.), 570
Estabrook country, 98–99
Eustis, William, 11
Evangelical Missionary Society, 623*n21*
Evarts, Jeremiah, 65–66, 81, 628*n42*
Everett, Edward, 33, 259–60, 265–66,
  288, 350; in Concord, 36–37, 39–41;
  Emerson, R. W., on speeches of, 391;
  on Freemasons, 299; Keyes, J., and,
  33, 691*n3*; on Kneeland, 494–95;
  Lexington speech by, 352; in SDUK,
  387; Shattuck, L., and, 694*n16*

Farmer, Jacob B., 175
"Farmers, Manufacturers, Mechanics,
  and others, interested in the
  Protection of American Industry"
  convention, 1832, 263–64
Farmers' Almanac, 173, 175

farmers and agriculture, in Concord,
165–83, 554–59, 572–73, 601–605,
786n69; Hunt family farm and
homestead, 150–59, 174, 658n6,
659n9, 660n12, 661nn19–20,
775n31, 776n41; Minot, J., farm and
homestead, 103, 147–49, 658n2; see
also Minott, George, and Moore, Abel
Farrar, Reuben, 655n46
Fay, Samuel P. P., 179, 290, 667n59
Federalists: on alcohol and
intemperance, 250; Boston, 27,
33, 35, 322; Emerson, R. W., and,
322–23; Merrick, T., and, 56–58; on
republicanism, 222, 322; Republicans
and, 11, 16–23, 26–30, 32–33, 35, 39,
58, 82, 231, 264–65, 292, 324, 613n5;
Ripley, E., and, 53
Feene, Case, 101–102
Fessenden, Thomas G., 170, 173
"Festus" (Bailey), 446, 740n80
Field, John, 608
financial crash of 1837, 401, 408, 421,
530
First African Baptist Church, 333–34
First Church, Boston, 305
First Church, Cambridge, 409
First Parish Church, Concord, 67,
143, 194, 282, 757n32; abolitionism
and, 531–32; ACS and, 330, 341,
713n49; Brooks, M. M., and, 515;
Bulkeley at, 622n12; Davis, Josiah,
and, 71; Emerson, M. M., at, 625n31;
Emerson, R. W., at, 314, 431, 483–84,
488, 491–93, 496; on Freemasonry,
297; Frost at, 373, 488–91, 496, 500;
Hoar, S., and, 27; Keyes, J. S., and,
484, 531–32; the Misses Thoreau and,
60–61, 65, 73–74, 502, 620n3, 655n48;
new members, 1778–1835, 625n32;
Prescott, M., on, 444; separation of
church and state, 483–84; Thoreau,
C., at, 502; Thoreau, H. D., and,
501–503; Transcendentalists and,
500; Trinitarian church and, 73–80,
484–85, 500, 515, 626n37; Unitarians
and, 484, 500; Universalists and, 500;
women as members of, 623n22; see also
Ripley, Ezra, at First Parish Church
First Universalist Society, 500, 757n31
Fischer, David Hackett, 735n35
Fiske, Clarissa, 213

Fiske, Isaac, 215
Fiske brothers, 251
Fitch, Zechariah, 642n42
Fitchburg, 541–43
Fitchburg Railroad: in Concord, 541–51,
553, 555–56, 559–61, 566, 575–77,
595; Concord Freeman on, 548, 551;
daily commuters, 771n18; Emerson,
R. W., on, 548, 550, 575–77; investors
in, 769n5; Irish immigrants building,
544–47, 576; Thoreau, H. D., on,
549–50
Fitchburg Sentinel, 543
Flannery, Michael, 546
Fletcher v. Peck (1810), 269
Flint, Abishai, 153
Follen, Karl, 752n73
Folsom, George, 212, 676nn55–56
Forbes, Abner, 209, 674n46
Forefathers' Day, 35
forensics, 214, 229, 232, 237, 240–41, 415
Formation of the Christian Character (Ware),
446
Formisano, Ronald P., 695n28
Foster, Comfort, 90
Fourth Report on the Agriculture of
Massachusetts, 164
Fox, George, 345–46
Franklin, Benjamin, 226
free Black citizens, of Concord, 333–34
freedom, religious, 318, 347, 356,
458–59, 494
Freeman, Brister, 100–101, 640n34,
642n42
Freeman, Fenda, 101
Freemasons, 138, 260–61, 277; Adams,
J. Q., on, 288, 298; Anti-Masonry
against, 261, 286–90, 292–301,
317, 321–28, 705n98; Atwill on,
287–92, 294–95, 297–98, 326–27,
334; Christianity and, 283–84, 286,
300; chronology of Masonic lodges in
Massachusetts, 699n56; in Concord,
37–38, 280–93, 297, 342, 700n66; at
Concord Fight monument, 37–38;
Emerson, R. W., on Anti-Masonry
and, 298, 328; Everett on, 299; First
Parish Church on, 297; Gourgas and,
328; Grand Lodge of Massachusetts
and, 394; Greenleaf on, 417; Jackson,
A., and, 283, 288; Keyes, J., and, 37,
284, 286, 289–91, 298; Ripley, E., and,

Freemasons (*cont.*)
283–87, 291, 295–98, 300, 348–49;
Royal Arch Chapter of, 285, 300,
417, 701*n73*; The Social Circle and,
280–82, 284, 299; Southmayd, D.,
and, 704*n90*; Thoreau, J., and, 284–85,
298; Trinitarians on, 296–97; *Yeoman's
Gazette* and, 287–92, 294, 325; *see also*
Anti-Masonic movement and party;
Corinthian Lodge, Concord
Freemasons' Hall, Concord, 283,
287–88, 297
French Revolution, 16, 400
Friends of the National Administration,
259–60
Frontier Thesis, of American history, 362
Frost, Barzillai, 375, 391, 460–61,
745*n30*, 766*n40*; on Brook Farm, 581;
Brooks, M. M., on, 532, 766*n41*; on
Bulkeley, 489; on Christianity, 488–89;
at Concord Lyceum, 533, 536, 596;
Emerson, R. W., and, 491–93, 496,
498, 580–82, 588, 755*n18*, 780*n28*; at
First Parish, 373, 488–91, 496, 500; at
Harvard, 488; Hawthorne, N., on, 563;
Keyes, J. S., on, 491, 755*n16*, 758*n38*;
on Moore, G., 732*n16*; on Phillips,
592; Ripley, E., and, 488–89, 505,
582; on social reform, 580–81; Stone
and, 754*n11*; "The True Principles of
Reform" by, 580–81
fruit farming, 172–73
Fruits of Philosophy (Knowlton), 317
Fugitive Slave Law of 1793, 534
Fuller, Elisha, 33, 232, 266
Fuller, Hiram, 406
Fuller, Margaret, xiv, 232; Alcott and,
379, 406, 431; at Brook Farm, 561;
at *The Dial*, 479, 589, 740*n80*; on
Emerson, R. W., 580, 586–87, 782*n36*;
at Greene Street School, 409; Moore,
G., on, 418; at School for Human
Culture, 379; Sturgis and, 440, 580
Fuller, Timothy, 32–33, 232
Furbish, James, 189, 670*n10*

Gallup, William, 766*n40*
Garrison, Ellen, 216, 359, 442, 444
Garrison, Jack, 103, 105–106, 149,
382, 395, 642*n41*, 729*n40*; Atwill on,
711*n35*
Garrison, Susan, 643*n43*

Garrison, Susan Robbins, 105, 333–34,
359, 395, 444, 510, 515
Garrison, William Lloyd, 335–37, 339;
assault on, 341–42, 521; on Concord,
535; at *The Liberator*, 328–29, 337, 525,
529–30; MCASS and, 529–30, 765*n38*;
militant abolitionism of, 422; Phillips
and, 494, 533
Garrison family, 104–106, 122–23, 515
*Geography of Middlesex County; for Young
Children, A*, 207
German idealism, 310–12, 314–15, 380,
412, 439, 504, 571–72, 752*n73*
German Romantics, 392
globalization, xx, 396, 572
Goethe, 385–86, 418, 446, 586
Goodhue, Isaac N., 359
Goodrich, Isaac W., 136
Goodwin, Hersey B., 72, 79–80, 204,
707*n6*, 730*n4*, 734*n24*; on alcohol,
256; on Concord bicentennial,
362–63, 720*n38*; at Concord Lyceum,
236, 238; death of, 372–73, 488; on
individualism, 447; Prescott, M., and,
444; Ripley, E., and, 204; on slavery
and abolition, 336, 340
Gourgas, Francis Richard, 327,
340–41, 359, 760*n7*, 769*nn4–5*; on
abolitionists, 530–31; at *Concord
Freeman*, 371–72, 466, 471, 476, 479,
543, 712*n43*, 749*n52*; Democrats and,
466–67; Freemasons and, 328; Keyes,
J., and, 541; on railroad, 541–43
Graham, Sylvester, 387–88
Graham's American Monthly Magazine,
782*n36*
Grand Lodge of Massachusetts, 394,
699*n56*
graphite, 5, 8, 129–30, 137
Great Awakening, the, 44, 49–50, 63,
229, 623*n20*; Emerson, R. W., on, 363;
Second, 61, 77–78; Shattuck, L., on,
357
Great Britain, U. S. naval hostilities with,
18–19
Great Famine of 1845–1851, Ireland,
544, 547
Great Field and Great Meadow, 103–105,
122–23, 156–57, 159–60, 180, 444
Great Migration, of 1630s, 18
Greeley, Horace, 533–34, 570, 590,
777*n4*

Green, Joseph C., 627*n39*, 632*n62*, 655*nn48–49*; Shattuck, D., and, 136; Trinitarian church and, 64–66, 73, 76–78, 135, 485

Green, Lucy Prescott, 77–78

Greene Street School, 406–407, 409

Greenleaf, Simon, 417

Grimké, Angelina, 509–11, 513, 523, 537, 759*nn2–3*, 760*n5*

Grimké, Sarah, 509–11, 513, 537, 759*nn2–3*, 760*n5*

Groton Academy, 210, 349, 564, 676*n56*

Grout, Henry M., 626*n37*

Hale, Edward Everett, 412

Hales, John G., *ix*

"Hall of Fantasy, The" (Hawthorne, N.), 565, 777*n4*

"Hamatreya" (Emerson, R. W.), 147, 165

Hamilton, Alexander, 16

Hamlet (Shakespeare), 786*n66*

Hammond, Charles, 645*n3*

Hanover Street Church, Boston, 63, 66, 630*n56*

Harding, Sewall, 67

Harding, Walter, 655*n46*

Harris, Robert Dalton, 648*n11*

Harrison, William Henry, 472–76, 480, 751*n62*

Hartford Convention of 1815, 11, 21–22, 26

Hartwell, Ephraim, 95–96, 627*n24*

Hartwell & Brown, 96, 638*n26*

Harvard College, 10, 169, 676*n56*; in American Revolution, 18; Andover Divinity School and, 62; Emerson, R. W., at, 305, 307, 314, 407–408; Frost at, 488; Hoar, E. S., at, 427–28; Hoar, S., family and, 24; Jarvis, E., at, 195, 198; Keyes, J. S., at, 426–28, 430, 445; Lafayette at, 30; Merrick, T., and, 56; Moore, G., at, 413–18, 456, 733*nn19–20*; Phi Beta Kappa society address, by Emerson, R. W., 404, 405, 407–12, 420, 429–30, 437–38, 449, 460, 509, 708*n8*, 724*n7*, 732*n13*; Quincy at, 409–10, 416, 427, 452, 462, 733*n20*; Ripley, E., at, 18, 45; Thoreau, H. D., at, 16, 180, 185–86, 209, 219, 376, 449, 452, 455–60, 465–67, 469, 500, 668*n3*, 741*n2*, 744*n17*; Unitarians and, 409, 495

Harvard Divinity School, 41, 489, 492–93; Emerson, R. W., address to, 315, 402, 405, 483, 493–500, 502–504, 538–39, 758*n39*

Harvard Law School, 414, 417

Harwood, Susannah, 642*n42*

Haskins, David Greene, 463

Hawthorne, Nathaniel, xiv, 305, 776*n39*; *The Blithedale Romance* by, 565; at Brook Farm, 562, 776*n42*; "The Celestial Railroad" by, 565–66, 777*nn43–44*; Channing, W. E., and, 563–64; on Concord, 565–68; Emerson, R. W., and, 562–63, 565, 777*n43*; Emerson, R. W., Thoreau, H. D., and, 590; on Frost, 563; "The Hall of Fantasy" by, 565, 777*n4*; *Mosses from an Old Manse* by, 566–68; *The Scarlet Letter* by, 563; Transcendentalists and, 568

Hawthorne, Sophia, 86, 562–63

Hayward, Jonathan P., 653*n34*

Hazewell, Charles C., 545–47, 563

Heald, Israel, 642*n42*

Healey, Caroline, 441

Hedge, Frederic Henry, 313, 315, 379, 569, 708*n13*, 709*nn17–18*, 711*n35*

Hemans, Felicia, 360–61

Hemenway, Bela, 116–17

Hemenway & Shattuck, 117

Henry, David, 140

Henshaw, David, 271, 324, 327

Herald of Freedom, 592

"Heroism" (lecture) (Emerson, R. W.), 440–41

Heywood, Abel B., 754*n8*

Heywood, Abiel, 10, 22, 67, 209, 616*n17*, 705*n97*; Concord Bank and, 91; as justice of the peace, 247, 249, 687*n63*; Thoreau, H. D., and, 187; as town clerk, 265, 295, 324, 349, 690*n79*

Heywood, George, 548

Hildreth, George and Jonathan, 155

Hildreth, Richard, 676*nn55–56*

Hill, Ralph, 646*n4*

History of Concord (Shattuck, L.), 355–57, 361–62, 364, 367–68, 718*nn16–18*, 720*n34*

History of England (Hume), 227–28

History of the Fight at Concord, 94

History of the Puritans (Neale), 227–28

Hoar, Ebenezer Rockwood, 159, 683*n39*,
  684*n43*, 685*n49*, 712*n43*
Hoar, Edward Sherman, 427–28
Hoar, Elizabeth, 307, 440, 445, 681*n19*
Hoar, George Frisbie, 227, 425, 451,
  681*n19*
Hoar, Rockwood, 214–15, 233, 241, 430,
  517, 524–25, 554
Hoar, Samuel, 24, 65, 72, 81, 616*n22*,
  620*n48*, 634*n8*; on abolitionists,
  535–36; in ACS, 341; Adams,
  J. Q., and, 298; anti-elitist mood
  against, 370; Anti-Masons on, 324,
  705*n96*; Brooks, N., and, 467–68;
  Concord Bank stock of, 693*n9*; on
  Concord Fight monument, 375–76;
  on Concord School Committee,
  676*nn53–54*; in Concord Temperance
  Society, 254; on Democrats, 375–76;
  on elimination of tax-supported
  religious establishment, 296;
  Emerson, C. C., and, 307–308;
  Emerson, R. W., on, 323, 370, 391,
  399–400; on fictional literature,
  227; First Parish Church and, 27;
  on Freemasonry and Anti-Masonry,
  298–99; *Gazette* on, 91, 270, 277, 298;
  on Grimké, A., 509–10; Keyes, J., and,
  23–31, 41–42, 92, 262–63, 267–68,
  270–71, 277, 370–71, 692*n8*, 693*n9*,
  697*n44*, 712*n44*; Munroe, W., and,
  133, 138; on Phillips, 535–36; for
  protectionism, 263; Ripley, E., and,
  27, 66, 271; Ripley, Samuel, and,
  331–32; Shattuck, D., and, 129; The
  Social Circle and, 698*n53*, 722*n43*;
  on South Carolina, slavery and,
  585–86; in temperance movement,
  552; Thoreau, H. D., on, 787*n76*; town
  improvements by, 91; Unitarians and,
  628*n42*; on Warren Bridge, 267–70,
  695*n27*; Whigs and, 298–99, 750*n60*;
  Wood, Ebenezer, and, 137
Hoar, Sarah Sherman, 451, 628*n42*
Holbrook, Josiah, 233–35, 238, 243–44,
  354, 387
Hollowell, Benjamin, 782*n38*
Hollowell, Samuel Green, 782*n38*
Hollowell, Sarah, 596, 782*n38*
Holmes, Oliver Wendell, 411–12
Hone, Philip, 366
Hopkinsianism, 70

Hornet, The, 471, 750*n53*
Hosmer, Ben, 79, 451
Hosmer, Cyrus, 237–38
Hosmer, George, 237–38
Hosmer, George Washington, 245–46
Hosmer, Horace, 464–65, 667*n60*, 679*n3*
Hosmer, Joe, 451
Hosmer, Rufus, 107, 138, 142, 159, 173,
  665*n45*
Howe, Peter, 381–82, 725*n8*
Howe, Phineas, 401, 772*n21*
Howe, Samuel Gridley, 318
Hubbard, Thomas, 660*n16*
Hudson, Frederick, 549, 559, 771*n17*
"Human Culture" (lecture) (Emerson,
  R. W.), 393–94, 440, 495
"Human Life" (lecture series) (Emerson,
  R. W.), 390, 420, 431, 580
Hume, David, 227–28
Hunstable, George, 486
Hunstable, Hannah, 764*n31*
Hunt, Almira, 228, 671*n23*
Hunt, Clarissa, 152–55, 158–59, 564,
  662*n21*
Hunt, Daniel, 160–61, 164, 167, 172,
  181, 236, 659*n8*, 666*n46*; Anti-
  Masonry of, 297–98; farming practices
  of, 558–59; at Hunt farm, 150–59,
  174, 658*n6*, 661*nn19–20*, 775*n31*; land
  of, 658*n6*, 661*n19*
Hunt, Martha, 563–65, 659*n8*
Hunt, Nehemiah, 150–51, 153–56, 158,
  172, 658*n6*, 660*n12*, 680*n11*; Hunt, D.,
  and, 659*n8*
Hunt, Nehemiah, Jr., 152
Hunt, William, 150
Hunt, William Henry, 154–55, 158,
  659*n9*
Hunt family farm and homestead,
  150–59, 174, 658*n6*, 659*n9*, 660*n12*,
  661*nn19–20*, 775*n31*, 776*n41*
Hurd, Isaac, 89, 112, 114, 116–18, 122,
  280, 634*n10*, 635*n12*, 662*n23*, 736*n36*
Hurd, Isaac, Jr., 114–16, 645*n3*, 646*n5*
Hutchinson, Peter, 334, 545
Hutchison, William R., 707*n7*

idealism: British, 314–15; Brownson,
  on Democrats and, 470; Emerson,
  R. W., on, 314–15, 317, 431; German,
  310–12, 314–15, 380, 412, 439, 504,
  571–72, 752*n73*; romantic, 385–86

immigrants: Black, to Boston, 640*n33*;
to Concord, 544–45; Irish, 20, 544–48,
565–66, 572–73, 576, 770*n11*, 771*n15*;
Ripley, E., on, 20–21; to US, 1845–
1854, 547–48
Independence Day, 10, 13, 16–17, 21–22,
613*n3*
Indian removal, 524–29
Indian Removal Act of 1830, 524, 749*n47*
individual, the: community and, 393,
574; democracy and, 392; education
and, 320, 393; Emerson, R. W., on,
xv–xvi, 319, 392–94, 397–99, 419, 438,
478, 480, 574; government and, 478;
institutions and, xv, 562; male and
female, 440; marriage and, 438; nation
and, 393–94; political parties and,
480; religion and, 503; Shattuck, L.,
on, 320, 357; Thoreau, H. D., on, xv,
503, 562, 591; Transcendentalism on,
404; Transcendentalists on, xv–xvi,
319, 434
individual freedom, xvii, 310–11, 365
individualism: American, xiii; in
Concord Transcendentalism, xvii;
economic, 269; Emerson, R. W., on,
xiii, 439, 505; of Emerson, R. W.,
and Thoreau, H. D., 220; Goodwin
on, 447; interdependence and, 320;
Romantic, 356, 458; Tocqueville on,
392, 505; Transcendentalist, xiv, xviii,
301; *Walden* and, 597; women on, 439
individuality, of Sturgis, 440
industrial capitalism, 598
industrial revolution, 7, 144, 262, 396,
568
interdependence, 394, 597; Bulkeley,
278; individualism and, 320;
Ripley, E., on, 278, 374–75; Society
of Middlesex Husbandmen and
Manufacturers on, 263–64; Thoreau,
H. D., on, 608; Transcendentalism on,
439
Ireland, 548; Great Famine of
1845–1851, 544, 547; independence
movement, 546–47
Irish immigrants, 20, 572–73, 576,
770*n11*, 771*n15*; to Boston, 544–45,
548; Brooks, M. M., on, 547; Catholic,
547–48; in Concord, 544–48; *Concord
Freeman* on, 545–47; Fitchburg
Railroad and, 544–47, 576; Moore, A.,

and, 546; Walden woods settlements
of, 545, 547, 565–66
Irving, Washington, 227

Jack, John, 106–107
Jackson, Andrew, 259–61, 271, 287–88;
in ACS, 332; Adams, J. Q., and, 259,
264–65, 277, 283; Anti-Masons and,
322; on banking system and national
economy, 298; *Boston Investigator* on,
317; Cherokees and, 523; Emerson,
R. W., on, 318, 328; Freemasons and,
283, 288; Indian Removal Act and,
749*n47*; Native Americans betrayed
by, 526; Van Buren and, 260, 300, 523,
526
Jackson, Charles T., 387–88, 534
Jackson, Lydia, 306, 308–309, 326, 337,
416–17; *see also* Emerson, Lidian
Jacksonian Democrats and Jacksonian
democracy, 261, 288, 300, 322–23,
327, 467, 779*n20*
Jarvis, Almira, 358
Jarvis, Edward, 332, 433, 723*n51*;
on alcohol and drinking, 686*n56*,
688*n69*, 690*n78*; Brooks, N., on,
195; on Charitable Library Society,
222; on Concord bicentennial,
346–47, 350–51, 358, 366, 717*n11*; in
Concord Debating Society, 231–32;
on Concord Fight monument, 369;
on Concord history, 356; in Concord
Lyceum debates, 685*n48*; on Concord
milldam, 86–87, 92, 194, 635*n12*;
Concord Social Library and, 228; on
Emerson, R. W., 314, 351, 726*n15*;
as grammar school master, 193–98,
227–28, 231–32, 460, 671*n24*, 676*n55*,
677*n63*; at Harvard, 195, 198; Hunt,
A., and, 671*n23*; Prichard, M., on,
195–96, 671*n24*; on school reform,
198, 208, 320; Shattuck, D., and, 217,
346–47, 678*n67*; Shattuck, L., and,
356, 672*n38*, 720*n34*; Thoreau, H. D.,
and, 197, 460, 462; *Traditions and
Reminiscences of Concord, Massachusetts
1779–1878* by, 678*n67*, 686*n56*,
688*n69*
Jarvis, Francis, 193–95, 245–46, 251–53,
645*n3*
Jefferson, Thomas, 6, 11, 17, 20, 95, 222;
expurgated letters, at Concord Social

Jefferson, Thomas (*cont.*)
  Library, 681*n17*; *Works of Thomas
    Jefferson* by, 225–26, 501, 681*n17*
Jeffersonian Republicans, 262
Jim Crow, 110
John Thoreau & Company, 136
Jones, Anna, 465, 471, 747*n38*
Jones, Elisha, Jr., 761*n13*
Jones, John, Jr., 747*n38*
Jones, Joshua, 6, 83, 85–88, 633*n1*
Jones, Mary, 4–5
Jones, Stephen, Jr., 646*n4*
Jones estate, 633*n1*, 634*nn7–8*

Kaestle, Carl F., 678*nn65–66*
Kant, Immanuel, 310
Kelly, Barney, 546
Kendall, James, 416
Keyes, Ann, 358
Keyes, John, 32–33, 35, 68–69, 77, 94,
    616*n19*, 617*n28*, 695*n28*, 769*n4*;
    Anti-Masonic Party against, 294–95,
    465, 704*n87*; Atwill and, 327, 702*n77*,
    704*n87*, 712*n42*; Barrett, J., and,
    349–50, 697*n44*; boardinghouse
    of, 452; Child, D. L., and, 272–76,
    696*n38*; children of, 424–25;
    committee on accounts, 280; at
    Concord Bank, 693*n9*; on Concord
    bicentennial committee chair,
    350, 358, 360; on Concord Fight
    monument committee, 722*n46*; on
    Concord Lyceum lecture by Phillips,
    534–35; *Daily American Statesman*
    and, 271–72; on elimination of tax-
    supported religious establishment,
    296; Everett and, 691*n3*; Freemasons
    and, 37, 284, 286, 289–91, 298;
    Frost and, 488; Fuller, E., and, 266;
    Garrison, W. L., assault witnessed by,
    342, 521; Gourgas and, 541; Henshaw
    and, 271; Hoar, S., and, 23–31,
    41–42, 92, 262–63, 267–68, 270–71,
    277, 370–71, 692*n8*, 693*n9*, 697*n44*,
    712*n44*; on Hoar, E. S., 428; Jarvis, F.,
    and, 195; as Jeffersonian Republican,
    262; Keyes, J. S., and, 424–34, 736*n46*;
    Massachusetts Journal on, 271–76; as
    Middlesex County treasurer, 261–62;
    in milldam redevelopment, 89, 91;
    on Mills, 695*n29*; Moore, A., and,
    162; Nelson and, 174; on Phillips,

534–35, 629*n47*; Prescott, T., and,
    441; Prichard, M., and, 696*n31*; for
    protectionism, 263; Shattuck, D., and,
    279, 290, 325, 335, 694*n16*; Todd on,
    628*n45*; Tuttle and, 118; on Warren
    Bridge, 270–71; on Webster, D., 271,
    695*n29*; Whigs and, 465–66, 712*n42*;
    Yeoman's Gazette and, 273, 276, 291,
    702*n78*
Keyes, John Shepard, 214–15, 238, 325,
    342, 542, 616*n19*, 618*n31*, 736*n36*; on
    Brooks, M. M., 784*n52*; on election of
    1840, 476; Emerson, A. F., on, 737*n57*;
    First Parish Church and, 484, 531–32;
    on Frost, 491, 755*n16*, 758*n38*;
    on Harrison rally, 474, 751*n62*; at
    Harvard, 426–28, 430, 445; on the
    Hawthornes, 563; Keyes, J., and,
    424–34, 736*n46*; on lectures of
    Emerson, R. W., 363, 430–34, 447,
    737*n51*; Moore, G., and, 736*n46*; on
    Phillips, 592; Prescott, M., and, 445–47,
    722*n46*, 740*n74*; racism of, 429; on
    shade trees in village square, 636*n16*;
    Thoreau, H. D., and, 432–33, 462, 489,
    746*n33*, 783*n42*; on Walden Pond, 433,
    446; *Yeoman's Gazette* and, 425–26
Keyes, Joseph Boyden, 464–65, 616*n19*
Keyes family, names of, 735*n35*
King Philip's War, 357, 361, 363–64
Kneeland, Abner, 471, 486–87, 497–99,
    754*n9*, 755*n22*; Emerson, R. W., on,
    317–18, 494–95; Everett on, 494–95
Knowlton, Charles, 317
Kurland, Susan, 703*n82*

Ladies' Sewing Society (LSS), 743*n11*,
    761*n11*
Lafayette, Marquis de, 15–16, 30–34,
    618*n32*, 618*nn31–32*
Lancaster, Joseph, 199–200, 212, 233
"Landing of the Pilgrim Fathers, The,"
    360–61
"Landlord, The" (Thoreau, H. D.), 590
Lathrop, Samuel, 332
Latimer, George, 534, 536
Lawrence, Luther, 215
Lawrence, Myron, 474
Lee, Joseph, 747*n38*
Lee, Ruth, 747*n38*
Lemire, Elise, 639*n31*, 640*n34*
Letters on the Entered Apprentice's Oath, 298

"Letters on the Equality of the Sexes, and the Condition of Women" (Grimké, S.), 511
Lexington: in American Revolution, 348, 352, 369 753n57; Concord and, 32, 34, 40–41, 352, 369, 717n14
libel laws, 273–76, 487, 696n36
Liberal Preacher, The, 72
liberal Protestantism, 61–62
Liberator, The, 330, 334, 523, 535–36, 761n12; Garrison, W. L., at, 328–29, 337, 525, 529–30; Thoreau, H., obituary in, 766n43; Thoreau, H. D., in, 592–93
Liberia, 329–30, 768n56
libertarianism, xv, 478–79
Liberty Party, 749n51
Library Company of Concord, 679n5
Life of George Washington (Moore, G.), 415–16
Lincoln, Levi, 41–42, 259–60, 270, 691n3, 695n28
Lincoln, Massachusetts, 24, 63, 98
Litchfield, Paul, 67
"Literary Ethics" (lecture) (Emerson, R. W.), 430–31
local democracy, 360, 364, 369–70
Locke, John, 311, 443, 445, 489–90
Loco Focoism, 469–70, 476, 479, 598, 749n48
Loring, David, 123, 769n4
Lowell, James Russell, 391, 463, 490–91, 498–99, 777n43
Lowell, Massachusetts, 95, 97–98, 107, 111, 123, 349, 371, 542, 723n50
Lowell Bank, 128
Lowell Journal, 549, 563, 692n7
Lowell Mercury, 692n7, 695n27
LSS, see Ladies' Sewing Society
Luther, Martin, 345–46
lyceum movement, 235, 241–43, 306, 354, 373
lyceums, 235–44, 255–56, 389, 417, 419, 570, 573; in Boston, 685n50
Lyman, Theodore, Jr., 696n36

Madison, James, 11, 17, 20–21, 283
Mann, Horace, 461
Mansfield, 171
"Man the Reformer" (lecture) (Emerson, R. W.), 752n74
Marie, or Slavery in the United States (Beaumont), 726n15

Marshall, John, 269
Marx, Leo, 777n44
Mason, Jeremiah, 739n69
Masons, see Freemasons
MASS, see Massachusetts Anti-Slavery Society
Massachusetts: geography and maps of, 207; liquor licenses in, 552; Masonic lodges in, 699n56; Native Americans of, 356–57; public entities in, 221; railroad projects, 541; schools and public education in, 189–92; slavery in, 99–100, 102, 104; see also specific cities and towns
Massachusetts Agricultural Society, 135–36, 655n46
Massachusetts Anti-Slavery Society (MASS), 511, 531, 582–83, 759n4, 760n7
Massachusetts Bay Colony, xvii, 347
Massachusetts Colonization Society, 333, 714n53
Massachusetts Constitution, 38, 296, 494, 542, 617n25, 617n27
Massachusetts General Court, 269, 272, 356, 553, 582, 613n5, 620n2, 670n15, 722n49, 723n50, 731n5
Massachusetts Historical Society (MHS), 354–55
Massachusetts Horticultural Society, 168–69, 558
Massachusetts Journal, 271–76
Massachusetts Mercury, 640n33
Massachusetts Missionary Society, 485
Massachusetts Register and United States Calendar, 692n8
Massachusetts Society for Promoting Agriculture (MSPA), 164–66
Massachusetts Society for the Suppression of Intemperance (MSSI), 250–52
mass society, 397–98, 463
materialism: Emerson, R. W., on, 323, 385, 390, 396, 401, 408, 421, 561; Minott, G., against, 183; in Panic of 1837, 421; slavery and, 584–85; Thoreau, H. D., on, 478
Mather, William L., 781n35
Mayhew, Jonathan, 49
MCASS, see Middlesex County Anti-Slavery Society
McCormick, Richard P., 751n63

MCTS, *see* Middlesex County
 Temperance Society
Means, James, 530, 766*n40*
Melvin, Emerson, 90
Melvin, Joshua, 655*n46*
Memoir of Ralph Waldo Emerson, A
 (Cabot), 760*n8*
Mercantile Library Association, 571,
 591, 779*n14*
Meriam, Ephraim, 732*n16*
Meriam, Joseph, 722*n45*
Meriam, Tarrant P., 646*n4*
Merino and Saxony sheep, 170
Merriam, John, 612*n16*
Merriam, Joseph, 612*n16*
Merrick, Mary, 56–58, 624*nn28–30*; *see
 also* Brooks, Mary Merrick
Merrick, Sally Minot, 624*n30*
Merrick, Tilly, 56–58, 332, 515–17
Merrimack Journal, 692*n7*
Merrimack River, 7–8, 95, 541, 594
Mexican War, 606–607
MHS, *see* Massachusetts Historical
 Society
Michelangelo, 345
Middle Passage, 438, 522, 538, 594
Middlesex agricultural fair, 169–70
Middlesex Agricultural Society, 165
Middlesex Bank, 9, 123, 210, 230
Middlesex Bible Society, 69, 110
Middlesex Canal, 8
Middlesex Canal Company, 157
Middlesex County Anti-Slavery Society
 (MCASS), 334–35, 340, 511, 519, 531,
 715*n66*, 760*nn5–6*; Brooks, M. M.,
 in, 530, 583, 593; Brooks, N., and,
 538; Emerson, R. W., address to,
 583–85, 593; Garrison, W. L., and,
 529–30, 765*n38*; Thoreau, H., in, 591;
 Thoreau, H. D., and, 593
Middlesex County Court of Common
 Pleas, 110, 289
Middlesex County court schedule,
 1820s, 691*n6*
Middlesex County Temperance Society
 (MCTS), 689*nn74–75*, 690*n80*
Middlesex Female Academy, 210,
 675*n48*
Middlesex Gazette, 103, 107, 166–67,
 173–74, 692*n7*
Middlesex Hotel, 37, 109–10, 119, 140,
 148, 169, 237, 687*n64*; conventions

at, 262–63; drinking at, 247–48, 417,
 690*n78*
Middlesex Institution for Savings,
 635*n13*, 693*n9*, 769*n5*
Middlesex Lyceum, 673*n43*, 685*n50*
Middlesex Mutual Fire Insurance
 Company, 90–91, 128, 251
Middlesex Observer, 10, 12–13, 176–77
Middlesex Republicans, 615*n14*, 615*n16*
Middlesex Whig, 325, 711*n37*, 713*n45*
Middleton, James, 334, 714*n56*
militant abolitionism, 422
Mill Dam Company, 92, 112, 161, 224,
 553, 635*n14*, 713*n45*; Concord Bank
 and, 129, 167–68, 284, 551, 693*n9*
Mills, John, 695*n29*
Milton, John, 345–46
Minot, Jonas, 5, 153, 180, 221, 285, 455,
 611*n4*, 667*n57*; census on household
 of, 642*n41*; as Charitable Library
 Society president, 679*n6*; on Minot
 farm, 103, 658*n2*; Thoreau, John, at
 homestead of, 147–49
Minot, Mary Jones Dunbar, 642*n41*
Minot, Timothy, 188
Minott, Abigail, 667*n58*
Minott, Ephraim, 178, 250, 667*n57*
Minott, George, 177–79, 382, 450–51,
 557, 667*nn57–58*; Channing, W. E.,
 on, 605; Emerson, R. W., and, 181,
 397, 668*n63*; against materialism, 183;
 Society of Middlesex Husbandmen
 and Manufacturers on, 180; Thoreau,
 H. D., on, 180–83, 605, 786*n73*;
 Transcendentalists on, 182; in War of
 1812, 181
Minott, Mary, 140, 177–81, 455, 667*n60*
Minutemen, xvi–xvii; Concord and,
 xvi–xvii, 35; at Concord North Bridge,
 93–94, 150, 454–55; descendants
 of, 236, 264; Transcendentalists and,
 xiv, xx
Minutemen and Their World, The (Gross),
 xviii–xx
Misses Thoreau, the, 81; First Parish
 Church and, 60–61, 65, 73–74, 502,
 620*n3*, 655*n58*; Trinitarian church and,
 63–65, 73–74, 77, 105, 135, 453, 485
"Model of Christian Charity, A"
 (Winthrop), 447
monitorial system, of education,
 199–200

Monroe, James, 9–10, 15, 22
Moore, Abel, 89, 91, 94, 159–65, 167,
    178–82, 702n80; alcohol and, 249;
    Concord Steam Mill Company and,
    554; Emerson, R. W., on, 164–65, 573,
    668n63; on English hay, 165, 172,
    604; farming methods, 159–65, 573,
    601, 604–605, 663n23, 664n24; Irish
    immigrants working for, 546; as jail
    keeper, 413; Keyes, J., and, 162; Moore,
    G., and, 413–14, 417–18; Patch, S.,
    and, 687n64; sons of, 732n16;
    Thoreau, H. D., and, 165
Moore, Clement Clark, 758n35
Moore, George, 162, 428; on Anti-Masons,
    417; at Cambridge Anti-Slavery Society
    meeting, 735n30; at Concord
    Academy, 732n17; at Concord
    Lyceum, 419; as divinity student,
    420–22, 498; Emerson, R. W., and,
    413, 417–23, 447, 494, 709n15,
    734nn23–26, 755n21; Frost on,
    732n16; on Fuller, M., 418; on God
    and nature, 422–23; at Harvard,
    413–18, 456, 733nn19–20; Keyes, J. S.,
    and, 736n46; Life of George Washington
    by, 415–16; Moore, A., and, 413–14,
    417–18; pacifism of, 417–18, 422; in
    Plymouth, 416–17; Prichard, F. J., and,
    501; Russell, E., and, 417, 422, 431; on
    social reform, 417–18; in temperance
    movement, 417; Unitarianism and,
    420–23; on universal mind, 734n25;
    on Ware, 420–21, 734n28, 735n30
Moore, Harriet, 413–14
Moore, Henry, 238, 420
Moore, John B., 162, 786n69
Morgan, William, 286–87, 289, 701n72
Morse, Jedidiah, 62–63, 65, 69–70, 207,
    623n23
Morton, Marcus, 274–75, 691n3
Moses Prichard & Company, 117
Mosses from an Old Manse (Hawthorne,
    N.), 566–68
Mount Airy, 331–32, 713n51
MSPA, see Massachusetts Society for
    Promoting Agriculture
MSSI, see Massachusetts Society for the
    Suppression of Intemperance
mulberry orchards, 171
Munroe, James, 777n4
Munroe, Mary, 144

Munroe, Nathan, 144
Munroe, Nehemiah, 133
Munroe, William, 7–8, 85, 95; on
    alcohol, 255; Burr, S., and, 143;
    capitalism and, 142; net worth of,
    657n61; in pencil-making industry,
    129–44, 167, 654nn38–39, 656n54–55,
    657n60, 706n100; real estate of,
    654n40; Shattuck, D., and, 142, 175,
    692n8; Thoreau, John, and, 5–6, 108,
    126, 129–30, 135–37, 139, 167–68,
    656n55; Wood, Ebenezer, and,
    705n97
Munroe family, 85–87
Murray, Lindley, 207
mutual education, 233–34, 237, 243–44

Napoleon, 140–41
National Intelligencer, 525
National Republican Party, 231, 239,
    260–68, 271, 287–88, 290, 298, 321,
    714n53
Native Americans: in Boston Commons,
    395; Christianity and, 357; Jackson
    and Van Buren betraying, 526; King
    Philip's War and, 357, 363–64; of
    Massachusetts, 356–57; removal of,
    524–29; on Trail of Tears, 523, 527
natural history lecture, by Emerson,
    R. W., 242–43
nature: civilization and, 458; Emerson,
    R. W., on, 361–62, 379–80, 383, 407,
    418–19, 495; God and, 422–23, 487;
    Moore, G., on God and, 422–23;
    Thoreau, H. D., on, 451, 458–60,
    588–89, 603; Thoreau, John, Jr., on,
    464–65; Thoreau family on, 451
Nature (Emerson, R. W.), xviii, 243, 379,
    382–83, 407, 419; composition of,
    504, 563, 567; Robinson on, 500–501;
    Thoreau, H. D., on, 449, 458–59,
    744n21; Transcendentalism and, 307,
    315, 380, 500–501
Neale, Daniel, 227–28
Nelson, Albert H., 174, 712n44, 724n6
New Divinity movement, 76, 409
Newell, John C., 140–41
New England: alcohol in, 244–45;
    Emerson, R. W., lectures on, 571–76,
    594, 600; railroads, 541–42; textiles,
    slavery and, 170; white villages of, 92;
    women, Ripley, E., on, 56

New England Anti-Slavery Society, 329, 337
New England Committee for the Relief of Ireland and Scotland, 548
New England Farmer, 164, 169–70, 173, 182, 604
"New England Reformers" (lecture) (Emerson, R. W.), 768n57
New England Spectator, 511, 759n3
new rum, 245–47
Newton, Isaac, 419
New York Herald, 549, 559
"Night Before Christmas, The" (Moore, C. C.), 758n35
Niles' Weekly Register, 125
nonresistance, 429, 478, 539, 783n42
North American Review, 367
Norton, Andrews, 497, 499
Nutting, Betty, 80

O'Brien, Michael, 547
O'Connell, Daniel, 546–47
O'Connor, Dick, 745n26
Oliver, Fatima, 104
O'Sullivan, John, 590–91, 779n20
Otis, Harrison Gray, 11, 22, 615n16

pacifism, 417–18, 422
Paine, Thomas, 221–22, 681n17
Palfrey, John G., 421
Panic of 1819, 4, 87, 95, 107, 115, 742n9
Panic of 1837, 401, 408, 421, 530
Panoplist, The, 62, 65
Paquette, Andrian, 637n25
Parker, Theodore, 479, 488, 497, 505, 534, 759n43
Parkman, William, 84, 648n11, 747n42
Park Street Church, Boston, 63–64, 317, 325–26, 627n39
Parmenter, William, 370, 467, 475–76, 538
partisanship: Adams, J. Q., on, 41; in American democracy, 476; of Atwill, 292, 325; in Concord, 17–19, 21–23, 41–42, 399, 471; Corinthian Lodge, as refuge from, 285; Emerson, R. W., on, 399; of Federalists and Republicans, 82; Ripley, E., against, 19; Thoreau, H. D., on, 458, 471–72; of Whigs and Anti-Masons, 298; of Whigs and Democrats, 466–67, 476
Patch, Ephraim B., 653n34

Patch, Stephen, 249, 653n34, 687n64
"Patriotism" (lecture) (Ripley, E.), 472, 487
Paul, Thomas, 105
Peabody, Elizabeth, 379, 439, 562
pencil-making: industry, 5–8, 15–16, 85, 108, 113, 129–44, 167, 656n55; of Munroe, W., 129–44, 167, 654nn38–39, 656n55, 656nn54–55, 657n60, 706n100; of Thoreau, John, 15–16, 43, 108, 113, 126, 129, 135, 137, 142, 144, 185, 219, 451–52, 655n46, 656n55
Penniman, Thomas, 642n42
Penobscot Indians, 115
Pestalozzi, Johann, 206, 234, 320, 408, 464, 673n41
Peterson's Guide, 11
Phillips, Wendell, 337; abolitionism of, 533–36, 586, 592; Brooks, M. M., and, 534–36, 586, 592; at Concord Lyceum, 533–36, 586, 592; Frost on, 592; Garrison, W. L., and, 494, 533; Hoar, S., on, 535–36; Keyes, J., on, 534–35, 629n47; Keyes, J. S., on, 592; Thoreau, H. D., on, 592–94
"Philosophy of Labor" (lecture) (Emerson, R. W.), 431
"Philosophy of Modern History, The" (lecture series) (Emerson, R. W.), 386–87, 389–90, 392–99, 406–407, 418–20, 458, 728n34
phrenology, 442, 444, 778n9
Pierpont, John, 719n30
Pilgrim's Progress, The (Bunyan), 565
Pioneer, The, 565, 777n43
Platt, Samuel, 86
pluralism, religious, 231, 300, 316, 357
Plymouth, 308–10, 346, 384, 416–17, 422
Plymouth Religious Society, 416
Plymouth Rock, 35, 309, 354
"Poet, The" (lecture) (Emerson, R. W.), 432
"Political, Moral, and Literary Character of a Nation" (speech) (Thoreau, H. D.), 459–60, 469
popular democracy, 370, 471
popular politics, 292, 472, 474–75, 477, 560
Power, Tyrone, 388
Pratt, Alvan, 7
Prescott, Abba Maria, 359

Prescott, Abigail, 178–79
Prescott, Martha, 105–106, 434, 441–47, 722n46, 739n71, 740n74
Prescott, Timothy, 434, 441–42, 446, 722n46, 732n13, 739nn70–71, 740n78
Prescott family farm, 160, 162–64, 178, 180, 662n23
"Present Age, The" (lecture series) (Emerson, R. W.), 393–97, 420, 431, 477–78, 730n49
Prichard, Frances Jane, 421, 501
Prichard, Jane, 501
Prichard, Lizzy, 518
Prichard, Moses, 116, 289, 358, 501; at Burr & Prichard, 118–19, 121, 123, 126–28, 135, 153, 174, 181; on Jarvis, E., 195–96, 671n24; Keyes, J., and, 696n31; Moses Prichard and Company, 117; in The Social Circle, 280; on Works of Thomas Jefferson, 225, 681n17
protectionism, 263
Protestantism and Protestants, xv, 225, 293, 318–19, 330, 360; Boston Investigator on, 486–87
Providence Daily Journal, 778n11
public education and public schools, 190–92, 208, 212, 216–17, 316, 359, 678n65
public speaking, 229–30, 240–41, 390–91
Puritanism: civic republicanism and, xv; Emerson, R. W., on, 538–39
Puritans, 61; Bulkeley and, 76, 81; clergy, 47–48; Concord and, xvi–xviii, 22, 81, 153, 360–64; Congregationalist Standing Order and, 23; Emerson, R. W., on, 572; Hunts as descendants of, 153; on licensing, 249; on local churches, 51; Minott family and, 178; Morse and, 63; practices of, 76; on religious freedom and slavery, 347; Ripley, E., and, 18, 20, 48, 52, 506; Thoreau, C., and, 43; tradition of, 80–81, 355; Trinitarians and, 80; on Walden woods, 99

Quincy, Josiah, 27, 29; Emerson, R. W., Thoreau, H. D., and, 449; at Harvard, 409–10, 416, 427, 452, 462, 733n20

racial egalitarianism, 444
racial equality, 339, 510, 586, 782n37

racism, 102, 106, 382, 610n7, 768n56; Concord bicentennial and, 359; Emerson, R. W., and, 538, 585–86; of Keyes, J. S., 429
railroad: Belknap and, 543–44, 553; Crocker on, 541–44; financing and building, 543–44, 553; Fitchburg Railroad, 541–51, 553, 555–56, 559–61, 566, 575–77, 595; Irish immigrants in building, 544–47, 576; in New England, 541–42; Western Railroad, 543; workers, 544–46
Rand, Asa, 66–67, 71, 629n51
Ratcliffe, Donald J., 703n82
reading: debating and, 230; Emerson, R. W., on, 398–99; social libraries and, 224–29; in social reform, 225
Redgauntlet (Scott), 227, 681n19
Regulations of the School Committee of the Town of Concord, 204–206
religion and morality, 18, 27, 312, 453, 675n48, 680n16
religious diversity, 80, 325–26, 483
religious establishments, Congregationalist Standing Order on, 23
religious freedom, 318, 347, 356, 458–59, 494
religious pluralism, 231, 300, 316, 357
religious sentiment, 338–39, 364, 491; Emerson, R. W., on, 507; Thoreau, H. D., on, 458, 502, 744n21; Transcendentalists on, 312–13, 315–17, 502
Report on the Agriculture of Massachusetts, 604
Republican, the, 475, 501, 505–506, 542, 758n41
republicanism, 21, 222, 285, 330; Catholicism and, 318; Charitable Library Society books on, 222; Christianity and, 18; civic, xv; classical, 28, 400; Federalists on, 222, 322
Republicans, Federalists and, 231, 324; in Concord, 11, 16–23, 26–30, 32–33, 35, 39, 58, 82, 613n5; partisanship, 82; in War of 1812, 264–65, 292
"Resistance to Civil Government" (Thoreau, H. D.), 469, 502–503, 607, 787n76
Revere, Paul, 4, 40, 299
Revolutionary War, see American Revolution

Rex, Samuel, 652n31, 687n60
Reynolds, Grindall, 626n37
Rice, Reuben, 774nn25–26
Richardson, James, Jr., 746n34
Ripley, Daniel, 331, 713n51
Ripley, Ezra, xviii, 202, 567, 630n53;
    on alcohol and drinking, 246–47,
    249–51, 255, 687n65; Alcott, A. B.,
    and, 758n40; American Revolution
    and, 18–19, 30, 36, 45, 348–49; on
    Anti-Masonry, 295–96, 348–49;
    Arminianism and, 49–50, 70, 623n20;
    Atwill and, 297, 348; on Calvinism,
    48–51, 61, 70, 486, 503; Charitable
    Library Society and, 221, 223; on
    Cherokees, 525; on Christ and
    Christianity, 47–53, 311, 330, 504; on
    community, 18–19, 47–48, 53, 82, 374,
    607; "Conscience, Its Design, Use,
    and Obligations," 62; at Corinthian
    Lodge, 283–84; Cushman and, 75;
    death of, 505–507, 539, 759n43;
    Emerson, M. M., and, 59, 71, 308, 504,
    596, 755n17; Emerson, R. W., and, xvii,
    18–19, 41, 48, 71, 305, 314, 322, 352,
    392, 394, 397, 499–500, 503–507;
    Emerson, William (father), and,
    629n50; on Emerson, William (father),
    347–48; in Evangelical Missionary
    Society, 623n21; Federalists and, 53;
    Freemasons, Anti-Masonry and,
    283–87, 291, 295–98, 300, 348–49;
    Frost and, 488–89, 505, 582;
    Goodwin, H., and, 204; at Harrison
    rally, 474; at Harvard College, 18, 45; in
    History of the Fight at Concord, 94; Hoar,
    S., and, 27, 66, 271; on immigrants,
    20–21; on interdependence, 278,
    374–75; Jarvis, F., and, 194–95; on
    Lexington, 352; MSSI and, 250–51;
    on New England women, 56; against
    partisanship, 19; "Patriotism" by,
    472, 487; Prichard, J., on, 501; public
    funding of religion and, 296; Puritans
    and, 18, 20, 48, 52, 506; Ripley, G., and,
    504–505, 708n13; Robbins, N., and, 75;
    slavery, abolition and, 99, 330–31, 341;
    on Smith, D., 652n29; Southmayd, D.,
    and, 81; to Thatcher, B. B., 721n42; to
    Thatcher, G., 621n8; on Thompson, G.,
    336; Thoreau, C., and, 43, 53, 56, 71,
    74–75, 453; Thoreau, H. D., and, 457;

on Thoreau, H. D., 487; on Thoreau,
    John, 248; Thoreau, R., and 54, 61,
    623n23, 624n24; Thoreau family and,
    53–54; Thoreau sisters and, 60–61, 63,
    74; on Transcendentalism, 504–505;
    Trinitarian church and, 74–78, 80,
    629n51, 637n21; Unitarianism and, 69,
    72; on Universalism, 486; on White, Z.,
    640n34
Ripley, Ezra, in Concord, 10, 17–22, 39,
    320; on bicentennial, 346, 349–50,
    360; on Concord Fight, 348, 352;
    on Concord Fight monument, 41,
    348–49, 368–69, 372–73, 375–77,
    717n8; Concord Lyceum and, 235–36,
    239–42, 321, 472, 487, 600; on
    Concord North Bridge, 368–69, 373;
    Concord Social Library and, 223;
    in Concord Temperance Society,
    254–55; on schools, 189, 208, 210,
    669n5; The Social Circle and, 279
Ripley, Ezra, at First Parish Church,
    59, 487, 626n37; on baptism,
    51–53; on Calvinism, 48–51, 61, 70;
    congregation of, 44–45, 47–48, 60–66,
    69–73, 78–79, 82, 231, 306, 314, 373,
    491–92, 502; on conversions, 55–56;
    Emerson, R. W., and, 314, 483–84,
    488, 491–92; Hoar, S., and, 27;
    liberal consensus at, 72; the Misses
    Thoreau and, 60–61, 65, 73–74, 502;
    orthodox preachers visiting pulpit
    of, 62; parishioners of, 45–47, 50,
    60, 80, 84, 491–92, 506; sermons by,
    47–48, 54–55, 62, 69–70, 72–73, 311,
    391, 487–88, 492, 503, 505, 614n9,
    624nn28–29, 758n41; Trinitarian
    church and, 74–78, 80, 629n51,
    637n21
Ripley, George, xvii, 318, 497, 758n39;
    Brook Farm of, 504, 561; Brownson
    and, 379–80; Hedge and, 313; on
    lectures of Emerson, R. W., 402;
    Parker and, 505; on religion and
    theology, 313, 315; Ripley, E., and,
    504–505, 708n13; Specimens of Foreign
    Standard Literature by, 384–85
Ripley, Samuel, 331–32, 499–500, 708n13,
    713n51, 715n63, 756n23, 758n39
Ripley, Sarah, 57, 70, 504, 756n29
Robbins, Caesar, 103–104, 333–34,
    642n42

Robbins, Dorothy, 642n42
Robbins, George, 642n42
Robbins, John, 642n42
Robbins, Nathan, 75, 77, 80, 642n42
Robbins, Peter, 104–105, 122–23,
    643nn43–44
Robbins, Susan, 103–104
Robinson, William S., 475, 563, 677n63,
    776n39; antislavery journalism of,
    216; *Gazette* purchased by, 713n45,
    749n52; on *The Hornet*, 750n53; in
    the *Republican*, 542; Thoreau, H. D.,
    and, 214–15, 471, 500, 749n52; on
    Transcendentalism, 500–501
Rogers, Nathaniel Peabody, 591–92,
    784n51
Rogers, Robert, 747n38
romantic idealism, 385–86
Romantic individualism, 356, 458
Romanticism, xv, 206, 308, 392, 439, 457
Rorabaugh, W. J., 686n56, 688n69
Rousseau, Jean-Jacques, 206
Roxbury, 85–86
Royal Arch Chapter of Freemasons, 285,
    300, 417, 701n73
Russell, Chambers, 639n31
Russell, Charles, 640n34
Russell, Elizabeth, 417, 422, 431, 733n21
Russell, Mary, 431–33, 445, 733n21
Russell, Shattuck & Co., 674n44

Safford, Ward, 366, 545, 598
Salem Lyceum, 389, 684n42
Sanborn, Franklin, 646nn4–5, 691n4,
    758n40
Scarlet Letter, The (Hawthorne, N.), 563
school and education: Alcott, A. B.,
    on, 379, 408; in Concord, 185–98,
    200–202, 204–18, 227–28; Concord
    Lyceum and, 219; corporal
    punishment in, 188–89, 460–62,
    509–10; Emerson, R. W., and, 320–21,
    381, 393, 398, 406–11, 710n29;
    funding for, 217; gender and, 409;
    Greene Street School, 406–407, 409;
    Holbrook on, 234–35; the individual
    and, 320, 393; Lancaster on, 199–200,
    212, 233; in Massachusetts, 189–92;
    monitorial system, 199–200; mutual
    education and, 233–34, 237, 243–44;
    Pestalozzi on, 206, 234, 320, 408, 464,
    673n41; public, 190–92, 208, 212,

216–17, 316, 359, 678n65; *Regulations
    of the School Committee of the Town of
    Concord* on, 204–206; Ripley, E., on,
    189, 208, 210, 669n5; schoolbooks,
    673n41, 674n44; self-education, 201,
    225–26; self-reliance in, 202–203;
    Shattuck, L., on, 198–208, 320,
    672n34, 673n43; Thatcher, B. B., on,
    710n29; Transcendentalists on, 464;
    women and, 439–40; *see also* Concord
    Academy; Concord grammar school;
    Harvard College
School for Human Culture, 379
school reform and reformers, 670n15,
    673n41, 745n26; in Concord, 20, 186,
    192–93, 217–18, 320, 462; against
    corporal punishment, 461–62;
    Emerson, R. W., on, 218, 320, 393,
    408; on funding, 217; Jarvis, E. on,
    198, 208, 320; on private academies,
    216; Shattuck, L., and, 202–204, 208;
    Thoreau, H. D., on, 193, 208, 218
Scott, Walter, 227–28, 681n19
Scottish Common Sense moral
    philosophy, 489
SDUK, *see* Boston Society for the
    Diffusion of Useful Knowledge
Second American Party System, 751n63
Second Bank of the United States, 261,
    265
Second Church, Boston, 305–306, 314,
    322, 383, 405, 407, 420, 493
Second Great Awakening, the, 61, 77–78
Sedgwick, Catherine, 227
Sedition Act of 1798, 274
self-culture: masculinity and, 438; social
    reform and, xvii; Unitarians on, 415
self-education, 201, 225–26
self-government, 14, 37, 202, 221, 225,
    281, 329, 365, 423
Self-Interpreting Bible (Brown, John),
    74–75, 630n57
self-reform, 399, 569
self-reliance: in education, 202–203;
    Emerson, R. W., and Thoreau, H. D.,
    on, 463; Emerson, R. W., on, 346,
    424, 429, 438, 447, 501; of farmers,
    175; Prichard, F. J., on, 501; Shattuck,
    L., and, 208; Thoreau, H. D., on, xiv;
    Transcendentalists on, 434, 463
"Self-Reliance" (Emerson, R. W.),
    522–23, 756n29, 764n27

separation of church and state, 296, 318, 357, 483–84, 487, 684*n44*

Sewall, Ellen Quincy, 588

Shakespeare, William, 418–19, 786*n66*

Shanley, J. Lyndon, 785*n59*

Shattuck, Daniel, 88–89, 91–92, 94, 116–18, 120; on alcohol and drinking, 247; Allen, J. C., and, 265–66, 694*n15*; annual financial statements, 650*n21*; Burr and, 121, 123–24, 128–29, 132, 262; Cheney and, 705*n97*; as Concord Bank president, 698*n50*; on Concord bicentennial, 346–47; on Concord Fight monument committee, 369; in Concord Lyceum debates, 685*n48*; estate of, 694*n15*; Freemasons and, 289–90, 298; Green, J. C., and, 136; at Harrison rally, 472–73; Hoar, S., and, 129; Howe, Phineas, and, 772*n21*; Hunt family and, 158; Jarvis, E., and, 217, 346–47, 678*n67*; Keyes, J., and, 279, 290, 325, 335, 694*n16*; Mansion House of, 129; Munroe, W., and, 142, 175, 692*n8*; printing shop of, 713*n45*, 749*n52*; for railroad, 543; Robbins, P., and, 122–23, 650*n23*; Shattuck, H., and, 551; in The Social Circle, 280; in Society of Middlesex Husbandmen and Manufacturers, 167; Thoreau, John, and, 122, 748*n46*; Thoreau family home and, 277, 600–601, 752*n66*; *Yeoman's Gazette* and, 265–66, 694*n16*

Shattuck, Henry, 551

Shattuck, Lemuel, 210, 225–26, 238, 266, 283; Atwill on, 718*n16*; at Brown, Shattuck, & Company, 352–53; on Concord history, 353–57, 361–62, 364, 367–68, 718*nn16–18*, 719*n22*, 720*n34*; on education and the individual, 320; Emerson, R. W., and, 208, 357–58, 361–62, 367; Everett and, 694*n16*; on the Great Awakening, 357; *History of Concord* by, 355–57, 361–62, 364, 367–68, 718*nn16–18*, 720*n34*; on the individual, 320, 357; Jarvis, E., and, 356, 672*n38*, 720*n34*; on school and education, 198–208, 320, 672*n34*, 673*n43*; on school reform, 202–204, 208; self-reliance and, 208; Thoreau, H. D., and, 208

Shattuck, Sarah, 455

Shattuck & Company, 124, 128, 201, 651*n24*, 694*n16*

Shaw, Lemuel, 754*n9*

Shepard, Ann Stow, 25

Shepherd, William, 109–10, 351, 358

Shepherd's Hotel, 248, 360, 690*n78*

Sherman, Roger, 25

Sherman, Roger Minot, 26

Sherman, Sarah, 25

silk industry and trade, 171–72

Silliman, Benjamin, 233–35, 388

Simmons, George F., 756*n23*

Slater, Samuel, 96

slavery: ACS on, 329–30, 339; American Revolution and, 99; Beaumont on, 726*n15*; Bliss on, 106–107; Brooks, M. M., on, 516–17; Channing, W. E., against, 417; Christianity and, 340–41; in Concord, 640*n34*, 642*n39*; Concord and, 99, 106–107, 395, 639*n31*; against democracy, 329; Democrats and Whigs on, 513; Emerson, C. C., against, 337–39; Emerson, L., on antislavery movement and, 438, 512, 514–15, 522, 538, 582–84; Emerson, R. W., and Thoreau, H. D., on, 522; Emerson, R. W., on, 329, 336, 393, 512, 522, 537–38, 583–87, 760*n8*; English campaign against, emancipation and, 583–84, 593; Goodwin on, 336, 340; Grimké sisters on, 509–10; *The Liberator* on, 328–29; in Massachusetts, 99–100, 102, 104; in Massachusetts Bay Colony, 347; materialism and, 584–85; Merrick, T., and, 516–17; Middle Passage and, 438, 522, 538, 594; New England textiles and, 170; Puritans and, 347; Ripley, D., on, 331; Ripley, E., and, 99, 330–31, 341; Shattuck, L., on history of, 364; South Carolina and, 585–86, 787*n76*; Unitarian church and, 532; U. S. Constitution and, 532, 534–36, 582, 591; women and, 510–11; *see also* abolitionism; antislavery

Slave's Friend, The, 359

Smith, Adam, 578

Smith, Daniel, 125, 128–29, 652*n29*

Smith School, 674*n46*

Smollett, Tobias, 679*n5*

Social Circle, The, 260–61, 278, 346, 358, 716*n4*, 722*n43*; Anti-Masons in, 705n97; average age of founders, 698n52; CFASS and, 761n13; CFCS and, 743n14; Concord Academy students and, 746n36; Concord Bank and, 279, 698n50; on Concord Fight monument, 369, 698n49; Concord Social Library and, 698n50; Corinthian Lodge and, 260–61, 280–81; Davis, C. B., in, 698n54; Emerson, R. W., in, 412, 580; Freemasons and, 280–82, 284, 299; Hoar, S., and, 698n53, 722n43; Prescott, T., in, 739n71; Prichard, M., in, 280; Ripley, E., and, 279; Shattuck, D., and, 280; Society of Middlesex Husbandmen and Manufacturers and, 698n50; Thoreau, C., and, 455; Thoreau, John, and, 277, 279

social equality, 106, 310–11, 392, 561

social ethic, xvii, 447

social libraries, 223–29

social reform: Concord Lyceum and, 220, 244; cosmopolitanism and, 220, 258; Frost on, 580–81; Hoar, S., and Keyes, J., on, 262; individual reform and, 316; intellectual innovation and, 220; Moore, G., on, 417–18; reading in, 225; self-culture and, xvii; self-reform and, 399; Walden on, 598–99; women in movement, 255, 513–14, 528–29, 537; see also temperance movement

social statistics, 356

Society for Christian Union and Progress, 394

Society of Free Enquirers, 317

Society of Middlesex Husbandmen and Manufacturers, 8–9, 207, 555, 664n38, 665n45; in Concord, 110, 165–68, 170, 172; on economic growth and interdependence, 263–64; on fruit and vegetable sales, 545; on Minott, G., 180; Shattuck, D., in, 167; The Social Circle and, 698n50; Thoreau, John, in, 219

solitude, 433–34, 450–51

South Carolina, 263–64, 585–86, 787n76

Southmayd, Daniel, 73–74, 76–81, 236, 452–53, 704n90, 743n11

Southmayd, Joanne Kent, 74, 77, 79, 630n57

Sparks, Jared, 415–16

Specimens of Foreign Standard Literature (Ripley, G.), 384–85

Spurzheim, Johann, 388

Stacy, John, 224, 227, 633n1

Staples, Sam, 606–607

Stearns, Samuel, 62, 67, 69

Stebbins, Rufus Phineas, 733n22

Sterne, Laurence, 679n5

Stetson, Caleb, 755n18

Stone, Elvira, 754n11

Story, Joseph, 224, 351, 407

Stow, Cyrus, 89, 400, 502, 634n10, 662n23, 769n4, 785n55

Stow, Nathan, 89, 662n23

Stowe, Harriet Beecher, 782n37

Sturgis, Caroline, 440–41, 443, 580

supernatural rationalism, 311

Swedenborg, Emanuel, 316, 422, 439, 503

Tariff of Abominations, 263–64

taxpayer suffrage, 27–29, 617n27

Tayloe, John, 25

Tayloe, John, III, 331

temperance movement: ATS in, 252; Bartlett, J., in, 253, 256; Concord Lyceum and, 244; Concord Total Abstinence Society in, 551–52, 557, 581, 772n22; CTS in, 254–55, 257–58, 689n75; Emerson, R. W., on, 399; growth of, 256–57; Hoar, S., in, 552; lyceums and, 243–44, 255–56; Moore, G., in, 417; MSSI in, 250–52; Thoreau family and, 220; Trinitarians in, 252–53, 256; War of 1812 and, 250

Temple of Reason, 317–18

textile factories, 7, 97–98, 170

textile mills, in Concord, 95–97, 262, 554

Thatcher, Benjamin B., 332, 367–68, 710n29, 721n42

Thatcher, George, 621n8

Therien, Alex, 608

Thompson, Aaron, 116

Thompson, George, 334–37, 340–43, 359, 509

Thoreau, Cynthia, 58, 72, 77, 81, 642n41; abolitionism and antislavery activism of, 103, 429, 522, 591, 764n25; boardinghouse of, 122, 452; Brooks, M. M., and, 591; on Calvinism, 453; in CFCS, 453–55, 464, 514, 547,

Thoreau, Cynthia (*cont.*)
  742*n9*, 743*n12*, 743*n14*; on Cherokees,
  525; on "Cold Friday," 103; at First
  Parish Church, 502; O'Brien and,
  547; Puritans and, 43; Ripley, E., and,
  43, 53, 56, 71, 74–75, 453; The Social
  Circle and, 455; on Thoreau, H. D.,
  452; Thoreau, John, and, 43–44, 56, 73,
  185, 219–20, 277, 285, 451–53, 502
Thoreau, David Henry, *see* Thoreau,
  Henry David
Thoreau, Helen, 193, 277, 532, 591,
  766*n43*
Thoreau, Helen Louisa, 56, 169
Thoreau, Henry David: on agricultural
  reform, 599, 601; Alcott, A. B., and,
  429; on American individualism,
  xiii; on antislavery and abolitionism,
  468–69, 522, 531, 591–93; birth of,
  115; on Brook Farm, 587; Brownson
  and, 457, 462, 469, 477, 481; on canal
  boats, 8; on community, 607–608; on
  consumerism, 119–20; on country
  parsons, 457–58; in debating society,
  232–33; in *Democratic Review*, 590–91;
  Democrats, Whigs and, 468–69,
  476–77, 481; in *The Dial*, 589–90, 592;
  on Dugan, E., 559–60; on election of
  1840, 476–77; to Emerson, L., 591;
  as farmer, 601–606; on Fitchburg
  Railroad, 549–50; on freedom,
  459–60, 469; on government, 588,
  607; at Harrison rally, 474; at Harvard,
  16, 180, 185–86, 209, 219, 376, 449,
  452, 455–60, 465–67, 469, 500, 668*n3*,
  741*n2*, 744*n17*; Hawthorne, S., and,
  86; Heywood, A., and, 187; Hoar, R.,
  and, 233; on Hoar, S., 787*n76*; on
  the individual, xv, 503, 591; on the
  individual, institutions and, xv, 562;
  on industrial capitalism, 598; on
  interdependence, 608; on Jacksonian
  democracy, 467; Jarvis, E., and, 197,
  460, 462; Jones, A., obituary by, 465,
  471; Keyes, J. S., and, 432–33, 462,
  589, 746*n33*, 783*n42*; "The Landlord"
  by, 590; on land ownership, 587; in
  The Liberator, 592–93; Mann and, 461;
  Massachusetts Board of Education
  on, 745*n27*; MCASS and, 593; on
  Middlesex fair, 168–69; on Minott,
  E., 667*n57*; on Minott, G., 180–83,

  605, 786*n73*; Minott, M., and, 667*n60*;
  Moore, A., and, 165; on nature, 451,
  458–60, 588–89, 603; in New York
  City, 589–91; on partisan editors, 458,
  471–72; on Phillips, 592–94; "Political,
  Moral, and Literary Character of
  a Nation" by, 459–60, 469; against
  political parties and process, 477;
  on politics, 468–69, 471–72, 476–77,
  480–81; on religion, 501–503; on
  religious sentiment, 458, 502, 744*n21*;
  "Resistance to Civil Government" by,
  469, 502–503, 607, 787*n76*; Ripley,
  E., on, 487; Robinson and, 214–15,
  471, 500, 749*n52*; on Rogers, N. P.,
  591–92; Russell, M., and, 432; school
  reform and, 193, 208, 218; on self-
  reliance, xiv; Shattuck, L., and, 208;
  on solitude, 450–51; Thoreau, C.,
  on, 452; on Thoreau, John, 108, 259;
  Transcendentalism and, 447, 458,
  481; Transcendentalists, Unitarians
  and, 61–62; on Walden Pond, 3, 99,
  101–102, 147, 588–89, 593–96, 600,
  607–608; in Walden woods, 596,
  607–608; *A Week on the Concord and
  Merrimack Rivers* by, 785*n61*; Weiss on,
  744*n17*; *see also Walden* (Thoreau, H. D.)
Thoreau, Henry David, Concord and,
  xiv, xvi–xvii, 3, 83–84, 86; boyhood in,
  451–52; as Concord Academy student,
  208–209, 214, 216, 232–33, 452; as
  Concord Academy teacher, 464–65,
  746*n34*; Concord Lyceum and, 219,
  463, 465, 533–34, 588–89, 592,
  596–602, 607, 783*n42*; Emerson, R. W.,
  and, 319, 449–51, 569–70; "Estabrook
  Country," 98; First Parish Church
  and, 501–503; as grammar school
  master, 460–62, 745*n30*; as grammar
  school student, 185–87, 189, 193, 197,
  208, 214, 216; at Minot homestead,
  147–49; Minott, G., and, 180; nature
  and, 588–89; North Bridge, 16, 456,
  459, 466; nostalgia for, 591; on society
  of, 462–63; trade and business, 113,
  115, 144–45; *Walden* on, 597–602, 608;
  Walden Pond and, 594–96
Thoreau, Henry David, Emerson, R. W.,
  and, xiii–xviii, xx, 108, 144, 165, 208,
  218, 301, 669*n6*; in Concord, 319,
  449–51, 569–70; at Concord Fight

memorial dedication, 376; on English poetry anthology, 589; Haskins and Lowell on, 463; Hawthorne, N., and, 590; ideal of the soul, Transcendentalism and, 447; on individualism, 220; living together, 587–90; *Nature* and, 449, 458–59, 744*n21*; Quincy and, 449; on school reform, 218; on self-reliance, 463; on slavery and antislavery, 522; social statistics and, 356; in Transcendental Club, 463; Transcendentalism of, 356, 447; in Transcendentalist movement, 569; Walden Pond, 593–94

Thoreau, Jean, 4, 53–54, 147, 458–59

Thoreau, John, 3–6, 8, 13, 87, 158, 634*nn8–9*; beans raised by, 602; Boston and, 220; at Burr & Prichard green store, 126; in Concord, 4, 6, 11, 15, 25, 34, 43, 114–15, 147; Concord Bank and, 748*n46*; on Concord Fight anniversary, 353–54; in Concord Fire Society, 259; in Concord Ornamental Tree Society, 91; Concord Social Library and, 223; in court, 646*nn4–5*; early business career, 114–15; Freemasons and, 284–85, 298; Hurd, I., Jr., and, 114–15, 646*n5*; at Minot homestead, 147–49; Munroe, W., and, 5–6, 108, 126, 129–30, 135–37, 139, 167–68, 656*n55*; as pencil maker, 15–16, 43, 108, 113, 126, 129, 135, 137, 142, 144, 185, 219, 451–52, 655*n46*, 656*n55*; political affiliations of, 259–60, 468; Ripley, E., on, 248; Shattuck, D., and, 122, 748*n46*; Smith, D., and, 125; The Social Circle and, 277, 279; in Society of Middlesex Husbandmen and Manufacturers, 219; Thoreau, C., and, 43–44, 56, 73, 185, 219–20, 277, 285, 451–53, 502; Thoreau, H. D., on, 108, 259; on Warren Bridge, 270, 695*n26*; Wood, Ebenezer, and, 139; at yellow store, 646*nn4–5*

Thoreau, John, Jr., 451–52, 464–65, 502, 587, 667*n60*; on Christmas celebrations, 758*n35*

Thoreau, Maria, 204, 530, 630*n57*, 743*n11*

Thoreau, Rebecca, 53–55, 61–62, 79, 221, 623*n23*, 624*n24*, 679*n6*

Thoreau, Sarah, 79, 502, 630*n56*

Thoreau, Sophia, 169

Thoreau sisters, *see* Misses Thoreau, the

"Times, The" (lecture series) (Emerson, R. W.), 570, 581

Tocqueville, Alexis de, 319, 392, 505, 575, 726*n15*, 779*n12*

Todd, Thomas, 628*n45*

Traditions and Reminiscences of Concord, Massachusetts 1779–1878 (Jarvis, E.), 678*n67*, 686*n56*, 688*n69*

Trail of Tears, 523, 527

Transcendental Club, 379, 439–40, 463, 494, 561, 569, 755*n18*

Transcendentalism: Alcott, A. B., on, 379; antislavery, abolitionism and, 512–13; in Boston, xvii; Concord and, xiv–xvii, 13, 319–20, 404, 417, 423, 560–61, 569–70, 580, 610*n7*; Dewey on, 708*n8*; Emerson, M. M., and, 308; of Emerson, R. W., 13, 307, 310, 315–16, 320, 343, 362, 385–86, 392; of Emerson, R. W., and Thoreau, H. D., 356, 447; Hunt, M., and, 564–65; ideal of the soul, 447; on the individual, 404; on individual freedom, xvii; interdependence and, 439; Keyes, J., and Keyes, J. S., on, 431–34; *Nature* (Emerson, R. W.) and, 307, 315, 380, 500–501; Norton on, 497; in political arena, 528; religious pluralism and, 316; Ripley, E., on, 504–505; Robinson on, 500–501; social statistics and, 356; Thoreau, H. D., and, 447, 458, 481; Unitarianism and, 413, 439; women and, 439–40

"Transcendentalist, The" (lecture) (Emerson, R. W.), 581–82, 588, 783*n43*

Transcendentalist individualism, xiv, xviii, 301

Transcendentalist movement: Brownson in, 457; *The Dial* in, 561, 569, 589; Emerson, R. W., and Thoreau, H. D., in, 569; Emerson, R. W., in, xiii, 379, 402, 412, 483, 497

Transcendentalists: at Brook Farm, 504, 561–62; Christianity and, 497; Democrats and, 470, 477–78; on education, 464; on "Festus," 446; First Parish and, 500; Hawthorne, N., and, 568; on the individual, xv–xvi, 319, 434; Minott, G., and, 182;

Transcendentalists (*cont.*)
  Minutemen and, xiv, xx; on religious
  sentiment, 312–13, 315–17, 502; on
  self-reliance, 434, 463; on solitude,
  433–34; Unitarians and, 61–62,
  72, 310, 312–13, 315–16, 421; on
  universal soul, 493
Treatise Concerning the Religious Affections
  (Edwards, Jonathan), 679n5
Treaty of New Echota, 523–24, 526
Trinitarian church, in Concord, 67–68,
  632n67, 753n5; on abolitionism, 531;
  ACS and, 330, 713n49, 716n67; on
  CFASS, 530; Davis, Josiah, and, 73,
  485–86; First Parish Church and,
  73–80, 484–85, 500, 515, 626n37;
  Green, J. C., and, 64–66, 73, 76–78,
  135, 485; on Heywood, A. B., 754n8;
  LSS, 743n11; the Misses Thoreau and,
  63–65, 73–74, 77, 105, 135, 453, 485;
  Ripley, E., and, 74–78, 80, 629n51,
  637n21; subscribers to, 631n59;
  women in, 485–86
Trinitarian churches and ministers:
  Calvinism and, 74, 312, 484–85; on
  Freemasonry, 296–97; secessions
  by, 62–63, 71, 252; in temperance
  movement, 252–53, 256
Trinitarian Ladies Sewing Society, 514
"True Principles of Reform, The"
  (lecture) (Frost), 580–81
Trumpet, 77
Turner, Frederick Jackson, 362
Turner, Nat, 336
Tuttle, John L., 26, 118, 615n13
Tyler, John, 592
Tyler, Orville, 722n48

Unitarian Advocate, 72, 486
Unitarians and Unitarianism, 69, 71, 74,
  78, 80, 252, 373, 753n5; on alcohol,
  256; antislavery of, 422; Boston, 380,
  506; Brooks, M. M., and, 515–16,
  532; against Calvinism, 312; *Christian
  Examiner*, 311, 313, 315–16, 379–80;
  Emerson, L., and, 439; Emerson,
  R. W., and, 310, 313–14, 380, 439,
  494–96; First Parish Church and, 484,
  500; on German idealism, 311–12,
  314–15; Harvard and, 409, 495; Hoar,
  S., and, 628n42; Locke and, 443;
  Moore, G., and, 420–23; Prescott, M.,

and, 444, 447; Ripley, E., and, 69, 72;
  on self-culture, 415; slaveholders and,
  532; on supernatural rationalism,
  311; Transcendentalism and,
  413, 439; Transcendentalists and,
  61–62, 72, 310, 312–13, 315–16, 421;
  Universalists and, 500; Ware and,
  420–21
*United States Magazine, and Democratic
  Review*, 469, 478, 563, 779n20
Universalist Palladium, 757n31
Universalists and Universalism, 484,
  486–87, 500, 757n30
universal mind, 392–93, 395, 410, 419,
  528, 734n25
universal soul, 392, 430, 437, 493, 495
universal suffrage, 28, 470

Van Buren, Martin, 370, 469–70, 472;
  Emerson, R. W., open letter to,
  525–29; Jackson, A., and, 260, 300,
  523, 526; Native Americans betrayed
  by, 526
View of Religions (Adams, Hannah), 70
Vinovskis, Maris A., 678nn65–66
Vose, Henry, 677n64
Vose, John, 65

Wade, John, 620n48
Wainwright, Jonathan M., 731n5
Walden (Thoreau, H. D.), xiv, xviii, 140,
  594, 782n38; "Bean Field" chapter,
  601–606; on Concord, 597–602,
  608; "Economy" chapter, 599–600;
  on English hay, as cash crop, 165;
  on farming, 601–606; individualism
  and, 597; on laborers, 597–98; as
  lecture and manuscript, 597–602;
  on orators, 233; on simple and
  sincere communication, 463; on
  social reform, 598–99; on trade and
  business, 113; "Where I Lived and
  What I Lived For" chapter, 599–601
Walden Pond, ix, xi; Keyes, J. S., on,
  433, 446; Thoreau, H. D., on, 3, 99,
  101–102, 147, 588–89, 593–96, 600,
  607–608; Thoreau family at, 1822,
  3–4, 451; in Walden woods, 98–99,
  553
Walden woods, 740n74; Emerson,
  R. W., on, 577; free people of color
  in, 99–102; Irish settlements in, 545,